Figure 11.3 Reframing Autoethnography

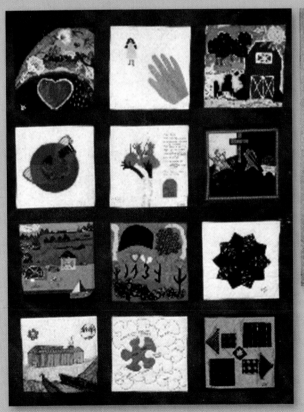

Figure 30.2 Source: Photograph by Helen Ball

Figure 30.1 Source: Photograph by Helen Ball

Figure 30.4 Source: Photograph by Helen Ball

Figure 30.5 Source: Photograph by Helen Ball

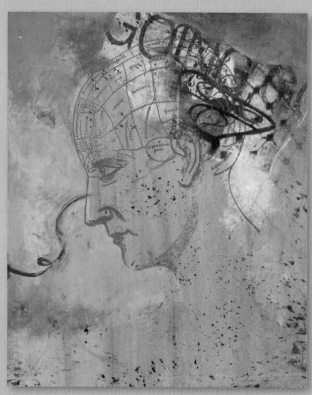

Figure 46.1 Going, Going, Gone
Source: Reproduced courtesy of Lou Horner

Figure 46.2 Desire
Source: Reproduced courtesy of Lou Horner

Figure 30.3 Source: Photograph by Helen Ball

Handbook of the
ARTS in
Qualitative
Research

J. Gary Knowles
Ardra L. Cole

*Ontario Institute of Education Studies,
University of Toronto, Canada*

Perspectives, Methodologies, Examples, and Issues

Handbook of the
ARTS in
Qualitative
Research

SAGE Publications
Los Angeles • London • New Delhi • Singapore

For information:

 Sage Publications, Inc.
2455 Teller Road
Thousand Oaks, California 91320
E-mail: order@sagepub.com

Sage Publications Ltd.
1 Oliver's Yard
55 City Road
London EC1Y 1SP
United Kingdom

Sage Publications India Pvt. Ltd.
B 1/I 1 Mohan Cooperative Industrial Area
Mathura Road, New Delhi 110 044
India

Sage Publications Asia-Pacific Pte. Ltd.
33 Pekin Street #02–01
Far East Square
Singapore 048763

Printed in the United States of America

Library of Congress Cataloging-in-Publication Data

Knowles, J. Gary, 1947-
Handbook of the arts in qualitative research: Perspectives, methodologies, examples, and issues/ J. Gary Knowles, Ardra L. Cole.
    p. cm.
Includes bibliographical references and index.
  ISBN 978-1-4129-0531-2 (cloth)
    1. Social sciences—Research. 2. Humanities—Research. I. Cole, Ardra L. II. Title.

H62.K6275 2008
300.72—dc22   2007021783

Printed on acid-free paper

07 08 09 10 11 10 9 8 7 6 5 4 3 2 1

Acquiring Editor:	Lisa Cuevas Shaw and Vicki Knight
Associate Editor:	Sean Connelly
Editorial Assistant:	Lauren Habib
Production Editor:	Sarah K. Quesenberry
Copy Editor:	Teresa Wilson
Proofreader:	Dennis Webb
Indexer:	Wendy Allex
Typesetter:	C&M Digitals (P) Ltd.
Marketing Manager:	Stephanie Adams
Cover Designer:	Bryan Fishman

CONTENTS

Visual Art

New Media

Folk Art and Popular Art Forms

PART IV: INQUIRY PROCESSES   369

PREFACE

The *Handbook of the Arts in Qualitative Research* is witness to the power of the arts in the lives and knowledge development of humans in a changing world of scholarship and research. The *Handbook* represents an unfolding and expanding orientation to qualitative social science research that draws inspiration, concepts, processes, and representational forms from the arts, broadly defined. The *Handbook* is designed as an exploration into a range of alternative researching possibilities that fuse the creative and imaginative possibilities of the arts with social science research. It is intended to provide a context, inspiration, and structure to facilitate new and experienced scholars' inquiries into elements or aspects of research methods appropriate to their current and future work.

The contents of the *Handbook* acknowledge the breadth of scholarship and burgeoning practice within a range of academic disciplines and contexts where the arts influence researching. At the same time it tells many stories about the way the arts frame and influence the inquiry theories and practices of renowned and emerging scholars. The contributing authors tell stories of engagement with the arts. Each, in her or his own way, evidences a history of learning from the arts, gaining inspiration from the arts, and/or a longstanding grounding and involvement in the arts. All of the authors proclaim the power of the arts for enhancing social science research. These authors give evidence of the movement of the arts into many, perhaps most (if not all), social science disciplines. Although not all disciplines are represented in the *Handbook* (and this has much to do with space limitations), it is difficult not to overlook the prevalence of the arts in human enterprise for making sense of the human condition and the surrounding world.

As editors of the *Handbook,* our paramount objective is to provide an accessible and stimulating collection of theoretical arguments and illustrative examples that delineate the role of the arts in qualitative social science research. So it is that the *Handbook* addresses many nuances and possibilities for infusing the arts into qualitative research as an alternative paradigm orientation and practice. Given the heightened interest in the possibilities of the arts for influencing qualitative social science research (especially as voiced by advanced graduate students and emerging scholars), a burgeoning body of work, and a sufficiently nuanced group of international scholars who address matters of the arts in social science research, the publication of the *Handbook* is timely.

The many fusions of the arts and qualitative inquiry are changing the face of social science research, opening possibilities for alternative perspectives, modes, media, and genres through which to understand and represent the human condition. The productive fusions and tensions among qualitative inquiry and the literary, fine, applied, performing, and media arts give rise to redefinitions of research form and representation as well as new understandings of process, spirit, purpose, subjectivities, emotion, responsiveness, and ethical dimensions of inquiry. Scholars use multiple ways to advance knowledge. They use, for example, the language, genres, and orientations of fiction, poetry, theatre/drama, and visual arts, including installation, film, and video. Communities of scholars articulate and engage in, for instance, arts-based research, arts-informed research, image-based research, A/R/Tography, and community-based activist art, to name some perspectives. The *Handbook* brings together a unique group of scholars for the purposes of putting forward this range of perspectives. Through the *Handbook* our purpose is to advance the field of qualitative methodologies and make alternative paradigm

research involving the arts more available to emerging and established social science researchers. In this way the *Handbook* is encyclopedic although not an encyclopedia; it is comprehensive but not all encompassing. It brings together, under one umbrella, as it were, a range of expressions of the arts in research. It serves as a reference point and marker for the development of alternative methodologies while providing points of reference regarding specific orientations and practices.

The *Handbook* is an acknowledgment that social science research involving the arts is an emerging, expanding research genre. There is much evidence of the appropriateness and, indeed, the acceptance of this approach to research within scholarly literature and professional organizations across academic disciplines of the humanities and social sciences, including health sciences and other applied disciplines. As a community of researchers, we are engaged in "efforts to map an intermediate space we can't quite define yet, a borderland between passion and intellect, analysis and subjectivity, ethnography and autobiography, art and life" (Behar, 1996, p. 174), and this represents both an exciting possibility and a challenge.

Given the burgeoning presence of the arts in research over the past two decades, it is safe to say that arts-related methodologies can be considered a milestone in the evolution of qualitative research methodologies. Those of us, including all the *Handbook* authors, who have been involved in charting new methodological territory have much to be pleased about by the place the arts has earned in contemporary research. Markers such as new online and print journals as well as theme issues of established journals, conferences involving and featuring the arts in research, book publications, conference sessions, and so on, all strongly suggest that arts-related approaches have found a place on the qualitative research map. The publication of this *Handbook* is another significant marker. We see this volume as a beginning.

Like all publications, this one reflects the temporal boundaries within which it was written and compiled. The process of locating contributing authors was often convoluted but members of the two advisory boards aided us. Although we intended to have a greater geographical spread of authors from beyond North America, that was not possible, especially given the production schedule constraints. The possibilities of and for the arts in research are limited only by the human imagination and commitment to pursue knowledge and knowing in its many forms. We trust that readers will engage with the works presented herein as members of a community of scholars who are provoked by and committed to the possibilities of the arts to reenchant (Gablik, 1991) research.

For readers the focus of the *Handbook* encourages a critical examination of the research process with a view to informing alternative scholarly perspectives and practices that draw on orientations, processes, and forms of the arts. Throughout, and within the many contributed chapters, the goal (sometimes foregrounded, sometimes backgrounded) is on:

- defining and exploring the role(s) of the arts in qualitative social science research;

- understanding the relationship between processes and representational forms of the arts and processes and representational forms of research;

- exploring features and qualities of research that is informed by or based in the arts, and related issues; and

- articulating challenges inherent in these alternative methodologies.

These, in fact, were the challenges given to the contributing authors.

As a way of guiding contributing authors, several questions were posed for the purposes of framing and shaping the development of their contributions to and, ultimately, the arrangement of the *Handbook*. These exact same questions may also be aids to reading the *Handbook:*

- Why and how do art and research come together to advance knowledge?

- What are some of the many and varied roles for the arts in social science research?

- What do art-research methodologies look like in practice?

- What is the place of the arts in various social science research contexts?

- What is the relationship of arts-related research to other forms of researching? . . . to the arts?

- What are features and characteristics of the various methodologies and genres of social science art-research?

- How is the quality of alternative genre research judged or determined?

- What are some key issues and challenges surrounding the bringing together of art and social science research?

At first glance, readers of the *Handbook* are likely to note its relatively conventional form. Like most academic print publications, this one is also constrained by the conventions of print media and, unfortunately, by costs associated with straying too far from those conventions. In an attempt to address some of the limitations of print media for presenting many of the art forms and ideas represented in this volume, Sage generously agreed to mount a Web site accompaniment to the *Handbook*. Although each chapter in the *Handbook* stands alone, many of the chapter authors make reference to supplemental material contained on the Web site. These references are clearly marked within the text of the relevant chapters. We invite readers to enhance their engagement with the ideas and materials presented in these chapters by spending time at the Web site (www.sagepub.com/knowlessupplement).

◆ References

Behar, R. (1996). *The vulnerable observer: Anthropology that breaks your heart.* Boston: Beacon Press.

Gablik, S. (1991). Introduction: Changing paradigms, breaking the cultural trance. In S. Gablik, *The reenchantment of art* (pp. 1–12). London: Thames and Hudson.

ACKNOWLEDGMENTS

The *Handbook of the Arts in Qualitative Research* is a community project, one centered on the work of scholars committed to articulating the place of the arts in researching. Those who have contributed chapters constitute one element of the community of researchers who believe in the power and potential of the arts to inform qualitative research. The community involves many others, however.

In some ways the heart of the community is best represented by our emerging scholar colleagues who, especially during their graduate school years, urged us to be true to ourselves and prodded and tugged at the more comfortable boundaries of traditional modes and orientations to qualitative social science research. Many were associated with the Centre for Arts-Informed Research at the Ontario Institute for Studies in Education of the University of Toronto and, within this circle of faculty and student associates, many of our notions about the arts in qualitative social science research were developed. These new scholars, who also participated in our qualitative and arts-informed research courses at the University of Toronto (as well as those graduate students at Mount Saint Vincent University, Saint Francis Xavier University, and the University of British Columbia, where we taught summer courses), asked hard questions about boundaries and constraints, about possibilities and pitfalls of infusing the arts into research. They voiced their wonderings about the facility of conventional methodologies to adequately portray the human condition. Many brought with them into our classrooms and the dissertation/thesis supervision process an array of experience and groundings in the arts. They were not afraid to criticize the bifurcation of knowledge development and everyday life. More holistic perspectives on knowledge generation, on how humans come to know/inquire, were at the heart of the thinking of this new generation of scholars. They dared to produce graduate research that pushed the boundaries of qualitative research, and their influence was, and continues to be, considerable.

Many of these graduate students (and others) moved on to become professors in institutions scattered over North America, and some of them are represented in the Emerging Scholar Advisory Board. Given that we also saw a key audience for the *Handbook* to rest in this population, we thought it entirely fitting for the development of the *Handbook* that we be guided by both relatively new, emerging scholars and those who are more senior, established, and well recognized in the field. The former group, individually and collectively, worked tirelessly in guiding the project and reviewing manuscripts. Their names and affiliations are listed on page ii.

We also are grateful for the significant, formative contributions of the International Advisory Board members. Some of them supported the initial *Handbook* proposal through critiques and reviews at the time of its presentation to Lisa Cuevas Shaw at Sage Publications. Moreover, many of these individuals have been colleagues over the last decade and a half, our lives often converging at doctoral examinations, academic conferences, related scholarly events, publications, or in the virtual world. We are privileged to have shaped the field together through our acts of teaching, research supervision, and discourse. Many members of this senior advisory board contributed a chapter to the *Handbook,* and most made multiple, insightful reviews of chapter manuscripts that helped forge this collection into its current shape. They come from a variety of academic disciplines and have made strong statements within their respective communities. The *Handbook* is stamped with their commitment to the

project. Their names and affiliations are listed on page ii.

Both advisory boards helped us identify many of the contributing authors; others we learned about through a rhizomatic process. Unfortunately, potential contributors continued to pop up long past the time when we had completed our list, and we were not able to include them. To these scholars we publicly extend our regrets. All of the authors we approached were enthusiastic about the project, and some, working in relative isolation from like-minded scholars, were surprised at the vibrancy of the broader field and the range of disciplines drawing on the arts to enhance qualitative researching theory and practices. We hope that the *Handbook* project served to create a sense of affiliation, encouragement, and inspiration for those authors in particular. The initial submission and revision processes were demanding and, we expect, at times, tedious; we thank authors for their patience, good will, and timely completions.

Ninety-seven reviewers (comprising members of both advisory boards in addition to scholars nominated by contributing authors and ourselves) helped us provide detailed commentaries that encouraged and guided chapter authors. Chapter contributions were reviewed by from two to five scholars besides us. The reviewers' names are listed at the end of this section, and this project could not have come to fruition without their close work. We are indebted to them. In addition, emerging scholars associated with the Centre for Arts-Informed Research aided in making sense of the reviews and resulting revisions. Particular thanks go to Tracy Luciani for helping us organize the reviews in readiness for authors, and to Dorothy Lichtblau, Indrani Margolin, and Mary Rykov for helping us respond to chapter revisions. The saying "The devil's in the details" crops up often toward the end of a project like this. Thanks to the keen eye, diligence, technical facility, and commitment of Sara Promislow (an artist-researcher herself and member of the Emerging Scholar Advisory Board), we were able to bring the *Handbook* to completion.

There are others who facilitated this project. Lisa Cuevas Shaw, acquisitions editor (Research Methods and Evaluation) at Sage Publications, recognized its potential and unwaveringly supported the project from the point at which it was merely a kernel of an idea. Her calmness and patience amid the whirl of manuscript preparation is much appreciated. Thanks to Lisa also for facilitating a smooth transition when she left Sage and put us in the very capable hands of Sean Connelly. Assuming a large project like this at midpoint is not easy; however, Sean stepped in and guided us the rest of the way with confidence, patience, and good humor. Sarah Quesenberry and Teresa Wilson and the rest of the Sage editing and production team have been fabulous to work with. Our sincere appreciation to everyone at Sage who had a hand in bringing the *Handbook* to fruition.

Our hope is that the *Handbook of the Arts in Qualitative Research* will serve as a vehicle to inspire, challenge, support, inform, and complement the qualitative research of well-established and emerging scholars alike.

Sage Publications gratefully acknowledges the contributions of the following reviewers:

Sharon Abbey
Kelly Akerman
Michael Angrosino
Laura Apol
Carl Bagley
Deborah Barndt
Tom Barone
Margaret Barrett
Donald Blumenfeld-Jones
Victoria Bowman
John M. Budd
James Burns
Leah Burns
Melisa Cahnmann
Greg Cajete
Mary Beth Cancienne
Deborah Ceglowski
Kathryn Church
Darlene Clover
Chris Cocoluzzi
Nancy Cooley
Alexis Cutcher
Elizabeth de Freitas
Nancy Davis Halifax
C. T. Patrick Diamond
Tim Diamond
Mary Doll
Robyn Ewing
Kathleen Fitzgerald
David J. Flinders
Arthur Frank
Charles Garoian
Pariss Garramone
Robyn Gibson
Douglas Gosse
Lenore Hervey
Lekkie Hopkins
Marianne Hulsbosch
Esther Ignagni
Rita Irwin
Barbara Jago
Allan H. Jones

Carolyn Kenny
Dorothy Kidd
Jean L. Konzal
Carl Leggo
Shawn Lennie
Dorothy Lichtblau
Lesa Lockford
Daria Loi
Teresa C. Luciani
Abbyann Lynch
Brenda McConnell Gladstone
Anne McCrary Sullivan
Maura McIntyre
Cathy Malchiodi
Indrani Margolin
Lina Medaglia
Jim Mienczakowski
Terry Mitchell
Matt Myer
Allan Neilsen
Lorri Neilsen
Joe Norris
Nicholas Paley
Susan Paterson
Lynette Plett
Sara Promislow
Laurel Richardson
Lena Richardson
Robert Rinehart
Carole Roy
Robert Runte
Mary Rykov
Johnny Saldaña
Pauline Sameshima
James Sanders
Brooke Shannon
Margaret Shone
Moneca Sinclaire
Christina Sinding
Patrick Slattery
Celeste Snowber
Stephanie Springgay

Andrew Stubbs
Jennifer Sumsion
Steve Taylor
Suzanne Thomas
Tanya Titchkowsky
P. Bruce Uhrmacher
Cheryl van Daalen-Smith

Christine van Halen-Faber
Jon Wagner
Rob Walker
Sandra Weber
Bob Willard
Natalie Zur Nedden

We dedicate this Handbook *to Elliot Eisner for his inspiring leadership and scholarship, his lifelong commitment to art, and his visionary advocacy for the place of art in research.*

PART I

KNOWING

Acknowledging art's place in qualitative research methodologies is, for some, long overdue—the argument unassailable, a "no-brainer." For others, the union of art and research is nothing short of paradoxical. Regardless, the alliance cannot be taken lightly. To welcome the arts into social science research, not as a subject or object of study but as a *mode* of inquiry, requires deep consideration. Seeing methodology through an artful eye reflects a way of being in the world as a researcher that is paradigmatically different from other ways of thinking about and designing research. And, as with any other significant undertaking, it behooves researchers to understand the many levels and implications of such a methodological commitment. Drawing from linguistic analysis we argue that understanding the deep structure of any methodology is a necessary starting point.

We begin the *Handbook,* therefore, by plumbing the very depths of methodological consideration—what it means to know. The two opening chapters provide a historical and epistemological context for exploring the relationship between the arts and knowledge. The authors illustrate and analyze the role of culture in shaping paradigmatic perspectives, and problematize the role of Western culture, in particular, in privileging into dominance a paradigm that has served as dictator over the production of scholarship, sanctioning what counts as knowledge and subjugating alternative perspectives. Taken together, the chapters provide a foundation for considering art, in its many forms, as a way of knowing, and knowing, in its many forms, as an art.

- Art and Knowledge, *Elliot Eisner*

- The Art of Indigenous Knowledge: A Million Porcupines Crying in the Dark, *Thomas King*

◆ 1

1

ART AND KNOWLEDGE

◆ Elliot Eisner

The idea that art can be regarded as a form of knowledge does not have a secure history in contemporary philosophical thought. The arts traditionally have been regarded as ornamental or emotional in character. Their connection to epistemological issues, at least in the modern day, has not been a strong one. Are the arts merely ornamental aspects of human production and experience or do they have a more significant role to play in enlarging human understanding?

The positivist tradition that has animated western philosophy during the first half of the 20th century viewed the arts as largely emotive rather than primarily informative. The arts are forms that you enjoyed, or felt strongly about, or savored for their delicacy. They had little to do with matters of knowledge. For knowledge of the empirical world you rely upon synthetic propositions whose truth value can be determined. And if you needed to know something about logical relationships, analytic propositions were the sources of data you would manage or manipulate (Ayer, 1952).

Part of the reason for the separation of the arts from matters epistemological pertains to the belief, a true one I would argue, that the arts are largely forms that generate emotion. We seek out the arts in order to take a ride on the wings that art forms provide: The arts are ways to get a natural high. This high is secured largely through our sensory response to the way sound is arranged, as in music; to the way colors are composed, as in visual art; to the ways in which the movement of a human body excites us as we experience its motion in time and space, as in dance. The sensory side of human experience is primary in the arts, or so it is believed. Plato himself regarded the senses as impediments to the achievement of that exalted state in which forms could be known (Plato, 1992). The weights and chains of the prisoners incarcerated in Plato's caves were really surrogates or proxies for the distractions that our senses imposed upon whatever our rational mind could possibly muster. Put most simply, the sensory systems that were stimulated through the arts were misleading; they lead one away rather than toward that form of critical rationality upon which truth depends.

Plato's ideas about mind, knowledge, and rationality are much more than ancient history. The model that they have provided has impacted our conception of intelligence and of rationality itself. It is not surprising, therefore, that it should have provided the model that has shaped our conception of science. That mathematics has been regarded as the queen of the sciences is a result of the legacy that Plato's theory of knowledge has left us.

Aristotle, however, had another view, and it is one that in many ways is closer to the most recent thinking done on methodology in social science research. Aristotle made distinctions between kinds of knowledge that people can secure. The three types he identified were the theoretical, the practical, and the productive (McKeon, 2001). The theoretical pertained to efforts to know things that were of necessity, that is, things and processes that could be no other way than the way they are. The processes and products of nature are prime examples. Practical knowledge was knowledge of

contingencies. What are the local circumstances that need to be addressed if one was to work effectively or act intelligently with respect to a particular state of affairs? The productive form of knowledge was knowledge of how to make something. How can this table be fashioned? How can this sculpture be shaped?

In differentiating types of knowledge, Aristotle comes closer than Plato to the kind of artistry that is relevant to arts-informed qualitative research. With Aristotle, we get an effort to draw distinctions in the service of conceptual clarity. This aim is wholly congruent with current efforts to make distinctions between types of research, even to redefine the meanings of research so that they are no longer singular, but multiple. Research differs in the ways in which it is conducted and in the products that it yields. What one needs to research in a situation must be appropriate for the circumstances one addresses and the aims one attempts to achieve. Such an aspiration acknowledges differences in the levels of precision that are achievable. Aristotle cautions us that an educated man expects only as much precision as the subject matter will admit. It is as foolish to seek approximations from mathematicians as exactitudes from poets (McKeon, 2001). What the term knowledge means depends on how inquiry is undertaken and the kind of problem one pursues. Even the term knowledge may be regarded as problematic. Knowledge as a term is a noun. Knowing is a verb. And knowing may be a much more appropriate descriptor of the processes of inquiry made in pursuit of a problem that will not yield to a set of rigidified procedures. Inquiry always yields tentative conclusions rather than permanently nailed down facts. The quest for certainty, as Dewey (1929/2005) pointed out, is hopeless.

What does it mean to know? Here, too, there are a variety of conditions under which the term *know* or *knowledge* can be used. One can know that something is the case.

One can know how something was done. One can know why something operates the way it does, and one can know how. For example, consider a medical relationship. "I remember this patient quite well, but I do not have a diagnosis for his illness." In this example, two types of knowledge emerge, the first pertaining to matters of recognition or recall, and the latter to theoretical or practical understanding. The doctor recognizes the patient, but doesn't know what is causing his problem. Clearly, one can know the former and not the latter, and one can know the latter without knowing the former. How one would find out which was which would depend on one's aims. Each variety of knowing bears its own fruits and has its own uses. The point here is that knowing is a multiple state of affairs, not a singular one. In pragmatic terms knowing is always about relationships. We need to know different things for different purposes, and sometimes we know some things for some purposes but not for others.

In traditional approaches to the conditions of scientific knowledge, the pursuit of certainty has been a longstanding ambition. Furthermore, knowledge is conceptualized as the ability to provide warranted assertions. *Warranted* refers to the provision of evidence regarding the truth or falsity of the assertion, and the term *assertion* itself belongs to a universe of discourse in which language is its representational vehicle. However, it has become increasingly clear since the latter half of the 20th century that knowledge or understanding is not always reducible to language. As Michael Polanyi says, we know more than we can tell (Polanyi, 1966/1983). Thus, not only does knowledge come in different forms, the forms of its creation differ. The idea of ineffable knowledge is not an oxymoron.

The liberation of the term knowledge from dominance by the propositional is a critical philosophical move. Do we not know what water tastes like, although we have very few words and virtually all of them inadequate for describing what water tastes like, or what music sounds like, or what someone looks like? Words, except when they are used artistically, are proxies for direct experience. They point us in a direction in which we can undergo what the words purport to reveal. Words, in this sense, are like cues to guide us on a journey. The utility of these cues depends upon their ability to help us anticipate the situation we wish to avoid or encounter.

The reason the deliteralization of knowledge is significant is that it opens the door for multiple forms of knowing. There are, indeed, propositions whose truth value is significant and whose claims are testable through scientific procedures. At the same time, there are utterances and images that are intended to be evocative of the situation they are designed to describe. Consider photography. Photographs can be powerful resources for portraying what cannot be articulated linguistically. We see this in the work of Edward Steichen, Dorothea Lange, Paul Strand, and other important photographers of the 20th century. But the ability to reveal is not limited to the talents of such photographers; it is available to those whose talents in photography are more ordinary. The point here is that humans have created within the context of culture a variety of forms of representation. These forms include the visual, the auditory, the gustatory, the kinesthetic, and the like. It includes forms of representation that combine the foregoing modalities as well. These forms of representation give us access to expressive possibilities that would not be possible without their presence. Technology provides new means during each generation for representational possibilities to be extended and diversified. The availability, for example, of neon tubes has made possible forms of sculpture that Michelangelo himself could not have imagined. Thus, technological advances promoted through scientific knowledge make new forms available to those who choose to use them.

This *Handbook* is an encomium to the use of new forms of representation in the service of improved understanding of the human condition. Rather than being constrained with criteria and methods formulated decades, indeed centuries, ago, this *Handbook* invites scholars to invent new ways through new means of representing what matters in human affairs. In this sense, the *Handbook* is something of a groundbreaking effort.

One should not conclude that new materials, technologies, and methods are the only innovative resources to be used to create arts-informed research. The way language is treated itself has a great deal to do with what it has to say. Consider, for example, Annie Dillard's book *Pilgrim at Tinker Creek* and focus upon the marriage between acute perception and artistically crafted prose.

It was sunny one evening last summer at Tinker Creek; the sun was low in the sky, upstream. I was sitting on the sycamore log bridge with the sunset at my back, watching the shiners the size of minnows who were feeding over the muddy sand in skittery schools. Again and again, one fish, then another, turned for a split second across the current and flash! the sun shot out from its silver side. I couldn't watch for it. It was always just happening somewhere else, and it drew my vision just as it disappeared: flash, like a sudden dazzle of the thinnest blade, a spark over a dun and olive ground at chance intervals from every direction. Then I noticed white specks, some sort of pale petals, small, floating, from under my feet on the creek's surface, very slow and steady. So I blurred my eyes and gazed upward toward the brim of my hat and saw a new world. I saw the pale white circles roll up, roll up, like the world's turning, mute and perfect, and I saw the linear flashes, gleaming silver, like stars being born at random down a rolling scroll of time. Something broke and something opened. I filled up like a new wineskin. I breathed an air like light; I saw a light like water. I was the lip of a fountain the creek filled forever; I was ether, the leaf in the zephyr; I was fleshflake, feather, bone. (Dillard, 1974, pp. 31–32)

This brief excerpt gives one a sense of what the artistic treatment of language makes possible. What, in this case, it makes possible is the writer's ability to give the reader a virtual sensory experience of nature in all its glorious richness and complexity. It is different from and, some would argue, more than a literal description; it is an artistic rendering, one that is evocative and that, psychologically speaking, gives us transport to another part of the world.

Let us distinguish for a moment between the descriptive and the evocative. Let the descriptive focus on the desire to create a mimetic relationship between something said and something done. The evocative has as its ambition the provision of a set of qualities that create an empathic sense of life in those who encounter it, whether the work is visual or linguistic, choreographic or musical. In all cases, emotion and imagination are involved. Art in research puts a premium on evocation, even when it has sections or aspects of it that are descriptive in character. Put another way, art is present in research when its presence enables one to participate vicariously in a situation.

Experiencing a situation in a form that allows you to walk in the shoes of another is one way to know one aspect of it. Empathy is a means to understanding, and strong empathic feelings may provide deep insight into what others are experiencing. In that sense, the arts in research promote a form of understanding that is derived or evoked through empathic experience.

At the same time, it should be recognized that answers to questions and solutions to problems might not be arts-informed research's long suit. This method of inquiry may trump conventional forms of research when it comes to generating questions or raising awareness of complex subtleties that matter. The deep strength of using the arts in research may be closer to the act of problematizing traditional conclusions than it is to providing answers in containers that are watertight. In this sense, the products of this research are closer in function to deep conversation and insightful dialogue than they are to error-free conclusions.

Attention to the relationship between the arts and knowledge has not been entirely neglected by aestheticians. One of the most prominent of them is Susanne Langer. Langer (1957) argues that works of art represent the artist's ability to create a structure of forms that are in their relationships analogs to the forms of feeling humans experience. Thus, what the artist is able to do is to provide a means through which feelings can come to be known. Langer (1957) writes:

> What does art seek to express? . . . I think every work of art expresses, more or less purely, more or less subtly, not feelings and emotions the artist has, but feelings which the artist knows; his insight into the nature of sentience, his picture of vital experience, physical, and emotive and fantastic. (p. 91)

Such knowledge is not expressible in ordinary discourse. The reason for this ineffability is not that the ideas to be expressed are too high, too spiritual or too anything else, but that the forms of feeling and the forms of discursive expression are logically incommensurate.

What we have here is a radical idea that the life of feeling is best revealed through those forms of feeling we call the arts; that is their special province, which is the function that they serve best. Langer (1957) claims that discursive language is the most useful scientific device humans have created but that the arts provide access to qualities of life that literal language has no great power to disclose. It follows, then, that an education of the life of feeling is best achieved through an education in and through the arts.

If one accepts Langer's argument, then the qualities of feelingful life expressed in human relationships, in the context of education, and in the wider conditions within which human beings live and work are perhaps most powerfully revealed when form is shaped artistically. The means through which those forms emerge is potentially infinite, that is, they might take place through poetry, they might be realized through music, they might be expressed through the visual arts; the options are as open as our imagination.

Of course, to use different media to effectively disclose what one has experienced emotionally requires the use of skills, knowledge of techniques, and familiarity with the materials themselves with respect to the way in which they behave when employed. The material must be converted into a medium, something that mediates the researcher's observations and culminates in a form that provides the analogous structure I mentioned earlier. What is created is the structural equivalent of emotions recollected in tranquility but expressing powerfully what an individual has undergone by virtue of the way the forms of the work relate to each other (Arnheim, 1974).

This process requires one to qualify qualities. That is, to create qualitative relationships among component qualities so that the expressive character of the total array of qualitative relationships actually helps reveal what the artist intended.

It is interesting to note the ways in which our language, riddled as it is with metaphors, describes affective states of affairs. We talk about being high or being low. We talk about being bright or being dull; we talk about being slow or being swift. Our personal attributes are captured in the metaphors we choose or invent to describe them. It is through such descriptions, at least in part, that we enable others to understand how we feel and, indeed, enable us to recognize our own feelings.

The capacity of metaphor to capture and express literally ineffable forms of feeling is related to Langer's (1957) conception of two kinds of knowing. Langer distinguishes between what she calls discursive and nondiscursive knowledge. The arts, especially music, occupy nondiscursive categories. Her basic argument is that the people we call artists have a conception of the structure of human feeling in its varieties. What they also have is the ability to create through the application of technique and skill forms whose empirical structure echoes the structure of a form of feeling. Thus, works of art enable us to know something about feeling that cannot be revealed in literal scientific statements. Put in Dewey's (1934) terms, science states meaning, art expresses it.

In talking about language, it is important to emphasize the point that language itself can be treated artistically. The meanings of poetry, for example, transcend what literal language provides. Indeed, it has been said that poetry was invented to say what words can never say. In other words, we should not confuse the nonliteral artistic character of language with its literal use. Each use performs its own distinctive functions.

I have been talking about that form of representation called language almost as though it were the only resource that could be used artistically to reveal the qualities and character of a state of affairs. The fact of the matter is that artistically rendered forms of representation can be created with virtually any material: film, video, dance, poetry, music, narrative, and so forth. Any talk about arts-informed research must take into account the characteristics of the particular art form or art forms that are being employed. Music, for example, does not have the kind of referentiality that realism in the visual arts possesses. One can come to know the countenance of an individual or the feel of a place by the features of a realist painting. There is no comparable analogue in music. Even program music, such as the William Tell Overture, is far less referential in character than what photo realists do in their work. Some art forms such as opera or theatre combine art forms. It is not unusual for a stage production to involve not only color and light, but speech and music. These synthetic art forms have different potentialities in the execution of research and need to be taken into account in planning a research agenda.

One might ask, if the arts are so diverse in their features and potentialities for research, do they have anything in common? Just what is it that enables us to refer to all of them as forms of art? For me, the defining feature that allows us to talk collectively about the arts is that art forms share the common mission of achieving expressiveness through the ways in which form has been crafted or shaped. The arts historically have addressed the task of evoking emotion. We sometimes speak of the arts as resources that can take us on a ride. The arts, as I have indicated elsewhere, provide a natural high. They can also provide a natural low. The range of emotional responses is enormous. These emotional consequences in relation to a referent color the referent by virtue of the character of the emotion that the artistically crafted form possesses. Through art we come to feel, very often, what we cannot see directly.

The views that I have just expressed are closer to a modern than to a postmodern conception of what the arts do. But I would argue that even successful postmodern art participates in the expression of emotion.

Recognizing the distinctive potential of various art forms and developing the skills and techniques to use them is a necessary condition for the achievement of effective arts-informed research.

There is, though, a serious complication in the use of nonliteral forms, and this complication has to do with precision of representation. The precision of representation I refer to is achieved by what Charles Peirce (1998) called the relationships between the referent, the symbol, and the interpretant. This triad is designed to describe a connection between an utterance and that to which it refers. If the interpretant is not clear, the referent to which a symbol refers might not be located. Thus, the more ambiguity or scope given for personal interpretation of the signified material, the less referential precision is achieved. If, however, one takes the view that the dominant function of arts in research is not necessarily to provide a precise referent for a specific symbol connected by a conventional interpretant, but rather to provide an evocative image that generates the conditions for new telling questions and for fruitful discussion, if its major function is to deepen and make more complex the conversation or increase the precision through which we vex each other (Peirce, 1998), then the need for consensus on what is signified might be less significant. But it is an issue that needs to be addressed. One can easily slip into an "anything goes" orientation that makes the research produced a kind of Rorschach test.

At the same time, to idolize precision if in the process it trivializes the questions one can raise, the problem still remains, only it is of another order. Obviously, what are needed are methods that have some significant degree of precision and, at the same time, do not reduce problems into questions that are trivial. One of the major weaknesses of the logical positivist movement was a tendency on their part to dismiss poetic and metaphorical language as meaningless utterances. This led them to regard as meaningful only propositions of an empirical kind that, in principle, could be proven through scientific procedures. For my taste, this is much too constrictive a conception of the kind of research criteria that are needed in the social sciences. If we indeed know more than we can tell, then we should try telling what we know with anything that will carry the message forward.

Bringing the message forward on new media—or even on old media for that matter—is no simple task. What are needed are skills and techniques to treat a material so that it *becomes* a medium of expression. One of the most formidable obstacles to arts-informed research is the paucity of highly skilled, artistically grounded practitioners, people who know how to use image, language, movement, in artistically refined ways. Schools of education, for example, seldom provide courses or even workshops for doctoral students to develop such skills. As a result, it is not uncommon to find this type of research appearing amateurish to those who know what the potentialities of the medium are. Furthermore, each medium requires, to some degree, its own set of skills and techniques. To be "multilingual" in this research means being able to use different media effectively to represent what one has learned.

One way to address this situation is to create teams of researchers in the social sciences who work closely with practitioners of the arts. It could be the case that such collaboration might provide a way to combine both theoretically sophisticated understandings and artistically inspired images. This too, as a putative solution, would require a new approach to not only the education of the researcher but to the kinds of dissertation projects that would be encouraged and supported. I can well imagine dissertations being prepared by groups of three or four individuals each of whom had major responsibility for some aspect of the work. It may be unrealistic to expect that someone without a background, say, in the visual arts, would be able to produce at a high enough level the quality of arts-informed research that was needed to warrant a doctoral degree. Furthermore, such work, in my view, should have both a theoretical or conceptual basis and should manifest sophistication in the arts as an achievement that I mentioned earlier. It is particularly in this sense of diverse competencies that arts-informed research is not easier, but more difficult, to do than traditional approaches to research in the social sciences.

Is there a future for arts-informed research? One can only speculate about the conditions that would create such a possibility. One of those conditions pertains to the vigor of those committed to the exploration of the arts and the means through which they help enlarge human understanding. Given the near revolutionary way in which the arts are being regarded as tools for research, I expect that there will be a variety of resistances to be encountered. These resistances need to be addressed by scholars committed to the idea and exploration of arts-informed research. Short-term enthusiasts are hardly going to be able to provide the kind of leadership, indeed the kind of courage, that such an enterprise will require. What will also be required are places in universities where young scholars interested in pursuing arts-informed research can find a sympathetic home. The Media Lab at MIT is a good example of how research might be pursued.

It is also likely that there will need to be collaborative connections made between, for example, schools of education and departments of the arts, photography, film, and videography. It takes a team to produce a docudrama, and it will take no less to create good examples of artistic inquiry. Yet the kind of collaboration I have in mind can be extremely intellectually exciting. Scholars can bring to bear under one collective umbrella ideas about matters of meaning and communication, matters of technique, and matters pertaining to theoretical knowledge that can enrich the environment and yield truly remarkable products. To encourage such activity will require a modification of promotion criteria that are typically employed in most American universities, particularly in research universities. We typically expect pre-tenure productions to be solo, yet in the hardest of the sciences, physics, work is very often collaborative. Indeed, without collaboration the work that needs to be done would not get done. The Stanford Linear Accelerator, for example, is employed by people living at the other end of the world for purposes that are jointly shared with Stanford University physicists. What this suggests is a new conception of who does research with whom, and what kind of research they do. The vision I am describing is considerably more collaborative, cooperative, multidisciplinary, and multimodal in character. Knowledge creation is a social affair. The solo producer will no longer be salient, particularly in the contexts for those wishing to do arts-informed research.

How can the discussion that has preceded be put in a summary form? Just what is it that makes possible a relationship between art and knowledge? It seems to me that the contributions of the arts to knowledge are several.

First, the arts address the qualitative nuances of situations. By learning how to read the images the arts make possible, awareness of those nuances is made possible. The examination or perception of a painting is as much a kind of "reading" as a text might be. One needs to learn how to see as well as learn how to read in the customary sense. Thus, in addressing what is subtle but significant, the arts develop dispositions and habits of mind that reveal to the individual a world he or she may not have noticed but that is there to be seen if only one knew how to look.

A second contribution the arts make to knowledge has to do with empathic feeling. Images rendered in artistically expressive form often generate a kind of empathy that makes action possible. One has only to recall images of war, whether created by Picasso as in "Guernica" or by a contemporary photographer addressing the war in Iraq, to realize that we are moved in ways that art makes. Art often creates such a powerful image that as a result we tend to see our world in terms of it, rather than it in terms of our world. Put another way, art does not always imitate life. Life often imitates art.

The ability to empathize with others is a way of understanding the character of their experience that, in some ways, is the first avenue to compassion. To achieve such an outcome, as I have indicated earlier, requires individuals skilled in the use of the medium with which they work and, of course, sensitive to the conditions they wish to render. No small task, but an extraordinarily important one.

A third contribution the arts make to knowledge has to do with the provision of a fresh perspective so that our old habits of mind do not dominate our reactions with stock responses. What we seek are new ways with which to perceive and interpret the world, ways that make vivid realities that would otherwise go unknown. It's a matter, as the anthropologists say, of making the familiar strange and making the strange familiar. To the extent to which we need to give up some of our old habits, the arts are willing and helpful allies in such a pursuit. It means, of course, relinquishing the ties that fetter the imagination. One

wants to encourage rather than to discourage the sweep of imagination in learning how to notice and understand what is not literally there. The arts contribute to the realization of such an aim.

Finally, for the purposes of this chapter, the arts tell us something about our own capacities to experience the affective responses to life that the arts evoke. If the arts are about anything, they are about emotion, and emotion has to do with the ways in which we feel. Becoming aware of our capacity to feel is a way of discovering our humanity. Art helps us connect with personal, subjective emotions, and through such a process, it enables us to discover our own interior landscape. Not an unimportant achievement.

All of the processes that I have described contribute to the enlargement of human understanding. We cannot take such conditions or characteristics or feelings into account unless they are available either by our volition or by the impact of others upon us. We come to understand the world in many ways; the arts are among these many ways. Their virtual absence in the methodology of educational research is a significant shortcoming in the ways in which we may be able to understand what goes on in classrooms and in schools, in conferences and in homes. The arts are a way of enriching our awareness and expanding our humanity. This, too, is not a bad consequence for a process so delicate but important.

Can such aims be achieved in the context of a competitive research environment? Let us hope so. But let us do more than hope. Let us embark on those studies of human action that reveal aspects of human experience and behavior that intuitively are difficult to deny. This is all to say that the quality of work done under the banner of research through the arts will be the most critical feature affecting its future. Let's hope that we are up to the task.

◆ *References*

Arnheim, R. (1974). *Art and visual perception: A psychology of the creative eye.* Berkeley: University of California Press.

Ayer, A. J. (1952). *Language, truth and logic.* New York: Courier Dover Publications.

Dewey, J. (1934). *Art as experience.* New York: Minton, Balch and Company.

Dewey, J. (2005). *The quest for certainty: A study of the relation of knowledge and action.* Whitefish, MT: Kessinger Publishing. (Original work published 1929)

Dillard, A. (1974). *Pilgrim at Tinker Creek.* New York: Harper's Magazine Press.

Langer, S. K. (1957). *Problems of art: Ten philosophical lectures.* New York: Scribner.

McKeon, R. P. (Ed.). (2001). *The basic works of Aristotle.* New York: The Modern Library.

Peirce, C. (1998). *Collected papers of Charles Sanders Peirce.* Bristol, UK: Thoemmes Continuum.

Plato (1992). *Republic.* Indianapolis, IN: Hackett Publishing Company.

Polanyi, M. (1983). *The tacit dimension.* Gloucester, MA: Peter Smith Publisher. (Original work published 1966)

2

THE ART OF INDIGENOUS KNOWLEDGE

A Million Porcupines Crying in the Dark

◆ Thomas King

There is a story I know. It's about the earth and how it floats in space on the back of a turtle. I've heard this story many times, and each time someone tells the story, it changes. Sometimes the change is simply in the voice of the storyteller. Sometimes the change is in the details. Sometimes in the order of events. Other times it's the dialogue or the response of the audience. But in all the tellings of all the tellers, the world never leaves the turtle's back. And the turtle never swims away.

One time, it was in Trois-Rivières I think, a man in the audience who was taking notes asked about the turtle and the earth. If the earth was on the back of a turtle, what was below the turtle? Another turtle, the storyteller told him. And below that turtle? Another turtle. And below that? Another turtle.

The man quickly scribbled down notes, enjoying the game, I imagine. So how many turtles are there? he wanted to know. The storyteller shrugged. No one knows for sure, she told him, but it's turtles all the way down.

Author's Note: A version of this chapter appeared in *The Truth About Stories: A Native Narrative* (2003). It is reprinted here with permission of the publishers.

The truth about stories is that that's all we are. "I will tell you something about stories," the Laguna storyteller Leslie Silko (1997) reminds us. "They aren't just entertainment/Don't be fooled/They are all we have, you see/All we have to fight off/Illness and death. You don't have anything/If you don't have the stories" (p. 2).

Over the years, I've lost more than my fair share of friends to suicide. The majority of them have been mixed-bloods. Native men and women who occupied those racial shadow zones that have been created for us and that we create for ourselves. The latest and greatest loss was the Choctaw-Cherokee-Irish writer Louis Owens, who killed himself in an airport parking garage on his way to an academic conference in Bellingham, Washington.

Louis was a fine novelist and an even better literary/cultural critic and theorist. But most especially, he was a good friend, more a brother, really. We were of a like age, shared much the same background, were haunted by the same fears. We loved fly-fishing and the solitude of quiet places. We understood in each other the same desperate desire for acceptance. And we were both hopeful pessimists. That is, we wrote knowing that none of the stories we told would change the world. But we wrote in the hope that they would.

We both knew that stories were medicine, that a story told one way could cure, that the same story told another way could injure. In his memoir *I Hear the Train,* Louis (Owens, 2001) tells the story of a summer that he spent picking tomatoes. It was 1965. The year before, the U.S. government had decided to end the Bracero Program that had brought half a million migrant workers up from Mexico each year to work in the fields of California. Faced with the continuing need for cheap labor and the prospect of a long, hot, politically dangerous summer—urban riots, Vietnam protests, and disillusioned youth had been the order of business the summer before—politicians at the state capitol came up with the bright idea of making field jobs—normally the domain of Mexican workers—available to Blacks from the inner cities and to the generic poor.

"The government men decided to call it an economic opportunity work program," Louis writes.

> Any lucky person with a sufficiently low income, they announced, could qualify to work in the fields for minimum wage. They advertised the program heavily and recruited in Los Angeles, Stockton, Compton, East Palo Alto, Oakland—those places where summer jobs for Black teens had never existed and where young Black males with time on their hands posed potential complications for the coming summer. Somehow we heard about it in Atascadero. It sounded like fun. (Owens, 2001, p. 20)

The labor camp where the workers were required to stay was an old military barracks left over from World War II that, over the years, had housed thousands of Mexican workers. Now it housed close to 300 young Black men and a handful of others. The barracks where the workers stayed were spartan at best. Old metal cots lined both sides of a long, narrow room, with mattresses flattened thin and hard as plywood by seasons of exhausted farm workers.

Best of all, a new 10-foot chain-link fence had been thrown up around the camp, topped with barbed wire to make sure no one wandered away. Each night the camp was locked and a guard stationed at the gate. Each morning Louis and the other workers were let out and taken to the fields. Each evening they were brought back and locked up again.

It was hard work. The food that was provided was inedible. Worse, the workers were charged for it. As well they were charged for their cots, for transportation to and from the fields, for insurance, and for anything else the growers could think up. And when the first payday rolled around, after all the expenses had been deducted, Louis discovered that he had spent more money than he had made. Twelve dollars to be exact.

This experiment in economic opportunity didn't last long. Three weeks. Given the rate at which the workers were going broke, it probably wouldn't have lasted much longer anyway, but halfway through the third week, a White mob from the nearby town of Merced attacked the camp with the intention of burning it down. The police held the mob off, and it contented itself with turning cars over and setting them on fire. Louis and the rest of the men stayed inside the fence, armed with metal cot legs and makeshift knives, waiting for the big fight.

But it never happened.

The mob eventually dispersed, and in the morning the workers came into the yard to find the front gate wide open, the supervisors and the guard gone. No trucks came to pick them up that day, and by afternoon, everyone began the long walk home. For many, that walk was over 300 miles, with little chance of catching a ride with a passing motorist.

In *I Hear the Train,* Louis (Owens, 2001) recalls that moment and wonders

> Where are those fellows today, the ones I picked tomatoes and played basketball and watched a mob with? Do they sit in midlife and wonder, as I do, whether it really happened at all? Whether their memories, like mine, are warped and shadowed far beyond reliability. Whether even trying to put such a thing into words is an absurd endeavor, as if such things are best left to turn and drift in inarticulate memory like those river pebbles that get worn more and more smooth over time until there are no edges. (p. 27)

Maybe this was the story Louis told himself as he sat in that airport garage. A story about poor young men walking home alone. Maybe it was another. Whichever one it was, for that instant Louis must have believed it.

Did you ever wonder how it is we imagine the world in the way we do, how it is we imagine ourselves, if not through our stories. And in the English-speaking world, nothing could be easier, for we are surrounded by stories, and we can trace these stories back to other stories and from there back to the beginnings of language. For these are our stories, the cornerstones of our culture.

You all know the names. Masculine names that grace the tables of contents of the best anthologies, all neatly arranged chronologically so we can watch the march of literary progress. A cumulative exercise in the early years, it has broadened its empire in the last few decades, sending scouting parties into new territory to find new voices. These days, English literature anthologies contain the works of women writers, Black writers, Hispanic writers, Asian writers, gay and lesbian writers, and, believe it or not, a few Native writers.

All in the cause of culture, all in the service of literacy, which we believe to be an essential skill. Indeed, the ability to read and write and keep records is understood as one of the primary markers of an advanced civilization. One of my professors at university argued that you could not have a "dependable" literature without literacy, that the two went hand in hand.

I'm sure he would have been buoyed by Statistics Canada's (1998) figures of Canadians' reading habits. According to the 1998 survey, which, so far as I can tell, was compiled through information that Canadians volunteered, approximately 80% of all Canadians from age 15 on read newspapers, 71% read magazines, and 61% read books.

Not bad.

Out of the 80% who read newspapers, 49% read a daily, which means that 39% of all Canadians read a daily newspaper.

I'm impressed.

Out of the 71% who read a magazine, 57% read at least one magazine weekly, which means that 40% of all Canadians read at least one magazine a week.

That's great.

And out of the 61% of all Canadians who read books, 31% read at least a book a week, which means about 19% of all Canadians read at least a book a week.

Fifty-two books a year.

Unless, of course, I've done the math wrong. Which is possible.

No doubt this includes students at high schools, colleges, and universities, who are "encouraged" to read. Still, if you look at just the self-confessed readers in the category of 25-year-olds and older, you'll find that the percentage stays exactly the same. Nineteen percent.

So how do they do that? Over four million Canadians reading a book a week, each and every week of the year. Well, some are parents reading to their children. Some are professionals who read for a living. Some are up at the cottage or on a beach somewhere, away from television and the phone.

And the rest?

Well, maybe it's true. Or maybe we Canadians just like to think of ourselves as more literate than we really are. Not that it matters. What's curious is that there are no statistics for oral literature. When I raised this question at a scholarly conference once, I was told that the reason we pay attention to written literature is that books are quantifiable, whereas oral literature is not. How can you quantify something that has sound but no physical form, a colleague wanted to know, something that exists only in the imagination of the storyteller, cultural ephemera that are always at the whim of

memory, something that needs to be written down to be . . . whole?

I understand the assumptions: first, that stories, in order to be complete, must be written down, an easy error to make, an ethnocentric stumble that imagines all literature in the Americas to have been oral, when in fact, pictographic systems (petroglyphs, pictographs, and hieroglyphics) were used by a great many tribes to commemorate events and to record stories, while in the valley of Mexico, the Aztecs maintained a large library of written works that may well have been the rival of the Royal Library at Alexandria. Written and oral. Side by side.

In the end, though, neither fared any better than the other. While European diseases and conflicts with explorers and settlers led to the death and displacement of a great many Native storytellers, superstitious Spanish priests, keen on saving the Aztecs from themselves, burned the library at Tenochtitlán to the ground, an event as devastating as Julius Caesar's destruction of the library at Alexandria.

In each case, at Tenochtitlán and at Alexandria, stories were lost. And, in the end, it didn't matter whether these stories were oral or written.

So much for dependability. So much for permanence. Though it doesn't take a disaster to destroy a literature. If we stopped telling the stories and reading the books, we would discover that neglect is as powerful an agent as war and fire.

In 1980, through a series of mishaps and happenstance, my 9-year-old son and I moved from Salt Lake City, Utah, to Lethbridge, Alberta. The details of the move—divorce, unemployment, depression—are too boring to explicate. The reason for the move, however, was simple. The University of Lethbridge had offered me a job. I had been to Lethbridge before. A good friend of mine, Leroy Little Bear, had brought me up as a speaker for Indian Days at the university. So I had seen the lay of the land. As it were.

And it was flat.

Flat, dry, windy, dusty. Nothing like the Northern California coast that I loved. And the last place on earth I wanted to work. But when you don't have a job, something always looks better than nothing.

So we moved. I bought an old step-side pickup from a government auction, packed everything I owned in the back, strapped my son into the passenger's seat, and headed north.

Just before we got to Sweetgrass and the border between Alberta and Montana, heavy rain turned into heavy hail, and we had to make a run for a freeway overpass. There, under the concrete canopy along with several other cars and trucks, we waited out the storm.

Which wasn't about to give up easily. The hail picked up pace, turning the road in front of us into a skating rink, and my son, who even at nine was not one to put sugar on sorrow, turned to me and said, "Just so we keep it straight, Dad, this was your idea."

The second assumption about written literature is that it has an inherent sophistication that oral literature lacks, that oral literature is a primitive form of written literature, a precursor to written literature, and as we move from the cave to the condo, we slough off the oral and leave it behind.

Like an old skin.

The Kiowa writer N. Scott Momaday (1968), in his novel *House Made of Dawn*, touches on the written and the oral, on the cultural understandings of language and literature. The White man, Momaday argues, takes

> such things as words and literatures for granted . . . for nothing in his world is so commonplace. . . . He is sated and insensitive; his regard for language . . . as an

instrument of creation has diminished nearly to the point of no return. It may be that he will perish by the Word.

But of his Kiowa grandmother, who could neither read nor write and whose use of language was confined to speech, Momaday says that

> her regard for words was always keen in proportion as she depended upon them . . . for her words were medicine; they were magic and invisible. They came from nothing into sound and meaning. They were beyond price; they could neither be bought nor sold. And she never threw words away. (pp. 95–96)

Perhaps it was this quality of medicine and magic that sent 19th- and 20th-century anthropologists and ethnographers west to collect and translate Native stories, thereby "preserving" Native oral literature before it was lost. As a result of these efforts, an impressive body of oral stories is now stored in periodicals and books that one can find at any good research library.

Not that anyone reads them. But they are safe and sound. As it were.

At the same time that social scientists were busy preserving Native oral culture, Native people were beginning to write. Depending on how far you want to stretch the definition of literature, you can begin in the late 18th century with Samson Occum, who collected hymns and spirituals, or you can wait until the 19th century and begin with George Copway's autobiography or Alice Callahan's novel or E. Pauline Johnson's poetry.

I'm tempted to say the names of all of the early Native writers aloud, though such a long and comprehensive list would probably put everybody to sleep. Still, such a name-dropping exercise might impress you and make me look scholarly and learned.

And truth be told, I can live with that.

Perhaps I could frame such a bibliography as a eulogy to remind myself of where stories come from, a chance to remember that I stand in a circle of storytellers, most of whom will never be published, who have only their imaginations and their voices.

That sounds rather romantic, doesn't it? Circles of storytellers. Oral voices in the night. You can almost hear the violins.

I mean the drums.

The point I wanted to make was that the advent of Native written literature did not, in any way, mark the passing of Native oral literature. In fact, they occupy the same space, the same time. And, if you know where to stand, you can hear the two of them talking to each other.

Robert Alexie's (2002) *Porcupines and China Dolls,* for instance, and Harry Robinson's (1989) *Write It On Your Heart,* along with Ruby Slipperjack's (1987) *Honour the Sun* and Eden Robinson's (2000) *Monkey Beach.* A novel, a collection of stories, and two more novels. Canadians all. Though the border doesn't mean that much to the majority of Native people in either country. It is, after all, a figment of someone else's imagination.

But I'll start this discussion of literature with an American example. Partly because I have to, and partly because I have a perverse streak and, at times, would rather annoy than placate.

So, the first thing to say about the advent of the modern period in Native written literature is that it begins with the publication of N. Scott Momaday's 1968 novel *House Made of Dawn,* a book that won the Pulitzer Prize. But what makes the novel special and what allows us to use it as a starting point are the questions that it raises and its concern with narrative strategies. As well as what it avoids.

With the long and problematic history that Native people have had with Europeans in North America, it would be reasonable to expect that, when Native writers took to the novel, they would go to the past for setting in order to argue against the rather lopsided and ethnocentric view of Indians that novelists and historians had created.

James Fenimore Cooper, for instance.

Cooper, whose sympathies lay with the wealthy, landowner class of 19th-century America, had a somewhat romantic view of Indians that saw them either as noble or savage. Noble Indians helped Whites and died for their trouble. Savage Indians hindered Whites and died for their trouble. A rather simplistic division. But Cooper took the matter further. What is it, Cooper asked himself, that makes Indians different from Whites? Why is it that Indians and Whites can never come together?

His answer was gifts. Indian gifts. And White gifts.

In *The Deerslayer* (Cooper, 1963), the first (chronologically, that is) of the five *Leatherstocking Tales,* Cooper's protagonist, Natty Bumppo, aka Deerslayer, later to be known as Hawkeye, gets into a running philosophical discussion with Henry March, a boorish frontiersman, on the matter of race. "Now skin makes the man," March tells Deerslayer.

This is reason—else how are people to judge each other? The skin is put on, over all, in order that when a creature or a mortal is fairly seen, you may know at once what to make of him. (Cooper, 1963, p. 50)

Here is the essence of racism. "Skin makes the man." A simple declaration that divides the world up quickly. March believes that anyone who is not White is inferior, but he's a bigot and a scoundrel whose morality is suspect, and readers have little sympathy for the man or his views. Deerslayer, on the other hand, objects to March's simple divisions and offers an explanation for difference that, on the surface, is more complex and balanced. Indians and Whites, Deerslayer argues, while having different-colored skin, are still both men, men with "different gifts and traditions, but, in the main, with the same natur'. Both have souls," he tells us, "and both will be held accountable for their deeds in this life" (Cooper, 1963, p. 50).

Though both are not necessarily equal.

"God made us all," Cooper says through Deerslayer,

> white, black, red—and no doubt had his own wise intentions in coloring us differently. Still, he made us, in the main, much the same in feelin's, though I'll not deny that he gave each race its gifts. A white man's gifts are Christianized, while a redskin's are more for the wilderness. (Cooper, 1963, p. 41)

As it turns out, March and Deerslayer are not arguing different points of view, they are arguing variations of the same view. Cooper isn't arguing for equality. He's arguing for separation, using some of the same arguments that 1950s America would use for segregating Blacks from Whites. Indians aren't necessarily inferior. They just have different gifts. Their skin color isn't the problem. It's their natures.

So what exactly are these gifts? What are these natures that mark out a people?

Well, according to Deerslayer, revenge is an Indian gift and forgiveness is a White gift. Indians have devious natures, while Whites believe the best of a person. "You were treacherous, according to your natur'," Deerslayer tells an Indian he has just mortally wounded, "and I was a little oversightful, as I'm apt to be in trusting others" (p. 116).

In the end, all Cooper is doing here is reiterating the basic propagandas that the British would use to justify their subjugation of India or the Germans would employ in their extermination of Jews, or that the Jews would utilize to displace Palestinians, or that North Americans would exploit for the internment of the Japanese, or that the United States military and the United States media would craft into jingoistic slogans in order to make the invasions of other countries—Grenada, Panama, Afghanistan, Iraq—seem reasonable, patriotic, and entertaining to television audiences throughout North America.

Reason and Instinct.

White gifts in Cooper's novel are gifts of Reason. Indian gifts in Cooper's novel are gifts of Instinct.

It would be reasonable to expect Native writers to want to revisit and reconstruct the literary and historical past, but oddly enough—with few exceptions such as James Welch's *Fools Crow* (1987) and *The Heartsong of Charging Elk* (2000), and Linda Hogan's (1992) *Mean Spirit*—contemporary Native writers have shown little interest in using the past as setting, preferring instead to place their fictions in the present.

And I don't have a good answer for why this is true. Though I do have some suspicions. I think that, by the time Native writers began to write in earnest and in numbers, we discovered that the North American version of the past was too well populated, too well defended. By 1968, the cowboy/Indian dichotomy was so firmly in place and had been repeated and re-inscribed so many times that there was no chance of dislodging it from the culture. Like it or not, it was a permanent landmark, and Native writers who went to that past ran into the demand that Indians had to be noble and tragic and perform all their duties on horseback.

What Native writers discovered, I believe, was that the North American past, the one that had been created in novels and histories, the one that had been heard on radio and seen on theatre screens and on television, the one that had been part of every school curriculum for the last 200 years, that past was unusable, for it had not only trapped Native people in a time warp, it also insisted that our past was all we had.

No present.

No future.

And to believe in such a past is to be dead.

Faced with such a proposition and knowing from empirical evidence that we were very much alive, physically and culturally, Native writers began to use the Native present as a way to resurrect a Native past and to imagine a Native future—to create, in words, as it were, a Native universe.

I had been teaching at Lethbridge for about a month when a couple of young men from the Blood reserve arrived at my office. Narcisse Blood and Martin Heavyhead. Both of them played basketball in an all-Native league, and they had come to talk me into playing for the team. I told them I was too old and too slow. I told them I couldn't dribble or shoot or block shots.

It's okay, Narcisse told me, you're nice and big and can get in the way.

So I said yes. I was lonely, wanted to be liked, wanted to be accepted. Even if I couldn't play, I could at least make the effort. But in the first game, I was amazing. Every time I lumbered to the basket, the other players got out of my way. When I took a shot, no one tried to stop me. I scored six points that night. The next game I scored eight.

The matter began to unravel in the third game. One of their guards drove the lane. I stepped in front of him, tried to block the shot, and both of us went down in a heap.

The guard who had run into me leaped up, concerned.

You okay?

Sure, I told him.

Nothing rattled loose, eh?

I have to admit, no one had ever asked me that. Rattled loose?

You know, the guard said, looking embarrassed. The plate.

Plate? I said. What plate?

In your head.

It turned out that Narcisse had told the other teams that when I had come up from Salt Lake City, I had run into a hailstorm, lost control of the truck, and flipped it. A serious accident that left me with a plate in my head. Everything was okay as long as I didn't get bumped, because if I did get bumped and the plated slipped, I would go berserk. It happened once during a practice, Narcisse had told everyone, and the guy was still in the hospital.

I don't have a plate in my head.

And with that imprudent remark, my basketball career went down the toilet. As soon as the rest of the teams in the league found out that they were in no danger from plate slippage, I was a marked man. I don't think I scored two points the rest of the season.

Now, where was I?

Oh, yes. Native writers creating a Native universe. For N. Scott Momaday (1968), the answer, in part, was to write a novel in which aspects of an unfamiliar universe stood close enough to parts of a known world so that the non-Native reader, knowing the one, might recognize the other. Ironically, Christianity, which had been a door barred against Native–non-Native harmony and understanding, suddenly became an open window through which we could see and hear each other.

House Made of Dawn, reduced to a Coles Notes blurb, is the story of a young Native man who returns from World War II to discover that he no longer has a place in the Pueblo world that he left. The return of the Native. No problem here. A common enough theme. Until Momaday begins to complicate it.

The protagonist's name is Abel, a name filled with import for a non-Native audience, conjuring up as it does a whole host of Christian concerns. Abel is Adam and Eve's son and Cain's brother, and it is Abel whom Cain kills.

Which should be the end of the story. But where Abel's story in the Bible ends, Momaday's story begins. And here is Abel's dilemma. When he returns from the horror and destruction of World War II, he discovers that he has no voice—not literally but figuratively—a condition that proves to be symptomatic of a larger confusion, a confusion surrounding the nature of good and evil, not just in the world that Momaday creates but in the world at large as well. In making parts of a Native universe visible, Momaday also examines the assumptions that the White world makes about good and evil. Using the occasion of the war and Abel's trial for killing an albino Indian, Momaday reminds us that within the Christian dichotomy, good and evil always oppose each other.

Which is why war, even with its inherent horror and destruction, can be presented and pursued as a righteous activity. And it's why Abel's trial is not concerned with the reasons he killed the albino but only with the simpler matter of whether or not he was responsible for the man's death. These questions, good/bad, guilty/innocent, are simple questions, their answers familiar and satisfying for Momaday's non-Native audience, and these moments of recognition allow him to re-ask the same questions, this time within a Pueblo context.

And here, the answers are not so familiar, not so easy, for within the Pueblo world, evil and good are not so much distinct and opposing entities as they are tributaries of the same river. In this world, old men in white leggings chase evil in the night, "not in the hope of anything, but hopelessly; neither in fear nor hatred nor despair of evil, but simply in recognition and with respect" (Momaday, 1968, pp. 103–104). And strong men on strong horses try to pull a live rooster out of the sand, only to destroy the bird by beating it to pieces against a fellow rider.

The runners after evil and the feast of Santiago. Strange moments in a strange world.

But not good and evil.

Rather, two ceremonies, ceremonies that describe a part of the complexity of the lives of the Pueblo people, ceremonies where the basic Christian oppositions have little meaning. For both of these moments are celebrations, acknowledgments, if you will, one of the presence of evil in the world while doing nothing to encourage or prevent it, the other of the need for sacrifice and renewal.

The temptation here, of course, is to dissect each scene, separate out the elements, and organize them according to color. The ceremonial run is good. The presence of evil is bad. The rooster pull is a form of competition and therefore good. The destruction of the rooster by beating it to death against another human being is cruel.

How we love our binaries.

But what Momaday and other Native writers suggest is that there are other ways of imagining the world, ways that do not depend so much on oppositions as they do on co-operations, and they raise the tantalizing question of what else one might do if confronted with the appearance of evil.

So just how would we manage a universe in which the attempt to destroy evil is seen as a form of insanity?

Relax. It's only fiction.

Besides, Native writers aren't arguing that evil isn't evil or that it doesn't exist. They're suggesting that trying to destroy it is misguided, even foolish. That the attempt risks disaster.

But you don't need Native writers to tell you that. Grab a copy of *Moby Dick* and consider the saga of Captain Ahab, wrapped in rage, as he roams the oceans in search of the great white whale, accomplishing little more than the destruction of his ship and crew; or turn on your television and watch a vengeful United States, burdened with the arms of war, bomb the world into goodness and supply-side capitalism, destroying American honor and credibility in the process.

Of course, Native writers are engaged in much more than a literary debate over the nature of good and evil. While writers such as N. Scott Momaday and Leslie Silko examine these tensions, other Native writers have taken on other concerns. Gerald Vizenor borrows traditional figures, such as the Trickster, re-imagines them within a contemporary context, and sets them loose in a sometimes modern, sometimes postapocalyptic world. James Welch looks at the question of identity, of place, and the value of names. Louise Erdrich explores the shadow land of resistance. Simon Ortiz captures the rhythms of traditional song and ceremony in his poetry. Tomson Highway handles the difficult matter of reserve community and gender and family relationships. Lee Maracle and Jeannette Armstrong show how traditional wisdom and customs can suggest ways to conduct oneself in the present.

But what is most satisfying is knowing that there are Native writers whose names I have never heard of, who are, at this minute, creating small panoramas of contemporary Native life by looking backward and forward with the same glance.

Not so differently from non-Native writers. The magic of Native literature—as with other literatures—is not in the themes of the stories—identity, isolation, loss, ceremony, community, maturation, home—it is in the way meaning is refracted by cosmology, the way understanding is shaped by cultural paradigms.

Narcisse Blood is a good friend. One time he took me out to visit his grandfather, who lived in a small house on the reserve. The old man had a garden, and he took me through it, showing me each plant. Later we had tea in his kitchen.

"Did I know about the big storm?" he asked.

I had to admit that I didn't.

"It was a big one," he said. "It came up quick and hard."

So I told him about my trip from Salt Lake City to Lethbridge and how we had been trapped under a freeway overpass by a storm.

"Yes, those storms can be tricky," he told me. "You see those tomatoes out there?"

From the kitchen window you could see his garden. The tomato plants were just beginning to produce fruit.

"When that storm came through, I was just getting ready to pick my tomatoes. They were big and red. Real ripe. But that storm beat me to it. First the rain. And then the hail."

And here the old man stopped and helped himself to more tea. And then he sat back and looked at the table.

I tried to be sympathetic. "You must have been upset," I said.

"Nope," said the old man, without even the hint of a smile. "Always good to have some ketchup."

During the 1960s, when many of us hoped that love would prove more powerful than hate, herds of young people—"hippies," if you were from Yorkville, or "flower children," if you were from Haight-Ashbury, or "bums," if you were from Pittsburgh—made their way to reserves and reservations throughout North America, sure that Native people possessed the secret to life. Or at least something middle-class North America didn't have.

That something turned out to be poverty. Or at least poverty was what they saw. And as quickly as they arrived, most left. After all, living simply was one thing, being poor was quite another.

What was not readily apparent at first glance from the window of a Volkswagen van or from the comfort of a refitted school bus was the intimate relationship that Native people had with the land. And here I am not talking about the romantic and spiritual clichés that have become so popular with advertisers, land developers, and well-meaning people with backpacks. Although the relationship that Native people have with the land certainly has a spiritual aspect to it, it is also a practical matter that balances respect with survival. It is an ethic that can be seen in the decisions and actions of a community and that is contained in the songs that Native people sing and the stories that they tell about the nature of the world and their place in it, about the webs of responsibilities that bind all things. Or, as the Mohawk writer Beth Brant (1990) put it, "We do not worship nature. We are part of it" (p. 119).

This is the territory of Native oral literature. And it is the territory of contemporary Native written literature. The difference is this: Instead of waiting for you to come to us, as we have in the past, written literature has allowed us to come to you.

I'd like to say that both efforts have been worth it. But I'm not sure they have. It seems to me that sharing our oral stories with ethnographers and anthropologists and sharing our written stories with non-Native audiences have produced pretty much the same results. And, at best, they have been mixed.

Some of the essential questions that Native storytellers and writers have raised about, say, the nature of good and evil have been ignored. The Trickster figure—a complex arrangement of appetites and desires—has been reduced to cartoon elements. The land as a living entity has become a mantra for industries that destroy the environment. Mother earth, a potent phrase for Native people, has been abused to the point where it has no more power or import than the word "freedom" tumbling out of George W. Bush's mouth.

It is true that scholars have taken on the task of considering Native literatures within a postcolonial context, and this, in and of itself, has been heartening, but most of us don't live in the university, and I can only imagine that the majority of Native people would be more amused by the gymnastics of theoretical language—hegemony and subalternity, indeed—than impressed.

All of which will sound as if I'm suggesting that Native writers should only write for Native readers, that these are our stories, that we should tell them for ourselves.

If only things were that simple.

Yet, truth be told, this is what it appears we are beginning to do. Remember those four writers I started to mention? The Canadians (if you believe in maps): Robert Alexie and Harry Robinson, Ruby Slipperjack and Eden Robinson? These four are creating their fictions, I believe, primarily for a Native audience, making a conscious decision not so much to ignore non-Native readers as to write for the very people they write about.

No, I can't prove it.

So it's lucky for me that literary analysis is not about proof, only persuasion. In our cynical world, where suspicion is a necessity, insisting that something is true is not nearly as powerful as suggesting that something might be true.

So allow me to suggest that we look at Robert Alexie's novel *Porcupines and China Dolls* just as an example. One of the more intriguing offerings in 2002, the book neither generated much critical acclaim nor made any of the shortlists for literary prizes. The blurb on the jacket of the Stoddart edition warns us that this is the "story of a journey from the dark side of reality . . . a story of pain and healing, of making amends and finding truth, of the inability of a people to hold on to their way of life."

Certainly sounds like the Indians we know.

The jacket copy also makes it sound as though *Porcupines and China Dolls* could be one of those depressing indictments of social policy and racial bias, a case study docudrama with all the romantic underpinnings and tragic disasters of a good soap opera.

But Alexie is not writing *that* story, and he is not writing for *that* audience.

"In order to understand this story," Alexie (2002) says in the first chapter, "it is important to know the People and where they came from and what they went through" (p. 5) and for the first two chapters, Alexie gives the reader a lightning-quick tour that includes a mention of creation, the arrival of Whites in 1789, the arrival of missionaries in 1850, and a brief history of life at a residential school.

All in the first sixteen pages.

For the non-Native reader, this briefing is too little to do much good. For the Native reader (and in this case, a particular Native reader) who knows the history and the way the weight of this knowing settles over the rest of the book, it is simply a way of saying "once upon a time."

In *Porcupines and China Dolls,* James Nathan and Jake Noland return from Aberdeen residential school, where the girls had been scrubbed and powdered to look like china dolls and the boys had been scrubbed and sheared to look like porcupines, and where each night, when the children cried in their beds, the sound was like "a million porcupines crying in the dark" (p. 12).

Native writers are particularly keen on the return of the Native. Momaday's (1968) Abel returns from World War II, as does Silko's (1997) Tayo. James Welch's (1986) unnamed narrator in *Winter in the Blood* returns from the city, as do June and Albertine in Louise Erdrich's (1984) *Love Medicine*. In *Slash,* Jeannette Armstrong's (1985) Tommy Kelasket comes home from jail, as does Garnet Raven in Richard Wagamese's (1994) *Keeper'n Me.* And, for that matter, in my first novel, *Medicine River* (King, 1990), Will also comes home.

These returns often precipitate a quest or a discovery or a journey. For James and Jake, their return involves simply a sorting out, an ordering of relationships, memories, and possibilities, an attempt to come to terms with the past, an attempt to find a future.

I suspect that many people who come to this book will leave it annoyed and/or puzzled and/or bored by the novel's biting satire, by its refusal to resolve the tensions that it creates, and by a narrative style that privileges repetition, hyperbole, and orality as storytelling strategies. Non-Native readers will probably tire of hearing about the sound of "a million porcupines crying in the dark" and cringe at the mantra of people growing 10, then 20, then 30, then 40 feet tall with pride as they "disclose" the sexual abuse they suffered at residential school or the relentless cycle of attempts and failures as characters try to put their lives in order. But in all this, there is a delightful inventiveness of tone, a strength of purpose that avoids the hazards of the lament and allows the characters the pleasure of laughing at themselves and their perils. For the Native reader, these continuing attempts of the community to right itself and the omnipresent choruses of sadness and humor, of tragedy and sarcasm, become, in the end, an honor song of sorts, a song many of us have heard before.

All Natives?

Of course not.

There's no magic in the blood that provides us with an ethnic memory. But there are more of us who know this song than there should be.

So what? What difference does it make if we write for a non-Native audience or a Native audience, when the fact of the matter is that we need to reach both?

Take Louis Owens, for instance. Maybe if *Porcupines and China Dolls* had been written earlier and more people had read the novel and understood the story, Louis and the rest of those workers wouldn't have had to walk home that summer.

I don't believe it, but then, I'm a cynic.

Maybe if Louis had had the chance to read Alexie's book, he would have gotten on that plane and gone to the conference.

I'm not sure I believe this, either.

Ironically, in many ways, Louis's story is Alexie's story. At the beginning and the end of *Porcupines and China Dolls,* James puts the barrel of a gun in his mouth and pulls the trigger. And in the novel, as in life, whether he lives or dies depends on which story he believes.

And this I do believe.

Which is why I tell those three stories over and over again. The story of the time my son and I came to Canada. The story of my short career as a basketball player. The story of an old man and his garden.

And there are others.

I tell them to myself, to my friends, sometimes to strangers. Because they make me laugh. Because they are a particular kind of story. Saving stories, if you will. Stories that help keep me alive.

Of course, you don't have to pay attention to any of these stories. Louis's story is not particularly cheery. Alexie's story doesn't have a demonstrably happy ending. Neither participates fully in Western epistemologies, and my three don't have a moral center nor are they particularly illuminating.

But help yourself to one if you like.

Take Louis's story, for instance. It's yours. Do with it what you will. Cry over it. Get angry. Forget it. But don't say in years to come that you would have lived your life differently if only you had heard this story.

You've heard it now.

◆ References

Alexie, R. (2002). *Porcupines and china dolls.* Toronto, Ontario, Canada: Stoddart.

Armstrong, J. C. (1985). *Slash.* Penticton, British Columbia, Canada: Theytus Books.

Brant, B. (1990). Recovery and transformation: The blue heron. In R. Brewer & L. Albrecht (Eds.), *Bridges of power* (pp. 118–121). Gabiola, British Columbia, Canada: New Society Publishing.

Cooper, J. F. (1963). *The deerslayer.* New York: New American Library.

Erdrich, L. (1984). *Love medicine: A novel.* New York: Holt, Rinehart & Winston.

Glancy, D. (1996). *Pushing the bear: A novel of the trail of tears.* New York: Harcourt Brace & Company.

Hogan, L. (1992). *Mean spirit: A novel.* New York: Ballantine Books.

King, T. (1990). *Medicine River.* Markham, Ontario, Canada: Viking.

Momaday, N. S. (1968). *House made of dawn.* New York: Harper & Row.

Owens, L. (2001). *I hear the train: Reflections, inventions, refractions.* Norman: University of Oklahoma Press.

Robinson, E. (2000). *Monkey beach.* Toronto, Ontario, Canada: Alfred A. Knopf.

Robinson, H. (1989). *Write it on your heart: The epic world of an Okanagan storyteller* (W. Wickwire, Ed.). Vancouver, British Columbia, Canada: Talonbooks, Theytus.

Silko, L. (1997). *Ceremony.* New York: Viking Press.

Slipperjack, R. (1987). *Honour the sun: Extracted and revised from the diary of the Owl.* Winnipeg, Manitoba, Canada: Pemmican Publications.

Statistics Canada. (1998). *General social survey of time use.* Retrieved August 25, 2005, from http://www40.statcan.ca/l01/cst01/famil36a.htm?sdi=reading

Wagamese, R. (1994). *Keeper'n me.* Toronto, Ontario, Canada: Doubleday.

Welch, J. (1986). *Winter in the blood.* New York: Penguin Books.

Welch, J. (1987). *Fools crow.* New York: Penguin Books.

Welch, J. (2000). *The heartsong of Charging Elk: A novel.* New York: Doubleday.

PART II

METHODOLOGIES

Incorporating the arts into research methodology involves much more than adding a splash of color or an illustrative image or an evocative turn of phrase or a new media track. There is much more to methodology than method. Carrying on with the idea that understanding the deep structure of any methodology is vital, this section includes a range of theoretical positions and approaches taken by those who involve the arts in qualitative research. Chapter authors from a variety of intellectual traditions and contexts define and describe research methodologies that employ the arts (conceptually and/or with respect to process or representational form). Each methodology has its own theoretical framework, unique elements, defining features, and procedural focus. It is not our intention to offer these as an exhaustive or comprehensive panoply or even to suggest that these methodologies, as described here, are themselves finite. As with all things qualitative, they are in perpetual, evolutionary motion. What we do intend, though, is to communicate, through these chapters, the depth and complexity inherent in employing the arts as a means to knowledge advancement through research.

- Art-Based Research, *Shaun McNiff*
- Visual Images in Research, *Sandra Weber*
- Arts-Informed Research, *Ardra L. Cole and J. Gary Knowles*
- Arts-Based Research, *Susan Finley*
- A/R/Tographers and Living Inquiry, *Stephanie Springgay, Rita L. Irwin, and Sylvia Kind*
- Lyric Inquiry, *Lorri Neilsen*

3

ART-BASED RESEARCH

◆ Shaun McNiff

◆ *The Domain*

I never made a painting as a work of art, it's all research.

—Pablo Picasso

Art-based research can be defined as the systematic use of the artistic process, the actual making of artistic expressions in all of the different forms of the arts, as a primary way of understanding and examining experience by both researchers and the people that they involve in their studies. These inquiries are distinguished from research activities where the arts may play a significant role but are essentially used as data for investigations that take place within academic disciplines that utilize more traditional scientific, verbal, and mathematic descriptions and analyses of phenomena.

The domain of art-based research, a more focused application of the larger epistemological process of artistic knowing and inquiry, has come into existence as an extension of a significant increase of studies researching the nature of the art experience in higher education and professional practice (McNiff, 1998a). As an artist, I began in the early 1970s to investigate artistic processes with the methods of psychology. Although I learned a great deal from these studies and continue to work closely with various human science disciplines, I realized with the assistance of my graduate students that the arts, with their long legacies of researching experience, could be used as primary modes of inquiry, especially when it came to exploring the nature of art and its creation. As colleges and universities offer master's and doctoral programs that combine the arts with other disciplines and artists look for ways to use their skills as researchers, the academic environment is becoming more responsive to new methods of investigation. These trends owe a great deal to Rudolf Arnheim (1954, 1966) and Susanne Langer (1951, 1953), who validated the cognitive aspects of the arts to large academic audiences and established the intellectual basis for approaching art making as serious inquiry.

Rather than just reflecting upon artistic phenomena in case studies, interviews, and other explanatory texts, students now ask if they can pursue the process of painting to learn more about a particular aspect of painting or elicit the creative imagination to let the characters in their expressions describe themselves and their experiences, and so forth. We are discovering how these art-based methods, making use of a larger spectrum of creative intelligence and communications, generate important information that often feels more accurate, original, and intelligent than more conventional descriptions.

I have been surprised by the enthusiastic way in which the idea of art-based research has been received. When I published *Art-Based Research* in 1998, informed by what I learned from my graduate students, primarily at the master's degree level, I was ready to have the work dismissed by the research community. Instead I discovered how the idea of researching human experience through the arts makes complete sense to people, especially those of us who long to

integrate art with service to others and revive partnerships between art and science.

I have always used the arts as primary modes of inquiry, but it was the simple action of naming this process "art-based research" that carried the work into major new dimensions of possibility. I advocate small "r" research and the demystification of the social science research enterprise that tends to separate research from practice.

In this chapter, I attempt to gather together many different examples and vignettes of what art-based research can be together with suggestions regarding methodology. I also try to show in working with a dream how knowing through the arts takes place in ways that are distinctly different yet complementary to more logical cognition and how artists throughout history can serve as models for art-based inquiry. My goal is one of inciting a sense of the vast potential that lies in this area.

◆ *Art-Based Inquiries*

My work as a researcher took a decisive new turn in 1989 when I used my own art as the primary mode of inquiry in *Depth Psychology of Art*. I felt that this more direct and firsthand approach enabled me to get closer to the artistic process than I could by interviewing others. I have great respect for the latter research method, but I wanted to explore something more experimental and empirical. I asked myself the kinds of questions that I had previously posed to others, and I responded through the artistic process as well as through words.

In *Art as Medicine: Creating a Therapy of the Imagination* (McNiff, 1992), I continued engaging my art as the basis of inquiry. I used my practice of responding to paintings with imaginal dialogue to perfect this method originating within the Jungian tradition (Chodorow, 1997; Hillman, 1977, 1978, 1979; Watkins, 1983) and make it more useful for others. I worked with a series of 26 paintings made over an extended period of time and responded to each through imaginal dialogue that I recorded, edited, and presented in the book as a demonstration of the process.

There is no better way to understand a particular aspect of creative practice than to research it in this direct way. Since I was also growing increasingly uncomfortable in using others to advance my ideas and methods, firsthand empirical experimentation offered a practical resolution to these ethical concerns. The focus of my research shifted away from experimenting with human subjects and toward the more direct examination of the artistic process. I want to emphasize how even though these artistic expressions may come from within me, I nevertheless attempt to study the art objects and the process of making them with as much objectivity as possible. I am intimately connected to what I make, and this relationship can further understanding, but it is still separate from me. The examination is both heuristic and empirical and thoroughly artistic.

I continue to expand this work with my ongoing explorations in which I respond to paintings through movement, vocal improvisation, performance, poetry, and ritual. I use my experimentation with these processes, as well as my experience with others as a "teacher-researcher" (Gallas, 1994), to learn more about how varied media can offer interpretations of art works that transcend the linear narratives that we conventionally use to respond to art. All of this research is part of my life-long examination of the process of interpreting art in more sensitive, imaginative, and accurate ways.

My teaching and personal artistic expressions have been the primary domains of my art-based research. In my studio classes we involve ourselves in particular forms of artistic expression, and then we systematically describe and reflect upon what we did, comparing our experiences to those of others in the group and to materials presented in published literature. We explore issues such as how movement improvisation offers something to the interpretation of art that cannot be accessed in words, how many people find it easier to have an imaginal dialogue with another person's painting than one of their own, and so forth.

For those who wonder how one of these ideas can be expanded into a research project, a study might focus on the process of making paintings and then responding to the pictures through movement with the objective of exploring how movement interpretations can further understanding in ways that are different from narrative description.

The artist-researcher might create a series of paintings over a period of time and then set up a research protocol whereby the artist interprets the image through spontaneous body movement in the presence of one or more witnesses. The paintings can be both large and small and in any medium and with totally open-ended subject matter (my personal preference), but individual researchers may wish to limit choices, variables of size, media, color, subject matter, and so forth, in keeping with the goals of the particular project. A study of movement interpretation can focus on paintings in a gallery made by others, although my interest as an artist, art therapist, and teacher has always focused on how different sensory expressions can help us to further relationships with our own art.

A specific and constant period of time might be given for the movement responses (i.e., 2 to 5 minutes), with the witness serving as timekeeper. Recorded dialogue and notes after the movement process can then focus on the unique features of the movement interpretations, new insights that they generate, how they affect a person's perception of the painting, whether or not the movement process helps the artist become more intimately connected to the painting, how fear and resistance to moving may influence the process, and so forth. These same questions can be explored systematically over a series of sessions.

The study might also engage the witness in responding to the painting before or after the artist moves. Other designs might involve both the witness and artist-researcher making paintings and responding to each other's work, or video documentation might be introduced—the variables and protocols are endless, and each direction offers new areas of research and learning. My recommendation as described later in this chapter is to keep the project design as simple, systematic, and constant as possible since the creative process will inevitably present variability and depth.

As someone with extensive experience working with both artists and beginners, I can report that in many forms of art-based research personal skills are essentially variables that need to be noted. In most art media, with the exception of playing musical instruments where expression requires technical ability, the absence of experience may even be viewed in a positive way as limiting bias. The persistent challenge that I face with both artists and beginners is the very universal resistance to new and unfamiliar modes of expressions that I embrace as a natural force that can draw attention to the need to let go and act with more spontaneity.

People often ask how the arts can research problems and questions outside the domain of artistic expression or how knowledge gained from artistic practice can be applied to experience within organizations and communities that might appear to have little direct

relation to art. In *Creating With Others: The Practice of Imagination in Life, Art, and the Workplace* (McNiff, 2003), I give examples of how the arts help us improve the way we interact with others by learning how to let go of negative attitudes and excessive needs for control, learning how to foster more open and original ways of perceiving situations and problems, gaining new insights and sensitivities toward others, learning how the slipstream of group expression can carry us to places where we cannot go alone, learning how to create supportive environments that inspire creative thought, and realizing that nothing happens in creative expression unless we show up and start working on a project, even with little sense of where we might ultimately go with it.

Using art-based research methods outside the circumscribed area of people already committed to artistic expression can be a challenging yet intriguing prospect. Let me try and give a possible example based on my experience with percussion in groups. We might ask how sustained rhythmic expression with drums can help people to transform conflict in organizations. The basic premise of this possible study might be that drumming and rhythm can connect people to forces of transformation and insight outside the realm of rational thought. How do the physical vibrations, energies, discipline, and physical expression of drumming alter our relationship toward particular phenomena? Can a creative process such as drumming be more effective in transforming a conflict than verbal interventions? How does the drumming activity further letting go, inspiration, focus, safety, and the power of the group slipstream?

As stated previously, the variable of the drummer's skill will influence outcomes. A person capable of creating a resonant and pure pulse with the drum is more likely to evoke the various influences and powers of this type of expression than someone who is self-conscious and unable to access the expressive qualities of the instrument and who experiences frustrations with the medium that might ultimately increase tension. The type of drum, the nature of its voice—deep and soothing versus sharp and penetrating—will also have an impact on the outcome. Therefore, the study might involve a leader who sets the pulse, provides quality instruments, and draws less experienced drummers into the rhythm. I predict that the skills of the leader in engaging others will have a significant impact on the quality of the experience.

The drumming process and the rhythms it generates offer many opportunities for verbal descriptions of effects on people. As a thoroughly empirical activity it also lends itself to different kinds of measurement. The sounds can be recorded with the goal of identifying patterns, variations, and other distinguishing features. I have always supported collaboration between art-based research and traditional scientific methods when questions and problems call for this kind of inquiry.

The simple question of how sustained rhythm in the practice of drumming can help us deal with a personal or group problem opens up numerous directions for inquiry and new learning. However, many people will instinctively say, "What in the world does drumming have to do with solving the problems I am having at work or with another person? I need more direct and practical help. I can't waste my time in a drum group."

Perhaps the perception of a drumming experiment being strange or irrelevant may be a key to its ultimate value since it offers different and new ways of thinking about and dealing with problems. In keeping with the dynamics of the creative process, what appears most removed from the problem at hand may offer a useful way of transforming it.

When difficulties in human experience become deeply lodged within individuals and groups, this is usually a sign that we are stuck in our ways of dealing with them. A shift in methodology can bring tremendous insight and relief. The process of drumming, and the use of our hands, bodies, and other senses as well as the activation of dormant dimensions of the mind, may offer ways of solving and re-visioning problems that are simply not possible through descriptive and linear language. The art-based researcher asks these questions and then sets out to design experiments and situations that will further understanding of the phenomena.

◆ *A Focus on Method*

Both art-based research and science involve the use of systematic experimentation with the goal of gaining knowledge about life.

I have discovered how easily art-based researchers can become lost and ineffective when inquiries become overly personal and lose focus or a larger purpose, or when they get too complex and try to do too many things. Therefore, I always focus on the creation of a clear method that can be easily described and then implemented in a systematic way that lends itself to the reporting of outcomes. Ideally, the method can be replicable and utilized by other researchers who may want to explore the problem separately. Experimentation with the method and learning more about it can even be a primary outcome of the research and an aide to future professional applications.

Perhaps a defining quality of art-based researchers is their willingness to start the work with questions and a willingness to design methods in response to the particular situation, as contrasted to the more general contemporary tendency within the human sciences to fit the question into a fixed research method. The art of the art-based researcher extends to the creation of a process of inquiry.

Sigmund Freud's method of psychoanalytic practice emphasized pure observation and attentiveness to the immediate situation. Paradoxically, Freud, who freely indulged himself in theoretical reductions after-the-fact, offers what I view as a most essential guide for the creation of methods of inquiry in art-based research. In 1912, he said

> Cases which are devoted from the first to scientific purposes and are treated accordingly suffer in their outcome; while the most successful cases are those in which one proceeds, as it were, without any purpose in view, allows oneself to be taken by surprise by any new turn in them, and always meets them with an open mind, free from presuppositions. (Freud, 1912/1958, p. 114)

Freud clearly understood how important it is to withhold conclusions of any kind when investigating human behavior, and it is unfortunate that the theories he developed have been so widely used to label expressions according to predetermined concepts.

In keeping with Freud's immersion in the present moment without judgment, students repeatedly tell me how confusing it can be to try and fit their vision into someone else's fixed system. They feel liberated when encouraged to establish their own ways of researching questions.

To freely observe and suspend judgment, the researcher needs a clearly defined structure of operation as with Freud, whose method is in many ways more lasting than his theories. My experience consistently reinforces the importance of establishing a relatively simple and consistent methodology for artistic inquiry. The simpler the deeper, I say as a guiding principle, and this direction is consistent with the way in which

science attempts to place controls on variables. Since artistic expression is essentially heuristic, introspective, and deeply personal, there needs to be a complementary focus in art-based research on how the work can be of use to others and how it connects to practices in the discipline. This standard of "usefulness" again corresponds to the values of science, and it protects against self-indulgence that can threaten art-based inquiries.

Emphasis on method helps the researcher avoid the confusion that may develop when the internal inquiry is not informed by clear, purposeful, and consistent organization. As with artistic expression, structure often liberates and informs the art-based researcher.

A colleague of mine describes how students pursuing more personal visions in research frequently initiate projects that cannot be replicated or even used by someone else. His guiding question with regard to research methodology is, "Can someone else do it?" (B. Logan, personal communication, May 17, 2005)

Where art-based research and science share this focus on a clearly defined method that can be used by others, the former process is by nature characterized by endless variations of style, interpretation, and outcomes. While many areas of science strive for replication and constancy of results in experiments, the arts welcome the inevitable variations that emerge from systematic practice. Science tends to reduce experience to core principles while art amplifies and expands, and I see the two as complementary within the total complex of knowing. Within what has become known as the "new science" of physics there is a widely recognized acceptance of this interplay.

As we compare the different domains of artistic and scientific knowing, it is essential to avoid the tendency to reduce one to the other and the assumption that one is more truthful. It is more intriguing and ultimately more productive to look at the similarities and differences between the approaches and how they can inform one another. Where science focuses on what can be objectively measured, art emphasizes the unique and immeasurable aesthetic qualities of a particular work. Yet art is characterized by consistent formal patterns and structural elements that can be generalized beyond the experience of individuals, and the new physics reveals how physical phenomena are far more variable and subject to contextual influences than once believed. Both art and science are thoroughly empirical and immersed in the physical manipulation of material substances that are carefully observed.

The translation of art experiences into descriptive language can present a number of challenges to the art-based researcher. The student who deeply believes in the power of arts to access realms of experience beyond the reach of descriptive language might ask: "Do we have to translate artistic insights into words? Didn't Merleau-Ponty (1962) say that the words of science and all other attempts at description are ways of 'concealing phenomena rather than elucidating them' (p. 21)? Isn't the pure art experience in movement, sound, or paint, the ultimate truth that is lost when we try to communicate it in another language? Aren't you contradicting the core premise of art-based knowing by attempting verbal descriptions?"

Although I agree that artistic knowing is not something that can always be reduced to language and that there is considerable truth to the phenomenological declaration that "the original text is perception itself" (Merleau-Ponty, 1962, p. 21), I do persist in the effort to speak and write about what I do in the arts. The original perception in this respect provides the stimulus for the unfolding of thought and the ongoing process of interpretation. My efforts to describe the process of art-based research in

words are also practical and motivated by a desire to convey information and ideas that are hopefully useful to others. Spoken and written language is thus a pragmatic tool, not a prerequisite of validity. I welcome and look forward to future inquiries by art-based researchers, working in artistic disciplines such as sound and movement, who strive to communicate outcomes in ways that may not rely on descriptive language. Perhaps these inquiries will draw artists even closer to researchers in science who similarly seek alternatives to the verbal description of outcomes.

As we develop new methods of art-based research, it is my hope that we can pursue our goals in ways that lessen the divide between art and science and between different kinds of research. I favor a simple focus on doing "research," systematically examining and passionately imagining phenomena in whatever ways address the needs of the particular situation.

◆ An Art-Based Exploration of a Dream

Let me give an example of how the ways of knowing that are unique to the creative imagination can work together with language and more conventional research methods. The object of this inquiry is a dream that itself offers unique insights into experience.

I wake in the morning with a dream that enacts a situation that I experienced the previous evening with a new twist. I gave a lecture that apparently went well, but in my dream about the lecture people were sleeping, talking, and heading for the restrooms. The dream embodied the uncertainty I sensed within myself about what had happened the night before and displayed it to me through striking and disturbing images. The unpleasant nature of these images got my attention, aroused fears and discomforts.

The dream is a way of knowing, and it stimulates responses and attempts to understand it that collaborate with other modes of cognition. I want to get to know the dream in a more complete way, so I discuss it with others and the conversations generate new insights. I discover how talking is a way of thinking and knowing and how important insights emerge from the flow of conversation focused on a particular experience. The process of speaking with another person naturally evokes different perspectives, and there is a spontaneity that does not occur when I try to collect my thoughts about something in isolation. Relating to the dream through conversation helps me realize how all of our senses and ways of communication play an integrated role in the process of understanding experience, and it offsets the idea that words and subsequent interpretations conceal the essence of an experience.

Stimulated by how talking about the dream expands my relationship to it, I respond creatively through movement, interpreting the dream through my body. As I move like one of the figures heading for the restroom, I feel an urgency to follow my instincts, to honor them and access their intelligence. I am surprised by the sense of relief that this brings and I feel energized, physically connected to the space, more relaxed, confident, and aware of how movement has contributed to my understanding.

I respond to the figures in the audience by enacting their postures and gestures with my body. To do this I have to envision them carefully and observe the details of their expression. I make use of the artistic and psychological tool of empathy to imagine myself as one of them, to project myself into their places and sense what they are feeling. As I enact their bodily expressions, aesthetic sensibilities help me get my expression as close as I can to theirs. I feel

a correspondence with their expression that is much nearer than before. I transcend my existing attitude toward them and start to see the scene in a completely different way. I feel comfortable and actually enjoy imagining the dream experience from the perspective of the sleeping audience members.

I decide to use the artistic device of personification as a way of entering into a dialogue with one of the sleeping figures, of trying to get even closer to it through poetic speech and maybe it will tell me something about itself. I personify the dream image, speak to it, and say how engaging it has changed my attitude and how differently I feel about it and the dream as a whole.

The personified figure speaks to me and says, "Relax. Go easy on yourself. Be like us and focus on breathing. Try to stop judging how you did in the lecture. Join us here and take it easy."

I pass up the temptation to ask the sleeping figure what it really thought about the lecture, sensing that it would just laugh at me and say, "There you go again. You've got to let go. We're just here, and we can teach you how to be more completely here too."

The dream is a way of knowing, and the same can be said about the process of describing it to another person, enacting it, dialoguing with dream figures, and so forth. We can continue to know it even better through painting, poetry, vocal improvisation, and various other expressive modalities, each offering its unique interpretation and understanding of the experience. This is an example of art-based knowing and inquiry, and to the extent that I engage the dream methodically and document the results, I am researching the experience. All of these responses to the dream make use of language and various forms of cognitive analysis.

The inquiry into the nature of the dream might simply stick with descriptions of how I engaged it with different expressive faculties and how they compare to one another.

It might be helpful to make comparative mathematical entries on a scale determining the degree to which a particular way of working helped me see new things about the dream or get closer to it. Or I might ask co-researchers to witness my expressions and rate their reactions that can be compared to mine. This relatively simple activity of exploring and documenting different ways of engaging a dream shows how the arts, spoken language, numerical analysis, and other modes of thought can interact naturally in the process furthering understanding.

The very ordinary dream that I just described can be viewed as an illustration that helps us understand how art-based knowing and inquiry take place. This example also suggests the largely unrecognized intelligence of dreams that many still see as meaningless and nothing but a discharge of excess energy. The artistic responses to the dream and the feelings of discomfort it evokes transform my relationship to the experience and take it to a new place. Making the effort to interact with the experience in different ways is thus a prerequisite for new learning.

All the methods that I have used to respond to the dream and get to know it better can be applied to knowing and researching a problem that I am having at work, to making a decision, to acquiring a better understanding of why a particular person or group of people act as they do, to gaining a new perspective on a seemingly irresolvable problem or conflict, to assessing what might be happening in a particular situation, and to planning future strategies. These art-based tools and ways of knowing take us out of our habitual responses to things.

In reaction to the preceding example it might be asked whether focusing on dream images and other distinctly personal phenomena is likely to encourage the self-absorption that I guard against in art-based research. I reply by suggesting that the way we treat the most mundane or apparently inconsequential experiences may have the most to offer in suggesting a larger vision of social transformation. One of the most valuable features of art-based research might be its potential for offering very different ways of approaching the most serious problems that we face in the world today.

Art embraces ordinary things with an eye for their unusual and extraordinary qualities. The artist looks at banal phenomena from a perspective of aesthetic significance and gives them a value that they do not normally have. This way of relating to things may have more social significance than one might at first imagine.

For example, when I give the dream image its autonomy and work with it as a creative partner, I convey a sense of respect for its existence. Can I do the same in my relations with others? Will I be able to extend the same compassion and desire for empathy to the person who constantly annoys me or who opposes everything I do? Is it possible for me to suspend judgment in tense situations with others and just do my best to interpret the encounters in more creative and new ways? Maybe I can try and just listen as openly as possible with the goal of learning something new about what the person is trying to say to me.

The work is always challenging since we are generally not easily disposed toward establishing creative relationships with the things we oppose and to possibly changing attitudes that have defined who we are. Most of us find it very difficult to let go of our habitual ways of viewing the world, and it is more than likely that we manifest the same tendencies in our dealings with others. Change and insight in the personal realm are increasingly being recognized as a key source of corresponding social change. Therefore, the way in which we treat the humble images of our art-based research may have a definite impact on how we engage the world.

Rather than trying to fix problems with our points of view, we might focus more on knowing them in creative ways as with the drumming example described above. This expanded comprehension of experience, and how we go about pursuing it, may be more helpful than proving our positions in an absolute sense. As with science, the validity of art-based knowing and inquiry is ultimately determined by the community of believers who experience firsthand what the arts can do to further human understanding.

◆ *Learning From Artists*

I encourage art-based researchers to immerse themselves in studies of how artists research personal and social experiences and how art has served as a primary agent of change in the world. It has been said writers are profound psychologists; the same can be said of artists as researchers.

My artist mentor Truman Nelson committed his life to writing novels dealing with revolutionary themes and figures. He described how his "revolutionary art is motivated by a desire to change American society" (Schafer, 1989, p. 275). Truman felt that through intensely personal and creative interpretations of historical events, the artist is able to go beyond facts and self-reflection to express conditions that are "interchangeable with other people" (p. 276). In writing his books Truman experienced a creative tension between art and reality, and he liked to cite Thoreau's effort to "make fact flower into truth." In describing this method he says: "There is an overruling psychological truth that can come out of my absorption of the total empirical substance that I am transmitting" (p. 276). The artistic or imaginal reality that emerges from this process was to him superior to the literal account of what occurred.

When people challenge the process of researching human experience through art, I like to describe Truman's belief that many of the greatest contributions to human understanding have been generated by the arts. He also reinforces the point that I make in *Art-Based Research* (McNiff, 1998a) about how fiction can take us even closer to experiences than verbatim descriptions and the tedious and formalistic literalism that pervades case study literature. Fictional explorations allow us to penetrate more freely and intimately into the particular subject matter, to identify with the characters and situations in new ways, and to speak from the perspectives of others. Methods such as fictional interviews, which can accompany literal ones in a research project, might also offer the most universally accessible forms of art-based research. One of my doctoral students (R. McGrath, personal communication, August 3, 2006) described how this method helped him to integrate a wide range of data gathered from many different interviews.

In the area of nonfiction, documentary films offer many examples of how carefully researched artistic projects can change society. Morgan Spurlock's (2004) *Super Size Me* is an exemplar for any person exploring how art and science can collaborate in examining a particular phenomenon with the goal of changing human behavior. Spurlock conducts an experiment in which he eats food only from McDonalds for 30 days and documents the physiological changes in his body—weight, cholesterol levels, and so forth. I was delighted when I saw this film, and I recommend it widely as a research model emerging from contemporary art and culture.

I also cite the work of Charlotte Salomon as an example of how art can plumb the depths of the personal soul while inciting others to creative action. After many personal tragedies and before being taken to

Auschwitz where she died in her mid-20s, Charlotte chose to explore the full spectrum of her life experiences through a series of 769 paintings with accompanying text. This work has been published as an autobiographical play, *Charlotte: Life or Theater?* (Salomon, 1981). In this extraordinary work Charlotte strives to transform her life into what her mentor, Alfred Wolfsohn, in the tradition of Nietzsche, described as "theater," a form of art that gives existence a greater meaning. I have never experienced anything that compares to this systematic, comprehensive, deep, and creative examination of a period of personal life through art.

The work of Wolfsohn in researching the range of human vocal expression, as furthered by Paul Newham (1993, 1998) and the Roy Hart Theater, is another of the great examples of recent art-based research.

I encourage students to study how artists operate instinctively as researchers who use whatever methods of inquiry and communication further their purposes. Nevertheless, I always encounter a certain reluctance to recognize and trust personal creative resources. In response to these doubts I say to students: "What particular artistic project or series of activities can you do to further your understanding of this issue? What can you do that is uniquely yours and that grows from the authority of your experience? What feels most natural to you? Where does your authentic expertise lie? What is it that you have done that others have not experienced with the same range and intensity?"

This approach to creating a method is much more challenging than following a standardized procedure. Even the published guides to phenomenological and heuristic research give unvarying stages that students everywhere are adopting without understanding the philosophical concepts and traditions that inform them. In addition to the reliance on formulas for inquiry, schools universally organize research courses by comparing preexisting types—sometimes art-based research is even listed as one of the options. The student is then expected to conduct research according to one of the existing approaches or in some cases to mix more than one. In my experience all of the different ways of inquiry have the ability to inform one another and help the researcher design a study that best serves the particular issue. Artistic knowing can be heuristic, phenomenological, hermeneutic, imaginal, archetypal, empirical, statistical, and more.

Within contemporary artistic training there is an assumption that one studies various traditions, but then builds upon them to create a new and personal method of inquiry. The search for a method, in art and research, is invariably characterized by a crucible of tensions, struggles, a certain degree of chaos, and even the destruction of cherished assumptions. I encourage "creating outside the lines" as contrasted to following the circumscribed procedures of a textbook approach to research. Invariably the encounter with this experience is the transformative engine that carries the researcher to significant new discoveries. My book *Trust the Process: An Artist's Guide to Letting Go* (McNiff, 1998b) was informed by these experiences and the realization that if a person stays with the creative process, it will generate unexpected results, the value of which are sometimes even proportionate to the degree of struggle.

Just as science assists art-based research through its emphasis on systematic inquiry, art enhances the process of discovery in science by its responsiveness to the unexpected. As W. E. Beveridge (1953) describes in *The Art of Scientific Investigation*, original knowledge occurs when ideas are placed in new relationships to one another, a process that typically requires crossing the boundaries of previously separated domains, such as those constructed between art and science.

Artistic inquiry, whether it is within the context of research or an individual person's creative expression, typically starts with the realization that you cannot define the final outcome when you are planning to do the work. As contrasted to scientific methods, you generally know little about the end of an artistic experiment when you are at the beginning. In the creative process, the most meaningful insights often come by surprise, unexpectedly, and even against the will of the creator. The artist may have a sense or intuition of what might be discovered or of what is needed, and in some cases even a conviction, but the defining aspect of knowing through art, as I try to demonstrate in the examples given in this chapter, is the emanation of meaning through the process of creative expression.

◆ *References*

Arnheim, R. (1954). *Art and visual perception: A psychology of the creative eye.* Berkeley: University of California Press.

Arnheim, R. (1966). *Toward a psychology of art.* Berkeley: University of California Press.

Beveridge, W. E. (1953). *The art of scientific investigation.* New York: Vintage.

Chodorow, J. (Ed.). (1997). *Jung on active imagination.* Princeton, NJ: Princeton University Press.

Freud, S. (1958). Recommendations to physicians practicing psycho-analysis. In J. Strachey (Ed.), *The standard edition of the complete psychological works of Sigmund Freud* (Vol. 12, pp. 109–120). New York: Norton. (Original work published 1912)

Gallas, K. (1994). *The languages of learning: How children talk, write, dance, draw, and sing their understanding of the world.* New York: Teachers College Press.

Hillman, J. (1977). An inquiry into image. *Spring,* 62–88.

Hillman, J. (1978). Further notes on images. *Spring,* 152–182.

Hillman, J. (1979). Image-sense. *Spring,* 130–143.

Langer, S. (1951). *Philosophy in a new key: A study in the symbolism of reason, rite, and art.* New York: Mentor Books.

Langer, S. (1953). *Feeling and form: A theory of art.* New York: Charles Scribner.

McNiff, S. (1989). *Depth psychology of art.* Springfield, IL: Charles C Thomas Publisher.

McNiff, S. (1992). *Art as medicine: Creating a therapy of the imagination.* Boston: Shambhala Publications.

McNiff, S. (1998a). *Art-based research.* London: Jessica Kingsley Publisher.

McNiff, S. (1998b). *Trust the process: An artist's guide to letting go.* Boston: Shambhala Publications.

McNiff, S. (2003). *Creating with others: The practice of imagination in life, art, and the workplace.* Boston: Shambhala Publications.

McNiff, S. (2004, Fall). Research in new keys: An introduction to the ideas and methods of arts-based research. *Journal of Pedagogy Pluralism and Practice, 9.* Retrieved May 21, 2007, from http://www.lesley.edu/news/publications/publications.toc.html

Merleau-Ponty, M. (1962). *Phenomenology of perception* (C. Smith, Trans.). London: Routledge & Kegan Paul.

Newham, P. (1993). *The singing cure: An introduction to voice movement therapy.* London: Rider Random House.

Newham, P. (1998). *Therapeutic voicework: Principles and practice for the use of singing as a therapy.* London: Jessica Kingsley Publishers.

Salomon, C. (1981). *Charlotte: Life or theater?* (L. Vennewitz, Trans.). New York: Viking.

Schafer, W. (Ed.). (1989). *The Truman Nelson reader.* Amherst: University of Massachusetts Press.

Spurlock, M. (Director). (2004). *Super size me* [Motion picture]. United States: Samuel Goldwyn Films.

Watkins, M. (1983). The characters speak because they want to speak. *Spring,* 13–33.

4

VISUAL IMAGES IN RESEARCH

◆ Sandra Weber

◆ *Seeing Image Worlds*

Seeing is believing.
A picture is worth a thousand words.
That's not how I see it.
I saw it with my own eyes.
I can't believe my eyes.
Do you see what I mean?
Oh! Now I see!
I can't bear to look.

Whether "natural" or designed, the environment demands to be seen. Just look around. We are born into a world of visual images projected onto our retinas, clamoring for the attention of our perceptual processes. Even before we can think, we can see.[1] Moreover, our sense of sight is so entwined with all our other senses that even with our eyes shut, we can see those inner images so often evoked by sounds, smells, words, feelings, or thoughts. When we plan, analyze, imagine, think, or critique, our thoughts are associated with and largely constituted by images (Bruner, 1984). And when we sleep, there are the images of dreams. For most people, this integration of the visual in daily life is a taken-for-granted, unexamined part of living and not a subject of systematic inquiry or an articulated part of scholarly methods. Seeing, being surrounded by the visual, doesn't always or necessarily mean that we *notice* what we see. It is the *paying attention,* the looking and the taking note of what we see that makes images especially important to art, scholarship, and research. Indeed the discourse of the academy is all about persuading others to see what we see. But of course, as Berger (1972) asserts, the relation between what we see and what we know is never settled (p. 7).

◆ *Image as Concept: A History of Multiple Uses*

The term *image* has often been used as the basis for distinguishing things from each other, to sort phenomena into categories. Strict definitions of image are thus used to make distinctions between the "original" and its image copy, or between the outer physical world and the inner imagined or psychological world, or between the "natural world" and a manufactured or designed (imaged) one, or, more recently, between analog, material space and digital, virtual space. But although these definitions have their uses in some circumstances, the dichotomies on which they depend or that they evoke do not usually hold up to close scrutiny or thoughtful argument. Baudrillard (1993), for example, posits that hyperrealism (the meticulous duplication of the real through another medium) is quietly erasing the boundary between real and imaginary. Contemporary uses of the term *image* are more likely to bridge or break down dichotomies, straddling both sides of "real– not real" questions, and offering ways to think about phenomena more holistically. Of course, all this discussion of image as a concept tends to ignore images themselves.

IMAGES AND SENSE-MAKING: HOW IMAGES MEAN

In our everyday lives, we interpret, create, and use images as a matter of course, often without much conscious attention and using whatever social codes and conventions we've picked up along the way. Whether they are visual or imagined; symbolic or literal; one-, two-, or three-dimensional; analog or digital; material or virtual; drawn with words or with lines; captured by the lens, the brush, the pen, or the poetic eye, images are constantly subject to reconstructions and reinterpretations. As Sturken and Cartwright (2001) point out, "The meanings of each image are multiple, created each time it is viewed" (p. 25).

What a specific image can mean or represent at any given time depends on a lot of factors, including who is doing the viewing and the context in which the image is viewed. Major scholars, from late 19th- and early 20th-century semioticians Charles Peirce (Merrell, 1997) and Ferdinand de Saussure (1915/ 1988) to later theorists such as Jean Baudrillard (1993, 1988), Roland Barthes (1981, 1983), and John Berger (1972) have addressed the slippery question of how images mean, providing a variety of sophisticated and nuanced models to guide the use of images in contemporary work. In considering the photographic image, for example, Barthes (1981, 1983) posits that images have two levels of meaning: denotative and connotative. The denotative meaning of an image refers to its literal, descriptive meaning—the apparent truth, evidence, or objective reality that the image documents or denotes. The same image or photograph also connotes more culturally specific meanings. Connotative meanings refer to the cultural and historical context of a specific image, as well as to the social conventions, codes, and meanings that have been attached to or associated with that image in a particular context. We learn these meanings through our personal experience (Sturken & Cartwright, 2001).

The distinction between an object (referent) and an image of that object (or signifier) is not always clear or even possible. As Baudrillard (1988) pointed out in his discussions of simulacra (signs that do not clearly have a real-life counterpart), images themselves act as objects and take on lives of their own, with no single object beyond the signifier as primary referent (consider images of a dragon, ogre, faerie, or even Mickey Mouse). An image can thus be "the thing itself"—the object of inquiry. Even in a post-postmodern era, there is a growing tendency to speak of images as part of both external and internal "realities" reflecting the relationship of image to the dialectics of human perception and sense-making, helping frame the concept more as a dynamic product of our interaction with the world than as an immutable and independent object in the world.

◆ Using Visual Images in the Social Sciences and Humanities

THE VALUE OF IMAGES TO RESEARCH

There are many kinds of image sources available to researchers and scholars. As this *Handbook* illustrates in detail, different kinds of images are central to arts-related approaches to social science research and lead to different ways of knowing (Allen, 1995; Denzin, 1995; Eisner, 1997; Greene, 1995; Paley, 1995). An image can be a multilayered theoretical statement, simultaneously positing even contradictory

propositions for us to consider, pointing to the fuzziness of logic and the complex or even paradoxical nature of particular human experiences. It is this ability of images to convey multiple messages, to pose questions, and to point to both abstract and concrete thoughts in so economical a fashion that makes image-based media highly appropriate for the communication of academic knowledge. A picture, Harnad (1991) reminds us, may not only be worth a thousand words, but it can also be apprehended almost instantaneously at a glance, whereas those thousand words require time to listen to or read.

In the last few decades of the 20th century, qualitative researchers in the social sciences began to pay serious attention to the use of image to enhance their understanding of the human condition (Prosser, 1998b). These uses encompass a wide range of visual forms, including films, video, photographs, drawings, cartoons, graffiti, maps, diagrams, cyber graphics, signs, and symbols. The fields of visual sociology and visual anthropology have done much of the pioneering work on image-based methodologies, and consequently, their Web sites (e.g., http://visualsociology.org and http://www.societyforvisualanthropology.org) and journals (e.g., *Visual Studies* and *Visual Anthropology Review*) remain valuable resources for researchers from other disciplines as well. For something more hip and artistic, I recommend the online e-zine *Stimulus* (http://www.stimulusrespond.com) as a possible harbinger of what some future image-based scholarship might look like. Similarly interesting journals, too numerous to mention, abound in the fields of education and communication. The sprawling field of cultural studies, with its vast array of journals, has also been home to highly relevant theoretical works on visual culture (e.g., Evans & Hall, 1999; Jenks, 1995;

Mirzoeff, 1998) that are very useful across a broad span of research contexts and methodologies. The problem is that academics are too seldom aware of the publications and methods outside their chosen field that could speak eloquently to their own disciplinary concerns.

Researchers seeking theoretical grounding for the use of the visual in their work often draw on the seminal theories of philosophers such as John Berger (1972), Gaston Bachelard (1964), Jean Baudrillard (1988), Roland Barthes (1981, 1983), Walter Benjamin (1969), Pierre Bourdieu (1990), Michel Foucault (1983), Susanne Langer (1957), and Susan Sontag (1977). The work of scholars such as Becker (1986), Chaplin (1994), Denzin and Lincoln (2000), Harper (1998, 2002), Hubbard (1994), Mirzoeff (1998), Paley (1995), Ruby (1996), and Steele (1998), as well as the useful reviews and updates of visual methodologies by researchers such as Banks (2001), Gauntlett (1997), Mitchell and Weber (in press), Prosser (1998a, 1998b), van Leeuwen and Jewitt (2001), and Weber and Mitchell (2004b) exemplify the burgeoning literature available to researchers seeking a firm base from which to venture forth. It is this theoretical grounding, as much as the images, that makes these research approaches so valuable and applicable to a variety of social sciences. The remainder of this chapter will focus on arts-related visual images, leaving literary images and science graphics to other authors to explore.

WHY USE ARTS-RELATED VISUAL IMAGES IN RESEARCH? TEN GOOD REASONS

There are many arguments that can be made for the use of visual images in research, all of them interlinked. Here are 10:

1. *Images can be used to capture the ineffable, the hard-to-put-into-words.* Some things just need to be shown, not merely stated. Artistic images can help us access those elusive, hard-to-put-into-words aspects of knowledge that might otherwise remain hidden or are ignored. Eisner (1995) argues that the use of images provides an "all-at-once-ness" that reveals what would be hard to grasp through language and numbers alone (p. 1). The use of visual images is not a luxury or add-on to scholarship but, in many situations, essential. A word and number description of the number of tons of toxic waste produced by a municipality and their short- and long-term effects on the environment simply does not have the same meaning as an image-based account would. Concepts such as poverty, pollution, racism, war, genocide, bureaucracy, utopia, and illness may require visual exemplars to give them breadth and depth, to point to an understanding that is connected to the world.

2. *Images can make us pay attention to things in new ways.* Art makes us look; it engages us. The reason we need and create art has to do with its ability to discover what we didn't know we knew, or to see what we never noticed before, even when it was right in front of our noses. Artistic uses of images can make the ordinary seem extraordinary—breaking through common resistance, forcing us to consider new ways of seeing or doing things. As Grumet (1988) observes,

> the aesthetic is distinguished from the flow of daily experience, the phone conversations, the walk to the corner store, only by the intensity, completeness, and unity of its elements and by a form that calls forth a level of perception that is, in itself, satisfying. (p. 88)

There was nothing extraordinary, for example, about the ubiquitous and familiar red and white Campbell soup can until pop artist Andy Warhol made it the focus of his work, thrusting it in the public eye on large canvas, interrogating common notions of art, commodification, and the popular. Giving a new symbolic visual twist to plain old things works well because we do not have our guard up against the mundane, allowing it to break through our everyday perceptions and get us to think outside of the theoretical box.

3. Images are likely to be memorable.
Some images are more memorable than academic texts, and therefore more likely to influence the ways we think and act. Images elicit emotional as well as intellectual responses and have overtones that stay with us and have a habit of popping up unbidden later on. Using images as representation thus increases the likelihood of making an impact on the reader/viewer/community, something granting agencies keep pestering the academy to do. The power of art helps get our research findings across to a much wider audience who may pay more attention because they can see what we mean, both literally and figuratively. Images tend not only to convey additional information but also to "burn themselves into our brain," forming internal memories that may be hard to erase.

4. Images can be used to communicate more holistically, incorporating multiple layers, and evoking stories or questions.
Images enable us to simultaneously keep the whole and the part in view, telling a story and helping us synthesize knowledge in a highly efficient way. Those who put up billboards or design magazine ads know that it is possible to convey a lot of things with just one image. Looking at a telling and artful juxtaposition of figures and objects in a photo can reveal as much information as several pages of written text, or convey a different kind of information that keeps a context always present. In other words, through the ways in which they are made and displayed, images can talk; they can have what Ong (1982) calls an "orality," a narrative quality or the ability to provoke or reconstruct conversations.

5. Images can enhance empathic understanding and generalizability.
Images literally help us to adopt someone else's gaze, see someone else's point of view, and borrow their experience for a moment. This enables a comparison with our own views and experience. Artful representation works well when it facilitates empathy or enables the viewer to see through the researcher-artist's eye. Hearing or seeing or feeling the details of a lived experience, its textures and shapes, helps make the representation trustworthy or believable. As Eisner (1995) writes, "artistically crafted work creates a paradox, revealing what is universal by examining in detail what is particular" (p. 3). The more visual detail that is provided about the context and phenomenon being investigated, the better able the audience is to judge how it may or may not apply to its own situation, models, or concerns, and the more trustworthy the work appears, leaving the readers to decide or "see" for themselves.

6. Through metaphor and symbol, artistic images can carry theory elegantly and eloquently.
The possibilities for using the visual to make effective and economical theoretical statements is, for the most part, dismally undertapped and undervalued in the humanities and social sciences. The advertising industry and political cartoonists seem to be way ahead of the academy in this regard. Some images (the double helix of DNA

comes to mind) are simultaneously the most simple yet the most effective knowledge statement possible. Others are less straightforward but nonetheless effective. I recall, for example, a picture on a magazine cover of a woman torn down the middle, the left half dressed in casual "mommy" clothes, the left hand reaching down to clutch a child. The right half was dressed for business, clutching a battered briefcase. Unidentified hands came clutching at both sides of the woman, trying to pull her in different directions. To me, at least, the image was making complex statements about the contemporary roles of women in industrialized societies, summing up in an instant what so many women felt or still feel.

7. *Images encourage embodied knowledge.*
Visual methods help researchers keep their own bodies and the bodies of those they study in mind. In a variety of disciplines, scholars are beginning to acknowledge the embodied nature of all knowledge. It is, after all, through their bodies that investigators conduct research. People are not ideas, but flesh and blood beings learning through their senses and responding to images through their embodied experiences. The visual disarms or bypasses the purely intellectual, leading to a more authentic and complete glimpse of what a particular experience is like or of what people think and feel. There is an unintentional but automatic and visceral identification with some images; we cannot escape contemplating or even, on some level, experiencing the situations depicted, even if they were previously unfamiliar to us.

8. *Images can be more accessible than most forms of academic discourse.*
Scholars such as Barone (1995), Cole (2001), and Greene (1995) assert that artistic forms of representation provide a refreshing and necessary challenge to prevailing modes of academic discourse. The use of widely shared cultural codes and popular images make many visual expressions far more accessible than usual academic language. To the degree that the mandate of the academy is to provoke discussion and thinking as well as communicate research to a broader audience (even within the academy), the use of images becomes significant. Many people who would never read scholarly texts are willing to engage with photography displayed on a Web site or a documentary on television.

9. *Images can facilitate reflexivity in research design.*
Using images connects to the self yet provides a certain distance. An image reveals at least as much about the person who took or chose or produced it as it does about the people or objects who are figured in it. Under the right conditions, using images can thus facilitate or encourage a certain transparency, introducing the potential for reflexivity into the research design. In a futile hope of maintaining "objectivity," researchers too often ignore the way their own viewpoints, personal experiences, and ways of seeing affect their research. By its very nature, artistic expression taps into and reveals aspects of the self and puts us in closer touch with how we really feel and look and act. Paradoxically, such self-revelation also forces us to take a step back and look at ourselves from the new perspective provided by the medium itself, increasing the potential that we will better understand our own subjectivity, leading to humbler and more nuanced knowledge claims.

10. *Images provoke action for social justice.*
No matter how personal or intimate they may seem at first glance, images, by the very nature of their provenance and creation, are also social. In an era when the relevance of research to questions of social justice is increasingly expected, few features can provoke critical questions and encourage

individual and collective action as well as images. Take, for example, the powerful photograph taken by Nick Ut during the Vietnam War of an obviously terrified young Vietnamese girl running naked down a street to flee a napalm fire bomb. It may have done more to galvanize the antiwar movement in the West than all the scholarly papers on the horrors of war. To the extent that various uses of images are authentic, nuanced, and contextualized, we can create bodies of visual work that may be useful in the service of changes for justice in social policies or cultural practices. This objective is central to a growing number of scholars in a variety of disciplines.

To sum up, this ability of images to evoke visceral and emotional responses in ways that are memorable, coupled with their capacity to help us empathize or see another's point of view and to provoke new ways of looking at things critically, makes them powerful tools for researchers to use in different ways during various phases of research.

◆ Visual Images and Research Processes

Images can be integral and essential components of different sorts of inquiries on a wide range of topics, and research questions may call for a visual component in one *or more* of the following ways:

PRODUCTION OF ARTISTIC IMAGES AS DATA

Images can be newly produced by participants or researchers; for example, the researcher may invite people to draw or paint or take photographs or make a short video or create an art installation that relates

to the research questions or the phenomena being investigated. Or the researcher might be the one making new images. Once the visual material is produced, the resulting collection might then be the basis of further discussion, interviews, and/or analysis, although the very process of creating images is often a major part of the research process itself.

Examples of the production of images for research include asking people to draw a teacher (Weber & Mitchell, 1995a, 1996) and, in another project, inviting girls to make a short film about their experiences of technology (Weber & Weber, 2007). As a further variation on the production of images, in *Secret Games: Collaborative Works With Children,* photographer Wendy Ewald (2000) bridges the gap between researcher-as-photographer and participant-as-photographer by inviting the children she was researching to suggest subject matter, poses, and props to give her direction for the artful photographs she took.

Wang's (1999) articulation of a visual methodology called "photovoice" illustrates how engaging and connected to social issues research can be when it is the participants themselves producing the images. This method is used in the service of social critique and involves group as well as individual interpretations of the photos produced by the participants. Hubbard's (1994) anthropological research on a Navajo reserve, where it was the residents who took the photographs, resulted in an artful book, *Shooting Back From the Reservation,* that brings out the "emic" point of view that is so often illusive in the usual volumes of written fieldnotes. Methods that put the production in the hands of nonprofessionals can project a credibility and authenticity that more polished and accomplished works of art cannot always achieve. It is the very lack of artifice in the not-always-technically-perfect images that sometimes makes them more convincing, more true to life.

USE OF EXISTING (FOUND) ARTISTIC IMAGES AS DATA OR SPRINGBOARDS FOR THEORIZING

The primary source of images on which the research question focuses may be *found material* or *already existing images*, whether from museum archives, books, billboards, film archives, videotapes, magazines, and so forth, or *images already created by or belonging to participants in the research project*, including photo albums, artwork, or artifacts. Langford (2001), for example, did a fascinating analysis of a family photo album she found in the archives of the McCord Museum that became a theoretical work on the orality of photo albums. Personal photographs from their own lives became springboards for the insightful work of scholars such as Chalfen (1987), Kuhn (1995), and Walkerdine (1990). Analyzing Hollywood "teacher movies" to see how teachers have been depicted in film over the years (Weber & Mitchell, 1995b) and speculating on the reproduction of cultural images through the phenomenon of school class photographs are two final examples of the use of the visual in different projects (Mitchell & Weber, 1998, 1999a, 1999b).

USE OF VISUAL AND OBJECT-IMAGES TO ELICIT OR PROVOKE OTHER DATA

Sometimes data that are the focus of an inquiry are elicited or obtained through the use of images or objects as memory prompts for writing or as points of departure for semistructured interviews. "Photo elicitation," for example, has become a frequently used method of data collection in conducting ethnographic studies.[2] As Harper (2002) describes it, the procedure involves asking people to take pictures and then looking at and discussing the photos with them during semistructured interviews. Giving people an image or object to talk about sparks multiple reactions, leading often to outpourings of all kinds of information, feelings, thoughts, and situation details. The concreteness, the *materiality* of photographs, artwork, and objects (see Winterson, 1995) seems to provide a versatile and movable scaffolding for the telling of life history, life events, life material. Things that might be too embarrassing or too painful to ask someone or to tackle head on are often brought to the fore incidentally and gently when the focus is on, for example, the shirt a departed loved one wore rather than on death and loss itself. In *Not Just Any Dress: Narratives of Memory, Body, and Identity* (Weber & Mitchell, 2004a), as a final example, items of clothing and photographs of dress provided the impetus for revealing narratives that give insight into many issues important to the social sciences, including professional and national identities, birth, marriage, aging, conformity, maternity, rebellion, body image, social codes, and death. Asking people to talk about visual images already in their possession is thus a very promising research method.

USE OF IMAGES FOR FEEDBACK AND DOCUMENTATION OF RESEARCH PROCESS

Researchers often visually document data collection by using a video or still camera to capture at least some of what happens throughout the project. Not only does this provide a visual running record, it provides another eye on the process as well as valuable feedback, helping researchers assess, adjust, and fine-tune. Image-ing the research process changes the research, making it more transparent, suggesting new directions, and facilitating self-critique. A telling example from my work concerns the reviewing of taped interviews with children. It was only when I saw those tapes, and noticed the children's facial expressions, body language, and, most embarrassing, my own rapid-fire delivery, that I realized how little time or space I was allowing for them to address the questions I was too intent on asking. As a result, I changed the questions and my manner of interacting and got much more meaningful data, all the while providing children with a more enjoyable and comfortable experience. Excerpts from those videos provided convincing "evidence" for subsequent conference presentations of my findings (Mitchell & Weber, in press; Weber, 2002; Weber & Mitchell, 1995b; Weber, Mitchell, & Tardiff, 2002).

USE OF IMAGES AS MODE OF INTERPRETATION AND/OR REPRESENTATION

As the norms and expectations for communicating research results change, a growing number of scholars are turning to image-based modes of representation, *creating art* to express their findings and theories (see Bagley & Cancienne, 2002a, 2002b; Cole & McIntyre, 2001; Jipson & Payley, 1997; and this handbook). Sociologist Cathy Greenblat (2005) comments creatively on Alzheimer's disease through carefully sequenced close-up photographs of small clear plastic "baggies" that contain a collection of things one would not ordinarily group together, for example, a straw, two pennies, an empty candy wrapper, and a valuable diamond ring. Many such bags were found stashed in various places in her mother's house shortly after she died of Alzheimer's. Greenblat uses her photographs of them to symbolically represent and examine the disease, giving us a peak at the world through her mother's eyes.

Jo Spence's seminal work (1995), as a further example, featured the careful constructing of symbolic images (for example, nude photographs of herself as "meat for sale") as *both* the method of inquiry and the mode of interpretation and representation, reminding us that any attempts to completely separate method from findings is artificial and somewhat arbitrary.

The importance of images to presenting research findings was never more apparent to me than when I tried to write about a project on the high school prom. Words alone just didn't do justice to the phenomenon. The studies involved so much visual detail— the dresses, the fabrics, the girls and boys all dressed up, the limos, the dances, the photographs, the disillusioned or happy facial expressions, and the dozens of teen movies— all of which simply refused to be flattened onto a page of scholarly text. A highly ritualized yet complex social phenomenon, the prom is known and portrayed largely through the visual language of popular culture. The question was how to keep all the layers of the phenomenon in view when communicating the results? And so I turned to artistic visual modes to theorize and represent some of our findings, directing two films, *Dress Fitting* (Weber & Mitchell, 2000) and *Canadian Pie* (Weber & Mitchell 2003), as well as a multimedia art installation, *I Am a Woman Now* (Weber, 2004).

◆ *Questions and Caveats Regarding the Use of Images in Research*

All of the preceding discussions do not mean, of course, that images per se are "good" or guarantee any sort of research outcome or automatically lead to deeper understanding or theoretical insight. Not all images are equal or equally effective or valid. Images, like words, can be used to twist and distort and mislead. Ethical issues (what is a responsible use of images of other people, who owns or controls them, loss of anonymity, and so on) can be very thorny and complicated. The effusive praise of image needs to be tempered by critical considerations and further explanation. As is the case with any other element of research, it is the quality and the judicious and knowledgeable choices and uses of images (see Tagg, 1993), the way they fit into the overall research design and dissemination, that likely determines how useful a specific image can be in any given situation.

Images are open to interrogation and interpretation, and there are so many questions to consider. How do images mean? What or whose reality, if any, do images represent? Whose gaze? What social, cultural, or political knowledge is required to be able to interpret specific images? What makes some images trustworthy and others less so? What constitutes a valid interpretation of images? Is there such a thing? What is the role of social and cultural context to interpretation? Individual experience? How does the visual genre used affect the research? In other words, how does the medium shape the inquiry and the message? What kinds of stories can images tell? When does image-ing become theorizing? What relationships are possible between visual images and words? There are no satisfactory universal answers to these questions, but they do provide useful criteria for the critique and evaluation of image-based research.

◆ Conclusion

Why use images? Images can spark research questions and inspire the design or presentation of an investigation. Images can be used as elegant and economical representation of

theoretical positions, can retain more of the whole within less space, can combine cultural and transcultural elements, can evoke but also sometimes transcend the specific context in which they are created, and can use specific instances to comment on or illustrate wider generalities. Images can simultaneously present multiple viewpoints or generate multiple interpretations, and can call attention to the everyday by making it strange or casting it in a new light. Given the centrality of image to culture and sense-making, social scientists are increasingly interested in developing more sophisticated understandings of image processes and are more routinely incorporating deliberate and rigorous uses of images as part of their research methods. Accordingly, we can expect the reporting of research findings in the social sciences and humanities to be more and more image-based, exploiting the power of images and imagery to communicate both theoretical and empirical meaning effectively.

◆ Notes

1. So much of my own and other people's thinking about images is influenced by John Berger's *Ways of Seeing*. First published in Britain by the BBC in 1972, it is based on a lecture series given by Berger, now available from Penguin Books. It is one of the seminal works on images. Even thought the ostensible focus is on art, its language and application are interdisciplinary. I recommend it highly to all social science researchers.

2. See, for example, Prosser's (1992) discussion of the role of photography in ethnography.

◆ References

Allen, P. (1995). *Art is a way of knowing*. Boston: Shambhala Press.

Bachelard, G. (1964). *The poetics of space* (M. Jolas, Trans.). Boston: Beacon Press.

Bagley, C., & Cancienne, M. B. (Eds.). (2002a). *Dancing the data.* New York: Peter Lang.

Bagley, C., & Cancienne, M. B. (2002b). Educational research and intertextual forms of (re)presentation: The case for dancing the data. In C. Bagely & M. B. Cancienne (Eds.), *Dancing the data* (pp. 3–19). New York: Peter Lang.

Banks, M. (2001). *Visual methods in social research.* London: Sage.

Barone, T. (1995). The purposes of arts-based educational research. *International Journal of Educational Research, 23*(2), 169–180.

Barthes, R. (1981). *Camera lucida: Reflections on photography.* New York: Noonday Press.

Barthes, R. (1983). *A Barthes reader* (S. Sontag, Ed.). New York: Hill & Wang.

Baudrillard, J. (1993). *Symbolic exchange and death.* London: Sage.

Baudrillard, J. (1988). Simulacra and simulations. In M. Poster (Ed.), *Jean Baudrillard: Selected writings* (pp. 166–184). Stanford, CA: Stanford University Press.

Becker, H. S. (1974). Photography and sociology. *Studies in the Anthropology of Visual Communication, 1*(1), 3–26.

Becker, H. S. (1986). *Doing things together: Selected papers.* Evanston, IL: Northwestern University Press.

Benjamin, W. (1969). *Illuminations* (H. Zohn, Trans.). New York: Schocken Books.

Berger, J. (1972). *Ways of seeing.* London: Penguin.

Bourdieu, P. (1990). *Photography: A middle-brow art.* Stanford, CA: Stanford University Press.

Bruner, E. M. (Ed.). (1984). *Text, play, and story: The construction and reconstruction of self and society.* Washington, DC: The American Ethnological Society.

Chalfen, R. (1987). *Snapshot versions of life.* Bowling Green, OH: Bowling Green State University Press.

Chaplin, E. (1994). *Sociology and visual representation.* London: Routledge.

Cole, A. (2001, November). The art of research: Arts-informed research. *University of Toronto Bulletin,* p. 16.

Cole, A. L., & McIntyre, M. (2001, Summer). Dance me to an understanding of teaching.

A performative text. *Journal of Curriculum Theorizing,* 43–60.

Denzin, N. K. (1995). The experiential text and the limits of visual understanding. *Educational Theory, 45*(1), 7–19.

Denzin, N. K., & Lincoln, Y. S. (Eds.). (2000). *Handbook of qualitative research* (2nd ed.). Thousand Oaks, CA: Sage.

de Saussure, F. (1988). *Course in general linguistics* (R. Harris, Trans.). Chicago: Open Court. (Original work published 1915)

Eisner, E. (1995). What artistically crafted research can help us to understand about schools. *Educational Theory, 45*(1), 1–13.

Eisner, E. W. (1997). The promise and perils of alternative forms of data representation. *Educational Researcher, 26*(6), 4–11.

Evans, J., & Hall, S. (Eds.). (1999). *Visual culture: The reader.* Thousand Oaks, CA: Sage.

Ewald, W. (2000). *Secret games: Collaborative works with children (1969–1999).* Berlin: Scalo.

Foucault, M. (1983). *This is not a pipe* (J. Harkness, Trans. & Ed.). Berkeley: University of California Press.

Gauntlett, D. (1997). *Video critical: Children, the environment, and media power.* Luton, UK: John Libby Media.

Greenblat, C. (2005). *Visual dimensions of a critical illness.* Paper presented at the annual meeting of the International Visual Sociology Association, Dublin.

Greene, M. (1995). *Releasing the imagination: Essays on education, the arts, and social change.* San Francisco: Jossey-Bass.

Grumet, M. R. (1988). *Bitter milk: Women and teaching.* Amherst: University of Massachusetts Press.

Harnad, S. (1991). *Back to the oral tradition: Through skywriting at the speed of thought.* Retrieved June 17, 2005, from http://www.cogsci.soton.ac.uk/%7Eharnad /Papers/Harnad/harnad/skyteaching.html

Harper, D. (1998). On the authority of the image: Visual methods at the crossroads. In N. K. Denzin & Y. S. Lincoln (Eds.), *Collecting and interpreting qualitative research* (pp. 403–412). Thousand Oaks, CA: Sage Publications.

Harper, D. (2002). Talking about pictures: A case for photo elicitation. *Visual Studies, 17*(1), 13–26.

Hubbard, J. (1994). *Shooting back from the reservation.* New York: New Press.

Jenks, C. (Ed.). (1995). *Visual culture.* New York: Routledge.

Jipson, J. A., & Paley, N. (Eds.). (1997). *Daredevil research.* New York: Peter Lang.

Kuhn, A. (1995). A credit to her mother. In A. Kuhn, *Family secrets: Acts of memory and imagination* (pp. 40–58). London: Verso.

Langer, S. K. (1957). *Problems of art: Ten philosophical lectures.* New York: Scribner.

Langford, M. (2001). *Suspended conversations: The afterlife of memory in photographic albums.* Montreal, Quebec, Canada: McGill-Queens University Press.

Merrell, F. M. (1997). *Peirce, signs, and meaning.* Toronto, Ontario, Canada: University of Toronto Press.

Mirzoeff, N. (Ed.). (1998). *The visual culture reader.* New York: Routledge.

Mitchell, C., & Weber, S. J. (1998). Picture this! Class line-ups, vernacular portraits, and lasting impressions of school. In J. Prosser (Ed.), *Image-based research: A sourcebook for qualitative researchers* (pp. 197–213). London: Falmer Press.

Mitchell, C. A., & Weber, S. J. (1999a). Picture this: Using school photographs to study ourselves. In C. A. Mitchell & S. J. Weber, *Reinventing ourselves as teachers: Beyond nostalgia* (pp. 74–123). London: Falmer Press.

Mitchell, C. A., & Weber, S. J. (1999b). *Reinventing ourselves as teachers: Beyond nostalgia.* London: Falmer Press.

Mitchell, C., & Weber, S. (in press). *Doing visual research.* Thousand Oaks, CA: Sage.

Ong, W. J. (1982). *Orality and literacy: The technologizing of the word.* London: Methuen.

Paley, N. (1995). *Finding art's place: Experiments in contemporary education and culture.* New York: Routledge.

Prosser, J. (1992). Personal reflections on the use of photography in an ethnographic case study. *British Educational Research Journal, 18*(4), 397–411.

Prosser, J. (Ed.). (1998a). *Image-based research: A sourcebook for qualitative research.* London: Falmer Press.

Prosser, J. (1998b). The status of image-based research. In J. Prosser (Ed.), *Image-based research: A sourcebook for qualitative research* (pp. 97–112). London: Falmer Press.

Ruby, J. (1996). Visual anthropology. In D. Levinson & M. Ember (Eds.), *Encyclopedia of cultural anthropology* (pp. 1345–1351). New York: Henry Holt & Co.

Sontag, S. (1977). *On photography.* New York: Doubleday.

Spence, J. (1995). *Cultural snipping: The art of transgression.* New York: Routledge.

Steele, B. (1998). *Draw me a story: An illustrated explanation of drawing-as-language.* Manitoba, Canada: Peguis Publishers.

Sturken, M., & Cartwright, L. (2001). *Practices of looking: An introduction to visual culture.* Oxford, UK: Oxford University Press.

Tagg, J. (1993). *The burden of representation: Essays on photographies and histories.* Minneapolis: University of Minnesota Press.

Van Leewen, T., & Jewitt, C. (2001). *Handbook of visual analysis.* London: Sage.

Walker, J. A., & Chaplin, S. (1997). *Visual culture: An introduction.* Manchester, UK: Manchester University Press.

Walkerdine, V. (1990). *Schoolgirl fictions.* London: Verso.

Wang, C. (1999). Photovoice: A participatory action research strategy applied to women's health. *Journal of Women's Health, 8*(2), 85–192.

Weber, S. J. (2002). *Using video in research: Methodological issues.* Symposium at the annual conference of the American Educational Research Association, New Orleans, LA.

Weber, S. (Director). (2004). *I am a woman now* [3-minute digital video loop for art installation]. Montreal, Quebec, Canada: Taffeta Productions.

Weber, S. J., & Mitchell, C. A. (1995a). More than words: Drawing out the gendered nature of teacher identity and work. In S. J. Weber & C. A. Mitchell, *"That's funny, you don't look like a teacher": Interrogating images, identity, and popular culture* (pp. 33–53.). London: Falmer Press.

Weber, S. J., & Mitchell, C. A. (1995b). *"That's funny, you don't look like a teacher": Interrogating images, identity, and popular culture.* London: Falmer Press.

Weber, S. J., & Mitchell, C. A. (1996). Drawing ourselves into teaching: Studying the images that shape and distort teacher education. *Teaching and Teacher Education, 12*(3), 303–313.

Weber, S. J. (Director), & Mitchell, C. (2000). *Dress fitting* [Documentary]. Montreal, Quebec, Canada: Concordia University and Image and Identity Research Collective.

Weber, S. J. (Director), & Mitchell, C. (2003). *Canadian pie* [Documentary]. Montreal, Quebec, Canada: Concordia University and Image and Identity Research Collective.

Weber, S. J., & Mitchell, C. (Eds.). (2004a). *Not just any dress: Narratives of memory, body, and identity.* New York: Peter Lang.

Weber, S. J., & Mitchell, C. A. (2004b). Using visual and artistic modes of representation for self-study. In J. Loughran, M. Hamilton, V. LaBoskey, & T. Russell (Eds.), *International handbook of self-study of teaching and teacher education practices* (pp. 979–1037). Dordrecht, Netherlands: Kluwer Press.

Weber, S. J. (Director), Mitchell, C., & Tardiff, C. (2002). *What can a researcher do with a video camera?* [Digital video]. Montreal, Quebec, Canada: Concordia University and Image and Identity Research Collective.

Weber, S. J., & Weber, J. (2007). A case study of technology in the everyday lives of tweens. In S. Weber and S. Dixon (Eds.), *Growing up on-line* (pp. 49–68). New York: Palgrave.

Winterson, J. (1995). *Art objects: Essays on ecstasy and effrontery.* London: Random House.

5

ARTS-INFORMED RESEARCH

◆ Ardra L. Cole and J. Gary Knowles

BEGINNINGS

Contemporary American artist Martha Rosler (cited in Gever, 1981) states, "[If you want to] bring conscious, concrete knowledge to your work . . . you had better locate yourself pretty concretely in it" (p. 11). We are life history researchers with deep roots in meaning making systems that honor the many and diverse ways of knowing—personal, narrative, embodied, artistic, aesthetic—that stand outside sanctioned intellectual frameworks. To begin this chapter we surface these roots.

ARDRA

As the youngest of three children and an only and much-wanted daughter, I grew up in the coddled environment of adults. Around kitchen tables, with my mother and her friends, I learned to make sense of the world. It was there that meaning was given to all that was good, bad, and indifferent in my mother's world as she and her friends philosophized and analyzed their way through bottomless teacups and countless packs of Black Cat cigarettes. Together for friendly visits, neighborly chats, weekly card games, domestic chores, or planning and preparing for community events, they'd tell stories, share opinions and confidences, gossip, give and receive advice and emotional support. I'd listen and watch as smoke, slowly but confidently released through crimson- and cotton candy–colored lips, enwreathed their spoken words. I took it all in, adding the knowledge to my accumulating understandings of my small but growing world. I formed (silent) opinions of my own, felt pleasure and pain, learned compassion, made promises to myself about how I would be in the world and what I would do. As a child of the 1950s and 1960s, at "the academy of the kitchen table" (Neilsen, 1998) in the company of women, I ground the lenses through which I see and understand the world.

After my mother's funeral, on the way to the cemetery, the silence of our inconsolable grief was finally broken by my niece who, between body-wracking sobs, pleaded with her father to tell some "Nanny stories." Telling stories of my mother, at a time when almost nothing made sense or seemed fair, was the only thing that did make sense to us. After all, "The truth about stories," says Aboriginal scholar Thomas King (2003, p. 2), "is that's all we are." They are who we are, who we have been, and who we will become.

I grew up in a working-class family, steeped in the Protestant work ethic, where actions spoke louder than words and "big feeling" people with "high falutin'" ideas didn't pass muster. What mattered most was the reward of a solid day's work and meaty ideas that produced tangible results and made a difference in the lives of everyday people. It was no surprise to discover in graduate school that William James's philosophy of pragmatism made inherent sense to me. Subsequently, the choices I made throughout my academic life and career naturally reflected the values and perspectives I grew up with.

GARY

I lived in the southernmost province of Aotearoa, New Zealand, for the first 22 years of my life. As an only child I often came to express and require the quietness of solitude in explorations of landscape and community. This fostered an ability to follow my own intuitions and dreams rather than those of siblings or peers. Also, for the first 13 years of my life, I grew head and shoulders above my peers in physical stature and this played out in some unexpected ways. For instance, I never experienced degradation at the hand of bullies and was most often the master of my own childhood games, fantasies, and explorations.

In a windswept, small, rural town I learned about the power of place and had the freedom to explore and express the learnings that resulted from being relatively unfettered in my day-to-day movements. Cycling throughout the community and beyond, I learned the powers of understanding that, perhaps, only finely tuned observations can bring. I learned experientially and geographically because I had the freedom to roam, sometimes by foot but, mostly, by bicycle.

Intergenerationally, strong women led my family and, to them, I attribute much learning about the order of the world around me. Everything that was done within the family had practical value borne of working-class roots and a quest for neo-middle-class status. Under these conditions and circumstances adults impressed upon me values and stories that afforded a glimpse into who I was and would become and where I came from. The power of personal and family stories was more than mildly obvious to me then as it is now. Like me, extended family members had both individual and familial scripts to follow but, unlike me, had little opportunity to deviate from them. Family stories, often about the context or experiences of labor, were told and retold in the context of yet more laboring work. Such was the source of my ingrained perspectives on the relationship between the purpose of one's life work and the public good.

Influenced strongly by a pragmatic, hard working mother, my emerging values were metered by an avocational artist father (whose dreams of daily existence seldom experienced joy in the mundane). Influenced by him, I gravitated toward the visual arts, eventually becoming involved in architecture. Not surprisingly, it was the technical, the pragmatic—the vernacular—that guided the emerging principles of design and aesthetics that I came to hold. A job needed to be accomplished, a building built, and there was always a bottom-line, functional element involved. Years later, having honed my drafting and painterly skills, I regularly exhibited work and came to see myself as a visual artist. This coincided somewhat with the process of becoming an academic, seeing myself as a scholar. Given these circumstances, it was natural that I sought ways to fuse artistry and artmaking with scholarship that evidenced a practical bent.

◆ Dissatisfaction and Disillusionment

Prior to assuming roles as academics and learning the language of the academy, we did not put names on how we (and others) came to know the world. But, as professors, we quickly came to know that our jobs were in large part defined by our abilities to attach words of explanation to phenomena, experiences, processes, contexts, and systems. We soon discovered, however, that the predominant language—or discourse—of the

academy did not ring true to us or how we perceived our task.

We quickly became disillusioned by the moat of science and mysticism built to keep researchers in and communities out of the ivory tower. Bolstered and challenged by our personal histories to build a bridge across the moat, we began to question the pragmatic value of our conventional-looking scholarship and imagine new possibilities. The language of the academy and all that it symbolized fell short in its ability to capture and communicate the complexity of human experience in all its diversity. Even challenging conventions of positivism and following qualitative research methodologies resulted in research representations wrung dry of life—of emotion, of sensuality, of physicality. Individuals and their lives were flattened into a form mostly unrecognizable to those directly and indirectly involved or represented. The result, with just the right academic ring, satisfied the academy but, with the extraction of life juices, those words became too light to take hold in the lives of the people and communities we researched.

We sought what we considered to be more appropriately inclusive approaches to inquiry processes and representation—methodologies that honored the diverse forms of knowing that were part of everyday experience and that paid appropriate respect to both research participants and those who "read" or might be interested in "reading" research texts. Our goals related to integrity, relevance, accessibility, and engagement. We wanted research to reach audiences beyond the academy and to make a difference.

◆ Enter the Arts

Within the broad paradigmatic framework containing qualitative methodologies, we began to experiment with process and form. We started in small ways, beginning, for example, by writing journal articles in alternative formats and in a personal narrative style with autobiographical elements. Our challenges to methodological convention got bolder as our experimentations with form brought color, texture, and life into work that had begun to seem grey, flat, and lifeless. These explorations, and the promises and possibilities they inspired, reawakened in us an excitement for our work. They reconnected us with our long-held epistemological roots and brought together elements of our personal and professional lives that had, to that point, been forced apart by academic orthodoxy. We continued to push boundaries of what was then possible in inquiry and representation (i.e., marginally acceptable as scholarship), trying to get closer and closer to human experience and to communicate it in a way that seemed truer to its original form and to those who may be involved.

Drawing on our artistic sensibilities, relationship to the arts, and respect for ways in which artists of all genres have, throughout history, tackled society's pressing sociopolitical concerns and confronted public audiences with their messages, we turned our attention to the relationship between art and research and the possibilities inherent in infusing processes and representational forms of the arts into social science inquiry. We began by dabbling with two- and three-dimensional art, performance, and fiction mainly for purposes of representation. At the same time we encouraged graduate students to explore media of poetry, literary prose, playwriting, visual arts, dance, and music as alternative approaches to knowledge representation and advancement.

By the early 1990s, a wave of change began to swell particularly in the educational research community where, perhaps because of its broad intellectual heritage or because of its interdisciplinary

nature or its broader commitment to practice and practical application of research, there is a history of methodological innovation. In 1993, Elliot Eisner gave a distinguished Presidential Address to the Annual Meeting of the American Educational Research Association (AERA) in which he speculated about the future of educational research witnessing an expanding array of research methods to acknowledge and account for the range of forms and modes of understanding that comprise human development. "Images created by literature, poetry, the visual arts, dance, and music," he states,

> give us insights that inform us in the special ways that only artistically rendered forms make possible. . . . [Beyond stories and narrative] film, video, the multiple displays made possible through computers, and even poetically crafted narrative are waiting in the wings. . . . We won't have long to wait until they are called to center stage. (pp. 7, 8)

Soon after, the Arts-Based Educational Research Special Interest Group of AERA was formed and quickly grew.

In 1997, Stefinee Pinnegar organized a groundbreaking session at the AERA Annual Meeting in which she invited several researchers to represent a set of conventionally gathered data each using a different art form such as painting, dance, creative nonfiction, readers' theatre, and poetry. At about this time a small but growing number of scholarly outlets (book and journal publications and professional and academic conferences) started to support "alternative" qualitative research. In 1998, at the Ontario Institute for Studies in Education of the University of Toronto, we started an informal working group of faculty and graduate students with a shared commitment to exploring, articulating, and supporting each other in bringing together art and social science research. As word got out and interest grew, the working group became formalized.

The Centre for Arts-Informed Research was established in 2000. It provides a context for promoting innovative research that infuses processes and forms of the arts into scholarly work for purposes of advancing knowledge and bridging the connection between academy and community. Those associated with the Centre continue to explore, encourage, and foster arts-informed research in a variety of ways through seminars, workshops, and works-in-progress series; exhibits, performances, and conference presentations; an active research and publishing program; and ongoing supervision and support of graduate students engaged in arts-informed research.

The time was right to forge ahead with formalizing and articulating the theoretical underpinnings, practices, and issues associated with the methodology that was emerging from our research and that of graduate students with whom we worked. It was also important to distinguish it from other companion methodologies established and evolving at the same time, such as arts-based research, art-based inquiry, image-based research, and visual sociology. This was important so as to, in Eisner's (1993) words, "achieve complementarity rather than methodological hegemony" (p. 9).

◆ *Arts-Informed Research*

Arts-informed research is a mode and form of qualitative research in the social sciences that is influenced by, but not based in, the arts broadly conceived. The central purposes of arts-informed research are to enhance understanding of the human condition through alternative (to conventional) processes and representational forms of inquiry, and to reach multiple audiences by making scholarship more accessible. The methodology infuses the languages, processes, and forms of literary, visual, and performing arts with the expansive possibilities of scholarly inquiry for purposes of advancing knowledge (Cole, 2001, 2004; Cole & Knowles, 2001; Knowles & Cole, 2002). Researchers working in this way might explicitly ground the processes and representational forms in one or several of the arts (see, e.g., Cole, Neilsen, Knowles, & Luciani, 2004; Knowles, Luciani, Cole, & Neilsen, 2007; Neilsen, Cole, & Knowles, 2001).

Arts-informed research is a way of redefining research form and representation and creating new understandings of process, spirit, purpose, subjectivities, emotion, responsiveness, and the ethical dimensions of inquiry. This redefinition reflects an explicit challenge to logical positivism and technical rationality as the only acceptable guides to explaining human behavior and understanding. Bringing together the systematic and rigorous qualities of conventional qualitative methodologies with the artistic, disciplined, and imaginative qualities of the arts acknowledges the power of art forms to reach diverse audiences and the importance of diverse languages for gaining insights into the complexities of the human condition.

The dominant paradigm of positivism historically has governed the way research is defined, conducted, and communicated and consciously and unconsciously defined what society accepts as Knowledge; however, it is not a paradigm that reflects how individuals in society actually experience and process the world. Life is lived and knowledge made through kitchen table conversations and yarnin' at the wharf or transit station or coffee shop or tavern, in the imaginative spaces created between the lines of a good book or an encounter with an evocative photograph, in an embodied response to a musical composition or interpretive dance. These moments of meaning making, however, are not typically thought of as Knowledge. "Knowledge," as society has learned to define it, dwells beyond the realm of the everyday. It is discovered by intellectuals—researchers and theorists—and held by them until its implications are determined and passed on for consumption. Knowledge is propositional and generalizable and Research is the process by which it is generated.

According to this paradigmatic view, Knowledge remains the purview of the academy where it can be carefully defined and controlled. But, as Eisner (1993, p. 6) states:

> Humans are sentient creatures who live in a qualitative world. The sensory system that humans possess provides the means through which the qualities of the world are experienced . . . [and] out of experience, concepts are formed. . . . Our conceptual life, shaped by imagination and the qualities of the world experienced, gives rise to the intentions that direct our activities.

Arts-informed research, with one of its main goals of accessibility (and breadth of audience), is an attempt to acknowledge individuals in societies as knowledge makers engaged in the act of knowledge advancement. Tied to moral purpose, it is also an explicit attempt to make a difference through research, not only in the lives of ordinary citizens but also in the thinking and decisions of policymakers, politicians, legislators, and other key decision makers.

Arts-informed research is part of a broader commitment to shift the dominant paradigmatic view that keeps the academy and community separated: to acknowledge the multiple dimensions that constitute and form the human condition—physical, emotional, spiritual, social, cultural—and the myriad ways of engaging in the world—oral, literal, visual, embodied. That is, to connect the work of the academy with the life and lives of communities through research that is accessible, evocative, embodied, empathic, and provocative.

Following Suzi Gablik (1991), arts-informed research is part of a larger agenda to reenchant research. According to Gablik, reenchantment

> means stepping beyond the modern traditions of mechanism, positivism, empiricism, rationalism, materialism, secularism and scientism—the whole objectifying consciousness of the Enlightenment—in a way that allows for a return of soul. . . . It also refers to that change in the general social mood toward a new paradigmatic idealism and a more integrated value system that brings head and heart together. (p. 11)

◆ Defining Elements and Form

- How can the arts (broadly conceived) inform the research process?

- How can the arts inform the representational form of research?

As a framework for inquiry, arts-informed research is sufficiently fluid and flexible to serve either as a methodological enhancement to other research approaches or as a stand-alone qualitative methodology. For example, as a methodological enhancement, one might conduct an arts-informed life history study (see, e.g., McIntyre, 2000; Miller, 2001; Promislow, 2005), an arts-informed phenomenological inquiry (see, e.g., Halifax, 2002; Rykov, 2006; Thomas, 2004), an arts-informed narrative inquiry (see, e.g., Kunkel, 2000), or an arts-informed ethnography (see, e.g., McIntyre, 2005). As a stand-alone methodology, situated within a qualitative framework, arts-informed research perspectives enhance the possibilities of information gathering and representation (see, e.g., brown, 2000; Cole & McIntyre, 2001, 2004, 2006; de Freitas, 2003; Gosse, 2005; Grant, 2003; Knowles & Thomas, 2002; Luciani, 2006; Mantas, 2004; Sbrocchi, 2005).

DEFINING ELEMENTS

Broadly grounded in assumptions that define a qualitative paradigm, arts-informed research has several defining elements:

• First and foremost, arts-informed research involves a *commitment to a particular art form* (or forms in the case of mixed or multimedia) that is reflected in elements of the creative research process and in the representation of the research "text." The selected art form or forms serve to frame and define the inquiry process and "text."

• The *methodological integrity* of the research, a second defining element, is determined in large part by the relationship between the form and substance of the research text and the inquiry process reflected in the text. In other words, the rationale for the use of photography, for example, as the defining art form guiding the inquiry or representation must be readily apparent by how and how well it works to illuminate and achieve the research purposes.

• Following the emergent nature of qualitative research in general, *the creative inquiry process* of arts-informed research is defined by an openness to the expansive possibilities of the human imagination. Rather than adhering to a set of rigid guidelines for gathering and working with research material, a researcher using arts-informed methodology follows a more natural process of engagement relying on commonsense decision making, intuition, and a general responsiveness to the natural flow of events and experiences. Serendipity plays a key role in the inquiry process much as it does

in life. Moreover, we infer that researchers can learn from artists about matters of process. That is, the processes of art making inform the inquiry in ways congruent with the artistic sensitivities and technical (artistic) strengths of the researcher in concert with the overall spirit and purpose of the inquiry.

• Also, as in most qualitative research, the subjective and reflexive *presence of the researcher* is evident in the research text in varying ways depending on the focus and purpose of the inquiry. In arts-informed research, however, the researcher's artistry is also predominant. By artistry, we include conceptual artistry and creative and aesthetic sensibilities, not only technical skills or an externally sanctioned title of "artist." Extending the idea from qualitative inquiry of "researcher as instrument," in arts-informed research the "instrument" of research is also the researcher-as-artist.

• Although we operate on the assumption that all research is inherently autobiographical—a reflection of who we are— arts-informed research is not exclusively about the researcher. In other words, although the focus of an arts-informed inquiry *may* be the researcher herself or himself, it is not necessarily so. Arts-informed research differs, for example, from autoethnography (see Scott-Hoy & Ellis, this volume) or autobiography, both of which focus on the researcher as the subject of inquiry. Arts-informed research has *strong reflexive elements* that evidence the presence and signature of the researcher, but the researcher is not necessarily the focus or subject of study.

• A sixth defining element of arts-informed research relates to *audience*. Consistent with one of the overarching purposes of arts-informed research, there must be an explicit intention for the research to reach communities and audiences including but beyond the academy. The choice and articulation of form will reflect this intention.

- Related to research relevance and accessibility to audience is the *centrality of audience engagement*. The use of the arts in research is not for art's sake. It is explicitly tied to moral purposes of social responsibility and epistemological equity. Thus, the research text is intended to involve the reader/audience in an active process of meaning making that is likely to have transformative potential. Relying on the power of art to both inform and engage, the research text is explicitly intended to evoke and provoke emotion, thought, and action.

FORM

To embrace the potential of the arts to inform scholarship is to be open to the ways in which the literary, visual, or performing arts—and the inherent methods and processes of those various art forms—can inform processes and representations of scholarly inquiry. The relationship between and among research purposes related to knowledge advancement and research communication, art form, and the artist-researchers' grounding in and developing expertise/competence with the chosen art form is key. Indeed, form is the main defining element of arts-informed research. Choice of art form that will guide inquiry processes and/or representation involves a consideration of form in its many manifestations.

- *Form as genre and/or medium* means the way or mode of presenting the text or concepts including text-based means such as fiction, creative nonfiction, and poetry; performative and time-sensitive approaches such as dance, performance, theatre, and music; and image-based approaches including painting, photography, collage, multimedia, sculpture, film/video, folk arts, and installation art. Important in decisions about

form as genre are prior experiences and familiarity with the particular genre or medium and how the use of that medium will contribute to knowledge production—in other words, how representation and inquiry process are unified.

- *Form as method* speaks to the relationship between the art form and the creative inquiry processes. Carl Leggo (2004) describes himself as living in the world as a poet, eager to rethink poetry into human life by engaging in a poetics of research. He describes poetry as a way of "making the world in words . . . a site for dwelling, for holding up, for stopping" (Leggo, 1998, p. 182). Carl's poetic research texts and the creative process they represent echo his way of being in the world as a poet. His work is a vivid example of how form and method can dwell in communion.

- *Form as structural element* refers to the literal or metaphorical arrangements of theoretical constructs, narratives, experiences, and their various representations, so that there is a coherent articulation of a particular perspective that illustrates knowledge production and purposeful communication. For example, Lois Kunkel's (2000) research about children of missionaries from their now adult perspectives is set in West Africa, where the author herself grew up as a child of missionary parents. West Africa is also the home of the mythological character, Anansi the Spider. Because, coincidentally, an epiphanal event in Lois's early life also involved a spider, she chose to work with a spider metaphor to define the structure of her research text. The result is an evocative and compelling arts-informed narrative, *Spiders Spin Silk,* with the Anansi stories providing the metaphorical structure for the research text.

- *Form as technical element* refers to the place of templates for designing the physical appearance of the document—how the text and media are presented on the page. In her book *Of Earth and Flesh and Bones and Breath: Landscapes of Embodiment and Moments of Re-enactment*, Suzanne Thomas (2004) uses languages of poetry and photography to create an intertextual space for phenomenological engagement with the natural world. Her intent is for the reader to "dwell in the intimacy of knowledge" and experience aesthetic representations "as a continuous unfolding of meanings" (p. 12). To create this kind of engagement, Suzanne developed a template for the aesthetic arrangement of visual and textual fragments—a skeletal frame to hold image and text in rhythmic patterns. The beauty, sensuality, and overall power of this work are in large part due to the author's attention to compositional arrangement and her use of an organizational template to "develop a symbiotic synergy between the elements of images/space/words" (p. 7).

• *Form as communication element* involves a consideration of both audience and research purpose to determine whether the form is optimal for full and rich communication of ideas and constructs. In other words, to paraphrase Elliot Eisner (1993), decisions about form as communication involve consideration of the question, "How and whom will the form inform?"

• *Form as aesthetic element* relates to how the work "should" look based on the aesthetic principles and conventions of the genre. By aesthetic we mean consideration of the enduring principles of form and composition, of weight and light, of color and line, of texture and tone, as when working in the painterly arts, for example. The aesthetic element reflects how central principles upheld in a variety of art forms—internal consistency and coherence, clarity and quality, authenticity and sincerity,

evocation and resonance—combine to contribute to the beauty of the work. Attending to aesthetics of form does not necessarily mean that researchers identify themselves as artists or have extensive background or experience in arts production. It does mean, though, that the researcher-as-artist must make a commitment to learning how the aesthetic elements of an art form can inform a research project.

• *Form as procedural element and emergent phenomenon* means that elements of form may change over time as the inquiry matures or develops and as ideas evolve. Inspiration for form may come at the outset and drive an inquiry. Inspiration may also present itself in various ways at any point in the research process; often it is because of implicit or metaphorical connections that become evident while immersed in the inquiry process. Inspiration may have rational, reasoned sources or it may be happenstance, serendipitous. It is at these times that the researcher's full depth of professional experience and perspective come into play. The researcher is, after all, the instrument of form.

• *Form as reflection of the qualities of goodness of inquiry* requires that, while the research must exhibit qualities of sound scholarship (focus, intensity, authority, relevance, substance, and so on), it must do so in a way that is congruent with the art form used. This speaks to the form being integral to research purposes and procedural approaches in conjunction with the potential of the work to influence the public good. The qualities of goodness (elaborated later in the chapter) are a set of broad principles that guide and define the qualities of arts-informed research. Under scrutiny it ought to be evident that the purposes, processes, orientations, literatures, and outcomes of the study work together in harmony.

◆ *Ways and Means of Finding Form*

FINDING FORM THROUGH DATA

During research conversations with professors of teacher education in a life history study, Ardra became vividly aware that some of the experiences being recounted were so imbued with emotion and such poignant illustrations of the often dysfunctional relationship between academic institutions and individual faculty members' goals and values that conventional forms of representing these experiences seemed inadequate. Frequently, the participants used graphic language to create images or metaphors to describe elements of their experience. They often struggled to find words to adequately convey the passion and emotion felt about certain issues and experiences. In an attempt to find a representational form that would more closely render the aesthetic of lived experience, however partial, and afford readers better opportunities for their own resonant interpretations, Ardra turned to the *tableau* art form, inspired by American contemporary artists Edward Kienholz and Nancy Reddin Kienholz.

The experiences recounted by the teacher educators, and the themes and issues embedded in those experiences and in the telling of them, inspired the conceptualization and creation of a series of three-dimensional representations entitled *Living in Paradox* (Cole, Knowles, brown, & Buttignol, 1999). In *Academic Altarcations* a conveyor belt carries symbols of personal sacrifice to the altar of the academy. *A Perfect Imbalance* is an unevenly weighted balance scale that depicts the dual mandate of teacher educators' work and the associated elusive pursuit of a balanced life. In *Wrestling Differences,* action figures set up in a toy wrestling ring depict the gender inequities that continue to define much of academic

life for women. Together, the images rely on shock value and exaggeration to draw viewers in to connect with the truths expressed, the ultimate goal being to precipitate the creation of a more humane and generous reality for teacher educators in the academy.

FINDING FORM BASED ON RESEARCHER'S ARTISTIC IDENTITY

During a visit to an art gallery, Gary came across the photographic and installation work of Canadian artist Marlene Creates. He was both intrigued and motivated by the resonance he felt with her art. The exhibit was a one-person, multi-installation, retrospective work entitled *Marlene Creates: Land Works 1979–1991* (Creates, 1992). The work portrays notions of space and place and humans' impressions and responses.

Two installations within the larger exhibit clearly expressed Creates's method of artistic inquiry. *The Distance Between Two Points Is Measured in Memories* (Creates, 1990) explored "the relationship between human experience and the landscape and, in particular, the ways in which landscape is richly and profoundly differentiated into 'places'" (Creates, quoted in Garvey, 1993, p. 20). The artist was primarily interested in how people remember place, and she used black and white photography, personal narratives, and graphite map drawings on paper with artifacts/found objects to articulate her artistic findings about individuals' memories of the landscape. *Places of Presence: Newfoundland Kin and Ancestral Land, Newfoundland, 1989–1991* (Creates, 1991) consisted of photographs, handwritten narratives, and hand-drawn memory maps, along with found objects as artifacts.

The complexities, yet also the simplicities, of Creates's life history-based, visual stories were obvious. She showed the personal strengths and attachments of her relatives to place and community and her own responses to them and their contexts. Her work reinforced Gary's intuitive feelings about the limitations of conventional, oral, and text-based life history work. Creates's work also offered insights into the creative art-making inquiry process. This happenstance encounter by one artist with the work of another gave rise to a program of research on "sense of place" that evolved over several years (see, e.g., Knowles & Thomas, 2000, 2002; Thomas & Knowles, 2002).

FINDING FORM BASED ON INTENDED AUDIENCE

In a research project on caregiving and Alzheimer's disease (Cole & McIntyre, 2004, 2006; McIntyre & Cole, 2006), the researchers identified public education and caregiver support as two of their goals. They created a seven-piece, two- and three-dimensional mixed media installation about caregiving and Alzheimer's disease that paid tribute to those with the illness and those in caregiving roles. One purpose of the exhibit was to make Alzheimer's disease more familiar to a wide public audience. Another aim was to provide opportunities for those directly affected by the illness to feel affirmed and supported. The Alzheimer's Project was displayed for several days in prominent public venues across Canada, and family caregivers were invited to view the work and share their experiences of Alzheimer's disease and caregiving through group and individual conversations and by contributing written responses and artifacts related to their experiences. Members of the general public responded through written comments and audiotape-recorded stories. Visitors to the exhibit were invited to participate in different ways. They could view the work; sit with others and enjoy conversation over a puzzle or game; share a thought, impression, or story by writing in a journal or speaking into a tape recorder; leave a memory (a poem, photograph, or memento) and be part of a collective remembering of care; and/or participate in a group conversation about issues of caregiving. Creating spaces for people to feel comfortable with the work was one of the central principles guiding the researchers' attention to form.

Regardless of how or when an art form is selected as a key methodological component, important in arts-informed research is the researcher's commitment to it in all of its manifestations.

◆ Qualities of Goodness in Arts-Informed Research

Arts-informed research, in process and representational form, is neither prescriptive nor codified. It is the creative meshing of scholarly and artistic endeavors. Nevertheless, like all research, studies following arts-informed research methodology must be subjected to scrutiny to assess, and perhaps help to explain, their worth or value as research. A broad assessment is guided by the two general questions: How do the arts inform the research process, and how do the arts inform the research representation? More specifically, a study imbued with the following qualities is one that is likely to both exemplify and contribute to the broad agenda of arts-informed research, that of enhancing understanding of the human condition through alternative (to conventional) processes and representational forms of inquiry, and reaching multiple audiences by making scholarship more accessible.

• **Intentionality.** All research has one or more purposes but not all research is driven by a moral commitment. Consistent with the broad agenda of social science research to improve the human condition, arts-informed research has both a clear *intellectual purpose* and *moral purpose.* Ultimately, the research must stand for something. Arts-informed research representations, then, are not intended as titillations but as opportunities for transformation, revelation, or some other intellectual and moral shift. They must be more than good stories, images, or performances. For example brenda brown's (2000) *Lost Bodies and Wild Imaginations* is a provocative tale about telling and "what it's like to tell about childhood sexual abuse through artistic enterprise." brown describes the intention of her work as "a testimony to lives lost and lives reclaimed, to the power of the imagination to . . . return these histories to their rightful place in the world" (p. ii). (www.sagepub.com/knowlessupplement)

• **Researcher Presence.** A researcher's presence is evident in a number of ways throughout an arts-informed research "text" (in whatever form it is presented and, by implication, throughout the entire researching process). The researcher is present through an explicit *reflexive self-accounting;* her presence is also implied and *felt,* and the research text (the representational form) clearly bears the *signature* or *fingerprint* of researcher-as-artist. Nancy Davis Halifax is a visual artist, poet, prose writer, and researcher in areas of health, disability, and homelessness. Her work (e.g., Halifax, 2002, 2007) is a vivid example of artist-researcher confluence. (www.sagepub.com/knowlessupplement)

• **Aesthetic Quality.** The central purpose of arts-informed research is knowledge advancement through research, not the production of fine art works. Art is a medium through which research purposes are achieved. The quality of the artistic elements of an arts-informed research project is defined by how well the artistic process and form serve research goals. Attention to the aesthetics of a particular genre are, therefore, important; aesthetics of form are integrally tied to communication. In *On Women's Domestic Knowledge and Work: Growing Up in an Italian Kitchen* (2006), Teresa Luciani combines fiction, autobiography, and photography in an exploration that celebrates the depth and complexity of domestic knowledge and makes visible women's domestic labor. The power and beauty of her work reflects rigorous attention to the aesthetic qualities of each art form and, in turn, how the art forms combine in an aesthetic whole. (www.sagepub.com/knowlessupplement)

• **Methodological Commitment.** Arts-informed research evidences attention to the defining elements and form of arts-informed research. As such the work reflects a methodological commitment through evidence of a *principled process, procedural harmony,* and attention to *aesthetic quality. Love Stories About Caregiving and Alzheimer's Disease* (McIntyre & Cole, 2006) is a 45-minute spoken word performance created from data gathered in a study of caregivers' experiences of caring for a loved one with Alzheimer's disease. Working with the data to identify substantive themes related to the research purpose, it became clear that, to preserve the integrity of and honor the caregivers' experiences, the form of representation needed to remain true to the narrative and emotive quality of what people contributed. (www.sagepub.com/knowlessupplement)

• **Holistic Quality.** From purpose to method to interpretation and representation, arts-informed research is a holistic process and rendering that runs counter to more conventional research endeavors that tend to be more linear, sequential, compartmentalized, and distanced from researcher and participants. A rigorous arts-informed "text" is imbued with an *internal consistency* and *coherence* that represents a strong and seamless relationship between purpose and method (process and form). The research text also evidences a high level of *authenticity* that speaks to the truthfulness and sincerity of the research relationship, process of inquiry, interpretation, and representational form. Gary Knowles's and Suzanne Thomas's research with high school students exploring sense of place in schools (Knowles & Thomas, 2000, 2002; Thomas & Knowles, 2002) is an example of holistic quality in research. The student-researchers in the project were at once information gatherers, portraiture artists, and interpreters of experience. The students' creations, made up of personal narratives, photographs, memory maps, and found objects, became at once "data" and representations indicative of the inquiry focus. (www.sagepub .com/knowlessupplement)

• **Communicability.** Foremost in arts-informed work are issues related to audience and the *transformative potential* of the work. Research that maximizes its communicative potential addresses concerns about the *accessibility* of the research account usually through the form and language in which it is written, performed, or otherwise presented. Accessibility is related to the potential for audience engagement and response. Such representations of research have the express purpose of connecting, in a holistic way, with the hearts, souls, and minds of the audience. They are intended to have an *evocative quality* and a high level of *resonance* for diverse audiences. In the Alzheimer's Project, described earlier, children, rural women, and men over 80—people who do not usually attend research presentations—came to see the

work and spend time at the various spaces in the exhibit created for social interaction, information exchange, or silent repose. (www.sagepub.com/knowlessupplement)

• **Knowledge Advancement.** Research is about advancing knowledge however "knowledge" is defined. The knowledge advanced in arts-informed research is generative rather than propositional and based on assumptions that reflect the multidimensional, complex, dynamic, intersubjective, and contextual nature of human experience. In so doing, knowledge claims must be made with sufficient *ambiguity* and *humility* to allow for multiple interpretations and reader response. Kathryn Church's research-based installation, *Fabrications: Stitching Ourselves Together,* is constructed around 22 wedding dresses that her mother sewed over 50 years. From 1997 to 2001, she exhibited the work in public venues to audiences who could immediately connect with the familiarity of the display and be challenged, perhaps for the first time, to think about some of the sociocultural complexities depicted. (www .sagepub.com/knowlessupplement)

• **Contributions.** Tied to the intellectual and moral purposes of arts-informed research are its theoretical and practical contributions. Sound and rigorous arts-informed work has both *theoretical potential* and *transformative potential.* The former acknowledges the centrality of the So What? question and the power of the inquiry work to provide insights into the human condition, while the latter urges researchers to imagine new possibilities for those whom the work is about and for. Researchers are not passive agents of the state, university, or any other agency of society. Researchers' responsibilities are toward fellow humans, neighbors, and community members. Ross Gray and Chris Sinding poignantly confront this issue in their research-based dramas on/with people living with cancer (see, e.g., Gray & Sinding, 2002). (www .sagepub.com/knowlessupplement)

The transformative potential of arts-informed research speaks to the need for researchers to develop representations that address audiences in ways that do not pacify or indulge the senses but arouse them and the intellect to new heights of response and action. In essence, and ideally, the educative possibilities of arts-informed work are foremost in the heart, soul, and mind of the researcher from the onset of an inquiry. The possibilities of such educative endeavors, broadly defined, are near limitless; their power to inform and provoke action are only constrained by the human spirit and its energies.

◆ References

brown, b. (2000). *Lost bodies and wild imaginations: Telling tales of childhood sexual abuse through artful inquiry*. Unpublished doctoral thesis, University of Toronto, Toronto, Ontario, Canada.

Church, K. (1997–2001). *Fabrications: Stitching ourselves together*. Curated exhibit installed in several museums across Canada.

Cole, A. L. (2001, November). The art of research. *The University of Toronto Bulletin*, p. 16.

Cole, A. L. (2004). Provoked by art. In A. L. Cole, L. Neilsen, J. G. Knowles, & T. Luciani (Eds.), *Provoked by art: Theorizing arts-informed inquiry* (pp. 11–17). Halifax, Nova Scotia, Canada: Backalong Books.

Cole, A. L., & Knowles, J. G. (2001). *Lives in context: The art of life history research*. Walnut Creek, CA: AltaMira Press.

Cole, A. L., Knowles, J. G., brown, b., & Buttignol, M. (1999). *Living in paradox: A multi-media representation of teacher educators' lives in context*. Artist statements from a three-part installation presented at the Annual Meeting of the American Educational Research Association, Montreal, Quebec, Canada.

Cole, A. L., & McIntyre, M. (2001). "Dance me to an understanding of teaching": A performative text. *Journal of Curriculum Theorizing, 17*(2), 43–60.

Cole, A. L., & McIntyre, M. (2004) Research as aesthetic contemplation: The role of the audience in research interpretation. *Educational Insights, 9*(1).

Cole, A. L., & McIntyre, M. (2006). *Living and dying with dignity: The Alzheimer's project*. Halifax, Nova Scotia/Toronto, Ontario, Canada: Backalong Books/Centre for Arts-Informed Research.

Cole, A. L., Neilsen, L., Knowles, J. G., & Luciani, T. (Eds.). (2004). *Provoked by art: Theorizing arts-informed inquiry* (Vol. 2, Arts-Informed Inquiry Series). Halifax, Nova Scotia, Canada: Backalong Books.

Creates, M. (1990). *The distance between two points is measured in memories, Labrador 1988*. North Vancouver, British Columbia, Canada: Presentation House Gallery.

Creates, M. (1991). *Places of presence: Newfoundland kin and ancestral land, Newfoundland 1989–1991*. St. John's, Newfoundland, Canada: Killick Press.

Creates, M. (1992). *Marlene Creates: Land works 1979–1991* (S. G. Garvey, Ed. & Curator). St. John's, Newfoundland, Canada: Memorial University of Newfoundland.

de Freitas, E. (2003). *The wrong shoe and other misfits: Fiction writing as reflexive inquiry within a private girls school*. Unpublished doctoral thesis, University of Toronto, Toronto, Ontario, Canada.

Eisner, E. (1993). Forms of understanding the future of educational research. *Educational Researcher, 22*(7), 5–11.

Gablik, S. (1991). Introduction: Changing paradigms, breaking the cultural trance. In S. Gablik, *The reenchantment of art* (pp. 1–12). London: Thames and Hudson.

Garvey, S. G. (Ed. & Curator). (1993). *Marlene Creates: Land works 1979–1991*. St. John's, Newfoundland, Canada: Memorial University of Newfoundland.

Gever, M. (1981). Interview with Martha Rosler. *Afterimage, 9*(3), 11.

Gosse, D. (2005). *Breaking silences: Marginality, resistance and the creative research process.* Unpublished doctoral thesis, University of Toronto, Toronto, Ontario, Canada.

Grant, C. (2003). *Getting it together: Relational learning in a jazz performance context.* Unpublished doctoral thesis, University of Toronto, Toronto, Ontario, Canada.

Gray, R., & Sinding, C. (2002). *Standing ovation: Performing social science research about cancer.* Walnut Creek, CA: AltaMira Press.

Halifax, N. V. D. (2002). *Another form of water: An aesthetic and oblique inquiry into dysbody, solace, and vulnerability.* Unpublished doctoral thesis, University of Toronto, Toronto, Ontario, Canada.

Halifax, N. V. D. (2007). Hidden narratives, intimate voices. In J. G. Knowles, A. L. Cole, T. Luciani, & L. Neilsen, & (Eds.), *The art of visual inquiry* (pp. 3–17). Halifax, Nova Scotia/Toronto, Ontario, Canada: Backalong Books/Centre for Arts-Informed Research.

King, T. (2003). *The truth about stories: A Native narrative.* Toronto, Ontario, Canada: House of Anansi Press.

Knowles, J. G., & Cole, A. L. (2002). Transforming research: Possibilities for arts-informed scholarship. In E. O'Sullivan, M. O'Connor, & A. Morrell (Eds.), *Vision and transformation: Emerging themes in transformative learning* (pp. 199–214). New York: Palgrave.

Knowles, J. G., Luciani, T., Cole, A. L., & Neilsen, L. (Eds.). (2007). *The art of visual inquiry.* Halifax, Nova Scotia/Toronto, Ontario, Canada: Backalong Books/Centre for Arts-Informed Research.

Knowles, J. G., & Thomas, S. (2000). Insights and inspiration from an artist's work: Envisioning and portraying lives-in-context. In A. L. Cole & J. G. Knowles (Eds.), *Lives in context: The art of life history research* (pp. 208–214). Walnut Creek, CA: AltaMira Press.

Knowles, J. G., & Thomas, S. (2002). Artistry, imagery, and sense of place. In C. Bagley & M. B. Cancienne (Eds.), *Dancing the data* (pp. 208–214). New York: Lesley College Arts and Learning Series and Peter Lang Publishing.

Kunkel, L. I. (2000). *Spiders spin silk: Reflections of missionary kids at midlife.* Unpublished doctoral thesis, University of Toronto, Toronto, Ontario, Canada.

Leggo, C. (1998). Living un/grammatically in a grammatical world: The pedagogical world of teachers and students. *Interchange, 29*(2), 169–184.

Leggo, C. (2004). The poet's corpus: Nine speculations. *Journal of Curriculum Theorizing, 20*(2), 65–85.

Luciani, T. (2006). *On women's domestic knowledge and work: Growing up in an Italian kitchen.* Unpublished doctoral thesis, University of Toronto, Toronto, Ontario, Canada.

Mantas, K. (2004). Becoming AIR-BORNe: Women coCREATING, informing & expressing . . . arias. Unpublished doctoral thesis, University of Toronto, Toronto, Ontario, Canada.

McIntyre, M. (2000). *Garden as phenomenon, method, and metaphor: An arts-informed life history view.* Unpublished doctoral thesis, University of Toronto, Toronto, Ontario, Canada.

McIntyre, M. (2005). *RESPECT: A reader's theatre about people who care for people in nursing homes.* Halifax, Nova Scotia/Toronto, Ontario, Canada: Backalong Books/Centre for Arts-Informed Research.

McIntyre, M., & Cole, A. (2006). *Love stories about caregiving and Alzheimer's disease.* Performance available on DVD from http://www.oise.utoronto.ca/research/mappingcare

Miller, E. (2001). *Closing time. Men, identity, vocation, and the end of work: A stage play as a representation of lives.* Unpublished doctoral thesis, University of Toronto, Toronto, Ontario, Canada.

Neilsen, L. (1998). *Knowing her place: Research literacies and feminist occasions.* San Francisco, CA/Halifax, Nova Scotia, Canada: Caddo Gap Press/Backalong Books.

Neilsen, L., Cole, A. L., & Knowles, J. G. (Eds.). (2001). *The art of writing inquiry.* Halifax, Nova Scotia, Canada: Backalong Books.

Promislow, S. (2005). *A collage of borderlands: Arts-informed life histories of childhood immigrants and refugees who maintain their mother tongue.* Unpublished doctoral thesis, University of Toronto, Toronto, Ontario, Canada.

Rykov, M. (2006). *Music at a time like this: Music therapy and cancer support groups.* Unpublished doctoral thesis, University of Toronto, Toronto, Ontario, Canada.

Sbrocchi, S. R. (2005). *Remembering place: Domicide and a childhood home.* Unpublished doctoral thesis, University of Toronto, Toronto, Ontario, Canada.

Thomas, S. (2004). *Of earth and flesh and bones and breath: Landscapes of embodiment and moments of re-eneactment.* Halifax, Nova Scotia/Toronto, Ontario, Canada: Backalong Books/Centre for Arts-Informed Research.

Thomas, S., & Knowles, J. G. (2002). In M. B. Cancienne & C. Bagley (Eds.), *Dancing the data too* [CD-ROM]. New York: Lesley College Arts and Learning Series and Peter Lang Publishers.

6

ARTS-BASED RESEARCH

◆ Susan Finley

Arts-based inquiry is uniquely positioned as a methodology for radical, ethical, and revolutionary research that is futuristic, socially responsible, and useful in addressing social inequities. By its integration of multiple methodologies used in the arts with the postmodern ethics of participative, action-oriented, and politically situated perspectives for human social inquiry, arts-based inquiry has the potential to facilitate critical race, indigenous, queer, feminist, and border theories and research methodologies. As a form of performance pedagogy, arts-based inquiry can be used to advance a subversive political agenda that addresses issues of social inequity. Such work exposes oppression, targets sites of resistance, and outlines possibilities for transformative praxis. From this perspective, arts-based inquiry can explore multiple, new, and diverse ways of understanding and living in the world. This chapter historically situates critical arts-based research, provides examples of its methodologies and representations, and suggests some ways to reposition arts-based research in order to better assure its usefulness as a tool of resistance against the politics of neoconservatism.

◆ *What Is Unique About Arts-Based Research in Relation to Various Forms of Postmodern Qualitative Inquiry?*

At the heart of arts-based inquiry is a radical, politically grounded statement about social justice and control over the production and dissemination of knowledge. By calling upon artful ways of knowing and being in the world, arts-based researchers make a rather audacious challenge to the dominant, entrenched academic community and its claims to scientific ways of knowing. In addition, arts-based methodologies bring both arts and social inquiry out of the elitist institutions of academe and art museums, and relocate inquiry within the realm of local, personal, everyday places and events.

From my reviews of the genre of arts and research (S. Finley, 2003; see also S. Finley, 2005), its most salient features include that arts-based research (1) makes use of emotive, affective experiences, senses, and bodies, and imagination and emotion as well as intellect, as ways of knowing and responding to the world; for example, arts-based researchers have explored the bounds of space and place with the artist's own body (for discussions and examples, see Blumenfeld-Jones, 1995; Cancienne, 1999; Cancienne & Snowber, 2003; S. Finley, 2001a, 2001b); (2) gives interpretive license to the researcher to create meaning from experience (e.g., for discussion in the context of poetics, see Brady, 2004, 2005); (3) attends to the role of form in shaping meaning (Eisner, 1981; see also Arnheim, 1954, 1971; Langer, 1951) by representing research in many different arrangements appropriated from the arts (e.g., dance, film, plastic arts, photography, drama, poetry, and narrative writing); and (4) exists in the tensions of blurred boundaries (Slattery, 2003).

These tensions create the open and dialogic spaces in which arts-based research *performs* social reconstructions (cf., Garoian, 1999; Houston & Pulido, 2002). Arts-based research involves processes of discovery and invention. These are the "moments of epiphany in the culture. Suspended in time, they are liminal moments. They open up institutions and their practices for critical inspection and evaluation" (Lincoln & Denzin, 2003, p. 377). They form the "contingency" spaces in which interpretations of cultural issues are performed (Garoian, 1999, p. 72). Arts-based research methodologies play out in what are often discontinuous and discordant social constructions; these are the contested sites that form the "zone of contention" (Garoian, 1999, p. 43) that take shape in negotiation between public and private worlds, forming liminal spaces in which relationships are made between people and politics, imagination and action, theory and activism. They are also the sites in which a critical arts-based research can unveil oppression (*discovery*) and transform praxis (*invention*).

Thus, arts-based inquiry creates and inhabits contested, liminal spaces. It takes form in the hyphen between art and social science research. It creates a place where epistemological standpoints of artists and social science workers collide, coalesce, and restructure to originate something new and unique among research practices. It forms in the tension between *truthfulness* and *artistic integrity* (Meyer & Moran, 2004). Other dialectics take form on the contested hyphen in arts-based research—they emerge in the thin lines of epistemological difference between plastic (visual) arts and performing arts and narrative forms of discourse. Another tension exists between artistic excellence and political effectiveness, and there is sometimes tension when a researcher's criteria for excellence do not harmonize with the standards for excellence held by artists for a particular art form (Saldaña,

2005). Similarly, there is tension between place-specific and sociopolitical goals for arts-based research, and between the primacy of ephemeral, rapid local change in dynamic communities and cultures and historically situated, cultural pride that enhances self-identity. Like the emancipatory teacher, the arts-based researcher is a "liminal servant" (Garoian, 1999, p. 43) whose responsibility is the creation of entrances to emotional, spiritual, and ephemeral spaces.

Arts-based research was initially constructed within a dialogue occurring in academic circles with regard to research—it was a product of a time in which researchers were actively rethinking the science behind social science research methodologies, while many researchers were trying to plot a futuristic vision of communal social science. Culturally, historically, and sensually, this contextualizing foundation was shared by artists working toward new genre public art in which artists deliberately functioned as social critics (Denzin, 2003). Thus, arts-based research emerged as a social construction that crossed the borders between science and art, and was contextualized by diverse efforts to revolutionize institutionalized classist, racist, and colonializing ways of experiencing and discoursing about human experience. These adaptations of artistic ways of collecting evidence to make meanings about the world and of arts-based forms for conveying those meanings to an ever-broadening, nonacademic audience marked a profound breaking away from academic research orthodoxy. To claim art and aesthetic ways of knowing as research is an act of rebellion against the monolithic "truth" that science is supposed to entail.

As an early proponent of arts-based research, Elliot Eisner (e.g., 1981, 1998, 2001) carefully spelled out the differences between scientific and artistic approaches to qualitative research in educational inquiry (Eisner, 1981). He encouraged social scientists to accept artistic ways of knowing as

complements to science and urged acceptance of narratives in the forms of novels as desirable manuscripts for doctoral dissertations, and he envisaged adaptations of music, dance, and poetry as forms of research representation.

In consequence of this wave of critical reflection about research methodologies, researchers implemented multiple, newly developed approaches to human inquiry and cast their narratives in an amazing variety of arts-based narrative forms, particularly poetry and drama. A smaller guild of "artists as researchers/researchers as artists" (S. Finley & Knowles, 1995) have chosen to document their inquiry as drama, dance, painting, collage, and other forms of visual and performing arts.

◆ Arts-Based Inquiry in the 21st Century: Engaging a Radical, Ethical, Political, and Aesthetic Qualitative Inquiry Useful in Addressing Social Inequities

The potential exists for arts-based research to enact inquiry in the social world as one feature of a people's pedagogy (S. Finley, 2003, 2005). Denzin (1997) calls for qualitative researchers to engage in ground-level "guerrilla warfare" (pp. 568, 572) as part of a revolutionary pedagogy to confront the oppressions of everyday life. Emancipation from colonizing human research that objectifies its participants (casting them as subjects) is not possible unless research is democratized and brought under the control of people in their daily lives. One objective the arts-based researcher can serve is to provide tools and opportunity for participants to perform inquiry, reflect on their performances, and preserve, create, and rewrite culture in dynamic indigenous spaces. Thus, in critical arts-based inquiry, the location of research changes from the isolated sanctuaries of the laboratory and constructed and bounded environments to places where people meet, including schools, homeless shelters, and working-class and minority neighborhoods. Socially responsible research for and by the people cannot reside inside the lonely walls of academic institutions.

In arts-based research, everyday living comprises its own aesthetic, characterized by vernacular language, cultural and historical aesthetics, and ephemeral moments in daily life (Barone, 2001a, 2001b; Barone & Eisner, 1997); that is, 21st century arts-based research enacts standpoint epistemologies that see the world from the point of view of oppressed persons of color, women, and gay, lesbian, bisexual, and transgendered persons, and research advances political movements based in critical race theories and social justice activism (Denzin, 2003). Thus, research becomes an available forum for advancing critical race theory and an aesthetic of artist-researchers and participant-observers belonging to oppressed groups and individuals traditionally excluded from established research locations.

In the current historical moment, arts-based researchers have an opportunity to consciously reject research practices that are implicated in colonialist traditions of objectivity and that treat production of knowledge as a function of social privilege. The grounding theory and methodologies for arts-based research approaches to human studies emerged in a historical epoch when the focus among qualitative researchers had turned to a particular set of questions, such as "What is research?" "How can we involve participants in research?" and "How

should research stories be told?" In response to current social pressures, focus is shifting to a different set of questions, such as "How can research generate social change?" and "How do we move arts-based research to progressive social action, to theory and method that connects politics, pedagogy, and ethics to action in the world?" (Denzin & Lincoln, 2005, p. x). Arts-based research is a political movement in the making and, as do all movements that challenge prevailing authority structures in attempts to broaden access to power, its future depends upon how effectively its defenders stand against aggressive assaults to its purpose.

◆ Restating the Purpose of Arts-Based Research: Performing a Public, Moral Enterprise

As we enter the 21st century, arts-based research is under siege, particularly in the United States, by neoconservative efforts to control access to information (e.g., Mayer, 2000, 2001). In this context, there is a pressing need to reorient arts-based research toward the conscious, considered articulation and performance of critical pedagogy. Arts-based researchers live in a new historical moment. It is imperative that its practitioners take a political, moral stance in this moment, because not taking such a stance allows the oppression of neoconservatism and the crisis of increasing social inequality to continue and grow (for discussion, see Lincoln & Canella, 2004). Wrote Freire (2001):

> Cultural action is always a systemic and deliberate form of action which operates upon the social structure, either with the

objective of preserving that structure or of transforming it. . . . Cultural action either serves domination (consciously or unconsciously) or it serves the liberation of men and women. (p. 180)

Time is passing for arts-based researchers to engage in deliberate "cultural action" to resist the tides of neoconservatism in service of liberation. It is time to affirm a people's pedagogy in which arts-based research is performed for the purpose of unveiling oppression and advocating social transformation. The opportunity exists for the discourse community of social science researchers to purposefully adopt arts-based methodologies in order to reject research practices that are implicated in paternalistic and colonizing traditions, or that treat production and acquisition of knowledge as a function of social privilege. To this end, arts-based researchers must focus on the inherent promise that artful representations have the capacity to provoke both reflective dialogue and meaningful action and, thereby, to change the world in positive ways that contribute to progressive, participatory, and ethical social action. Yet several transformative discourses and actions need to be undertaken in order to construct a social norm that arts-based research should be activist, engaged in public criticism, and resistant to neoconservative discourses that threaten social justice. Specifically, taking this political and moral stance requires that arts-based researchers

(1) revisit and even restate the goals of arts-based research, with renewed emphasis on arts-based research as a public, moral enterprise;

(2) revitalize practices in which arts-based researchers renounce the role of expert and fully accept the communities of participants and audiences

as coequal collaborators in doing research;

(3) develop a passionate respect for the insights of street critics (and street artists);

(4) reorient discussions about quality from their current inward focus on assessments of structural form and toward assessments that place value in diversity, inclusivity, dialogic creativity, and openness to the participation of an ephemeral, dynamic community of participants, and that promote the dialogic and performative qualities of research events and representations;

(5) intensify attention to the important roles of research audiences and plan for the roles of the audiences of the research in the research design; and

(6) reassert openness to diverse art forms and media while contextualizing arts-based research in its relationship to art, rather than defining it in contrast to science.

If the purpose of arts-based research is to unveil oppression and transform unjust social practices, then it needs to connect with the everyday lives of real people. The tasks of unveiling and naming oppressors will cause the arts-based researcher to challenge the assumptions behind social constructions that are engrained in everyday experience. This transformation of practice requires imaginative reordering of what seems to be the natural order of things. Most often, reformation of a participatory democracy will be achieved in small, local steps, through community-based projects.

From the perspective of a social revolutionary, Freire (2001) used the terms *cultural invasion* and *cultural synthesis* to describe these types of pedagogical, community interactions. In cultural invasions, "actors draw the thematic content of their action from their own values and ideology: their starting point is their own world, from which they enter the world of those they invade" (p. 180). By contrast, in cultural synthesis,

> the actors become integrated with the people, who are coauthors of the action that both *perform* [italics added] upon the world. . . . They do not come to teach or to transmit or to give anything, but rather to learn, with the people, about the people's world. (p. 180)

From the perspective of a community-based artist, Lippard (1998) similarly argues for a conceptualization of community art as cultural synthesis. Wrote Lippard

> If the skilled muralist continues to probe for the hidden histories, the politics, and the underlying tensions of a place and its people, a more real story begins to emerge, based in lived experiences rather than imposed ideas, revealing the stress lines, and, ideally, suggesting ways to approach them that will not only present problems but suggest solutions. (p. xiv)

In the context of arts-based research, it is the arts-based researcher's role to integrate herself into the community of participants as learners, and to initiate introspection, reflection, and representations that teach. Thus, the critical, revolutionary arts-based researcher needs to develop passionate respect for the insights of street artists and street critics. The forms of art that are indigenous to a community might be the best forms in which to tell a particular story. Artist-researchers might also introduce their own "tellings" that, in turn, might be brought back into the community for the purpose of open, critical critique. Arts-based researchers should ask: Does the representation seem authentic to the community of participant-practitioners?

◆ Why Arts-Based Research Cannot Tolerate Expertism: Valuing Diversity, Inclusivity, Dialogic Creativity, and Performative Qualities in Arts-Based Research

If the basic fundamental values for doing arts-based research include respect for indigenous knowledge and vernacular utterances, then researcher-artists must follow through with antipaternalistic and anticolonialist principles that forbid the researcher from speaking for people who are capable of making political assertions and social observations for themselves (see Delgado, 1995; hooks, 1981, 1994).

Diversity of worldview, of media, of levels of preparation to perform "arts" is potentially one of the strongest features of critical arts-based research. Diversity defies standards. Indigenous or locally generated arts situate research in community. Not all community researchers will be educated in the specifics of research methodology, and not all community researchers will be trained artists. Instead, the performative, arts-based researcher needs to facilitate community-based inquiry without taking the stance of either expert researcher or expert artist. Equalizing the roles of researcher and participant is one way to value diversity and inclusivity in field-based research. Debunking the need for researchers to be experts who stand above and outside the community of participants is a good place to begin. The role of the "artist as expert" draws undue attention to form and distracts from meaningful conversation about social issues brought to light by the research. "Sociologist as expert" imposes one worldview on another.

By contrast, many arts-based researchers have argued that quality representations of research require that the researcher possess fundamental "technical skills" necessary to the arts they employ (e.g., Eisner, 2001; Saldaña, 2005; see S. Finley, 2003, for a review of literature focused on representational quality in arts-based research). Other writers seek ways to legitimate arts-based research in the culture of science (e.g., Piantanida, McMahon, & Garman, 2003). These urges to legitimize arts-based research by standardizing the qualities of form have deleterious effects on efforts to use arts-based inquiry in a larger project of social resistance and reform. The need for recognition in the academy and the desire to remain a person of standing in a powerful role in a community of scholars has created undo emphasis on procedure and role. Concentration on form grows out of an attempt to legitimize the work of arts-based researchers.

Writing in counterpoint to Piantanida and colleagues, Slattery (2003) asked the rhetorical question, "What is the purpose of legitimate [arts-based] research: to predict, to understand, to empower, or to evoke" (p. 195)? In a people's pedagogy forged for the purposes of social reform and social justice, arts-based research unveils oppression and evokes social transformation.

The first level of reference is the community in which the research occurs. Among the avenues to social transformation is the empowerment and performance of research by communities of involved participants. Here, the role of artist-as-researcher is to facilitate the production of knowledge in community. However, in representing what the researcher learns, facility with specific research methodologies as well as specific

artful forms of representation may allow the arts-based researcher broader audience—diversifying discourse communities beyond the immediate place in which inquiry occurs for representation among academic, policy-making, and other audiences who have political power and the potential for advancing social change that will benefit the community in which research occurred. Yet through evocations of events of everyday life, researchers can raise questions about biases, presuppositions, and worldviews that play out in those events. Arts-based researchers can then take on the responsibility of creating spaces where "unjust practices are identified and interrogated" (Madison, 1998, quoted in Denzin, 2003).

Moreover, the "power of form to inform" multiple, diverse audiences calls for expanded collaborations—a researcher-artist may not have the agility to equally utilize the various forms of painting, dance, and poetry, but may recognize that a topic or audience calls for one of these forms not readily available to her. (There have been many exemplary productions of interdisciplinary multimedia representations by arts-based researchers, e.g., S. Finley, 2006; S. Finley, Cole, Knowles, & Elijah, 2000; Preisinger, Schroeder, & Scott-Hoy, 2000.) Susanne Langer (1951) suggested that interdisciplinarity among the arts would expand human intellect and bring about more complex, more imaginative ways of understanding human experience. "Scholars in ethnography have much to contribute to those initially educated as artists, and artists well versed in the creative process and products of theatre have much to offer ethnographers" (p. 29).

An example is *Street Rat* (Saldaña, Finley, & Finley, 2005), in which dramatist Johnny Saldaña guided the theatrical adaptation of S. Finley and M. Finley's arts-based, educational ethnographies from their fieldwork and experiences with homeless youth in New Orleans. Previous incarnations of this work included more or less "traditional" ethnographic narratives (e.g., S. Finley, 2001a, 2001b) as well as representations in various art forms, including short story (e.g., "Roach's Story" by Susan Finley, in S. Finley & Finley, 1999), reader's theater (S. Finley & Finley, 1998), and poetry (M. Finley, 2000, 2003; S. Finley, 2000). It would have been impossible for the original researchers, of which I was one, to bring this work to the stage as a full-scale theatrical production. Most of the dialogue came directly from the previously published pieces, and in particular, it presented the poetry selections as "poetic dialogue," but Saldaña rearranged the excerpts into a single storyline. Moreover, Saldaña possessed the tools to stage the production—including his access to actors and his ability to direct them in their performance of the script. In this project, story, poetry, paintings, and reader's theatre were shared with the actual participants in the research project and with other unhoused street youths for several purposes, including (1) to check for authenticity and (2) to facilitate activism and create continuing dialogue.

If arts-based researchers can reorient discussions about quality from their current inward focus on assessments of structural form and instead restate the values of diversity, inclusivity, and openness to the participation of varied communities of participants, then they should be able to assess arts-based research according to its propensity to promote dialogic creativity and its performative qualities. Saldaña (2005) offers that, in his experience of writing research data into dramatic performances, "there are no established or standardized criteria for what constitutes 'good' ethnodrama. The success of work is jointly constructed and determined by the participants, the artistic collaborators, and their audiences" (p. 14).

Whereas Saldaña holds open the question of standards, he re-centers the discussion in the context of communal interactions. In this construction, the arbiters of arts-based research would no longer inhabit the "inner circle" of academics but would instead reside in the "people's world" (Freire, 2001, p. 180). We (arts-based researchers) would seek affirmation for our research from the collaborators who inhabit the spaces of the people's world and who have been both our teachers and our coauthors of actions that we *coperform* upon the world.

These would be emancipatory performances, enriched by intertextual references to popular culture performances. This is an arts-based research that invokes vernacular symbols, mythologies, and storytelling traditions. It takes multiple representational forms—music, movies, poetry, paintings, murals, plays, dance, and so on. Further, "these performances record the histories of injustices experienced by the members of oppressed groups. They show how members of local groups have struggled to find places of dignity and respect in a violent, racist, and sexist civil society" (Denzin, 2003, p. 123).

If arts-based researchers actively create a body of work that tells the stories of local groups and individuals, while it exposes injustices people have experienced as subjects to the tyranny of the majority, and in which diverse forms of art are used as a means to draw attention to citizens' articulations of oppression, arts-based research can retrace and expose the common threads of racism, sexism, and discrimination that form the social contract to which Delgado (1995) referred. Citation to dialogue and actions taken by individuals and discourse communities in the forms of artworks can "give minority viewpoints and literature the full consideration due" (p. 53). This is especially true when the people are collaborating artists or coauthors working in the context of cultural synthesis. "In cultural synthesis—and only in cultural synthesis," wrote Freire (2001),

> it is possible to resolve the contradiction between the worldview of the leaders and that of the people, to the enrichment of both. Cultural synthesis does not deny the differences between the two views; indeed, it is based on these differences. It *does* deny the *invasion* of one *by* the other, but affirms the undeniable *support* each gives to the other. (p. 180)

It is, of course, possible to produce research as a product, to have the *goal* be (re)presentations of characters, or (re)productions of epiphanic life events that characterize some aspect of the human condition. But if this is the end of research, the outcomes could be only to entertain or to eroticize the lives of those persons portrayed in the research representation. In looking for higher purpose, such work could offer insight or intentionally expose audiences to life experiences that they would not encounter except vicariously, through their adaptation to an art medium. But to reach an even higher aim of transformative praxis, arts-based researchers need to revisit the importance of the power of form, not only to inform, but also to promote dialogic, performative, activist responses among audience participants. A particularly important phase in the process of doing research is left out of the research process when the "end" is strictly informational, rather than provocative.

I believe that the arts make more forms of communication available to people and provide opportunities for self-expression. It is then my role as a researcher to facilitate learning the skills and providing the technological support for making art available to community participants. This role emphasizes that equity and access to learning are also important values that should guide the construction of research designs in arts-based research.

◆ Performing Arts-Based Research

Arts-based research describes an epistemological foundation for human inquiry that utilizes artful ways of understanding and representing the worlds in which research is constructed. Arts-based research is difficult to characterize because its forms and methods vary according to location, diversity of participants, and the range of ways through which researchers, artists, and participants describe, interpret, and make meanings from experiences, as well as by multiple forms of representation available to the artist-as-researcher—e.g., novel, poetry, film, dance, photographic portfolios, visual art installations, or dramatic performance. Arts-based research makes use of diverse ways of knowing and experiencing the world. As such, the term *arts-based research* cannot be reduced to a prescriptive set of methods for generating and representing empirical materials. It is more of an "umbrella term" for many methodologies that follow from a constructivist, emotive, empiricist research aesthetic.

When arts-based research is grounded in a critical performance pedagogy, it can be used to advance a progressive political agenda that addresses issues of social inequity. *Performance* opens contested spaces and liminal sites for community dialogue used to "critique dominant cultural assumptions, to construct identity, and to attain political agency" (Garoian, 1999, p. 2). The power of performance moves the arts-based researcher "from interpretation and emotional evocation to praxis, empowerment, and social change" (Denzin, 2003,

p. 133). *Performativity* is the quality criterion I emphasize as being necessary to achieve arts-based approaches to inquiry that is activist, engages in critical reflection, resists neoconservatism in preference of social justice, and purposefully facilitates imaginative thinking about multiple, new, and diverse ways of understanding and living in the world.

◆ *References*

Arnheim, R. (1954). *Art and visual perception.* Berkeley: University of California Press.

Arnheim, R. (1971). *Visual thinking.* Berkeley: University of California Press.

Barone, T. (2001a). Science, art, and the predispositions of educational researchers. *Educational Researcher, 30*(7), 24–28.

Barone, T. (2001b). *Touching eternity: The enduring outcomes of teaching.* New York: Columbia University, Teachers College Press.

Barone, T., & Eisner, E. (1997). *Handbook on complementary methods for educational research* (R. Yeager, Ed.). Washington, DC: American Educational Research Association.

Blumenfeld-Jones, D. S. (1995). Dance as a mode of research representation. *Qualitative Inquiry, 4,* 391–401.

Brady, I. (2004). In defense of the sensual: Meaning construction in ethnography and poetics. *Qualitative Inquiry, 10,* 622–644.

Brady, I. (2005). Poetics for a planet: Discourse on some problems of being-in-place. In N. K. Denzin & Y. S. Lincoln (Eds.), *Handbook of qualitative research* (3rd ed., pp. 979–1026). Thousand Oaks, CA: Sage.

Cancienne, M. B. (1999). The gender gaze: Rethinking gender through performance. *Journal of Curriculum Theorizing, 15*(2), 167–175.

Cancienne, M. B., & Snowber, C. N. (2003). Writing rhythm: Movement as method. *Qualitative Inquiry, 9*(2), 237–253.

Delgado, R. (1995). The imperial scholar: Reflections on a review of civil rights literature. In K. Crenshaw, N. Gotanda, G. Peller, & K. Thomas (Eds.), *Critical race theory: The key writings that formed the movement* (pp. 46–57). New York: The New Press.

Denzin, N. K. (1997). *Interpretive ethnography: Ethnographic practices for the 21st century.* Thousand Oaks, CA: Sage.

Denzin, N. K. (2003). *Performance ethnography: Critical pedagogy and the politics of culture.* Thousand Oaks, CA: Sage.

Denzin, N. K., & Lincoln, Y. S. (Eds.). (2005). *Handbook of qualitative research* (3rd ed.). Thousand Oaks, CA: Sage.

Eisner, E. W. (1981). On the difference between scientific and artistic approaches to qualitative research. *Educational Researcher, 10*(4), 5–9.

Eisner, E. W. (1998). *The enlightened eye: Qualitative inquiry and the enhancement of educational practice.* Upper Saddle River, NJ: Prentice Hall. (Original work published 1981)

Eisner, E. W. (2001). Concerns and aspirations for qualitative research in the new millennium. *Qualitative Research 1*(2), 135–145.

Finley, M. (2000). *Street Rat.* Detroit: Greenroom Press, University of Detroit Mercy.

Finley, M. (2003). Fugue of the street rat: Writing research poetry. *International Journal of Qualitative Studies in Education, 16*(4), 603–604.

Finley, S. (2000). "Dream child": The role of poetic dialogue in homeless research. *Qualitative Inquiry, 6*(3), 432–434.

Finley, S. (2001a). From the streets to the classrooms: Street intellectuals as teacher educators, collaborations in revolutionary pedagogy. In K. Sloan & J. T. Sears (Eds.), *Democratic curriculum theory and practice: Retrieving public spaces* (pp. 113–126). Troy, NY: Educators International Press.

Finley, S. (2001b). Painting life histories. *Journal of Curriculum Theorizing, 17*(2), 13–26.

Finley, S. (2003). Arts-based inquiry in QI: Seven years from crisis to guerrilla warfare. *Qualitative Inquiry, 9,* 281–296.

Finley, S. (2005). Arts-based inquiry: Performing revolutionary pedagogy. In N. K. Denzin & Y. S. Lincoln (Eds.), *Handbook of qualitative research* (3rd ed., pp. 681–694). Thousand Oaks, CA: Sage.

Finley, S. (Author/Editor). (2006). *At Home At School (AHAS) Toolkit.* [Digital video/ DVD-ROM]. Gaston, OR: Kwamba Productions.

Finley, S., Cole, A., Knowles, J. G., & Elijah, R. (2000). Making "Mindscapes": Continuing reflections of a community of researchers. *Journal of Critical Inquiry Into Curriculum and Instruction, 2*(2), 7–14.

Finley, S., & Finley, M. (1998). *Traveling through the cracks: Homeless youth speak out.* Paper presented at the annual meeting of the American Educational Research Association, San Diego, CA.

Finley, S., & Finley, M. (1999). Sp'ange: A research story. *Qualitative Inquiry, 5,* 313–337.

Finley, S., & Knowles, J. G. (1995). Researcher as artist/artist as researcher. *Qualitative Inquiry 1*(1), 110–142.

Freire, P. (2001). *Pedagogy of the oppressed* (30th anniversary ed.). New York: Continuum.

Garoian, C. R. (1999). *Performing pedagogy: Toward an art of politics.* Albany: State University of New York Press.

hooks, b. (1981). *Ain't I a woman: Black women and feminism.* Boston: South End Press.

hooks, b. (1994). *Teaching to transgress: Education as the practice of freedom.* New York: Routledge.

Houston, D., & Pulido, L. (2002). The work of performitivity: Staging social justice at the University of Southern California. *Environment and Planning D: Society and Space, 20,* 379–504.

Langer, S. (1951). *Philosophy in a new key: A study in the symbolism of reason, rite, and art.* New York: Mentor Books.

Lincoln, Y. S., & Cannella, G. S. (2004). Dangerous discourses: Methodological conservatism and governmental regimes of truth. *Qualitative Inquiry, 10,* 5–14.

Lincoln, Y. S., & Denzin, N. K. (2003). The revolution in presentation. In Y. S. Lincoln & N. K. Denzin (Eds.), *Turning points in qualitative research: Tying knots in a handkerchief* (pp. 375–378). Walnut Creek, CA: AltaMira Press.

Lippard, L. (1998). Foreword to the 1998 edition. In E. Cockcroft, J. P. Weber, & J. Cockcroft (Eds.), *Toward a people's art: The contemporary mural movement* (pp. xi–xv). Albuquerque: University of New Mexico Press. (Original work published 1977)

Mayer, R. E. (2000). What is the place of science in educational research? *Educational Researcher, 29*(6), 38–39.

Mayer, R. E. (2001). Resisting the assault on science: The case for evidence-based reasoning in educational research. *Educational Researcher, 30*(7), 29–30.

Meyer, M. J., & Moran, K. J. K. (2004). *Evidence and artistic integrity in arts-based research: Necessity with a bit of folly.* Paper presented at the annual meeting of the American Educational Research Association, San Diego, CA.

Piantanida, M., McMahon, P. L., & Garman, N. B. (2003). Sculpting the contours of arts-based educational research within a discourse community. *Qualitative Inquiry, 9*(2), 182–191.

Preisinger, M. A., Schroeder, C., & Scott-Hoy, K. (2000, February). *What makes me? Stories of motivation, morality, and me.* Interdisciplinary art performance at the 2000 American Educational Research Association Arts-Based Research Conference, Albuquerque, NM.

Saldaña, J. (2005). An introduction to ethnodrama. In J. Saldaña (Ed.), *Ethnodrama: An anthology of reality theatre* (pp. 1–36). Walnut Creek, CA: AltaMira Press.

Saldaña, J., Finley, S., & Finley, M. (2005). *Street Rat* [Adaptation]. In J. Saldaña (Ed.), *Ethnodrama: An anthology of reality theatre* (pp. 139–179). Walnut Creek, CA: AltaMira Press.

Slattery, P. (2003). Troubling the contours of arts-based educational research within a discourse community. *Qualitative Inquiry, 9*(2), 192–198.

7

A/R/TOGRAPHERS AND LIVING INQUIRY

◆ Stephanie Springgay, Rita L. Irwin, and Sylvia Kind

C ommunities are peculiar places, both inclusive and perverse. They are inclusive insofar as they can only ever make sense of, or reference, what is excluded. Understood as having something in common, community becomes an inside, a within, an interior. Yet communities are also perverse, deviating from the common path, refusing to be contained or constrained by their insides. Thus, the outside itself becomes a community that one can never fully or completely occupy because the outside of something is always the inside of another (Grosz, 2001). It is this temporality and interpenetration between inside and outside that Elizabeth Grosz (2001) believes enables criticality and evaluation. What exists in the space between inside and outside is an unknown relationship between self and other, a relationship that is itself a community of understanding. Similarly, in theories of visual art and culture, scholars are reexamining community from the perspective of *situation* rather than defining it as a physical, geographical, or locational place (Doherty, 2004). In this sense, community is re-imag(e)-ined as a set of circumstances that are not fixed but are ever evolving (Agamben, 1993). Emphasizing experience that is constituted through social, economic,

◆ 83

cultural, and political processes, *site* (as in learning, community, location, identity, art work) becomes *relational* (Bourriaud, 2002; Kwon, 2002). Thus, art, both the process of creation and its outcomes, is marked by social engagements that break down conventional distinctions between artist, artwork, and audience. Irit Rogoff (2004) maintains that we need to find a critical language to talk about artistic meaning making beyond the specifics of time and place. For instance, scholars need to examine art not from the perspective of when it was made and where it is located, but rather unravel the implications of the work relationally. It is this relational understanding of community, art, and research that shapes the methodology of a/r/tography.[1]

A/r/tography is a methodology that resides in the space of the in-between and in doing so redefines community, knowledge, and research by unsettling perception (Irwin & de Cosson, 2003, 2004). As an arts-related methodology, a/r/tography interfaces the arts and scholarly writing through living inquiry. In a/r/tographic practices the identities, roles, and understandings of artist/researcher/teacher are intertwined in an approach to social science research that is dedicated to perceiving the world artistically and educationally (Irwin, 1999). It is an inquiry process that lingers in the liminal spaces inside and outside—the between—of *a(artist) and r(researcher) and t(teacher)*. Vacillating between intimacy and distance, a/r/tography constructs research and knowledge as acts of *complication*. Rather than reassuring a reader/viewer with an easily shared idea or a commonly held belief, a/r/tography recognizes that meaning making can be disturbing, unexpected, and hesitant.

This chapter develops the conditions for enacting a/r/tography as relational. The first section draws on educational uses of complexity theory in order to articulate what relational acts of teaching and learning through living inquiry might look like. In the second section we frame our discussion using an example from contemporary art. The third and final section examines the relational practices and understandings of artists, researchers, and teachers. In doing so we will argue that a/r/tographical research, although concerned with the artistic products or representations of arts-based educational research, is committed to an enactive space of living inquiry in and through singular time and space.

◆ Relational Acts of Living Inquiry

Complexity theories of learning (Davis, Sumara, & Luce-Kapler, 2000) describe learning as participatory and evolutionary. Rather than being concerned with the acquisition of information, learners are concerned with one's changing and evolving circumstances. "Learning is coming to be understood as a participation in the world, a co-evolution of knower and known that transforms both" (p. 64). As such, learning and knowing can never be predictable. Complexity theories of learning emphasize learning as nonlinear, dynamic, and relational. Learning occurs within communities of practice (Lave & Wenger, 1991) and within a social world and webs of interconnection (Capra, 1996). Learning environments, such as classrooms and schools, are viewed as relational, interconnected, interdependent living systems that adapt themselves to changing circumstances. Generally classrooms, teachers, students, and caregivers have been viewed as distinct, separate, and discrete elements in the larger whole of schooling and learning viewed as an individual matter between teacher and student. However, within complexity theory, learning events occur not in isolation but in relation and within a complex system of action and reaction. Even small things matter and profoundly influence the learning community. Linda Laidlaw (2004) illustrates this as she recounts the story of an elementary school deciding not to punctuate the school day with electronic bells. The simple act of turning off bells prompted many other interconnected changes.

Laidlaw describes how, on a typical school morning since eliminating the use of bells, children enter the school foyer, sit in comfortable chairs, read, play board games, dance to music in the library, engage in activities in the hallways, or work on computers. It is also common for parents and caregivers to join in the morning activities, creating an easier transition between home and school and a more porous relationship. Rather than the jarring interruption of bells, typical outdoor line-ups, morning scuffles, and disturbances, the school day emerges more peacefully and gradually. She describes how it is the small things, and the relationships between things, that matter. The simple acts of turning off bells and inviting children and caregivers to gather together at the beginning of the day had profound, continuing effects, much like concentric waves that are created when a pebble is tossed into a pond. Other rituals, such as singing to send children off to classrooms at the beginning of the school day, are spontaneous events that evolve into more elaborate patterns and responses. Thus, the nature of the school community is shaped differently from one "structured by bell time and linear waits at the door" (p. 4). It keeps a different pace and brings forth a different set of relations and structures. There is a rhythmic and fluid flow within open systems and a continual relational process of response and change.

◆ Relational Inquiring: Exploring the Methodological Conditions of A/R/Tography

During the winter of 2003, on the public streets of icy Montreal, artist Rachel Echenberg enacted a series of performative gestures that placed her body heat against the winter cold. Incorporating homemade ice blocks that she positioned throughout the city—at bus stops and metro stations, near busy restaurants and bars, and in the quiet corners of the darkened night—Echenberg's body heat transformed each ice sculpture. Lying on a bench in the stillness of falling snow, her body heat molded the ice blocks buried beneath her. In other interventions she melted snowballs with her breath, or lay for hours letting the snow pile up on and around her—processes of interaction with the elements and time and space.

Art critic Nicolas Bourriaud (2002) states that postmodern art is marked by interventions that require viewers to be called to a particular time and place, unlike the Great Masters' paintings, for example, which hang throughout time in museums and are accessible continuously. Both the accessibility and continuity of these "master works" and of museums could be highly contested. According to Bourriaud (2002), contemporary artists who challenge fixed notions of "site" operate from a position that he calls *relational aesthetics*. The meaning of the work emerges not from the work itself (the inside), nor an assigned value given to it by the artist, curator, or institutional framework (outside), but through a movement *between* and an encounter *within* the exhibition space. In other words, a work of art becomes meaningful only through interactions and engagements with an audience.

Art becomes a socially useful activity. Relational aesthetics turns the apparatus of viewing and meaning making from something that is done to an art work (deconstructive critique) into a situation where subject (art) and subject (viewer) are confronted and mutually interrogated. For instance, Echenberg's body heat gestures exist only in the moment of encounter and exchange between her actions and the actions of viewers as they make meaning of such actions. Her art resides in the seemingly contiguous and unstable moments of interaction that her work generates.

Many of Echenberg's body–time interventions exist without the ruse of formal audiences (those that are called to witness this event as an art exhibit), and they remain, transforming and mutating long after the artist has disappeared. Echenberg's artistic interventions, like many other contemporary artists working in the space of relational aesthetics, question the ways that art has traditionally been viewed and decoded. This is not to say that in the future all artists must take to the streets in the dead of night in the icy chill of winter, but rather educational scholars devoted to acts of interpretation can learn from such artists. Interpretive engagements are not methods applied to a phenomenon (something from the outside brought to bear on the inside in order to make sense of it), nor does a phenomenon embody meaning simply within itself that needs to be unleashed (an inclusive inside that fails to recognize the influences of social, political, and cultural power structures); rather, interpretation exists in the interstitial space between inside and outside. Feminist art activist Suzanne Lacy (1995) states, "What exists in the space between the words public and art is an unknown relationship between artist and audience, a relationship that may itself be the artwork" (p. 19).

Relational aesthetics suggests that meaning is not external to action. Meaning is not separated from the gestures and the encounters that produce and change it. Relationality insists that the phenomena being studied and their assemblages of interpretation are embodied, intercorporeal, and folded with, in, and through each other. Similarly, patterns of relationality are perceived as interpenetrative between beings. Each ice block, frozen, heated, and molded, becomes a momentary grouping of relationships alluding to the effects of climate, geography, location, identity, body heat, pressure, and change. Whether encountering Echenberg's performance as a gallery event, or stumbling upon her in the velvet hours of snow-lit nights, each experience poses an encounter between being(s)-in-relation, shaping participation and meaning making simultaneously (Springgay, 2005a, 2005b). A transformed ice block, imprinted with the artist's tongue, folds the subject–object relationship such that we, the viewers, become embedded in her actions. Merleau-Ponty (1964) writes of this intertwining between self and other, inside and outside, where the seer and seen become folded together in a porous encounter: "The bodies of others are not objects; they are phenomena that are coextensive with one's own body" (p. 118). This active and dynamic body shapes experience through lived encounters, where participation becomes an exposure, an opening up toward the other.

A/r/tography is a methodology of relational aesthetics where patterns exist not as predetermined identities but as "co-appearance"—a being with-one-another. Meaning thus circulates, moving in all directions simultaneously. According to Nancy (2000) this co-appearance is both unity and uniqueness, the singular plural of being. In other words, each individual identity is brought to being through encounters *with* other beings, and it is the *with* that maintains both the contiguity and the distinctiveness of each pattern. Relational aesthetics does not represent a theory of art with an implied statement of origin and destination, but a theory of form where art is part of an overall series of existing forms. Forms come into being through encounters between and the collective elaboration of meaning. Likewise, we might understand relationality in terms of the act of folding and unfolding—a movement, a hesitation, and a stuttering.

Deleuze (1993) translates the fold as sensuous vibrations, a world made up of divergent series, an infinity of pleats and creases. Un/folding divides endlessly, folds within folds touching one another. A fold is not divisible into independent points, but rather any un/folding results in additional folds; it is the movement or operation of one fold to another. Thus, perception is not a question then of part to whole but a singular totality "where the totality can be as imperceptible as the parts" (p. 87). Perception is not embodied in perceiving the sum of all parts; rather, it is distinguished by and within the fold. Both Deleuze (1994b) and Grosz (2001) exemplify this act of folding through another metaphor—*stuttering*. When language (meaning) reaches a limit, it begins to stutter, to murmur and reverberate. This stuttering may provide a point of mobilization and destabilization and enable educational scholars to think of inquiry—the stuff of art, research, and teaching—as a "wrenching of concepts away from their usual configurations, outside the systems in which they have a home, and outside the structures of recognition that constrain through to the already known" (Grosz, 2001, p. 61). A/r/tography forces us to search for the unknown, to think while making, to think *as* doing (Grosz, 2001).

◆ Artist, Researcher, Teacher as Relational

In addition to the reconstruction of inquiry and interpretation from the perspective of relationality, a/r/tography reassembles the relationships between artist, researcher, and teacher. For example, one form of research is to investigate artists and the work they do. This mode of inquiry posits already existing theories onto the activities and work of an artist. Similarly, educational research often examines what teachers do in order to support theoretical claims and hypotheses. In both instances there is a fixed entity—a given. An artwork that now needs to be deconstructed in order to provide the public (or at least the academic public) with its meaning. In education one might research a pedagogical strategy and frame it by existing educational theories and practices. This top-down approach to research has of course been troubled by a host of postmodern methodologies, including a/r/tography. However, a/r/tography troubles the structures of research through aesthetic, artistic, and creative means.

If we take what we have learned from relational aesthetics and apply it to the interrelationships between artist, researcher, and teacher, we begin to see new patterns of knowledge production emerge. In one instance we are arguing that a/r/tographers need to be attentive to their artist, researcher, and teacher selves. A/r/tographers don't simply research phenomena in the arts using qualitative means; they are artists-and-teachers-and-researchers who examine educational phenomena through an artistic understanding and inquiry process. It is thinking as doing that produces a/r/tographical knowledge. This calls for a slippage in "time."

A/r/tographical time is not linear. It is not the time of clocks and schedules. It is not a time of codification and systematization. In a/r/tographical research, time is singular (Deleuze, 1994a; Nancy, 2000). Singular refers to the complexities that are assembled and contained with one. For example, "we" is the singular plural of the first-person "I." "We" is often used to describe a universal quality, a generalization—as in we—the entire field of educational research. A singular approach to we would understand we as containing within it divergent multiplicities, dividing endlessly into itself—extraordinary, remarkable, and uncommon. The singular is distinguished from the plural. It is a unit of measurement that denotes one, a peculiarity. However, singularity in the Deleuzian sense is not a universalizing one, where difference is consumed by the common or the same; it is a one that embodies within it the uniqueness of difference. Nancy (2000) writes that

> the touch of meaning brings into play its own singularity, its distinction, and brings into play the plurality of the "each time" of every touch of meaning, "mine" as well as all the others, each one of which is "mine" in turn, according to the singular turn of its affirmation. (p. 6)

A/r/tographically speaking, singularity refers to the question, How are we experiencing lived experience? By implication, Echenberg's art can be regarded as a singular endeavor within a larger context, which is a complex collective of dynamic, interacting systems. Her interventions become relational moments provoking deeper understandings within and between other assemblages. For a/r/tographers these implications prompt a number of questions regarding the nature of art making, teaching, learning, and researching as relational. What might we uncover if we consider learning through a singular understanding of time? Echenberg's icy gestures force us to interrogate assumptions and demand that we not stand on the outside gazing in as passive viewers. Instead, we become active producers in and through singular time.

Another facet of time in a/r/tographical research has to do with the way in which meaning unfolds or evolves over time. In modern Western society, time is metaphorically understood to be immutable and uniformly flowing without regard for individuals or the actions they take. Likewise, space is metaphorically seen as a container or even the vast emptiness of the universe. Space becomes something to be filled or acted upon. Postmodern configurations of space and time shift these understandings. For instance, feminist theories argue that space is linked with how one encounters, constructs, and performs identity, thereby mapping the relationship of space to subjectivity, corporeality, and ways of knowing (Ahmed & Stacey, 2001). In other words, a body is not simply *in* space (an object placed in a particular location), but rather the body *is* spatial itself. Knowledge and space shape and define one another.

Many contemporary artists like Rachel Echenberg explore such connections between inquiry, learning, and space. Their vocabulary for time includes such language as pausing, enduring, changing, slowing, interruption, cycles, haste, and pacing, while space may be seen as open, vast, expansive, fragmented, and connected. A/r/tographers see time and space as singular and as conditions for living inquiry that is relational. Moreover,

> meaning arises not just in the fact of action, and the type of action, but also in the how. How is that action or activity performed: more slowly or more quickly, rarely or often, all at once or in fits and starts, in a small space or across a large one, in one place or in many, with the grain of the place or against it? (Lemke, 2004)

Exploring singular perceptions of time and space offers artists, researchers, and teachers opportunities to know the world in different ways.

Perceptions of time and space are also bound by our thoughts and memories. Roland Barthes (1981) names the phenomenon of an intense personal experience while viewing a photograph to be a punctum. The punctum gives the viewer insights that are particularly personal and profound. While viewing a photograph of his mother, Barthes at once felt an awareness of her when he was a child, while simultaneously knowing of her death beyond the time of the photograph. In this moment of viewing the photograph, he experienced the past and the future alongside the recognition of her character as a woman. Barthes's punctum is particular to his life experience. Through photographs, forms of art, or living attentively in the world, individuals may experience their own punctum. Echenberg's art, which continues to evolve through the folds of space and time, captures this notion of the punctum. The punctum is not just memory or an anticipation of loss; it is a singular moment in which the uniqueness of one's being is experienced as multiple and expansive. For a/r/tographers, the punctum exists within the realization that it is the phenomenon of life that calls us to be engaged in artistic ways of knowing, doing, and being. A/r/tographers transform perception into an experience and experience into perceptions, complicating things in the process.

A/r/tographers are concerned with relational acts of living inquiry in and through singular space and time. Opening out art, research, and teaching to acts of complication enables a/r/tographers to find and explore new patterns of meaning.

An exploration of these singular assemblages is important if we are to conceptualize what a/r/tographical research might look like and how it could be enacted among communities of artists, researchers, and teachers.

◆ **Note**

1. For other essays that conceptualize the field of a/r/tographical research, see Cole, Neilsen, Knowles, & Luciani, 2004; Darts, 2004; de Cosson, 2000, 2001, 2002, 2003; de Cosson, Irwin, Grauer, & Wilson, 2003; de Cosson, Irwin, Kind, & Springgay, in press; de Cosson, Wilson, et al., 2003; Irwin, 1999, 2003, 2004; Irwin & de Cosson, 2003, 2004; Irwin, et al., 1998; Irwin, Mastri, & Robertson, 2000; Irwin, Stephenson, Robertson, & Reynolds, 2001; Springgay, 2002, 2003, 2004, 2005a, 2005b; Springgay & Irwin, 2004; Springgay, Irwin, & Kind, in press; Wilson, 2000; Wilson et al., 2002. For other information on a/r/tography, please check the Web site http://m1.cust.educ.ubc.ca/Artography

◆ **References**

Agamben, G. (1993). *The coming community.* Minneapolis: University of Minnesota Press.

Ahmed, S., & Stacey, J. (2001). *Thinking through skin.* London, UK: Routledge.

Barthes, R. (1981). *Camera lucida: Reflections on photography* (R. Howard, Trans.). New York: Hill and Wang.

Bourriaud, N. (2002). *Relational aesthetics.* Paris: Les presses du réel.

Capra, F. (1996). *The web of life.* New York: Anchor Books.

Cole, A., Neilsen, L., Knowles, J. G., & Luciani, T. (Eds.). (2004). *Provoked by art: Theorizing arts-informed inquiry.* Halifax, Nova Scotia, Canada: Backalong Books.

Darts, D. (2004). *Visual culture jam: Art, pedagogy, and creative resistance.* Unpublished doctoral dissertation, University of British Columbia.

Davis, B., Sumara, D., & Luce-Kapler, R. (2000). *Engaging minds: Learning and teaching in a complex world.* Mahwah, NJ: Lawrence Erlbaum.

de Cosson, A. (2000). Following the process: A non-modern inter(face). *Educational Insights, 6*(1). Retrieved November 1, 2005, from http://www.csci.educ.ubc.ca/publication/insights/archives/v06n01/

de Cosson, A. (2001). Anecdotal sculpting: Learning to learn, one from another. *Journal of Curriculum Theorizing, 17*(4), 173–183.

de Cosson, A. (2002, Fall). The hermeneutic dialogic: Finding patterns amid the aporia of the artist/researcher/teacher [article on CD-ROM insert]. *Alberta Journal of Educational Research, XLVIII*(3).

de Cosson, A. (2003). *(Re)searching sculpted a/r/tography: (Re)learning subverted- knowing through aporetic praxis.* Unpublished doctoral dissertation, University of British Columbia.

de Cosson, A., Irwin, R. L., Grauer, K., & Wilson, S. (2003). Hanging identities: Artist's dancing interruptions into corridors of learning. A performance/paper presented at the International Conference on Imagination and Education, Vancouver, Canada. July 16–19, 2003. Retrieved November 1, 2005, from http://www.ierg.net/pub_conf2003.html

de Cosson, A., Irwin, R. L., Kind, S., & Springgay, S. (2007). Walking in wonder. In J. G. Knowles, A. Cole, & T. Luciani (Eds.), *The art of visual inquiry* (pp. 135–152). Halifax, Nova Scotia, Canada: Backalong Books.

de Cosson, A., Wilson, S., Irwin, R. L., Adu Poku, S., Penti, P., Stephenson, W., et al. (2003). The pedagogy of performative liberation: A multilectic inter/intrastanding [Article on CD-ROM]. In P. Sahasrabudhe (Ed.), *The 31st InSEA World Congress Proceedings, 2002, International Conversations Through Art.* New York: International Society for Education Through Art.

Deleuze, G. (1993). *The fold: Leibniz and the baroque.* Minneapolis: University of Minnesota Press.

Deleuze, G. (1994a). *Difference and repetition.* New York: Columbia University Press.

Deleuze, G. (1994b). He stuttered. In C. V. Boundas & D. Olkowski (Eds.), *Gilles Deleuze and the theatre of philosophy* (pp. 23–29). New York: Routledge.

Doherty, C. (2004). *From studio to situation.* London: Black Dog Publishing.

Grosz, E. (2001). *Architecture from the outside: Essays on virtual and real space.* Cambridge, MA: MIT Press.

Irwin, R. L. (1999). Listening to the shapes of collaborative art making. *Art Education, 52*(2), 35–40.

Irwin, R. L. (2003). Towards an aesthetic of unfolding in/sights through curriculum. *Journal of the Canadian Association for Curriculum Studies, 1*(2), 63–78. Retrieved November 1, 2005, from http://www.csse.ca/CACS/JCACS/V1N2/PDF%20Content/07._Irwin.pdf

Irwin, R. L. (2004). A/r/tography: A metonymic métissage. In R. L. Irwin & A. de Cosson (Eds.), *A/r/tography: Rendering self through arts-based living inquiry* (pp. 27–40). Vancouver, British Columbia, Canada: Pacific Educational Press.

Irwin, R. L., & de Cosson, A. (2003). A/R/T as metonymic métissage [Article on CD-ROM]. In P. Sahasrabudhe (Ed.), *The 31st InSEA World Congress Proceedings, 2002, International Conversations Through Art.* New York: International Society for Education Through Art.

Irwin, R. L., & de Cosson, A. (Eds.). (2004). *A/r/tography: Rendering self through arts-based living inquiry.* Vancouver, British Columbia, Canada: Pacific Educational Press.

Irwin, R. L., Mastri, R., & Robertson, H. (2000). Pausing to reflect: Moments in feminist collaborative action research. *The Journal of Gender Issues in Art and Education, 1,* 43–56.

Irwin, R. L., Stephenson, W., Neale, A., Robertson, H., Mastri, R., & Crawford, N. (1998). Quiltmaking as a metaphor: Creating feminist political consciousness for art pedagogies. In E. Sacca & E. Zimmerman (Eds.), *Women art educators IV: Herstories, our stories, future stories* (pp. 100–111). Boucherville, Quebec, Canada: CSEA.

Irwin, R. L., Stephenson, W., Robertson, H., & Reynolds, J. K. (2001). Passionate creativity, compassionate community. *Canadian Review of Art Education, 28*(2), 15–34.

Kwon, M. (2002). *One place after another: Site-specific art and locational identity.* Cambridge, MA: MIT Press.

Lacy, S. (1995). *Mapping the terrain: New genre public art.* San Francisco, CA: Bay Press.

Laidlaw, L. (2004). On the importance of little details: Complexity, emergence, and pedagogy. *Educational Insights, 9*(1). Retrieved November 1, 2005, from http://www.ccfi .educ.ubc.ca/publication/insights/v09n01/ articles/laidlaw.html

Lave, J., & Wenger, E. (1991). *Situated learning: Legitimate peripheral participation.* New York: Cambridge University Press.

Lemke, J. L. (2004). *Space, time, and the chronotopes of learning.* Paper presented at the American Educational Research Association Conference, San Diego, CA. Retrieved November 1, 2005, from: http://www.per sonal.umich.edu/~jaylemke/papers/aera_20 04.htm

Merleau-Ponty, M. (1964). *Signs.* Evanston, IL: Northwestern University Press.

Nancy, J. L. (2000). *Of being singular plural.* Stanford, CA: University Press.

Rogoff, I. (2004). In conversation. In C. Doherty (Ed.), *From studio to situation* (pp. 81–89). London: Black Dog Publishing.

Springgay, S. (2002). Arts-based educational research as an unknowable text [article on CD-ROM insert]. *Alberta Journal of Educational Research, XLVIII*(3).

Springgay, S. (2003). Cloth as intercorporeality: Touch, fantasy, and performance and the construction of body knowledge. *International Journal of Education and the Arts, 4*(5). Retrieved November 1, 2005, from: http://ijea.asu.edu/v4n5/

Springgay, S. (2004). *Inside the visible: Youth understandings of body knowledge through touch.* Unpublished doctoral dissertation, University of British Columbia.

Springgay, S. (2005a). An intimate distance: Youth interrogations of intercorporeal cartography as visual narrative text. *Journal of the Canadian Association of Curriculum Studies.* Retrieved November 1, 2005, from: http://www.csse.ca/CACS/JCACS/index .html

Springgay, S. (2005b). Thinking through bodies: Bodied encounters and the process of meaning making in an email generated art project. *Studies in Art Education, 47*(1), 34–50.

Springgay, S., & Irwin, R. L. (2004). Women making art: Aesthetic inquiry as a political performance. In A. Cole, L. Neilsen, J. G. Knowles, & T. Luciani (Eds.), *Provoked by art: Theorizing arts-informed inquiry* (pp. 71–83). Halifax, Nova Scotia, Canada: Backalong Books.

Springgay, S., Irwin, R. L., & Kind, S. (in press). A/r/tography as living inquiry through art and text. *Qualitative Inquiry.*

Wilson, S. (2000). *Fragments: An art-based narrative inquiry.* Unpublished master's thesis, University of British Columbia.

Wilson, S., Stephenson, W., Springgay, S., Irwin, R. L., de Cosson, A., & Adu Poku, S. (2002). Performative liberation: A multilectic inter/intrastanding of pedagogy. In T. Poetter, C. Haerr, M. Hayes, C. Higgins, & K. Wilson Baptist (Eds.), *In (Ex)clusion (Re)Visioning the democratic ideal (Papers from the 2nd Curriculum and Pedagogy Group's Annual Conference, University of Victoria, BC).* Troy, NY: Educator's International Press. Retrieved November 1, 2005, from http:// education.wsu.edu/journal

8

LYRIC INQUIRY

◆ Lorri Neilsen

I speak of the body, the spirit,
the mockingbird, the hollyhock, leaves opening in the
rain, music, faith, angels seen at dusk—and seven
more people leave the room and are seen running
down the road. . . .

—Oliver, 2002, p. 4

Being is the interconnectedness, the resonant ecology of
things . . . to be wise is to grasp another form of life without
abandoning one's own; to be able to translate experience in
and out of two original tongues . . . one can no more hope to
understand metaphor if one is not sure the "real world"
exists, than one can hope to understand music if one does not
have a body.

—Zwicky, 2003, p. 43

Author's Note: The author wishes to thank the following for conversations
that contributed to the writing of this chapter: Lekkie Hopkins, Jan Zwicky,
Don McKay, Carl Leggo, and Gary Rasberry.

Lyric inquiry draws upon nonrationalist and nondiscursive ways of knowing in order to engage in inquiry practices and to produce written forms that have, up to now, been undervalued or ignored in scholarly discourses. Lyric inquiry is informed by aesthetic and philosophical principles of writing; it is based on a conviction that using expressive and poetic functions of language creates the possibility of a resonant, ethical, and engaged relationship between the knower and the known. Because it often strikes deep, lyric inquiry can move us, in all senses of that word.

The term *lyric inquiry* refers both to the engagement in inquiry (the process) and the outcome of this engagement (the written work). Such research foregrounds the personal and the aesthetic. As a scholar, researcher, and poet who has both undertaken and taught lyric inquiry practices for several years, I provide here a description of the impetus and rationale for lyric inquiry, as well as its implications for rethinking research in education and the social sciences. Research I have undertaken over the last 15 years has informed my belief that our researching and writing selves—both individual and collective—seek the language that best creates intimate and ethical connections with one another.

Characteristic of lyric inquiry and its written works are features such as the following: liminality, ineffability, metaphorical thinking, embodied understanding, personal evocations, domestic and local understanding, and an embrace of the eros of language—the desire to honor and experience phenomena through words, ambiguous and inadequate as they might be, and to communicate this experience to others.

The term *lyric* is a term with the roomy capacity to include the expressive, the poetic, and the phenomenological in our scholarship without returning to the false distinctions or choices our enterprises often invite: literary or academic, subjective or objective, science or art, humanities or social sciences. To understand the scope of lyric inquiry, we must abandon disciplinary distinctions and look at the broader field of writing in life, learning, and scholarship. The primary point of this chapter is twofold: to offer the idea that lyric inquiry is one of many legitimate methodologies available to us in the social sciences, and to argue that lyric inquiry has profound possibilities for addressing issues in research such as the quality of our relationships and the relevance and inclusiveness of our work.

The irony in a statement about "the point of a chapter on lyric inquiry" is obvious: We typically associate propositional language, not lyric language, with the academy. And so the writing of this chapter becomes an example both of the challenge and the opportunity facing us as social science researchers. To invite the reader into an understanding here of lyric inquiry, I primarily use conventional academic discourse. But to reach and engage the reader, I could also write a letter (expressive), a poem (rhetorical, lyric, or narrative), tell a story (fictional or personal anecdote), or choose any of the increasingly blurred genres across the spectrum of written communication. As this chapter unfolds, I will explore the linguistic means necessary to describe this perspective on inquiry; as a scholar and poet, I balance a tension: to tell and to show using language that addresses through art. For the reader to embrace the ideas, she must be as willing as the writer to be comfortable with uncertainty. Lyric inquiry is marked by the willingness to let go, and with the recognition that aesthetic writing *is* the inquiry. Impact, in other words, can be achieved with resonance as much as with report.

Phenomenology, Or Later, that same day
The cat comes back, the doctor calls,
things happen in ways you can only
begin to imagine. The story
comes after, remember? You turn

the strange into familiar with what is
at hand. Most of your life is like this:
memory, mercy, the ballast
of desire, heavier for the words
you've wrapped around them,
and lighter too. (Glenn, 2007)

Increasingly, scholars are choosing to
explore phenomena in ways that fuse their
scholarship with their aesthetic perspectives;
the resulting scholartistry (Neilsen, 2001) has
created room for a discussion that is long
overdue. To advocate for lyric inquiry and
expression requires that we reconsider what
counts as knowledge. We cannot, like Mary
Oliver's audience (above), come undone and
leave the room. We must also rethink the
purposes of our research, of coming to know.
Poets typically understand that written language is merely a finger pointing at the moon
(McKay, 2001); discursive practices that
adhere in social science research, however,
seem to perpetuate our use of language to
land on the moon, name and categorize it,
and perhaps claim and populate it as well.

◆ What Is Lyric?

*Lyricism, a singing self, empathetic,
embodied.*

—Lee, 1998, p. 31

The word *lyric* refers to "any fairly short
poem expressing the personal mood, feeling,
or meditation of a speaker" (Burchfield,
1996, p. 473). *Lyric* and *lyrics* also refer to
the words of a song. Greek myth reminds us
that Hermes, the trickster, created the lyre by
scooping out the shell of the tortoise and
stringing the instrument with gut; in this
way, music was born. Any spoken or written
language can be described as "lyrical," often
taken to mean song-like, personal, and,

generally, "poetic." The term sometimes
connotes the pathetic, sentimental, or—as in
the term "waxing lyrical"—highly enthusiastic. The specific, concrete, sensory, and often
intimate language of poetry and narrative
marks those genres as lyrical. Lyric language
is often grounded in the particular and has
been described as resonant and embodied
(Cixous, 1991; Kirsch, 1993; Kristeva, 1981;
Neilsen, 1998a, 2002a, 2002b, 2002c,
2004). Because lyric language is associated
with the personal and with the imaginative,
it is often segregated or marginalized. What
Zwicky argues, however, is that we need to
recognize that imagination allows us to enter
the experience of another without appropriation, ownership, or reductiveness (Zwicky,
2003). Or to phrase it another way, lyric
language allows us to hear the music of
the other.

As Abram (1996) notes, the birth of the
alphabet was a step toward a cognitive, disembodied relationship with the landscape.
In indigenous oral cultures, nature speaks;
landforms have presence; humans, just one
of many forms of life on the planet, are of
the earth, not separate from it. When the
sensory experience of living reveals itself in
language, each of us—bird, animal, river,
human—sings the world. Feminists have
long spoken of such connection among and
between humans and the environment as
embodiment. Lyric, whether song, expressive language, or poem, is embodied language: the self (and selves) of our personal
landscapes embodied in aesthetic forms of
writing. In other words, as Abram suggests,
the flesh of language and experience are
mutually constitutive.

◆ What Is Lyric Inquiry?

Lyric inquiry marries lyric with research. It
is a methodology that acknowledges the role
of the expressive and poetic in inquiry and

in the aesthetics of communicating the results of such inquiry, regardless of discipline. Lyric inquiry acknowledges the processes and demands, as well as the tropes, conventions, and semiotic and sensory interplay involved in the creation of an aesthetic work. To engage in this inquiry is to engage in all manner of nonrationalist writing—narrative, poetry, fiction and creative non-fiction, journals, prose poetry, dialogue, and monologue (among other forms usually thought of as written artistic expression)—to explore and to communicate to others an issue, dilemma, or phenomenon. Lyric inquiry, as a term, has greater scope than narrative inquiry (more genres and options are available) and lyric poetry (usually thought of as expressive, meditative). It is a phenomenological process and practice that embraces ambiguity, metaphor, recursiveness, silence, sensory immersion, and resonance, creating forms of writing that may become art, or may simply create an aesthetic experience for the writer.

Lyric inquiry aims for such an effect on the reader as well. The process and the work are such that their conceptual and aesthetic integrity create a resonant, or what reading theorist Louise Rosenblatt (1976) has called an aesthetic effect, on the reader/audience. Having undertaken the inquiry process through language (a process that is neither linear nor amenable to imposed structure) and having produced a written work of artistic merit, the inquirer brings the artistic work of writing to light not as proof, as with our conventional practices in social science, but as illumination and connection.

Lyric inquiry has an uneasy relationship with knowledge as product, commodity, or "trump card." Knowing, instead, is an experience of immersion and expression rather than one of gathering data only to advance an argument. A researcher who

creates lyric forms to communicate to readers such engagements emphasizes concrete, specific, located language; concise, artful word choice; and metaphorical, allegorical, or analogical approaches. She emphasizes language that aims to create an aesthetic experience, transporting a reader into a world, a mind, a voice (her own, or others') in the same way as does a fiction writer, a songwriter, or a poet. She apprentices herself to the craft of expression. The effect is not, to use Rosenblatt's (1976) term, efferent: A reader does not take away three key points or five examples. A reader comes away with the resonance of another's world, in the way we emerge from the reading of a poem or a novel, from a film screening or a musical event—physically transported or moved, often unaware of the architecture or structure that created the experience, our senses stimulated, our spirit and emotions affected. Emily Dickinson (1976) knew good poetry when the words made her hair stand on end. "Take me there" is a phrase I have often used with students writing in lyric forms: Rather than tell me or summarize for me or editorialize or judge—show me. Use vivid, sensory language that I can fall into, that makes the world come alive.

◆ Why Lyric Inquiry?

Language theorists and linguists have argued since the middle of the 20th century that human linguistic and intellectual development hinges on participation in a range of linguistic forms and functions. James Britton and Janet Emig (Neilsen, Jessome, Horsfall, & Hollis, 2000), among others, argued for the use of all modes of writing in education: expository (telling), argumentative (arguing), transactional (doing) modes, expressive, and the poetic (imaginative, personal, reflective). The result—increased attention to "creative" forms of writing for children in schools—is that we associate the expressive and poetic with the early years; in high school and college, the emphasis has remained on transactional and argumentative writing.

Personal responses to readings or journal keeping seem to be the only forms of lyric writing in postsecondary education—those and literary writing produced in creative writing programs. It is rare, except in circles of arts-informed or arts-based researchers, to see lyric forms used as legitimate scholarly discourse across disciplines. Literary writing (fiction, poetry, and plays), according to traditional academic beliefs, belongs to the humanities, alongside criticism (argument, expository); social science writing, however, does not share this diverse repertoire of expression—argument and expository remain the primary genres through which social scientists communicate. Despite the introduction of narrative inquiry into the research community, that form of research is still primarily used as a vehicle for rationalist thought (for using story to make a point). To date, whether they include poetic epigrams, narrative accounts, or snippets of journals or researcher diaries, most theses, dissertations, and scholarly articles are written to build an argument or to get things done.

Our need to delineate categories prevents us from drawing upon all linguistic resources across all disciplines, allowing for the possibility of poetry alone, for example, as being sufficient "evidence" of inquiry and of knowing. Further, this segregation of linguistic practices by discipline blunts the knowledge in the discipline, prevents it from being explored in new ways, producing ontological stagnation and creating a climate of self-referential and self-justifying structures of knowing.

In a climate where concern for the protection of individual rights and privacy is at an all-time high, lyric inquiry provides new possibilities: Poetry related to place, for example, or fiction or a script as an account allow the researcher or scholartist to enter into an experience in the only way any researcher can (regardless of method)—as herself, observing and recording. She does not presume to speak for another. But there is a difference, and that difference is primarily one of perspective on knowing.

◆ Liminality and Knowing

My text is flawed not when it is ambiguous or even contradictory, but only when it leaves you no room for stories of your own.

—Mairs, 1994, p. 74

That knowledge is and must be proof, proposition, muscle for prediction and control is bound inextricably with our Western belief in the individual as a separate, autonomous being and with our fear of the unknown (Neilsen, 1998a, 2002b). In the social sciences, our preference for propositional knowledge may be a result of a collective perception that society wants research and practices that *know* and *prove* with certainty. This ontological bias toward foundational knowledge has prevailed, regardless of the testimonies we hear from scientists and theorists in a spectrum of disciplines who describe their own knowledge-creating processes as fertile, imaginative states with intuitive leaps and places of indecision and liminality.

Literary writers commonly refer to the state of liminality in some variation of the question attributed to E. M. Forster: "How do I know what I think until I see what I say?" Language is always inadequate: We are always struggling with the space between and among perceptions, ideas, and words. Poet Don McKay (2001) refers to this state "before, under, through the wonderful terrible wrestling with words" as poetic attention. McKay says that "poets are supremely interested in what language can't do" and "to gesture outside, they use language in a way that flirts with its destruction" (p. 32). Liminality is "a space that invites anomaly, and relishes ambiguity" (Neilsen, 1998a, p. 273), a place where we "perceive patterns in new ways, find sensuous openings into new understandings, fresh concepts, wild possibilities," a place where we "subvert the ordinary and see the extraordinary" (p. 274). Where liminal and lyric meet is a place of play, fluidity, and imagination. It is also a means of connection. As poet Jane Hirshfield (1997) writes:

The liminal is not opposite to, but the necessary companion of, identity and particularity—a person who steps outside her usual position falls away from any singular relationship to others and into oneness with the community as a whole. Within the separateness of liminality, separateness itself is remade . . . entire societies, as well as individuals, at times enter the condition of threshold for renewal. (p. 204)

In social science research, liminality and uncertainty seem antithetical to a discipline that looks for answers and is founded on practices of studying and then attempting to represent others. Yet although a threshold space can be uncertain, its redeeming quality is curiosity, a desire to learn. It is a space that is in love with the questions. In exploring and expressing identity through language, lyric inquiry creates a space both

for questions and for connection—for finding the universal in the particular and for rethinking any belief that suggests we can know the other.

In this way, poetic language can be a transgressive and powerful tool, especially for women and others who prefer to write outside rationalist forms of language—"to let go, to explode forms, and create fantastic transgressions" (Neilsen & Clifford, 1996, p. 1)—and who often have had little opportunity to see their experiences through their own lens or write them in the forms in which they want to be represented. Lyric forms, in this sense, are political; they challenge the status quo of accepted academic language, and they remind us of the inherent biases in speaking for others. Writing the personal can be risky, because of the folk-historical association of women with the forces of unreason; yet writing the personal can also be seen as courageous (Rogers, 1993). Expressive and poetic writing is often dismissed as "merely subjective," a charge that is based on the mistaken assumption that disembodied and distanced language carries more weight or is owed more authority. Yet consider what we know from studies in technology: When encountering the liminal space of new media, women and girls typically opt for lyric forms of communication (expressive, personal) over rationalist discourse (Neilsen, 1997). Literary writers write about the transformative power of writing. Nancy Mairs (1994) claims writing didn't help her find her voice; it helped her find Nancy. Nadine Gordimer (1995) turned to writing "as a means to find what my truth was" (p. 123). Bronwen Wallace (1987) writes of remapping her life, all her "selves incomplete and ambiguous" (pp. 108–109).

Further, we know from our encounters with the everyday that when provided with information that is locally situated, specific, and embodied (for example, a news feature or a magazine or journal article in print and visual media), consumers of information typically remember the "color" stories—the grounded particulars. The news media provide consumers with a range of linguistic options—the "color" of the personal, the narrative, the imagistic, as well as argument and persuasion and exposition. Why do we, as researchers and scholars whose work needs to have more community currency than ever before, remain wedded to telling rather than showing or imagining? As our research increasingly reaches into the public domain to investigate a myriad of social phenomena, a reaching that is often motivated by a desire for social justice, we can look to lyric inquiry to make the research accessible and memorable and, we hope, to foster agency and action.

◆ *Body Writing*

Write your self. Your body must be heard.

—Cixous, 1991, p. 335

When narrative forms and writing as inquiry were introduced to social science research about 20 years ago, a struggle ensued to wrest the methodology from criteria associated with rationalist discourse and positivist assumptions about research. The struggle continues today with questions about whether literary works can be accepted as dissertations and theses, and the degree to which these documents must adhere to rationalist forms of dissemination in order to be considered "knowledge." Again, the issue is ontological: How do we know, and how do we tell?

Lyric forms make connections among intellect, emotion, spirit, and the body.

Lyric inquiry returns us to pre-Cartesian beliefs about our connection to the landscape that carries us. According to Abram (1996), "the world of our direct, unmediated interactions is always local . . . the sensuous world is the particular ground on which we walk." He further claims that we, as humans, are shaped "by the places (we) inhabit, both individually and collectively. Our bodily rhythms, our moods, cycles of creativity and stillness, and even our thoughts are readily engaged and influenced by shifting patterns in the land" (pp. 266–267). Yet our technologically mediated experiences—using language and other systems that lift us away from the local—have inspired and reinforced the belief we are separate from the environment that carries us. Language as a uniquely human tool has also reinforced the belief that our thoughts reside in an otherworldly place called our mind. Ackerman (1990) and others, however, claim that the mind "travels the whole body in caravans of hormone and enzyme, busily making sense of the catalogue of wonders we call touch, taste, smell, hearing, vision" (p. xix).

Helene Cixous's (1991) work explores the relationship of body with language, women's bodies in particular. Because language is part of a symbolic structure that is largely male in invention and influence, she argues that women must learn *l'ecriture feminine,* writing that springs from the body and subverts the given structures and available forms. This writing is typically sensory and poetic in nature. Yet writing from the body, in spite of feminist arguments about the patriarchal nature of language, is not a practice or a possibility limited to women. Our educational conventions in postsecondary institutions have simply reinforced that belief by denying all students and scholars opportunities for—and legitimization of—embodied writing.

◆ A Lyric Ontology

Social science research and writing have historically embraced the hypostatic—finding truths, laws, and principles that we can count on that add up, perhaps, to a wholeness or a summary of *what is*. The pursuit of the hypostatic is important, but so, too, is the pursuit of the ineffable. For alongside the pursuit of laws and principles is the ontological perspective of knowledge as particular and present, and often impossible to pin down. Ontological attention, as Zwicky (2003) refers to it, is a position of awe—of honoring what we see through the inadequate language resources we have available. For her, this ontology is fundamentally an ethical position. Zwicky (2003) writes:

> Ontological attention is a response to particularity; *this* porch, *this* laundry basket, *this* day. Its object cannot be substituted for, even when it is an object of considerable generality ("the country," "cheese," "garage sales"). It is the antithesis of the attitude that regards things as "resources," mere means to human ends. In perceiving *this*ness, we respond to having been addressed (In fact, we are addressed all the time, but we don't always notice this). (p. 52)

Research undertaken through and informed by the arts challenges what counts as legitimate knowledge and considers research to be a form of address. Lyric inquiry, in particular, because of its reliance on language, challenges both the impulse for pursuing universal truths or laws and the attendant agonistic practices of argument and persuasion that bring them to the fore. Although binaries run the risk of reinforcing essentialist categories, it might be worth considering the ways we can pursue the kind of inquiry that opens up knowledge and knowing to include both the rationalist (objective, linear, foundational, hypostatic, analytical) and embodied (relational, fluid, sensory, experiential, located, "personal") and all their myriad intersections and overlaps—allowing for the full range of linguistic expression, and thus firing our thinking, our knowing, and our imagination in well-rounded ways.

◆ Lyric Inquiry and Possibility

Current thought in philosophy and poetics considers the resonant, metaphorical, and elusive (as well as allusive) dimensions of language. Lyric forms of writing draw on the immediate and the material, and recognize the power of the particular to invoke the universal. In Zwicky's (1992) terms, "analysis is a laser; lyric is a bell" (p. 284). Lyric inquiry's embrace of resonance is connected to its tolerance for ambiguity and liminality, all characteristics of the development (and reception) of literary works. The implications of this perspective on language are both ethical and ontological. To name, categorize, and judge, one might argue, are a form of control, appropriation, or dominance. Yet lyric inquiry, following Levinas's philosophy (McKay, 2001), is a means of recording and honoring phenomena, often translating this "listening" or "being with" into prose that makes no claim to knowledge or power over; it aims only to create resonance and aesthetic impact through address. Lyric inquiry is "an invitation to begin to live poetically in the work, to embrace the suspended moments inside which words dangle us—elusive, mysterious, fecund states which our controlling selves have traditionally been schooled to master, define, name, or categorize" (Neilsen, 1998a, p. 273).

Lyric inquiry practices are especially appealing to women and girls (Neilsen,

1996, 1998a, 1998b, 1998c, 2002b, 2002c), affording them opportunities to both engage with academic work and resist it, even as they use lyric inquiry for epistemic growth and understanding. Less than 150 years ago, women and other traditionally underrepresented groups had little access to university study; they now comprise the majority of the postsecondary student population. It seems timely, then, to extend the reaches of our inquiry to include forms of written expression that are both inclusive and representative. Social scientists across disciplines are, increasingly, a gender-balanced and culturally diverse group. The continued use of primarily rationalist discourse in the academy is a source of imbalance, not only epistemologically, but culturally and linguistically (McCann, 2002). Attention to the development of lyric inquiry allows us, as human users of language, to develop linguistic muscles that are, in many cases, our natural preferences or strengths and, in other cases, muscles we have allowed to become atrophied. When we increase the richness and diversity of our scholarly writing, we expand our possibilities: We do not replace one form for another or eliminate any form that has served well.

Lyric inquiry, as I have learned in my research into inquiry itself, results in at least three benefits. First, this entry into research has the capacity to develop voice and agency for both researcher and participants, many of whom have found that their work has been ignored inside mainstream social science practices. Second, lyric inquiry foregrounds conceptual and philosophical processes marked by metaphor, resonance, and liminality, all processes that ignite the imagination and have a strong heuristic effect for both researcher and reader/audience. Finally, lyric inquiry reunites us with the vivifying effects of imagination and beauty—those long-forgotten qualities that add grace and wisdom to public discourse.

Lyric inquiry as a means of studying and communicating phenomena in social science research recognizes that the only linguistic tool we have—human language—is more than a blunt instrument with which we gather or claim or control knowledge; it is a powerful mix of art and the phenomenological, honoring not only phenomena under our gaze, but the epistemic possibilities of writing in a new key.

References

Abram, D. (1996). *The spell of the sensuous.* New York: Vintage Books.

Ackerman, D. (1990). *A natural history of the senses.* New York: Vintage Books.

Burchfield, R. W. (Ed.). (1996). *New Fowler's modern English usage* (3rd ed.). Oxford: Clarendon Press.

Cixous, H. (1991). The laugh of the medusa. In R. R. Warhol & D. Price Herndel (Eds.), *Feminisms: An anthology of literary theory and criticism* (p. 335). New Brunswick, NJ: Rutgers.

Dickinson, E. (1976). Linscott, Robert (Ed.). *Selected poems and letters of Emily Dickinson.* New York: Bantam Doubleday Dell.

Glenn, L. N. (2007). Phenomenology. In L. N. Glenn, *Combustion* (p. 69). London, Ontario, Canada: Brick Books.

Gordimer, N. (1995). *Writing and being.* Cambridge, MA: Harvard University Press.

Hirshfield, J. (1997). *Nine gates: Entering the mind of poetry.* New York: Harper Perennial.

Kirsch, G. (1993). *Women writing the academy.* Carbondale: Southern Illinois University Press.

Kristeva, J. (1981). Women's time (Alice Jardine and Harry Blake, Trans.). *Signs, 7*(33–34), 42–43.

Lee, D. (1998). *Body music.* Toronto, Ontario, Canada: Anansi Press.

Mairs, N. (1994). *Voice lessons: On becoming a (woman) writer.* Boston: Beacon Press.

McCann, H. (2002). *Other lives, other learning.* Unpublished doctoral dissertation, James Cook University, Australia.

McKay, D. (2001). *Vis a vis: Fieldnotes on poetry and wilderness.* Wolfville, Nova Scotia, Canada: Gaspereau Press.

Neilsen, L. (1996). Reclaiming the sign, remaking sense: Feminist metaphors for a literacy of the possible. In J. Flood, S. Brice Heath, & D. Lapp (Eds.), *A handbook for literacy educators: Research on teaching the communicative and visual arts* (pp. 203–214). New York: Macmillan.

Neilsen, L. (1997). Email/Fe-mail: Gender and the semiotics of telecommunications. In C. Laudano (Ed.), *Mujeres en el fin de siglo: Desafinios y controversias* (pp. 151–168). La Plata: Red de Editoriales Universitarias.

Neilsen, L. (1998a). *Knowing her place: Research literacies and feminist occasions.* San Francisco and Big Tancook Island, Nova Scotia, Canada: Caddo Gap Press and Backalong Books.

Neilsen, L. (1998b). *Writing our foremothers: Grand/mother lines.* Paper presented at the conference on Qualitative Research in Education (QUIG), Athens, GA.

Neilsen, L. (1998c, May). *Writing our foremothers: Women, re/search, writing.* Paper presented at the XV Inkshed Conference, Oak Island, Nova Scotia, Canada.

Neilsen, L. (2001). Scribbler: Notes on writing and learning inquiry. In L. Neilsen, A. L. Cole, & J. G. Knowles (Eds.), *The art of writing inquiry* (p. 258). Halifax, Nova Scotia, Canada: Backalong Books.

Neilsen, L. (2002a). Learning from the liminal: Fiction as knowledge. *Alberta Journal of Educational Research, 48*(3), 206–214.

Neilsen, L. (2002b, Spring). *Lyric inquiry: Line breaks and liminal spaces.* Invited address at the University of Alberta.

Neilsen, L. (2002c, February). *Write of passage: Women and writing.* Keynote address at the Teaching and Learning Conference, Edith Cowan University, Western Australia.

Neilsen, L. (2004). Learning to listen: Data as poetry, poetry as data. *Journal of Critical Inquiry Into Curriculum and Instruction, 5*(2), 41–43.

Neilsen, L., & Clifford, P. (1996, December). *Making sense: Fantastic transgressions into research as literacy.* Paper presented at the National Reading Conference, Charleston, SC.

Neilsen, L., Jessome, R., Horsfall, H., & Hollis, H. (2000). *Women writing learning.* Paper presented at the Conference of Atlantic Educators, Halifax, Nova Scotia, Canada.

Oliver, M. (2002). *What do we know.* Cambridge, MA: Da Capo Press.

Rogers, A. (1993). Voice, play, and a practice of ordinary courage in girls' and women's lives. *Harvard Educational Review, 63*(3), 265–295.

Rosenblatt, L. (1976). *Literature as exploration* (3rd ed.). New York: Noble and Noble Publishers.

Wallace, B. (1987). *The stubborn particulars of grace.* Toronto, Ontario, Canada: McClelland & Stewart.

Zwicky, J. (1992). *Lyric philosophy.* Toronto, Ontario, Canada: University of Toronto Press.

Zwicky, J. (2003). *Wisdom and metaphor.* Kentville, Nova Scotia, Canada: Gaspereau Press.

PART III

GENRES

B ringing the arts into research to advance knowledge means that research no longer looks a particular way. Bringing the arts into research throws into disarray the set of shared and accepted beliefs, values, techniques, discourses, and so on about research that academics (including many qualitative researchers) have come to accept as paradigmatic givens. And, like any paradigm shift, a fundamental change at the level of deep structure takes time (a long time). Even entertaining the prospects and possibilities of such a shift is perhaps best begun with examples of what such research might look like. The chapters in this section are the heart of the *Handbook*. Individually and collectively, the many chapters both show and tell how specific arts genres advance knowledge in ways that are different from conventional social science research methodologies. Authors describe what research employing different art forms might look like. They discuss some of the main issues and challenges associated with using various art forms so as to illuminate their possibilities in qualitative research methodologies. Because of the many different art forms and genres, chapters in this section are clustered in subsections: literary forms, performance, visual art, new media, and popular and folk art forms.

◆ *Literary Forms*

- Métissage: A Research Praxis, *Cynthia Chambers and Erika Hasebe-Ludt with Dwayne Donald, Wanda Hurren, Carl Leggo, and Antoinette Oberg*
- Writing as Theory: In Defense of Fiction, *Stephen Banks*
- Astonishing Silence: Knowing in Poetry, *Carl Leggo*

◆ Performance

- Dance, Choreography, and Social Science Research, *Donald Blumenfeld-Jones*
- Performative Inquiry: Embodiment and Its Challenges, *Ronald J. Pelias*
- Ethnodrama and Ethnotheatre, *Johnny Saldaña*
- Readers' Theater as a Display Strategy, *Robert Donmoyer and June Yennie Donmoyer*
- The Music Lesson, *Liora Bresler*

◆ Visual Art

- Painting as Research: Create and Critique, *Graeme Sullivan*
- Photographs and/as Social Documentary, *Claudia Mitchell and Susan Allnutt*
- Collage as Inquiry, *Lynn Butler-Kisber*
- Textu(r)al Walking/Writing Through Sculpture, *Alex F. de Cosson*
- Installation Art-as-Research, *Ardra L. Cole and Maura McIntyre*

◆ New Media

- Digital Content: Video as Research, *Janice Rahn*
- Blogs, *Robert Runte*
- Zines: Individual to Community, *Troy R. Lovata*
- Radio in/for Research: Creating Knowledge Waves, *Christine McKenzie*

◆ Folk and Popular Art Forms

- Touching Minds and Hearts: Community Arts as Collaborative Research, *Deborah Barndt*
- Quilts, *Helen K. Ball*

9

Literary Forms

CREATIVE NONFICTION AND SOCIAL RESEARCH

◆ Tom Barone

A chasm between scientists who have claimed the ability through rigorous methods to approach "objective truth" and literary/artistic types who valorize texts of fiction has long divided them into what C. P. Snow (1959/1998) called two cultures. Snow identified these two polar groups as the literary intellectuals and the scientists. These two cultures, with their dramatically different epistemological stances and ways of viewing the world, still exist today. The associated scientific/literary dichotomy remains apparent as we search for works labeled "fiction" or "nonfiction" in the library, on Internet bookseller sites, or in segregated best-seller lists.

These classifications are meant as guidance for an intended readership about how to regard and use the contents of a particular work. Without such guidance, notes the literary theorist Wolfgang Iser (1993), "inappropriate reactions will ensue" (p. 12). The post-positivist Phillips (1994) agrees with the seemingly commonsensical notion that there is indeed danger in mistaking fiction (or fantasy) for fact, even (or especially) in storied accounts: "If an action is taken on the basis of an incorrect narrative, even if disaster does not always ensue, we [will likely] end up with consequences that we neither anticipated nor desired" (p. 17).

For Phillips, actions that rely upon non-fictional ("correct") accounts of events—events that "actually happened"—are more likely to be "successful" than those based on stories that are "incorrect," not literally "true."

Within this dualistic mindset, stories classified as fictional may serve certain non-research purposes, but not the purposes of social science. They may not be considered legitimate as social research. This dichotomizing supports a "single drop of blood" perspective regarding the purity of social research texts. Stories categorized as non-fictional, and therefore as correct and useful, must at least strive toward "truth" as a regulative ideal. They must aim to consistently, directly, and precisely mirror the "real world."

In our Western culture, fiction continues to be associated with the fantastic, and as such, "remain[s] a no-no, a mode of expression . . . that is simply off-limits in conventional academic discourse" (Banks & Banks, 1998, p. 17). And to the extent that "nonfictional stories" tolerate ambiguity, imagination, or creativity—indeed, subjectivity of any sort—they may be seen as diminished in terms of the reliability, validity, and objectivity so important for conventional forms of research, and therefore are still reviled as tainted, dismissed as illegitimate half-breeds.

◆ *Creativity in Nonfictional Social Inquiry Texts: Origins*

Despite the dominance of the dichotomy identified by Snow (1959/1998), some scholars have suggested that the line between science and art (including the literary arts) and the line between fiction and nonfiction have never been easily discernible. Although most would admit to sufficiently distinct identifying marks to warrant the use of the labels of "art" and "science," "fiction" and "nonfiction," many have emphasized the commonalities between the two terms in each of these apparent dyads (Latour, 1987; Nisbet, 1976; Vattimo, 1988).

Before the 17th century, these dualisms were nowhere to be found. As Levine (1985) notes: "Surely no one in the West before 1600 intended to cast the discussion of human affairs in the language of precise propositions" (p. 1). It took an "assault on ambiguity" by the mathematical and physical sciences, with their emphases on theoretical rigor and metric precision alluded to above, to devalue the then prevailing "natural" forms of discourse through the erection of a hierarchy of language genres.

Since that time, however, some social scientists and artists have transgressed against the conventional hierarchy and boundaries between these separate domains. As early as the 19th century, literary types (especially novelists) could be found engaging in the close scrutiny of the world that was supposedly the exclusive hallmark of science, while social scientists (and journalists and other writers professionally betrothed to the "factual") began to creatively employ metaphorical, evocative language and the storied formats that reside ostensibly within the realm of imaginative literature.

This transgression occurred in various sorts of texts, including mid-19th-century British literary criticism, 18th-century travel literature, certain early forms of autobiography, confessional life stories (including the first by Rousseau), and social realist novels advocated by the likes of Honore de Balzac and Emile Zola.

In the 20th century, the most brazen moves (outside of the academy) to problematize the boundaries between fact and fiction occurred within the New Journalism movement (Barone 1980; Johnson, 1971). New Journalism emerged in the 1960s in magazines such as *Esquire* and *The New Yorker,* as well as in books by Tom Wolfe

(1969, 1973, 1979), Joan Didion (1969), Hunter S. Thompson (1973), Michael Herr (1968), and others. Most notably, Truman Capote (1963) published *In Cold Blood,* a work that he called a "nonfiction novel." Norman Mailer (1968) subtitled his *Armies of the Night,* an award-winning account of a protest march on the Pentagon, "History as a Novel, The Novel as History." Elizabeth Hardwick's (1979) acclaimed *Sleepless Nights* was described as an "autobiographical novel." And Alex Haley (1976), refusing the fact/fiction dualism, insisted instead upon the hybrid term *faction* as more accurately descriptive of his book *Roots.*

The New Journalists shared a preference for accounts that defied the entrenched notion of the reporter as a detached and "objective" recorder of events in favor of one who, employing an evocative and metaphorical language of description, also moves to interpret and evaluate those events from an obvious point of view. Or as Johnson (1971) put it, "New Journalists aimed for novelistic or impressionistic reconstructions of actual events" (p. 40). The sort of literary nonfiction espoused and practiced by the New Journalists survives in the form of New Journalism (Boynton, 2005).

◆ Three Pioneers in Academia

Concurrent with the advent of literary style journalism, similar stirrings could be felt within the walls of the academy. The movement was gradual and broad-based, pushing the culture of the scientist ever closer to that of the author of literature. The movement occurred within what has been characterized as the rhetorical, narrative, literary, and performative "turns" during the last three decades of the 20th century. Among the scholars in the humanities and social sciences whose works of the late 1970s were enormously influential in, and emblematic of, the "turnings," were the sociologist Robert Nisbet, the anthropologist Clifford Geertz, and the educationist Elliot Eisner.

Nisbet's (1976) book *Sociology as an Art Form* argued persuasively for the dissolution of Snow's dualism, claiming that sociology was/is not only one of the sciences but also one of the arts. He suggested that a close affinity of sociology with the world of art could be found in various features: the themes explored within each field, the styles in which each reveals itself, the modes of representation that each employs.

Although Nisbet focused primarily on the historical similarities between the two intellectual domains, his recognition of common features within their means of representing reality—portraiture, landscape, and a dynamic sense of temporal and spatial flow—may have promoted a kind of literary sociology. Similarly, Clifford Geertz both described and advocated for the storytelling and poetic qualities of ethnography.

The ethnographic essays of Geertz, a self-described anthropologist/storyteller, are both aesthetically and substantively impressive; indeed, they are accomplished literary essays. Moreover, Geertz (1973) argued they are, in a certain sense, like all ethnographies, works of fiction, at least in the "sense that they are 'something made,' 'something fashioned'" (p. 16). Geertz (1983), moreover, is credited with coining the term *genre blurring,* suggesting a recognition and acceptance of the use of artistic design elements in crafting works of ethnography and those within the other fields of the human sciences.

In the field of education, a similar champion of creative nonfiction was Elliot Eisner of Stanford University. An arts educator, curricularist, and qualitative research methodologist, Eisner (1979) theorized about the possibilities of bringing the talents of the art critic to bear in the fields of educational research and evaluation. Eisner noted that art critics often employed a language that is highly vivid, evocative, and metaphorical, while adequately referring to the phenomena being observed, studied, and represented. Similarly, the *educational critic* was conceived by Eisner (1979, 1991) as someone who could artfully disclose subtle and important facets of educational phenomena. Taking Eisner's lead, several educational researchers explored the utility of educational criticism for writing about the realms of teaching (Greer, 1973), curriculum materials (Vallance, 1977), classroom life (McCutcheon, 1976), and the parallels between this sort of creative nonfiction and literary journalism (Barone, 1979, 1980). Later, Barone and Eisner (1997) began to refer to research that contained a number of aesthetic design elements in the research and compositional process as *arts-based research.*

◆ *Tropisms and Dialectics*

These and other scholars in fields often identified with social science challenged the traditional fact/fiction dualism in creative ways. Still, their work was/is often qualified and characterized as creative or literary, *nonfiction.* Does this terminology signify that the fact/fiction dichotomy has managed to persist and survive the strong movement toward genre blurring? Yes, conventions of all sorts die hard.

Since the 1970s, cultural texts or documents of social research that might conventionally be characterized as creative nonfiction have indeed burgeoned. In the various fields and disciplines of the social sciences and humanities, these works have taken on various literary forms (Denzin & Lincoln, 1998; Ellis, 1995, 2004; Ellis & Bochner, 1996; Richardson, 1997). These include, but are not limited to, the following: life stories, life histories, literary style essays, autoethnographies, ethnodramas, performance ethnographies, documentary films and videos, nonfictional novels and short stories, educational criticism, and reader's theater. Richardson (2000, p. 930) has provided a list of "creative analytical practices" in ethnography, fiction-stories, polyvocal texts, responsive readings, aphorisms, comedy and satire, visual presentations, allegory, conversation, layered accounts, writing-stories, and mixed genres.

Why has creative nonfiction proliferated in light of the well-established fact/fiction dichotomy? Is it because works of creative nonfiction serve a purpose that is somehow distinct from texts that are more easily classified as either fictional or factual? Perhaps they claim a space between fact and fiction in which a different sort of textual dynamic is played out, the same sort of dynamic present in the viewing of books and films that claim to be "based on a true story" or "inspired by actual events" or that are described as follows:

> Though this is a work of nonfiction, I have taken certain storytelling liberties. . . . When the narrative strays from strict nonfiction, my intention has been to remain faithful to the characters and to the essential drift of events as they really happened. (Berendt, 1994, p. 389)

Like the term *creative nonfiction,* these authorial declarations seem to signal to the reader the coexistence of two apparently conflicting reasons for reading a particular text. The first is to secure a proximity to the truth, the "essential drift of events as they really happened"; and the second reason is one often associated with the reading of a work of fiction imbued with "storytelling liberties." I will elaborate on this point by extrapolating from the ideas of the literary critic Wolfgang Iser.

Two opposing forces or tendencies may be seen operating in all human discourse, including the reading of inquiry texts. These forces may be identified as the *centripetal* and the *centrifugal*. In the reading of texts in which centripetal forces dominate, one senses design elements that serve as stimuli or cues to adopt a certain epistemological attitude toward the text. This "pull" or "tropism" honors the ultimate aim of human inquiry that Rorty (1979) described as a "quest for truth." The kind of text in which centripetal forces strongly dominate suggests a final, standard, authoritative, unambiguous, conventionally truthful rendition of events. It honors a correspondence theory of truth wherein language is meant to mirror the objects of a real world. Texts of this sort aim to be maximally denotative, purely factual, strictly nonfictional, highly valid, literally true.

Those texts in which centrifugal forces dominate lean in an opposite direction, as Iser (1993) would argue, toward fantasy and formlessness, toward the territory of the scattered, the incoherent, the impossibly distant, the absolutely arbitrary. They would tend to be chaotic, nonsensical texts that partake of what Iser (1993) calls the "imaginary." This imaginary "tends to manifest itself in a somewhat diffuse manner, in fleeting impressions that defy our attempts to pin it down in a concrete and stabilized form" (p. 3).

This chaotic realm of the fantastic is often associated in the traditional paradigm of Western thought with that of fiction. That is unfortunate—a mistake. Indeed, Iser (1993) argues that it is precisely in the act of fictionalizing that these opposing forces—the tropisms toward literal truth and a formless imaginary—are successfully harnessed into a productive dialectic. In an act of fictionalizing, "reproduced reality is made to point to a 'reality' beyond itself, while the imaginary is lured into form." In the production of a work of fiction, "extra-textual reality merges into the imaginary and the imaginary emerges into reality" (p. 3).

The prevailing binary of truth and fiction (or fantasy) is thereby replaced with a complex conception of the act of reading as one in which a delicious dialectic tension between actuality and imagination may be experienced. Indeed, a boundary between fact and fiction has never been, itself, an objective, strictly "factual" entity. Rather it is a human (social) construction, an artifact of convention, one born out of a general need for an unambiguous classification of otherwise indeterminate entities.

A persistent yearning for the resolution of ambiguities regarding what constitutes fiction and nonfiction may indeed be viewed as an ongoing manifestation of an ancient desire to reduce anxiety about the indefinite. But an adequate understanding of the manner in which texts of creative nonfiction operate requires an acceptance of the inevitability of ambiguity. To illustrate this point, we return to the notion of opposing centripetal and centrifugal forces operating within texts.

◆ *Reading Creative Nonfiction as Fiction? Three Examples*

Just as ethnography may be, on the one hand, described as an "artful science" (Brady, 1991), some social research that has been described as arts-based may, on the other hand, claim a "nonfictional" rather than "fictional" status. Indeed, arts-based research texts, like those labeled sociological or ethnographic or journalistic, exhibit varying degrees of centripetal and centrifugal tropisms. Some may lean toward the promotion of a privileged, "correct" version of behaviors and events. For example, a text may be advertised as a summative evaluation, a terminal, overall appraisal of a public program. Or a text may purport to offer an accurate depiction of auto/biographical or historical phenomena. Texts of these sorts, with strong centripetal tendencies, may indeed be prestructured to promote certainty rather than ambiguity and thus suggest a desire to be regarded as valid, literally true, trustworthy, and (in one sense) useful.

But within the very same text, literary dimensions and devices may also be discerned. These devices are usually the ones that serve to justify the modification of the nonfictional text as "creative." Among these may be the following: expressive, connotative language; contextualized, vernacular language; the presence of an aesthetic form, perhaps a story or quasi-storied format; composite characters; inner dialogue; complex characterization; invented dialogue; obvious point of view; plot; narrative drive; metaphor; allusions; flashbacks and flash forwards; synecdoche; tone shifts; and so on. The presence of these literary attributes serves as a countervailing, centrifugal tendency.

This centrifugal tendency may be so strong that, regardless of the presence of opposing linguistic cues, or the apparent desire of the author or readers to label, categorize, or classify the text unambiguously as nonfiction, one is enabled to read the text as *either fiction or nonfiction, or as both*. To illustrate this point, I offer, from an enormous array of possibilities, three examples, each representing a different form of creative nonfiction.

◆ *Street Rat*

The first example is the ethnodrama *Street Rat* (Saldaña, Finley, & Finley, 2002). *Ethnodrama, performance ethnography, ethnoperformance, ethnodrama,* and *reality theatre* are all terms used to identify a form of literary nonfictional data representation in which the qualitative researcher "playwrites with data" (Saldaña, 2005, p. 2), creating a play out of an ethnographic text

usually meant to be performed on stage. The ethnodrama is a kind of performance text (Denzin, 1997). In other sorts of performance texts, poems, short stories, diary entries, and interview texts are re-crafted into dramatic presentations.

Street Rat may be considered a work of creative nonfiction that focuses on the lives of some homeless youths in New Orleans. The play was adapted by Johnny Saldaña, Susan Finley, and her son, Macklin, from a research story composed by the Finleys (S. Finley & Finley, 1999; Saldaña, 2005) and from poetry written by Macklin (M. Finley, 2000). I attended a production of this ethnodrama directed by Saldaña.

The script, based on participant-observer Macklin's experiences with his informants, was based on the lives of "real characters." It moved briskly from an introduction of the two main characters, Roach and Tigger, to complications arising partly from their relationships with each other and their homeless friends, to a dramatic climax as violence nearly erupts, and finally a touching denouement, a scene in which Tigger and Roach, obviously filling a void in each other's lives left there by others, declared in their garbage-strewn living quarters that they were, at least for the time being, home. The narrative drive of the story was punctuated by the recitation of poems of various lengths, composed by Macklin, who thereby became, himself, a character in the play.

Other theatrical touches added to the production's effective *mise en scène*. Absent a proscenium arch, audience members were seated in a black-draped, rectangular room, its floor shared with the actors. The minimal props, authentic costuming, and background music were all carefully designed and selected to advance the vision of the director and his collaborators.

The formal attributes of *Street Rat* were matched by its content. The telling details in the lives of Roach, Tigger, and their comrades enabled me to dwell within an otherwise largely unavailable world of homeless young people. Through an array of concrete images, particular forms of intelligence were revealed to me, the structure of moral codes laid bare. Through a cascade of specific utterances and gestures, I was granted access to their personal hopes, dreams, and motivations.

◆ *Fields of Play*

My second example is *Fields of Play* by Laurel Richardson (1997). This remarkable book represents a creative reshaping of the genre of collected scholarly works. Instead of offering the usual chronological or thematic arrangement of individual writings published over a portion of a scholar's academic career, Richardson crafts a compelling personal/professional autobiography that is melded with theory.

Her most prominent experimental writings (including poems, literary essays, an ethnographic drama, and other experimental writings) themselves exhibit artful elements of design as well as deeply personal revelations and so become integral parts of the plot of her life story. Indeed, these previously published works serve as flashbacks of a sort, placed into a temporal relief through her reflective present-day commentary.

Her previously published "selections" for this book are situated among what she calls *writing-stories*. These "forewords" and "afterwords" envelop each of the earlier pieces, thereby serving as elegant bridges that connect those textual islands and providing a kind of continuity to the lived experiences. They enable the reader to experience vicariously the arc of the academic life of a sociologist whose creative nonfictional works defied traditions and contributed significantly to the literary turn in sociology. The arc is completed as

Richardson concludes the book with a powerful personal essay that circles back to her early life as a child, focusing on an incident at the age of eight that may have served as a starting point in the history of her desire to write.

◆ *Touching Eternity*

The third example is my own book entitled *Touching Eternity: The Enduring Outcomes of Teaching* (Barone, 2001). This book investigates the work of a high school arts teacher named Don Forrister. The book first presents an evaluative essay of the teacher initially published in 1983. Part II of the book consists of a set of nine life stories of his former students, elicited and composed by the researcher more than a decade after their graduation, life stories in which the former students describe what they perceive are Forrister's long-range influences on their lives. Part III highlights what Forrister perceives, in turn, as the influences of his former students on his own life story.

Most of the first three parts of the book are written in a language that is vernacular in character, while also often vivid, metaphorical, and evocative. Its narrative and story-like features, as well as its variegated formatting, are meant to contribute to an experimental, postmodernist biography of a teacher. Moreover, most of the stories of Forrister's former students suggest certain enduring outcomes of his teaching, pointing to the possibility that he had indeed "touched eternity" though them. But in Part IV the voice of the author/researcher is heard analyzing the contents of the life stories through two incommensurate and conflicting theoretical frameworks: one from phenomenology, one from critical theory. In so doing, the text raises doubts about whether Forrister was indeed able to have a lasting impact on his students' lives.

In each of these three examples, the author of the text seems to claim a kind of creative nonfictional status for the work (without necessarily using that term). In each case, the authors have entered into a tacit contract with the reader that the work is (at least partly) meant to focus on actual incidents in the lives of specific individuals. (In two of the cases—the Barone and Richardson books—actual names were used for the two protagonists; in *Touching Eternity,* as in the ethnodrama *Street Rat,* pseudonyms were used for the youthful characters; *Fields of Play* is autobiographical.) In each case, centripetal forces operate to direct the attention of readers inward, signaling that they are becoming privy to truths (or at least partial truths—truths as seen from a particular perspective) about central characters and events.

In that sense, these works seem to earn the appellation of nonfiction. Readers may perceive themselves as coming to know (better) these particular individuals. And if the "real" characters in the text are recognized as direct acquaintances of the reader, the text may serve as a basis for judgment as to how to regard and act toward them. In that sort of reading, Phillips's (1994) caution about the need for "correct" information in narratives seems quite appropriate.

But often the reader is not familiar with the actual people, events, or settings portrayed within a social research text. In that case, the reader may nevertheless still retain an inward focus, regarding the text in a strictly literal fashion. Iser (1993) has noted that the "real world" elements portrayed in a text, inscribed in an attempt at mimetic replication, may indeed serve merely to point to an actual individual involved in purportedly "real-life" experiences.

But the centrifugal forces within a text may allow for an additional or alternative reading, a *fictional* one. Then the mimicry of the conventionally real in the text "is not present [only] for its own sake, but [also]

refers to something else" (Iser, 1993, p. 15). That "something else" is the figurative—places and events that are analogues of those inscribed within the text.

This may, in fact, be viewed as a central activity within the crafting of a work of fiction—the creation by the author, and recreation by the reader, of an "as if" world, albeit a credible, believable one. Iser (1993) suggests this recreation is promoted through an author's purposeful (and inevitable) selection and combination of elements "from a variety of social, historical, cultural, and literary systems outside the text" (p. 10). In the production of a work of fiction, such real world elements are indeed needed to bring the imaginary into form.

Texts that are prestructured in this manner tend to promote a different kind of reading than that offered by a nonliterary text with centripetal tendencies. In the former, the reader is more likely to momentarily bracket off the text from the ordinary stream of consciousness. In so doing she may simultaneously view it as *both* representing an actual world *and* presenting a hypothetical "as if" or, in Iser's sense of the word, *fictional* world. Because of the inherent ambiguity in this sort of textual experience the reader may then be free to search for a *reference* (Ricouer, 1976) for the text, to take the text home into the world of her daily experiences to see what it might say about familiar conditions, conventional practices, and the values and ideologies that support them.

So are these three works really examples of creative nonfiction, and not something else? My answer to that question is—an ambiguous one. The texts do purport to document reality, even as they evidence forms of creativity, experimenting with writing strategies and textual design elements that can be aptly characterized as literary. Several of these serve to entice the reader into experiencing the internal world of the text, into leaving her own, nearby, extra-textual world, in order to dwell vicariously within the (presumably) actual world being portrayed, and there to imagine the lives of the "real" characters of Don Forrister, Laurel Richardson, and the homeless youths of New Orleans.

But despite the cautionary label of "nonfiction," these same literary devices and constructions may lure the reader outward from a literal construal of textual content, enabling her to read the texts figuratively, as something other or more than a mirror image of reality. While accepting, to a degree, the "reality" of the portrayals, readers are nevertheless encouraged to put the text to use as an imaginary, as an opening into a possible world.

So in all three examples described above, the reader may construe the textual world not only as an actual one about which to learn the facts, but simultaneously as a hypothetical world that abandons the circumscribed territory of the "real" and moves into the vast realm of the possible. In providing the contract details of her own life story, Richardson surely intends the outcome suggested by Carolyn Ellis on the book's back cover (Richardson, 1997): "to evoke academic readers to critically assess the taken-for-granted paths they have chosen for themselves." Likewise, Saldaña does not intend to only present the real worlds of the particular street kids whose lives were carefully researched by Macklin Finley. His play also suggests the travails and tribulations of youths who are living similar lives in nearby neighborhoods. And my book concerns not only the pedagogical attributes of a single Appalachian high school teacher. Indeed, my intent in *Touching Eternity* was not to bring readers closer to an answer to the question of what constitutes good teaching. Instead, it was meant to disturb and puzzle, to promote reflection about what constitutes quality in teaching. It ponders the likelihood of success of a hero-teacher's single-handed attempts at

combating a powerful array of pervasive cultural formations that serve to undercut the impact of his work.

◆ The Textual Dance

In choosing to adopt a kind of binocular vision for regarding works characterized as creative nonfiction, the reader moves constantly back and forth, reverberating between the world of the text and her own fund of extra-textual "realities." This requires a willingness on the part of the reader to be, herself, creative in the reading of the text, to engage in a kind of textual play that is premised on the understanding that there are no final meanings inscribed within the text. The meanings are, rather, ambiguous ones that are brought into being within negotiations between the text and the reader.

For so very long social researchers considered ambiguity to be a disreputable quality, an unwanted problem child whose dirty hands threatened the presumed purity of their textual accounts. Social researchers were engaged in a quest to eliminate all forms of contamination from their inquiry texts lest, they feared, they slide down a slippery slope from the safe, reassuring hard-high-ground of the literally true into the dangerous abyss of subjective fictions, the fantastic, even hallucinatory, realm of the madman.

But time passes and conditions change. Nowadays ambiguity has become, for many social researchers, an intriguing characteristic whose healthy presence in their accounts has been not only accepted as inevitable, but openly celebrated as desirable and even useful.

Within this celebration, social researchers can be found dancing back and forth across what was once a clearly delineated and closed border between the true and the false, the factual and the fictional. They dance in what may be seen as a fiesta of textual possibilities, even as works of social research, although qualified as "creative," remain conventionally classified as "nonfictional."

◆ *References*

Banks, A., & Banks, S. (1998). *Fiction and social research: By ice or fire*. Walnut Creek, CA: AltaMira Press.

Barone, T. (1979). *Inquiry into classroom experiences: A qualitative, holistic approach*. Stanford, CA: Stanford University Press.

Barone, T. (1980). Effectively critiquing the experienced curriculum: Clues from the "new journalism." *Curriculum Inquiry, 10*(1), 29–53.

Barone, T. (2001). *Touching eternity: The enduring outcomes of teaching*. New York: Teachers College Press.

Barone, T., & Eisner, E. (1997). Arts-based educational research. In R. M. Jaeger (Ed.), *Complementary methods for research in education* (2nd ed., pp. 75–116). Washington, DC: American Educational Research Association.

Barone, T., & Eisner, E. (2006). Arts-based educational research. In J. Green, G. Camilli, & P. Elmore (Eds.), *Handbook of complementary methods in education research* (3rd ed., pp. 93–107). New York: Lawrence Erlbaum.

Berendt. J. (1994). *Midnight in the garden of good and evil*. New York: Random House.

Boynton, R. (2005). *The new new journalism*. New York: Vintage Books.

Brady, I. (1991). Harmony and argument: Bringing forth the artful science. In I. Brady (Ed.), *Anthropological poetics* (pp. 3–30). Savage, MD: Rowman & Littlefield.

Capote, T. (1963). *In cold blood: A true account of a multiple murder and its consequences*. New York: Random House.

Denzin, N. (1997) *Interpretive ethnography: Ethnographic practices for the 21st century*. Thousand Oaks, CA: Sage.

Denzin, N., & Lincoln, Y (Eds.). (1998). *The landscape of qualitative research: Theories and issues*. Thousand Oaks, CA: Sage.

Didion, J. (1969). *Slouching towards Bethlehem*. New York: Delta Books.

Eisner, E. W. (1979). *The educational imagination*. New York: Macmillan.

Eisner, E. W. (1991). *The enlightened eye*. New York: Macmillan.

Ellis, C. (1995) *Final negotiations: A story of love, loss, and chronic illness*. Philadelphia: Temple University Press.

Ellis, C. (2004). *The ethnographic I: A methodological novel about autoethnography*. Walnut Creek, CA: AltaMira Press.

Ellis, C., & Bochner, B. (Eds.). (1996). *Composing ethnography: Alternative forms of qualitative writing*. Walnut Creek, CA: AltaMira Press.

Finley, M. (2000). *Street rat*. Detroit: Greenroom Press, University of Detroit Mercy.

Finley, S., & Finley, M. (1999). Sp'ange: A research story. *Qualitative Inquiry, 5*(3), 313–337.

Geertz, C. (1973). *The interpretation of cultures*. New York: Basic Books.

Geertz, C. (1983). *Local knowledge: Further essays in interpretive ethnography*. New York: Basic Books.

Greer, D. (1973). *The criticism of teaching*. Unpublished doctoral dissertation, Stanford University.

Haley, A. (1976). *Roots*. Garden City, NY: Doubleday.

Hardwick, E. (1979). *Sleepless nights*. New York: Random House.

Herr, M. (1968). *Dispatches*. New York: Avon Books.

Iser, W. (1993). *The fictive and the imaginary: Charting literary anthropology*. Baltimore: Johns Hopkins University Press.

Johnson, M. (1971). *The new journalism: The underground press, the artists of nonfiction, and changes in the established media*. Lawrence: University of Kansas Press.

Latour, B. (1987). *The pasteurization of France*. Cambridge, MA: Harvard University Press.

Levine, D. (1985). *The flight from ambiguity: Essays in social and cultural theory*. Chicago: University of Chicago Press.

Mailer, N. (1968). *Armies of the night: History as a novel, the novel as history*. New York: New American Library.

McCutcheon, G. (1976). *The disclosure of classroom life*. Unpublished doctoral dissertation, Stanford University.

Nisbet, R. (1976). *Sociology as an art form.* New York: Oxford University Press.

Phillips, D. C. (1994). Telling it straight: Issues in assessing narrative research. *Educational Psychologist, 29,* 13–21.

Richardson, L. (1997). *Fields of play: Constructing an academic life.* New Brunswick, NJ: Rutgers Academic Press.

Richardson, L. (2000). Writing: A method of inquiry. In N. Denzin & Y. Lincoln (Eds.), *Handbook of qualitative research* (2nd ed., pp. 923–948). Thousand Oaks, CA: Sage.

Ricoeur, P. (1976). *Interpretation theory: Discourse and the surplus of meaning.* Fort Worth: Texas Christian University Press.

Rorty, R. (1979). *Philosophy and the mirror of nature.* Princeton: Princeton University Press.

Saldaña, J. (Ed.). (2005). *Ethnodrama: An anthology of reality theatre.* Walnut Creek, CA: Alta Mira Press.

Saldaña, J., Finley, S., & Finley, M. (2002). *Street rat.* Unpublished manuscript.

Snow, C. P. (1998). *The two cultures.* Cambridge, UK: Cambridge University Press. (Original work published 1959)

Thompson, H. (1973). *Fear and loathing in Las Vegas.* New York: Popular Library.

Vallance, E. (1977). The landscape of "The Great Plains Experience": An application of curriculum criticism. *Curriculum Inquiry, 7*(2), 87–106.

Vattimo, G. (1988). *The end of modernity: Nihilism and hermeneutics in post-modern culture.* London: Polity.

Wolfe, T. (1969). *Radical chic and mau-mauing the flak catchers.* New York: Bantam Books.

Wolfe, T. (1973). *The new journalism.* New York: Harper & Row.

Wolfe, T. (1979). *The right stuff.* New York: Farrar, Straus & Giroux.

10

INTERPRETIVE BIOGRAPHY

◆ Norman K. Denzin

The subject matter of interpretive research is meaningful biographical experience. Interpretive studies are organized in terms of a biographically meaningful event or moment in a subject's life. This event, the epiphany, how it is experienced, how it is defined, and how it is woven through the multiple strands of a person's life constitute the focus of interpretive biographical research (Denzin, 2001).

◆ Epiphany and the Sting of Memory

The biographical project begins with personal history, with the sting of childhood memory, with an event that lingers and remains in the person's life story (Ulmer, 1989). Interpretive biography, or autoethnography, re-tells and re-performs these life experiences. The life story becomes an invention, a re-presentation, a historical object ripped or torn out of its contexts.

In writing a life story, I create the conditions for rediscovering the meanings of a past sequence of events (Ulmer, 1989). In so doing, I create new ways of performing and experiencing the past. To represent the past this way does not mean to "recognize it 'the way it really was.' It means to seize hold of a memory as it flashes up at a moment of danger"

(Benjamin, 1968, p. 257) to see and rediscover the past, not as a succession of events but as a series of scenes, inventions, emotions, images, and stories (Ulmer, 1989).

In bringing the past into the autobiographical present, I insert myself into the past and create the conditions for rewriting and hence reexperiencing it. History becomes a montage, moments quoted out of context, "juxtaposed fragments from widely dispersed places and times" (Ulmer, 1989, p. 112). Thus are revealed hidden features of the present as well as of the past (Ulmer, 1989). I want to invent a new version of the past, a new history. This is what interpretive biography does. Here is an example, an excerpt from an ongoing project (Denzin, 2005, 2007).

SCENE ONE: THE PAST

Voice 1: Narrator As Young Boy

When I was little, in the 1940s, living in south central Iowa, my grandmother would tell stories about Indians. She loved to tell the story about the day a tall Indian brave, with braided hair, came to her mother's kitchen door and asked for some bread to eat. This happened when grandma was a little girl, probably around 1915.

Voice 2: Grandmother

This Indian was so polite and handsome. Mother said his wife and children stood right behind him in a straight row. The Indian said his name was Mr. Thomas. He said that he and his wife and his children were traveling to the Mesquaki Reservation near Tama, Iowa, to visit relatives. Mother believed him. He said that they had run out of money and did not like to ask for hand-outs, but this looked like a friendly farm house. Mother said it

is a crime in this country to be hungry! I believe that too!

Voice 3: Grandmother As Young Daughter

Mother made lunch for Mr. Thomas and his family. They sat under the big oak tree in the front yard and had a picnic. Later, when they were leaving, Mr. Thomas came back to the kitchen and thanked mother again. He gave her a small hand-woven wicker basket as a gift. I treasure to this day this basket. It has become a family heirloom.

SCENE TWO: REAL INDIANS

Voice 4: Narrator As Young Boy

When I was not yet 10, one Sunday Mother and Dad took my brother and me to Tama, to the Mesquaki Reservation, to see a powwow. I wondered if we'd see Mr. Thomas, if I would even recognize him if he was there. We walked through the mud past teepees to the center of a big field. Indians in costumes with paint on their faces and long braids of hair were singing, and dancing. Some were drumming and singing. At the edge of the field tables under canvas tents were set up. Dad bought some Indian fry bread for all of us, and bottles of cold root beer. We took the fry bread and pop back to the dance area and watched the dancers. Then it rained some more and the dancing stopped and we got in the car and drove home.

SCENE THREE: MADE-FOR-MOVIE INDIANS

Voice 5: Narrator As Young Boy

The next time I saw an Indian was the following Saturday night when Grandpa took me to a movie at the Strand Theater in Iowa City, and we watched *Broken Arrow* with Jay Silverheels, Jimmy Stewart, Debra Paget, Will Geer, and Jeff Chandler, who played Chief Cochise. Those Indians did not look like the Indians on the Tama Reservation. The Tama Indians were less real, they kind of looked like everybody else, except for the dancers in their costumes.

◆ Selves, Narratives, and Sacred Places

We live in a performative moment. The dividing line between person and character, performer and actor, stage and setting, script and text, performance and reality has disappeared. Illusion and make-believe prevail.

We live in stories, like the story above about my grandmother, and my visit to the Tama Indian reservation when I was 10 years old. We need larger narratives, stories that connect us to others, to community, to the morality, and the moral self.[1] In the first decade of a new century we need new stories, new narratives that embed the self in storied histories of sacred spaces and local places. We need to re-narrate the past. We need to tell the past and its stories in ways that allow us to disrupt conventional narratives and conventional history. Such disruptions help us to better understand how racism and social injustice have been seamlessly woven together, as in the story of Mr. Thomas, in our family histories.

◆ Process and Performance

The emphasis on self, biography, history, and experience must always work back and forth between three concerns—the concerns of performance, of process, and/or of analysis. A focus on performance produces performance texts, like the narrative above. A focus on process examines a social form or event, for example, epiphanies. The focus on analysis looks at the specific lives of individuals who live the process that is being studied.

Building on Pollock (2006), Madison (2006), and Thompson (1978), interpretive, biographical materials may be presented in four different ways. First, complex, multileveled performance texts may be written, staged, and performed, for example, the performance narratives assembled by Pelias (2004). Second, following Spry (2006) single, personal experience narratives may be presented and connected to the life story of a given individual. Spry writes that after she lost her son in childbirth

> things fell apart. The shadowlands of grief became my unwanted field of study. . . . After losing our son in childbirth, writing felt like the identification of body parts, as if each described piece of the experience were a cumbersome limb that I could snap off my body and lay upon the ground. (Spry, 2006, pp. 340–341)

Third, a collection of self and personal experience stories may be collected and grouped around a common theme. Stewart (2005) does this in her recent essay on cultural poesis. She records and performs episodes from mundane, everyday life, including making trips to day care and the grocery store and picking up the sick dog at the vet. Fourth, the researcher can offer a cross-case analysis of the materials that have been collected, paying more attention to the process being studied than to the persons whose lives are embedded in those processes. Glaser and Strauss (1964) did this in their famous analysis of the awareness contexts (open, closed, suspicion, pretense) that surround death and dying in the modern hospital.

I recommend that all biographical-interpretive studies incorporate each of the above modes of presentation. Because any individual can tell multiple stories about his or her life, it must be understood that a life will consist of multiple narratives. No self or personal experience story will encompass all the stories that can, or could, be told about a single life, nor will any personal history contain all the self-stories that could be told about that life's story. Multiple narratives, drawn from the self-stories of many individuals located in different points in the process being interpreted, must be secured. This triangulation, or combination of biographical methods, ensures that history, structure, and individuals receive fair and thorough consideration in any inquiry.

◆ Interpretive Assumptions

A life refers to the biographical experiences of a named person. A person is a cultural creation. Every culture, for example, has names for different types of persons: male, female, husband, wife, daughter, son, professor, student, and so on. These names are attached to persons. Persons build biographies around the experiences associated with these names (i.e., old man, young man, divorced woman, only daughter, only son, etc.).

These experiences have effects at two levels in a person's life. On the *surface level,* effects are barely felt. They are taken for granted and are nonproblematic, as when a person buys a newspaper at the corner grocery.

Effects at the *deep level* cut to the inner core of the person's life and leave indelible marks on them. These are the *epiphanies* of a life. Interpretive researchers attempt to secure self and personal experience stories that deal with events that have effects at the deep level of a person's life.

Experience can only be studied through performance (Bruner, 1986, p. 6). However, what counts as experience is shaped by a politics of representation and hence is "neither self-evident nor straight-forward; it is always contested and always therefore political" (Scott, 1993, p. 412). Representations of experience are performative, symbolic, and material. Anchored in performance events, they include drama, ritual, and storytelling.

This view of experience and the performative makes it difficult to sustain any distinction between "appearances and actualities" (Schechner, 1998, p. 362). Further, if, as Butler (1993) reminds us, there are no original performances, then every performance establishes itself performatively as an original, a personal and locally situated production.

An extended quote from Goffman (1959) summarizes my position:

> The legitimate performances of everyday life are not "acted" or "put on" in the sense that the performer knows in advance just what he [she] is going to do, and does this solely because of the effect it is likely to have. The expressions it is felt he [she] is giving off will be especially "inaccessible" to him [her] . . . but the incapacity of the ordinary individual to formulate in advance the movements of his [her] eyes and body does not mean that he [she] will not express him [her] self through these devices in a way that is dramatized and pre-formed in his [her] repertoire of actions. In short, we all act better than we know how. (pp. 73–74)

Behind and in front of their masks and performances, persons are moral beings, already present in the world, ahead of themselves, occupied and preoccupied with everyday doings and emotional practices (see Denzin, 1984, p. 91).

◆ Liminality, Ritual, and the Structure of the Epiphany

The postmodern world stages existential crises. Following Turner (1986), the ethnographer gravitates to these narratively structured, liminal, existential spaces in the culture. In these dramaturgical sites, people take sides, forcing, threatening, inducing, seducing, cajoling, nudging, loving, living, abusing, and killing one another (see Turner, 1986). In these sites, ongoing social dramas occur. These dramas have complex temporal rhythms. They are storied events, narratives that rearrange chronology into multiple and differing forms and layers of meaningful experience (Turner, 1986).

The critical autoethnographer enters those strange and familiar situations that connect critical biographical experiences (epiphanies) with culture, history, and social structure. He or she seeks out those narratives and stories people tell one another as they attempt to make sense of the epiphanies, or existential turning point moments, in their lives.

Here is an example. Yvonna S. Lincoln writes about grieving immediately after the attacks on the World Trade Center Towers and the Pentagon on September 11, 2001:

YVONNA LINCOLN: GRIEF IN AN APPALACHIAN REGISTER

> For two weeks now, we have watched the staggering outpouring of grief, shock and horror as a nation struggles to come to terms with the attacks. . . . And I, too, have sat numb with shock, glued to the television screen, struggling with the incomprehensibility of these acts, overwhelmed by the bewildering worldview which could have led people to commit such atrocities. But I have been numb for another reason, and it will be important to see my reasons as another part of the phenomenon which has struck so deeply at the heart and soul of the United States. I sat numb because my reactions to grief are always usually private. They are always delayed. . . .
>
> My people—my family (of English and Dutch and Scottish stock) were born and raised, as were their parents before them, in the southern Appalachian mountains. . . . Mountain people . . . keep their emotions to themselves, especially those of a most private nature. . . . The end result, I have come to realize, is a human being who lives with his or her grief for all their days. The future, like tears, never comes. (Lincoln, 2002, p. 147)

Epiphanies, like reactions to September 11, are experienced as social dramas, as dramatic events with beginnings, middles, and endings. Epiphanies represent ruptures in the structure of daily life.[2] Turner (1986) reminds us that the theater of social life is often structured around a four-fold processual ritual model involving *breach, crisis, redress, reintegration,* or *schism.* Each of these phases is organized as a ritual. Thus, there are rituals of *breach, crisis, redress, reintegration,* and *schism.* Americans sought rituals of reintegration after September 11, ways of overcoming the shocks of breach, crisis, and disintegration.

Many rituals and epiphanies are associated with life-crisis ceremonies, particularly those of puberty, marriage, and death. Turner (1986) contends that redressive and life-crisis rituals "contain within themselves a liminal phase, which provides a stage . . . for unique structures of experience" (p. 41). The liminal phase of experience is a kind of no-person's land, "on the edge of what is possible" (Broadhurst, 1999, p. 12), "betwixt and between the structural past and the structural future" (p. 41).

Epiphanies are ritually structured liminal experiences, connected to moments of breach, crisis, redress, reintegration, and schism, crossing from one space to another.

Mary Weems reads this sign, as she crosses the state line between Indiana and Illinois:

"The People of Illinois Welcome You"
comes right after the LYNCH ROAD sign
and the LYNCH ROAD sign comes right after
I see a thin road strung with the bodies
of black men like burned out lights
their backs twisting in the wind,
the road littered with try out ropes,
gleaned chicken parts, and cloth napkins
soiled wiping the lips of the audience.
I know roads don't hang,
but the welcome sandwiched between
the words like bread
cuts off my air
and I pull to the side of the road
loosen my collar
and search for bones. (Weems, 2002, p. xx)

The storied nature of epiphanic experiences continually raises the following questions: Whose story is being told (and made) here? Who is doing the telling? Who has the authority to make their telling stick (Smith, 1990)? As soon as a chronological event is told in the form of a story, it enters a text-mediated system of discourse where larger issues of power and control come into play (Smith, 1990). In this text-mediated system new tellings occur. The interpretations of original experience are now fitted to this larger interpretive structure (Smith, 1990).

The reflexive performance text contests the pull of traditional "realist" theater and modernist ethnography wherein performers and ethnographers reenact and recreate a "recognizable verisimilitude of setting, character and dialogue" (Cohn, 1988, p. 815) where dramatic action reproduces a linear sequence, a "mimetic representation of cause and effect" (Birringer, 1993, p. 196). An evocative epistemology demands a postmodern performance aesthetic that goes beyond "the already-seen and already-heard" (Birringer, 1993, p. 186). This aesthetic criticizes the ideological and technological requirements of late-capitalist social realism and hyperrealism (Birringer, 1993).

Performances always return to the lived body (Garoian, 1999). The body's dramaturgical presence is "a site and pretext for . . . debates about representation and gender, about history and postmodern culture" (Birringer, 1993, p. 203). At this level, performance ethnography answers to Trinh's (1991) call for works that seek the truth of life's fictions, where experiences are evoked, not explained. The performer seeks a presentation that, like good fiction, is true in experience, but not necessarily true to experience (Lockford, 1998).

Whether the events presented actually occurred is tangential to the larger project (Lockford, 1998). As dramatic theater, with connections to Brecht (Epic Theater) and Artaud (Theater of Cruelty), these texts turn tales of suffering, loss, pain, and victory into evocative performances that have the ability to move audiences to reflective, critical action, not just emotional catharsis (on Brecht's theater, see Benjamin, 1968).[3]

The performed text is lived experience, and this is in two senses (Pelias, 1998). The performance doubles back on the experiences previously represented in the writer's text. It then re-presents those experiences as an embodied performance. It thus privileges immediate experience, the evocative moment when another's experiences come alive.

◆ Mystory as Montage[4]

The mystory, for example, the excerpts from my family story above, is simultaneously a personal mythology, a public story, a personal narrative, and a performance that critiques. It is an interactive, dramatic performance. It is participatory theater, a performance, not a text-centered interpretive event; that is, the emphasis is on performance and improvisation, and not the reading of a text.

The mystory is a montage text, cinematic and multimedia in shape, filled with sounds, music, poetry, and images taken from the writer's personal history. This personal narrative is grafted onto discourses from popular culture. It locates itself against the specialized knowledges that circulate in the larger society. The audience co-performs the text, and the writer, as narrator, functions as a guide, a commentator, a co-performer.

The mystory text begins with those moments that define the crisis in question, a turning point in the person's life. Ulmer (1989, 1994) suggests the following starting point:

> Write a mystory bringing into relation your experience with three levels of discourse—personal (autobiography), popular (community stories, oral history or popular culture), [and] expert (disciplines of knowledge). In each case use the punctum or sting of memory to locate items significant to you. (Ulmer, 1989, p. 209)

The sting of memory locates the moment, the beginning; once located, this moment is dramatically described, fashioned into a text to be performed. This moment is then surrounded by those cultural representations and voices that define the experience in question. These representations are contested, challenged.

Focusing on epiphanies and liminal moments of experience, the writer imposes a narrative framework on the text. This framework shapes how experience will be represented. It uses the devices of plot, setting, characters, characterization, temporality, dialogue, protagonists, antagonists, showing, not telling. The narration may move through Turner's (1986) four-stage dramatic cycle, emphasizing breach, crisis, redress, reintegration, or schism.

Jameson (1990) reminds us that works of popular culture are always already ideological and utopian. Shaped by a dialectic of anxiety and hope, such works revive and manipulate fears and anxieties about the social order. Beginning with a fear, problem, or crisis, these works move characters and audiences through the familiar three-stage dramatic model of conflict, crisis, and resolution. In this way, they offer kernels of utopian hope. They show how these anxieties and fears can be satisfactorily addressed by the existing social order (Jameson, 1990). Hence the audience is lulled into believing that the problems of the social have in fact been successfully resolved.

The mystory occupies a similar ideological space, except it functions as critique. The mystory is also ideological and utopian; it begins from a progressive political position stressing the politics of hope. The mystory uses the methods of drama and personal narrative to present its critique and utopian vision. It presumes that the social order has to change if problems are to be successfully resolved in the long run. If the status quo is maintained, if only actors and not the social order change, then the systemic processes producing the problem remain in place.

◆ Notes

1. In the aftermath of the crisis of September 11, 2001, we need a platform for rethinking, "What is meant by democracy and freedom in America today?" "Can we revise our dominant mythologies about who we are?" "Can we fashion a post-9/11 narrative that allows us to

reinvent and reimagine our laws in ways that express a critical pedagogy of hope, liberation, freedom, and love?"

2. The next three paragraphs draw from Denzin (2001, pp. 38–39).

3. Benjamin (1968) contends that Brecht's Epic Theater is didactic, and participatory because it "facilitates . . . interchange between audience and actors . . . and every spectator is enabled to become a participant" (p. 154).

4. The following section reworks Denzin (1997, pp. 115–120).

◆ References

Benjamin, W. (1968). What is epic theater? In W. Benjamin, *Illuminations* (H. Arendt, Ed., H. Zohn, Trans.; pp. 149–156). New York: Harcourt, Brace & World.

Birringer, J. (1993). *Theatre, theory, postmodernism.* Bloomington: Indiana University Press.

Broadhurst, S. (1999). *Liminal acts: A critical overview of contemporary performance and theory.* New York: Cassell.

Bruner, E. M. (1986). Experience and its expressions. In V. M. Turner & E. M. Bruner (Eds.), *The anthropology of experience* (pp. 3–30). Urbana: University of Illinois Press.

Butler, J. (1993). *Bodies that matter.* New York: Routledge.

Cohn, R. (1988). Realism. In M. Banham (Ed.), *The Cambridge guide to theatre* (p. 815). Cambridge, UK: Cambridge University Press.

Culler, J. (1981). *The pursuit of signs.* Ithaca, NY: Cornell University Press.

Denzin, N. K. (1984). *On understanding emotion.* San Francisco: Jossey-Bass.

Denzin, N. K. (1997). *Interpretive ethnography.* Thousand Oaks, CA: Sage.

Denzin, N. K. (2001). *Interpretive interactionism* (2nd ed.). Thousand Oaks, CA: Sage.

Denzin, N. K. (2005). Indians in the park. *Qualitative Research, 3,* 9–33.

Denzin, N. K. (2007). *Searching for Yellowstone: Performing race, nation, and nature in the new West.* Walnut Creek, CA: Left Coast Press.

Garoian, C. R. (1999). *Performing pedagogy: Toward an art of politics.* Albany: State University of New York Press.

Glaser, B., & Strauss, A. (1964). *Awareness of dying.* Chicago: Aldine.

Goffman, E. (1959). *The presentation of self in everyday life.* New York: Doubleday.

Jameson, F. (1990). *Signatures of the visible.* New York: Routledge.

Lincoln, Y. S. (2002). Grief in an Appalachian register. *Qualitative Inquiry, 8*(2), 146–149.

Lockford, L. (1998). Emergent issues in the performance of a border-transgressive narrative. In S. J. Dailey (Ed.), *The future of performance studies: Visions and revisions* (pp. 214–220). Annadale, VA: National Communication Association.

Madison, D. S. (2006). The dialogic performative in critical ethnography. *Text and Performance Quarterly, 26*(4), 320–324.

Pelias, R. J. (1998). Meditations and mediations. In S. J. Dailey (Ed.), *The future of performance studies: Visions and revisions* (pp. 14–22). Washington, DC: National Communication Association.

Pelias, R. J. (2004). *A methodology of the heart.* Walnut Creek, CA: AltaMira Press.

Pollock, D. (2006). Making new directions in performance ethnography. *Text and Performance Quarterly, 26*(4), 325–329.

Schechner, R. (1998). What is performance studies anyway? In P. Phelan & J. Lane (Eds.), *The ends of performance* (pp. 357–362). New York: New York University Press.

Scott, J. W. (1993). The evidence of experience. In H. Abelove, M. A. Barale, & D. M. Halperin (Eds.), *The lesbian and gay studies reader* (pp. 397–415). New York: Routledge.

Smith, D. E. (1990). *The conceptual practices of power: A feminist sociology of knowledge.* Boston: Northeastern University Press.

Spry, T. (2006). A "Performative-I" copresence: Embodying the ethnographic turn in performance and the performance turn in ethnography. *Text and Performance Quarterly, 26*(4), 339–346.

Stewart, K. (2005). Cultural poesis: The generativity of emergent things. In N. K. Denzin & Y. S. Lincoln (Eds.), *Handbook of qualitative research* (3rd ed., pp. 1027–1043). Thousand Oaks, CA: Sage.

Thompson, P. (1978). *Voices of the past.* Oxford, UK: Oxford University Press.

Trinh, T. M. H. (1991). *When the moon waxes red: Representation, gender, and cultural politics.* New York: Routledge.

Turner, V. (1986). Dewey, Dilthey, and drama: An essay in the anthropology of experience. In V. M. Turner & E. M. Bruner (Eds.), *The anthropology of experience* (pp. 33–44). Urbana: University of Illinois Press.

Ulmer, G. (1989). *Teletheory.* New York: Routledge.

Ulmer, G. (1994). *Heuretics: The logic of invention.* Baltimore, MD: Johns Hopkins University Press.

Weems, M. (2002). *I speak from the wound in my mouth.* New York: Peter Lang.

11 *Literary Forms*

WORDING PICTURES

Discovering Heartful Autoethnography

◆ Karen Scott-Hoy and Carolyn Ellis

◆ *Researching With Passion*

Swallowing hard to contain my tears, I look with dismay at my professor's blue handwriting in the margin of the first draft of my dissertation. "Leave this out. Even tho' I am sure you mean it, others are cynics!" and "For your book, not the dissertation".

I reread the offending paragraph:

> The process of knowing involves a "passionate contribution" (Polanyi, 1962) hence my research incorporates altruistic values. I have not emerged from my fieldwork the same person. Everything about me has been challenged. I have come to agree with Peter Berger (1974) that, "it is necessary to act quietly and disbelievingly out of that compassion which is the only credible motive for any actions to change the world" (p. 231).

Author's Note: The authors wish to thank Arthur P. Bochner and Kelly Clark/Keefe for helpful comments on earlier versions of this paper.

Why can I, Karen Scott-Hoy, an Australian mum, scholar, and health worker, write about passion in a book but not in my dissertation? Having collected data using action research, in-depth interviews, and participant observation, I need to come to grips with my experience as an involved and situated researcher who is an integral part of the research and writing process. I don't feel neutral or authoritative about my project; I feel part of it, vulnerable and aware of the things I still don't know or understand. Surely experience and subjectivity are important parts of understanding what happened and why?

I've heard about the "crisis of representation" opening up new styles of research and writing. Could I be part of this move away from realist research, which privileges theory generation, typicality, and generalization to a wider world, over evocative storytelling, detailing concrete experience, and multiple perspectives that include participants' voices and interpretation (Bochner, 1994)?

A number of authors (Denzin, 1997; Ellis, 1995b; Punch, 1994) have pointed out that during the writing stage, it's easy to feel a sense that you are betraying your subjects and "selling somebody out"(Didion, 1968, in Denzin, 1997, p. 287). That's how I feel—as if I'm betraying the people of the small Pacific nation of Vanuatu, where I designed and conducted a preventative eye care project (Scott-Hoy, 1997).

I want to show in my dissertation the relationships that grew through the research process, to include the contributions of the participants in their own voices, not tell about them. I want to share what it feels like to do health care research in a cross-cultural setting. I want to record my research in a way readers can know and feel the complexities of the concrete moments of lived experience in their bodies (Ellis, 2004).

In an emotional quandary, I set off to browse the library shelves. Pushing through the heavy glass doors, I make my way to the sociology section. To continue writing up this research, I have to find something helpful and soon. A bright blue book catches my eye. Reaching up, I push my fingers deep into its spine and remove it from the crammed bookshelf. *Composing Ethnography: Alternative Forms of Qualitative Writing*, Carolyn Ellis and Arthur P. Bochner, editors, 1996. I flick open the pages, and in the dim, quiet space between the oppressively high shelves, my heart leaps. I am drawn to the words of the introduction: "Let readers know . . . that they've come to the right place, that we've got something useful and different for them to read" (p. 16).

These words are part of a script of a conversation between the two editors, Carolyn and Art. As I read, I feel as if I'm in the room with them, learning about how they want to *"reach people who are looking for alternatives, who want to write differently, and who see an opportunity to expand the boundaries of ethnographic research"* (p. 16). That's me, I think, as a tear rolls down my cheek. That's me.

Before class, I pick up trash strewn on the floor and move extra chairs to a corner of my classroom. After the usual housekeeping chores, I say, "Let's contextualize autoethnography within ethnography."

In answer to a student who asks, "Professor Ellis, what is ethnography and what led you to it?" I reply, "Ethnography is a perspective and framework for thinking about the world. This perspective reflects a way of viewing the world—holistically and naturalistically—and a way of being in the world as an involved participant. Buddy Goodall (2000) observes that you don't really choose ethnography; it chooses you."

I've always been an ethnographer, from the time I was a kid trying to figure out my parents' relationship and the hidden—or not so hidden—dramas in my small town.

I watched and listened carefully, often—or maybe especially—when I was not supposed to. "What's going on here?" I often asked of contradictory situations. Being nosy and a good listener are two primary prerequisites of a good ethnographer.

The same student then asks how I got involved in autoethnographic story writing. "It started when I tried to write about losing my partner, Gene, who died in 1984," I respond. "At first, I planned to do a traditional study on grief and storytelling. But then I decided to write from the stack of field notes I had kept on his illness, hospitals, caregiving, our relationship, our conversations, my thoughts and feelings. What came out was an evocative, scenic, and unfolding story of what happened. I became committed to personal storytelling as a way of doing social science research.

"Stories are the way humans make sense of their worlds and are essential to human understanding. Given their importance, stories should be both a subject and a method of social science research. Now I feel a greater calling to narrative ethnography and autoethnography than I did to traditional ethnography. I love to tell and write stories (see Ellis, 2004)."

◆ Autoethnography Meets Art

My hand trembles as I look at the program advertising The First International Conference on Advances in Qualitative Methods to be held in 1999 in Edmonton, Canada. Carolyn Ellis is the keynote speaker and is conducting a workshop (Ellis, 2001). My heart races as I recognize her name.

Having read her stories (Ellis, 1993, 1996; Ellis & Bochner, 1992) and those of her colleagues and students, such as Richardson (1992, 1996), Rambo Ronai (1992, 1996), and Tillmann-Healy 1996), I love the way she practices ethnographic writing as a form of creative nonfiction, taking expressive liberties associated with the arts, and feels the ethical pull of converting data into experiences readers can use. She opens ethnography to a wider audience, not just academics but all people who can benefit from thinking about their own lives in terms of other people's experiences.

I want to record my research like that, but can I write well enough? Can I cope with what colleagues and other readers may say and assume about me? I'm still struggling with the dilemma of how to position myself within my research project to show aspects of my own tacit world, challenge my assumptions, locate myself through the eyes of the Other, and observe myself observing. If I write an autoethnography, I'll have to struggle to position myself within academia, as well as in the research.

I note the submission dates for abstracts, and resolve to go to this conference whether the paper I submit is accepted or not. I fill in the form and fax it off. The workshop will be very expensive, but I feel a connection to this woman, and I desperately need a sense of community to validate my feelings and work. Will I find it on the other side of the world?

I enter the small conference room attached to the aptly named Fantasyland Hotel in Edmonton, Canada, and write "Auto-ethnography Workshop, Carolyn Ellis, Professor" on the whiteboard in front of the participants seated at the grey laminated desks. Pushing to one side the pages of my forthcoming lecture, *Heartful Auto-ethnography* (Ellis, 1999a, 1999b), I arrange my introductory notes on the lectern.

As the last of the participants hurriedly find seats, I take a deep breath and begin. "Welcome to this workshop on doing autoethnography. I want to divide our time today into two parts: First, I'll define and outline some methodological issues in autoethnographic writing, and second, we'll discuss any personal stories and ethnographic narratives you may have brought with you." I sit on top of the large table at the front, my purple, blue, and red titanium earrings jingling noisily. I clear my throat, noting the slight quiver that always occurs in a new teaching situation. No matter how long I teach and do workshops, I'll still feel the anxiety and exhilaration of beginning a new relationship with people in the audience.

"Ethnography is part art and part science, but it is also something all its own," I say. "Viewing autoethnography, a form of ethnography, like this, gets us out of either/or thinking. Autoethnography overlaps art and science, but is also part *auto* or self and part *ethno* or culture. Yet it is something different from both of them, or greater than its parts," I say. "That's what we're going to look at here, what that something is."

A student from the back asks for a definition. "Autoethnography," I begin, "refers to the process as well as the product of writing about the personal and its relationship to culture. It is an autobiographical genre of writing and research that displays multiple layers of consciousness. Usually written in the first-person voice, autoethnographic texts appear in a variety of forms—short stories, poetry, fiction, novels, photographic essays, scripts, personal essays, journals, fragmented and layered writing, and social science prose. Autoethnographers showcase concrete action, dialogue, emotion, embodiment, spirituality, and self-consciousness. These features appear as relational and institutional stories affected by histories and social structures that are dialectically revealed through actions, feelings, thoughts, and language."

I take a breath and look at the mix of workshop participants, some taking notes, looking wide-eyed and interested, others looking a bit lost or tired, perhaps fighting jetlag. Since I want to spend the afternoon allowing students to work in small groups on their own, I feel the need to press on. I always seem to be fighting this battle between emotional sensitivity to students and the need to cover as much of the material as possible.

Later, when I interact with small groups, I find myself drawn to a woman from Australia. Writing an ethnography of a health project in Vanuatu, she has come to this workshop to seek direction. She shows me a photo of her participants and a poem she has written.

◆ Art as Autoethnography/ Autoethnography as Art

The cobalt blue oozes from the tube as my fingers push into its soft metal casing. Its smell awakens my consciousness. The knife guides the thick oil paint around on the canvas, giving images color, shape, and texture, in the process of interpretive creation. How can I give similar texture and multiple layers to the interpretive creation of my research?

"Go home and paint," he had said. What sort of advice is that? I had hoped for something more concrete from an academic mentor. Returning from the conference in Edmonton, with renewed confidence and hope, and armed with my new knowledge of autoethnography, I contacted the Research Degrees' coordinator and aired my frustration and fears. He suggested meeting another academic, Peter Willis (Willis, Smith, & Collins, 2000), who might be interested in supervising an autoethnographic dissertation. Now here I am with a palette knife in my hand.

"You are all written out," he said. "Go home and paint."

Paint what? As I mix the paint, a flash of reflected sunlight from the blade of the palette knife catches my eye and is mixed with flashes of inspiration and insight and the picture portraying my methodology takes shape.

"Back and forth autoethnographers gaze: first they look through an ethnographic wide angle lens, focusing outward on social and cultural aspects of their personal experience," I hear Carolyn's distinctive voice lecturing in my head.

> Then they look inward, exposing a vulnerable self that is moved by and may move through, refract, and resist cultural interpretations. As they zoom backward and forward, inward and outward, distinctions between the personal and cultural become blurred, sometimes beyond distinct recognition. (Ellis & Bochner, 2000, p. 739)

Carolyn's words resonate in my heart as well as my head. I stand back to look at the images on the canvas; then I move in again to add a detail. In this moment it occurs to me how similar research and painting are. If you look at one little aspect, you don't see the bigger picture. Looking at the bigger picture, it is easy to miss the smaller details. Back and forth I move in the creation of the painting, as back and forth I had moved in focus and thought during the creation of knowledge in the field.

"If the visual arts teach one lesson," Eisner (1991) writes, *"it's that seeing is central to making. Seeing, rather than mere looking, requires an enlightened eye: this is as true and as important in understanding and improving education as in creating a painting"* (p. 1).

I become sensitive to the social tones, the moods and feelings that colored daily life, the worldview and cosmos that shaped action and interaction. I begin to look at myself, to try and take off my "colored" glasses and observe the impact different personal and cultural lenses have on what we see.

The knife moves across the canvas, back to the palette and to the canvas again, creating images, composing a picture, mixing elements using contemplation and intuition transposing the experience of being a health worker in Vanuatu onto a canvas. The work is emotional and cognitive, deep and spiritual. Can this be called ethnography?

My painting, like others' writing, reveals my personality, historical roots, and spiritual, moral, and ethical beliefs. My physical body and senses are present, as are integral parts of my interaction with and interpretation of the world. I sit opposite the creation on the canvas, like a director watching actors in a performance, and catch my breath. The act of painting has taken me back into experiences buried under my conscious reasoning, and teaches me things about the experience and culture I have begun to absorb, the people I have come to know, and myself.

Carefully I align the painting, which I have called *Autoethnography*, in the lens of my camera and click.

(See Figure 11.1 at the front of this book for a color reproduction.)

I print photo and place it in a manila envelope with the abstract for the 2000 Couch-Stone Symposium, titled "Ethnography for the Twenty-first Century: Alternatives and Opportunities," that Carolyn Ellis and her partner, Art Bochner, are convening.

The envelope sits on my dressing table for two weeks though the deadline is drawing near. I pick up a pen to write an accompanying note then hesitate. Should I say "Dear Professor Ellis" or "Dear Carolyn"? I am sending her a painting that exposes myself, my inner thoughts, and my ways of relating to the world. I feel I know her well from reading her work. But she doesn't know me, except for a brief interaction at the workshop.

As I wander into the mailroom in the middle of a busy and stressful day, I dread opening all the manila envelopes stuffed in my mailbox, knowing most will add to my workload. One package catches my eye, and I open it first. I remove the layers of wrapping, bypassing the neatly typed pages of the submission to our conference, and go directly to the small, white package inside. I open it, ignoring the attached letter. My heart pounds as I view the photograph inside. I am surprised at the depth of my feeling—my bodily reaction. I can hardly breathe.

I am drawn into the rich pink and turquoise colors on the partially clothed woman in the center of the painting. Her reflection in a mirrored image of her back, a reflection I can see that she herself cannot, the other parts of her hidden from my view. She is connected through flowing lines to a darker, partially formed and partially dressed figure. I do not ask myself what any part of this means; instead, I am caught up in the swirls of paint connecting the two women and my overwhelming emotions connecting me to them.

As I look at the painting, my body feels autoethnography. The feeling shares elements with the emotionality I experience when I read and identify with an evocative autoethnographic piece, but the feeling is more physiological and involves more sensory and less cognitive knowing than I am used to acknowledging. This painting represents what I've been trying to put into words, though I do not have the words to describe what I see and feel. Just now I doubt words will ever be sufficient.

Walking back to my office, clutching the photograph to my chest, I can't stop looking or feeling. I don't want to talk or show the photograph to anyone, except my partner Art, and he isn't around. My heart feels so open and vulnerable, like the belly of the woman in the picture, and I embrace my response as an integral part of autoethnography.

Inside my office I open the accompanying letter.

"Dear Professor Ellis, Thank you for your workshop.

Here is a gift for you. I've called it *Autoethnography.*

I hope you like it," Karen Scott-Hoy

She hopes I like it? What an understatement. I feel elated, hyperventilating almost and chills passing through my body. At that moment, I realize how defensive I have been about autoethnography and how that posture has stood in the way of my experience. No more. I place the picture in a prominent place on my desk. Then I notice Karen's submission to the SSSI Couch-Stone Conference we are organizing.

◆ Learning to See/ Transcending Vision

As I look out the window, the white sand and waves rolling in from the Gulf of Mexico seem unreal. Growing up in South Australia, I gained much of my knowledge of the world through TV, and American police shows on Australian television had made me scared of traveling alone to Florida. Now here I am half a world away from the quiet country town where I live. Our total population would fit into a few of the high rises crowded along the beach.

My attention is drawn back to the five original oil paintings I have brought to St. Petersburg, Florida, for my presentation, "The Visitor" (Scott-Hoy, 2002a), at the 2000 SSSI Couch-Stone Symposium. Using a consciousness that did not rely on words, I studied my experience and produced these "visual texts" free from constraints of language and culture-specific words, important because my research involved English and non-English speaking and illiterate people. Until now I'd been apprehensive about returning to the written word, afraid I would lose some of the spontaneity and fluidity of the images, the aesthetic essence present in the paintings, but at this symposium I've seen and heard how performance, visual arts, and embodied narration can give ethnography more evocative power and encourage empathy and engagement on the part of its audiences, as people purposefully merge the arts, social sciences, and literature.[1] Now, I feel ready to write stories from and about the paintings. I no longer feel the need to "explain" the paintings, but rather I want to write stories that help the audience to find meaning in what they see.

I have just one more scheduled discussion before flying home and that is with Carolyn Ellis. Seeing "Autoethnography" propped against the bed makes me think about a new painting "Form Carries Experience" (Scott-Hoy, 2003), which continues to explore the relationships depicted in "Autoethnography" but portrays them as more fluid, building one upon another. I realize then that in developing this work, I have moved to a greater understanding of autoethnography as a process, not just a product, and I have taken my first few sure-footed steps along the road to becoming an autoethnographer.

A sharp knock on the door echoes down the hall outside and sets my heart racing.

As I enter Karen's room, my eyes are drawn as if by a magnet to the painting leaning against the bed. Karen seems pleased I am here, but moves and talks somewhat anxiously. I sit in a chair opposite the bed while she sits on the edge of the bed next to the painting. Gradually Karen and I are drawn into conversation with each other and it seems with the painting, which adds its silent voice to ours.

I am glad that Karen is willing to talk about the painting, since I want to hear her interpretations and hesitantly voice mine. Mesmerized by the painting, I am conscious that I don't have an eye that immediately takes in deeper meanings in art.

"You learn to see," Karen assures. "It's like the reading process. I often read your stories over and over, unpacking the layers and finding new challenges with each reading." I nod, gaining confidence that I too can "see." I understand, as Irigaray (1985) says, that this kind of knowing "transcends pure vision and specularity" (p. 103) and "plunges the reader into the interior, feeling, hearing, tasting, smelling, and touching worlds of subjective human perception" (Denzin, 1997, p. 46; see also Ong, 1977, p. 137).

Karen and I talk about perspective and how the painting reveals and conceals: The researcher sees parts of herself that we, the viewers, cannot; yet we see parts of her that she cannot, and the darker-skinned woman has yet another view. We look over the woman's shoulder into the mirror, which reflects back to her and to us yet another view. Karen points out how the mirror in the painting allows viewers to be positioned in the story wherever they want to be. I ask Karen about the black object in the woman's hand, wondering what it is that each of us hangs onto or carries with us into our research. We talk about blending different worlds in ethnographic research and about reaching across boundaries to make connections. "Our worlds can never be that of the Other," Karen says. "Nor theirs ours," I respond.

Overwhelmed by the connection I feel to Karen and the painting, a wave of vulnerability sweeps over me. The feeling is enlivening; yet I hold back tears. Hesitantly I express my desire to buy the painting. When Karen agrees, I carry the painting out to my van and retrieve and sign copies of *Final Negotiations* (Ellis, 1995b) and *Investigating Subjectivity* (Ellis & Flaherty, 1992). When I see Karen walking by in the foyer, I hurry over to give her the books. Karen smiles appreciatively, runs her hand gently over the covers, and quickly reads the inscriptions in each book. We embrace.

Reluctantly, Art and I depart. As we drive home, we feel the spirit of "Autoethnography" watching over us, beckoning us to look deeper into our lives and the lives of those around us, enticing us to extend ourselves more caringly to those in the painting and those looking at the painting, to turn and look directly into the mirror, and to handle the black box with care.

Climbing off my stool, I rush outside to the sound of the kookaburras and the smell of eucalyptus leaves crushing beneath my feet. My restlessness comes not from the hours of typing, but the emotional strain of recording experiences so close. I am fearful of inadvertently hurting my participants by what I write about them. I know that they, like I, will change over the time their story is told (Ellis, 1995a; Flemons & Green, 2002). Will I be, as Rod Stewart sings, "just another writer trapped within my truth" (Stewart, 1996)?

Writing the story of the Vanuatu forces me to again face things that confront me and generate fear and self-doubt. Have the experiences my children had in Vanuatu hurt them or helped them? My youngest son doesn't want to return. He recalls the people pinching his cheeks and stroking his straight blonde hair. I never realized how much this scared him. What kind of mother am I? Did I put my work ahead of my son's welfare (Scott-Hoy, 2002b)?

Returning from my walk, I pass my art room. The paintings beckon me inside.

The images are emotive and challenging to me. I continue to imagine, reflect, grieve, and rejoice, expressing the energies that the act of painting releases, behaving—not rationally, yet very "sens"-ibly; employing, experiencing, and embracing all senses in the search for a better, more honest, engaged, lifelike, and transforming ethnographic form.

As I return to my computer, the words flow more easily and soon the whirr of the printer signals the end of my writing. I send an e-mail to Carolyn confirming my arrival dates for the workshop and exhibition she has planned at her university.

The sound of metal lids clunking against the saucepans in the kitchen tells me my children are searching for food and hoping that tea is ready on time tonight.

◆ Arts-Based Research: Unmasking the Artist/Storyteller

"After the break in class tonight, we'll be attending a presentation by Karen Scott-Hoy on art and autoethnography," I announce. "To get ready for Karen's talk, I'd like to briefly review literature on arts-based autoethnography.

"Arts-based inquiry experiments with alternative ways to transform what is in our consciousness into a public form that others can take in and understand (Eisner, 1997)," I say without taking a breath. "Many arts-based researchers are now examining the intersections of art, education, qualitative, and/or autoethnographic research (e.g., Clark/Keefe, 2002; Finley & Mullen, 2003; Saarnivaara, 2000, 2003; Saarnivaara & Bochner, 2003).

"Educational researchers, such as Tierney and Lincoln (1997), have argued that these multiple approaches 'may represent both the complexity of the lives we study, and the lives we lead as academics and private persons' (p. xi). Though arts-based research includes multiple venues such as dance (Ylonen, 2003), film (Barone, 2003), poetry (Pelias, 2004; Richardson, 1994), performance (Gray, 2003; Pelias, 2002), and others, tonight we'll focus on painting and art installations, and their relationship to autoethnography.

"Slattery (2001) makes a case for what he calls arts-based autoethnography, which uses material generated from one's unconscious. In collaboration with Craig Richard Johanns, an independent artist, he presented an installation that used conscious and unconscious experiences about his elementary classrooms in Catholic school in the 1960s to deconstruct ideas about the body and regulation of sexual practices in schools. For example, he included artifacts from scrapbooks, yearbooks, and family closets, as well as photographs of bodies from *Playboy,* their erotic body parts covered with communion wafers.

"In line with autoethnography, arts-based researchers include the artist's subjectivity and present their work as embodied inquiry: sensuous, emotional, complex, intimate. They expect their projects to evoke response, inspire imagination, give pause for new possibilities and new meanings, and open new questions and avenues of inquiry (Bochner & Ellis, 2003).

"Many arts-based researchers combine their art with story. The art part of the project, which creates moods and images, combines with writing, which is better at directing emotion. In many cases, published words are used more to explain the art, rather than enhance the emotional mood (e.g., Barone, 2003; Slattery, 2001). Others combine evocative pictures and words. For example, Inkeri Saava and Kari Nuutinen (2003) start with words, then finish with words mediated by pictures, positioning themselves in the spaces between texts and drawings. Karen Scott-Hoy's (2000a, 2000b) work is also an example of arts-based autoethnography that uses evocative stories to intersect with the evocative images she paints of her research process (see also Clark/Keefe, 2002; Scott-Hoy 2002a, 2003).

"Speaking of Karen," I say, looking at my watch, "we better go to the performance lab for her presentation." Without much talk, we grab our books and hurry down the hall.

As the students from Carolyn's qualitative methods class move into the performance lab, I hand out programs that give them clues as to what each painting placed around the room seeks to portray. Music plays in the background and a large, blank easel is set up in front of the room with lights directed towards it. Pieces of brightly colored paper are lying on the adjoining table.

Tonight I'll use performance to recreate for my audience the experience of painting. I hope to take them vicariously inside the process and allow them to see the decisions I made and why. Carolyn indicates it's time to start. I raise the lights, she introduces me, and I begin.

I reach out and pick up the cut-out of the first image. Using Velcro, I place it on the blank "canvas" on the easel, telling as I do, why I decided to incorporate the image. I recall what moved me to autoethnography as I begin with the storyteller behind the mask: me. "I feel it is important that the audience see me; that I not hide behind the mask of storyteller, distant and protected from my audience," my voice is soft and relaxed as I become the storyteller on and off the canvas.

As the painting takes shape before them, I feel the eyes of the students on me. Some of the students recognize the painting from their text book cover.[2] I invite the students to ask themselves what each piece means to them. I slow the pace of the performance, allowing their sighs, mutterings, and silence to become part of the whole being created here. I am conscious that we have now all become part of this story. Placing the final piece on the board, a hush fills the room.

(See Figure 11.2 at the front of this book for a color reproduction.)

I nod to Carolyn and she turns the lights down and starts the music softly. I want to allow my audience time to feel, before they try to articulate thoughts and reactions, and I need some space too.

◆ *Framing and Reframing Autoethnography: Life and Work*

Dear Karen,

Have I told you recently how much I love my painting? I still stop to look at it almost every day. Other times, I feel its presence and just know it's there. Also I am so happy with the cover of *The Ethnographic I* (Ellis, 2004). Now I not only get to see "Autoethnography" framed on my living room wall, I get to see it every time I review my book for a class. Students always ask me to bring the original "Autoethnography" into school when we talk about the art chapter, and I happily oblige.

In a recent undergraduate class, the students said the painting and the interview we co-constructed about it helped them to understand the autoethnographic perspective (Ellis & Scott-Hoy, 2004). They suggested that next time I teach the course, I start with the painting, and now I do.

I am amazed by the power of the combination of art and personal story, words and pictures—what happens when we let go of our categories and open up possibilities. I see it all the time in my classes and in my life. I'm delighted to be able to connect my life and work, to connect our stories and our pictures and, hopefully, inspire others coming after us to cross boundaries and try new things.

I'm starting to feel a role change now from one hoping to lead the way with a new perspective to one who wants to expend more energy on supporting younger folks who carry the autoethnographic torch. Guess that's what happens with age. The prospect of occupying the role of Crone or elder is strangely exhilarating, and I am pleased with all the new forms of autoethnography—from fiction to artwork—that others are producing.

Don't get me wrong; I still have a lot of work in me and new ideas to explore. But more and more, I'm reframing my life. Family, our dogs, our North Carolina mountain cabin, and the relationships we've developed there attract my time and attention. I also want to travel and hopefully get back to Australia one more time.

Well, it's time to turn my attention to the three dissertations on my desk. I miss you. Hope all is well. Love Carolyn

Hi Carolyn,

Thanks for your e-mail. I am excited and encouraged to think that our interview chapter and my painting helped your students understand more about autoethnography, but I must confess I also felt some sadness in response to your students' feedback. If something as simple as a painting and a conversation between two friends can help clarify a methodology, epistemology, and ontology, why are these elements not used more frequently in our teaching?

Why do academics have to make research so complex with all our " . . . ologies"? Is it that social scientists are scared of being honest about the messy, complicated, and uncertain phenomena that we study (Bochner, 2000)?

I am not ungrateful for or bitter about my experience in the academy. I feel privileged to have had the opportunity to explore the wonderful literature available and to share others' theories and ideas and those ideas have enriched my thought processes. But I feel sad that some people may have been put off by the jargon and complexity. What have we as feeling and thinking members of communities missed out on, because we have alienated others who wanted to contribute?

Recently (see Byron, 2005) there has been a lot of debate here about social science producing boring "grey" manuscripts nobody will read, versus subordinating scholarly rigor to ensure "colorful," "ready to wear" books for the general market. It seems the dilemma they are debating is something I faced nearly 10 years ago, while searching for a methodology that was accessible to those outside of academia and yet would still provide a vehicle for my research and dissertation.

The appeal of autoethnography for me is the way the method values the stories of "ordinary" people, which reminds me of a presentation I heard several years ago, *Searching for Autoethnographic Credibility: Reflections From a Mom With a Notepad* (Jenks, 2002). My work in our optometry practice involves taking patient histories. When asked their occupation, many women reply almost apologetically, "Oh, I'm just a mum." I also am "just a mum." I have no academic position, partly because I live in a rural area, but also because I work in the family business and I have stayed home with my four sons. This has caused me angst at times as I felt I was losing my identity.

Discovering autoethnography and applying ethnographic methods to my life and tasks (see Dietz, Prus, & Shaffir, 1994) helped me feel more comfortable with who I am. I study life, I paint life, and I write about life. I can be a researcher and a mum, because mums are researchers and storytellers. Mums tell stories written by others as well as our own. We tell stories to calm our children when they are sick, to help prepare them for situations they haven't faced before, and to reassure them of their importance and value in the world.

I hope I pass onto my kids and others my passion for people and justice. Sometimes I worry that I won't get down everything I want to. There doesn't seem to be enough hours in the day. As I've hit 46, I can no longer see without glasses and am concerned that will affect how I see colors, and my ability to paint and interpret the world. Maybe I'll have to move to more tactile means of expression if that happens! Perhaps that's where I should end, with autoethnographic expression evolving and being reframed and interpreted according to people's needs and responses, because it's time for this mum to go prepare tea and change over a load of washing.

Hope all is well, Karen.

P. S. I've sent you a photograph of a painting, *Reframing Autoethnography*, stimulated by our current discussions.

(See Figure 11.3 at the front of this book for a color reproduction).

◆ Notes

1. See Bochner and Ellis (2002), for a reflexive volume of these conference pieces.

2. *Ethnographically speaking: Autoethnography, literature, and aesthetics* (Bochner & Ellis, 2002).

◆ *Appendix*

Also see Scott-Hoy's paintings online (www
.sagepub.com/knowlessupplement) to accompany this chapter:

1. *Autoethnography*
2. *The Storyteller*
3. *Reframing Autoethnography*

◆ *References*

Barone, T. (2003). Challenging the educational
imaginary: Issues of form, substance, and
quality in film-based research. *Qualitative
Inquiry, 9,* 202–207.

Berger, P. (1974). *Pyramids of sacrifice.* New
York: Basic Books.

Bochner, A. P. (1994). Perspectives on inquiry II:
Theories and stories. In M. Knapp & G. R.
Miller (Eds.), *Handbook of interpersonal
communication* (2nd ed., pp. 21–41).
Thousand Oaks, CA: Sage.

Bochner, A. P. (2000). Criteria against ourselves.
Qualitative Inquiry, 6(2), 266–272.

Bochner, A. P., & Ellis, C. (2002). *Ethnographically speaking: Autoethnography, literature, and aesthetics.* Walnut Creek, CA:
AltaMira Press.

Bochner, A. P., & Ellis, C. (2003). An introduction to the arts and narrative research: Art as
inquiry. *Qualitative Inquiry, 9*(4), 506–514.

Byron, J. (2005, February 9). Hawking our
wares. *Higher Education Supplement, The
Australian Newspaper.*

Clark/Keefe, K. (2002). A fine line: Integrating
art and fieldwork in the study of self-
conceptualization and educational experiences [CD-ROM]. *Alberta Journal of
Educational Research, XLVIII*(3), 1–27.

Denzin, N. (1997). *Interpretive ethnography:
Ethnographic practices for the 21st century.*
Thousand Oaks, CA: Sage.

Didion, J. (1968). *Slouching towards Bethlehem.*
New York: Farrar.

Dietz, M. L., Prus, R., & Shaffir, W. (Eds.).
(1994). *Doing everyday life: Ethnography
as human lived experience.* Toronto, Ontario,
Canada: Copp, Clark Longman Ltd.

Eisner, E. (1991). *The enlightened eye: Qualitative inquiry and the enhancement of educational practice.* New York: Macmillan.

Eisner, E. (1997). *The educational imagination:
On the design and evaluation of school programs* (3rd ed.). New York: Macmillan.

Ellis, C. (1993). "There are survivors": Telling a
story of sudden death. *Sociological Quarterly, 34,* 711–730.

Ellis, C. (1995a). Emotional and ethical quagmires in returning to the field. *Journal of
Contemporary Ethnography, 24,* 68–98.

Ellis, C. (1995b). *Final negotiations: A story of
love, loss, and chronic illness.* Philadelphia,
PA: Temple University Press.

Ellis, C. (1996). Maternal connections. In C. Ellis
& A. Bochner (Eds.), *Composing ethnog-
raphy* (pp. 240–243). Walnut Creek, CA:
AltaMira Press.

Ellis, C. (1999a). *Heartful autoethnography.*
Keynote address, First Annual Advances in
Qualitative Methods Conference, Edmonton,
Alberta, Canada.

Ellis, C. (1999b). Heartful autoethnography.
Qualitative Health Research, 9(5), 669–683.

Ellis, C. (2001). *My mother/my baby: Reading
and writing an autoethnography of aging
and caregiving.* Plenary talk, University of
Miami, SSSI Couch-Stone Symposium.

Ellis, C. (2004). *The ethnographic I: A methodological novel about autoethnography.*
Walnut Creek, CA: AltaMira Press.

Ellis, C., & Bochner, A. P. (1992). Telling and
performing personal stories: The constraints of choice in abortion. In C. Ellis &
M. Flaherty (Eds.), *Investigating subjectivity: Research on lived experience*
(pp. 79–101). Newbury Park, CA: Sage.

Ellis, C., & Bochner, A. P. (Eds.). (1996).
*Composing ethnography: Alternative forms
of qualitative writing.* Walnut Creek, CA:
AltaMira Press.

Ellis, C., & Bochner, A. P. (2000). Auto-
ethnography, personal narrative, reflexivity:
Researcher as subject. In N. Denzin &
Y. Lincoln (Eds.), *The handbook of qualitative*

research (2nd ed., pp. 733–768). Thousand Oaks, CA: Sage.

Ellis, C., & Flaherty, M. (Eds.). (1992). *Investigating subjectivity: Research on lived experience.* Newbury Park, CA: Sage.

Ellis, C., & Scott-Hoy, K. (2004). Art as autoethnography/autoethnography as art. In C. Ellis, *The ethnographic I* (pp. 184–192). Walnut Creek, CA: AltaMira Press.

Finley, S., & Mullen, C. (Eds.). (2003). Arts-based approaches to qualitative inquiry [Special issue]. *Qualitative Inquiry, 9.*

Flemons, D., & Green, S. (2002) Stories that conform/Stories that transform: A conversation in four parts. In A. P. Bochner & C. Ellis (Eds.), *Ethnographically speaking: Autoethnography, literature, and aesthetics* (pp. 87–94). Walnut Creek, CA: AltaMira Press.

Goodall, H. L. (2000). *Writing the new ethnography.* Walnut Creek, CA: AltaMira Press.

Gray, R. (2003). Performing on and off the stage: The place(s) of performance in arts-based approaches to qualitative inquiry. *Qualitative Inquiry, 9,* 254–267.

Irigaray, L. (1985). *Speculum of the other woman* (G. G. Gill, Trans.). Ithaca, NY: Cornell University Press.

Jenks, E. (2002). Searching for autoethnographic credibility: Reflections from a mom with a notepad. In A. P. Bochner & C. Ellis (Eds.), *Ethnographically speaking: Autoethnography, literature, and aesthetics* (pp. 170–186). Walnut Creek, CA: AltaMira Press.

Ong, W. J. (1977). *Interfaces of the world.* Ithaca, NY: Cornell University Press.

Pelias, R. (2002). For father and son: An ethnodrama with no catharsis. In A. P. Bochner & C. Ellis (Eds.), *Ethnographically speaking: Autoethnography, literature, and aesthetics,* (pp. 35–43). Walnut Creek, CA: AltaMira Press.

Pelias, R. (2004). *A methodology of the heart: Evoking academic and daily life.* Walnut Creek, CA: AltaMira Press.

Polanyi, M. (1962). *Personal knowledge.* London: Routledge & Kegan Paul.

Punch, M. (1994). Politics and ethics in qualitative research. In N. Denzin & Y. Lincoln (Eds.), *Handbook of qualitative research* (pp. 83–98). Thousand Oaks, CA: Sage.

Rambo Ronai, C. (1992). The reflexive self through narrative: A night in the life of an erotic dancer/researcher. In C. Ellis & M. Flaherty (Eds.), *Investigating subjectivity: Research on lived experience* (pp. 102–124). Newbury Park, CA: Sage.

Rambo Ronai, C. (1996). My mother is mentally retarded. In C. Ellis & A. Bochner (Eds.), *Composing ethnography* (pp. 109–131). Walnut Creek, CA: AltaMira Press.

Richardson, L. (1992). The consequences of poetic representation: Writing the other, rewriting the self. In C. Ellis & M. Flaherty (Eds.), *Investigating subjectivity: Research on lived experience* (pp. 125–137). Newbury Park, CA: Sage.

Richardson, L. (1994). Nine poems: Marriage and the family. *Journal of Contemporary Ethnography, 23,* 3–14.

Richardson, L. (1996). Speech lessons. In C. Ellis & A. Bochner (Eds.), *Composing ethnography: Alternative forms of qualitative writing* (pp. 231–239). Walnut Creek, CA: AltaMira Press.

Saarnivaara, M. (2000). The boundary within me: Reflections on the difficulty of transgression. *Auto/Biography, 8*(1&2), 56–61.

Saarnivaara, M. (2003). Art as inquiry: The autopsy of an [art] experience. *Qualitative Inquiry, 9,* 580–602.

Saarnivaara, M., & Bochner, A. P. (Eds.). (2003). The arts and narrative research [Special issue]. *Qualitative Inquiry, 9*(4).

Saava, I., & Nuutinen, K. (2003). At the meeting place of word and picture. *Qualitative Inquiry, 9*(4), 515–34.

Scott-Hoy, K. (1997). Dialogue not monologue: Preventative eye care and research in Vanuatu. *Pacific Health Dialog, 4*(2), 138–145.

Scott-Hoy, K. (2000a). *Eye of the other within: Artistic autoethnographic evocations of cross-cultural health work in Vanuatu.* Unpublished doctoral dissertation, University of South Australia.

Scott-Hoy, K. (2000b). With people, passion, paint, and palette: Artistic autoethnography. In P. Willis, R. Smith, & E. Collins

(Eds.), *Being, seeking, telling: Expressive approaches to qualitative adult education research* (pp. 322–344). Flaxton, Queensland, Australia: Post Pressed.

Scott-Hoy, K. (2002a). The visitor. In A. P. Bochner & C. Ellis (Eds.), *Ethnographically speaking: Autoethnography, literature, and aesthetics* (pp. 274–294). Walnut Creek, CA: AltaMira Press.

Scott-Hoy, K. (2002b). What kind of mother . . . ? An ethnographic short story. *Qualitative Inquiry, 8*(3), 273–279.

Scott-Hoy, K. (2003). Form carries experience: A story of the art and form of knowledge. *Qualitative Inquiry, 9*(2), 268–280.

Slattery, P. (2001). The educational researcher as artist working within. *Qualitative Inquiry, 7*(3), 370–398.

Stewart, R. (1996). *Sometimes when we touch* (Barry Mann & Dan Hill, Composers). WEA International.

Tierney, W., & Lincoln, Y. (Eds.). (1997). *Representation and the text: Re-framing the narrative voice.* Albany, NY: State University of New York Press.

Tillmann-Healy, L. (1996). A secret life in a culture of thinness: Reflections on body, food, and bulimia. In C. Ellis & A. P. Bochner (Eds.), *Composing ethnography: Alternative forms of qualitative writing* (pp. 77–109). Walnut Creek, CA: AltaMira Press.

Willis, P., Smith, R., & Collins, E. (Eds.). (2000). *Being, seeking, telling: Expressive approaches to qualitative adult education research.* Flaxton, Queensland, Australia: Post Pressed.

Ylonen, M. (2003). Bodily flashes of dancing women: Dance as a method of inquiry. *Qualitative Inquiry: The Arts and Narrative Research, 9*(4), 554–568.

12

MÉTISSAGE

A Research Praxis

◆ Cynthia Chambers and Erika
Hasebe-Ludt with Dwayne Donald,
Wanda Hurren, Carl Leggo,
and Antoinette Oberg

This chapter is organized into three parts, emulating the strands of a traditional braid. The introduction traces the roots and routes of métissage as a linguistic artifact, a theoretical construct, a literary strategy, and a research praxis. This introduction answers the questions: What is métissage? What does it contribute to social science research? The braid interweaves the texts and images of individual authors into the three strands of the braid. This braid addresses the question: What does métissage look like?

Métissage comes from the Latin word *mixtus* meaning "mixed," primarily referring to cloth of two different fibers. Its Greek homonym is *metis,* a figure of skill and craft, as well as wisdom and intelligence (Harper, 2001). Metis, the wife of Zeus, was gifted with powers of transformation. Thus, métissage carries the ability to transform and, through its properties of mixing, opposes transparency and has the power to undo logic and the clarity of concepts. In various colonial contexts, such as Canada, métis became a racial category translated as "mixed-blood" or "half-breed" with the negative connotations of animals (and humans) breeding across species.

Métissage is not only a theory but also a praxis (Haug et al., 1987; Lionnet, 1989; Zuss, 1997). It is a thoughtful *political* praxis that resists "heterophobia" (Memmi cited in Lionnet, 1989) or the fear of mixing, and the desire for a pure untainted space, language, or form of research. Métissage is also a *reading* praxis that engages the world as dialogic and heteroglossic (Bakhtin, 1981) and invites readers to attend to the interreferentiality of texts. Also, métissage is a *writing* praxis that enables researchers and their audiences to imagine and create plural selves and communities that thrive on ambiguity and multiplicity. Métissage affirms, rather than polarizes, difference (Lionnet, 1989). As a conscious textual act, métissage "resists fixed categories and ideological closure of racial, ethnic, and gender identities and their performance within a culture" (Zuss, 1997, p. 168). As a *research* praxis, métissage seeks cross-cultural, egalitarian relations of knowing and being. It respects the historical interrelatedness of traditions, collective contexts, and individual circumstances while resisting 19th-century scholarly conventions of discrete disciplines with corresponding rhetorics for conducting and representing research. It is committed to interdisciplinarity and the blurring of genres, texts, and identities.

What does métissage look like in practice? Single authors/researchers use métissage as a theoretical construct and textual practice (Lionnet, 1989; Zuss, 1997). They weave the repressed languages and traditions of local cultures and vernaculars (particularly incorporating autobiographical material and local oral traditions and stories) with the dominant (often colonial) languages and traditions of literacy. Authors of this chapter

have used métissage, in this way, in their individual work (Chambers, 2005; Donald, 2003; Hasebe-Ludt, 2004). However, they have also worked collectively to juxtapose their texts in such a way that highlights difference (racial, cultural, historical, sociopolitical, linguistic) without essentializing or erasing it, while simultaneously locating points of affinity (Haraway, 1985/1990) or rhizomean connections (Deleuze & Guattari, 1980/1987) among the texts.

In keeping with the commitment to creativity that is inherent in métissage, the authors have collaborated to mix their individual writings into a script for live performance and publication. In these collaborative pieces, individual authors assume responsibility for writing a longer piece, segmenting it into three to five sections, and sometimes selecting accompanying images and sound. This writing takes the form of such literary genres as poetry, narrative, memoir, and postcard essay, as well as the blurring of these genres. One or two authors assume responsibility for purposefully mixing the segments, using points of affinity, to create individual strands much like acts in a dramatic play.

The lead authors then braid the strands in such a way that retains the integrity and distinctiveness of the individual texts/voices and at the same time creates a new text, one that illuminates the braided, polysemic, and relational character of our lives, experiences, and memories, as well as the interconnections among the personal and the public realm. Thus, collective métissage both attends to difference and generates something new (Deleuze & Parnet, 1977/1987) in the same movement—one that addresses the past while imagining new relations and solidarities.

Editing of the final script is a collective responsibility; drafts are circulated either face-to-face or electronically for comments and revisions. In performance (live or electronic), we have mixed audio and video clips with still images and oral renditions of text (Chambers, Donald, & Hasebe-Ludt, 2001; Chambers, Fidyk, Hasebe-Ludt, Hurren, Leggo, & Rahn, 2003; Chambers, Hasebe-Ludt, Hurren, Leggo, & Oberg, 2004). Below is a *short* exemplar of this practice.

◆ *The Braid*

FIRST STRAND OF THE BRAID

Where Are You From? Dwayne Donald

"Where are you from?"[1] the question is asked with a tone of familiarity and *camaraderie* that distracts me and leaves me not wanting to answer. "I'm from Edmonton," I reluctantly reply, and then I wait for the looks of confusion, wonderment, the slow, half-hearted nodding of the head. These work together to give one message: "I thought this guy was an Indian, but I guess he's not . . ."

When Aboriginal people meet each other for the first time, "Where are you from?" is the most common question. The question seeks identity through location of your roots, your family, your ancestors, your relations, your home, your place, your tribe, your Reserve. I don't come from a reserve, nor do any of my immediate relatives. I don't have a *place* in the Aboriginal sense of traditional territory or sacred land.

I descend from a cabin on Hastings Lake, Alberta. My family didn't choose that place; rather, it was chosen for them through the various events of colonialism that could be called acts of displacement. The "spatial and ideological diaspora" that characterizes the displacement of many Aboriginal families has caused them to become alienated from their stories and has disrupted the links connecting one generation to the next (McLeod, 1998, p. 52). However, some stories have been revitalized and told again.

A Theory of Research, Antoinette Oberg

Research: (L. *re* again + OF. *cerchier* from L. *circare* to go around) to go around looking for something, a topic, to begin with. Students are generally advised to read the literature and find something not yet studied. The implication is that not having been studied makes a topic worthy.

It is more reasonable that a research topic would emerge from the place (Topic: Gk. *topos* 1. place) where we are positioned in life, from the propositions with which we prop up our lives and compose the narratives that tell how we live.

Out of the narrative depths a topic emerges (L. *e* out of + *mergere* to plunge) and thereby comes into the view afforded by our position. This view is a theory (Gk. *theorein* to look at). A theory is a way of looking at the world rather than a form of knowledge of how the world is (Bohm, 1983). Thus, every topic statement, being from a point of view, implies (L. *implicare* to enfold a theory) a way of seeing (Topic: Gk. *topos* 2. Commonplace way of seeing).

Once aware that looking is always from a place, a position, a point of view, the possibility arises that we could look differently and hence see differently, thereby changing our prospects.

Wiseman's Cottage, York Harbor, Carl Leggo

While on sabbatical leave, my wife Lana and I lived in the town of York Harbor, Newfoundland. In 1767, Captain

James Cook sailed into the Bay of Islands, and with the self-possessed enthusiasm of 18th-century European explorers, he charted, mapped, and named this ancient, wild, tangled space before sailing off to inscribe other locations. Probably running out of seemingly suitable words, Cook apparently named York Harbor after one of his ships.

Figure 12.1

in the Wiseman's cottage
rented at the end of Main Street
in York Harbour faraway
on the edge of the Atlantic
I learned in slow ways
how to live sabbatically,
drawing silence like
the sun calls the sea

In this place of solitude and stillness, I learned to hear the heart's rhythms. A couple of centuries after Captain James Cook, I sought the heart's cartography, sought to live with attention to poetry, embodiment, sensual experience, imagination, wellness, and connection to the earth. During bike rides through the forest, runs around the arc of York Harbor, snowshoeing across the bog to Wild Cove Pond, and hikes along narrow mountain trails through tuckamore carved by caribou and moose, I sought embodied and emotional connections with the earth's landscape, seascape, mountainscape, and skyscape. And I finally learned that I have lived far too long in my head alone, compelled by a scholar's crazed presumption.

Battle River, Wanda Hurren

I will begin with a photograph. I am standing in the Battle River Pioneer Museum, holding a local history book. The large book is opened to a page revealing a photograph of a woman standing in front of birch trees. The woman is Christina Robertson, my great grandmother. She is 56 years old in the photograph. I am 47 as I stand looking at her image for the first time. (Wanda Hurren. b. Torquay (CAN), 1957. *Battle River.* 2004. Chlorobromide print)

When I opened the history book, randomly choosing a spot to enter, I swear to God, I opened the book to the very page of my great grandmother's photograph. Underneath the photo, a local writer noted that Christina Robertson was "referred to by many as 'the mother of the North.'"

She was also the mother of six children. Only five are mentioned in this history book. Missing from the account is her firstborn child. Mary was born in Scotland, before Christina married George Robertson and came to Canada. Mary was my grandmother.

Walnuts, Erika Hasebe-Ludt

are geographic
rifts compost
in family trees?

—Roy Miki, 2001, p. 56

The walnut tree stood in my mother's garden in Saarbrücken for over two hundred years. Every autumn, my family labored to gather the nuts, dry them on racks, compost the leaves. Each year, the tree shot higher, until it was taller than the house next door. Every spring my father pruned the tree. After his death, my brothers took up the saws and ladders. When one brother became ill with cancer and the other's visits hard to arrange, an arborist was hired. But the tree kept producing its copious crop. After I moved to Canada, there were bundles of walnuts stuffed in my mother's annual Christmas parcel.

Last year, my family instructed the arborist to saw down the branches and cut back the strong furrowed trunk to a bare pole. On my last visit home, I gazed into the space where once a rich canopy of leaves and branches had reigned. I mourned its loss, just as I mourned the fading of my mother's memory. And then, suddenly, I was startled by the new space that opened around the tree trunk.

"The tree will grow again in time," my mother told me. "We will not lose its memory."

But this Christmas there will be no parcel from my mother, no bundle of walnuts under the tree.

Native Speaker, Cynthia Chambers

There was this woman, Margaret Lamouche. She spoke Cree, but she was really Métis—that meant no Indian status, one of those complicated situations where history mixed up languages and families, land and stories, too. Margaret and my daughter, they were friends. And they took a Cree language class together—helped each other out and the professor, too. More than once, Margaret said to me, "I love that daughter of yours."

And then one spring, Margaret Lamouche took a course from me: "Issues in Native Education." She never came to my office, except that once, 5 minutes before class. I feared her visit would make me late, and it wouldn't be the first time. But I invited her

to sit anyways. Then I sat down, too, and waited for her to speak.

SECOND STRAND OF THE BRAID

How Topics Emerge Where Researchers Are. . . . Antoinette Oberg

Figure 12.2

SOURCE: Photo by Antoinette M. Alexander. Reprinted with permission.

Beginning in the place where they are, student researchers write autobiographically about what interests them (L. *inter esse* to be in the midst of). They construct then deconstruct the narratives of their lives. Abstracting (L. *abstrahere* to draw away) allows them to see the ways of seeing (i.e., the theories) that give their narratives the illusion of truth.

These theories pattern not only the researcher's life, but also the lives of others in the culture at large. At different levels of abstraction, different patterns emerge.

Articulating these patterns eventually produces a statement of topic cum theory;

for example, self-judgment as a technology of self, ecoharmonious living as an ecology of mutual adaptation, women's compliance and resistance as an effect of discourse.

Articulating topic and theory keeps research moving. Being a process of seeing, theory—or should we say, theorizing—continuously changes what is seen as well as the seer.

(See Figure 12.2 in color at the front of this book)

Seeing how the self judges itself, Rasmussen[2] became more confident in talking back to the inner critic. Seeing the tensions in a high school classroom, Drew became more congruent by changing his site of teaching from the classroom to the roundpen. Seeing how compliance could include resistance, Kimpson came to be able to resist the designation "unemployable" imposed by the language of disability income assistance forms.

Family Re(as)semblances, Wanda Hurren

Back to the photograph. Christina is wearing a dress, belted at her waist. Her hair is dark and combed back from her face. Her chin is my grandmother Mary's chin, my aunt Maudie's chin, my cousin Mary's chin. I wonder if I look like Christina. I smile.
(Wanda Hurren. b. Torquay (CAN), 1957. *Family Re(as)semblances*. 2004. Sepia print)

In the local history book, there is only one photograph of my great grandmother with her husband, George. It is actually two separate photographs, one of Christina and one of George, pasted together so that it looks like they are both in the same photograph. They are each smiling, but not at the same camera.

They are buried in separate graveyards. George is buried in Fort Smith, North West Territories. Christina is buried along with five of her children, in the Vale of Peace Cemetery, in Notikewin, Alberta.

My great grandmother married George some time after her first child, Mary, was born. The name given for Mary's father (my great grandfather) on her birth certificate is James Horn. My aunt Maudie thinks James was a migrant worker, who travelled to Scotland with a shipment of horses. He worked in the stables with Christina's father. They met when Christina was very young.

Cabin at Hastings Lake, Dwayne Donald

Figure 12.3

SOURCE: Photo by Allen Donald. Reprinted with permission.

From the time he was an infant, my dad lived with his grandma in a cabin beside Hastings Lake, Alberta. He was 18 years old when she died, and he made the decision to move to the nearby city of Edmonton. This meant leaving the cabin and the community behind.

A few years ago, my dad led our family on a visit back to his childhood home. I saw the land had been turned into a private campground. Trees, bushes, and grass had grown up around the old cabin, creating an artifact. My brother and I approached the cabin and began poking around the inside of it. Campers from nearby sites, curious themselves, were drawn to us. Then, a woman arrived who explained that the cabin had been the home of an old Cree woman and her grandson. In that moment, my dad became an artifact of his own history on the very land that bears his memories and stories. What we did not realize at the time was that the uncovering of these family stories and memories, while helping us make sense of where we are from, would also eventually lead us back to the place we now know as Edmonton.

Dragon Slayer, Cynthia Chambers

Figure 12.4

SOURCE: Copyright © Margaret Lamouche.

And when that Métis woman finally spoke she said, "I got evaluated today."

Now, Margaret had eight kids and she'd volunteered in all their classrooms. And that's when she wasn't cooking, sewing, raising kids, and going to school, first that adult upgrading, then college. Then her family moved down south so Margaret could be a teacher. She was an artist, too. Once she drew a picture of a warrior with her broadsword raised against a housefly, because "la mouche" means *housefly* and "Margaret" means *dragon slayer.*

But no matter all that: Margaret had to repeat that student teaching.

Margaret, she was a published poet but her talk—well—that was a real métissage. Her poems were in English, but the Cree was never silent, more like the music for the song. And when she told stories—like the one about her mother who walked out into a blizzard and never came back—Cree was always the story behind the words. Now, Margaret, she never raised her voice, even with those students. She didn't make those kids look her in the eye when she talked to them. Or glare and give the "evil eye" so those kids would listen. No sir. And Margaret, she didn't smile—not unless she really meant it.

And because of all that, Margaret had to repeat that student teaching.

Space Into Place, Blow-Me-Down Mountain, Carl Leggo

Figure 12.5

SOURCE: Photo by Antoinette M. Alexander. Reprinted with permission.

on snowshoes I tramped a trail
up Blow-Me-Down Mountain,

twisted amidst ancient dead trees,
gray scrawny lost corpses
like sea-washed driftwood,
still held in the earth, rooted
in stories long ago forgotten

Scott Walden (2003) points out an intriguing difference between *place* and *space:*

> The world of place is the world of subjective human experience and significance. The world of space is the objective world of points in space–time that are meaningless to humans, abstractions that can be represented in mathematics or physical geography. Space ordinarily comes first, developing aspects of place with the onset of human habitation. A rock takes on significance by becoming the rock that took the bottom out of Gus's boat. A tree takes on meaning by becoming the one in which the children play. (p. 18)

In York Harbor I learned to translate space into place. I engaged creatively with the expansive earth that filled my senses and imagination; I was constantly left both breathless and speechless. In my poems I seek to hold light glimpses of the world that can only be charted and mapped in words. But I know that the world always exhausts words, drives language to the limits of distraction.

Figure 12.6

SOURCE: Photo by Carl Leggo. Reprinted with permission.

snow more snow
will come and erase
the line we wrote
yesterday, we'll clear
more paths like drafts
of writing, impermanent
transitory traces, both
visible and invisible.

Rhododendrons, Erika Hasebe-Ludt

In Berlin in 1989, there was a no-man's land separating East and West, a danger zone of deserted fields and armed border guards behind the Berlin Wall. Standing in my friend Ina's backyard you could see the barbed wire atop the Wall. When you left the gate you entered a narrow trail that paralleled the Wall. When I lived in Berlin, Ina and I often walked this path but we could only travel west, north and south, never east. Yet as I walked within arm's length of the *Mauer*, I did not know the horrible truth about the deaths of those trying to escape from behind the eastern side of the Wall.

After the Wall fell, Ina's family was able to purchase a parcel of the old border zone. She built a garden with a new border, a living wall of rhododendron trees. Their dense foliage and magenta blossoms protect Ina and her family from the reality of the old and the new Berlin where there is the freedom to travel in all directions.

An extension of the *Autobahn* covers the ground where the Wall once stood and offers easy access from East to West, and West to East, but not so easy questions about what this opening signifies to people on both sides.

THIRD STRAND OF THE BRAID

The Question of Methodology. . . . Antoinette Oberg

Graduate student researchers are generally advised to find a research topic and then to find a methodology to match. I tell them that methodology is a way of seeing knowledge, knowers, and knowing, and that this theory is already there, implicit in their writings-toward-topic: in narratives about their interests, researchers construct and display their theories.

Now deconstructing my own theory of methodology, I adjust my ways of seeing. I begin to focus on relating, responding, and resonating rather than knowledge, knowers, and knowing. I theorize a researcher is a node in a nested network of relations among social and intellectual processes of production (Capra, 1996, p. 168). The researcher's responses, like the responses of any living organism to its environment, change both the researcher and the environment in cycles sometimes novel, sometimes repetitive, sometimes dissonant, sometimes resonant.

This autopoietic (Gk. *auto* self + *poiesis* making) process of researching is the topic that emerges from my autobiographical writing about what interests me in my position as instructor of research methodologies.

"Where is That?" Dwayne Donald

My ancestors, led by Chief Papasschayo, agreed to the terms of Treaty Six at Fort Edmonton in 1877. Papasschayo selected an area for their Reserve across the river from the growing settlement of Edmonton. Trouble started soon after. Settlers in the Edmonton area argued that the Reserve would impede the development of the town by denying the settlers access to valuable resources and fertile land. A newspaper of the time advocated that the Papaschase Band "be sent back to the country they originally came from" (Maurice, 2001, p. 4).

In the end, the settlers got their wish. The members of the Papaschase Band were denied their Treaty rights and left destitute and hungry for several years after the negotiation of Treaty Six and the disappearance of the buffalo. Eventually, they lost their rights to the Reserve land. My relations moved to Hastings Lake.

The current leaders of the reestablished Papaschase Band have filed court documents seeking compensation for the wrongful removal of Treaty and land rights. My family could receive some form of "official" recognition as Indians with membership in the Papaschase Band. Finally, I could offer an unequivocal reply to the question that has been plaguing me for so many years:

"Where are you from?"
"Papaschase."
"Where's that?"
"Edmonton."

Notikewin, Wanda Hurren

Figure 12.7

SOURCE: With compliments of Wanda Hurren.

maybe
because of the way an evening breeze
played with a lock of hair just so
she could see his eyes smiling his chin tilted
just so she decided he would be the one then
and now I am standing here on the banks of
the Notikewin River
maybe
because of the way an evening breeze
played with a lock of hair just so
(Wanda Hurren. b. Torquay (CAN), 1957.
Notenaygewn Cepe. 2004. Gelatin silver print)

In my search through photographs and words, I want to find out about Christina traveling to northern Canada to meet up with James. Maybe he returned to his home in northern Canada, to wait for Christina to join him. Instead, I found out there were five more children, all born after her marriage to George. Why did Christina settle in Notikewin? What happened to James? Where did he come from? Where did he go?

My first son was born with a bruise on his lower back that would not fade away. I believed the bruise was a result of his difficult birth. "Oh, no," the doctor informed me, "that is a Mongolian spot—very common for babies of northern indigenous heritage to be born with that spot."

Notenaygewn Cepe
Battle River
Land of the Mighty Peace
Robertson's Crossing
George Robertson and his dog Caesar
Jim Robertson on Midge
John on Lady
she came to live on the banks
of the Notikewin River
the weather was so severe
she whispered to me
with a chuckle
the past is being erased
(Wanda Hurren. b. Torquay (CAN), 1957. *Found in Notikewin*, 2004, Gelatin silver print)

Low Grade, Cynthia Chambers

"Yeah, I got evaluated," that Métis woman said and then added, as if to console me, "but it's okay."

I waited.

"The evaluation of my teaching . . ." she explained, "it was okay; but that first part on the form. . . ."

"Communication skills?" I'd supervised student teachers with that form for 15 years, so I filled in the blank. Now that's a bad habit—filling in the blanks—hard to stop so I didn't often try.

"Yah, they marked me so low on that and I know. . . ." Another pause. "Its because of. . . ."

Margaret's eyes welled up so I jumped in again. "Your Cree accent?"

"Yah. . . ." she said. This time I waited. I knew Margaret had to talk for herself from now on and I had to listen, bite my lip maybe.

Margaret went on. "I can change all those other things. I can plan better lessons; I can manage the classroom better. But what, what am I gonna to do about the way I talk? I can't change that."

"And that low mark, I feel it." She pressed the heel of her hand into her heart like she could stop it from bleeding. "Right here," she said. "Because I can't change it; the Cree language that's who I am, and it's my language, my people, we're all getting a low mark."

I said nothing but I thought about my class and the students waiting. Margaret stood up and I followed.

"So today, I'm prayin' in Cree," she said and then laughed. "Usually I mix Cree and English when I pray; but today—I'm just prayin' in Cree."

I walked to class with Margaret. And although I didn't ask, I wanted her to pray for me. And forgive me, too.

Japanese Maples, Erika Hasebe-Ludt

Figure 12.8

Two Japanese maples stand on either side of the path in my garden in Vancouver. My husband, Ken, planted these trees almost twenty years ago. One he left untouched, the other, he shaped, into a different tree. Using wires and tape, he sculpted this maple with a sensibility nurtured by Japanese genes soaked in Hiroshima soil and Canadian upbringing weathered by the Pacific Ocean. For many years, I could not see what he imagined for the trees. But he told me to be patient, that you cannot hurry a tree. I had to trust a Japanese Canadian gardener.

Recently, to my surprise, I noticed that each maple, in its own way, harmonizes with the surrounding cedar, pine, fire thorn, and rhododendron. Ken nurtured them so the maple on the East grew vertically, and the maple on the West horizontally. Now with the ocean breeze, the leaves move up and down, back and forth, in an aesthetic wave of yin yang.

Soon the autumn storms will scatter the rust-colored abundance of maple leaves. Then, only the braveness of the bare branches will remain, waiting, patiently, for snow and the return of spring, eventually. I learned to trust a Japanese Canadian gardener.

"You're Not From Around Here," Carl Leggo

York Harbor is a mysterious, enchanted place inhabited by only a few hundred people and countless gulls, crows, moose, caribou, lobsters, cod, and a tangled menagerie of wild life, earth life, ocean life, and sky life beyond all counting and telling. While biking, I met a man on the trail. He was gathering peat moss for his gardens. He said, *"You're not from around here."* I just nodded, but I knew I too am a part of this landscape, this space, this place that can't be named or tamed. I will carry the memories, emotions, and poetry with me forever. I am changed. Like the ancient trees and driftwood and beachstones, I too have dwelled in this place. Lana and I have lived the circle of seasons, turning and turning, knowing we will not return to this place, but also knowing we will carry the tangled rhythms of this hallowed place with us wherever we go.

Figure 12.9

SOURCE: Photo by Carl Leggo. Reprinted with permission.

as the sun rises in the harbor
I make poems, and find sustaining
places of stillness and stability,
but like the countless beachstones,
I can't tell you all the stories I have
lived and will live in this place.

KNOTTING THE BRAID

In this chapter, we have both (1) *illustrated* métissage as a research praxis and (2) *illuminated* issues and challenges métissage offers social science research. We mixed binaries such as colonized with colonizer, local with global, East with West, North with South, particular with universal, feminine with masculine, vernacular with literate, and theory with practice. We braided strands of place and space, memory and history, ancestry and (mixed) race, language and literacy, familiar and strange with strands of tradition, ambiguity, becoming, (re)creation, and renewal into a métissage.

By way of knotting the braid, we respond to a possible critique that this approach is simply an aesthetic literary practice. We assert that our collective praxis of métissage is a way of speaking and acting that is both political and redemptive. Our métissage offers a rapprochement between alternative and mainstream social science discourses and seeks a genuine exchange among the writers, and between the writers and their various audiences. Our aim is to go out into the world, to embrace it and love it fiercely (Arendt, 1958; Galeano, 1991), always returning home with the gifts of new knowledge, new hope that it is possible to live well in this particular place, at this time, with ourselves and with all our relations (King, 1990).

◆ Notes

1. An earlier version of Donald's text was published in Goyette and Jakeway (2005, pp. 382–385).
2. Rasmussen, Drew, and Kimpson recount their experiences in Oberg, Drew, Montgomery, Rasmussen, and Kimpson (2002).

◆ References

Arendt, H. (1958). *The human condition.* Chicago: The University of Chicago Press.

Bakhtin, M. M. (1981). *The dialogic imagination: Four essays.* Austin: University of Texas Press.

Bohm, D. (1983). *Wholeness and the implicate order.* London: Ark Paperbacks.

Capra, F. (1996). *The web of life.* New York: Anchor Books.

Chambers, C. (2005, April). *"Where do I belong?" Canadian curriculum as passport home.* Keynote address to Annual Conference of the American Association for the Advancement of Curriculum Studies, Montreal, Quebec, Canada.

Chambers, C., Donald, D., & Hasebe-Ludt, E. (2001). Creating a curriculum of métissage. *Educational Insights, 7(2).* Retrieved December 2, 2004, from http://www.ccfi.educ.ubc.ca/publication/insights/v07n02/toc2.html

Chambers, C., Fidyk, A., Hasebe-Ludt, E., Hurren, W., Leggo, C., & Rahn, J. (2003). Dis(e)rupting syntax: Curriculum as (dis)composure. *Educational Insights, 8(2).* Retrieved December 2, 2004, from http://www.ccfi.educ.ubc.ca/publication/insights/v08n02/contextual explorations/curriculum/index.html

Chambers, C., Hasebe-Ludt, E., Hurren, W., Leggo, C., & Oberg, A. (2004). *The credible and the incredible in autobiographical research: A Canadian curriculum métissage.* Performed at the American Educational Research Association Annual Conference, San Diego, CA.

Deleuze, G., & Guattari, F. (1987). *A thousand plateaus: Capitalism and schizophrenia* (B. Masumi, Trans.). Minneapolis: University of Minnesota Press. (Original work published 1980)

Deleuze, G., & Parnet, C. (1987). *Dialogues* (H. Tomlinson & B. Habberjam, Trans.). New York: Columbia University Press. (Original work published 1977)

Donald, D. (2003). *Elder, student, teacher: A Kainai curriculum métissage.* Unpublished Master's thesis, University of Lethbridge, Lethbridge, Alberta, Canada.

Galeano, E. (1991). *A book of embraces* (C. Belfrage with M. Schafer, Trans.). New York: W. W. Norton.

Goyette, L., & C. Jakeway R. (2005). *Edmonton in our words.* Edmonton, Alberta, Canada: University of Alberta Press.

Haraway, D. (1990). A manifesto for cyborgs: Science, technology, and socialist feminism in the 1980s. In L. J. Nicholson (Ed.), *Feminism/Postmodernism* (pp. 190–233). New York: Routledge. (Original work published in 1985)

Harper, D. (2001). *Online etymology dictionary.* Retrieved October 27, 2004, from http://www.etymonline.com/

Hasebe-Ludt, E. (2004). We talked freely of many things: Writing home/away from home. In A. L. Cole, L. Neilsen, J. G. Knowles, & T. C. Luciani (Eds.), *Provoked by art: Theorizing arts-informed research* (pp. 203–213). Halifax, Nova Scotia, Canada: Backalong Books.

Haug, F., et al. (1987). *Female sexualization: A collective work of memory* (E. Carter, Trans.). London: Verso. Retrieved from http://www.ualberta.ca/NATIVESTUDIES/LegalPDF/papaschase.pdf

King, T. (Ed.). (1990). *All my relations: An anthology of contemporary Native fiction.* Toronto, Ontario, Canada: McClleland & Stewart.

Lionnet, F. (1989). *Autobiographical voices: Race, gender, and self-portraiture.* Ithaca, NY: Cornell University.

Maurice, R. S. (2001). Statement of claim: The Papaschase Indian Band No. 136. *Pimohtewin: A Native Studies E-Journal.* Retrieved October 2, 2001, from: http://www.ualberta.ca/NATIVESTUDIES/LegalPDF/papaschase.pdf

McLeod, N. (1998). Coming home through stories. *International Journal of Canadian Studies, 18,* 51–66.

Miki, R. (2001). *Surrender.* Toronto, Ontario, Canada: The Mercury Press.

Oberg, A., Drew, D., Montgomery, P., Rasmussen, P., & Kimpson, S. (2002). *Shape/shifting: The articulation of topic in the midst of ongoing autobiographical inquiry.* Paper presented at the International Human Science Research Conference, Victoria, British Columbia, Canada.

Walden, S. (2003). *Places lost: In search of Newfoundland's resettled communities.* Toronto, Ontario, Canada: Lynx Images.

Webster's seventh new collegiate dictionary. (1963). Springfield, MA: G. & C. Merriam.

Zuss, M. (1997). Strategies of representation: Autobiographical métissage and critical pragmatism. *Educational Theory, 47*(2), 163–180.

13

Literary Forms

WRITING AS THEORY

In Defense of Fiction

◆ Stephen Banks

Humanity has but one product, and that is fiction.

—Dillard, 1982, p. 1

This chapter advocates using literary fiction as a mode of expression in reporting scholarly research. I will not argue that conventional social science must be transformed or that standards for research reports be jettisoned in favor of fiction, nor will I attempt to repudiate any other aspect of scientific writing, except to challenge its failure to engage writing as a theoretical activity and to question its practical utility in some instances. Rather, this chapter sets forth a defense of the position that writing literary fiction can be a productive, even revelatory, practice for communicating scholarship, and as such fiction writing should be taught, used, and appreciated as a form of research reporting. I will make a distinction between reporting as a conveyance of findings and reporting as relating a story of the research experience.

Certainly the zone between the practices of fiction writers and nonfiction writers is blurry. In an interview with National Public Radio journalist Steve Inskeep, Seattle author and librarian Nancy Pearl

(2005) said this about spy fiction writer Robert Littell's novel *The Company:* "If you want a fictional history, lightly fictionalized history of the CIA, 'The Company' is the book to read." Pearl expressed an ambiguity commonly felt about fiction, that is, it is only more or less "fictional." As Morroe Berger (1977) amply demonstrated, fiction strives for a social science–like verisimilitude as a condition of its being. British novelist A. S. Byatt (2001) calls this "fiction's preoccupation with impossible truthfulness," and she connects it "with modern scholarship's increasing use of the techniques and attitudes of art" (pp. 98–99). To achieve that verisimilitude, creative writers conduct rigorous, extensive research. Many novelists conduct in-depth interviews, historical investigations, legal searches, media content analyses, participant observation, and similar fieldwork. They often have "research assistants." In *A Writer's Reality,* Mario Vargas Llosa (1991) says, "I did a great deal of research. I went to the newspapers and magazines of that year. I read everything that had been written and tried to interview the participants. . . . The interviews helped me considerably in writing my novel" (p. 151). A lack of research invites comment:

Mark Twain (1918/1994) savagely criticized James Fenimore Cooper for his "absence of the observer's protecting gift" in *Deerslayer,* saying Cooper's "eye was splendidly inaccurate" (p. 70). Twain took Cooper to task for poor research concerning the shapes of streams, the size of an ark, the behavior of Indians, the visibility of a nail head, even the sounds of conversations.

On the other side, a small clan of social researchers has sensed there is something in the logic and practice of fiction that invites the construction of a "bridge" (Watson, 2000) between social science and literary writing. In the past two decades they have presented diverse arguments for using alternative modes of expression for reporting scholarly investigations, mainly in ethnographic research. In some cases they have made their points by creating provocative examples of experimental writing in scholarly research. Prominent among such scholars, Norman Denzin has championed publication of new forms of writing in the journals *Qualitative Inquiry, Qualitative Research,* and *Studies in Symbolic Interaction,* and more recently in *Culture & Communication,* as well as in numerous books.

These innovations in scholarly expression have established, either by explicit argument or indirectly by example, four foundational premises upon which this chapter builds its position. First, writing must itself be theorized as a generative research practice. Laurel Richardson (1990) concludes that the "crisis of representation" in postfoundationalist social science is an uncertainty about what constitutes adequate depiction of social reality. "How do we write (explain, describe, index) the social?" (p. 19) she asks. Similarly, Susan Krieger (1984) says we need to theorize writing so as to bring into our purview the "inner world" of experience that is anchored in subjective meanings. To theorize writing means not to take writing for granted but to account reflexively for its foundational principles. If, as communication scholar Steven Corman (1995) has argued, theories basically are ways people explain things, then those expressive techniques by which social scientists explain motives, rationalize methods, and communicate findings are themselves theories. If the expression reflexively accounts for itself, then writing *is* theory. And those accounts are always and only grounded in the genre, form, and content of our expression.

Building on the imperative for a self-reflexive practice of writing, a second premise says theorizing writing also invites a critique of the received practice. Against the growing body of critical and experimental work on new forms of scholarly expression there stands a huge, monolithic and overwhelmingly conventionalized canon of ideas that govern research writing. That dictatorial canon rests on the foundational assumptions of science. It assumes the possibility and necessity for objectivity; it demands and simultaneously assumes writerly authority; and it prescribes textual uniformity and positions scholarly writing as a distinctive, nonliterary mode of expression.

Third, in research writing, as in any human expression, "narrative is unavoidable" (Richardson, 1990, p. 20). Mark Freeman (1998) points out that narrative is unavoidable because, "the phenomenology of human temporality requires it as a condition of the very intelligibility of experience" (p. 457). He argues further that the possibilities for constructing selves, enacting human agency, and sharing social meanings are grounded in narratives. Narratives also are used to diagnose medical conditions, to assess cognitive and social development, to convict criminals as well as to free the innocent, and other practical applications, reflecting an understanding that narrative "captures" experience as an immediate and true metric (see Lieblich, Tuval-Mashiach, & Zilber, 1998, pp. 3–5).

The last premise is that one of the key modes of narrative—literary fiction—can profitably be used for scholarly writing tasks. This is not an unprecedented point, since numerous scholars have begun to express themselves in literary productions,[1] and critics have for many years turned to literary resources to bolster scholarly arguments, such as Joshua Landy's (2004) use of Proust to develop a philosophy of mind and aesthetics, and Robert Hopper's (1998) use of fictional materials to examine such social rituals as flirting and teasing. The rest of this chapter explores the latter three of these premises in order, as elaborations on theorizing scholarly writing. I conclude with a discussion of what can serve as standards of acceptability for scholarly fiction writing.

◆ The Conventional Research Report

Open any current textbook on social research and examine the material about how research activity is to be communicated to audiences. With rare exception, research is assumed to culminate in (i.e., to produce) "findings" or "results" (e.g., Keyton, 2001, p. 343). I place these words in scare quotes to highlight them as terms of art that embody assumptions about what research is and what it does. To ground this part of my discussion, I examined 10 textbooks in research methods across the social science disciplines, all of which included sections on qualitative research. Only one allowed for any deviation from traditional ways of presenting the conclusions of research projects. Structurally, "findings" inevitably are presented as if they occur in the research protocol upstream of the creation of the research report. The positioning of research as something that "produces" likens it to a knowledge factory, a device for generating expected, planned, or epiphenomenal outputs. "Findings" entails the idea that something preexists to be found, and the planned output is the discovery and revelation of the phenomenon assumed to preexist the search to find it. Articulation of the "findings" or "results" is a closing of the episode, an ending of the activity, and the use of the term belies an underlying assumption that the goal of a quest has been achieved, a question definitively answered, or a once elusive relationship found.

Like "findings" and "results," the idea of data as naturally occurring phenomena is another assumption of the standard research report. Yet what are counted as "data" invariably are selected and named by the investigator; in most cases the phenomena under analysis are created by the investigator. Elinor Ochs (1979) has demonstrated that even in the most empirical research involving recorded spontaneous talk, the data worked on are never the in vivo talk: Almost always analysis is performed on transcripts created when researchers reproduce those conversations through auditing and transcribing the tape recordings. Ochs argues that transcribing is always theoretical work, since the researcher decides what to include and what to exclude. If everything were to be transcribed, she says, one would be transcribing into infinity. But the conventional view is that data are either evoked by experimenters or produced by nature, and all the researcher does is observe it, harvest it, and analyze it. This process produces "findings," which, as John Reinard cautions, should be presented "without comment on their substantive importance" (Reinard, 2001, p. 136).

The canons of style include the requirement for clear, well-organized expression (Schutt, 2001), the advisability of writing drafts and revisions (Booth, Colomb, & Williams, 2003), and in qualitative research reports, the fitting of a conventional narrative form to a standard organizing scheme (Baxter & Babbie, 2004). Only in Lindlof and Taylor's (2002) book on qualitative communication research methods is found encouragement to think about and experiment with "alternative writing formats" (p. 287).

As encoded in the language used to discuss methods, then, research is understood as an autonomous procedure in quest of a conclusive discovery about self-presenting natural data that is subsequently related in an omniscient, transparent text. Ben Agger (2000) points out, however, that "what is distinctive about much positivist sociological writing is that it suppresses the fact that it is writing at all" (p. 2). The text calls no attention to itself, even while it struggles to appear as an automatic and faithful reproduction of an a priori reality. The *Publication Manual of the American Psychological Association*

specifically discourages literary writing, as it "might confuse or disturb readers of scientific prose" (American Psychological Association [APA], p. 32). Agger (2000) argues to the contrary that any method is argument, a rhetorical positioning of the research act that "polemicizes quietly for a certain view of the world" (p. 2), so that the *Publication Manual*'s striving for "writing that aims for clear and logical communication" (APA, p. 31) itself argues for a particular worldview in scholarship.

For many years authorship has been problematized among qualitative researchers and particularly among ethnographers. What is the role and responsibility of the author, if reading constructs the meaning of a text? If there is an implied reader in a text, is the author a textual prognosticator? A puppeteer? A lagniappe? In whose voice does and should the report speak? From Barthes to Eco, the question of authorial reality, power, and legitimacy has depended on whether a text is thought to be able to mirror another, different reality or is a creation of a partially or entirely new one. It has become almost a cliché to say that the text as an object is meaningless without a reader yet inevitably has an author. Indeed, texts don't write themselves (films don't imprint themselves; dances don't choreograph themselves): Authors exercise consequential agency and intentionality in creating texts.

◆ *The Narrative Alternative*

Reflecting on the social science research report, Donald Polkinghorne (1988) says researchers should change their voices from logicians to that of storytellers, so that they can reveal more profitably the narrativity in the research experience. The format of the research report, Polkinghorne argues, is an artifact of the social sciences disciplines and (quoting Calvin O. Schrag) as such it needs to take into account the "web of delivered discourses, social practices, professional requirements, and daily decisions" within which the research practice takes place (Polkinghorne, 1997, p. 22; see also Harré, 1990). Polkinghorne points to the practical uses of research reports beyond the stated purpose of making knowledge claims, uses such as establishing the prestige or reputation of scholars and departments, the establishment and perpetuation of scholarly publications, the promotion and tenuring of writers, and the improvement of lives of participants and their communities. These uses also are parts of the larger narrative of the research act.

Narrative theorists, like Polkinghorne, Laurel Richardson, William Tierney and Yvonna Lincoln, and Arthur Bochner and Carolyn Ellis, theorize all writing as having essential narrative qualities. This move goes beyond the usual perspective of narrative analysis, by which texts can be analyzed as sorts of conventional stories, with plot, setting, character development, action, and a beginning–middle–denouement–ending structure, for example. Narrative theory in the poststructuralist view, says Denzin (1997), asserts that all texts encode stories with a "narrative logic concerning discursive authority, sexual difference, power, and knowledge" (p. 232). Such elements are embedded but not always obvious in texts.

The Italian philosopher Adriana Cavarero (2000) says the very idea of sentience, of selfhood and personal identity, is grounded in narrative. The self is not fabricated within a project of opportunistically matching one's identity to situational or mass-mediated circumstances, but is instead an aspect of our unavoidable exhibiting of ourselves to others. We present ourselves to others from birth on, and others cumulatively tell us who we are. Only when others tell our stories do we know our identities,

she says. Cavarero counterposes the ancient question *What am I?* as against the pragmatic *Who am I?* The first question is a categorical inquiry: What class of objects do I belong to? This is the sort of question found in science writing. To say *what* a person is is to place persons into nomothetic categories. But even philosophical inquiry cannot say *Who* a person is, in all his or her singularity, according to Cavarero. Fortunately, philosophical discourse is only one of many forms of expression we humans are capable of using, she points out. Narrative gives life its figuration and each individual's life its figure, not only its uniqueness but also its unity, its coherence over time. So scientific and philosophical discourses unitize humanity, while narratives unify an individual autobiography.

More to the point of research writing is the theoretical observation that narrative, in moving from the *what* to the *who* of characters, shifts from representing persons as units in categories to unique existents (Cavarero's term) in a constitutive relationship with others, a move from radical individualism to a more relational, socially communitarian view of subjectivity (and the characters can be any phenomenon, from Melville's whale to a soup can in Tom Robbins's *Skinny Legs and All*). From this perspective, then, narrative is fundamental to human understanding, selfhood, and sociality.

But recall my opening quotation from Annie Dillard's *Living by Fiction*: "Life has but one product, and that is fiction." What can she possibly mean by that? The pragmaticist philosopher and semiotician Charles Saunders Peirce (1958) argued that what is taken as factual is actually an agreement of beliefs. Peirce held that truth is decided within interpretive communities and that disagreements over truth represent diverse interpretations of narratives, which have their own logics, evidence, and styles. This means that truth, as Denzin (1997) has argued, is a social construct and is judged not as a correspondence to external events but is judged according to its internal cohesiveness and correspondence to a world we recognize in other narratives.

◆ *From Narrative to Fiction*

Fiction per se, however, still struggles for legitimacy in the academy as scholarly writing. In their introduction to *Composing Ethnography,* Carolyn Ellis and Arthur Bochner (1997) write:

> Gregory Bateson knew there was no way to guarantee objective truth, but he didn't think that meant the end result had to be make-believe. . . . That's the danger of going too far with the notion of ethnographic fiction. We ought to treat our ethnographies as partial, situated, and selective productions, but this should not be seen as license to exclude details that don't fit the story we want to tell. [It's not the same as] saying the impossibility of telling the whole truth means you can lie. (p. 21)

This view shortchanges the uses and purposes of fiction, as I discuss below. Moreover, lying isn't the point of fiction. Fiction is the selective ordering of experience rendered in a unique story. Paraphrasing Denzin (1997), a fiction is a narrative that deals with real and imagined facts and how they might be experienced, made up stories fashioned out of real and imagined happenings, and that tells a truth. Indeed, psychiatrist and story advocate Robert Coles (1989) argued that researchers shouldn't be concerned about whether we present our subjects as real or fictional characters, but whether we can capture and well express the interiority of those persons.

Even when fictions are deemed as lying, or are seen as purely works of the writer's imagination, they nonetheless have several strong utilities for reporting scholarly research. If two of the main purposes of social science research include instructing others about social life and sharing understandings, then part of the teaching and sharing might (some would argue *must*) include the expressive–emotional dimensions of the researcher's relationship with participants. An example of how this dimension can be conveyed is found in Phil Smith's part story, part poem called "Food Truck's Party Hat" (Smith, 1999). He could have written a report that explored the lives of developmentally disabled, middle-aged men, and layered those lives under various social theories, perhaps correlated their degree of disability with various aspects of social functioning or dysfunction, and reported his "findings." Instead, Smith was interested in the persons themselves, as defined by the particularities of their lived experience. He chose to privilege the voices and lives of his participants and "let the story write itself." He accounted for himself this way:

> As I sat down a month or so after my morning with Food Truck in the donut shop, I did not have a clear picture in my mind of what the resulting text about him would end up being. I wanted it to be what Neal Stephenson calls a *nam-shub,* a Sumerian word that he says is "a speech with magical force" . . . capable of infecting those who hear it with a virus that will affect how they think and act and understand the world. I wanted to write a nam-shub that would begin to change how people think and act and understand what they call developmental disability. (Smith, 1999, p. 248)

This is a positive use of fiction, instructing readers by evoking an awareness of the subjective aspects of participants' experience. In addition, the uses of fiction might include attempts to share with audiences the researcher's own subjective response to participants' experiences and other research materials, as I have advocated in my fictional renditions of holiday letters (S. P. Banks, 2000).

Several of the strongest arguments for using fiction in scholarly writing are offered by former sex worker and ethnographer Katherine Frank (2000). She says fiction can reach audiences that are broader and larger than those within the academic tribe of readers. In addition, fiction provides immediacy—an artfully strategic evocation of sights, smells, sounds, and other contextual factors—far beyond what conventional writing conveys. Moreover, fiction writing is a form of practice that often is pre-theoretical in the sense that the writer can write into and out of problems of representation without the more cumbersome and constraining language of academic discourse. Frank (2000) also cites a related utility: Fiction, she says, helps "work out problems for which I am unable to find the appropriate theoretical language or framework" (p. 484). Accordingly, she writes about characters as a way of interrogating the social scene she is studying and to learn about her own relation to it and how to locate her research experience in the existing literature. Inevitably, fiction allows writers and readers the freedom to remain open to new interpretations and to avoid closure on any research project.

Finally, in any advocacy of fiction writing as scholarly production, the problems, threats, and inhibiting factors must be confronted. Frank points to the threshold problem of audience expectations. Academic readers, editors, and university review committees overwhelmingly expect research to be communicated in the traditional mode of reporting and to address standards of validity and reliability. The politics of publication are a significant concern to those who would use fiction: What editor will accept a short story in lieu of a scientific report or a conventional realist ethnography? More to the point, how would editorial reviewers judge the quality of a research report written as fiction?

A special issue of *Qualitative Inquiry* (June, 2000) was devoted to this question about criteria for judging in "alternative representations," which is about as close to a confrontation with fiction as academe moves, and the responses of the contributors were varied and mostly cautious. Emphasizing verisimilitude, Richardson (2000) seeks ethnographies that correspond to a lived truth. Focusing on thematic content, Denzin (2000) looks for work that advances social movements and offers a blueprint for cultural criticism. Ellis (2000) would review an experimental text by using the same criteria she applies to any scholarly report. And Clough (2000) seeks theoretical rigor and fidelity in any experimental text. Only Bochner (2000) takes an expansive enough perspective on alternative modes to be responsive to fiction: He seeks persuasive details of fact and emotion, structural and emotional complexity, a plot that shows transformation of character, ethical self-consciousness and commitment, and finally, "a story that moves me, my heart and belly as well as my head" (p. 271). In my own work, I have held that the standards of quality for scholarly fiction should be the same as any other literary fiction, because it seeks to evoke the same responses within its audiences: aesthetic pleasure, understandings derived from narrative coherence and verisimilitude, and an enhancement of emotional resources.

Fiction as research reports, however, needs something more: Because fiction until recently has been rooted entirely in the spaces of literary art or popular entertainment, it is necessary for scholarly fiction to declare itself to have a specialized purpose for its own creation. Likewise, when fictions are created so as to share with readers a research experience, it is necessary for them to declare their fictional nature. In this limited sense I agree with Tony Watson (2000), who advocates setting fictional reporting within a larger text that explicates the writer's research methods, including an explicit identification of the fiction, and relates the fiction to established theory and research literature. Watson's "ethnographic fiction science" formulation, however, drifts away from the principle earmarks of fiction as he strives to retain the aims and standards of science in the fictional report. Those qualities are the centrality of story, the use of figurative language, and imagination. Vargas Llosa (2002) identified thematically driven story as fiction's core and emphasized coherence and persuasiveness as story's defining properties. Eugène Ionesco insisted on a distinction between invention and imagination, arguing that imagination is the foundational resource of the "honest" writer (see Weiss, 1991). Watson (2000), on the contrary, says ethnographic fiction writers should "draw on the language of the social sciences, reflexively and tentatively, when appropriate [and] make some formalized generalizations about social life in the ways we expect of sociologists or psychologists" (p. 503). This view brings to mind novelist John Banville (1993), who quipped, "the word *psychology* when it is applied to art makes me want to reach for my revolver" (p. 107). Using the language and explicit conceptual frameworks of the social sciences repudiates the very reasons moving a scholar to turn to fiction for expression in the first place.

The practical reality of writing scholarly fiction is that the leap must be total and transparent. The natural history of conventional social science is that of a real world being articulated in imagined details; the natural history of fiction is that of an imaginary world being articulated in real details. The former helps us understand what people are, while the latter helps us understand who people can be.

◆ Note

1. A partial list of representative work includes Anzaldua, 1987; Angrosino, 1998; S. P. Banks, 2000; Diversi, 1998; Ellis, 2004; Lingis, 1994; Lyotard, 1997; Schaviro, 1997; and Stoller, 1999.

◆ References

Agger, B. (2000). *Public sociology: From social facts to literary acts.* Lanham, MD: Rowman & Littlefield.

American Psychological Association. (2001). *Publication Manual of the American Psychological Association* (5th ed.). Washington, DC: Author.

Angrosino, M. (1998). *Opportunity house: Ethnographic stories of mental retardation.* Walnut Creek, CA: AltaMira Press.

Anzaldua, G. (1987). *Borderlands/La frontera: The new Mestiza.* San Francisco: Spinsters/Aunt Lute.

Banks, A., & Banks, S. P. (Eds.). (1998). *Fiction and social research: By ice or fire.* Walnut Creek, CA: AltaMira Press.

Banks, S. P. (2000). Five holiday letters: A fiction. *Qualitative Inquiry, 6*(3), 392–405.

Banville, J. (1993). Making little monsters walk. In C. Boyland (Ed.), *The agony and the ego: The art and strategy of fiction writing explored* (pp. 107–112). New York: Penguin.

Baxter, L., & Babbie, E. (2004). *The basics of communication research.* Belmont, CA: Wadsworth.

Berger, M. (1977). *Real and imagined worlds: The novel and social science.* Cambridge, MA: Harvard University Press.

Bochner, A. (2000). Criteria against ourselves. *Qualitative Inquiry, 6*(2), 266–272.

Booth, W. C., Colomb, G. G., & Williams, J. M. (2003). *The craft of research* (2nd ed.). Chicago: University of Chicago Press.

Byatt, A. S. (2001). *On histories and stories: Selected essays.* Cambridge, MA: Harvard University Press.

Cavarero, A. (2000). *Relating narratives: Storytelling and selfhood* (P. A. Kottman, Trans.). New York: Routledge.

Clough, P. T. (2000). Comments on setting criteria for experimental writing. *Qualitative Inquiry, 6*(2), 278–291.

Coles, R. (1989). *The call of stories.* Boston: Houghton Mifflin Company.

Corman, S. (1995). That works fine in theory, but.... In S. R. Corman, S. P. Banks, C. R. Bantz, & M. E. Mayer (Eds.), *Foundations of organizational communication* (2nd ed., pp. 3–10). White Plains, NY: Longman.

Denzin, N. (1997). *Interpretive ethnography: Ethnographic practices for the 21st century.* Thousand Oaks, CA: Sage.

Denzin, N. (2000). Aesthetics and practices of qualitative inquiry. *Qualitative Inquiry, 6*(2), 256–272.

Dillard, A. (1982). *Living by fiction.* New York: Harper & Row.

Diversi, M. (1998). Glimpses of street life: Representing lived experience through short stories. *Qualitative Inquiry, 4*(2), 131–147.

Ellis, C. (2000). Creating criteria: An ethnographic short story. *Qualitative Inquiry, 6*(2), 273–277.

Ellis, C. (2004). *The ethnographic I: A methodological novel about autoethnography.* Thousand Oaks, CA: Sage.

Ellis, C., & Bochner, A. (Eds.). (1997). *Composing ethnography: Alternative forms of qualitative writing.* Walnut Creek, CA: AltaMira Press.

Frank, K. (2000). "The management of hunger": Using fiction in writing anthropology. *Qualitative Inquiry, 6*(4), 474–488.

Freeman, M. (1998). Experience, narrative, and the relationship between them. *Narrative Inquiry, 8,* 455–466.

Harré, R. (1990). Some narrative conventions in scientific discourse. In C. Nash (Ed.), *Narrative in culture: The uses of storytelling in the sciences, philosophy, and literature* (pp. 81–101). New York: Routledge.

Hopper, R. (1998). Flirtations: Conversation analysis from fiction and life. In A. Banks & S. Banks (Eds.), *Fiction and social research: By ice or fire* (pp. 33–50). Walnut Creek, CA: AltaMira Press.

Keyton, J. (2001). *Communication research: Asking questions, finding answers.* New York: McGraw-Hill.

Krieger, S. (1984). Fiction and social science. *Studies in Symbolic Interaction, 5,* 269–286.

Landy, J. (2004). *Philosophy as fiction: Self, deception, and knowledge in Proust.* New York: Oxford University Press.

Lieblich, A., Tuval-Mashiach, R., & Zilber, T. (1998). *Narrative research: Reading, analysis, and interpretation.* Thousand Oaks, CA: Sage.

Lindlof, T. R., & Taylor, B. C. (2002). *Qualitative communication research methods* (2nd ed.). Thousand Oaks, CA: Sage.

Lingis, A. (1994). *Abuses.* Berkeley: University of California Press.

Lyotard, J.-F. (1997). *Postmodern fables* (G. Van den Abbeele, Trans.). Minneapolis: University of Minnesota Press.

Ochs, E. (1979). Transcription as theory. In E. Ochs & B. Schieffelin (Eds.), *Developmental pragmatics* (pp. 43–72). New York: Academic Press.

Pearl, N. (2005, February 2). Nancy Pearl talks about her favorite spy novels. *Morning Edition*, National Public Radio.

Peirce, C. S. (1958). *Collected papers.* Cambridge, MA: Harvard University Press.

Polkinghorne, D. E. (1988). *Narrative knowing and the human sciences.* Albany: State University of New York.

Polkinghorne, D. E. (1997). Reporting qualitative research as practice. In W. G. Tierney & Y. S. Lincoln (Eds.), *Representation and the text: Reframing the narrative voice* (pp. 3–22). Albany: State University of New York.

Reinard, J. (2001). *Introduction to communication research* (2nd ed). Boston: McGraw-Hill.

Richardson, L. (1990). *Writing strategies: Reaching diverse audiences.* Newbury Park, CA: Sage.

Richardson, L. (1994). Writing as a method of inquiry. In N. K. Denzin & Y. S. Lincoln (Eds.), *The handbook of qualitative research* (pp. 516–529). Thousand Oaks, CA: Sage.

Richardson, L. (2000). Evaluating ethnography. *Qualitative Inquiry, 6*(2), 253–255.

Schaviro, S. (1997). *Doom patrols: A theoretical fiction about postmodernism.* New York: High Risk Books.

Schutt, R. K. (2001). *Investigating the social world* (3rd ed). Thousand Oaks, CA: Pine Forge Press/Sage.

Smith, P. (1999). Food Truck's party hat. *Qualitative Inquiry, 5*(2), 244–261.

Stoller, P. (1999). *Jaguar: A story of Africans in America.* Chicago: University of Chicago Press.

Tierney, W., & Lincoln, Y. S. (Eds.). (1997). *Representation and the text: Re-framing the narrative voice.* Albany: State University of New York.

Twain, M. (1994). *Literary essays.* New York: Harper & Brothers. (Original work published 1918)

Vargas Llosa, M. (1991). *A writer's reality.* Syracuse, NY: Syracuse University Press.

Vargas Llosa, M. (2002). *Letters to a young novelist* (N. Wimmer, Trans.). New York: Farrar, Straus and Giroux.

Watson, T. (2000). Ethnographic fiction science: Making sense of managerial work and organizational research with Caroline and Terry. *Organization, 7*(3), 489–510.

Weiss, J. (Ed.). (1991). *Writing at risk: Interviews in Paris with uncommon writers.* Iowa City: University of Iowa Press.

14

Literary Forms

ASTONISHING SILENCE

Knowing in Poetry

◆ Carl Leggo

I live in the world as a poet. I spend a part of most days in reading and writing poetry, in the practice of poetry, even in the experience of poetic living. I am constantly vigilant about seeing the world with a poet's senses and heart and imagination. I didn't write poetry in school. I didn't even like poetry very much. I was long out of school when I began to write poetry, well into my twenties when I discovered the pleasures and possibilities of poetic language. For the past two decades I have been writing poetry as a way to know the world, as a way to be and become in the world.

Poetry invites us to experiment with language, to create, to know, to engage creatively and imaginatively with experience. Winterson (1995) makes a bold claim that "it is the poet who goes further than any human scientist" (p. 115). As a poet, I am eager, in some ways, to embrace Winterson's claim, but I don't really want to argue that the poet goes further than the human scientist because I prefer to make the claim that the poet *is* a human scientist. I am interested in examining the places where poetry and human science research intersect, especially regarding philosophies, perspectives, and practices. Where many human science researchers focus on research questions and methods, conclusions and implications, as a poet I am often more intrigued with how language works to open up possibilities for constructing understanding. Therefore, I work with language in the kinds of ways that a sculptor works with stone, wood, bone, ice, steel, and bronze.

This essay is shaped out of citations, exposition, narration, poetry, and rumination in order to evoke a textual space for both invitation and provocation. It is my hope that this essay, by performing an artful work of words, will invite readers to ruminate on their conceptions of experience and researching experience, especially in the tangled complexity of each day's demands.

As a poet and social science researcher, the most pressing question I know is the epistemological question, "How do I know what I know?" Winterson (1995) reminds me that language lives, and she warns that "a writer must resist the pressure of old formulae and work towards new combinations of language" (p. 76). Like all language use, poetry is epistemological and ontological. Poetry reminds me that everything is constructed in language; our experiences are all epistemologically and ontologically composed and understood in words, our words and others' words. Mills (1997) notes that "the only way we have to apprehend reality is through discourse and discursive structures" (p. 54). We write the world, individually and corporately. Poetry reminds me to challenge the dominant discourses that are typically propagated and supported by school and university curricula and pedagogy. Inspired by poetry, I seek to write in diverse discourses that are alternative, creative, and unconventional.

I am committed to exploring the lively intersections between critical discourse and creative discourse. Too often in the academy, the creative arts are separated from the social science disciplines. My goal is to open up spaces for the creative arts to inform social science research. As a poet-educator-scholar,

I research and teach the composition and rhetoric of poetry as creative writing, and the curriculum and pedagogy of poetry as literature, as well as how to use poetry in social science research.

Like Pelias (2004), my research and writing begin "in the desire to write from the heart" and to practice research that does not hide "behind the illusion of objectivity," but instead seeks to create "an emotionally vulnerable, linguistically evocative, and sensuously poetic voice" (p. 1). And like Pelias, I "want a scholarship that fosters connections, opens spaces for dialogue, heals" (p. 2). Therefore, much like Whyte (1994), who seeks "to bring the insights of the poetic imagination out of the garret and into the boardrooms and factory floors of America" (p. 10), I am part of an extensive network of poets and researchers who are working to bring the wisdom of poetry and poetic knowing into human science research (Brady, 2000; Butler-Kisber, 2002; Cahnmann, 2003; Cannon Poindexter, 2002; Dunlop, 2004; Finley, 2000, 2003; Glesne, 1997; Hayes-Percer, 2002; Hurren, 1998; Luce-Kapler, 2003; Moody, 2001; Neilsen, 2004; Norman, 2001; Öhlen, 2003; Piirto, 2002a, 2002b; Prendergast, 2006; L. Richardson, 1992, 1994, 1997; M. Richardson, 1998; W. Smith, 2002; Sullivan, 2000; Thomas, 2004).

◆ What Is a Poem?

Poetry (from the Greek *poiein*, to make) creates or makes the world in words. Poetry calls attention to itself as text, as rhetorical device and stratagem. Poetry does not invite readers to consume the text as if it were a husk that contains a pithy truth. Poetry is not a window on the world. Poetry invites us to listen. Poetry is a site for dwelling, for holding up, for stopping. Poetry prevails against hermeneutic exhaustion, hermeneutic consumption, hermeneutic closure, hermeneutic certainty. Poetry is not hermetic. A poem is a textual event, an "act of literature," an experience of spelling and spells. Derrida (1992) suggests that "every poem has its own language, it is one time alone its own language, even and especially if several languages are able to cross there" (p. 409).

Poetry is about rhythm (from the Greek *rhythmos:* measure or measured motion). Rhythm is the relation of part to part and of parts to the whole. It is balance, the flowing of blood, breath, breathing, not breathtaking but breathgiving. Rhythm is the measure of speech, of the heart, of dancing, of the seasons, knowing the living word, the energy of language to inscribe, inspirit hope, even in the midst of each day's wild chaos. As Haase and Large (2001) propose, "in the informational model of language, the spoken or written word is merely a vehicle for the meaning that it conveys" (p. 27), but "in literature it is not only the meaning of words which matters, but their texture, which is to say their rhythm, color and style, none of which can be reduced to an item of information" (p. 28). For so much of my life I have hurried here and there, out of breath. In poetry I am learning to breathe. As Kingston (2002) concludes, "I've discovered what stanza breaks are for. In the space, breathe. Before and after the poem, breathe" (p. 80). Instead of living breathlessly, I am learning to live breath-fully.

Poetry creates textual spaces that invite and create ways of knowing and becoming in the world. Poetry invites interactive responses—intellectual, emotional, spiritual, and aesthetic responses. Poetry invites a way of uniting the heart, mind, imagination, body, and spirit. As a poet I grow more and more enamored with the echoes of wonder, mystery, and silence that I hear when I attend to the words and world all around me.

Steffler (1995) claims that poetry "reorganizes and deepens our awareness of our past experience and kindles our appetite for future experience. It sharpens our sense of vitality and mortality" (p. 49). In a similar way, Griffin (1995) contends that "poetry does not describe. It *is* the thing. It is an experience, not the secondhand record of an experience, but the experience itself" (p. 191). Steffler (1995) asks:

What, ideally, can poetry offer that other types of writing cannot offer, or at least not so directly or purely? It seems to me that at its best—and this is what we search for in poems all the time—poetry approximates, through the powerful use of language, our fundamental, original sense of life's miraculousness, its profound and mysterious meaning. (p. 47)

The poet always understands that she or he is located in a complex space and time. The poet's commitment entails a zeal for attending, and questioning, and perceiving.

Poetic knowing has been too much ignored in human science research. Labouvie-Vief (1994) presents a useful perspective on philosophy as constructed in Western scholarship:

Western intellectual tradition has brought us a separation of two aspects of mind and self. On the one hand, there is the realm of *logos*—the realm of logic and objectivity, of all that can be stated in terms of rational truths, of our hope that life can be reduced to laws that are mechanical and precise. On the other hand, there is the realm of *mythos*—the realm of all that is felt and organic, of all that appeals to the inner world of emotions, of our tendency to leap out of the constraints of analytical precision and to seize the novel. (p. 1)

Woolf (1976) echoes this perspective:

> I feel that strong emotion must leave its trace; and it is only a question of discovering how we can get ourselves again attached to it, so that we shall be able to live our lives through from the start. (p. 67)

Poetry involves seeking ways to attach ourselves to strong emotion. As a poet, I know that I live consciously and constantly in my emotions. I am seeking to live poetically, and that means living emotionally with my feelings in motion and commotion.

My poems are part of an ongoing engagement with living in the world. As Mills (1997) notes, "discourses structure both our sense of reality and our notion of our own identity" (p. 15). Our understanding, interpretations, responses, thoughts, and actions are all constructed and constrained by the discursive patterns and frames that society permits and authorizes, on the one hand, and excludes and prohibits, on the other. Our life work, our living work is to challenge these discursive patterns in well-crafted and courageous writing, to recognize "how singularly words, speech, language, and phrase shape consciousness and define reality" (Brueggemann, 2001, p. 64). We need imagination to break out of the stereotypes and to create other possibilities. Freire (1997) echoes my convictions regarding the creative potential of all people to compose their lives with imagination. Freire reminds us that "a total denouncement of fatalism is necessary. We are transformative beings and not beings for accommodation" (p. 36). Effectively we are presented with images of who we are and who we can become, but we are not constrained to imitate those images in a slavish way like we are painting a portrait with a paint-by-numbers kit. We have far more

freedom and will and energy for inventing ourselves and our places in the world.

As Lee (1995) confesses, "if you knew what a given poem was, you could just write it down. But you're responding to something you feel claimed by, but can't yet articulate, or maybe even identify" (p. 31). Poetry is a way of knowing, being, and becoming in the world. Poetry begins with attentiveness, imagination, mystery, enchantment. Poetry invites researchers to experiment with language, to create, to know, to engage creatively and imaginatively with experience. The poet-researcher seeks to live attentively in the moment, to know the momentousness of each moment, to seek to enter lived experiences with a creative openness to people and experiences and understandings.

In poetry I am not trying to close anything down; I am not trying to understand everything; I am not seeking control. Instead, I am open to the world, open to process and mystery, open to fragmentariness, open to understanding as an archipelago of fragments. This does not mean I am not trying to make connections in understanding, but I am no longer pretending that I understand what I do not know. I am fundamentally *agnostic,* knowing above all that there is much I do not know and will never likely know.

◆ How Does Poetry Inform Social Science Research?

The only way I can answer a question like "How does poetry inform social science research?" is to invite readers to attend to exemplars of the many ways that poetry has been used in social science research. Of course, in the creative and imaginative ways of poets, there will be many more uses of poetry in future research as well. I am currently collaborating with M. Prendergast, who is conducting a postdoctoral research project (funded by the Social Sciences and Humanities Research Council of Canada, May 2006 to April 2008) into poetic inquiry practices in qualitative research in the social sciences.

One goal of Prendergast's research is to compose *a critical anthology of poetic forms of inquiry* (an explanation of this timely and comprehensive research project is available at http://www.ccfi.educ.ubc. ca/people/M_Prendergast.html). Prendergast reports that she plans to complete the project by the spring of 2008, but already (in 2006) she has compiled an annotated bibliography of almost 200 citations of research publications that include poetry in a wide range of disciplines including education, anthropology, sociology, psychology, cultural studies, geography, social work, nursing, health, administration, and urban planning.

Prendergast notes that researchers engaging in poetic forms use a *diverse number of terms* to describe their methods: research poetry (Cannon Poindexter, 2002); data poetry (Commeyras & Montsi, 2000); poetic representation (L. Richardson, 1994, 1997); poetic transcription and poetic narrative (Glesne, 1997); anthropological poetry (Brady, 2000); narrative poetry (Tedlock, 1983); aesthetic social science (M. Richardson, 1998); poetic, fictional narrative (P. Smith, 1999); ethnopoem (W. Smith, 2002); transcript poems (Santoro & Kamler, 2001); map-poems (Hurren, 1998); poetic condensation of oral narratives (Öhlen, 2003); and fieldnote poems (Cahnmann, 2003).

Not only is Prendergast documenting the surprising robustness of poetry in social science research, but she is also contributing significantly to understanding the critical questions and challenges that poet-researchers are addressing in this relatively recent but rapidly evolving research enterprise.

In my collaboration with Prendergast, I am again and again reminded that poetry is a discursive practice, a learned craft that uses language. As a discursive practice, poetry often seems alien to many researchers because most of us have had few opportunities to write poetry. Simply, most researchers have learned the craft of the five-paragraph expository essay built firmly on a logical and linear structure, but they have not learned how to write poetry. Like any discursive practice, poetry is constructed and constrained by conventions, rules, expectations, devices, and tropes. A useful starting place for understanding poetry is that everything in a poem can have significance. Where prose often seems transparent and is taken for granted, poetry invites the writer and the reader to pay attention to the semiotics of figurative language, sound effects, texture, voice, rhythm, shape on the page, line breaks, and stanzaic structure. In a poem, everything signifies.

As a poet and language educator, I am often asked, "*Is this a good poem?*" as if I carry some kind of standard measuring device for assessing the value of poems. But perhaps the important question is not "*Is this a good poem?*" but instead "*What is a poem good for?*" Kingsolver (2002) claims that "poems are everywhere, but easy to miss" (p. 229). We bear the rhythms of poetry in our blood, constantly in motion with the heart's beating. Poems tell stories, reflect on lived experiences, express political manifestos, recount versions of history, and tease the imagination to distraction.

With keen insight Griffin (1995) asks, "What is it that makes poetry different than prose" (p. 189)? She writes:

It is said that poetry has rhyme, and rhythm, and line breaks, that it uses metaphor. But these distinctions have never seemed sufficient to me. They seem instead only to be symptomatic of a deeper-lying purpose. It is said that prose is rational and poetry is not. And yet, on one level, poetry is quite rational. (p. 189)

Researchers who want to learn the craft of writing poetry need to make the same kind of commitment to reading and writing and studying poetry that they have typically made to learning the craft of writing prose. And above all, they need to be ready to play with the possibilities of language. Poetry is always transcending rhetorical patterns, forms, and designs.

With regard to the use of poetry in research, there are many questions and issues to be addressed, and these issues are being addressed by many researchers, especially those connected with arts-based research (Barone, 2001; Barone & Eisner, 1997; Bochner, 2000; Butler-Kisber, 2002; Cahnmann, 2003; Cole & Knowles, 2001; Cole & McIntyre, 2004; Dunlop, 2004; Eisner, 1997, 2004; Finley, 2000, 2003; Hayes-Percer, 2002; Irwin & de Cosson, 2004; Leggo, 1999, 2003, 2004; Luce-Kapler, 2003; Neilsen, 2004; Norman, 2001; Piirto, 2002a, 2002b; Prendergast, 2006). The kinds of questions addressed by these social science researchers include: (1) What does poetry as research look like? (2) What does research informed by poetry look like? (3) What kinds of questions does poetry as research help to ask, perhaps even answer? (4) How does poetry as research complement or contradict other sorts of social science research? (5) What are some of the main issues and challenges associated with poetry as a research genre? (6) Is any poetry also necessarily research? (7) How can poetry speak to social science inquiry in ways that will have integrity and credibility to others in the field?

These are significant and complex questions, and they will continue to generate lively discussion, but it is not possible to address adequately all these issues in this brief essay. Certainly there are no simple answers. Instead, social science researchers who use poetry in their research will continue to define and transform their theorizing, crafting, and researching with each new project. Piirto (2002a, 2002b) argues insightfully that researchers who are going to use poetry need to learn the craft and art of poetry. I absolutely agree, and I also claim with Piirto that we can learn the art and craft of poetry if we devote ourselves to it. In this regard, perhaps learning to write poetry is not so different from learning to use statistical procedures in research. Each approach assumes that the researcher will learn the tools, strategies, and language to conduct valuable and defensible research.

If researchers want to include poetry in their writing, then they should. And they should work hard at crafting the poems in the same way they work hard at crafting a strong prose sentence. All researchers need to be more attentive to their writing as craft and art. I often recommend to graduate students who want to use poetry in their research to enroll in courses in a creative writing program. And I always encourage all researchers to read lots of poetry. But at the same time, I am concerned that some researchers put poetry on a pedestal as an object for awe-inspiring reverence. I like to stress that poetry is earthy, rooted in everyday experiences, connected integrally to the flow of blood in our bodies, expressed constantly in the rhythms of our speech and embodied movement. So, I claim that we are all poets, but sadly many of us have lost our confidence as poets. We have lost our creative energy for living poetically. Of course, we all need more guidance—all the time.

Scholarly research depends on an extensive network of support and peer review and collaboration. When I submit my essays and poems for publication, they are frequently returned with advice for revision. I look forward to advice from peers. I will never learn all there is to learn about the craft of poetry—not in this short lifetime! Learning the craft is a life-long apprenticeship that involves lots of writing and reading and living. If we think about the prefix "re" in researcher, we understand that our questing/questioning is always a returning, a turning again. This is a ruminative process. In my experience, the poetic process is an experience of lingering with memory and emotion and heart and story, a process of leaning on language in order to seek understanding and wisdom, a process of attending sensually and sensitively to life. The poetic process is a verb, a journey, a flow. Like life; like living. Poetry fosters curiosity, quest(ion)ing, imagination. Too many researchers are looking for answers, and often researchers shape their research goals in ways that can be answered with a sense of resounding conclusion. I prefer to live in/conclusively. Perhaps the questions frequently asked aren't really worth answering!

Poetry is a way of knowing and living, a way of examining lived experiences by attending to issues of identity, relationship, and community. Poetry acknowledges how the heart and imagination are always integral parts of human knowing. Poetry seeks the truth about human experience. The evaluation of the knowledge generated in poetic research will include: a critical investigation of the craft and aesthetics of poetry, a creative examination of the ways that poetry evokes responses and connections, a careful inquiry into the methods that poetry uses to unsettle ossified thinking and provoke imagination, and a conscientious consideration of the resonances that sing out from word to world.

I am caught up in language, in word making, in meaning making, constantly striving to create the world, or at least a sense of place in the world. Like Kingsolver (2002), "my way of finding a place in this world is to write one" (p. 233). Writing is then "about finding a way to be alive" (Kingsolver, 2002, p. 233). Writing does not enable the writer to hammer down secure truth; writing enables the writer to explore possibilities for meaningful living in the world.

As a part of this chapter on poetic knowing in research, I include (and conclude with) an autobiographical poem about the vocation of the teacher. "Left Turns" was written as part of my response to a researcher's question regarding my experience of vocation. I end with the poem because the poem represents, even performs, my researching process. I don't want to explicate the poem. I trust that the poem will invite readers to consider their experiences of vocation, to examine with keener insight the complex convolutions that frequently comprise the surprising twists and turns of lived experience. Poetry is a practice of language and literacy that can foster hope and wisdom for living more effectively and productively in the world. Simply, my claim is that attention to words can open up possibilities for attending to the world and becoming in the world. As an educator and researcher, I am convinced that all of us need to attend to multiple ways of knowing and becoming. We need to acknowledge how we are all interconnected in creating the world by exploring and composing possibilities for living. Poetry offers significant ways for learning and practicing our living in the world. This is my research; this is my poetry.

═ **Left Turns** ═

Corner Brook 1970, 1989
My high school principal said,
You ought to be a teacher.
I said, No way. Almost two
decades faded away. I

circled back to my old school,
the principal was retired, long
gone. I was a teacher, surprised.

St. John's 1970–1976
I never wanted to be a teacher.
I wanted to be an astronomer
and watch the heavens, or
even a poet and write the heavens.
I took a vocational interests inventory.
I learned I ought to be a farrier,
even though I am scared of horses.

Robert's Arm 1976–1978
Broke, I slipped into teaching.
My first year I taught grade seven
with forty-eight students.
I woke up in an alien world,
a small place where everybody
knew God's mind on everything.
I tried to fit in. I didn't fit. I left

Toronto 1978–1979
for the big city, a world alone.
I planned to be a pastor, but
after two months of seminary
like a cemetery, the call passed, now
sure a pastor had to be pasteurized
when I wanted to be impure rough
germy germinating. So, I left

Stephenville 1979–1985
for a little school in a town
on the ocean, a small farm
perhaps, an avocation and a vocation,
where I was determined to fit,
but taught with fire in my eyes
and heart till the school committee
called me dangerous. I was. I left

Fredericton 1985–1987
and left

Edmonton 1987–1989
and left

Corner Brook 1989–1990
and left.

Vancouver 1990–present
Still teaching, I have turned
a circle, round and round,
to know I am a teacher,
a farrier even, who shoes students
in order to shoo them away
with warnings to look both ways
before making left turns.

◆ References

Barone, T. (2001). Science, art, and the pre-dispositions of educational researchers. *Educational Researcher, 30*(7), 24–28.

Barone, T. E., & Eisner, E. (1997). Arts-based educational research. In R. M. Jaeger (Ed.), *Complementary methods for research in education* (2nd ed., pp. 73–99). Washington, DC: American Educational Research Association.

Bochner, A. P. (2000). Criteria against ourselves. *Qualitative Inquiry, 6*(2), 266–272.

Brady, I. (2000). Three Jaguar/Mayan intertexts: Poetry and prose fiction. *Qualitative Inquiry, 6*(1), 58–64.

Brueggemann, W. (2001). *The prophetic imagination.* Minneapolis, MN: Fortress Press.

Butler-Kisber, L. (2002). Artful portrayals in qualitative inquiry: The road to found poetry and beyond. *Alberta Journal of Educational Research, XLVIII*(3), 229–239.

Cahnmann, M. (2003). The craft, practice, and possibility of poetry in educational research. *Educational Researcher, 32*(3), 29–36.

Cannon Poindexter, C. (2002). Research as poetry: A couple experiences HIV. *Qualitative Inquiry, 8*(6), 707–714.

Cole, A. L., & Knowles, J. G. (2001). Qualities of inquiry: Process, form, and "goodness." In L. Neilsen, A. L. Cole, & J. G. Knowles (Eds.), *The art of writing inquiry* (pp. 211–219). Halifax, Nova Scotia, Canada: Backalong Books.

Cole, A. L., & McIntyre, M. (2004). Research as aesthetic contemplation: The role of the audience in research interpretation. *Educational Insights, 9*(1). Retrieved October 1,

2006, from http://www.ccfi.educ.ubc.ca/publication/insights/v09n01/articles/cole.html

Commeyras, M., & Montsi, M. (2000). What if I woke up as the other sex? Batswana youth perspectives on gender. *Gender & Education, 12*(3), 327–347.

Derrida, J. (1992). *Acts of literature* (D. Attridge, Ed.). New York: Routledge.

Dunlop, R. (2004). Lector in fabula: The poet's notebooks. *Language and Literacy, 6*(1). Retrieved October 1, 2006, from http://www.langandlit.ualberta.ca/archivesDate.html

Eisner, E. (1997). The new frontier in qualitative research methodology. *Qualitative Inquiry, 3*(3), 259–273.

Eisner, E. (2004). What can education learn from the arts about the practice of education? *International Journal of Education and the Arts, 5*(4),1–12. Retrieved October 1, 2006, from http://ijea.asu.edu/v5n4/

Finley, S. (2000). Dream child. *Qualitative Inquiry, 6*(3), 432–434.

Finley, S. (2003). Arts-based inquiry in *QI*: Seven years from crisis to guerrilla warfare. *Qualitative Inquiry, 9*(2), 281–296.

Freire, P. (1997). *Pedagogy of the heart* (D. Macedo & A. Oliveira, Trans.). New York: Continuum.

Glesne, C. (1997). That rare feeling: Representing research through poetic transcription. *Qualitative Inquiry, 3*(2), 202–221.

Griffin, S. (1995). *The eros of everyday life: Essays on ecology, gender, and society.* New York: Doubleday.

Haase, U., & Large, W. (2001). *Maurice Blanchot.* London: Routledge.

Hayes-Percer, L. (2002). Going beyond the demonstrable range in educational scholarship: Exploring the intersections of poetry and research. *The Qualitative Report, 7*(2). Retrieved October 1, 2006, from www.nova.edu/ssss/QR/QR7–2/hayespercer.html

Hurren, W. (1998). Living with/in the lines: Poetic possibilities for world writing. *Gender, Place, and Culture, 5*(3), 301–304.

Irwin, R. L., & de Cosson, A. (Eds.). (2004). *A/r/tography: Rendering self through arts-based living inquiry.* Vancouver, British Columbia, Canada: Pacific Educational Press.

Kingsolver, B. (2002). *Small wonder: Essays.* New York: HarperCollins Publishers.

Kingston, M. H. (2002). *To be the poet.* Cambridge, MA: Harvard University Press.

Labouvie-Vief, G. (1994). *Psyche and eros: Mind and gender in the life course.* Cambridge, UK: Cambridge University Press.

Lee, D. (1995). Poetry and unknowing. In T. Lilburn (Ed.), *Poetry and knowing: Speculative essays and interviews* (pp. 29–44). Kingston, Ontario, Canada: Quarry Press.

Leggo, C. (1999). Research as poetic rumination: Twenty-six ways of listening to light. *Journal of Educational Thought, 33*(2), 113–133.

Leggo, C. (2003). Backyard quest(ion)s written in stone and water: Alchemic possibilities in the space of the heart. In E. Hasebe-Ludt & W. Hurren (Eds.), *Curriculum intertext: Place/language/pedagogy* (pp. 131–148). New York: Peter Lang.

Leggo, C. (2004). Tangled lines: On autobiography and poetic knowing. In A. L. Cole, L. Neilsen, J. G. Knowles, & T. C. Luciani (Eds.), *Provoked by art: Theorizing arts-informed research* (pp. 18–35). Halifax, Nova Scotia, Canada: Backalong Books.

Luce-Kapler, R. (2003). Melopoeia: Syncope, interruption, and writing. *Educational Insights, 8*(2). Retrieved October 1, 2006, from http://www.ccfi.educ.ubc.ca/publication/insights/v08n02/contextualexplorations/voices/lucekapler.html

Mills, S. (1997). *Discourse.* London: Routledge.

Moody. R. (2001). Three poems. *crossXconnect, 5*(2). Retrieved October 1, 2006, from http://ccat.sas.upenn.edu/xconnect/v5/i2/t/contents.html

Neilsen, L. (2004). Learning to listen: Data as poetry, poetry as data. *Journal of Critical Inquiry Into Curriculum and Instruction, 5*(2), 40–42.

Norman, R. (2001). *House of mirrors: Performing autobiograph(icall)y in language/education.* New York: Peter Lang.

Öhlen, J. (2003). Evocation of meaning through poetic condensation of narratives in empirical phenomenological inquiry into human suffering. *Qualitative Health Research, 13*(4), 557–566.

Pelias, R. J. (2004). *A methodology of the heart: Evoking academic and daily life.* Walnut Creek, CA: AltaMira Press.

Piirto, J. (2002a). The question of quality and qualifications: Writing inferior poems as qualitative research. *International Journal of Qualitative Studies in Education, 15*(4), 421–445.

Piirto, J. (2002b). The unreliable narrator, or the difference between writing prose in literature and in social science. *International Journal of Qualitative Studies in Education, 15*(4), 407–415.

Prendergast, M. (2006). *Audience in performance: A poetics and pedagogy of spectatorship.* Unpublished doctoral dissertation, University of Victoria, British Columbia, Canada.

Richardson, L. (1992). The consequences of poetic representation: Writing the other, rewriting the self. In C. Ellis and M. Flaherty (Eds.), *Investigating subjectivity: Research on lived experience* (pp. 125–137). London: Sage.

Richardson, L. (1994). Nine poems. *Journal of Contemporary Ethnography, 23*(1), 3–13.

Richardson, L. (1997). *Fields of play: Constructing an academic life.* New Brunswick, NJ: Rutgers University Press.

Richardson, M. (1998). Poetics in the field and on the page. *Qualitative Inquiry, 4*(4), 451–462.

Santoro, N., & Kamler, B. (2001). Teachers talking difference: Teacher education and the poetics of anti-racism. *Teaching Education, 12*(2), 191–212.

Smith, P. (1999). Food Truck's party hat. *Qualitative Inquiry, 5*(2), 244–261.

Smith, W. (2002). Ethno-poetry notes. *International Journal of Qualitative Studies in Education, 15*(4), 461–467.

Steffler, J. (1995). Language as matter. In T. Lilburn (Ed.), *Poetry and knowing: Speculative essays and interviews* (pp. 45–51). Kingston, Ontario, Canada: Quarry Press.

Sullivan, A. M. (2000). The necessity of art: Three found poems from John Dewey's *Art as experience. International Journal of Qualitative Studies in Education, 13*(3), 325–327.

Tedlock, D. (1983). *The spoken word and the work of interpretation.* Philadelphia, PA: University of Philadelphia Press.

Thomas, S. (2004). *Of earth and flesh and bones and breath: Landscapes of embodiment and moments of re-enactment.* Halifax, Nova Scotia, & Toronto, Ontario, Canada: Backalong Books & Centre for Arts-Informed Research.

Whyte, D. (1994). *The heart aroused: Poetry and the preservation of the soul in corporate America.* New York: Doubleday.

Winterson, J. (1995). *Art objects: Essays on ecstasy and effrontery.* Toronto, Ontario, Canada: Alfred A. Knopf Canada.

Woolf, V. (1976). *Moments of being* (J. Schulkind, Ed.). New York: Harcourt Brace Jovanovich.

15

Performance

DANCE, CHOREOGRAPHY, AND SOCIAL SCIENCE RESEARCH

◆ Donald Blumenfeld-Jones

In this chapter, I explore the potential of the art of dance for practicing social science research. Given that mentioning dance automatically brings to mind the body, it is important to note that the body is already present in social science research in a strong line of social science research dealing with and through the body as a social object and a locus of experience. Although this research does not deal with the body as a dance person might, it has brought the body, as a subject worthy of study, into inquiry focus such that there is no need to argue for the place of the body in the social sciences.

Dance as an art form for performing social science research is distinctive from more standard forms of social science research. A dance person focuses on the body not only as an object of inquiry and gaze, but also as the mode of inquiry itself, working from "inside" the body. That is, the dance person doesn't merely analyze bodily action, but puts that analysis into action with her or his own body and studies the actions as a personal affair of motion. Through this "personal affair of motion" the dance person may gain new insights into the meanings in the social scene under investigation, insights available as a direct outcome of having thought through motion. This "thinking through" can be subsequently choreographed and performed for others. These three arenas of dance life (studying human motion through motion, organizing motion into choreography, and performing the choreography for others) comprise the world of being a dance artist. The notions forwarded in this chapter are based on this arena.

For the dance person, being both an analytic instrument and an analyst and being concerned with art are of greatest importance. Although other social scientists, such as the ethnographer, may also be understood in this way, the dance person also manipulates motion in the pursuit of art. In this regard, there is a lessening of the usual distance between the researcher and what is researched. And even in cases such as Frigga Haug and her colleagues' memory work (1987) investigating their own bodily experiences in learning to become women, which makes their work highly personal and similarly begins in the personal, they are not concerned with art. So, the dance person is unique in focusing upon aesthetics and the personal as well as social understanding.

What does "inside the body" mean? In dance terms, the person functions from an interior working of bodily material for the purpose of understanding both the movement being performed and the meaning of the movement within the context of the "topic" of the dance. Perhaps the dance researchers are interested in understanding what it is like to navigate the terrain of an office space. They would study how various people move in that space and would take the movement back to the studio and begin to dance that material as dance material. They would objectify their stance toward the material in order to be able to work with it, understanding how body weight is used, how long sitting might

affect mobility, how some people are always moving rather than sitting, and so forth.

The movement/bodily material with which they are working is ultimately experienced as both an inside state of awareness and an outside view of what dancers are doing with their body. Because it is their body, the material is simultaneously personal, and they do not claim the people in the setting are experiencing in this way. They develop understanding about states of mind and body as the movement unfolds in them. The scene is recreated not to represent experience but to find aesthetic insight about the experience that is different from other sorts of insights. If, during the making and performance of the work, they reflect upon their own culture and how this is affecting the dance that is being made and performed, then they have, once again, stepped outside the movement to understand it.

This inside-experiencing/outside-observing vibration is the interaction between bodily experience and objective art making, primarily body based, that brings forth the dance. Both poles of experience are needed. It is this complexity that makes using dance for social science inquiry distinctive. As a demurral to an insistence upon art, it is possible to cultivate a dance sensibility as a supplement to standard forms of research. This will be discussed later in this chapter.

◆ The Terrain of Dance

In this section, the practice of dance is considered in more detail. In particular, analogies are made between the practice of choreography and the practice of research. In this way, the potential for dance and choreography is examined.

CHOREOGRAPHY AS A VENUE OF RESEARCH

Although I have written of "dance," the potential of dance for research lies not in dancing but in the act of choreography. The fact is that dancers represent a choreographer's ideas to the choreographer, but it is the choreographer who composes, either creating movement to be performed or shaping movement that is elicited from the dancers. The line between dancer and choreographer is, to be sure, blurred. As dancers move, they bring new ideas to the choreographer and, in making real the choreographer's movements that were previously in the mind or were worked out on the choreographer's body, the choreographer sees what is actually possible as opposed to what is only, originally, conceptually possible. Only through this actualization does knowledge emerge; form and knowledge are inseparable. In this account, therefore, the relationship is: The dancers' dancing is crucial, and it is the choreographer who decides what is in and what is out, how to perform something and how not to perform it and so on.

The choreographer researches a theme at hand, either by performing standard background research (literature review, examination of primary documents including photographs, film, etc.) or by spending time within an environment and responding motionally to it, or both. Having done this preparatory work of paying attention in other than a dance setting, the choreographer develops the motional, spatial, and temporal themes of the dance either alone or with dancers, and then begins to compose the movements for the dance. How might this be used in social science research?

Returning to the office experience, the choreographer stylizes motions found in the office, experimenting with forms of exaggeration: changing a normal walk covering normal space to small steps and covering no space, moving everything very quickly to staying frozen in a chair for what seems an interminable amount of time. Through such space, time, motion manipulations the choreographer seeks motions that will feel right to her or him within the context of the dance being conceptualized. In brief, the choreographer analyzes the observed world, has a motional response, and interprets and rearranges the world through motion. Finally, the choreographer teaches the movements to the dancers.

The research process continues. The choreographer watches the dancers' movements and makes alterations until the dance meets the choreographer's interpretation of the phenomenon in which she or he is interested. The choreographer may ask the dancers to compose some movements, but in the end the choreographer determines what to use, what to discard, and how to shape what is used. As an example, Phyllis Lamhut, in composing one of her dances, asked us to improvise a "pile of grief." We didn't know what that meant, and Lamhut had only a vague idea. We made motions together that, we hoped, would carry some essence of a "pile of grief." After we had done some work, she asked us to repeat motions together that she thought were particularly what she sought. She watched, we danced, she saw, she and we remembered, we re-danced, and so, we built up together a "pile of grief." It was her conception ("a pile of grief") that began the work; it was she who saw what worked in reference to that conception; they were her instructions that guided us to shape the material until we had achieved what she sought, a "pile of grief."

Certainly we were crucial to the process, the practice was rewarding, and we felt quite central to her work. Nevertheless, she made the work, and we provided material for her to shape. We provided the data, she performed the analysis, and she made the final conclusion: Ah yes, that's it, a "pile of grief." She needed to understand how to dance, and dancing is certainly pertinent to our discussion, but the actions we associate with research (data gathering, data analysis, data patterning, and so forth) lie in the hands of the choreographer, not the dancers. It is to the choreographer that we should be turning our attention, with the understanding that the choreographer is also a dancer who understands movement in time, space, and shape.

MOVEMENT AS THE CENTRAL MODE OF DANCING

Although it may seem obvious to state that movement is what makes dance a unique art form, it is worth explaining this idea in more detail.

All dance is based in everyday movement. Whether it is a balletic *pas de chat*, Martha Graham's contraction series, or Luigi's jazz style, all these highly complex and difficult movements are based on the natural capacities of the human body to bend in certain ways and not in others. A dancer's extraordinary movements are achieved either because of natural capacities beyond the reach of many people or because she or he has cultivated the normal capacities through strenuous work. In both cases, the dancer is only exaggerating what is already potentially possible. Further, the *battement* of ballet, Graham's twisted fourth position of Graham technique, and the Balinese stylization of arms are no different from a casual stroll down the street, if while strolling, the walker is paying attention to motion in time and space and the shape of the body and the energy being used. That is, dancing is not

about specialized movement: Dancing is about paying attention to movement in a thorough manner within these four areas: space, time, shape, and motion (Blumenfeld-Jones, 2004a).

Dancers and choreographers develop refined understandings of these basic elements. As dancers walk forward in space, covering space in a specific manner, they must be conscious of this fact and show that consciousness as opposed to simply moving forward. As dancers walk forward, they do so through time. Time is nothing more than duration: how long it takes to perform a certain action. Dancers pay attention to such duration, whether in a music environment or in silence. Time can be rhythmically experienced. It can also be experienced as slow or fast motion in which all of the ratios of speed of movements, one to the other, are correct in time, but the people observing the movements are living at a different overall speed and observe, therefore, perceiving the dancer as if underwater or in a Keystone Cops chase scene. Time can be fast time and slow time: Both the viewer and the dancer are living in the same time frame, but time feels as if it has slowed down. From everyday life we have the adage "time flies when you're having fun." Conversely, we experience boredom, and time, suddenly, slows down and inches along microscopically.

Shape and motion are linked ideas. Shape, in dance terms, is arrested motion. In holding a shape, dancers must always have the feeling that they could move at any moment; a vibratory tension keeps the shape alive and ready and is experienced by the viewer as such. In terms of social science research, this can be a valuable idea since, as we observe people in a setting who are not moving, we can discern the kind of energy with which they are occupying their bodies and which can, in turn, help us understand something about what is occurring. If people have a "dead" look about them while not moving, we can distinguish this from an engaged look about them as they are not moving. This references Rudolph von Laban's (1975) idea of energy.

Motion focuses not on movements but rather on the "itinerary of movement" (Alwin Nikolais in Siegel, 1971). Movement is moving from point A to point B, but motion is paying attention to the many ways to get from point A to point B. Applying this to social science research, it matters very much how the subject of a study moves from the table in a restaurant to the bar area, which affects the possible implications of that motional itinerary for the experience of the social scene. It matters very much how legislators move through their legislative buildings and deliberation spaces, and who arrays themselves where and the kind of "body language" they employ as they pursue their negotiations.

DANCE AS A
FORM OF RESEARCH

Social science researchers and choreographers are both interested in extending our understanding of some aspect of our social experience (politics, social groupings, culture, and more). Choreographers do so, however, against the taken-for-granted notion that the inquirers should, as much as possible, remove themselves from the object of their inquiry in order to prevent their prejudices from interfering with understanding (Cancienne & Snowber, 2003). In recognizing that the dances they make are very much their view of the social scene, they are under no constraints to be either "true" to the scholarship around the scene or fairly represent various viewpoints. Their task is to compose choreography that, to the best of their abilities, offers the viewer an understanding of the viewpoint informing the

presented dance. However, it would be wrong to think that the heart of dance making is the promotion of a viewpoint per se. At the heart of dance making is the kinesthetic response the choreographer has to the social scene and what Barone (2006) felicitously terms "enhancing ambiguity." That is, the best dances help us think about a phenomenon without telling us what to think about the phenomenon.

The kinesthetic response is also important for the audience. Viewing dance is not an intellectual experience (even though the intellect may be engaged at some points by the choreography) but an immediate, sensory experience of and through movement encounter. What knowledge eventuates from experiencing the dance is nondiscursive, even if the dance may be discussed postperformance. What is "at work" in the dance is the motion and how it feels as one creates it, performs it, and watches it.

The kinesthetic response is at the heart of how we must think about the uses of dance for social science research. Without considering the centrality of the kinesthetic experience, dance has no unique place in social science research. What could be garnered through dance could be more effectively garnered without it through other means. What dance has to contribute to social science research is an understanding of the meaning of human movement as a phenomenological experience and as a way of making sense of what the researchers encounter in the field that cannot be made sense of in other ways. That is, what can be discovered by the researcher as dancer can only be discovered through the agency of dancing and organizing dancing (choreographing).

There are immediate implications in the above for using dance to perform social science research. At the very least, researchers must develop their kinesthetic capacities in order to "see" the kinesthesia of the situation. To use dance beyond this, they must develop the skill of dancing and choreography in order to find meaning in the situation and to communicate their understanding through the choreography, just as persons who would perform sociological or anthropological research must develop themselves as sociologists or anthropologists. Dance is no less a rigorous practice of inquiry into the world than are the more standard forms of social science research. Rigor requires study and the development of good judgment based on experience and education (either formal or informal or a combination of the two). Dance, no less than other forms of research, should be pursued as a practice, vigorously.

◆ Social Science Research and Dance

In this section two directions are offered for the use of dance in social science research. First, dance may be used as supplemental knowledge for social scientists as they explore events in a social scene by sensitizing them to the movement and the ways in which space, time, and dynamics are played out in the scene. Second, social scientists may actually use dance activity to explore meanings from the social scene and to represent the research in formal, public displays. In both cases, the focus is on what can be termed "pedestrian movement," meaning the "everyday" movement we use to live our lives.

The supplementalist explores the everyday movement for understanding and the choreographer transforms it into dance. Choreographically, the movement may be changed into more stylized forms or not changed at all but only closely attended and performed; both are dance. As already stated, this is at the heart of the dance art: paying attention to our motion. This suggests

that forms of dance art that rely on already existing motion vocabularies (ballet, Graham, Humphrey-Weidman, jazz) are not useful for social science research (although they might make great art). Since the data for dance social science research are the movements of people in the social scene under investigation, it follows that you must begin with that material. Everything that follows in this chapter is based in that premise.

DANCE AS SUPPLEMENTAL KNOWLEDGE

The use of movement as raw data for understanding human beings is not a new idea. Ray Birdwhistell (1970) studied human movement cross-culturally, treating such movement as equally "cultural" with clothing, language, food, shelter, and so on. Hugh Mehan (1992) videotaped children in reading groups and then analyzed their movements to better understand how they negotiated the learning that was occurring. The basic datum was motion, key to cultural life (Birdwhistell, 1970) or states of mind (Mehan, 1992). A social scientist can use dance understanding to become sensitized to motion as part of a meaning making apparatus utilized to negotiate the terrain of social life.

In order to accomplish such awareness of the possible meanings of various body states, social scientists might study dance, as a practice and experience, to become aware of the possible kinds of bodily states associated with various emotional states of affair. From within their own cultural frame they can learn experientially about the physical dynamics of bodily experience: the weight of the body, how the body moves (fluidly, haltingly, aggressively, timidly, lightly, breathily, etc.), how bodies interact with each other, how time is experienced (as described earlier), how stillness versus moving is experienced, and more. Through this learning, social scientists are sensitized to include such "information" in their "data set." This is both a psychological matter and allows cultural knowledge to surface that might ordinarily escape notice.

If, as Bourdieu (1971) asserts, culture permeates our very bodies, then understanding bodies becomes an important component of the repertoire of knowledge that a social scientist possesses. At the same time, a focus upon the limitations of one's own cultural understanding in making sense of another is crucial. Birdwhistell (1970) noted that there are no universal human movements that mean the same thing no matter what the culture. Great care must be taken lest facile psychological conclusions are developed. Dance, as with any other form of social science research, cannot stand alone in developing understanding. Inquiries of interlocuters must be made. However, even these inquiries cannot assure that the conclusions made will be "correct." Boddy (1990), in studying pharonic circumcision in the Sudan, showed that what the Sudanese professed to be the meaning of the practice did not reveal the deeper ways in which the practice functioned as a summative symbol of their lives. It remained central to their lives despite international pressure to desist. In like fashion, although there might be no final conclusions about the meaning of movement, dance can contribute a sensitization to the ways in which movement means.

DANCE TO EXPLORE SOCIAL MEANINGS

In the supplemental approach, the social scientist, through personal practice and other sorts of study, becomes conversant with how to look at a social scene from a movement perspective. New data emerge through this looking. Similarly, using dance as a means of exploring meanings in a social scene begins in such looking. These observed movements become the basis for enacting, in one's own body, the movement of another. There is no pretence that the dancer is actually replicating the experience of the other. Rather, the dance artist is making sense of what she or he experiences, and if that sense-making begins to deliver insights into the other person who is the original maker of the motion (albeit an unwitting maker in that, for the most part, people do not think about how they are moving and what their bodily movements might mean), then something new is discovered about that original movement that was not previously available.

The work of the choreographer was discussed in an earlier section. In this section, a more intimate look at choreography is necessary. In the German expressionist tradition of modern dance (developed by Mary Wigman, Hanya Holm, Rudolph Laban, and Kurt Joos) the choreographer's task is to find the essence of a human experience in its motional life. Rather than making a dance about "young love" by having dancers mime the relationship, the choreographer begins with recalling her or his young love, speaking with others about their young love and then placing her- or himself in that inner state of young love. Composing motion begins out of that inner state. Bodily decisions are made (rather than intellectual decisions), building phrases of dancing and linking those phrases together for longer action. Having developed a motional vocabulary appropriate to the situation, the choreographer begins actually making motions that the dancer or dancers will learn and reproduce, organizing the moving dancers in space, either aligning the dance with sound accompaniment or working through silence and bringing in sound later (or not).

Attending to the emerging ideas about "young love," the choreographer focuses equal amounts of attention on the motion as motion, on spatial placement as spatial placement, on how time is used (rhythmic time, other sorts of duration). The dance does not merely reproduce the actions of young lovers but reorganizes actions and motions within aesthetic choices having to do with the elements of dance itself. "I am making a dance having to do with 'young love.' Whatever I do, as long as I keep that in mind, my choices are bound to speak to 'young love' even if they are not obvious or conventional choices."

Writing of choreography in this way returns us to consider how dance might be used to make sense of a social phenomenon. At this point, my own experience as a choreographer may be pertinent for the discussion. Allow me, therefore, to describe two of my dances.

The first dance was entitled *Sneakers*. I had observed the importance of sneakers to the generation of students I was teaching and decided to create a dance about sneakers. I began with that insight and the knowledge that young people were stealing other young people's shoes, extorting the shoes, or even killing someone for their shoes. As I began to choreograph, I developed the image of people jealously guarding their sneakers by having the dancers in the wings make a quiet roar that rose in loudness until the sound exploded and the dancers threw their sneakers out of the wings, so that they landed in a scattered pile. The dancers stalked out (I invited them to invent their own version of "stalking out"), glared at each other and looked for their own sneakers by circling and moving around the pile. Once found, they all stood rigidly, still glaring at each other, and then returned quickly back to the wings. This event was repeated, and then

upon retrieving their sneakers, they began a dance of a strong herd of animals, carrying their sneakers in their hands, moving on a diagonal in the space, using thrusting actions, then circling back to the top of the diagonal and doing it again.

In another section, two of the dancers performed a duel with their sneakers in hand while the others sat at the edge of the performing space, encouraging them with animal sounds and strong gestures. In the last section, I constructed a very large wooden sneaker upon which one dancer stood, rooted in her feet to the sneaker while the other dancers performed a ritual of homage, fear, and finally, exhaustion, collapsing in a circle on the edges of the wooden sneaker, with the dancer on the sneaker collapsing forward in a sprawl as if dead.

This dance dealt with the ritualization of clothing as social marker, the guarding of identity situated in the sneakers, and the ferocity of contemporary social life. In the beginning I didn't know that the dance would deal with those ideas; they emerged through the process of choreography. The ferocity manifested itself on a very personal level and came to me during the composing of the dance. Although I was aware of the news stories about people being killed for their sneakers, the understanding of what this meant on a more personal level only became available through the practice of choreography. The movement vocabulary was mostly "pedestrian" movement, but then organized through space/time/shape/energy considerations.

The dance was done in silence except for dancers vocalizing and the sound of their bodies and the sneakers falling and the like. I had the dancers carry the sneakers and not wear them in order to give greater focus on the sneakers by displacing them from their normal use. In so doing, I was afforded greater inventiveness about what I could do with the sneakers. This dance is an example of an art form being used to explore a social phenomenon, focused on a contemporary situation of the time (my interest in sneakers stemmed from the news stories about sneakers).

A second dance is entitled *Passing Away.* This solo dance dealt with the death of my grandparents within 6 months of each other. Initially I struggled for many weeks, unable to make motion that spoke of what I felt. I had been shocked by my grandfather's death and not so by my grandmother 6 months later but, nevertheless, deeply saddened. One day I came upon the idea of recreating the phone call from my father telling me of my grandfather's death. It was a brief scenario: The phone rang, my father asked me if I was sitting down, told me my grandfather had died, I was speechless, thanked him for calling, hung up, and sobbed.

The motions and words became the basis for part of the dance. I began by walking down stage toward a table, dressed in street clothing carrying a bag with dance clothing. I sat at the table, heard the phone ring (there was no real phone on the table), answered the phone, enacted the scenario and left immediately into the wings. I proceeded up to the far end of the wings, emerged, walked down stage and repeated the scenario. I did this over and over again but each time I altered the scenario, using fast time, slow time, and the like. I exaggerated motions and changed dynamics, making the dance increasingly abstract.

After the second iteration I emerged from the wings dressed in dance clothing, not even carrying the bag. Over and over again I did this, and then crossed to the top of the other side of the stage and performed an abstract sequence of motion that, in the German Expressionist tradition, derived from what it felt like to grieve. This, too, I danced over and over in different time and energy frames.

I alternated (now never leaving the stage) from one side of the stage to the other, doing the scenario or the abstract sequence in unpredictable order. Finally, for the end of the dance, I crossed to the table from the abstract side of the stage, grabbed the imaginary phone while standing, yelled into it "I don't want to hear it" and the lights blacked out. This dance dealt with the grinding, repetitive character of grief.

I consider both of these dances to be examples of how a choreographer can explore a social phenomenon and discover new elements about it.

◆ Conclusion

It was mentioned earlier that for dance to be useful, the researcher must pursue a vigorous education in dance. I would argue that this education must be of a certain kind. As written earlier, most dance traditions are not useful for social science research because they are circumscribed by a specific vocabulary. This may make them good for making art but not necessarily for understanding human motion in general. Such understanding is crucial; otherwise, the motion of the social scene is invisible. For dance to be useful, the researcher must be dedicated to developing a kinesthetic sense. This sense can only be developed outside of a concern for making beautiful art.

In a contradictory sense, using dance as a primary mode of social science research involves, in this author's estimation, a focus on art. Dance is, first and foremost, an art form. To reap the benefits from employing an art form, the art needs to be practiced. It is not necessary for every "dance as social science research" to be great art (in terms of aspiring to a professional life on the stage), but it is necessary that the focus be on the art aspect, not on the research aspect, of the idea. The insights discovered through the practice of dance as an art form are only available through that practice, and the practice focuses on making art, not on coming to understand. To consider using dance as a primary mode of research, persons must first develop themselves as artists, understanding that the practice of art is, in many ways, no different from the practice of research (Blumenfeld-Jones, 2002, 2004a, 2004b). There are not many social scientists who are also well-educated dance artists, and without such grounding, the concern is that the emerging art will be poor and nothing significant can be gained from it. This chapter ends on a strong cautionary note, but it is hoped that, taken seriously, there might be those who persist in their interest and develop an approach consonant with these ideas.

◆ References

Barone, T. (2006). Making educational history: Qualitative inquiry, artistry, and the public interest. In G. Ladsen-Billings & W. F. Tate (Eds.), *Education research in the public interest* (pp. 213–230). New York: Teachers College Press.

Birdwhistell, R. (1970). *Kinesics and context: Essays on body motion communication.* Philadelphia: University of Pennsylvania Press.

Blumenfeld-Jones, D. S. (2002). If I could have said it, I would have. In C. Bagley and M. B. Cancienne (Eds.), *Dancing the data* (pp. 90–104). New York: Peter Lang.

Blumenfeld-Jones, D. S. (2004a). Bodily-kinesthetic intelligence and the democratic ideal. In J. Kinchloe (Ed.), *Revisiting Gardner.* New York: Peter Lang.

Blumenfeld-Jones, D. S. (2004b). Hogan dreams. *Qualitative Inquiry, 10*(3), 316–388.

Boddy, J. (1990). *Wombs and alien spirits: Women, men, and the Zar cult in northern Sudan.* Madison: University of Wisconsin Press.

Bourdieu, P. (1971). *Outline of a theory of practice.* Cambridge, UK: University of Cambridge Press.

Cancienne, M. B., & Snowber, C. (2003). Writing rhythm: Movement as method. *Qualitative Inquiry, 9*(2), 237–253.

Haug, F. (Ed.). (1987). *Female sexulation: A collective work of memory.* London: Verso.

Laban, R. von (1975). *Laban's principles of dance and movement notation* (2nd ed., R. Lange, Ed.). Boston: Plays.

Mehan, H. (1992). Why I like to look: On the use of videotape as an instrument in educational research. In M. Schratz (Ed.), *Qualitative voices in research.* New York: Falmer Press.

Siegel, M. (Ed.). (1971). *Nik: A documentary.* New York: Dance Perspectives.

16

Performance

PERFORMATIVE INQUIRY

Embodiment and Its Challenges

◆ Ronald J. Pelias

I n the long history of theatrical discussion, scholars have approached performance from three general stances. First, scholars have viewed performance as a cultural and artistic object worthy of investigation. Within this logic, scholars have most frequently explored how performance functions within certain historical and cultural contexts, how performance is best theorized and accomplished, how a given performance might best be understood as a communicative act and as a moment within theatrical practice, and how performance fosters meaning making and social change. Such studies borrow from a wide range of theoretical and methodological approaches from the arts, humanities, and social sciences.

Second, scholars have called upon performance as a generative vocabulary for understanding human behavior. In this sense, people are best seen not as *homo sapiens* or *homo luden*, but as *homo histrio*— performing creatures who are created and maintained through enactment, through doing what they do. Kenneth Burke's (1945) dramatistic scheme, Irving Goffman's (1959) notion of the presentation of self, Victor Turner's (1982) model of social dramas, and Judith Butler's (1990) conceptualization of stylized repetitive acts are familiar examples.

Foundational in this perspective is the belief in the explanatory power of the life/drama analogy.

Third, scholars have operated from the assumption that performance itself is a way of knowing. This claim, axiomatic for performers, rests upon a faith in embodiment, in the power of giving voice and physicality to words, in the body as a site of knowledge. It is this last stance that I hope to address in this chapter, for it insists upon a working artist who engages in aesthetic performances as a methodological starting place. It finds its epistemological and ontological heart in performers enacting their own or others' words on stage. In short, performative inquiry, from this perspective, is an embodied practice.

I proceed by discussing the nature of performance as an embodied practice. In doing so, I trace how embodiment entails a knowing, participatory, empathic, and political body. Next, I turn to three representative forms (literature in performance, performance ethnography, and autobiographical performance) to show a range of embodied inquiry and to point toward their respective methodological demands. Finally, I identify several challenges that performers confront when calling upon embodiment as a methodological tool. In particular, I will look at the presenting, lying, assuming, and intervening body.

◆ Performance as Embodied Practice

To embody a self on stage, the performer must develop a flexible and responsive body, a body ready to function as a methodological tool. Just as mathematicians increase their methodological competence as they move from simple arithmetic to the highest forms of mathematical calculation, performers

expand their procedural repertoire as they develop as artists. As the performers' skills increase, they gain greater capacity in using the body as an exploratory instrument that probes and ponders what it encounters.

With training, the performer's instrument becomes increasingly attuned and generates more productive insights. Over time, the performer learns to trust what the body teaches. It is useful to remember, however, that not all bodies move through the world in a similar manner. Some bodies possess limited agility, some not; some live in constant pain, some not; some feel disassociated from a sense of self, some not; some bodies are labeled disabled, some not. Regardless of the performer's body, embodied practice calls upon the performer to employ a knowing, participatory, empathic, and political body. Each of these bodies is necessarily implicated in any performative act and, hence, is fundamental to performative inquiry.

The performer's knowing body relies upon the physical and vocal behaviors brought forth in rehearsal and public presentation. The performer listens to what the body is saying and, based upon what the body has come to know, makes judgments about performance choices. More specifically, it involves a process of selecting what text to stage, playing with possible vocal and physical behaviors, testing the various possibilities against the givens in the text, choosing among the viable options for the best artistic choice, repeating each choice so that it becomes fine tuned for performance, and presenting the performance before an audience (Pelias, 1999). At each step in the process, the performer relies upon the body as a location of knowledge.

Performers are always trying to separate the good from the bad, the magical from the mundane. The knowing body serves to negotiate the multiplicity of options a performer faces. It helps the performer decide what seems right. It tells the performer what it knows about what is being said and how it is being said. Its telling comes forward cognitively, providing the performer with a clear understanding of why a particular decision might be right. In such cases, the performer can articulate the reasons for a given choice. The body's telling also comes forward affectively, giving the performer emotional knowledge, offering a sense of the attitudes, sentiments, and passions of what is being performed. And its telling comes forward intuitively, initiating a felt but ineffable sense of what appears true. The knowing body, then, finds its power in the cognitive, affective, and intuitive coming together to form a sense of what it has to say.

The knowing body gains support from the empathic body. On the most fundamental level, the empathic body recognizes points of view other than its own. It understands that multiple perspectives always exist. More importantly, the empathic body has the capacity to understand and share in the feelings of others, to take on another sensibility. This methodological skill helps situate performers to create characters, including their own character in an autobiographical text. The empathic task, to use Stanislavski's (1952) familiar terms, demands that the performer take into account the "given circumstances" of a character and employ the "magic if": If I were in that situation, what would I do and feel? In this construction, performers project themselves into the life circumstances of others and use themselves to determine the nature of the experience. Alternatively, as Parrella (1971) first pointed out, performers may attempt to become others, adopting the characteristics of others as their own. The question here is not how the performer might feel in a certain situation but how the other might feel. This process of taking on others, of letting one's own body be open to others, provides

performers an entry, albeit always incomplete, into others' life worlds. The empathic body, because of its ability and willingness to coalesce with others, is essential to embodiment and to performance as a method.

The participatory body learns by doing. The performer's task is located in action. By doing the actions called forth by a given role, the performer comes to a sense of what those actions entail. As suggested above, the performer tries on various actions before settling into the actions that seem right. It is, in part, the repetition of those selected actions that is the most telling for the performer. Living with specific actions over an extended period of time allows the performer's body to make those actions the performer's own. This may require performers to reach well beyond their typical ways of being in the world, and as they reach out, they come to understand what it may be like to be another body. Performative inquiry cannot be accomplished from an observational stance; it demands participation. It asks performers to become others, to commit to others' ways of being. Performers, of course, seldom forget that they are performers. Keeping in touch with their performing selves allows them to do the work they must do on stage. Yet part of the performers' power is the ability, to use Wilshire's (1982) helpful phrasing, "to stand in for others."

Standing in, as Conquergood (1995) suggests, may be viewed as an act of mimesis (faking), poiesis (making), or kinesis (breaking and remaking). Whether performers see themselves as participating in order to replicate, construct, or provide alternatives to current constructions, their task remains constant: They are to perform actions that are available for others and for themselves to read. And, in the doing, they come to know how embodiment reifies, insinuates, destabilizes, interrogates, and alters their own and others' ways of seeing the world.

Conquergood's scheme is a reminder that in any act of embodiment there is always a political body. All performance is ideologically laden. Performers' bodies are not neutral. They carry, among other markers, their gender, sexuality, ableness, class, race, and ethnicity with them. They signal cultural biases—beauty and blond hair, handsome and tan, jolly and round, and so on. Such claims imply that the performer's body is always a contested site. Efforts at color-blind casting, for example, only demonstrate that directors can attempt to erase issues of race but cannot eliminate how audiences might interpret what they see. The identities that are put on stage come with and without cultural endorsement. Performers who are interested in interventionist work find their political bodies a rich methodological source for exploration and advocacy.

It would be misleading, however, to imply that any body could come on stage without being a body of advocacy. Bodily presence reifies or argues against a way of being. Questions of what bodies have access to the stage, what bodies are privileged, and what bodies are used for what ends swirl around every performance. Such questions may remain implicit, but increasingly, such issues have become explicit, sometimes in textual form and sometimes in staging. Dolan's (1996) desire to use performance for activist work comes, in part, from its potential to display "the connectedness of bodies to themselves and each other, the demonstration of bodies in relations that are clearly political, deeply marked with power and with danger" (p. 12). The political body recognizes how power functions, dares to explore and expose it, and welcomes the opportunity to subvert it in the name of social justice.

Embodiment, then, is "an intensely sensuous way of knowing" (Conquergood, 1991, p. 180). The experiencing body, situated in culture, is its methodological center. Unlike traditional scholarship where the body seems to slip away, performers generate and present their insights through the body, a knowing body, dependent upon its participatory and empathic capacities and located in contested yet potentially liberating space. As Conquergood (1991) puts it, performative inquiry "privileges particular, participatory, dynamic, intimate, precarious, embodied experience grounded in historical process, contingency, and ideology" (p. 187).

◆ Representative Forms of Performative Inquiry

Performers may focus their inquiry in a number of different directions, but the three most common sites for exploration are the literary, cultural, and personal, known generically as literature in performance, performance ethnography, and autobiographical performance. These labels, of course, blur, crisscross, leak, but they do point toward distinct orientations and place certain methodological issues in the foreground.

Staging literature (i.e., drama, poems, prose fiction, nonfiction) has consumed the bulk of performers' energies. Literary texts, some specifically written for presentation on stage and some not, carry their own aesthetic dimensions, situating the performer in a position of either trying to feature or to resist what a given text asks. The delicate negotiation between literature's art and the performer's art is an ongoing process, informed by the performer's motives for presenting a given work. For some performers, their task is to offer a credible rendering of a literary text; for others, their aim is to discover in literature places for innovation and critique. Not surprisingly, these goals are in keeping with the objectives of various literary and critical theories—some positions, to use Booth's (1979) helpful terms, encourage readers to strive for "understanding" and some for "overstanding" (pp. 235–257). A central consideration performers face when working with literary texts is their stance, whether it will be one of consent or one of dissent. Depending upon the stance the performer elects, performative inquiry may be textually driven or textually detached.

For the performers who are driven to give consent to a literary work, their methodological task is to seek entry into the textual world and, in so doing, come to know the characters that live there. Much of actor training is involved with giving performers the skills to gain access, to allow others to speak through them, and to inhabit worlds other than their own. For the performers who wish to detach themselves from textual dictates, their procedural charge is to discover how to keep present a given literary work while they spin away from or comment upon it. The text, functioning as a launch point for what the performer wants to say, might be approached metaphorically to establish a conceptual overlay that guides an audience's reading. Shakespeare's plays, for instance, are often placed in surprising contexts (e.g., *The Merry Wives of Windsor* in the United States suburbia in the 1950s *The Merchant of Venice* in Nazi Germany). Or a text might be inserted with the performer's political commentary, encouraging an audience to reflect upon what is being said. Such postmodern stagings, perhaps most frequently associated with the Wooster Group, often interweave their own intertextual observations and connections. Performers who elect such strategies put into play the power of their own readings. Methodologically, their embodied enactments tilt toward their own stamp upon a literary work.

Performance ethnography places cultural understandings on stage. Performers, following ethnographic procedures, gather data from the field, but instead of turning that data into a traditional written report, they script and stage their findings. Informed by the early work of Turner (1986) and Schechner (1993), performance ethnographers believe that the rich array of cultural practices can best be represented, not on the page, but through embodied presentation. By presenting cultural others on stage, performers display living bodies who participate in the ongoing process of making culture. In their representations, performance ethnographers strive to avoid shallowness and exploitation, a desire that is not easily accomplished when reaching across cultures.

Equally tricky is how performance ethnographers decide to script themselves. In some shows, the ethnographer is implied but not embodied on stage. In others, the ethnographer functions as a narrator who provides an interpretive frame for the audience. In still others, the ethnographer becomes a central character, a participant in ongoing cultural practices. Another issue facing performance ethnographers is how they see their task. For some, the performance functions as a report, an account of what they found in the field that reaches toward objectivity. For others, performance serves as a site of advocacy, an opportunity to intervene on behalf of cultural others. Such considerations call forward different methodological procedures and, hence, alter the nature of the performative inquiry.

Autobiographical performance traffics in the details of a particular life, featuring either one's own personal life experiences or another's autobiographical tale. More often than not, it features texts of exceptional wit, extraordinary events, and/or oppressed or historical individuals. As for the performance ethnographer, the autobiographical performer engages in a process of selection and shaping, of deciding what to share. Both are always making a rhetorical case, and in doing so, they face issues of truthfulness: What information can be buried, minimized, or altered? What particulars can be dropped or added to create aesthetic interest? What details about others can be included without their consent? The autobiographer performer, unlike the performance ethnographer, however, takes as the primary aim to create a particular speaker that tells of life lived. The autobiographical performer shares intimacies and, at times, indignities. The performer establishes a persona that audience members may admire or abhor, embrace or resist, identify with or dismiss.

Such an interest leads performers to be keenly aware that there are personal consequences to every telling. Making public occurrences that are often kept private carries risks. The man who in performance self-identifies as gay, for example, may soon find himself in danger of physical harm beyond the site of the performance. The woman who discloses her anorexia, for instance, may discover that in her social life she has become reduced to that identity marker. The autobiographical performer, then, is always in an ongoing negotiation between authenticity and rhetorical efficacy, between the desire for honesty and the need to protect. With autobiographical performances, inquiry maneuvers between the told and untold. Its strength, however, derives from telling the untold. As Lockford (2001) argues,

> it is often dirty work, this digging into the rich soil of humanity. Digging into our humanity, we cannot keep the soil out from under our nails, the clay off our faces, and the sand away from the folds of our skin. We write with humility about that which makes us remember our humanity, that which makes us humble, that which makes us human. (p. 118)

◆ Some Challenges for Performative Inquiry

I have been arguing that the performative method is powerful and carries some particular methodological demands as it moves across genres. Like other methods, it also confronts certain challenges. In this next section, I outline some risks that performers face when embodiment functions as their method of inquiry. These risks might best be addressed as the presenting, lying, assuming, and intervening bodies. The performer's body is engaged in an act of live presentation.

Through physical and vocal behaviors, performers attempt to put on display what they wish to communicate. There may be, however, slippage between what the body knows and what it can say and between what the body says and what an audience can interpret. Performers may have intense bodily feelings but lack the competence to translate those feelings into meaningful communicative acts for either themselves or an audience. Moreover, performers and an audience may recognize a given act as highly meaningful but remain unable to articulate what it might be saying. In this case, the presenting body is communicative, speaking through the intuitive and the felt, but performers cannot always formulate into words the body's meaning. In addition, performers may have difficulty determining whether or not what they know has come from bodily enactment or from some other source of insight. Park-Fuller (1983) offers a rich explanation of these dilemmas:

> Because the language of performance is a sensual language, it does not constitute knowledge by naming; it constitutes knowledge by sensing. Thus, when called upon to describe an insight gained in the process of production, the reporter

must translate sensed knowledge to conceptual knowledge and, since any translation involves change, the translation from sensed knowledge to conceptual knowledge changes the nature of the insight. (p. 72)

The presenting body sees the stage as its site of publication. It offers what it knows not on the page but in live performance. But because performance is ephemeral (once given, then lost), performance scholars have tried to document in print form what the body knows. Such attempts, more often than not, have been frustrating. Seldom does a printed account capture the feel for a performance. In recent years, scholars (e.g., Miller & Pelias, 2001; Pollock, 1998) have turned to performative writing as a strategy for providing a richer sense of the presenting body. Recognizing language's representational limitations, performative writing often deploys the poetic as the best strategy for entering into and reporting what the body might know. Even when doing so, print accounts remain limited, a diminished rendering of what occurred on stage.

The lying body is a reminder that the body is a habituated site that carries its historical and cultural markings. The fact that I gag at the sight of mayonnaise tells more about my unfortunate encounter with some rancid mayonnaise in my childhood than it does about the nature of mayonnaise. This trivial example calls to mind examples of much larger consequence: the disgust the Nazi body may have felt toward Jews, the repulsion the straight body may feel when seeing two men kissing, the loathing one political party may feel for another political party. As Gingrich-Philbrook (2001) notes, the body offers "an opportunity for error as much as wisdom" (p. 7). This suggests that what the body knows requires critical reflection, a constant ethical testing, a reflexive turn.

Such a move keeps bodily claims where they belong, connected to a particular body. The habit of speaking of "the body" can obscure the fact that performative inquiry always takes place in an individual body, a body enriched and scarred by its lifelong facts. Rich's (2001) call for using "my body" over "the body" in her discussion of identity politics is applicable here:

Perhaps we need a moratorium on saying "the body." For it's also possible to abstract "the" body. When I write "the body" I see nothing in particular. To write "my body" plunges me into lived experience, particularity. . . . To say "the body" lifts me away from what has given me a primary perspective. To say "my body" reduces the temptation to grandiose assertions. (p. 67)

And it reduces the potential confusion between what performing bodies might know and what a particular, situated body might assert. Whatever lies or truths our bodies might tell, they are our own.

The assuming body falls prey to the intimacy of embodiment. Coming to know others by taking on their physical and vocal qualities, their attitudes and circumstances, and their historical and cultural situations may lead performers to believe that they fully understand others. But understanding is always partial. Moreover, in the belief of full understanding, they may feel an obligation to speak for others, particularly given their communicative skills. But a difference can be drawn between "speaking for" and "speaking with." When speaking for, performers offer a monologue on behalf of another. The monologue comes forward as a "what is." When speaking with, performers engage in a dialogue, an ongoing conversation between a performer and another, even though the performer may be the only speaker. Instead of suggesting "what is," dialogic performance stages "what might be." The difference between a performance that asserts "what is" and one that poses "what might be" becomes particularly loaded when a performer wishes to "overstand," to offer a critique of another's way of being. The challenge for performers is to recognize the nature of what they know, its partiality, its presumptive and political dangers.

The intervening body sees performance as an opportunity to work for social justice. It is politically engaged, committed to productive change. In its desire to affect social life, it strives to reach constituencies that have a stake in what it has to say. As Dolan (2001) explains, performance can be a "participatory forum in which ideas and possibilities for social equity and justice are shared" (p. 456). Performance can "offer us glimpses of utopia" (p. 456), "imaginative territories that map themselves over the real" (p. 457). This "utopian performative" plays against performance practices that reify cultural logics and obstruct alternative expressions, often by means of commodification and control of resources.

The intervening body, regardless of the obstacles it might confront, runs a number of methodological risks. In addition to reifying what it may hope to question, the intervening body may offer possibilities but no course of action, or conversely, may call for action without posing sufficient possibilities. In the first case, embodiment may propose so many speculative possibilities that it is difficult to imagine what action to take. In the second case, embodiment posits an action that appears to solve a problem without recognizing the complexity of a situation.

Despite the challenges of the presenting, lying, assuming, and intervening bodies, performative inquiry stands as a highly productive method. Across various forms, performance is an embodied practice, dependent upon participatory and empathic skills and situated politically, that trusts the body as a site of knowing. It insists that performers

who surrender themselves to the bodily stance of others will come to understand in a most profound way: sensuously, human to human, fully present, open, ready to take in what others have to offer.

◆ *References*

Booth, W. C. (1979). *Critical understanding: The powers and limits of pluralism.* Chicago: University of Chicago Press.

Burke, K. (1945). *The grammar of motives.* New York: Prentice Hall.

Butler, J. (1990). *Gender trouble: Feminism and the subversion of identity.* New York: Routledge.

Conquergood, D. (1991). Rethinking ethnography: Towards a critical cultural politics. *Communication Monographs, 58,* 179–194.

Conquergood, D. (1995). Of caravans and carnivals. *The Drama Review, 39,* 137–141.

Dolan, J. (1996). Producing knowledges that matter. *The Drama Review, 40,* 9–19.

Dolan, J. (2001). Performance, utopia, and the "utopian performative." *Theatre Journal, 53,* 455–479.

Gingrich-Philbrook, C. (2001). Bite your tongue: Four songs of body and language. In L. C. Miller & R. J. Pelias (Eds.), *The green window: Proceeding of the Giant City conference on performative writing* (pp. 1–7). Carbondale: Southern Illinois University.

Goffman, E. (1959). *The presentation of self in everyday life.* New York: Doubleday.

Lockford, L. (2001). Talking dirty and laying low: A humble homage to humanity. In L. C. Miller & R. J. Pelias (Eds.), *The green window: Proceeding of the Giant City conference on performative writing* (pp. 113–121). Carbondale: Southern Illinois University.

Miller, L. C., & Pelias, R. J. (Eds.). (2001). *The green window: Proceeding of the Giant City conference on performative writing.* Carbondale: Southern Illinois University.

Park-Fuller, L. (1983). Understanding what we know: Yonnondio—from the thirties. *Literature in Performance, 4,* 65–74

Parrella, G. C. (1971). Projection and adoption: Toward a clarification of the concept of empathy. *Quarterly Journal of Speech, 57,* 204–213.

Pelias, R. J. (1999). Becoming another: A love song for J. Alfred Prufrock. In R. J. Pelias, *Writing performance: Poeticizing the researcher's body* (pp. 97–108). Carbondale: Southern Illinois University Press.

Pollock, D. (1998). Performing writing. In P. Phelan & J. Lane (Eds.), *The ends of performance* (pp. 73–103). New York: New York University Press.

Rich, A. (2001). *Arts of the possible.* New York: W. W. Norton.

Schechner, R. (1993). *The future of ritual: Writing on culture and performance.* New York: Routledge.

Stanislavski, C. (1952). *An actor prepares* (E. R. Hapgood, Trans.). New York: Theatre Arts Books.

Turner, V. (1982). *From ritual to theatre: The human seriousness of play.* New York: Performing Arts Journal Publications.

Turner, V. (1986). *The anthropology of performance.* New York: Performing Arts Journal Publications.

Wilshire, B. (1982). *Role playing and identity: The limits of theatre as metaphor.* Bloomington: Indiana University Press.

17

Performance

ETHNODRAMA
AND ETHNOTHEATRE

◆ Johnny Saldaña

The purpose of this chapter is to provide a brief overview of the scripting and performance of ethnographic research known as *ethnodrama* and *ethnotheatre*, respectively. From *Ethnodrama: An Anthology of Reality Theatre* (Saldaña, 2005), the following definitions apply to this review:

> Ethno*theatre* employs the traditional craft and artistic techniques of theatre production to mount for an audience a live performance event of research participants' experiences and/or the researcher's interpretations of data. This research—meaning, to investigate in its broadest sense—can be conducted by artists, scholars or even by the participants themselves in such diverse fields of study as sociology, anthropology, psychology, education, health care, women's studies, justice studies, ethnic studies, cultural studies, political science, journalism, human communication, performance studies and theatre. The goal is to investigate a particular facet of the human condition for purposes of adapting those observations and insights into a performance medium. Simply put, this is preparatory fieldwork for theatrical production work.

An ethno*drama,* the written script, consists of dramatized, significant selections of narrative collected through interviews, participant observation field notes, journal entries, and/or print and media artifacts such as diaries, television broadcasts, newspaper articles and court proceedings. Simply put, this is dramatizing the data. (pp. 1–2)

The umbrella term commonly applied to presentations of this genre is "arts-based research." The phrase suggests that art receives priority or is used as the springboard for research. But I propose that ethnodrama and ethnotheatre are "research-based art" since the forms are in service to the content.

◆ *The Performance of Research*

How do ethnodrama and ethnotheatre advance knowledge in ways different from conventional social science research methods?

We all tell stories in one form or another, but some of us are more effective at it than others. Some of the best tellers of tales have rich, fluent voices, expressive faces, well-chosen gestures, and consummate timing. Their narrative texts seem polished with well-chosen words and strong, linear progression. As listeners we become emotionally engaged with their evocative presence, commit to memory the impact and aesthetic of the event, and even derive more significant meaning from their oral rendering of the stories than if we were to read them silently on our own. This is the power of live performance—the ability to enhance the written word. Performed dramatic literature, like social science, examines the human condition. Ethnotheatre's goal is much the same and can achieve powerful results, assuming a well-written script,

high production values, and a receptive audience. Beyond the text, the immediacy and live phenomenon of ethnotheatrical performance heightens and crystallizes the representation of the participants' culture and lived experiences for its audiences (Denzin, 2003; Mienczakowski, 2001).

"Performance" as a construct is applied quite liberally in the social sciences today: Culture and gender are "performed"; teaching is "performance"; we live in a "performative" society. If these theories are substantive, then theatre is not just around us, theatre is within us. It took approximately 2,500 years for anthropologists, psychologists, and sociologists to discover what western theatre practitioners since the golden age of ancient Greece have known all along. Performance is innate to humans and ubiquitous in our social interactions. Humans are socialized from childhood (if not genetically predisposed) to imitate, to pretend, to role play, to ritualize, and to storytell. It is thus a simple transition to act on our performative impulses by developing artistically rendered work that reflects our dramatic nature.

Ethnotheatre is also a presentational form of research in harmony with our contemporary visual and performative cultures. In these societies, project work is exhibited, displayed, showcased—the medium shows" us as well as "tells" us about phenomena in nonverbal symbols that supplement oral and written language. The late Miles and Huberman (1994) encouraged researchers to "think display"—meaning that the complexity of qualitative data analysis and a study's findings could be essentialized through readable charts, matrices, and graphics. An ethnodrama is a written, artistically composed arrangement of qualitative data using such dramatic literary conventions as monologue, dialogue, and stage directions. Ethnotheatre is the synchronous, three-dimensional, mounted performance display of the ethnodrama for spectators.

◆ *Ethnodramatic Forms and Ethnotheatrical Staging*

What are the most common forms of ethnodrama and selected methods for staging the play ethnotheatrically?

The Academy of Motion Picture Arts and Sciences honors writers for screenplays adapted from literary sources. This prestigious Oscar acknowledges that adaptation is a special skill and hard work. You must find a new way of telling an established story by transforming it from one medium to another while maintaining the integrity and spirit of the piece. If possible, the goal is to make the work even better than its original source. Narrative must be transformed into monologue and dialogue while the director, actors, and designers find ways to realize the writer's words. Thus, ethnotheatrical production begins with a potentially dynamic ethnodramatic script.

Following are examples from selected ethnodramas rather than extensive prescriptions for writing them. It is hoped that these serve as models for the genre and catalysts for your own creative work. Use the accompanying production photographs as stimuli for your mind's eye to imagine how these scenes might be performed live on stage.

MONOLOGUE

Professional one-person shows offer audiences an evening with such personalities as Mark Twain, Emily Dickinson, and Gertrude Stein. Most recently, the 2004 Pulitzer Prize and Tony Award were given to Doug Wright (2004) for *I Am My Own Wife*, a one-man ethnodrama showcasing the life of German gay transvestite Charlotte von Mahlsdorf. Through an actor's extended monologue the audience witnesses the performance of a life story peppered with informative, amusing, and poignant anecdotes and vignettes. These plays are their playwrights' biographical *case studies* of historic figures, composed in the first person, to render a seemingly autobiographical solo performance through theatrical storytelling. The individual's narrative includes carefully selected life history details extracted from interviews (when possible), period materials such as newspapers, other historians' biographical works, or autobiographical materials such as journals and diaries. These are adapted and woven together through the playwright's conjecture of how the subject him- or herself might have spoken, with comparable attention paid to solid dramatic structure.

Ethnodramatic monologue provides opportunities for the character-participant to reveal not just autobiographical factual details, but inner thoughts, feelings, attitudes, values, and beliefs through spoken narrative. From Saldaña, Finley, and Finley's (2005) *Street Rat*, an adaptation of fieldwork with homeless adolescents in New Orleans, one of the young men speaks to a female newcomer at their squat:

Tigger: My dad kicked me out when I was just seventeen. When I graduated from high school, he said "Congratulations." Then he gave me two weeks to get out. That was six years ago. When I first left home, I lived in Chicago, in the subway. I did what I had to do to survive. It's all about survival. You either survive or you die. . . . People who live here, the professionals, the fucking little yuppie people, they don't even see this side of life. They don't see it,

Figure 17.1 Jess Sari, as Tigger, Looks for Food in the New Orleans French Quarter in Saldaña, Finley, and Finley's *Street Rat*

SOURCE: Photo by Lyle Beitman. Reproduced by permission of Herberger College of the Arts, Arizona State University.

they're blind to it. That's why they ignore me when I ask them for change. But how am I going to stay fed, other than asking people for money? I hate it. I'm free, but things aren't free. I need things so I have to get money. I want a regular job. *(stands)* When I go job hunting I dress smart, wear button downs most of the time. If I had a tie, I'd wear it. But, I mean, just look. Who the fuck is going to want some nasty lookin', dirty lookin', someone who hasn't taken a shower in God knows how long, handling their food, or ringing them up on a cash register, or whatever? I've got over a hundred goddamn applications out in this city. I've got a voice mail number. Nobody ever calls. I make plans, but anytime I make plans they always fall through. *(sits)* So, I take things day by day, don't make plans too far in the future. Every minute of my life is another minute of my life. (pp. 171–172)*

*SOURCE: From Saldaña, J., Finley, S., & Finley, M., Street rat, in *Ethnodrama: An anthology of reality theatre*, pp. 139–179, copyright © 2005. Used with the permission of Rowman & Littlefield Publishing Group.

DIALOGUE

Dialogue emerges from field notes, focus group interviews, or fictive constructions (yet firmly grounded in the data) of plausible interactions among two or more participants. The back-and-forth nature of dramatic dialogue, however, is more than conversational sharing of differing perspectives. Dialogue consists of the character-participants' negotiations over an issue, an opposition of wills, or a tense, conflict-laden exchange.

Again, from *Street Rat*, the playwrights drew from multiple data sources and genres of reporting (e.g., short story, poetry, reader's theatre script) to reconstruct the possible dialogue that might have occurred between the participant-characters. In the scene below, Roach, a 19-year-old runaway, has just been demeaned by a gay leather-man pitching pennies at his feet after asking for spare change. Roach's best friend joins him as they wait for more generous passers-by on the street:

Roach: People try and trick with me for money all the time. I just say, "Fuck off, I'm not a whore." People figure that if you're in the gay district, you *are*. I'm not going to sell my ass.

Tigger: I know plenty of fucking straight up prostitutes. They're cool as hell, but that's not something I'm going to do.

Figure 17.2   David Ojala (left) as Roach and Jess Sari as Tigger Dialogue in the French Quarter in Saldaña, Finley, and Finley's *Street Rat*

SOURCE: Photo by Lyle Beitman. Reproduced by permission of Herberger College of the Arts, Arizona State University.

Roach: It makes you compromise yourself. People who do it have to be comfortable with doing it. Sometimes people get caught up in it, when they aren't comfortable doing it, but they do it anyway. That causes so many problems.

Tigger: That, and the simple fact that people who hustle—not the people who hustle, but the people who hustle them—it's like, the only reason why these rich fuckin' guys are doing this shit, lots of times, the simple fact is they know they can grab a guy off the street and just say, "Come home and fuck me!," "Come home, do this with me," and just take control. I don't know; it's just fucked up.

Roach: And then they act all disgusted when you tell them, "No." Like you're nothing if you don't do something like that to earn money.

Tigger: Like you don't have any choice in the matter.

(A WAITRESS on her way to work passes by)

Roach: Spare change?

Tigger: Spare change?

Waitress: (smiles at them, pulls a coin from her apron pocket, and puts it in ROACH's outstretched hand) There you go. (exits)

Roach: Thanks.

Tigger: Thanks.

(ROACH and TIGGER leer at the WAITRESS as she leaves)

Roach: Now, if a woman wanted to pay me to have sex with her, I would.

Tigger: Well, depends on the woman.

Roach: Yeah. If it's some Nancy Reagan–looking woman, then no.

(a GAY TOURIST enters, wearing Mardi Gras necklaces and with a clear plastic cup of beer in hand, walks past the boys)

Roach and Tigger: Spare change?

(the TOURIST glances quickly at ROACH, shakes his head "no," and sets his half-empty cup on the sidewalk by a trash can; exits; TIGGER goes for the beer)

Roach: Fuck him. Sneakin' peeks at my facial tat. (as TIGGER gets the beer, ROACH smiles and starts a private joke between them) Just say "No!"

Tigger: No! (he drinks from the cup, offers ROACH the last swig). . .

Tigger: (rooting through the trash can for food) We better make quick work of the schwillies, man. We gotta sp'ange enough for all weekend today; it's gonna rain tomorrow.

Roach: How do you know that? Are you a weather man now?

Tigger: I read it in the paper. Town is gonna be packed and we can make bank. The Clover has a sign welcoming some conference, so there's plenty of green around. We just gotta get it while the weather holds.

Roach: *(looks down the street)* I've gotta meet that guy in a couple hours. *(pulls out some partially-smoked cigarettes from his pocket, gives one to TIGGER; they both light up)*

Tigger: *(worriedly)* Right. I don't buy it. I don't trust him, Roach.

Roach: *(tries to reassure TIGGER but sounds doubtful)* I'm not going to have anything on me. The guy holds the stuff. I just go find customers. I take them to him and he gives me a runner's fee. I'm not going to have the stuff on me.

Tigger: Never in my life have I fucked with the needle.

Roach: *(insistent)* I'm not using it, Tigger. I'm just running it.

Tigger: You've done it before, now you'll want to do it again.

Roach: No! It's only a job. I'm going to get money so we can get a place and we can eat. *(TIGGER does not look at him; impatiently as he sits)* I'm a fuckin' slinger, man. I sell drugs on occasion.

Tigger: Being around the needle, talking about the needle, makes me very uncomfortable. Fucks with my head. But if someone's gonna do it, they're gonna do it. I've seen it—friends dead.

Roach: You snort coke with me, but if I try heroin with the guy I'm going to sell it for, that makes it wrong? You're such a fucking hypocrite!

Tigger: No I'm not! You know what I think's going to happen? You're going to start slammin' it again.

Roach: *(singing the end of Neil Young's song to TIGGER)* "I've seen the needle and the damage done, a little part of it in everyone, but every junkie's like a setting sun." *(laughs; pulls TIGGER by the arm)* C'mon, let's get outta here.

Tigger: *(yanks his arm away from ROACH's grip)* You do what you gotta do, I'll catch ya later.

Roach: Tigger, . . .

Tigger: *(as he exits)* I'll be on the Square. Hook up with me when you're through.

Roach: Tigger! Damn. *(shouts after TIGGER)* I hate it when we fight! We fight just like a couple of fucking married people! (pp. 146–148)

The italicized stage directions included throughout the dialogue above illustrate another critical element of theatre: The art form is both verbally and *physically* enacted on stage.

STAGE ACTION

"Show it, don't tell it" is sage advice from those who develop theatrical productions for audiences because we become engaged with visual spectacle—from the smallest hand property to the largest scenic change—on stage. But "showing it" is not just the designer's job, it is also the collaborative responsibility of the playwright, director, and actor. Directors and actors apply the principle when they realize the playwright's words during rehearsal through movement, gesture, facial reactions, hand properties, and other stage devices. Italicized stage directions are one of the most distinguishing textual features of contemporary dramatic literature. The playwright intersperses these throughout monologue and dialogue because it encourages him to think both verbally and visually.

In Vanover and Saldaña's (2005) *Chalkboard Concerto: Growing Up as a Teacher in the Chicago Public Schools,* Vanover's original autoethnographic article, "Attunement" became the foundation for a one-man ethnodramatic adaptation. The monologue below is extracted verbatim from the original source—a narrative originally read while Charles sat on a chair behind a table in a conference setting. When Saldaña co-adapted and directed the ethnodrama, the staging possibilities were almost inherent in the narrative since the text is active and richly descriptive. In this excerpt, Charles describes the energy inherent in an inner-city grade school classroom. Note how the stage directions specify the theatrical elements of sound, settings, voice, and physical actions for Charles to "show" during performance:

> (*sound effect: noisy children in a classroom; CHARLES rises from his desk and paces back and forth quickly as he speaks to the audience*)

CHARLES: Children create an emotional energy. They change the way that you move and the way that you feel. Thirty poor kids, sixty eyes looking up at you, sixty hands, three hundred fingers, there's so much going on, there's so much happening, it never stops, the classroom never slows down!

(*sound effect out*)

If you can ride with it, if you can move with it, if you can figure out that

(*in a gentle voice, looking downward*)

Figure 17.3   Charles Vanover Begins Class in Vanover and Saldaña's *Chalkboard Concerto: Growing Up as a Teacher in the Chicago Public Schools*

SOURCE: Used with permission of Charles Vanover.

this kid needs to be talked to in this way

(*in a harsh voice, looking at another child*)

and that kid needs to be talked to in that way,

(*in his regular voice, to the audience*)

if you can communicate, if you can join together, there's no better feeling. You become part of a whole, you create a dance, the classroom has a life of its own.

You're not in control, but you are conducting. You fly!

(*crosses to chalkboard*)

You stand there in front of the chalkboard and look at each of those faces. You glance into each of those eyes.

(*he picks up a copy of Dr. Seuss's One Fish, Two Fish, Red Fish, Blue Fish from the desk, stands in front of the audience to show them the book cover*)

Energy travels from them into you and then out and back again:

"One fish, two fish, red fish, blue fish."

(*he looks at the book admiringly and turns to a page*)

Just holding the yellow book in my hand and showing the pictures to the Head Start kids and reading those words:

(*holds the book to point at and show the illustrations to the audience*)

"This one has a little star. This one has a little car."

(*he closes the book, looks at the audience*)

They were poor children. They were very poor children. (p. 68)

Goodall (2000) writes that the best lens for fieldwork views human action "dramatistically" (p. 116). Elsewhere (Saldaña, 2003) I noted that ethnodrama becomes a valid mode of research representation and ethnotheatre a valid mode of research presentation when the art forms are *the* most effective way of documenting the lived experiences of participants. If you know from the beginning of a project that the representation and presentation of the research will be ethnotheatrical, fieldwork proceeds with dramatization of the social setting as one of its primary goals. Individual interviews and personal documents, such as journals, are not only for obtaining the participants' worldviews, but also sources for monologic foundations. Focus group interviews and observations of multiple participants interacting in a social setting provide the stimuli for dialogue and group scenes. Artifacts from the environment hold the potential for transfer onto the stage as scenic elements and properties.

◆ Issues and Challenges

What are major issues and challenges facing writers and producers of ethnotheatre?

First, the legitimacy of ethnotheatre as a credible genre of research reportage remains suspect to many scholars in the social sciences. Most of us have been indoctrinated through the culture of university coursework and scholarly publishing to write (and think) in certain standardized ways. Creative works such as poetry and drama that deviate from the entrenched traditions of mainstream academic prose might be considered "alternative" or "experimental" diversions with no validity or rigor. The doubtful can be convinced if they read an engaging play script or witness an outstanding performance. The burden of proof, then, is on those who write and produce ethnotheatre to not only publish or propose and showcase their work at professional gatherings and in journals, but to create the best play script and production possible.

Second, journal and conference proposal reviewers without ethnodrama or theatre experience often make uninformed judgments about submissions whose mode of reporting is performance. Nontheatre people are applying qualitative research criteria not applicable to dramatic literature, with some placing too much emphasis on such aspects as missing "theoretical frameworks" or the researcher's "positionality" about the piece. Those knowledgeable about the art forms should volunteer as readers, reviewers, and evaluators of arts-based conference proposals and journal article submissions for professional associations.

Third, unlike the published ethnodramatic play script in a book or scholarly journal which can potentially reach thousands of readers, the experience of live ethnotheatrical performance is limited to the audience members in attendance, sometimes amounting to fewer than 100 people. Productions like Vanover and Saldaña's *Chalkboard Concerto* and Chapman, Swedberg, and Sykes's (2005) *Wearing the Secret Out*—a two-person ethnodrama on nonheterosexual physical education teachers—were deliberately produced from the beginning to tour accessibly to other locations. Touring generates additional audiences to see the work in performance rather than simply read the script with sometimes accompanying photographs. Some ethnotheatrical productions have been documented in media formats. Gray and Sinding's (2002) *Standing Ovation: Performing Social Science Research About*

Cancer is accompanied with a studio-quality videotape of two ethnotheatrical performances. Commercially produced ethnodramas such as *The Laramie Project* (Kaufman & Members of the Tectonic Theater Project, 2001) and *The Exonerated* (Blank & Jensen, 2004) are also available in media formats, but it should be noted that original stage scripts are sometimes altered for television broadcast.

Fourth, there are some scholars lacking basic theatre training exploring how to structure their research into ethnodramatic form. As a result, their play scripts often exhibit didactic content—intellectual debate rather than participant/character-driven action. The best ethnodramas I've read have been developed by those with theatrical experience, and their work stands as models for other ethnodramatists (See Saldaña, 2005). I do not want to discourage anyone from writing an ethnodrama if they are inspired to do so yet have no fine arts experience. I offer instead the ethic that any playwright should seek and be open to honest, constructive feedback from peers on the quality of their work. The ultimate merit and success of a play are constructed by the audience in attendance—the final arbiters of a play and its production.

◆ Closure

A "closet drama" is a theatrical term for a play written to be read but not mounted on stage for performance. This is comparable to writing an exceptional research article but not bothering to get it published. Writing an ethnodrama is a vital first step, but the next is getting the script, at the very least, read aloud by a group of colleagues—and at best, mounting it on stage for performance in front of an audience. This is the true test of a play's effectiveness.

Mounting theatre is not easy. Those not formally trained in the art sometimes believe that the technical elements of a production (e.g., lighting, scenery, sound) can be quickly and effortlessly assembled, and they most often underestimate the time needed for rehearsals. Some of the most impressive theatre I've witnessed has been elegant. Less *is* more. The focus on the actors and not the scenographic trappings places more demands on the performers, but if they are at optimal performance, the results can be outstanding.

If the audience is receptive; if the director, designers, and performers are good at their craft; and if the script's content is meaningful to us in some way, then ethnotheatre "works" as research representation. These conditions are necessary prerequisites for the genre to be engaging and effective. This brief chapter cannot possibly include everything one needs to know about writing and staging ethnodrama. The References below will provide you with titles for additional reading. If you are interested in exploring this genre of research, but are not directly involved in theatrical production or performance studies, you are encouraged to contact and collaborate with artists at a university or professional venue who study and practice the art form. Each person will bring his or her own expertise to the venture to create original work that entertains ideas as well as its audiences.

◆ *Ethnodramatic Exercises*

I've long thought that teaching and learning anthropology should be more fun than they often are. Perhaps we should not merely read and comment on ethnographies, but actually perform them. . . . How, then, may this be done? One possibility may be to turn the more interesting portions of ethnographies into playscripts, then to act them out in class, and finally to turn back to ethnographies armed with the understanding that comes from "getting inside the skin" of members of other cultures. (Turner, 1982, pp. 89–90)

A standard playwriting exercise is to adapt and transform an existing nondramatic literary piece into a dramatic work. Several published titles in ethnography possess exciting dramatic potential and, as a practical conclusion, I offer the following sample exercises for novices to ethnodrama.

ALAN PESHKIN'S (1986) GOD'S CHOICE: THE TOTAL WORLD OF A FUNDAMENTALIST CHRISTIAN SCHOOL

Objective: To capture the essence and essentials of an extended interview into a concise monologue for the stage.

Exercise: Read Chapter 1 ("Introduction: The Setting, the Author, the Times") and reduce Pastor William Muller's "first-person account" to a 7- to 10-minute monologue. Delete what is unnecessary for an audience member to know about the pastor and the school. Maintain what is vital and salient. Explore the rearrangement of text for a more logical flow and dramatic impact. List the best scenic pieces and hand properties (e.g., desk, chair, Bible) for the performance of this monologue on stage.

Assessment: Recruit a university or professional actor to read aloud the monologue and ask him to assess its effectiveness from a performer's perspective. Reflect on the legitimacy of the reduced monologue as a credible and trustworthy representation of Pastor Muller.

LISA M. TILLMANN-HEALY'S (1996) "A SECRET LIFE IN A CULTURE OF THINNESS: REFLECTIONS ON BODY, FOOD, AND BULIMIA"

Objective: To adapt a prose narrative into a multiple-character scene portrayed by one actor.

Exercise: Select a scene from Tillman-Healy's chapter with two or more character-participants (e.g., "Cellulite," "Weighing In," "The Spaghetti Feed (and Other Meals)," "An Open Door," "Common Bathroom"). Develop monologic text, with stage directions, for a solo actor to portray the multiple character-participants included and described in the scene.

Assessment: Recruit a university or professional actor to read aloud the monologue and ask her to assess its effectiveness from a performer's perspective. Reflect whether Tillman-Healy's story can be effectively performed by a solo actor, or whether multiple actors are needed for the dramatization and staging of the work.

JENNIFER TOTH'S (1993) THE MOLE PEOPLE: LIFE IN THE TUNNELS BENEATH NEW YORK CITY

Objective: To adapt and transform narrative prose into dialogic form for the stage.

Exercise: Select a chapter from Toth's account with multiple character-participants in narrative dialogue (e.g., "Hell's Kitchen," "Harlem Gang," "J. C.'s Community"). Adapt and dramatize an excerpt from the chapter into a 10- to 15-minute scene for the stage. Create original dialogue for the character-participants when Toth describes, rather than quotes, what they told her:

[Ali M.] says he has studied literature, philosophy and writing. He has been a member of the working class, and he has experienced poverty. His anger comes from being "left out of society." He has not rejected society, but it has rejected him, he says, cast him out because of his black skin. . . . He still suffers from the "conditioning" he received aboveground, conditioning that still causes him to doubt his self-worth and question his own "validity," he says. (pp. 199–200)

Explore how Toth, as a character, can be woven into the scene without narrating to the audience.

Assessment: Recruit university or professional actors to read aloud the scene and ask them to assess its effectiveness from a performer's perspective. Reflect on the challenges of dramatizing a scene with multiple character-participants. Also reflect on the challenges of dramatizing an ethnographic account as a "secondary source" for an ethnodramatic adaptation, and the legitimacy (i.e., ethics, credibility, and trustworthiness) of inventing dialogue not documented in the original account.

◆ References

Blank, J., & Jensen, E. (2004). *The exonerated*. New York: Faber and Faber.

Chapman, J., Swedberg, A., & Sykes, H. (2005). Wearing the secret out. In J. Saldaña (Ed.), *Ethnodrama: An anthology of reality theatre* (pp. 103–120). Walnut Creek, CA: AltaMira Press.

Denzin, N. K. (2003). *Performance ethnography: Critical pedagogy and the politics of culture*. Thousand Oaks, CA: Sage.

Goodall, H. L., Jr. (2000). *Writing the new ethnography*. Walnut Creek, CA: AltaMira Press.

Gray, R., & Sinding, C. (2002). *Standing ovation: Performing social science research about cancer*. Walnut Creek, CA: AltaMira Press.

Kaufman, M., & Members of the Tectonic Theater Project. (2001). *The Laramie project*. New York: Vintage Books.

Mienczakowski, J. (2001). Ethnodrama: Performed research—limitations and potential. In P. Atkinson, A. Coffey, S. Delamont, J. Lofland, & L. Lofland (Eds.), *Handbook of ethnography* (pp. 468–476). Thousand Oaks, CA: Sage.

Miles, M. B., & Huberman, A. M. (1994). *Qualitative data analysis* (2nd ed.). Thousand Oaks, CA: Sage.

Peshkin, A. (1986). *God's choice: The total world of a fundamentalist Christian school*. Chicago: University of Chicago Press.

Saldaña, J. (2003). Dramatizing data: A primer. *Qualitative Inquiry, 9*(2), 218–236.

Saldaña, J. (Ed.). (2005). *Ethnodrama: An anthology of reality theatre*. Walnut Creek, CA: AltaMira Press.

Saldaña, J., Finley, S., & Finley, M. (2005). Street rat. In J. Saldaña (Ed.), *Ethnodrama: An anthology of reality theatre* (pp. 139–179). Walnut Creek, CA: AltaMira Press.

Tillmann-Healy, L. M. (1996). A secret life in a culture of thinness: Reflections on body, food, and bulimia. In C. Ellis & A. P. Bochner (Eds.), *Composing ethnography: Alternative forms of qualitative writing* (pp. 78–108). Walnut Creek, CA: AltaMira Press.

Toth, J. (1993). *The mole people: Life in the tunnels beneath New York City*. Chicago: Chicago Review Press.

Turner, V. (1982). *From ritual to theatre*. New York: PAJ Publications.

Vanover, C., & Saldaña, J. (2005). Chalkboard concerto: Growing up as a teacher in the Chicago public schools. In J. Saldaña (Ed.), *Ethnodrama: An anthology of reality theatre* (pp. 62–77). Walnut Creek, CA: AltaMira Press.

Wright, D. (2004). *I am my own wife: Studies for a play about the life of Charlotte von Mahlsdorf*. New York: Faber and Faber.

18

Performance

READERS' THEATER AS A DATA DISPLAY STRATEGY

◆ Robert Donmoyer and
June Yennie Donmoyer

During the second half of the 20th century, a number of social scientists looked to the arts and literature for inspiration. Some even began to borrow and adapt various artistic and literary techniques. Anthropologist Clifford Geertz (1983) provided a name for this sort of borrowing: He characterized the second half of the 20th century as an era of *blurred genres*. This handbook, which is being assembled in the first decade of the 21st century, is a legacy of the blurred-genre era.

It is possible, however, that by the time this handbook is published, the ideas in it may already be out of date (or at least out of vogue). In the United States (a country that for better or worse often influences the rest of the world), high-profile initiatives have attempted to "un-blur genres" and reverse the inroads that the arts and literature have made in at least one field in which arts-influenced social science research had been quite influential. The field is educational research. The bulk of this chapter focuses on arts-based educational research and recent attempts to minimize its influence.

To avoid painting with brushstrokes that are too broad, we will focus on one arts-based research strategy: readers' theater. Our choice of readers' theater as a focal point was not arbitrary; nor was it made simply

◆ 209

because we personally have explored the potential of using the readers' theater strategy in research. Rather we selected readers' theater as our focal point because the strategy represents a relatively conservative form of arts-based inquiry. As used here, at least, the term *readers' theater* refers to a data display technique that, unlike some other forms of arts-based inquiry (see, e.g., Eisner & Barone, 1997), does not appreciably impact the processes of data collection and analysis.

Here, in other words, we intentionally are framing the discussion narrowly. Our goal is to demonstrate that merging the arts with the social sciences is not *inherently* problematic. The same points *might* be able to be made for more radical forms of arts-based research, but the tendency, in the past, has been to differentiate arts-based research from scientific inquiry (Eisner, 1991/1998). These attempts were duly noted by the authors of the National Research Council's (2002) influential book *Scientific Research in Education* and used as a justification for cavalierly dismissing all forms of arts-based educational research as nonscientific (there will be more about this in the final section of the chapter). Thus, here, we have opted to take a more modest tack and o tackle a clearly achievable—but still important—task: to demonstrate that at least some forms of arts-based research are no less scientific than other forms of qualitative research that, historically, at least, have been viewed as being part of science.

This chapter will be divided into three sections. The first focuses on the emerging interest in the arts and literature among social scientists in general and educational researchers in particular. The second section discusses the readers' theater strategy that is being used here as an exemplar of relatively conservative forms of arts-based inquiry in the educational research field. The third reviews and critiques recent thinking that moves even the readers' theater strategy to the margins of the educational research enterprise.

◆ Social Scientists' Growing Interest in the Arts and Literature During the Era of Blurred Genres

THE ARTS AND LITERATURE IN SOCIOLOGY AND ANTHROPOLOGY

In 1976, sociologist Robert Nisbet began his book, *Sociology as an Art Form*, by noting that "none of the great themes which have provided continuing challenge and also theoretical foundation for sociologists during the last century was ever reached through anything resembling what we are today fond of identifying as 'scientific method'" (p. 3). Nisbet (1976) went on to demonstrate that the great themes that influenced—and continue to influence—sociology were prefigured in the iconic imagery of great works of art and literature, sometimes decades before sociologists embraced them as central constructs in their field. He concluded:

> Sociology is . . . one of the sciences, but it is also one of the arts—nourished . . . by precisely the same kinds of creative imagination which are to be found in such areas as music, painting, poetry, the novel and drama. (p. 9)

Other sociologists have made similar points and, in fact, have demonstrated that the impact of artistic and literary elements extends well beyond the discovery or hypothesis-generating phase of the research process. Gusfield (1976), for instance, demonstrated that the impact of a highly influential study in criminology about drinking drivers had much more to do with the language the researcher employed to characterize his data than with the measures of blood alcohol content that constituted the study's data. Throughout the research report, the author referred to his subjects as *drunken drivers* rather than as, say, *drinking drivers*. Gusfield noted that the researcher's terminology conjures up a pathological, out-of-control subject unlikely to be deterred by stiff penalties. It was this imagery—rather than the numerical data—that justified the study's influential recommendation that drinking drivers should be treated therapeutically rather than punitively.

Interestingly, Gusfield (1976) was not critical of the researcher's use of emotion-laden imagery. Indeed, he argued that social scientists' operational definitions always must be linked with commonsense images if social science is to have any utility in the policy domain. For Gusfield, in short, social science is inevitably "a form of action with meanings derived from its Art as well as its Science" (p. 31).

More recently, some sociologists have moved beyond simply acknowledging the impact of artistic and literary elements and have begun to employ artistic and literary forms such as poetry and drama to report research findings (see, e.g., Richardson, 1992, 1994). The conscious use of artistic and literary form has had an even longer history in the anthropology field (see, e.g., Bandelier, 1890/1971, as well as more recent work by Clifford and Marcus (1986) and Holmes and Marcus, 2005). Arguably, however, the artistic and literary techniques have been used most extensively in the field of educational research.

THE ARTS AND LITERATURE IN EDUCATIONAL RESEARCH

In 1993, for example, Elliot Eisner (1979, 1998), the person who developed and has been the chief advocate for arts-based educational research, was elected president of the American Educational Research Association (AERA), and in 1997, he and Tom Barone were invited to coauthor a chapter on arts-based research for the AERA publication, *Complementary Methods for Research in Education*. Also in 1993, *performance* became a session format option for those submitting research proposals for AERA's annual meeting; in subsequent years, proposals for various performance sessions survived the review process and were placed on the annual meeting program. Some people, quite literally, were even seen dancing their data.[1]

There are a number of explanations for the relatively strong impact of the arts and literature on the educational research community. Much of the credit must be given to Eisner, an articulate spokesperson for integrating the arts into educational inquiry, and to an earlier AERA president, Maxine Greene, an educational philosopher who conjures up literary and artistic allusions in her writing as easily as she cites the philosophy field's canon. For many years, Greene championed the arts and literature as unique ways of knowing that were especially useful in confronting the value issues that were embedded in educational questions (see, e.g., Greene, 1995).[2]

There also were situational factors that made the education field fertile ground for incorporating artistic and literary techniques into empirical inquiry. For instance, the value issues Greene continually wrote about could not be resolved with empirical evidence alone; consequently, there was an incentive to explore other forms of human understanding, including those associated with arts and humanities. Also, educational practitioners must confront and make sense of considerable contextual variation, and this contextual variation both limited the utility of social scientists' abstract generalizations and theories (see, e.g., Cronbach, 1975, 1982) and led for calls for contextualized knowledge that practitioners could use heuristically rather than formulaically (see, e.g., Lincoln & Guba's 1985 discussions of transferability). Context, of course, is often front and center in artistic and literary form, and both the arts and literature provide ways to "theorize in the concrete" (Simon & Dippo, 1980).

Finally, education is an applied field, and consequently educational researchers do not have the luxury of working within a simplified, ideal typical world of their own creation, as researchers in traditional academic disciplines do. It is no accident, for instance, that the field's initial interest in and exploration of the arts in empirical inquiry occurred in the application-oriented subfield of program evaluation. During the 1970s, evaluators became frustrated by the inability of traditional quantitative evaluation designs to accommodate the complexity of the phenomena they were assessing. This frustration led to the development of alternative evaluation "models." One of these "models" was Eisner's (1979) notion of educational criticism, an evaluation approach that used art criticism as a model for assessing educational programs.

Thus, for a variety of reasons, efforts to integrate artistic and literary techniques into empirical inquiry found a reasonably firm foothold in the educational research field. Over the years, this integration effort has taken a variety of forms, including using readers' theater for the purpose of qualitative data display.

◆ Readers' Theater: An Example of Arts-Based Educational Research

Initially the *educational* criticisms produced by Eisner (1971) and his students (see Barone, 1983) read like traditional case studies—albeit with more literary language—but, in time, arts-oriented researchers became more adventuresome. Some (e.g., Barone, 1997; Glesne, 1997), for instance, followed sociologist Laurel Richardson's (1992) lead and

began using poetry to represent their data, while others (Tierney, 1993) behaved like early novel-writing anthropologists such as Bandelier (1890/1971) and experimented with a genre of research reporting they labeled *ethnographic fiction*. There also was considerable experimentation with the use of drama to represent the results of research. This last type of experimentation mirrored—albeit from a different starting point—the experimentation with documentary forms of drama that were occurring in the theater world at about the time. (see, e.g., *The Laramie Project*, Kaufman & Members of the Tectonic Theatre Project, 2001, and two works that were researched, written, and performed by Anna Deavere-Smith, 1993, 1994).

Within the academic community, documentary forms of drama went by a number of names—for example, ethnodrama (Mienczakowski, 2000; Saldaña, 2005), performance ethnography (Denzin, 2003; McCall, 2003), performed ethnography (Goldstein, 2002), performance science (McCall & Becker, 1990), research-based theater (Gray, Ivonoffski, & Sinding, 2002), reality theater (Saldaña, 2005), applied theater (Taylor, 2003), and data-based readers' theater (Donmoyer & Yennie-Donmoyer, 1995; Finley & Finley, 1998; Konzal, 1995). These different names often signal subtle—and at times not so subtle—differences in goals and/or technique. The focus here is on work bearing the readers' theater label. Specifically this section will (1) indicate what readers' theater is, (2) describe selected examples of the genre, and (3) discuss the rationale for reporting data by constructing and performing a readers' theater script.

READERS' THEATER: WHAT IS IT?

In the field of drama, readers' theater has been defined in a number of ways (Coger & White, 1982; Pikering, 1975). Here it refers to a staged presentation of qualitative data performed by an individual or ensemble of performers. Staging is simple; scenery is normally limited to things like stools and ladders; props are used sparingly, if at all, and theatrical lighting is not required (though, of course, even modest lighting effects can enhance the dramatic effect of any theatrical presentation).

Probably the most obvious difference between readers' theater and some of the other versions of presenting data as drama mentioned above is the convention of having actors hold and read from scripts during performances. The fact that performers do not have to memorize scripts makes it possible to stage a script at a research conference or within a school or university classroom without an extended rehearsal period, and this certainly is one of the things that makes the readers' theater genre attractive to researchers.

But the convention of holding scripts is not employed in readers' theater productions merely for pragmatic reasons, and pragmatic concerns were not the only considerations that led us, at least, to select the readers' theater genre when we decided to experiment with displaying data in dramatic form. The holding of scripts, in fact, is one of a number of Brecht-like distancing devices used in readers' theater productions to stylize what happens on stage (Kleinau & McHughes, 1980). If a character exists during a scene in a readers' theater performance, for instance, it is unlikely that the actor will literally leave the stage; rather the actor, more often than not, will simply turn his or her back to the audience.

Why stylize? Brecht (1992) provided at least one answer in his critique of traditional so-called realistic forms of drama, which, Brecht argued,

> always aim at smoothing over contradictions, at creating false harmony, at idealization. Conditions are reported as if they could not be otherwise; characters

as individuals, incapable by definition of being divided, cast in one block, manifesting themselves in the most various situation, likewise for that matter existing without any situations at all. If there is any development it is always steady, never by jerk; the developments always take place with a definite framework which cannot be broken through. (p. 277)

Brecht added: "None of this is reality, so a [truly] realistic theatre must give it up" (p. 277).

For Brecht, in other words, theater should never be escapist or tie things up in neat and tidy packages; rather it should encourage thought as well as emotion, and provoke analysis, not just empathy. Brecht, in fact, employed various distancing strategies to break the spell created by the illusion of reality on stage and to ensure that people will think as well as feel in response to the "epic theatre" he was attempting to create.[3] Readers' theater employs similar techniques to insure that people watching a readers' theater production continue to think, analyze, and co-construct with the actors onstage the meaning of what they are watching.

In addition to employing the sorts of distancing techniques used in the theater world, readers' theater scripts developed in the educational research field often present data in montage rather than narrative form. Script construction, in other words, is more akin to creating a review (in this case, a review of ideas and life experiences) than a well-made play with a beginning, middle, and end. Or, to use the research-world language of Polkinghorne (1995), script construction is built around *the analysis of narrative* rather than *narrative analysis*. The analysis-of-narrative strategy is the strategy traditionally used in qualitative social science; it involves coding and presenting data in categorical form. Narrative analysis, on the other hand, entails reconfiguring a researcher's narrative data into a kind of metastory with its own plot and literary-like themes.

Although the montage form is not a defining property of readers' theater in the theater world (e.g., theater folks are more than willing to stage short stories, novels, and chronologically organized plays in a readers' theater format), educational researchers' tendency to use it is one reason we are able to characterize data-based readers' theater as a relatively conservative form of arts-based inquiry. Indeed, as was suggested at the outset of this chapter, the script construction process is not appreciably different from the data collection and analysis process employed in traditional forms of qualitative research. Of course, the montage format also functions as yet another distancing device to ensure that emotional engagement does not overpower thinking when audiences respond to staged presentations of research results.

This emphasis on thinking and analysis made readers' theater, for us at least, an especially appropriate dramatic form to use in a research context. In contrast to more realistic forms of drama, we saw readers' theater as an appropriate way to achieve the dual goal that Denzin talks about when he discusses the potential of ethnographic performance: that is, "to recover *yet interrogate* [italics added] the meanings of lived experience" (Denzin, 1997, p. 94). There will be more on this below. At this point, however, it seems appropriate to discuss some examples of the use of readers' theater in educational research.

EXAMPLES

We begin this section by discussing one of the first readers' theater scripts to be staged at a research conference. For the 1994 annual meeting of the AERA, the two of us created a readers' theater script and recruited nine colleagues—some with and some without prior acting experience—to perform the script during a conference session. As its title implies, the script, "In Their Own Words: Middle School Students Write About Writing" (Yennie-Donmoyer & Donmoyer, 1994), was constructed from middle school students' essays about the conditions in schools and elsewhere that facilitate and inhibit their development as writers.

One of our goals in doing this work was to explore the potential of dramatic form in general, and the readers' theater form in particular, for data display purposes. After the production, we wrote a paper about our experiences. The paper, "Data as Drama: Reflections on the Use of Readers' Theater as a Mode of Qualitative Data Display" was published in *Qualitative Inquiry* (Donmoyer & Yennie-Donmoyer, 1995).

In that article we noted, among other things, that much to our surprise the script construction process mirrored the coding and thematic analysis procedures traditionally used in analyzing qualitative data for the purpose of creating "thick descriptions" (Geertz, 1973). To be sure, aesthetic considerations came into play and, on occasion, influenced how (and which) data were represented on stage. But these considerations seemed no greater than the influence of rhetorical considerations (e.g., the need to simplify and compress findings and limit complexity in the interpretation of findings so as not to confuse and tire the reader) that inevitably come into play when writing traditional research reports. Indeed, as we reflected on the staging of our script, we realized that, in our production, stage directions functioned in much the same way as punctuation and other style-manual conventions (e.g., the use of headings and subheadings) function in traditional research reports (Donmoyer & Yennie-Donmoyer, 1995).

We also noted that the montage-like format we used in this particular script allowed us to display a plethora of perspectives rather than merely juxtapose antithetical points of view as is normally done in expository texts. To state this point another way: The montage format helped us avoid the sort of either–or binary thinking that scholars from Dewey to postmodernists suggest is both problematic and a characteristic of expository discourse.

We have restaged the *In Their Own Words* scripts many times since its original presentation at a research conference; most of these subsequent "productions" were done with and for groups of teachers. We also have used readers' theater to display other data from other studies when it seemed appropriate to do so. For example, in 2002 Robert and his colleague, Fred Galloway, transformed interview data collected for an evaluation of an educational reform initiative sponsored by a foundation/school district partnership into the readers' theater script *Voices in Our Heads* (Donmoyer & Galloway, 2002). Teachers and administrators who had been involved with the reform helped stage the script, and the staging was presented to foundation and school employees in lieu of the two evaluators presenting a traditional "talking heads" oral report on their findings (a traditional written report was also prepared, but the two evaluators suspect that few read it). The response to *Voices in Our Heads* was so positive that foundation officials employed the team to evaluate their annual conference with the stipulation that they report the evaluation findings in a readers' theater format.

Others also have explored the potential of readers' theater for reporting research findings. Jean Konzal, for example, was in the process of completing her doctoral dissertation when she attended an Arts-Based Educational Research workshop sponsored by AERA. We both participated in that workshop, and, in fact, the script we had constructed for the 1994 meeting of AERA

was performed during the workshop by a troupe of volunteer workshop participants (including Jean). After the experience, Jean decided to structure the findings chapter of her dissertation as two readers' theater scripts (Konzal, 1995).

The scripts are interesting for a number of reasons. Konzal, for instance, uses an *Our Town*–type narrator to provide the sort of contextual exposition expected in qualitative doctoral dissertations (she also uses the pseudonym, Grovers Corner, the name of the town in Wilder's play, for her study site). In addition, noted theorists become characters in her script to ensure that she met committee members' expectations about linking her findings to the existing literature. Konzal's dissertation went on to win the Outstanding Dissertation Award from AERA's Division D (Research Methodology) and her scripts have also been published (Konzal, 1996, 2001).

Susan Finley was another emerging scholar who participated in the staging of *In Their Own Words* during the research workshop mentioned above, and she too has gone on to develop a number of readers' theater scripts from a range of data sets. In 1998, for example, she and her son, Macklin Finley, staged a production of a readers' theater script (Finley & Finley, 1998) that they developed from data that Macklin had collected by interviewing homeless youth in New Orleans in the mid-1990s. The data the Finleys dramatized were inherently dramatic and virtually required that they be represented through some sort of dramatic or literary form.

Since their initial staging of the data, one or both of the Finley's have reconstructed the homeless youth data in a number of ways including a story built around composite characters (Finley & Finley, 1999), a book of poetry also called *Street Rat* (Finley, 2000), and with the assistance of theater professor Johnny Saldaña, a more or less conventional play also called *Street Rat* (Saldaña, Finley, & Finley, 2005). The latter script is included in Saldaña's (2005) anthology of "reality theatre" pieces.

Another readers' theater script that has the distinction of being published in a mainstream academic journal—in this case *Qualitative Studies in Education*— is *Womentalkin': A Readers' Theater Performance of Teachers' Stories* (Adams et al., 1998). The journal's editors also published critiques of the work that focused on both the substance and the readers' theater form of the work (Donmoyer & Yennie-Donmoyer, 1998; Torres, 1998).

One impressive example of the growing (but uneven) collection of conference presentations that have employed the readers' theater data display technique is a script, *Voces y Visiones: Portraits of Bilingual Education Teachers' Journeys,* presented at the 2003 meeting of the University Council of Educational Administration. The script was constructed by Anabel Montoya-Tanabe (2003), a student enrolled in a special New Mexico State University principal preparation program overseen by faculty members Maria Luisa Gonzales and Elsy Sutmiller. The program was designed to transform bilingual teachers into principals of schools with large numbers of English language learners (ELL). Montoya-Tanabe constructed her script from her own and her fellow students' autoethnographic reflections.

A number of the students who had provided the data from which the script was constructed performed the script at the conference session.[4] After the performance, they indicated that the script construction process had helped them recall and learn from their own and their fellow cohort members' experiences as English language learners in American schools. The performance itself helped audience members, who had never been in this sort of situation,

understand intellectually—but also in more visceral ways—what being an English language learner in an American school was like. It is unlikely that anyone in the audience will ever see ELL students in quite the same way again.

THE RATIONALE FOR REPORTING DATA IN READERS' THEATER FORM

Implicit in what was just said about the script prepared and performed by students from the New Mexico State program is one reason some researchers display their data in readers' theater form: Dramatic form of any sort allows one to retain, at least somewhat, the human dimensions of the life experiences qualitative researchers attempt to study. The *New York Times* critic Margo Jefferson, for example, has written that theater gives us something that nothing else can: "It gives us human beings in three dimensions: bodies that live in front of us, that move, speak, change shape, create tension or bestow peace" (p. H-5).

Although we emphasized above that we were attracted to the specific readers' theater genre in part because it did not require that we totally abandon the analytical and critical dimensions of doing and reporting research, it is also the case that our initial search for some sort of dramatic form with which to display data had a great deal to do with a desire not to lose the people in our data or to transform them into dehumanized concepts, abstract constructs, or mere ideal types that are always, to some degree, stereotypes. Indeed, we ended up deciding to report the middle school student data about writing in dramatic form because when we initially attempted to analyze the data through traditional content analysis procedures, we found that we were losing too much of the students we knew so well and for whom we had great affection. These students were insightful, emotional, and, invariably, very funny. When students are transformed into the ideal types that populate the traditional research report, much of this is lost.

Arguably the most important reason for displaying data in a readers' theater format, however, is its potential for generating discussion. Well-done readers' theater productions invariably provide the sort of communal experiences that lead to deep and deeply animated conversations about what should be done in the particular contexts in which audience members work. The role of research as a conversation starter—and as a source of new frames within which new conversations can occur—should not be underestimated.

Indeed, those who study research utilization[5] have suggested that this sort of generative role is the only viable one for research to play in a field like education. Particular contexts are simply too idiosyncratic and value issues too omnipresent and too entangled with "empirical" questions (Donmoyer & Kos, 1993) to expect research to provide anything like definitive, value-free solutions to educational problems. Rather, research can only play a heuristic role in decision making about what specific courses of action to pursue at any point in time in any particular setting. It does this by sensitizing decision makers to new ways of seeing and new ways of framing the problem to be addressed (Donmoyer, 1990; Weiss, 1982). The stylized dramatic form of readers' theater, when used for the purpose of data display, has the potential to be an especially useful source of frames and perspectives—and, also, an effective conversation starter—because it can present new ideas in an engaging way while keeping theoretical abstraction at least somewhat tethered to human beings and human situations (Moran, 2006).[6]

◆ The Marginalization of Readers' Theater in an Era of "Scientific Research in Education"

CURRENT THINKING

Unfortunately, in recent years, influential policymakers and educational researchers have chosen to minimize and even, at times, totally ignore both the difficulties posed by contextual factors and the impact of values on "empirical" research. In the process, they have, in effect, moved even relatively conservative versions of arts-based research to the margins of the field.

Grover Whitehurst (2003), the head of the Institute of Education Sciences (IES), the federal agency charged with funding educational inquiry, for instance, has declared randomized trials (i.e., experimental studies in which research subjects are assigned to control and experimental groups by chance) the new "gold standard" in educational inquiry. Unlike those who spend time staging their data because they assume that research findings can only function heuristically (e.g., as sources of working hypotheses, Lincoln & Guba, 1985; new ways of framing problems, Weiss, 1982; and/or more sophisticated cognitive schemas, Donmoyer, 1990), Whitehurst's (2003) expectation is that educational researchers will tell policymakers, in relatively definitive terms, "what works" so that policymakers can replicate "what works" throughout the nation (e.g., see the Institute of Education Sciences' *Request for Applications*, 2006).

Prominent academics have aided and abetted policymakers' efforts to marginalize even relatively conservative forms of arts-based inquiry. The National Research Council (NRC, 2002) committee set up to define what constitutes "scientific research in Education," for instance, explicitly declared all forms of arts-based research nonscientific (and by implication ineligible for federal funding). As noted above, the NRC committee could easily hoist advocates of arts-based educational research on their own petard on this point because advocates themselves often had emphasized differences rather than similarities between arts-based and scientific inquiry (Eisner, 1991/1998). Yet even if the arts-based researchers' rhetoric had been different, the NRC committee defined science in such a way that all arts-based strategies fall outside of the scientific domain.[7] The committee, for instance, stipulated that to be considered scientific (and, consequently, fundable from the federal government's perspective) research must, among other things, be oriented toward the generation and validation of theory that applies across a variety of places and times (NRC, 2002).

PROBLEMS WITH CURRENT THINKING

Current thinking in both the academic and policy communities is problematic for a number of reasons. The NRC committee's equating of science with theory construction, for instance, not only puts readers' theater and other forms of arts-based research outside the domain of science; it also does the same for many other forms of qualitative research, including the bulk of research conducted by cultural anthropologists. After all, Clifford Geertz (1973, 1983), one of cultural anthropology's intellectual leaders, has argued that

> theoretical formulations hover so low over the interpretations they govern that they don't make much sense or hold much interest apart from them. This is so, not because they are not general

(if they are not general, they are not theoretical), but because, stated independently of their applications, they seem either commonplace or vacant. (p. 25)

Geertz, in fact, viewed theory as a tool for doing—rather than an end product of—research. For Geertz and other thick description–oriented anthropologists, in other words, theory is, in essence, a rhetorical device employed "to make thick description possible" (Geertz, 1973, p. 26).

Thus, if researchers who engage in even relatively conservative forms of arts-based inquiry such as readers' theater are to be banished from the enterprise of science, they are, at least, in very good company. That company includes researchers from the academic discipline of cultural anthropology, a discipline that historically, at least, was thought to be engaged in a form of scientific work (Geertz, 1973).

The NRC committee's thinking also seems out of sync with the history of educational research in the 20th century. There is, after all, a historical precedent for the NRC committee's emphasis on theory construction in the so-called theory movement that flourished in the educational administration field during the 1950s and 1960s. In time, members of that field recognized not only that the focus on developing empirical theories obscured important value questions but also that the general theories they sought were not particularly helpful—except, perhaps, as heuristics—for practitioners who must confront and manage the complexity of real—as opposed to the theoretician's ideal typical—settings (Donmoyer, 1999). The authors of *Scientific Research in Education* (NRC, 2002) say nothing about why their emphasis on theory will succeed while a similar 20th-century initiative failed; indeed, there is no evidence that they are even aware that there is a precedent for the vision of education research they articulate.

Whitehurst's comments also seem surprisingly ahistorical. The title of his 2003 AERA address was "New Wine in New Bottles." In it he never discussed how his approach to experimental design will overcome past difficulties with experimental studies; indeed, he never even alluded to past problems. He never acknowledged, for instance, the limited payoff of process–product studies of teaching, studies that taught us that the more time students spend engaged in a task, the more likely they will master it (Tickunoff, Berliner, & Rist, 1975) and that students who have teachers who communicate clearly are likely to do better on tests that measure what was communicated than students who have teachers who communicate less clearly (Bush, Kennedy, & Cruickshank, 1977). These findings give new meaning to Geertz's (1973) notions of "commonplace" and "vacant" knowledge.

Even more surprising, Whitehurst (2003) never even alludes to the government's previous attempt to use large-scale research studies—the so-called planned variation studies of the 1960s and 1970s—to determine what works and, consequently, what should be replicated throughout the nation. A host of problems was uncovered by a team of scholars assembled by the Ford Foundation to review data from one of these studies, Project Follow Through (ABT Associates, 1977), a study that was supposed to tell, once and for all, which of a number of models of early childhood education (e.g., the basic-skills and affective-education models) was most effective. Among other things, the team noted that the study focused only on a limited number of easy-to-measure goals and that the goals that were measured were emphasized more by the supposedly most effective models and less by the models judged least effective. The study's limited (but still statistically significant) aggregate findings, therefore, appeared tautological.

Even more problematic was the fact that, even with the study's apparent measurement bias, aggregate-level results could not predict what had occurred at particular sites: Some sites that implemented the model that appeared at the aggregate level most effective (and, of course, most consistent with the measures employed) produced some of the least impressive results, while in certain places supposedly ineffective models were highly effective despite the model–measurement mismatch. The review team concluded: "Local schools do seem to make a difference. The peculiarities of individual teachers, schools, neighborhoods and homes influence pupils' achievement far more than whatever is captured by labels such as *basic skills* or *affective education*." The team added that this insight "should be honored widely and serve as a basis of educational policy" (House, Glass, McLean, & Walker, 1978, p. 462).

The arts-based research movement, of course, was fueled, in part, by a desire to honor this insight about the importance of what happens at the local level. Now, however, even practitioners of conservative forms of arts-based inquiry must confront the fact that the insight is often ignored not only by key policymakers but also by influential academics.

◆ *What to Do?*

There is no reason to believe that Whitehurst's (2003) randomization strategy will even address—much less effectively manage—the measurement and contextual complexity problems that plagued the earlier planned variation studies, just as there is no reason to believe that contemporary social scientists' theories will be any more adept at overcoming the value-related and relevance problems that plagued the earlier theory movement. Thus, it seems certain that, sooner or later, the limitations of current thinking will be recognized.

The problem is that such recognition is likely to come later rather than sooner. Once again, history has lessons to teach: For nearly three quarters of the 20th century, the thinking that supported both process–product studies of teaching and planned variation studies of policies and programs dictated both the methods educational researchers used (and did not even consider using) and the types of scholars universities hired, promoted, and tenured. Furthermore, the mere promise that educational researchers could produce scientific knowledge that definitively linked specific organizational and pedagogical practices with desired educational outcomes helped legitimate a range of policies and practices in schools—everything from top-down decision making to teacher-proof curricula to competency-based teacher education (Donmoyer, 2005).

There is a certain irony in the fact that scientific researchers' "spin" rather than their "commonplace" and "vacant" findings influenced policy and practice. There is no reason to believe, however, that this irony of the past will not occur in the future. Indeed, in his 2003 AERA address, Whitehurst made clear that he planned to leverage the power and resources of his agency to promote his vision of educational inquiry and its role in dictating educational practice, and there is now ample evidence that this leveraging activity is underway (e.g., Viadero, 2006).

So, it seems time for those who remain committed to integrating the arts into educational research to actively challenge the "reality" that currently is being constructed (or, to be more precise, reconstructed) in both the policy and the academic communities. The

need to do this certainly influenced the writing of this chapter.

◆ Conclusion

This chapter, in fact, intentionally framed the case for integrating the arts into social science research narrowly. Our goal was modest: to demonstrate that integrating the arts into social science inquiry is not *inherently* problematic, or at least no more problematic than the sort of research that is done in a discipline such as cultural anthropology. We attempted to accomplish this goal by focusing on the use of readers' theater for data display purposes. With this approach, data collection and analysis are not appreciably different from the data collection and analysis strategies used in any other thick description–oriented qualitative research (including the bulk of research conducted in cultural anthropology). Furthermore, even the readers' theater data display method incorporates a range of distancing devices to ensure that audiences respond intellectually as well as emotionally to the data on stage.

We are not naïve; we understand that pointing out the similarities between work that displays data in a readers' theater format and other thick description–oriented qualitative research will not persuade either academics who equate being scientific with the construction of abstract theory or policymakers to provide research results that can be used to create programs that can be replicated with predictable results. Still, it is a bit more difficult to cavalierly write-off the thinking and research procedures of virtually an entire academic discipline, especially one that historically was viewed as operating within the domain of science, than it is to dismiss a small band of arts-oriented educational researchers. In the arena, it is always helpful to have allies!

◆ Notes

1. The most recent example of this is Blumenfeld-Jones's high-profile 2006 AERA Annual Meeting Vice-Presidential address.

2. Interestingly, Greene has not been especially supportive of arts-based educational research. She prefers the richness and complexity of actual literary and artistic works to any artistic or literary products that educational researchers—who lack real artists' sensibility and training—might produce.

3. For example, he used a variety of conventions from the German expressionist movement such as masks, songs, verse, and direct rhetorical address to the audience as well as a number of techniques that he had created (e.g., lantern slide projections, asides to the audience encouraging them to develop their own points of view, and lowering lights so visible wires and pipes would remind audiences that they were watching a construction of reality rather than reality itself).

4. Performers included J. Moncada, S. Pando, D. Deschamps, U. Chavira, and A. Montoya-Tenabe.

5. See, for example, Weiss's (1982) seminal work on this topic.

6. The emerging literature on transforming qualitative data into various forms of drama suggests additional reasons for using dramatic form in the context of research. These reasons include everything from emancipating audience members from politically problematic conceptions of reality and ways of operating in the world (Mienczakowski, 1995) to promoting confrontation and catharsis as a means of developing collective action (Mienczakowski, Smith, & Sinclair, 1996). At least some of these rationales might also be used to justify the use of the specific genre of readers' theater. The rationale discussed in this chapter, however, is the one

that motivated our explorations of readers' theater as a data display method. This rationale contrasts directly with the thinking of policymakers and certain members of the research community, a topic that will be discussed in the next section.

7. The authors of the NRC report also write off Lawrence-Lightfoot's portraiture method as nonscientific, even though Lawrence-Lightfoot and her coauthor Davis (1997) suggest their method combines elements of art and science.

◆ References

ABT Associates. (1977). *Education as experimentation: A planned variation model* (Vol. IVA-D). Boston: ABT Associates.

Adams, N., Causey, T., Jacobs, M., Munro, P., Quinn, M., & Trousdale, A. (1998). Womentalkin': A readers' theater performance of teachers' stories. *Qualitative Studies in Education, 11*(3), 385–395.

Bandelier, A. (1971). *The delight makers.* Orlando, FL: Harcourt Brace & Company. (Original work published 1890)

Barone, T. (1983). Things of use and things of beauty: The Swain County High School Arts Program. *Daedalus, 112*(3), 1–28.

Barone, T. (1997). Among the chosen: A collaborative educational (auto)biography. *Qualitative Inquiry, 3*(2), 222–236.

Blumenfeld-Jones, D. (2006). *The shattered mirror: Curriculum, art, and critical politics.* Division B Vice-Presidential Address presented at the American Educational Research Association, San Francisco, CA.

Brecht, B. (1992). *Brecht on theatre: The development of an aesthetic* (J. Willet, Trans.). New York: Hill and Wing.

Bush, A., Kennedy, J., & Cruickshank, D. (1977). An empirical investigation of teacher clarity. *Journal of Teacher Education, 28*(2), 53–58.

Clifford, J., & Marcus, G. (1986). *Writing culture: The poetics and politics of ethnography.* Berkeley: University of California Press.

Coger, L., & White, M. (1982). *Readers' theater handbook*. Glenview, IL: Scott, Foresman.

Cronbach, L. (1975). Beyond the two disciplines of scientific psychology. *American Psychologist, 12*, 671–684.

Cronbach, L. (1982). Prudent aspirations of social inquiry. In W. Kruskal (Ed.), *The Social sciences: Their nature and lines* (pp. 42–54). Chicago: University of Chicago Press.

Deavere-Smith, A. (1993). *Fires in the mirror.* New York: Anchor Books.

Deavere-Smith, A. (1994). *Twilight, LA. 1992.* New York: Anchor Books.

Denzin, N. K. (1997). *Interpretive ethnography: Ethnographic practices for the 21st century.* London: Sage.

Denzin, K. N. (2002). *Interpretive ethnography.* Thousand Oaks, CA: Sage.

Denzin, K. N. (2003). *Performance ethnography.* Thousand Oaks, CA: Sage.

Donmoyer, R. (1990). Generalizability and the single case study. In E. Eisner & A. Peshkin (Eds.), *Qualitative research in education: The continuing debate* (pp. 175–200). New York: Teachers College Press.

Donmoyer, R. (1999). The continuing quest for a knowledge base. In J. Murphy and K. Seashore Louis (Eds.), *The handbook of research in educational administration* (pp. 25–43). San Francisco: Jossey-Bass.

Donmoyer, R. (2005). Science as scriptwriters: How educational researchers influence public policy without ever producing definitive results. In B. Alexander, G. Anderson, & B. Gallegos (Eds.), *Performance theories in education* (pp. 239–262). Mahwah, NJ: Lawrence Erlbaum.

Donmoyer, R., & Galloway, F. (2002). *Voices in our heads.* Glencoe, IL: The Ball Foundation.

Donmoyer, R., & Kos, R. (1993). At-risk students: Insights from/about research. In Donmoyer, R., & Kos, R. (Eds.), *At-risk students: Portraits, policies, programs, and practices* (pp. 2–35). New York: State University of New York Press.

Donmoyer, R., & Yennie-Donmoyer, J. (1995). Data as drama: Reflections on the use of readers' theater as a mode of qualitative data display. *Qualitative Inquiry, 20*(1), 74–83.

Donmoyer R., & Yennie-Donmoyer, J. (1998). Reader's theater and educational research— Give me a for instance: A commentary on Womentalkin.' *Qualitative Studies in Education, 11*(3), 397–402.

Eisner, E. (1971). *English primary schools: Some observations and assessments.* Stanford, CA: Stanford University. (ERIC Document Reproduction Service No. ED093471).

Eisner, E. (1979). *The educational imagination.* New York: Macmillan.

Eisner, E. (1998). *The enlightened eye: Qualitative inquiry and the enhancement of educational practice.* Upper Saddle River, NJ: Prentice Hall. (Original work published 1991)

Eisner, E., & Barone, T. (1997). Arts-based educational research. In R. Jager & T. Barone (Eds.), *Complementary methods for research in education* (pp. 36–116). Washington, DC: American Educational Research Association.

Finley, M. (2000). *Street Rat.* Detroit: Greenroom Press.

Finley, S., & Finley, M. (1998). *Traveling through the cracks: Homeless youth speak out.* Performance presented at the annual meeting of the American Educational Research Association, San Diego, CA.

Finley, S., & Finley, M. (1999). Sp'ange: A research story. *Qualitative Inquiry, 5*(3), 313–337.

Geertz, C. (1973). *The interpretation of cultures: Selected essays.* New York: Basic Books.

Geertz, C. (1983). *Local knowledge.* New York: Basic Books.

Glesne, C. (1997). That rare feeling: Re-presenting research through poetic transcription. *Qualitative Inquiry, 3*(2), 202–221.

Goldstein, T. (2002). Performed Ethnography for representing other people's children in critical educational research. *Applied Theatre Researcher, ISSN 1443–1726, Number 3, Article No. 5.*

Gray, R., Ivonoffski, V., & Sinding, C. (2002). Making a mess and spreading it around: Articulation of an approach to research-based theater. In A. Bouchner & C. Ellis (Eds.), *Ethnographically speaking: Autoethnography, literature, and aesthetics* (pp. 57–75). Walnut Creek, CA: Altamira Press.

Greene, M. (1995). *Releasing the imagination: Essays on education, the arts, and social change.* San Francisco: Jossey-Bass.

Gusfield, J. (1976). The literary rhetoric of science. *American Sociologist, 41,* 11–33.

Holmes, D., & Marcus, G. (2005). Refunctioning ethnography: The challenge of an anthropology of the contemporary. In N. Denzin & Y. Lincoln (Eds.), *The SAGE Handbook of qualitative research* (3rd ed.; pp. 1099–1114). Thousand Oaks, CA: Sage.

House, E., Glass, G., McLean, D., & Walker, D. (1978). No simple answer: Critiques of the project follow-through evaluation. *Educational Leadership, 35,* 462–464.

Institute of Education Sciences. (2006, April 7). *Research grants request for applications IES-NCER-2007–01.* Washington, DC: U.S. Department of Education. Retrieved July 20, 2006, from www.ed.gov/about/offices/list/ies/programs.html

Jefferson, M. (1995, April 23). Perfectly tuned actors hit a high note. *The New York Times,* p. H5.

Kaufman, M., & Members of the Tectonic Theatre Project. (2001). *The Laramie Project.* New York: Vintage Books.

Kleinau, M., & McHughes, J. (1980). Theaters for literature: A practical aesthetic for group interpretation. Sherman Oaks, CA: Alfred.

Konzal, J. (1995). *Our changing town, our changing school.* Unpublished doctoral dissertation, The University of Pittsburgh.

Konzal, J. (1996). Our changing town, our changing school. *School Community Journal, 6*(2), 93–130.

Konzal, J. (2001). Our changing town, our changing school. In S. Redding & L. Thomas (Eds.), *The community and the school* (pp. 63–82) Lincoln, IL: Academic Development Institute.

Lawrence-Lightfoot, S., & Davis, J. (1997). *The art and science of portraiture.* San Francisco: Jossey-Bass.

Lincoln, Y., & Guba, E. (1985). *Naturalistic inquiry.* Beverly Hills, CA: Sage.

McCall, M. (2003). Performance ethnography: A brief history and some advice. In K. N. Denzin & Lincoln, Y. (Eds.), *Strategies of qualitative inquiry* (pp. 421–434). Thousand Oaks, CA: Sage.

McCall, M., & Becker, H. (1990). Performance science. *Social Problems, 37,* 116–132.

Mienczakowski, J. (1995). The theater of ethnography: The reconstruction of ethnography into theater with emancipatory potential. *Qualitative Inquiry, 1,* 360–375.

Mienczakowski, J. (2000). Ethnodrama: Performed research—limitations and potential. In P. Atkinson, S. Delamont, & A. Coffey (Eds.), *Handbook of ethnography* (pp. 468–476). Thousand Oaks, CA: Sage.

Mienczakowski, J., Smith, R., & Sinclair, M. (1996). On the road to catharsis: A theoretical framework for change. *Qualitative Inquiry, 2,* 439–462.

Montoya-Tanabe, A. (2003). *Voces y visiones: Portraits of bilingual education teachers' journeys.* Readers' theater script presented at the annual meeting of the University Council of Educational Administration, Portland, OR.

Moran, C. (2006). *How teachers use feedback received from students, parents, and peers in the 360-degree evaluation system.* Unpublished doctoral dissertation, University of San Diego, CA.

National Research Council. (2002). *Scientific research in education.* Washington, DC: National Academy Press.

Nisbet, R. (1976). *Sociology as an art form.* London: Oxford University Press.

Pikering, J. (1975). *Readers' theater.* Encino, CA: Dickenson.

Polkinghorne, D. (1995). Narrative configuration in qualitative analysis. *Qualitative Studies in Education, 8*(1), 5–23.

Richardson, L. (1992). The poetic representation of lives: Writing a postmodern sociology. *Studies in Symbolic Interaction, 13,* 19–29.

Richardson, L. (1994). Writing: A method of inquiry. In N. Denzin & Y. Lincoln (Eds.) *Handbook of qualitative research* (pp. 516–529). Thousand Oaks, CA: Sage.

Saldaña, J. (Ed.). (2005). *Ethnodrama: An anthology of reality theatre.* Thousand Oaks, CA: Sage.

Saldaña, J., Finley, S., & Finley, M. (2005). Street rat. In Saldana, J. (Ed.), *Ethnodrama: An anthology of reality theatre* (pp. 139–179). Thousand Oaks, CA: Sage.

Simon, R., & Dippo, D. (1980). Dramatic analysis: Interpretive inquiry for transformation of social settings. *Journal of Curriculum Theorizing, 2,* 109–134.

Taylor, P. (2003). *Applied theater.* Portsmouth, NH: Heinemann.

Tickunoff, W., Berliner, D., & Rist, R. (1975). *An ethnographic study of the forty classroom of BTES known sample.* San Francisco: Far West Regional Lab.

Tierney, W. (1993). The cedar closet. *Qualitative Studies in Education, 6*(4), 303–314.

Torres, C. (1998). Six authors in search of four characters. *Qualitative Studies in Education, 11*(3), 409–413.

Viadero, D. (2006, February 1). New group of researchers focuses on scientific Study [Electronic version]. *Education Week.* Retrieved June 26, 2007, from http://www.edweek .org/ew/articles/2006/02/01/21research.h25. html?tmp=1538939125

Weiss, C. (1982). Policy research in the context of diffuse decision making. *Journal of Higher Education, 53,* 619–639.

Whitehurst, G. (2003). *The institute of education sciences: New wine in new bottles.* Invited address to the Annual Meeting of the American Educational Research Association, Chicago.

Yennie-Donmoyer, J., & Donmoyer, R. (1994). *In their own words: Middle school students write about writing.* Script performed at the annual meeting of the American Educational Research Association, April 1999, New Orleans, LA.

19

Performance

THE MUSIC LESSON

◆ Liora Bresler

I n the conversation about the arts in research literature, visual art and
drama have taken a leading role. The voice of music has been relatively mute. Can music offer anything to social science research within
postmodern research paradigms that are primarily verbal and visual?

The Viennese philosopher of music and conductor Victor
Zuckerkandl (1956) proclaimed that the majesty of vision in the epistemology of Western thought stems from our traditional emphasis on
the observation of material things within a field of vision. "In seeing,
touching, tasting, we reach through the sensation to an object, to a
thing. Tone is the only sensation not that of a thing" (Zuckerkandl,
1956, p. 70). Along similar lines, David Burrows (1990), the American
musicologist, stated that "we see the world as a noun and hear it as a
verb" (p. 21). Following on this theme and expanding it, I suggest in
this chapter that learning to hear cultivates sensitivities essential to
social science inquiry. As Sorko Seyni, a healer among the Songhay in
Niger, West Africa, cautioned the anthropologist Paul Stoller (1984):
"Without sight or touch, one can learn a great deal. But you must learn
how to *hear,* or you will not learn about our ways" (p. 560).

Author's Note: Many thanks to Tom Barone, Nancy Ellis, Jason Helfer, Rita
Irwin, Saville Kushner, Jana Mason, Koji Matsunobu, Regina Murphy, Philip
Silvey, and Su-Jeong Wee for their insightful comments on early drafts.

◆ 225

The literature on research methodology has enormously expanded knowledge and understanding of inquiry. Still, there are areas at the core of qualitative research that are not addressed in this literature. They include: (1) attention to live interactions in the inquiry process and its communication, (2) the polyphonic nature and dynamics of collaborative research, and (3) finer conceptualizations of the personal and communal flow of experience.

In this chapter I explore ways in which the various musical processes of listening, performing, composing, and improvising can inform the processes of social science research. Specifically, I will focus on: relationships to participants, coresearchers, and the audience of research and meaning making and conceptualizations in observations, data analysis, and writing. Specific themes that run contrapuntally across these domains include: systematic improvisation; disciplined empathy, and embodiment.

Building on Zuckerkandl (1956) and Sorko Seyni (in Stoller, 1984), I suggest that both the personal and cultural dimensions of lived experience can be better understood by greater attentiveness to states, relations, and tendencies. Musical experiences can help reveal important dimensions of qualitative inquiry that have not been explored. Where sight gives us physical entities, the heard world is phenomenally evanescent, relentlessly moving, ever changing, writes Burrows (1990). Involvement in music as creators, performers, and listeners[1] requires that we engage in the evanescent aspects of world, cultivating sensibilities that apply to ways of doing as well as ways of *becoming*.[2] These are the very same sensibilities that are needed for researchers of human sciences.

Often it is the "ah-hah" of personal experiences, rather than only the abstracted concept, that generates insights and motivation to deepen exploration. I was hit by the notion of musical dimensions as useful lenses for conceptualization in social research in an environment far removed from music. Two months after finishing a thesis in musicology, I began work with Elliot Eisner on a research project that involved classroom observations. Since I had no background in education and lacked a conceptual framework from which to generate descriptions and questions, I was baffled about what to attend to in the barrage of classroom activities. In desperation I turned to my one area of expertise—music—and drew on (internalized) tools for musical analysis. Suddenly, classroom life assumed meaning. It transformed from blurred chaos to a coherent form (introduction to the lesson, its development, closure) that was visibly orchestrated (teacher as a conductor) and had distinct dynamics, texture, and rhythm. The power of using musical lenses to make sense of educational settings was palpable for me.

It took me several more years to acknowledge the bodily aspect of the *chaotic* versus *focused* observations. Initially, I was immobilized and overwhelmed by my classroom experience, responding to it as a cacophony of sound. Equipped with ways to conceptualize classroom activities and a channel to attune to, in the process of "tuning into" and attending, my body and mind became focused and directed. A third stage, years later, involved the aural communication of this research (including this story), now processed and rehearsed, on a meta-level. That *public* communication of scholarship resembled a solo performance in a "by-heart" mode,[3] bodily as well as intellectually. Each of these three stances—the "noise" stage, the making-sense stage, and the communication stage—had its distinct characteristics, corresponding to my musical experiences as a performer.

The second sets of experiences where musical lenses illuminated research processes occurred when I was heading a research group. Teamwork, like jazz ensembles, I realized, consisted of individual voices, each with its own timbres and characteristics, yet all interacting to create a composition. Indeed, the intensity of our research group conversations, the conflicts and their resolutions (sometimes as agreements, at other times as acknowledgment of the validity of others' points of view), were experienced by us as embodying aesthetic quality. That quality emerged as a part of a focused, attentive listening and sharing, targeted toward common goals and endeavors, yet integrating a variety of perspectives and voices. In addition to the predefined aspects and structures of our research goals, it was the emerging, improvisatory aspects that gave our group discussions their flavor: developing and presenting a topic to the group, cultivating a particular way of listening, probing, interacting[4] (Bresler, Wasser, Hertzog, & Lemons, 1996).

Within education, the scholar who first framed the arts explicitly as models not only for knowledge but for the *process* of inquiry was Elliot Eisner. In his conceptualization of connoisseurship and educational criticism, Eisner, drawing on the visual arts, expanded the modes of inquiry beyond the verbal and numerical to the sensory. His notion of the *enlightened eye* (Eisner, 1991) propelled me to explore the possibilities and implications of an enlightened *ear*, in research and beyond, to perceive the world. In this chapter, I expand the ear to a larger set of musical sensitivities—oral, kinesthetic, cognitive—all grounded in musical experience, to reflect on their power for social science research.

A couple of qualifications are in order. The sensitivities discussed here, ways of being and doing, are epitomized in music but are also present in other areas (e.g., dance, drama). A second caution concerns implications for researcher development, our own and others'. Although musical experiences cultivate these sensitivities, it takes an *active* transfer to apply them to social science research.[5]

◆ Dialogic Relationships With Participants: Learning to Hear

Sorko Seyni's (in Stoller, 1984) admonition about learning to hear refers to a particular "tuning," a sensitized, nuanced quality of relationship. This tuned-in quality of relationship is powerfully articulated by Martin Buber (1971) in his description of "I–Thou" relationships, as distinct from other types of relationships ("I–I," "It–It," "We–We," "Us–Them"). Indeed, interactions in research can take many forms. Because in the social sciences researchers attend to participants' descriptions and interpretations of their lived experience, researchers must listen as though they were within an "I–Thou" relationship. Stoller (1989) remarked that when a musician or an apprentice Songhay healer learns to hear, he begins to learn that sound allows for the interpretation of the visible and the invisible, the tangible and the intangible. Indeed, hearing attends to much more than literal content. It attends to tone, mood, rhythm, and dynamics. Sound has the power to bond. In contrast to a person's spatialized "gaze," which creates distance, sound penetrates the individual and creates a sense of communication and participation (Stoller, 1984, p. 563).

Engaged listening, rather than background listening, is crucial to qualitative interviews; yet it is not part of our busy, rushed culture (where the question "how are you?" is typically meant as "hi," where a real answer is not expected). As I elaborate later in this chapter, interviewing requires attentive and empathetic listening, and the juxtaposition of both "efferent" and "aesthetic" qualities.

The act of interviewing can be conceptualized as accompaniment that requires intense attentiveness to the other's voice. The interviewer is not in the limelight but uses her aural sensitivities to create a structure for the interviewee's reflection and communication. Mutuality is part of the process. Schutz (1951) has pointed out that it is the mutual tuning-in relationship by which the "I" and the "Thou" are experienced by both participants as a "We" in vivid presence.

DIALOGIC RELATIONSHIPS IN COLLABORATIVE RESEARCH: JAZZ ENSEMBLE

Attentiveness to others' voices is also at the core of collaborative research. There is increasing recognition in the social sciences of the collective nature of knowing and social theories of development, but little about the role that researchers' interactions with other researchers play in the co-construction of knowledge.[6] The metaphor of "ensemble research" highlights these important transactions. Jazz ensembles consist of several voices, each with its own timbre and melodic line, yet all interacting closely, building on and responding to each other's themes to create a polyphonic performance.[7] Driven by a common goal, musicians seem to work together like "the different organs in a living body, with each individual action taken tuned to and affecting the actions of all others" (Stubley, 1998, p. 95).

Jazz ensemble provides the metaphor for an "interpretive zone," the intellectual realm in which researchers work collaboratively. The concept of zone assumes more than one party—at least two if not more—negotiating and interacting from different perspectives (Bresler, Wasser, Hertzog, & Lemons, 1996; Wasser & Bresler, 1996).[8] Thus, the term zone, more than the term interpretation, moves us away from the traditional image of the researcher as a soloist working independently to that of a socially embedded researcher grounded in social interactions. The notion of zone implies dynamic processes—exchange, transaction, transformation, and intensity. In the interpretive zone researchers bring together their distinct voices—various areas of knowledge, experience, and beliefs—to forge new meanings through the process of the joint inquiry in which they are engaged. Harmonies range from neutral (scaffolding) through conflict (struggles) to amicable (negotiations). It is the unexpected meeting between different ideas and perspectives that often breaks new intellectual ground.

◆ Three-Pronged Communication

The communication of both music and research is three pronged. Musical performance focuses on the music to be played, on the self,[9] and on the audience. Communication in musical performance is judged not only by its correctness, but also by its depth and the resonance it creates in others. The differences among these three gestures are striking: Correctness has a specific, accurate focus; self-inquiry is characterized by depth; public communication, traversing personal and spatial boundaries, creates an expanded, broader space. During the performance of music, these three gestures are not mutually exclusive; rather they coexist, support, and intensify each other.

Qualitative research is similarly tridirectional: reaching toward the phenomenon under study to understand it accurately and fully, reaching within oneself, and reaching out to an audience. As in music, the awareness of the potential audience in conducting research is present at various stages, well before the actual communication. The process of research, like getting to know music, typically involves the discovery and shaping of meaning for oneself as well as for *others*. Much as a performer anticipates an audience when rehearsing, in fieldwork what is observed is shaped by the prospect of its communication to others. Researchers are propelled by intellectual–emotional curiosity, intensified by the commitment to an outside audience. The act of communication intensifies meaning. The expectation of a potential audience, essential to both music performance and research, heightens perception, rendering it into an articulated, communal act. The communication embodies expressivity with its specific aesthetics and interplay of cognition and affect.

◆ *The Polyphonic Nature of Lived Experience*

A central feature of music in particular, and the arts in general, is its unique ability to convey complexity and ambiguity. Traditionally, in social sciences, we strive for simple, precise, and consistent models (which, one can argue, are artificial products of verbal and mathematical languages). Still, complexity and ambiguity are at the heart of human experience, including the processes of inquiry. In this section, I examine the oxymorons of *systematic improvisation, disciplined empathy,* and *embodiment* as they operate within dialogical relationship in fieldwork, analysis, and communication. Although presented here separately for clarity, they are interwoven within each other.

◆ *Systematic Improvisation*

Musical improvisation, central to many musical genres and cultures, has a long history. Indeed, it is likely that the earliest forms of music making were created through improvisatory activity, possibly incorporating sounds of the natural world (McMillan, 1999). In improvisation, performers are expected to respond appropriately to unforeseen challenges and opportunities (cf. Blum, 1998). Improvisation is central to some genres (e.g., jazz, African, Indian) and not to others (e.g., classical). Western, "serious" music is traditionally associated with discipline, reliability, and predictability and tends to look down on what is perceived as the lack of discipline associated with improvised genres (Nettl, 1998, pp. 6–7).

Academic research, like Western classical music, demands sophisticated skills, technical and theoretical knowledge, and systematicity. Its evaluation, just like classical music, is framed against well-established traditions of research communities. In both music and research, the interplay between tradition and innovation, script and exploration, is made complex by the expectation to be groundbreaking, adhering to rigorous traditions. The emphasis on systematic inquiry distinguishes research from myths and "folk theories" (Bruner, 1996), often perceived as undisciplined.

Creating a dichotomy out of systematicity and improvisation is, as every jazz player and experienced researcher is fully aware, false. Even though improvisation is not addressed by research textbooks, it is evident in accounts of the inquiry processes, an integral part of the conduct of research. This is true in the natural sciences (e.g., in the discovery of DNA, Watson, 1968) and in the social sciences (e.g., Gottlieb & Graham, 1994; Myerhoff, 1978). Improvisation is present in data collection. The use of open-ended observations and interviews in qualitative research implies the need to respond to unforeseen challenges and opportunities. Improvisation is also central to conceptualization (elaborated below) and in data analysis. The phenomena we study interact with our preconceived ideas, inviting us to attend to new data sources, grapple with unexpected issues, and, in this process, sometimes branch into new intellectual (and emotional) territories. Improvisation in research involves the cyclical processes of identifying emergent issues in response to fieldwork, generating a corresponding design to explore them, and embarking on additional data collection. Responsiveness is key to data analysis, when new categories emerge in response to new knowledge and deepened understanding (cf. Miles & Huberman, 1984).

In that process, improvisation is never capricious. George Steiner has commented that we lack the right word for the "ordered enlistment of intuition" (Steiner, 1989, p. 12). Indeed, research, like playing jazz, involves the systematic cultivation of sophisticated skills on the one hand and intuitive response on the other. Improvisation allows us to get out of an "automatic pilot" mode, treating the unexpected as opportunities to expand and redirect our attention. As I discuss in the next section, improvisation is "tuned" empathy.

◆ *Disciplined Empathy*

What distinguishes the aims and processes of human sciences from other forms of research is the quest for verstehen— *empathic understanding* (cf. Bresler & Stake, 1992; Kvale, 1996; van Manen, 1990; von Wright, 1971). However, empathy has not been part of the academic culture, traditionally characterized by objectivity and distance. Another practical hindrance to empathy is the fact that academia increasingly becomes as rushed as the outside life, whereas empathy requires a slower rhythm, responsive to participants. Even within qualitative research, Eisner's (1991) notion of *connoisseurship,* for example, is primarily a discernment of a detached expert. In contrast, empathy involves putting oneself in another's place.

Empathy is dialogic (Buber, 1971; Gadamer, 1988). In that dialogue, the researcher/performer is touched and expanded, not just in terms of factual knowledge, but also in her resonance to the world. Musical performances involve a dedicate balance: empathic connection and resonance to the music, within aesthetic controlled distance of the performance. The challenge of qualitative research is trying to understand the other empathically while maintaining disciplined scholarship.

Empathy is essential to all the arts but is achieved differently in each. Because most instrumental music is not mimetic, empathy or resonance is not based on a story (as it is in literature and drama) but on a connection to a mood, an emotional quality. The literal is irrelevant. In research, the near enemy of empathic listening is literal judgment—obvious, practical, and prompt— apt to judge before the entire content has been absorbed. Louise Rosenblatt's (1978) notions of *efferent* and *aesthetic* transactions, not distinct but interdependent, are useful in qualitative research as well as in literature. A practical, efferent transaction— reading for cognitive utilitarian understanding—is inarguably at the forefront of observations and interviews, just as it is essential in analyzing and performing music. An aesthetic and empathic transaction, I argue, is equally important at the interview stage, aiming to absorb, withholding evaluation. Empathic listening in an interview, similar to the engaged way that we listen to music, is open, present, following closely and caringly, attending to nuanced qualities, much as an accompanist is present for the soloist.

We learn to hear the expressive in its complexity. Jazz or classical musical contents are never simple in their expression; note the serene intensity of Bach, or the pained exquisiteness of Abbey Lincoln. Likewise, the complexities of lived experience that we aim to capture in interviewing require an empathic listening mode as well as critical analysis. As I elaborate in the next section, this mode is highly embodied.

EMBODIMENT

Thinking and feeling, traditionally perceived as dichotomous, are now recognized as interdependent. This interdependence is a core characteristic of art, as various scholars, from John Dewey and Susanne Langer to Harry Broudy and Elliot Eisner, have articulated extensively.[10] More recently, ethnographies, as reflected in the detailed self-descriptions of researchers, acknowledge thinking and feeling as fundamental to the ways we respond to the world (cf. Myerhoff, 1978; Stoller, 1989; Wikan, 1991). Another layer, integral to both thinking and feeling, involves *embodiment* (cf. Bresler, 2004a; Damasio, 2003; Johnson, 1999; Lakoff & Johnson, 1999). Embodiment can be defined as the "integration of the physical or biological body and the phenomenal or experiential body," suggesting "a seamless though often-elusive matrix of body/mind worlds, a web that integrates thinking, being, doing and interacting within worlds" (Varela, Thompson, & Rosch cited in Hocking, Haskell, & Linds, 2001, xviii). To work in a paradigm of embodiment is not to study anything new or different (Csordas, 1993) but, as I do in this chapter, to address familiar topics—observing, interviewing, performing music, presenting a research paper—from a different perspective.

Embodiment is at the core of music. Music is produced by physical movement—the voice or an instrument that functions as the extension of the body, where the performer unites with the instrument to produce sound. Embodiment is manifested differently in sight and sound. Whereas we see things "out there," the experience of sound, like touch and taste, is internal, "in here" (cf. Burrows, 1990; Rasmussen, 1999; Zuckerkandl, 1956). Sound penetrates us, engaging us on a bodily level in ways fundamentally different than the visual. This is why, I believe, that learning to hear takes so much, and gives so much.

Interestingly, until recently, aesthetic discourse (including that of the aesthetic of music) contained few references to the body. Richard Shusterman (2004) points out that when Alexander Baumgarten founded the field of aesthetics as a theoretical but also practical discipline aimed at beauty, he excluded somatic study from this enterprise, probably because of religious and rationalist influences. The body has entered scholarship, mostly through phenomenology, in the writing of French philosophers (cf. Bourdieu, 1990; Foucault, 1977; Merleau-Ponty, 1962; Sartre, 1956/1966), infiltrating aesthetics (cf. Peters, 2004; Shusterman, 2000) and the various disciplines of arts education (Bowman, 1998, 2004; Bresler, 2004a).

Equally crucial, yet relatively unexplored, is the notion of embodiment in qualitative research. The body/mind presence is crucial to creating an interview "space," in which participants are invited to reflect, interpret, and communicate. The body is central in the conduct of observations and interviews; yet there has been little reflection from a methodological perspective on the body. Tom Csordas (1993) introduced the notion of *somatic modes of attention* as culturally elaborated ways of attending to and with one's body in surroundings that include the embodied presence of others. Csordas observes that even though our bodies are ever-present, we do not always attend to and with them. Somatic modes of attention are present with the acquisition of any technique of the body—for example, in learning to play an instrument or to dance—but recede into the horizon once the technique is mastered. Clearly, the activities of observations, interviews, and the aural communication of research involve a similarly elaborated somatic mode of attention.

The specific manifestations of body/mind attentiveness in interviews interact with cultural conventions (note, for example, the closer physical proximity and intense eye contact in Israeli culture as compared to the United States, Bresler, 2002). The body is present in various roles—perceiving, interpreting, communicating. Our voices, intonations, and postures as observers convey messages shaping interactions with participants. The aloof "professorial from the podium" posture is not conducive to connected relationship and learning from participants (since the podium serves to distance rather than connect, this posture is not effective for engaging public presentations either).

◆ Musical Dimensions as Illuminating Lived Experience

In the sections above, I discussed issues of connection and relationships in creating dialogic relationships with participants, coresearchers, and audience. In this section, I focus on musical dimensions in attending to personal and social lived experience. In the opening story about my initiation into educational research, musical lenses provided tools for perception and analysis that were relevant to me. Their power refers to their ability to capture the dynamic. As Zuckerkandl (1956) observed, musical laws refer to "states not objects" (p. 364). Analysis of a lesson or a social ritual through musical lenses can deepen our perception and understanding of fluid experiences. States and relationships are captured by the dimensions of form, rhythm, melody, and dynamics, illuminating central aspects of social life and their expression.

As we learn in Genesis, the creation of order comes first. Noise has all the characteristics of music except its order. This is the notion that underlies Dewey's (1934) distinction between ordinary, "anesthetic" experience and "an experience," with its pronounced, intensified form and aesthetic qualities. Similarly, the act of research organizes the "noise" of everyday life into meaningful coherent experiences. This aesthetics of form is shared with all research and scholarship, in both social and natural sciences. Relating to *perception* and *conceptualization* of phenomena in fieldwork and data analysis, these dimensions are also key to *communication* (written and verbal) of research.

How is creating order in the aural domain different from the visual? Sound and music, like life itself, are always in flux. Sound does not have the stability that color does; it passes by as soon as it is created. This aural flow is represented by musical concepts (e.g., form, rhythm, harmony). As with all concepts, they are abstract, masking the fluid quality of musical experience. Yet as my first educational research encounter taught me, they can capture important aspects of the "flow" of social life, the processes of teaching and learning.

Below, I outline some musical dimensions that I found particularly useful in social science research.[11]

Musical form is a dynamic form (Langer, 1957). Form relates to the organization of parts and whole, arrangement of repetition and variation, unity and variety. Form is fundamental to social life. A number of educational models point to the importance of form in teaching: setting up introductory anticipation, development and closure, the creation of suspense, a dramatic climax, and resolution as the summing up of a topic. Similarly, rituals, in their broadest sense, draw on formal qualities (Moore & Myerhoff, 1977; Turner, 1982). In social science we ask, What are the forms of lessons and rituals? Do they follow a Baroque suite—a series of short, loosely related movements, or a classical sonata form, developed, tightly organized, and well-balanced? Qualitative researchers, like improvisers and performers, attend to these fleeting, dynamic "lived experiences" of situations and people.

Central to lived experience and dynamic form is rhythm, defined as "the ordering of movement" (Sparshott, 1995). If tempo is the pace, quick and slow and all the gradations in between, rhythm refers to relationships of tempi over time as well as to temporal patterns. What are the rhythms and paces of social encounters? How fast do the ideas flow in a lesson? How quickly does a teacher change a topic, focus, and assignment? How does this rhythm raise anticipation or a sense of development? How does rhythm shape rituals and social gatherings? A lesson? A school year?

The rhythms we create are partly personal, partly cultural, carrying implicit messages and powerful values. Some cultures thrive on explicit undulated energy, whereas others hold a more even-pace ideal. Perception of rhythm is shaped not only by the "absolute" tempo, but also by the context in which it is embedded. Likewise, the "same" social phenomena are heard and interpreted differently, depending on where they are situated.

As in rhythm, the perception of dynamic, loud and quiet, exists in relationship. A particular tone quality sounds different when it follows a softer versus louder tone. Silence feels differently just before the music starts, as compared to immediately following a climax or as closure. Likewise, the dynamics and silences of social encounters are ever-present, creating a sense of anticipation, tension, confrontation, and resolution.

Melody refers to the individual plot line of the voice, its direction, ascending, descending, or flat. In the analysis of discourse, we examine the unit of thought. Long or composed of shorter units? What are the interrelationships of the shorter idea units to the whole lesson? Are they complementary? Autonomous? Unified?

Texture refers to the interrelations of simultaneous lines and their development over time during the lesson. The coexistence of multiple voices, polyphony, is central to both vocal and instrumental music, as it is to social life. A board meeting, for example, can be homophonic or contrapuntal, with several voices echoing, confronting, or ignoring each other. Indeed, life consists of simultaneously multiple voices, sometimes silent, always present—thinking, interacting, experiencing, creating the texture of life.

Musical styles, like educational settings, have codified conventions regarding harmonic progressions, tolerance for how much dissonance, where and when. The harmonic conventions of blues are different from those of Baroque style, just as the conventions and goals of early childhood education may be different from secondary. Some societies aspire toward harmonious, elegant textures. Others embrace clashes and dissonances, attaching different meanings to them. As researchers, we attend to the dissonances versus consonances of social life, often appreciating the interplay between dissonant moments and their resolutions (or lack of), mindful of their social and political ramifications.

Orchestration refers to the character of the interplay among players or participants. What is the character of interplay between teachers and students? How does a political leader or teacher cultivate more (or less) initiative? Solos, orchestras, and small ensembles offer different social opportunities. These dimensions provide a backbone to perception, documentation, and data analysis. They are equally present in the communication stage, following different conventions for popular stories and more formal papers. The form, rhythm, and texture of the presentation are part of its message, shaping expressivity and impact.

Rhythms, dynamics, and form are also central to researchers' interactions with the participants. A postpositivist paradigm acknowledges the researcher's inquiry process as constructing and shaping the data. A similar process that happens with "getting to know music" (cf. Silvey, 2002) occurs when researchers embark on a research project. Various points of entry (e.g., literature review and fieldwork) facilitate or hinder tuning to a setting or a culture. The resulting journey, with its unique rhythms, forms, and dramatic moments, changes a preordained map to a highly interactive, improvisatory process.

CODA

In contrast to the eye's promise of clarity and distinctness, the ear's world offers us ambiguity and mystery, writes Burrows (1990). As researchers and scholars, attending to fluid phenomena, we strive to capture it in numbers or words, aspiring toward clarity and distinctness. Yet a postmodern consciousness acknowledges the complexity of research and the fluidity of process. It is the dialectical tension between the quest for the permanent versus the inevitably evanescent, I believe, that propels and energizes scholarship, just as a musical score attempts to fix something that defies fixation.

I noted earlier that music's lack of reference to specific objects makes it particularly well-suited to express processes in their fluidity. Thought, writes Burrows, and I would add, the activity of writing (for example, this chapter), may be inspired by the quest to capture ideas with the clarity and stability of visual experience. However, thinking, like breathing, talking, lecturing, advising, and writing a chapter, is fluid, constantly moving. The fluidity of sound and music sensitizes us to the ephemeral, to the ebb and flow of lived and researched experience. Therein lie lessons from music.

◆ Notes

1. Music is a broad category. Different musical genres and ensembles (e.g., jazz ensemble, choir, or solos) highlight different sensibilities, as do the range of musical activities (e.g., performing, analyzing, arranging, and improvising). Still, there are commonalities relating to the nature of sound and people's interactions with it. The discussion of the various activities will address their specificity as well as the interrelationships and commonalities among these activities.

2. I am indebted to Jason Helfer for this distinction.

3. In that communication stage, the score of paper, essential as starting point to formulate thoughts, would have been a hindrance rather than help.

4. There were additional experiences: realizing the extent to which my "interview listening"

drew on "musical listening" or analyzing qualitative data in ways typical of traditional music analysis.

5. Implications to researcher education, beyond the scope of this chapter, are addressed in Bresler (2004b).

6. This includes theoretical and practical work on the nature of groups and interpretation in diverse fields, including anthropology, the sociology of science, and clinical psychology.

7. Polyphony, as an anonymous reviewer has pointed out wisely, is not the sole preserve of ensembles, as Bach's solo keyboard works testify admirably.

8. We drew on scholarly uses of the term, including Vygotsky's (1986) *zone of proximal development* and Giroux's (1992) *border zones.*

9. I am indebted to Rita Irwin for pointing out to me the essential aspect of self-inquiry.

10. Broudy (1980), for example, captured this interconnectedness well when he stated: "The arts . . . should supply what no other discipline does: the strange and wonderful synthesis we call knowledgeful feeling and feelingful knowledge" (p. 7).

11. These ideas were first presented in Bresler (2005).

◆ *References*

Blum, S. (1998). Recognizing improvisation. In B. Nettl (Ed.), *The course of performance: Studies in the world of musical improvisation* (pp. 27–45). Chicago: University of Chicago Press.

Bourdieu, P. (1990). *The logic of practice* (R. Nice, Trans.). Stanford, CA: Stanford University Press. (Original work published 1980)

Bowman, W. (1998). *Philosophical perspectives on music.* New York: Oxford University Press.

Bowman, W. (2004). Cognition and the body: Perspectives from music education. In L. Bresler (Ed.), *Knowing bodies, feeling minds: Embodied knowledge in arts education and schooling* (pp. 29–50). Dordrecht, Netherlands: Kluwer.

Bresler, L. (2002). The interpretive zone in international qualitative research. In L. Bresler & A. Ardichvili (Eds.), *International research in education: Experience, theory, and practice* (pp. 39–81). New York: Peter Lang.

Bresler, L. (Ed.). (2004a). *Knowing bodies, moving minds: Towards an embodied teaching and learning.* Dordrecht, Netherlands: Kluwer.

Bresler, L. (2004b). *Research education: From music to research.* A keynote address presented in CIC, Northwestern University, Evanston, IL. (To be published in *Council of Research in Music Education*)

Bresler, L. (2005). What musicianship can teach educational research. *Music Education Research, 7*(2), 169–183.

Bresler, L., & Stake, R. (1992). Qualitative research methodology in music education. In R. Colwell (Ed.), *The handbook on research in music teaching and learning* (pp. 75–90). New York: Macmillan.

Bresler, L, Wasser, J., Hertzog N., & Lemons, M. (1996). Beyond the Lone Ranger researcher: Teamwork in qualitative research. *Research Studies in Music Education, 7,* 15–30.

Broudy, H. (1980). On the third realm-Aesthetic schooling. *Journal of Aesthetic Education, 14*(2), 5–9.

Bruner, J. (1996). *The culture of education.* Cambridge, MA: Harvard University Press.

Buber, M. (1971). *I and Thou.* New York: Simon and Schuster.

Burrows, D. (1990). *Sound, speech, and music.* Amherst: University of Massachusetts Press.

Csordas, T. (1993). Somatic modes of attention. *Cultural Anthropology, 8*(2), 157–168.

Damasio, A. (2003). *Looking for Spinoza: Joy, sorrow, and the feeling brain.* New York: Harcourt.

Dewey, J. (1934). *Art as experience.* New York: Perigee Books.

Eisner, E. (1991). *The enlightened eye: Qualitative inquiry and the enhancement of educational practice.* New York: Macmillan.

Foucault, M. (1977). *Discipline and punish: The birth of the prison.* New York: Vintage Books.

Gadamer, H. (1988). *Truth and method* (G. Barden & J. Cumming, Trans. & Eds.). New York: The Crossroad Publishing Company.

Giroux, H. (1992). *Border crossings.* New York: Perigee Books.

Gottlieb, A., & Graham, P. (1994). *Parallel worlds.* Chicago: University of Chicago Press.

Hocking, B., Haskell, J., & Linds, W. (2001). *Unfolding bodymind: Exploring possibility through education.* Brandon, VT: Foundations for Educational Renewal.

Johnson, M. (1999). Embodied reason. In G. Weiss & H. F. Haber (Eds.), *Perspectives on embodiment: The intersections of nature and culture* (pp. 103–120). New York: Routledge.

Kvale, S. (1996). *InterViews.* Thousand Oaks, CA: Sage.

Lakoff, G., & Johnson, M. (1999). *Philosophy in the flesh: The embodied mind and its challenge to Western thought.* New York: Basic Books.

Langer, S. K. (1957). *Problems of art.* New York: Charles Scribner's Sons.

McMillan, R. (1999). "To say something that was me": Developing a personal voice through improvisation. *British Journal of Music Education, 16*(3), 263–273.

Merleau-Ponty, M. (1962). *The phenomenology of perception.* London: Routledge & Kegan Paul.

Miles, M. B., & Huberman, A. (1984). *Qualitative data analysis.* Beverly Hills, CA: Sage.

Moore, S., & Myerhoff, B. (1977). Introduction. In S. Moore & B. Myerhoff (Eds.), *Secular rituals* (pp. 3–24). Amsterdam: Van Gorcum.

Myerhoff, B. (1978). *Number our days.* New York: Simon & Schuster.

Nettl, B. (1998). (Ed.). *In the course of performance: Studies in the world of musical improvisation.* Chicago: University of Chicago Press.

Peters, M. (2004). Education and the philosophy of the body: Bodies of knowledge and knowledges of the body. In L Bresler (Ed.), *Knowing bodies, moving minds: Towards an embodied teaching and learning* (pp. 13–28). Dordrecht, Netherlands: Kluwer.

Rasmussen, S. (1999). Making better "scents" in anthropology: Aroma in Tuareg sociocultural systems and the shaping of ethnography. *Anthropological Quarterly, 82*(2), 55–73.

Rosenblatt, L. (1978). *The reader, the text, the poem: The transactional theory of the literary work.* Carbondale: Southern Illinois University Press.

Sartre, J. (1966). *Being and nothingness: A phenomenological essay on ontology* (H. Barnes, Trans). New York: Pocket Books. (Original work published 1956)

Schutz, A. (1951). Making music together: A study in social relationship. *Social Research, 18*(1), 76–97.

Shusterman, R. (2000). *Performing live: Aesthetic alternatives for the ends of art.* Ithaca, NY: Cornell University Press.

Shusterman, R. (2004). Soma aesthetics and education: Exploring the terrain. In L. Bresler (Ed.), *Knowing bodies, moving minds: Towards an embodied teaching and learning* (pp. 51–60). Dordrecht, Netherlands: Kluwer.

Silvey, P. E. (2002). *Learning music from the inside: The process of coming to know musical works as experienced by four high school choral singers.* Unpublished doctoral dissertation, University of Illinois, Urbana–Champaign.

Sparshott, F. (1995). *A measured pace: Toward a philosophical understanding of the arts of dance.* Toronto, Ontario, Canada: University of Toronto Press.

Steiner, G. (1989). *Real presences.* Chicago: University of Chicago Press.

Stoller, P. (1984). Sound in Songhay cultural experiences. *American Technologist, 11, 559–570.*

Stoller, P. (1989). *The taste of ethnographic things: The senses in anthropology.* Philadelphia: University of Philadelphia Press.

Stubley, E. (1998). Being in the body, being in the sound: A tale of modulating identities and lost potential. *Journal of Aesthetic Education, 32*(4), 93–105.

Turner, V. (1982). *From ritual to theater.* New York: Performing Arts Journal Press.

van Manen, M. (1990). *Researching lived experience*. New York: State University of New York Press.

von Wright, G. H. (1971). *Explanation and understanding*. London: Routledge and Kegan Paul.

Vygotsky, L. (1986). *Thought and language* (A. Kozulin, Trans. & Ed.). Cambridge, MA: MIT Press.

Wasser, J., & Bresler, L. (1996). Working in the interpretive zone: Conceptualizing collaboration in qualitative research teams. *Educational Researcher, 25*(5), 5–15.

Watson, J. (1968). *The double helix*. New York: New American Library.

Wikan, U. (1991). Toward an experience-near anthropology. *Cultural Anthropology, 6*, 285–305.

Zuckerkandl, V. (1956). *Sound and symbol: Music and the external world* (W. Trask, Trans.). Kingsport, TN: Kingsport Press.

20 *Visual Art*

PAINTING AS RESEARCH

Create and Critique

◆ Graeme Sullivan

At an exhibition in Egypt in 2005, Austrian artist Richard Jochum's artwork showed three easily recognized international symbols.[1] A colon and an arrow are each overlaid with a divided circle suggesting that the meaning of these ubiquitous symbols cannot be trusted. What Jochum implies is that statements do not easily lead to firm conclusions. As a readily understood punctuation mark, the colon is used to divide distinct but related elements in a statement so that the second part helps to explain the first. As a device used in titles, the colon separates and joins meaning in a way that assumes there is finality to what is said—in this sense a title of a text is like a contract with the reader as it defines what is covered. But when a simple graphic mark such as a colon or an arrow is seen as an *image,* meaning is opened up as evidence found in the form or the context can suggest other possible and plausible interpretations. As Jochum suggests, perhaps we should stop drawing simplistic conclusions.

There is a close connection these days between creative and critical practice such as that pursued by Richard Jochum. The edges that once defined differences among worlds of artists, critics, historians, teachers, and their audiences are much more blurred. Therefore, the manner by

◆ 239

Figure 20.1 *No Colon, No Conclusions!*

SOURCE: Richard Jochum. (2004–2005). *No Colon, No Conclusions!* New York. C-print, each 15 in. × 15 in. Reproduced courtesy of the artist.

which art is created, critiqued, and communicated is more seamless than ever with art objects, ideas, and issues being debated and exchanged in many ways as artists become theorists and critics become creators.[2] In taking on the additional communicative role of an art writer, Richard Jochum (2003) describes the situation this way:

> Theory considers treating a painting as painting as obsolete and treating an object as object as historical. And so do the artists. Answering the historicizing (and discriminating) tendency of the theorist, the artist has developed a series of self-reflective strategies. As a result, 20th century art, to a large degree, cannot be understood without critical theory. Art now serves the additional function of providing interpretation. To warrant putting everyday items in a museum requires an intellectual analysis of those items. Duchamp was an intellectual, as is Beuys, as is Haacke. *The artist has become a theorist* [emphasis in the original]. (p. 102)

In considering what it is to "make" a painting within the context of research, there are different perspectives to ponder.

The study of painting as an inquiry process takes into account more than the physical and formal practices of creating images on surfaces. Not only is the artist involved in a "doing" performance, but this also results in an image that is a site for further interpretation by viewers and an object that is part of visual culture. Before looking at the contexts surrounding painting as research, there is a need to examine more closely the perspectives that inform our understanding of painting as a form of individual inquiry, as a means of critical engagement, and as an instance of cultural practice.

◆ *Theorizing Painting as a Research Practice*

Painting Practices as Research (Figure 20.2) describes a framework for thinking about painting as research. The figure is drawn around three elements that characterize painting as a cultural practice, namely, structure, agency, and action. Painting, like all forms of visual art, involves giving form to thought in a purposeful way. Painting also embodies meaning that is negotiated in many contexts. The relationship among painterly

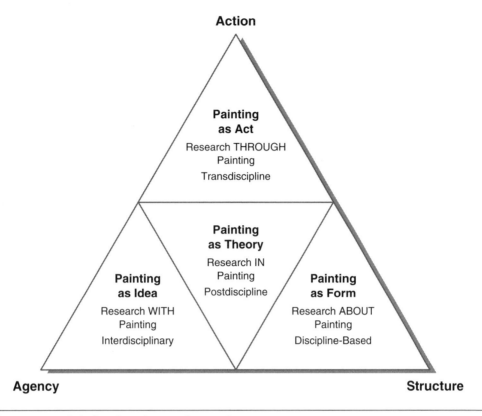

Figure 20.2 Painting Practices as Research

structures, self-initiated ideas, and thought-ful actions resists any fixed notions. A useful way to think about this seemingly elusive aspect of painting is to consider the word "painting" as both a noun and a verb. As a noun, there is ready acceptance that paint-ing, as an object, has creative and material form, provenance, and a host of interpretive outcomes it generates. However, when painting is seen as a verb, we get a better sense of the way that painting as a practice is determined by the act of doing it. In this way, distinctions between terms such as painter, object, and viewer melt away as the circumstance or setting influences the meanings invoked in artistic efforts and encounters. What this does *not* mean is that painting, as a means of creative and critical investigation, is too ephemeral to consider within the context of research. Whether seen as process or product, the practice of painting can be argued to be a robust form of human engagement that has the potential to reveal new insights and understandings. To argue this point further, the following discussion describes aspects that are embod-ied within painting as a research practice that involves painting as theory, form, idea, and action.

◆ *Painting as Theory*

Painters have always been deep thinkers. A historical characteristic of art practice shows that artists periodically "think in a medium," "think in a language," and "think in a context" (Sullivan, 2001). By this I mean that the creative and critical intent changes as interests shift from an emphasis on the structural and expressive properties opened up by new media to the interpretive richness offered as art experience is enhanced through discourse, and to the cultural relevance highlighted as critical artistic encounters change the way we think about things around us. The argument that painting practice *can* be a theoretically grounded form of research offers more than just rhetorical appeal. If the broad intent of research is seen to be the creation of new knowledge and the theoretical quest is to explain things, then art practice achieves this goal in a distinctive way.

The methodological conventions of mainstream research rely on the confirmatory methods of the quantitative paradigm or the interpretive approaches of the qualitative paradigm. Both research traditions seek to construct theory, with the former relying on causal claims of probability, and the latter on relational arguments of plausibility. Further, both research regimes help us explain phenomena, either by clarifying how things are different in degree or different in kind. What is often missing from debates is that "explanation" as an outcome of inquiry is a limited description of the kind of knowledge we need. There is a "making" or productive feature that links knowledge and understanding whereby new insights are enacted in some conceptual and concrete way. As such, it is "understanding" rather than mere explanation that is of central interest in research activity.[3] As a research methodology, art practice is premised on the need to "create and critique," which opens up the possibility of achieving new understanding. In many instances there is merit in stepping outside what is known so as to see more clearly what is not. Normalized practices may help locate theories and approaches within existing knowledge structures, but these can be a constraint if seen mostly as a place for privileged information. The capacity to look beyond what is known to seek the possibility of new understanding is what artists do. Knowledge may be power, but insight makes a difference.

Conceiving painting as theory within a framework of inquiry sets in place the prospect of doing research *in* painting. When used as a site for research, painting brings into play the seamless relationship between the "researcher" (painter) and the "researched" (painting practice), and this builds on arguments that disrupt untenable dichotomies such as the fictive subjective–objective divide, or presumptions that form and content can somehow be separated. Another way to think about this is the idea that the artist is not only embodied in the making of images and objects, but these artworks also exist within a wider space of critical discourse that is partly directed by the scope of the research project, and partly by the field at large. Griselda Pollock describes an outcome of this expanded notion of inquiry as a "visual field." She adds:

> I'm very interested in images of people making paintings, for here we have a new form of documentation that privileges the act of art making, of the painter's body in action over time. The product of that activity is a visual field, not just necessarily a visual object. But in terms of painting or whatever, you are creating a field that calls to the visual fantasy of the viewer, but also speaks to the visual fantasy of the embodied maker. (cited in Raney, 2003, p. 131)

As is shown in Figure 20.2, if theoretical processes are central to painting practice, then the emphasis can be seen to involve research *in* painting. This core practice takes on a different perspective when other research interests are pursued and wider visual fields encountered. When structural and formal interests are central to the artistic inquiry, then research *"in"* and *"about"* painting is important. Similarly, if the relationship among the artist, artwork, and viewer is vital to the ideas and responses sparked by an artistic encounter, then research *"in"* and *"with"* painting is crucial. Further, if the context surrounding purposeful artistic inquiry helps give meaning to the critical role painting can play as a form of social action, then research *"in"* and *"through"* painting is significant.

In these interactions, the artist changes the field and the field changes the artist. The field that Pollock describes above, however, is not the hierarchical model we normally associate with traditional disciplines with their conceptual and cultural centrisms. Rather, there is a "postdiscipline" feature to domains of inquiry and content fields that the visual arts inhabit. The interpretive orbit that surrounds any artistic knowledge construct created by a painter-researcher intermixes with various discipline content and allows us to see in new ways. Therefore, it is not the discipline knowledge that helps create the interpretive space; rather, it is the disciplines themselves that become open to critique, for what is of interest is not what *is* there, but what is *not there*. This is what it is to "create and critique."

If the quest is to move beyond the boundaries of disciplines and to see them as places of meaning making rather than objects of knowledge, then there is a need to consider what a postdiscipline structure might look like. A feature of the structure shown in Figure 20.2 is that it is nonhierarchical. This is not a form that is a foundation structure, which supports more complex systems. Rather, this is a structure that has no scale at all. Whether viewed on a micro (local), meso (regional), macro (continental), or mega (global) scale, the basic structure stays the same.[4] This feature is called "self-similarity"

(Mandelbrot, 1983), and the form stays basically the same across scale. Elsewhere I explain self-similarity thus:

> Reductionism and Euclidean notions of space are powerful systems that guide inquiry in both the sciences and the arts. The assumption is that a change in scale brings about new kinds of information so that the more things can be reduced to their basic essence, the better the chance of figuring out how they work. But nature and humans resist such simplistic design. (Sullivan, 2005, p. 106)

I argue that a postdiscipline environment would display features of self-similarity whereby art research practice is independent of scale, and would have a similar structure if undertaken during the painting process or in the studio, in the community, within cultures, or within the virtual space of the Internet. The self-similarity shown in Figure 20.2 can be seen to be a braided structure[5] (see Figure 20.3) where strands shown as various kinds of painting appear to neatly fit together—much like four strands of rope viewed end-on. In this sense, theories, forms, ideas, and actions are compatible and fit together. However, if the braided "rope" is unraveled, separated, and twisted, what initially appeared to be in close proximity can be seen to be far apart. What is congruent in content may now be irreconcilable, and vice versa. This has more than metaphorical interest as it reflects the fluid capacity of knowledge to mean different things in different contexts. Consequently, meaning is not static but open to multiple views and compatible contradictions. Whether exploring painting as form, ideas, or act, a process that is both complex and simple becomes dislodged and braided as knowledge is created and critiqued, and assumptions about normative structures and behaviors are questioned.

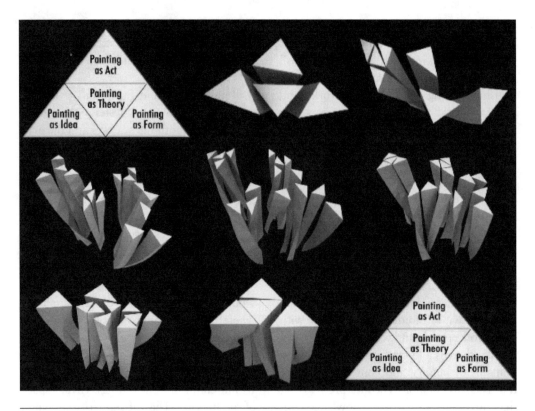

Figure 20.3   Postdiscipline Structure as Self-Similar Form

◆ *Painting as Form*

Although the mind is the medium that most clearly shapes art practice, for many artists, art materials are still the most tangible means that give form to imaginative thought. Therefore, when undertaking research *"in"* and *"about"* painting, where there is a focus on structural qualities among other interests, the artist really does think in a medium. In this process the artwork becomes the primary site of knowledge and painting becomes the source of questions, problems, and insights, which emerge as part of practice. Visual problem finding and problem solving are characteristic of this kind of inquiry whereby forms, materials, properties, and qualities become the means by which concerns are explored and expressed. As a result new forms and images are created, and these open up the possibility of new meanings. A crucial element of art research is that understanding emerges during the process of media experimentation, and this performative knowledge can be likened to more traditional research strategies such as observation and empirical confirmation.

Consider the media exploration that characterizes the art practice of David Hockney. His visual experiments with space and perspective using Polaroid photography during the 1980s helped reconfigure ideas about pictorial illusion and reality. This interest was sparked earlier when he curated an exhibition for the National Gallery in London, which was part of a series called

The Artist's Eye, where he was invited to select works from the collection that had some connection to his art. It was part of a series of shows that sought to help museum visitors get a sense of what it is that an artist notices. Hockney (1981) wrote about this in a catalogue essay, *Looking at Pictures in a Book at the National Gallery,* in which he raised questions about the modernist dilemma posed by mechanically reproduced images and the different experience to be had when encountering original works of art as against viewing reproductions. For Hockney, the issue was best exemplified in photography, for although photographs create an image that is an illusion of real time and space, if photographs are used to take pictures of paintings, then there is some element of truth in the reproduced image. He explains:

Now I think the best use for photography, the *best* use for it, is photographing other pictures. It is the only time it can be true to its medium, in the sense that it's real. This is the only way that you can take a photograph that could be described as having a strong illusion of reality. Because on the flat surface of the photograph is simply reproduced another flat surface—a painting. (Hockney, 1981, p. 8)

In his later camerawork assemblages, Hockney composed "walls of images" made from single Polaroid pictures, each taken as one aspect of an overall scene and then carefully aligned and joined to depict a panoramic view of the space or object photographed. These visual compositions described scenes in a rather curious way because each photographic print reduced a section of three-dimensional time and space into a seemingly flat surface. Consequently, the capacity to create an illusion of perspective that was believed to be on one of the most enduring features of photography was

questioned. In Hockney's montages he "painted" pictures with photographs that severely compressed the picture plane whereby perspective was almost reversed. He described the image making process as a way to make a "photograph without perspective" (Hockney, 1993, p. 100), and this inverted a prime characteristic seen to be a magical part of the mechanical picturing process. This is what it is for artists to think in a medium in a way that extends discipline knowledge through the mindful use of media.

◆ Painting as Idea

Artists whose focus of inquiry can be described as having an interest *"in" and "with"* painting invoke a somewhat different set of practices and perspectives. There is an acknowledgement that artistic practice is not only a personal pursuit but also a public process that can change the way we understand ourselves in the world we inhabit. Consequently, the ideas expressed and communicated have an interpretive utility that assumes different textual forms as others make sense of what it is artists have to say through what it is they see. Painting as "idea" builds on the rich conceptual traditions associated with image making whose purpose is to open up dialogue between the artist and viewer, and among an interpretive community whose interests may cut across disciplines. Painters whose work explores conceptual issues that seek to open up a dialectical exchange tend to do their artistic "thinking in a language" as this best describes the interactions that occur as relationships are found and formed among artists, artworks, and viewers.

In exploring the research practices that surround "painting as idea," the work of David Hockney again proves helpful. As a conceptualist, Hockney's art practice has, at times, opened up an interpretive space that relies on the participation of others to complete the aesthetic process. Yet this interactive element has the capacity to disrupt accepted practices for "new ideas often seem to go against common sense" (Hockney, 1993, p. 104). Hockney's notion of photography and mechanical reproduction described in the section above uses the medium in a way that is somewhat different from much of the discourse (Benjamin, 1968). Although a photograph of a painting cannot exist unless an artist creates an original in the first place, Hockney (1981) maintains that even if the quality of a reproduction is poor, a picture retains the capacity to give "immense pleasure." In acknowledging that a reproduction cannot hope to capture evidence of the artist's use of the "spirit" of media to represent forms, he does concede that a photograph of it has the capacity to give enjoyment "in strange ways that go on and on" (p. 8).

Hockney's aesthetic and conceptual interest makes use of the capacity of artworks to withstand continual revisiting and clearly illustrates how images can be interpreted in multiple ways. Within the hermeneutic tradition of Habermas (1971) and Paul Ricoeur (1981) interpretation can be seen to be a uniquely human process of making meaning. An important part is experience as it is lived and felt, reconstructed and understood. Consequently, meanings are made in encounters with artworks. From Ricoeur's (1981) notion of textual interpretation comes the idea that when a written text is read it takes on a level of autonomy and "what the text signifies no longer coincides with what the author means" (p. 139). This serves the visual arts well as it opens up the interpretive space among the artist, the artwork, and the setting as different interests and perspectives are embraced. As Arthur Danto (1981) notes, "in art, every new interpretation is a

Copernican revolution, in the sense that each new interpretation constitutes a new work" (p. 125). However, he reminds us "you can call a painting anything that you choose, but you cannot interpret in any way you choose, not if the argument holds that the limits of knowledge are the limits of interpretation" (p. 131).

In his interpretation of reality using photographic images, Hockney required others to be involved in the process, both technically and aesthetically. He used mechanical reproduction techniques much like a photocopying machine, which merely recreates flat images. This is precisely the kind of image that most viewers see when they learn about art. Only a relatively small proportion of the population regularly visit museums or galleries to view artworks "in the flesh." For many, it is through the printed reproduction that is the most pervasive way that we see, for "most people know about painting now through printing of some kind, some reproductive process." Hockney (1993) continues:

> Even with a printed thing on a page each of us sees something different because each brings a different memory to it. . . . Images on a printed page evoke different memories. Even in a reproduction there's nothing that is objective. (p. 114)

Using his extensive knowledge of printmaking that involved making composite images built up in layers, what Hockney did in the mid 1980s was to create photographic collages, which he then photographed and made color copies scaled to a different size. These were made using a photocopy machine, and he created prints that were not reproductions at all. Hockney made photocopies in layers where each could be recopied several times to build up surfaces and forms much like the multicolor process of block printing. He called these "home made prints," and they were made without the use of a preexisting image. Today we would scan an image and manipulate it in Photoshop© to achieve the same thing Hockney did. What Hockney was doing was painting and printing with photographic images and not merely copying things as was widely assumed at the time. As such, these homemade prints carried an intriguing conceptual and aesthetic problem. These mostly still lifes and domestic scenes not only questioned ideas about artistic (re)production, but also sharpened Hockney's expectations of viewers in that he wanted them to become the human subjects in the scenes by remaking the art experience for themselves.

◆ Painting as Act

Another perspective that informs painting as a form of research is the critical tradition that has always been part of the history of art practice. There is an enactive or "doing" element here, for critical action implies both a reactive and proactive stance, which is responsive to circumstances and contexts that require attention. Painting has long been used as an instrument of social and political action, yet artists are sometimes hard pressed to show what their actions actually achieve. Similarly, complaints made about those who advocate a critical perspective in educational debates often make the claim that theory does not always match practice. Achieving an effective blend where theory informs practice and practice informs theory is sometimes an elusive goal in educational praxis. A similar challenge exists for cultural practitioners who make use of artistic inquiry as a form of social critique. Powerful visual statements may serve as provocative political and rhetorical devices; however, if any

artistic appeal is to go beyond iconic status, it requires profound theoretical and inter-disciplinary support to back it up.

For an artist-researcher inspired by a call to critical action, inquiry is undertaken *"in" and "through"* art practice. Painting in this sense is a means and an end. This suggests that any quest for change has both personal and public relevance. On the one hand there is an aesthetic interest as the outcomes of any imaginative inquiry can lead to self-realization and understanding. On the other hand there is an educational purpose that has a social utility. As a site for the embodiment of the social imagination (Greene, 2003), the practice of painting takes on a critical focus and responds to meaningful issues and contexts. A questioning attitude that is socially and culturally directed readily maps onto methods of inquiry and research protocols that are responsive and exploratory. Yet the most crucial element within this inquiry process is the need to be able to create forms from which critical options can be addressed. This may require moving in and beyond the comfort of prescribed discipline knowledge, as issues and concerns demand a "transdiscipline" approach to support the new perspectives opened up. Consequently it is the creation of new opportunities to see beyond what is known that has the potential to lead to the creation of new knowledge.

Disrupting privileged knowledge or challenging accepted practices is a critical outlook shared by many artists. Again, the art practice of David Hockney provides a useful example. In his text, *Secret Knowledge: Rediscovering the Lost Techniques of the Old Masters* (2001), Hockney makes the provocative claim that many of the European masters most likely used lenses and mirroring devices to draft many of their paintings. What is crucial to appreciate is that this controversial assertion arose as a consequence of Hockney's art making. For many artists, an enduring quest is to understand how other artists create the things they do. Artists look very closely at artworks in a way that others do not. It was as a result of looking intensely at the line work in sketches by Jean-Auguste-Dominique Ingres in the 19th century, and some traced drawings by Andy Warhol in the mid-20th century, that Hockney noticed a distinct similarity. The quick and confident lines that captured an uncanny representational accuracy in Ingres's quick sketches bore the same quality as the bold and deft line work created by Andy Warhol. Hockney knew that Warhol used an overhead projector to create his images. Maybe, he surmised, Ingres also used some kind of mechanical device to quickly capture the scenes he drew.

Hockney's text, *Secret Knowledge,* documents in depth his relentless quest to support his hypothesis that many European master painters used lenses and other mechanical devices for reproducing images. As a fellow painter, he directed his research at the paintings themselves, convinced that the visual images held the necessary evidence. It is not surprising that Hockney's claims raised the ire of historians and critics who had their own, less secret knowledge upon which to ground their arguments. A common response was to question Hockney's motives on the basis that an artist with less skill than a European master may have good reason to suggest that such artistic fluency could only be achieved using a visual trick. The late Susan Sontag was reported as saying, "if David Hockney's thesis is correct, it would be a bit like finding out that all the great lovers of history have been using Viagra."[6]

That art historians did not notice what Hockney did is not surprising as in this case they did not draw on the same kind of knowledge because practice-based understanding is not normally part of a curatorial skill set. Hockney observed these things because he was able to create connections

based on experience and accumulated evidence, and this is at the heart of what research is about. For Hockney, however, the significance of his observations, borne in the first instance from a creative insight, will remain moot unless further evidence from independent sources is obtained to confirm his findings. *Any* research strategy, therefore, has to be as systematic and rigorous as it is imaginative, irrespective of the method used.

A central feature of painting is that knowledge is embodied in the process of making artworks. Like the research process, which begins with an integrated focus on problems and methods and proceeds to break things up through analysis before drawing conclusions, painting *as* research exhibits a similar structure. Not unlike the self-similar structures described in Figure 20.3, painting as theory, form, idea, or act begins with a nested set of problems, concepts, and issues, which lead to an exploratory, intertwining search before reaching a resolution, from which new pathways open up. Irrespective of the informing sources, media preferences, or image base, the artist exercises imaginative control over the creation and presentation of forms of knowledge. Further, the images and ideas created have the capacity to not only change the artist's conceptions of reality, but also influence the viewer's interpretation of issues generated from encounters with paintings. Consequently, the practice of painting can be seen as a form of intellectual and imaginative inquiry, and as a place where research can be carried out that is robust enough to yield reliable insights that are well grounded and culturally relevant.

◆ Conclusion

This chapter took its cue from Richard Jochum's cautionary visual statements presented at the beginning to help argue that painting *as* research is based on the assumption that the outcomes of inquiry are focused *and* open-ended; conclusive *and* open to conjecture, beyond doubt *and* open to question. This does not contradict the accepted notion that research is supposed to come up with unequivocal results. On the contrary, the task of any rigorous intellectual and imaginative inquiry is not only to produce new insight, but also to realize how this can transform our knowledge of things we assume we already understand. Within fields such as the visual arts this research approach involves a creative and critical process whereby imaginative leaps are made into what we do not know, as this can lead to crucial insights that can change what we do know. To *create* in order to *critique* in this way captures the reflexive quality of art practice as research. Artist-researchers create critical insights that are germane and current, and the viewer creates meaning within the critical contexts that inform the artistic encounter. This view asserts that the task of artistic or scientific inquiry is to create and apply new knowledge; however, these goals can be achieved by following different but complementary pathways.

◆ Notes

1. Richard Jochum, from *Playground* exhibition, by Richard Jochum. El Sawy Center, Zamalek, Egypt, February 11–19, 2005. See http://richardjochum.net/playground-e.html (retrieved August 12, 2005).

2. For another example of Richard Jochum's art practice where he explores the role of critics as creators, see his Dis-Positiv series where art critics are placed inside a Plexiglas enclosure in a museum setting and observed as they create their artwriting. See http://www.dis-positiv.org/welcome/dispositiv-e.html (retrieved September 2, 2005).

3. See Chapter 3, "Explanation, Understanding and Beyond," in *Art Practice as Research* (Sullivan, 2005) for a more detailed discussion of theorizing art practice within the frameworks of research.

4. I am indebted to Liora Bresler for clarifying these spatial descriptions.

5. The painter Jean Dubuffet (1988) refers to a braided relationship as a way to critique what he sees as the fickle views of art critics. He describes art criticism as being like strands of rope where in some instances the judgment expressed can be seen to be in close connection to the artwork itself—and here the braided strands are tightly woven together. On the other hand, a judgment might be made that has little apparent connection to the artwork itself—and here the rope has unraveled with strands representing the artist's work and the critic's view now seen to be far apart. Another way to consider Dubuffet's conundrum is to see it in a positive light as it highlights the context-dependent nature of interpretation and opens up the possibility of considering multiple perspectives and compatible contradictions.

6. See http://www.koopfilms.com/hockney/articles.html (retrieved January 18, 2004).

◆ References

Benjamin, W. (1968). The work of art in the age of mechanical reproduction. In W. Benjamin, *Illuminations* (H. Arendt, Ed., & H. Zohn, Trans.; pp. 219–253). New York: Schocken Books.

Danto, A. C. (1981). *The transfiguration of the commonplace: A philosophy of art.* Cambridge, MA: Harvard University Press.

Dubuffet, J. (1988). *Asphyxiating culture and other writings* (C. Volk, Trans.). New York: Four Walls Eight Windows.

Greene, M. (2003). The arts and social justice. In P. Sahasrabudhe (Ed.), *Art education: Meaning dimensions and possibilities* (pp. 21–25). Keynote addresses, The 31st InSEA World Congress, August 2002. New York: Center for International Art Education, Teachers College, Columbia University.

Habermas, J. (1971). *Knowledge and human interest.* (J. J. Shapiro, Trans.). Boston, MA: Beacon.

Hockney, D. (1981). *The artist's eye: Looking at pictures in a book at the National Gallery.* Exhibition at The National Gallery, London, July 1, 1981–August 31, 1981.

Hockney, D. (1993). *That's the way I see it.* San Francisco: Chronicle Books.

Hockney, D. (2001). *Secret knowledge: Rediscovering the lost techniques of the old masters.* New York: Viking Studio.

Jochum, R. (2003). Dis-positiv as role model. In H. Fassbinder (Ed.), *Through the 'net: Studies in Jochen Gerz "Anthology of art"* (pp. 101–106). Cologne, Germany: Salon Verlag.

Mandelbrot, B. (1983). *The fractal geometry of nature.* New York: W. H. Freeman.

Raney, K. (2003). *Art in question.* London: Continuum, The Arts Council of England.

Ricoeur, P. (1981). *Hermeneutics and the human sciences: Essays on language, action, and interpretation* (J. B. Thompson, Ed. & Trans.). Cambridge, UK: Cambridge University Press.

Sullivan, G. (2001). Artistic thinking as transcognitive practice: A reconciliation of the process–product dichotomy. *Visual Arts Research, 27*(1), 2–12.

Sullivan, G. (2005). *Art practice as research: Inquiry in the visual arts.* Thousand Oaks, CA: Sage.

21

Visual Art

PHOTOGRAPHS AND/AS SOCIAL DOCUMENTARY

◆ Claudia Mitchell and Susan Allnutt

Imagine a world without things. It would be not so much an empty world as a blurry, frictionless one: No sharp outlines would separate one part of the uniform plenum from another; there would be no resistance against which to stub a toe or test a theory or struggle stalwartly. Nor would there be anything to describe, or to explain, remark on, interpret, or complain about—just a kind of porridgy oneness. Without things, we would stop talking.

—Daston, 2004, p. 9

We are interested in some of the ways in which photographs talk. Working with photographs—both photographs *found* as in the case of the Elsie and Dolly project (C. Mitchell, 2005) and photographs *taken*

Author's Note: We gratefully acknowledge the contributions of the Honors, Master's, and Doctoral students in several courses: Textual Approaches to Research, 2002 (McGill University); Cinematic, Documentary, and Television Texts, 2004 (University of KwaZulu-Natal); and Visual Methodologies and Social Change, 2005 (McGill University). We would also like to acknowledge our colleague Jean Stuart who co-taught the course at UKZN and who has been keenly interested in the work on photo documentary.

(as described elsewhere in the photo-voice[1] projects of Ewald, 1992, 1996, 2001; Lykes, 2001a, 2001b; C. Mitchell, Stuart, Moletsane, Delange, & Buthelezi, 2005; Wang 1999; Wang, Morrel-Samuels, Hutchison, Bell, & Pestronk, 2004)—offers fascinating possibilities for engaging in what W. J. T. Mitchell (2004) describes as "a new materialism" in social science research. We take our title from Daston's work with things. Studying and producing photographs and photo albums, we can begin to get a sense of the power of photographs as objects and as things in social science research—and of their capacity for talk.

Clearly much has been done already on family albums, particularly in the area of the visual arts and art history. These studies range from work on one's own family album(s) (Faber, 2003; Kuhn, 1995; C. Mitchell & Weber, 1999; Spence, 1986; Spence & Holland, 1991; Weiser, 1993), to the work of Arbus (see Chalfen, 1987, 1991, 2002; Hirsch, 1997; Langford, 2000; Lee & Pultz, 2004; and Willis, 1994, to name only some of the scholars who examine other people's albums). These various album projects have highlighted the personal in looking at or working with one's own photographs, but there is also, as in the case of Langford (2000), the idea of explicitly looking at "other people's photo albums" through a sociocultural lens. The issues that they have explored range from questions of cultural identity and memory through to what Spence (1986) has described as "reconfiguring" the family album. In this chapter we extend these explorations into work on producing albums, focusing in particular on the ways in which the process of producing small photo documentaries helps to deepen an understanding of the power of photographs as objects. We start with an example of "showing" where Claudia narrates an account of working with a small collection of family photographs. We then go on to describe a series of photo album projects produced by a group of graduate students. These we draw on to highlight how photographs can exist as objects and as social documents in social science research.

◆ What Dolly Sent Elsie: Photographs Found

Claudia finds a collection of photographs sent to her mother Elsie as a young married woman in Manitoba, Canada, by Dolly, a young woman working in a milk top factory in York, England.

A set of snapshots and letters is exchanged by two young women, one from York, England, and the other from Gopher Creek, Manitoba, in Canada between 1938 and some time into the mid-1950s. The two women "meet" (at least through letters) when my mother Elsie, a farm woman working alongside her husband, Bill, on a dairy farm in the middle of Canada, opens up a box of milk bottle tops and finds the name and address of Dolly who works in the factory in York which produces the cardboard tops for milk bottles. Dolly, it seems, has put her name and address in the box; it is a version of the glass bottle with the message in it being flung into the sea. The farm woman, Elsie, finding the name and address, must have sent off a reply, though what she said we don't know—but so begins a correspondence that lasts for 20 years or more.

Dolly only really comes alive for me, however, after my mother's death about five years ago, when my two brothers and I find ourselves sorting photographs in the apartment Elsie moved into after my father died. Dolly manages to get herself into the burial night by appearing over and over again—in tiny black and white snapshots, in wallet-sized studio portraits of herself by the sea (Figure 21.1) or putting on make-up (Figure 21.2).

commercial "children on a donkey photo" (Figure 21.4).

All of this is, of course, very one sided and uni-dimensional. We are missing Elsie's photos to Dolly. We are also missing Dolly's letters to Elsie and Elsie's letters to Dolly. And then there are stories that are only implied by the photographs. In many of the Dolly-by-the-sea photos, for example, we are left wondering who actually took these photos. Who was Dolly posing for as she puts on her make-up? Why were Dolly's parents on holiday with her? But there is another set of questions about Elsie. What could Elsie have been thinking when she opened up that carton of bottle tops and discovered Dolly's name and address? Did she exclaim and show it to

Figure 21.1

Figure 21.2

Dolly also becomes visible through her inscriptions on the backs of most of the snapshots; these are overlaid by Elsie's inscriptions as we see in Figure 21.3.

I know I must have missed some, but by the end of the evening I have a good 25 or more of these photos, photos which can be pieced together at least in a chronological way which documents Dolly by herself, Dolly with her fiancé, Dolly married, and Dolly with children as we see in the

Figure 21.3

Figure 21.4

her mother-in-law or Bill her new husband or would they both think it frivolous? She had moved into their house, their farm—was this some way of keeping something for herself? How long did she wait before she responded? What did she write. . . ." I am living on this farm in the middle of nowhere and I am bored out of my mind, and I hate living with my mother-in-law." What if I set out to construct a photo documentary around Elsie's life using Dolly's photographs as the base? The photo genres of the day were quite well established, which is why people's albums from a particular era so often look so much alike; it is all about clothing, hair, photo-finishing, the normative poses, and so on. Take Dolly's photo where she is posed with "friends on the rocks" (Figure 21.5).

Elsie's photo with her sister and two friends is quite similar only instead of the sea as backdrop there is a prairie and the Pipestone Creek (Figure 21.6) *(C. Mitchell, 2005, p. 5)²*.

Figure 21.6

Figure 21.5

◆ *Photo Albums and Documentary Studies*

What the Dolly–Elsie project sets up is a "frame" for studying the use of photo albums in social science research that we have taken up through the Centre for Visual Methodologies for Social Change at the University of KwaZulu-Natal and the International Visual Methodologies Project at McGill University (www.ivmproject.ca).³ These studies were organized around a class "photo documentary project." This endeavor was initially conceived of as a prelude to video documentary work and focuses on participants working on their own family albums.

The approach is quite simple:

- Find (not take) seven or eight photos that appear (to you) to be linked to some sort of theme or narrative.

- Organize the seven or eight photos into a small photo album.

- Provide a title, a short curatorial statement of 150–200 words, short captions with each photo, and acknowledgements (where appropriate).

- Contain each aspect of the text material (curatorial statement and captions) to what can be placed within an album window.

The themes that people address in these photo-album documentaries have been fascinating. Some are very personal and almost confessional, and others, although personal in the sense of representing the passion of the documentarian, have a broader social context. In a set of albums produced in South Africa, Tembinkosi (now also documented in a video *My Photos, My Video, My Story,* Mak, Mitchell, & Stuart, 2005) uses the album project to explore one of the stark realities of life in rural KwaZulu-Natal in the age of AIDS—death and dying, silences, and "the after life" (as in how the survivors deal with all of this). In this case, he documents the story of his sister who in her early 20s dies mysteriously, leaving behind her 6-year-old son to be raised by Tembinkosi and the grandmother. Tembinkosi uses the project to explore the silences, not just about the cause of his sister's death and the importance of naming the disease, but also the position of AIDS orphans—in this case, his young nephew. In Tembinkosi's "performing"[4] of the album when he presents it to the class, he offers the image of his mother falling asleep with the album under her arm. It is a poignant representation of what the album project means to his family in terms of breaking silences.

Then there is Grace, a Black teacher in her late 20s who, as the daughter of a domestic worker, is more or less adopted into the White family for whom her mother works. As Grace goes back through the family photos, she looks at the ways in which she is dressed the same as the little White girl in the family and the fact that they are sometimes given identical toys. The culminating event is her graduation photo—or is it? Grace's documentary is an interrogation of privilege—her own to a certain extent, but not without questioning. There is Bongani, whose photographs of his daughter (born in 1994), are organized around the theme of the "decade of democracy" babies, as they have come to be called. His documentary takes us up to 2004 and, like Grace's album, is not without questioning about a postapartheid South Africa. Is it better? How have the hopes of April 1994 for a new beginning been fulfilled? And which ones haven't?

One documentary study submitted as a final project in the Canadian class, which emerged from its photo-album beginning, was conceived by Ran Tao as an examination of Chinese women's contemporary history. Using only eight photographs of Ying, the mother of a friend of hers, she manages to chart not only an individual woman's life in China from the 1940s to the present but also the sweeping changes that have occurred in Chinese society during those years. Ran does this by identifying and culturally locating the dress and body manners in the photographs. These eight images show early 1940s pre-liberation, the People's Liberation Army era of the 1950s, the Cultural Revolution, the 1980s "spring comes to China," the 1990s and China's Open Door Policy, the beginning of the 21st century, and the opportunities of Ying's daughter, Yu, to travel to Canada. Though not a constructed photo-album project in the same way as those noted above, *Listening With Our Eyes: Ying's Photographic Memories and Chinese Women's Contemporary History* (Tao, 2005) emanated from a photo album. The shorthand of the photographs, excavated by the "reader" Ran with her implicit knowledge, and "transcribed" for us as Western viewers, makes instantly explicit the vast divides this woman (known to us only as Ying's mother) has traveled. These photographs, shown out of their family photo-album context, now act as an index of social change.

The titles of the documentaries and actual curatorial statements that participants include are also fascinating because they give the artist-narrators an opportunity to position themselves in the work. In fact we have come to think of them as another type of photo-voice, not that different from the work of Wendy Ewald and Caroline Wang. The curatorial statements as tightly worded, single-paged texts sit as aesthetic pieces unto themselves as do their titles: "Transmutations of a Girl"; "Country Folk, City Folk"; "Breaking the Silences: Sexual Abuse in Families"; "Methods for Felling a Tree"; "Through the Lens: The Changing Face of Canadian Classrooms"; "What Does Freedom Mean (to my Children)?"; "Class and Status Changes Through One's Life Time"; and "Generations."

◆ *Looking in on the Process*

What album projects offer are some intriguing questions about creating and viewing, about meaning and materiality and the way photographs can exist as objects and social documents in social science research.

1. PHOTO DOCUMENTARY AND METHOD

What the photo documentary project highlights is method: a set of practices for *doing*—and in particular, the significance of participatory process in working with photographs—and a set of practices around *engaging* with the thing that is produced. Several authors, but particularly the sociosemiotician Stephen Riggins (1994), offer useful ways of thinking about method in working with objects in the social sciences. Riggins looks at the denotative and connotative meanings of objects. Using the case of his parents' living room, he methodically

photographs each object (starting at the door and ending up back at that door): the wall hangings, lamps, television set, easy chairs, and so on. For each object there is its denotative meaning (the first television set exhibited in the forties; the purchase of the particular television set), and then its connotative meaning, the stories of that particular television set, or the narration that accompanies it.

Riggins (1994) uses the term "mapping" to describe the ways in which objects serve as entry points for the telling of stories about the self. Of this mapping, he writes:

> meaning by this that the self uses the displayed objects (gift, heirlooms, photographs, etc.) as a way of plotting its social network, representing its cosmology and ideology, and projecting its history onto the world's map, its spatial spread so to speak. (p. 109)

The taking of the photographs is central to the process of visual ethnography:

> Many of the subtleties of domestic artifacts will elude the researcher unless it is possible to closely examine photographs. Consequently each room must be thoroughly photographed. Unlike the practice followed by the professional photographers employed by decorating and architectural magazines of removing all ephemeral traces left by users and inhabitants in order to avoid dating the photographs, ethnographers should make an effort to include the permanent as well as the ephemeral. Both are relevant to the research. (p. 110)

In *Researching Children's Popular Culture*, C. Mitchell and Reid-Walsh (2002) draw heavily on Riggins to read children's bedrooms. But in the context we are describing here, we see how this work can be applied to producing albums. In the case of photo documentary, there is the process of locating and selecting the photographs, followed by producing "the thing" of the album. Many family albums, as Langford (2000) and others have pointed out, have a "keeper," a person who is responsible for organizing and arranging, adding transcriptions, dating, and so on. Denotatively, the albums in the project can reflect this same tradition. Connotatively, though, in their making, they conjure up stories based on "looking for" and "looking at." Indeed, many of the students with whom we have worked comment on how doing this assignment becomes a family affair. Several of the students have had to direct their families in some other city to locate and send specific photos that they want to use in the album. Another student speaks of the time she spent with her parents going back through a set of school pictures. In fact, it is her mother who helps her decide on the theme. In this regard, the photographs both "are" and "do."

2. HOW WE LOOK/ HOW WE LOOK AT

Richard Chalfen (2002) discusses the phrase "how they looked" in his exploration of home media. He suggests that the domestic snapshot is more concerned with how we look than how we *look at*. More specifically in the usual creating/looking of a family photo album, the focal point would be on the familial, on relationship, on dress, hair . . . how we looked. As Chalfen says, "Family members are much *less* likely to make evidentiary claims for how they looked *at* their lives than how they appeared *to* people in their lives" (p. 143). Social scientists on the other hand bring a different perspective; they seek the "social and cultural practices and processes" (p. 143) embedded in the snapshots. Although Daniel Miller (1998) suggests that objects are mute and thus it is important to obtain ethnographic information, Chalfen (1991) notes the feedback function of photographs—how they

act as a form of communication. The photo album projects take advantage simultaneously of both the muteness and the communicative aspects of photographs, and speak to the "social biography" of the album (see Edwards, 2002, and number 3 of this chapter).

Chalfen (2002) suggests there may be resistance to being "critical viewers of our own family pictures. . . . People may experience a kind of security in not having to treat their own snapshot collections as problematic" (p. 144). None of the students appeared to have a problem with this; they were, however, not problematizing their families in this exercise, but rather charting social transitions or change by identifying shifts in material objects, dress, and so on. One exception to this was the narrative identification of a family recently fragmented by incest and sexual abuse. This photo album was an example of the dissonance Hirsch (1997) talks about in her discussion of the domestic photos of Holocaust survivors. The photos themselves speak of family. The context, into which we as viewers/readers must put our imagination, is one of abuse and destruction. This particular project speaks of social change in and of itself; it carries what is not seen—the invisible trauma. But the mere telling of this "domestic" story in the context of social change shows the distance from the historically invisible "not spoken" to the possibility now of the invisible being spoken. The bridging of the distance between the personal and the societal, through this participant's photo-album project, appears to have been an empowering experience for her; there was in addition a forceful impact on the viewers of this album.

3. PERFORMANCE

Elizabeth Edwards (2002) puts forward the idea of performance in talking about the materiality of photos. Our experience of photographs, she observes, is situated in space and time and mediated by the presentational format and the context of looking. Thus, the photograph, in and of itself, carries meaning prior to even considering the content of the image. Edwards and Hart (2004) highlight this with Roland Barthes' (1984) famous description of a photograph, which is first and foremost about the materiality of the object and only then includes a reference to the actual image:

> The photograph was very old, the corners were blunted from having been pasted in an album, the sepia had faded, and the picture just managed to show two children standing together at the end of a little wooden bridge in a glassed-in conservatory, what was called a Winter Garden in those days. (p. 67)

Edwards (2002) suggests that we need to address this materiality, which has not been forefronted in visual studies' concentration on the semiotic and representational aspects of the photograph. Materiality is "closely related to social biography," as Edwards says, and any object "should be understood as belonging in a continuing process of meaning, production, exchange and usage" (p. 68). The participants in the two album projects noted above presented their album projects to each other. Having the participants "perform" the album project (and at the very beginning of the class prior to the delivery of theoretical standpoints) moves them to a different place very quickly. As Hirsch (1997) says, "to step into the visual is not to engage in theory as systematic explanation of a set of facts, but to practice theory, to make theory just as the photographer materially makes an image" (p. 15). Interestingly, many of the participants in the photo-album projects found this new perspective on their domestic photos, admittedly in an academic situation, to be challenging, freeing, and expansive. It

pointed them to their own backyard—an often overlooked source of material. They understood that "kitchen studies" (C. Mitchell & Reid-Walsh, 2002) can reduce some ethical concerns.[5] It freed them to think differently about their own lives—in a compact yet concrete manner.

The photo albums document what stretching the family photo album can bring to the surface. Hirsch (1997) speaks of how the family photo is a naturalization of cultural practices that thus disguises "their stereotyped and coded characteristics" (p. 7). Doing this form of photo-album creation takes the family photo out of its context and forces the participants to move out of the familial, personal genre to acknowledge the cultural practices embedded there, to identify change through objects and rituals (ritualizations) present in the photos. It is a representation of a point of view, demanding a stepping back, a stepping away. This project makes visible what Hirsch calls "private, familiar and virtually invisible" (p. 10) aspects of family photos, bringing them into the wider social context in which they were taken, preserved, and viewed.

4. PHOTO DOCUMENTARY AS VOICE IN SOCIAL CHANGE

Photo-voice, as Ewald (1996, 2001), Hubbard (1994), Lykes (2001a, 2001b), C. Mitchell et al. (2005), Stuart (2004), Wang (1999), and Wang et al. (2004) have noted, relies on giving research participants cameras to document their own lives. The actual "prompt" can vary from something very specific, even initiated by the researcher (e.g., taking photographs of problems and solutions in addressing HIV and AIDS, taking photographs of safe and not so safe places in school), to a more open-ended type of self-representation as in the case of Wendy Ewald's work with children. What is interesting, we think, is to look at the photo-album projects noted above as a type of "voicing" project as well. The photographs we choose and the process of putting them into a documentary album serve to give voice.

Interestingly, many of the teachers with whom we have worked who have engaged in photo-album projects using "found" photos have often gone on to create with their own students albums that are based on the photos that children themselves take. In one school in rural South Africa, for example, a teacher who has acknowledged that most of her learners are too poor to have many photographs to engage in such a project, much less purchase an album to put them in, nonetheless adapts the pedagogical intervention by making little albums for each student out of four or five A4 sheets of paper stapled together. Children who don't have photographs draw their own pictures. The children produce drawings that look like posed photographs. In another school, Lindiwe decides to do an adaptation by having children become photographers first. Each of the first-grade students looks through the lens of a camera and carefully composes a picture that he or she describes to the teacher. The camera, though, as Lindiwe points out, has no film. There is no money for film or developing, but the idea of framing and "a gaze" is there and a story is still told.

This stands in contrast to a photo-voice/photo-album project done by a Canadian course participant and teacher in which each of her Grade 6 students had his or her own disposable camera to take photos of their view of the transition from elementary to secondary school. They then created photo albums with titles and brief curatorial statements. The identical photo albums made by the children with the assistance of their teacher were small-format albums, about 5 in. by 7 in., with a black cover and photos mounted on black pages, professionally coil-bound. Elegant and compact,

they were presented by the teacher as her final class project, lined up in a plastic box. We don't have access to the children's perceptions of their projects, only the teacher's view of the process. But it would be interesting to discuss the differences in perceptions of the students in this Canadian project and those of the students in the South African project. Is the idea of framing "universal"? Is the camera an extension of the eye, when the camera is not known? Here we are reminded of Sarah Pink's (2001) story about Tomas, a man of Guinea Bissau, who didn't recognize himself in a playback seen in the viewfinder of the video camera, even though he had seen television in a different context.

5. PHOTO DOCUMENTARY AND SOCIAL CHANGE

"Can the visual arts make a difference?" asks Marilyn Martin (2004) in relation to addressing HIV and AIDS in South Africa, highlighting the ways in which various artists and art projects (including artistic interventions, memory quilts, and memory boxes) have contributed to AIDS activism and engagement. In this regard photographs might be read as documents (Hodder, 1997) and, as such, representative of change. He is referring to a range of documents, including historical writings, but we might also look at photographs and other objects as documents and thus as representational agents of change. A good example can be seen in the work of Susan Schwartzenberg (2005) when she combines photos, documents, children, and disability. Her multilayered documentation looks at children and disability in Seattle over 40 years, using material from family photo albums and linking it with other historical records. In doing this work, she connects the domestic photo album expressly to its temporal and geographical as well as geopolitical locations. Understanding the multilayered ways in which social change can occur lays bare any idea that revolution/evolution is or can be straightforward. The iterative nature of social change, spiraling up, down, and across social spheres, in time and place, reminds us of the structural nature of our cultures, no matter how naturalized geopolitics wants us to believe them to be. Schwartzenberg (2005) says of the stories of change she documented on disability, that through them, she "saw a matrix of ideas flooding society during the past century" (p. 80). Charting change in this way reminds us of the possibility of change and is a concise history lesson in empowerment. In the case of Tembinkosi's album, noted above, and the image of his mother falling asleep with the album under her arm, it is difficult to resist the idea of "the power of objects" both to study change and to bring about change.

6. PHOTO DOCUMENTARY AND IMAGINATION

Finally, we return to the idea of things and the imagination in the social sciences. Looking to Annette Kuhn (1995), it is hard to avoid the imaginative potential of this kind of research. Writing that uses photography as a central metaphor can contribute to our understanding of the power of both the object of the photograph and its connotative meanings (Lively, 2003; Modjeska, 1990; Oakley, 1996). One might also think about the imaginative potential of contesting "what was" or "what is" and to suggest "what could be." Jo Spence and Rosy Martin (Spence, 1995) engaged in staged photography wherein they "re-took" the kinds of photographs that they thought should have been taken of them as schoolgirls, or which would provide for an embodied investigation of issues of school and the expectations

of working-class parents. In an imaginative study of "what Dolly sent Elsie," it may be possible to reconfigure the family album to create the kinds of photos Elsie and Dolly might have wanted to exchange as opposed to the socially sanctioned photos of birthdays and holidays: images of Elsie "stepping out" beyond the world of the farm, perhaps packing to go on a romantic Shirley Valentine holiday to England, or having Dolly and Elsie reenact their work sites (Valerie Walkerdine, personal communication, November 10, 2005).

◆ *Conclusion*

In this chapter we have attempted to locate work on objects and things within the field of visual studies more generally. Each has its well-established literatures as we see in the work of Brown (1998), Haworth-Booth (2004), and Miller (1998), for example, on things and material culture, and the vast range of research on working with photographs within visual studies (e.g., Banks, 1998, 2001; Higonnet, 1998; Knowles & Sweetman, 2004). Here we simply wish to see how these works, taken together, can deepen an understanding of the perspectives of participants on a particular phenomenon and at the same time engage participants more actively in the process of both researching their own lives and offering "ways forward." In a photo project with young people in South Africa on addressing issues of stigma in relation to HIV and AIDS, many of the participants spontaneously play with the idea of staging as part of representation (Moletsane et al., 2005). One of the most poignant staged images is of a 16-year-old boy with a noose around his neck. As difficult as it is to look at it, the photo is one that "matches" one set of scenarios for young people in South Africa where the prevalence rates for HIV infection are high and where there is the association that (unprotected) sex = death. Studying and exploring both the materiality of the photograph and the image itself suggests, we think, new possibilities for creating images of hope rather than despair and, in so doing, suggests a place for photographs as things and as objects in the process of social change. Although this is not an area that has been foregrounded in the work on objects and things in visual studies more generally, mapping out a variety of visual methods can suggest pathways for change. In this way we think that this "new materialism" offers pathways for hope.

◆ Notes

1. Well elaborated by Caroline Wang and Mary Brinton Lykes, among others, photo-voice is a method that "is based on the understanding that people are experts in their own lives" (Wang, Morrel-Samuels, Hutchison, Bell, & Pestronk, 2004) and uses photography as a tool for both individual empowerment and broader social change (see number 4 in this chapter).

2. A version of the section "What Dolly Sent Elsie" was first presented by Claudia Mitchell as part of a keynote address at the Annual Conference of the Literacy Researchers of Canada, Canadian Society for Studies in Education, May 27, 2005. A version of this paper was also presented at the International Visual Sociology Association Conference by Susann Allnutt, Claudia Mitchell, and Jean Stuart (2005). The "What Dolly Sent Elsie" component of the paper was later expanded by Claudia into a talk at the Power of Objects Seminar Series, Cardiff University, November 10, 2005.

3. For further information about the Centre for Visual Methodologies for Social Change and the International Visual Methodologies Project, see www.ivmproject.ca

4. Edwards (2002) says "photography is not merely the instrument of indexical inscription, it

is technology for visual display experienced as meaningful" (p. 67). Thus, the display of the albums becomes a performance of meaning, which is understood as such by the other participants in the class.

5. It raises other ethical concerns, however, not the least of which is positioning as "other" those with whom you are intimate.

◆ References

Allnutt, S., Mitchell, C., & Stuart, J. (2005). *Photo documentary and reconfiguring the family album: Studies in Canada and South Africa.* International Visual Sociology Association Conference, Dublin, August 3–5.

Banks, M. (1998). Visual anthropology: Image, object, and interpretation. In J. Prosser (Ed.), *Image-based research: A sourcebook for qualitative researchers* (pp. 9–23). London: Falmer Press.

Banks, M. (2001). *Visual methods in social research.* London: Sage.

Barthes, R. (1984). *Camera lucida* (R. Howard Trans). London: Fontana.

Brown, B. (1998). How to do things with things. *Critical Inquiry, 24,* 935–964.

Chalfen, R. (1987). *Snapshot versions of life.* Bowling Green, OH: Bowling Green State University Popular Press.

Chalfen, R. (1991). *Turning leaves: Exploring identity in Japanese American photograph albums.* Albuquerque: University of New Mexico Press.

Chalfen, R. (2002). Snapshots "r" us: The evidentiary problematic of home media. *Visual Studies, 17*(2), 141–149.

Daston, L. (Ed.). (2004). *Things that talk: Object lessons from art and science.* New York: Zone Books.

Edwards, E. (2002). Material beings: Objecthood and ethnographic photographs. *Visual Studies, 17*(1), 67–75.

Edwards, E., & Hart, J. (Eds.). (2004). *Photographs, objects, histories on the materiality of images.* New York: Routledge.

Ewald, W. (1992). *Magic eyes: Scenes from an Andean girlhood.* Seattle: Bay Press.

Ewald, W. (1996). *I dreamed I had a girl in my pocket.* New York: W. W. Norton.

Ewald, W. (2001). *I wanna take me a picture: Teaching photography and writing to children.* Boston: Beacon Press.

Faber, P. (Compiler). (2003). *Group portrait South Africa: Nine family histories.* Cape Town, South Africa: Kwela Books.

Haworth-Booth, M. (Ed.). (2004). *Things: A spectrum of photography, 1850–2001.* London: Jonathan Cape, Victoria and Albert Museum.

Higonnet, A. (1998). *Pictures of innocence: The history and crisis of ideal childhood.* London: Thames and Hudson.

Hirsch, M. (1997). *Family frames: Photography, narrative, and postmemory.* Cambridge, MA: Harvard University Press.

Hodder, I. (1997). Always momentary, fluid, and flexible. Towards a reflexive excavation methodology. *Antiquity, 71,* 691–700.

Hubbard, J. (1994). *Shooting back from the reservation.* New York: New Press.

Knowles, C., & Sweetman, P. (Eds.). (2004). *Picturing the social landscape: Visual methods and the sociological imagination.* London and New York: Routledge.

Kuhn, A. (1995). *Family secrets: Acts of memory and imagination.* London and New York: Verso.

Langford, M. (2000). *Suspended conversations: The afterlife of memory in photographic albums.* Montreal, Quebec, Canada: McGill-Queen's Press.

Lee, A., & Pultz, J. (2004). *Diane Arbus: Family albums.* New Haven, CT: Yale University Press.

Lively, P. (2003). *The photograph.* New York: Viking.

Lykes, M. B. (2001a). Activist participatory research and the arts with rural Mayan women: Interculturality and situated meaning making. In D. L. Tolman & M. Brydon Miller (Eds.), *From subject to subjectivities: A handbook of interpretive and participatory methods* (pp. 183–199). New York: New York University Press.

Lykes, M. B. (2001b). Creative arts and photography in participatory action research in Guatemala. In P. Reason & H. Bradbury (Eds.), *Handbook of action research: Participative inquiry and practice* (pp. 363–371). Thousand Oaks, CA: Sage.

Mak, M., Mitchell, C., & Stuart, J. (2005). *My photos, my video, my story.* Documentary produced by Taffetta Production, Montreal, Canada.

Martin, M. (2004). HIV/AIDS in South Africa: Can the visual arts make a difference? In K. D. Kauffman & D. Lindauer (Eds.), *AIDS and South Africa: The social expression of a pandemic* (pp. 120–135). New York: Palgrave Macmillan.

Miller, D. (Ed.). (1998). *Material cultures: Why some things matter.* London: UCL Press.

Mitchell, C. (2005). *What Dolly sent Elsie: Objects as social documents in social science research.* A presentation at the Power of Object Invited Lecture Series, School of Social Sciences, University of Cardiff, November 10, 2005.

Mitchell, C., & Reid-Walsh, J. (2002). *Researching children's popular culture: The cultural spaces of childhood.* New York: Routledge Taylor Francis.

Mitchell, C., Stuart, J., Moletsane, R., Delange, N., & Buthelezi, T. (2005). Giving a face to HIV and AIDS: On the uses of photo-voice by teachers and community health care workers working with youth in rural South Africa. *Qualitative Research in Psychology, 2,* 257–270.

Mitchell, C., & Weber, S. (1999). *Reinventing ourselves as teachers: Beyond nostalgia.* London: Falmer.

Mitchell, W. J. T. (2004). [Cover notes]. In L. Daston (Ed.), *Things that talk: Object lessons from art and science.* New York: Zone Books.

Modjeska, D. (1990). *Poppy.* Ringwood, Victoria, Australia: McPhee Gribble.

Moletsane, R., De Lange, N., Mitchell, C., Stuart, J., Buthelezi, T., & Taylor, M. (2005). *Photo-voice as an analytical and activist tool in the fight against HIV and AIDS stigma in a rural KwaZulu-Natal School.* Kenton Conference, Mpekweni Resort, October 27–30.

Oakley, A. (1996). *Man and wife: Richard and Kay Titmuss—My parents' early years.* London: HarperCollins.

Pink, S. (2001). *Doing visual ethnography.* London: Sage.

Riggins, S. H. (1994). Fieldwork in the living room: An autoethnographic essay. In S. H. Riggins (Ed.), *The socialness of things: Essays on the socio-semiotics of objects* (pp. 101–147). Berlin, Germany: Mouton de Gruyer.

Schwartzenberg, S. (2005). The personal archive as historical record. *Visual Studies, 20*(1), 70–82.

Spence, J. (1986). *Putting myself in the picture: A political, personal, and photographic autobiography.* London: Camden Press.

Spence, J. (1995). *Cultural sniping: The art of transgression.* London: Routledge.

Spence, J., & Holland, P. (Eds.). (1991). *Family snaps: The meanings of domestic photography.* London: Virago.

Stuart, J. (2004). Media matters: Producing a culture of compassion in the age of AIDS. *English Quarterly, 36*(2), 3–5.

Tao, R. (2005). *Listening with our eyes: Ying's photographic memories and Chinese women's contemporary history.* Unpublished manuscript, Department of Integrated Studies, McGill University.

Wang, C. (1999). Photovoice: A participatory action research strategy applied to women's health. *Journal of Women's Health, 8,* 85–192.

Wang, C., Morrel-Samuels, S., Hutchison, P., Bell, L., & Pestronk, R. M. (2004). Flint photovoice: Community building among youths, adults, and policymakers. *American Journal of Public Health, 94*(6), 911–913.

Weiser, J. (1993). *Phototherapy techniques.* New York: Jossey-Bass.

Willis, D. (Ed.). (1994). *Picturing us: African American identity in photography.* New York: New Press.

22

Visual Art

COLLAGE AS INQUIRY

◆ Lynn Butler-Kisber

*The symbol evokes imitations, language can only explain.
The symbol touches all chords of the human heart at once,
language is always forced to keep one thought at a time.*

—Bachofen, 1967, p. 49

The overall purpose of this chapter is to define and explore the potential of collage in qualitative research. It will show how the use of visual inquiry, in this case collage, can mediate understanding in new and interesting ways for both the creator and the viewer because of its partial, embodied, multivocal, and nonlinear representational potential. It will examine collage as a form of qualitative inquiry from historical, theoretical, and practical perspectives to provide a context, strategies, tools, and examples. In addition, it will articulate the inherent challenges in this type of work and suggest some future directions. For the purposes of this discussion, collage is defined as the process of cutting and sticking found images and image fragments from popular print/magazines onto cardstock.

◆ Personal Context

My interest in collage as inquiry grew out of my initiation into arts-informed qualitative research that occurred about a decade ago when

I attended my first American Educational Research Association Winter Institute on Arts-Based Qualitative Research directed by Elliot Eisner in Palo Alto, California. The use of art as a form of communication/inquiry was not new to me. For many years I had encouraged artful ways in my classroom teaching, initially in the elementary school, and then later at the university level in language and literacy courses (Butler-Kisber, 1997). I had witnessed many instances of how artful approaches can elicit communicative talents that otherwise remain hidden (Gardner, 1983, 1999), increase the connectedness with and engagement in learning (Belenky, Clinchy, Goldberger, & Tarule, 1986), and encourage new ways of understanding (Eisner, 1991). I was fascinated and excited to learn on one hand what seemed so novel and on another what seemed so expected, that a growing number of qualitative researchers were incorporating artful ways into their work, and I resolved to do the same. I began using found poetry in my research (Butler-Kisber, 2002) and encouraged graduate students in my research courses to explore an array of artful approaches and pursue those best suited to their propensities and contexts. When Donna Davis, a collage artist, announced one night in class how in doing a collage for an exhibition for which she was preparing, she had unexpectedly seen how the collage portrayed a research dilemma she was facing, I suddenly realized the analytic potential in collage (Davis & Butler-Kisber, 1999). With her help, I introduced students to collage in subsequent courses. Several years later, I began using collage as an inquiry approach in my own research (Butler-Kisber, 2007).

♦ History of Collage

The term collage comes from the French verb *coller*, meaning to stick. In the world of

art, collage refers to a genre in which "found" materials that are either natural or made are cut up and pasted on some sort of flat surface. The roots of paper collage extend back at least 1000 years in folk art such as in examples of Japanese texts where the calligraphy was augmented by sticking on torn scraps of paper. Mary Delany (1700–1788) has been identified as the inventor of "paper mosaic" or "plant collage" (Warden, 2000). Her method was to cut the petals and leaves from colored paper, and paste them on a background of black paper. Some unusual tints were created from paper on which color had run, and occasionally she added touches of watercolor and even real leaves (Goldman, 1988, p. 19).

In the 19th century, collage was used to create German greeting cards, and interestingly, families in the Victorian era produced parlor scrapbooks that were collages of the everyday life of the time (Atkinson, 1996). Perhaps this was a foreshadowing of the scrapbooking trend that is currently sweeping North America (Browning, 2000; Hart, Grossman, & Dunhill, 1989).

Lyons (1998), as part of a yearly, tongue-in-cheek "Centaur Symposium" at the University of Tennessee, has suggested that collage can be traced back to an even more ancient time when the earliest use of zoomorphic juncture, or the practice of "collaging" two or more animal parts to produce a hybrid such as a centaur, occurred. He playfully argues that if these mythical collages have actual biological roots, citing the platypus as a possible example, a counterargument exists for evolutionary theory.

Collage made its debut in the art world in the early part of the 20th century, mainly in the art movements of Cubism (1907–1925), Futurism (1909–1915), Constructivism (1913–1930), and Dadaism (1916–1925) (Onley, 2004). Pablo Picasso and George Braque are most often cited as the founders of collage. Brockelman (2001) argues it is the intention in the work that "differentiates

Figure 22.1   Paper Mosaic by Mary Delany

their work from earlier examples of folk practices" (p. 2). The intention of the Cubists in using the medium of collage was to challenge the long-held conventions of painting, oppose the 19th-century notion of a single reality or truth by portraying multiple realities, and merge art with the more banal, everyday aspects of life as a critique of the elitist nature of "high art." Although Brockelman's attribution of intention to what separates earlier folk art practices from collage art may be a persuasive interpretation, it is interesting, and perhaps not coincidental, that the introduction of collage as art came from circles of well-known and mostly male artists, while its antecedents remain as categories of folk art, hobbies, and practices that were carried out largely by women.

The collages of the Futurists incorporated the energy of the machine age into their art,

while the Constructivists attempted "to create harmonic structures with abstract, geometric forms" with materials that reflected industrialized society in order to "lead mankind to harmony and a better society" (Onley, 2004, p. 2).

After the mid-19th century, it was not unusual for artists to integrate photographs into their work. However, it was the Dadaists who coined the term "photomontage," a photographic equivalent of collage. Their canvases were created from cut up photographs and print used to portray the violence of society and critique the capitalism and militarism that they felt were inherently connected (Ades, 1993). Dadaism was an anti-art movement that rejected the term collage in favor of photomontage to distinguish itself from the materialism of the Cubists (Ades, 1993).

Kurt Schwitters (1887–1948), a painter who was profoundly influenced by the Dada movement, is known as the "father" of collage. He defined the creative process as inseparable from everyday life and used discarded fragments from the past to show the discontinuities of war and industrialized society of the time. He is attributed with having had one of the most profound influences on the creative arts since then, opening the way for the collage principle to permeate all types of artistic expression (Dietrich, 1993). Thus, these four movements pushed the boundaries of representational form and laid the groundwork for the 20th-century art that followed, foreshadowing the postmodern notions we currently embrace. "With collage we have a postmodern intertwined with the modern, a postmodern crisis of the modern announced from within modernity" (Brockelman, 2001, p. 6).

◆ Collage in Qualitative Research

It is not surprising that collage is gaining prominence in qualitative research. There is a burgeoning interest in using arts-informed research to counteract the hegemony and linearity in written texts, increase voice and reflexivity in the research process, and expand the possibilities of multiple and diverse realities and understandings. The search for more embodied and alternative representational forms where meaning is understood to be a construction of what the text represents and what the reader/viewer brings to it, and the realization that we live in an increasingly visual/nonlinear world, have naturally led researchers to explore the potential of visual texts, collage being one possibility. "[C]ollage reflects the very way we see the world with objects being given meaning not from something within themselves, but rather through the way we perceive they stand in relationship to one another" (Robertson, 2000, p. 2).

Qualitative researchers, who for the reasons mentioned above are pursuing arts-informed approaches, are most often researchers who have turned to artful ways, rather than the reverse. In terms of a visual medium, then, collage is an attractive one. Even a novice has grasped at a young age the fundamentals of cutting and sticking and, with a willingness to experiment, can engage in creative and inventive collage work that can push the boundaries of understanding. That being said, there is much that can and should be learned about collage as an art form if it is to acquire a reputable and acceptable place in qualitative research circles.

Collage can contribute to qualitative research in several profound ways. The potentially evocative power of art forms, in particular visual ones, produces a sensory or embodied response that can help the viewer/responder generate meanings in very concrete ways. In collage a single, coherent notion "gives way to relations of juxtaposition and difference" (Rainey, 1998, p. 124), and these fragments "work against one another so hard, the mind is sparked" (Steinberg, 1972, p. 14) into new ways of knowing. The ambiguity that remains present in collage provides a way of expressing the said and the unsaid, and allows for multiple avenues of interpretation and greater accessibility. "The collage-making process inherently uses metaphor (similarity or comparison) metonymy (contiguity or connectedness) and . . . challenges the dichotomy of the intellect and the senses" (Irwin, 2003, p. 9). Novel juxtapositions and/or connections, and gaps or spaces, can reveal both the intended and the unintended. The collage process reduces "conscious control over what is being presented which contributes to greater levels of expression, and in turn greater areas for examination and subsequent clarification" (Williams, 2000, p. 275).

Usually in writing up research, the researcher first delineates the ideas and then finds the words and particular ways of expressing these ideas to get at nuances and more embodied ways of representing the work. Even in arts-informed work such as found poetry, the researcher typically distils the "found" words/ideas from transcripts and then uses poetic structures to express the ideas in more compelling and sensory ways (Butler-Kisber, 2002; Richardson, 1994). The reverse is true for collage. This process moves from intuitions and feelings to thoughts and ideas. Image fragments are chosen and placed to give a "sense" of something rather than a literal expression of an idea and, as a result, the process "honours the unconnected and inexplicable" and allows for "reseeing, relocating, and connecting anew" (Mullen, 1999, p. 292).

Finally, written qualitative texts go through a number of drafts/interpretations before being completed. The analytic process involves trying to become successively more definitive and clearer about an interpretation. The collage process, on the other hand, may go through a number of iterations before the images are actually glued into place, but it results in a metaphorical product that is then subject to or available for different responses (Allnutt, Butler-Kisber, Poldma, & Stewart, 2005), providing alternate ways for interpreting both conscious and unconscious ideas.

◆ Collage as Inquiry

The increasing interest in collage as inquiry is producing a growing body of research that describes instances of collage use across a number of disciplines. A library or Internet search quickly reveals that collage is not just relegated to research. It is used quite frequently as a pedagogical approach for students from elementary to tertiary levels of education in many different curricular areas, as a means of portraying a visual synthesis of a process, and as a way of interrogating identity and values because "images enable meaning to travel in ways that words cannot" (Burns, 2003, p. 9) and assumptions emerge that may not otherwise be either conscious or apparent. It is also used as a way of scaffolding/eliciting a creative process such as writing (Olshansky, 1994).

Although not exhaustive, nor mutually exclusive, there are three approaches for using collage described here that have proven to be useful in the inquiry process in both the analysis and subsequent representation. In what follows I emphasize the analytic possibilities but would suggest that these forms of collage, as well as others, can be used in the final representational product to enhance understanding, show poignancy, open avenues for discussion and further reflection, and contribute to persuasiveness, as shown in the doctoral dissertations of Finley (1998), Promislow (2005), and Steeves (2000).

These three approaches are collage as a memoing/reflective process (Butler-Kisber, 2007; Davis & Butler-Kisber, 1999; McDermott, 2002), collage as a conceptualizing approach (Butler-Kisber et al., 2005), and collage as an elicitation for writing or discussion (Butler-Kisber, Rudd, & Stewart, 2007; Williams, 2000).

◆ Memoing/Reflecting Process

Memoing is used in qualitative research to help researchers reflect on some aspect of the research process (Miles & Huberman, 1994). The researcher writes a memo in order to examine the data in new ways and to "grapple with ideas . . . set an analytic course . . . and define relationships among various categories" (Charmaz, 2000, p. 518–519). Memos can potentially produce important insights that have profound effects on the analytic process. However, memo writing is a very linear process in spite of the ideas that may emerge. When collage is used as a memoing or reflective process, it is just the opposite. The researcher works in an intuitive and nonlinear way using disparate fragments and joining them in ways that can produce associations and connections that might otherwise remain unconscious.

To create a collage memo, the researcher focuses on some aspect of the research process and then cuts and pastes found images onto cardstock to visually portray this focus. In essence the creator works by reviewing different images and then selecting ones or pieces of some that resonate with or "feel like" the particular focus. It is useful to work conceptually rather than literally choosing images that stand metaphorically for an idea (James, 2000), and to experiment with size, color, texture, overlap, and spaces to portray the nuances of the focus. Frequently, the outcome reveals an important new idea that helps to refine the focus of the research and/or move the analytic process further. As described elsewhere, Donna Davis was able to identify and understand a power struggle she had with a participant. Her collage depicted a jungle and represented the ambiguity that exists between an aggressor and defender. She saw it as reflective of her relationship with her participant. It helped her to decide that it would be best to sensitively withdraw from her work with this person (Davis & Butler-Kisber, 1999). Pam Markus was able to move from a binary view of collaboration manifested as a tension between the individual and the group that she had depicted in her collage to a unified perspective, one where she understood that the individual and the group can complement each other.

This insight helped to redirect her research focus (Butler-Kisber, 2005).

In a similar way, McDermott (2002) had pre-service teachers create collages to help unearth their values and discover their "teacher identity." One of her participants, Jessica, "used various objects, images and colors in her collage to serve as metaphors for her own beliefs about teaching, and the role her personal identity plays in the ongoing formation of her teacher self" (McDermott, 2002, p. 61). As a result of the work, Jessica was able to name things she came to know about herself and raise questions about some of her assumptions, as well as those of others.

In the final public products, collage memos such as these can be used in much the same way that reflective comments and/or data excerpts are inserted into text to show rather than just tell, and bring the research process to life.

◆ *Conceptualizing Approach*

Collage can also be used as a helpful way of conceptualizing a response to a research question. Once a research question is articulated, a series of collages can be created to respond to the question. Then the collages can be interrogated to get at the themes that cut across the work. For example, as part of my work in the Artful Analysis and Representation in Research Collective (AARRC), made up at any one time of five to eight researchers who have come together to work once a month over the last 4 years, the collages below were a response to one of our research questions, "What does working in the research group mean to me?" In this exercise a series of "artcards," small-scale collages constructed on cardstock the size of hockey trading cards, were produced. I worked in a largely intuitive way selecting images and fragments that seemed to best express what working in our collective felt like. When completed, I examined them carefully to choose titles that represented the essence of each one. As a result, I titled them "Serenity," "Camaraderie," "Challenge," and "Energy." Then I examined this cluster together and in so doing began to see other possibilities. By looking at the colors, shapes, composition, and content (Rose, 2001), I identified the recurring shades of red and the repeated use of spheres. I realized that in each collage there is a suggestion of a vortex that threatens to submerge the lips, swallow the birds, and erase the tree. Thus, a deeper interpretation was that working in this group creates a tension between the serenity, camaraderie, challenge, and energy that the group provides, and the potential loss of individuality and personal voice that occurs as a result.

Similarly, when working as a team, each of the researchers can produce a collage in response to a research question. Then the results can be analyzed using an iterative process of viewing, discussing, and writing in order to tease out commonalities and differences across the collages, to

Camaraderie

Figure 22.3 Camaraderie

Challenge

Figure 22.4 Challenge

Serenity

Figure 22.2 Serenity

Energy

Figure 22.5 Energy

conceptualize the nuances of a phenomenon (Allnutt et al., 2005). In either situation, it is the production of multiple responses to the same question that produces a "kaleidoscopic representation" of a phenomenon and helps to reveal interpretations that otherwise might not emerge.

In the public presentation of this group work, the collages were reduced from their original 8.5 by 11 in. size so that they could be juxtaposed side by side in the written text to elaborate the written word in much the same way that tables and/or figures are used in texts as illustrative of the discussion.

◆ Elicitation For Writing

Collage making can also be used as a way of eliciting writing and/or discussion. Pam Markus, mentioned earlier, is a doctoral candidate and collage artist who has found it useful in writing her autobiographical dissertation to make a collage before she begins a specific section of writing.

This collage/writing process is a way of mapping subjectivity. The spontaneous and intuitive method of collage draws out more complex notions about experience, disrupting and challenging safer, more traditional textual routes, leading to learning that is both personal and significant (Butler-Kisber et al., 2007).

Williams (2000) has described how in nursing collage can be used as a helpful medium for guided reflection in clinical supervision. During each session, a collage furnishes the focal point for the discussion and helps to elicit the conversation that ensues. As Williams (2000) indicates:

> This medium is used as a starting point for discussion in the supervision setting where reflective questioning by the supervisor is framed around the collage

images in order to clarify relationships of the issues presented and the personal meanings and values of these to the supervisee. (p. 273)

Including elicitation in the final representation collages can provide a very useful visual trail of a thinking or reflective process that is otherwise difficult to make explicit. It allows the reader/viewer to relate to the text differently and enhances the trustworthiness of the work. In summary, whether used as a reflective, conceptualizing, or elicitation approach in the analysis, representation, or both, collage has the potential of providing new and different ways of thinking about phenomena and revealing aspects about everyday life and identity that are unconscious or implicit.

◆ Articulating Challenges

There are some challenges that exist for qualitative researchers who wish to use collage to enhance rather than detract from the final, public representations of their work. These include how collage expertise can be developed, how to know when collage should be used, how collage work should be evaluated, and how collage work can be carried out ethically when using found images created by others.

Like any other skill, work in collage requires technical knowledge, such as an understanding of the role of color, texture, size, directionality, space, and position in composition. It also requires practice. Immersion in viewing the art form and reading about it no doubt helps, and there are some very useful books on the "how to" of collage art (see Atkinson, 1996). One strategy we found useful in our AARRC group is what we call inkshedding. It is an adaptation of the inkshedding writing process (Hunt, 2004) to collage work and helps to focus attention on collage techniques. In collage inkshedding (Butler-Kisber, 2007), the participants agree on a focus/topic, and then each member begins a collage with the focus in mind. The collages are circulated around the group and images are added until the cardstock is covered or the topic seems saturated. Adding images to those of others helps to focus attention on the compositional details and as a result improves technique. Workshopping with a collage artist, however, is probably the best way to develop the technical skill and confidence necessary for collage making. Unfortunately, workshops are not always readily available to researchers who wish to pursue this or other kinds of arts-informed work. Aside from increasing the availability of workshops at conferences such as the Annual Meeting of the American Educational Researchers Association, it would be a good idea for universities to make the necessary changes to include arts-informed workshops or courses as part of the preparation for becoming a qualitative researcher, and to encourage interdisciplinary exchanges between artists and others.

There is no definitive answer for when to use collage in the inquiry process. The three approaches—memoing, conceptualizing and elicitation outlined earlier—provide ways of thinking about when collage might be used. There are some who think that collage making should be left to artists who also are researchers, as in the cases of Donna Davis and Pam Markus. Others would respond that this is elitist and exclusionary. On the other hand, there is potential for inadequate work to detract from the recent, positive strides made in arts-informed research. I would suggest that because the analytic and representational potential of collage is so powerful that no one should shy away from exploring this avenue if it seems appropriate. There may be times when a decision should be made to relegate collages to the

analytic process, including them only as an example of this process, perhaps in the appendices, rather than using them as a final representational form. A decision of this kind requires ways of evaluating collage in research, to which I now turn.

Barone and Eisner (1997) and Richardson et al. (2000) have offered some helpful criteria for evaluating arts-informed qualitative research. These criteria are more applicable to written forms of arts-informed work such as narrative, ethno-drama, and poetry than to visual ones. Kress and van Leeuwen (1996) and Rose (2001) have provided useful ways of how to read/evaluate visual images. Their work, however, is more applicable to photographs and paintings. In the visual/digital arena, Bamford (2005) has suggested that the characteristics of "quality form" such as unity, organic integrity, semblance, and sentience, to mention a few, might provide an alternative conception for validity. The scope of this chapter does not permit a summary of these perspectives. What is needed, however, is an integration of the criteria for evaluating arts-informed research with those for evaluating visual images, with a particular focus on collage. Although this is no easy task, it would be a worthwhile endeavor, and one that would be well received in the field. It would be particularly helpful for dissertation committees who wish to encourage graduate students to push the inquiry boundaries but worry about how the results will/should be evaluated.

In collage work, as in all other qualitative research, the ethical issues of voice, reflexivity, and trustworthiness are always of prime importance because of the proximity between participants and researchers and the attention that must be paid to building trust and relationships that arise as a result. One other ethical aspect that is particularly relevant to the collage work described here is that of copyright. When using pictures or fragments from public/popular magazines, it is difficult to give credit when frequently no attribution is apparent. However, according to law there are restrictions. Works of art in Canada are protected for the duration of the artist's life plus 50 years. In terms of photographs, as of 1998, the same rule applies and similar rules apply in other countries. There are some who suggest that the principle of fair use, or use without gain or profit, should apply when images are used for educational purposes including work done in classes, presented at conferences, and/or published in educational journals (Rolan, 1996). Of course, the question of what constitutes gain is a complicated one and merits attention. There are companies that provide licensing for the use of a piece of an image or a whole one, and they have more modest rates for those who are using images for nonprofit work. To avoid this ethical issue entirely, collage researchers can simply use images from public picture banks, several of which are available on the Internet, and can search out old, found images that are no longer protected or make their own. A useful task, however, would be for the American Educational Research Association or another research association to generate ethical guidelines for using found images in collage research work. This would provide researchers with helpful parameters before a project is underway, and it would also help to unearth any ethical concerns that have yet to become apparent.

◆ Future Directions

Future directions for collage are exciting. The high level of interest in such work, the increasing presence of it at research conferences and in theses, and the burgeoning technologies that can support the work suggest that it is a form of inquiry that is here to stay.

More public accounts of researchers' explorations with the medium, more opportunities for exchanges between researchers and artists, and efforts to make available lists of exemplary work are needed.

◆ References

Ades, D. (1993). *Photomontage*. London: Thames and Hudson.

Allnutt, S., Butler-Kisber, L., Poldma, T., & Stewart, M. (2005, April). *Doing, sensing, knowing*. Paper presented at the annual meeting of the American Educational Research Association, Montreal, Quebec, Canada.

Atkinson, J. L. (1996). *A step-by-step guide and showcase*. Gloucester, MA: Rockport.

Bachofen, J. J. (1967). *Myth, religion, and mother right*. Princeton, NJ: Princeton University Press.

Bamford, A. (2005). *The art of research: Digital theses in the arts*. Retrieved February 20, 2006, from: http://www.adt.caul.edu.auetc2005/papersw/123Bamford.pdf

Barone, T., & Eisner, E. (1997). Arts-based educational research. In R. M. Jaeger (Ed.), *Complementary methods for research in education* (pp. 73–114). Washington, DC: American Educational Research Association.

Belenky, M. F., Clinchy, B. M., Goldberger, N. R., & Tarule, J. M. (1986). *Women's ways of knowing*. New York: Basic Books.

Brockelman, T. P. (2001). *The frame and the mirror: On collage and the postmodern*. Evanston, IL: Northwestern University Press.

Browning, M. (2000). *Handcrafted journals, albums, scrapbooks, and more*. New York: Sterling Publishing.

Burns, D. (2003, September). *Whole systems action research in complex governance settings*. Keynote address at the 10th World Congress of Participatory Action Research, Pretoria, South Africa.

Butler-Kisber, L. (1997). The practical: Classroom literacy through stories, questions, and action. In V. Froese (Ed.), *Language across the curriculum* (pp. 183–213). Toronto, Ontario, Canada: Harcourt Brace.

Butler-Kisber, L. (2002). Artful portrayals in qualitative inquiry. *Alberta Journal of Qualitative Research, XLVII*(3), 229–239.

Butler-Kisber, L. (2005). The potential of artful analysis and portrayals in qualitative inquiry. In F. Bodone (Ed.), *What difference does research make and for whom?* (pp. 203–217). New York: Peter Lang.

Butler-Kisber, L. (2007). Collage as analysis and representation in qualitative inquiry. In J. G. Knowles, A. Cole, L. Neilsen, & C. Luciani (Eds.), *The art of visual inquiry* (pp. 265–280). Halifax, Nova Scotia, Canada: Backalong Books.

Butler-Kisber, L. Allnutt, S., Furlini, L., Kronish, N., Markus, P., Poldma, T., et al. (2005, April). *Collage as inquiry: Sensing, doing, and knowing in qualitative research.* Paper presented at the Annual Meeting of the American Educational Association, Montreal, Quebec, Canada.

Butler-Kisber, L., Rudd, C., & Stewart, M. (in press). Creating spaces for artful ways in qualitative research. In J. G. Knowles, S. Promislow, & A. Cole (Eds.), *Creating scholartistry: Imagining the arts-informed thesis or dissertation.* Halifax, Nova Scotia, Canada: Backalong Books.

Charmaz, K. (2000). Grounded theory: Objectivist and constructivist methods. In N. K. Denzin & Y. S. Lincoln (Eds.), *Handbook of qualitative research* (2nd ed., pp. 509–535). Thousand Oaks, CA: Sage.

Davis, D., & Butler-Kisber, L. (1999, April). *Arts-based representation in qualitative research: Collage as a contextualizing analytic strategy.* Paper presented at the annual meeting of the American Education Research Association. Montreal, Quebec, Canada. *Resources in Education, 34*(11), 1–10. (ED 431 790)

Dietrich, D. (1993). *The collages of Kurt Schwitters: Tradition and innovation.* Cambridge, England: Cambridge University Press.

Eisner, E. W. (1991). *The enlightened eye.* New York: Macmillan.

Finley, S. (1998). *Teacher education faculty as researchers: Composing lives in context,* *a blend of form and content.* Unpublished doctoral dissertation, University of Ann Arbor, Michigan.

Gardner, H. (1983). *Frames of mind: The theory of multiple intelligences.* New York: Basic Books.

Gardner, H. (1999) *Intelligence reframed: Multiple intelligences for the 21st century.* New York: Basic Books.

Goldman, P. (1988). *Looking at prints, drawings, and watercolors: A guide to technical terms.* London: British Museum Publications (in association with the J. Paul Getty Museum, Malibu, CA).

Hart, C., Grossman, J., & Dunhill, P. (1989). *A Victorian scrapbook.* New York: Workman.

Hunt, R. (2004). *What is inkshedding?* Retrieved July 15, 2004, from http://www.tthomasu.ca/~hunt/dialogic/whatshed.htm

Irwin, R. (2003, April). *Curating the aesthetics of curriculum/leadership and/or caring for how we perceive walking/guiding the course.* Paper given at the University of Alberta. Retrieved April 27, 2005, from http://www.cpinfolder/papers/Rita_Irwin.pdf

James, P. (2000). Working toward meaning: The evolution of an assignment. *Studies in Art Education, 41*(6), 146–163.

Kress, G., & van Leeuwen, T. (1996). *Reading images: The grammar of visual design.* New York: Routledge.

Lyons, B. (1998). *Zoomorphic structure and the true origin of collage.* Knoxville: University of Tennessee.

McDermott, M. (2002, Fall). Collaging preservice teacher identity. *Teacher Education Quarterly,* 53–67.

Miles, M., & Huberman, M. (1994). *Qualitative data analysis* (2nd ed.). Newbury Park, CA: Sage.

Mullen, C. A. (1999). Carousel: A metaphor for spinning inquiry in prison and education. In C. T. P. Diamond & C. A. Mullen (Eds.), *The postmodern educator: Arts-based inquiries in teacher development* (pp. 281–309). New York: Peter Lang.

Olshansky, B. (1994). Making writing a work of art: Image-making within the writing process. *Language Arts, 71*(5), 350–356.

Onley, T. (2004). *Collage through the history of modern art.* Retrieved February 12, 2005, from www.evergreenculturalcentre .ca/toncollagehist.htm

Promislow, S. (2005). *A collage of "Borderlands": Arts-informed life histories of childhood immigrants and refugees who maintain their mother tongue.* Unpublished doctoral thesis, University of Toronto, Ontario, Canada.

Rainey, L. (1998). Taking dictation: Collage poetics, pathology, and politics. *Modernism/ Modernity, 5*(2), 123–153.

Richardson, L. (1994). Nine poems: Marriage and the family. *Journal of Contemporary Ethnography, 23*(1), 3–13.

Richardson, L., Denzin, N., Bochner, A., Ellis, C., Clough, P., & Finley, S. (2000). Special Focus. *Qualitative Inquiry, 6*(2), 251–265.

Robertson, B. (2000). *Why collage?* Retrieved April 5, 2004, from http://www.collagetown .com/history01.shtml

Rolan, C. (1996, March). *Fair use: Section 107 of the copyright act.* Paper presented at the National Association of Art Education Conference, San Francisco, CA.

Rose, G. (2001). *Visual methodologies.* Thousand Oaks, CA: Sage.

Steeves, P. (2000). *Crazy quilt: Continuity, identity, and a storied school landscape in transition: A teacher's and a principal's work in progress.* Unpublished doctoral dissertation, University of Alberta, Edmonton, Alberta, Canada.

Steinberg, L. (1972). *Other criteria: Confrontations with twentieth-century art.* New York: Oxford University Press.

Warden, G. (2000). Mary Delany: Artistic ingenuity in 18th century England. *Masters Abstracts International, 38*(4), 813. (IMI No. MQ47289)

Williams, B. (2000). Collage work: A medium for guided reflection in clinical supervision. *Nurse Education Today, 20*(4), 273–280.

23

Visual Art

TEXTU(R)AL WALKING/WRITING THROUGH SCULPTURE

◆ Alex F. de Cosson

◆ *Building a Textu(r)al Sculpture*

Through a process of literal, metaphorical, and metonymic cutting (Aoki, Low, & Palulis, 2001), I build a sculpture out of text. This text is textu(r)al, a hybrid of text and texture, built from words and print fonts. I conceive of fonts as similar to various bits of string or wire that I use to build a sculpture. These are visual connecting devices and help compose the texture (a fundamental sculpture reality) of the page.

I consider the question of how to gather the data needed to build a textu(r)al sculpture (Carson & Sumara, 1997) within the context of methodologies based in journaling (Janesick, 1999) and autoethnography (Ellis & Bochner, 1996, 2000). Many methodologies could be adapted once an understanding of the fundamentals of sculpture are grasped. In this chapter I utilize an overarching methodology of a/r/tography (Irwin & de Cosson, 2004; see Chapter 7 in this volume) to allow for *form* to develop.

The praxis of my comfort in noncomfort is studio-based art practice

I am well trained in the serendipity of trusting (McNiff 1998a, 1998b) implicitly in the process of art making's ability to lead me (Csikszentmihalyi, 1990). I am comfortable within the house of qualitative research and agree with Rhonda Watrin's (1999) succinctly stated similarities between the two modes of working: "Creating art, like qualitative research, is a problem-solving process, a combination of thinking and sensing intuitively that leads to insight. In qualitative research and artistic creation the end product is determined by the means" (p. 95).

An artist knows that a point of disjuncture is a point of learning

"No walk, no work."

The concept of *"the walk,"* as a pedagogical place to unravel and reflect on personal understandings, *forms* one of the multiple spines of the practice of sculpture as a social science research methodology. To walk, one must be a part of the world; the world as three-dimensional reality that is a fundamental understanding of sculpture.

(This is all a lie—this is not sculpture, how can it be? This is an impression of sculpture; it is, as we can all attest, two-dimensional space. This, then, is a conceptual exercise. And until the conceptual leap is taken, whereby IT IS a sculpture [because you, dear reader, embrace the three-dimensional space of your reading as dynamic] it remains static. This is what must be done! As Louwrien Wijers (1996) alludes to in Writing as Sculpture, *"It was Joseph Beuys who made us think of thinking as sculpture," which allowed her to conceive of her written text as "'mental sculpture' you are holding in your hands" (p. 7). I concur with the conceptual notion of this object as form, and*

the thinking transference from page/text-textu(r)ality to you, dear reader, creates a new space/(s)p(l)ace that has no boundaries and is akin to contemporary artists' notions of sculptural work.

IT IS THIS DYNAMIC, LIVING SPACE—a (s)p(l)ace (de Cosson, 2003)—an in-between space and place—a hybrid of breathing reality where sculpture grows. It is in this conceptual framework that walking/writing is housed as sculpture.)

The British artist Hamish Fulton (1999), whose foundational philosophy to his work is *"No walk, no work,"* states, when writing his syllabus for an advanced course in visual arts, *Is it Today, Yesterday, or Tomorrow?* (viewed at the Fondazione Antonio Ratti, Como, Italy) that "we have focused our research on the idea that the only anthropological and physically complete way to adhere to reality, what Merleau-Ponty called 'the flesh of the world,' is walking" (p. 115).

Figure 23.1

It is through *walking/writing in sculpture* that understanding surfaces (it is the texture of sculpture that embodies its surface). It is through the building process, inherent to the practice of sculpture, that meaning is made. Meaning grows out of the working process; the blocks (or units of text in this case) placed, the text forced into shape to take *form* on the page, a (reflective) reflection of praxis-in-action.

We come to understanding as
we move
forward through praxis

I walk

to see

(in/side a visuality

a world enacted)

Another walking artist, Richard Long (Haas, 1988), exclaims, "I see things I've never seen before."

I walk

to think . . .

I walk to find meaning through my step-
ping body.

One after another

my strides define

who I am becoming

opening me

to that which is yet to come.

"We must lay in waiting for ourselves. Throughout our lives. Abandoning the pretense that we know" (Pinar & Grumet, 1976, p. viii). This strikes me as the root of all inquiry; if we know before we commence, why commence at all?

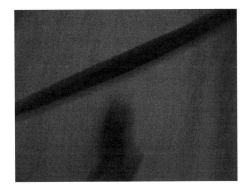

Figure 23.2

The results of following the process of artistic praxis-in-action.

I must write to capture the fleeting moments as they drift by, as the sun slowly but deliberately drops below Gadamer's (1965/1986) horizon.

I am *imagining* a sculpture that illustrates a new research methodology so as to illuminate (wondrous) possibilities in social science research grounded in the arts.

I have imagined its finished state knowing full well it will twist and turn down a roadway to fruition (de Cosson, 2003).

◆ *Tension of the Physicality of Sculpture Building*

My mind's eye foresees a completed project. My body anticipates tension in worked muscles (Cancienne & Snowber, 2003), the gripping and pulling, tying and threading (Wilson, 2004). It contains multiple negative spaces allowing its *form* to be both open and closed, a multiplying binary that transcends itself, defying the binary it suggests. It remains open (Eco, 1989) and standing, its upright *form* defying the very foundation it is built upon. It circles back on itself in a hermeneutic (Gadamer, 1965/1986) of self (and "other"), no closed connections, all is allowed to "be" (Ram Dass, 1971) in a space of inter(intra)connectedness.

A sculpted imagining works with/in intellectual ruminations of problem solving before, and in the midst of, (*form*)ation through *walking/writing.*

These initial ruminations are but glimpses into a multilectic process; there is no knowing where it may lead. It foregrounds a research methodology that employs the in-between space of knowing/not knowing—it is neither this nor that. However its process, it is a known entity.

> *Just as we listen for a sound*
>
> *to emanate from a wind-chime*
>
> *(all its potential awaiting but a breath of air),*
>
> *so too a methodology based in sculpture*
>
> *awaits the fluidity of forms*
>
> *forming,*
>
> *its being becoming.*
>
> *It is fluid,*
>
> *always forming,*
>
> *(re)forming*
>
> *once formed*
>
> *always awaiting new trans(form)ations.*

◆ Need for Attention

Simone Weil (1978) explains, "A work of art is something which is unlike anything else. It is art which, best of all, gives us ideas of what is particular" (p. 59).

The sculpture is now in process. I have many choices. I have no choices. I must pay attention. Weil (1951) emphasizes the need to *have attention* for an object and to not be

fearful of an unknown. Her belief in learning *through looking,* as a way to understanding, is akin to hermeneutics and Gadamer's (1965/1986) understanding of an art object. Weil (1951) says that an object will "talk back," that interpretation comes out of *being with attention,* that there is no need to smother with intellect, and "whoever goes through years of study without developing this attention within himself [*sic*] has lost a great treasure" (p. 114). That understanding, and thus meaning, comes if enough time is given for an object to speak. "It is a question of uprooting our readings of things, of changing them, so as to arrive at non-reading" (Weil, 1956, p. 312).

◆ Process Proceeding

Once started there is the dreaded knowledge that there is no escape until completion. Indeed, sometimes not wanting to start (de Cosson, 1996) precisely because of this knowledge.

I do not necessarily like this *being in praxis* even though I know it as part of the process of beginning. I am reminded of one of my first research projects—a qualitative analysis of taped interviews with four established artist/teachers. How forcefully one participant illustrated this point:

> I know that personally, I put all kinds of things in my own way. Like I've got to do the laundry, I've got to water the plants, and I've got to pick every f***ing scale off every leaf on the plant; I can invent a million zillion reasons why I can't work. But eventually I have to do it. (de Cosson, 1996, p. 107)

The artist also knew that this part of the process, however painful, must be gone through to reach a place of beginning—that, in fact, the process of cleaning is the beginning. It is the hermeneutic circling, around and around within the problem, that is *walking/writing through sculpture.*

HOW ABOUT A PHILOSOPHICAL *understanding* OF THIS WRITING THROUGH SCULPTURE: A WHAT IS IT SECTION. I AM SURE I HAVE ALREADY WRITTEN IT—NO IT'S ABOUT SHOWING IT, REMEMBER, IT'S THE ONLY WAY FOR PRAXIS TO MANIFEST ITSELF, FOR THE "FLESH OF THE WORLD" TO BECOME REAL.

I know the three-dimensionality of space. I feel it resonating within my body. I know its progression. There is a flow (Csikszentmihalyi, 1990) in which I am immersed (Cawelti, Rappaport, & Wood, 1992). I map and plan; in my mind, on paper, on the bus, in line-ups, while shopping, at the bank, driving; it is a joyous point of intellectual stimulation. It consumes my thinking with intricate possibilities; day-to-day concerns get tossed aside and the rhythms of life are disturbed.

A researcher is constantly "disturbed" to find new ways into subject(s) and subject matter. In using sculpture (three-dimensional form illustrated through fonts on a two-dimensional surface of text on paper) to unravel thoughts, to allow new insights to surface, I am allowing the tacit knowledge of my body to come into the equation. I cannot *build* sculpture without this interacting. It pulls and pushes, finding ways to insert itself into the mix.

"NEVER CUT A THREAD UNTIL YOU ARE SURE YOU DON'T NEED IT" I ALWAYS INSIST TO MY STUDENTS

I know the physicality of the work (Springgay, 2004). I know I will reach places of exhaustion. Sculpture is the world; to move within it takes real time, real effort. It is a phenomenology (Merleau-Ponty, 1971) in action. All of it changes, but still it is the same; trust the process (de Cosson,

2004; McNiff, 1998b). A problem emerges that must be dealt with.

I reach points of disillusionment.

My entire self is lost in the doing of the work. I tie one element to another and the structure grows, sometimes slowly, sometimes very fast. Meaning flows outward, configuration takes hold.

◆ Interludes of Autoethnography

I have always been this way; that is why I am a sculptor. Not to build large objects for other people but to understand my own world. As Ross Laird (2001) laments, "spoken *through*" (p. 63), the craft of wood working, "without a spirit of discovery, the work is just a technical exercise" (p. 31).

A Memory in Action 1:

(I hated to go to her desk, as she had an over powering smell [from my young impressionable perspective] an old person smell to which I reacted strongly. I remember staying away from her as much as possible).

My Grade 2 teacher would order me to empty my pockets as I always had them full of bits of string, wire, cork, and other (useful) bits and pieces, so that I could build desktop wonders behind a raised book, their creation related to the lesson at hand. My teacher, however, only saw stuff to confiscate as I wasn't paying attention to what she wanted me to learn. She,

not seeing what I was paying attention to.

Those spaces in-between that she could not see, as Schoemperlen (2001) helps us understand in her contemplation:

Ordinary Time is all these days that blend one into the next without exceptional incident, good or bad; all those days unmarked by either tragedy or celebration. Ordinary time is the spaces between events, the parts of a life that do not show up in photo albums or get told in stories. In real life, this is the bulk of most people's lives. But in literature, this is the part that doesn't make it into the book. This is the line space between scenes, the blank half-page at the end of a chapter, and the next one begins with a sentence like: Three years later he was dead. (p. 160)

◆ (S)p(l)aces to Take Advantage Of

I am intrigued with how many (s)p(l)aces turn up (in-between a space and a place), how attracted I am to them, to these nothing areas, and how I am almost jealous when others talk about them. I want them to be all mine and I do not want to share. These are enigmas that I understand and yet do not understand. It is that *calling to* spaces that have no clear boundaries, that are not definable precisely because they are only spaces and spaces have no defined area. Or rather, the defined area is subjected to what surrounds them. By moving one, the space will change. It is a negative that is created by a positive, that always exists but also never exists or, rather, cannot be controlled in the same positivistic manner that a *known* can.

This is the attraction,
this is what pulls
this is a thread
not to be cut

How to get closer to that *negative* space and not be confined by a positive? It is what is *not* seen that is important. I hear Canadian sculptor Krzysztof Wodiczko (May, 1989) saying, in response to a New York City poverty activist's negative understanding of his poverty-inspired Vehicle Project, "This is precisely what it should be, in that it should not be, it is in its impossibility as an answer that its meaning lies." I also strive for an impossibility. I do not want to be confined by a known, but how, then, to write and produce an unknown?

It rains a peaceful drumming on the roof. I realize this is the first writing on the new computer. The keyboard is pleasant, and I also realize I will not be able to do extensive writing at this position, I can feel my wrist already tightening. Lying in the hammock may never be a writable position, but it is a sculptural position. What to do with that knowledge? Now there is a good question.

Figure 23.3

A Memory in Action 2:

One of the strongest memories from my Grade 2 class shines through; I vividly remember a picture hanging on the wall by the counter with the pencil sharpener. A picture of a path meandering up a mountain, rocks and boulders stopping the way, the symbolism clear; a rocky path we tread but we can get there. That was a reassuring picture, one that talked to me. I instinctively understood that journey. I already saw various rocks and precipices that I would encounter on my way. The picture spoke of a peaceful journey, that it was not in gaining a mountaintop but in the walking through/with/in one's life, that understanding is engendered. For my Grade 2 soul this was a reassurance; I always looked back and saw that image as a place of hope. The image of a path walked, however rocky, was worth walking for its own sake,

to walk

is to walk

is to walk/write

sculpture

My Grade 2 teacher was an ogre who stifled creativity in her classroom and in me. There was, however, that classroom image that I clung to as she drew the class's attention to my misbehavior as, once again, she confiscated something buildable from me. She never inquired what my materials might be for, or how they may have been significant to me. I would most probably have been unable to answer her anyway. It was not about language, it was about the doing that I was involved in. I was not trying to articulate with words, either written or spoken. I was articulating through my doing, almost an autistic's instance of another language, that no one, it seemed, wanted to understand.
Not until much later, in university, did I discover there was another language, one that demanded expression in something other than words written or spoken.

Oh the tyranny of the text, the power of letters to hold attention as they make quick linear connections to cognition cells that eagerly eat them up.

And now I choose these symbols to wrestle with, *to play with,* in a tangled dance of metaphor and metonymic spaces *to crack some new space of seeing, of learning, of understanding.*
I was never encouraged to *build* an answer to a problem in any material other than pencil and paper, my natural medium relegated to the rubbish bin.
Art allows for communication that can continually change and fragment anew.
Text can also do this, but so often it is hijacked to serve the hegemonic hierarchies of the status quo.
I call for us to walk care(fully)
stealth(fully)
forward
walking carefully,
a/r/tfully
with freedom
I set a walk   to lead
a journey of discovery

A PLACE OF GROWTH FOR ALL

"Sometimes, all we need is the willingness and our inner process will do the rest" (Schaef, 1998, p. 131).
This is what I am endeavoring to provide,
a (s)p(l)ace
to collect
(data)
as
sculpture through text,

which is then a subject of work
(a physical reality embodied).
I am drawn to quote Ellis & Bochner
(2000)
*"to show how important it is to make
the researcher's own experience
a topic of investigation in its own right"*
(p. 733).

To show the importance of textu(r)al sculpture as writing in which the "flesh of the world" is made real

"I'd rather move forward, yet I'm
aware that in my creative work there are
times when the momentum departs, energy
dwindles, the safe passage vanishes,
and all comes to shuddering halt"
(Laird, 2001, p. 80).

*Oh the sun grows hot
This not that—that not this
To get to the nub—to brush the surface*

◆ Site of Resting Resolutions

The finished sculpture stands, a hybrid (Minh-ha, 1992) of forms, a third space (Bhabha, 1990) of visual complexity, a (s)p(l)ace of mixing and matching, slipping and sliding, through metonymic and metaphorical nuances.

The finished sculpture defines itself through itself; it references the world as a living embodiment of its surroundings, comprehensible by all who give attention. Its simplicity transcends "boundaries imposed by outmoded discipline-based structures" (Gude, 2004). It has a multiplicity of meanings through the lenses of postmodernism, a pluralistic understanding contextualized by its location and the prior knowledge of a viewer who engages in a dialogic relationship.

Figure 23.4

The sculpture is engaged in its own (re)creation as nature claims for itself the very twines of its existence.

A *walking/writing sculpture* is temporal.

I have *walked* through (metaphorically) *writing* a *sculpture* as social science research embedded in an understanding of a/r/tography utilizing autoethnography and journaling as touchstones that engage a framework for building meaning out of textu(r)al writing, creating new (s)p(l)aces of inquiry. As Susan Finley and J. Gary Knowles (1995) write, I, too,

asked myself whether doing art improves my research. And I am emphatic in saying that it does. I am not merely looking, I am seeing. . . . That what I write, the end product, responds, not corresponds, to what I see and understand. (pp. 131–132)

In the same vein I appropriate Laurel Richardson's (2000) words, "I write because I want to find something out. I write in order to learn something that I didn't know before I wrote it" (p. 924). Substituting *build sculpture* in place of *write*:

> I *build sculpture*
> because I want to find something out.
> I *build sculpture*
> in order to learn something
> that I didn't know before I *built* it.

"It is important to remember that writing begins . . . in the way we are consciously embodied—the way we breathe, think, and feel in our bodies. Writing is essentially attention" (Cancienne & Snowber, 2003, p. 248). It is this attention to the daily rhythms of living and seeing through the arts in Elliot Eisner's (2002) words as "a means of exploring our own interior landscape. When the arts genuinely move us, we discover what it is that we are capable of experiencing. . . . They provide resources for experiencing the range and varieties of our responsive capacities" (p. 11).

◆ *References*

Aoki, T., Low, M., & Palulis P. (2001, April). *Rereading metonymic moments with/in living pedagogy*. Paper presented at the meeting of the American Educational Research Association, Seattle, WA.

Bhabha, H. (1990). The third space. In J. Rutherford (Ed.), *Identity: Community, culture, difference* (pp. 207–221). London: Lawrence and Wishert.

Cancienne, M. B., & Snowber, C. (2003). Writing rhythm: Movement as method. *Qualitative Inquiry, 9*(2), 237–253.

Carson, T., & Sumara, D. (Eds.). (1997). *Action research as a living practice*. New York: Peter Lang.

Cawelti, S., Rappaport, A., & Wood, B. (1992). Modeling artistic creativity: An empirical study. *Journal of Creative Behavior, 26*(2), 83–94.

Csikszentmihalyi, M. (1990). *Flow: The psychology of optimal experience*. New York: Harper & Row.

de Cosson, A. F. (1996). *Creativity and the working artist/teacher: The relationships*. Unpublished master's thesis, Brock University, St. Catharines, Ontario, Canada.

de Cosson, A. F. (2003). *(Re)searching sculpted a/r/tography:(Re)learning subverted-knowing through aporetic praxis*. Unpublished doctoral thesis, University of British Columbia, Canada.

de Cosson, A. F. (2004). The hermeneutic dialogic: Finding patterns amid the aporia of the artist/researcher/teacher. In R. L. Irwin & A. de Cosson (Eds.), *A/r/tography: Rendering self through arts-based living inquiry* (pp. 127–152). Vancouver, British Columbia, Canada: Pacific Educational Press.

Eco, U. (1989). *The open work*. Cambridge, MA: Harvard University Press.

Eisner, E. (2002). *The arts and the creation of mind*. New Haven, CT: Yale University Press.

Ellis, C., & Bochner, A. (Eds.). (1996). *Composing ethnography: Alternative forms of qualitative writing*. Walnut Creek, CA: AltaMira Press.

Ellis, C., & Bochner, A. (2000). Autoethnography, personal narrative, reflexivity: Researcher as subject. In N. K. Denzin & Y. S. Lincoln (Eds.), *Handbook of qualitative research* (2nd ed., pp. 733–768). Thousand Oaks, CA.: Sage.

Finley, S., & Knowles, J. G. (1995). Researcher as artist/artist as researcher. *Qualitative Inquiry, 1*(1), 110–142.

Fulton, H. (1999). Hamish Fulton. In A. Daneri, G. Di Pietrantonio, & A. Vettese (Eds.), *Is it today, yesterday or tomorrow?* (pp. 109–115). Milan: Edizioni Charta.

Gadamer, H. G. (1986). *Truth and method* (G. Bardon & J. Cumming, Trans. & Eds.). New York: Cross Roads Publishing. (Original work published 1965)

Gude, O. (2004). Postmodern principles: A 21st century art education. *Art Education, 57*(1), 6–14.

Haas, P. (Director). (1988). *Stones and flies: Richard Long in the Sahara* [Film].

(Available from http://www.milestonefilms
.com/movie.php/stones/)

Irwin, R. L., & de Cosson, A., F. (Eds.). (2004). *A/r/tography: Rendering self through arts-based living inquiry.* Vancouver, British Columbia, Canada: Pacific Educational Press.

Janesick, V. (1999). A journal about journal writing as a qualitative research technique: History, issues, and reflections. *Qualitative Inquiry, 5*(4), 505–575.

Laird, R. A. (2001). *Grain of truth: The ancient lessons of craft.* Toronto, Ontario, Canada: Macfarlane Walter & Ross.

May, D. (Director). (1989). *Krzysztof Wodiczko: Projections* [Film]. (Available from The National Film Board of Canada, Ottawa, Ontario, Canada)

McNiff, S. (1998a). *Art-based research.* London: Jessica Kingsley Publishers.

McNiff, S. (1998b). *Trust the process: An artist's guide to letting go.* Boston: Shambhala.

Merleau-Ponty, M. (1971). *Phenomenology of perception.* New York: Humanities Press.

Minh-ha, Trinh T. (1992). *Framer framed.* New York: Routledge.

Pinar, W., & Grumet, M. (1976). *Toward a poor curriculum.* Dubuque, IA: Kendall/Hunt.

Ram Dass, B. (1971). *Be here now.* San Cristobal, NM: Lama Foundation.

Richardson, L. (2000). Writing: A method of inquiry. In N. K. Denzin & Y. S. Lincoln (Eds.), *Handbook of qualitative research* (2nd ed., pp. 923–948). Thousand Oaks, CA: Sage.

Shaef, A. W. (1998). *Living in process: Basic truths for living the path of the soul.* New York: Ballantine Wellspring.

Schoemperlen, D. (2001). *Our lady of the lost and found.* Toronto, Ontario, Canada: HarperCollins.

Springgay, S. (2004). *Inside the visible: Youth understandings of body knowledge through touch.* Unpublished doctoral thesis, University of British Columbia, Vancouver, Canada.

Watrin, R. (1999). Art as research. *Canadian Review of Art Education, 26*(2), 92–100.

Weil, S. (1951). *Waiting for God* (E. Craufurd, Trans.). New York: Putnam's Sons.

Weil, S. (1956). *Notebooks 1* (A. Wills, Trans.). London: Routledge & Kegan Paul Ltd.

Weil, S. (1978). *Lectures on philosophy* (H. Price, Trans.). London: Cambridge University Press.

Wijers, L. (1996). *Writing as sculpture.* London: Academy Group LTD.

Wilson, S. (2004). Fragments: Life writing in image and text. In R. L. Irwin & A. de Cosson (Eds.), *A/r/tography: Rendering self through arts-based living inquiry* (pp. 41–59). Vancouver, British Columbia, Canada: Pacific Educational Press.

24 *Visual Art*

INSTALLATION ART-AS-RESEARCH

◆ Ardra L. Cole and Maura McIntyre

*My art has always tried to resist a position in which we're
supposed to be passive consumers of culture. . . . The viewers
complete the work. They're the other half of the making of
meaning.*

—Joseph Kosuth speaking about *The Play of the Unmentionable*
installed in the Brooklyn Museum's Grand Lobby in 1990
(Putnam, 2001, p. 156)

Join us in a look at installation art as one of the many art forms that
has found its way into social science research as a methodological
challenge to modernist perspectives on knowledge and knowing. Our
chapter is a virtual tour of several research installations including our
own. Through our experiential rendering of this art form, we consider
how our work and the work of other installation artist-researchers
advances knowledge in unique ways, paying particular attention to the
qualities of accessibility, inclusion, audience engagement, and sociopolitical commitment. During the journey we explore some issues and
challenges peculiar to installation art-as-research. We also make particular reference to the role of installation art as articulated by a number
of contemporary artists whose work reflects intentions and "attitude"
that echo some of the qualities of installation art-as-research. We invite

you to dwell in our "thick description" of these installations and to join us in reflecting upon and theorizing the methodology.

We begin on a beach in sunny Sydney, Australia, with Marianne Hulsbosch's and Robyn Gibson's work in the annual exhibition *Sculpture by the Sea*. From there we cross the equator and fly north into Albuquerque, New Mexico, where Patrick Slattery's *Knowledge (De)Constructed and (Re)Embodied: An Art Installation That Disrupts Regulations of the Body in Classroom Practices* is exhibited at a conference on arts-based research. Continuing north we begin the Canadian leg of our journey in Hull, Quebec, at the Canadian Museum of Civilization where Kathryn Church's exhibit *Fabrications: Stitching Ourselves Together* has just opened. From there we head for Sherbrooke, Quebec, and another conference to see *Living in Paradox,* a teacher education project mounted by Cole, Knowles, brown, and Buttignol. Finally, ending up on the east coast, at Pier 21 National Historic Site in Halifax we see *The Alzheimer's Project,* our installation about caregiving. (See www.sagepub.com/ knowlessupplement.)

◆ *In Your Own Backyard*

SYDNEY, AUSTRALIA (HULSBOSCH & GIBSON, 2002)

Touching Down Under you make the transition from tarmac to salt water by taking off your shoes. Walking along the spectacular coastline of the Pacific Ocean from Bondi to Tamarama Beach, you take in the beauty and drama of the incessant, rhythmic cresting and breaking of towering waves against expansive stretches of white sand. This is surfers' paradise, and the surfers are out today in full force, riding the waves, dotting the beaches with their colorful

"boardshorts," wetsuits, and surfing paraphernalia. As a first-time visitor to Sydney, you have noted its urban and multicultural landscape, intrigued by the blend of cultural symbols that help to form its identity. Continuing your walk you cast your eyes toward a townscape of colorful shops, restaurants, and houses at the edge of the beach. At first, you look beyond what you assume is just a line of laundry hanging in someone's backyard. But this is no ordinary laundry line. You move closer to investigate.

A rotary clothesline is set up so as to create a boundary between urban and seascape. Hanging around the full perimeter of the line are numerous pairs of the ubiquitous boardshorts that you have come to recognize as a cultural beach-fashion icon. But these are not just any boardshorts you discover. They are made from national flags of the world— 55 in all—for many of the national groups now living in Australia. You see that this is an outdoor art piece created and installed by two artist-researchers from the University of Sydney as part of a large, annual outdoor exhibition of contemporary sculpture. The installation invites viewers "to move beyond the passive spectator role and respond, engage, even touch the work" (Gibson & Hulsbosch, 2007, p. 175) and contemplate their own notions of self and collective identity. It is intended to speak of the authors' "personal, lived experiences and those of new and would-be Australians—immigrants, refugees and displaced persons who like us, felt like outsiders" (p. 174).

You like the way the researchers have aired the topic of immigration and pluralism in a public place, confronting it where it lives. You wonder how many people actually have responded to the researchers' invitation to engage, touch, and contemplate, and how the exhibit and the issues it represents are taken up in this location of sun and surf. As you prepare to retrace your steps, you wonder about the many possible responses to the sculpture and begin to imagine the range of conversations sparked by the presence of this work in this space.

Getting settled on the plane for another unimaginably long journey, you take out your research journal and make a few notes about what you have seen so far and how it relates to what you know about installation art and its origins.

By definition, "installation art is art made for a specific space exploiting certain qualities of that space" (Delahunt, 2007). Because one intention of much of installation art-as-research is to make research more accessible to diverse audiences including but beyond the academy, the work is exhibited in a variety of venues atypical to academic work. The interactive nature of most of the work also renders it responsive and dynamic. Each time it is exhibited in a different venue, the work is changed to suit the space.

Marcel Duchamp, with his 1917 work *Readymade*, is often considered to be the first artist to use everyday objects, usually found cast-offs, to create works of art. He did so as a statement against "the 'aura' of value and prestige that traditionally accrues to the art object" (Putnam, 2001, p. 12).

Well-known contemporary artist Martha Rosler uses art as a form of political action, to move people forward in their thinking rather than to engage them passively with an art work as a representational truth. With her installations, as with all her work, Rosler intends to challenge high art culture by moving her work out into communities and inviting everyday citizens to engage with it. She "unravel[s] conventional narrative structures and representational forms" (Alberro, 1998, p. 85) to both communicate and engage her audience on a social topic. Rosler's work is an interactive, open text where "the art is a continuous and ongoing practice, a conversation in which images, text, and fragments all take part" (p. 86). She

seeks to confuse or challenge opposites of "everyday life and high art, museum objects and art works" (p. 84). For example, as a strategy to widen the audience for art, Martha Rosler advertised her 1972 *Monumental Garage Sale* in flyers and local bulletins as an ordinary garage sale and in newspapers as an art event. Describing Martha Rosler's work, Elizabeth Macgregor and Sabine Breitweiser (1998, Foreword) state: "Accessibility has always been a major concern of hers, as is the role of the viewer in constructing the meaning of the work. She presses viewers to rethink the boundaries between the public and the private as well as the social and the political." Rosler's use of multiple forms signifies "her aspiration to reach beyond the limits of aesthetically enfranchised high art publics to a wider audience" (Alberro, 1998, p. 90).

You think about the clothesline of boardshorts near the beach and note how the researchers' choices of venue and materials combine to bring a broad sociocultural issue into the lives and thoughts of ordinary citizens. You wonder how the meaning might change in another location.

◆ Knowledge (De)Constructed and (Re)Embodied

ALBUQUERQUE, NEW MEXICO (SLATTERY, 2000)

Stepping into the coolness of the air-conditioned building, you welcome the relief from the intense desert sun. After your eyes adjust to the dim light, you follow directional signs pointing the way to an exhibition space. Partway there you hear the haunting sounds of melodious religious chanting. As you approach the open exhibit area, a contemporary protest song, *Take the Power Back,* competes with the harmonic voices of the Monks of Taize. You feel unsettled by the contrast and curious to know more. At the entrance to the installation *Knowledge (De)Constructed and (Re)Embodied,* a disclaimer is posted warning you that you are about to be exposed to religious, violent, and sexual images that may disturb you. "In an educational research conference?" you think. You enter the area that has been transformed into a Catholic junior high school classroom of the 1960s. The exhibit, you discern, is a critical representation of the regulation and oppression of the adolescent body by religious institutions. Using an array of artifacts, visual images, and religious symbols and icons, the artist-researcher has recreated a monastic atmosphere.

Candles and incense burn on a makeshift altar fashioned from a wooden classroom bench, and you are invited to view the exhibit while kneeling on an antique Catholic confessional *prie-dieu.* You decline. A 1962 sixth-grade Baltimore Catholic catechism pictures a comparison of holy lifestyles with the word "best" inscribed under the drawing of angelic celibate priests and nuns. Part of the exhibit titled *10,000 Ejaculations* depicts images from the artist-researcher's own childhood catechism. You learn that ejaculations are short and spontaneous prayers that the nuns instructed students to call out in times of temptation. In another part of the installation juxtapositions of sexual and religious symbols invite the viewer to reexperience the confusion and guilt of adolescence. Nude male and female bodies are partially covered with communion wafers that you could easily remove if you chose to. Knowing that you are in a public place, you suppress the urge. You smile at the clever way the artist-researcher has drawn you in to illustrate the theme of the piece.

An old, wooden school desk holds textbooks and personal memorabilia. A decorated greeting card—a spiritual bouquet—from the child artist-researcher to his mother

lists a quantity of prayer offerings. A calendar and photograph of a young man masturbating are "hidden" under the desk. The desk and surrounding floor are littered with communion hosts doubling as globs of semen. In the bottom corner of the desk is a cardboard artwork completed by the researcher's father on the morning of his death by suicide.

The weight and pain of the installation are almost too much to bear. Even though the work is explicitly based in the artist-researcher's own experience, you know that it speaks of the experiences of many. With this in mind, and your physical response to the work settling deep in your body, you leave the exhibit longing for the warmth and light of the out-of-doors.

Some time alone with your notebook in the bland surroundings of the plane en route to your next destination helps you process the intensity of this experience.

Using salvaged objects, artists Edward Kienholz and Nancy Reddin Kienholz also constructed and displayed freestanding, full-size sculptures of reconstructed spaces, human forms, and assemblages. Their bold cultural and political statements about societal conditions and contradictions rely on human inclinations toward voyeurism; they often coerce the viewer to become an active participant in the representation. Says Harten (1996, p. 45),

> For Edward and Nancy Kienholz, to be committed through art means to engage the beholder too—to surprise a person with an artistic device much as with a hello, and then to draw that person in . . . and better still to force the viewer to a position of self-identification.

Part of the power of the Kienholz's art is in the demands it makes on the audience. As Ross (1996) says:

> It is not the work's shocking truthfulness or the artists' willingness to explore

intricate and delicate societal issues, nor is it merely their ability to create extreme dramatic impact through the use of assembled found objects. The Kienholz' works are forever lodged in our memory because they remain fresh wounds, scars that will never heal. (p. 22)

You ponder the Catholic school room and how the artist so effectively drew you in to experience the work. You can still feel it in your body.
According to Ruskin (1996), Kienholz's

realism is our collective fears and the social responsibility from which [they] will not allow us to escape. . . . We are invited to judge our present social condition and then we are begged, through a visual scream, to create another reality, one which celebrates human dignity. (pp. 42, 43)

You think about the power of the work you have just seen and try to recall the last academic journal article that had a comparable impact. This search occupies your thoughts for the remainder of the flight. Upon landing you still haven't come up with an answer. You wonder how many people visited the exhibit and how they were affected by it. You think about the artist-researcher and wonder about his vulnerability.

◆ Fabrications

HULL, QUEBEC (CHURCH, 1999)

Arriving at the Museum of Civilization, you are wowed by the grandeur of the place and the prestige of the venue. This is an internationally acclaimed museum and social science research as installation art is on display! Overcome by the feeling of quiet reverence

that seems to envelop you in aesthetically constructed spaces, you are already in a contemplative mood when you emerge into the gallery that displays Church's work.

A collection of wedding dresses is displayed individually and, occasionally, in groups. The bodily form of a simple mannequin mounted on a sturdy wooden base animates each dress. You smile at the weathered white picket fences that protect the dresses from the curious hands of the general public. You wonder at the choice of barrier and feel certain that it was carefully chosen to convey a series of meanings that relate to the dresses and the institution of marriage—properness, domesticity, and property. Reading only the titles you struggle to keep your promise to save the detailed text panels for later.

The colors are appropriate—pastel backdrops that speak of traditional femininity, shades of white and ivory that connote various degrees of purity. The textures of silks and satins make your skin yearn for contact; the crinkled lace makes you flinch. Associated wedding day paraphernalia, such as an eyelet veil and lace-covered, spike-heeled ankle boots accompany some of the gowns. Several exercise books with drawings of the dresses and the seamstress's notes look clearly like original artifacts. By the time you encounter a reproduction of the sewing room, complete with wood paneling, TV, and plush toys, your guess is confirmed that one woman made all the dresses in the cracks between her responsibilities to her own family.

The lighting, dimmer than you expected, serves to create a mood of ambiguity. The disembodied dresses are highly evocative, at times almost eerie. The atmosphere is not simply jolly and celebratory; the dresses somehow emanate a fuller story than anticipation, artistry, and beauty. You wonder at the story behind the dress behind each woman behind the artist/seamstress. You are aware that the dresses are not ordered chronologically and are curious about what narrative the overall shape of the exhibit tells. You are awed by the magnitude of the exhibit in its entirety, the fragility of the dresses, the weight of the associated materials (like the wooden picket fences) and both the simplicity and the complexity of the exhibit's conceptualization.

Heading back to the station to catch the train for the next stop on the tour you find yourself looking forward to the in-between time of travel as a space of sense-making.

Richard Jackson (1996, p. 283), a lifelong friend of contemporary American assemblage artist Edward Kienholz, concisely summarizes the power and possibility of installation art in/as research. "The thing I like about Ed [Kienholz] and Nancy's [Reddin Kienholz] art," he says, "is that it's real democratic. It doesn't take a Ph.D. to understand it. So it kind of spoke to everyone. Not highbrow or exclusive."

You think about how the wedding dress exhibit brings the invisible labor of the artist/seamstress out of the basement work room and into full view of a public audience, who can immediately connect with the familiarity of the display and be challenged, perhaps for the first time, to think about some of the sociocultural complexities depicted. You also are mindful of the technical and logistical complexities of the project and long to talk about the process with the artist-researcher (see Church's discussion of Fabrications in Chapter 35 of this volume).

◆ *Living in Paradox*

SHERBROOKE, QUEBEC
(COLE, KNOWLES,
BROWN, & BUTTIGNOL, 1999)

Arriving in Sherbrooke you dodge the conference registration and head straight to the installation. Halfway across the expansive foyer of the building your attention is grabbed once again by the haunting sounds of melodious chanting that leads you to an altar. This time the recreated setting is a university instead of a junior high school classroom. Carefully placed on a cloth-covered table are burning candles and a black mortarboard. Behind the altar painted on two large canvases are familiar symbols—a blackboard covered with faint traces of erased words, an office door with appointment schedule and posted notices to students, an ivy-covered wall. A chronology of academic garb—school uniforms of different sizes and an academic gown—hangs on pegs under the sign "Men's Room." You smile at the subtle statement. All of this is backdrop to the centerpiece of the assemblage. Lined up on an electrically driven conveyor belt are several tiny, white, satin pillows that laboriously climb their way to the altar. You feel a stabbing pang of recognition as though the symbols positioned on the pillows and passing before your eyes are of your own life: a torn family photograph, gold wedding band, empty pill bottle, ticking clock, money, and on it goes. You recognize the sacrifices religiously made at the altar of the academy. You are mesmerized by the rhythmic movement and sound of the conveyor belt, the monks' voices, and another familiar chant that, for a moment, you think is coming from your own inner voice. In contrast to the beautiful and harmonious male voices are the recorded, spoken words of rationalization— "But I love my work. I really, really love my work." "Too close to home," you think as you walk a few feet away to another part of the exhibit.

A Perfect Imbalance is a simple balance scale. Your curiosity is immediately aroused because, although the scales seem balanced, the items on each side of the scale are clearly unmatched. A small sign invites you to try to balance the scale. Knowing that achieving balance between the personal and professional sides of your life has always been an elusive pursuit, you decide to try. You topple the high tower of blocks from one side of the scale. Each foam block is labeled to represent a different activity or role required of professors of teacher education (teaching, service, professional development, community development, in-service education, family, recreation, exercise, etc.). From the other side you remove a single, much heavier, multifaceted block labeled with activities the university deems most meritorious. You catch on. You know that, according to the values and standards of the university, activities that have mainly local or personal implications and that demand inordinate time and energy do not carry much weight. The heavy weights from the university's perspective are those activities that result in intellectual and financial prestige and international acclaim. You know that the scales will only balance when the entire pile of blocks defining teacher educators' work is in place. As you replace the last block at the top of the teetering tower, you reflect on how imperfect the balance really is.

A miniature version of a wrestling arena is set up on a nearby table. A toy wrestling ring sits in the middle of a simulated set of bleachers filled with jeering onlookers. Standing menacingly in the middle of the ring are three World Wrestling Federation-syndicated toy action figures. Up against the ropes, appearing vulnerable but in a defiant pose, is a much smaller female figure. Poignant narrative excerpts are projected onto the spot-lit and smoke-filled painted backdrop of the arena. More phrases are written on the bleacher-like supports. "The academy, as a bastion of patriarchy built on norms and values of rugged individualism, competition, and hierarchy, is an adverse arena for many women faculty members" says the descriptive statement, under the title *Wrestling Differences*, posted nearby. "Amen," you mutter as you finish reading and turn away, aware of your strong emotional response to the work.

You notice that the foyer has filled with people and set off for a bite to eat and to think some more about what you have just seen and experienced.

Graeme Sullivan, in his book *Art Practice as Research* (2005), describes visual art exhibitions as sites of inquiry and learning where "meaning can be seen to take place through enactment and action. . . . The learning space disrupts distinctions among artist-objects, viewer-audience, and time-space, such that the encounter is direct and engaging." "This reflexive encounter," he says, is a form of "performative interpretation" (p. 210).

Claes Oldenburg, who created a series of works from found and altered objects wrote, "I am for art that is political-erotical-mystical, that does something other than sit on its ass in a museum" (quoted in Putnam, 2001, p. 13).

Reworking this quote you add "and for research accounts that do more than gather dust on a shelf!"

Feeling rejuvenated once again through time spent in quiet reflection and contemplation, you set off for the train station and the final stop on the research tour.

◆ *The Alzheimer's Project*

HALIFAX, NOVA SCOTIA
(COLE & MCINTYRE, 2003)

The moist sea air of a port city infuses your pores with life as you step off the train and head toward Pier 21 National Historic Site. Located on the harbor front of Halifax, the building was gateway to Canada for over a million immigrants between 1928 and 1971. The restored building is now a museum and tribute to those people. *The Alzheimer's Project* occupies an expansive space outside the main exhibit hall. You remember that installations displayed "outside" permanent museum or gallery collections are called "museum interventions" (Kosuth, in Putnam, 2001). Their purpose is to provide a commentary on the permanent collection or to "refresh" the permanent display. Typically displayed in museum entrance halls or large, "non-art" spaces, these installations, often arresting in their subject matter or form, capture the attention of passersby, thus broadening the audience beyond the usual museum or gallery patrons.

A large Plexiglas sign grabs your attention: "*The Alzheimer's Project.*" A floral arrangement on an adjacent table invites you to take a closer look. You stop at the table to look over information about the display, about Alzheimer's disease, and about the artist-researchers and their work. A fact sheet positioned on a small easel reveals some startling statistics about Alzheimer's disease.

Your curiosity is piqued when you look to your left and see three freestanding refrigerator doors arranged in chronological order, each reminiscent of a different era. The front of each door is partially covered with photographs secured by magnets. "Just like my fridge at home," you think to yourself as you step closer. You study the black and white images on the first door and see snapshots of a young mother and daughter— baby, toddler, adolescent—involved in a variety of everyday activities. You study the images long enough to get a sense that the relationship depicted looks quite ordinary. You move to the next fridge and notice that some years have passed: The refrigerator door is more modern, the images are in color, and mother and daughter are older. You see snapshots of two adult women enjoying life and each other. You take in the story told and feel like you are almost part of it. You move on to the third and final door and immediately realize that the mood of the story has changed and that the

characters in the story have switched roles. Daughter is now feeding, bathing, and caring for mother whose illness is very apparent. You step back and do a visual sweep to read the relationship narrative laid out before you. You pause to reflect, looking out over the calm waters of the harbor, and then walk along a few steps further.

A short distance away you spot a series of large black and white photographs of another mother–daughter relationship, As your eyes sweep from left to right you read a visual narrative across a life span— mother holding newborn baby to baby-now-adult holding ill mother. On a table beneath the photographs is a set of eight small handmade books, each resting on an individual stand. It seems that they are meant to be read so you pick one up. On each page, in hand-printed, silver lettering, is written one or a few words. You savor each word, slowly turning each page. Each book tells a different relationship story, of the intimacy of human connection. As you replace the last book on its stand, you pause to look again at the photographs.

The partition has two sides, and so you move to see a set of eight large framed photographs hanging in a row. The matted and framed black and white photographs appear normal from a distance. As you step up to them, however, you realize that the images appear out of focus. A closer look reveals that there is another image superimposed on each that is creating a distortion and obscuring your view. It is a transparent image of an aging and ill woman with a vacant, gaunt look. Her haunting eyes draw you in, fix your gaze. It is difficult to get past that look, to see beyond to the background image. When you do, you see a little girl in old-fashioned attire standing in what might be the backyard of her home. The next image, also overshadowed by the ill woman, is of a young woman perhaps in her late teens.

With chin resting on crossed hands she leans over a high fence, a piece of straw clenched in her broad, confident smile. You fill out the rest of the story in your mind. Each image captures a moment in a woman's life as she grows through childhood, adolescence, adulthood, marriage, motherhood, and grandmotherhood. This is herstory but you have difficulty keeping it in focus; the ill woman commands your attention.

As you reach the end of the partition, you encounter another image of an aging and ill woman; this one is larger than life and affixed to a mirror suspended less than a meter above the floor. She is obviously in an institutional context, and you recognize that same steady gaze demanding your attention. As you respond to her demand, you realize that you have entered the picture. Beside her image you see your own reflection. You pause to take it in. Herstory/Yourstory the title says. You wonder.

A full-sized clothesline of undergarments intrigues you. You move closer and slowly walk its length. You trace the line of laundry from baby's diaper to lace garter belt to multihooked brassiere to adult diaper. The over-washed, white, female undergarments mark the shift in personal power and changing nature of dependence across a life span. You are tempted to move closer to the adorable baby's undershirt to see if it smells like powder; you giggle to yourself as you imagine slipping away to try on the padded push-up bra; you groan as you recognize the full-size nylon panties with the elastic waist-band slightly stretched; and you pause in silence in front of the adult size diaper hanging heavily at the end of the life line. A small basket of tiny, brightly colored clothespins sits on a small table at the end of the clothesline. You choose one, pin it to your lapel in a gesture of solidarity, and continue.

Off to your right you spot a warm and inviting scene—a welcome respite from the emotional intensity of the earlier pieces. Three vintage card tables and folding chairs are clustered around a bright red, wool rug with a large heart at its centre. "*Loving Care*" the sign reads. You notice that a couple seated at one of the tables is hovered over a Scrabble™ game: C-A-R-E; L-O-V-E; R-E-L-A-X; S-O-F-T. You catch on to the theme. Another table is set up with pencils and tear-off pads of word puzzles. "Why not?" you think to yourself as you pull out a chair and take a seat close to the full dish of candy.

At the final piece you are met with an invitation to: *Help us Remember. . . . Leave a memory (a poem, story, picture, memento, etc.) about caregiving.* You see a corkboard and cloth-covered table set up to collect and display memories of care and caregiving. Affixed to the corkboard and within a memory box and scrapbook are photographs, recipes, poems, scribbled reminders, torn fragments of notes and letters from different people and places. The objects on the table— a doll, a string of beads, a Wandering Registry bracelet—give you pause. You remember your Aunt Min and start thinking about a memento that you might bring back to add to the collection. For the time being you open the journal and write her name.

You think back to the beginning of the tour and how much you have traveled and taken in; you have the strange sensation that the entire experience has been etched in your psyche/body/spirit. Feeling inspired and provoked, you wonder at how you will integrate this experience into your own academic work. Like Rosler, who looked "for ways to bend the frames of the art world, slip past its boundaries, and fill its silences" (Alberro, 1998, p. 85), and Kienholz and Reddin Kienholz, who "believed passionately that art should be accessible to everyone" (Brooks & Hopps, 1996, p. 115), these artist-researchers in the academic realm have similar aspirations. Beginning to reflect on some possibilities for your own work, you start a list of questions and issues to follow up on:

- *How do the researchers manage the practical issues of time and portability, not to mention finding materials and actually constructing the pieces?*

- *What about funding? What kind of support is available for this kind of research?*

- *Is it actually considered to be research? How might a research-based installation "count" in terms of academic merit?*

- *What might a proposal for one of these projects look like, especially the methodological rationale?*

- *What about the creative process? How did each of the pieces unfold?*

- *What is it like for the researchers to see their work on public display? Is it different from a published article?*

- *And what about vulnerability? Are there particular ethical concerns associated with using installation in research?*

You know that many more questions will emerge over the next few days as you continue to think back over the tour. Right now, the hour is late and your mind and body crave rest.

◆ References

Alberro, A. (1998). The dialectics of everyday life: Martha Rosler and the strategy of the decoy. In C. de Zegher (Ed.), *Martha Rosler: Positions in the life world* (pp. 72–112). Birmingham, UK/Vienna, Austria: Ikon Gallery/Genarali Foundation.

Brooks, R., & Hopps, W. (1996). Plates and commentaries. In W. Hopps (Ed. & Curator), *Kienholz: A retrospective—Edward and Nancy Reddin Kienholz* (pp. 55–247). New York: Whitney Museum of American Art/Distributed Art Publishers.

Church, K. (1999). *Fabrications: Stitching ourselves together.* Installation exhibited at the Canadian Museum of Civilization, Hull, Quebec.

Cole, A. L., Knowles, J. G., brown, b., & Buttignol, M. (1999). *Living in paradox: A multi-media representation of teacher educators' lives in context.* Installation presented at the Canadian Society for the Study of Education Annual Conference, June 1999, Sherbrooke, Quebec.

Cole, A. L., & McIntyre, M. (2003). *The Alzheimer's project: A seven part multimedia exhibit.* Pier 21 National Historic Site, May 26–June 3, Halifax, Nova Scotia, Canada.

Delahunt, M. R. (2007). Installation. *Artlex art dictionary.* Retrieved August, 2006, from http://www.artlex.com

Gibson, R., & Hulsbosch, M. (2007). Creation, collaboration, and quiet conversations. In J. G. Knowles, T. Luciani, A. L. Cole, & L. Neilsen (Eds.), *The art of visual inquiry* (pp. 167–178). Halifax, Nova Scotia, and Toronto, Ontario, Canada: Backalong Books/Centre for Arts-Informed Research.

Harten, J. (1996). Universal life (1989). In W. Hopps (Ed. & Curator), *Kienholz: A retrospective—Edward and Nancy Reddin Kienholz* (pp. 44–47). New York: Whitney Museum of American Art/Distributed Art Publishers.

Hulsbosch, M., &. Gibson, R. (2002). *In your own backyard.* Installation exhibited at Sculpture by the Sea, Tamarama, Australia.

Jackson, R. (1996). A few words about Ed Kienholz. In W. Hopps (Ed. & Curator), *Kienholz: A retrospective—Edward and Nancy Reddin Kienholz* (p. 283). New York: Whitney Museum of American Art/Distributed Art Publishers.

Macgregor, E. A., & Breitweiser, S. (1998). Foreword. In C. de Zegher (Ed.), *Martha*

Rosler: Positions in the life world. Birmingham, UK/Vienna, Austria: Ikon Gallery/Genarali Foundation.

Putnam, J. (2001). *Art and artifact: The museum as medium.* New York: Thames & Hudson.

Ross, D. A. (1996). Director's foreword. In W. Hopps (Ed. & Curator), *Kienholz: A retrospective—Edward and Nancy Reddin Kienholz* (pp. 22–23). New York: Whitney Museum of American Art/Distributed Art Publishers.

Ruskin, M. (1996). Ed Kienholz and the burden of being an American. In W. Hopps (Ed. & Curator), *Kienholz: A retrospective—Edward and Nancy Reddin Kienholz* (pp. 38–43). New York: Whitney Museum of American Art/Distributed Art Publishers.

Slattery, P. (with Johanns, C. R.) (2000). *Knowledge (de)constructed and (re)embodied: An art installation that disrupts regulations of the body in classroom practices.* Installation exhibited at the Arts-Based Educational Research Association Conference, February 2000, Albuquerque, New Mexico.

Sullivan, G. (2005). *Art practice as research: Inquiry in the visual arts.* Thousand Oaks, CA: Sage.

New Media

DIGITAL CONTENT

Video as Research

◆ Janice Rahn

◆ *Background*

My first experience with video as a tool for cultural research was as an arts educator in 1982 in Iqaluit, a tiny Nunavut arctic town known at the time by the name of Frobisher Bay. I was teaching music and drama to high school students. My friends working for Inuit Broadcasting Corporation (IBC) were always looking for a local story, and I accommodated them by having students stage cultural events or by borrowing the equipment required to have students make their own video productions. Within this context it was obvious how revolutionary the portapack video camera was in allowing students to participate in representing their culture rather than consume television controlled by southern advertisers and corporations.

While working up north, I was introduced to Paul Apak and Zak Kanuk, who had learned their trade from IBC and went on to form their own company called Isuma Productions in the small community of Igloolik. They began making their own videos as a way to record elders dressing up "like the old days" and telling stories. Isuma Productions created a cottage industry by hiring elders to make authentic sets, clothing, and artifacts for these videos. This was different than the salvage paradigm of museums that seek to preserve cultures that are becoming lost. Instead, these videos were being made by the Inuit for the Inuit of Igloolik.

Isuma built an international reputation with a mission to produce independent community-based media videos in all genres (documentary, fiction, TV series, etc.), and the approach has proven to enrich their community and beyond. In 1999 they produced the first Aboriginal-language Canadian feature movie called *Atanarjuat,* which has won over two dozen international awards, and can be rented and purchased on mainstream video. Paul died of cancer halfway through the making of this film, but his legacy to the Inuit and the world is his grassroots approach to video production that culminated in *Atanarjuat.*

Isuma Productions represents and continues to inspire my research and instruction of new media: to model and to facilitate others to take the means of production into their own hands and to believe in the potential for media to locate the regional within a massive, revolutionary, communication network. Their productions are a phenomenal success on many levels as entertainment, education, economic resource, and contemporary art.

As Berger (1982) wrote: "The effect of mass reality should not be mistaken for reality" (p. 49). Video production helped my northern students separate the reality that was being projected into their homes from the reality of their own rich cultural heritage. Artistic creation and the sensitive adaptation of media to a community's needs can restore individual voice and identity. Alternative media can communicate new insights and paradigms. However, the increased accessibility of video production can also be problematic. As a visual language, video has unique formal considerations. As a research tool, the medium raises issues of subject and audience. I speak from personal experience to explore the tensions and behind-the-scene

complexities of video production that are not visible to an outside audience.

◆ *Introduction*

In this chapter I describe the process, social relationships, audience, and personal reflections about my own agenda as an artist and educator in the making of four video documentaries as research into urban subcultures. Furthermore, I present a theoretical discussion about problems of visual representation associated with the ubiquity of media.

In 1998, I first gravitated toward digital video when I was preparing the defense of my doctoral thesis on hip-hop graffiti culture. Although I had completed my written thesis, it seemed inadequate to fully represent a visual culture. I had slides but felt uncomfortable narrating about graffiti writers. I noted that people would often be surprised at how articulate graffiti writers were in the interview segments that I included in my thesis. Some even assumed that I had cleaned up the grammar and added my own words since the interviews didn't fit assumptions about graffiti writers as deviants. I wanted people to experience a more direct encounter with the subtle nuances of place, facial expressions, voice, and other characteristics of the interesting people who drove this research. At this time I was offered a chance to make a digital video.

◆ *"LOST" Performance in Public Space*

In the spring of 1999, two months before my thesis defense, Emmedia, a Calgary video resource center, came to Lethbridge with a portable editing suite to offer training sessions on how to produce a digital video. My main objective was to present a performance of graffiti in action, and to explore the assumption that representation in public space is reserved for only those who have the money to buy it.

I emailed graffiti writer DAES (DAZE) from Calgary, to ask if he was interested in painting an old minivan to make a video about graffiti. He agreed and told me which colors of spray paint to buy. I documented him painting his new tag name "LOST" in big letters filling both sides of the van. He was excited to talk to me about graffiti and to spend a day painting. He wanted me to video-tape him painting a wall since the smooth surface of the van had caused unwanted drips. We drove to an abandoned fire station outside of Canmore (near Banff) where he used to practice painting. He talked about his dissatisfaction with college, mainly about people going to school just to earn a degree, and about the ugly urban sprawl outside of Calgary. I recognized in him the critical awareness and honesty I had seen in many graffiti writers toward contemporary culture.

As I returned home to Lethbridge, I videotaped the van in a variety of contexts, such as under the yellow arches of McDonald's, beside a bus painted with large advertising slogans, a car painted with super graphics, and railroad cars full of graffiti. Like the graffiti on freight trains, my van was now like a billboard traveling across the country connecting with an audience in chance encounters.

The van provoked communication with people through a range of conversations about their experiences with hip-hop graffiti. For example, I filmed a group of teenagers who skateboarded up to me to ask about the van. They told me where to find graffiti locations in Lethbridge. This is where I met a young graffiti writer from Cranbrook who was visiting Lethbridge. He talked to me about what it was like to be a teenager in a small western town. His main preoccupation was memorizing the train schedule to spot graffiti pieces painted

by his mentors, traveling from Vancouver and Montreal on the moving gallery of freight trains. He knew about many graffiti artists through Web sites on the Internet and wanted to see them in real life.

For 2 years, until the van finally died in eastern Ontario, I met young people in rural towns throughout Canada who gave me the thumbs up, saying "that's stylin'," or stopped me to talk about graffiti. The van became a catalyst for meeting people to talk about graffiti and to document graffiti within the everyday context of advertising and other forms of representation in public space. I ended up producing a 13-minute video beginning with me talking to LOST about his name. The next section is an uninterrupted performance showing his concentration and skill in painting both sides of the van, with close-ups of hand movements and amplified rhythmical sounds of the spray nozzle. This is followed by traveling with the van to typical graffiti locations through an overgrown road to an abandoned fire station that is covered with graffiti. LOST chooses his wall and begins to paint. The video shows the beginning and end of his piece. We get back in the van, and the rest of the video shows the van in different locations cutting between interviews with people who approach me to talk about the van and their knowledge of graffiti. I later reconnected with LOST and gave him a video in exchange for his participation in the video research. I rarely show this video since it was shot with extreme limitations of time and access to equipment and lack of technical skills. However, it showed me the potential and the need to communicate through a visual medium in an academic institution where text ruled in research.

My written thesis research in Montreal analyzed the evolution and changes in a regional hip-hop subculture. My ongoing investigation with the van gave me first-hand experience with youth who were participating in the increasingly global culture of hip-hop through the Internet.

◆ *Relationships*

The sharing of information in public space is key to developing relationships and evolving a culture. In graffiti culture the Internet was quickly adopted as the optimum medium for disseminating images and networking within a global community. The egalitarian yet ego-driven entrepreneurial spirit of graffiti writers lent itself well to grassroots video productions and net communities that existed outside of the gallery-museum establishments. My interest in video production was immediately accepted and opened doors for me as a member of the community. Video fit the agenda of communicating within the World Wide Web that includes an ever-increasing number of graffiti sites that link cities, names, and images like a gallery and reference manual. Graffiti conventions are being announced and writers are easily located, facilitating a network within an ever-emerging organizational structure. Although the Internet may not be accessible to everyone, it is certainly to the people within the graffiti community or to those interested in the community. People from all over the world who would never open an academic journal watch the videos and write me to learn more.

A central subject in the investigative process in social science research is the relationship between people.

> Consider man with man, and you see human life, dynamic, twofold, the giver and the receiver . . . the nature which investigates and the nature which supplies information, the request begged and granted—always both together, completing one another in mutual contribution. (Buber, 1992, p. 41)

In planning and shooting documentary, one is always conscious of the line between the constructed cinematic setup and the opportunity to go beyond oneself in a quest

for the authenticity and multiplicity in social interactions. Video has the capacity to investigate what is surprising and unexpected; it heightens awareness of situations and people as unique. Video as a "form" or type of relationship can create and represent a third space beyond "the dichotomy in sociological analysis" (Buber, 1992, p. 19).

Although the act of qualitative research requires one to be completely present in the moment in relation to the experience, video can distance the observer behind the camera. It is important to be conscious of this tension between the camera as a means to provoke connections and to sharpen perception and as a potential barrier between the subject and researcher behind the camera. As in any investigation the process is directed by an open curiosity and questions informed by preliminary research. I never speak to people from behind the camera. I either position the camera on a tripod beside me or zoom in from a distance, camera on my shoulder, or Michael my husband videotapes while I feel free to directly engage in conversation. The camera can create a performative element that fits in with hip-hop culture, where events are constantly being staged for an audience. However, I became increasingly aware of how subtle nuances within social relationships were not communicated.

The editing process is a more distant, objective process of structuring video as a language. When I had finished shooting *LOST*, I arrived with a bag of tapes to edit in a few sessions with a technician who had little experience with video editing. We worked together to help figure things out as we went along. The first thing that excited me about digital editing was the highly visual, graphically displayed sound waves and images that could be moved around, like cutting and pasting sentences into endless varieties of reconfigurations. I had an immediate attraction to the flexibility of digital information as opposed to the rigidity of analogue videotape. This one experience in producing a video completely changed my awareness of how videos are constructed.

There is a play-off between the idea of the truthfulness of photographic documentation that dates back to the beginning of photography and the sophisticated understanding in our digital age that all images can be appropriated, manipulated, and constructed. On the one hand, there are the pleasures of losing our critical awareness and getting lost in the magic of conventional narrative cinema. On the other hand, there is the moralized documentary imperative to be true to your subject, expressed by players such as the dogme 95 films, which devised 10 rules called "The Vow of Chastity" (http://www.dogme95.dk/menu/menuset.htm). However, in the end both these approaches can be developed into stylized tropes that need to be questioned.

In video research, it is more important to maintain an authentic relationship with the participant than it is to upstage that moment with stylized camera or editing work.

Ideally one is conscious of a privileged relationship where both parties learn something in the exchange.

◆ *Video as a Research Method*

LOST was my first video essay. I had much to learn technically and had extreme limitations of having to shoot and edit the entire production in 2 weeks. However, I knew it was the method that best fit the particular problem and context being studied. Video fit with my research into hip-hop culture for many reasons. It allowed me entrance into the community as a participant: I was viewed as a fellow practitioner, and I actively participated in the shareware philosophy of giving it back to the community by giving everyone a copy of the video. I can talk to my students about how many graffiti writers and DJs are an off-shoot of early punk culture with its

do-it-yourself (DIY) attitude in taking control over the means of production, but students learn more from modeling my method of working with video and the Internet.

Video was more efficient than written notes or even audio tape for investigating and engaging a theoretical discussion about the context of the hip-hop community. Video showed the dynamic, continually evolving, interdisciplinary production processes, the verbal exchange of ideas, the visual transfer of skills, and the interaction with an audience in a public arena.

I encourage researchers to use video in their struggle to find new forms for their work to better address the cultural shift from print to electronic media, especially when researching popular culture. Both are intricately linked in their methods of circulating knowledge and information within public space.

Video as a research method can be used instead of audiotape to collect data, planning from the beginning of the process to produce a video, while writing to develop the theoretical analysis and arguments. What seems most important is to apply the same critical attention to research and craft in structuring the video medium as in the writing process.

Academic research is now being informed by interaction with artistic disciplines. This cross-disciplinary position brings into question the relationship of art as a specific autonomous language and the role and purpose of art in its larger social context. The art discipline contributes a vocabulary and a variety of nonconventional approaches to using video, as well as an evolved critique of mass media. Experimental videos offer a vast semiotic vocabulary, including various storytelling devices, editing techniques, and visual styles.

PROBLEMS PRESENTED BY VIDEO AS A RESEARCH METHOD

Video is a relatively young and complex form of visual communication. It has large potential for dissemination. Because of its reproducibility and the channels of distribution, it can potentially access an audience of millions. Where academic journals are expensive and mainly circulate among other researchers, video has a populist appeal. With the present state of the Internet, video research data can reach everyone who has a computer online. However, the ubiquity of video in our culture also presents problems and complex issues.

If video is to be recognized as a legitimate tool for academic research, it has to be applied with the same rigor as text. It has to be substantiated by taking a historical and cultural perspective to distinguish the specific characteristics of video. What are the difficulties and challenges in understanding and applying video's time-based audio/visual form? How important is it to understand video's unique codes, references, genres, language structure, background, and even development as a mass communication system? What are the multiple ways to adopt the video camera for research purposes? Are video and digital technology becoming inextricably linked? How does one maintain a critical position to a medium that is continually evolving and renewing itself?

One of the fundamental precepts is that images exist within a language system—a complex network of codes in reference to the history of photography, cinema, advertising, art, and television. Although there may be the assumption that images are universal in that anyone can recognize them, there will always be an intellectual process in "reading" the resonance of images that often leads to different and even opposing interpretations of even the most stable signifiers. Take for example, a 1999 advertisement that I clipped out of a *Vanity Fair* magazine. The woman lounges in the odalisque position wearing only her underwear and gazes out at the viewer. The caption says "The Good Life." The advertiser intends the audience to simply desire the sexuality offered up along with its

promise of social status in the hope that this will translate to a desire for the product. But from a feminist art historical perspective the same image is recognized as a persistent stereotype of the passive near-naked women referenced in so many paintings purchased by wealthy male patrons. The gaze signifies submission and ownership of the patron over the painting and the woman.

Although people increasingly consume and produce more and more images with immediate ease (think here of the recent arrival of affordable digital cameras), there is often little conscious, let alone critical, understanding of how we construct and read images. The facility in identifying images and the desire for plot-driven narratives invariably distract from any analysis of visual communication, often resulting in reductive, essentialist interpretations.

VIDEO FORMAT AND VISUAL LITERACY

Before researchers consider video production as a research method, they should enrich their visual literacy. One of the most important aspects is to be critically aware of the authority and hegemony of mass media visual codes, and to possess a good grasp on the academic tools for deconstructing these. It means to be trained to go beyond the cliché in the production of images and to critique the material processes of constructing and viewing images as a viewer. Surrounded by ritual responses to images such as passive viewing of television, one falls unwittingly into formulaic conventions without identifying and interpreting them. In schools, images are rarely analyzed critically as language but are accepted as support to illustrate the main text. Carol Becker (2003) argues that visual illiteracy is perpetuated by the educational system.

The root of the problem is the way that the visual is being taught. . . . Even when art is taught within the school system, those who teach it rarely stretch beyond the traditional humanistic goals of art education which focuses on genius, masterpieces, divine inspiration, and predominantly white western art that ends with impressionism. (p. 107)

Video media brings new questions to address in visual education. For example, how does the intent of the filmmaker and the materiality of video mediate between reality and its representation (Cubitt, 1993)? What is the process of production and the changing role of video in society? What is unique about moving images as a poetic language and malleable material, beyond its most obvious ability to illustrate a narrative or document an event? The most literate readers have more experience and knowledge of visual cultural conventions (Monaco, 2000, p. 125). If one ignores the relationship between materials and ideas in the communication process, it is impossible to disassociate the video support from data when engaging in and teaching video research methods.

Inquiry in the arts is defined as critical observation and playful experimentation with materials and ideas. So, although it is important to be aware of genres related to video, such as documentary, fiction, and art video, it remains important to the video researcher to remain critical of these categories. In the last few years, for example, I have been happy to see that the boundaries between video art and social documentary video have eroded. I am being asked more and more to present my videos across disciplines in art, gender issues, education, and new media. Academia has become more interested in visual representation, and fine arts has become less rigid in categorizing experimental versus documentary. As in hip-hop culture, the innovation is in the mix. This cross-fertilization is hopeful for it means that more people will be creating alternatives to an increasingly commercialized social agenda and the prescriptive

thinking that accompanies video and other new technologies.

I continue to have concerns about researchers using video as a tool who have not been trained in the visual. I often see images used superficially to illustrate a more complex written thesis. If the visual is to stand alone as a mode of academic research and communication, it must be produced with an understanding of visual literacy resources. It is imperative that practitioners think deeply about the use of video in their work as a primary text, rather than an illustrative prop.

It is important, for example, to consider why one is shooting video as research and whether it fits as a form of communication, the agenda of both researcher and participants. As video is becoming more commonplace as a research method, it is important to understand the value of forming a relationship with and being aware of the ethical considerations of "giving back" to the subjects. In hip-hop culture, video fits the spirit of the shareware and do-it-yourself philosophies. I was encouraged by participants to broadcast the video and to make it available to anyone who wanted it for the cost of dubbing or free on the web.

◆ You Have to Watch to Learn

After making *LOST* I purchased my own camera and video editing equipment so that I could be in direct control of the production process in the same way as I am in direct control of the writing process. The more I mastered using the video camera the more critically aware I became of the ways I was framing my subjects. Digital video editing becomes more intuitive with ease in using the software and because playback of changes is immediate. The graphical interface makes it easy to continually view, move things around, layer images and sounds. As in writing, digital processes allow decisions to be made in the doing, and ideas are developed and put together to make a coherent proposition.

You Have to Watch to Learn documented *Under Pressure,* a hip-hop event in Montreal in August 1999. Graffiti writers, DJs, and break-dancers came from around the world to paint a section of wall in downtown Montreal, spin records, and dance for the crowd of onlookers and participants. The event was staged for the media and the general public to showcase what the tradition of hip-hop graffiti culture was all about. My camera was welcomed as part of the event; temporality of performance is part of the culture, but documentation is revered.

SEAZ, who had been my main contact throughout my research on graffiti, was the organizer of the event. He first began organizing "graffiti jams" in 1995 as a participant and later as an "administrator," "to show the public what we are all about.... Now that I have some fame and notoriety, it's my turn to give back to the graffiti community" (Rahn & Campbell, 1999). Video documentation fit with SEAZ's purpose of reaching out to a public outside of hip-hop culture and of giving a record of the event back to the graffiti community.

I interviewed people throughout the day and documented the process of setting up during a rainstorm at 7 a.m. through to midnight when the scaffolding was dismantled while group photos were taken. I promised everyone that they would receive a copy of the tape in a release form that described in detail what I planned to do with the video. My questions were informed by prior research about personal motivation, ways of learning, and issues of community, public space, and commercialization of the culture.

Time became the conceptual frame for editing the interviews and footage documenting the evolution of the event. Mural paintings progress from blank walls to completed works at the end. Break dancing is juxtaposed on top of or beside close-ups of graffiti

painting to show the interdisciplinary nature of the culture centered on music. For the first time, I was happy with the pacing and rhythm of video cuts using breaks, dissolves, duration shots, and juxtapositions. A slow motion dissolve of a young boy practicing spins on his BMX bicycle cuts to a man watching from the audience who suddenly starts to dance. Close-ups of spray painting, interviews, DJs, break dancing, tattoos on different body parts, homemade bikes, and writers who paint characters instead of letters are edited to the flow of the music. My favorite sequence was a series of slow-motion close-ups of a DJ's hands as they scratched and spun records. This sequence is the most successful in the formal relationship of image to audio. The interdisciplinarity of my subject taught me how to video-edit.

The other half of video format that is chronically neglected is audio. A conventional solution to audio within video is to overlay music in the form of a music video or popular film. I wanted to show how music drives and unifies the culture, and it became the pulse of the video. After this video project, I consciously analyzed the editing process in relation to audio.

◆ Broadening the Experience of Video Media

There is much to be learned from the tradition of video art when approaching video as a research tool. Teachers have to dig a little further than the mainstream Hollywood fare offered by their local video stores or even their school libraries to find examples of this work to broaden their repertoire. University libraries tend to contain collections of resources compiled by specialists. More experimental videos would include Goddard, Murnau, Fritz Lang, Lars Von Trier, Truffaut, Bill Viola, Mia Derin, and

Chris Marker, among others. Secondary schools are usually limited to mainstream Hollywood models to reference video production. This can be a problem if the researcher using video as a research method does not broaden their experience of video.

Early video artists Frank Gillette and Nam June Paik believed that they could "enter the communication process" to change passive viewing (Rush, 2003, p. 17). Although this belief may now seem naive, their work presents examples of how to break from standardized stylized devices and how to question the relationship of form and content in video as communication. Historically, video developed from within three separate systems of communication—photography, cinema, and television—but they interconnect and distribute visual references to a media-saturated audience (Cubitt, 1993). Technically, cinema developed from photography and video evolved from radio and television. Photography and cinema were immediately picked up by artists such as Man Ray and later Fluxus who were not as interested in techniques or formalistic concerns as they were in ideas and in the potential of the medium to actively engage an audience. Their approach to video was often interdisciplinary, informed by conceptual contemporary arts/design/communications traditions in two-dimensional, three-dimensional, performance, installation, audio, and other time-based practices.

Early video artists broadened the potential of the medium through experimentation. Their goal was to privilege conceptual intent in the interplay with aesthetic formalism and technical possibilities. In other words, an arts approach to video is not determined by technological skills but driven by conceptual and material strategies. Both video and cinema are a process of composing an audio/visual language that is predominantly used in a much more literal way by mass media to tell stories. By the time artists were broadening the potential of the medium through experimentation, video as television was integrated

into the social environment. For example, Bruce Nauman and Nam June Paik played with the realities and values of a culture dominated by ubiquitous advertising and entertainment media (Sturken, 1986). These artists, in the early utopian development in the 1960s and 1970s, believed that video art could infiltrate and counter its commercial application in television long before artists such as Stan Douglas inserted video shorts on television to defamiliarize commercials.

◆ The Limits of Video Art

Although the exploratory and conceptual approach of video art is a rich source of critical vocabulary for the researcher, the final product is by definition hermetic, involved as it is in its antagonistic stance toward the mainstream or in the subjective explorations of the author. I did not want to speak in a dialect common to a secluded group. I wanted a relationship with a general audience, while resisting assimilation into standardized methods of video production. My challenge when I first started making video research essays was figuring out how to bridge the gaps between the general public, academia, and the contemporary art community. How could I produce something that was entertaining, experimental, and critically analytical?

I was drawn to a whole other body of cultural production for my answer to these questions. I found models of documentary filmmakers who experimented with video as an audio/visual language yet spoke to a wide audience.

Visual literacy comes by critically viewing many different styles of video editing to find mentors who express themselves in ways that may not be seen in mainstream videos. For example, when I first watched *Fast Cheap and Out of Control* by Errol Morris (1997), I recognized him as a documentarian to emulate. His content, interview style, camera work, and editing made me consciously aware of my relationship to the subject, the subject in relation to the camera, and the rhythm and pacing of the filming and editing process. Morris was obviously drawing on stylistic and narrative devices being explored by video artists, but he used them in a way that communicated artistic intent, a critical understanding of the medium and insight into his film's subjects. Errol Morris's documentaries play with the tension between the controlled rational intent of inquiry and the pursuit of the unknown. In *The Believer* (Poppy, 2004), Morris talks about how his films are more "truthful" when he allows the chaos of the unknown to happen in human actions and relations, since one never really knows what people will say.

B-GIRL

Although I was happy with the editing of *You Have to Watch to Learn,* and it did frame the passion and energy of this one-day event, I was aware that it seemed to celebrate the macho culture of hip-hop. Even during the process of shooting the traditional graffiti event I was aware of the absence of women. Afterward I sought out women who were not invited to participate in this event and who felt marginalized in trying to break into this subculture. So, I turned my attention to this problem.

The more I learned about hip-hop culture, the more it seemed defined by contradictions that continually disrupted common suppositions. For example, although it was an inclusive culture that crossed disciplines and categories of styles in painting, music, and dance, it had a tradition that was based on hierarchy of skills and machismo working-class values. During my research of hip-hop, I met women graffiti writers, DJs, and breakdancers who were becoming part of a "New School" group of graffiti who came more out of punk culture than hip-hop. They shared similar attitudes, but New School was more inclusive of women and did not care as much for the "Old School" ethics of competition, showmanship, and "getting the most work up." I made *B-Girl* in pursuit of a whole picture of the complex, continually evolving phenomenon of hip-hop. Again this video was about passion, active agency, and self-directed learning among peers, but the *B-Girl* video modeled a different determination to participate on their own terms within a culture dominated by "guys."

I had known the lead dancer, Katie Alsterlund, for about 5 years since she had been my student in an interdisciplinary course at Concordia University. It was typical of the New School group to cross over between the university, the contemporary art community, and the street/club culture of hip-hop. Again the tight network and interest in media production made it easy for me to meet people, and the artists saw the video as an opportunity to assert their identity and opinions and to document their work.

I went into this video with a clearer idea of what questions I would ask. I knew that there would be a lot of footage, and I needed some kind of conceptual logic to guide my questions and editing process. I structured my questions to link dance, graffiti writing, and DJing across issues of identity, tradition/innovation, ways of learning, gender, and motivation. This was the first video where I felt satisfied that I had included voices from different perspectives of race, class, and gender through a process of inquiry to present a critical view and analysis of hip-hop culture. I documented women from divergent backgrounds with a common interest in hip-hop and a feeling of exclusion within a macho subculture. The broader theme of gender bias and exclusion makes this video popular across disciplines from physical education to women studies courses.

The video opens with the theme of naming in relation to identity construction, which is characteristic of traditional hip-hop culture. The women all introduce themselves by talking about the name they have given themselves and what it means. For the graffiti writers, their tag name is chosen for formal reasons—they like the way it looks and sounds—whereas the dancers and DJs choose names like "short circuit," "agent lynx," and "kilojule" because they reference movement and the energy of the music. They demonstrate traditional skills, followed by deviations through the development of personal style, followed by ways of learning. In the next section, called *Gender,* they all talk about their experiences as a woman in a masculine culture. Finally, the last theme, *Love,* is about motivation: their "love for the music."

The editing of this video was similar to other qualitative research methods. I worked from a knowledge base of the community to loosely structure interview questions and to organize the video into themes. This could not have occurred without prior knowledge and a relationship with the subject. Otherwise, I took an exploratory approach since I had my own equipment and didn't need the approval of a funding agency. When applying for video grants, one must have the entire video described in detail for the jury to visualize and to believe in the person's ability to finish the video. Equipment is becoming economical enough for the general researcher, but the quality of the video will depend on prior research like a literature review, personal relationships, and on-camera and editing skills. Like writing, video has the potential to be engaging, informative, and innovative, but it can also present its subject superficially and buried in derivative representation and irrelevant narrative detail.

◆ *Other and the Problems of Ethnographic Video*

It is necessary to assume a critical attitude in order to break from historical ethnographic videos that represented "the other" as a

voyeur that was touristic and colonialistic. In the making of the last three videos, I was conscious of my relationship with the subject and tried to engage with the culture as a participant. However, in all three I felt restricted by a time limit for shooting the video and by my conscious attempt to "capture" their stories on video. The process in my next video was completely different. It happened organically in that it was not planned but made in response to a situation. At the time I was thinking of Isuma production videos, where the pacing is slow as if the camera just happened to be on to capture a moment in everyday life.

You Have to Watch to Learn is a compressed series of action-packed events paced with an energetic rhythm. *B-Girl* was filmed on the run, mainly in Montreal, to different locations to capture practices at home, community centers, and in clubs to film evening performances. I also traveled to Calgary and Vancouver to visit a break-dancer and DJ.

My next video on graffiti was a departure from the previous videos in the way it was filmed and in the calm pacing of the edit. "Other" is the name of a graffiti writer, his name literally meaning an *other* kind of graffiti. The video is about his work and our exploration of urban art together in Berlin. Other heard that I was traveling to Berlin to shoot a video about squatter communities in Berlin and asked if he could work as my assistant in exchange for room and board and money for his airline ticket. He said that he spoke German so I agreed. I met Other for the first time in the Berlin airport, and I soon found out that he didn't speak German. However, he was very likeable and he soon became part of the family.

Every morning Other would get up early to find some interesting object as a surface to draw something from his bank of found images. His choices were random. It was the occupation of retrieving, transforming, and discarding. I had no intention of shooting a video about graffiti at this time, but my husband, Michael Campbell, and I had been collaborating on a series about obsession. After a few days of observing Other draw or paint on abandoned surfaces, I asked if I could turn on the camera. The process was diaristic, recording the daily ritual of drawing followed by a search for a location to leave the work on the street. I recorded our excursions biking throughout the city and our conversations as we stopped to talk about the stencil art pasted throughout the city like the layers of peeling posters. Other knew most of the artists and explained the meaning of their symbols. For example, the stencil print of a surveillance camera meant "designated graffiti area." Once it was put up, other stencil artists would paint in that area in response. I started to bike to different locations throughout the city to document certain images. For example, the numeral 6 was painted everywhere along with a Web site address on top of advertising posters, four sides of a cement block, a sweater found on the street and tied taut across a fence at a construction site, and high up on the walls of abandoned warehouses. This research reminded me of my early documentation of graffiti in Montreal, which began as a way to explore neighborhoods.

The previous summer in Berlin, I had passed through many of the same streets looking through the guide book for museums to visit. Now I was looking at the street itself through Other's eyes, decoding and recording the networking signs of traveling graffiti writers. A touristic, tentative approach to the world is to be outside the language, trying to glean what one can through didactic panels or guide books. From this vantage point it is difficult to even know what questions to ask. It was not a situation of simply following Other, for everything seemed worth investigating. It was like breaking through the limitations of language set up by tourism to interact spontaneously with genuine curiosity to a new place and culture. Tourism is an interesting metaphor to reflect critically upon ethnographic research.

When editing the video, I consciously tried to express the intimacy of drawing as a daily ritual and the leisurely pace of exploring a city by foot or bicycle. I showed long shots of Other looking at buildings and drawings, and time-lapsed shots showing the hours spent drawing on a piece simply to leave it on the street, never knowing who, if anyone, picked it up. There was no formal interview as in the last two videos but often a voice-over of our conversations as he worked.

One is always conscious of the camera frame because it is often still, with the subject moving in relation to it or things moving in and out of the frame. This is a method I am growing to like more, especially as I see students constantly move the camera, zooming in and out or nervously moving around as if in search of a subject. The still camera is not anxious as it quietly respects the subject framed in real time and space.

This video taught me a different relationship with the subject that expressed Other's meditative way of working. The method of shooting and editing should respond to the uniqueness of the situation. The making of *Other* will inform my next video when I will more consciously consider this relationship between the subject and the camera.

◆ *Conclusion*

My motivation to make videos as research was (1) to allow one to see and hear the interdisciplinary culture of hip-hop and for participants to narrate their own lives along with examples of their work, (2) to form authentic relationships with participants through an interest in their background and motivation, (3) to experiment with an audio/visual language in a research method that crosses between art and academic disciplines, (4) to interpret themes that emerged from the audio/visual data throughout the editing process, (5) to disseminate and communicate the data as research within an academic culture that was predominantly text-based, and (6) to provide documentation in the media as advocacy for the arts.

I would never have considered making a documentary if I had not been dissatisfied with print as a way to represent a visual culture in my doctoral dissertation on hip-hop graffiti subculture. Although I included interviews in my book, *Painting Without Permission* (Rahn, 2002), I knew that people still had assumptions about how graffiti writers looked and talked. The phenomenon of graffiti is best understood when viewed as a performance: an acting out of identities within a context that cannot be appreciated until seen and heard in the music, images and dance, and demeanor of the participants.

My intent to recover fresh perspectives on beliefs and opinions that had not been questioned opened doors for me into the culture. Also, I was welcomed as a participant-observer because self-publication and alternative media were such an important part of hip-hop culture. There was a genuine entrepreneurial curiosity in what I was doing and in my tools of the trade, such as the DIY (do-it-yourself) freedom of traveling with a small handheld camera and laptop to experiment with shooting and editing video without the assistance of camera crews. Hip-hop, like new media, is always being redefined because it is part of the culture to embrace new forms and to learn from other people within a network. Video as a method of research can be more than a means to collect data. Like the culture I was documenting, it can also involve an audience in a process of change.

I show my videos, not to encourage young people to become graffiti writers or to normalize a subculture, but to show the curiosity and passion of learning among peers within a network. I try to model this by streaming segments of my videos on the Web

and setting up a database to communicate with instructors of new media.

The most important issue is that every video is a relationship with the participants. Otherwise, ethnographic video can too easily slip into the pleasures of voyeurism, which forces subjects into the predetermined social norms of dominant culture. However, if video is regarded as a language that involves the researcher, the subject, and an audience in constructive dialogue, it opens up possibilities for fluidity, communication, and therefore personal and political change (Cubitt, 1993; Gallagher, 2001).

◆ References

Becker, C. (2003). [Keynote address]. Interdisciplinary Conference, Regina University, Regina, Saskatchewan, Canada.

Berger, R. (1982). Video in the modern world. In *Artistic creation and video art* (Documentary dossier 25–26, pp. 31–70). Paris: UNESCO Cultural Development.

Buber, M. (1992). *On intersubjectivity and cultural creativity.* Chicago: University of Chicago Press.

Cubitt, S. (1993). *Videography: Video media as art and culture.* New York: St. Martin's Press.

Gallagher, M. (2001). The push and pull of action and research in feminist media studies. *Feminist Media Studies, 11*(1), 11–15.

Monaco, J. (2000). *How to read a film: The world of movies, media, and multimedia—Language, history, theory* (3rd ed.). New York: Oxford University Press.

Morris, E. (Director). (1997). *Fast, cheap, and out of control* [Documentary film]. United States: Sony Pictures

Poppy, N. (2004). An interview with Errol Morris. *The Believer, 12*(2&3), 57–64.

Rahn, J. (2002). *Painting without permission.* Westport, CT: Bergin & Garvey, Greenwood Press.

Rahn, J., & Campbell, M. (Creators, Producers, Editors). (1999). *You've got to watch to learn* [video]. Montreal, Quebec, Canada: SCRAB: A Rahn/Campbell production.

Rush, M. (2003). *Video art.* London: Thames and Hudson.

Sturken, M. (1986). Paradox in the evolution of an art form: Great expectations and the making of a history. In D. Hall & S. J. Fifer (Eds.), *Illuminating video: An essential guide to video art* (pp. 101–121). San Francisco: Aperture/Bay Area Video Coalition (BAVC).

26 *New Media*

BLOGS

Robert Runte

Most people are aware of blogs as sites of social and political commentary, but the role of blogs in the arts and the emergence of blogging as an art form may not be immediately apparent. Although blogs may serve many purposes, a growing number have been created by writers and artists to serve as venue, to build community, or simply to experiment with the potentialities of this rapidly evolving modality. As blogging technology becomes increasingly flexible and accessible, entirely new genres are beginning to emerge, engaging a significant proportion of the population.

For researchers in the arts, blogs offer unique opportunities. First, as increasing numbers of artists blog about their work, post examples of their work directly to their blogs, and otherwise use their blogs as continually updated online portfolios, a vast storehouse of source material is now readily (if not always ethically) available to the researcher. Second, as artists create and sustain close-knit virtual communities through their blogs, the potential for analyzing issues and identifying trends within any of the various genres represented is greatly facilitated. Third, as a significant proportion of the general population blogs, the public attitude toward particular artists, art forms, genres, policies, and so on, can be readily ascertained and continually updated through an analysis of this spontaneous expression. Finally, although there are no reliable figures on the number of bloggers, it is clear that *millions* of individuals are posting regularly; for many of these, blogging has become the preferred outlet for their artistic expression, whatever their particular genre. Correspondingly, researchers in the arts must begin to address this emergent aspect of popular culture.

Even researchers for whom blogs are unlikely to represent useful source material are finding blogs an inexpensive and efficient alternative to project management software. As with writers and artists, blogs allow researchers to establish virtual communities with those sharing their specialization, track developments in their field, manage sources, brainstorm with colleagues, document their priority in the formulation of key ideas, pace their own work, and rapidly disseminate results.

However, a cautionary note: Blogs and blogging raise a number of new ethical dilemmas and pose potential pitfalls for researchers. Human subjects research overseeing committees are only now beginning to come to grips with the thorny issue of whether blogs should be considered public "published" documents—and so exempt from ethical review—or "private spaces," and therefore subject to various protections (Bell, 2005).

◆ Blogs as Art

Blogs are both a new medium through which to express existing genres and a new set of genres in their own right.

BLOGS AS MEDIUM

Blogs serve at least three purposes in the arts.

Publishing Venue

First and most obvious, many people use blogs to publish their photography, music, artwork, videos, fiction, poetry, essays, or journal entries. In this, blogging technology is doing for the literary, visual, and performing arts what Napster did to the music industry: short-circuiting the gap between producer and consumer to create a democratic, synergistic, anarchic, publishing environment.

Since there are no gatekeepers, and entry into this public marketplace is relatively inexpensive, many more individuals can participate than could through traditional publishing, performance, or exhibition venues. Consequently, a much greater proportion of the population may now self-identify as participating in the arts. Although critics may decry the quality of much of this self-publishing, many bloggers attract significant audiences, and some few have even made this a paying proposition through hardcopy sales, the direct solicitation of donations, or through carrying advertising on their blogs (Rowse, 2004).

Similarly, many established artists use blogs as an extension of their regular exhibitions, providing additional commentary, supplementary material, or exhibiting directly through the blog. As artists push the limits of how and what can be presented online, the traditional divisions between genres are sometimes blurred, as the emergent multimedia modalities become their own medium of expression.

Marketing Strategy

Many established artists and writers maintain blogs about their careers and work as a marketing tool. A survey by Spier New York, for example, found that 23% of readers polled (35% under age 35) have visited an author's site (PW Daily, 2006). Similarly, in the visual and performing arts, complex networks of mutually referential blogs create discourse networks in which self-promotion, reviews, commentary, and responses create not only "buzz" but a synergistic environment in which influence can rapidly evolve into virtual trends and artistic movements. For the researcher, such blogs not only provide a constantly updated stream of current information, but also often include considerable autobiographical commentary about both the artist and the evolution of his or her work.

Virtual Community

There are many reasons why writers and artists seek out community, but the most compelling is simply that most work alone, without the job-place interactions others take for granted. Consequently, many writers and artists use blogs to establish community, either through private networks of peers (such as available through Live Journal.com) or by attracting regular subscribers (many of whom will correspond through the blog's comment function) to their public blog. The asynchronous nature of the medium allows artists to put down tools and take a social break at their convenience, with minimal reciprocal commitment. Although all of the authors and poets interviewed in my current research commented on the need to strictly ration the time allotted to writing, reading, and responding to blogs—lest their real writing not get done—most considered blogging fundamental to maintaining their sense of connectedness within a community of writers.

Additionally, many artists use the networking potential of blogging to stay atop developments in their field, identifying marketing and grant opportunities, and so on. Collaborative efforts are also greatly facilitated by such online communities (as these benefits are also available to the researcher, they are discussed in some detail later).

Others use communities of bloggers in specific ways to move their projects forward. For example, many novelists, poets, and playwrights maintain semiprivate blogs accessible only to peers who serve as first readers and a focus group for early drafts. Such writers often motivate themselves by publicly committing to some deadline or quota, post scenes they are struggling with to their blog for feedback, direct esoteric questions to the encyclopedic knowledge contained within the collegial network, and so on. Similarly, many beginning writers use blogging software to establish on-line writers' workshops.

One perhaps surprising application in the literary arts, though typical of the many latent functions of blogging, is the rant blog. Several authors I interviewed in the current study mentioned maintaining a blog for the expressed purpose of providing a venue in which to rant *other than* in their current work for publication. These authors expressed that prior to blogging, they had had difficulty in keeping themselves from pursuing personal hobbyhorses within their fiction or documentary work, even where they knew this to be inappropriate. The rant blog provides a safety valve through which "to get it off their chest" without contaminating the work at hand.

THE MEDIUM AS MESSAGE

As new genres emerge, the blog and its descendents have to be taken seriously as art forms in and of themselves.

The video blog (vlog), for example, is a new but increasingly popular art form with members of the digital generation, who take access to digital video recorders and video cell phones for granted. Constantly making the conscious choice whether to "roll tape" as they move through the environments and events of their lives, they are essentially engaged in interpreting their lives through the lens of their camcorders. Here the vlog serves not just as a convenient venue for the distribution of short videos (*YouTube* would serve that function better); rather, the implicit continuity and ongoing commitment renders the vlog its own particular art form, and the vlogger an artist.

With *millions* blogging daily, a significant portion of the population has now taken up creative documentary as a filter through which to view their own lives (Runte, 2000), thanks to their regular blog/podcast/vlog. This would be a fascinating sociological phenomenon were these narratives merely private diaries, but given the expectation of audience, and the critique implicit in number and responsiveness of subscribers, this new interactive genre is clearly an art form, duly subject to review and research.

As one delves deeper into the popular culture of blogging, as blogging technology continues to evolve, and as the online community continues to grow and diversify, the temptation is to identify each new subcategory as its own genre. The key, however, is simply to recognize that blogging is more than merely the sum of its roles as a medium for the transmission of the arts; rather, the gestalt of these roles, and the blogger's self-identification as writer, artist, or performer, renders blogging an art form.

◆ Blogs as Source Material

For researchers in the arts, the rapid spread of blogging provides an abundance of formerly unavailable source material. Better yet, all this material comes pre-typed, formatted, date stamped, archived, and *indexed*. Researchers can identify and then efficiently track very large numbers of relevant blogs, as freely available software informs the researcher when any of the blogs under study are updated, thus eliminating the need to monitor each blog individually.

Until now, diary-based research has been a relatively minor methodological stream, limited by the logistical difficulties of obtaining sufficient diaries for review. With the emergence of blogging as a mass phenomenon, this has changed, and an explosion in the number of studies using anecdote, journal entries, autobiography, photographs, vlogs, and the like may be anticipated.

Another factor that makes blog-based research so attractive is that postings are date stamped and archived, facilitating comparisons over time. Cohn, Mehl, and Pennebaker (2004), for example, were able to bypass the usual methodological obstacles in trauma research to provide a detailed analysis of the time line of trauma response by analyzing the linguistic differences in 1,084 American blogs for a period of 4 months spanning the 2 months prior to and after the September 11th attacks. Researchers could similarly track trends and issues in the arts.

Blog-based research is facilitated by the highly searchable and cross-referenced nature of the medium. Public blogs are indexed by Internet search engines like any other Web page; bloggers typically self-identify key themes by titling each post, for which Google can "advance search" separately; bloggers often register their blogs by type, topic, or interest with one or more of the many blog-specific indexing services, and they often include a detailed personal profile. Each of these provides the researcher a way of defining and identifying the target sample. On Blogger.com, for example, any phrase entered into the "interest" field of the blogger's profile automatically becomes clickable, so that one can pull up the profiles of all other Blogger.com clients who also listed that interest, which can be literally *anything*, from "photography" to "left handed" to the title of a particular exhibition.

Thus, just as diary research takes on renewed importance with the emergence of blogging as a mass phenomenon, snowball sampling takes on an entirely new functionality. Once having identified a few relevant blogs, those blogs are likely to provide leads to other blogs sharing the target characteristics: First, bloggers usually make explicit reference (with clickable links) to other blogs they find relevant, which are therefore also likely of potential interest to the researcher. These blogs can then lead the researcher to further relevant blogs, until one with the precisely desired characteristics has been identified, or the sample has "snowballed" to the desired critical mass. Second, most blogs invite comments, and most comments include a link to that individual's own blog, thereby allowing researchers another way to identify members of their target community. Finally, some blogs incorporate a "trackback" feature that automatically links to any other blog that makes direct reference to the current entry, thus providing a third avenue to identify or expand one's sample.

Notice that this indexed and interconnected environment provides access to three different types of samples: those defined by blog content, those defined by the characteristics of the blogger, and those defined by the linkages between blogs/bloggers. For example, a researcher interested in Chopin could sample discussions *about* Chopin, or could sample *individuals* who have self-identified as Chopin enthusiasts in their profiles, or could study how often blogs about Chopin or by Chopin fans include *links* to blogs about Metallica. Even if the Chopin devotee never comments directly on Chopin, the researcher may gain insights into the relationship between classical music and, say, political orientation, by observing how often and with what slant politics turn up in their blog.

Because the blog entries are not produced within a research context, the commentary may be considerably more forthright and revealing than when directly solicited. Van House (2004) notes, for example, that "the norms of blogging promote a high degree of self-disclosure" (p. 2), even where bloggers were using their real identities. The effect, therefore, may be even more pronounced where bloggers retain anonymity or conceive their primary audience to be contained within a sympathetic discourse network.

◆ *Ethical Issues*

At first glance, blog-based research does not come under the purview of human subjects research review committees because blogs constitute "published" material. This interpretation is supported by four key aspects of blogging software: Bloggers can remain anonymous, can designate the level of privacy they wish to maintain, can choose whether to include syndication, and can choose whether to register with various indexing services.

ANONYMITY

Anonymity becomes a somewhat slippery concept within the context of the World Wide Web, however. Whereas it is often sufficient with interviews or surveys to simply remove identifying names from a quotation, this is clearly *not* the case with blogs: Any unique phrase from the quotation typed into Google will immediately yield a link to the original posting. Thus, researchers must proceed on the assumption that anonymity cannot be guaranteed, or limit the use of quotation to sufficiently brief or generalized comments that cannot be traced through search engines, or include only anonymous or clearly pseudonymous blogs in their sample.

Even when pseudonyms are used, however, anonymity is less well protected than might be assumed. First, many bloggers repeat their aliases from other contexts (such as online role-playing games, chatrooms, etc.) and so are known to peers, even though the obvious pseudonym may suggest to the researchers that the blog is anonymous.

Second, the cumulative detail provided in hundreds of postings over time is often sufficient to give the blogger's identity away (Electronic Frontier Foundation, 2005). Third, most bloggers fail to take advantage of anonymizing technologies, exposing them to identification (Electronic Frontier Foundation, 2005). For example, deconstructing the file address of photographs or artwork contained within a blog will often reveal the blogger's home campus, organization, or regional computer network. Consequently, researchers may not be able to guarantee respondent anonymity.

INFORMED CONSENT

Most blogging software allow the blogger to indicate who should have access. Blogger.com, for example, asks new bloggers if they wish their blog to be "public" or "private"; if they choose "private," the software adds invisible tags to their blogs that prevent them being indexed by search engines. Consequently, it could be argued that if a blogger chooses the "public" option, registers the blog with one or more blog lists or indexing services, and includes syndication, then the blogger's explicit intention is to make the blog accessible to the public, and researchers may therefore make use of these blogs without further consent.

There are, however, several difficulties here. First, many bloggers may not adequately understand the implications of the "public" tag and be unaware that it allows their postings to be indexed by various search engines.

Second, bloggers routinely quote, refer, and link to other blogs without necessarily respecting, or even being aware of, whether the cited blog is public or one to which there is only limited access. Thus, researches following a series of links in an expanding snowball sample could easily, if inadvertently, include blogs or postings that the originator believed to be private.

Third, many bloggers erroneously believe that if they delete a blog posting it disappears from the net. This is often not the case: Google and other search engines may still include access to pages as they existed when initially indexed through the "cache" button; archival sites attempt to preserve a significant proportion of the net, and so may retain permanent records of deleted postings; and other bloggers may have quoted extensively from material the originator subsequently retracts but cannot then remove from others' blogs. Consequently, ethical researchers need to attend to whether postings have been subsequently deleted and to treat such deletions as the subject withdrawing from the study.

Finally, it is not clear that choosing the "public" software setting is synonymous with "agreeing to participate" in a particular research project. It is therefore arguably well within the purview of ethical review committees to ensure that bloggers are informed and willing participants in any study using even their "public" materials, lest abuses lead to the emergence of norms within the blogging community that forestall any future research participation.

And that is just for explicitly "public" blogs. Researchers accessing "private" postings would obviously have to obtain informed consent.

◆ Blogs as Research Tool

RESEARCHER-INITIATED METHODOLOGIES UTILIZING BLOGS

So far the discussion has focused on blogs as preexisting sources, but of course blogs can also be used to create or solicit material. The "sustained asynchronous focus group," in which researchers initiate their own topical blog to solicit postings or comments, and "directed journal entries," in which researchers identify a sample population and require them to keep a topical online diary, are two examples. Both approaches retain all the logistical advantages of blog sources (pre-typed, date-stamped, automatically archived and threaded responses, accessible asynchronously from any computer with an Internet connection) and may even encourage a similar degree of self-disclosure if respondents have had previous experience with blogging norms. Hessler et al. (2003), for example, noted that even though the daily journal entries in their study had been solicited,

> in the absence of direct questioning from the researchers, the respondents seemed to write what was on their minds. Theoretically, the behaviors and issues that got the most attention would be the most salient parts of the respondents' everyday lives. (pp. 122–123)

Another possible application would be in ethnographies or other qualitative approaches that require the researcher to go back to the research site to allow study participants to respond to the researcher's initial interpretations. Where the participants have Internet access, a blog could provide a vehicle for the researcher to present, and the participants to respond to and discuss (with each other as well as with the researchers), (re)interpretations through several iterations, each stage automatically documented, archived, and validated.

Blogs may also have a role in heuristic and narrative approaches, as the software lends itself to generating and interrogating autobiographical and collaborative texts. By keeping a journal online, one not only

gains the logistical advantages of instant archiving and convenient access, but one can also grant access to colleagues whose observations and queries in the comments section may facilitate the identification of confabulations, selective recall, or other manifestations of false consciousness, and so allow the researcher to dig deeper.

Finally, blog sampling techniques could be combined with traditional data gathering methodologies, that is, using Internet searches and snowball sampling within the blogging community to quickly identify a sample of, say, left-handed musicians, to whom one could then e-mail relevant surveys or requests for in-depth interviews.

PRIVATE RESEARCH BLOGS AS PROJECT MANAGEMENT TOOLS

Whatever the potential for identifying sources, the widest applicability of blog software in research may be for knowledge management, both for oneself and as a collaborative tool. Researchers dissatisfied with expensive, overly complex project management software may find the research blog the answer to their needs.

Most blogging software may be set to allow more than one individual to post, such that all members of the research team can be given access to the same private research blog. The software can be set to notify team members when any member posts to the blog, allowing everyone to stay in touch efficiently; indeed, Reichardt and Harder (2005) argue that because blogs are archived, searchable, and continually accessible to all team members, blog communication eliminates many of the frustrations of e-mail correspondence.

The daily research blog allows team members to report what they have accomplished each day; to back up their work on a remote (blog host) server; to pose questions, make suggestions, or debate issues with the rest of the team; and to track their progress toward projected targets.

Many researchers also find that blogging "forces them to write" as "the periodicity of the blog helps to establish a rhythm for writing" (Nardi, 2004, p. 17). This in turn facilitates analysis and theory construction, as blogs serve as "an 'outlet' for 'thinking by writing'" (Nardi, 2004, p. 17). As one posts one's thoughts to one's blog, and ideas begin to build one upon the other, the evolution of one's thinking becomes more explicit, and thereby facilitated (Efimova, 2003).

As each team member observes what everyone else is doing on a regular basis, it not only motivates everyone to meet their project commitments, but also generates a synergistic energy: The continual exchange of ideas and information between collaborators can turn the team blog into a permanent online brainstorming session. Since everyone's contribution is automatically date stamped and archived, it is easy to track and credit who came up with which ideas first, thus ensuring that credit is retained where due. Thus, the daily research blog encourages a high level of trust and commitment among team members (for the same reasons, the team blog can be an effective discussion and student project tool in seminar courses).

Similarly, the daily blog allows one to motivate and monitor graduate research assistants without constantly hovering at their shoulders. The graduate assistants are in turn mentored in the actual thinking and research processes of their supervisor through access to their privately shared blog.

PRIVATE RESEARCH BLOGS AS PERSONAL KNOWLEDGE MANAGEMENT TOOL

Even working alone, however, one can benefit from the research blog. Researchers use their blogs as their commonplace book to file online searches, citations, relevant quotations, conference notes, musings, Web bookmarks, charts, photographs, and so on (Efimova, 2003). The attraction of a private online diary is the convenience of accessibility from any computer, and that it is categorizable and searchable—in contrast to paper notes, which may be harder to keep organized, which are never with one when one needs them, or which simply go missing.

PUBLIC RESEARCH BLOGS AS NETWORKING AND DISSEMINATION TOOL

The greatest benefits are realized, however, when the research blog is public. In this case, one's methodological and analytical musings can generate useful feedback from colleagues, peers, graduate students, practitioners in the field, and so on. Indeed, it is not unusual for researchers faced with a particular conundrum to pose it in their blog, triggering a productive brainstorming session with input from across the Internet.

Such exchanges represent a "non-intrusive emergent collaboration" (Efimova, 2003) unique to the blogging community. Each researcher may begin by making notes on some esoteric subject for their *own* purposes, but by making them public, the notes are likely to quickly attract the attention of others working in the same specialty. As one notes breaking news, grant opportunities, links to relevant blogs, interesting quotes, and so on, in one's working blog, other academics may come to rely on these postings so that *they* may stay on top of developments in a field in which they have an interest but may not be as current. As these researchers become, first, regular readers and then either occasional or regular contributors (through the comment function), vast collegial networks—unconstrained by geography, funding, or status—can rapidly emerge. Indeed, using free sites such as Bloglines, one can track any number of colleagues' blogs from a single Web page, a more efficient networking tool than previously available.

Since blogs emphasize work in progress, one can track trends and be aware of significant developments long before they appear in published journals. In the future, establishing a virtual presence on the Web may become key to documenting the research process and so legitimizing the research product (Majava, 2005). Consequently, to not monitor relevant colleagues' blogs is to be left behind.

Of course, the objection can be raised that the self-published blog cannot replace the authority of a refereed journal, and there is obviously still a need for journal publication as the final "version of record," in contrast to the preliminary musings of the research blog. Nevertheless, blogs also undergo an informal peer review through the simple mechanism that readers only return to those blogs they find worthy. Readership is therefore one key measure of relevance, credibility, and utility; the other relevant measure is how often a particular blog is cited and linked to by fellow academics. Peer filtering quickly identifies emergent opinion leaders through citation and direct linking (Efimova, 2003), whereas unworthy blogs attract few readers and so languish in obscurity.

Indeed, researchers may "test" their ideas by posting them in their blogs: Worthy innovations may flow across the Internet to become commonly cited knowledge within hours (Efimova, 2003); flawed reasoning is likely to receive useful feedback in one's comment section, but excite little comment in others' blogs. Nardi's (2004) study of bloggers, for example, found that highly charged negative comments, such as an accusation of racism regarding one post, were quickly taken out

of public view and resolved privately through e-mail while the disputants continued to present a civil face in their public postings.

Naturally, one has to exercise reasonable care to ensure that postings neither betray confidential information nor slander colleagues (through citation out of context or too vitriolic a review), but as these norms are part of professional socialization, they should not prove overly burdensome.

Whenever one advocates taking research blogs public, the initial reaction from colleagues is inevitably the objection that someone might "steal" their ideas. This is exactly the opposite: Posting an idea to one's blog automatically date stamps and therefore documents one's priority. Posting to the Web is the quickest way to disseminate and establish credit for worthy ideas, as academics worldwide read and cite one's blog, or the blogs of others cite one's original posting. In contrast to valid ideas languishing unread in too specialized journals, blog postings may disseminate much more rapidly and to a more diverse academic community.

◆ Summary

I have tried to make a case in this chapter for the utility of blogging as both research tool and source material. Blogging makes supervising, coordinating, and documenting research activities easier; I know of no better tool for personal knowledge management, data transfer, and collaborative brainstorming. Blogging creates a "visible web of interpersonal trust" (Paquet, 2002) and is a more efficient networking tool than e-mail, the telephone, or sporadic contacts at conferences. Depending on the nature of one's research, blogs may also provide an unlimited source of anecdotal, life history, or narrative materials, or a similarly rich vein of exemplars from the visual or performing arts. At a minimum, blogs represent an emergent art form that engages a significant proportion of the population and so is deserving of attention.

◆ References

Bell, B. L. (2005). *The ethics of researching weblogs: Public or private spaces?* International Congress of Qualitative Inquiry, May 2005, University of Illinois, Urbana–Champaign.

Cohn, M. A., Mehl, M. R., & Pennebaker, J. W. (2004). Linguistic markers of psychological change surrounding September 11, 2001. *Psychological Science, 15*(10), 687–693.

Efimova, L. (2003). *Weblogs, research, and knowledge management.* Netherlands: Telematica Instituut. Retrieved June 10, 2005, from http://www.telin.nl/index.cfm?language=en&handle;=33962&type;=doc

Electronic Frontier Foundation. (2005). *How to blog safely (about work or anything else).* Retrieved May 2005 from http://www.eff.org/Privacy/Anonymity/blog-anonymously.php

Hessler, R. M., Downing, J., Beltz, C., Pelliccio A., Powell M., & Vale W. (2003). Qualitative research on adolescent risk using e-mail: A methodological assessment. *Qualitative Sociology, 26*(1), 111–124.

Majava, J. (2005). *Weblogs in research-based teaching.* LERU Seminar, Helsinki, March 22–23.

Nardi, B. A (2004, June). *Blogging: Past, present, and future.* Paper presented at the Institute for Software Research Forum, University of California, Irvine.

Paquet, S. (2002). *Personal knowledge publishing and its uses in research.* Retrieved June 10, 2005, from http://radio.weblogs.com/0110772/stories/2002/10/03/personalKnowledgePublishingAndItsUsesInResearch.html

PW Daily. (2006, December 11). *One-fifth of readers visit pub/author sites.* Retrieved January 1, 2007, from http://www.publishersweekly.com/article/CA6398771.html?nid=2286

Reichardt, R., & Harder, G. (2005). Weblogs: Their use and application in science and technology libraries. *Science & Technology Libraries, 25*(3), 105–116.

Rowse, D. (2004, December 6). How bloggers make money from Blogs. *Problogger.* Retrieved January 2007 from http://www.problogger.net/archives/2005/12/06/how-bloggers-make-money-from-blogs/

Runte, R. (2000). Why publish? A sociological analysis of motivation in youth avocational subcultures. *Broken Pencil, 1*(12), 12–15.

Van House, N. (2004). *Weblogs: Credibility and collaboration in an online world.* Paper prepared for CSCW Workshop on Trust, October 2004.

27

New Media

ZINES

Individual to Community

◆ Troy R. Lovata

Z ines and the processes behind their creation offer specific opportunities for qualitative research. They give people expressive control and, thus, are a pathway for applied research that empowers individuals in contrast to corporate-controlled media. Zines also allow individuals to interact with like-minded people and form communities based on their own terms and shared interests. These expressions of community are fodder for exploring informal and subjective viewpoints not always apparent in people's daily lives or the formalized channels of communication associated with their work.

◆ Definitions and Histories

Attempts can be made to identify or separate zines from other expressive genres based on physical form or intellectual content, but it is a fallacy to push any system of categorization too far. Zines have too long a history and have involved too many people to keep to strict guidelines about either morphology or subject matter. Zines have an essence, but they've ranged widely in practice. Thus, the actions of those who discover them, and then attempt to claim ownership, are often defied by the history of zines themselves. Consider William Safire's (1996) arbitrary decisions about how to properly pronounce and spell zine and the responses it provoked (Rowe, 2002). Or note the oft repeated (Austin & Gregg, 1993; Collins, 1999), but mistaken, claim that the form was first born in the punk rock scene of the 1980s. Zines have changed with shifts in production technology, and the topics at hand have followed changing politics and fashion. Recognizing diversity and history is a key to understanding not just what zines entail, but the form's power in different contexts. Some (Marr, 1999; Yorke, n.d.) have declared, after a particular topic or format falls from favor, that "zines are dead." Yet zines persist beyond individual creations and direct lines of influence because time passes and new generations find fertile ground in the act of creating them (Holdaway, 2004).

Zines, at their core, are self-published periodicals. Periodic, in this instance, must be understood generously. Many zines fail to last beyond a single issue. If they do make a run, they rarely keep to strict schedules. This is often due to the exigencies of self-publication that zines share with the genres they have roots in and helped promulgate—underground high school newspapers, fan fiction, literary small presses, underground comics, and mini-comics (Dodge, 1995). The process of self-publication both reflects and facilitates very specific ideologies and goals. It allows ownership in the face of a seemingly monolithic media environment. The process lets individuals bypass the tenuous world of money-making publishing and the demands of a profit motive (Dodge 1995). It allows individuals to free themselves from the confines of a job title, like author, artist, editor, proofreader, or publisher, and act as creators from start to finish. Yet this is not an individualistic enterprise. The underlying goal is not to separate oneself from the world at large. The act is one of community building, sharing oneself with an audience, and finding a cadre of like-minded readers to interact with. Self-publishing is still publishing, and the goal is to be read.

The periodic nature of zines facilitates a critical bridge between the individual and the community. Stephen Dumcombe (1997) finds that "the form of zines lies somewhere between a personal letter and a magazine" (p. 10). After reading a zine, many people are apt to respond by crafting something of their own. Zines often spur, even with infrequent publication schedules, contributors who send in material or create whole new zines in response (Stoneman, 2001). The constructive reply certainly includes the typical letter to the editor (see Figure 27.1). But it often extends further and builds stronger links between individuals when the response is creatively demanding and personally revealing (Wright, 2001). The cycle of reading and response is key in community building and one of a zine's most powerful attributes.

The word *zine* is derived from the fanzine, which itself is a contraction of fan magazine (Gunderloy & Janice, 1992). Fanzines are amateur publications—as opposed to paying, professional magazines—but they have a rich history (see Moskowitz 1974). They were originally produced by fans of science fiction writing (and later science fiction films, comic books, and television) in the golden pulp age of the 1930s and 1940s (Wright, 2001). These fans found missing any discussion of the writing they loved. Bruce Southard (1982) notes that "professionals in the fields of science and literary criticism tended to ignore the genre; its analysis was left to the fan" (p. 19). So fans created a medium in which they could share their own stories, offer critical commentary, create visual representations, discuss the nuances and rules of science fiction, and form

Letters

Dear Shovel Bum,
My husband and I were taking a scenic drive on the newly finished Highway 71 through Mena, Arkansas, when we stumbled across a quaint little watering hole called "The Fish Net". We stopped in to wet our whistle and were both impressed by the "Arkansas Martini". Could *Shovel Bum* acquire the recipe?

Thirstin' in Thurston County

Dear Thirstin',
The fine folks at the Fish Net were a bit reluctant to divulge their recipe at first. You see, Mena's in a dry county and you shouldn't have been able to get a drink with any kick whatsoever. But with a little prodding, the famed Arkansas Martini formula is ours!

The Arkansas Martini
8 oz. Moonshine, chilled
1 pickled egg
Strain moonshine for any "floaters".
Pour quickly into a Mason canning jar.
Serve with pickled egg for garnish.
Bon Appetit!

Dear Shovel Bum,
My buddy and I want you to settle an argument -- he thinks that CRM companies should provide the crew with all the tools they'll use on a project, including basics like trowels, tape measures, and even compasses. I think that a real shovel bum should already own all that stuff. What do you think?

Taking Pride

Dear Taking Pride,
I hope you put money on that argument, because that money is yours. Just like a mechanic owns his own wrenches and a tattoo artist owns his own guns, so should a shovel bum own his own dig kit. Sure, CRM companies are to be expected to provide tools like the transit, screens and shovels, the field vehicle, and so on, but a true shovel bum will not stray far from his dig kit. Isn't this common knowledge?!!

Figure 27.1   Letters Sent to *Shovel Bum,* Issue 5, a Zine About the Life of Contract Archaeology Workers and the Travails of Digging Up the Past

SOURCE: From de Boer, T. (2004). *Shovel bum: Comix of archaeological field life.* Walnut Creek, California: AltaMira Press. Used with permission of Trent de Boer.

communities of like-minded individuals. Fans turned to self-publication.

Over time, fanzines changed with larger social trends. The 1960s and 1970s saw countercultural pushes to break down, or at least defy, conformist and confining institutions. There was also a drive to build up new groupings in their place. Fanzines followed this trend along with the underground press (publications like *Ramparts, The Realist,* or *The Whole Earth Catalog*) and underground comics (like *ZAP!* and the works of Robert Crumb). Science-fiction fanzines themselves reflected burgeoning fan interest in newer series like *Star Trek* or *Dr. Who.* But fanzines also grew beyond science fiction to include music and movies—often in direct response to a perceived misrepresentation or lack of representation in the mainstream press for genres like slasher/horror films or punk rock music (Stoneman, 2001). Stephen Duncombe (1997) notes that the shifts from science fiction to music and movie fanzines was followed by moves away from fandom itself. Sometime early in the Reagan years, in which corporate power was further entrenched in American life, large numbers of people found a voice that had less to do with fan fawning and more of a connection to self- and scene-sufficiency. Zines were created with a focus on producing alternatives to the passive consumption of mass media. People began publishing about their personal lives as a whole—jobs, schooling, family, private actions, politics, even deviancies—instead of just their hobbies or pop culture tastes. Zines were allowed to tell stories from typical definitions of newsworthiness, such as the lives of infamous serial killers, to the most mundane activities of day-to-day existence, such as how office workers kill time. At this point, as they extended beyond fandom, zines came into their own.

The mid-1980s to mid-1990s saw zine popularity grow enormously. Traditional news outlets and social commentators started taking notice of the existence of zines. Librarians began asking how they could collect and catalog them (Dodge, 1995). Academics started using them as source material in the study of culture at large and began finding ways in which zine production could be incorporated into pedagogy. The popularity of zines rose so quickly that there appeared entire zines, like *FactSheet5*, that simply reviewed other zines.

The shift away from fandom (not a complete shift—fan-oriented publications still persist) ushered in a decade of zine production that matched the heights of science-fiction fanzine popularity. The connections weren't necessarily evolutionary—since there were few who had been tutored by golden age predecessors—but, rather, responses to similar methods of production and reactions to similar cultural currents. Science-fiction fans had previously faced a divide between hobbyists and those so firmly committed that they used the genre to shape and direct their lives. Bruce Southard (1982) recorded acronyms in use during this time, "fiawol" and "fijagh," that reflected a difference between those for whom, "fandom is a way of life" and for whom "fandom is just a goddamned hobby" (p. 26). The number of zines increasing, book deals were signed with mainstream publishers and television rights to works were acquired (Dodge, 1995). However, zine creators were becoming increasingly distrustful of popularity and the less-than-fully-committed hangers-on it attracted (Chu, 1997). It was after this point that a "zines are dead" undercurrent arose in response to perceived over saturation and co-option by commercial forces (Marr, 1999; Yorke, n.d.).

◆ Formats and Methods of Distribution

Falling popularity was also driven by the emergence of the Web and the rise in computer-mediated communication. The mid-1990s marked the beginning of dramatic growth in Internet users and new accessibility in the tools for Web page creation. People began to realize, and fantasize about, how powerful the Web could be in spurring alternative forms of communication. The e-zine and webzine were envisioned as a way to leave behind traditional, paperbound forms (Wright, 2001). But along the way something happened to Web-mediated production that seems to have run counter to the self-published and community-driven aspects of zines. So many people could use the Web that most had no connection to the roots of zines. The Web generated its own forms and terminologies, like webcams and blogging, and Web users did not affiliate themselves with e-zines. The essence of a zine was there, but the name was not. At the same time the dot-com collapse soured many to idealistic uses of the Web. Web pages became standardized, commercialized, and market driven (McCloud, 2000). E-zines were eschewed from both sides and simply never reached the mass popularity and recognition that paper zines had commanded a few years earlier. E-zines do persist. But, nowadays, the Web is used primarily in the assistance of their paper counterparts. They have a curatorial role in sites like grrrlzines.net or zinebook.com. They collect histories and information about zines rather than act as distribution.

Yet concerns about form and popularity help define zines in as much as content. They show why, even after a change in popularity, Matt Holdaway (2004) finds the "lack of mainstream attention created a fresh, new, open environment" in which "many zine publishers have returned to almost-forgotten printing methods" (p. 3). Most people envision zines as only a stapled set of photocopied pages that use cut-and-paste layout to juxtapose images and text (see Figures 27.2 and 27.3).

Figure 27.2 *Upward Bound,* a Literary Zine Created by High School Students Participating in a College Preparatory Class Run by the University of New Mexico

SOURCE: Used with the permission of Maxine Roush Marks.

The proliferation of photocopiers that began in the 1980s is credited with fomenting zine popularity as much as their content (Dodge, 1995). Zines once relied on now forgotten, cumbersome, and restrictive technologies like mimeographs, hectographs, and ditto. Cost was a major factor in production runs and, thus, hindered the ability of people to widely distribute their works and reach like-minded individuals. Bruce Southard (1982) has recorded fanzine subgenres, like the "cardzine" (a zine printed on a postcard) and "carbonzine" (a zine created by typing on carbon paper, which, of course, limited a run to three or four copies), that were early, creative attempts to affordably duplicate and distribute one's work (p. 7).

Photocopying changed the process dramatically. It is relatively affordable and copiers are widely distributed. Photocopying allowed the zine to blossom beyond text-based forms. Images have been a cost-based bane to publishing since the beginning of printing. Early zines and fanzines used images, but they also faced their expenses. However, for all these restrictions images are undeniably powerful tools in critical commentary. Alone they are stockpiled and used as memes with which people approach new ideas and new situations (Greenblatt, 1991). In concert with text they allow for multiple readings and the reforming of meaning within a single panel or page (McCloud, 1993). The concept of literacy has given way to the recognition of multiple literacies, and we live in a world not just saturated with images, but in which people skillfully and routinely use images as currency (Faigley, George, Palchick, & Selfe, 2004). Zines, willfully or by circumstance operating at the economic fringes, have thrived on the photocopier's ability to cheaply scavenge, reformat, and recontextualize found images. At the same time, wholly original images, including comics and mini-comics, are so distributable because the photocopier allows image quality just good enough for do-it-yourself publication.

Flatbed scanners have come to rival the photocopier in its ability to collect and manipulate individual images, and inkjet printers enable computer owners to produce high-quality originals. The photocopier is replaceable, but the standards it set for distribution and image acquisition are not. E-zines may have run their course at the turn of this century as much as carbon copies 30 years previous, but other means of production are certainly yet untapped or waiting to be retapped in the process of reaching the photocopier standard. History shows zines to be a series of form-dependent undertakings with tangible breaks between technologies and those who implement them. The "zines are dead" calls of the likes of John Marr (1999) and Chris Yorke (n.d.) came at such a juncture. But zines did not die—other individuals found them to be fertile ground, discovered in them a chance to constitute new social relations, and began to deploy both new and old forms of production. Thus, the form of self-publication, as much as the factors driving the desire to self-publish, defines zines.

◆ *Youth and Education*

The librarian's attempt to collect and preserve zines (e.g., Perris, 2004) and the historian's charting of their trajectory (e.g., Moskowitz, 1974) have been most valuable undertakings. The history and definitions herein are possible because of such work. But zines can also offer much to a wider and more diverse array of scholars. Zines have been successfully used in qualitative research, especially as an applied research tool. Some have turned to zines in contexts that deal with the empowerment and education of youth.

Youths and students are often skilled at asking "why" and are more open to building alternative networks with each other than adults entrenched in their thinking and encumbered by monetary responsibility. Zines are often irreverent in title and content and firmly connected to the underground and the subversiveness of the young (Dodge, 1995). Zines are often associated with youth even when their creators have moved well into adulthood and have other media outlets opened to them (Lovata, 2004). Thus, zines have a role in applied research that addresses youth.

Anthropologist Julie Chu (1997) has produced a vivid picture of how youths use zines as a form of claiming their place within the media environment. Her work shows how zines can make things relevant and make things happen for youth. When the young are in charge, as opposed to being catered to by adults, they produce tangibly different works than expected. Julie Chu (1997) notes that "the media as an environment for youths looks tremendously different and *richer* when zine publisher's own perceptions are center stage" (p. 83). She perceptively asks not how one generation can dictate to the next, but "how *we* [as adults and social scientists] can involve *ourselves* in the projects young people are initiating on their own" (pp. 82–83). Hence, she calls for an applied research that facilitates, not just works upon, youth.

Educators and those interested in curriculum development have learned the value of the projects Julie Chu espouses. The zine *Upward Bound* (Figures 27.2 and 27.3) was created by ninth-grade high school students from a college preparatory summer class offered by the University of New Mexico. The teacher behind the publication, Maxine Roush Marks, was given the leeway to incorporate zines into the syllabus and saw the value of self-publication.

The course had goals of empowering high school students through their literacy— primarily poetry and prose—and, as the poem in Figure 27.3 reflects, the students found an individual and relevant voice in their writings. A similar voice was reflected in their images and design, which included original drawings (of fantasy animals), sketches of wider culture motifs they had connected with (such as *Manga* characters), original photographs (of their city and each other), and appropriated and recontextualized images (like the wrapper from a set of the television series *M*A*S*H* trading cards).

The production of a physical and enduring product was at the core of the curriculum. The teacher's role included the traditional duties of assigning and correcting the student's writing, but in relation to the zine itself she acted more as a facilitator than lead editor. Although few beyond those in the class and their friends and family will ever see the zine, *Upward Bound* offered a public forum not found in the typical secondary-level essay read only by those who've assigned it. Students were pushed toward refinement because they knew they would be in the public eye. They also gained a personal foothold in the media environment.

◆ Work, an Adult Undertaking

Zines also have a role in qualitative research that continues beyond youth or the claiming of an individual voice. Zines can reflect upon one of the most adult undertakings of all—work. Publications focusing on work can serve as primary data in sociological or anthropological attempts to take the pulse of a community. Zines have been a place for expressing informal views about work and for people to interact based on shared work experiences. How people are able to discuss their work tells much about how a field operates and how people attempt to fulfill basic social responsibilities. Zines offer a view into groupings that broach traditional

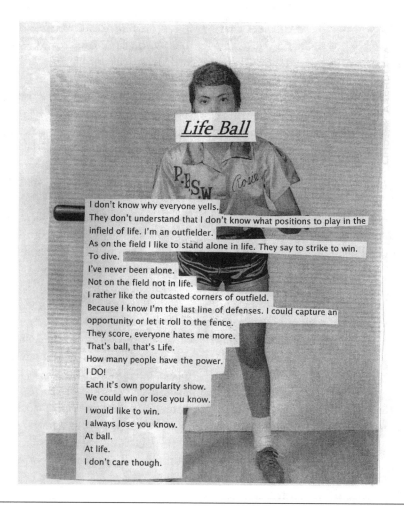

Figure 27.3 A Page From *Upward Bound*. This zine, created in 2004, exhibits what could be labeled as classic zine attributes: cut-and-paste layout, sampled images, photocopy reproduction, and personalized writing.

SOURCE: Used with the permission of Maxine Roush Marks.

and traditionally accessible assemblages of workers based on things like geographic boundaries or formal communication.

When zines shifted away from fandom, many came to focus on work. Employment simply encompasses too much of most people's lives to fall outside the introspection that zines offer (Duncombe, 1997). Publications like *Temp Slave,* produced by the burgeoning pool of temporary workers, and *Dishwasher,* which followed one man's goal to wash dishes, were popular in the 1990s (Duncombe, 1997). They brought

a sense of community into the socially isolated workplace and made the process of earning a living understandable, if not palatable. Stephen Duncombe (1997) explains something of this sentiment when he posits:

Between the cracks of the system new— and very old—ideas and ideals of what work should be emerge. . . . Zines are a medium through which to express these new ideals, but, more important, they are actual embodiments of a type of work and creation that runs counter to the norm within our capitalist society. (p. 94)

The zine *Shovel Bum* (Figures 27.1, 27.4, and 27.5) is a clear example of how work generates self-publication and how scholars can fruitfully approach work based on this genre.

Shovel Bum began in 1997 when Trent de Boer, a contract archaeologist then working in Arkansas, began sharing his experiences with friends and family who had questions about his relatively unique mode of employment. The moniker "shovel bum" refers to skilled, but primarily itinerant, workers who actually move dirt, generate data, and write field reports, but don't always have a say in what questions about the past are worth pursuing. Sketches about how work affected Trent's life—how he talked, what he ate, how he dressed, who he met, where he slept—were collected from his field notebook, redrawn, photocopied, and distributed through direct contact.

Figure 27.4 The Introduction to the First Issue of Trent de Boer's *Shovel Bum*. The zine began with the true story of a single contract archaeologist, but others in the field soon sent in their own stories and comics. Subsequent issues have been built around a community of workers and offered a multivocal account of the work of uncovering the past.

SOURCE: From de Boer, T. (2004). *Shovel bum: Comix of archaeological field life*. Walnut Creek, California: AltaMira Press. Used with permission of Trent de Boer.

Figure 27.5   The Cover of *Shovel Bum,* Issue 3, the "Egg Issue." Thematic issues, which collect a variety of perspectives on single topic, have become the norm for this zine as more people contribute.

SOURCE: From de Boer, T. (2004). *Shovel bum: Comix of archaeological field life.* Walnut Creek, California: AltaMira Press. Used with permission of Trent de Boer.

Copies of the comic-based zine were slowly traded among an ever widening network. Other archaeologists noted that he was presenting a little recorded, but informally mentioned, narrative that mirrored their own lives. They began comparing their experiences to Trent's, and some felt compelled to respond with pictures and words. With each new issue something more about the life of an archaeologist was discussed, more people became involved, and more stories were shared. Archaeologists used region overlap, study of similar sets of artifacts, or shared teachers to network. They now use *Shovel Bum* to form relationships based on

the fact that simply doing archaeology had shaped their daily lives. People across the field came to know each other through a discussion of work itself and the realization that doing archaeology as a job not only changes one's perspective about the past, but one's lifestyle.

Eight years on, eight issues have appeared. In 2004 they were collected into a book by academic publisher AltaMira Press (de Boer, 2004). This anthology included a foreword and afterword that began to examine the role of *Shovel Bum* within the discipline of archaeology itself, and in the spring of 2005, it formed the basis for a symposium on comic book and cartoon archaeology at the Society for American Archaeology's 70th Annual Meeting (Society for American Archaeology, 2004). *Shovel Bum* functions as a device to form community—a role many other zines have played—but it also allows the discipline of archaeology itself to take a reflexive turn and examine how it operates.

Archaeologists like Ian Hodder (1995) noted a decade ago that writing within their field leaves out significant descriptions of what happened in the process of uncovering the past. The last hundred years has witnessed a trend toward increasingly formalized writing—away from a first-person narrative of the context of discovery. Moreover, the structure of archaeological communication tends to neglect the collective nature of research—that numerous individuals contributed to the collection and interpretation of stories about the past.

Authorship is cited and credit is given primarily to the individuals in charge. The laborers who take shovels in hand are often unnamed and lack the opportunity, in formal and academic discourse, to provide context, describe what it was like to uncover evidence, articulate what choices they made in their labors, or even comment upon what it meant to be ordered to dig. Archaeologists, though they are a visual lot, also tend to discount the role of visual communication within their field (Lovata, 2000, 2004). The discipline has created a formalized mask that has caused archaeologists like Bill Sillar (1992) to make a plea for funny images that expose incongruities in our ideas about the past and open up the field to self-reflection.

Shovel Bum answered Bill Sillar's (1992) call. It helped the discipline take an introspective turn and lets it recognize the place of the archaeology worker. It is certainly not the first or only attempt at this, but it has been successful in formalizing observations about work. *Shovel Bum* helped interject images into the discussion and the images

themselves, sometimes crude comics and cartoons (Figure 27.4), provide a necessary contrast to objective communications. Moreover, the zine is rife with the kind of context that dates it—names and nicknames of specific people, makes of field vehicles, descriptions of the food workers eat, and accounts of the clothes archaeologists wear. This datable context, which lets the material eventually become out of date, is a good thing. It provides a record that keeps statements about the discipline from seeming self-evident, timeless, and beyond history because it eschews neutral, universal, or impersonal terms. *Shovel Bum*, through its own small community, attempts to offer validity to the work of its creators. *Shovel Bum*, in its own small way, is living up to Stephen Duncombe's (1997) vision of zines as an embodiment of what work should be.

◆ Future Directions and Challenges

Zines can serve as a fruitful foundation for many diverse types of qualitative scholarship. The proceeding examples are but two of the many paths such research may take. However, by no means should either they or the definitions and histories of zines contained herein be considered exhaustive. More historical accounts are needed. Consider that in the late 1990s Julie Chu (1997) estimated there were between 10,000 and 50,000 zines printed. These sheer numbers should serve as a cautionary tale for anyone intending to use them in their research. The physical problems facing those hoping to find, collect, and organize zines are all too obvious. Yet perhaps the more significant challenges are the restraints researchers must place on themselves. Zines do form communities and do have tangible impacts, but it is easy to overestimate any particular publication. Zines are fleeting, and any claims about their function must provide a detailed context that clearly spells out their spread, influence, and limitations. Self-publishing often lets the ego run unfettered—this is one reason this genre offers such clear insights into their creators. But the researcher has to check how far any particular zine has actually reached. Even the most basic of zine histories show as many breaks between creators as connections, and the dynamic nature of zines must set the stage for any critical examination.

◆ References

Austin, S. B., & Gregg, P. (1993). A freak among freaks: The zine scene. In A. Stein (Ed.), *Sisters, sexperts, queers: Beyond the lesbian nation* (pp. 81–95). New York: Penguin Books.

Chu, J. (1997). Navigating the media environment: How youth claim a place through zines. *Social Justice, 24*(3), 71–85.

Collins, D. (1999). "No experts: guaranteed!" Do-it-yourself sex radicalism and the production of the lesbian zine "Brat Attack." *Signs: Journal of Women in Culture and Society, 25*(1), 65–89.

de Boer, T. (2004). *Shovel bum: Comix of archaeological field life.* Walnut Creek, CA: AltaMira Press.

Dodge, C. (1995). Zines and libraries: Pushing the boundaries. *Wilson Library Bulletin, 69*(9), 26–30.

Duncombe, S. (1997). *Notes from underground: Zines and the politics of alternative culture.* London: Verso.

Faigley, L., George, D., Palchick, A., & Selfe, C. (2004). *Picturing texts.* New York: W. W. Norton and Company.

Greenblatt, S. (1991). *Marvelous possessions.* Chicago: University of Chicago Press.

Gunderloy, M., & Janice, C. G. (1992). *The world of zines: A guide to the independent magazine revolution.* New York: Penguin Books.

Hodder, I. (1995). *Theory and practice in archaeology.* London: Routledge.

Holdaway, M. (2004). *A student's guide on what a zine is and tips on how to make one* (Version 2.0). Retrieved January 30, 2005, from http://grrrlzines.net/writing/student%20zine%20guide.pdf

Lovata, T. (2000). *An exploration of archaeological presentation: People and the domestic dog on the great plains of North America.* Unpublished doctoral dissertation, The University of Texas, Austin.

Lovata, T. (2004). Putting Shovel Bum in context: Why a view from the shovel handle matters. In T. de Boer (Ed.), *Shovel Bum: Comix of archaeological field life* (pp. 115–127). Walnut Creek, CA: AltaMira Press.

Marr, J. (1999). Zines are dead. *Bad Subjects, 46.* Retrieved January 30, 2005, from http://www.eserver.org/bs/46/marr.html?source=zinebook

McCloud, S. (1993). *Understanding comics: The invisible art.* New York: Harper Perennial.

McCloud, S. (2000). *Reinventing comics.* New York: Perennial Currents.

Moskowitz, S. (1974). *Immortal storm: A history of science-fiction fandom.* Westport, CT: Hyperion Press.

Perris, K. (2004). *Unearthing the underground: A comparative study of zines in libraries.* Unpublished master's thesis, London Metropolitan University, England.

Rowe, C. (2002). Zeens and mags. *The Zine & E-zine Resource Guide.* Retrieved January 30, 2005, from http://www.zinebook.com/resource/safire.html

Society for American Archaeology. (2004). Society for American Archaeology, 70th Annual Meeting, March 30–April 3, 2005, Salt Lake City, Utah. *Preliminary Program of Annual Meeting of the Society for American Archaeology, 9*(1), 20.

Safire, W. (1996, November 10). On language: Take the DARE. *New York Times Magazine, 32,* 3.

Sillar, B. (1992). Digging for a laugh: Archaeology and humor. *Archaeological Review From Cambridge, 11*(2), 203–211.

Southard, B. (1982). The language of science-fiction fan magazines. *American Speech, 57*(1), 19–31.

Stoneman, P. (2001). *Fanzines: Their production, culture, and future.* Unpublished master's thesis, University of Stirling, Scotland.

Wright, F. A. (2001). *From zines to ezines: Electronic publishing and the literary underground.* Unpublished doctoral dissertation, Kent State University, Ohio.

Yorke, C. (n.d.). Zines are dead: The six deadly sins that killed zinery. *Broken Pencil, 12.* Retrieved January 30, 2005, from http://www.brokenpencil.com/features/feature.php?featureid=46

28

New Media

RADIO IN/FOR RESEARCH

Creating Knowledge Waves

◆ Christine McKenzie

R adio was the first art form widely accessible to the masses. It connected people over extended geographic areas and allowed them to share experiences and create cultural reference points.

Since radio's inception in North America in 1895, there has been controversy over who has access to creating and disseminating information using this technology. Initially its use was limited to meeting state and corporate interests, despite the fact that most early development of radio technology happened through the experimentation of amateurs. In the early days radio was a "force for popular representation and mobilization . . . and the articulation and negotiation of crucial economic and social policies" (Kidd, 1992, p. 99). By 1906, competition among world governments made it necessary to assign broadcast frequencies, which had the effect of legalizing the dominance that existing imperial powers had over the airwaves.

Tensions between amateurs and state/corporate interests over the use of airwaves mounted over time. In 1927, amateurs made testimony to the U.S. Congress, arguing that the people were the rightful owners of the radio waves. Despite their plea, the Radio Act was imposed requiring amateurs to hold broadcasting licenses (Kidd, 1992). Similarly, throughout the world, grassroots communities have struggled for access and control of the radio waves (Reeves, 1993). Although radio is ideal for knowledge creation, the power struggles over whose knowledge is developed through the airwaves continues to be a central issue.

Still, radio holds many possibilities within the realm of social science research. As an arts-related approach, the medium of radio enables innovation, both artistically and in terms of what constitutes research. Research has been conceptualized as "a careful or diligent search . . . the collection of information about a particular subject . . . examination aimed at the discovery of new knowledge" (*Webster's New Explorer Dictionary and Thesaurus*, 1999, p. 447). For the purposes of this writing, I consider radio as integral to both sending and receiving information, as well as to connecting those participating in the process of discovering or creating (new) knowledge. Therefore, for radio to have a role in/for research, it must be used as a tool in the discovery or creation of new knowledge. In this way only radio broadcasters or educators using radio as part of a process of critical inquiry are considered radio researchers.

To illustrate how radio may be a tool in/for research I draw an example from my work using radio in participatory action research in Nicaragua. Through this case I outline how radio is an ideal form for processes of inquiry and action using the arts. I also illustrate the art forms embedded in radio that surface ways of knowing and a few of the technical and structural elements associated with radio broadcasting. I then outline radio as a means to transfer knowledge, enable learning, and facilitate participation in research. Finally, I explore what I see as the future possibilities for radio waves to deepen and challenge processes for knowledge creation and dissemination.

◆ Methodologies of Radio in/for Research

INQUIRY AND ACTION: RADIO SURFACING WAYS OF KNOWING/BEING

As a methodology, radio production can become an act of co-construction, rupturing the barrier between audience and broadcasters if the production process is inclusive to community members beyond the experts normally involved. Using such a process, communication is not just the transmission of ideas but also a process of constructing meaning together (Rahim, 1994; Rosas in Rodriguez, 2003). More specifically, radio produces knowledge as participants who are producing the communications use their way of seeing things, their worldviews—their ideologies—to construct meanings (Rahim, 1994). This gives both producer and receiver a role in the "creation of the represented world" (Folch-Serra, 1990).

Example: Popular Communications in Nicaragua

The CAMP-Lab project, named after the community-based Coastal Area Monitoring of natural resources located on the Atlantic Coast of Nicaragua, involved working with members of fishing communities to collectively produce a weekly broadcast. The work was modeled after the popular communication tradition, which uses the word "popular" in the Latin American sense meaning coming from and working for the interests of the (everyday) people. In this case local interests were to manage the use of natural resources, such as fish and forests, and protect against their exploitation in order to maintain the livelihood and way of life for the majority of the area's population.

Using radio as a form of popular communication is part of a broader practice of popular education, which challenges the dominant idea that life and research are two separate things (Jara, 1997). Specifically, popular education is

> carried out with a political vision that sees women and men at the community and grassroots level as the primary agents for social change. It equips people to define their own struggles and have their voices heard. It involves a process whereby a group collectively analyses its problems and works collectively to solve them, including identifying the resources and skills they need. Popular education develops within this process of consciousness of and

commitment to the interests of the most marginalized. (Nadeau, 1996, p. 4)

This methodology has roots in the work of Paulo Freire (1970) and is conceptualized through the spiral model, depicting a fluid interaction between action and reflection, as seen in Figure 28.1.

The radio initiative in Nicaragua was part of a larger research and action process that came about as an outside researcher teamed up with local community members to pose questions and engage in dialogue about the area's natural resource and land claims issues.

This was a method of participatory action research (PAR) that challenged the hierarchical power relationships between the "researcher" and the "researched" to

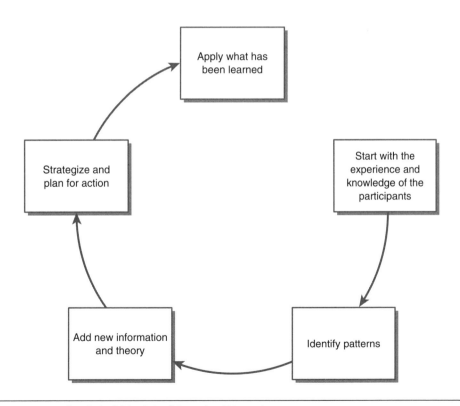

Figure 28.1 The Spiral Model of Popular Education

create an alternate research paradigm. As a form of research, PAR blurs the distinctions between education, activism, and social science research, engaging research participants in the constant praxis of action and reflection (Fals-Borda, 1991; Hall, 1994). The intention was to develop a critical understanding (in this case of local and foreign involvement in natural resources) so we could take action and transform the inequities.

As the PAR process took shape and momentum grew, participants formed a project through the support of the International Development Research Centre (IDRC) and a local research center, the Centre for the Documentation and Investigation of the Atlantic Coast (CIDCA). To broaden participation, community members requested assistance to start a radio program that would enable a larger number of people to shape and participate in the dialogue and research process. I became involved when I assisted with initiating the radio program with community members. Together we used the art form of radio to explore opinions and develop new understandings about the situation of natural resources in the region.

A radio committee was formed to guide the process. The committee brainstormed generative themes related to natural resource management that would resonate with others, and consulted with community members through both formal and informal meetings. The themes became the focus of popular education activities (such as brainstorming through theatre role plays, drawing, or singing) that engaged more community members in posing further questions and solutions. This dialogue and its art forms produced the content of the radio programs. The content drew on the three main art components that can be utilized in radio in/for research: music, spoken word, and drama.

◆ Art Component: Surfacing Ways of Knowing in Radio in/for Research

MUSIC

Music was central to the radio programming, as it communicated ideas and culture. This is true particularly on community radio where local and diverse programmers play a wide range of music (Kidd, 1992). Music draws people together to engage critical thought, expression, and memory (Gardner, 1983). The meaning and knowledge contained in music are culturally situated and historically specific and, as with other art forms, have a form and message that are highly contextual and, usually, accessible.

SPOKEN WORD

We most often used spoken word, which for radio comes in the form of interviews, news commentary, or poetry, that draws on the community's more traditional forms of spoken word such as storytelling, oral history, and testimony. Commentary, such as monologue or conversation between announcers and poetry, was often coupled with background music. Together they conveyed a story using voice(s) as the instrument to portray metaphors and symbols. On our show *Living in Progress* the use of rhythm in poetry was used to persuade the listener to continue listening. The poems were also appealing because they were written by local people and expressed local views.

Storytelling similarly drew people in, connecting listeners to one another as we learned and taught from everyday experiences (Gardner, 1983; Kavanagh, 1998; Levanthal & Green, 2002). Some of the storytelling we used was oral history or testimony, often conveyed through an interview by someone who participated in or observed significant historical events, bearing oral witness by sharing their perspectives (Gluck & Patai, 1991; Randall, 1985).

Some of the drawbacks we experienced were that any form of spoken word conveyed over radio lost some of its impact as the audience missed out on the storytellers' energy and visual cues. Also, listeners did not always necessarily share the culturally situated meanings.

DRAMA

Through the radio program we also used sociodramas as a form of collective knowledge creation. Sociodramas are produced through dialogue with nonprofessional actors who explore questions and social issues, presenting alternative ways to consider and solve problems. Whereas radio dramas are scripted and didactic, sociodramas aim to have listeners think critically and act for social change (Sternberg & Garcia Praege, 1990).

Radio soap operas can also facilitate the discovery of knowledge, as in the case of the exchange with Bolivian communicators' indigenous communities of Atikamekw, Montagnais, and Cree. Together they effectively used radio soap operas as a tool for inquiry and social change with one another, combining "the creative imagination of drama with the intimacy of radio to create programs dealing with a wide range of social, political, historical and cultural themes" (Nutaaq, 2005).

Using these forms through a dialogical process, community members produced the radio program as a means to explore issues related to natural resource management in the region, such as cutting of trees for export or local cattle farming, shrimp farming, sand mining, trawling for fish, water quality, and land claims issues. Listeners became part of the dialogue as they responded and became integral to the process of questioning, hypothesizing, and acting, and critical consciousness continued to rise.

◆ Technical and Structural Aspects of Radio Broadcasting

For us, radio was a vehicle that enabled a culturally relevant and critical learning exchange through the dialogue that took place over the airwaves and as we produced the program together. Technology created the space to search for common ground and solutions to ensure the livelihood of local indigenous people. Given that technology shapes what is possible, it is important to consider the mechanisms of broadcast.

In this program we used a regular FM-band radio broadcast, which has the strongest signal if multiple signals appeared on the same frequency. This gives it a higher reliability than an AM band, and for this reason, it is considered the standard in broadcasting. More specifically, our program was broadcast by a micro-powered station, which, if unlicensed, is known as a "pirate radio" station. In either case these stations usually operate at frequencies of less than 100 watts. Regulatory bodies claim this is trespassing on other signals whereas groups such as Prometheus Radio defend pirate radio on the grounds that "access to communications for all citizens is at the heart of a democratic society" (*Prometheus Radio*, n.d.). Micro-powered broadcasters represent the full range of the political spectrum but commonly provide an intimate address between neighbors (Rodriguez, 2001).

Our broadcast was part of a campus-community radio station network, funded by a local indigenous university and operated by student groups with a few paid staff. This type of station offered quasi-professional programming, but broadcasters were frequently volunteers from local community grassroots or citizen groups without formal training in sound editing or other production skills. This made our program much more accessible and created a means by which broadcasters and listeners from the same community shared identity and common values. This also overlapped with indigenous and ethnic community radio stations regarding setup to maintain cultural spaces for groups not adequately represented in other forms of media.

The station was set up by the local indigenous university as part of the project to promote and celebrate the cultural diversity of the region and to work toward autonomy (*University of the Autonomous Regions of the Caribbean Coast of Nicaragua*, n.d.). The program was developed by members of the Miskito and Creole communities to explore the use of natural resources and land tenure, which are the basis of the communities' livelihoods. Indigenous radio in Latin America has transformed the use of radio, not only to transmit indigenous languages but also to meet cultural needs. It is beginning to transform the radio to "transmit greetings, to facilitate community gatherings, to educate and finally to account for diversity and power it recreates" (Vilar & Villegas, 1988, p. 133).

In our case, although the frequency was not strong as in other rural settings, the radio became a sort of a community telephone between geographically isolated areas since access to other means of communication was limited. For these reasons radio is the most widespread communication tool throughout the world and is considered the ideal medium for change (Gumucio Dagron, 2002). In this way, regardless of the radio technology used, it is distinct from other media for communication because it is generally affordable and easy to use and can, therefore, reach large numbers of people in ways that other media cannot.

Through these channels radio is a widely accessed medium and has a unique ephemeral quality that weaves into the daily fabric of the listeners' lives, allowing them to imagine and create concurrent stories and ideas as they listen. This makes radio quite different from other mass media communication forms such as the often frenetic and mesmerizing visual experience of video or television or written word that requires viewers' or readers' fixed attention.

As an arts-related methodology, radio has the potential not only to reach broader audiences than other media but also to engage listeners and producers in constructing different ways of knowing by virtue of these unique qualities.

◆ Facilitating Participation in Research: Radio as a Tool for Outreach

The second methodology within radio in/for research is participatory communications, which is conceptualized as a move from informing or persuading people to address a common problem to bring about change within a community. This methodology engages community members in radio production and derives from the trend in international development work to involve and empower communities instead of imposing projects upon them (Deza, 1994; Servaes, 2001). However, this methodology emerges from the dominant paradigm in which experts define what community subjects and which community members should participate in producing over the radio and how they should go about producing these messages. In this way this process is distinct from popular communications in which local grassroots interests drive the program's form, content, and production process.

Participatory communications follows the stages of developing a research relationship with a local community and negotiating a mandate, problem identification or goal setting, planning, intervention and implementation, integrating, monitoring, evaluation and assessment and utilization of results (Bessette, 2001).

Example: Banana Farmers in Uganda

Banana farmers in Uganda were asked to participate in radio production in an effort to help farmers improve their yield. This methodology was helpful in introducing farmers to new technologies and encouraging them to experiment with their adoption, as well as fostering farmer-to-farmer training with the help of communication tools developed in a participatory manner (Odoi in Bessette, 2005).

By nature of its methodology, participatory communications reinforce hegemony or dominant ways of knowing because, although the focus of strategies is two-way interaction with information flowing from the top (institutions and development experts) down and the bottom (communities) up, the message is controlled by the information source (Riaño, 1994).

Through this format listeners receive information or knowledge through an art form. Although they may create their own interpretation of the broadcast they receive, they are not engaged as artists or cocreators of the original message itself or invited to engage in dialogue or reflection about what they have heard.

KNOWLEDGE TRANSFER: RADIO AS A WAY TO SHARE INFORMATION

The third means by which radio can be used in/for research is to share information didactically, in the case where a researcher has knowledge to share. Although many names have been assigned to methodologies that use radio in this way, *social communications* is

one that is widely used. Social communications messages originate from outside a community and encourage individuals to change their current practices, actively support a program, and mobilize the community for (future) mass campaigns. These cases are most often documented in "development communications" (Riaño, 1994).

Example: Hamari Awaz (Our Voice) in Pakistan Faisalabad

The program *Hamari Awaz (Our Voice)* at Radio Pakistan Faisalabad has the objective of promoting changes in attitudes and social behavior and helping communities identify sustainable opportunities and development solutions that are within their reach (Zia, 2003). Zia notes *Hamari Awaz* aired voter education programs for women to show the different problems women faced, to provide them with accurate information, and to give solutions to their problems, using clear language. The educational methodology used radio listening groups. Groups comprised of 15–20 members from each of eight union councils met with a coordinator who facilitated the group and raised issues for discussion based on the program content. Feedback questionnaires from the group discussions were passed on to the radio programmers at *Hamari Awaz*. In this way audience perceptions were central to informing how future programming was conducted, while the women were not directly producing the content themselves (Zia, 2003).

ENABLING LEARNING: RADIO AS NONFORMAL EDUCATION

The final methodology within radio in/for research illustrates another way that radio has related to research and knowledge creation as it helps participants reflect on and digest the information that they hear over the airwaves. In this way research findings shared over the radio waves take a deeper hold in affecting opinions and social change. At times this type of process takes on the form of "distance learning," where students follow along individually from home with a lesson being taught by a teacher over the radio.

In other cases radio broadcasts have facilitated group learning using radio listening groups, which adapts the Swedish pedagogical tradition of study circles where students follow a lesson broadcast over the radio and together reflect on what they understood. Although there is much strength to this type of methodology for information and learning, it has been criticized for failing to critique structural issues and local norms (Fraser & Restrepo-Estrada, 1998).

Example: Accion Cultural Popular (Popular Cultural Action) in Colombia

In Colombia, Radio Sutatenza established the program *Accion Cultural Popular*, which provided basic literacy skills for those living in the rural Andean region from 1947 until 1990. This basic education took place as a 4-month course in which students met in one another's homes to listen to the daily 30-minute broadcast lessons, with past student mentors who helped guide the learning. This model of learning has been followed throughout Latin America (Eshgh, Hoxeng, Provenzano, & Casals 1988). The vision of Father José Salcedo, "The Invisible Professor," became much more than a way to broadcast to his parish but also for listeners to explore the principles of health, alphabet, numbers, work, and spirituality (Communications Initiative, n.d.).

◆ Future Directions for Radio in/for Research and New Technologies

Similar to its beginnings, the possibilities for radio in/for research are shaped by the existing and potential technology. In this regard there are as many directions for the future of radio in/for research as there are curious minds interested in engaging in creative inquiry. In the following section I outline the recent technological developments that impact radio usage and then consider both how these innovations are being utilized and how they could be further developed for radio in/for research.

Radio and related technologies are developing at an ever-increasing speed, making new innovation for radio in/for research possible through both new technologies and the combination of technologies. For example, satellite technology has been used to upgrade or complement many shortwave broadcasts due to the fact that it is less vulnerable to atmospheric conditions and radio signals can therefore reach further distances.

Perhaps more significant is the advent of the Internet, which has enabled live-streamed radio. According to Lee (1998) it was in 1994 that radio broadcasting really took off, as a result of the introduction of RealAudio free streaming software. The development of free radio streaming on the Internet began with Internet Talk Radio, the first radio station developed by the Internet Multicasting Service (IMS) (Ginsburg, 1997). Quickly afterward other Internet broadcasters such as broadcast.com and net.radio were established by entrepreneurs, expanding the field (Alexander in Sahney & Lee, 2005). Since then an even greater capability for information sharing via radio and Internet technology has taken place thanks to the music file sharing system Napster, which "let the genie out of the bag" in terms of many people accessing information using the Internet (Sahney & Lee, 2005). Still new opportunities present themselves with Internet-enabled cellular phones and handheld devices such as the Blackberry (Ghini, Pau, Roccettti, Salomoni, & Gerla, 2005).

These new technologies can be used to further any of the aforementioned methodologies such as inquiry and action, facilitating participation in research, knowledge transfer, or enabling learning. As Sahney and Lee (2005) note, "new communication technology connects individuals across space and makes the emergence of new communities possible" (p. 393). This echoes Girard's (2003) observation that the combinations of Internet and broadcast radio offer great possibilities for communication projects, within which research projects can be included. The following examples illustrate the ways that technology has enabled information sharing and forums for connection via the combination of Internet and radio technology.

Example: Broadcasting Events—Feminist International Radio Endeavour (FIRE)

Internet/satellite connection has been used effectively to enable people to connect and learn around the world, such as through the Feminist International Radio Endeavour (FIRE), which plays an important role in the global women's movement by broadcasting local and international dialogue about women's human rights (Suárez Toro, 2000).

Example: Sharing Radio Content—A-Infos Radio Project

The Internet enabled the formation of the A-Infos Radio Project in 2006 by grassroots broadcasters, free radio journalists, and cyber-activists who can sign on and upload any radio content they wish to share. "The archived material is available to anyone who wants it free of charge . . . to enable the free expression of creativity" (A-Infos Radio Project, n.d.).

Example: Online Forums

Finally, the radio coupled with the Internet has created the ability for online forums such as Myspace.com, and Last.fm (among many others), enabling users to share and upload music through peer-to-peer networks, as well as engage in chatting with other users and posting information to blogs.

◆ Challenges and Ongoing Issues: Appropriate Technology

Although the quality of all types of radio broadcast is improved by satellite transmission and Internet access, these technological developments have not necessarily meant an equal improvement in the quality of, or access to, participation via these mediums. Girard (2003) notes that the digital divide hinders many poor countries (and individuals) who do not have access to the Internet and that the rate of Internet usage is as follows:

> 62 percent are in North America or Western Europe, home to ten percent of the world's population. The Asia/Pacific region accounts for almost 31 percent, almost two-thirds of them concentrated in a few countries. Barely five percent are in Latino America. Sub-Sahara Africa, with roughly the same population as North America combined, has about one percent of the world's Internet users. (p. 3)

Although the nonprofit organization One Laptop per Child (*One Laptop per Child*, n.d.) is aiming to change this by developing a 100-dollar laptop for use by children around the world, radio practitioners and those using radio in/for research still need to be mindful of how the use of technology, and technological gaps resulting in new technologies, may inadvertently perpetuate dominant paradigms and hegemonic ways of knowing. This is a particular challenge, as Vandana Shiva (in Rodriguez,

2003) points out, especially when it may be that those producing community media only know and relate to the monocultures of dominant paradigms that shape what we know, how we see, and (therefore) what we can produce.

◆ Conclusion

Although currently new innovations in technology such as Internet live-streaming and audio file sharing are used mainly for recreational purposes, avenues for dialogue or generating ways of knowing could be further explored for radio in/for research. For example, dialogue can be shared in real time on a large scale, such as at a conference or on a small scale as in the case of study circles. Through these technologies increased possibilities also exist to involve participants in research. For example, radio listening groups taking part in participatory action research could connect in real time and could also participate through blogging, thus increasing potential research participants' ability to take part in collective inquiry at a time when they are available. Finally, there are possibilities to (re)generate ways of knowing, using technology in more dialogical and/or counterhegemonic ways, for example, connecting indigenous peoples in nation-building exercises through satellite radio networks and online language or "cultural rescuing" projects (*AIROS Native Radio Network*, n.d.; Buchtmann, 2000).

To use and bridge these modalities researchers will have to be as innovative and creative as those amateurs who pioneered the media themselves. As Sahney and Lee (2005) note about radio itself, for innovations to come about, groups of people in conversation and who share camaraderie are needed to generate knowledge about the use of the tool or other topics of mutual interest.

This "cannot be willed into existence by design. It is a process of individual interests intertwined in a bottom-up process" (p. 407). In a similar way, through exploring arts-related and hybrid forms of research or inquiry, new avenues can be paved in the information highway.

◆ Suggested Resources

COMMUNITY RADIO

Fraser, C., & Estrada, S. R. (2001). *Community radio handbook*. Paris: UNESCO.
http://www.community-media.com/startfm.html (starting a community radio station)

RADIO LEARNING GROUPS

Crowley, D., Etherington, A., & Kidd, R. (1978). *Mass media manual: How to run a radio learning group*. Germany: Drukhaus Gottington.

RADIO-ASSISTED, COMMUNITY-BASED EDUCATION

Eshgh, R., Hoxeng, J., Provenzano, J., & Casals, B. (1988). *Radio-assisted community based education*. Pittsburgh, PA: U.S. Agency for International Development, Office of Education Bureau for Science and Technology, Duquesne University Press.

PARTICIPATORY RADIO PROGRAMS

http://www.comminit.com/radio

RADIO ACTIVISM

http://www.prometheusradio.org

RADIO NETWORKING

- OurMedia Network, http://ourmedia net.org

A global network of activists, academics, and radio practitioners working to strengthen the role of citizens' media through collaboration, policy advocacy, and research.

- World Association of Community Radio Broadcasters, www.amarc.org

An international nongovernmental organization serving the community radio movement, with a goal to support and contribute to the development of community and participatory radio along the principles of solidarity and international cooperation.

◆ References

A-Infos Radio Project. (n.d.). *Broadcasting quality programming via the Internet*. Retrieved May 14, 2006, from http://radi04all.net/

AIROS Native Radio Network. (n.d.). Retrieved September 1, 2006, from http://www.airos. org/audio.html

Bessette, G. (2001). *From information dissemination to community participation: A facilitator's guide to participatory development communications*. Ottawa, Ontario, Canada: International Development Research Centre.

Bessette, G. (2005). Participatory development communications: Reinforcing the participatory NRM research and action process. In J. Gonsalves, T. Becker, A. Braun, D. Campilan, H. de Chavez, E. Fajber, et al. (Eds.), *Participatory research and development for sustainable agriculture and natural resource management: A sourcebook* (pp. 94–103). Ottawa, Ontario, Canada: International Development Research Centre.

Buchtmann, L. (2000). Digital songlines: The use of modern communication technology by an Aboriginal community in remote Australia. *Prometheus, 18*(1), 59–74.

Burke, B., Geronimo, J., Martin, D., Thomas, B., & Wall, C. (2003). *Education for changing unions*. Toronto, Ontario, Canada: Between the Lines Press.

Communications Initiative. (n.d.). *Making waves: Stories of participatory communication for social change: Radio Sutatenza*. Retrieved September 1, 2006, from http:// www.comminit.com/strategicthinking/pds-makingwaves/sld-1856.html

Deza, A. (1994). Media production and the process of becoming in the context of community development. In S. A. White (Ed.), *Participatory communication: Working for change and development* (pp. 420–445). London: Sage.

Eshgh, R., Hoxeng, J., Provenzano, J., & Casals, B. (1988). *Radio-assisted community based education, U.S. Agency for International Development*. Philadelphia PA: Duquesne University Press.

Fals-Borda, O. (1991). *Action and knowledge: Breaking the monopoly with participatory action research*. New York: Apex Press.

Folch-Serra, M. (1990). Place, voice, space: Mikhail Bakhtin's dialogical landscape. *Environment and Planning D: Society and Space, 8*, 255–274.

Fraser, C., & Restrepo-Estrada, S. (1998). *Communicating for development: Human change for survival*. New York: I. B. Tauris Publishers.

Freire, P. (1970). *Pedagogy of the oppressed*. New York: Herder and Herder.

Gardner, H. (1983). *Frames of mind*. New York: Basic Books.

Ghini, V., Pau, G., Roccettti, M., Salomoni, P., & Gerla, M. (2005). For here or to go? Downloading music on the move with an ultra reliable wireless Internet application. *Computer Networks, 49*(1), 4–26.

Ginsburg, L. (1997). Contrarian libertarian: Carl Malamud, defender of civil liberties, wants more—not less—government on the Internet. *Wired*, July, 130–131.

Girard, B. (Ed.). (2003). *The one to watch: Radio, new ICTs, and interactivity*. Rome: Friedrich Ebert Foundation, the Communication for Development Group Research, Extension and Training Division Sustainable

Development, Department Food and Agricultural Organization.

Gluck, S., & Patai, D. (1991). *Women's words: The feminist practice of oral history*. New York: Routledge.

Gumucio Dagron, A. (2002). Radio: Small waves, giant changes. In A. Gumucio Dagron, *Making waves: Stories of participatory communications for social change* (pp. 12–16). New York: Rockefeller Foundation.

Hall, B. (1994). Participatory research. In T. Husen & T. N. Postlethwaite (Eds.), *International encyclopaedia of education* (2nd ed., Vol. 7, pp. 4330–4336). Tarrytown, NY: Elsevier Science Ltd.

Jara, V. (1997). *Para sistemizar experiencias*. Guadalajara, México: Mexican Institute for Community Development.

Kavanagh, A. (1998). *The power of the story: Proceedings of the University College of Cape Breton's first annual storytelling symposium*. Cape Breton, Nova Scotia: University College of Cape Breton Press.

Kidd, D. (1992). Offbeat, in-step: Vancouver cooperative radio. In B. Girard (Ed.), *A passion for radio: Radio waves and community*. Retrieved May 13, 2007, from http://www.comunica.org/passion

Lee, S. (1998, August). *The convergence of the web and television: Current technological situation and its future*. Paper presented at the Association for Education in Journalism and Mass Communication conference, Baltimore, MD.

Levanthal, R., & Green, K. (2002). Introduction to the second edition: Ten reasons to tell stories in the classroom. In E. Brody, J. Goldspinner, K. Green, R. Leventhal, & J. Porcino (Ed.), *Spinning tales, weaving hope: Stories, storytelling, and activities for peace, justice and the environment* (2nd ed., pp. x–xv). Philadelphia: New Society Publishers.

Nadeau, D. (1996). *Counting our victories: Popular education and organizing*. Vancouver, British Columbia, Canada: Repeal the Deal Productions.

Nutaaq. (2005). *Radio novelas*. Retrieved August 12, 2005, from http://www.nutaaq.com/novelas.html

One Laptop per Child. (n.d). Retrieved May 1, 2006, from http://laptop.org/

Prometheus Radio Project: Freeing the Radio from Corporate Control. (n.d.). Retrieved October 7, 2006, from http://www.prometheusradio.org

Rahim, S. (1994). Participatory development communications as a dialogical process. In S. White, K. Sadanandan Nair, & J. Ashroft (Eds.), *Participatory communication: Working for change and development* (pp. 118–137). New Delhi, India: Sage.

Randall, M. (1985). *Testimonios: A guide to oral histories*. Toronto, Ontario, Canada: The Participatory Research Group, International Council for Adult Education.

Reeves, G. (1993). *Communications and the Third World*. New York: Routledge.

Riaño, P. (Ed.). (1994). *Women and grassroots communication: Furthering social change*. Thousand Oaks, CA: Sage.

Rodriguez, C. (2001). *Fissures in the mediascape: An international study of citizens' media*. Cresskill, NJ: Hampton Press.

Rodriguez, C. (2003). The Bishop and his star: Citizens' communication in Southern Chile. In N. Couldry & J. Curran (Eds.), *Contesting media power: Alternative media in a networked world* (pp. 177–194). Boulder, CO: Rowman & Littlefield.

Sahney, H., & Lee, S. (2005). Arenas of innovation: Understanding new configurational potentialities of communication technologies. *Media, Culture, & Society, 27*(3), 391–414.

Servaes, J. (2001). Participatory communications research for democracy and social change. In M. Richards, P. N. Thomas, & Z. Nain (Eds.), *Communication and development: The Freirian connection* (pp. 13–32). Cresskill, NJ: Hampton Press.

Sternberg, P., & Garcia Praege, A. (1990). *Sociodrama: Who's in your shoes?* New York: Praeger.

Suárez Toro, M. (2000). *Women's voices on FIRE: Feminist International Radio Endeavour*. Austin, TX: Anomaly Press.

The University of the Autonomous Regions of the Caribbean Coast of Nicaragua (URRACAN). (n.d.). Retrieved August 20, 2006, from http://www.yorku.ca/cerlac/URACCAN/URACCAN.html

Vilar, J., & Villegas, T. (1988). *El sonido de la radio: Ensayo teorico practico sobre produccion radiofonica* [The sounds of radio: Teaching practical theory of radio production]. Mexico City, Mexico: Universidad Autonimo Metropolitana-Xochimilco, Instituto Mexicano de la Radio & Plaza y Janes.

Webster's New Explorer Dictionary and Thesaurus. (1999). Springfield, MA: Merriam Webster.

Zia, N. (2003). *Our voice: Radio for social change.* Unpublished manuscript. Lahore, Pakistan: Sarsabz.

29

Folk Art and Popular Art Forms

TOUCHING MINDS AND HEARTS

Community Arts as Collaborative Research

◆ Deborah Barndt

◆ *Roots and Strands of Community Arts*

Community arts, as a term and recognized field of practice, only came
into currency in the latter part of the 20th century. But the process it
refers to—the engagement of people in representing their collective identities, histories, and aspirations in multiple forms of expression—is as old
as cave paintings and ritualistic chanting. Gregory Cajete (1994) describes
art in North American Aboriginal contexts as "an expression of life"
practiced by all the people, usually an "anonymous activity expressing
a unique cultural perspective of living" (p. 154). Thus, art was/is integral to life, totally democratized, and reflecting a community rather
than an individual identity. Art was/is also a means of visioning, used
within rituals and ceremonies, and integrating "myth, dream, art, ecological philosophy, communality, and spirit" (p. 146). Certainly for many
Aboriginal peoples art is synonymous with community, whereas for the
mainstream Western art world, "community" as a descriptor may connote something of lesser quality when judged against the work of individual geniuses of "high art."

The separation of "art" from "community" perhaps has its roots in
both a body/mind and a nature/culture split in Western consciousness

◆ 351

emerging from certain streams of the European scientific revolution of the 1700s (Griffin, 1995) and in the commodification of art and knowledge associated with industrial capitalism of the 1800s (Berger, 1972). This has intensified in recent decades with commercialized and individualistic practices of art and media in the context of corporate cultural globalization, often "reducing culture to commerce" (Adams & Goldbard, 2002, p. 20). This process is paralleled by and integral to the commodification of knowledge, which emphasizes knowledge transmission and accumulation rather than the knowledge production process and frames learning as a personal and primarily mental undertaking rather than a social relation and holistic experience (Barndt, 1990).

Besides the resistance of Aboriginal peoples to fragmented ways of knowing often implicitly promoted in Western schools, media, and institutions, there have been many forms of education, art, and activism that have also challenged these dominant paradigms (Freire, 1982). In the North American context, the *cultural workers* of the 1930s, for example, promoted collective production of the arts through the mural movement and film, theatre, and dance workers' leagues associated with socialist politics and supported by U.S. President Roosevelt's New Deal programs (Adams & Goldbard, 2001). *Community development* and *community animation* in the radical 1960s (and the related *animation socioculturelle* in Quebec) linked the organizing of marginalized communities with the expression of their issues through theatre (Teatro Campesino was linked to organizing Chicano farmworkers in California; see Rose-Avila, 2003), video (the Canadian National Film Board's Challenge for Change program documented and represented video portraits back to Maritimes communities; see Marchessault, 1995), and music (Black spirituals were transformed into hymns of the United States–based civil rights movement; see Sapp, 1995).

In the Latin American context, *popular education, popular communications,* and community arts were linked to the building of social movements in the 1960s and 1970s to challenge military dictatorships, United States intervention, and extreme disparities between the rich and the poor in the southern hemisphere (Kane, 2001; Nadeau, 1996; Nuñez, 1999). Art and media forms such as community radio, popular theatre, *nueva cancion* (new song), slide shows, and video were democratized and used to engage an exploited majority in naming and challenging current power relations while envisioning utopias of more just and equitable societies (Arnold & Burke, 1983). In this context, the critical and the creative were wed. As popular education promoted the collective production of knowledge, popular art offered both a mode of collective inquiry and a form of communicating that knowledge to the poor majority in ways that touched hearts as well as minds. It was understood that change would not happen unless the majority not only understood the root causes of their oppression and the necessity of struggle but also felt a deep commitment to working for change and a growing sense of their own power to make a difference. The arts were not only tools in education and organizing but engaged people more fully, moved their spirits, and inspired collective action. Participatory research was part and parcel of popular education, and so the processes of art-making and popular communications were also about people researching their own lives (Barndt, 2004).

In the past 20 years, the term "community arts" has become more common in North America, but its meaning remains as diverse as the contexts in which it is practiced. At its most conservative, it refers to the dissemination of elite or classical arts to rural communities that have been marginalized by the large (and more heavily funded) urban cultural centers. Many municipal or provincial community arts councils, for example, were responses to this disparity. Adams and Goldbard (2001), U.S. consultants in community arts for the past 30 years, eschew the term because of this connotation and prefer instead the concept of *community cultural development,* which they define as "a range of initiatives undertaken by artists in collaboration with other community members to express identity, concerns and aspirations through the arts and communications media, while building cultural capacity and contributing to social change" (p. 107).

In the Canadian context, this new institutional space, however, has also been claimed by more political artists, who work collaboratively with diverse communities of interest and location. Honor Ford-Smith (2001), Jamaican Canadian community artist and cultural theorist, assesses both the potential and the dangers revealed in a new surge of public and private funding for community arts. Concerned that funders might hijack community agendas, she argues for

> an increasingly hybrid definition of community and community arts, one that allows for diversity of practice, rigorous critique of practice and that challenges the essentially conservative dichotomy between professional and amateur and between product and process. (p. 13)

Among activists of the new millennium, there has also been a resurgence of participatory production of the arts, often in response to commodified culture of global capitalism and the promotion of passive consumption rather than active citizenship (Starr, 2001). It is evident in the proliferation of puppets, masks, and performance artists in street protests (Hutcheson, 2006), as well as in the adoption of culture jamming practices (Liacas, 2005), theatre of the oppressed techniques (Boal, 2002), hip hop music, reclaim the streets movements (Jordan, 2002), and Web-based activisms (Kidd, 2005).

Community arts is often implicitly a critique of the domination of Western mass media and popular consumer culture. It is also a response to migration and diasporic populations claiming and creating diverse and multiple identities. In global cities such as Toronto, a cauldron of diverse cultural practices, new cultural fusions are drawing on traditions that challenge both the Eurocentric content and individualism of hegemonic White Western culture (Fung & Gagnon, 2002).

In choosing to use the term *community arts* here, then, I recognize its multiple connotations and the contestations about who does it, in what contexts, for what, and how. I like the juxtaposition of the two terms—art and community—in part because it challenges our commonsense notions of both complex concepts. It behooves us to constantly interrogate how we understand art (as most of us are socialized in a more colonial and capitalist notion of the term) as well as how we understand community—whether it be defined by place, tradition, intention, practice, or spirit.

Cleveland (2002) suggests that community arts can nurture four different kinds of purposes:

To educate and inform us about ourselves and the world;

To inspire and mobilize individuals and groups;

To nurture and heal people and/or communities;

To build and improve community capacity.

I would add that the process of engaging in community arts is in itself a research process, a collaborative process of producing knowledge. The social experience of art-making can open up aspects of peoples' beings, their stories, their memories and aspirations, in ways that other methods might miss. When people are given the opportunity to tell their own stories—whether through oral traditions, theatre, visual arts, music, or other media—they bring their bodies, minds, and spirits into a process of communicating and sharing their experiences; they affirm their lives as sources of knowledge, and they stimulate each other in a synergistic process of collective knowledge production.

◆ Key Elements of Community Arts

In my own framing of community arts as a research process, I emphasize four key interacting elements: collaboration, creative artistic practices, critical social analysis, and commitment.

COLLABORATION

Community arts is infused with a spirit of collaboration at many different levels, whether it's collaboration between an artist or facilitator and a particular community, collaboration among participants in a community arts project, or collaboration with an audience. Animators of community arts, as research facilitators, must be able to draw out the issues, talents, and energies of people they are working with and help them spark each other's strengths. In contrast to most conventional art practices, this is basically a collaborative process; it may involve the artist ceding some control as it empowers the participants. This is a fluid dynamic, in that levels and forms of collaboration may shift from one moment to the next, depending on the context, the people, and the purposes of the project.

This intersubjective approach to research counters positivist thinking and objective knowing that until recently has dominated both science and art and, according to Suzi

Gablik (1995), is "attuned to the interrelational, ecological, and interactive character of reality." Gablik promotes this "connective aesthetics after individualism" that sees human nature as "deeply embedded in the world" (p. 86), similar to the reciprocity at play in an ecosystem.

CREATIVE ARTISTIC PRACTICES

What distinguishes this kind of research from other collaborative forms is the centrality of the arts as tools of inquiry and collective expression. This involves a reclaiming of art forms considered the exclusive domain of professionally trained artists and nurturing the creative capacities of everyone in a community-based process. One of the first challenges is to counter our own internalized sense that "I can't draw." Chris Cavanagh (2006, p. 71) evokes Gramsci's notions of common sense to explain how in the Western world we have bought into this powerful notion of art that acts "to exclude the vast majority of people from the identity of 'artist.'"

In contrast with conventional research tools that have been primarily individual, verbal, and text based, community arts taps sense-based, intuitive, and relational ways of knowing (Belenky, Clinchy, Goldberger, & Tarule, 1986) through nonverbal forms such as images, movement, and music. The arts are powerful catalysts for unearthing different kinds of knowledge and moving people to participate more fully in the knowledge production process. There are, however, ongoing debates about the extent of the participation of ordinary people in the art-making and how much professional control of the art-making is necessary.

CRITICAL SOCIAL ANALYSIS

Community arts is often identified with marginalized groups and communities, offering them a space for articulating their own perspectives on the social conditions of their lives. The art-making process thus becomes a collaborative process of naming and challenging current power relations, of digging into the root causes of current injustices. By representing their lives in artistic forms, the social contradictions are made more visible and visceral. Part of the animator's role is to help groups engage those contradictions, to deepen their critical social analysis. There will, of course, be differences in the perspectives brought to such a discussion, and the differences within a group or community (based on gender, race, class, age, etc.) will likely come to the fore through this process. Rather than avoiding or flattening internal contradictions, these differences complicate and enrich the analysis, promoting a critical self-reflexivity.

Different understandings of power inform the social analysis that emerges from a group research/art-making process. For some, community arts should represent the major social schisms with a clear sense of the powerful social, economic, and political forces that perpetuate injustice. Others advocate a more subtle reading of power as "something that is circulated and dispersed throughout society rather than being held exclusively or primarily by certain groups" (Strega, 2005, p. 225). Whether framed by a Marxist, Gramscian, Foucauldian, or more liberal analysis of power, community art processes offer a critical edge over other approaches.

COMMITMENT

One goal of community arts is to help groups move from collective analysis to collective action, to become active participants in shaping a more democratic and just society. Community arts involves a questioning of the status quo and a commitment to social change. More than a purely ideological stance, this commitment must be

deeply identified with the aspirations of the community, while recognizing the many contradictions within. On the part of the artist or research facilitator, then, it is not a rigid adherence to some predetermined vision or outcome but rather a deep commitment to accompany people in a process of exploring their own histories, identities, struggles, and hopes—not knowing where it will lead. Such a commitment is based on respect and humility, an openness to learn and to be transformed in the process. Again though, commitments will conflict, and visions will not always be shared; so this is something that is constantly renegotiated as well. There is sometimes a clash of utopias and differences over strategies; the art-making process can help both to illuminate these tensions and to work through them.

◆ The Role of the Artist or Research Facilitator

In considering community arts as a form of qualitative research, there are several possible entry points. One frames community arts practice in itself as a research process. In this case the artist or organizer of collaborative projects is also a research facilitator. Another approach sees researchers adapting community arts as a tool within the context of community-based research, in which case the research facilitator becomes an animator of the arts but not necessarily an artist whose vision shapes the project. It's important to acknowledge many different potential roles for the artist or research facilitator, which will be determined ultimately by the main purposes of the project, the nature of the issue, the community participants, and the orientation of the artist/facilitator herself.

The role of the artist/facilitator can also vary tremendously, along a continuum, from one who gathers stories (data) from the community and represents them through her own artistic creations to one who engages community members in producing their own art as part of the process of gathering, analyzing, and synthesizing the data. Most projects fall somewhere between these two extremes: the artist/facilitator taking more control at one moment or another while ceding control through participatory processes at other moments.

◆ Some Community Arts Stories

The ideas underlying community arts practice and its potential as a research process come alive in all their complexity through five stories of projects/processes in different contexts and times. All projects have integrated some form of participatory research, an approach that honors the subjects of research as participants in naming the issues to be explored, developing the analysis, communicating results, and often acting upon them. Participatory research has a deep tradition of using art and media tools as ways to engage people directly, drawing them into the process and offering them multiple forms of expression.

SNAPSHOT 1: PARTICIPATORY RESEARCH (TORONTO IN THE 1970s)

The Participatory Research Group of the International Council for Adult Education undertook local projects using art and media in participatory processes as well as linking with groups around the world creating alternatives to conventional research. I worked with a Chilean exile, Raul Rojas, on a participatory research project to examine the causes of immigration among an emerging Latin American community in Toronto. We sometimes started interviews in living rooms with family albums, the images serving as catalysts for their own storytelling.

A slide show I produced on the emigration of Ecuadorians to Toronto was transferred to video and shown on personal television sets to generate conversations about the various forces that compelled immigrants to leave their homelands (political, economic, war, etc.). Video became the common medium that carried their stories outside the home; we edited the interviews and returned them to community events for further discussion. In this project then, we retained some control of the artistic process but brought in community members' images (from albums) and returned our visual representations of their histories to the community to generate further collective analysis.

A process that involved people more directly in art-making was the collective song-writing of the activist troubadour Arlene Mantle, who also joined the Participatory Research Group for a short time. In a community gathering called "Songs for People," Arlene offered a song-writing workshop, inviting the group to first brainstorm the issues that were most pressing to them, and then to choose one to focus on. The discussion about how this issue played out in their daily lives became the raw material for collective song-writing. Arlene offered a simple tune and worked with the group to generate lyrics that not only reflected their stories but also their own words or ways of speaking, developing their sense of ownership of both the ideas and the song. The process of creating the song collectively created the space for group members to share their analyses and to deepen their understanding of the issues they were singing about.

SNAPSHOT 2: COMMUNITY MURAL PRODUCTION (CALIFORNIA IN THE 1980s)

Building on the Mexican mural movement of the 1930s, a new mural movement instigated by Chicano and African American artists blossomed in the 1960s, in particular in Chicago and Los Angeles. In the late 1970s and early 1980s, Chicana artist Judy Baca, a cofounder of the Social and Public Art Resource Centre, coordinated a major project that involved over 400 youth, 40 historians, 40 artists, and thousands of residents in the production of the longest mural in the world, the half-mile long Great Wall of Los Angeles (Baca, 2002). The youth were charged with researching the hidden histories of the many ethnic communities in California and making the results of their research visible in this monumental wall that followed a flood control channel. Thus, youth developed research and artistic skills, while learning about the rich multicultural history of the region and coming together across different ethnic and gang cultures.

In the late 1980s, Baca facilitated a participatory research process in Guadalupe, California, a primarily agricultural and Mexican American community. Again she hired teenagers from Chicano and Filipino farm families to collect historical information and develop a time line of the town's history. She took Polaroid photos of the farmworkers, which she returned to them, and then culled photos from local scrapbooks and school yearbooks that they lent to her. A town meeting involved discussing the key moments in the history and choosing imagery for the panels of a large public art piece, turning the art-making process into a forum for civic dialogue (Doss, 1995). The final product revealed Aboriginal roots of the area, the early Hispanic settlers, the arrival of Chinese and Japanese farmers, and the organizing of farmworkers in the 1970s—again contributing to a deeper social consciousness.

SNAPSHOT 3: COMMUNITY RADIO (NICARAGUA IN THE 1990s AND 2000s)

A community-based research management project initiated in the mid-1990s on the Atlantic Coast of Nicaragua chose to create a community radio program and a newsletter as tools in the participatory action research process undertaken with support from the International Development Research Centre in Canada and coordinated by York University (Barndt, 2004). The pluri-ethnic coast is comprised of Creole, Mestizo, Miskitu, Garifuna, Sumu, and Rama peoples, who make their living from fishing, mining, and forestry. Community radio is the most accessible medium in these communities, which may not have electricity and which are steeped in oral traditions. With the support of a then York University graduate student (see Christine McKenzie in Chapter 28 of this volume), a new radio program became a tool of participatory action research, as youth interviewed community folks about encroachment on their agricultural lands by Mestizos, shrimp farming that threatened the ecology of the area, and forestry companies that flagrantly ignored state regulations. The youth also gathered or created poems, songs, riddles, and other popular cultural forms to include in the radio program. As they became skilled in engaging people in critical discussion, they developed confidence and skills in both participatory research and radio production.

SNAPSHOT 4: MULTIMEDIA PROJECTS AND COMMUNITY THEATRE (TORONTO IN THE 2000s)

The Laidlaw Foundation initiated a series of pilot projects in community arts in 2000, among them The Garbage Collection, which brought together four sanitation workers, four environmentalists, and four community artists to produce murals on municipal garbage trucks with environmental messages. A two-day workshop created the space for these 12 participants to examine their own relationship to garbage, through an activity called "tracing the trash." Using storytelling as a tool, the artists revealed their complicity in creating trash from the toxic materials they use, the garbage workers exposed the dangers they face as they pick up our garbage, and the environmentalists unearthed the impact current garbage disposal systems have on the planet. These distinct relationships to the trash were represented in drawings as well as stories. A second activity uncovered key environmental conflicts of recent decades through a popular theatre activity known as "sculpting." Finally, everyone contributed to a graphic brainstorming that fed collective processes of designing the murals for three garbage trucks. In this process, then, people who had not considered themselves artists nonetheless used the arts (storytelling, theatre, and drawing) to articulate their distinct knowledges and collectively designed and painted murals that integrated their diverse vantage points. This project was clearly a participatory action research process as well as a community arts production and culminated in the city whitewashing one of the murals depicting a controversial deal proposed for diverting Toronto garbage to a rural northern native community.

Also using multiple forms of art, Toronto-based Jumblies Theatre mounted a community play in 2004 that was built on 4 years of research in a west-end neighborhood of Toronto. Led by artistic director Ruth Howard, based at the Davenport-Perth Neighborhood Centre, the process started with the gathering of oral histories of residents from diverse cultural backgrounds. Stories of immigration were expressed in the construction of miniature boats that carried mementos reflecting pasts left behind. Groups in the centre claimed their own particular space in the process. A Latin American seniors group, for example, offered traditional dance to the dialogue.

Several smaller theatre productions were performed over the 3 years leading up to the final culminating community play,

Once a Shoreline. The story was a composite of the oral histories and reflected two generational perspectives on immigration— a way of synthesizing and feeding back a preliminary analysis to the community. The final production involved over 100 residents of all ages, three choirs, dancers, stiltwalkers, aerial acrobats, and puppeteers. Of particular interest was the integration of professional artists (e.g., two singers, a composer, and instrumentalists) into the participatory production.

The quality of the final production was critical to Jumblies' director Howard and did not diminish but rather enhanced the participation of community members. Seeing their stories represented in such magnificent and powerful form no doubt affirmed their identities while ingraining the ideas as powerful images in their minds. In this case, the results of early oral history research were transformed into a composite play that fed their stories back to local residents.

SNAPSHOT 5: THE VIVA! PROJECT AND EXCHANGE

Jumblies Theatre is one Canadian partner in a transnational research project, the VIVA! Project coordinated through York University, involving eight nongovernmental organization and university partners in exploring creative tensions of community arts and popular education in the Americas. Whereas participatory action research is a common methodology for North American collaborators, Central American partners have adapted a process they call *sistematización*, which involves project participants in a historical recovery and collective analysis of their shared experience with a selected focus.

Partners associated with CEASPA, the Panamanian Social Education and Action Centre, applied the systematization methodology in revisiting the Kuna Children's Art project, assessing how involving Kuna youth in a wide range of creative art practices (theatre, painting, poetry) had contributed to their cultural and environmental awareness. In Nicaragua, the Intercultural Communications Institute of URACCAN, the Regional Autonomous University on the Carribean Coast of Nicaragua, has created a community cable television station to produce stories drawn from the daily lives and struggles of the pluri-ethnic coastal peoples. Run by eight young people, Bilwivision has as its slogan "Less Hollywood, More Local Stories" and operates in three languages: Creole, Miskitu, and Spanish.

A Mexican partner in the VIVA! Project exchange has developed through UAM, the Autonomous Metropolitan University, a training program in community-based mural production, titled Painting by Listening. It involves potential animators of mural projects in a community research process to ensure that the murals represent the issues of the community and contribute to an ongoing process of community development. Another Canadian project, the Personal Legacy Project based in Montreal, involves individuals exploring through a collective process their ancestral histories. Using both archival research and body work, they recover and recreate characters based on specific ancestors. The resulting performances are based on embodied knowing as well as creative group processes.

◆ Blurring the Boundaries Between Research and Art

In the examples offered above, it is clear that the purposes of each project were distinct. Not all were framed as research, yet research was very integral to their processes. The selection of the art forms or tools to be used in any of these contexts depended on a variety of factors: what was culturally appropriate to the participants, the overall goals and objectives of the project, the talents and interests of the artists and facilitators, and so on.

Stanley and Wise (1990) make the important distinction between method, methodology, and epistemology: "Methods" include specific techniques or research practices (surveys, interviews, or artistic practices such as storytelling, popular theatre, photo-story production, songwriting, etc.), "methodology" refers to a broader theoretically informed framework (e.g., participatory research), and an "epistemology" is a theory of knowledge, an understanding of how we know and what counts as knowledge. There is always a danger of art-making processes being reduced to tools or techniques when using them as integral to qualitative research, making them devoid of meaning in relationship to the deeper purposes of the research.

The kind of community arts-informed research process I've been describing here is built on an epistemology that challenges the relationship between knowledge and power, that aims to democratize and collectivize knowledge production, and to engage people fully, as individuals and as groups, in expressing their identities, recovering their histories, articulating their visions, deepening their analyses, and developing their capacities to create history. The arts, when applied appropriately and facilitated sensitively, can involve participants as full human beings, touching minds AND hearts, healing the body/mind split inherent in Western scientific research methods.

◆ What Makes a Good Researcher/Community Artist?

Engaging people in research and representing their lives in artistic forms involves a very special set of skills. Singer/educator Jane Sapp (1995) includes in her list of key practices: listening, listening, listening. She is referring to what is called deep listening or active listening, meaning that a facilitator of research using community arts must go beyond the kind of self-expression often associated with art to expressions that are collective and community-driven. Community artist Suzi Gablik (1995) calls this listener-centered rather than vision-oriented art, which "can only come into its own through dialogue, as open conversation, in which one listens to and includes other voices" (p. 83).

When artists/researchers listen, they not only hear others' stories but they also discover other forms of storytelling that emerge from the group/community with whom they work. Ruth Howard, Toronto-based community play animator, described how she discovered sewing as a medium important to a group of women in a new community art project and basketball as a key entry point for the young men. Careful listening can unearth other forms of expression, but it is yet another skill to tap the creative powers lying within people of all ages. Animating the creativity in everyone requires patience, daring, and belief in peoples' capacities, even when they may not have that belief in themselves.

One of the ways that people become more confident in their own abilities to express themselves is when their ideas or symbols are fed back to them in forms that affirm and inspire. Community-based researchers/artists bring their own skills of synthesis and artistic expression to feed back or re-present to community members the ideas and images that have come from them. This may involve identifying tensions or contradictions uncovered in collective discussions and creations, but that ring true with participants. It also helps move from the level of individual concerns to issues of common import.

Finally, this kind of research and art requires a willingness to share power and to embrace processes that may be beyond one's control. Community artists talk about this tension between holding on and letting go. The researcher/artist may structure processes to engage participants in creative inquiry, but if the process is to draw on the knowledge, skills, and visions of community members, there must be space for that to happen. It can be unsettling for people who like to be in control of all aspects of the process. One must learn to live with uncertainty, become comfortable with discomfort, and be excited by the insights and creativity that can emerge from both silent and sticky moments.

Community artist Leah Burns (2006) summarizes this spirit when she suggests that coordinating community art and participatory research requires healthy doses of honesty, humility, and a good sense of humor.

◆ References

Adams, D., & Goldbard, A. (2001). *Creative community: The art of cultural development.* New York: The Rockefeller Foundation.

Adams, D., & Goldbard, A. (2002). *Community, culture, and globalization.* New York: The Rockefeller Foundation.

Arnold, R., & Burke, B. (1983). *Popular education handbook.* Toronto, Ontario, Canada: Canadian University Service Overseas and the Ontario Institute for Studies in Education.

Baca, J. (2002). Birth of a movement. In D. Adams & A. Goldbard (Eds.), *Community, culture, and globalization* (pp. 107–125). New York: The Rockefeller Foundation.

Barndt, D. (1990). *To change this house: Popular education under the Sandinistas.* Toronto, Ontario, Canada: Between the Lines.

Barndt, D. (2004). By whom and for whom? Intersections of participatory research and community art. In A. L. Cole, L. Neilsen,

J. G. Knowles, & T. C. Luciani (Eds.), *Provoked by art: Theorizing arts-informed research* (pp. 221–237). Halifax, Nova Scotia, & Toronto, Ontario, Canada: Backalong Books & the Centre for Arts-Informed Research.

Belenky, M. F., Clinchy, B. M., Goldberger, N. R., & Tarule, J. M. (1986). *Women's ways of knowing.* New York: Basic Books.

Berger, J. (1972). *Ways of seeing.* London: Penguin Books.

Boal, A. (2002). *Games for actors and non-actors* (2nd ed., A. Jackson, Trans.). New York: Routledge.

Burns, L. (2006). "Seriously . . . are you *really* an artist?" Humour and integrity in a community mural project. In D. Barndt (Ed.), *Playing with fire: Art as activism* (pp. 25–36). Toronto, Ontario, Canada: Sumach Press.

Cajete, G. (1994). Seeing the voices of our heart. In G. Cajete, *Look to the mountain: An ecology of Indigenous education.* Kyland, NC: Kivaki Press.

Cavanagh, C. (2006). The strawberry tasted so good: The trickster practices of activist art. In D. Barndt (Ed.), *Playing with fire: Art as activism* (pp. 68–76). Toronto, Ontario, Canada: Sumach Press.

Cleveland, W. (2002). *Mapping the field: Arts-based community development.* Retrieved August 3, 2004, from http://www.communityarts.net/readingroom/archive/intro-develop.php

Doss, E. (1995). Raising community consciousness with public art: The Guadalupe Mural Project. In E. Doss, *Spirit poles and flying pigs: Public art and cultural democracy in American communities.* Washington, DC: Smithsonian Institution Press.

Ford-Smith, H. (2001). Whose community? Whose art? The politics of reformulating community arts. In M. Fernandez (Ed.), *No frame around it: Process and outcome of the A Space Community Art Biennale* (pp. 11–27). Toronto, Ontario, Canada: A Space Gallery.

Freire, P. (1982). *Pedagogy of the oppressed.* New York: Continuum.

Fung, R., & Gagnon, M. (2002). *13 conversations about art and cultural race politics.* Montreal, Quebec, Canada: Prendre Parole.

Gablik, S. (1995). Connective aesthetics: Art after individualism. In S. Lacy (Ed.), *Mapping the terrain: New genre public art* (pp. 74–87). Seattle, WA: Bay Press.

Griffin, S. (1995). *The eros of everyday life: Essays on ecology, gender, and society.* Toronto, Ontario, Canada: Doubleday.

Hutcheson, M. (2006). Demechanizing our politics: Street performance and making change. In D. Barndt (Ed.), *Playing with fire: Art as activism* (pp. 79–88). Toronto, Ontario, Canada: Sumach Press.

Jordan, J. (2002). The art of necessity: The subversive imagination of anti-road protest and reclaim the streets. In S. Duncombe (Ed.), *Cultural resistance reader* (p. 348). London: Verso.

Kane, L. (2001). *Popular education and social change in Latin America.* London: Latin American Bureau of Education.

Kidd, D. (2005). Linking back, looking forward. In A. Langlois & F. Dubois (Eds.), *Autonomous media: Activating resistance and dissent* (pp. 151–161). Montreal, Quebec, Canada: Cumulus Press.

Liacas, T. (2005). 101 tricks to play with the mainstream: Culture jamming as subversive recreation. In A. Langlois & F. Dubois (Eds.), *Autonomous media: Activating resistance and dissent* (pp. 61–74). Montreal, Quebec, Canada: Cumulus Press.

Marchessault, J. (1995) Reflections on the dispossessed: Video and the "Challenge for Change" Experiment. *Screen, 36*(2), 13–146.

Nadeau, D. (1996). *Celebrating our victories: Popular education and organizing.* New Westminster, British Columbia, Canada: Repeal the Deal Productions.

Nuñez, C. (1999). *La revolución ética.* Guadalajara, Mexico: Mexican Institute for Community Development.

Rose-Avila, M. (2003, Fall). Homegrown revolution. *ColorLines: Race, Culture, Action.* 10–12.

Sapp, J. (1995). To move and to change. *ARTS: The Arts in Religious and Theological Studies.* 7(2), 30–33.

Stanley, L. & Wise, S. (1990). Method, methodology, and epistemology in feminist research processes. In L. Stanley (Ed.), *Feminist praxis:*

Research, theory, and epistemology in feminist sociology (pp. 20–60). New York: Routledge.

Starr, A. (2001). Art and revolution: Revitalizing political protest. In N. Welton & L. Wolf (Eds.), *Global uprising: Confronting the tyrannies of the 21st century* (pp. 33–37). Gabriola Island, British Columbia, Canada: New Society Publishers.

Strega, S. (2005). The view from the poststructural margins: Epistemology and methodology reconsidered. In L. Brown & S. Strega (Eds.), *Research as resistance: Critical, Indigenous, and anti-oppressive approaches* (pp. 199–236). Toronto, Ontario, Canada: Canadian Scholars' Press.

30

Folk Art and Popular Art Forms

QUILTS

◆ Helen K. Ball

T he dominant discourse of social science writing is driven by textual styles that, in their commitment to authority, remove most traces of humanity, vulnerability, complexity, and uncertainty. The text is asocial. These textual styles privilege the voice of the external, positionless expert through constitutive conventions that in "analysis and writing . . . create a structure subduing the voices of those with whom they talked" (Smith, 1989, p. 55). By remaining positionless in their texts, conventional social science writers recreate the authority, position, and power they gain as a result of the roles they hold in institutions. Oddly, in Western society, the positionless voice in the text is equated with authority, power, and influence. The separation of the self from the world, or the circumstances of which social scientists write, has come to mean that scholars have more insight, objectivity, and, thus, more authority than a more personal account.

If traditional social science writers are writing about social issues, then why is it that they continually remove the social from their texts? Are there things that they don't want to see? Words that they don't want to hear? Kincheloe (1997) suggests:

> For traditional narrative to retain its coherence, the silencing had to be done. As an act of power, this silence excluded dangerous meanings, echoes of resistance, and clips of alternative realities, that at

some level of dominant perception posed a threat. (p. 72)

According to Kincheloe (1997), maintaining this tradition, while not overtly acknowledging it, allows conventional social science writers the potential and opportunity to act in oppressive and destructive ways in deciding who is heard, what is published, and what is considered knowledge.

◆ *Knots*

The question now arises of how to study social phenomena and re-present them in ways that do not perpetuate the positionless, invisible, disengaged authority. How can discourse become more engaged, present and honest (Richardson, 1993)?

These questions are threads in the fabric of re-presentation—issues common within the knot of postmodernism (Denzin, 1994; Gordon, 1993). They twine themselves around postmodern critiques that complain that modernist representation "finalizes and excludes complexity" (Rosenau, 1992, p. 94) and upholds an assumption that there is no "loss of content or intention" (p. 93) in the representational process. I am concerned with textual construction that does not acknowledge how the experiences of those studied are "transformed into textual representations that are only stand-ins for the actual experience being described" (Denzin, 1992, p. 20).

What is needed are texts with people in them—social texts.

Poststructuralists regard power as a "productive force that creates meaning" (Shapiro, 1985/1986, p. 212) and meaning as a force that constructs identities and positions within society (Shapiro, 1985/1986; Weedon, 1987). A number of poststructuralist texts focus on the manifestations of power through readings of conversation (Stenner, 1993), identity (Widdicombe, 1993), and illness

(Orr, 1993). Poststructuralist authors create self-conscious texts that draw attention not only to the textuality of the work but also to the manifestations of power both in how they are writing and what is being written about. Writers achieve a self-conscious text through the use of nontraditional textuality (Ellis, 1997; Lather, 1997), nontraditional presentation of information (Michalowski, 1993; Richardson, 1992, 1993), and through the use of language that disrupts and interrupts traditional discourse (Orr, 1993; Ronai, 1996). The intent of these methodologies is to remind readers of the partiality of information presented, how it is circumscribed by the author, and of the constant intersection of power in the text.

Social texts could be similar in style to some poststructuralist writing, such as the work of Pfohl (1993) and Richardson (1992), who experiment with different formats and writing styles. The creation of a social text would also be responsive to much of the work in feminist methodology (Baker, 1998; DeVault, 1990, 1996, 1997; Ellis & Bochner, 1996; Lather, 1997; Lincoln, 1993; Spender, 1980; Weedon, 1987). These researchers and theorists identify writing as one of the few ways that are left to disrupt the dominant discourses in society that silence and marginalize. The social text finds support among those who have challenged the idea of prose as the only way to represent experience in the research text. These innovators have experimented in representing their research, for example, as poetry (Richardson, 1994a, 1994b) and as performance (Ellis & Bochner, 1992; McCall, Becker, & Meshejian, 1990; Paget, 1990). And this volume abounds with other examples.

The current structure of traditional social science texts can be transformed by preparing readers and audiences for new styles wherein the intent is to disrupt, interrupt, re-interrogate, and break down hegemonic textual styles. Through teaching and collaborating with participants in the creation of a research process, it is possible to "challenge disciplinary technologies that affect us, write themselves on and through our bodies, and also fracture those bodies powerfully" (Gordon, 1993, p. 322).

Acts of writing and reading, however, are more than the creation and acquisition of knowledge. They are the construction (or maintenance) of a particular convention of reality and the incorporation (or rejection) of a position within a discursive field. The acts of writing and reading are exquisitely intertwined at a level that is deeper than the mere writing of a report. These acts are social, components of the DNA of the culture in which they were created. Like DNA, they reveal the imprints of the biases, interests, weaknesses, strengths, and social structures that can ultimately be traced to a particular time and place in the history of a culture. Just as altering DNA will alter the development of an organism, altering our textual styles and discursive practices will alter the culture.

Situating social texts among the work of feminist writers and methodologists, they are revealed as having engaged and presented authors, who create the texts to reflect the intersection of prevailing sociocultural forces. They are characterized by a self-conscious textuality within which authors, researchers, knowers, and knotknowers are cocreators. For their creation, social texts require a space within which multiple voices can comment on experience.

◆ Quilts

Quilts offer the opportunity to explore the creation of a social text. They have been used for hundreds of years to document family stories, for example, in the form of wedding quilts, baby quilts, and mourning quilts (Federico, 1983; McKendry, 1979). They have been used to represent/document social issues in the form of commemorative

quilts such as the quilts created in World War I and World War II and the American Civil War. More recently, the AIDS Memorial Quilt (Howe, 1991) was created and displayed as a memorial to people who died of AIDS. A murder trial at the turn of the 20th century was represented in a quilt (Neyman, 1996); numerous family losses were represented in the Graveyard Quilt in the 1700s. There are hundreds of examples of quilts being used to represent social experiences. Moreover, women have used quilting, and the creation of a quilt, as a legitimate way to come together to work on what seems, at first glance, a utilitarian task.

In the past, quilts were mainly functional objects for the home; yet through the images and symbols used, women were able to tell stories of their lives. The quilt is a communicative expressive form or sign (Roach, 1985). Quilts contain symbolic messages and stories that are told and that exist beyond the life of the quilter. In some cases quilts are used as subversive acts—as a medium for the expression of resistance, rage, grief, and celebration. The irony is that, while these stories were created, not a word needed to be said.

For many, quilts are merely beautiful presentations of colors and patterns, but to those who know how to read them, they contain complex stories and meanings.

◆ Quilters

The people who made the quilts in the first project in which I explored this methodology were participants in an inpatient treatment program for trauma recovery. A more detailed discussion of that project can be found in two earlier works (Ball, 2000, 2003). Trauma survivors often struggle with issues of invisibility and silence. The concerns of what is not being said, of what is not being seen, are similar to the concerns discussed earlier of the silencing effects that traditional academic writing can have on the representation of experience.

Participants interested in the quilting groups were invited to create a quilt block representing their experience of survival, as well as maintain a journal that described their experience of creating the quilt block. How their experience was defined and interpreted was determined by each participant. Those who chose to participate in the quilting group met weekly over a 6-week period. The quilting group was open in the sense that new members joined at different points and each member determined her or his own level of participation. The group was not established for therapeutic purposes. It was clearly defined as an exploration of different ways to represent experience.

Participants made their quilt blocks from a choice of provided fabrics. Having a variety of materials/media available to the participants, as well as welcoming the use of their own materials, facilitated the process of creativity. It was not necessary for participants to know how to quilt or sew or have any particular artistic ability. The purpose was not to create a perfect quilt but, rather, to provide a safe space within which to explore the creation of a social text. That creation was determined by the participants.[1]

Twenty people made quilt blocks. Some made as many as three blocks. Some participants chose to work on their quilt blocks at home or at times outside of the scheduled quilt meetings. Once the quilt blocks and the accompanying journals were completed, the quilt blocks were sewn together into a quilt top. When the quilt top was completed it was quilted (sewn together with backing and batting) by a local quilting group. Three quilts were produced in the first group. (See Figures 30.1–30.3 at the front of this book for a color reproduction.)

The quilts carry messages and information into places (settings) that would not normally be receptive. In this sense they are subversive. Working with quilts somehow

gets between language and image to a place that does not express either and yet expresses both. As one of the participants wrote:

> Using this media to express myself and [my] experiences allowed me to express more of myself than I do in words and voice alone.

(See Figure 30.5 at the front of this book for a color reproduction.)

With regard to the quilts taking messages to places that they would typically go unheard, another participant wrote:

> It's a graphic way of saying, "We have a voice and we will be heard. We have a lot to say! Listen and learn! To those of you who work with survivors, I want to say that, even as we learn from you and honor your facilitation in our journey, you can learn from us. LISTEN TO US! We are the ones who have not died, who continue to heal and grow. We can also teach you."

(See Figure 30.5 at the front of this book for a color reproduction.)

It is the constructing of the quilt—the actual making of the blocks—that creates this space, journey, opportunity, opening. It is the time involved. It is slow. The images are not as immediate as they might be in drawing or painting. The quilts create movement, interactions, and thinking in nonlinear ways. It is important to see past the content into the realm of process and deep knowing. This methodology requires that both the linear and nonlinear are spun together, while maintaining a focus on how different types of combinations of perceptions can move understanding ahead to new places. This is the value of an arts-based methodology.

Pursuing arts-based methodologies and alternative methods of representation is difficult work, even brutal at times (Aisenberg & Harrington, 1988). It may be easier to remain within traditional discursive practices. If new knowledge and new understandings are to be created, then an openness to innovative methodologies is required.

Reexamining what is and can be known and how to know it, challenging discursive practices, looking for new ways to represent experience is exciting and sometimes painful work. In spite of the pain, or perhaps because of it, the knowing that comes from this type of methodology is much richer. The realities that are revealed are rendered in such exquisite detail that they are unforgettable. Social scientists now have the opportunity to create texts that matter inside and outside of the academy. Texts that provoke, evoke, disturb, challenge, make the reader laugh, gasp, or cry; texts that allow us to catch our breath and find our voices; texts that remind us that we are all together in this social world.

◆ Note

1. When working with quilts in this way, it is helpful to work with at least one person who knows how to quilt. This person can assist group members with the construction of their creations.

◆ References

Aisenberg, N., & Harrington, M. (1988). *Women of academe: Outsiders in the sacred grove.* Amherst: University of Massachusetts Press.

Baker, P. (1998). Hearing and writing women's voices. *Resources for Feminist Research*, 26(1&2), 31–53.

Ball, H. K. (2000). *Quilts as social text.* Unpublished doctoral dissertation, Wilfrid Laurier University, Waterloo, Ontario, Canada.

Ball, H. K. (2003). Subversive materials: Quilts as social text. *Alberta Journal of Educational Research*, XLVIII(3).

Denzin, N. K. (1992). The many faces of emotionality: Reading Persona. In C. Ellis &

M. G. Flaherty (Eds.), *Investigating subjectivity: Research on lived experience* (pp. 17–30). Newbury Park, CA: Sage.

Denzin, N. K. (1994). The art and politics of interpretation. In N. K. Denzin & Y. S. Lincoln (Eds.), *Handbook of qualitative research* (pp. 500–515). Thousand Oaks, CA: Sage.

DeVault, M. L. (1990). Women write sociology: Rhetorical strategies. In A. Hunter (Ed.), *The rhetoric of social research: Understood and believed* (pp. 97–110). New Brunswick, NJ: Rutgers University Press.

DeVault, M. L. (1996). Talking back to sociology: Distinctive contributions of feminist methodology. *Annual Review of Sociology*, 22, 29–50.

DeVault, M. L. (1997). Personal writing in social research: Issues of production and interpretation. In R. Hertz (Ed.), *Reflexivity and voice* (pp. 216–228). Thousand Oaks, CA: Sage.

Ellis, C. (1997). Evocative ethnography: Writing emotionally about our lives. In W. G. Tierney & Y. S. Lincoln (Eds.), *Representation and the text: Reframing the narrative voice* (pp. 115–139). Albany: State University of New York Press.

Ellis, C., & Bochner, A. P. (1992). Telling and performing personal stories: The constraints of choice in abortion. In C. Ellis & M. G. Flaherty (Eds.), *Investigating subjectivity: Research on lived experience* (pp. 79–101). Newbury Park, CA: Sage.

Ellis, C., & Bochner, A. P. (Eds.). (1996). *Ethnographic alternatives series: Vol. 1. Composing ethnography: Alternative forms of qualitative writing.* Walnut Creek, CA: AltaMira Press.

Federico, J. (1983). American quilts: 1770–1880. In C. Robinson (Ed.), *The artist and the quilt* (pp. 16–25). New York: Alfred A. Knopf.

Gordon, D. A. (1993). Worlds of consequences: Feminist ethnography as social action. *Critique of Anthropology*, 13(4), 429–443.

Howe, L. (1991). A text of the times: The names project. *Uncoverings*, 12, 11–31.

Kincheloe, J. (1997). Fiction formulas: Critical constructivism and the representation of reality. In W. G. Tierney & Y. S. Lincoln (Eds.),

Representation and the text: Reframing the narrative voice (pp. 57–79). Albany: State University of New York Press.

Lather, P. (1997). Creating a multi-layered text: Women, AIDS, and angels. In W. G. Tierney & Y. S. Lincoln (Eds.), *Representation and the text: Reframing the narrative voice* (pp. 233–258). Albany: State University of New York Press.

Lincoln, Y. S. (1993). I and thou: Method voice and roles in research with the silenced. In D. McLaughlin & W. G. Tierney (Eds.), *Naming silenced lives: Personal narratives and processes of educational change* (pp. 29–47). New York: Routledge.

McCall, M. M., Becker, H. S., & Meshejian, P. (1990). Performance science. *Social Problems, 37*(1), 117–132.

McKendry, R. (1979). *Quilts and other bed coverings in the Canadian tradition.* Toronto, Ontario, Canada: Van Nostrand Reinhold Ltd.

Michalowski, R. J. (1993). (De)Construction, postmodernism, and social problems: Facts, fictions, and fantasies at the "end of history." In J. A. Holstein & G. Miller (Eds.), *Reconsidering social constructionism: Debates in social problems theory* (pp. 377–401). New York: Aldine de Gruyter.

Neyman, G. (1996, March–April). The murder quilt. *Piecework,* pp. 30–33.

Orr, J. (1993). Panic diary: (Re)constructing a partial politics and poetics of disease. In J. A. Holstein & G. Miller (Eds.), *Reconsidering social constructionism: Debates in social problems theory* (pp. 441–482). New York: Aldine de Gruyter.

Paget, M. A. (1990). Performing the text. *Journal of Contemporary Ethnography, 19*(1), 136–155.

Pfohl, S. (1993). Revenge of the parasites: Feeding off the ruins of sociological (de)construction. In J. A. Holstein & G. Miller (Eds.), *Reconsidering social constructionism: Debates in social problems theory* (pp. 403–440). New York: Aldine de Gruyter.

Richardson, L. (1992). The consequences of poetic representation: Writing the other, rewriting the self. In C. Ellis & M. G. Flaherty (Eds.), *Investigating subjectivity: Research on lived experience* (pp. 125–137). Newbury Park, CA: Sage.

Richardson, L. (1993). Poetics, dramatics, and transgressive validity: The case of the skipped line. *Sociological Quarterly, 34*(4), 695–710.

Richardson, L. (1994a). Nine poems: Marriage and the family. *Journal of Contemporary Ethnography, 23*(1), 3–13.

Richardson, L. (1994b). Writing: A method of inquiry. In N. K. Denzin & Y. S. Lincoln (Eds.), *Handbook of qualitative research* (pp. 516–529). Thousand Oaks, CA: Sage.

Roach, S. (1985). The kinship quilt: An ethnographic semiotic analysis of a quilting bee. In R. A. Jordan & S. J. Kalcik (Eds.), *Women's folklore, women's culture.* Philadelphia: University of Philadelphia Press.

Ronai, C. R. (1996). My mother is mentally retarded. In C. Ellis & A. P. Bochner (Eds.), *Ethnographic Alternatives Series, Vol. 1. Composing ethnography: Alternative forms of qualitative writing* (pp. 109–131). Walnut Creek, CA: AltaMira Press.

Rosenau, P. M. (1992). *Postmodernism and the social sciences: Insights, inroads, and intrusions.* Princeton, NJ: Princeton University Press.

Shapiro, M. J. (1985/86). Metaphor in the philosophy of social sciences. *Cultural Critique, 2,* 191–214.

Smith, D. E. (1989). Sociological theory: Methods of writing patriarchy. In R. A. Wallace (Ed.), *Feminism and sociological theory* (pp. 34–64). Newbury Park, CA: Sage.

Spender, D. (1980). *Man made language.* London: HarperCollins.

Stenner, P. (1993). Discoursing jealousy. In E. Burman & I. Parker (Eds.), *Discourse analytic research: Repertoires and readings of texts in action* (pp. 114–134). London: Routledge.

Weedon, C. (1987). *Feminist practice and poststructuralist theory.* Cambridge, MA: Blackwell Publishers.

Widdicombe, S. (1993). Autobiography and change: Rhetoric and authenticity of "Gothic" style. In E. Burman & I. Parker (Eds.), *Discourse analytic research: Repertoires and readings of texts in action* (pp. 94–113). London: Routledge.

PART IV

INQUIRY PROCESSES

Chapters in this section focus on the pragmatics of doing research grounded in the arts. They are not intended as definitive statements about process but rather as "think-aloud" pieces that make transparent the messiness of the creative process. These chapters are both practical and inspirational in the sense of casting new possibilities for many readers. Because the process of art-research is inherently creative—dynamic, fluid, open, nonlinear—this section on process reflects this. Authors, each actively working in one of the genres discussed in Part III, both describe and reflect on how they engage in the creative research process. In a sense, these authors provide a close-up look at the creative inquiry process so that readers can gain insights into how elements of the creative/artistic process and elements of the research process (developing focus, situating research, data gathering, analysis, and representation and theorizing) come together as a whole and play out in scholarship.

- An Indigenous Storywork Methodology, *Jo-ann Archibald (Q'um Q'um Xiiem)*

- Literacy Genres: Housecleaning—A Work With Theoretical Notes, *Lorri Neilsen*

- From Research Analysis to Performance: A Choreographic Process, *Mary Beth Cancienne*

31

AN INDIGENOUS STORYWORK METHODOLOGY

◆ Jo-ann Archibald (Q'um Q'um Xiiem)

I have stood in many different circles of people, praying for guidance from the Creator, to help us make a better world for younger and future generations. I speak from the heart, and from the teachings and experiences of the Coast Salish peoples of British Columbia, in particular the Sto:lo of the Lower Fraser River.[1] Sto:lo means "river." We are strongly connected to the river systems in our traditional territory and to the resources of the river. My Indian name is Q'um Q'um Xiiem, which means "strong clear water." I am named after a particular place.

The teachings that I speak of have persisted since "time immemorial" and were vibrant when contact with non-Indigenous peoples occurred 500 years ago in Canada (Canadian Royal Commission on Aboriginal Peoples, 1996, p. 36). In many of the aforementioned circles, the Elders of the Indigenous[2] communities share their perspectives, knowledges, and insights gained from many years of learning, teaching, and reflection.

I am an Indigenous educator who values the power and beauty of our stories to educate and heal people. I have had the privilege of learning from Indigenous Elders for over 30 years. In this chapter, I highlight some important understandings that I gained from Indigenous Elders about an Indigenous storywork methodology. I talk about Elders and their teachings as examples of Indigenous traditional, ecological, and cultural knowledges. Then I introduce the concept of *storywork* and an important Indigenous character, the Trickster, and show the relationship between Indigenous teachings and storywork. Stories of working with Indigenous Elders and learning *Indigenous Storywork* comprise a substantial part of this chapter. The Trickster gets the last word.

◆ *Indigenous Elders: Teachings About Traditional, Ecological, and Cultural Knowledges*

Indigenous Elders possess wisdom and insight gained from their traditional, ecological, and cultural knowledges (TEC) and lived experience. Age is not the sole determining factor for achieving Elder status. Usually, people who are not Elders determine or name individuals to Elder status. Elder Ellen White, from the Snuneymuxw First Nation (around Nanaimo, British Columbia) Coast Salish Nation, said this about Elder characteristics: "To be an elder you first have to be accepted, listened to and not laughed at. You have to be a good speaker. . . . You always know where it's [knowledge] going to be in your memory, in your mind" (cited in Neel, 1992, p. 107). Elder Beatrice Medicine (1987) of the Lakota/Sioux Nation says: "Elders are repositories of cultural and philosophical knowledge and are the transmitters of such information" (p. 142). As noted in Ellen White's definition, respect from others and possessing cultural knowledge are critical characteristics.

I have heard Indigenous people say that what matters is how an individual "carries" her- or himself. They mean that an Elder must treat TEC knowledges respectfully and demonstrate responsibility or care in the process of sharing or teaching these forms of

knowledge. *Traditional knowledge* is a timeless type of knowledge that includes values and philosophies that have been transmitted from generation to generation. *Ecological knowledge* relates to place-based knowing and environmental knowledge. *Cultural knowledge* focuses on ways of living and combines contemporary with traditional ways of knowing. These three forms of knowledge are interrelated and shaped by Indigenous language. They are not the only Indigenous ways of knowing.[3] Elders have various knowledges or "gifts" to pass on to others. These include knowledge about spirituality, healing, medicine, history, storytelling, and language.

The term *teachings* includes the notion of combining forms of knowledge with values such as respect and responsibility. In this chapter I talk about Elders who live their good traditional teachings and carry on the tradition of compassionately and mindfully teaching others. Not all older people live good traditional teachings; therefore, they are not Elders.[4] Gregory Cajete (1994), a Tewa Indian from the Santa Clara Pueblo, New Mexico, provides a definition of the "goodness" I am promoting:

> The Indigenous ideal of living "a good life" in Indian traditions is at times referred to by Indian people as striving "to always think the highest thought." . . . Thinking the highest thought means thinking of one's self, one's community, and one's environment richly. This thinking in the highest, most respectful and compassionate way systematically influences the actions of both individuals and the community. It is a way to perpetuate "a good life," a respectful and spiritual life, a wholesome life. (p. 46)

I am fortunate to have learned from Elders who have upheld and "carried" their cultural responsibility by passing their teachings to others in ways that are heartfelt and mindful of traditional, ecological, and cultural knowledges, cultural protocols, and oral tradition. In the next section I introduce Indigenous storywork and the tribal Trickster, who will journey along with us.

◆ Introducing Indigenous Storywork and a Tribal Trickster

During a Sto:lo cultural gathering, one of the organizing speakers tells the guests, *"My dear ones, it is time to start the work."* When these words are spoken, it is time to give serious attention to what is said and done; this is the "cultural work." The words *story* and *work* together signal the importance and seriousness of undertaking the educational and research work of making meaning through stories, whether they are traditional or lived experience stories. Seven principles comprise storywork: respect, responsibility, reverence, reciprocity,[5] wholism, interrelatedness, and synergy (Archibald, 1997).

The four Rs of *respect, responsibility, reverence,* and *reciprocity* are traditional values and teachings demonstrated toward the story, toward and by the storyteller and the listener, and practiced in the storywork context. The other three principles of *wholism, interrelatedness,* and *synergy* shape the quality of the learning process. Indigenous wholism comprises the spiritual, emotional, physical, and intellectual domains of human development. Wholism also addresses the relationships among the self, family, community, wider world, and the environment. Effective storywork grows out of the actions of interrelatedness and synergy formed by the storyteller, the story, the listener, and the context in which the story is used. A transformative learning experience occurs by working with Indigenous stories and these seven principles. Storywork is also an Indigenous research methodology.

The research process of learning to make meaning through stories reminds me of a basket weaving experience. Sto:lo women weave cedar root baskets with their own trademark designs. During the basket making process, the pieces of cedar sometimes stand alone and sometimes they lose their distinctiveness and form a design. Similarly, the processes of research and learning to make story meaning are distinguishable as separate entities and sometimes they seem bound together, losing their distinctiveness. The basket designs that relate to research are the four Rs of *respect, reverence, responsibility,* and *reciprocity.*

The Trickster character helped me appreciate each of the storywork principles through an experiential approach of learning by feeling, thinking, and doing. In British Columbia, Aboriginal cultures have Trickster characters such as Raven and Coyote. In our stories, the multifaceted Trickster changes form and shape. The forms may range from human to any element of nature to a more sacred form. The Trickster often gets into trouble by ignoring good teachings such as sharing, caring, taking responsibility, and being fair and letting negative emotions such as greed and envy take over. Trickster's separation from cultural teachings and emotional connectedness to family, community, land, and Nation provide many life lessons as Trickster tries to reconnect to these teachings. Trickster is usually in motion, traveling and learning life lessons. Once in a while, Trickster surprises by using supernatural powers to help others. It is important not to be fooled by thinking that Trickster will use obvious "tricks" to get his/her/its way. I have learned to value Trickster's humorous learning ways and the process-oriented nature of teaching and learning through Indigenous stories.

Gerald Vizenor (1987) of the Minnesota Chippewa Nation also helped me appreciate the role of the tribal Trickster. He said that the Trickster is a "doing, not an essence, not a museum being, not an aesthetic presence" (p. 13). The notion of Trickster as a "doing" rather than a "being" fits with how I have come to appreciate the process of learning through Trickster stories. Trickster as a doing can change and live on through time as people interact with Trickster through stories. One does not have to be too concerned about what the Trickster looks like if he/she/it is a doing rather than a being. This notion of the tribal Trickster lets me interact with him/her/it. Coyote, then, helps me to reflect and gain understandings. He challenges and comforts me just like a critical friend.

Eber Hampton, Oklahoma Chickasaw Nation, told the following story to a gathering of researchers to whom he was talking about the relationship between research motives (why) and research methods (how). During his story and subsequent talk, I sensed there was much more to storytelling, and I knew that I had to rethink how I was going to find a meaningful place for stories in educational systems. Eber gave me permission to use this story and encouraged me to adapt it for storywork purposes.[6] I renamed the Trickster "Old Man Coyote" because Coyote, in all its forms, has become my Trickster of learning. The name "Old Man Coyote" called out to be named in this story.[7] In the background, we hear one of our Elders say, *"My dear ones, the work is about to begin."*

Old Man Coyote had just finished a long hard day of hunting. He decided to set up his camp for the night. After supper, he sat by the fire and rubbed his tired feet from the long day's walk. He took his favorite moccasins out of his bag and noticed that there was a hole in the toe of one of them. He looked for his special bone needle to mend the moccasin but couldn't feel it in the bag. Old Man Coyote started to crawl on his hands and knees around the fire to see if he could see or feel the needle. Just then Owl flew by and landed next to Old Man Coyote and asked him what he was looking for. Old Man Coyote told Owl his problem. Owl said that he would help his friend look for the bone needle. After he made one swoop around the area of the fire, he told Old Man Coyote that he didn't see the needle. Owl said that if it was around the fire, then he would have spotted it. He then asked Old Man Coyote where he last used the needle. Old Man Coyote said that he used it quite far away, somewhere in the northern direction, to mend his jacket. Then Owl asked him why he was searching for the needle around the campfire. Old Man Coyote said, "Well, it's much easier to look for the needle here because the fire gives off such good light, and I can see much better here."

I have behaved like Old Man Coyote many times, wanting to stay close to a cozy fire, wanting to continue to think, feel, and act in ways that are comfortable, familiar, and easy. But mentors like the Owl or the Elders come into my life to make me seek the bone needle—perhaps a solution for improving Indigenous education or finding a culturally appropriate research methodology. The search for the bone needle may mean going back to knowledge territories established by the Ancestors to gain clearer insights or find effective ways to bring heart and mind together in a modern-day educational context. Maybe the bone needle symbolizes something that could become a useful research tool. With the story Eber made me think and raise questions about the purpose and benefit of research. I challenged myself to find a culturally relevant way to carry out inquiry in order to make intellectual space for Indigenous methodology in academe. I also turned for help[8] to three Coast Salish Elders: Simon Baker, Vincent Stogan, and Ellen White. They taught me important research lessons about the four Rs of *respect, responsibility, reverence,* and *reciprocity.*

◆ *Taking Direction From Elders: Chief Khot-La-Cha, Dr. Simon Baker*

I have known Simon Baker since 1985 but have known about him for many more years in his role as Chief of his reserve, speaker for the Squamish people and ambassador for First Nations.[9] When I became the Supervisor of the Native Indian Teacher Education Program (NITEP) at the University of British Columbia, our group invited Simon Baker to speak to students on many occasions. He eventually became our NITEP Elder. Simon carries out his Elder teaching responsibilities with humor and life experience stories about cultural, political, social, and economic survival. My relationship with Simon took on a different teaching and learning dimension when he became one of my research advisors.[10]

I invited Simon to breakfast one day in the winter of 1990. We talked for quite a while. He spoke about his past life experiences. He always talks about his Ancestors and what they have taught him. Our talks are often like this. He readily agreed when I asked him to be one of my research advisors. I talked to Simon Baker many times from 1990 until his death in 2001. In the earlier years, I voiced my concerns about story representation and appropriation of stories. He helped me work through this concern by teaching me to appreciate the cultural concept of reciprocity. In the beginning stages of the research process he also helped me to conduct a pilot interview and data analysis. His guidance led me to use a storytelling interview approach.

Simon's determination to mentor others and to ensure that First Nations' cultural knowledge and values continue has helped me deal with "guilt" feelings associated with academic research. These feelings have not entirely disappeared, but now I am able to make space in academe to deal with ethical research issues and actions. Simon's latter years of life were devoted to sharing and teaching cultural knowledge that brought healing and good life to people. I have come to believe that bringing together cultural knowledge and research can create a better life for us and future generations.

Even though I am First Nations and have some initial understandings about various First Nations cultures, I become like an outsider when I use the "tools" of literacy to record my research observations and reflections on oral traditions and practices through fieldnotes and now through this publication. One of my journal entries states

> I felt tension in doing my first ethnographic observations at an Elders' gathering for a fieldnote exercise. Tension/uneasiness because I had to record people's behaviours, their words in key phrases, the physical setting, the chronological order of events, which is antithetical to the way I normally participate in this type of cultural gathering. Even if I hadn't taken notes during the event, I viewed everything with different eyes. Tension/anxiety because I had to become and see like an outsider. To do this, I visualized the event within a circle, and I stood outside it and I looked in. The act of writing notes also made me feel like an outsider. Tension/resistance because I knew I would eventually be writing for others about what I had seen and interpreted, thus transforming myself and culture. (J. Archibald, journal entries, May 27, June 20, and July 5, 1991)

The legacy of disrespectful research methods of early anthropologists, linguists, and health academics still looms over Indigenous communities. Community members are often skeptical of any researcher who comes to the community. Their concerns include the appropriation of Indigenous stories, knowledge, and even DNA (Menzies, 2004; Smith, 1999; Wuyee Wi Medeek, 2004). My affiliation with a research-intensive university shadows my First Nation identity and position. Simon helped me realize, though, that taking time to establish trusting relationships with research participants is critical. Once he illustrated the ethical issue of appropriation with an example of a time when someone used his words and knowledge without acknowledging him:

> In my den, I have many tapes in there. A lot of them say, "Why don't you let us use it?" I say "No, unless you people invite me to do something. I'll be glad to do it. But I'm not going to give you what I got so that you can use it and say I did this." That's what [so and so] did to me. Oh [so and so] sure used me. I don't mind it if you come, like you did. I gave you permission, that's good. I respect you for that and I know a lot of it will come out for good use. That's very good. (S. Baker, personal communication, February 18, 1992)

When Simon said those words, I felt very honored that Chief Simon Baker had agreed to be my guide and teacher. I also understood the importance of the responsibility that research should "come out for good use." From these anxious ponderings, I began to realize that respect and responsibility must be an integral part of the relationship between the Elder and the researcher: respect for each other as human beings; respect and responsibility for the power of cultural knowledge, and respect and responsibility for cultural protocol, for honoring the authority and expertise of the Elder teacher. The principles of respect and responsibility include trust and being culturally worthy.

Floy Pepper, an Elder of the Choctaw Nation and one of my mentors, read an early draft of this chapter and told me that she was tired of reading about my anxious feelings and that what she thought I meant was that I was not feeling worthy and ready to receive the Elders' cultural knowledge and teachings. Her point was well taken and, upon reflection, I agreed that not feeling culturally ready or culturally worthy was another dimension to the complex ethical feelings that I experienced. Now I understand that being culturally worthy means being intellectually, emotionally, physically, and spiritually ready to fully absorb cultural knowledge. Getting ready in this wholistic way is like participating in a "cultural protocol" that Walter Lightning (1992) describes:

> That term, protocol, refers to any one of a number of culturally ordained actions and statements, established by ancient tradition that an individual completes to establish a relationship with another person from whom the individual makes a request. The protocols differ according to the nature of the request and the nature of the individuals involved. The actions and statements may be outwardly simple and straightforward, or they may be complex, involving preparation lasting a year or more. The protocols may often involve the presentation of something. It would be a mistake to say that what is presented is symbolic of whatever may be requested, or the relationship that it is hoped will be established, because it is much more than symbolic. (p. 216)

In addition, the researcher must trust and have patience that the Elder is guiding the learning process in a culturally appropriate way. The Elder must also be culturally trustworthy. When I talk about trust, I do not mean that one should have "blind" trust, but one must know when an Elder is also worthy of trust and respect. In the background, I hear Old Man Coyote asking for the easy answer to how one knows.

◆ Telling Stories as a Way of Interviewing

Sit down and listen, and that's the thing, our Ancestors used to say.

— Chief Simon Baker (personal communication, February 17, 1992)

Sources of fundamental and important Indigenous knowledge are the land, our spiritual beliefs and ceremonies, traditional teachings of Elders, stories, and our lived experiences. Knowing the values and interrelated actions of responsibility, respect, reverence, and reciprocity are essential to understanding Elders' teachings. Understandings and insights also result from lived experiences and critical reflections on those experiences. Many Aboriginal people have said that, in order to understand ourselves and our situation today, we must know where we come from and know what has influenced us. The historical and intergenerational effects of colonization and assimilation still affect our people and communities today. Elders' life stories can show how we, as Indigenous Peoples, can keep our cultural knowledges intact.

In my early interviews with Simon, I used a reflexive approach—as discussed by Hammersley and Atkinson (1983)—to explore issues that bothered me. I wanted some general direction about how to start the research process. I wanted to ask Simon's advice about whom I might approach and how I should start my research work. I also needed to discuss ways of getting people to work with me and to discuss ethical concerns about research such as appropriation of cultural knowledge.

As I continued to work with Simon, our talks (interviews) moved from an issues-based process to "research as conversation" to "research as chat" (Haig-Brown, 1992, pp. 104–105) and then to "research as storytelling." Research as conversation is characterized as an open-ended interview with opportunity for both sides to engage in talk. Research as chat occurs when the researcher is very familiar with the participant(s) and they interact on a frequent basis. As I reflect upon the interview process many years later, I characterize the talking process as one during which Simon, the Elder, maintained control over the knowledge he wanted me to know. But he also was interested in what I thought about various matters and what issues I was concerned about in my role (at the time) as Director of the First Nations House of Learning at the University of British Columbia. On many occasions, Simon told life experience stories to exemplify leadership and political strategies that had implications for me: thus, research as storytelling.

I stopped using the taperecorder early on in our research relationship. Instead, I took written and "oral and heart memory" notes after discussions. Leilani Holmes (2000) realized the importance of blood memory and heart knowledge in her research work with Hawaiian Elders: "As I listened to the *kupuna* [Elder], it seemed as if through them, knowledge lodged in the heart of the listener, memory flowed through blood lines, and the land was given voice and agency" (p. 40). For me, the experience of taking oral and heart memory notes has similar meaning.

Simon stressed the importance of living honorably and showing respect to everyone because "in time," he said, "that respect could be returned to you" (S. Baker, personal communication, February 17, 1992). Simon's teachings guided me to seek out those Elders who continue to practice and pass on their cultural teachings. The cycle of reciprocity and reverence toward the spiritual are more dynamics of storywork.

◆ *Tsimilano, Dr. Vincent Stogan, Musqueam Elder: Tsimilano's Teaching of Hands Back and Hands Forward*

My dear ones, form a circle and join hands in prayer. In joining hands, hold your left palm upward to reach back to grasp the teachings of the Ancestors. Hold your right palm downward to pass these teachings on to the younger generation. In this way, the teachings of the Ancestors continue and the circle of human understanding and caring grows stronger.

During the process of learning about interviewing, I experienced similarly valuable lessons about respect, responsibility, and reciprocity between teacher and learner from another respected cultural teacher of the Musqueam people, Dr. Vincent Stogan, Tsimilano, which means "A Great Man." I also learned more about the principle of reverence. Vincent Stogan is a Spiritual Healer who works with many people across Canada and the United States. He and his wife, whom everyone calls "Mom," carry on the traditional healing and spiritual work passed down to him by his relatives. One day he told me how they got this important responsibility.

> A lot of Elders wanted me to take my grandfather's place. . . . He was a great healer, that old man. He was blind but he said when I was little. . . . "You are the one that's going to take my place and do this kind of work." I never thought of it until I was old enough. . . . I was about 45 years old I guess when we [Mom and I] noticed that our Elders were going fast, so we made up our minds that we had better do the work they want us to do.

We put our minds to it and then started the healing work. (V. Stogan, personal communication, August 16, 1994)

Vincent Stogan's relatives trained him in the spiritual ways. The spiritual dimension of the wholistic paradigm I mentioned earlier became more evident with my interaction with Elder Vincent Stogan. I had known Vincent since 1990 and watched him work at numerous gatherings, until his death in 2000. He was also an Elder Advisor to the students, staff, and faculty of the First Nations House of Learning at the University of British Columbia where I worked.

I started my conversations about oral traditions and began a research learning relationship with Vincent Stogan in 1991. In our first session, Vincent immediately became the teacher and I the learner (similar to the relationship between Simon Baker and me). Sto:lo cultural ways guided our teacher–learner relationship. I approached Vincent Stogan, a respected keeper of the culture, because I wanted to learn about a topic I did not know very much about. As an insider of the culture, I observed a cultural learning protocol: The Elder determined where we should meet, I ensured that there was sharing of food and tea, and I created unhurried time and talking space so that we could get to the topic of discussion at the "right" moment. It would have been disrespectful to ask my questions immediately. During breakfast we talked about many things. I told Vincent about my research interest in our oral traditions. I also spoke about the kinds of things I wanted to know, such as the way people learned to be storytellers and how people learned from stories. As he began to talk, he assumed the role of teacher and I understood that he was agreeing to teach me. His comments show how he intended to direct the learning process:

> Another way that I can help you get to know these things—it won't be just like

us talking now, it'll take time. I can go just so far and maybe we carry on some other time . . . because this is the teaching that we got that we can't hurry everything. . . . Well, I think knowing you this long, I know your parents now, where you're from, I'm willing to help you. I trust you and I know you're our kind. (V. Stogan, personal communication, May 17, 1991)

When Vincent talked about knowing my parents and knowing where I am from, I understood him to mean that our culture bonded us together in important ways. He felt responsible to help me because of our cultural bond. His decision to help me by becoming my teacher, and our subsequent talks made me realize that, as a learner, I too have responsibilities. Our relationship as teacher and learner had to be based on respect for each other and respect for the traditional cultural ways of teaching and learning, and reverence for spirituality. I also realized that reciprocity was essential to our working together. As learner, I needed to listen carefully and think "hard" about the meanings in Vincent's personal stories and his words. I could then check my knowledge and understandings with him to ensure their accuracy. Vincent carried out his Elder responsibility by teaching and also ensuring the correctness of the learning. My part then included acquiring and validating my understandings and eventually sharing them and becoming a teacher to others. This reciprocal action has a cyclical nature that is embedded in the "hands back, hands forward" teaching noted earlier.

Vincent also carried out important spiritual cultural work. He opened gatherings with prayer and sometimes song. He taught the "younger" ones the spiritual ceremonies in Sto:lo territory. The importance of addressing spiritual needs and asking for spiritual guidance from the Creator became

an important teaching for me and continues to guide my work. One time Vincent told me: "We always pray first to the Creator. . . . I think in your kind of work using [spirituality] will help you a lot. It's no shame to pray to the Creator" (V. Stogan, personal communication, May 17, 1991).

Elder Vincent Stogan provided me with guidance about how to conduct story research, and he taught me more about traditional spiritual teachings and cultural knowledge. He often telephoned me or dropped by the First Nations Longhouse to ask how things were going, or to say that he and Mom were going traveling. He called me his niece, although we are not directly related by kinship. I stopped taping and interviewing him and followed, for a while, the research as chat approach. I then switched to a traditional approach of learning from Tsimilano, as he first directed me: learning pieces at a time and not hurrying the learning. I watched him speak many times and at many different gatherings. We shared many private talks. What he taught me is in my oral memory and an important part of my heart knowledge and my spiritual being. His teachings are reflected on the pages of this publication and often guide my interactions with others.

Vincent Stogan also made a significant impact upon the work of the First Nations House of Learning by teaching us the importance of beginning our work, especially events, with prayer. He often opened many of the general university gatherings with prayer. His prayers said in the Halq'emeylem language helped to create a respectful atmosphere in which to interact. Tsimilano's teachings about the importance of the spiritual for learning continue in various forms throughout many First Nations learning and research environments today.

Establishing relationships within the storywork research context has become a way of establishing and sustaining lasting friendships with deep caring and endless stories and talk. Learning to listen with patience, learning about cultural responsibility toward the oral tradition, learning to make self-understandings, continuing the cycle of reciprocity about cultural knowledge, and practicing reverence are some of the lessons I experienced with Chief Simon Baker and Elder Vincent Stogan. These lessons and others are inherent in my relationship with Kwulasulwut, Elder Ellen White, who is from the Coast Salish, Snuneymuxw people. Kwulasulwut means "Many Stars." Elder Ellen White is my mentor, teacher, and dear friend. Ellen helped me gain a deeper appreciation of the teachings about respect, responsibility, reverence, and reciprocity that I applied to storywork for educational and research purposes.

◆ The Teachings of Kwulasulwut, Ellen White

I met Ellen White in 1991, but I knew about her long before that. For many years I admired Ellen's work as storyteller, writer, and healer. She has published storybooks (1981, 1995) and currently has one in press. I attended a public lecture given by Ellen at the Museum of Anthropology, University of British Columbia. She used stories, humor, song, and drum to engage listeners. Being there, hearing her words, took me back to another time and place when I listened to the Sto:lo Elders. After her talk, I introduced myself and acknowledged her good words, a teaching that I remember from Chief Simon Baker. He often said, "Go speak to the Elders. It feels good when someone acknowledges your work." This was the first time that I followed his teaching with someone I did not know. During our short talk, Ellen said that she thought she knew me from other times. I knew immediately that I wanted to work with and learn from her.

Our storywork relationship began when Ellen participated in a curriculum project in which Aboriginal students from across Canada wrote about their Aboriginal heroes. They wrote life experience stories, and some recounted traditional cultural stories. Ellen also agreed to participate in an interview and talk with me about the voices/teachings of the Ancestors for educational purposes. Our talk was taped, transcribed, cooperatively edited, and published in the *Canadian Journal of Native Education* (White & Archibald, 1992) with Ellen as the lead author. The following story exemplifies research issues about analyzing and representing cultural knowledge that emerged during our talk.

I traveled to Ellen's and her husband Doug's home to work on the journal article. When I arrived, Ellen served salmon chowder and bannock. As we ate, Doug and I teased each other about who drank the strongest coffee—me from the Sto:los or him from the Snuneymuxw Coast Salish. In a way we are related by the Halq'emeylem language. We come from the same cultural traditions. I felt accepted and at home there; I felt like a member of their extended family. Before we began working, I offered Ellen a Star blanket as a gift from the First Nations House of Learning, to thank her for helping us with this important work. When her husband left, I took out the tape recorder, and we sat at the dining room table. I reviewed the intent of the talk, the purpose of the publication, and the process of how we could work together: I would record and transcribe the talk, review the written transcript with her, and get her approval before the text— her story, her words, and her work—would be published (similar to the process used by Cruickshank, Sidney, Smith, & Ned, 1990; Wickwire & Robinson, 1989, 1992). Ellen asked what I would add to her words. I said that I wanted to write about what I had learned from her words and that our article would be cooperative: she and I would be the authors. Ellen said that she liked that approach because I could question what was not clear and add parts that were missing. Then Ellen began talking about some of her Ancestors; after a few minutes, she said to turn the tape recorder on.

I remember feeling excited and challenged emotionally, spiritually, and intellectually after I left the White's home. My journal entry notes:

> I feel almost overwhelmed! What a rich experience—to be involved at so many levels. . . . I get immersed in her stories. When Ellen talks about her Ancestors, it is as if she is "there with them"—her voice changes and she sounds as if she is her granny. I recall the power of her metaphors: trees, baskets, canoes, hair, paths, air/body. I see these images so vividly and, when I do the comparison and connection of them to life, considerations are so clear, so evident. (J. Archibald, journal entry, September 18, 1992)

The metaphors visually reinforce one teaching that has guided me since that day: Begin learning with the "core" of knowledge starting from the inside and going to the surface, the outside. Ellen said:

> They said, "You learn the base, the very basic, the inside, the stem, and the core." It sort of sounds like it when you translate it, the core of what you are learning and then expand out. The teacher will already know that—"It is like a big tree, never mind the apples or flowers, we're going to learn inside first and then out," they said, "never from outside first." (E. White, personal communication, September 18, 1992)

Ellen's Ancestors also said that it is important to take time to sit and think about and feel what we have learned. Until my encounter with Ellen, I had thought more about uncovering the layers of meaning

from story—going from the outside surface to the depths. Now, I had to completely rethink this approach and to go once more to the unknown to find this particular "bone needle."

On subsequent visits with Ellen, we reviewed the written transcripts for editing purposes. I suggested this process in response to Ellen's question about how I was going to use her talk and what was going to be put in print. My journal notes

> Ellen is so good to work with. She knows what words and information she wants kept in, what might be inappropriate for the readers, and what is culturally inappropriate for this article (i.e., particular healing and spiritual practices). (J. Archibald, journal entry, November 11, 1992)

This research experience with Ellen made me realize some of the complexities of cooperative research work with Elders such as requiring a lot of time to record, listen to, and transcribe recordings verbatim; examining together the correctness of English words that become public cultural record for future generations; and ensuring that the cooperating research partners are both satisfied with an article before it is published.

Ellen took the lead at the beginning of the transcription work, deciding what words and sections to keep and what to leave out. I gave her feedback on her directives and, by the end of the transcript, I could tell that our process was similar to that described by Walter Lightning (1992) and Carl Urion (personal communication, December 1, 1992) as "mutual thinking": When we came to certain parts, we simultaneously identified them. I think our process of getting to know one another, sharing the same cultural traditions, and establishing a consensual working approach led to mutual thinking.

Out of the complexities I gained an appreciation for four principles: respect for each other and for the cultural knowledge;

responsibly carrying out the roles of teacher and learner (a serious approach to the work and being mindful of what readers/other learners can comprehend); practicing reciprocity where we each give to the other, thereby continuing the cycle of knowledge from generation to generation; and reverence toward spiritual knowledge and one's spiritual being.

◆ *Hands Back, Hands Forward*

In the process of learning how to make meaning through stories, which is a core part of Indigenous knowledge, I reached back to the Elders of the Coast Salish communities to receive their teachings. I spent considerable time trying to understand these teachings. Ellen's thoughts about learning the Ancestors' knowledge are worth repeating here: "You could study the [A]ncestors, but without a deep feeling of communication with them it would be surface learning and surface talking" (cited in Neel, 1992, p. 108). Over many years, I learned about the storywork principles of respect, responsibility, reverence, reciprocity, wholism, interrelatedness, and synergy for educational and research applications. My research-learning relationships with three Elders, Khot-La-Cha, Tsimilano, and Kwulasulwut, also resulted in an intimate understanding of the four Rs of storywork research as an example of Indigenous methodology: respect, responsibility, reverence, and reciprocity. I purposefully detailed the four Rs because I want readers to understand these teachings. The four Rs can also become too comfortable, like staying close to Old Man Coyote's fire, and they can become a cliché, thereby losing their power. There is much more to the storywork research process and to the topic of Indigenous methodology[11] that remains unsaid, waiting for the next chance to tell a story.

In Coast Salish tradition, I hold my hand out to share my storywork methodology with you. For anyone who is interested in using this storywork methodology, I echo Chief Khot-La-Cha, Simon Baker's words, "Take what is useful," when learning something new. I also echo what Thomas King, Cherokee storyteller, scholar, and writer cautions: "Stories are wonderous things. And they are dangerous" (2003, p. 9). The danger exists when we do not have a deep understanding of the power and beauty of Indigenous stories. As Old Man Coyote joins the circle of Indigenous methodology, he holds out his palm and smiles, wondering how we and future generations will look for the bone needle.

◆ *Notes*

1. The term Coast Salish is used to describe the First Nations along the southwest coast of British Columbia. Sto:lo is one of the Coast Salish Nations. Sto:lo means "river" in the Halq'emeylem language. The lower Fraser River, and its tributaries between Yale and the Strait of Georgia, are the river boundaries of the Sto:lo cultural area.

2. The terms Indian, Indigenous, Aboriginal, and First Nations are used interchangeably, even though First Nations in some contexts is limited to mean Status Indian people. For the purposes of this article, Indian, Indigenous, Aboriginal, and First Nations refer to a person of Aboriginal ancestry. Indigenous will also signal that the matters affecting Aboriginal people are global: We share a history of colonization, and we strive to revitalize our knowledges and regain self-governance. Even though I write about a specific Indigenous culture and the geographical area of British Columbia, Canada, the storywork principles have relevance to territories beyond Canada.

3. See Marie Battiste (2002), Gregory Cajete (2000), Marlene Brant Castellano (2000), Fyre Jean Graveline (1998), Eber Hampton (1995), Oscar Kawageley (2001), Carolyn Kenny (1998), Jane Mt. Pleasant (2001), and Cora Weber-Pillwax

(2001) for diverse discussions about Indigenous knowledge.

4. Aboriginal communities and organizations across Canada have various ways of identifying and working with Elders, and their criteria may differ from mine.

5. I am thankful to Verna J. Kirkness and Ray Barnhardt (1991) for pointing out the importance of the "four Rs" (respect, relevance, responsibility, and reciprocity) for Indigenous postsecondary education in their milestone article "First Nations and Higher Education: The Four R's—Respect, Relevance, Reciprocity, Responsibility."

6. There are many complex issues concerning appropriation of First Nations stories, culturally appropriate times to tell particular stories, and who has authority to tell stories. The solutions to the issues are diverse and reflect the diverse nature of Aboriginal Nations in Canada. In this chapter, basic examples of ethical practices for storywork are introduced. Asking or getting permission to tell a story, and stating the name and nation of the person from whom the story is acquired, are examples.

7. I share the "Old Man Coyote and the Bone Needle" story because it is one of the stories that connected to me on an emotional level first, and made me shift my thinking and challenged me to continue learning about the educational significance of Sto:lo and Indigenous stories by going on a research journey.

8. These Elders have worked with numerous people in a diverse ways. Often an Elder will determine the learning approach based on the needs and interests of the learner. These approaches may be very different from the story approach that I have discussed in this chapter.

9. Verna J. Kirkness (1994) worked with Simon Baker to document his life story. See *Khot-La-Cha: The Autobiography of Chief Simon Baker.*

10. At the time of my request, I was undertaking my doctoral research at Simon Fraser University, Faculty of Education. I completed my dissertation in 1997.

11. See the following sources for critical discussions about Indigenous research: Marie Battiste and James (Sa'ke'j) Youngblood Henderson (2000), Karen Swisher and John Tippeconnic III (1999), Canadian Royal Commission on Aboriginal Peoples

(1996), Linda Smith (1999), and Shawn Wilson (2003).

◆ References

Archibald, J. (1997). *Coyote learns to make a storybasket: The place of First Nations stories in education.* Unpublished doctoral dissertation, Simon Fraser University, Burnaby, British Columbia, Canada.

Battiste, M. (2002). (Ed.). *Reclaiming Indigenous voice and vision.* Vancouver, Canada: University of British Columbia Press.

Battiste, M., & Henderson, J. (S.) Y. (2000). *Protecting Indigenous knowledge and heritage: A global challenge.* Saskatoon, Saskatchewan, Canada: Purich Publishing.

Cajete, G. (1994). *Look to the mountain: An ecology of Indigenous education.* Durango, CO: Kivaki Press.

Cajete, G. (2000). *Native science: Natural laws of interdependence.* Santa Fe, NM: Clear Light Publishers.

Canadian Royal Commission on Aboriginal Peoples. (1996). *Report of the Royal Commission on Aboriginal Peoples: Vol. 1. Looking forward, looking back.* Ottawa, Ontario: Canada Communication Group.

Castellano, M. B. (2000). Updating Aboriginal traditions of knowledge. In G. S. Dei, B. Hall, & D. Rosenberg (Eds.), *Indigenous knowledges in global contexts: Multiple readings of our world* (pp. 21–36). Toronto, Ontario, Canada: University of Toronto Press.

Cruikshank, J., Sidney, A., Smith, K., & Ned, A. (1990). *Life lived like a story: Life stories of three Yukon Elders.* Vancouver, Canada: University of British Columbia Press.

Graveline, F. J. (1998). *Circle works: Transforming Eurocentric consciousness.* Halifax, Nova Scotia, Canada: Fernwood Publishing.

Haig-Brown, C. (1992). Choosing border work. *Canadian Journal of Native Education, 19*(1), 96–116.

Hammersley, M., & Atkinson, P. (1983). *Ethnography: Principles in practice.* London: Tavistock Publications.

Hampton, E. (1995). Towards a redefinition of Indian education. In M. Battiste & J. Barman

(Eds.), *First Nations education in Canada: The circle unfolds* (pp. 5–46). Vancouver, Canada: University of British Columbia Press.

Holmes, L. (2000). Heart knowledge, blood memory, and the voice of the land: Implications of research among Hawaiian Elders. In G. J. S. Dei, B. L. Hall, & D. Goldin Rosenberg (Eds.), *Indigenous knowledges in global contexts: Multiple readings of our world* (pp. 37–53). Toronto, Ontario, Canada: University of Toronto Press.

Kawageley, O. (2001). Tradition and education: The world made seamless again. In K. James (Ed.), *Science and Native American communities: Legacies of pain, visions of promise* (pp. 51–56). Lincoln: University of Nebraska Press.

Kenny, C. (1998). The sense of art: A First Nations view. *Canadian Journal of Native Education, 22*(1), 77–84.

King, T. (2003). *The truth about stories: A Native narrative. CBC Massey Lecture Series.* Toronto, Ontario, Canada: House of Anansi Press.

Kirkness, V. J. (Ed.). (1994). *Khot-La-Cha: The autobiography of Chief Simon Baker.* Vancouver, British Columbia, Canada: Douglas & McIntyre.

Kirkness, V. J., & Barnhardt, R. (1991). First Nations and higher education: The four R's—respect, relevance, reciprocity, responsibility. *Journal of American Indian Education, 30*(3), 1–15.

Lightning, W. (1992). Compassionate mind: Implications of a text written by Elder Louis Sunchild. *Canadian Journal of Native Education, 19*(2), 215–253.

Medicine, B. (1987). My Elders tell me. In J. Barman, Y. Hebert, & D. McCaskill (Eds.), *Indian education in Canada: Vol. 2. The challenge* (pp. 142–152). Vancouver, Canada: University of British Columbia Press.

Menzies, C. (2004). Putting words into action: Negotiating collaborative research in Gitzaala. *Canadian Journal of Native Education, 28*(1/2), 15–32.

Mt. Pleasant, J. (2001). The three sisters: Care for the land and the people. In K. James (Ed.), *Science and Native American communities: Legacies of pain, visions of promise* (pp. 126–136). Lincoln: University of Nebraska Press.

Neel, D. (1992). *Our Chiefs and Elders: Words and photographs of Native leaders.* Vancouver, Canada: University of British Columbia Press.

Smith, L. (1999). *Decolonizing methodologies: Research and Indigenous peoples.* London: Zed Books.

Swisher, K., & Tippeconnic III, J. (Eds.). (1999). *Next steps: Research and practice to advance Indian education.* Charleston, WV: Clearinghouse on Rural Education and Small Schools.

Vizenor, G. (1987). Follow the Trickroutes: An interview with Gerald Vizenor. In J. Bruchac (Ed.). *Survival this way: Interviews with American Indian poets* (pp. 287–310). Tucson: University of Arizona Press.

Weber-Pillwax, C. (2001). Orality in Northern Cree Indigenous worlds. *Canadian Journal of Native Education, 25*(2), 149–165.

White, E. (1981). *Kwulasulwut: Stories from the Coast Salish* (New ed.). Penticton, British Columbia, Canada: Theytus Books.

White, E. (1995). *Kwulasulwut 11: More stories from the Coast Salish.* Penticton, British Columbia, Canada: Theytus Books.

White, E., & Archibald, J. (1992). Kwulasulwut Syuth: Ellen White's teachings. *Canadian Journal of Native Education, 19*(2), 150–164.

Wickwire, W., & Robinson, H. (1989). *Write it on your heart: The epic world of an Okanagan storyteller.* Vancouver, British Columbia, Canada: Talonbooks/Theytus.

Wickwire, W., & Robinson, H. (1992). *Nature power: In the spirit of an Okanagan storyteller.* Vancouver, British Columbia, Canada: Douglas & McIntyre.

Wilson, S. (2003). Progressing toward an Indigenous research paradigm in Canada and Australia. *Canadian Journal of Native Education, 27*(2), 161–178.

Wuyee Wi Medeek. (Lewis, J.). (2004). Forest for the future: The view from Gitkxaala. *Canadian Journal of Native Education, 28*(1/2), 8–14.

32

LITERACY GENRES

Housecleaning—A Work With Theoretical Notes

◆ Lorri Neilsen

The challenge in arts-informed inquiry has always been epistemo-logical: How do we come to know and how do we express or con-vey that knowing? What does it mean to know? Novelists, playwrights, poets, and creative nonfiction writers not engaged in social science research are typically immune to the debates: Fiction (or poetry, or—) is a form of knowing (Neilsen, 2003); so, what's the problem?

In the literary world, the scientific enterprise rarely applies. What use would it serve to ask, for example, as Louise Rosenblatt (1980, p. 386) did, "What facts does this poem teach you?" Imagine an enterprise in which knowledge construction applied to the literary world resulted in an argument about whether Carol Shields's representation of women's lives supplants Margaret Laurence's representation.[1] Supplants—for what pur-pose: To replace a current theory? To be cited first and often in the liter-ature? Why? In literary genres, authenticity, aesthetic expression, and resonance are the primary concerns. In the case of Shields and Laurence, both authors (and their texts) create legitimate, credible, memorable descriptions of the lives of strong women characters. If critics (the scientists of the literary world) want to engage in qualitative evaluation and theoretical pigeonholing, certainly we cannot stop them. But readers and authors looking to find credible (and sometimes aesthetically exciting) representations of lives are there for the experience—both of the writing and the reading—that moves them to understanding, to insight, to the enjoyment of the aesthetic. There is no literature review to be created afterward, no invitation to current arguments about the merits of Morag's world (Laurence, 1974) over Daisy Goodwill's (Shields, 1993). Only critics (and those who develop book club discussion questions) seem to enjoy that enterprise. Literary writers and readers, it seems, prefer to watch the red-winged blackbird fly rather than pinning the bird to a board and dissecting it to analyze flight.

As language users, we have a range of communication modes available to us. In social science research, we use far fewer than is healthy for the growth of our profession and of our capacity to engage with the world. We have strengthened our muscles for argument, propositional discourse, hortatory expression, categorizing, and creating hierarchies. In social science, and particularly in education, we have let our other muscles languish (see Neilsen, Chapter 8 in this volume, for further discussion). The work of Roman Jakobson (Jakobson, 1960) and James Britton (Britton, Burgess, Martin, McLeod, & Rosen, 1975) among others has argued for schooling that allows students to use their expressive, aesthetic, and descriptive powers as language users. This call has been taken up by arts-informed researchers who argue for research and teaching at all levels to embrace diversity in our expression. The increased appearance of literary genres as literary genres—works of art as works of art—in the social sciences is an indication that we are ready to "know" in ways that perhaps we are unable to tell. We

are ready to embrace ambiguity, liminality, the quiddity of a work (its *thisness*) for its own sake. A work's utility has never been as simple as the cause and effect relationships we hold dear in the social sciences. Literary genres show us in powerful ways that we can be moved (shaken, awaken, aesthetically, emotionally and psychologically altered) and that is enough.

This chapter provides an exemplar of literary writing. "Housecleaning"[2] is a published creative nonfiction piece that includes poetry, dialogue, and prose poetry. The work was created over a period of several years. Pushed to say what it is about, I might answer, "It's about the body, about loss, about letting go"; but pushed to describe its theoretical underpinning or the knowledge it conveys, I would turn the question back to the reader because in the way that literary genres work, it's the reader, finally, who decides.

The work appears in its entirety below. To highlight the qualities of literary genres, the preoccupations of authors, and any craft issues that apply in the writing, I have added notes for the reader. These are not meant as prescriptive, but the aim is certainly for the notes to offer a glimpse into the decisions that created the work. At the end of the chapter, the reader will find a list of reference works pertaining to "Housecleaning" itself, and to the art and craft of writing in literary genres.

◆ *Housecleaning*

The body itself is a dwelling place, as the Anglo-Saxons knew in naming it banhus (bonehouse) and lichama (bodyhome).

—Mairs, 1989, p. 7[3]

Dust. Stale smoke. I wrestle another box from the back of the top shelf.[4]

— Good grief, Mom.

— I know. I have no idea what's in there. When he left, everything was tossed into boxes and I put them away. Up and away.

— Hang on. It's too heavy. I'll get down off this chair.[5]

Under the white scrub brush of hair I see her scalp is pink, a shock of youthful skin unlike her tea-brown hands and finely wrinkled face. She is bent as she beetles from the closet to the living room with one item after another. My mother, walking through the world in italics. But that line of rough red skin that arcs from the nape of her neck to her shoulder—is it getting worse? The place where her fingers are drawn, sweep, sweep, like she is strumming a guitar behind her. Something under the skin, she insists: a fungus, and the doctors can't figure it out.

— Oh, I've needed to do this for years. What a jumble. What's in that white one? Whoof—so much dust in the air.

Fungus schmungus, say my brothers. It's OCD—eighty years of anxiety funnelling through her hand and writing pain on her body.[6] Dirty Thirties. Father dies. Mother leaves. War years. Marriage; children. Major surgery several times. Twenty moves across the Prairies in 37 years. Divorce. Left for a bit of nookie my age who'd followed him around for years. Heart attack. Then: blindness. How much can a body take? This morning, when I woke her up—Oh, my, have I slept that long? Oh, my, I never sleep-in, I'm always up by six—her eyes looked as though she'd been travelling deep. No finger-sweeping so far today. It has to be nerves.

— Spatula. Old electric knife. Colander. Cheese grater. Tupperware thingees. An extension cord. Old Christmas

cards—blank. They're pretty yellowed, Mom.

— Oh, my. I'll never use those. Millie's coming on Thursday to clean and shop for me. She'll want those for her daughter. She's on her own now, with the kids.

— This old can of Silvo should just be thrown out, I think. Remember that?

— What?

— The Silvo. This finger. Baby finger. I was—what—five, maybe six? I figured if you can get it in, you can get it out. You can't see the scar, but it's right there, right across the knuckle.

— You were always curious. And bad. They made those spouts with metal then.

— Sometimes it amounts to the same thing for a kid, doesn't it? They haven't improved much on packaging. Cornstarch boxes, for one—If they can put a man on the moon—

— Did you find the pictures up there? I swear he took the pictures, you know. I keep hoping I'm wrong. Yes. Or honey containers. Cornstarch. Honey. Silvo's the worst.

This is a different tone, I think. Not: "If he doesn't want the family, why would he want the pictures? Just for spite, that's what. Selfish. Arrogant. It was always about him, always about his needs." The rants have abated these last few years. He is still He—no name. But language no longer seems to open the wound. Yesterday, when I mentioned I ought to call him to say I am in town, her comment was sincere: "I think he would appreciate that." No acid leaking from the words. No sudden rising from the chair to slam the cup on the counter.

— Let's get all these down in one swell foop and see what's inside. Do you want to put the kettle on for some tea? I'll put these in the living room.

* * *

Women haven't had eyes for themselves. They haven't gone exploring in their house.

Through writing her body, a woman may reclaim the deed to her dwelling.

—Mairs, 1989, p. 7

— CJOB traffic watch. Twenty-eight below, exhaust fog. Car stalled on Bishop Grandin. Icy out there, folks, so take it easy.

Still dark. We're falling toward winter solstice, shortest day of the year. From the fifteenth floor, one floor above Mom's, I can see a stream of lights—prairie ocean of cars—and fog. Not a phrase I hear at home in Nova Scotia. Ice pellets, black ice, plain ordinary fog, sea smoke, yes. But not exhaust fog. The hum of traffic like a low growl. I wonder how she can stand the noise.

Long day yesterday. She'd hardly slept the night before, waiting for me to come.

She's probably exhausted, and sleeping in. Either that or still wired, up at five a.m. listening to American talk shows on the radio, sitting by an open window in her bedroom, smoking. Angry at "that stupid man George Bush." When she arranged for the guest suite for me, neither of us knew it would be only a floor away from hers. She was thrilled to be able to take the stairs. One at a time and slowly.

Today she wants to go through her closet, to send me home with things. I've always spouted some far-fetched fantasy that I could free myself from all worldly possessions—everything in a backpack—to teach myself impermanence. What a load—I'll never do it. If you have time on your side you can indulge in playing at principled behaviour. When

you're walking in that valley of the shadow—I want you kids to have these, so there are no fights or hard feelings when I'm gone—when you know you will never again make a large spread of jellied salads, baked ham, scalloped potatoes and an assortment of pickles, you don't need the Silver Birch. It just collects dust. It's not a principled decision. It's practical. Serious housecleaning—getting ready to have only a body. Thirty years from now, will I be ready to be that realistic?

Eight a.m. I looked for some tea. The kitchen was well-equipped for guest quarters. Microwave, tea pot—broken handle but it worked. A lot of frill and floral around, a lot of plastic. Mom had carried up a poinsettia last night, a real one. A petal lay on the floor now, curled. I needed to leave it there. She had balanced a plate of fruit in the other hand: tangerines, an apple, and grapes with all the stems removed. A couple of them rolled off the plate as she wrestled the door open, but she managed. She always knows where to feel. Proprioception, I think it's called. How the body feels itself in space, knows how far to reach, what angle to shift. She's become a curved five-foot antenna. Human radar. A lightning rod.

A couple of years ago, the morning after she called to say that the macular degeneration had suddenly swept away the last veil of light and shadow, I woke up, closed my eyes. Used the washroom, brushed my teeth, tried to make tea, find a banana, the oatmeal in the cupboard and the switch on the stove. I lasted fifteen minutes. What would I do? My body knows so little. Most of what I take in is with my eyes: a novel, a poem, a street sign, facial expressions, where I last left my hairbrush. All my senses, and still I'm handicapped.

Nearly thirty below out there. Shirtsleeves weather at home. When I arrived at the Winnipeg airport, I lay my coat on the luggage cart and walked outside to the rental kiosk. Foolish. It may be a dry cold here, but it's bloody cold. I'd forgotten about the clap of ice in your throat as you breathe, the hollow sound of boots on frozen ground. I'd forgotten what every cell in my body had learned all those years on the prairie—from Northern Alberta to Saskatoon to The Pas, to Dauphin, to Winnipeg. The real Canadian winter. The baseline winter, against which my body has measured all other winters. But this exhaust fog—that's new, and not exactly what I'd call progress.

By now, Mom should be up. When I hugged her last night, she felt like a wire cage. I kissed the red scar on her neck, rubbed her back. You need a good, long sleep, I said.

* * *

When we were children, we formed an enclosure of hands linked into arches and sang: Go in and out the window, as you have done before. *Writing my past as a body enacts that circle game. I invite you through my openings because I have been schooled in hospitality . . . writing itself is space. It is a populated house.*

—Mairs, 1989, p. 10

— Oh. My. God. Mom, this is the pattern you used to make David's sweater.

— And yours, you know. I'd saved that from when you were in high school. You had to have that sweater. Had to; had to. You came home and said "We're all going to Regina on the bus for the drama finals and everyone has a Cowichan except me." I had a three-year-old, a ten-year-old, an eleven-year-old—and you—I was working for the VON part time, and I still did a whole sweater in less than a week. I don't know how I did it.

— I don't know why you did it. Oh, here we are. A box of pictures.

* * *

═ Cowichan[7] ═

at sixteen we tumble on the bus to the provincials, props folded, capes and gilded gowns tucked in trunks, greasepaint and pompadour wigs, clamour in the belly of the night-riding coach, merry troupe of tender thespians, delectable tomorrow under our ribs, a time to make old Willy proud, out-perform the others, our lanky limbs wrapped in splendour, lungs inhaling the excitement of the small-town crowd, hear them now—*imagine, this old gym, transformed, just like that, in no time*—but tonight, we ride, ninety-nine bottles and boys at the back, girls, the front and our Native-knit sweaters a roll call in a glance: Pat's, browner, Mardi's narrow pattern edged in black, Wayne's high collar, smaller weave, mine homemade and Dale's worn, shredded at the elbow and the sleeve. Oiled wool, stitches purled and turned, patterning the night, knitting our bodies, imprinting days unravelling, singular, pile them on the floor before rehearsal and find yours after with the ease of an old dance, just as you know a face in a photo years from now, how you lift it whole from blur and grey, how you wear it like a talisman inside your skin, how its heat makes you shiver—*transformed, just like that, in no time.*[8]

* * *

— Oh, my. Are they in—

— frames, envelopes. And dust. We'll sort them. Some here from Alberta, from Edson. Some from Strathclair, when you were a girl. Look, this must be Jean. Have you talked with her since last summer? How's she doing?

— Viv died, you know. Stroke.

— Oh Mom, I'm sorry. Oh, I didn't know. When? Did you tell me and I forgot?

— Maybe. It doesn't matter. I'm glad I got to see her last summer. I'm glad you met her.

— How's Doug?

— Not so good. Jean says he won't last. I introduced them, you know. Viv and Doug. I was going out with Doug's brother and we used to double-date. Donald Beamish. He never came back from the war. By then, I'd met your—

— That was a great trip, Mom. Viv was so frail. Your best friend. Well, your first best friend. I can't believe that Jean is eighty-five.

— Hot as Hades and she still made me smoke outside!

— You and those smokes. I have no idea where that Cowichan is now. Are these round needles for socks?

* * *

The past itself is an oneiric house: the house we were born in. You can't get into it in real time, or in real space . . . there's no place to go to get there. . . . Nor can you relive it, even in imagination, if by that you mean re-experience it exactly as it occurred. You are now another person.

—Mairs, 1989, p. 14

=== Home Stretch[9] ===

Febrile air, Portage la Prairie PetroCan
and the restaurant boarded up. Only a till,
a restroom. Trucks swarm like flies
around the rich draw of pumps
and on the east side, in shade,
a shiny hog, black as a roach
and a biker's tan body stroked by shredded jeans.
He holds a lighter at the end of a long brown
fresco of tattoo and leans toward the
woman's tiny frame,
his ponytail whipping in the fetid exhalation
of traffic on the Trans-Canada, this long
hot summer road. Snaps
his thumb, flame pops out like a tongue.
She curls around it, curves into a promise
of smoke, late afternoon hit, one of the few
     remaining

pleasures, she always says. Her hair white
as stripped bone, too near the flame I notice,
and her hand shakes, steady now, steady, the glare
of prairie sky beyond glancing off her shades—
We're pariahs, you know.

She spits it out like a blown piston, barks
her Dunhill-and-scotch laugh and the trucker
at the pump nearby startles, notes
the rumpled face, white cane, body like
a divining rod, tremulous and twisting,

but grounded.
She nods her thanks, the biker
smiles, they are nose to nose now—
We get it where we can, you bet.
They giggle, inhale with satisfaction.
I have emerged from the restroom
into the fullness of the sun and waited within
     earshot until
she has tossed the smouldering inch
next to the Harley wheel. He flicks his next
to hers. They look out beyond the shimmer of
     road
ahead, huddled,
silence reaching.

I join them, grind the fires out with my heel
and they look at me as through a dream. Smile.

Take it easy now: whisper, fingers light on her
sleeve. My mother grins at us, gives me her arm,
warm and fragile as ash, lifts her cane
in salute and we open the door
for the last leg home.[10]

* * *

— I'm so glad you found those pictures. Her voice from the bathroom.

— I'll make copies of them for Brian and Ron.

— I wish I could see them. Even the shapes. For a long time I could still see shapes.

— We'll sit down and I'll describe them to you.

Her hair, flat against her skull like the down of a wet cat. The room is steamy, and I catch a glimpse of her belly—the cup that poured five children into the world. Only three of us around now. One stillborn, and one who seems to have disowned us all—both long gone. Her breasts are flat against her chest, and as she snugs the tie of her dressing gown, I see they hang at her waist. First food. First body of knowledge. I flash to an image of Playboy cartoons of the 1960s and 1970s, caricatured images of old women. Every young man's worst fear; everyone's cruel joke—even women laughed. The story of a woman's body: Madonna, whore, and then hag. Woman disintegrates into a disposable joke—we've come a long way, baby. I find a dry towel on the rack and begin to rub her head.

— Fuzzy wuzzy wasn't very fuzzy, was he?

— Did you find the crème? She laughs.

— Yes, and it's aloe vera, too. Should work great. It'll soften the skin, at least. Give you some relief.

Her skin is like a sponge. The crème goes on easily and I find myself wincing at the angry raw abrasion on her neck. The memory of Sheryl.

— You remember my friend Sheryl, Mom?

— You taught with her. Went on trips. Does she still have her travel agency?

— No. She's gone. Pancreatic cancer. About a month ago. I had a long talk on the phone with her daughter, Kelly, before I came here. She's a doctor, an AIDS researcher, in Toronto now. She took time off work to be with her mom for the last few weeks.

— Oh. Oh, my.

And I rubbed crème on her everyday, Kelly had said when I called. Pancreatic is the worst, you know. You starve to death and you're in pain constantly. I had to monitor the morphine. Slept in a chair by her bed. She was curled in a ball like a malnourished child. All the body fat gone—her backside was flat and her buttocks concave. Massaging her gave her a bit of relief. It was a gift, really. It was all I could do. That, and sit there as she drifted in and out. As Kelly talked, I thought of all the burial rituals that honour the body of the dead with water, lotions, perfume. Even the bodies of emaciated old hags. Especially them.

— It happened so fast that Kelly wasn't even able to contact everyone to let us know she was sick.

— This is the best present I could ever have.

— Good. I'm glad.

— I mean you being here.

* * *

Like all children, except perhaps orphans, my memories begin before I have the capacity for remembering, coded for me in the tales adults, and Mother in particular, recount over and over, joined in time by stuttering images that gradually become surer, more continuous, until I can say on my own: "I remember!"

—Mairs, 1989, p. 16

= Combustion[11] =

And so the nuns put my brother Jack into the
    furnace, and
that's that. My mother doesn't know until she
    wakes up, the
white shoes a whisper by her bed, my father's
    voice cold sand
in her ear. And I, at home, curled near the heat
    register

on the floor, Gram despairing that I won't eat.
Won't eat.
Waiting for the baby. Snowball sits on the back
of the chesterfield, watching what wind does in
the claws
of bare trees, the drifts outside too high and
wilding for her
paws, too high for me and my snowsuit. Too
high, too cold.
And the black phone on the wall. And no baby.
Fine then,
no soup. *They decided*, she says now, fifty years
away, as we sit
on the deck, our skin inhaling summer-waning
sun. *The Holy*
Trinity. Doctor, nun, husband. Dead of winter.
They could have
waited until I saw my son's face. Dead. Of winter. She stuffs out
her cigarette, rolls her head back. That distance.
Where she
goes. I reach, grasp only the howl of storms in
the small
railway town, fist of cold at the door in winter,
maw of
streets under high clouds and summer dust. My
father's voice at supper—*they fired the sta-*
tionmaster today: image of a man
tied to a pole over a bonfire. A July parade.
Crepe paper, my
white peaked hat and apron, the Old Dutch
cleanser woman.
Joey, hobbling beside me, brown fringed hat
and holster. The
water tower the highest thing in the world at
the end of
Main Street. Drums. And the Switzer girls, on
their tricycles
ahead of us, gone the next winter. Fire, the
whole house
down. Clang
of our coal stove, my father shovelling early in
the morning.
Heat. Cold. Mother. Gram. Cat. And the empty
space where
a baby was going to be. Old shadows, smoke of
memory. I
could pull out the old Brownie photos, crisp
and snapping
from their little crow-wing tabs, I could burn
those into my

mind. But how to go back on my own. How to
go where she
goes, even to the edge. She pulls out her lighter
again.
The DuMaurier, a small white finger in her
mouth, sparks.
Ash. *Lying there, cut from my gut to my ribs.*
Sick from ether. Out
cold. And he comes home from Hinton in time
to tell them to go
ahead. Dispose of the body. Small town. Small
hospital. And you
at home, waiting. Stillborn. A brother. Out of
the chimney into
the air. The whole town breathing him. Her
smoke drifts off
the deck toward the trees, a wavering white
line.[12]

* * *

— CJOB Weather. Warming up out there, for those of you headed out to do some Christmas shopping. Ten below, no snow in the forecast, but watch out, the mercury is dipping ver-rrry low tonight, so bundle up. Minus 30, and that will stay with us for the next couple of days.

I pack my great-grandmother's crocheted bedspread into my suitcase—each time I push with my hand, the smell of smoke escapes. I dust off the mirror and brush set, wrap them inside a sweater to protect them. Yesterday I spent at a Mailboxes outlet, having Gram's few remaining pieces of Limoges packed in about nine square feet of bubble wrap and Styrofoam. Why do I keep these things? Because Mom wants me to have them? Because I know they were touched by bodies no longer here? Because I want to imagine the stories, perhaps even re-create the stories that trail behind them? How do we carry stories forward except in bodies? on bodies? through bodies? Will my sons care that their great-grandmother bought herself one piece of Limoges per year before the war? That their great-great-grandmother's hands were the crucible through which this bedspread was formed? The alchemy of hands.

No, that doesn't work—words fail. The body can never tell all it knows.

* * *

My body is going away/It fades to the transparency of rubbed amber held against the sun/It shrinks. It grows quiet.... Who will have it/when it lies/pale and polished/as a clean bone?

—Mairs, 1989, p. 240

— Have you got everything? In her housecoat, misbuttoned. Sleep in her eyes. Coughing. Her bunions poking from her soft slippers like aberrant thumbs. I should have made you breakfast. You can't go out like that, without eating.

— I finished up the fruit, Mom. Thank you for that. And thanks for everything. I loved being here. I'm just sorry I wore you out.

— Oh, no, I'm all filled up. Cheered me up. I'm good for a few months now. And that damned closet is finally clean. Oh, my, that was bothering me.

— I don't like that cough. Take it easy. Be careful in your bedroom with those cigarettes.

Her small warm body. I kiss the top of her head.

— I'm fine. They did an X-ray, you know. He said my lungs are like a twenty-year-old's.

— Uh, huh. Well. My fingers on her cheek. My brother says I'm starting to look like her.

The thought used to scare me.

— I hope that storm doesn't hold you up in Toronto. Call me when the plane lands.

— I promise.

One body. Then another. Cell division over time and over land. Bodies propelled through frigid air, so natural, so unnatural. Tin cans full of stories and connections. Cargo—crocheted bedspreads. A hairbrush. An old photo of us at 1019 15th Street, before my brother was born. If we crashed in the Arctic, who could match bodies with belongings, pictures with stories, bodies with knowledge? What do I fear? Not leaving something of what my body knows, has learned. Erasure.

The suitcase wheels squeak along the corridor, past the mistletoe on 1428, the large red sock on the door of 1418. I press the down button on the elevator turn to wave one last time. At the end of the hall, her hand, a small tree branch shaking through the crack in the door.[13]

◆ *Notes*

1. Carol Shields and Margaret Laurence are highly regarded Canadian novelists whose works include *The Stone Diaries, Unless,* and *Larry's Party* (Shields) and *The Stone Angel, A Bird in the House,* and *The Diviners* (Laurence).

2. "Housecleaning" was first published in 2004 in the *Journal of the Canadian Association for Curriculum Studies, 2*(1), 101–112. Copyright © Lorri Neilsen Glenn. Reprinted with permission.

3. Unless otherwise noted, all quotes in italics at the beginning of sections are from Mairs (1989). This work includes epigraphs such as this one throughout. Epigraphs are common in literary works as they can set the stage for the work and provide context, tone, or location. Sometimes their purpose is explanatory; other times, epigraphs can create catalytic tensions—ideas rubbing up against one another—in the way that bricolage itself does. Bricolage is a form of improvisatory writing as this work demonstrates, using materials at hand to create a work that subverts the linear, presenting pieces as they come to mind or as they "talk" to one another.

4. I chose to bring a moment into sharp focus by using present tense and short phrasing (to

simulate thought) and by abandoning quotation marks. Readers over the last 20 years (the sociological explanations are many and varied) seem to follow distilled material easily. In fact, poetic economy and precision are often found in contemporary prose.

5. The dialogue here is reconstructed, aiming for the "truth" of the conversation, not literal fact. All the exchanges and details in this "nonfiction" account are based on what I know to have "really" happened. Yet obviously, it is my perspective. Triangulation of data is not necessary. Resonance and believability are. The line between fiction and nonfiction is blurred: Author Fred Stenson (2002) suggests writers use the "purport" test: If the writer intends the work to be fiction, it is; to be nonfiction, it is. Journalists must pay attention to verifiable fact (although there have been spectacular lapses in the profession in that regard). However, fiction writers use verifiable fact as well as fantasy and whole-cloth implausibility, and nonfiction writers use techniques (e.g., dialogue, description) we expect fiction to demonstrate. Fictionalized accounts of historical figures' lives are common on the fiction shelf. Some challenge historians for the degree to which they fictionalize accounts of events and people. Lines in the sand are drawn and redrawn, and the debates continue; for this reason, I find Stenson's distinction helpful.

6. My mother has heard and approved of the material; however, the issue of informed consent is rarely addressed in literary works, unless the material is such that it invites a lawsuit.

7. From Neilsen Glenn (2007).

8. This is an example of a prose poem. Again, drawing the line to distinguish prose poem from poem is difficult. Typically, the language of poetry is condensed, language reaching for the impossible, and, as though the reader must leap from one peak to another—one phrase or image to another—highly charged, abbreviated, and semiotically potent. Poetry does not always lay out the explanation of a feeling or event in the way prose typically does. Poet Don McKay (personal communication, May 12, 2004; see also McKay, 2002) claims that we can lay language on a continuum between song and speech. Lyric poetry (personal expression, usually short—see Chapter 8 in this volume for discussion) is on the one end, conversation on the other. If we use

McKay's criteria, this prose poem is closer to speech, and thus prose, than it is to the lyric poem. The next poem in this piece, "Home Stretch," is closer to the lyric end of the spectrum.

9. Neilsen, L. (2003). *All the perfect disguises*. Fredericton, New Brunswick: Broken Jaw Press. Copyright © Lorri Neilsen Glenn. Reprinted with permission.

10. This poem, like most, underwent a dozen or more revisions. The challenge for poetry in arts-informed research is to work on image, intention, and tone. Language, rhythm, and line breaks, among other almost inarticulable features, and how they work in concert are critical to the effect of the poem. Using phrases of rendered data in plenty of white space—with frequent and random line breaks to give the appearance of poetry on the page—is not enough. Here the issue of quality rears its unpleasant face: If we, as arts-informed researchers are to embrace literary genres, we owe it to ourselves and to the field to apprentice ourselves to the craft (and the art), not simply adopt its most obvious features. Consider the lines "body like/a divining rod, tremulous and twisting/but grounded." I chose to keep "a divining rod, tremulous and twisting" in its own line. It pulls from "body" (which will be described as divining rod), but also takes its own place as an image—the divining rod itself. This is meant to provide more power and propulsion than leaving the line to describe the body alone. Line breaks in poetry often are hinges, leaning back, craning ahead. The line space after "twisting" intends to embody the idea of "grounded" by using the space on the first line of the next stanza as a place to land. For more information on poetry as data, see Lynn Butler-Kisber and Anne Sullivan (2004). This publication is devoted to the practice of rendering poetry in research.

11. From Neilsen, L. *Combustion.* Copyright © Lorri Neilsen Glenn. Reprinted with permisson.

12. This prose poem was several years in the making. As an apprentice poet (who will always be apprenticing), I began with several poems about my early childhood in a Northern Alberta town (this is, apparently, common for writers and poets—to begin with what they know and either fictionalize it or render it into poetry— some argue that researchers have the same impulse to research aspects of their lives that want

resolution). Although moments in that time were romanticized in my memory (the parade on the first of July, my friend with spina bifida, my cat, my grandmother), shadows lurked behind the memories. The poet Jane Hirshfield (1997) says that poetry is always the union of Mnemosyne and Hermes, memory and communication. Memories of childhood are often most vivid because we were highly impressionable, both emotionally and physiologically (we had proportionally less Mnemosyne than when we are older). The process of coming to this poem, then, was a process using writing as re-membering in many threads and through many lenses, particularly from my mother's perspective and through at least a half dozen related poems. This is a form of triangulation that seems to be a cousin of the processes in social science research, but is phenomenological and remains so—memory as a construction we're willing to renovate as we age and as we gather other sources of information. As Mairs (1989) suggests, we never re-member "on our own." Grief and loss are key to this poem, as they are to the larger piece. Although I could have chosen more romantic versions of experience that appear in the earlier poems, they did not ring true here. The gravity of life in a small town in the fifties was critical to a story of bodies and aging. As well, because this piece needed a fuller and deeper description of my mother's character, it called for material about her that pierces (to use a term from Hausherr, 1982), material that doesn't sentimentalize, divert its gaze, or back down. In my ongoing apprenticeship as a reader and writer, I am learning that writing that compels doesn't dot its i's with hearts. I must do what I can and leave the thinking and feeling to the reader.

13. The ending of this piece is conventional: I've used the organizing structure of a visit, right to the leaving at the end, as a vehicle for the stories and layers of experience. As the author, I'm still struggling with whether the piece is too sentimental: The challenge in literary writing always is restraint. As Hirshfield (1997) says, we must tell stories with "the compassion that comes when the self's deepest interest is not in the self, but in turning outward and into awareness" (p. 222).

◆ References

Britton, J., Burgess, T., Martin, N., McLeod, A., & Rosen, H. (1975). *The development of writing abilities*. London: Macmillan Education Limited.

Butler-Kisber, L., & Sullivan, A. (Eds.). (2004). *Journal of Critical Inquiry Into Curriculum and Instruction, 5*(2).

Hausherr, I. (1982). *Penthos: The doctrine of compunction in the Christian east.* Kalamazoo, MI: Cistercian Publications.

Hirshfield, J. (1997). *Nine gates: Entering the mind of poetry:* New York: HarperPerennial.

Jakobson, R. (1960). Linguistics and poetics. In T. A. Sebeok (Ed.), *Style in language* (pp. 130–144). New York: Wiley.

Laurence, M. (1974). *The diviners*. Toronto, Ontario, Canada: McClelland and Stewart.

Mairs, N. (1989). *Remembering the bone house*. New York: Random House.

McKay, D. (2002). *Vis a vis: Field notes on poetry and wilderness*. Kentville, Nova Scotia, Canada: Gaspereau Press.

Neilsen, L. (2002). Learning from the liminal: Fiction as knowledge. *Alberta Journal of Educational Research, 48*(3), 206–214.

Neilsen, L. (2004a). Housecleaning. *Journal of the Canadian Association for Curriculum Studies, 2*(1), 101–112.

Neilsen, L. (2004b). Learning to listen: Data as poetry, poetry as data. *Journal of Curriculum Inquiry Into Curriculum and Instruction, 5*(2), 41–43.

Neilsen Glenn, L. (2003). *All the perfect disguises*. Fredericton, New Brunswick, Canada: Broken Jaw Press.

Neilsen Glenn, L. (2007). *Combustion: Poems*. London: Brick Books.

Rosenblatt, L. (1980). What facts does this poem teach you? *Language Arts, 57*, 386–394.

Shields, C. (1993). *The stone diaries*. Toronto, Ontario, Canada: Random House.

Stenson, F. (2002). *Thing feigned or imagined: The craft of fiction*. Banff, Alberta, Canada: Banff Centre Press.

33

FROM RESEARCH ANALYSIS TO PERFORMANCE

The Choreographic Process

◆ Mary Beth Cancienne

◆ Moving Data

I am often asked the question, how does one move from an analysis of an educational qualitative study to a performance? Another way to think about this question is to ask, what is the process of moving from written language to body language? There are three main areas that I draw from in moving from a discursive symbolic system (words) to a presentational symbolic system (movement). The first area concerns the role of image and metaphor. The second is the role of dance technique and choreography, and the third is the role of childhood educational experience. For more than 15 years, I have choreographed dance performances based on literary pieces, curriculum theory writings, and autobiographical reflections (see Cancienne & Snowber, 2003) within an educational setting. More recently I have begun to choreograph based on educational qualitative data analysis. Performance doesn't necessarily entail representing experience through movement. In general, when someone thinks of the word "performance," theatre is the art form that comes to mind. Because my artistic training originates from modern dance technique, my performances are movement oriented. This means that I intentionally use movement as a symbolic system to represent or influence the words that are spoken on stage.

To look more closely at how image, metaphor, choreography, and educational experience function in process, I use examples from one qualitative research study that I performed several times and have also presented on a CD-ROM (Cancienne & Bagley, 2002). In the article "Educational Research and Intertextual Forms of (Re)Presentation: The Case for Dancing the Data," Carl Bagley and I argued for the use of dance as a medium for representing educational qualitative research (Bagley & Cancienne, 2001). In that article, we describe the performance that represented a section of the research data on school choice, markets, and special educational needs. The article also includes questions and concerns that I raised with Bagley, the researcher, about the interview data, the performance script, and the opportunities and challenges that we faced when we presented the performance at the American Educational Research Association (AERA) in 1998. The description of the study follows.

◆ School Choice, Markets, and Special Educational Needs

The article "School Choice, Markets, and Special Educational Needs" by Bagley and Woods (1998) presented data from a qualitative longitudinal research study (1994–1996) conducted in the United Kingdom. The Education Act of 1993 in the United Kingdom states that all state schools must have a code of practice and must publish information about their policies for serving children with special educational needs. To help parents identify an appropriate school for their child, the local educational authorities enforcing this act are responsible for informing the parents of the different types of ordinary and special schools in their area. The act is designed to help parents make informed decisions about their children's education in terms of school choice, diversity, and site-based management.

Whereas data were collected for 5 years in three case study areas, I included interview data gathered in only one case study area (Northern Heights). These findings represent 11 interviews with parents whose children were identified as having special educational needs. Parents had a possible choice of three different schools that their children could attend. The following themes emerged from the analysis of the interviews: lack of information, traumatic and stressful negotiation, fact-finding exercise, school visits, friends' advice, a headmaster's speech, and protection and happiness.

I now explain the three main categories that I used as a method of choreographing based on a qualitative research analysis. The first category draws from my personal experience as a child, the second category uses images and metaphor, and the third category shows how I use the elements of choreography and image and metaphor. Three of the eight sections of this performance are explained below. It is important to note that this performance was choreographed for an audience of educational researchers who, in general, were not choreographers or dancers. Since few educational researchers other than Blumenfeld-Jones (1995) and Cole and McIntyre (2001) had previously represented research through the medium of movement/dance at the American Educational Research Association, I was very cautious. For this purpose, I chose to choreograph movements that were mostly literal and closely represented the words of the research participants. Sometimes the movements are so literal that they are mimed. At the end of this chapter, I provide a critique of this performance, which includes alternative scenarios to this work.

◆ *Choreographic Process*

Performer 1 (Carl Bagley, the researcher) sits at the back left-hand side of the stage. Performer 2 (Mary Beth Cancienne, the choreographer) stands upright center stage. As Bagley reads the themes from the analysis of the study in a nonexpressive, straightforward manner, Cancienne speaks the voices of the parents who were interviewed and interprets their meaning through voice and movement. The following script is excerpted from Bagley and Cancienne (2001).

THEME: LACK OF INFORMATION

Performer 1 (*researcher reading from cue cards*): "The knowledge of parents of their child's special educational needs remained relatively limited and unclear."

Performer 2: *Standing in the front left-hand corner of the stage, the performer pretends to open a book [while trying to sound out a word] and says,* "I know my child is poor at reading." *Walking to the back right-hand corner of the stage, the performer writes a name with her foot, then looks up and says,* "I know my child can't really write." *Walking to the front right-hand corner of the stage, she paces back and forth, places her right hand on the right-hand side of her face, and says,* "But to be honest, I really don't know what *all* (emphasis) my child's needs are when looking for a school." (Bagley & Cancienne, 2001, p. 229)

Sometimes there are themes within educational data that will connect to a choreographer's childhood educational experience. Such is the case with the passage stated above. The theme of "inadequate or missing information" regarding a child's special educational need reminded me of the frustration that my siblings and I experienced in the educational system in southern Louisiana, where we lived. My two brothers, who were not diagnosed with dyslexia until they were in their 20s, had a difficult time reading and writing. At the time educators knew very little about dyslexia as a special need. As a result, my brothers did not receive the kind of attention that they needed, and I saw their ongoing frustration with school. My mother was also frustrated by not being adequately informed about why her two sons were not doing well in school.

In addition to drawing from my brothers' frustration, I recalled my own problems with reading and writing in school. Though I was an "A" student and read and wrote well, I enjoyed reading with my book turned upside down and writing stories starting from the right-hand side of the page moving to the left-hand side. Teachers would hold a mirror to my work to read my papers. Many were very upset when they saw that I read with my book turned upside down. I was placed in a lower reading group as a form of punishment.

Drawing from personal experience and connecting that experience to the section entitled "Lack of Information," I chose to read from an imaginary book turned upside down and also to write my name on the floor with my left foot from the right-hand side to the left-hand side. The images of the upside-down book and the unconventional right-to-left writing not only highlight my own personal experience but also serve as powerful representations of the "Lack of Information" theme. I drew from this experience to connect the parents' voices with the movement choices that I made on stage.

Although choreographers may draw from childhood experience to connect to a written text, they also draw on or recall images and use metaphor to translate words into movement. Alma Hawkins (1991) writes:

Images, both memory images and newly imagined ones, are basic ingredients in the creative process. They feed the process and play a significant role in bringing about innovative connections between bits of sensory data. The emergent synthesis from this process provides the germinal material for choreography. (p. 42)

In one section of the performance entitled "Traumatic and Stressful," I portrayed a tightrope walker to represent the experiences of parents who did not receive a sufficient amount of information in choosing a school for their child. The tightrope walker metaphor powerfully illustrates the words of one parent, who described her experience as "difficult, rough, and nightmarish" (Bagley & Cancienne, 2001, p. 229). In this way, the metaphor of the tightrope walker conveys in concrete terms the parents' frustration and sense of trauma.

THEME: TRAUMATIC AND STRESSFUL

Performer 1 *(researcher reading from cue cards):* "The experience of choosing a secondary school is particularly traumatic and stressful for parents with children who have special educational needs."

Performer 2: *Walks on an imaginary tightrope with arms stretched, she says,* "I found it difficult picking a school for my children who didn't have problems." *She appears to lose her balance with her upper torso leaning side to side. With her back leg in the air, she takes a step forward and, regaining her balance on the tightrope, says,* "But because he has got so many different special needs, it was really, really hard. It was a really tough time, really rough." *She loses her balance and falls and with her hands and feet walks backwards frantically, breathing*

heavily, and then suddenly stops, faces the audience and with a look of anguish she says, "It was a nightmare, literally." (Bagley & Cancienne, 2001, p. 229)

Just as the tightrope walker feels nervous and stressed because she has to walk a thin rope with little support, the parents experience stress because they have to choose a school for their child even though they lack information about their child's special needs.

Choreographers use elements of choreography whether or not they are conscious of it. For instance, all dances have elements of energy, rhythm, and space. In this next section, I specifically used elements of choreography based on the theme "Fact-Finding Exercise" by identifying the elements that I wanted to include.

THEME: FACT-FINDING EXERCISE

Performer 1 *(researcher reading from cue cards):* "The middle-class parents tended to be the ones who had spent the most time in planning and preparing for a school visit and making a choice."

Performer 2: *Repetitively moving her arms and legs back and forth in a stiff, machine-like pattern and in a monotone voice she says,* "I conducted a fact-finding exercise. I phoned up all the schools before I visited them, drew up a short list, prepared a set of questions, then visited the school with my child during school hours." (Bagley & Cancienne, 2001, p. 229)

The parent stated that he chose the best school for his child by "conducting a fact-finding exercise" (Bagley & Cancienne, 2001, p. 229). I used these words as the theme for this section. The parent described his process in a logical, mechanical manner. His words made me think of a robot that was completing a task. In thinking of how to portray this image, I turned to the basic elements of choreography, which are concepts of space, time, force, body, movement, and form (Gilbert, 1992). Using the parent's words, I decided to move in general space using a straight pathway and with a singular focus. Additionally, I decided to move at a medium speed with sharp, sustained energy.

In the preceding paragraphs, I took three sections from a performance and explained the process by which I transformed words into movements. In creating this process, I drew from images, metaphors, the elements of choreography, and personal experience. The following is the overall framework that I used to choreograph this study.

Hawkins's (1991) explanation of the creative process of choreography is very much in agreement with my own understanding. She identifies a developmental pattern that, though unique for each choreographer, includes the following stages: taking in, feeling, imaging, transforming, and forming. Hawkins describes taking in information as "a constant flow of sensory data (visual, aural, tactile, and kinesthetic)" (p. 5) that one takes in from the outer world and makes sense of internally through organizing fragmented experiences into a meaningful relationship.

Choreography can be seen as the process of giving out, which is the expression of how one has made sense of data. One of the first steps in the creative process of translating the findings of the United Kingdom study on school selection was to take the data from the external world and bring it into my internal world. First, I read the representative quotes from parents and the researcher's analysis of them. I also read the transcripts of the parental interviews several times. After reading these data, I began to attend to the qualities of the information by working to absorb the educational research analysis on a daily basis.

The next step of the choreographic process involved focusing on the "felt" experience of these data. Felt experience includes both physical and emotive responses to stimuli. While reading the text and immersing myself in the data, I became aware of my own bodily sensations as well as personal memories and new images in order to make more conscious decisions about the entire work.

As recollected images or new images entered into my consciousness, I recorded them on paper and began to move/dance to the images. The fourth stage of the choreographic process is when the choreographer transforms feelings and images into movements. Whereas in the beginning stages the choreographer takes sensory data from the outer world and brings it into his or her inner world, in the transforming stage the inner world is projected metaphorically to the outer world through movement/dance. Hawkins (1991) writes, "This means that images and felt experiences are transformed into movement elements and qualities in such a way that the movement event presents an objectification of inner experiencing" (p. 41). In the transforming stage, the choreographer works and reworks the patterns of motion—energy, flow, spatial patterns, and rhythmic structure.

Since initial movements can inspire other movements, I continued to move until I felt that I had incorporated all of the parents' words into the movements. I readjusted my movements if something did not feel right physically or did not represent parents' words based on my interpretation. Finally, I recorded the movements on paper. Forming or synthesizing inner experience is the final step in the choreographic process. When the dance is formed, the choreographer has used artistic expression to make sense of data to share with others. All five steps—taking in, feeling, imaging, transforming, and forming—are essential to the choreographic process.

RESEARCH QUALITIES WITHIN CHOREOGRAPHY

Reflecting on this process, I noticed a few important similarities between qualitative research and choreography, one of which involves the use of themes. Since the researcher organizes qualitative data analysis around themes, it seems logical to start with thematic discursive language (data analysis) and move to presentational language (choreography). A qualitative researcher organizes data analysis thematically just as a choreographer organizes movement thematically. Therefore, I use themes from the data analysis as motivation for my movements. *In the Art of Making Dances*, Doris Humphrey (1959) writes

> The choreographer must behave as though the theme were of the highest significance, for if he [sic] does not, the fire goes out, the piece becomes routine and the public will know that nothing has happened when it is finally on view. (p. 28)

Humphrey believes that a choreographer should develop a theme-centered work and then the appropriate movements will follow. In the case of the United Kingdom study, the themes generated from the data inspired the choreography.

Another way in which the choreographic process is similar to the research process is the centrality of interpretation. Researchers gather and make sense of the data using an interpretive framework (Denzin, 1997), and then they share their findings with an audience. Just as the choreographer may draw from technique, theory, personal/cultural experience, feelings, images, and metaphors to shape sensory data from the outer world, the researcher may draw from technique, theory, personal/cultural experience, feelings, images, and metaphors to shape the analysis of the data.

Dewey (1938) writes, "An experience is always what it is because of a transaction taking place between an individual and what, at the time, constitutes his [sic] environment" (p. 43). As such, Dewey's "transactive account" sounds very similar to Hawkins's (1991) description of the choreographic process as first an immersion in sensory input (taking in) and then an outward projection indicating an interaction. The performance can be viewed as the transaction among the choreographer, researcher, and the research data. A researcher's data analysis can be viewed as the transaction between the researcher and participants. In the case of this performance, I interacted with the research by means of a choreographic process and then presented a synthesis of this interaction through a performance.

This process constitutes what Dewey (1934) would call "an experience." It is important for educational arts-based researchers like myself to engage in an in-depth process of interpretation for the purpose of making an educational statement about the research for audiences, to move them to think critically and ultimately to take action based on the research findings.

FROM PROCESS TO CRITIQUE: A POSTMODERN PERSPECTIVE

In the final section of this chapter, I make a radical leap from process to critique. Although the performance described above drew more from the literal than the abstract, I critique my creative process by making suggestions based on what I currently think about this performance. I use a postmodern perspective drawn from participatory critical action research as well as feminist critical dance and performance studies for the purposes of thinking about my future research and its representation. It is important to note that this longitudinal qualitative research study (Bagley & Woods, 1998) employed interviews and surveys and was not a participatory critical action research study. I chose to represent the study in the form in which it was conducted. I have chosen to critique this performance using a postmodern perspective; however, I do not want to devalue the form in terms of its intended purpose. In many ways, the performance was a success. For example, the performance allows the representation of the research participants to express more emotion and interpersonal connection than is possible in conventional scholarly writing.

Participatory critical action research and the performance of that research seek to disrupt traditional power relationships by showing the complexity of the relationship. In the *Dancing the Data* performance, the roles of the researcher and the participants are not blurred. The dialogue does not show the participants as researchers and the researcher as a participant. By failing to address the complexity of the relationship between the researcher and participants, the performance may be viewed as reinforcing stereotypes of traditional research methods.

From the perspective of participatory critical action research, I reinforce stereotypes of traditional research methods in two ways. First, I draw a sharp distinction between the researcher and participants to show concretely the distance between the researcher's supposed objectivity and the participants' emotionality and subjectivity. The researcher and participants do not speak to one another or even make eye contact. Another example of how I reinforce stereotypes is that the researcher sits in the back corner in a director's chair in an elevated position and higher than the participants. He towers over the person who portrays the parents' voices (the participants). In many ways, I made choices in staging the performance that reinforce the stereotype of the researcher as an omniscient

figure and the participants as essentially powerless. In this performance, I chose to make this power distinction apparent instead of questioning this uneven power relationship.

In the larger context of this performance, one of the purposes of arts-based representations at the American Educational Research Association's annual meetings is to represent the emotional lives of participants in a more meaningful way than in a traditional academic paper, thus bringing the lives of the participants center stage. At the same time that arts-based representations are connecting the educational community to the emotional lives of research participants, the arts-based community must also ensure that well-rounded, complex lives are portrayed.

If I were to choreograph this performance using a postmodern perspective, I would need to consider including the gaps, omissions, and absences in the performance as well as incorporating a disruption technique throughout the performance. One way to include omissions would be for Bagley, the researcher, to explore on stage his "psychological and emotional states before, during, and after the research experience" (Finley, 2003, p. 282). This would place the researcher and participants in a more complex relationship with one another and challenge notions that the researcher is omniscient.

I could incorporate the disruption technique in two ways. I could use subtitles in the performance video to show that it is a critique of traditional research methods. Another approach would be to have the researcher begin to dance while the performer, who represents the participants' voices, sits in the director's chair and becomes the researcher.

To move the discussion further, I continue to critique this performance from a variety of theoretical perspectives, including feminism, critical dance, and performance studies scholarship. I am particularly interested in exploring the following questions about the body, identity, and its representation in performance: What is at stake when the body is brought into discussion about representation and identity? Are gender stereotypes reinforced by this performance?

Much is at stake when bringing the physical body into the center of a discussion about representation in research performance. Traditionally, Western philosophy has separated mind from body, and socially this separation extends to how audience members view women on stage. Albright (1997) writes, "We need to interrogate and deconstruct ideas that situate the body as preculture, as the 'natural' ground onto which society builds its own image" (p. 7). For instance, the White heterosexual European male researcher is viewed as the "I," the rational being, and everyone else (women, people of color, people with disabilities, and homosexual males) has been tied to the material conditions of their body. Connecting Albright's theory of the body as nonrational with my own desire to represent research data through performance is problematic. I am a woman who historically has been marginalized socially and considered only a "body," and I am representing research data through literal movements and voice, a supposedly nonintellectual, entirely physical art form (Albright, 1997). Creating postmodern performance to represent educational research data becomes paramount if I wish to disrupt traditional notions of the body and identity and how it is played out on stage.

In the United Kingdom study performance, the researcher is male and the dancer, who represents the participants, is female. From this perspective, this performance could unintentionally be seen as a reenactment of gender stereotypes. Many postmodern and feminist theorists suggest that a role reversal between the researcher and dancer would help to disrupt gender stereotypes. That is, Carl, the researcher, should dance, and I, the

dancer, become the analyst who cites the research themes. Changing roles at certain points during the performance is one way to move beyond traditional notions of gender. This role reversal challenges the stereotypes of the researcher as the White European heterosexual male researcher and a strictly rational being who can transcend his physicality and of woman as a purely emotional self who is imprisoned by her physicality.

Arts-based researchers (in my case, a choreographer/performer/researcher/writer) have the opportunity through written word and performance to construct different representations of identity and the body in regard to gender, race, class, sexuality, and disabilities. Exploring postmodern performance techniques is a way to rethink and reconstruct the body in performance. The Bill T. Jones and Arnie Zane Dance Company is one professional dance company that asks audiences to question traditional notions of race, class, gender, and body image by choreographing postmodern performances (Banes, 1994).

Representing research data through performance as an inquiry process has had both intended and unintended outcomes. Bagley and I were successful in our goal of experimenting with performance to highlight the emotional quality of the participants. Likewise, using performance as a method of representing qualitative data was also successful. However, it was never our intention to reinforce either the power relationships between the researcher and participants or gender stereotypes.

◆ Conclusion

I undertook the performance of the United Kingdom study to communicate data from a qualitative research study and, in doing so, to stimulate discussion within the educational research community about the potential for performance as a beneficial form of data representation. The notion of using expressive bodies/performance to represent qualitative research in education is very innovative. For arts-based researchers, teachers, and graduate students who are drawn to this way of working, performance is a powerful form of representation that expands the resources available to educational researchers. Arts-based researchers should reflect on their innovative work by documenting their process as a means to enlarge the body of knowledge that contributes to the arts-based educational research field.

◆ References

Albright, A. C. (1997). *Choreographing difference: The body and identity in contemporary dance.* Hanover, NH: Wesleyan University Press.

Banes, S. (1994). *Writing dancing in the age of postmodernism.* Hanover, NH: Wesleyan University Press.

Bagley, C., & Cancienne, M. B. (2001). Educational research and intertextual forms of (re)presentation: The case for dancing the data. *Qualitative Inquiry, 7*(2), 221–237.

Bagley, C., & Cancienne, M. B. (2002). Educational research and inter-textual forms of (re)presentation: The case for dancing the data. In C. Bagley & M. B. Cancienne (Eds.), *Dancing the data* (pp. 3–19). New York: Peter Lang.

Bagley, C., & Woods, P. A. (1998). School choice, markets, and special educational needs. *Disability and Society, 13*(5), 763–783.

Blumenfeld-Jones, D. S. (1995). Dance as a mode of research representation. *Qualitative Inquiry, 1*(4), 391–401.

Cancienne, M. B., & Bagley, C. (2002). Parents' voices on school choice concerning students with special educational needs [CD-ROM]. In M. B. Cancienne & C. Bagley (Eds.), *Dancing the data too.* Charlottesville, VA: 2flydesigns.

Cancienne, M. B., & Snowber, C. (2003). Writing rhythm: Movement as method. *Qualitative Inquiry, 9*(2), 237–253.

Cole, A. L., & McIntyre, M. (2001). Dance me to an understanding of teaching: A performative text. *Journal of Curriculum Theorizing, 17*(2), 43–60.

Denzin, N. (1997). *Interpretive ethnography: Ethnographic practices for the 21st century.* Thousand Oaks, CA: Sage.

Dewey, J. (1934). *Art as experience.* New York: Perigee Books.

Dewey, J. (1938). *Experience and education.* New York: Collier Books.

Finley, S. (2003). Arts-based inquiry in QI: Seven years from crisis to guerrilla warfare. *Qualitative Inquiry, 9*(2), 281–298.

Gilbert, A. G. (1992). *Creative dance for all ages.* Reston, VA: American Alliance for Health, Physical Education, Recreation, & Dance.

Hawkins, A. (1991). *Moving from within.* Pennington, NJ: A Capella.

Humphrey, D. (1959). *The art of making dances.* Princeton, NJ: Dance Horizons.

34

IMAGE-BASED EDUCATIONAL RESEARCH

Childlike Perspectives

◆ Jon Prosser and Catherine Burke

Anew approach to researching childhood experience has become established whereby researchers are seeking out ways of giving voice to children and young people by "close listening" and engaging them in the research process. In this way, researchers can choose to adopt a childlike perspective, to recognize and pay due attention to children's multiple ways of "seeing" childhood in particular and the world in general. Visual research is well placed to access, interpret, and give voice to children's worlds. This is achieved by adopting child-sensitive research methods and by recognizing that children's experience and agency are important and worthy of study.

This chapter empathizes with children's visual culture in two ways. The first is a matter of empowerment: Words are the domain of adult researchers and therefore can be disempowering to the young. Images and their mode of production, on the other hand, are central to children's culture from a very early age and are therefore empowering. Put simply, children often feel more confident in creating drawings, photographs, and videos than words. Second, children's visual culture is central to any study of childhood. Children's everyday creative enthusiasms and aesthetic capacity for visualizing, space sharing, mobile technology, doodling, graffiti, sketching, dreaming, blogging, video, and photography are all expressions and representations of childhood. They are pivotal to understanding children's meaning making in their taken-for-granted lives. Striving to engage in children's lives by combining participatory research with children's visual culture is a worthy endeavor.

◆ *Methodological Background*

Observation of children has always played a pivotal role in researchers' endeavors to understand their physical, cognitive, and social worlds. Sociologists at the turn of the 20th century used photographs to record and document observations of children's working and living conditions (e.g., Hine 1932; Riis, 1971). This body of work can now be viewed as lacking academic rigor and integrity. It was regarded by some as merely using images for political ends and therefore "muck-raking" (Stasz, 1979, p. 134). However, the status of image-based research across the disciplines was significantly enhanced following the publication of Bateson and Mead's (1942) anthropological study *Balinese Character*. They made more than 25,000 photographs of Balinese culture, some of which critically documented children's lives, and organized them under emergent categories, such as "parents and children," "siblings," "stages of children's development" and "rites of passage." The next significant phase of development followed the publication of Collier's classic 1967 methodological text *Visual Anthropology: Photography as a Research Method* (updated and revised

1986) and Wagner's sociologically orientated *Images of Information* (1979). Currently, a gamut of texts, for example, Prosser (1998), Banks (2001), Rose (2001), Van Leeuwen and Jewitt (2001), and Pink (2004) provide insightful, varied, and rigorous discussion of contemporary visual methods, which can legitimately be applied to working with children. Child-focused researchers have adopted, adapted, and further developed these approaches for their own needs in child-centric visual studies, such as *Seeing Kid's Worlds* (Wagner, 1999), *Seeing Beyond Violence: Children as Researchers* (Egg, Schratz-Hadwich, Trubwasser, & Walker, 2004), and *The School I'd Like* (Burke & Grosvenor, 2003).

In the past, adults and children were seen as passive objects of research. Researchers' thinking has changed to encompass the general view that the subject of study has "the right as well as the ability to enter into discourse about the construction of their lives" (Banks, 2001, p. 9). Coupled with these philosophical changes are shifts in theory within the discipline of sociology of childhood. The long-held position that children should be viewed as being in a stage of transition to adulthood and therefore lacking worthwhile cognitive skills is no longer tenable. The current view is that children are active participants in their own social worlds and, given the means, are able to articulate and construct their own unique perspectives. This democratic and empowering model, which is personified as research "on, for and with" (Cameron, Frazer, Harvey, Rampton, & Richardson, 1992, p. 22), recognizes children as dynamic members of the community with their own agendas. Hence, methodological advances in themselves are insufficient to understand children's increasingly complex lives. There is a requirement that researchers embrace an "on, for, and with children" mentality.

For social scientists an image-based approach is a pivotal element in understanding children's visual culture—its production, consumption, and meaning. Visual researchers have evolved methods and techniques that are collaborative, participatory, and insightful. Particular advances have been made, even involving very young children, in design-based visualization and planning. In sum, image-based research methods offer a powerful tool for realizing children's ways of seeing the designed present and imagining the designed future, capturing the visual culture of schools and other formal or informal edu-care environments in which children are placed, communicating to a wider audience the creative capacities of children in informing from their own experience, and shifting dominant paradigms of practice from research *with* children toward research *by* and *for* children.

◆ *Visual Methods*

Accessing children's visual culture inevitably means understanding their perspectives. Children develop visual skills early in life, and visual methods draw on this strength. Children from as young as 2 years of age can explore feelings about their worlds, assisted by an adult photo-ethnographer. Older children can make their own photo-essays designed to explore and communicate their own experiences of, for example, the built school environment. Photo-collage techniques can be conducive to evaluative participation among those for whom lack of language or literacy is an impediment to communication. Children's views can be sought via diaries, drawings, modeling, and still and video camera work. The Internet can allow children to communicate visually about their lives from all

continents, creating new visualizations and challenging assumptions by means of the photo-voice. All these possibilities have been achieved in practice by projects designed to recognize the implications of new ways of seeing children and childhood as a consequence of legal, theoretical, and social changes in the decades following the United Nations Convention on the Rights of the Child in 1990.

◆ *Photo-Elicitation With Children*

A common data gathering technique is *photo-elicitation*. Here photographs (or film, video, drawings, or objects) are introduced as part of an interview. The aim is to explore the significance or meaning of the images or objects with the respondent. The images can be created by the researcher specifically for the purposes of photo-elicitation; they can be drawn from archives, magazines, or newspapers; or they can belong to the interviewee. Photo-elicitation has been used by visual anthropologists since the 1950s and is extensively used by a wide range of contemporary visual researchers (see Harper, 2002, for examples). However, it has no agreed protocol, and few studies have been undertaken to establish its validity as a research method. Nonetheless, the feeling is that "if it works, use it," and it is a technique that if used appropriately with children is capable of producing insightful data.

Researchers choose to use images or objects during initial discussions with young people because they are useful "icebreakers" and help to break down the power differential. Of course building bridges is important since potentially it leads to cooperation and engagement, but using visuals merely as a quick "way in" is to underplay the potential of the technique. Stand in a playground and point to objects or places, and bold children, generous with their time and knowledge, enthusiastically shower you with their insights—pleased you are taking an interest in what they do. Moreover, they are visually astute and enjoy talking about images they or others have constructed, and photo-elicitation builds on this enthusiasm.

Photo-elicitation protocol in its simplest and most common form entails inserting a photograph into a research interview with the aim of drawing out the viewer's response. Interviewing children is a key method for data gathering, and interviewing with images or objects aids this approach in a number of ways. Banks (2001), for example, points to photographs acting as a neutral third party facilitating a more relaxed atmosphere for interviewing since eye-to-eye contact need not be maintained. This role for imagery is particularly worthwhile where children are interviewees and adults the interviewers since there are inescapable differences in status and power. The potential tension generated by face-to-face contact is lessened by mutual gazing at a photograph or the act of exploring an object together.

Children's willingness to pass comment on images depends on the image's content, their relationship to the content, and the context of viewing. It makes sense to young people and they feel more comfortable in sharing their insights if they are depicted since the image acts as an aide-mémoire, and they can more readily appreciate the researcher's need to gain their insights since they are visibly central actors. The timing, territory, membership, and nature of a photo-interview session are also important if children are to feel sufficiently confident and comfortable to pass on their ideas and beliefs.

Accessing a child's perceptions through image-elicitation may work by taking an indirect route. For example, rather than exploring a child's feelings about family relationships by looking through their family album, there is potential in using comics, magazines, or paintings depicting family relationships as a starting point, thereby allowing the child to dictate the pace and direction the interview takes. Children may feel less pressured if they don't speak directly to a researcher about a sensitive topic and may prefer working through a toy or doll. This approach, commonly used to build rapport or for diagnostic reasons, is a "projective technique" and requires careful, sometimes specialist handling (see Wakefield & Underwager, 1998).

Video-elicitation was not popular in the past because it required cumbersome and nonportable equipment. Photo-elicitation was more popular since photographs are easily picked up, dropped, and rearranged in another sequence. However, portable DVD players are now the norm and widely accepted as part of a visual researcher's toolkit. This makes viewing of moving imagery more practical for empirical work, and one would expect to see an increase in the use of video-elicitation. There are many different but valid ways of conducting visual-elicitation. Whatever approach is taken, the media and topic should be part of children's everyday culture.

◆ Giving Children Still Cameras

During the late 1960s experimental participatory visual studies were carried out by Worth and Adair (1972). They provided inner city teenagers, students, and representatives of the Navajo with movie cameras and film in an attempt to circumnavigate the problems caused by "outsiders" determining the form, content, and cultural context of filmmaking. In short, Worth and Adair attempted to shift away from the orthodox researcher–researched relationship by getting participants to act as the critical agents of data collection and interpretation. This approach was taken up by still photographers in the 1980s who emphasized the empowerment aspect of giving cameras to children. Jim Hubbard,[1] a professional photographer, gave cameras to homeless children, children at risk, and American Indian children through a project called "Shooting Back." Ewald (2001), a photographer/educator[2] working around the same time, gave children cameras to aid self-expression and language development. In the 1990s numerous studies adapted Worth and Adair's (1972) approach and provided children and young adults with movie cameras or a combination of movie and still cameras (see Rollins, 1995).

Giving cameras to children and inviting them to photograph aspects of their lives gives children the freedom to create their own agenda in two ways: If the images are used later for photo-elicitation, it is their priorities that are the focus, and as narrative and a vehicle for personal expression (as, for example, in Caroline Wang's, n.d., work). The research community generally underestimates children's media abilities. Children of the 21st century are familiar and adept with the technology of image production to such an extent that they are capable of being significant image makers themselves.

Sharples, Davison, Thomas, and Rudman (2003), in their systematic study of children as photographers, aged 7, 11, and 15 from five European countries, provide an insight into children's photographic interests and capacities. The study found that children across the age groups showed an increasing ability to distinguish the properties of images from the world they represent. This suggests that children should not necessarily be viewed as apprentice adult photographers since they exhibit their own distinctive intentions and products. Since children display critical capacities through their photography and are able to access physical and mental territory not available to adults, there is a case

for perceiving them as fellow researchers. Given a particular focus and scenario, children will, driven by their innate imagination, create a "picture-led" narrative of their world (see, for example, Burke, 2005). At the center of giving children cameras is the idea of passing control to them—what Dell Clark (1999) calls "auto-driving."

There is a danger that the process of instructing children in what is required of them will perpetuate the unequal power relationship. Researchers will always have to make judgments about the need to "guide" students and take account of the intentionality of researchers and informants. A common strategy, based on the assumption that children and young people are experts in their own lives, is to invite them to photograph their own special or everyday environments. The Mosaic Approach (Clark & Moss, 2001) adopts standard research methods like observation but in addition suggests providing 2- to 4-year-old children with single-use cameras to photograph what was important to them in their nursery setting. The researcher is taken on a "tour" of the setting by children who also provide a running commentary on their regular activities. The children were responsible for deciding what and how to record, either by photograph, drawings, or tape recorder. Clark and Moss (2001) make an important point arguing that cameras offer young children the opportunity to produce a finished product in which they can take pride and that they know is valued. Children who have seen the members of their family take photographs, pored over family albums, or looked at photographs in books and comics know that photographs have a value in the "adult world." This is not always the case with children's own drawings and paintings.

Another approach is to ask older children to work collaboratively (child-to-child) to record the lives of younger children. So, for example, a 4-year-old would be asked to use a camera to record the everyday events of an

8-month-old in "the baby room." The photographs produced by the children are later used as discussion points with the older children, the staff in the setting, and the younger children's parents. As this approach shows, age is rarely a barrier to giving young people single-use cameras in research settings, although underestimating their capacities is.

◆ Giving Children Digital Video Cameras

Word-based research tends to reproduce hierarchies exacerbating differences between researchers and the researched. Image-making technologies have the potential to reduce the distance between researchers and children, producing a more democratic model. Providing children with digital video cameras, often called "participative video," offers transformative potential when the practice of "looking at" becomes "looking alongside." Nonetheless, sensitive and reflexive negotiation of research relationships is critical if hierarchical power relations are not to be reproduced through researcher-dominated procedures leading to subjugated children's imagery. The balance between the responsibilities, needs, and intentions of researchers and informants is difficult to achieve but needs to be transparent to all parties. Where video technology remains physically and metaphorically in the hands of the researchers and is used to capture, document, or note-take a scene, it remains an extension of adult gaze and should be understood as such.

A central aim of the participatory video process is to create a video narrative that conveys what children want to communicate in the manner they wish to communicate. Of course pragmatic decisions about what should be framed and how the sequences are to be organized to tell a story bring into question the negotiation roles. Critical reflection on two elements is fundamental to producing

trustworthy outcomes. First, participatory video demands attention to the exercise of power within sets of dynamic research relationships reflected in both researcher–children and children–children groupings. Second, children are looking and sense-making before they can walk or talk and quickly adapt to contemporary pervasive visual culture, and adults should accept that children have substantial filmmaking potential.

Young people are often familiar with the technology of image production and capable of becoming image makers themselves following basic instruction. They may mimic adult filming methods even to the extent of adopting a preplanned storyboard approach. However, they are merely embracing generic visual culture, and this should not be a signal for heavy-handed researcher involvement with the express aim of creating an adult notion of a "good," that is, technically proficient film reflecting adult intellectual concerns. Where practicable, children's own unique filmic visual subculture should prevail over researchers' conventions, which are traditionally aligned with documentary film or scientific observation.

A wide range of children-centered topics and research questions are predisposed to the participatory video process. It may be that young people's social class, culture, and situation influence what they want to film (Rich & Chalfen, 1999). Nonetheless, focusing on their everyday lived experience takes advantage of the time-based properties of film. Quite specific contexts are useful as a starting point. Children's homes or social lives, for example, provide situations where they are confident in their own knowledge and that act as a "springboard" for filming. Moreover, key insights could be gained when children and young people film the changing nexus of activities and spheres of influence as they undergo significant transitions in their lives, for example, an illness they are experiencing, leaving school and going to work, or as a means of creating a record of their own physical and emotional space.

◆ Concept Mapping

One important approach to identifying and visually representing children's perspectives on a range of complex topics is through concept mapping. This is defined by Novak and Gowin (1984) as "a visual road map showing some of the pathways we may take to connect meanings of concepts in propositions" (p. 15). It is most commonly used for tracking the development of children's learning, as a diagnostic tool for evaluating their progress, and as an aide to help children learn how to learn (Georghiades, 2000). These approaches are premised on a constructivist notion of learning and on the idea that learners frame their understanding of new knowledge on preexisting beliefs. However, importantly, concept mapping can be used as a tool to articulate children's perceptions, promote reflection, and generate and communicate complex ideas on a range of topics. An example of a child-created concept map in which the starting point is "food" and the subconcepts need to be related to one another is given in Figure 34.1.

A search of the Internet for "concept mapping" will uncover a plethora of commercially available word-graphic tools. A simple version of a concept map, sometimes referred to as a "mind map," consists of a central word or concept around which about 5 to 10 main ideas are drawn, and then an additional 5 to 10 ideas are drawn that relate to each of those main ideas (Buzan, 1995). Whereas mind maps have only one main concept represented like a (family) tree, concept mapping

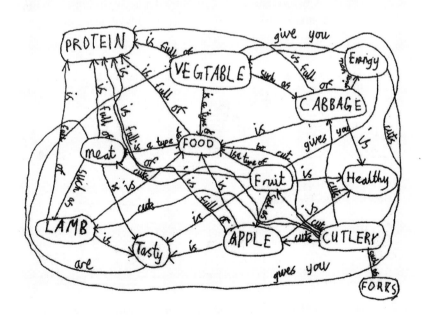

Figure 34.1   An Example of a Concept Map From Georghiades and Parla-Petrou (2001)

SOURCE: From Georghiades, P., & Parla-Petrou, E. (2001). *Diverse use of concept mapping across two domains: The cases of primary food and science education.* Presented at the British Educational Research Association Annual Conferences, University of Leeds, 13–15, September. Used with permission of Petros Georghiades.

may require a network of representation. Concept maps may take various forms. Novak and Gowin (1984) propose a hierarchical form in which key concepts are placed at the top and lesser concepts positioned lower down on a page. Others prefer a "spider" map in which the trigger word or pivotal concept is placed centrally (see Figure 34. 1) and participants are asked to provide additional linked concepts.

Since children will be unfamiliar with concept mapping; important terms like *concept*, *mapping*, and *linking words* will need explanation, discussion, and activities. A useful approach may be to involve a group of children in a joint construction of a concept map and to provide examples of concept maps of unrelated themes.

◆ Draw and Write

Many of the above methods use visuals as a stimulus for communication. Images that have meaning for children may be used within orthodox research methods such as questionnaires to identify and differentiate between levels of response. Figure 34.2, for example, illustrates how Snoopy, a widely known cartoon character, is depicted in various poses and children are asked to circle the pose that corresponds to their feelings. However, the "draw and write" approach is based on the notion that "starting where the children are," that is, children's *own* drawings and words, is of fundamental significance.

Children have the ability to capture feelings and emotions through drawings and paintings while lacking an equally expressive written or spoken language. This opens up a range of active participation in research to disadvantaged children. Special educational needs (SEN) children have been habitually and systematically excluded from discussions about their education. The underlying assumption has been that they are neither well informed nor sufficiently articulate to contribute. To be a child and disabled is to be doubly disadvantaged in terms of voice.

1. **How do you feel when your teacher reads a story aloud?**

2. **How do you feel when someone gives you a book for a present?**

Figure 34.2 Snoopy Questionnaire

SOURCE: From Hopkins, D. (1985). *A Teacher's Guide to Classroom Research 3/e*, published by Open University Press, Milton Keynes, UK. Reproduced with the kind permission of the Open University Press Publishing Company.

There are many visual methods and techniques that help SEN children to learn and that can be used to understand their experiences of the world. The "draw and write" method was used to help Jane, a young girl with a fire phobia who was experiencing recurrent nightmares with a fire theme. She was autistic and aphasic with learning difficulties, experienced problems relating to others, and was unable to speak or write expressively. Jane was asked to draw her nightmare (Figure 34.3), and a more able peer, her only friend, helped her to write a prayer to accompany the image. It became apparent from the drawing and words and later interviews that Jane had seen TV footage of the New York 9/11 disaster. She was deeply disturbed by the experience, particularly by the sight of people leaping from the World Trade Center building to avoid the fire. Later, counseling based on the visual data enabled Jane to escape the nightly replay of the film loop in her mind that caused the nightmares to recur.

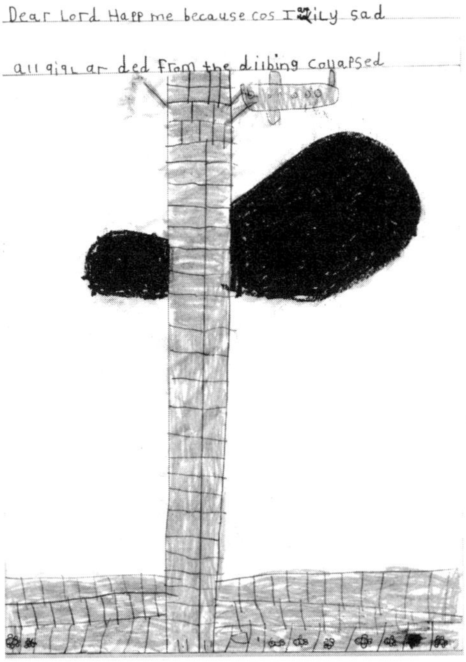

Interpreting children's drawings is particularly difficult but rewarding. Diem-Wille (2001), adopting a psychoanalytical perspective, argues that drawings show a child's emotional state better than verbal descriptions since they are "expressions of the unconscious emotional aspects of a person" (p. 119). Adopting the view that children's drawings are expressions of their "inner world," Figure 34.3 gains significance suggesting that in addition to distinguishing likes and dislikes, it represents Jane in terms of an emotional map.

Figure 34.3   Drawing and Words by Jane (Name Changed) With Help From a Friend

◆ Visual Research as a Vehicle for Change

Cameras can be employed in imaginative ways to enable children and young people to confront difficult aspects of their lives. "Seeing Beyond Violence: Children as Researchers" (Egg, Schratz-Hadwich, Trubwasser, & Walker, 2004) is a research project that foregrounds children and young people's photography. Children's understanding of violence in Colombia, Thailand, India, and Nicaragua was explored through a methodological device that required that they use digital cameras to photograph the opposite of violence. Adult researchers were in the background and acted as "assistants" to the children. This repositioning of the adult in the research field is an important shift if children are to wear the mantle of researcher. A combination of "digital ethnography" with symbolic interactionism was intended to give children more than a voice but also provide the opportunity to build visual evidence of their social reality. Here the images are the priority; they are not merely present as a tool to elicit language or to illustrate a report.

Cameras are now becoming used quite commonly as part of a method to allow the very youngest children to express their views. Sometimes the adult researcher will take the photograph for the child from the child's own height; sometimes they will leave the camera with professionals to allow them to record activities. Polaroid cameras were used with the youngest children in a study on children's views on child-care quality, allowing instant conversations about the photographs to be recorded. The children took the researcher on a tour of their childcare setting and then took photographs of what they liked or disliked (Clark & Moss, 2001). The reports of such research rarely if ever present the photographs created by children or include these nontextual views of children in their summaries and conclusions. They appear to be tools to create engagement and participation while the language—what the child says—is all important.

International nongovernmental organizations such as UNICEF are employing visual means of empowering children. Drawing allows the youngest children to "speak." At the United Nations' Special Session on Children (May 8–10, 2002; http://www.unicef.org/specialsession), the voices of nearly 34,000 children from more than 125 countries were heard through their paintings. In another project, more than 500 children and young people from 45 countries captured images of their lives on camera as part of "Imagine: Your Photos Will Open My Eyes," a joint youth photography project of the German Agency for Technical Cooperation (GTZ) and Philip Abresch, a journalist in Berlin. Such projects illustrate and realize the potential available through information and communication technology (ICT) as digital photo exhibitions and image-based online conversations can enable cross-cultural collaboration between and among young people. Save the Children's "Eye to Eye" project does just this. The project enables Palestinian children living in refugee camps in Lebanon to record their lives using cameras and video. The result is a vivid and accessible online resource for communities of children and their teachers throughout the world (http://www.savethechildren.org.uk/eyetoeye). Photovoice (Wang, n.d.) is an organization committed to the principle of enabling those traditionally not the subject of photography to be its creator and thus works with street children throughout the world, allowing them control over ways of seeing them. They have worked in Vietnam, Afghanistan, the Congo, Nepal, and the United Kingdom. A key intention of this initiative is to enable participants to become advocates for change.

◆ The Dilemmas of Visual Ethics

Research with children is fraught with complex ethical issues. A visual dimension adds to the list of potential dilemmas and deserves more space than encapsulated within this brief review. The most common principles that underpin ethical codes of practice have been referred to as "mutual respect, non-coercion and non-manipulation, and support for democratic values and institutions" (House, 1993, p. 167). This is a useful starting point, but visual ethical principles are best discussed in concrete situations (Pink 2004; Prosser 2000; Simons & Usher, 2000).

Participatory research by its nature is ethical—potentially. Just as action research shifts power to practitioners, an ethical participative epistemology empowers the disempowered and suggests a shift in the power balance away from researchers toward respondents. The notion that research is solely concerned with finding out about the world and is essentially politically neutral is rejected by emancipatory research. An aim of emancipatory and participatory research is to reduce discrimination, marginalization, and inequality and increase empowerment through social action, that is, the participation of children within a child-centered methodology.

Informed consent is central to good ethical practice. With all forms of longitudinal ethnographic and emergent studies with children, the notion of informed consent is problematic since direction and outcomes are variable. The notion of "provisional consent" may be appropriate in these circumstances. Here, the ongoing relationship between researcher and children is seen as evolving and dependent on reciprocal trust and collaboration. This enables ethical problems to be explored and resolved as they emerge within specific contexts and provides the possibility for children (and parents) to opt in or out at different phases.

Anonymity, unless participants choose to be identified and are fully aware of potential repercussions, is common practice in social science research. It is possible to blur or "cloak" children's faces in photographs using a relatively simple pixel reduction technique, thereby blurring their faces and protecting their identity. Where data are intended for reproduction and wider consumption, it is possible to restrict access to video data on CDs and Web sites using encryption. However, using visual images of young people or created by them makes issues of anonymity problematic. In America, for example, where restrictive research codes of practice operate, authors of artwork or those depicted in the artwork of others may be assured of anonymity, but in doing so they are denied the choice to be named and their work celebrated. This is questionable ethical practice.

There are times when children are happy for their work to be displayed publicly (and the researcher is keen to publicize their achievements) but wish to remain anonymous (for example the author of Figure 34.3). Equally, there are occasions when a researcher decides, against the author's wishes, not to name the creator because in the researcher's judgment, the author may be damaged or put in danger. These dilemmas are only the tip of the ethical "iceberg" and not easily resolved. Adult visual researchers with child visual researchers will need to make decisions and resolve ethical problems as they arise. This is not an avocation of ad hoc decision making since knowledge, planning, and awareness of potential problems prior to conducting visual research are central to ethical practice.

◆ Conclusion

In this chapter, we explored the possibilities of image-based research with children. Childlike perspectives, we hope we have demonstrated, are worthwhile pursuing, necessary to include in ethical practice, and complex to attain. Images, art, and interpretation of the visual in the research approach can facilitate childlike perspectives and empower the child participant as researcher or as subject in research. Seeing the world through the eyes of a child means literally getting down to the eye level and realizing the difference that scale makes in a person's view of the world. Image-based research approaches, principles, and practices, illustrated in this chapter, can bring the adult closer to the view of the child in the research process. An ethical practice will not only realize the usual agreed conventions on consent and protection of rights but also be sensitive to the particular status and position of the child in its social and cultural context.

This is a rich and complex seam of knowledge that can be constructed via imaginative and skillful practice—so rich and attractive a field that we should be wise to the possibilities and careful of the consequences of realizing childlike perspectives in educational research.

◆ Notes

1. Jim Hubbard's work can be found at http://www.shootingback.org. He teaches photography to street youth and conducts workshops around the world through universities and government agencies.

2. Ewald works through Duke's Center for Documentary Studies, Durham, NC. Her Web site is http//globetrotter.berkley.edu/Ewald/

◆ References

Banks, M. (2001). *Visual methods in social research*. London: Sage.

Bateson, G., & Mead, M. (1942). *Balinese character: A photographic analysis*. New York: New York Academy of Sciences.

Burke, C. (2005). "Play in focus": Children researching their own spaces and places for play. *Children, Youth, and Environments, 15*(1), 23–53.

Burke, C., & Grosvenor, I. (2003). *The school I'd like*. London: RoutledgeFalmer.

Buzan, T. (1995). *The mind map book*. London: BBC Books.

Cameron, D., Frazer, E., Harvey, P., Rampton, M. B. H., & Richardson, K. (1992). *Researching language*. London: Routledge.

Clark, A., & Moss, P. (2001). *Listening to young children: The mosaic approach*. London: The National Children's Bureau & Joseph Rowntree Foundation.

Collier, J. (1986). *Visual anthropology: Photography as a research method* (Rev ed.). Albuquerque: University of New Mexico Press. (Original work published 1967)

Dell Clark, C. (1999). The autodriven interview: A photographic viewfinder into children's experience. *Visual Sociology, 14,* 39–50.

Diem-Wille, G. (2001). A therapeutic perspective: The use of drawings in child psychoanalysis and social science. In T. Van Leeuwen & C. Jewitt (Eds.), *Handbook of visual communication* (pp. 119–133). London: Sage.

Egg, P., Schratz-Hadwich, B., Trubwasser, G., & Walker, R. (2004). *Seeing beyond violence: Children as researchers*. Innsbruck, Austria: Herman Gmeiner Academy.

Ewald, W. (2001). *I wanna take me a picture: Teaching writing and photography to children*. Boston: Lynhurst Books and Beacon Press.

Georghiades, P. (2000). Beyond conceptual change learning in science education: Focusing on transfer, durability, and metacognition. *Educational Research, 42*(2), 119–139.

Harper, D. (2002). Talking about pictures: A case for photo-elicitation. *Visual Studies, 17*(1), 13–26.

Hine, L (1932). *Men at work*. New York: Macmillan.

House, E. R. (1993). *Professional evaluation: Social impact and political consequences*. London: Sage.

Novak, J. D., & Gowin, D. R. (1984). *Learning how to learn*. New York: Cambridge University Press.

Pink, S. (2004). *Doing visual ethnography*. London: Sage.

Prosser, J. (Ed.). (1998). *Image-based research: A sourcebook for qualitative researchers*. London: Falmer Press.

Prosser, J. (2000). The moral maze of visual ethics. In H. Simons & R. Usher (Eds.), *Situated ethics in educational research* (pp. 116–132). London: Routledge Falmer.

Rich, M., & Chalfen, R. (1999). Showing and telling: Children teaching physicians with visual narrative. *Visual Sociology, 14,* 51–71.

Riis, J. A. (1971). *How the other half lives*. New York: Dover.

Rollins, T. (1995). Kids of survival. In N. Paley (Ed.). *Finding art's place* (pp. 92–98). London: Routledge.

Rose, G. (2001). *Visual methodologies: An introduction to the interpretation of visual materials.* London: Sage.

Sharples, M., Davison, L., Thomas, G., & Rudman, P. D. (2003). Children as photographers: An analysis of children's graphic behaviour and intentions at three age levels. *Visual Communication, 2*(3), 303–330.

Simons, H., & Usher, R. (2000). *Situated ethics in educational research.* London: Routledge Falmer.

Stasz, C. (1979). The early history of visual sociology. In J. Wagner (Ed.), *Images of information: Still photography in the social sciences.* Beverly Hills, CA: Sage.

Van Leeuwen, T., & Jewitt, C. (Eds.). (2001). *Handbook of visual analysis.* London: Sage.

Wagner, J. (Ed.). (1979). *Images of information: Still photography in the social sciences.* Beverly Hills, CA: Sage.

Wagner, J. (Ed.). (1999). Seeing kid's worlds [Special issue]. *Visual Sociology, 14.*

Wakefield, H., & Underwager, R. (1998). The application of images in child abuse investigations. In J. Prosser (Ed.), *Image-based research: A sourcebook for qualitative researchers* (pp. 176–194). London: Falmer Press.

Wang, C. (n.d.). *Photovoice.* Retrieved May 24, 2007, from http://www.photovoice.com/index.html

Worth, S., & Adair, J. (1972). *Through Navajo eyes: Explorations in film communication and anthropology.* Bloomington: Indiana University Press.

35

EXHIBITING AS INQUIRY

Travels of an Accidental Curator

◆ Kathryn Church

From 1997 to 2001, I curated a museum exhibit that featured my mother's work as a dressmaker. Entitled *Fabrications: Stitching Ourselves Together,* it was constructed around 22 wedding dresses that Lorraine sewed over 50 years for women in and around her community. In this chapter, *Fabrications* is a touchstone for my reflections on using material objects to investigate and render social relations. My account focuses not so much on meanings—a preoccupation of much qualitative research—as on the activities of exhibiting and how that work extended and complexified my relationship to objects.

By most standards, *Fabrications* was a success. Created in partnership with a museum in central Alberta, it was supported primarily by internal resources with some supplemental grant funding. The exhibit toured five other Canadian sites, including two national museums, and was viewed by 200,000 visitors. It received good media coverage through local and national papers and over radio and television (Church, 1998; Shorten, 1998). I made numerous public and academic presentations about the project and have published in academic books and journals. Any proficiency I might claim with arts-informed inquiry stems from this work.

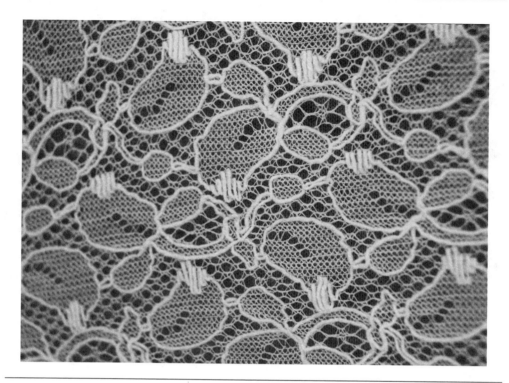

Figure 35.1   "I always loved lace." Fabric From Lorraine Church's 1951 Wedding Dress

That said, the contribution I offer here is a step-by-step deconstruction of "proficiency." Having become a curator by accident, I want to foreground the tentativeness of my performance—and the strength of that stance—in order to reveal some of the problems and dilemmas that I encountered in the museum. A primary aim of the chapter is to make transparent the "messiness" of creative inquiry in this modality for the sake of enhancing learning and practice in this area (Denzin, 1997; Ellis & Bochner, 1992; Gray, Ivanoffski, & Sinding, 2002).

◆ Sewing Scribblers

Fabrications did not begin as an academic project shaped by scholarly concerns and literature. It began with my life as a daughter and the need I felt in my forties to address a rift I experienced between my mother and me (Church 2002; Church & Church, 2003). Our distance was not the result of argument. It was a more subtle schism that became pronounced during the years of my doctoral studies in Toronto. When that process was over, I felt a strong urge to probe the differences that Lorraine and I had come to embody. So, although *Fabrications* can be read through multiple disciplinary lenses—material and/or visual culture (e.g., Kuchler & Miller, 2005), dress studies (e.g., Crane, 2000; Green & Banim, 2001), and museum studies (e.g., Hooper-Greenhill, 1992, 2000), to name three obvious examples—it actually began in personal history. And it took its bearings from emotions: alienation, sadness, yearning, hope.

As an adult, I seldom return to the prairie town in which I grew up: At least, that is the story my parents tell. On one brief visit, I watched my mother relaxing at the kitchen table as the sun set behind the neighbors' trees. The fading rays fell over her white hair and onto her hands. In front of her sat a cup of tea and a small stack of books. Selecting a single copy off the top, she laid it on the table. She opened it and gently smoothed back the tattered, lumpy pages. She smiled. And with that gesture, my mother launched a project that would consume me for the next 5 years.

The notebooks Lorraine opened that evening were her "sewing scribblers"—a scrapbook record of 50 years of labor. They had originally belonged to my three brothers and me, their covers marked with school-kid scrawl. At the point where we stopped laboring over arithmetic and spelling and social studies, she turned our unused pages to her own purpose. Each time someone brought her a sewing project, my mother recorded the woman's name and her body measurements along with the style number and company of the pattern (or patterns) that the woman had chosen. She sketched the garment and pinned scraps of fabric to the page. Sometimes, she penciled a brief comment: "lovely fit," for example, or "beautiful dress."

I knew these scribblers well. As a child, I watched my mother create them while she measured and pinned, chatted and laughed with the women who came and went from her basement sewing room. Perched quietly in the corner, I came to understand Lorraine's sketching and jotting as an integral feature of dressmaking. Indeed, she measured and charted my own body as it grew and matured; many of the garments in my girlhood wardrobe are documented in her records. Thus, the scribblers were enmeshed in domestic life; they inscribed my bodily difference in a family of boys.

It is this subjective history that cracked open that fateful evening. Without planning or preparation, the taken-for-grantedness

Figure 35.2 "My mother kept a record of her sewing." Fabric Scraps and Pencil Sketches From Lorraine Church's Sewing "Scribblers"

of the scribblers disappeared. What had been familiar suddenly seemed strange: the scribblers, and my mother along with them. What she held in her hands was a detailed account of an activity that, although largely invisible, has been part of women's domestic lives for many generations (Barber, 1994; Burman, 1999; Gamber, 1997). Kept by the woman at the hub of the exchange, it documented the construction of a range of garments through a work form based on her skills with tape measure and tissue paper, pins and needles, scissors and seam binding, fabric and form. Lorraine's reasons for keeping these notes were practical and emotional. She did not see herself as practicing and preserving knowledge that was publicly significant.

I have always been proud of my mother's dressmaking abilities. However, until that kitchen-table moment, I had never fully understood that she is most present, communicative, and instrumental in and through objects. And I had never fully admitted how clumsy and ill at ease I feel in the modality where she is strong and comfortable. Here was one of the roots of our "trouble." More than a matter of mismatched personal styles, our disconnection pointed to larger social and political struggles around what counts as knowledge and who counts as a legitimate knower.

This insight was a turning point for me as a daughter but also as an interpretive methodologist. What would happen if I leaned into rather than pulled away from my discomforting ignorance in the material realm? I decided to find out by taking my mother's scribblers seriously. When she and I looked through them together, we quickly noticed the recurrence of the wedding dress. Given its dominance, I decided to "follow" this object as the next step in the unfolding of my research. This decision established a general pattern. One "thing" led to another in continual discovery until the study became a circle of intersecting objects: from scribblers to wedding dresses to the built forms of an exhibit.

When I look back now, what I value most about this process is coming to trust what felt like a procedural "free fall." My previous research was much more planned, structured, and textual—partly to calm my anxieties but also to satisfy the scrutiny of university and/or community organizations. When I sat down beside my mother to explore the world of her sewing, I stepped off the edge of my existing practice. I stepped into a three-dimensional world inhabited by actual bodies, with tangible height, depth, width, and weight. I stepped into a sensual world constituted by colors and patterns, fabric and thread, seams and hems, satin and lace. And in that world, I did not know what I was doing.

◆ Dresses

In the winter of 1997, I spent a month in my old hometown interviewing my mother and her brides. Finding them turned out to be relatively easy. Despite the passage of time, my mother was no more than two phone calls away from any of her "customers." Twenty-two agreed to participate. I met most of them face-to-face in environments of their choosing. Where a personal visit was not possible, I interviewed by phone. My questions were quite simple: "Tell me about your dress," for example, or "Why does the dress look this way?" I was curious about each bride's negotiations with the traditional elements of this garment: color, length, volume, type of fabric, bodice and sleeve style, and headpiece.

Hodder (2000) points out that, typically, the people who made, used, and/or wore the objects of material culture research cannot be asked about them because they are either long dead or "curiously inarticulate" (p. 703). My project differed here because all but one of Lorraine's brides are very much alive. The meanings of their dresses were "tacit and implicit" (Hodder, 2000, p. 707) only because no one had bothered to ask about them. When questioned, these women were capable not just of remembering the original conception of their "look" but of reinterpreting it into the present (Church, 2003).

As we talked, the dresses themselves emerged from the attics, closets, and trunks in which they had been stored. Their reappearance highlighted an issue that I had not anticipated, namely, whether and/or how to clean and preserve a garment that has social significance.

My mother's oldest friend and first "customer" washed and starched the cotton lace dress that Lorraine made for her wedding. Stored casually in a shoebox for five decades, it was retrieved in pristine condition. By contrast, my mother's last "customer" had her dress specially treated by a drycleaner. Made in 1995, this Grace Kelly–inspired creation was one of the most beautiful in the collection.

"Would you like to see it?" asked the owner.

"Of course!" I urged.

Off she went down the hall, returning in a few moments not with a dress but with a medium-sized box.

"Here it is," she declared, proudly.

And, sure enough, peering through the cellophane window I could see the lace bodice of the dress mounted on what turned out to be a plastic torso. The cardboard tomb was sealed to prevent the escape of a preservative gas.

"You've gone to a lot of trouble here," I observed, taken aback. "Are you willing to have the dress become part of the exhibit?"

She was. So we broke the seal and set the "mummy" free. Ironically, because the drycleaner had not used acid-free paper, the collar was already yellow around the edges.

In a rural suburb north of Red Deer, one of the older brides handed me just the underslip and lace bodice from her 1957 gown. Years previous, she had cut off the lace skirt to make curtains for her daughter's playhouse. For similar reasons, I was lucky to retrieve a 1968 dress from one of the brides who attended our church. In true prairie fashion, her mother planned to cut the high-quality bridal satin into strips for reuse as blanket binding. Fortunately, she never got around to it.

The 1979 wedding photographs of a high school classmate of mine had been destroyed in a basement flood. Divorced, she was thinking about selling her square-dance style dress for some much-needed cash. My letter arrived before she had the chance, and the exhibit process renewed her relationship with the garment. "I never knew how much it meant to me until we started talking," she confessed.

Lorraine made wedding dresses for one mother–daughter pair: the mother in 1958, her daughter in 1980. Both garments were touched by tragedy as the mother died of cancer and the daughter's husband was killed in a construction accident. It took many months and several awkward phone calls before the younger woman delivered these garments. "Seeing my own wedding dress again after it had been tucked away for 12 years at a time in my life when I had decided to remarry brought back sadness," she admitted.

Married in 1969, a local acquaintance had Lorraine make her a full-length, *peau-de-soie* sheath overlaid by a Chantilly lace coat with lily-point sleeves.

"It was better than perfect . . . a wonderful dress that I felt elegant in all day," she recalled.

Unfortunately, she no longer had it.

"Did you give it away?" I asked, carefully, over coffee in her mother's kitchen.

"I *threw* it away!" she replied, signaling the finality of her divorce. "It is too bad you didn't arrive in time because you certainly could have had it."

"Will you allow me to feature your story with an empty mannequin?" I ventured hopefully.

"Better leave well enough alone," she concluded.

One of my sisters-in-law also discarded her dress. Lorraine discovered it lying in a dirty heap on the basement floor of my brother's home, a clear sign that the owner had departed. Distressed at finding her handiwork in such a state—it can hardly have been an accident—my mother tossed the dress in the laundry. The relationship could not be fixed, but the dress came out as good as new and was successfully reincarnated in the museum.

Another sister-in-law had a similar if less loaded experience. Encased in plastic, this dress hung for some months in her parents' closet. To her horror, she discovered that the fabric had been badly discolored by cigarette smoke. She feared its ruin, but this dress, too, emerged triumphant from the washing machine.

◆ A Prototype

Barone (2006) has argued that arts-informed researchers have to push against

our own perceived lack of talent for crafting meaningful works of arts-based research, and against an academic culture that refuses to support the fostering of those talents in the next generation. . . . [However, we] need not necessarily match the high art of the masters in order to make history. (p. 228)

These are reassuring words for researchers wondering how to acquire the technical skills and artistic sensibilities that an arts-informed project demands. After I had assembled all of the dresses, I felt the full impact of this dilemma. I was seduced by what I had called to life, but mystified about how to touch, manipulate, and arrange these garments for public presentation. At every turn in the project, the sharpest edge of my learning curve was relating directly to exhibit materials—whether fabric, foam, plastic, wood, or metal.

Panicked, I signed up for a weekend workshop on exhibit design that was held in a drafty old fort clinging to the Lake Ontario shoreline. The major assignment was to construct a foam core box that replicated a room in the Fort: its window and door placement, ceiling height, pillars, and fireplaces. Inside the box, each group was to build a scale model for an exhibit on a topic randomly selected by the instructor. My group's topic was particularly dull. I can no longer recall what it was. I do know that it was a topic-in-the-abstract, intended to generate a history-for-everyone, and silent around the particularities and subjectivities that I longed to hear.

The workshop also touched off the frustration I felt as a child living with parents who worked easily with their hands. Minute by sweating minute, I struggled with my inability to conceptualize three-dimensional space. I could neither imagine nor build the little props that members of other groups were swiftly and even laughingly producing to illustrate their designs (it is for precisely these reasons that I never learned to sew). So I did not enjoy the training, but I did come away with a slightly better sense of how to proceed with my own project.

Several months later, in a back room at the Red Deer Museum, I worked with a battered foam core box that represented the Donor's Gallery: a single room measuring 47 ft by 33 ft with a high ceiling. Inside were miniature partitions and cut-out figures stuck upright onto old spools. In one afternoon, I used these materials to mock-up the *Fabrications* design. I was gaining some skill, but more importantly, I began to understand that "messing around" was part of the work. While designing renovations to the Hermitage Museum in Moscow, for example, Dutch "starchitect" Rem Koolhaas worked from a model that fit into a shoebox.

It was a blunt geometric form, suggesting, in profile, the lid of a grand piano.

It was also brazenly shoddy. Pieces of blue foam, orange posterboard, and Plexiglas had been glued together in the manner of a child's craft project. The model had been hastily assembled the previous night . . . "Often my most important role is to undo things," [Koolhaas] later explained—and there had not been time to make a more polished prototype. (Zalewski, 2005, p. 110)

As this anecdote demonstrates, much can be accomplished with supposedly slap-dash models.

More helpful than training workshops were the museum professionals who collaborated with me on exhibit design, production, and management. I tapped their expertise particularly in Red Deer where the project began. Wendy Martindale became the museum's executive director just shortly before I walked in the door to "sell" my idea. I came to know her as an astute observer, a superb manager, and an ally in feminism. Exhibits coordinator Diana Anderson had definite ideas about how to display objects. Although I sometimes felt restricted by her opinions, I also relied on her strong organizational and practical knowledge. For two years, using e-mail, telephone, and on-site meetings, the three of us consulted over the exhibit's development. The end product emerged from these negotiations.

◆ *Mannequins*

Mannequins come in a range of styles, materials, and prices. Early on, my mother and I visited a beautiful set created by the Canadian Museum of Civilization for a historical costume display. Custom-made at a cost of one thousand Canadian dollars per garment, the mounts were sculpted from a wire foundation followed by layers of plaster and/or papier-mâché. They were then painted to match the inside of the dress. Hollow and invisible, these mannequins gave the impression that the garments they supported actually stood lightly on their own.

The Red Deer Museum could not afford anything so discrete or elegant. Limited resources meant that we had to be economical with our design and resourceful in assembling our props. The Museum owned some mannequins that had been used for a story of Alberta nuns; we borrowed more from a nearby university. These mannequins had torsos covered in beige-colored cloth and impaled on plastic-covered steel rods mounted on round bases. Their heads were hairless with silhouette features and a rather disturbing row of stitching that ran laterally across the crown. When the exhibit reached the Museum of Civilization, to my relief, one of the textile specialists sewed satin headbands, like belated bandages, to cover these "incisions."

Our major problem, however, was that the mannequins were too bulky and shapeless to accommodate bridal gowns. Wielding a hot knife, a volunteer spent several days carving away pounds of plastic "fat" to give them waists. And so the Brides of Christ became the brides of men.

"This way, we make them look 20 years old instead of middle-aged," Wendy reported, wryly. "Although it is a smelly business, envy has been voiced by some observers."

◆ *The Fence*

O give me land, lots of land
Under starry skies above . . .

Don't fence me in? A nice idea but we needed a spatial organizer and some kind of

Figure 35.3   "Don't fence me in?" The white picket fence was both practical and highly symbolic.

protective barrier around the dresses. I suggested a picket fence. The image conjured up backyard friendliness and neighborly conversation of the sort that my mother and her brides enjoyed. It invoked gossip and the fact that people in small towns often know more about you than you might like. Although I expected her to scoff, Diana embraced this homely idea. Soon, a carpenter in sawdust-covered jeans was at work with hammer and saw to create the interlocking sections of a hinged fence. He built podiums to slide in place between the short pickets—one in front of each dress. Here we mounted the text of each bride's story accompanied by a reproduction of her wedding picture.

My simple notion turned out to be not so simple after all. Like wedding dresses, picket fences only seem obvious and familiar. Beyond their bucolic façade, they communicate ownership and private (often male) property, excluding some people both legally and on the basis of informal standards of civility. On the prairies, they have marked tiny oases of "polite" society carved with difficulty out of what White settlers experienced as a wild, even hostile, environment (Laird, 1998). To surround the brides with fences joined them with these conflicting meanings, suggesting wifely constraint as well as safety and the possibility of yearning for open spaces and different race relations.

Practically speaking, the fences traveled sturdily and were easy to install and almost indestructible; in fact, they were actually enhanced by wear and tear. However, the whole arrangement did very little to protect the garments from the 15 brides who attended the Red Deer opening. They climbed right over the pickets to be photographed—grinning broadly—with their arms clutched firmly around their former bodies.

◆ The Text

My "personal signature" (Barone & Eisner, 1997) on *Fabrications* is most obvious in the text, a working through of 300 pages of interview transcripts. Rejecting an abstract orientation toward objects in general, I drew on autobiography (Church, 1995/2004) to produce a first-person narrative about the work of a small-town dressmaker.

Fabrications could have been organized chronologically. This would have given primacy to its dominant artifact and reinforced a familiar narrative of changing fashion. But I wanted to tell a different story. As I studied my mother's transcript, I discovered that her sewing activities were heavily shaped by relationships with my grandmother and myself, schoolgirl friends, children, neighbors, daughters-in-law, and other local women. I wrote the text to reveal these connections. I wrote it as a daughter who knew her mother's work intimately, who had been deeply affected by, but had also taken issue with, how it was shaped

Afton

I wanted to get married in boots and faded blue jeans. But there were the grandparents to consider. So I created this mix-and-match outfit to express three sides of my personality: hippie, cowgirl, and biker. The bolero jacket was important because its lace sleeves disguised the tattoos on my arms. The look was a break with tradition. I loved this outfit. It suited my character.

Figure 35.4 "Not smothered in bride." Afton Partlow's 1994 Wedding Ensemble

around touchy matters such as getting paid for her labor.

I amplified the exhibit's primary storyline with short paragraphs about each dress. I worked these up from interview transcripts to highlight what I considered to be the most dramatic features of each bride's story but framed in such a way that she could comfortably identify with it in public. Avoiding thematic analysis, I condensed each bride's remarks to capture her particular "spark" or angle. I used words and phrases from the transcripts to link the woman's story with features of her dress. Each bride had the final say on this description.

Writing for an exhibit meant imagining readers looking forward through space rather than down at a page, mobile rather than stationary readers, visitors reading speedily as they walked or rolled through a room. Diana's instructions were to create three levels of description: a "headline" for each text panel that would catch the visitor's attention; a substatement that would provide more information, and a final short paragraph that would fill in the details. I was happy with my first draft but she noted a number of novice errors.

Titles and subtitles should be submessages, not isolated, unrelated thought fragments. They have to have meaning on their own, add up to a complete idea when read with each other, and be able to stand alone. Most of the language you use is easy to understand, but even if you were writing at a Grade 8 or 10 level, some words, such as "discourse" or "sociologist" may not be understood. Your text alone includes 2,107 words and would take over 14 minutes to read, not looking at anything else. You need to shorten it, make it more succinct.

These comments gave me a jolt. For years I had been preoccupied with writing plain language documents. How could I have forgotten? Nursing bruised feelings, I condensed substantive chunks of the first draft into punchy titles and subtitles and pared the rest to bare essentials. In this way, I was able to sharpen my presentation while preserving important details. It was a compromise that satisfied both Diana and me. Minor revisions later, we reached agreement on the final draft.

◆ Text Panels

Diana commissioned the carpenter. He built the text panels: 10 wooden sandwich boards with smoothly rounded corners. Five feet tall and three feet wide, each was designed to stand independently or be hung on the wall depending on the demands of the room. Diana then painted the panels: pink, mauve, yellow, blue. Using a level to keep the adhesive-backed letters straight, she glued on my words. Into the heavy boards, she nailed reproductions of family photos and transparent plastic pouches containing

pages from the sewing scribblers, pattern pieces, magazine images that had inspired two dresses, and a letter Lorraine wrote to me in which she sketched the garments she made for an entire wedding party.

None of this seemed controversial until the museum entertained a Toronto-based radio journalist who covered our story just before the Red Deer opening.

"Pastel colors are *far* too Martha Stewart! They refeminize the dresses—and the women," our guest declared with authority. "The exhibit is too celebratory. What about the sadness inherent in the dresses? Must they be done up so stiffly? Could they not float, suspended on rods, with a bit of breeze to ruffle their skirts? And what are you going to do about those ugly beige walls and that horrible blue floor?!"

The critique stung. It took me awhile to recognize the journalist's outsider privilege in making these judgments. Engaged as a

Figure 35.5   Diana Anderson positions one of the small podiums built to display "dress stories" and photos.

daughter, a sister, a neighbor, a friend, and a researcher, my relation to the project was fractious. I was torn between shaping it myself and allowing it to be shaped by local people, skills, and points of view. Significantly invested in both my small town and big city selves, I slid back and forth depending on the situation or interaction. I produced myself differently in different contexts. I struggled for balance.

"What other colors could you possibly use for a bridal show?!" puzzled Diana.

She had researched the exhibit from the same magazines she used to plan her own wedding. The two events were linked in her mind from the beginning.

"This is the first direct challenge we have had to our interpretation," I noted, white-knuckled. "I take it seriously, especially where it overlaps with questions I've had from the beginning."

"The comments are fair—within limits," nodded Wendy. "There isn't much we can do about the walls or the floor. Even if we wanted to, we don't have the money."

"True," I agreed. "But somehow, we need to give the exhibit an edge of darkness. We are overcome by sweetness and light!"

And yet the logic of pastels was difficult to escape. Delicate shades formed the palette in which my mother worked, the colors most closely associated with the feminine in Western cultures. In the end, we muted the color scheme by doing the photos in black and white. The carpenter painted the fences a weather-beaten gray and museum staff pounded the pickets to roughen their edges.

These adjustments affirmed my commitment to doing what was possible with local resources. In keeping with the rich legacy of prairie women, *Fabrications* would be homespun. It would be central Alberta not Toronto. Although the decision split me, I was determined not to deny my roots. The exhibit would be an act of recuperation; my

way of saying—finally—"What is here is good enough."

◆ Sewing Machines

Eight thousand visitors toured *Fabrications* during its 9-week summer run in Red Deer. Most were women; many were not regular museum-goers. On the strength of this affirmation, the museum organized and managed a tour that lasted for 3 years. The exhibit was packed up, shipped, and received at each new location as a ready-made package complete with assembly instructions. The fences and panels fit snugly into custom-made wooden crates. My mother's sewing scribblers traveled with them, as did a framed illustration created for an article I published in *Elm Street* magazine (Church, 1998). Already dressed, the mannequins were encased in large muslin bags with drawstring tops. At each installation, with increasing familiarity, I spent time loosening and bending their doughy arms into some semblance of grace and curving their fingers—stiff and pudgy—around the dried flowers that grew increasingly ratty in their grasp.

In Red Deer, we included a small replica of Lorraine's sewing space complete with wood paneling and objects from her workroom.

"Surely you don't want that!" she exclaimed, as I loaded up several boxes.

"Oh yes I do!" I insisted, and made off with patterns, plush animals, balls of wool, an ironing board that my father had made, an iron, my mother's college diploma with the broken glass in one corner, and a hooked rug for which she won first prize at the county fair.

Then, just before the opening, my father dismantled Lorraine's Singer sewing machine, wrapped the pieces in blankets, loaded them into the Pontiac, drove to Red Deer, and unloaded everything through the museum's back door.

"I haven't taken it apart since I bought it in 1948," my mother wailed, wringing her hands.

It was clear that we had moved not just an object but a tangible piece of her identity. For days she wandered around her basement looking lost—almost frightened. Wisely, she reclaimed the machine prior to the tour. Other venues displayed similar vintage machines drawn from their collections or someone else's sewing room.

Because the spaces were all different, each museum modified and contributed to the design according to its needs and resources. To present the text in French as well as English, the Museum of Civilization built their own text panels, each topped with a wooden cut-out of a dancing dress. The introduction was screened onto fabric and draped over a hanger attached to a coat stand. Designers from the Glenbow in Calgary used Japanese screens to divide *Fabrications* from other displays. They suspended text panels from the ceiling by giant metal coat hangers made in the museum's workshop. These became a popular decorative element in other venues and were a source of amusement to airport security.

In a sense, then, *Fabrications* kept evolving until its final closing in 2001. The crates were shipped back to the Red Deer Museum for the last time: The dresses returned wearily to their owners; the mannequins—now youthfully slender—await other garments; the text panels and fences readily found other work.

Figure 35.6　The author's parents, Lorraine and Stuart Church, prepare to carry her 1950s Singer sewing machine through the back door of the museum.

◆ Conclusion

In this chapter, I have made a case for taking objects seriously, encountering them directly, proceeding object by object to unfold a study, tracking back and forth in the dialogic space between objects and their makers/users, and working reflexively with our limitations, confusions, and discoveries. A methodological "free fall," this process raises major questions for arts-informed researchers as we move to establish, legitimize, and formalize the tradition through definitive texts. Will we recognize the disjunctures of our own lives as exciting starting points for creative work? Will we value the "accidental" quality of the journey that they open up for us? Can we lose control over how we come into knowing? Or will we turn creative inquiry into a familiar order: a step-wise and predictable set of practices, planned and tidy, learned as part of a formal curriculum?

The answers, personal and institutional, will profoundly affect the ways in which we find jobs, secure grant funding, and create credibility. Even as I articulate this issue, I catch myself in a contradiction. In mapping the "travels" that shaped my own project, I have also made a case for tried and true qualitative methods: for asking questions, listening to and collecting stories, observing what happens, making notes, and (somehow) writing what we come to know. Learning fresh skills for an emergent practice does not necessarily mean leaving old skills behind.

As a novice creative researcher in a three-dimensional medium, I was thrown off of what I knew, invariably falling on strange ground, seeing afresh or askew. At this point in the history of arts-informed research, many of us are in this position. As we acquire the skills we need to produce artistically "credible" work, I want to argue that our liminality is illuminating. My imbalance was a resource for *Fabrications*.

It ensured my reciprocity with other people: my mother, the brides, my Red Deer collaborators, and other museum professionals across the country. These cross-disciplinary and cross-country exchanges were a big part of what worked well. As arts-informed researchers, do we want to be in a position to do it all by ourselves? Or might multiple conjunctions of knowledge through the meshing of different people's skills become a hallmark of this emerging mode of inquiry? Perhaps we always do our best work just on the verge of knowing.

◆ References

Barber, E. B. (1994). *Women's work: The first 20,000 years—Women, cloth, and society in early times.* New York: W. W. Norton and Co.

Barone, T. (2006). Making educational history: Qualitative inquiry, artistry, and the public interest. In G. Ladson-Billings & W. F. Tate (Eds.), *Education research in the public interest: Social justice, action, and policy* (pp. 213–230). New York: Teachers College Press.

Barone, T., & Eisner, E. (1997). Arts-based educational research. In M. Jaeger (Ed.), *Complementary methods for research in education* (pp. 36–116). Washington, DC: American Educational Research Association.

Burman, B. (Ed.). (1999). *The culture of sewing: Gender, consumption, and home dressmaking.* Oxford, UK: Berg.

Church, K. (1998, Summer). The dressmaker. *Elm Street,* 54–62.

Church, K. (2002). The hard road home: Towards a polyphonic narrative of the mother/daughter relationship. In C. Ellis & A. Bochner (Eds.), *Ethnographically speaking: Autoethnography, literature and aesthetics* (pp. 234–257). Walnut Creek, CA: AltaMira Press.

Church, K. (2003). Something plain and simple? Unpacking custom-made wedding dresses of Western Canada (1950–1995). In H. Foster

& D. Johnson (Eds.), *Wedding dress across cultures* (pp. 5–21). Oxford, UK: Berg.

Church, K. (2004). *Forbidden narratives: Critical autobiography as social science.* London: Routledge. (Original work published 1995)

Church, K., & Church, L. (2003). Needles and pins: Dialogue on a mother–daughter journey. *Journal of the Association for Research on Mothering, 5*(1), 148–156.

Crane, D. (2000). *Fashion and its social agendas: Class, gender, and identity in clothing.* Chicago: University of Chicago Press.

Denzin, N. (1997). *Interpretive ethnography: Ethnographic practices for the 21st century.* Thousand Oaks, CA: Sage.

Ellis, C., & Bochner, A. (1992). Telling and performing personal stories: The constraints of choice in abortion. In C. Ellis & M. Flaherty (Eds.), *Investigating subjectivity: Research on lived experience* (pp. 79–101). Newbury Park, CA: Sage.

Gamber, W. (1997). *The female economy: The millinery and dressmaking trades, 1860–1930.* Urbana: University of Illinois Press.

Gray, R., Ivonoffski, V., & Sinding, C. (2002). Making a mess and spreading it around: Articulation of an approach to research-based theatre. In C. Ellis & A. Bochner (Eds.), *Ethnographically speaking: Autoethnography, literature, and aesthetics* (pp. 57–75). Walnut Creek, CA: AltaMira Press.

Green, G., & Banim, M. (Eds.). (2001). *Through the wardrobe: Women's relationships with their clothes.* New York: Berg.

Hodder, I. (2000). The interpretation of documents and material culture. In N. K. Denzin & Y. S. Lincoln (Eds.), *Handbook of qualitative research* (2nd ed.; pp. 703–715). Thousand Oaks, CA: Sage.

Hooper-Greenhill, E. (1992). *Museums and the shaping of knowledge.* London: Routledge.

Hooper-Greenhill, E. (2000). *Museums and the interpretation of visual culture.* London: Routledge.

Kuchler, S., & Miller, D. (Eds.). (2005). *Clothing as material culture.* Oxford, UK: Berg.

Laird, G. (1998). *Slumming it at the rodeo: The cultural roots of Canada's right-wing revolution.* Vancouver, British Columbia, Canada: Douglas & McIntyre.

Shorten, L. (Producer). (1998, May 31). Behind the scenes at the Red Deer Museum. *This Morning (The Sunday Edition)*, Canadian Broadcasting Corporation, CBC Radio One.

Zalewski, D. (2005, March 14). Intelligent design: Can Rem Koolhaas kill the skyscraper? *The New Yorker*, 110–125.

36

NO STYLE, NO COMPOSITION, NO JUDGMENT[1]

◆ Janice Jipson and Nicholas Paley

When we were invited to contribute a chapter to the *Handbook of the Arts in Qualitative Research*, the editors asked us to reflect on what had brought us to doing educational inquiry from an artistic perspective. They further suggested that since we had collaborated in working with artistic forms of data display for nearly two decades we might, as part of our reflection, consider some of the key understandings that had emerged from—and characterized—our thinking and research practice. Seemingly straightforward, the invitation was for us to put down into words the unsayable—why we sought to reinvent our work outside the conventions of academic research.

Our initial reaction to this opportunity was simultaneously hesitant and welcoming. On the one hand, we have long maintained that our work should stand without explanation—resisting any form of universalizing narrative. On the other, we found the challenge of articulating our thinking about the development of our method intriguing. Thus, the notion of conceptualizing our work discursively was tantalizing, precisely because it challenged our resistance to objectivity and analytic territorialization.

Across the range of our work together—from textual analysis to policy critique, from personal history to conceptual representation—we have been insistently led by the necessity of letting the subject find its own

◆ 435

form. Much of our past work (but not all of it), and most of our newer work (but not all of it), was not intended to advance any one line about teaching strategy, learning theory, or research practice. Rather, we saw our collaborative, singular projects always as

> catalysts for departure to somewhere else in our understanding of [the research] experience—somewhere that offers a fresh perspective on experience that would allow us to . . . use new understandings of experience to create concepts and pedagogies capable of making more of the experience of the learning self. (Ellsworth, 2004, p. 3)

Our recent examinations continue our diversified explorations of the educational concrete. For example, responding to the U.S. legislation embodied in the *No Child Left Behind Act,* we wrote and produced a one-act play built around the narrative reflections of practicing teachers whose voices were nowhere present in the debate and formation of this policy. We wanted to dramatize shifts in relations of power that have increasingly diminished the personal and the local in educational thinking. We situated our play in the experimental, politically committed traditions of the Berliner ensemble and the work of Helene Weigel and Bertholt Brecht, intending to articulate the many tensions experienced by teachers around issues of assessment and standardization (Jipson & Paley, 2004).

In another example of our recent work, *Outsider Research: 6 Concepts,* we created an unsponsored presentation that we exhibited as an alternative to the 2004 American Educational Research Association (AERA) Roundtable Colloquium, A Gallery of Aesthetic Research Practices. In our unauthorized session, we displayed—in a vacant hallway just outside the room where an official roundtable session was being held—a collection of intermedia representations and textual commentary of six concepts that had personal reference for our own evolving research practice (Paley & Jipson, 2004).

Surveying these recent and other previous examples of our collaborations, we have selected three understandings around which to organize our reflections about the work we've been doing together for the past 15 years. At this point in our collaborative work, we think of these understandings as "No style," "No composition," "No judgment"—and we use these terms here in a positive, independent way to analyze the collective, different aspects of our work as they relate to notions of arts-related inquiry. There are two important points to consider about our organizing terminology here. First, we view these three understandings not as taxonomies for imposing any kind of order on our research work. Gilles Deleuze (Rajchman, 2000) has shown us a way to unthink such terminologies. We see them as what Deleuze might call "images of thought" (pp. 32–47) that might help us generate ideas and languages for recasting our work as a set of problems that need to be worked through from new angles "so that we can find a way out of them" (p. 33).

Second, these three understandings require a particular art of seeing—not to be confused with any "transparency" of explanation but, rather, of seeing as a process of absorbing the material at hand *in order to think how and what we do not yet know.* To see this way means to think in other ways. So, in discussing "No style, No composition, No judgment," this process means frequently working from intuitive rather than propositional impulses as we try to map out the interrelationships of what is both already there and what is yet to be reconstructed.

◆ *No Style*

To think of "No style" as a key understanding in the work we do is to immediately plunge into different territory. It is something not easily captured in language, and we struggle with its precise articulation because we may not yet know what it fully is. To clarify its relation to the work of our analytic practice is even more challenging. If anything, the term seems counterintuitive—simultaneously calling to mind the enterprise of research methodology itself (i.e., "style"), or its unfortunate lack. "No style" also suggests numerous definitional associations—no distinctiveness, no cohesiveness, no consistency. No manner or custom. Even further, "No style" doesn't readily fit in any accustomed modes of analytic thinking—artistic or otherwise. A brief scan of its textual/conceptual presence draws a blank across all major reference bases in qualitative social inquiry.

To resolve this, it might be helpful here to perhaps speak about the term "style," but we prefer to pass over this without comment. Methodology has been thoroughly discussed already across many disciplinary landscapes. Those interested enough in its histories can refer to any number of excellent texts that chart its various interpretations. So we frustrate this reading expectation by remaining silent on the topic, since we're not interested in creating a Kabuki-like theater of formalized oppositions, or a kind of doubled text in which "no style" could be analyzed in relation to "some style" in the histories of artistic production—our own or someone else's.

Rather, we prefer in this section to sometimes think of the term "No style" in certain ways, sometimes in others—defying gravity, so to speak—recasting the conventional definitions of terminology for our own purposes in this chapter. In taking this kind of approach, we find a strong and powerful borrowing in the analytic practice of bell hooks (1994), who similarly experiments with familiar terminologies and definitions in her writing in order to construct spaces for thinking "an education of freedom." Although we recognize that she is clearly addressing a different set of critical realities, we appreciate her admirable courage "to make English do what we want it to do . . . liberating ourselves in language" (hooks, 1994, p. 175) in order to construct a learning self.

Much of the production (and analysis) of imaginative creations has been contradictory and provocative. "The world of art," as Herbert Marcuse (1978) reminds us, "is that of another *Reality Principle,* of estrangement—and only as estrangement does it fulfill a *cognitive* function; it communicates truths not communicable in any other language; it *contradicts*" (p. 10).

In the following section, then, we offer some speculations about how it is within precisely the conditions and circumstances of "No style" that we do our work—and how this understanding has a productive potential in helping us think about arts-related analytic work today. To get at all of this in a more concrete way, we provide three brief snapshots of our collaborations—some of which have been identified as "arts-related," some of which have not. So what follows is an attempt to access, through the concrete and the particular, and through the image of "No style," a way of thinking about certain fundamental questions of doing contemporary qualitative research—to light up, as it were, and from this specific angle, a wider range of research issues that others, perhaps, might also find useful to ponder. And although it is always difficult to know how far back to go in charting a particular course of practice, we feel that a good place to begin is with the first intentionally collaborative research project we undertook.

◆ The Selective Tradition

The Selective Tradition in Teachers' Choice of Children's Literature: Does it Exist in the Elementary Classroom? was our first collaborative research project (Jipson & Paley, 1989). Begun in 1988, just after completing our doctoral programs, it was a study of how practicing elementary teachers selected trade and children's books for classroom use, and of the dynamics of their decision making. We grounded our inquiry in the theoretical literature that argued that text selection in educational settings was never a neutral curricular decision but one that was inherently part of a political and ideological process—since in choosing books for classroom use, individuals were essentially selecting for or against the representations of particular kinds of cultural experience and value in their classes. In this project, we followed the methods we learned in graduate school, and we took seriously the ordained script for research production. Our study, for example, was divided into familiar sections: Introduction, Design, Data Analysis, Findings and Discussion, Conclusion. Listen to (and not just read) the cadence of some of our wording from the section on data analysis:

> Initial data analysis involved our independently sorting out the books listed by the teachers according to author's name. In a similar way, each author's and main character's sex and ethnic background was coded. Poetry books, information books without human characters, and animal stories with main characters of unspecified sex or ethnic background were coded as separate categories. . . . Coding of reasons for selecting each of the books was completed by sorting questionnaires for each of the books named according to apparently similar explanations. Three general categories of reasons emerged from this process. . . . (Jipson & Paley, 1989, pp. 150–151)

The processes of both conducting and presenting this research observed the formats we had been taught. Hiding ourselves as individuals in the process, we objectively gathered and examined the data, closely reading it for patterns and categories, condensing and enumerating the experiences of classroom teachers. Our research at that time employed a positional language. It had a syntax and a sequence. It referenced an emancipatory politics and pronounced our affiliation with it. It was straightforward. It was objective. It had a style—the coding of which could be seen and the doing of which could be learned. We presented our study at the AERA conference in 1989 and published it in the content literature soon after (Jipson & Paley, 1989, 1991).

◆ Animals and Curriculum Masters

One of our first intentionally arts-related projects began at the annual conference of American Association of Colleges of Teacher Education (AACTE) in Chicago, Illinois, in February 1996. We had each been sent by our deans to represent our respective institutions and gather data about recent developments related to teacher education program certification and licensure, but after one full morning of conference participation, we felt the need to address familiar forms of discourse about teacher education in a new way in order to sharpen the intensity related to the making of such discourses. To accomplish this goal, we embarked on a site-specific, spontaneous research study that collected data using available print and visual resources from, at, and near the conference on that day.

Neither the process of conducting this research nor the process of presenting it followed any of the formats for inquiry that we had previously been taught, heard, or seen. The processes we did employ emerged from our feelings at the conference presentations on that morning (resistance to systems of conference language, control, and power) and from our commitment to social responsibility (service of the spirit and of the subversive imagination). After lunch, we left the conference hotel, having already gathered a collection of AACTE display materials, and returned to our own hotel a few blocks away. There, we similarly gathered a number of tourist brochures of Chicago that were exhibited in the hotel lobby. We asked the front desk staff for material and technical support—scissors, glue, paper, and tape—then took the elevator up to one of our rooms.

For the next few hours—working over each other's shoulders and in each other's way—we tore texts from contexts, ideas from images, and specificities from totalities, remixing the data we'd collected according to our own personal and aesthetic preferences. The remixing that we did was done intuitively—until we arrived at a series of images that seemed to us to be the most sincere and evocative. We then arranged these images into page format, and then on the hotel room floor, we intuitively placed the pages in a sequence that told a story for which there was no narrative. After this, we created a cover page with the title *Animals and Curriculum Masters* to convey some of the multiple, contradictory associations that reflected exactly what we felt.

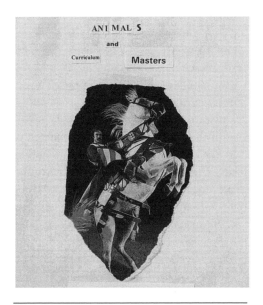

Figure 36.1

Figure 36.2

By evening, we were finished with our project. Since there was no prior research literature within which to situate what we had done, there was nothing more to do. And having no desire to say anything more than what we had made, we presented our work nowhere. There was no reference to any emancipatory ideology on our part, even though we were very much interested in language and language policies in a changing world. What we made lived in service of a particular spirit. Several years later, "Animals" (Jipson & Paley, 1999), was published in Patrick Diamond and Carol Mullen's (1999) book *The Postmodern Educator: Arts-Based Inquiries and Teacher Development,* although we did not consider ourselves in any way post-anything.

◆ Duplications

"Duplications" (Paley & Jipson, 1997) began in 1997 as a response to an increasingly standardized world. It was part of a series of our own arts-related interventions that emerged from our teaching and research need to address issues of standardization in the discourses of "scientifically based" educational research and the impact of such languages on educational life. In this multisited series of interventions, we experimented, both inside and outside of our classes, with creating what Foucault (1988) has termed "fracture areas" (pp. 36–37) in established systems of organized thinking and practice in order to open up spaces of possible transformation of such thinking and practice.

These arts-based interventions were generally text and image based, and one or two pages in length. They drew their support from Maxine Greene's rich and varied urging for educators "to engage in new kinds of questioning and problem posing" (Greene,

1978, p. 52) that might challenge the many kinds of "taken-for-grantedness of much of what is taught" (p. 171). Central to many of these interventions—but perhaps most intentionally explicit in "Duplications"—was a threefold interest: (1) to confront the pervasiveness of repetitive analytic structures and ritualistic research representation; (2) to critique such efforts from perspectives that accessed aspects of the aesthetic, the visual, and/or the conceptual; and (3) to do so in ways that themselves were never repetitive and always different.

We originally disseminated these interventions informally—preferring to have them suggest their analytic connections conceptually and in their own magnetic way. "Duplications" was a two-page intervention. On the left page was an infrared satellite image of Hurricane Andrew at 922 millibars of air pressure, 50 miles southeast of the Florida coast on August 23, 1992. On the right side of the page was the following text:

> Duplications are the most lethal storms known. They destroy more things on earth than everything else added together. Some duplications have the potential to extend over thousands and thousands of miles, and the destructive power produced by some of them is so intense, it is like a thousand lasers exploding at once. When duplications form, they exert tremendous pressure, moving with incredible speed until their force crashes into whatever is in their way. The resulting devastation can be awesome, and their effects can be felt long after they have disappeared from view. During the height of some of these phenomena, the violence is unreal, and the whole world howls in obliteration. At the center of most duplications is the eye—a clearly defined location of light and air so pure that it could almost be a symbol for something else. Inside the eye, everything is still as death, and the sun

shines in a sky of clear blue. (Paley & Jipson, 1999, p. 269)

Our "Duplication" making had few precedents to benefit from. It was a spontaneous creation, a *sui generis* project. It was inspired, in part, by the book *Storms* by Seymour Simon (1992)—a children's trade book that we had been invited to read by one of our own children to help with a science assignment. As we read one evening, we were immediately struck by Simon's observations of the phenomenon of hurricanes. We intuitively substituted the word "duplications" for the word "hurricanes" in some of his text—and found that the entire passage took on a potentially fresh and powerful set of meanings, albeit in a different part of the educational world—our own. We then "duplicated" several passages of Simon's text in developing our intervention and mixed it with our own wordings until "Duplications" said what we wanted it to say. The National Oceanic and Atmospheric Administration kindly provided us with a set of digital images of recent hurricanes, from which we chose an image to match with our text. Although "Duplications" had little impact on developing educational policy, it was appreciated by several of our colleagues and by some of our students. In 1998, "Duplications" eventually found a semipermanent home in *Taboo: The Journal of Education and Culture* (Paley & Jipson, 1997).

In an essay written several years ago—partly in order to help us trace the social and analytic terrain in which we lived—we wrote

When we work now, we don't know where we're going to end up. We start with something, and end up with something else. We begin with an idea that interests us, but very quickly it becomes many ideas. It splits apart into pieces.

Our one idea becomes a kind of jumble. . . . So there's an idea which almost immediately becomes an impossibility. A tangle of internal logic. Systems of competing voice. . . . And then long moments of silence when we wonder: How to put things together now? (Jipson & Paley, 1997a, p. 221)

And:

When we work now, no top, no bottom. No back, no front. No under, no over, no symmetry. No yard we own. Heap ideas on top of ideas until they give us their own shape anywhere. Sometimes this can be startling—sometimes a mess. . . . Refusing to be a building. Refusing their destiny to be an architecture. Their density is what really attracts us. We often wonder now: What else possibly could? (p. 230)

As we consider these words again, we are reminded that all analytic works are, to paraphrase Gilles Deleuze (Rajchman, 2000), "*singular* creations." Each individual who thinks creates *a* research "indefinite for there to be others" (p. 32). Each recasts what it means to ask, to think, given the circumstances of the moment.

There are two things that the above passages help us think about. The first is the idea of *supervision*—metapractices "that set or keep the rules for others"—as when an attempt is made to set down a model to stylize inquiry—arts-related or otherwise. Again, as Deleuze points out, not only might inquiry not always benefit from rules to follow, but it often evolves in ways that are emergent and that aren't predictable in advance (Rajchman, 2000, p. 46), therefore not necessitating a distinctive style of thinking about it that's the same for everyone, everywhere, every time. The second thing that these passages help us think about is the idea of *imitation*—notions of "no top, no bottom," "no back, no front" may well interrupt the duplication (naturalization?) of method—perhaps enabling individuals to venture into new territories where they are then forced to think how and what they do not yet know.

So for us, borrowing here and borrowing there, we have tried to make each inquiry a singular creation. An invention where each questioning itself is a unique becoming, a something-always-in-the making, a *some-one*-always-in the-making. So to speak of "No style" is to think of doing things experimentally, intuitively—before style itself becomes a matter for conscious debate.

In *The Daily Practice of Painting*, the artist, Gerhard Richter (1998), speaks of the continuous task of his craft: "To try out what can be done with painting: how I can paint today, and above all what. Or, to put it differently: the continual attempt to picture to myself what is going on" (p. 92). This (albeit from a different disciplinary perspective) is a challenge that we feel we share, too—continuing to work together at what we do together—sometimes dramatically shifting from one project to another, sometimes only to return again—struggling to produce works of irreducible particularity in "No style"—all of which are grounded in the constantly changing, sensuous aspects of our daily existence—in order to construct "a kind of paradigm of what a non-alienated mode of cognition might look like" (Eagleton, 1990, p. 2).

◆ No Composition

Research work in the post–20th century increasingly seems to be situated within a narrowed terrain of hyper-determined formations, partially established by U.S. federal government mandates that serve to reduce the forms and expressions that knowledge can take to standardized protocols easily represented graphically and readily determined by "scientific" assessment. In many ways, arts-related research is able to provide a resistance to such universal forms of knowledge production and reproduction while simultaneously creating variant spaces for the expression of educational knowledge. After all, Walter Benjamin (1978) has urged us to intervene in the means of artistic production—to change the "technique" of the traditional to transform the "apparatus" of bourgeois culture.

Questions of "What knowledge is of most worth?" "Whose knowledge is it?" and "Whose interests are served, whose needs are met?" have framed contemporary critically informed educational research. Our work together has sought to explore the contested nature of these questions, to deepen our understanding of the nature of social inquiry, and to provide insight into the problems of thought that arise when individuals experiment with *formerly* static representations of knowledge.

When we speak then of "No composition" in our work, we are not addressing the mechanical processes of composing but issues we have with representation in a post–20th century time. Like many educators, we have wondered about what forms knowledge might take in this series of historical moments, and this questioning has prompted us to experiment with responses to it in ways that are meaningful to us. During the past decade, this experimentation has increasingly been represented in nondiscursive forms of research work, and we have similarly encouraged our graduate students to invent ways of sharing research findings that resonate with their research questions rather than with formally authorized modes of representation (Paley, Crawford, Kinney, Koons, & Mendoza, 2004).

Although this approach has generated much enthusiasm among students, it has also been met with significant confusion and often direct dismissal by our peers, generating repeated questions about converting research representations into transmittable form. In our own work, we have continued to address questions regarding alternative modes of representation within educational research from the frame of internal critique and to explore the theoretical and empirical complexities of nonstandard representations and formations in research. Asking the question "What forms can knowledge take?" we have also examined the implementation of nonstandard representations within curriculum practice and the relational implications of such formations across educational communities—classrooms, schools, universities, state governing agencies, and professional organizations.

One question that continues to puzzle us, however, is this: In doing educational research that incorporates alternative forms of representation, how can we be certain that our formations are not just analytic diversions or aesthetic entertainment? We take our struggles with form seriously, and we work to respond to questions of educational practice in ways "that do not duplicate other narratives" (Greene, 1994, p. 217). We try very hard to get the tone, the shape, the phrasing to match the ideas we wanted to address, but we are unsure if any of this has the same meaning to anyone else.

Two years ago, for example, we constructed an outsider research project (briefly alluded to in the introduction to this chapter) for AERA in which we explored the personal meanings of six concepts that had implications for our research practice: Hiding, Alone, Enough, Else, Convention, and Sans (Paley & Jipson, 2004). The project was unauthorized in that it had neither been submitted to AERA for acceptance nor was it presented in the approved AERA venue. Rather, we set up our collection of Joseph Cornell–like, shadow-box, conceptual configurations in a darkened hallway, as a complement to the large roundtable

meeting "A Gallery of Aesthetic Research Practices." For us, it was clear that our constructions represented carefully explored understandings of our own meanings related to specific, perhaps unexamined conceptual issues of research, but we could not respond as certainly to the question of whether they communicated any meanings (or, perhaps, "our" meanings) for anyone else. The "audience" that unexpectedly wandered into our nonsession had no expectation of what they might encounter—and although several of them documented their responses in a log that we had made available, we were not sure how our session substantively contributed to questions of art and educational research.

That raised, for us, another set of key questions. Were these constructions we had assembled "representations" of our ideas in the sense of being outcomes of our research process, or were they "formations," actively constructing their own meaning as they were encountered? Had we merely constructed a nondiscursive shrine to our analysis and interpretation? Or were these representations, in fact, actively enshrining knowledge as they were viewed and consumed, thereby assuming a meaning apart from our own understandings? In his own (musical) experiments with aesthetic practice as social inquiry, David Byrne (1995) has spoken of similar tensions:

> I often sing with all my might, and I find that all I've accomplished is to convey a sense of energy being expended and a desperate need to communicate something. Often, no one is able to figure out exactly what it is I'm trying to communicate. I myself often feel that I've touched something deep as my voice rises into a painful, sudden sharp edge. And I assume and hope that the exact same feelings are reconstructed in the minds and hearts of the listeners, but that isn't always true.

By disputing the predictability and uniformity of research representation, and by asserting that its composition need not encompass a perfect and transmittable replication of certain educational knowledge but rather a singular mode of representational practice, we accentuate the variance possible within research practice. In contrast, by relying on the traditions of the successful standardizers of educational research practice, researchers are limited in the analysis of their own work.

To the extent to which research is knowledge production, the construction of a research representation is a process of interpretation, a physical making of meaning. Affirming the "right way" to conduct and present research always risks doing it the wrong way, thus invalidating the results. Rather than participate in such a circular venture, we have chosen to promote local, specific representations and formations that extend from the knowledge itself. For example, in our earlier research into the process of selecting and setting standards for education in the public schools (Jipson & Paley, 1999), the text of our research report echoed the plaint, "One of the X is missing, the one where XX." The abrupt, arbitrary, and incomplete form of the text mirrored what we had determined to be the imposition of curricular standards in our local schools.

We have tried to get at the issue of the meanings carried by forms of research representation more directly in the invited, arts-based project "Double-Bind" (Paley & Jipson, 2001). In this piece our text is literally bound on both sides into the *Journal of Curriculum Theorizing*, making it impossible to access without destroying the research object itself. Calling into question the process of accessing research knowledge, "Double-Bind" invites the research consumer to actively become a part of the research representation act by violating the object and thereby creating a different object in its place—one that is literally torn open or out of its context.

So then, to reengage our own questions about the construction of alternative forms of representation: Are we just composing design modifications on the surface of the meaning? Are we merely engaged in stylizing . . . changing the surface experience while keeping the underlying knowledge structures the same? Or are we responding to the issue of internal construction—the shifting meanings within the knowledge that inform and suggest the representation? We continue to wonder, can you ever change the surface without changing the meaning?

And even given that understanding, as researchers are we defeated when we sometimes reach the point where it is difficult to develop new external forms, so that we come to rely on older forms that we reinterpret, recycling our good old ideas, with direct reference to their past forms? But then, why do some of our representations prevail, but not others? And if you recycle the representation often enough, does indifference set in? Or have you just created your own colossus? And then where do you go?

Paul Valery (cited in Walter Benjamin, 1968) suggests that "great innovations transform the entire technique of the arts, thereby affecting artistic invention itself and perhaps even bringing about an amazing change in our very notion of art" (p. 217). But new representations do not themselves solve all research problems, especially the problem of creating new knowledge. Thus, instead of making alternative forms of representation an end in itself, we consider its value as a strategy allowing maximum diffusion within difficult methodological work where everything needs to be considered. It becomes our own kind of standardization, adapted in infinite variation.

◆ *No Judgment (A Nonsynchronous Reflection)*

Is it Art? Is it Research?
Research isn't research until someone says it is
So who gets to do the saying? Certainly, not me—
I have always had trouble thinking of our "scholarly" work
As either art or research.
For me, it is something else—
Something about bringing insight to form,
Based on distraction and passion
and the excitement of the ideas
that always seem to crackle between us.
Maybe it's the remnants of my empirical training,
Maybe it's my indolence,
Maybe it's my evasion of connoisseurship
(how could I, a rural, working-class kid from Wisconsin,
ever presume to be an expert on anything?)
but I tend to think of our work as play
and our productions as a sly resistance
(to what? to whom?)
to whatever it is that is
the fashion of the moment.
So perhaps I am trapped in
that dreadful circle of judgment . . .
on one hand, I refuse the invitation to classification
(which is, of course, as much a judgment as the parodies we produce)
but then, on the other hand,
I do decide—our work is *not* of that sort
Not belonging in the art/research taxonomy
so I create my own elusive category
(Certainly not research, about which I know a little
and probably not art, of which I know nothing),
One more stubborn than anything—
The disruption of expectation.

Is it art? Is it research?
I once heard that art isn't art

until someone says it is.
But I've never imagined our work as either.
It's something else
Another kind
Another sort
Fabrications
That have developed in and despite time
Passions of companionship and curiosity
Of both matter and spirit.
My small town Wisconsin experience
Did not prepare me for this either.
What we do together
Who can say exactly?

Funny.
You wrote earlier about "Animals and Curriculum Masters"
Which was an intuitive project if there ever was one
but then it was put in a book
and someone talked about it in an AERA session,
asking "Is it research?"
It must have been (research? art? interesting?)
Or they wouldn't have bothered with it.
But we didn't know it was happening,
didn't know whether they decided it was research or not.

But the question that occurred to me was
how can you evaluate something that has no context?
And in our stand-alone position,
context is what we refuse to offer. . . .
Walter Benjamin (1968) writes:
"The presence of the original is the prerequisite
to the concept of authenticity" (p. 220).
And later, when "the instance the criterion of authenticity
Ceases to be applicable to artistic production,
the total function of art is reversed. . . .
it begins to be based on another practice—
politics" (p. 224).

When we imagined the idea for "Double-Bind"
I initially visualized it as a book that questioned
The categories of arts-related research

But that resisted any conventional reading.
If you wanted to enter into it, you had to
*   destroy what it was*
In order to find what you were looking for.
I liked the idea that we would be producing a
*   text that wasn't*
Meant to be read in the usual way.
When invited to talk about "Double-Bind" and
*   other examples of our work*
And their connection to social inquiry
At an informal doctoral research seminar this
*   semester*
I fumbled around.
I confessed that I did not know
Much about inquiry.
Much less about aesthetic practice.
Is it research?
Is it art?
Is it useful?
The expert tangle
Of still another double-bind.

Paraphrasing Benjamin's concern about art,
What matters about research?
Its existence? Or its being on view?
Think again about "Double-Bind," which was
packaged in such a way that the printed text
    could not be accessed
without violating and destroying it.
So when I was asked to explain it
to doctoral students at my university,
I had to interrupt its meaning with logic and history,
creating the very context that permitted the
    judgment.
Creating for us all "the silence of displace-
    ment" (Rich, 2001, p. 151).

What's really difficult is this:
What do individuals need to know
In order to make art?
In order to make research?
(Again, I don't think of our work as any of
*   these things,*
but it's something.)
Perhaps it would have been better
To consider more carefully
Some aesthetic qualities
In producing arts-related research.
Yet as much as I admire
systems designed to qualify
inquiry

I've always been uncomfortable
With them—
Artistic or otherwise.
I prefer Rajchman (2000):
"[Thought] is free
in its creations not when everyone agrees
or plays by the rules, but on the contrary,
when what the rules and who the players are
is not given in advance, but instead
emerges along with the new
concepts created and the new problems posed"
*   (p. 38).*

But maybe it is indifference, after all,
The desire to create knowledge in anonymous form
And yet, obsessively self-referential,
(No sentence without an "I")
The presumption of power embedded
Within its elusiveness
Our own little knowledge-production factory.

Prefer instead how the painter
Jean-Michel Basquiat's tagged the "qualifica-
*   tions"*
For his artistic practice:
Pay for soup.
Build a fort.
Set it on fire.
Wonder, though, if this is just another
system of a different kind,
A different vision,
A different sort?

So when we talk about judgment, are we really
Talking about the commodification of art?
of research?
To judge one must classify, qualify. . . .

When we did the "Inquiry" project
Ten years ago
I saw it partly as an attempt to explore
The life and the underlife of collaborative
*   work*
One lived thing after another.
The questions of emotion
Huge and small
That interested us
And that influenced what we thought.
It was a project that swirled
From an inside out:
How can you frame experience?

Take a look at Adrienne Rich's (2001) *Arts of the Possible*.
She quotes Eduardo Galeano's essay "In Defense of the Word":

"The prevailing social order perverts or annihilates the creative capacity of the immense majority of people and reduces the possibility of creation—an age-old response to human anguish and the certainty of death—to its professional exercise by a handful of specialists."

He asks the good questions:
"How many 'specialists' are we in Latin America?
For whom do we write, whom do we reach?
Where is our real public?" (p. 160)

Push "beyond judgment
to an invention . . .
That precedes it"—
An experimentation
"For which there exists
No method
No doctrine
No School"
No avant-garde
But for which there might be
"Only a kind of friendship"? *(Gilles Deleuze, cited and reworded in Rajchman, 2000, pp. 27–28)*

It brings to mind the question,
dare we ask,
Does the language of inquiry ever become too abstract?
As in the jumbled-up text we created (Jipson & Paley, 1997a)
with the help of the scanner
Or the dispersed images of "Curriculum and Its Unconscious." (Jipson & Paley, 1997b)
(And notice how "the question" invariably calls forth a judgment)
As Hal Foster (1996) frames it,
An "abstraction already reduced to design" (p. 100–101)
Or "reality as an effect of representation" (p. 146).

Might this be one of the reasons
We've struggled so hard
Not to specify the classification
Of the work we do?
After completing "Animals,"
I remember you saying this:
"Take a position.
Then get away from it."

I'm asked again by my best critic
"When are you going to do something socially useful?"
The ultimate judgment, at least in my house.
But, after all, Adrienne Rich (2001) suggests,
"For what we are, anyway, at our best,
but one small, persistent cluster in a greater ferment of human activity—
still and forever turning toward, tuned
for the possible, the unrealized and irrepressible design" (p. 167).

Produce the work then,
So that it has no face.
So that it disperses itself
As it scatters.
That does not mean you have produced
The absence of the work (Blanchot, 1981).[2]

◆ Notes

1. The title of this chapter is a reconstructed borrowing from personal notes taken related to several paintings by Gerhard Richter exhibited at the Tate Museum of Art, London, September 22, 2004.

2. Here, a remix and paraphrase of the original text: "Produce the book, then, so it disengages itself as it scatters. That does not mean you have produced the absence of the book . . ." (Blanchot, 1981, p. 149).

◆ References

Benjamin, W. (1968). *Illuminations*. New York: Schocken.
Benjamin, W. (1978). *Reflections*. New York: Harcourt, Brace, Jovanovich.

Blanchot, M. (1981). *The gaze of Orpheus.* Barrytown, NY: Station Hill Press.

Byrne, D. (1995). *Strange ritual: Pictures and words.* San Francisco: Chronicle Books.

Diamond, C. T. P., & Mullen, C. A. (Eds.). (1999). *The postmodern educator: Arts-based inquiries and teacher development.* New York: Peter Lang.

Eagleton, T. (1990). *The ideology of the aesthetic.* Chicago: University of Chicago.

Ellsworth, E. (2004). *Places of learning: Media, architecture, pedagogy.* New York: Routledge Falmer.

Foster, H. (1996). *The return of the real.* Cambridge, MA: MIT.

Foucault, M. (1988). Critical theory/intellectual history. In L. Kritzman (Ed. & Trans.), *Politics, philosophy, culture: Interviews and other writings 1977–1984* (pp. 17–46). New York: Routledge.

Greene, M. (1978). *Landscapes of learning.* New York: Teachers College Press.

Greene, M. (1994). Postmodernism and the crisis of representation. *English Education, 26*(4), 206–219.

hooks, b. (1994). *Teaching to transgress: Education as the practice of freedom.* New York: Routledge.

Jipson, J., & Paley, N. (1989). *The selective tradition in teachers' choice of children's literature: Does it exist in the elementary classroom?* Paper presented at the annual meeting of the American Educational Research Association, San Francisco, CA.

Jipson, J., & Paley, N. (1991). The selective tradition in teachers' choice of children's literature: Does it exist in the elementary classroom? *English Education, 23*(3), 148–159.

Jipson, J., & Paley, N. (1997a). Method: Who am I? In J. Jipson & N. Paley (Eds.), *Daredevil research: Re-creating analytic practice* (pp. 218–232). New York: Peter Lang.

Jipson, J., & Paley, N. (1997b). Personal history: Researching literature and curriculum (literal, alter, hyper). *English Education, 29*(1), 59–69.

Jipson, J., & Paley, N. (1999). Animals and curriculum masters. In C. T. P. Diamond & C. A. Mullen (Eds.), *The postmodern educator: Arts-based inquiries and teacher development* (pp. 409–422). New York: Peter Lang.

Jipson, J., & Paley, N. (Directors & Producers). (2004). *No teacher left standing* [Play]. Washington, DC: Lisner Theater, George Washington University.

Marcuse, H. (1978). *The aesthetic dimension: Toward a critique of Marxist aesthetics.* Boston: Beacon Press.

Paley, N., Crawford, J., Kinney, K., Koons, D., & Mendoza, C. (with Hansen-Knight, A., & Price, T.). (2004). Experiments in teaching: Re-imagining the spiral curriculum. *Journal of Curriculum and Pedagogy, 1*(2), 122–147.

Paley, N., & Jipson, J. (1997). Duplications. *Taboo: The Journal of Education and Culture, 6*(2), 269.

Paley, N., & Jipson, J. (2001). Double-bind. *Journal of Curriculum Theorizing, 17*(2), 73–80.

Paley, N., & Jipson, J. (2004, April). *Outsider research: 6 concepts.* An unsponsored non-session presented at the annual meeting of the American Educational Research Association in conjunction with the roundtable session, A Gallery of Aesthetic Research Practices, San Diego, CA.

Rajchman, J. (2000). *The Deleuze connections.* Cambridge, MA: MIT.

Rich, A. (2001). *Arts of the possible.* New York: Norton.

Richter, G. (1998). *The daily practice of painting.* London: Thames & Hudson.

Simon, S. (1992). *Storms.* New York: HarperTrophy.

PART V

ISSUES AND CHALLENGES

B ecause involving the arts in qualitative research represents a challenge to convention, inherent issues arise from the "borderland" quality of the work. Chapters in this section focus on the tensions, challenges, and issues associated with working between and across academic and nonacademic cultures, discourses, and communities. Probably one of the most pressing institutional issues for alternative genre researchers located in the academy relates to the legitimacy (i.e., acceptance as scholarship) of research that challenges academic convention. This issue is so significant because it has direct implications for individuals' job security, progress through the ranks, research funding, and publishing possibilities. Throughout the evolution of qualitative methodologies, researchers have been challenged to defend the rigor and quality not only of their own research but also of an entire methodological approach. As qualitative methodologies have become increasingly alternative, the demand for methodological accountability also has increased. With the recent burgeoning of arts-related methodologies, variations on the question "Yes, but (how) is it research?" have become a commonplace. Artist-researchers, out of necessity, often take on an educative role to respond to doubts, questions, and concerns about the quality of their work and how it "measures up" as research. Just as it was in the early days when qualitative research made its debut on the research stage and researchers had to develop and argue for criteria other than what Kvale (1995, p. 20) calls "the methodological holy trinity of psychological science"—validity, reliability, generalizability—to assess research quality, so it is now with arts-related approaches to research.

Alternative genre researchers face challenges with respect to the dissemination of their work. The conventions of most scholarly journals are not well suited for the publication of art-research. Researchers using nonprint art forms face particular challenges because of the currency value of the printed word in scholarly circles. There is an intangible quality to many of the art forms that make reproduction and communication challenging. Methodological issues germane to most qualitative research (e.g., reflexivity and artist-researcher presence, intersubjectivity, ethics, rigor) take on another dimension with the involvement of the arts. In addition, when research is intended for multiple and diverse audiences, researchers grapple with how to effectively communicate in multiple forms of literacy. Related to this are challenges and issues associated with achieving standards of both methodological and artistic rigor. Authors explore these and other issues in this section.

- Performing Data With Notions of Responsibility, *Jim Mienczakowski and Teresa Moore*

- Ethical Issues and Issues of Ethics, *Chris Sinding, Ross Gray, and Jeff Nisker*

- Interrogating Reflexivity: Art, Research, and the Desire for Presence, *Elizabeth de Freitas*

- Art and Experience: Lessons From Dewey and Hawkins, *Valerie Janesick*

- Going Public With Arts-Inspired Social Research: Issues of Audience, *Tom Barone*

- Between Scholarship and Art: Dramaturgy and Quality in Arts-Related Research, *Kelli Jo Kerry-Moran*

- Money Worries: Challenges of Funding Arts-Related Research, *Ross Gray and Ardra L. Cole*

- Using an Arts Methodology to Create a Thesis or Dissertation, *J. Gary Knowles and Sara Promislow*

◆ Reference

Kvale, S. (1995). The social construction of validity. *Qualitative Inquiry, 1*(1), 19–40.

37

PERFORMING DATA WITH NOTIONS OF RESPONSIBILITY

◆ Jim Mienczakowski and Teresa Moore

E thnodrama is a utilitarian concept used in understanding experiences of others and has wider impetus than health education (Saldaña, 2003). Ethnodrama, for us, is a method and methodology synthesizing health and education fields where we combine qualitative research processes with action research, grounded theory, and narrative (Denzin, 1997; Gray & Sinding, 2002) to provide data from which a script can be written that, in turn, becomes the basis of health theatre. This form of performance offers accountability and autonomy to the informants and validity for the researchers. Performed data have an empathetic power and dimension often lacking in standard qualitative research narratives (Mienczakowski, Smith, & Morgan, 2002). Essentially ethnodrama relies upon the voices, lived experiences, and beliefs of its subjects to inform its content, shape, and intent.

◆ Personal Dilemmas: Tensions Among the Academic, Aesthetic, and Creative

Autoethnographers, visual artists, and fictional playwrights see themselves located in their works. They are "look at me, hear me" artists[1] often concerned with the relationship between their self-exploration and more conventional notions of aesthetic performance values. As the constructors of ethnodramatic narratives, we are not, in our view, explaining *our* singular perspectives. Ethnodrama is not about a tradition of artistic endeavor but explanation and emotional evocation. Ethnodrama, we suggest, is a tool for drawing attention to specific issues, with one side critical and emancipatory (we also realize that these are large claims here), the other side evocative, self-expressing, and intentionally creative. We are more comfortable with "hands-on" intervention and health promotion.

Recent recognition (within Australian governmental health and welfare agencies) of increasing youth suicide trends has resulted in a proliferation of suicide prevention strategies with a corresponding aggregation of mainstream and "fringe" theatre groups adopting a suicide theme and associated health-issue based works. The problem or concern here for us is limited evidence or research regarding the impact of such works (Morgan & Mienczakowski, 1999). We believe there are some ethical and moral dilemmas for those performance groups that fail to anticipate any potentially harmful effects on the recovery of health consumers who may be in their audiences. Sometimes, to us, it appears that research work in mental health promotion areas often satisfies academic protocols rather than makes an actual difference to individual health consumers.

At times we have strongly felt the tension between the aesthetic and creative urges associated in performance and keeping the integrity of our informants' data intact. Increasingly we became aware that we were in need of a new aesthetic—one valuing the accurate interpretation of content over the style, mode, and traditions of the theatrical presentation form. In *Busting: The Challenge of the Drought Spirit* (Mienczakowski & Morgan, 1993), we removed as many of the aesthetic tensions as possible and brought the piece forward as a documentary-style presentation of experiences with the data doing the talking. It was played as a conversation piece with and to the audiences in a Stanislavskian style.[2] The audiences often comprised those with a close relationship to or lived experience of the themes, and their anticipation of "performance" and "entertainment" were proven to be secondary to their expectations of "theatrical engagement." The overall performance becomes a shared context that the actor and audience member intimately construct and relate to because of their own emotional links to the topic of the research/performance. The audience and the issues are our theatre.

There have been many ethnodrama projects since our first fully fledged foray into data as theatre with *Syncing Out Loud: A Journey Into Illness* (Mienczakowski, 1992/1994) concerning experiences of schizophrenia, and *Busting: The Challenge of the Drought Spirit* (Mienczakowski & Morgan, 1993), concerning detoxification processes. However, we keep returning to these works because of their performance scale. Each production involved very large casts, up to 35 players and crews of similar dimensions, and played to large public and health consumer/industry audiences in theatres. Ethical concerns were raised with our large-scale interactions with audiences that made us more cautious in our performance endeavors and are the focus of this chapter. We also illustrate the relationship between the work of educators in the arts and their counterparts in the world of research and present a framework for considering and determining the possible unwanted (or less desirable) impacts and implications of ethnodrama and other critical interventionist approaches.

◆ Performing Risk: Dramatizing Research

Performing data is an immensely powerful way of presenting research. There is potential to reach within both the individual actors and individual audience members and elicit an emotional, potentially epiphanal (Denzin, 1989) response to the topic being targeted; thus, as a process it can be seen as possibly emancipatory and cathartic. This interaction may in effect transcend the boundary between concrete reality and reality as interpreted by both the actor and audience member. Performing ethnographic texts has been an innovative way to challenge readers and audiences over dominant stereotypes and myths concerning both the lived realities of certain marginalized groups and the workers who deal with these groups on a daily basis. Although they are increasingly gaining "voice" in the public domain, many healthcare workers remain on the fringe of the workplace. It is, in all reality, not glamorous working in a detoxification unit or working with the survivors of sexual abuse and domestic violence.

Prior to producing *Busting: The Challenge of the Drought Spirit* (Mienczakowski & Morgan, 1993) to further understand the culture and marginalization of the workers, extensive fieldwork was done at a local detoxification "Unit." For the healthcare workers at this particular Unit, the silencing of their voice in the public sphere meant that one group of patients, namely, women alcoholics, have been further marginalized when it comes to resources and treatment. Although the staff at the Unit perceive this gap, their lack of voice in the public sphere has meant that they, rather than government services, are attempting to remedy this situation as Ginny, a senior nurse with the Unit, explains:

There are a lot of things wrong with the system. . . . Very few places in town for women in crisis—loads of flop houses for men but they don't accept women. Look, I mean I've rung around every place I know to find a place for a woman in crisis—be it alcohol or drug abuse or even just domestic violence coupled with

the other two, and there is sweet F. A. available for women in this town, we tend to think of alcoholics as "deros"[3] on the street—but it can be a woman who can run a house, albeit piece-meal. She may be good at it one minute and "hit the piss"[4] the next day. With women it is a hidden problem because she is not supposed to get drunk . . . women are meant to be role models, if they are drunks . . . they are seen as immoral. (Mienczakowski & Morgan, 1993)

Despite gaining some public awareness, those who work with these subcultures remain less socially acceptable than their counterparts in other areas of healthcare delivery. This is demonstrated in another scene from *Busting: The Challenge of the Drought Spirit* where Max and Lisa, two nurses in the Unit, are discussing their work, and as Max walks onto the stage, he begins the scene by stating:

Sometimes I feel all right about it, it's just, you know, the pointlessness of it all. Sometimes, you know, the lack of respect and job satisfaction. . . . I'm thinking of going back into the psychiatric wards for a while or just doing something else.

Lisa:

I've had other jobs, Max. I use to work in a cake factory. Four years of it—part time—no responsibilities and I loved it. But I'm always pulled back into nursing. I fell into alcohol and drug rehab when I couldn't stick the acute admissions in psych nursing anymore. . . . Dealing with acutely psychotic schizophrenics who are terrified by whatever they are hearing or seeing can be more frightening—because you're more of a threat to them. That's the big difference for me. It is intimidating here because they have chosen to be here, and I like most of the regulars too. (pp. 20–21)

In this scene Max struggles with the fact that he sees the same people returning to the Unit, whereas Lisa sees some comfort for the patient in that at least they are seeking help. Although the scripts can present the multiple subjectivities of various healthcare workers, this is also a chance for the health workers to get an understanding of their own "selves" in the context of the work that they do and that forms part of their identity.

This lived experience is contextualizing the authentic knowledge of the healthcare consumers and healthcare workers. With this come multiple dimensions that make research an ethical dilemma; as Moore (2004) declares, one dimension refers to how researching becomes a personal involvement and personal investment as researchers give of themselves as they develop a shared intimate understanding of their informants' lived experiences and pursue reciprocity, thus making the public pursuit of a specific research topic personal. The intent is to develop a performance of lived realities that is empowering for informants: This isn't always the outcome. Another dimension refers to the "rich and thick" data given by the informants who open up their lives, exposing the personal life of the informant to public scrutiny. Therefore, researchers need to continually ask "who benefits" from and what are the effects of our research (Moore, 2004). That is, effects beyond benefits for academic researchers and their own specific discourse interests.

◆ *Interpreting the Self or Self-Interpretation: Potential Risks for Actors and the Audience*

One unintended dilemma and potential risk has to do with using health consumers as performers. In our conception and presentation of scripts, we have perhaps underestimated the extent to which some of our audience and participants have continued to travel on ethnodramatic and nomadic journeys (Braidotti, 1994) after the "end of the show." As Braidotti (1994) states:

> Though the image of "nomadic subjects" is inspired by the experience of peoples or cultures that are literally nomadic, the nomadism in question here refers to a kind of critical consciousness that resists settling into socially coded modes of thought and behaviour. Not all nomads are world travellers; some of the greatest trips can take place without physically moving from one's habitat. (p. 5)

Through this ethnodramatic genre, healthcare consumers are able to illustrate an experiential interpretation and portrayal of "self" via a trip of self-discovery. This expression of self is a way for the person to create and legitimate an identity. Mienczakowski and Smith (2001) believe that it is this experiential understanding and evolving construction of self that ethnodrama draws on.

Aside from the favorable outcomes and cathartic experiences associated with ethnodrama (Mienczakowski, 1995, 1996; Mienczakowski, Smith, & Sinclair, 1996), we argue the need to take account of a range of unwanted and unintended outcomes that may arise directly through unforeseen emotional responses to the performance. Remaining true to the rich data comes with ethical dilemmas. As Conquerwood (2003) points out, ethnodrama enables us "to see performance with all its moral entailments . . . moral and ethical questions get stirred to the surface because ethnographers of performance explode the notion of aesthetic distance" (p. 398). What this means for us is that we must be mindful of the response that our performance text has on vulnerable or "fragile" audiences (Mienczakowski et al., 2002).

An example is illustrated in the following feedback, given after a performance of *Syncing Out Loud* (Mienczakowski, 1992/1994), from an audience member who was also a mental health consumer:

As a patient I thought the first scene with the female doctor to be very intense, and very factual. The reason behind the audience responding (during the validatory performance members of the audience came on stage and argued with the actor/doctor as if the actor was actually a doctor) was both very therapeutic and enlightening in some parts. . . . I didn't find it frightening but it did give me a great deal of insight.

Performing this work took place inside a secure psychiatric facility and subsequently stimulated a significant amount of discussion and concern for us. Audience members joined the young actors on stage, mid speech, to argue about how the medical profession had dealt with their own diagnoses. We were not in anyway in control of the performance, its messages, or its progress at that stage. Nor could we assist the cast in their discomfort. Until audience members were gently ushered from the stage, the interactions and exchanges continued; it certainly intimidated some of our cast—it also gave rise to the public voicing we had claimed we wanted but were unprepared for!

Another example concerns suicide prevention, a health care area that has moved from the margins of health promotion to become a highly visible campaign with a number of theatre groups using ethnodrama to reach out to youth. Mienczakowski (Mienczakowski & Morgan, 2001; Morgan, Rolfe, & Mienczakowski, 1999), along with various colleagues, has evaluated health theatre performances. In one such performance a cast of young university students became subjected to a great deal of criticism from an increasingly hostile audience. This hostility grew from an audience perception of the performance as stereotypical and as a "Hollywood style" presentation of mental illness rather than a more authentic recreation of their lived experiences.

Attention has been drawn previously to how impromptu events and interactions during a performance have sensitized us to the potential harm that can occur by conversing with unsuspecting or uninformed audiences and/or actors (Mienczakowski, Morgan, & Smith, 2000; Morgan et al., 1999). Performing research texts allows actors to cross boundaries and, in doing so, potentially open up new understandings and provide new discourses that can resist rigid and narrow stereotypes (Braidotti, 1994). However, there is a potential risk that our informants could continue to be marginalized, precisely because of *performing their "selves"* in public. In an extreme situation the "show" has the potential to continue in the mind of the informant and for them to relive their lived experience in negative or harm-producing ways, which is precisely why we have *never* used health consumers as performers.

With these potential risks comes a social responsibility for the care of our informants and participants. Mienczakowski, in an e-mail discussion concerning the scene Talking with the Devil, from *Syncing Out Loud* (Mienczakowski, 1992/1994), highlights his concerns about the potential impact and the very fine line that researchers and producers of ethnodrama are required to negotiate and questions whose responsibility this should be.

But as the constructors of cathartic encounters, as educators we surely are responsible for the morality and ethics of what we produce. We seek catharsis as a catalyst for therapeutic encounters, therefore we must also take ownership of the implications . . . look at Carolyn Ellis' work on the emotional quagmires of returning to the field . . . (and other evidence) of how researchers are impacted by their emotional responses to, basically, working with other human beings. I understand our aim to be the construction of a form of cathartic encounter which has implications for specific audiences [and since] we do all of this with the validation and good will of our informants we acknowledge that . . . we are not alone in creating these consensual representations. (p. 238)

With this in mind it is useful to have a set of guiding practices to assist when making decisions about what data to include; we are not censuring the data or the lived experience of the informants but rather consider this as a methodological approach.

◆ Writing the Rules as We Go: Risk Management

The participation of all health informants in these works, we believe, requires careful risk management. If the experience of the performance is outside *suspended disbelief* (the notion that audiences, in order to become engaged with a theatrical performance suspend their disbelief that all in the theatre is not actually real), it becomes about *self* and possibly *real*. Professional therapists have compulsory guidelines and clearly defined protocols to which they must refer and also the benefit of peers from whom they can gain advice and share their concerns (Australian Psychological Society, 1994). In spaces where ethnodrama is being developed, refined, and used as an experimental genre, we do not have the luxury of such references (Mienczakowski et al., 2002).

Being in an emergent space, we write the rules as we go; this is exciting and sometimes

troubling; therefore, some guiding principles that we have found useful are:

- It is vital to have healthcare professionals present to counsel members of the audience when, and if, required at the performance and postperformance debriefings.

- Ethical clearance from university human ethics committee, including relevant health support groups, or approval from the relevant research association, is obtained.

- Researchers engage in ongoing reflexive and reflective practice during the performance construction process.

- Overtly choose data that reveal themes that are positive and full of hope for the future rather than dwelling too much on despair.

- Carefully negotiate these data so that the informants consensually retain a sense of ownership and authenticity about their lived experiences mindful of the potential risks that this authenticity brings to the performance text.

◆ Conclusion

Ethnodrama has been used with Australian government initiatives to promote intervention strategies with so-called "at risk" groups such as young people suffering from depression and those using excessive alcohol. Ethnodrama is a powerful way of presenting issues usually relegated to the private sphere, such as mental illness, an area often marginalized in the hierarchy of health consumption and where caregivers are frequently silenced. Ethnodrama is a new aesthetic through which the arts can make a contribution to human understanding and seek new research values. But as researchers and script collaborators, we walk a fine line when validating and, necessarily, selecting what data are included. When doing any kind of research, the first aim is to "do no harm," and to continue as researchers in marginalized health care environments, such as mental health, drug and alcohol dependency, and suicide prevention, we have a social, moral, and ethical responsibility to "take care" in and of the field.

◆ Notes

1. Not for a minute do we perceive self-location in an artistic work as unimportant or a less defensible position than our unprovable claim that we are not located in the intention of our ethnodramas. We are simply drawing attention to different purposes that, inevitably, form different positions. See also Bagley and Cancienne (2002).

2. Stanislavskian approaches to acting relate to an understanding of characterization that marries empathy, emotional experience, and emotional identification between the actor and the role being played. A truthful portrayal requires the actor to identify with and, in some circumstances, emulate the lived realities of fictional characters' lives. In the case of *Busting* several nursing/theatre students voluntarily joined a group of homeless people, living rough for a winter's weekend, in order to gain insight into the experiences of the alcohol abusers they were portraying in the project.

3. The term *dero* is a shortened version of the word *derelict* referring to someone who is often homeless, dirty, alcoholic, and perceived as drinking solvents in place of alcohol.

4. The phrase "hit the piss" refers to bingeing on alcohol.

◆ References

Australian Psychological Society. (1994). *Code of professional conduct, principle 3*. Melbourne, Victoria, Australia: Australian Psychological Society.

Bagley, C., & Cancienne, M. B. (2002). *Dancing the data*. New York: Peter Lang.

Braidotti, R. (1994). *Nomadic subjects*. New York: Columbia University Press.

Conquerwood, D. (2003). Performing as a moral act: Ethical dimensions of the ethnography of performance. In Y. Lincoln & N. Denzin (Eds.), *Turning points in qualitative research: Tying knots in a handkerchief* (pp. 397–413). Walnut Creek, CA: AltaMira Press.

Denzin, N. (1989). *Interpretive interactionism*. Newbury Park, CA: Sage.

Denzin, N. (1997). *Interpretive ethnography: Ethnographic practices for the 21st century*. Thousand Oaks, CA: Sage.

Gray, R., & Sinding, C. (2002). *Standing ovation: Performing social science research about cancer*. Walnut Creek, CA: AltaMira Press.

Mienczakowski, J. (Artist). (1994). *Syncing out loud: A journey into illness* [script]. Brisbane, Australia: Griffith University Reprographics. (Original work published 1992)

Mienczakowski, J. (1995). The theatre of ethnography: The reconstruction of ethnography into theatre with emancipatory potential. *Qualitative Inquiry, 1*(3), 360–375.

Mienczakowski, J. (1996). An ethnographic act: The construction of consensual theatre. In C. Ellis & A. Bochner (Eds.), *Composing ethnography* (pp. 244–266). Walnut Creek, CA: AltaMira Press.

Mienczakowski, J., & Morgan, S. (1993). [Culture and marginalization of healthcare workers in a detoxification unit]. Unpublished research transcript.

Mienczakowski, J., & Morgan, S. (Artists). (1993). *Busting: The challenge of the drought spirit* [script]. Brisbane, Australia: Griffith University Reprographics.

Mienczakowski, J., & Morgan, S. (2001). Ethnodrama: Constructing participatory, experiential, and compelling action research through performance. In H. Bradbury (Ed.), *The handbook of action research* (pp. 219–227). London: Sage.

Mienczakowski, J., Morgan, S., & Smith, L. (2000). An act of subversion: Night workers on the fringe of dawn—From bow wave to deluge. In K. Gilbert (Ed.), *Emotional nature of qualitative research* (pp. 179–194). Boca Raton, FL: CRC Press.

Mienczakowski, J., & Smith, L. (2001). Ethnodrama: Analysis in action. In B. Knight & L. Rowan (Eds.), *Researching in contemporary educational environments* (pp. 97–112). Flaxton, Queensland, Australia: Post Pressed.

Mienczakowski, J., Smith, L., & Morgan, S. (2002). Seeing words, hearing feelings: Ethnodrama and the performance of data. In C. Bagley & M. B. Cancienne (Eds.), *Dancing the data* (pp. 34–52). New York: Peter Lang.

Mienczakowski, J., Smith, R., & Sinclair, M. (1996). On the road to catharsis: A theoretical framework for change. *Qualitative Inquiry, 2*(4), 439–462.

Moore, T. (2004). (En)gendering risk: Reflecting on risks and dilemmas when researching academic women in a hostile terrain. In P. Coombes, M. Danaher, & P. Danaher (Eds.), *Strategic uncertainties: Ethics, politics, and risk in contemporary educational research* (pp. 105–115). Flaxton, Queensland, Australia: Post Pressed.

Morgan, S., & Mienczakowski, J. (1999). *Extreme dilemmas in performance ethnography: Unleashed emotionality of performance in critical areas of suicide, abuse, and madness.* Paper presented at the Couch Stone Symposium, University of Nevada, Las Vegas.

Morgan, S., Rolfe, A., & Mienczakowski, J. (1999). Exploration! Intervention! Education! Health promotion! A developmental set of guidelines for the presentation of dramatic performances in suicide prevention. In S. Robertson, K. Kellehear, M. Teeson, & V. Miller (Eds.), *Making history, shaping the future: The 1999 mental health services conference* (pp. 227–229). Rozelle New South Wales, Australia: Standard Publishing House.

Saldaña, J. (2003). Dramatizing data: A primer. *Qualitative Inquiry, 9*(2), 218–236.

38

ETHICAL ISSUES AND ISSUES OF ETHICS

◆ Christine Sinding, Ross Gray, and Jeff Nisker

The social science turn toward alternative forms of research representation is prompted in no small part by the reporting conventions of the academy. Usual publishing forms and outlets tend to thwart the desires that draw us to art: desires to have our senses activated, to be personally engaged, and to reach audiences beyond our academic peers (McIntyre, 2004; Richardson, 1992). Adrienne Rich (1978) describes poetry as a criticism of language, a vital sifting-through of the words we are using and that are using us, a process of rejecting and selecting and artfully forging text and images to create new relationships among words, among ideas, among people. What does this mean to us as researchers? What are the ethical consequences of criticizing familiar language, concentrating the power of words from qualitative studies, rendering them artistically, and sending them into the world?

In this chapter we explore questions of informed choice, harm, privacy, and anonymity salient to the artistic representation of research findings. We consider these questions in relation to three constituencies: the people who create the representation, audiences, and research participants. Although we rely on insights from friends and colleagues engaged in similar projects, we draw examples primarily from our research-based dramas: *Handle with Care? Women Living with Metastatic Breast Cancer* (Ivonoffski & Gray, 1998), *Ladies in Waiting? A Play About Life After Breast Cancer* (Ivonoffski, 2002),[1] and *Sarah's Daughters* (Nisker, 2004).[2]

◆ Ethics in Relation to the People Who Create the Representation

Louisa May's Story of Her Life is a poem that Laurel Richardson fashioned from a transcript of a research interview in a project about unwed mothers. Over the course of innumerable revisions to the poem, says Richardson (1992), "Louisa May moved into my psychic interior in a way that no interviewee of mine ever had. She moved in the way poetry does. She's not yet moved out" (p. 133). Louisa May's "moving in" changed Richardson's life. Richardson outlines how her self has been rearranged by the artful representation of qualitative research. Several of the consequences she describes resonate for us, including a sense of being better able to appreciate the situation of "the other." This is an ethically relevant outcome for qualitative researchers.

Yet this "moving in," this reorganization of the self that may emerge from arts-informed engagement with research findings, may have much more difficult implications.

It is our first creative meeting about the drama *Ladies in Waiting?* Ten cancer survivors, many of them long-time advocates in the cancer community, are explaining cancer survivorship to Vrenia Ivonoffski, artistic director of Act II Studio. The women describe the worry that cancer will return, their powerlessness to prevent its return, and the difficulty of speaking openly about these lived realities. They

offer examples of survivors who, years after a diagnosis, find themselves weeping or enraged for no apparent reason. Their words have a vaguely didactic quality. They have said this all before.

Two meetings later, the conversation is markedly different. The women speak a few words, then stop, or speak all in a rush. Certainty has given way. They are groping now, reaching for words and pulling back from them, struggling.

In response to Vrenia's insistence that the experience of survivorship became available to her in a way she can internalize (a prerequisite, in her training, for its dramatic representation) someone has offered the word "dread." We have focused on dread, attending slowly to it, testing its adequacy and its power. We have acted it: one woman crouching on the ground covering her ears, the rest circling around, rocking back and forth and keening, pressing in toward her.

The process is taking a toll. One woman describes nightmares in which she is trapped in a fiery maze. Another speaks of having participated in an 8-week therapeutic group dedicated to exploring survivorship; nothing about that experience generated the kind of feeling she is having now.

There is, it seems, something about the process of representing things artistically— of undoing the familiar language, of reaching for new words, of distilling the experience into an image, of embodying it—that is especially powerful, and especially disruptive.

Vulnerability in a creative process is linked to our relationship with the topic at hand. Some of the women who took part in the creation of *Handle With Care?* have had breast cancer. In focusing intently on the experience of advanced cancer and in working closely with Mary Sue and Jan (both of whom had it), these women engaged with their possible futures. This can happen in other research settings—a series of focus groups held over time, for instance, or participatory research projects. Yet in our experience, the intense collective search for images and language that conveyed the experience of advanced disease called for something different, and something more than is required in most research endeavors. As actors, the women with breast cancer studied and performed a part. As understudies in a more symbolic (but, we would argue, linked) sense, they were asked to step into the role of "woman with metastatic disease" and to anticipate—in a particularly visceral, embodied way—the possibility that they will someday be required to live it. Anxiety and distress (recognized risks for participants in qualitative research; Richards & Schwartz, 2002) were virtually inevitable. In both of the dramas about breast cancer with which we have been involved, members of the script development team have had difficulties sleeping as a result of our work together.

A process leading to informed choice outlines risks and enables potential participants to assess and express their willingness or not to take them. We entered our first research-based drama projects with considerable naiveté (gall, say some); alerting others involved in the creative process to the risks ahead of time was out of the question. Working with an artist did not merely call for approaches or generate insights unanticipated at the outset, as is common in qualitative studies. We spent most of our time utterly baffled about what would happen next and what it would take from the group in emotional terms, and in terms of time and energy.

In subsequent research-based drama projects, we have described to potential participants the experiences we and our collaborators have had. We have acknowledged how intense the creative process was and talked about the surprising and profound ways it spoke to our experiences and worries about illness. Thus informed, everyone has the option of avoiding the project entirely. Among those who do take part, having made an informed choice does not foreclose distress; indeed, anyone paying any kind of attention suffers in some way. Our description of previous creative work does, perhaps, allow participants to gauge their levels of emotional involvement. Certainly our talk normalizes and collectivizes the suffering, which in our experience is no small thing.

Arts-informed processes offer unique ways to respond to distress when it emerges. Beyond the usual strategies (skipping a difficult interview question, treading lightly with probes, pausing the interview, etc.) we also had play and movement. Wrung out from a particularly intense discussion about family members' responses to illness, we moved on to creating commercials and lists: an ad gushing the merits of a cancer diagnosis; a list of 10 things you "shouldn't oughta" say to someone with cancer. When the drama became intense, we retreated to discussion; when the discussion became intense, we stood up and moved—opportunities paralleled in drama therapy (Mulkey, 2004).

It is true that all of the people involved in creating these artful representations struggled emotionally over the course of our work together and that these struggles matter in ethical terms. It is equally true that we laughed, often—that we delighted in the achievement of the dramas and became immensely fond of one another. After several months of traveling with *Handle With Care?* the ethical question had turned on its head: Where we had wondered about the ethics of proceeding with the work, we were now confronted with the ethics of ending it. Some of the people involved in creating the drama, perceiving its benefit to audiences and loyal to Mary Sue's and Jan's memories, felt it simply wrong to call a halt to the tour.

◆ Ethics in Relation to Audiences

Linda Park-Fuller (2000) suggests that, insofar as audiences take the risk of witnessing artistic testimony, creators and performers of that testimony must make an effort to stand in with the audience, to anticipate their needs, concerns, and expectations. In taking up this responsibility to "stand with" audiences, we find ourselves teetering between imperatives. We want both to recognize and to avoid exaggerating our power or the power of our art; likewise, we want both to recognize and to avoid overstating the vulnerability of people who witness our work. When people are tearful while witnessing an exhibit or reading a research-based short story, it is usually because the art has spoken to losses or yearnings in their lives. The losses and yearnings were there before they witnessed the representation, and we do not wish, with excessive warnings or interventions, to render the experience or expression of emotion problematic. We also do not want to stand between audiences and the representation. When we offer art rather than a traditionally constructed scholarly manuscript as our form of research publication, we deliberately invite audiences to craft their own meanings (Cole & McIntyre, 2004). To make the process consent-heavy up front (to ask potential audience members to sign a form that specifies exactly what they will encounter and anticipates their responses) or to imply a significant need for follow-up support is at odds with the context and purposes of the endeavor and risks foreclosing its possibilities.

That said, the artful presentation of research findings does invoke particular ethical challenges. As we have noted, art "moves in," rearranges our understandings of ourselves and the world, and goes home with us in ways that traditional social science representations rarely do. Arguably, then, artful research representations have a particular

potential to do harm (Nisker, Martin, Bluhm, & Daar, 2006; Nisker & Daar, 2006). The subject of artful representations, like that of qualitative research generally, is often Hard Life Stuff. Artistic representations are commonly presented to people directly affected by the subject at hand. Such audiences are more fully in harm's way than are researchers' usual audiences. Venues are community settings that may be awkward to leave; the right to withdraw from participation may be difficult to exercise. Community settings may also carry expectations of what will (and will not) be seen and heard there. The intersection of art, audience, and venue is an ethically complex space.[3]

In general terms, we encourage arts-informed researchers to anticipate ways that their representations may harm people witnessing them, especially people most affected by the subject matter. So, for instance, ethical principles around privacy suggest that our audiences may require protection from receiving unwanted information. In *Handle With Care?* although loathe to deny the medical realities of metastatic cancer, we realized that some women might hear the word "incurable" applied to their diagnoses for the first time. The potential of artful representations to either undermine or bolster hope is, we believe, a central ethical concern. A much crafted and agonized-over line was included in the introduction: "While metastatic disease is rarely curable, it can be treated, and many people in communities around the world are living with it today." The line attempts to speak the medical truths while also leaving space—space for hope—around those truths.

It makes sense that research-based art be promoted in ways that reflect principles of informed choice. Publicity material for *Sarah's Daughters,* for instance, notes that the drama is "about living with the fear of hereditary breast cancer," so that people can choose with awareness whether or not to attend. Promoting *Handle With Care?* we made clear that the drama spoke to the experiences of women with *metastatic* breast cancer, and defined metastatic. In this particular case, people who had seen the drama eventually became its ambassadors, and the responsibility we felt for ensuring people understood its focus diminished. Conversely, as *Ladies in Waiting?* toured, we learned that some audience members were caught off guard by its representation of cancer survivorship. We responded by letting local organizers know what we were hearing, allowing them to acts as gatekeepers as they saw fit. Over time, then, researchers may continue to assess the need for more (or less) information up front about the content of the representation, or additional or different strategies to convey it.

Art, some theorists contend, lends boundaries to what is difficult to witness and endure in "real life" (Gilman, 1988). That art is avowedly constructed, and that it is contained (on the page, on the stage, in the gallery), arguably minimizes risk: Audience members have their cathartic moments and leave safe in the knowledge that it was not real and need not spill into daily life. Yet in our experience the social agreements that distinguish reality from art do not always hold. Audience members have believed that all of the actors in our dramas are cancer survivors and that relationships portrayed on stage are actual relationships, despite information to the contrary. A man attending Mienczakowski's drama *Syncing Out Loud* walked up on stage and confronted an actor as if she were a psychiatrist. We are not suggesting that anyone was harmed in these moments (see Mienczakowski & Morgan, 1998, for thoughtful reflection on this question), merely that we cannot assume an artistic form allows all audience members distance from the subject matter.

Expectations associated with the venue operate as well and merit attention in the informed choice process. The drama *Ladies in Waiting?* was usually presented in the

regular meeting spaces of local cancer support groups, where the physical and emotional chronicity of cancer is often obscured by efforts to fully support people newly diagnosed with the disease (Gray, Fitch, Davis, & Phillips, 1997). The distress some audience members experienced in watching the drama may have emerged in part from its challenge to the social conventions of the setting. Similarly, audiences for *Sarah's Daughters,* arriving at a traditional theatre venue, do not expect to receive medical information and are likely not braced for it as they might be in a clinical setting.

Of course we cannot always anticipate what will happen when art is presented. Sometimes our worries were quite off base; occasionally an audience member was unsettled or angered by an aspect of the production we found quite benign. Opportunities for audiences to debrief or "talk back" to arts-based representations can be useful in this regard. Postperformance discussions, writing spaces, notebooks, and e-mail contacts allow researchers to understand how audiences are engaging with, and affected by, the representation. Again, however, such processes are not without their own challenges. Following *Sarah's Daughters,* audience members' disclosures of their genetic status have sparked yet more disclosures. In at least three cases, young women learned during postperformance discussion that their mothers carry a genetic mutation that considerably increased their risk of the disease— information likely unwanted in that setting. It may be that artful representations "end run" people's usual defenses, leading audiences to say things they might not usually, and may later regret. In this situation we chose to have a consistent team facilitating postperformance feedback, familiar with the dynamics that can emerge and able to judge the necessity of redirecting or commenting on the discussion; as well, specialized counseling resources were on hand (see also Chapter 51 in this volume).

Although we encourage researchers to understand and anticipate potential distress for audience members, we want to caution against any easy equation between distress and harm.

Our first community showing of the video *Ladies in Waiting? Life After Breast Cancer* has just ended. The facilitator welcomes a woman to speak from the audience. "Can we have a show of hands to see how many people found that depressing?" the woman asks. About half the audience raises their hands. "And how many found it uplifting?" Not a single hand. And then a woman speaks from the back of the room. "It was depressing," she says. "It hit home."

"It hit home" was a theme reflected many times over: The representation's distressing effect was, it seemed, part and parcel of its resonance with audience members' experiences. Distress was evoked, yet the association of distress with negative evaluations of the production, or a desire not to have seen it, was extremely rare. Some audience members spoke, in fact, of the merits of being upset. More commonly, viewers who acknowledged they had been upset by the production affirmed, unprompted, the production's realistic portrayal of survivorship, and expressed interest in having family members see it (Sinding, Gray, Grassau, Damianakis, & Hampson, 2006). The benefit of the production was not separate from distress; indeed, it was in a certain sense embedded in it. We suspect this holds true for many artistic research representations. This does not mean, of course, that a representation's resonance with audiences trumps harm to them: Rather, it means that we must distinguish between efforts to minimize and mitigate harm, and efforts to eliminate distress. The latter may be inimical to the integrity and effectiveness of many artful representations.

Worries about harm and undue distress are sometimes addressed more gracefully by art than science. One woman who saw *Handle With Care?* remarked on the ways its choreography drew people into difficult emotions, then carried them away as the next scene transformed the tone and the players. "You got sad," she said, "but you didn't stay there." Something of the same effect is achieved in Ardra Cole and Maura McIntyre's (2004) installation about Alzheimer's disease. At the edge of the exhibit area a life-sized image of an aging and ill woman is affixed to a mirror; as viewers move to stand directly in front of the woman's image, we appear in the mirror. We are directly and dramatically implicated in the illness or in caregiving or both. And yet nearby is a fridge—daily, ordinary, filled with images of a mother and daughter over time, enjoying life and each other. We get sad, unsettled, distressed—but we don't (only) stay there.

◆ Ethics in Relation to Research Participants

Participants in qualitative research risk being identified (by themselves and others), and they risk being misrepresented (Richards & Schwartz, 2002); they also risk witnessing their lives and struggles analyzed and objectified (Larossa, Bennett, & Gelles, 1981). Each of these risks takes on particular texture when research is represented artistically.

In a photovoice project about mothers with learning difficulties (Booth & Booth, 2003, p. 435), a "serious problem" emerged that "should perhaps have been foreseen": Participants, alert to the surveillance of statutory authorities, were unwilling to have their photos posted on a project-mandated supportive parenting Web site. The researchers responded by severing the link between image and identity, including only photos without people in them or without any identifiable link to the women. Some artistic representations partially sidestep the risk of identification by creating composite characters, organizing representations by theme, situation, or plot rather than the narratives of individuals.

In other projects research participants have chosen visibility. The Web site *Things That Matter* (www.storiesthatmatter.com), created by Nancy Viva Davis Halifax, features creative nonfiction and photographs founded on stories told by people with colorectal cancer, and participants' faces are recognizable in several images. One woman, for instance, had searched for a photograph of a person with a stoma before her own surgery, "not a photograph that isolated a piece of the body, but that showed a whole being" (Halifax, Gray, & Jadad, 2004, p. 765). Unable to find one—and determined that others not be so alone—she chose to post on the Web site images of her daily life alongside a photo in which she is emptying her colostomy bag over the toilet. She did not, however, wished to be named.

The woman's representational decisions emerged over several conversations— conversations to which Halifax brought her own lived understanding of the consequences of public exposure. Images of Halifax, her mastectomy, and illness narrative appear in the book *My Breasts, My Choice: Journeys Through Surgery* (Brown, Aslin, & Carey, 2003). She knows the sense of surprise— and vulnerability and delight—that comes with seeing herself in public spaces. One of the consequences of her visibility is her daughter's pride; another, her daughter's increased sense of risk for cancer. Halifax makes these experiences, in all their ambiguity and complexity, available to research participants considering the implications of "going public."[4]

Salient to the risk of misrepresentation is the intent to produce a research product that has aesthetic merit and audience appeal. Johnny Saldaña (1998) worried that his case study about a young man's dreams of becoming an actor lacked sufficient crises

and conflicts to maintain a suitable flow of tension: "As a playwright, my anxiety motivated me to include lengthy 'monologues' sparingly, and to interweave the participants' voices frequently for variety" (p. 186). These choices are not misrepresentations, but Saldaña usefully alerts us to the ways misrepresentation—in the sense of overemphasizing "the juicy stuff"—may happen.

As Saldaña's (1998) account also makes clear, however, research participants themselves (like any of us) may be less concerned about being misrepresented than about being represented unfavorably. How research reports are experienced by the communities they portray is a question little examined, in part because academics so often speak only to one another. When research results are presented as art, and public access to the work is both enabled and deliberately arranged, our recontextualizations of research participants' stories and lives become audible, visible, felt by them, in visceral and potentially lasting ways. To the extent that we have objectified them, they will know this objectification and experience it in public. Working all of our own dramas, we have, in Denzin's (1997) terms, "improvised on" research transcripts (see also Gray & Sinding, 2002). We can imagine the possibility that the creative transformation of participants' stories becomes *about* improvising—about the artistic experimentation, with participants' narratives mere props.

As with much in the world of artful research representation, the lines are fuzzy, the territory largely unmapped. In the most general way, we suggest, representations must respect the sensibilities of the people represented. This does not mean that we advocate for "feel-good" images devoid of edge or critique.[5] However, we do encourage researchers to enable the people and communities represented to engage with the art before it goes public. Endorsing such a process implies not that each suggestion or demand be taken up but rather that persistent concerns or critiques have a platform: either as changes to the representation or as a counternarrative presented alongside the researcher's work. In this way, researchers' representations are required (and have the opportunity) to "listen . . . very carefully for the counsel of [their] kin" (Gingrich-Philbrook cited in Park-Fuller, 2000, p. 33).

◆ Notes

1. *Handle With Care?* and *Ladies in Waiting?* emerged out of a collaboration with Act II Studio, a theatre school for adults over age 50 at Ryerson University in Toronto, Ontario. Interview transcripts and articles written from them (Gray, Fitch, et al., 1998; Gray, Greenberg, et al., 1998) inspired and grounded the dramas. Under the leadership of Artistic Director Vrenia Ivonoffski, cancer survivors, members of the research team, and amateur actors participated in a series of half-day meetings to explore themes in the transcripts, drawing on personal experiences and engaging in a series of improvisation exercises. Working from the images and dialogue generated in this process and the transcripts, Ivonoffski wrote the dramas (Ivonoffski, 2002; Ivonoffski & Gray, 1998).

2. The Dora Award–winning actor Liza Balkan will perform J. Nisker's play *Sarah's Daughters*, exploring the fears of a young woman whose mother and grandmother died at a young age of breast cancer, "who lives with the knowledge it will happen to her." *Sarah's Daughters* surfaces the ethical issues inherent to breast cancer (BRCA) gene testing, indeed all genetic testing, and begins the conversation toward compassionate appreciation of genetic risk and sensitive understanding of the consequences of genetic testing.

3. *Handle With Care?* was barred from the keynote space at a conference because the organizer felt it would be hard to watch, and because she perceived the audience as captive.

4. Alongside the knowledge about public exposure that researchers bring to such conversations, participants' knowledge about the possible implications of visibility in their own life contexts is essential. Risks and benefits (and the balance between them) may also change over time, and unexpected consequences may emerge. Sustained conversation—an ongoing process of choice, rather than a one-time event—is required. At the same time, representations at some point slip into the public sphere; participants must be aware of the limits of the researcher's control over images and text, and thus the limits of our capacities to respect a wish to withdraw consent late in the life of the project. Any person's choice to "go public" has, as well, consequences for others in her or his life; *Sarah's Daughters,* dealing as it does with an inheritable genetic mutation, makes this point especially clear and speaks to the value of ethics frameworks organized around communities and social networks rather than only individuals (Hoeyer, Dahlager, & Lynoe, 2005).

5. See Church (2002) for a compelling account of the tensions between celebrating, and bringing a critical analysis to, her mother's life and work.

◆ References

Booth, T., & Booth, W. (2003). In the frame: Photovoice and mothers with learning difficulties. *Disability and Society, 18*(4), 431–442.

Brown, B., Aslin, M., & Carey, B. (2003). *My breasts, my choice: Journeys through surgery.* Toronto, Ontario, Canada: Sumach Press.

Church, K. (2002). The hard road home: Toward a polyphonic narrative of the mother–daughter relationship. In C. Ellis (Ed.), *Ethnographically speaking: Autoethnography, literature and aesthetics* (pp. 234–257). Walnut Creek, CA: AltaMira Press.

Cole, A. L., & McIntyre, M. (2004). Research as aesthetic contemplation: The role of the audience in research interpretation. *Educational Insights, 9*(1). Retrieved January 29, 2007, from http://www.ccfi.educ.ubc.ca/publication/insights/v09n01/pdfs/cole.pdf

Denzin, N. (1997). *Interpretive ethnography.* Thousand Oaks, CA: Sage.

Gilman, S. L. (1988). *Disease and representation: Images of illness from madness to AIDS.* Ithaca, NY: Cornell University Press.

Gingrich-Philbrook, C. (1998). What I "know" about the story: For those about to tell personal narratives on stage. In S. J. Dailey (Ed.), *The future of performance studies: Visions and revisions* (pp. 298–300). Annandale, VA: National Communication Association.

Gray, R. E., Fitch, M., Davis, C., & Phillips, C. (1997). A qualitative study of breast cancer self-help groups. *Psycho-Oncology, 6,* 279–289.

Gray, R. E., Fitch, M., Greenberg, M., Hampson, A., Doherty, M., & Labrecque, M. (1998). The information needs of well, longer-term survivors of breast cancer. *Patient Education and Counseling, 44,* 245–255.

Gray, R. E., Greenberg, M., Fitch, M., Sawka, C., Hampson, A., & Labrecque, M. (1998). Information needs of women with metastatic breast cancer. *Cancer Prevention and Control, 2*(2), 57–62.

Gray, R. E., & Sinding, C. (2002). *Standing ovation: Performing social science research about cancer.* Walnut Creek, CA: AltaMira Press.

Halifax, N. D., Gray, R., & Jadad, A. R. (2004). Self-portraits of illness: The gift of the gaze. *Canadian Medical Association Journal, 171*(7), 764–765.

Hoeyer, K., Dahlager, L., & Lynoe, N. (2005). Conflicting notions of research ethics. The mutually challenging traditions of social scientists and medical researchers. *Social Science & Medicine, 61*(8), 1741–1749.

Ivonoffski, V. (2002). *Ladies in waiting? A play about life after breast cancer.* Toronto, Ontario, Canada: Toronto Sunnybrook Regional Cancer Centre.

Ivonoffski, V., & Gray, R. E. (1998). *Handle with care? Women living with metastatic breast cancer.* Toronto, Ontario, Canada: Toronto Sunnybrook Regional Cancer Centre.

Larossa, R., Bennett, L. A., & Gelles, R. J. (1981). Ethical dilemmas in qualitative family research. *Journal of Marriage and the Family, 43*(2), 303–313.

McIntyre, M. (2004). Ethic and aesthetics: The goodness of arts-informed research. In A. Cole, L. Nielsen, J. G. Knowles, &

T. C. Luciani (Eds.), *Provoked by art: Theorizing arts-informed inquiry* (pp. 251–261). Halifax, Nova Scotia, Canada: Backalong Books.

Mienczakowski, J., & Morgan, S. (1998). Finding closure and moving on: An examination of challenges presented to the constructors of research performances. *Drama, 5*(2), 22–29.

Mulkey, M. (2004). Recreating masculinity: Drama therapy with male survivors of sexual assault. *The Arts in Psychotherapy, 31,* 19–28.

Nisker, J. (2004). She lived with the knowledge. *Ars Medica, 1*(1), 75–80.

Nisker, J., Martin, D., Bluhm, R., & Daar, A. (2006). Theatre as a public engagement tool for health-policy development. *Health Policy, 78*(2/3), 258–271.

Nisker, J., & Daar, A. (2006). Moral presentation of genetics-based narratives for public understanding of genetic science and its implications. *Public Understanding of Science, 15,* 113–123.

Park-Fuller, L. (2000). Performing absence: The staged personal narrative as testimony. *Text and Performance Quarterly, 20*(1), 20–42.

Rich, A. (1978). Power and danger. In J. Grahn (Ed.), *The work of a common woman* (pp. 7–21). Freedom, CA: The Crossing Press.

Richards, H. M., & Schwartz, L. J. (2002). Ethics of qualitative research: Are there special issues for health services research? *Family Practice, 19,* 135–139.

Richardson, L. (1992). The consequences of poetic representation: Writing the other, rewriting the self. In C. Ellis & M. Flaherty (Eds.), *Investigating subjectivity* (pp. 125–137). Newbury Park, CA: Sage.

Saldaña, J. (1998). Ethical issues in an ethnographic performance text: The "dramatic impact" of "juicy stuff." *Research in Drama Education, 3*(2), 181–196.

Sinding, C., Gray, R., Grassau, P., Damianakis, F., & Hampson, A. (2006). Audience responses to a research-based drama about life after breast cancer. *Psycho-Oncology, 15,* 694–700.

39

INTERROGATING REFLEXIVITY

Art, Research, and the Desire for Presence

◆ Elizabeth de Freitas

I n *Lolly: The Final Word* (Clough, 2002) an irate man confronts and accuses the social science researcher Doctor Clough of writing the script—"the rich piece of research"—that caused the eventual demise of his delinquent brother. The story is situated in the home office of the researcher, on an otherwise quiet evening, interrupted by the unexpected visitor.

> You killed that boy. Mm? Do you think he'd have been pissing about like that if he hadn't had you for an audience? D'you think? D'you think he'd have punched that teacher? Do you think he'd have been expelled if you hadn't . . . if you hadn't been there? If you hadn't written the script for him? Eh? (p. 58)

Doctor Clough finds himself cornered in an overstuffed armchair, gripped by fear and guilt, subjected to a set of intrusive questions, while the Other looms over him. Suddenly, the privileged academic is the object of the Other's gaze, and now it is *his* family and home that are at risk. The unanticipated *return of the researched* incites terror in the scholar, and like a trapped animal, he spontaneously relieves himself, then and there, all too aware of how the others will see the patch of wet across his groin.

Peter Clough wrote this "research fiction" in response to ethical concerns about the art of storying other people's experiences. Clough uses fiction-based strategies to craft research narratives so as to increase the capacity to convey, evoke, provoke, and persuade. In *Lolly*, which he describes as a "complete fiction," he invites the reader to examine the ethical implications of narrative research. The story is deliberately disturbing because it fails to resolve the confrontation between the two men, and it refuses to exonerate the researcher for his complicity in the boy's death. Peter Clough names the demoralized researcher "Doctor Clough," and thus invokes a double reading of the text, demanding that the reader speculate on the intersection between the responsibility of the author and that of the narrator. This attention to the responsibility of the researcher-as-author speaks to the reflexivity of the work. The author locates himself in the narrative through the shared signifier "Clough" and through the use of the first-person singular voice, and yet there is an overwhelming sense that the craftedness of this narrative complicates its claim to reflexivity. The reflexive presence of the author is problematized precisely because this is a work of fiction that troubles the very notion of reference.

This chapter examines reflexivity and the desire for presence in qualitative research. I argue that our desire for presence often reduces the Other to categories of sameness, and that arts-informed research practices can productively disrupt this tendency. Although reflexivity effectively counters positivist paradigms that extol the virtue of objective distance in the research process, the desire for presence is never innocent; reflexive researchers, like any others, inscribe silence and absence while simultaneously making themselves visible. This chapter explores the ethical and theoretical implications of deconstructing "presence" in reflexive research practices. I use radical hermeneutics to theorize an alternate notion of presence, drawing from the writings of Jacques Derrida, John Caputo, and Maggie Maclure. Each of these postsructuralist thinkers has examined the role, purpose, and impact of art in coming to know the Other. I analyze a case study—the installation artwork of Ardra Cole and Maura McIntyre—in search of a research model that interrogates our desire for presence.

◆ Reflexivity

Reflexivity in research is meant to trace the presence of the researcher onto the research context, marking their interference, their participation, their desire (Creswell, 2003). It is both an epistemological statement about the connected nature of knowledge and a political statement about the noninnocence of research. Reflexive writing practices dispute the positivist claim that researchers should maintain an objective distance between subject and object. The reflexive researcher, claims Deborah Ceglowski (2002), assumes a "relational or connective notion of the self" (p. 15) for whom knowing is an intimate caring relation in which self and Other fuse. By locating knowledge claims within the subjective language of the first person, and situating researchers in their frame of research, the text aims for a more ethical relation to that which it names as Other.

Reflexive researchers front their signature in the texts they create, evoking a feeling of immediacy and self-presence. Readers of reflexive narratives are often led to believe, through the rhetoric of reflexivity, that they have unfettered access to the interior thoughts of the researcher. Ellis and

Bochner (2000) suggest that the distinction between "the personal and the cultural" is blurred in such work. "I" statements that mark reflexive texts, however, are often read as transparent indices of the researcher's motives (p. 739). By rhetorically crafting the research text as emanating from or filtering through their own experiences and interpretations, the reflexive researcher hopes to claim the power of the "inside" through introspection.

The reliance on the transparency of language, and the tendency to see the self as the unitary signifier, underscore a tacit metaphysical assumption that prizes presence over its deferred and distorted representations. Indeed, the reflexive text often maintains the binary between the essence of experience and its artful traces if it fails to problematize representation in general. There is often still hope that the materiality of writing will disperse and disappear when good reflexive writing achieves its goal of transparency. Reflexive researchers aim to accurately represent their true motives, while the vagaries of language and interpretation are seen as interference. If, on the other hand, writing cannot render itself transparent, and the attempt to do so is a kind of delusion grounded in the "metaphysics of presence," and if the difference between sign and signifier is irreducible, and the outside is always already inside (the one breaching the other in the play of differences), then what becomes of the goal of reflexive research? What happens when the research text embraces its own textuality and artfulness? Can a self-consciously artful approach to research tackle our desire for presence?

Peter Clough's (2002) story does precisely that in two different ways. First, by embedding ambiguity into the signifiers "Clough" and "I," the reader is asked to speculate on the difficulty of naming a reference outside the text. By complicating the referential nature of the story, and

problematizing the relation to outside-the-text, presence itself is put into play. Second, the moment of crisis within the story is a moment of presence in which the written text returns in the angry flesh of a face-to-face encounter. The very notion of "face" validity, which is obviously lacking in Doctor Clough's case, rests on the ranking of presence over and above its flawed representations.

The character Doctor Clough is thoroughly disarmed by the presence of Lolly and his demand for some sort of reciprocity and justice. The story asks the reader to critically and emotionally respond to the prospect of a radical vulnerability on the part of the researcher. The scene depicts a far more disturbing vulnerability than that which is often touted as a consequence of reflexive writing. Doctor Clough's vulnerability results from his having allowed the Other into his home and having risked his own presence and status. His vulnerability is not a result of his acts of reflexive self-disclosure. The story asks the reader to imagine what exactly it means to put oneself at risk. Might it mean more than tracing the presence of the self? Might it involve a vulnerability that is deeper than that which emerges in reflexive research practices that lay claim to the possibility of self-presence? If, as Maclure (2003) claims, "the point is to interrupt, or disrupt, the processes by which research knowledge is customarily produced, and treated by those who read it as self-evident" (p. 81), can arts-informed research create a space for critical reading practices that productively problematize the goals of reflexive writing, while ethically contributing to our understanding of research? The question Patti Lather (1991) asked a decade and a half ago is still relevant to the project of reflexive research practices: "How do we explore our own reasons for doing the research without putting ourselves back at the center?" (p. 91)

◆ *The Desire for Presence*

The desire for communion with the Other, and the goal of transparency and presence, are grounded in "the promise of community that is immediately present to itself, without difference, a community of speech where all the members are within earshot"(Maclure, 2003, p. 102). This dream of communion, of the erasure of any distance or difference between self and Other, is a dream we have inherited from Gadamer and the hermeneutic tradition. It is a dream in which understanding is seen as the fusion of distinct horizons, where alignment to the ideal of self-presence and unfettered immediacy marks the objective. It is a dream that strives for a community without difference, a community of consensus, in which the radical alterity of the Other is erased. The dream is lived through a desire for presence, argues Derrida (in Kearney, 2004), which pervades our cultural heritage and saturates the meaning of *essence, truth,* and *being* in Western philosophy. Troubling the "metaphysics of presence" is a crucial strategy for the poststructural critique of Western "logocentrism"—a term Derrida uses to describe the master narrative that uncritically privileges reason's mastery and the transparency of language.

Radical hermeneutics, in contrast to its own heritage, aims to trouble the desire for presence and maintain the "structural non-knowing" (Caputo 2000, p. 56) of the Other. This revisioning of hermeneutics is a strategy for recognizing and nurturing a radically different space of learning, where distinct horizons are not fused, and where the unanticipated is invited, and indeed demanded. I draw from John Caputo's work on radical hermeneutics in which hermeneutic inquiry is coupled with deconstruction. Caputo (2000) demands that we bracket all humanist dreams of fusing our

horizons and focus instead on the displacement of the subject and the "infinite slippage" of meaning. He rehabilitates the facticity of hermeneutics, claiming that

> Deconstruction pushes facticity to its limits, radicalizing it, remaining rigorously loyal to our factical limits, ruthlessly, without pity, without appeal, without nostalgia, without a desire for presence, right on up to speaking of an experience of the impossible. (p. 56)

The aim of deconstruction is to carve out a new nonphilosophical space where the desire for presence is questioned. "To deconstruct a text is to disclose how it functions as desire, as a search for presence and fulfillment which is interminably deferred" (Derrida in Kearney, 2004, p. 156). Although Derrida argues that we can never be outside of the language of metaphysics because, in a certain irreducible way, we are always within such a language, he does claim that it is still possible to think of another space or location (*topos*) from which we can problematize the appearances of limits in our language, beginning with the limit of presence (Derrida in Kearney, 2004, p. 142).

Maggie Maclure (2003) applies this notion of phonocentrism to educational research, showing how issues of method and data collection "can be seen as the attempt to control the threat posed by writing" (p. 105). The custom of obscuring the textuality or writtenness of research texts reflects a metaphysical binary that forever demotes writing as a mere trace of the site of immediate and unsullied self-presence. Exposing the writtenness of research, explains Maclure, threatens to disrupt the boundaries that separate words from meaning, play from seriousness, and art from research. Deconstruction is an attempt to disrupt these binaries and generate a philosophical nonsite, a location from which both art and research can see itself as Other, a site where we can interrogate and reflect upon our desire for presence.

In *More Radical Hermeneutics: On Not Knowing Who We Are,* John Caputo (2000) describes the "domesticative gestures" that tame the radical alterity of artwork. He criticizes Gadamer for imposing an essence of unity onto all artwork, and for insisting that the modern artist, in disrupting forms of representation, is merely obscuring her or his intended meanings.

> It appears thus to be a fundamental metaphysical assumption on Gadamer's part that the modern artwork cannot be aimed at the disruption of perception itself, that it cannot mean to effect a deeper disturbance than merely to make perception more difficult. (p. 48)

It is through art that Gadamer hopes we can touch eternity. Art is thus trapped in the relation of representation to presence, trapped in the metaphysics of the temporal delay of meaning, deferring to an ideal entity that is always more present, more authentic, more real than the art that scrambles after it.

Hermeneutics is bound to the notion that representation is a function of presence; the hidden metaphysics of hermeneutic interpretation presumes a pure space of nonsignification, which is itself the source of all signification. Caputo demands that we move further toward a disruption of this binary relation and posit presence as an effect of representation. The modern artwork, the apparent trace of an artist's intentions, is in fact the play of indefinitely deferred meaning, circulating and forever shifting all stable references, enacting the imprint of an always absent presence. Deconstruction, argues Caputo, demonstrates a greater fidelity to the facticity of the Other, thereby generating an ethical relation that brings self and Other together in noncoercive and responsive ways.

I am not suggesting that all arts-informed research must embrace a postmodern aesthetic and interrogate its desire for presence, but I do believe that certain arts-informed inquiries can show us how to do this. In the particular case that I examine below, the artwork troubles its capacity to represent something outside of itself, including its capacity to represent the reflexive self.

◆ The Alzheimer's Project

The Alzheimer's Project is an arts-informed research program exploring experiences of Alzheimer's disease and caregiving. The principal investigators, Ardra Cole and Maura McIntyre, created an installation art show that toured Canadian galleries, civic centers, public broadcasting buildings, and shopping malls in 2003. The show consists of installation artwork that traces the ways in which lives are erased by the degenerative impact of Alzheimer's disease. Visitors are invited to move through the show in a nonlinear path. Many of the installation locations have been lobbies or open connecting corridors where visitors pass through the show on their way somewhere else. One wall displays a series of photographs that document the reversal of the care relation between mother and daughter as time progresses, functioning as a testimony to the ways in which relations of temporal development are overturned. Another set of photographs, arranged in an array, traces the "natural" development of a young woman. Each of these appear out of focus. As viewers readjust their vision so as to make meaning of the images, a second faintly superimposed image of an "aging and ill woman with a vacant, gaunt look" (Cole & McIntyre, 2004, p. 7) becomes visible.

In another corner, three detached fridge doors are arranged in a semicircle, each from a distinct style and era, and each functioning as the frame for various images, tickets, and "ordinary" notes. The dislocation of the fridge door from its domestic context and purpose provokes a visceral anxiety about the disappearance of sustenance, comfort, and familiarity. A clothesline carrying a line of women's white underwear, from androgynous diapers through to padded push-up bras, and onward to maternity wear, stretched nylon panties, and an adult-size diaper, underscores the irony of displaced intimacy and disclosure in the context of Alzheimer's disease. The laundry line of "intimate" apparel is shockingly clean, "hanging outside" for all to see, hailing the glaring absence of the Self.

On a table lies a series of small books marking the devolution of writing from the polished and expressive words of an accomplished educator to the chaotic scratches and haphazard words found in a note pad. These last missives do not intentionally obscure their meaning, but are evidence of an absence of meaning. They trace a silence, and point to the disturbing absence of the one who was presumed to be once there. The artwork underscores the radical unknowability of the lived experience of Alzheimer's disease.

♦ Conclusion

Derrida argues that it is only through a relation to alterity, to the absolute singularity of the Other, that a text can even begin to engender a political and ethical urgency. Although the Alzheimer's Project is directly based on the experiences of Cole and McIntyre in caring for their mothers, both of whom died of Alzheimer's disease, the installation refrains from statements such as "My mother. . . ." and contains only one direct reference to the artists' relationships with their mothers, inviting the audience to speculate, to respond, and to intervene by

contributing their own story in the notebooks provided. This moment of response, when the unanticipated appears, when the Other enters the work and leaves the trace of their own caregiving experiences, or surprises the researchers by writing something and then scratching it out, captures the urgency of the present moment in ways that mere reflexive writing cannot do. Arts-informed research is a radical way of thinking presence, precisely because it aims to prepare for the unexpected, and it is only the unexpected that is truly urgent and warranted by that urgency to become present. The Alzheimer's Project demonstrates how research can put itself at risk in generating a space that is a radical "openness towards the other."

This chapter has shown how arts-informed research might foster a more ethical reciprocity between self and Other, by carving out a space of indeterminacy and thereby troubling our incessant desire for presence. In the Alzheimer's Project, as in the stories of Peter Clough, the power of reflexive practice is put into play, drawing on audience empathy, emotional connection, and the desire for presence, while insisting on the radical alterity of the unknown, and generating a space where critical reading practices can emerge.

♦ References

Caputo, J. D. (2000). *More radical hermeneutics: On not knowing who we are.* Indianapolis: Indiana University Press.

Ceglowski, D. (2002). Research as relationship. In N. K. Denzin & Y. S. Lincoln (Eds.), *The qualitative inquiry reader* (pp. 5–24). Thousand Oaks, CA: Sage.

Clough, P. (2002). *Narratives and fictions in educational research.* Philadelphia, PA: Open University Press.

Cole, A. L., & McIntyre, M. (2004). Research as aesthetic contemplation: The role of the audience in research interpretation [Electronic version]. *Educational Insights, 9*(1). Retrieved December 15, 2005, from www.ccfi.educ .ubc.ca/publication/insights/vo9no1/articles/ cole.html

Creswell, J. C. (2003). *Research design: Qualitative, quantitative, and mixed methods approaches* (2nd ed.). Thousand Oaks, CA: Sage.

Ellis, C., & Bochner, A. P. (2000). Autoethnography, personal narrative, reflexivity: Researcher as subject. In N. K. Denzin & Y. S. Lincoln (Eds.), *The handbook of qualitative research* (2nd ed., pp. 733–768). Thousand Oaks, CA: Sage.

Kearney, R. (2004). *Debates in continental philosophy: Conversations with contemporary thinkers.* New York: Fordham University Press.

Lather, P. (1991). *Getting smart: Feminist research and pedagogy with/in the postmodern.* New York: Routledge.

Maclure, M. (2003). *Discourse in educational and social research.* Philadelphia, PA: Open University Press.

40

ART AND EXPERIENCE

Lessons From Dewey and Hawkins

◆ Valerie J. Janesick

Art begins with resistance—at the point where resistance is overcome. No human masterpiece has ever been created without great labor.

—Andre Gide (1869–1951)

As a choreographer, photographer, historian, scholar, and qualitative researcher, I write this chapter looking back. I am looking to John Dewey's (1859–1952) views on art as experience as well as Erick Hawkins's (1909–1994) views on experience as central to modern dance. Taken together, they are remarkably congruent and foreshadow ways to understand social science research. These two thinkers, artists, change agents, philosophers-in-action, and social scientists have much to offer qualitative researchers in terms of understanding and interpreting human experience.

I studied at the Erick Hawkins studio in the West Village of New York City earlier in my life and was profoundly influenced by his thinking and technique. Likewise, in my study of John Dewey's writings on art, education, and experience in graduate school, and continuing in my life as a scholar, I came to realize that the work of the artist is very much like that of the qualitative social science researcher and vice versa. In dance, the body is the instrument through which the story is told. In the arena of qualitative research, the researcher is the research instrument. Both qualitative researcher and dancer refine their instruments in order to pursue their art and craft. Both tell a story of some sort, a narrative of a person's life, a major event or trauma. As the narrative unfolds, the artistic process becomes the inquiry process. Designing a project, seeking evidence, communicating an idea or story to a relevant audience, and receiving feedback is a recurring cycle for artists and qualitative researchers. For the artist, in dance for example, the dancer receives constant feedback from the choreographer, other dancers, and the audience. For the qualitative researcher, feedback is regular and sustained from the participants in the study, and eventually many participants become coresearchers as a result.

Both Dewey and Hawkins refused to separate the aesthetic from ordinary experience. Both located the emergence of the aesthetic in humans' capacity to live life, to connect with individuals in community, and to recognize interaction and communication as the cornerstone to understanding any human endeavor. Thus, I describe and explain how art, experience, and inquiry interrelate and provide a basis for critical engagement in social science qualitative research.

◆ Dewey's Theory of Art, Experience, Nature, and Meaning

John Dewey was born in 1859, in Burlington, Vermont. He was a writer, teacher, scholar, lecturer, and philosopher. He is most often remembered as a pragmatist educator. After Dewey graduated from the University of Vermont, he was a high school teacher for 2 years. He went on to graduate school at Johns Hopkins University and received a doctorate in 1884. He took his first academic job at the University of Michigan where he stayed for 10 years, with 1 year at the University of Minnesota within that period. Next he went to the University of Chicago where he founded and directed the experimental University Lab School—a testing ground for his ideas on experience and education, art as deeply imbedded in education, and the school as an integral part of a community. He rejected rote and repetitive learning in favor of experience and practice. Dewey left Chicago in 1904 for the Department of Philosophy at Columbia University in New York. There he wrote many of his most renowned books and articles. He came into contact with Eastern philosophy through many of his international students and studied it. Through extensive travels as a visiting scholar in North America and Asia, his ideas became known worldwide. He continued to work after his retirement from Columbia University till his death on June 2, 1952, at the age of 92.

In the winter and spring of 1931, Dewey gave 10 lectures at Harvard University. The lectures became the text *Art as Experience* (1934). This was one of Dewey's most profound contributions to understanding the relationship between art and experience. In it Dewey asserts that to understand the nature of art requires expanding conceptions of art beyond that which hangs in museums. He explains more fully that the art of human experience simply cannot be separated from the human experience of art. For Dewey, there is no work of art apart from experience. He wrote that the physical object of art, such as a painting, a dance, a song, is the "art product," whereas the actual work of art is what "the product does with and in experience" (1934, p. 3). Thus, art is a process within a given experience. It exists within a context of a given history, culture, language, and vernacular. It is about a lived experience. Furthermore, for Dewey, creativity and vision are part of an aesthetic experience of both artist and spectator. Both feel and see something in the product or work of art.

The following passage from Dewey (1981) resonates with ideas on contemporary choreography:

> The pervasively qualitative is not only that which binds all constituents into a whole but it is also unique; it constitutes in each situation an individual situation indivisible and unduplicable. . . . Distractions and relations are instituted within a situation; they are recurrent and repeatable in different situations. (p. 74)

It would be difficult to find a choreographer who disagrees with Dewey. Perhaps dance, of all art forms, is the clearest example of this point. For even with a choreographed dance, every performance of that dance is one of a kind and changes with each performance. Dancers' bodies exhibit differences and uniqueness everyday; one day stiff, another fluid; one day a leg or arm may be in pain, another day pain free. Movement on a pain-free day looks and feels very different from movement on a day of sore or pulled muscles. The nature of an experience is unique, whole, and able to be characterized aesthetically or, in some ways, is aesthetic.

Dewey explains that any work of art or any experience of art "moves as we move." He adds, "We are never wholly free from the something that lies beyond. . . . This sense of the including whole, implicit in ordinary experiences is rendered intense within the frame of a painting or a poem" (1934, pp. 193–194). Dewey acknowledges the "exquisite intelligibility and clarity we have in the presence of an object that is experienced with aesthetic intensity" (1934, p. 195). Thus, mentioned regularly in Dewey's work is the belief that the qualities

of art include the temporality or time of the art work in history, the intensity, understanding, clarity, and intelligibility of the art product.

◆ Hawkins's Theory of Art, Experience, Nature, and Meaning

Erick Hawkins was born in 1909 in a small town in Colorado. This put him in contact with Native American culture that, later in his career, influenced his thinking and choreography. He studied the classics at Harvard University, which sharpened his interest in dance and storytelling. In 1934, Hawkins was one of the first students to enroll in George Balanchine's School of American Ballet in New York City. In 1938, he studied at the legendary American Dance Festival in Bennington, Vermont. It was there that he became interested in the work of Martha Graham. A complicated artistic and personal relationship with Graham resulted in Hawkins becoming the first male dancer in Graham's company. He was also her counselor, partner, husband, and collaborator. While evolving as a dancer, he rejected both the rigidity of ballet and some of the "Graham technique." Consequently, in 1951, Hawkins founded his own school and company. He was insistent upon using newly created music in live performance, which put him at odds with many modern dancers and choreographers.

The term "modern dance" refers to the dance and form apart from ballet that evolved in reaction to strictures of ballet. For example, the inorganic foot and leg movements that resulted in excessive injuries in ballet were one thing modern dancers disavowed. Hawkins considered modern dance as evolving from the late 1920s, and most dance historians would agree. He explains in this way why ballet "went down":

The reason why it is inevitable, sitting in the seats as spectators or we as dancers, composing and dancing new dances, need the revolution, the direction called "modern dance," and the reason why it is inevitable is because the tradition of dance which grew out up in the Renaissance in Europe, which we now call ballet, is theoretical. It is based on a concept of movement which is essentially diagrammatic and opposed to the immediate apprehended kinesthetic sense of movement. (Hawkins, 1992, p. 23)

Hawkins saw the naturally occurring revolution in dance as paralleling changes in society, new ways of understanding the world, the body, and society from an organic, not a mechanistic, perspective.

Like John Dewey, Hawkins was a pioneer in many ways. For example, he collaborated with the musical community and worked with many modern composers. Hawkins stressed the Dewey-like theme of collaboration and connection to a given community. He believed in the free expressive form of dance based on human experience. Late in his life, Hawkins wrote his now famous text *The Body Is a Clear Place* (1992), which consists of chapters based on lectures while artist-in-residence at various universities and colleges, and interviews given to various professionals on the topic of his dance and choreography. In this text, he passionately explains his philosophy of dance in action.

Erick Hawkins has been described as a true dance radical. His theory of art and dance are similar to Dewey's theory of art as experience in more than superficial ways. Hawkins was radical because he went to the root of dance, saying that dance should be totally free movement. By this he meant that dance should not separate thought and action. He believed choreography and the resulting dance should be immediate and freed from space. He believed dance should explore movement in and for itself. The pure fact of movement is the poetic experience of the present "now" moment. He wanted to throw away all crutches, so to speak, and find the deep physicality, intensity, and passion of the experience in the dance. He wanted to see the audience not just "look" at a dance with their eyes but with their whole body (Hawkins, 1992). Throughout a lifetime in dance and choreography, Hawkins tested the boundaries of understanding of dance as experience, as art, and as a form of inquiry into both art and experience.

Hawkins believed a teacher does not actually "teach" a student. Rather, a teacher supports the student to uncover basic movement principles. Ultimately the student/learner is the best teacher. Hawkins believed that any information a teacher may have is accessible to anyone who will seek it out. Hawkins was a student of Zen Buddhism and often used Buddhist techniques to illustrate his ideas. For example, he often recalled

When the Ten Thousand things
Are viewed in their oneness
We return to the origin
and remain where we have
Always been.

Sen T'Sen (2004, p. 74)

For Hawkins, the student of dance needed to understand movement in order to be free of movement. One way to view Hawkins's ideas about dance is to revisit his now famous 1962 response to questions posed by the editor of *Wagner College Magazine*. Hawkins was asked: What do you consider the most beautiful dance? Hawkins remarks in this abbreviated list (for a full text see Hawkins, 1992)

Dance that is violent clarity;

Dance that is effortless;

Dance that lets itself happen;

Dance that loves the pure fact of movement;

Dance that does not stay in the mind, even the avant-garde mind;

Dance that loves gravity rather than fights it;

Dance that never ignores either audience, or music . . . or fellow dancers;

Dance that is grown up;

Dance that reveals the dance and the dancer;

Dance that knows dance is and should and can be a way of saying NOW.

Hawkins captures his belief in a postmodern description of modern dance. As a teacher, philosopher, and choreographer he was very much like John Dewey in terms of valuing aesthetics, all art forms, and experience.

◆ *Points of Resonance*

The points of connection and resonance between Dewey and Hawkins are remarkable. These points include life histories, as well as major points of convergence in philosophy and practice, all of which have implications for qualitative social science research. The first obvious connection is that, as in qualitative social science research, the researcher cannot be a bystander. This central theme is also evident in the writings and lives of Dewey and Hawkins. One cannot be a bystander in a dance any more than one can be a bystander in education or art. The many similarities in Dewey's and Hawkins's work indicate agreement that

Loose ends and open-ended situations are a fact of life;

All art connects to the community—local or global;

Dualisms of mind and body make no sense;

Experience is the basis for knowledge and understanding;

Ethical matters are important;

Narrative and storytelling are part of any art work;

Art stands as a reminder of life as it is lived and celebrated;

All art has social implications;

Art is part of culture;

Art and education are inseparable.

Working with international professionals and in international settings was critical to the development of their work. Furthermore, Dewey and Hawkins also converge on the following: Both were educators and conducted their own schools. Both men acknowledged that the senses play a key role in art and education. Both emphasized active engagement of student and/or audience. Both saw matter and form as side by side and connected. And both left lasting legacies in the areas of aesthetics, experience, art, and community.

◆ *Experience, Lessons Learned*

To make sense of the contributions of John Dewey and Erick Hawkins to art, experience, and inquiry, I refer to the third chapter of *Art as Experience* titled, "Having an Experience." Dewey begins: "Experience occurs continuously because the interaction of live creature and environing condition is involved in the very process of living" (Dewey, 1934, p. 35).

Whereas Dewey speaks in theory, Hawkins writes in the movement of an actual dance in progress. Hawkins (1992) sees the body as the perfect instrument of the lived experience:

> Several times so called critics have judged the dancers of my company as being "too graceful." How can you be too graceful? How can you obey the laws of movement too much?.... The answer is a kind of feeling introspected in the body and leads one into doing the correct effort for any movement. The kinesiological rule is to just do the movement.... The tenderness in the mind takes care of the movement in action. (p. 133–134)

Hawkins (1992) also writes:

> One of the reasons we are not accustomed as a culture to graceful movement is because we do not treasure it. The saying among the Greeks of the Athenian supremacy was that the body was to be treasured and great sensitivity was used in the observation of movement. They treasured the body by having many statues of deity . . . maybe they understood that the body is a clear place. (p. 134)

Dewey and Hawkins teach about the critical importance of experience, imagination, and the resulting artifact as layered and connected. Both emphasize the power and value of subjective experience in interpretation of art and artifact. They recall that the landscape of feelings and emotions cannot and should not be avoided when expressing art or artifact. For a researcher to "have the experience" of telling someone's story, the researcher must acknowledge the experience component of empathy, understanding, and the story itself. Just as do qualitative social science researchers, both Hawkins and Dewey celebrate narrative storytelling in many forms.

As cultural workers, teachers, and artist/philosophers Dewey and Hawkins have left an important legacy. They also continue to teach us a great deal about the importance of the arts. For example, both have written that through the arts, a larger audience is most likely reached than in any other curricular or cultural area. Regularly in their writing and speeches, they say that the arts can meet the needs of nearly every person no matter who that person is and no matter where that person is in the world. Both write of how the power of experience, art as experience, and artifacts resulting from experience transcend the day-to-day moments of life. In other words, art illuminates experience.

> The direction of discovery called modern dance can be inept, it can fail, it can flounder, it can compromise, it can be not very bright, it can lose impetus and courage, but it has to exist. It will not be swallowed by the old 19th-century European ballet foisted on America, because a larger principle cannot be included in a smaller one. A salmon cannot be swallowed by a goldfish. (Hawkins, 1992, p. 42)

Thus, qualitative social science researchers, like salmon, must move ahead to claim niches for arts' place in inquiry without fear of being swallowed by goldfish.

Hawkins's and Dewey's idea of a "consciousness of experience" allows for all the things they wrote about in terms of experience, art, and inquiry into the human condition. For Dewey and Hawkins, art and experience are inseparable. Every art work tells a story. For qualitative social scientists as well, it is nearly impossible to separate art from experience. The critical engagement of qualitative social science researchers in the research act is illuminated by understanding art as experience and, indeed, having an experience, as Dewey would say. To conclude, Hawkins's (1992) appraisal of his choreographed piece, *Eight Clear Places*, seems appropriate: "Each dance becomes a ceremony of awareness . . . of violent clarity, seeing and hearing at the same time, beautiful collaboration in poetry, . . . seeing the music, sensing duration between events of timbre" (p. 43).

◆ *References*

Dewey, J. (1934). *Art as experience.* New York: Capricorn Books.

Dewey, J. (1981). *The later works 1925–1953.* Carbondale: Southern Illinois University Press.

Hawkins, E. (1992). *The body is a clear place and other statements on dance.* Pennington, NJ: Dance Horizons, Princeton Book Co. Publishers.

T'Sen, S. (2004). The third patriarch of Zen. In A. Huxley (Ed.), *The perennial philosophy* (pp. 56–80). New York: Harper and Row.

41

GOING PUBLIC WITH ARTS-INSPIRED SOCIAL RESEARCH

Issues of Audience

◆ Tom Barone

The potential audiences for works of arts-inspired social research are no doubt more varied than the actual audiences for quantitative and qualitative social science have been in the past. In the academy, hopes for career advancement, along with sheer habit, have ensured that social scientists write primarily toward professional colleagues, fellow members of circumscribed discursive communities who converse in what Toulmin (1953) called the *participant languages* of those who work in specialized fields.

But in recent years certain cultural observers have expressed discomfort with this narrow audience for scholarly work (Agger, 1990; Jacoby, 1987). The concerns of these critics about the tendency of academic writing in a variety of fields to alienate readers unprepared to penetrate the opaque prose of disciplinary specialization may suggest a rethinking of research audience. These critics imagine the possibilities of academics directly addressing those who think and talk in the vernacular languages of not participants but *onlookers* (Toulmin, 1953). When that shift in audience is achieved, scholarly writing will have been, as Nash (2004) put it, "liberated," and then scholars may have enhanced their influence through *audience blending* (Barone, 2002), opening up their work to a larger community of percipients and readers.

The presence of this volume is testimony to the fact that, in the last few decades, some researchers have moved to complement the traditional premises, procedures, protocols, and modes of representation of the social sciences with those of the arts. And since many of these researchers identify themselves as artists rather than social scientists, one might expect a sense of freedom regarding the issue of audience. But while arts-inspired researchers have thus far only rarely abandoned the traditional conception of research readership, some stirrings toward "liberation" can be detected. Toward that hope, in this chapter I am wondering: For arts-based scholars who no longer wish to disclose their research findings only to their "participant" colleagues, who might their additional audiences be? Might they also directly address "onlooker" members of the public? And if so, how? What are some of the sticky issues involved in achieving successful audience blending?

◆ Moving Outward: Categories of Research Audiences

One sort of audience ("additional" because it is not generally considered as legitimate for traditional sorts of social research projects) may be the researcher herself. Drawing upon phenomenologist philosophers, some researchers highlight the self-emancipatory potential of engaging in arts-based projects. Catharsis, therapy, self-awakening, self-transformation, self-empowerment, personal growth—these are available subjectivist aims for social inquiry espoused by methodologists who are willing to brave the epithets of self-indulgence, self-absorption, narcissism, and navel-gazing inevitably hurled at them.

Instead of moving directly outward to a wider audience, these researchers first move inward, if often with the assumption that the personal meanings they uncover and disclose will ultimately be appreciated by others. Of course, insofar as writing is inner dialogue, the author of any text may be rightfully seen as its initial audience, the first beneficiary of the personal insights, change, and growth that it fosters. And changing the course of history may indeed occur by first changing oneself.

Most arts-based researchers are, however, not unaware of the intersubjective nature of their enterprise, understanding the artistic gesture, like a speech utterance, as primarily a social act, a moving outward into communion with others. And she herself may be one of those "others." Indeed, the arts-based-researcher-as-her-own-audience may defy dichotomization into self and other. Postmodernist scholars have succeeded in casting doubt on the notion of a totally unified, integrated, consistent self-identity. Instead, they have resurrected Nietzsche's (1887/1968) idea of the multiple self in a form that is fluid, fragmented, and only semistable (if, hopefully, still engaged in some degree of coherent self-dialogue). This view of the self affirms a human capacity to adopt multiple social roles, to compose alternative (even conflicting) versions of one's autobiography. It accommodates the possibility of participating in more than one form of discourse or manner of being. Indeed, I often find my own multidimensional self quite capable of engaging with cultural texts that employ languages and imagery both academic and popular, technical and vernacular. I realize that, when it comes to projects of social inquiry, I can be, like my colleagues, simultaneously specialist *and* layperson, participant *and* onlooker.

Still, those (including academics) who have not been initiated into the particular idiom employed within a scholarly text may remain frozen out of a participation in its consumption. One set of such onlookers may be the informants whose lives have been represented in the research text. This irony has not been lost on a few social researchers. One is Patti Lather, whose book *Troubling the Angels* (Lather & Smithies, 1997)— a postmodern, if not exactly arts-based, work—is aimed at engaging people with AIDS who are not academics, the kind of people whose lives are revealed in its pages. Similarly, Denzin (1997, p. 101) has identified a lay audience of ethnographic performance texts as those "whose experiences are being performed," those whose life experiences are similar to those of the researcher's informants.

Yet another kind of "foreign" audience might consist of those who commission arts-based researchers to produce evaluations of social programs. For example, Elliot Eisner's (1979) notion of educational criticism imagined an audience of consumers of arts-based evaluation reports of educational programs. And, as with other forms of qualitative research, some arts-based projects have yielded research texts friendly to those involved in professional training programs, as well as those in positions to make policy regarding those programs.

Finally, there is the possibility of sharing the fruits of social research with sets of onlookers who have often been viewed as residing in` a realm quite distant from the world of the researcher. This is an audience of the lay public or, better, the various *publics-at-large*.

◆ Reaching Various Publics Through Art

Currently, the results of social research studies that do not employ arts-based methods are often translated and broadly disseminated to the general public through the mass print and electronic media. But some commentators have noted that a translation of social science research texts into linguistic forms more familiar to lay onlookers is not an easy task (McNergney, 1990). In the rewriting process meanings can be distorted, information lost. Enormously complex issues may be oversimplified and important ones ignored. Trenchant questioning of subtle but significant assumptions and premises upon which the research project rested may be tacitly discouraged.

For arts-based researchers in particular, a rethinking of audience might result in an elimination of the need for journalistic middlemen. Instead, their research texts might be composed for members of various lay publics as *immediate* audiences, made more formally and substantively accessible, and even alluring, to a wider array of discursive communities.

How might arts-based researchers accomplish this feat? How might arts-based researchers diminish the discursive distance between themselves and their fellow citizens? Through what venues might target audiences of onlookers be reached? To answer these questions, we might seek out inspirational exemplars. We might consider the works, not only of arts-based social researchers, but of nonacademic professional artists who have reached out to a variety of publics. Activist artists, in particular, have in recent decades achieved some degree of success in communicating with nonacademic audiences.

◆ From Outside the Academy

What has come to be called activist or public art is a form of cultural practice begun in the 1970s, and then expanded and institutionalized. Activist artists drew from the earlier birth and growth of conceptual art and performance art. Felshin (1995) described activist art as a "hybrid cultural practice" insofar as it maintained "one foot in the art world and the other in the world of political activism and community organizing" (p. 9). Arts-inspired social researchers interested in addressing a wide audience might learn much from the aspirations and dissemination strategies of this portion of the art world.

Consider venues and locales. Performance-based artistic activities in the last quarter of the 20th century took the form of media events, installations, public demonstrations, and exhibitions (Felshin, 1995). And prior to the revolution in electronic media, activist artists exhibited their works on billboards, through subway and bus advertising, as newspaper inserts, as photo-narratives, as wall murals and graffiti, and so on.

Currently, public art remains available both as interventionist performance and as exhibitions. Sometimes called *public performance art* or *political pedagogical performance,* these efforts include slam poetry, street festivals, and creative mixed media combinations of all sorts. Moreover, the onset of new technologies has meant opportunities for digital and computer-based artistry. The Internet is rife with sites devoted to artistic expression related to a myriad of social and political causes. On the Internet can be found many art galleries of digitalized artworks, online journals, zines, and weblogs. Groups such as Adbusters and Planned Parenthood solicit artwork to be displayed online, and Adbusters often underwrites artists.

Public artists with varying degrees of social commitment have employed, in addition to the electronic media, films, videos, and still photography in their attempts to address segments of the general public. Playwrights and theatrical artists have also managed to engage the public in their exploration of important social issues. Those who perform most like qualitative researchers write and stage what, within the academy, have come

to be called *ethnodramas*. Prominent non-academics among this group include Anna Devere Smith and Moises Kaufman. Smith is most famous for her plays *Fires in the Mirror* (1993) and *Twilight: Los Angeles, 1992* (1994). The former is a serious exploration of Black–Jewish relations in America, and the latter surrounds the civil disturbances following the Rodney King verdict. Kaufman's (2001) stage play *The Laramie Project* about the 1988 murder in Wyoming of gay college student Matthew Shephard became a movie made for cable television.

◆ From Inside the Academy

University scholars, as artists and storytellers, have not explored as wide a range of venues for dissemination as have professional artists. Some, however, are sallying forth into the discursive spaces of the lay onlooker. Just as nonacademic activist artists are performing and displaying (even creating) their works in public sites away from museums, theaters, and other traditional "art-world" venues, some academy-based arts-inspired social researchers are choosing venues for their work that reach a diversified audience over the usual academically oriented presses and scholarly journals. I will mention a few examples.

Johnny Saldaña is one ethnodramatist who has declared his work to be a form of arts-based research. A notable example is *Street Rat* (Saldaña, 2005), a play about homeless youth in New Orleans based on ethnographic work by Finley and Finley (1999). In research approach, form, and content, Saldaña's work closely resembles that of the abovementioned socially conscientious playwrights who reside outside of the academy and who tend to reach much larger audiences. Indeed, while his work is often presented in campus locales, its themes often attract members of the public into the audience.

University arts-based researchers working in other narrative and literary genres are also reaching toward that goal. Banks and Banks (1998) have discussed at length the possibilities of using fiction as social research. In the field of education, novels (especially as dissertations) are becoming much more common (Dunlop, 1999; Poetter, 2006; Saye, 2002). One such educational novel-as-dissertation by Gosse (2005) became the first to be published in Canada. The Edge of Each Other's Battles Project (N. Smith, 2005) employs poetry, narrative, filmmaking, and storytelling as a means for bringing together social justice academics and scholars who are members of local communities to learn from each other and to plan strategies for social action. These are goals similar to those adopted by advocates for and practitioners of *applied theatre* (Taylor, 2003).

◆ Seducing the Onlooker

For arts-inspired scholars, seducing onlookers into encounters with their work may not be easy. Indeed, any arts-based researcher (especially those working outside of the popular or vernacular arts) may find that nonartists (both academic and lay) lack a strong desire to engage with their works, the products of their efforts merely replicating the disinterest that members of the public have traditionally held for social science research manuscripts. For, like the traditionalists, they too may be employing participant languages that relegate some potential audience members to the status of outsiders.

For those arts-based researchers who attempt politically overt activist art, occasionally the problem may be a heavy-handed delivery of an intended message, a stridency that hinders efforts at reaching their target audiences. Carol Becker (1994) suggests that a kind of alienation may be the result of some (although certainly not all) activist art:

> Art may be focused directly on the issues of daily life, but, because it seeks to reveal contradictions and not obfuscate them, art works which should spark a shock of recognition and effect catharsis actually appear alien and deliberately difficult. Art easily becomes the object of rage and confrontation. [And artists], frustrated by the illusion of order and well-being posited by society . . . [may] choose rebellion as a method of retaliation. . . . In so doing, they separate themselves from those with whom they may actually long to interact. (p. xiii)

But popular art, including activist varieties, can be inviting and challenging without being off-putting or alienating. Creating a "lay friendly" work might require that arts-based researchers enter into the comfort zones of members of an intended audience, enabling them to identify with facets of the work. The artist must manage to pull the lay onlooker into the world of the work, coaxing him or her to participate in a reconstruction of its meaning. The percipient can then place this reconstructed meaning into analogous contexts found in the familiar "real" world outside of the text. If this reading and viewing process results in previously unimagined questions or insights about facets of that "outside" social world, then artistic success is at hand.

◆ Bypassing or Penetrating the Culture Industry?

But must arts-inspired researchers aspire to interact with everyone within and outside of the academy? Does "going public" with arts-inspired research texts mean reaching as large a portion of the citizenry as have, say, *Star Wars* or *The DaVinci Code* or *Desperate Housewives*? Even connecting with a more modest slice of the citizenry might require dissemination though the mass media, a move that raises additional questions about the character of the arts-based work to be produced.

The possibility of reaching the masses in this fashion would require more than simply peeling away from the text its coating of what William James (1975) once called privileged meaning. Additional compromises might be required. What are they? Commentators on the popular media have noted the stranglehold on the commercially driven media market by the large corporations who comprise the culture industry. To observers such as Agger (1990), this corporate ownership and control of the media has meant a displacement of imaginative, vibrant, challenging, transgressive literature and art. This in turn, he argues, has produced a decline in public discourse.

If Agger is correct, then it is not merely stridency or mystification through technical jargon that cuts against the possibility of a broad dissemination of the work by the artist-scholar-researcher. Because the culture market squeezes out works that compete poorly in terms of mass appeal, all that fail to attract an audience out of an unwillingness to sensationalize and titillate are in jeopardy. So can broadly based arts-inspired research texts ever be educational in a profound sense? Can they penetrate the center of the public sphere, intellectually and emotionally touching large numbers of people and pulling them toward an enhanced understanding of—or least deeper curiosity toward—important social and political issues?

Might we look to models of great artists throughout history—Dickens? Shakespeare?—whose complex and edifying work has been revered by both the intelligentsia and the working classes? What are more recent examples—in the last half century—of simultaneously thought provoking and entertaining artworks that have managed to slip past the blockades erected by the gatekeepers of the culture industry to activate the imagination of the masses? The televised adaptation of Alex Haley's (1976) *Roots*? Green Day's punk rock opera *American Idiot*? Films such as *Platoon, Brokeback Mountain, An Inconvenient Truth*, or *Fahrenheit 9/11*? Or do some or all of these more recent examples of provocative art fail the stridency test, their appeal and impact thereby diminished?

Ultimately, all arts-inspired researchers, like other artists and writers, must understand that the scope of their audience will always be finite. Referring to literature, the novelist Nadine Gordimer (1989) noted that

> [Any text] will be understood only by readers who share terms of reference formed in us by our education—not merely academic but in the broadest sense of life experience: our political, economic, social, and emotional concepts, and our values derived from these: our cultural background. (p. 59)

Indeed, the general population should never be imagined as a homogeneous mass, nonvariegated by cultural background and personal life experiences. And it is obvious that the Zeitgeist can never be transformed by any single arts-based research effort. But that is not to suggest that social researchers inspired by the arts should abandon their arduous quest to maintain their scholarly identity and develop their artistic virtuosity while (à la independent filmmakers, playwrights, aspiring novelists, and other storytellers) moving to infiltrate the consciousness of the populace. Nor is it to disparage the strategies pioneered by activist artists to bypass the corporate apparatus of the communications industry, as they target more circumscribed communities within the larger population through the Internet, applied theater, and other localized efforts. Indeed, my hope is that all arts-based social researchers will continue to experiment with various ways to move their work into the public domain, generating trenchant questions about prevailing societal conditions that might otherwise remain largely unasked outside of the walls of the academy.

◆ References

Agger, B. (1990). *The decline of discourse: Reading, writing, and resistance in postmodern capitalism.* New York: Falmer.

Banks, A., & Banks, S. (1998). *Fiction and social research: By ice or fire.* Walnut Creek, CA: AltaMira Press.

Barone, T. (2002). From genre blurring to audience blending: Reflections on the field emanating from an ethnodrama. *Anthropology and Education Quarterly, 33*(2), 255–267.

Becker, C. (1994). Introduction: Presenting the problem. In C. Becker (Ed.), *The subversive imagination: Artists, society, and social responsibility* (pp. xi–xx). New York: Routledge.

Denzin, N. (1997). *Interpretive ethnography: Ethnographic practices for the 21st century.* Thousand Oaks, CA: Sage.

Dunlop, R. (1999). *Boundary Bay: A novel.* Unpublished doctoral dissertation, University of British Columbia, Vancouver, Canada.

Eisner, E. (1979). *The educational imagination: On the design and evaluation of school programs.* New York: Macmillan.

Felshin, N. (1995). *But is it art? The spirit of art as activism.* Seattle, WA: Bay Press.

Finley, S., & Finley, M. (1999). Sp'ange: A research story. *Qualitative Inquiry, 9*(2), 254–267.

Gordimer, N. (1989). The gap between the writer and the reader. *New York Review of Books, 36*(14), 59–61.

Gosse, D. (2005). *Jackytar.* St. Johns, Newfoundland, Canada: Jesperson.

Haley, A. (1976). *Roots.* Garden City, NY: Doubleday.

Jacoby, R. (1987). *The last intellectuals: American culture in the age of academe.* New York: Basic Books.

James, W. (1975). *The meaning of truth: The works of William James.* Cambridge, MA: Harvard University Press.

Kaufman, M. (2001). *The Laramie project.* New York: Vintage Books.

Lather, P., & Smithies, C. (1997). *Troubling the angels: Women living with AIDS.* Boulder, CO: Westview Press.

McNergney, R. F. (1990). Improving communication among educational researchers, policymakers, and the press. *Educational Researcher, 20*(10), 3–9.

Nash, R. J. (2004). *Liberating scholarly writing: The power of personal narrative.* New York: Teachers College Press.

Nietzsche, F. (1968). *The will to power.* New York: Vintage. (Original work published 1887)

Poetter, T. (2006). *The education of Sam Sanders.* Lanham, MD: Hamilton Books.

Saldaña, J. (2005). *Ethnodrama.* Walnut Creek, CA: AltaMira Press.

Saye, N. (2002). *More than "once upon a time": Fiction as a bridge to knowing.* Unpublished doctoral dissertation, Georgia Southern University, Statesboro.

Smith, A. D. (1993). *Fires in the mirror: Crown Heights, Brooklyn, and other identities.* Garland City, NY: Anchor.

Smith, A. D. (1994). *Twilight: Los Angeles, 1992.* Garden City, NY: Anchor Books.

Smith, N. (Ed.). (2005). *Newsletter I: The edge of each other's battles project.* Oakland, CA: The Edge of Each Other's Battles Project.

Taylor, P. (2003). *Applied theatre: Creating transformative encounters in the community.* Portsmouth, NH: Heinemann.

Toulmin, S. (1953). *Philosophy of science.* London: Hutchinson University Library.

42

BETWEEN SCHOLARSHIP AND ART

Dramaturgy and Quality in Arts-Related Research

◆ Kelli Jo Kerry-Moran

It is the red that I remember most vividly. The year was 1997 and I was participating with several other researchers in a most unique conference presentation. We had all been given the same set of raw data—interview transcripts from a study of newly-wed couples. Our task was to create artistic (re)presentations of the data. I worked with Jean Konzal (Konzal & Kerry-Moran, 1997) in crafting and performing a readers' theater script, but my most compelling memory from that session is viewing the large, panoramic painting created by J. Gary Knowles (1997). The mammoth proportions, colors, textures and content of the painting evoked aspects of the data that gave visual form to emotional undercurrents; it moved me. And I still cannot translate into words what I then understood in images.

—Notes after an arts-based inquiry session at a meeting of the
American Educational Research Association, April 1997

Author's Note: Thank you to the anonymous reviewers and the editors, Ardra L. Cole and J. Gary Knowles, for their insightful feedback and suggestions. This chapter is adapted from a paper presented at the American Educational Research Association Annual Meeting (Kerry-Moran, 2003).

◆ 493

This aesthetic experience is one of the most powerful and passionate academic moments of my career. It was a marriage of the emotional and intellectual that shaped my perception and increased my understanding. Since that 1997 American Educational Research Association meeting, I have had many opportunities to read, hear, view, participate in, and create arts-related research. While the forms, formats, and quality have varied, each piece, regardless of discipline, has represented a search for knowledge and contributed toward a more expansive view of inquiry. Artist/researchers champion multiple ways of doing and representing social science research. One consequence is perplexity in how arts-related research should be evaluated.

Research communities arrive at shared perceptions of good research through discussions, debates, and exploration over time. This cycle continues, and the last few decades have seen growth in the development of language and concepts used to assess quality in arts-related research. This chapter contributes to this dialogue. Others have suggested qualities, commitments, and frameworks for evaluating arts-related research that focus on the research product (see Barone & Eisner, 1997; Finley, 2003; Piirto, 2002). My aim is different.

The focus of this chapter is the evaluator. This in no way shifts responsibility away from researcher/artists. Those creating arts-related work retain sole responsibility for its quality. Rather, it addresses the need for evaluators to weigh qualities that are both arts and research related. Quality, both artistic and otherwise, is of such great consequence that those judging arts-related research must strive to be as fluent in discussing and discerning artistic merit as they are in social science. Improving the quality of evaluation will lead to better arts-related research while supporting the spirit of risk, play, and exploration that runs through all things artistic.

I begin by discussing the meaning and potential of evaluation followed by an outline of the dramaturg[1] as one possible metaphor for the critical analysis of research-based artistic work. Using the dramaturg metaphor, I describe the dispositions that evaluators should possess and the questions that should be considered in assessing the quality of arts-related research. Finally, I suggest strategies for the layperson in approaching and exploring issues of quality in arts-related social science research.

◆ What Is Evaluation?

Evaluation holds different meanings in different contexts. The bulk of this chapter deals with more formal evaluation contexts in which comparisons or judgments of quality are made, such as publication or presentation decisions. Program evaluators break evaluation into two types: summative and formative. Summative evaluation is designed to assess the quality of an end product. It is final and is typically used in high stakes situations such as standardized testing, publication decisions, and bestowing honors or awards. It is not aimed toward ongoing improvement, at least in the short term. Summative evaluation is about having the last word. As Barone (2001) describes it, summative evaluation is declarative, emerging from that same epistemology that seeks to reduce uncertainty by uncovering life's absolute truths through scientific research.

By contrast, formative evaluation focuses on continuous improvement. Its purpose is to assess current strengths and weaknesses with an aim toward improving the ongoing project. Whether it is an essay, painting, thesis, preschool program, or community food bank, formative evaluation is about reaching an as yet unrealized potential. Barone (2001) describes this type of evaluation as exploratory and claims that its epistemological foundation is an "epistemology of ambiguity that seeks out and celebrates meanings that are partial, tentative, incomplete, sometimes even contradictory, and originating from multiple vantage points" (pp. 152–153). While summative evaluation is necessary, exploratory evaluation is a better philosophical fit for arts-related research. At its best, exploratory evaluation can be the muse that inspires the artist/researcher to new heights. However, arts-related research holds many unique characteristics that make evaluation problematic.

◆ *Evaluation Challenges*

Most, perhaps even all, research involving the arts emerges from qualitative work. Consequently, the criteria and concepts with which research communities evaluate qualitative inquiry are applicable to many of the designs and methodologies from which arts-related research emerges. There are differences, however, and these differences stem from the inclusion of the arts.

The forms that research takes and the multiple ways it is perceived and interpreted are different for arts-related work than other forms of qualitative research and require different considerations of quality. The 1997 American Educational Research Association Annual Meeting session highlighted at the beginning of this chapter is one example. That Chicago convention center ballroom was filled with artistic representations of the same data: painting, collage, poetry, theatre, all focused on one set of interview transcripts but through very different forms. If form cannot be separated from content (Eisner, 1997),

then each artistic representation within that session was not saying the *same* thing differently; each representation was saying a related, yet *different* thing. If form cannot be separated from content, then evaluations of arts-related work must consider both content and form, both research and art.

Arts-related inquiry remains virgin territory: broad, largely undefined, and uncharted. Although educational researchers, anthropologists, sociologists, and other social scientists have been engaging in arts-related research for several years, these explorations are isolated from much of mainstream research. Additionally, the fields making up social science are widespread so that artist/scholars in one area may be unaware of artistic explorations in other disciplines. Certainly the reasons for this isolation are many, but at least one contributing factor is diversity among arts-related research itself. Narrative, drama, dance, poetry, collage, fiber arts, portraiture, storytelling, and many other formats rest comfortably beneath the wide umbrella of arts-related research, yet these forms differ in voice and approach. The quality of arts-related formats cannot be adequately considered without a mind attuned to each particular form. Excellent poetry is certainly different from excellent drama, and the two must be evaluated differently to be evaluated well. This problematizes the evaluation of arts-related research because any single person may be ill equipped to assess arts/research works that cross discipline boundaries such as those between visual art and social science.

Those performing formal or high stakes judgments of arts-related research must be competent evaluators both in terms of art and social science. Some may view this assertion as advocating elitism. Individuals evaluate works of art on a daily basis and know their own minds when deciding that a song is good or a sculpture is powerful. Who has the right to say otherwise? Certainly personal opinion has value, and the opening example of my engagement with Knowles's (1997) painting is an apt example. The painting moved me; it resonated with me and helped me to understand differently particular aspects of the data. I intuitively know that this piece of arts-informed research works, yet I lack the language, experiential background, and knowledge of visual arts to effectively explore *why* and *how* the painting moved me. My visceral response can do little to move the evaluation beyond good–bad dichotomies and generalizations. With few exceptions, perceiving and articulating the shades of gray that lie between labels like good and bad requires experience and training particular to the art form. I lack the visual design skills to critically evaluate painting. Perhaps most importantly, I lack the skills to help the visual artist improve the work. Like a diner enjoying a fine meal, one can take pleasure in the food yet be unable to make recommendations to the chef.

◆ *Evaluation: Muse or Siren?*

Formal evaluation requires something more, a sort of connoisseurship and criticism similar in theory to what Eisner (1995, 1998) advocates for school contexts. It is the rare individual who can fully describe *why* a song is good or *what* makes a sculpture powerful without some training and experience, without an eye, ear, or touch conscious of what needs noticing. It is not enough to appreciate arts-related inquiry; quality evaluation demands the development of the language and skills to describe, explore, and explain arts-related work and the reactions it elicits. Doing so will require diverse efforts and may include things like: working as part of an interdisciplinary team of artists and social scientists; consulting with artists and other arts-people; and pursuing training, experiences,

and perspectives outside the traditional fields of social science. This type of evaluation is challenging and demands evaluators with great skill, commitment, and flexibility. Dramaturgy provides an appropriate metaphor in part because dramaturgs are widely experienced in the theater arts.

◆ *Dramaturgy as Evaluation Metaphor*

The dramaturg must be able to move from one perspective to another as the situation demands, constructing lines of communication that facilitate production planning. To use a French term, the dramaturg must be a *bricoleur,* someone who builds using the various materials at hand. (Lutterbie, 1997, p. 224)

The tradition of dramaturgy emerged from Germanic theater in the 18th century (Cohen, 1988); however, dramaturgy has been widely practiced in America only over the last 30 to 40 years. A dramaturg may be described in many different ways by many different people, with each description being equally correct yet equally incomplete. Dramaturgs are chameleons of the theater, most often possessing a background in theater history, theory, criticism, acting, directing, and other theater crafts. Contemporary applications of dramaturgy include non-Western conceptions of art and aesthetics (Jonas, Proehl, & Lupu, 1997), and the definition of dramaturgy is in constant motion. The role of a dramaturg is fluid, and the responsibilities and contributions of dramaturgs vary with their relationships with directors, producers, and other key members of the theatrical team. A shapeshifter, the dramaturg may be used at virtually all levels of theatre: historical consultant, critic, reviewer, acting coach, literary manager, or a number of other roles as needed to educate an audience or strengthen a production. The dramaturg is a "jack of all trades," and this approach addresses at least one troublesome area in evaluating arts-related research: the diversity of the field and its forms.

Often, when dramaturgs are invited and allowed to play a key role in theatrical production, the line between dramaturg and playwright or director blurs so that the resultant production is a collective work (Jonas et al., 1997). This marriage of "critic" and "author" provides parallels and possibilities for arts-related research and social science research in general. If the evaluation of arts-informed work is to be more formative and exploratory than summative, then evaluation should include collaborative relationships. In *Art and Experience*, Dewey (as cited in Barone, 2000) describes good criticism as that which extends conversations, leading to growth rather than stagnation. Good editors and reviewers do this by providing feedback that researchers and writers use to improve their work, as in the suggestions that a doctoral student might expect from a mentor. When the reviewer is experienced in the field, he or she is prepared to provide specific and insightful feedback. Within arts-related research this will mean seeking out reviewers experienced in both art and social science.

Yet it may not be possible to find one person with an appropriate mix of qualifications and experience. Review teams composed of both social scientists and artists can fill the evaluator's role, functioning similarly to dissertation committees where each member represents a valued expertise or perspective. While I am unaware of an example in which an interdisciplinary team has evaluated an arts-related work, such teams have created arts-related research. The performance of "Have Script Will Travel: Readers' Theater for Social Change" at the 2004 American Educational Research Association Annual Meeting emerged from a collaboration between educational researchers and theater educators (Donovan, Diaz, Salvatore, & Taylor, 2004). The result was an artistically

and educationally sound piece of research that refreshingly stood out from its peers in both script and performance quality. This interdisciplinary group possessed the skills necessary to provide excellent analysis, feedback, and support for a work of drama-based educational inquiry.

Regardless of whether arts-related research is judged by a single qualified reviewer or an interdisciplinary team, feedback can be enriched if reviewer(s) and researcher(s) dialogue. Although the standard of blind review makes this difficult, a more reciprocal interchange is desirable between authors/artists and academic reviewers. This type of formative exchange is one of many approaches that distinguish dramaturg from theater critic. Dramaturgs often work with the theatrical team throughout the production, and their presence and feedback serve to improve and strengthen the performance. Conversely, theater critics simply judge, and their evaluation usually comes too late to result in any real improvement of the drama. Likewise, evaluation and assessment are more effective, offering greater opportunity for improvement, when they are done with us rather than to us.

Yet academic convention runs counter to formative evaluation procedures in the areas that matter most: dissertations, publication, promotion, and tenure. The stakes are high. However, even within a high stakes arena, the attributes of the dramaturg, as broadly prepared in the field while actively researching and developing skills appropriate to each project, provide a model of the way in which evaluators, reviewers, editors, and dissertation committees might approach arts-related research.

◆ Considerations for Making Judgments

One of the concepts basic to evaluation is that one first must have a framework or criteria from which to make an evaluation. This holds true for all types of research, including arts-related research. I propose three contexts that the evaluator should consider in making a judgment of arts-related work: goals, arts approach, and audience.

KNOWLEDGE OF GOALS

A restrictive list of arts-related research goals is inappropriate for this diverse and changing field. Current goals seem to include: social activism and giving voice to the powerless and silenced (Barone, 2000; Finley & Finley, 1999); making connections between research and lived experience (Garoian, 1999); making meaning through multiple senses and sensibilities (Norris, 2000); enhancing meaning, provoking thought and questions, even reducing certainty in long-standing beliefs (Barone, 2001; Finley, 2003); and extending the influence of scholarship beyond the academy to the reaches of policymakers and the general public (Barone, 2002). These are worthy goals, and within current circumstances, it is difficult to imagine "good" arts-related research that does not touch on at least one of these purposes. However, perspectives, climates, cultures, and goals change. Any attempt to evaluate the quality of the arts in research must balance shared perspectives of arts-related inquiry with the unique attributes and purposes of particular approaches, projects, or products. Those judging arts-related research should know what is current in the field and what the aim of the artist/researcher is. This is not to say that all goals are equally worthwhile. Evaluators might well contest the value of the research goals as they address the quality of the research itself. But evaluators must know and understand the individual goals and purposes of each piece of arts-related research before they can adequately evaluate it.

KNOWLEDGE OF ARTS APPROACH

Current practice suggests at least two general arts approaches in arts-related research (Finley, 2003; Kerry-Moran, 1998). First, arts-related research as product: indicating that research results are communicated in an artistic format (i.e., readers' theater, data poem, collage, rap, etc.). Arts-related research taking this approach has obvious and apparent goals that are communicated and achieved through an artistic representation. Thus, a piece of arts-related research intended to inspire activism and consequently provoking its audience achieves its major goal. A second approach is arts-related research as process or methodology, in which the researcher and/or participants use an artistic format to develop, explore, analyze, or collect data. A nursing student studying women of childbearing age who are diagnosed with multiple sclerosis might compose poems as one way of exploring emergent themes. The poems are successful if they serve the researcher's purpose of informing her scholarship. Just as creative dramatics is designed to give participants particular experiences rather than to create a polished performance, process-oriented arts-informed research uses artistic formats to frame and enrich the research process rather than to create an artistic product. Of course there are many variations, and perhaps most arts-related inquiry is a combination of the two; however, an arts approach does influence how something should be evaluated.

AUDIENCE

Lastly, the intended audience must be considered. Whether a piece is to be presented/performed for an audience of social scientists, the general public, students, research participants, or policymakers greatly influences the approach to artistic integrity (Meyer & Moran, 2005) and the forms and format through which the art/research is presented (Barone, 2003). Each person brings something to the table, and personal experiences, preferences, and long-standing beliefs shape what one sees or experiences when interacting with an artwork or a piece of arts-related research. Consequently, audience, and the biases and expectations the audience possesses, influence how arts-related research will be perceived, understood, and assessed.

For example, much of the arts-related research produced within academia is meant for an audience of social science researchers. Within the field of arts-based research, there has been considerable debate concerning the use of explanatory pieces to accompany arts-based work. Some scholars support such pieces as playing an important role in providing explanatory information and adding legitimacy to the arts-based research (Coe & Strachan, 2002; Feldman, 2003). Other artist/researchers have argued against these texts on the grounds that good art, and good arts-based research, stands on its own (Blumenfeld-Jones & Barone, 1997; Piirto, 2002).

This debate exists in part because of the audience. Social science researchers care about things such as methodology and theoretical orientation. At least some of these researchers feel inadequately prepared to fully engage with, or consider the quality of, pieces of arts-based work without knowledge of the research background and theoretical basis. It seems unlikely that similar concerns would be raised by a group of nonresearchers. Similarly, artists are often extremely discriminating participants of the arts, and their greater knowledge of the art field may result in higher expectations for artistic quality (Piirto, 2002). It also has been noted that a frequent aim of arts-related work is to persuade participant/viewers to take action, and audience characteristics greatly influence

what approaches and presentations will be most persuasive. Different audiences have different needs, hold different expectations, and are best served through different approaches.

◆ What of the Layperson or Naïve Reader?

Thus far, this chapter has focused on more formal evaluations of arts-related work and approaches that a formal or "professional" evaluator should take. But what of the layperson or naïve reader who has little knowledge of arts-related work and no particular experience or background with art? How is this person to consider an arts-related piece as research, engage with the work, and consider its quality?

First, any person approaching arts-related work, novice or not, is well served by a willingness to consider inquiry as an organized quest for knowledge and understanding. Research holds many connotations, and although the term has been widely adopted by the arts-related research community, many of those connotations do not fit arts-related research. Broadly defined, research can include modes of inquiry with multiple interpretations and questions without definitive answers. It can also include works that seek to elucidate the emotive and ineffable aspects of human experience. Arts-related research is not meant to replace other forms of social science research but to contribute to the tools and methods through which social science can advance. Consequently, individuals newly encountering arts-related research should try to envision it as an additional way of "doing" social science research and not a replacement of any other method or framework.

Second, any person approaching arts-related work for the first time will do well in trying to engage with the work on an emotional level, remaining open to the feelings and impressions the work might invite. Arts-related research links the emotional with the scholarly and places emotional learning on even ground with scientific understanding. This is in direct contradiction to the notion that science, and by extension, good research, is devoid of emotion. Neumann's (2006) work on the role of emotion in scholarship indicates that research and scholarly work are an emotional and even passionate undertaking. Arts-related research brings emotion to the forefront of the research experience and celebrates the emotional and sensual in the research process. Researchers using the arts enlist a variety of the senses in seeking to comprehend and communicate human experiences. Qualitative researchers seek to understand things and people in their daily settings and to make interpretations based on the meanings people find in their own lives and activities (Denzin & Lincoln, 1994). Life is emotional, and art provides a means for communicating and exploring emotions and emotive things.

Finally, a reader unfamiliar with arts-related research can enlist the same questions or contexts of goals, arts approach, and audience when considering the quality of an arts-related research work. This might involve discussions with the artist/researcher, and this in itself is likely to enhance one's experience with the arts-related research piece. In addition, seeking out opportunities to explore arts-related works and actively engaging in arts experiences on a regular basis will help increase perceptivity and one's ability to think and "read" artistically.

◆ Scholarship? Art? Or Something in Between?

Arts-related research is a field in flux. Although many discussions focus on research

involving the arts as something between art and science, it is a different entity. As Finley (2003) states, "arts-based research may simply be one among many systemic studies of phenomena undertaken to advance human understanding, not exactly art and certainly not science" (p. 290). When a baby is born, we never speak of the child as being something "in between" the parents. Regardless of the characteristics inherited from mother and father, each child is a unique human being. Arts-related research is much the same. Although it retains characteristics of both art and social science research, it is different. Its purposes, aims, and methods cross disciplines and forge uncharted territory. Surely the means of determining quality and visions for evaluation should follow suit.

◆ Beyond in Between

Judging arts-related research may seem daunting. Rigid criteria and approaches tailored to either social science or art are outdated, for what is not entirely science is not fully art and is not really something in between. Arts-related research is still becoming. It is changing; it is unique, and as such it cannot be adequately evaluated through ill-fitting frameworks. The task at hand requires gaining perceptibilities and skills outside the research canon. It requires cross-disciplinary collaboration, conferring with and learning from artists who are masters of their craft and adept at creating works of art for audiences beyond the academy (Barone, 2002). It requires revisioning concepts like evaluation, and it requires a willingness to take risks. Judging arts-related research is daunting, but failure to define appropriate processes and criteria will only lead to the establishment of criteria by others less informed and less conscious of the challenges, peculiarities, and vision of this work.

◆ Note

1. My use of dramaturgy as metaphor should not be confused with the sociologist Erving Goffman's (2001) dramaturgical model of human life and communication. Goffman uses drama and theater as metaphors for analyzing human interaction. While I also use a theatrical metaphor, my focus is on the actions, responsibilities, roles, and preparation of dramaturgs.

◆ References

Barone, T. (2000). *Aesthetics, politics, and educational inquiry: Essays and examples.* Washington, DC: Peter Lang.

Barone, T. (2001). *Touching eternity: The enduring outcomes of teaching.* New York: Teachers College Press.

Barone, T. (2002). From genre blurring to audience blending: Reflections on the field emanating from an ethnodrama. *Anthropology & Education Quarterly, 33*(2), 255–267.

Barone, T. (2003). Challenging the educational imaginary: Issues of form, substance, and quality in film-based research. *Qualitative Inquiry, 9*(2), 202–217.

Barone, T., & Eisner, E. (1997). Arts-based educational research. In M. Jaeger (Ed.), *Complementary methods for research in education* (2nd ed., pp. 73–116). Washington, DC: American Educational Research Association.

Blumenfeld-Jones, D., & Barone, T. (1997). Interrupting the sign: The aesthetics of research texts. In J. Jipson & N. Paley (Eds.), *Daredevil research: Re-creating analytic practice* (pp. 83–107). New York: Peter Lang.

Coe, D., & Strachan, J. (2002). Writing dance: Tensions in researching movement or aesthetic experiences. *Qualitative Studies in Education, 15*(5), 497–511.

Cohen, R. (1988). *Theatre* (2nd ed.). Mountain View, CA: Mayfield Publishing Company.

Denzin, N. K., & Lincoln, Y. S. (1994). Introduction: Entering the field of qualitative research. In N. K. Denzin & Y. S. Lincoln (Eds.), *Handbook of qualitative research* (pp. 1–17). Thousand Oaks, CA: Sage.

Dewey, J. (1958). *Art as experience.* New York: Capricorn Books.

Donovan, L. M., Diaz, G. R., Salvatore, J., & Taylor, P. (2004, April). *Have script will travel: Reader's theater for social change.* Performance presented at the meeting of the American Educational Research Association, San Diego, CA.

Eisner, E. W. (1995). What artistically crafted research can help us understand about schools. *Educational Theory, 45*(1), 1–6.

Eisner, E. W. (1997). The promise and perils of alternative forms of data representation. *Educational Researcher, 26*(6), 4–10.

Eisner, E. W. (1998). *The enlightened eye: Qualitative inquiry and the enhancement of educational practice.* Upper Saddle River, NJ: Merrill.

Feldman, A. (2003). Validity and quality in self-study. *Educational Researcher, 32*(3), 26–28.

Finley, S. (2003). Arts-informed inquiry in QI: Seven years from crisis to guerilla warfare. *Qualitative Inquiry, 9*(2), 281–296.

Finley, S., & Finley, M. (1999). Sp'ange: A research story. *Qualitative Inquiry, 5*(3), 313–337.

Garoian, C. R. (1999). *Performing pedagogy.* Albany: State University of New York Press.

Goffman, E. (2001). The presentation of self in everyday life [Electronic version]. In J. M. Henslin (Ed.), *Down to earth sociology: Introductory readings* (11th ed., pp. 113–123). New York: Free Press.

Jonas, S., Proehl, G. S., & Lupu, M. (Eds.). (1997). *Dramaturgy in American theater: A source book.* Philadelphia, PA: Harcourt Brace College Publishers.

Kerry-Moran, K. J. (1998). *Secrets of the self: The reconceptualization of gender-role identity in contemporary Latter-Day Saint women.* Unpublished doctoral dissertation, Iowa State University, Ames.

Kerry-Moran, K. J. (2003, April). *Valuing, evaluating, and re-viewing the aesthetic.* Paper presented at the meeting of the American Educational Research Association, Chicago.

Knowles, J. G. (1997, March). *Marriage and/as/in/of/to perspective.* Painting presented at the annual meeting of the American Educational Research Association, Chicago.

Konzal, J., & Kerry-Moran, K. J. (1997). *Change of heart: An insider/outsider view*. Readers' theater presented at the annual meeting of the American Educational Research Association, March 1997, Chicago.

Lutterbie, J. H. (1997). Theory and the practice of dramaturgy. In S. Jonas, G. D. Proehl, & M. Lupu (Eds.), *Dramaturgy in American theater* (pp. 220–224). Philadelphia, PA: Harcourt Brace College Publishers.

Meyer, M. J., & Moran, K. J. (2005). Evidence and artistic integrity in arts-informed research: The place of artistic quality. *Arts & Learning Research Journal, 21*(1), 37–62.

Neumann, A. (2006). Professing passion: Emotion in the scholarship of professors at research universities. *American Educational Research Journal, 43*(3), 381–424.

Norris, J. (2000). Drama as research: Realizing the potential of drama in education as a research methodology. *Youth Theatre Journal, 14,* 40–51.

Piirto, J. (2002). The question of quality and qualifications: Writing inferior poems as qualitative research. *Qualitative Studies in Education, 15*(1), 431–445.

43

MONEY WORRIES

Tackling the Challenges of
Funding Arts-Related Research

◆ Ross Gray and Ardra L. Cole

N o handbook on research methodologies would be complete without at least a nod to money matters. But because the "starving artist" phenomenon is just as apt a description of researchers who variously incorporate the arts into their work, we did not see ourselves writing a guide to successful procurement of pots of money; nor did we imagine writing an issues-based essay on the "whys," "wherefores," and "whethers" of seeking funding for alternative genre research.[1] Rather, we were more interested in getting a sense of the overall funding picture in the small but growing international community of artist-researchers.

Although we both have had some success in finding money to support our arts-related projects, we came to our first planning meeting worried. Did we know enough about funding issues to write this chapter? Acquiring funding is a struggle, and the pathways we have chosen have not always been straightforward or easy. The rejections have been many. Maybe other social scientists have strategies that work better? Maybe funding is more accessible in other countries? Surely somebody else must know the secrets to making money flow on demand.

We sent out a call for help via e-mail, asking what strategies others have used to try to garner support for their projects. Would they share with us their rejections and successes, along with comments they have received from reviewers? We heard back from 22 researchers from around the world, most of them prolific scholars and seasoned veterans in linking research and the arts.[2] It was quickly apparent that we were not alone in our struggles to find funding. We read many comments and stories that revealed an unwelcoming political and academic context slow to flow funds to support arts-related research. Below are three examples of such comments from our respondents.

Funding is extremely hard to find. The federal government mostly only funds quantitative or mixed method design studies, and private corporations have been hit hard by the recession.

We have a system here where large grant requests that may be attractive sources for faculty go to centralized university committees in a pre-proposal evaluation. The university then selects which faculty can apply for funding. I have never been selected to submit my work, and the reasons are always tied to comments like "This is interesting scholarship but not research" and "How will you measure improvements?"

We were thrilled to be invited to make a special presentation to the funding agency. This was a really big team grant, and they'd short-listed us and expressed interest in our arts[-related] approaches. But our expectations for being well received were misplaced. We dramatized our introductory remarks, trying to spice things up and make the presentation consistent with our program of innovation. It was about the worst audience you could hope for. Not a flicker of response across their impassive faces. And then the same old questions started in a consistently hostile tone. The underlying question was whether this should be counted as real research. We were there for over an hour, but we knew after 10 minutes that they had no intention of funding us.

So this is where we begin—with the acknowledgement that funding is a challenge. We could go on for a long time in this chapter about this hard luck reality, moan and complain with complete justification. But we choose to move on to a consideration of how alternative genre researchers have been able to survive, sometimes thrive, in a predominantly hostile environment. There are lessons to be learned. And positive changes in the making.

◆ *Bringing in the Money*

One of the strategies commonly described by researchers incorporating the arts into their work is diverting funds from other research projects or nonresearch sources. For example, "We're now using a little funding from an actual community project to assist with our research work."

Sometimes researchers use money from a conventional research project to support their more innovative work. One of our respondents finally succeeded in obtaining funding for a project by including it "as part of a very large proposal where the arts [-related] details were well hidden." Other researchers conducted conventional projects but then communicated findings through the arts without asking their funders for permission. For example

I've always couched my research proposals in terms of conventional social science—it's only the written end-products that have taken on fictional or other alternative forms. As long as there's a conventional academic report as well, the funding agencies don't care.

Researchers wrote to us about being strategic about which competitions they decided to enter. One person commented, "I go around the system by applying for small grants." Others reported getting most of their support within their academic institutions and avoiding seeking external funds where they thought the odds of success were low. For example, "at the department and college levels I've been able to generate some research dollars, but for the most part the corporate and foundation grantors are hesitant to give money for arts-based research." Some researchers keep their expectations for funding low, pursuing only the avenues that seemed most promising. "Generally, we don't apply for many grants or get much money. We tend to only apply where we think people will be sympathetic to our approaches."

Several respondents noted that they had been able to be more successful in obtaining funds as time went on and they developed a reputation for their work. They stressed the importance of creating a context where people controlling money can feel safe in investing in arts-related projects. For example

My motto is to persevere, and when I get turned down, I learn from it and try again. It helps to start small, have some success, and build incrementally. People respond well to completing research and disseminating it. Once you have a record, it is easier to get the funding.

Another said

Track record is the number one concern for reviewers. So as long as you can demonstrate that you have had success in

obtaining funding and are a productive scholar, they seem more willing to support you. Going back to the same agency also seems helpful. If they awarded you before and you produced "good results," they seem inclined to want to build on that.

Given that the major pots of research money are often not easily accessible to arts-related researchers, there sometimes may need to be a greater reliance on the good will of individuals who control smaller pots of money and exercise power. One of our respondents described how important it is to cultivate such relationships.

X provides most of the money for my work. So I thank him by name in any publications, give him copies of my publications with his name highlighted, invite him to my performances, keep him informed of how the productions went, who and how many attended, where it was presented, etc.

Several of the researchers who wrote to us noted that they had received funds from private foundations. Although foundations vary in size and mode of operation, they are more likely than scientific research organizations to be controlled by one or a few individuals. One respondent described how he pursued a wealthy patron over many months, sending her written materials and videotapes, phoning her at the odd hours she requested, and staging a special performance for the benefit of her and her family. When she eventually provided a smaller-than-hoped-for donation, the researcher was chagrined to overhear her laughing comment to a colleague that she gave the money because "he was such a good beggar."

One enterprising research team consistently approached local individuals and organizations for support for arts-related projects. After seemingly exhausting this strategy, they decided to raise the stakes.

> We wrote a list of all agencies, members of health services and government offices who hadn't contributed or supported our health promotion research and then leaked it to a friendly news agency. Each individual and agency was approached with the potential of their non-support of our work being made public, and surprise, surprise most of them made good. . . . It isn't something we'd advise trying more than once.

Most of the researchers who wrote to us did not attempt to secure private sector funding for their work. Several did explore the possibilities and were successful, but not without some harrowing experiences along the way. One researcher described how he had to turn down the requests of pharmaceutical company representatives to insert the names of their cancer drugs into dramatic scripts. And how he subsequently ended up in the middle of a controversy where sponsoring pharmaceutical companies attempted to set up product displays at public performances against the wishes of local support groups. And then there was the following scenario from another respondent, likely much more entertaining to read about than to live through.

> We got a major brewery to provide funding for our research into clinical experiences of alcohol abuse. They provided free alcohol for the intermissions and were keen to promote a safe-drinking message. On the other hand, and not surprisingly, the health agencies dealing with alcohol recovery temporarily withdrew their support for the project. The local police services became the circuit breaker—giving penalty-free alcohol breath tests to audience members and showing how alcohol-impaired individuals believed they'd

not drunk enough to be over the safe limit. Health agencies provided counseling advice and health information literature during these intermission events.

◆ *Paying Our Own Way*

Although many of the researchers we heard from found ways to access project money, others did most of the financing themselves, or were able to do their work without much financial expenditure. Sometimes the costs of being funded, including threats to artistic integrity, outweighed the benefits of support.

> One reviewer wanted there to be a more upbeat ending to the tragic stories [of the participants]. Was I to rewrite/fabricate an upbeat ending to the play or keep the drama as it really happened to these adolescents? I opted for the latter.

Securing external funding most often involves having to wait a considerable time for project implementation. Researchers have to balance the satisfaction of moving the creative process forward with the possible implications for their own pocketbooks.

> Out of pocket costs for one project were due to me not thinking far enough in advance. This taught me not to be too spontaneously "inspired" and to not try and work too quickly to put up an arts-based research project, but to plan at least 18 months in advance.

A few researchers wrote that they had no funding for their projects, but that this was not a problem for them due to other positive circumstances.

> I have neither sought nor received research funding. I have been fortunate to have had support from publishers over the years, and all of my art-based

research is the basis for what I do in my books, essays, lectures, etc.

One researcher felt that she could never have undertaken her arts-related project if she had been in a full-time academic position, where it would have been difficult to find both funding and time for the work. But she nevertheless found it ironic that she was unpaid for her labor.

I was unpaid as the primary person developing the exhibit. So, here I was going around the country talking about how odd it was that my mother made wedding dresses over 50 years for about $500 total . . . And I was, with every step, mirroring those same relations. It was the only way of getting the work done. I was in a couple relationship at the time and would not have been able to make this grand gesture outside of that financial context.

Sometimes researchers' need to create took precedence over the material conditions of their labor. They did what they needed to do to support their creative process and lived as best they could while they were doing it.

I did most of my early work, and much of my most interesting work, while living for seven years in a microscopic, one bedroom rented condo with peeling paint, temperamental plumbing, and an oven that didn't work. Steinbeck stuff.

While it is unfortunate that more financial support is not available, artist-researchers often go into debt with their wide eyes open, preferring to pay their own way than to compromise their work or turn away from what they most want to achieve.

I went into debt for about two years by paying for our project. The total cost of the project was $25,000 . . . I do plan on

funding another project like this in the future with my own money. I don't know if the projects will ever pay off in any monetary value, but it will give me personal satisfaction in pursuing my dreams in higher education.

Another commented

Often the costs cannot be anticipated or easily described to fit budget lines or justification required by funding agencies so you do end up out-of-pocket a lot. Having said that, however, it is also true that in our first large (and successful) grant proposal we included a budget for shopping, studio space, construction materials, etc.

◆ *Things Are Getting Better*

Although the environment for arts-related research has been predominantly difficult, there are signs that this is changing, at least in some circumstances. Many individuals using arts-related approaches to research have been able to develop their own programs over time, building a sense of credibility for themselves and for the field. "I have now gained a credible research reputation within my college and am given an annual research/creative activity budget for my work."

I was heartened when a reviewer of one of my grant proposals made a point of acknowledging my "success" in using arts-based methods to challenge the status quo in qualitative research methodology.

With the visible growth of arts-related research over the past decade, institutional administrators are more likely to see alternative genre work as legitimate, sometimes resulting in their fair-minded support of individual scholars.

The recent chairs of our department, as well as the dean, have been fairly responsive to the case I've made that alternative research in the social sciences doesn't have access to the financial largesse available to science, math, etc., and so requires institutional support.

One researcher described her experience at a recent qualitative, arts-focused research conference in Georgia, commenting how she became aware that there is now a generation of successful arts-influenced researchers available to mentor students. And a collective track record of funded projects and publications has been laid down over time, establishing the legitimacy of the field, and making it much more possible for up and coming researchers to be competitive for funds.

There also have been some remarkable successes in recent times, where arts-informed researchers have secured major funding from mainstream scientific organizations. One of us (Ardra with coresearcher Maura McIntyre) received a large grant to tour an exhibit related to Alzheimer's disease across Canada, gathering new data along the way. The second phase of the project also received substantial funding from the same social science research funding agency. The other (Ross) received funding from a very conservative cancer research organization to evaluate a research-based drama about issues facing couples after prostate cancer treatment. And at the Centre for Arts-Informed Research at the University of Toronto, with which we are both affiliated, several graduate students and postdoctoral researchers have received external funding to develop arts-related research programs. Such stories are islands of hope in the larger sea of unfriendliness. But every year there are more such stories/islands. Will reports like the ones below ever become commonplace?

I was largely unsuccessful in receiving grants for arts-based and creative research projects. Then we received two grants. What is really amazing to me is that after so much rejection, the reviews for both these successful grants were glowing.

In our most recent successful large-scale funding award one reviewer described our "demonstrated commitment to innovative ways of dissemination" as "the major strength of the proposal."

◆ *What Can Be Done?*

How can the momentum that is building for arts-related research continue to grow? What are some steps that will lead to greater acceptance from peers and funders, and that will provide easier access to money necessary for this work? Here are our best guesses:

- The efforts at networking that have been developing among artist-researchers need to continue and intensify so that researchers can learn from each other and create more group visibility. A strong chorus has a better chance of being heard louder and further than several solo voices.

- At conferences, in written correspondence and publications, and in everyday interactions within faculties and institutions, artist-researchers need to promote the importance and relevance of alternative genre research.

- Research units/organizations with an explicit focus on the integration of research and the arts make arts-related research visible and viable within academic and research institutions. The art-research community needs more such structures.

- Experienced artist-researchers have important roles in shaping future decision making via serving on grant review panels, tenure and promotion committees, student award committees, editorial boards, and so on. The acceptance of alternative genre research is linked to the willingness and commitment of senior faculty to advocate within formal structures/processes.

- Organizations/institutions concerned with arts and research (such as the Society for Arts in Health Care or the Arts-Based Educational Research Special Interest Group or AERA) could produce documents that detail processes, standards, agreements, and values that inform the work of artist-researchers. Similarly, artist-researchers could make a commitment to publishing works that focus on epistemological and methodological issues associated with arts-related research. The existence of such documents will help to provide greater legitimacy for researchers seeking approval for research proposals and ethics protocols.

- Building on their successes, experienced artist-researchers could develop grant-writing workshops to inform students and new scholars, as well as funding organizations, about how arts-related research is conducted, how it can be articulated clearly, and why/how it should be funded.

- Artist-researchers, particularly those who have had success with funding agencies, could advocate for special competitions that focus on the linkage between research and the arts.

◆ Wrapping Up

We believe there will be better times ahead for artist-researchers seeking funding for their work. As noted above, there are encouraging signs and a strengthening momentum generated by first-wave social scientists. It is even possible to imagine a day when arts-related research could be a fully accepted and routinely funded feature of mainstream social science. We want to pause, however, and consider the price of too much success. Drawn as we are to the fringes and to the excitement of making things appear out of thin air, we are well aware of the significant disadvantages associated with becoming mainstream. Nipping at the heels of institutional acceptance are demands for standardization and other regulatory measures of proof that have the potential to undermine the creative thrust of arts-related work. We thus seek a perfect balance in which systemic structures support our work but do not infringe too much on the creative process and the excitement of artistic work. Perhaps we ask too much?

◆ Notes

1. We recommend Julianne Cheek's (2000) chapter, "An Untold Story? Doing Funded Qualitative Research," in the *Handbook of Qualitative Research* for both guidelines and an excellent discussion of issues related to funding of qualitative research.

2. We thank those who so generously shared with us their stories, strategies, and standpoints.

◆ References

Cheek, J. (2000). An untold story? Doing funded qualitative research. In N. K. Denzin & Y. Lincoln (Eds.), *Handbook of qualitative research* (2nd ed., p. 401–420). Thousand Oaks, CA: Sage.

44

USING AN ARTS METHODOLOGY TO CREATE A THESIS OR DISSERTATION

◆ J. Gary Knowles and Sara Promislow

There is a certain pleasure in leaving one of the first footprints of the day on the sand of a sun-, wind-, and water-washed deserted beach. Similarly, the act of making one of the first morning prints on fresh snow laid in a forest during a quiet, snow-falling night embodies a kind of magic. So it is that opportunities to forge new ground in the academy create similar pleasures for new and more experienced researchers alike. Traversing uncharted territories opens up exciting new possibilities. The growing number of English language, artful theses and dissertations completed over the last 15 years is witness to this (for a very small sampling see Knowles, Luciani, Cole, & Neilsen, 2007; Knowles, Promislow, & Cole, in press). In pockets of creativity and artful energy in far-flung places and disciplines there are new and more experienced scholars making space for the arts to inform scholarly work. Such new work, invariably, contributes to the development of artful methodologies, strengthening

Author's Note: This chapter includes information gleaned from conversations Antoinette Oberg had with Thomas Barone, Noreen Garman, Rita Irwin, and Carl Leggo about their experiences and insights in supervising arts-inspired educational research.

and expanding existing communities of arts-related researchers around the globe.

We write this chapter with two main audiences in mind: The first is new researchers, usually graduate students, who are making their way through the labyrinth of institutional requirements and an array of methodologies but have a growing interest in arts-related qualitative research (we also expect that more advanced peers will gain some solace here as well); the second is university faculty who may potentially support the work of new researchers infusing the arts into their research. In this chapter we explore contexts, processes, issues, and challenges associated with developing artful theses and dissertations. To do so, we draw on reflexive accounts by emerging artist-researchers and their supervisors. These comprise excerpts from some of the chapter contributions to *Creating Scholartistry: Imagining the Arts-Informed Thesis or Dissertation* (Knowles, Promislow, & Cole, in press).

◆ What Do Arts-Related Works Look Like?

Alma Fleet (in press) from Macquarie University in Australia describes her first impressions after browsing through a dozen or so theses on the occasion of a visit to the Centre for Arts-Informed Research at the Ontario Institute for Studies in Education (of the University of Toronto). Since the mid-1990s more than 50 doctoral theses employing arts-related methodologies were completed under the guidance of scholars in several departments within the Institute:

> Physical format varied from the traditional (hard bound in strong red, navy blue, or apple green with single coloured lettering), presenting a solid academic front,

to those with small metaphoric individual messages on the cover or frontispiece, to those with fully illustrated covers creating an invitation to the reader to become involved in the text. . . . Opening pages led to a discovery of individuality in the Tables of Contents. For example, each piece included an analytic frame for an artistic piece, either independently or integrated in the body of the work, depending on the forms being used for representation. Page layouts moved from the straightforward to the poetic, with page placements and white space carrying particular messages, including the use of different fonts and iconic features to guide or challenge the reader.

Fleet's account speaks of the multiplicity of form and the multilayered nature of research indicative of arts-related theses, where researchers conform to the traditional text-based, bound form of the thesis or dissertation. There are also those who choose to include sound and visual CDs or DVDs (perhaps illustrating elements of the research, making data accessible, or providing some other complementary function). Sometimes these elements accompany more conventional work. Other researchers mount visual exhibitions and performances of various kinds, or develop radio or film documentaries or features or other media productions, and these become the thesis or dissertation itself. The ongoing debate about the extent to which these alternative art forms may be or are the thesis is far from being expressed. A central question relates to whether or not all arts-related scholarship needs to be translated into "book form."

Throughout the chapter, we refer to (and sometimes describe) a number of works. Nearly all of these authors choose to stay close to bound text. The examples are merely illustrative of the diversity of such graduate work in select disciplines. (They are, however, limited in displaying the range of forms/genre as well as procedural and representational possibilities.) Descriptions of three arts-related doctoral theses/dissertations (completed in three different countries) provide a glimpse of form and content.

Douglas Gosse's (2005a) award-winning thesis[1] *Breaking Silences: An Inquiry Into Identity and the Creative Research Process* incorporates an experimental novel-as-thesis (later, partly published as a trade book novel entitled *Jackytar;* Gosse, 2005b). Employing the genre of the *Bildungsroman* to write his fictional novel, Gosse explores intersectional identities in education along the lines of ethnicity, class, gender, sexual orientation, geographical location, language, culture, and disability. He problematizes notions of self, group, and community and gives voice to those often silenced. Like others, such as Dunlop (1999) and de Freitas (2003) before him, his work offers a model, guidance, and inspiration for scholars interested in writing a thesis as novel.

Christina Marín's (2005) research focused on how forms of theatre and performance give voice and agency to populations often marginalized and discounted. Her award-winning dissertation[2] *Breaking Down Barriers, Building Dreams: Using Theatre for Social Change to Explore the Concept of Identity With Latina Adolescents* employs techniques expressed in Theatre for Social Change and those derived from Theatre of the Oppressed (Boal, 1982) to explore concepts of language, immigration, and teenage pregnancy with a bilingual, youth theatre group in Phoenix, Arizona.

A groundbreaking thesis, unique in form and content, is Daria Loi's (2005) *Lavoretti per bimbi: Playful Triggers as Keys to Foster Collaborative Practices and Workspaces Where People Learn, Wonder, and Play.* It is a "thesis-as-suitcase" completed at the School of Management at the Royal Melbourne Institute of Technology University, Australia. A 13-kilogram, medium-sized, black, apparently well-traveled, cardboard suitcase filled with artifacts and text, Loi's work explores "how to foster organizational spaces where collaborative activities can be undertaken" (Loi, in press). It is about collaborative practices, participatory design processes, and the active involvement of people. The thesis-as-suitcase emerged from a goal to reach wide and diverse audiences, to embody theory and practice, and to enable collaborative practice through active engagement with the many, diverse elements of the work. Loi's suitcase has "written content and nontextual elements that use metaphorical,

Figure 44.1 A Thought per Day: My Traveling Inside a Suitcase.
SOURCE: Photo by Daria Loi.

tactile, audio and visual means to express meaning," specifically, employing visual images, CDs, found objects, game-like and sculptural elements, and gifts for readers.

Each of the three above-mentioned doctoral researchers came to the development of their scholarship with sound theoretical and practical groundings in their respective disciplines (education, English literature, and the literary arts; theatre/drama; architecture, design, and management). But they also came to the process with a vision and a determination to create a thesis or dissertation that, in process and representational form, expanded conventional notions of knowledge and knowing. Their acts of arts-related qualitative researching called upon a range of individual knowledge and experience and also demanded the support of peers and supervising faculty within their institutions.

It would be comforting to imagine that this kind of developmental work is plain sailing. But often it is not. In large institutions—even where the arts in qualitative research is supported by a cluster of faculty—it is not uncommon for thesis and dissertation proposals involving the arts in research to be rejected or watered down, or for the new researcher to flounder around in efforts to find a supervisor and supervising committee to support the work. More often than not these new researchers take on educative roles with prospective guides of their work before the thesis or dissertation gets underway.

◆ *Supportive Contexts?*

Putting aside the complexities of completing any thesis or dissertation, an artful thesis may be developed within the context of any university—and be sanctioned by it—where there are enough advocating or sympathetic scholars to comprise a supervising and examining committee. Such conditions exist at numerous universities within Canada, the United States, Australia, Great Britain, and Ireland, for instance. In this section we focus primarily on a few North American examples of contexts that support emerging scholars who decide to take roads less traveled.

The institutional contexts from which arts-related thesis and dissertation research have emerged comprise groups of like-inspired individuals—faculty and graduate students alike. In North America five contexts bear special mention primarily because of the volume of work supported or sponsored by them. Four are universities, although the first mentioned is a research organization comprised of like-minded scholars that, since the mid-1990s, has been a major source of support for many new and emerging scholars, many of whom work in relative isolation.

The Arts-Based Educational Research (ABER) Special Interest Group of the American Educational Research Association attracts international interest and membership. Graduate students and emerging scholars comprise a large segment of its membership. ABER "provides a community for those who view education through artistic lenses, who use a variety of arts-based methodologies, and who communicate understandings through diverse genres." It sponsors a variety of sessions, symposia, and workshops at the annual meeting of its parent body, as well as stand-alone conferences and publications, and is supported by a Listserv, Web site, and newsletter (http://abersig.org/). Each year it names and makes an award for outstanding dissertations. (There are similar, burgeoning special interest groups associated with conferences and research bodies of other disciplines, say sociology, visual sociology, anthropology, social work, for example.)

The A/R/Tography Research Group at the Faculty of Education, University of British Columbia, advocates a particular arts-related methodology collaboratively developed by visual artist Rita Irwin and her graduate students, many of whom are art educators (see Springgay, Irwin, & Kind, Chapter 7 in this volume). Faculty and students alike participate "through an ongoing process of art making . . . and writing not separate or illustrative of each other but interconnected and woven through each other to create additional and/or enhanced meanings" (http://m1.cust.educ.ubc.ca/Artography). Like other supportive contexts, the A/R/Tography group

> gather[s] together to work on publications, conference presentations, dissertations and theses, research projects and art exhibitions as a way of supporting one another's academic journey [which is seen as] . . . an integral part of creating and articulating an a/r/tographical methodology. (Springgay, de Cosson, & Irwin, in press)

Within the Department of Communication at the University of South Florida, Carolyn Ellis, Arthur Bochner, and colleagues have, over the last decade, created a context for alternative and arts-related qualitative research. They have fostered inquiry and scholarship at the intersection of literature, ethnography, autoethnography, narrative inquiry, and social and cultural theories. Their *Ethnographic Alternatives Series*, published by AltaMira Press, for example, provides a venue for new scholars to express elements of their creative scholarship. Recent dissertations from this context include: Moreman (2005), *Performativity and the Latina/o-White Hybrid Identity: Performing the Textual Self;* Curry (2005), *Communicating*

Collaboration and Empowerment: A Research Novel of Relationships With Domestic Violence Workers; Baglia (2003), *Building Masculinity: Viagra and the Performance of Sexual Health;* and Leoutsakas (2003), *The Orphan Tales: Real and Imagined Stories of Parental Loss.*

Graduate researchers associated with the Centre for Arts-Informed Research (CAIR) at the Ontario Institute for Studies in Education of the University of Toronto have produced a sizable body of work since the late 1990s. CAIR is a community of faculty and graduate students with a shared commitment to exploring, articulating, and supporting "alternative forms of qualitative research and representation which infuse elements, processes, and forms of the arts into scholarly work." The Centre sponsors colloquia, workshops, gallery exhibits, performances, seminars, and conference presentations. It also sponsors a book series and an online publication and is the academic home of funded research projects. One of the Centre's goals "is to provide a context for promoting exciting, innovative, 'scholartistry' that forges new shapes of academic discourse" (http://home.oise.utoronto.ca/~aresearch).

The Image and Identity Research Collective (IIRC; www.iirc.mcgill.ca) was initiated by Sandra Weber (Concordia University) and Claudia Mitchell (McGill University). Its collaborators include faculty and graduate students from both institutions and from other universities, as well as independent artists and researchers. Collectively they share "an interest in developing interdisciplinary, image-based research methodologies as well as exploring artistic forms of representation for the Humanities and Social Sciences . . ." (Derry, 2003, pp. 24–25).

To imply that bold, creative, arts-related research only takes place in these contexts is incorrect: These particular university contexts and the Special Interest Group are merely indicative of the availability of sustained support and advocacy for the arts in qualitative research. Many authors in this *Handbook* teach regular or occasional arts-related graduate courses and workshops, relative to their disciplines and interests, and likely have institutional colleagues who support alternative qualitative researching. In addition, various research organizations and conferences offer occasional methodology courses and workshops. To become aware of conferences, exhibitions, and publications that support alternative scholarship is to also network with like-minded new and experienced scholars. Reference lists associated with the chapters of this volume are a good place to start because they evidence glimpses of intellectual paths taken by respective scholars.

New scholars who know in advance that they want to do arts-related research locate supportive institutional contexts and supporting faculty before making graduate school applications. But the reality is that most new researchers do not have such foreknowledge. Most of those who come to use the arts in their qualitative research do so because of inspiration gleaned from peers, networks of various kinds, academic texts, performances, attending conferences, and simply by happenstance. This *Handbook* also provides a range of support and perspectives to enable arts-related researchers and further develop the expression of knowledge and methodologies involving the arts. The resources of the *Handbook* and the various contexts previously mentioned are mere starting points to help emerging scholars prepare for their arts-related researching.

◆ New Scholars Employing the Arts?

Sara's doctoral research journey provides some insights into how individuals and contexts

serve to inspire and support the use of arts-related, qualitative research methods. In her thesis, *A Collage of Borderlands: Arts-Informed Life Histories of Childhood Immigrants and Refugees Who Maintain Their Mother Tongue* (Promislow, 2005), she explores the experiences of four adults in and through languages, cultures, and identities. The research representation includes literary genres, scholarly discourse, and the art form collage. Sara's initial exposure to arts-related research was through advanced qualitative research courses with Ardra Cole at the University of Toronto. Without possessing a substantial background in the arts, her curiosity was piqued and she became involved in the activities of the Centre for Arts-Informed Research. Through the Centre's seminars and events and, later, becoming the editor of the Centre's online publication, *arts-informed*, Sara was inspired to infuse arts-informed approaches into the life history method, convinced that the arts would contribute to her work in process and representation.

Decisions about the influence of an art form may be complex, but they may also be inspired by happenstance events or circumstances. Three brief examples suffice. Sara started with the notion of employing diverse textual genres to explore and represent research participants' experiences. At an academic conference workshop (Butler-Kisber, Bodone, Meyer, & Stewart, 2003) she learned about and experimented with the art form collage. With her supervisor's encouragement and support she analyzed collected information through collage making. Eventually the collages became integral to the research analysis and representation.

I had gained much insight and understanding through the art form collage and was able to move forward with the conceptualization of my research analysis, with the images I juxtaposed at times when I was unable to move

Figure 44.2 *Reconciling Worlds,* Collage, Mixed Media, 11 × 9.6 in.

SOURCE: Sara Promislow, 2005.

forward with words. My participants' experiences defied words and fixed categories. Linear analysis served only to block my way. In order to do justice to their experiences I knew that I needed to go beyond . . . habitual linear thinking and take risks. (Promislow & Cole, in press)

Lynn Fels's (1999) thesis *In the Wind Clothes Dance on a Line: Performative Inquiry as a Research Methodology* employs performative writing to conceptualize performance as an action/site of learning and research. Based on her experiences as a drama educator, Fels examined the possibilities of performance such as role drama, visualizations, and improvisation for learning and research. Wanting her thesis representation to reflect the unique qualities of her research, Fels struggled to find form. "I didn't want to explain what happened. . . . I wanted to textually perform moments of learning that emerged from my performative work with my students" (Fels, Linds, & Purru, in press). After 6 months of dwelling with her thesis, unable to write, Fels had a breakthrough during a lecture by Jaques Daignault. Inspired by him she felt "[I am] not alone. This too is possible." Her difficulties with writing transformed into the challenge of "writing a performative text that listens, interplays between absence and presence, and welcomes the not yet known."

performative inquiry
a mapping-exploration of space-moments of
   learning
through which action-process occurs utterly
   through form and
simultaneously through the destruction of form
chaos disorder absence possibility
unknown world(s) not yet realized
and in a moment of hesitation (Fels, 1999)

Sharon Sbrocchi's (2005) thesis *Remembering Place: Domicide and a Childhood Home* "focuses on the relationship between self and place in a rapidly urbanizing world" (p. iii). Sbrocchi's exploration of childhood experiences of a place (which now no longer exists) is structured within and around a simple device—a series of pencil lines on paper, "mind maps" that capture her and friends' memories of their childhood neighborhood. Sharon developed a methodological device and form serendipitously during a meeting with her supervisor. They discussed her childhood home. "Then in mid-conversation, [my supervisor] suggested I draw a 'sense of place' map. 'Right now. At this moment!' He handed me a sharpened pencil. I looked perplexed. 'Now?' I asked. I drew it with ease. I know the place" (Sbrocchi, in press). So began an articulation of place. Drawing the map precipitated a flow of memories and helped Sbrocchi "focus a broad range of stories, emotions and general information from within. . . . It took less than two minutes to draw the memory map and three more years to complete the thesis." Moving back and forth from the mind map, Sbrocchi's thesis became

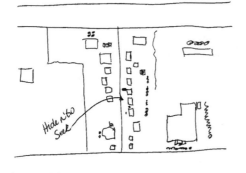

Figure 44.3 Map 16. Zorra Street Memory Map: *Hide 'n' Go Seek.*

SOURCE: Sharon Rylko Sbrocchi, 2001. Reprinted with permission.

a multilayered text that also included photographs and archival material.

◆ To Employ the Arts?

Because of the extensive commitment of energy required, arts-inspired inquiry is something researchers choose to do; they do not take it up by default as the single available methodological possibility (as was often the case in the past with conventional, empirical research). Are the arts seen as a possibility for enhancing scholarship and research? If so: Is the research process and the mode of telling the research story the most effective form given the subject matter, audience, and purpose of the research? It may be appropriate to infuse the arts into researching when

- it is congruent with one's worldview, an acknowledgment that knowing through the arts is more than mere knowledge about the arts;

- it makes inherent sense given the focus and substance of the research;

- it fits one's artistic skills and expertise;

- there is an obvious potential to develop exceptional insights and knowledge; and

- it presents opportunities to reach audiences that are not normally very accessible to academic researchers.

◆ How Is It Possible?

To conduct research infused by the arts is to break out of the conventional (as defined by each qualitative research tradition or orientation). It is also to be inspired by the arts, especially, with regard to process and representation. Such inspiration may be serendipitous (see Knowles & Thomas, 2000). To engage in the process of this work is to act as a visual artist, poet, painter, photographer, dancer, dramatist, performer, and so on. Process is informed not only by bringing to bear one's creativity given that art form but also by knowing how it is that artists in that sphere or genre may work. It is about incorporating both the inspiration of an art and the processes that an artist might use. For example, how does the fiction writer work? How does a fiction writer inform herself about the work she is about to do? What are some of the processes involved in readying to write, developing storylines, plot? How does the photographer work? Is it possible to get inside the photographer's mind to bring to bear the intellectual frames for shooting? And the filmmaker? How does the playwright work? How does the dancer work?

These questions help reveal the essence of what it means to do arts-related research. And so, this knowledge of process is infused into the researching procedures in ways that make inherent sense and enhance the possibilities for gathering a different quality of information and interpreting and presenting it creatively. Although the very questions we ask reveal our orientations, the various chapters of Parts II and III of this *Handbook* provide a sense of the possibilities.

Is it necessary for researchers infusing the arts into their work to consider themselves "artists"? Being a researcher who draws on the arts implies a willingness to come to know the art form (or forms) in some depth and to the degree that makes inherent sense for the purposes of the project at hand. For instance, in preparation for researching there may be no preordained "arts" coursework. Nor are there "standard measures of artistic abilities." Certainly there are no set paths to becoming competent as an arts-related researcher—although one may do "coursework" or seek guidance from practicing artists of various kinds (who may well be located beyond the confines of academic institutions). Ultimately, knowing how

artists of a specific genre engage with and represent subject matter is paramount. To become a researcher who fuses the arts into research processes and representations is to possess a creativity and artfulness. It is to have a willingness to be creative and to not be bounded by traditions of academic discourse and research processes but, rather, to be grounded in them.

Teresa Luciani's (2006) thesis *On Women's Domestic Knowledge and Work: Growing Up in an Italian Kitchen* explores the knowledge and work of Italian immigrant women through her experiences as a second-generation immigrant and the experiences of the women in her family. The work comprises autobiographical and fictional short stories, lively with detail, affording readers vivid, vicarious experiences of growing up and being a woman in an Italian immigrant family in Canada. Integral and important to the development of her work, Luciani expanded and honed her skills as a short story writer through creative writing courses that afforded critical feedback from a professional writer.

To complete a thesis or dissertation is a formidable task in itself, and new scholars and their supervisors working with arts-related approaches face additional challenges that make the thesis/dissertation journey all the more full of uncertainty and surprises. Risk taking, courage, openness to unknowing, and tolerance for ambiguity—on the part of both emerging scholars and their supervisors—are prerequisites for developing an arts-related project. Securing a supportive supervisor (and committee) is not always an easy task for new scholars. As for completing such a project, there are no models and maps to follow. Indeed, research projects drawing on the arts are likely to be entirely idiosyncratic endeavors, especially with regard to process, form, and representation.

Creativity is at the heart of the enterprise. This may be scary for a novice researcher unsure of her step and whose first socialized action is to seek reassurance from completed theses already stacked neatly on university library shelves. "It is not easy to work against the grain. The usual tensions get tenser, and new ones add sparks. Responses at times vary wildly" (Norman, in press). Such circumstances may even evoke nervousness on the part of a novice supervisor who questions: "How do I judge the work?" "What will my colleagues think?" and "Will 'the institution' approve?" Pat Thompson says of the experience of the first arts-infused thesis she supervised: "I was worried about the conservatism of the university in considering alternative thesis forms" (Baskwell & Thompson, in press), a not uncommon position. Those forging new ground will need to be able to respond to the question "How is this research?" and to take on an educative role with some committee members or faculty.

◆ To Supervise?

> The journey towards becoming a helpful, challenging and creative supervisor of arts-informed inquiry seems to me to contain two elements. Firstly, there is the essence of being an empowering, nurturant, informed supervisor, and secondly, there is the extension of that role into a way of being in relationship to a graduate student interested in alternative representation. (Fleet, in press)

Supervisors come to the role with different perspectives. In his role as thesis supervisor, for example, Gary is interested in supporting new researchers who show confidence in research traditions that intersect with his own research expertise (such as phenomenology, life history, ethnography, narrative inquiry, or, say, a qualitative interview study) and his disciplinary interests, broadly defined. He gets excited when new researchers have visions of

stepping out of their comfort zones and of forging new approaches to the topic at hand. In essence this means that creativity and confidence are forefront. He sees one of his roles as being a supportive curator and guide. The fine line walked is between that of nurturer of creativity and conceptual editor. Ultimately, though, the emerging researcher has to be trusted.

Antoinette Oberg has a unique perspective. Her pedagogy and coursework orientation, "inquiry-without-method," is productive for supporting artful inquiries:

> This pedagogy begins with the question, What interests you? and proceeds by means of an ongoing series of written exchanges between teacher and student as the student seeks to articulate her not-yet-imagined interest. Each piece of student writing calls for (and calls forth) an imaginative response from the teacher intended to provoke a further act of imagination by the student. (Oberg & Cranmer, in press)

An illustration of the potential of Oberg's pedagogy in supervision is her work with Laura Cranmer (2002), whose master's degree thesis, *DP's Colonial Cabaret*, is a two-act play. The action follows DP's struggle with substance abuse and ends with a confrontation between Anomie and Mother Bond, two characters competing for his allegiance. Led by Oberg's question "What are you in the midst of?" Laura explored forces that contributed to her identity as a colonized 'Namgis woman. With Oberg's initial "patient, non-judgmental acceptance of whatever students write," she opened "a space of possibility for creative processes to unfold" (Oberg & Cranmer, in press). Her ongoing affirmations enabled Cranmer to be confident in pushing the boundaries of her comfort zone. Oberg's reflective questions inspired Cranmer to move more deeply and explore alternative possibilities for the representation of pain and hurt. "The process of writing the play became [Cranmer's] way of rewriting, in essence, purging [her] blood and bone of the colonial script."

Bronwyn Davies "provoked, inspired, cajoled and challenged" doctoral student Suzanne Gannon. Of this Gannon said, "Most of all, she trusted me. Sometimes she frustrated me. Sometimes I wanted simple answers, shortcuts or linear thinking. She answered my questions clearly and promptly, but always refusing binaries and clichés" (Davies & Gannon, in press). Gannon's (2003) work is an exploration of the possibilities of poststructural theory in writing and research. Her own textual performances and processes of writing are at the root of her inquiry and its representation. The work weaves creative and analytical genres of writing around each other in textual performances. Davies recognized that Gannon began as a practiced writer and saw her role "as lending active support for [Gannon's] initiatives; as giving strong encouragement for thinking outside the usual bounds of what a 'thesis' might be . . . what a thesis will look like." Integral to the supervisory role, Davies facilitates "collective biography" workshops where she and her students write and share memory stories and learn a range of writing skills through collaborative projects. "Arts-informed practices such as voice work, assemblage and visual arts practice became a part of our way of working together."

One aspect of supervision not discussed thus far is the role of external examiner. Many North American universities do not require such a role for the completion of master's and doctoral degrees; however, in other national contexts it is not the case. Most Canadian and Australian universities (in addition to English language universities in many other countries), for example, require the work of a supervising committee to be supplemented by an external examiner's report. Such a report makes a critique of the research, providing an examining committee with an outsider's point of view. It highlights the strengths, weaknesses, and contributions of the work and is usually written by "an expert from the field," someone of renown. A challenge for new supervisors is to help locate suitable scholars matched with the research being examined. Given that their contribution to the successful completion of a thesis or dissertation is pivotal, this reasonable match is essential.

◆ *There Are Issues and Obstacles?*

There are numerous obstacles and challenges to those choosing to incorporate the arts into their research methodology. Some are individual and others institutional. Individual obstacles and challenges include

- becoming confident about stepping into the unknown;

- melding research methods with processes and representations;

- developing related artistic skills and knowledge; and

- having the energy, time, skill, and technical and, perhaps, financial means associated with "doing" the work.

Others obstacles and challenges are institutional. They include

- locating a suitable supervisor who resonates with arts-related approaches who can, perhaps, suspend judgment and trust the process; and

- negotiating real and imagined institutional constraints such as perceptions that the form, structure, and medium for graduate thesis and dissertation work is solidified and preordained by universities.

The persistent dominance of conventional views of empirical research is, perhaps, the greatest obstacle to arts-related research. Despite the fact that alternative research methodologies proliferate, books are available on arts-related inquiry, and journals increasingly publish articles employing alternative approaches to qualitative research, incoming graduate school students enter with limited notions of what constitutes research or knowledge of the range of epistemologies and methods possible. In some institutions, where faculty actively support arts-related research, there are concerted attempts to make known alternative possibilities, but for the most part, this is sporadic. In other places, students may become independently aware of arts-related research and seek out supportive faculty. In the latter cases, faculty may not promote arts-related work either because they think it not credible or appropriate at their institution or because they lack the expertise needed to supervise sound arts-related research. Consider, for example, a music professor's wonderings about the arts and research

> [Arts-related inquiry] seems somewhat . . . subversive. . . . Research needs to be systematic. . . . There must be a sense of rigor, a clearly defined purpose and problem, a certain structure—an introduction, a literature review, a methodology and tangible results and conclusions, and all of those components linked through various substructures in the thesis . . . I mean, how can you hand in a thesis that's merely a series of stories? (Gouzouasis & Lee, in press)

Taken from a reconstructed conversation with Karen Lee (2004), a doctoral student (now graduated), Peter Gouzouasis (who, at the time, was "new" to the idea of arts-related research but now employs it himself) voices common concerns about alternative forms of dissertations that draw on the arts. The paradox is, however, that the very elements of traditional research and resulting theses that Gouzouasis implies are the "standards" for judgment are also the essential qualities of a thesis or dissertation informed by the arts. In other words, the hallmark qualities remain, but the process, structure, form, and representation may be quite diverse depending on the art genre involved. Possibilities abound because the range of methodologies available for new researchers has multiplied in recent decades. So, also, has the available literature within which to theoretically ground new innovative work.

◆ *Creation Completed?*

One of our hopes for this chapter is that it may assist in making it easier for emerging scholars to complete arts-inspired theses and dissertations. We see it as a reference point offering a checklist of sorts, highlighting relevant issues important for researchers to consider. In providing snapshots of what some arts-related research looks like, we are mindful of the myriad examples of innovative work completed and not acknowledged here. There is no one model to follow. It is evident that the distinguishing features of this work relate to the qualities of researchers: vision, perseverance, and commitment to form. There is support for arts-related work, whether it be in universities or professional/research networking organizations although, often, new researchers have their work cut out as they locate and often educate supervisors, and debate the value, process, structure, and form of their work.

The paths taken by arts-related researchers are largely idiosyncratic but often hinge on serendipity, exposure to other like-inspired scholars, grounding, or experience in the arts so that the art or arts become as a catalyst and vehicle for the work. To employ the arts in research is for the arts to make inherent sense in researchers' orientations and for the purposes of the work. New researchers may need to look beyond universities for opportunities to develop their familiarity and competence with art forms although questions about judgment of the place of the arts are likely to be highly debated. Concerns about judging the quality of theses are often concerns of thesis and dissertation supervisors who have to nurture and foster creativity in new researchers yet make decisions about quality—a demanding, difficult, and sometime confusing task. The ultimate criteria for judging the quality of arts-inspired theses and dissertations may be the responses of audiences to whom the work is directed. Perhaps this is the greatest challenge and hope for arts-related work whose authors are driven to make a difference.

◆ Notes

1. Gosse's doctoral thesis received the Arts-Based Educational Research (ABER) Outstanding Dissertation of the Year Award for 2005.

2. Marín's doctoral dissertation received the Arts-Based Educational Research (ABER) Outstanding Dissertation of the Year Award for 2006.

◆ References

Baglia, W. J. (2003). *Building masculinity: Viagra and the performance of sexual health.* Unpublished doctoral dissertation, University of South Florida, Tampa.

Baskwell, J., & Thompson, P. (in press). Jane and Pat think and do: A basal reader. In J. G. Knowles, S. Promislow, & A. L. Cole (Eds.), *Creating scholartistry: Imagining the arts-informed thesis or dissertation.* Halifax, Nova Scotia, & Toronto, Ontario, Canada: Backalong Books & Centre for Arts-Informed Research.

Boal, A. (1982). *The theatre of the oppressed.* New York: Routledge Press.

Butler-Kisber, L., Bodone, F., Meyer, M., & Stewart, M. (2003). *Artful analysis and representation in qualitative inquiry using poetry, theatre, and collage.* AERA Pre-Conference Workshop, Chicago.

Cranmer, L. (2002). *DP's colonial cabaret.* Unpublished master's thesis, University of Victoria, British Columbia, Canada.

Curry, E. (2005). *Communicating collaboration and empowerment: A research novel of relationships with domestic violence workers.* Unpublished doctoral dissertation, University of South Florida, Tampa.

Davies, B., & Gannon, S. (in press). Hanging on and flying. In J. G. Knowles, S. Promislow, & A. L. Cole (Eds.). *Creating scholartistry: Imagining the arts-informed thesis or dissertation.* Halifax, Nova Scotia, & Toronto, Ontario, Canada: Backalong Books & Centre for Arts-Informed Research.

de Freitas, E. (2003). *The wrong shoe and other misfits: Fiction writing as reflexive inquiry within a private girls school.* Unpublished doctoral thesis, University of Toronto, Ontario, Canada.

Derry, C. (2003). An update and greetings from the Image and Identity Research Collective. *arts-Informed, 3*(1). Retrieved January 16, 2007, from http://home.oise.utoronto.ca/~aresearch/artsinformed3.pdf

Dunlop, R. (1999). *Boundary Bay: A novel as educational research.* Unpublished doctoral thesis, University of British Columbia, Vancouver, Canada.

Fels, L. (1999). *In the wind clothes dance on a line: Performative inquiry as a research methodology.* Unpublished doctoral thesis, University of British Columbia, Vancouver, Canada.

Fels, L., Linds, W., & Purru, K. (in press). Performing impossibility. In J. G. Knowles, S. Promislow, & A. L. Cole (Eds.), *Creating scholartistry: Imagining the arts-informed thesis or dissertation.* Halifax, Nova Scotia, & Toronto, Ontario, Canada: Backalong Books & Centre for Arts-Informed Research.

Fleet, A. (in press). Re-becoming a supervisor. Extending possibilities. In J. G. Knowles, S. Promislow, & A. L. Cole (Eds.),

Creating scholartistry: Imagining the arts-informed thesis or dissertation. Halifax, Nova Scotia, & Toronto, Ontario, Canada: Backalong Books & Centre for Arts-Informed Research.

Gannon, S. (2003). *Flesh and the text: Poststructural theory and writing research.* Unpublished doctoral dissertation, James Cook University, Townsville, Queensland, Australia.

Gosse, D. (2005a). *Breaking silences: An inquiry into identity and the creative research process.* Unpublished doctoral thesis, Ontario Institute for Studies in Education of the University of Toronto, Ontario, Canada.

Gosse, D. (2005b). *Jackytar.* St. Johns, Newfoundland, Canada: Jesperson Publishing.

Gozouasis, P., & Lee, K. V. (in press). Sticky knot danish. In J. G. Knowles, S. Promislow, & A. L. Cole (Eds.), *Creating scholartistry: Imagining the arts-informed thesis or dissertation.* Halifax, Nova Scotia, & Toronto, Ontario, Canada: Backalong Books & Centre for Arts-Informed Research.

Knowles, J. G,. Luciani, T., Cole, A. L., & Neilsen, L. (2007). *The art of visual inquiry.* Halifax, Nova Scotia, & Toronto, Ontario, Canada: Backalong Books & Centre for Arts-Informed Research.

Knowles, J. G., Promislow, S., & Cole, L. (Eds.). (in press). *Creating scholartistry: Imagining the arts-informed thesis or dissertation.* Halifax, Nova Scotia, & Toronto, Ontario, Canada: Backalong Books & Centre for Arts-Informed Research.

Knowles, J. G., & Thomas, S. (2000). Insights and inspiration from an artist's work: Envisioning and portraying lives-in-context. In A. L. Cole & J. G. Knowles, *Lives in context: The art of life history research* (pp. 208–214). Walnut Creek, CA: AltaMira Press.

Lee, K. (2004). *Riffs of change: Musicians becoming music educators.* Unpublished doctoral thesis, University of British Columbia, Vancouver, Canada.

Leoutsakas, D. (2003). *The orphan tales: Real and imagined stories of parental loss.* Unpublished doctoral dissertation, University of South Florida, Tampa.

Loi, D. (2005). *Lavoretti per bimbi: Playful triggers as keys to foster collaborative practices and workspaces where people learn, wonder, and play.* Unpublished doctoral thesis, School of Management, RMIT University, Melbourne, Victoria, Australia.

Loi, D. (in press). A thought per day: My traveling inside a suitcase. In J. G. Knowles, S. Promislow, & A. L. Cole (Eds.), *Creating scholartistry: Imagining the arts-informed thesis or dissertation.* Halifax, Nova Scotia, & Toronto, Ontario, Canada: Backalong Books & Centre for Arts-Informed Research.

Luciani, T. (2006). *On women's domestic knowledge and work: Growing up in an Italian kitchen.* Unpublished doctoral thesis, University of Toronto, Ontario, Canada.

Marín, C. (2005). *Breaking down barriers, building dreams: Using theatre for social change to explore the concept of identity with Latina adolescents.* Unpublished doctoral dissertation, Arizona State University, Tempe.

Moreman, S. (2005). *Performativity and the Latina/o-White hybrid identity: Performing the textual self.* Unpublished doctoral dissertation, University of South Florida, Tampa.

Norman, R. (in press). Imaginative energy: Artistic and autobiographical dreams. In J. G. Knowles, S. Promislow, & A. L. Cole (Eds.), *Creating scholartistry: Imagining the arts-informed thesis or dissertation.* Halifax, Nova Scotia, & Toronto, Ontario, Canada: Backalong Books & Centre for Arts-Informed Research.

Oberg, A., & Cranmer, L. (in press). Mirroring at the borders: Strategies for methodless method. In J. G. Knowles, S. Promislow, & A. L. Cole (Eds.), *Creating scholartistry: Imagining the arts-informed thesis or dissertation.* Halifax, Nova Scotia, & Toronto, Ontario, Canada: Backalong Books & Centre for Arts-Informed Research.

Promislow, S. (2005). *A collage of borderlands: Arts-informed life histories of childhood immigrants and refugees who maintain their mother tongue.* Unpublished doctoral thesis, Ontario Institute for Studies in Education of the University of Toronto, Ontario, Canada.

Promislow, S., & Cole, A. L. (in press). Collaging borderlands. In J. G. Knowles, S. Promislow, & A. L. Cole (Eds.), *Creating scholartistry:*

Imagining the arts-informed thesis or dissertation. Halifax, Nova Scotia, & Toronto, Ontario, Canada: Backalong Books & Centre for Arts-Informed Research.

Sbrocchi, S. (2005). *Remembering place: Domicide and a childhood home.* Unpublished doctoral thesis, Ontario Institute for Studies in Education of the University of Toronto, Ontario, Canada.

Sbrocchi, S. (in press). Sketchy lines. In J. G. Knowles, S. Promislow, & A. L. Cole (Eds.), *Creating scholartistry: Imagining the arts-informed thesis or dissertation.* Halifax, Nova Scotia, & Toronto, Ontario, Canada: Backalong Books & Centre for Arts-Informed Research.

Springgay, S., de Cosson, A., & Irwin, R. (in press). Liminal (s)p(l)aces of writing and creating. In J. G. Knowles, S. Promislow, & A. L. Cole (Eds.), *Creating scholartistry: Imagining the arts-informed thesis or dissertation.* Halifax, Nova Scotia, & Toronto, Ontario, Canada: Backalong Books & Centre for Arts-Informed Research.

PART VI

ARTS IN RESEARCH ACROSS DISCIPLINES

C hapters in this section are divided according to discipline. Authors provide an overview, analysis, and brief examples of the current and potential role of the arts in research in a variety of disciplines. They also speculate about the future of the arts in qualitative research in their particular discipline or field. In many ways this is, for us, the most exciting part of the *Handbook* because it underscores the presence of the arts in research across many social science disciplines and signifies a hopeful future of challenge and change. Perhaps more important, though, gathering together in one place the range of disciplines represented here renders the collective workings of a group of individuals in a way that helps to create a sense of community among researchers in disparate geographic and disciplinary places. And it is in and through community and collective action that individual efforts are supported and significant change can occur.

- Anthropology: Ethnography and the Book That Was Lost, *Ruth Behar*

- Psychology: Knowing the Self Through Arts, *Graham E. Higgs*

- Women's Studies and Arts-Informed Research: Some Australian Examples, *Lekkie Hopkins*

- A History of the Arts in Educational Research: A Postmodern Guide for Readers-Flâneurs, *Christine van Halen-Faber and C. T. Patrick Diamond*

- Social Work and the Arts: Critical Imagination, *Adrienne Chambon*

- Nursing Research and the Transformative Value of Art, *Vangie Bergum and Dianne Godkin*

- Health-Policy Research and the Possibilities of Theater, *Jeff Nisker*

- Disability Studies and the Ties and Tensions With Arts-Informed Inquiry: One More Reason to Look Away? *Esther Ignagni and Kathryn Church*

- Business Studies: Vivifying Data and Experience Through Artful Approaches, *Laura Brearley and Lotte Darsø*

- Sport and Physical Education: Embracing New Forms of Representation, *Andrew C. Sparkes*

45

ANTHROPOLOGY

Ethnography and the Book That Was Lost

◆ Ruth Behar

◆ *A Book That Was Lost*

Ethnography began as a method—discovered, perfected, and institution-alized in Western centers of power—for telling stories about the margin-alized populations of the world. It has its origins in the flagrant colonial inequalities from which modernity was born and in the arrogant assumptions that its privileged intellectual class made about who has the right to tell stories about whom. Knowing this history, how can ethnography still be practiced today in an age of unprecedented global intercon-nectedness, in which continuing inequalities have only served to heighten awareness of the politics of all storytelling? What can be salvaged from the original vision of ethnography to make it a project of emancipation?

Author's Note: This essay was originally prepared as a presentation for the "Ethnografeast" conference held at the University of California, Berkeley, in September of 2002. I am grateful to Loïc Wacquant for the invitation to par-ticipate in a most inspiring conference and for his warm encouragement of my writing. I offer my most sincere thanks and appreciation to Paul Willis, whose careful and generous reading of an earlier version of this essay pushed me to confront the implications of my position as an ethnographer. This essay in a longer form was first published in 2003 in *Ethnography*, 4(1), 15–39.

Must every use of ethnography in the present inevitably be an act of apology and grief for the shamefulness of what ethnography was in the past? Or is there still some lingering shame even in today's self-conscious pursuit of ethnography?

These are issues that have been hotly debated in recent years (Behar & Gordon, 1995; Clifford & Marcus, 1986; Fox, 1991; Harrison, 1991; Sanjek, 1990). Contrary to expectations that ethnography would become an anachronism, it has in fact proliferated as a method, an epistemology, a field practice, and a form of writing and performance across the social sciences and humanities (Clifford, 1988; Ellis & Bochner, 1996; Geertz, 1989; Gupta & Ferguson, 1997). There is a strange hunger for ethnography in the contemporary world, which is shaped by concepts of the "really real" and the desire for stories based on the truth and urgency of witnessing. Ethnography, rather than becoming extinct, has become a necessary way of knowing. Even though the pioneering writers of ethnography themselves often treated it as a "second-fiddle" genre, current practitioners have come to cherish it (Behar, 1999). And yet to engage with this method is to be conscious of the contradictions of such knowing and the history of shame that precedes and marks all of our efforts to still want to be there ethnographically.

I came to ethnography because I wanted to be a storyteller who told stories about real people in real places. I was seduced by the notion of fieldwork, the idea of going some place to find a story I wasn't looking for. Of course, ethnographic journeys are always taken with the knowledge that the "field" has already been theorized by precursors of various sorts (Limón, 1994). But the beauty and mystery of the ethnographer's quest is to find the unexpected stories, the stories that challenge our theories. Isn't that the reason why we still go to the field—even as we question where the field is

located—in the 21st century? We go to find the stories we didn't know we were looking for in the first place.

This idea, that ethnography is about finding stories we don't know we have lost, became clear to me after I accidentally came across a gem of a short story one night while I was roaming through the literature section at a Borders bookstore. Reading it brought me to tears. The story, which is exceedingly brief and concise, is called "A Book That Was Lost." It was written by S. Y. Agnon (1995, pp. 128–135), a Polish Jewish writer who won the Nobel Prize for Literature in 1966 for his fictional writing in Hebrew. The title alone is already enough to awaken the curiosity and even, I would say, the most morbid fear of all of us who, in one way or another, have come to ethnography through a love of books and the desire to write our own books.

At the beginning of the story we learn about Rabbi Shmaria, who lived in a small town in Poland and spent 12 years preparing a detailed commentary on another commentary written by another rabbi of an earlier generation on the laws concerning daily ritual. Convinced that he has "left no difficult passage uninterpreted," he calls in the bookbinder to print and publish his book. But while the bookbinder is attending to Rabbi Shmaria's pages, the rabbi notices that the bookbinder happened to have brought along another manuscript for binding, and he asks to see it. That manuscript, written by a scholar and rabbi more prominent than he, impresses Rabbi Shmaria so profoundly that he sighs and says, "I have been preceded by another; there is no need for my work." He sends the bookbinder home and leaves his work "where it was . . . neither bound nor published." Several generations later, the manuscript is found by a student poking around in the attic of the town's synagogue where the worn-out religious books are kept before being taken to the graveyard for burial, as is customary in Jewish tradition.

The student immediately sees that Rabbi Shmaria's text has "nice distinctions" and "innovations." He is further persuaded of its value after he shows the text to his father, a teacher, and to other scholars, all of whom agree that the rabbi's voice deserves to be heard.

Pondering how best to prevent the text from falling into oblivion, the student decides to send it to Jerusalem where a Jewish national library is being created to house the scattered texts of the Jewish diaspora (this is in the 1920s, before the existence of the state of Israel). The student saves his lunch money for many months, going hungry in order to send the book by mail from Poland to Jerusalem. Some time later, he ends up settling in Jerusalem, arriving on the Ninth of Av the day of mourning the destruction of the Temple. After the Ninth of Av, his friends show him around Jerusalem and they take him to the great library where he has sent Rabbi Shmaria's manuscript. The librarian shows them various books, and about each he says, "It's the only one in the world, unique, a gift from so-and-so." Finally, the rescuer of Rabbi Shmaria's manuscript tells the librarian about the book he sent from Poland. The librarian searches and searches to no avail, but he promises to keep looking. Over the years the book's rescuer keeps returning to the library, and every time the librarian expresses the sincere hope that the book will be found. The years continue to pass. Eventually both the librarian and the one who succeeds him pass away and still the book isn't found. The story ends with the simple but devastating admission, "What a pity the book was lost."

◆ The Poignant Politics of Love and Rescue

I imagine every person who hears this story brings a story of loss and fear of loss to the

reading. I will try to elucidate some of the meanings, specific and general, that this story called up in me in terms of both my personal history and my aims as a storyteller and ethnographer. I believe the story is haunting because it is about the horror of self-erasure. In reading the story I identified fully with Rabbi Shmaria because I have often felt the terrible uselessness of my own writing. I approach ethnography as a form of blurred-genre writing that mixes reportage with memoir, travel writing, theoretical reflection, accounts of dramatic encounters, the storytelling techniques of fiction, and sometimes even the lyricism of poetry.

Since for me ethnography is most of all a method for converting lived experience into memorable, even beautiful, writing, I frequently wonder whether it might not be best to leave the writing to the "professional writers," to those who truly know the craft of writing, like journalists, fiction writers, playwrights, and poets. Are all my labors in vain? Does it matter if I write or not? Will my writing always be just a poor second-fiddle rendition? Or are there "innovations" I can offer as an ethnographer that make my efforts worthwhile?

In many ways, ethnographers are similar to the rabbinical scholars portrayed in Agnon's story. We write commentaries about the commentaries that our informants share with us about their lives and their societies. Most crucially, we listen to other people's stories, especially to the stories of those whose voices often go unheard. We believe that by listening to these stories and then retelling them, displacing these stories to other places and audiences, we can help to save the world. I know that it was with that faith that I went into cultural anthropology as a young woman 20 years ago.

But the fact is we cannot know the true value of our work in our own lifetime. It is the future generations, those who will come after us, whose task it will be to decide whether our work is worth keeping. It is well known that what tends to become out-dated first in ethnographies is the theory. As paradigms shift, an ethnography that once was a cutting edge demonstration of the merits of a theory of structural-functionalism, or a theory of social drama or a theory of communitas, quickly loses its punch. What remains valuable in ethnographies after their theories become stale is precisely those aspects of lived experience that the ethnographer's theory could not harness, could not squeeze into the box. Long after the theoretical plat-forms of ethnographies have been super-seded, what still makes them interesting as texts is the chronicle they offer of a society observed in a given historical moment; and the fictions they often unwittingly embrace, the fiction of who the ethnographer thought she or he was in the field, the fiction of how that society was constructed by the ethnog-rapher, whether harmoniously or conflic-tively, depending on the nuances of the ethnographer's sensibility and the historical moment in which the ethnographer hap-pened to be present as an observer.

It is exactly such an extended temporal and historical arc that gives Agnon's story its bite. The story doesn't stop at Rabbi Shmaria's loss of faith in the worthiness of his intellectual journey. It follows the thread of the story a few generations later and inserts it into a longer history. In this way, the story reaches down into a deeper level of sorrow and bereavement. Although the book was lost in its historical moment, it was almost saved in a subsequent moment. The irony is that it is precisely the heroic effort to save this old European Jewish book and give it a new home in the library in Jerusalem that leads to its more perma-nent loss. Not only is the book doubly lost, but it is denied proper burial in the Jewish cemetery in Poland, where it might have been given holy rest among other sacred religious books and objects. The book is condemned to forever be in transit, to remain in limbo, never to arrive at its destination in the promised land.

Agnon's story asserts that sometimes knowledge can be lost, that even the wor-thiest of books can vanish without leaving a trace, as if they never existed. And yet, of course, what is important is that the story itself constructs a home for the lost book. The story creates a site to mark the absence of the lost book and in that way preserves a memory of it. Just as the Temple was lost, the book is lost. They are irretrievable. But marking the loss of the book in a story—or in the case of the Temple, in the constant reference to it in Hebrew liturgy—is a way of resisting its loss.

Nevertheless, the story cannot bring back the lost book. Agnon's take on modernity, like Walter Benjamin's, is suffused with an ambivalent awareness that to cross into modernity is to live in a world of translations without originals. A closer Jewish reading of this story adds another troubling level of meaning. Jerusalem is revealed as an incom-plete and flawed repository of Jewish learn-ing and history. Much is lost in the transition from a diasporic Jewish existence to a centralized modern Zionist homeland. The Jewish past reaches the Jewish future only in fragments. And if we add to our reading, as we can't help but do in the current historical nexus, our knowledge of the embattled situ-ation in Jerusalem, and in Israel and Palestine right now, the story is prophetic. It seems to be an infinitely sad warning that even the most far-reaching of Jewish efforts not to lose the promised land, the land that, indeed, was promised to the Jews for centuries by the Torah, the quintessential "Jewish Book," could result in yet more destruction and loss.

Loss has been a classical trope of ethnog-raphy. The practice of ethnography origi-nates in the desire to salvage the fragments of societies that were seen as being on the verge of extinction. Ethnography engaged in a language of loss, of preventing loss, of mourning loss, of arriving there just in time to save the old books of culture from a total and permanent loss. Bringing the lost books to "civilization," to the central library of Western culture for preservation, ethnographers have classically tried to stem the tide of social transformation in which they themselves have been implicated. Ironically, like the savior of the lost book in Agnon's story, they have engaged in the act of bringing about further loss, being complicitous with loss, enacting what has been called "imperialist nostalgia" (Rosaldo, 1993, pp. 68–87).

In my effort to understand why Agnon's story brought me to tears, I realized that it touched me deeply because it spoke to me both personally and as an ethnographer. I was born a Jew in Cuba and consider myself a daughter of two homelands, Cuba and Israel, which I lost as a child. My four Jewish grandparents left Poland and Turkey in the 1920s, escaping growing anti-Semitism, and settled in Cuba where they thought they had found their promised land in the tropics. Instead, diaspora followed upon diaspora, loss upon loss. In the next generation, not only my grandparents but my Cuban-born parents felt their economic livelihood was threatened by the revolution, and they decided to leave Cuba. We left Cuba in 1961. My parents didn't have passports since they had never traveled outside of Cuba and the United States Embassy had shut down, but as Jews we were permitted by the Cuban government to be "repatriated" in Israel. We went to live on a kibbutz that one of my mother's uncles, the only socialist in the family, had helped to found. But after a year, my parents chose to uproot again and go to New York.

I grew up in the United States, where I always had to explain who I was as a Cuban Jew. And so my understanding of loss will always be associated with the names of two countries, Cuba and Israel, and the child I cannot remember being in these two abandoned homelands. That child is a lost book. I know I was that person. I have seen the pictures. Family members and family friends who knew me then tell me who I was as a child in Cuba. But I have never been able to find that child again. I only remember from the time our ship docked in New York. Everything before then is gone from my memory.

By becoming an ethnographer I acquired an intellectual and philosophical framework for my explorations of identity, memory, home, and the crossing of borders. The dislocations and relocations that are at the heart of the ethnographic imagination—that are part of the lived experience of those who dwell in diasporas—have become the method by which I have been able to join my personal quest for the lost book of my childhood with my professional interest in understanding the interplay between subjective meanings and cultural meanings. It was through the pursuit of ethnography, as well, that I was able to undertake the magical, and also politicizing, journeys into the everyday reality of people living in the Spanish-speaking world, the world I longed to reclaim.

Agnon's story also made an impact on me as an ethnographer whose work in the Spanish-speaking world has continually raised questions about my often submerged Jewish identity. As I write this essay, I am worried by Israel, as I am worried for Israel, and I no longer know what to think or even how to think about the situation we are living at this time, which has world historical implications and will have world historical consequences. A story about the loss of one book by a provincial rabbinical scholar who suffered from low self-esteem is certainly of minor relevance given everything that is at stake now in Israel and Palestine.

And yet I'm drawn to it as an argument or metaphor, in support of the only kind of ethnographic storytelling I'm able to engage in now, which is storytelling that enacts what anthropologist Virginia Dominguez (2000, p. 361) has called "a politics of love and rescue."

What moves me most about Agnon's story is not simply the pathos I experience as I identify with the rabbi who was willing to erase his scholarship out of a misguided sense that the world did not need his book. I am moved even more by the love of the man who tried to rescue the lost book, the love he felt for a book that was not his. I am moved by the gift that is at the story's core, the gift of wanting to save a book felt to be unworthy by the writer who produced it, the gift of loving someone who lacked self-love.

◆ Bringing Back Stories From the Places Where I Have Dwelled

As ethnographers we are expected to travel somewhere, even if that somewhere is a return trip to a lost home, but always with the commitment to bring back a story. When I think about the places where I have dwelled as an anthropologist—in a small mountain village in northern Spain, in a town in Mexico 12 hours from the U.S. border, and most recently in my native Havana—I could not have accomplished anything without the generosity of those who trusted me enough to let me take their stories from them so they could find a place in my books. The truth is the ethnographer cannot enact "a politics of love and rescue" unless and until her informants choose to love and rescue her first.

I think of all the gifts I have received in my work as an ethnographer, and I realize I cannot ever repay those who have given away their stories to me without asking for anything in return. Although fables of rapport are routinely dismissed in contemporary anthropology as romantic and naive, I have not yet become jaded enough to cease thinking that the ability to do our work as ethnographers depends on people being willing to talk to us freely and give us the gift of their stories. Of course, the stories are given in a context of complex intersubjective negotiations and exchanges, mutual expectations and desires informed by obvious power differences in which the ethnographer, at a minimum, promises to maintain the social obligation of staying connected to her informants.

I may be unusual in having been able to maintain a certain innocence about the increasing commodification of ethnographic encounters, not to mention the refusal of such encounters by would-be informants who have decided they no longer want anything to do with story-extracting ethnographers, even those who have owned up to their imperialist nostalgia. For better or worse, my ethnographic encounters have filled me with hope rather than despair and have given me faith in the emancipatory possibilities of a pursuit that I never forget is rooted in shame. Perhaps this is the inevitable result of my ethnographic practice being so closely interwoven with my personal quest as a woman of the Spanish-speaking diaspora.

Although as a budding ethnographer I wanted to work in Cuba, and traveled to the island in 1979 to try to make the necessary arrangements, the political moment had not yet arrived that would have made it possible for a Cuban American anthropologist to be trusted to do fieldwork in her abandoned homeland. When I suggested to my advisors that I might instead do a study of the Cuban American community, I was told that this project was too close to home and that I should travel abroad to truly experience the rite of passage of fieldwork. And so I was advised to go to Spain, a place that had already fascinated me as a young literature student, and where I would be able to use "my Spanish" and still be immersed in a different culture. It wasn't bad advice.

In Santa Maria del Monte, the village in Spain where I first went in 1978 when I was 21, not knowing who I was, let alone knowing what I was to do there as an anthropologist, I came to an early recognition that everything depended on the ungrudging generosity of the strangers who let me live among them. And it was in that village, to which I returned in 1987, a year after finishing my book about its history, that I lived through the fundamental crisis that allowed me to become the only kind of ethnographer I could bear to be: a brokenhearted ethnographer.

That crisis came about because my return to Santa Maria in 1987 coincided with the moment when my beloved maternal grandfather was dying of cancer in Miami Beach. I had been told by my family to pursue my studies, that it was not good to be waiting for my grandfather to die, that surely he would still be there when I returned from my trip. Ironically, my reason for returning to Spain was to carry out research on attitudes toward death for a paper I had promised to deliver at the annual American anthropology conference. While in Spain, knowing that my grandfather was dying, I listened to people tell stories of grief about the loss of their loved ones, and it was as if the volume was turned way up high in my heart. And then when the news came that my grandfather had died and that I could not get back to Miami Beach in time for the funeral, it was as if my heart was screaming. Comfort came from the strangers in Santa Maria who offered me words of consolation and sympathy, and I realized that hearing about their sorrow for the loss of their loved ones had prepared

me to face the ache of death's merciless finality.

But afterward I was stricken by guilt, rage, and moral confusion. I suddenly found the displacement of anthropology to be cruel and senseless. Why had I been in Spain talking with strangers about death rather than being at my grandfather's side gently offering him my last goodbye? Why was it that over the course of my work as an anthropologist I had become an expert on popular Catholicism and could recite the rosary in Spanish from memory, but I knew nothing of Jewish mourning rituals and had no idea how to honor my grandfather within the traditions of my own heritage? Haunted by these questions, I struggled with how to write my paper for the conference.

And then it became clear to me that the loss of my grandfather in Miami Beach and my research findings about how Spanish villagers felt about the subject of death could not be separated. They were, they had to be, the same story. Identification and connection rather than distance, difference and otherness is what I would seek as an ethnographer. And I would use not only the observational and participatory methods of classical anthropology but the subtle forms of knowledge found in ineffable moments of intuition and epiphany. This was the basis for my essay "Death and Memory," which became the opening piece of my book *The Vulnerable Observer: Anthropology That Breaks Your Heart* (Behar, 1996).

After writing that essay, there was no turning back for me. I knew that I wanted to keep searching for ways to evoke how intersubjectivity unfolds as a fundamental part of the representation of social reality. And I wanted, most importantly, to discover the deep conjunctures that inform any effort to know the world beyond the self. For it was these conjunctures that could most fully reveal the process by which ethnographic knowledge is attained in the highly charged moments of our fieldwork encounters. I came to see that in writing "Death and Memory" I mixed together levels of experience that are not usually mixed. I created a counterpoint between the ethnographic stories of death in rural Spain, which required my objective presence as an ethnographer, and my own grandfather's death in Miami Beach, which had taken place in my pained absence.

This unique convergence, with all its friction, poignancy, and contradiction, had a certain musicality. It conveyed a faith in the surrealist principle that joining together incongruous things can bring about an unexpected awareness, a slant of sharp, sublime light, an edgy form of knowing that dares to surprise the knower too. Curiously, in these situations you yourself the knower didn't know fully what you knew until you wrote it down, until you told the story with you yourself included in it.

I went on to Mexico and found myself smack in the middle of the resentment and hurt that so many Mexicans feel when they reflect on what the Chicana writer Gloria Anzaldúa (1999, p. 1) has called "the open wound," which is the border between the United States and Mexico. As a Cuban immigrant with an American passport, I had gained the privilege of being able to cross back and forth. But I didn't know at first that this was a privilege. My hosts in Mexquitic, the Mexican town where my husband and I lived for 3 years, opened my eyes and politicized me, showing me how distinctions of race and class made it impossible for them to make the same crossing, the crossing that allowed me to do my ethnography. Esperanza Hernandez, a street peddler from Mexquitic who mesmerized me with her stories about her life, gave me a necessary education not only about borders but about the possibility of seeking connection in spite of them. Even though there were other women who were easier to like, it was the tough and unforgiving Esperanza who stole my heart. She not only helped me to know my politics better but restored my faith in the power of stories to create bonds between strangers.

I wrote my book *Translated Woman* (Behar, 1993) in awe of the possibility of our relationship, of a Cuban American anthropologist and a Mexican street peddler being drawn together by the twisted threads of an interconnected colonial and neocolonial history that had left Esperanza impoverished and borne me across the border from Cuba to the United States. Our relationship further inscribed an uneasy desire for womanly intimacy in which were conjoined the stirrings of an international feminist desire, on my side, and the promise of our becoming *comadres,* spiritual kin with mutual obligations, on her side.

The result of our shared production of knowledge was a book that Esperanza initially demanded only exist in the English language and only circulate "on the other side," among the *gringos* of the United States, the mythical land across the border that she did not expect to ever set eyes upon. So maligned was Esperanza in her hometown that she feared her female neighbors would ridicule her if they heard she'd told her life story to her *comadre* from the United States. And yet she was convinced of her need for justice and hoped that by telling me her story and having it be heard "on the other side," she would ultimately find redemption. Her life story became a lost book that could only be found in translation.

Aware of the importance of being able to assess the theoretical lessons of Esperanza's story, I made a point in *Translated Woman* of turning to the literary texts of Chicanas, Latinas, African American women, and Latin American writers as frameworks for reading her story. I deliberately tried to connect her story to more locally relevant frameworks out of a sense that ethnography needs to question what constitutes theory. The writings of Durkheim, Weber, Marx, and Foucault, among other works classified as "theory," are essentially ethnographic texts that have been anointed as theoretical. My sense is that we tend to automatically reach for the work of such European theorists, which our canon has legitimated as translocal and applicable to myriad situations beyond their original settings, without always thinking about the way this reproduces Eurocentric prestige hierarchies of knowledge in the academy.

As part of my musing on textual relations of power, I also felt the need to attempt something that was taboo for classical anthropology: I not only presented Esperanza's life story, but in the very last chapter I explored my own interpretations and responses to her story, including the consequences that thinking about her story had for my own life. I wrote of my struggles to become an educated woman. I wrote of the awkward way that tenure was dished out to me at my university because my identity as both Cuban and Jewish made me difficult to classify.

Anthropologists are supposed to keep quiet about their lives, so that their focus on "the other" won't become obscured. But I thought it was important for readers to know how I came to be the one with the power to transport Esperanza's story across the border. The last chapter of the book was full of raw emotions about my own upward mobility and the uncertainty and ambivalence it reaped. Coming into power is neither easy nor pretty. I chose not to remove the thorns from my story. Not surprisingly, the chapter made some of my colleagues uncomfortable. Yet Latino and Latina students felt that it spoke to their own anxieties about entering the academy and praised me for my courage. Ultimately, the chapter became an indelible part of the book. Whatever its shortcomings, by shining the spotlight back on me as ethnographer, the chapter provoked important conversations

about what can and can't be said in an ethnography that was perhaps its most significant contribution.

◆ *Adio Kerida: Daring to Come Out of the Jewish Closet*

As an ethnographer I had found it difficult to announce my "Jewishness" openly in the small places in Spain and Mexico where I spent so many years of my life, speaking my native Spanish, being accepted as a Latina. In those places where I was "almost home," I often felt like a *conversa*, a 15th-century Jew-in-hiding. My "Jewishness" always separated me from the people I wanted to claim affinity toward. Finding myself in places where various forms of popular Catholicism were the only forms of acceptable religious identity, I kept quiet about being Jewish. Additionally, what has come to be known as the "Jewish closet" in anthropology played an unconscious role in encouraging me to remain silent about Jewish issues and my own "Jewishness" (Dominguez, 1993; Frank, 1997). In Cuba, I was finally able to "come out" as a Jew, to embrace my Jewish identity in a Spanish-speaking country and to begin to work on Jewish issues as an ethnographer.

The secular tolerance instilled in the population by the Cuban revolution, together with Cuba's long historical tradition of cultural pluralism, allowed me to emerge from the Jewish closet in my native land. I was, for the first time, staying in a major city, in Havana, rather than in the countryside as I had been in Spain and Mexico. This made it easy for me to make my way to the Patronato Synagogue, located just a stone's throw from the apartment building where I lived as a child. I had been photographed in front of the synagogue as a child and been the flower girl there at the wedding of my mother's cousin the very night before we left Cuba, so it was a space resonant with meaning for me. The secretary and librarian of the synagogue remembered my family. I didn't know what I would find there, but every time I was in Cuba I felt compelled to attend Jewish services at the Patronato, even though I rarely attended Jewish services back in Michigan.

Over time, I came to know the members of the small but vibrant community of a thousand Jews still left on the island. I found it striking that most of them were Sephardic rather than Ashkenazi Jews, and so I began to explore the traces left by the Sephardic Jews in Cuba. This was a moment in which I was making contact with a circle of Sephardic intellectuals in the United States who were formulating a critique of the narrow definitions of Jewish identity produced by the dominant Ashkenazi American majority. Jewish multiculturalism was at last coming into prominence. Suddenly I didn't need to explain my identity all the time. The new "multiracial" box on the United States census officially acknowledged the possibility of cultural and ethnic mixtures. A diasporic consciousness began to be part of public culture in the United States, and this had an important general impact on the rethinking of identity.

In the case of the two identities that I know best, I was aware of how both Jews and Latinos were working to break out of the boxes of the way their identities had been formulated. This convergent search for new self-constructions of their communities reached a public level and even led to the organization of a Latino-Jewish summit in Washington, to which both Latino and Jewish political and intellectual leaders were invited. I was asked to attend as a Jewish Latina who might act as a bridge between the two communities, and I began to see that I had a unique contribution to make as a Jewish ethnographer of the Spanish-speaking world. Within this newly discovered Latino-Jewish convergence, I learned that the Sephardic Jews were playing an important role because they are Jews of Spanish heritage. The Sephardic Jews are a living reminder of the repressed and hidden Jewish heritage of the Latino community. These Spanish-speaking Jews were expelled from Spain in 1492 because they refused to convert to Catholicism. They resettled in the former countries of the Ottoman Empire, where they lived peacefully among their Muslim neighbors and were warmly accepted, maintaining Spanish traditions until the early years of the 20th century. When the welcome mat grew thin, they began to migrate in large numbers to the Americas and later to Israel. And some of them, especially from the small towns around Istanbul, found their way to Cuba, among them my paternal grandparents.

Growing up with a Cuban mother who is Ashkenazi and a Cuban father who is Sephardic, I learned early on that there is more than one way of being Jewish. But this appreciation of Jewish multiculturalism did not come easily nor harmoniously. In my mother's family, my father was known as *"el turco,"* the Turk, not only because his parents were from Turkey but because he was hot tempered and unforgiving. When my mother would get angry at me, she'd say I was just like my father, just like the *"turcos."* And yet even though I was like the *"turcos,"* the Sephardim were mysterious to me. I grew up closer to my mother's Yiddish-speaking side of the family, and the Jewish education I received in Hebrew school was always oriented toward Ashkenazi traditions.

As I entered my teenage years, my Sephardic identity became a vexed issue because that identity came to me from my father and we were locked in a contest of wills. In our life together, my father was usually either absolutely furious at me or not speaking to me at all. As a young woman I upset him deeply by going to college against his will, and as a grown woman I upset him by writing stories about him and my mother that he thought dishonored them. When I began to travel regularly to Cuba in the 1990s, I further upset him by returning to the country from which he had fled in the early 1960s, and he viewed my desire to reconnect with Cuba as yet another manifestation of my ingratitude and disrespect.

So naturally, given this history of heartbreak between my Sephardic father and me, I knew I had to prepare a gift for him that would allow both of us to share in the Sephardic Cuban legacy with joy and with pride. That gift became my documentary film *Adio Kerida [Goodbye Dear Love]* (Behar, 2002), which I dedicated to my father. Although I couldn't convince my father to go to Cuba with me, I made a film for him, to show him what kind of people we are, we the Sephardic Jews, with our strong tempers and our inability to forgive. For despite the years of conflict with my father, I had never given up the Behar last name, the name I inherited from my father, the Béjar, which is still the name of a town in northwestern Spain. And as I embarked on the making of *Adio Kerida*, it is this name that I would find all over Cuba, both among the living Sephardic Jews I met and the many departed Sephardic Jews whose tombs abound in the cemeteries of the island.

The film is structured as a journey that begins in Havana with an exploration of my longing for memory. It then moves to a series of encounters with Jews currently living on the island, continues in Miami with a focus on Jewish Cubans there, including my father's relatives, goes on to New York, where I go with my parents to various sites of our immigrant passage, and then moves to Philadelphia, where my brother gently pokes fun at my need to travel to places left behind. The film ends in Michigan, where

I reflect on my uncertainty about knowing where home really is. It is at once personal and ethnographic, another way of telling a counterpointed story.

The story, I gradually came to realize, was rooted in the fundamental conflict between my father's idea that all goodbyes are final and you should never look back, and my own desire, as an immigrant daughter and an ethnographer, to search for memories and meaning in our abandoned Cuba. As I edited, I began to structure the film in terms of layers of goodbye and return, focusing on the way Sephardic identity was maintained while Cuban culture was also adopted by those who had been "*turcos.*"

The entire project was an act of faith as people on both sides of the ocean border dared to entrust me with their stories. Many of those who participated on the United States' side, like my father, won't go back to Cuba, while those on the Cuban side often stated that they would never leave Cuba, but all agreed to participate in the same film because they had faith that I would not harm them, that their stories were safe with me. Working on any project that concerns Cuba, especially if you are Cuban American, is always a matter of walking a tightrope, if you want to hold on to the privilege of being allowed to keep returning to Cuba to do research and you don't want to burn your bridge to Miami either.

There were provocative topics I chose not to address. Instead, I focused on the durability of the "culture," because everyone could feel good about the cultural survival of the Sephardic Jews of Cuba, everyone could agree that the culture united them, however loosely, across political and economic borders. The film balanced the nostalgia and longing for Cuba felt by those who left with a sense of humor about the remembered island. And music in the film, ranging from Sephardic songs to Spanish flamenco to American jazz to Argentine tango to

Cuban boleros, offered a lush sense of comfort for the melancholia of diaspora. The risks I took were in showing how widely intermarried people are within the community and therefore how diverse the community is in real life. The use of filmic images allowed me to make the strong visual point that not all Jewish Cubans are White and middle class, that in fact, they now include Afro-Cubans on the island. The community also emerges as diverse politically and holding different positions about the revolution. My critical gaze was directed most openly at the uncertain impact that well-meaning Jewish American organizations and visitors have had on the Jewish community in Cuba, which feels it is now constantly on display to these outsiders.

It has been very fulfilling to receive positive responses to the film by the Jewish community in both Havana and Miami. Even my father likes it! As the film now travels to both Latino and Jewish film festivals all over the United States, and finds a Spanish-speaking audience through airings on Spanish and Latin American television, it is being embraced as a vivid portrayal of the way complex, mixed identities are shaped through the interplay of subjectivity and history. Through the film, I am being pushed into the public arena in new and challenging ways that are forcing me to think about how ethnographers need to be more active players in debates about identity and culture.

◆ In Defense of Popularization

Several years ago I worked with a New York Latino theater group, PREGONES, to create a stage adaptation of *Translated Woman* (Behar, 1993) and found that to be an exciting way to bring anthropological ideas about translation and border crossing to a broader audience. Making *Adio Kerida* (Behar, 2002)

has likewise given me a fresh perspective on the possibility of communicating our ideas to audiences who might not otherwise learn of our research. While we often speak of applying anthropology to public policy, I think we can also apply anthropology to the arts in the widest sense of the term, to the different arts of representation. If we can get our stories out there, in readable books, in theater, in film, and on television, I believe we can make a significant contribution to public knowledge and public debate.

I have come to believe strongly that in order for ethnography to survive, we must learn to produce ethnographic work that is more accessible than it has been in the past and work that is also artistically satisfying. If we don't get our ethnographies out there, I do fear that they will become lost books. In the meantime, the ethnography that does flourish in public spaces is being produced by people working outside of the academy who typically are not credentialed ethnographers. I think of the amazing work that dedicated documentary filmmakers are doing, that investigative journalists are doing, or of how a performance artist like Anne Deveare Smith gathers stories from real people in all their rich diversity in order to create ethnographically grounded theatrical vignettes. Ethnography is not the property of anthropology, sociology, the social sciences, or the academy. It seems to me that ethnography is flourishing in a wide variety of contexts, but it flourishes not by its name, but as the invisible genre, as the lost book.

As I see it, one key failing in the way we approach ethnography is that we tend to teach courses in which ethnographies are read but rarely do we teach students how to write ethnography. Is ethnography a form of creative nonfiction? If it is, shouldn't we be able to teach courses that focus on the craft of ethnography? How can people write interesting ethnographies if they don't pay attention to craft? Could we agree on the fundamental elements of a good ethnography?

What kind of relationship needs to exist in ethnography between characters, plot, voice, place, observer, critique, theory, and previous scholarly literature? We teach courses on methods, on theory, on specific areas of the world, but ethnography itself remains elusive, which is why ethnography ends up having to be figured out by each ethnographer when her or his time comes to write one.

But even if we teach ethnography as writing, perhaps in the end ethnography will still remain elusive, because every ethnography emerges from a unique encounter between an ethnographer and those who become the subjects of the ethnography. These encounters are not repeatable, not easily verifiable. And so we must ultimately accept ethnographies on trust, and hope that the ethnographer was listening well. Every ethnographer, to some extent, has to reinvent the genre of ethnography to make it fit the uniqueness of his or her fieldwork experience. In a sense, this is true for writing across the genres. We can recognize a novel when we see one, but James Joyce, Virginia Woolf, and Ernest Hemingway approached the writing of fiction from different perspectives, so even though their fictions are all described as novels they do not resemble one another.

Yet there is probably more agreement on how to evaluate a novel than there is on how to evaluate an ethnography. Perhaps because ethnography, as a self-conscious literary pursuit, is a relatively new genre compared to autobiography, poetry, and fiction, we have yet to know exactly what the criteria should be for assessing its value and meaning. But I don't think we're going to arrive at these criteria until we can get over our fear of "going popular" and dare to let our ethnographies be read in the harsh glare of the public eye, which may well be the most grueling but necessary and enlightening way to discover if what we have to say is significant beyond the safe space of our academic homes.

◆ *Not Alone*

I have learned that I am not alone in my resolve to find a way to do scholarship that refuses anonymity and authority and instead seeks connection, intimacy, and passion. Scholars in numerous fields, including literature, music, film, history, anthropology, law, medicine, mathematics, psychology, and the natural sciences, have been grappling with the sense of exasperation and frustration they feel with classical forms of uncovering and relaying knowledge. By the end of the century, a wide range of scholars, especially in the United States, were consciously blurring the illusory line between "hard" and "soft" disciplines and experimenting with diverse and compelling first-person forms of writing (Freedman & Frey, 1993; Kaplan, 1994; Limón, 1994; Miller, 1991; Okeley & Callaway, 1992; Rosaldo, 1993; Steedman, 1987; Suleiman, 1994; Williams, 1991). This movement wasn't simply a spillover from the "memoir boom." Deep, critical self-examination turned out *not* to be an escape, a vacation, from the complexities of the world we live in but a way of being more present in this world that is our world now. The common project came out of a burning need to be present, to be there, unflinchingly, facing up to who we are as we keep daring to know the world.

Our world now draws us closer to one another but leaves each of us in peril of becoming ever more anonymous, ever more identified with our social security numbers and our frequent flyer numbers and our credit cards. Such anonymity, I must hasten to add, is the price of privilege. The sadder anonymity, the truly tragic vulnerability, is that of the large populations around the world mired in hunger, poverty, oblivion, and underdevelopment. And yet despite the finer quality of life for the privileged few, humanity has never been so fragile, so susceptible to massive car crashes, explosions, the killing hatred of the excluded, so susceptible to ravaging illnesses like AIDS and cancer, so susceptible to the nasty fallout of an environment that we ourselves have damaged more relentlessly in the past century than in the thousands of years that preceded our existence on this planet.

Our world now is characterized by increasing anonymity, increasing suffering, increasing uncertainty, increasing recognition of too many far-away others who cannot be helped all at once. As the globalized world beckons and terrifies simultaneously, there will be ethnographers who will say that this is the time to return to the detached voice of authority of the past. They will say that the reflexive musings of brokenhearted ethnographers is nothing more than solipsism and the palm reading of gypsies. They will say that it is time to address the serious issues at hand, with proper distance and severity. But I would argue that assuming uncritically the mask of objectivity again, as if the reflexive turn had never happened, will only give us a false security. I say that more than ever, if ethnography is to realize its emancipatory promise, what we are going to need are strong, personal, heartfelt voices, the voices of love, trust, faith, the gift.

One thing remains constant about our humanity—that we must never stop trying to tell stories of who we think we are. Just as important, we must never stop wanting to listen to each other's stories. If we ever stopped, it would all be over. Everything we are as human beings would be reduced to a lost book floating in the universe, with no one to remember us, no one to know we once existed.

SOURCE: From Behar, R. (1999). Ethnography: Cherishing our second-fiddle genre. *Journal of Contemporary Ethnography,* 28(5), 472–484. Sage Publications, Inc. Reprinted with permission of the publisher

◆ References

Agnon, S. Y. (1995). A book that was lost. In S. Y. Agnon, *A book that was lost and other stories* (pp. 128–135). New York: Schocken.

Anzaldúa, G. (1999). *Borderlands: La frontera* (2nd ed.). San Francisco: Aunt Lute Books.

Behar, R. (1993). *Translated woman: Crossing the border with Esperanza's story.* Boston: Beacon.

Behar, R. (1996). *The vulnerable observer: Anthropology that breaks your heart.* Boston: Beacon.

Behar, R. (1999). Ethnography: Cherishing our second-fiddle genre. *Journal of Contemporary Ethnography, 28*(5), 472–484.

Behar, R. (Director). (2002). *Adio kerida* [Goodbye dear love] [Motion picture]. Cuba: Women Make Movies.

Behar, R., & Gordon, D. A. (Eds.). (1995). *Women writing culture.* Berkeley: University of California.

Clifford, J. (1988). *The predicament of culture: Twentieth-century ethnography, literature, and art.* Cambridge, MA: Harvard University.

Clifford, J., & Marcus, G. E. (Eds.). (1986). *Writing culture: The poetics and politics of ethnography.* Berkeley: University of California.

Dominguez, V. (1993). Questioning Jews. *American Ethnologist, 20,* 618–624.

Dominguez, V. (2000). For a politics of love and rescue. *Cultural Anthropology, 15*(3), 361–393.

Ellis, C., & Bochner, A. P. (Eds.). (1996). *Composing ethnography: Alternative forms of qualitative writing.* London: Sage.

Fox, R. G. (Ed.). (1991). *Recapturing anthropology: Working in the present.* Santa Fe, NM: School of American Research.

Frank, G. (1997). Jews, multiculturalism, and Boasian anthropology. *American Anthropologist, 99*(4), 731–745.

Freedman, D. P., & Frey, O. (Eds.). (1993). *The intimate critique: Autobiographical literary criticism.* Durham, NC: Duke University.

Geertz, C. (1989). *Works and lives: The anthropologist as author.* Stanford, CA: Stanford University Press.

Gupta, A., & Ferguson, J. (Eds.). (1997). *Anthropological locations: Boundaries and grounds of a field science.* Berkeley: University of California.

Harrison, F. V. (Ed.). (1991). *Decolonizing anthropology: Moving further toward an anthropology for liberation.* Washington, DC: American Anthropological Association.

Kaplan, A. (1994). *French lessons: A memoir.* Chicago: University of Chicago.

Limón, J. E. (1994). *Dancing with the devil: Society and cultural poetics in Mexican-American South Texas.* Madison: University of Wisconsin.

Miller, N. K. (1991). *Getting personal: Feminist occasions and other autobiographical acts.* New York: Routledge.

Okely, J., & Callaway, H. (Eds.). (1992). *Anthropology and autobiography.* New York: Routledge.

Rosaldo, R. (1993). Imperialist nostalgia. In R. Rosaldo, *Culture and truth: The remaking of social analysis* (pp. 68–87). Boston: Beacon.

Sanjek, R. (Ed.). (1990). *Fieldnotes: The makings of anthropology.* Ithaca, NY: Cornell University.

Steedman, C. K. (1987). *Landscape for a good woman: A story of two lives.* New Brunswick, NJ: Rutgers University.

Suleiman, S. R. (1994). *Risking who one is: Encounters with contemporary art and literature.* Cambridge, MA: Harvard University.

Williams, P. J. (1991). *The alchemy of race and rights.* Cambridge, MA: Harvard University.

46

PSYCHOLOGY

Knowing the Self Through Arts

◆ Graham E. Higgs

I have kept a journal, recording poems and stories and drawings, since I began a reflective practice, which developed out of necessity for my psychological health during my sophomore year of high school. At the time, I was struggling to adapt to a new culture in the United States, a culture drastically different from the rural village and small town environment of the Shona-Manyika speaking people of Zimbabwe where I was born and spent my childhood. I know from direct experience that to know the Shona people it is necessary to understand the spiritual connection they have to each other and to their ancestry as it is expressed through their arts. Music, dance, storytelling, sculpture, pottery making, and fabric arts and crafts are so much a part of the natural expression of the culture that, to understand a Shona individual's psychology, one must at least be aware of this sustaining, creative, cultural expression. In my own reflective practice I have found that writing poetry, drawing, painting, and creating sculpture has enabled me to transcend difficulties, solve problems, and imagine a future when the reality of the world is difficult. Life in a Shona village is far from easy, yet the people are filled with a creative, expressive voice. My journal and the Shona people's art serve a common purpose. Art is an expression of time and place, of experience, perception, and existence.

While working on a master's degree in counseling psychology, I was introduced to qualitative research and critical theory, which had somehow been neglected in my undergraduate coursework in psychology. It was during this time that I began working with artists as a psychological counselor and as a qualitative researcher. In those days, I spent several hours each day in the studios of artists, observing their working habits and discussing with them their creative practices and the personal histories that led them to choose art as a vocation. The creative process has always fascinated me, and this opportunity allowed me to explore how various theoretical perspectives in counseling psychology would relate to artists' ways of knowing.

Prior to graduate school, I had worked as a protective services social worker and teacher in rural Appalachia. It was at this time that I began to understand the theoretical value of my naturally other-centered philosophy. My research as a counseling practitioner led me to support the integration of art therapy into the alternative schools in Appalachia where I worked with seriously emotionally disturbed teens. I began to understand the power of art as a means to circumvent the resistance that marginalized youths have toward traditional schooling practices; I used art successfully in individual therapy with children whose emotional adaptation seemed hopeless. These experiences ultimately led me to work on a doctorate in educational psychology, with an emphasis in psychological interventions in schools and community settings.

Since 1997, I have been teaching psychology in the setting of a small liberal arts college. Psychology, for the most part, is still a traditional social science discipline struggling with the popular misconception of its mysticism and countering with a positivistic standard for research. The reality, however, of social change, globalization, the influence of technology, and the character of a postmodern condition presents the discipline with unprecedented transformative challenges (Kidd, 2002; Sampson, 1989). As a result, psychology attempts to straddle, and is subsequently divided by, two mutually exclusive ontologies (views about the nature of reality) that provide the foundation for the postpositivist and constructivist paradigms (Denzin & Lincoln, 2000).

As I set out to write this chapter, I wondered what the scope of arts-based inquiry in psychology would include. A review of the literature has shown a limited body of work, but some of these works, as we shall see, are exemplary and inspirational. I tried my own hand at arts-based qualitative research in 1996, writing a novel for my dissertation. Three weeks before defending my dissertation as a fictional narrative analysis, I attended the American Educational Research Association annual conference in New York City. Imagine my surprise and excited angst as I listened to a debate between Elliot Eisner, Howard Gardner, and others about writing a novel for one's dissertation (Donmoyer, Eisner, & Gardner, 1996). The idea alone of such a debate left me feeling that I at least had some basis for argument of my risky project.

Now, 11 years later, I have a more mature perspective on the whole enterprise of using arts in qualitative research in psychology. In this chapter, I will share my view of what I believe is possible, why it is important to use the arts to expand the base of qualitative research methods, and how these methods can broaden our understanding of human behavior and mental processes. I will share some exemplars and conclude with some thoughts about the potential of the arts in qualitative research in the future.

◆ Ways of Knowing

To begin the discussion of how the arts inform qualitative research in psychology, it is necessary to start with epistemology (how knowledge is constructed), methods of inquiry, and the domains most suited to those methods. To date, qualitative research in psychology has been used most extensively in clinical, developmental, sport, community, vocational, and organizational psychology (Kidd, 2002). A rift has always existed between basic research and clinical practice, and the discipline finds itself somewhat divided along this line. The major perspectives in psychology that potentially define epistemological models suitable for qualitative research that draws on the arts are the humanist/existential, psychodynamic, cognitive, and social perspectives. These research methods, I believe, can be used effectively in these domains to contribute to the knowledges relative to each.

Some of the first qualitative methods in psychology used narrative forms of analysis and presentation (Polkinghorne, 1988). More recently, fictional narratives and the arguments for their epistemological value to education and psychology have appeared (Higgs, 1996; Kilbourn, 1998, 1999). Poetry has also been used by researchers in education (Piirto, 1998, 1999a, 1999b, 2000, 2002a), sociology (Richardson, 1994), and psychology (Rogers, 2001) to both create and present research understandings. The boundaries of qualitative research traditionally evident in the social sciences have been expanded by these unique methods of creating and reporting human experience.

Qualitative research in psychology has evolved through a number of different approaches. Carla Willig (2001) outlines several traditional approaches in her chapters on grounded theory, interpretative phenomenology, and case study. She then moves into more postmodern territory, exploring

methods of discursive psychology, Foucauldian discourse analysis, and memory work. These methods form a progressive move subtly closer to the acceptance of new creative ways of knowing and representing understanding in studies of human psychology. A similar progression can be seen in Camic, Rhodes, and Yardley's (2003) text of qualitative research in psychology. The paradigm gradually shifts toward a more relativistic mode of knowing, seeking subjective and intersubjective understanding in psychology.

Creative qualitative research methods may be considered new approaches, having their own epistemological and methodological designs, explained earlier in this handbook. Criticism exists within the qualitative research community concerning quality in developing arts-based research practices (Percer, 2002; Piirto, 2002b), but similar means for deciding what is good in traditional qualitative research should be employed in arts-based qualitative research. The arts, used in research, provide an opportunity to broaden the scope of qualitative design and add dimension to the constructivist paradigm.

◆ Three Questions About Epistemology

In the following section of this chapter, I will introduce examples of arts-based qualitative research in psychology and discuss their relationship to the larger project of human understanding that is psychology's goal. I will begin by addressing three questions related to epistemology.

1. WHAT COUNTS AS ARTS-BASED RESEARCH IN PSYCHOLOGY AND WHY?

Art is a unique expression of the artist. Because psychology is the study of behavior and mental processes of the individual, it is then conceivable that art can be studied for its psychological meaning. The arts have, in fact, been applied to inform culture of psychological truth for at least as long as humans have had literature. The ancient Greek narratives ascribed to Homer were great recitations, the purposes of which were to inform and guide the psychological health of the people. An enduring mystery is the philosophical question of whether the creator was constructing psychological truths in the process of writing a narrative, or reporting on folk wisdom that existed in the culture as knowledges reified in an oral tradition. Regardless, the narratives provided a means of constructing and reconstructing meanings and relative truths in the complex drama of human cultural evolution.

Homer's mythology suggests how one should manage emotions and know the self. Certainly, Shakespeare was also among the great creators and translators of psychological knowledge through his poetry and drama, and the audiences of his art are more informed about the human condition and about themselves. Using broad criteria such as these, the list of contributors to psychological knowledge through the arts would be unlimited. But a literature search for the arts in qualitative research reveals a severely limited pool of academic contributions to professional psychology journals (Kidd, 2002). Considering the contribution to psychological knowledge that the arts provide in teaching and building culture, a vast domain exists and is yet relatively unexplored.

2. WHO IS THE RESEARCHER IN ARTS-BASED RESEARCH, THE OBSERVER OR THE ARTIST?

In all qualitative research, the researcher is inseparable from the process (Hertz, 1997). The researcher in research based in the arts may be a witness to the creative process or be the artist involved in the research that explores the psychological aspects of the process. In either case, the researcher is heavily involved and must possess both expert understanding of the artistic process and the research methods most suited to the domain of psychology under investigation. Several useful critiques of poetry as qualitative research in education are provided by Jane Piirto (2002b) and Liza Hayes Percer (2002). Piirto and Percer suggest an efficacy in the use of poetry as research method but warn that respect for the craft and quality in the practice are as important as the degree of sophisticated understanding of theoretical knowledge in the studied discipline. Other writers on arts-based research suggest that, from a policy perspective, changes in the paradigm for conducting and displaying research findings are profound and that researchers "using artistically treated forms to conduct research ought to have a firm foundation in the relevant philosophical literature so that the process of doing that work becomes more than a technical achievement" (Barone & Eisner, 1997, p. 92).

Psychologists who are skilled artists and who would also like to conduct research using the arts will be confronted with the challenge of blending alternative epistemologies, a process that can create cognitive dissonance. Shaun McNiff (1999) acknowledges the discomfort presented by such a challenge as he discusses the work he is doing in his art studio and how it differs from the psychological research he conducts. "I did not realize how my slight discomfort with the early forms of art-based research was an expression of the separation between my artistic and psychological identities" (p. 69). Other therapists wanting to conduct relevant research note the same schism between research and clinical practice (Aigen, 1993).

While voices on both extremes suggest that the ontological differences between positivism and constructivism make collaboration impossible, I disagree. I believe these poles do serve unique purposes, but there is an abundant middle ground, and researchers and practitioners need to be aware of the demands, constraints, and potentials of both extremes. Taking a stronger collaborative stance allows us, as psychologists, to situate our research practices relative to their purposes and not necessarily according to the authority of tradition. In my view, then, the researcher should intentionally engage in art as psychological research and have qualified experience in both.

3. OF WHAT VALUE IS THE KNOWLEDGE CREATED BY ARTS-BASED RESEARCH TO PSYCHOLOGY'S TELOS?

In general, qualitative researchers in psychology are interested in the individual's lived experiences in the world and how one interprets those experiences in behavior and mental processes (Kidd, 2002; Marecek, Fine, & Kidder, 1997). Traditional qualitative research reports are presented as texts—descriptive narratives, interpretive or analytic essays, transcripts of interviews, or other forms of writing. Arts-based research, on the other hand, may break the mold of how to conduct research as well as present findings. Because using the arts in research provides new ways of knowing—ways of knowing that cannot be articulated through traditional practices or methods of reporting—the results potentially provide a richer context and practice-dependent understanding of the experience of the subject being investigated. Subjective and intersubjective knowing emerge in the act of making art and also later in observers who engage with the presentation of the work.

All arts-based research is psychological because it involves the reflexive subject engaged in psychophysical processes related to the psychological construction of self and world. Psychophysical processes include all aspects of sensory perception leading to cognition, emotion, and proprioception. The psychological questions of interest to arts-based researchers in psychology would most likely relate to some phenomenon of the subject's experience. Art making, as a research method, allows the researcher to experience directly through the senses (empirically) the dialectical interactions between the self and the medium of expression. The artist "sees" the world and uses skill to render the qualities in a way that evokes a truth about experience.

Lou Horner is an artist whose oeuvre is established (Watson-Jones, 1986). She has been a painter, sculptor, and multimedia artist for more than 25 years and has a long resumé of work in private collections and exhibitions in established galleries. There is no doubt that her works are portraits of meaning about being human. In 1991, when her mother was diagnosed with Alzheimer's disease, it became clear that Horner would have to adapt to the reality of watching the disease take her beloved from her. She used mixed media of collage and painting as a way to understand and communicate her own felt experience of observing the process of her mother's mental and physical decline. Using the arts as research, the artist as researcher may, as in Horner's case, conduct multiple interviews, do repeated observations, and engage in a long period of artifact collection and reflection.

This process is not unlike that used in ethnographic case studies where multiple interviews are standard (Kotre, 1984; Vaillant, 1977). In discussing ethnographic case study research as it applies to studies of the impact of chronic illness, Mishler (1999) suggests

Adaptation to trauma does not follow a linear, progressive course that is projectible from a one-shot interview at any point in the process. Successive interviews—their number and spacing depending on what happened and the aims of the study—are necessary to understand how identities change as alternative modes of adaptation and strategies for living are explored and tested. (p. 151)

Horner (2002) used arts-based qualitative research to attend to the progressive course of her mother's illness. She began recording her observations and writing introspective notes. She collected artifacts, using them as metaphors, attempted new forms of communication, and sketched changes in her mother's features. She employed a creative process to depict the progress of the disease, as therapy for her self to recover, to guide her own strategy for adapting, and as a means of communicating to others. *Going, Going, Gone* (See Figure 46.1 at the front of this book for a color reproduction) is one of Horner's paintings from a series that evokes the loss of mind in memory, identity, and connections with others.

In discussing the work, Horner describes her research process. "An artist is always researching, collecting artifacts, creating data, observing the world and conditions and emotions to use in their portrayal of the meaningful." I asked Horner to explain her art to me and she flatly stated that she could not. "The art speaks for itself," she said (Personal communication, July 29, 2004). In talking about art elements, though, Horner is more specific. The use of color to understand and shape the meaning of her felt experience is expressed eloquently in her painting Desire (See Figure 46.2 at the front of this book for a color reproduction.) and in her words (Horner, 2002).

Color, in this piece is used to create soft atmospheric surfaces that suggest hazy moments of memory. The use of color here creates an atmosphere that is nostalgic and evocative of memories, often foggy, or ambiguous. . . . The lean application of paint creating a transparent surface with veils of color and fragile, thin lines and small decorative elements, suggest emotional reserve and the betrayal felt in uncertain memories. Color is an element that is consistently expressed across my oeuvre. My pallet over time has contained a unique set of distinctive colors, which serve to identify my personal expression of emotion and connection with the world. (Horner, 2002, p. 11)

As a researcher, Horner is an artist first and a student of human psychology second. Her way of constructing knowledge and representing meaning in psychological subjects is through a mixed medium of collage, printmaking, and painting.

What value does Horner's work on the felt experience of watching her mother die of Alzheimer's disease contribute to psychology's *telos*? As an observer of her research work in progress and its products, I am taught lessons about human emotion, adaptation, and creative resilience that I might never have understood as a therapist. The opportunity to see through artists' eyes has provided new knowledge of human potential to adapt. It has taught me more about empathy and has given me an understanding that the art of therapy may be enriched by the use of arts in process and as artifacts of felt experience. I also understand that art products represent unique expressions of psychological truth that cannot be translated into traditional textual representations. Other observers of artists engaged in psychological research through their painting and drawing have observed that "the generative powers of a creative expression need to be fed with a corresponding consciousness which appreciates and keeps their mysteries" (McNiff, 1999, p. 74). The art itself is an adequate expression of meaning.

◆ *Three Psychological Characteristics of Arts-Based Qualitative Research*

Arts-based research has much to contribute to our understanding of individual psychology. Using examples from the professional literature, I will explore three characteristics: reflexivity, metaphor, and generativity. I believe these characteristics support the validity of arts-based qualitative research as a tool for investigating highly subjective aspects of human behavior and mental processes.

1. REFLEXIVITY

Artists, by training, become experts of observation and masters of translation, presenting their vision of the world through the processes and products of their work. Art making, by its nature, is a transformative process in which the artist and the medium are both changed. Artistic expression is frequently at the leading edge of change, defining a reality unseen by the language of objectivity. The artist, using special training, creative sensibility, and the willingness to move and be moved in a reflexive act, creates a way of knowing. The reflexive, transformative act of making art has many benefits, not the least of which include cognitive exercise, emotional catharsis, creation and explication of imaginative potential, theory building, perspective shifting, and many others. Arts-based qualitative research enjoys the same benefits of this reflexivity. The researcher, using

the craft skills of their art, is transformed in the process of discovering qualities of the subject under study, and a type of knowledge about each is created.

One of the key characteristics of human psychology is adaptive behavior through imaginative potential. In uncritical acts of living, people engage in a dance with experience and are changed as a result. In more critical or self-conscious acts, humans create change and respond to the environment or change it and are changed in the process. Dance therapist Maarit Ylonen (2003), in her hermeneutic analysis of dancing as a research method, effectively illustrates the reflexive nature of the relationship between researcher and participant, a process in which researcher becomes a participant and the method for producing knowledge is transformed. She reports

> Increasingly, the act of dancing itself, its physical nature, touch and closeness, and dance as nonverbal interaction with research participants have become the main methods of inquiry in my research. (p. 555) . . . I have used myself as a research instrument and learned to sense bodily dialogue, which has made dance a story, interpreted and reinterpreted over and over again. . . . The dancing person is like a reflective mirror, simultaneously revealing something about her self and about the other. (p. 565)

Arts reflect the dynamic self of the artist and the artist's perspective on experience. They are a personal expression of an understanding of the world, and they evoke the distilled experience of being in the world of the individual. As researchers, artists are attuned to the self-knowing reflective practice. The artist as researcher creates meaning.

Research in educational, health, and clinical psychology has shown benefits of the reflexive process of artistic engagement. In children, creative play and artistic expression are essential for cognitive development and academic achievement (Cesarone, 1999; Eisner, 1986; Gwathmey & Mott, 2000; Hamblen, 1993). Expressive arts therapies are also employed because of their capacity to respond to human suffering (Levine & Levine, 1999). The arts create a context in which the reflexive act of perceiving and expressing through various sensory modalities is made possible, and psychology's ideal goal, improving the quality of life, can be accomplished. Arts encourage a transcendental capacity. They allow the creator and the viewer to imagine possible ways of being, encourage the individual to move personal boundaries, and challenge resistance to change and growth.

2. METAPHOR

Much of psychology deals with the inner and intersubjective world of emotion and cognition related to experience. One of the greatest challenges of research in psychology is effectively describing inner states or experiences. Metaphors are widely used in therapeutic practice to allow clients and therapists to characterize and communicate often difficult-to-describe felt experience. Arts, as creative acts, provide a perfect opportunity to create new metaphorical models to illustrate the subject or question under study. Howard Stein (2003) provides a salient example of how arts can be used in applied psychology. As a consulting psychologist working with organizations to prevent and solve workplace problems, Stein has found that art can be a "useful vehicle for cultivating the imagination and thereby giving greater breadth and depth of access to the experienced world of organizations" (p. 84). His thesis is that arts, in the broadest sense, reflect deep inner experience, and as metaphors they can be used to reflect the meaningful inner life of organizations. The

arts are metaphorical—they allow the researcher/consultant to see into the organization to "identify organizational themes, narratives (story lines), secrets, conflicts, implicit structure, and the like" (p. 85). Stein's practice demonstrates the utility of metaphors as research tools for consultants and also as working tools within organizations that facilitate communication processes.

In what may be one of the more beautiful and powerful uses of poststructural theory, Annie Rogers (2001), a developmental psychologist, uses the craft of poetry as a metaphor to unwrap the profound effects of culture and gender on the lived experience and adaptive development in girls and young women. With remarkable clarity, Rogers identifies the effect of gender as a negative status and its influence on girls' development. Poetry, like painting, she suggests, depends on negative space to support and define the focal content. Trauma, for Rogers (2001), can be compared to poetic processes:

> I'm crafting a poetics of trauma in girls' and young women's lives through metaphors of memory, voice, and body. I follow both what is said and what is unsaid in girl's conversations and play, in dreams, in reenactments, in their writing and drawing. Rather than conceptualizing trauma as a cluster of symptoms, I consider trauma as a poetic process. I draw on fifteen years of research and clinical work with girls and young women to create a psychology of trauma, attending to conscious and unconscious processes of the mind and body that can be understood in the same way that we interpret poems.

Her remarkable research method, interpretive poetics, is used to read the "unsaid" that is a backdrop for the said in counseling interviews. The sensitive and creative approach of Rogers et al. (1999) employs a multilayered narrative analysis of interview texts and uses figurative associations to interpret the "not-said" (negative space) in counseling interviews with children and young women. In what can be described as the use of poetics to bridge the gap between what can be empirically known and the phenomena of highly subjective, lived experience, for the purpose of listening to the sometimes unspeakable in a therapeutic alliance, Rogers et al. (1999) provide counseling psychologists valuable tools for training in how to listen to the unsaid in their clients' communications.

Artists have always used their work to show the culture what it does not see otherwise. Art often exposes the negative space that forms a background, allowing the objective to stand out. Annie Rogers (2001) has seen this powerful tool in poetry and is using it in therapy. Those of us who read her work understand that the message is not just for the children with whom she works, but she is teaching us to listen to those who are oppressed by their languaged position in the narrative of being. Dance, music, poetry, and other arts all provide metaphors for lived experience, allowing us to see new ways to live and grow and new ways to know.

3. GENERATIVITY

I use the term generativity to describe the real potential that arts-based qualitative research has to create understanding, perspectives, and theory, unlike the traditional experimental methods used in psychology that simply seek to confirm existing theory and perspective. Good research, even in science, begins with informed imagination. The arts may create the spark that ignites further inquiry. The process of making art can nurture the intellectual flame that pushes the inquiring mind into a quest for new knowledge. Imagination and information

provide the basis for the further quest for knowledge in psychology. Much of the discipline of psychology is founded on basic science research, but even basic science involves improvisation and can be inspired by the arts and acts of making art. Scientists who do not see the connection between their practice and the world in which they struggle to live are only potentially accidental contributors to the puzzle.

In an innovative collaboration between Bobby Baker, a performance artist and recipient of cognitive behavior therapy (CBT), and psychotherapist Richard Hallam (Baker & Hallam, 2003), a creative video training tape of a CBT technique, Acting Opposite, was compared with a Good Manners training video. In a process that involved both quantitative and qualitative data collection and analysis methods, Baker and Hallam, intending to measure the effects of different CBT training methods, invited subjects who had previously completed questionnaires measuring their mood states to view the two instructional videos. This was followed by a formal tea party where participants were asked to select their choice of mouth-watering tea cakes from a menu, after which a randomly selected half of the participants were given their choice and the other half were served only dry biscuits.

By provoking emotion, Baker and Hallam (2003) hoped to be able to observe if the training tapes had influenced behavioral self-management in participants. The entire process was filmed by video and still cameras. After the tea party, participants were asked to complete mood scale exercises and engage in a focus group to discuss their experience of the event. In this exemplar, a psychologist and a performance artist collaborated to conduct research to explore the efficacy of self-help training videos of certain CBT constructs on human emotion and therapeutic practice. Baker's performance art in the innovative training videos and the research collaboration between artist and therapist generated new ways to use the therapeutic tools of cognitive behavioral therapy, normally a highly prescriptive, therapist-directed intervention.

Arts-based research creates a discursive space in which possible new ways of knowing are fostered and imaginative, creative processes are fueled. Inherent ambiguity in artistic processes creates cognitive dissonance, which often sparks growth and learning. Because there are no fixed truths, no final judgment can be made, and the therapeutic environment is enhanced. Clients are encouraged to find or create their own solutions. Growth potential is enhanced. Adaptation is piqued, and the generative spirit is given free reign.

◆ Conclusion

Much of what qualifies as arts-based qualitative research in psychology is currently found in its applied domains: education, counseling, clinical, and industrial and organizational psychology. The applied domains of the discipline are areas in which a reflective practice and practical improvisation are essential. The practice of applied psychology is naturally reflexive. Teachers, therapists, clinicians, and consultants must be empathic, creative, and imaginative, and also must be able to translate the understanding gained in practice using metaphors, narratives, representations, and nontraditional tools that can be imagined and created through arts-based research. Practitioners who engage in personal reflection through creative expression are more likely to be the ones who provide new direction and vitality to treatment, consulting, and pedagogical practice. In the nexus between basic research in human psychological processes and the therapeutic application of these understandings, we are offered a range of opportunity to conduct arts-based qualitative research in psychology.

As the traditional discipline of scientific psychology further defines the norms for acceptability and adaptation in social and cultural contexts, and thereby establishes the labels for difference and pathology, the search for the meaning of being and the individual self is crowded into a known space. This very process is found by many to be stultifying and antithetical to the human impulse to create and to know what is unknown. Psychology, as a discipline, has always struggled with this dilemma: how to unleash the creative potential in human nature and, at the same time, name and treat the pathologically deviant to guard the heart of the social norm. To hold on and to let go—this is the task of development, adaptation, intelligence, and survival. A diverse and intelligent psychology, embracing its qualitative roots, will be able to accomplish these seemingly disparate missions.

◆ References

Aigen, K. (1993). The music therapist as qualitative researcher. *Music Therapy, 12*(1), 16–39.
Baker, B., & Hallam, R. (2003). How to live. In B. Arends & D. Thackara (Eds.), *Experiment: Conversations in art and science* (pp. 62–95). London: The Wellcome Trust.
Barone, T., & Eisner, E. W. (1997). Art-based educational research. In R. M. Jaeger (Ed.), *Complementary methods for research in education* (pp. 73–94). Washington, DC: American Educational Research Association.
Camic, P. M., Rhodes, J. E., & Yardley, L. (Eds.). (2003). *Qualitative research in psychology: Expanding perspectives in methodology and design.* Washington, DC: American Psychological Association.
Cesarone, B. (1999). Benefits of art and music education. *Childhood Education, 76*(1), 52–53.
Denzin, N. K., & Lincoln, Y. S. (2000). *Handbook of qualitative research* (2nd ed.). Thousand Oaks, CA: Sage.
Donmoyer, R., Eisner, E., & Gardner, H. (1996). *Can a novel be a dissertation?* Panel

presented at the annual meeting of the American Educational Research Association, New York.

Eisner, E. W. (1986). The role of the arts in cognition and curriculum. *Journal of Art and Design Education, 5*(1–2), 57–67.

Gwathmey, E., & Mott, A. M. (2000). Visualizing experience. In N. Nager & E. K. Shapiro (Eds.), *Revisiting a progressive pedagogy: The developmental-interaction approach* (pp. 139–160). Albany: State University of New York Press.

Hamblen, K. A. (1993). Theories and research that support art instruction for instrumental outcomes. *Theory Into Practice, 32*(4), 191–198.

Hertz, R. (Ed.). (1997). *Reflexivity and voice.* Thousand Oaks, CA: Sage.

Higgs, G. E. (1996). Jordan: An allegorical novel exploring meaning in education and psychology. *Dissertation Abstracts International, 57*(01). (UMI No. 9636536)

Horner, M. L. (2002). *Recording the impermanence of experience.* Unpublished master's thesis, University of Missouri, Columbia.

Kidd, S. A. (2002). The role of qualitative research in psychology journals. *Psychological Methods, 7*(1), 126–138.

Kilbourn. B. (1998). *For the love of teaching.* London, Ontario, Canada: The Althouse Press.

Kilbourn, B. (1999). Fictional theses. *Educational Researcher, 28*(9), 27–32.

Kotre, J. (1984). *Outliving the self: Generativity and the interpretation of lives.* Baltimore, MD: Johns Hopkins University Press.

Levine, S. K., & Levine, E. G. (Eds.). (1999). *Foundations of expressive arts therapy: Theoretical and clinical perspectives.* Philadelphia: Jessica Kingsley Publishers.

Marecek, J., Fine, M., & Kidder, L. (1997). Working between worlds: Qualitative methods and social psychology. *Journal of Social Issues, 53*(4), 631–644.

McNiff, S. (1999). Artistic inquiry: Research in expressive arts therapy. In S. K. Levine & E. G. Levine (Eds.), *Foundations of expressive arts therapy: Theoretical and clinical perspectives* (pp. 67–88). Philadelphia: Jessica Kingsley Publishers.

Mishler, E. (1999). *Storylines: Craftartists' narratives of identity.* Cambridge, MA: Harvard University Press.

Percer, L. H. (2002). Going beyond the demonstrable range in educational scholarship: Exploring the intersections of poetry and research. *The Qualitative Report, 7*(2). Retrieved June 14, 2004, from http://www.nova.edu/ssss/QR/QR7–2/hayespercer.html

Piirto, J. (1998). *Understanding those who create* (2nd ed.). Tempe, AZ: Gifted Psychology Press.

Piirto, J. (1999a). A different approach to creativity enhancement. *Tempo, XIX*(3), 1–23.

Piirto, J. (1999b). *Talented children and adults: Their development and education* (2nd ed.). Columbus, OH: Prentice Hall/Merrill.

Piirto, J. (2000). Krishnamurti and me: Meditations on India and on his philosophy of education. *Journal for Curriculum Theorizing, 16*(2), 109–124.

Piirto, J. (2002a). *My teeming brain: Understanding creative writers.* Cresswood, NJ: Hampton Press.

Piirto, J. (2002b). The question of quality and qualifications: Writing inferior poems as qualitative research. *International Journal of Qualitative Studies in Education, 15*(4), 431–445.

Polkinghorne, D. (1988). *Narrative knowing and the human sciences.* Albany: State University of New York Press.

Richardson, L. (1994). Nine poems: Marriage and the family. *Journal of Contemporary Ethnography, 23*(1), 3–13.

Rogers, A. G. (2001). Alphabets of the night: Toward a poetics of trauma. *Radcliffe Quarterly.* Retrieved January 5, 2005, from http://donhanlonjohnson.com/annierogers.html

Rogers, A. G., Casey, M. E., Ekert, J., Holland, J., Nakkula, V., & Sheinberg, N. (1999). An interpretive poetics of language of the unsayable: Conceptions of the said and the not-said. In D. McAdams (Series Ed.) & R. Josselson & A. Lieblich (Vol. Eds.), *The narrative study of lives: Vol. 6. Making meaning of narratives* (pp. 77–106). London: Sage.

Sampson, E. E. (1989). The challenge of social change for psychology: Globalization and psychology's theory of the person. *American Psychologist, 44*(6), 914–921.

Stein, H. F. (2003). The inner world of work-places: Accessing this world through poetry, narrative literature, music, and visual art. *Consulting Psychology Journal: Practice and Research, 55*(2), 84–93.

Vaillant, G. E. (1977). *Adaptation to life.* Boston: Little, Brown.

Watson-Jones, V. (1986). *Contemporary American women sculptors.* Phoenix, AZ: Oryx Press.

Willig, C. (2001). *Introducing qualitative research in psychology: Adventures in theory and method.* Philadelphia, PA: Open University Press.

Ylonen, M. (2003). Bodily flashes of dancing women: Dance as a method of inquiry. *Qualitative Inquiry, 9*(4), 554–568.

47

WOMEN'S STUDIES AND ARTS-INFORMED RESEARCH

Some Australian Examples

◆ Lekkie Hopkins

Research in women's studies is inevitably interdisciplinary, frequently drawing on the arts to critique existing knowledges about cultural and social phenomena and to make new knowledges about a host of topics, including the body, sexuality, interpersonal violence, constructions of femininity and masculinity, ways of seeing, representations of women, women's health issues, ecofeminist issues, philosophy, cultures, the arts, the sciences. . . . The list is long. Research in women's studies is also inevitably political, making, as it must, connections between the activist practices and lived experiences of women out there in the world, the political and cultural discourses that constrain and shape them and with which women in turn interact, and the academic arena. And because it has frequently taken a position on the margins of academia, research in women's studies is sometimes experimental, exciting, risk-taking research that challenges the very foundations of established knowledge-making practices. Judy Chicago's (1979) controversial installation, *The Dinner Party,* provides an early example of such work.

These characteristics of research in women's studies—its interdisciplinarity and its highly political nature, in combination with its frequent occupation of the margins of academia—have implications for the ways it is conducted. For example, the politics of women's studies knowledge-making and the consequent desire for transparency in the research endeavor have ensured that the author herself is often placed firmly at the center of inquiry. Reflective collections such as Gayle Green and Coppelia Kahn's (1993) *Changing Subjects* draw attention to the intense pleasure and sometimes painful growth experienced by a number of feminist literary critics as they grapple with questions of location and identity emerging from the new knowledge-making processes they are swept up in. Closely linked to this kind of reflective investigation of the interconnections between one's scholarship and one's identity is an ongoing fascination within feminist scholarship with questions of the body and of the mind/body connection (excellently reviewed in such collections as that by Price & Shildrick, 1999). Of particular interest to this chapter are questions of embodied ways of knowing (theorized variously, for example, by Cixous & Calle Guber, 1997; Curti 1998; Davies, 1994; Diprose, 2002; Jaggar & Bordo, 1989; Neilsen, 1998). Such interest in the bodily impacts of knowledge is not new. Indeed, Moira Gatens (1996) draws on the rather remote figure of the philosopher Spinoza to remind us that he, too, was aware of the interconnections between epistemology and ontology. To know is to be, not to have, she argues. When we know differently, we are different.

Because the arts are crucial in their appeal to the senses, much of the experimental, risk-taking work in women's studies is arts-informed. Such work is not without tensions: Canadian scholar Lorri Neilsen (1998) writes of the delights and challenges in knowing and articulating one's ideas in relation to the ideas of others. She cites Yeager in stressing that

> the practice of following method and taking stances on methodological theorising can create a Bakhtian tension: ideas and methods invite focus, centring, normalising, cohering, reifying and replicating practices, often dangerously. Yet inquiry itself, its products and its processes, spin outward, multiply, refuse to mesh with a hegemonic centre. (Neilsen, 1998, p. 262)

And here, suggests Neilsen, in the movement towards the uncertain territory of the as-yet-undiscovered, is where the excitement lies:

> It is this centrifugal force, a destabilising force, which researchers have feared and which we now invite. Whether we call it feminist or postmodern . . . the inclination is to openness and growth, to take risks, to create critical spaces. . . . We can learn more when our pen is a tool of discovery, not domination. (Neilsen, 1998, p. 262)

In Australia, after four decades of women's studies scholarship, we find an ongoing fascination with the politics and processes of feminist, risk-taking knowledge making. Nowhere is this more obvious, perhaps, than in scholarship about the body and/or embodied knowledge. Readers will no doubt be familiar with the distinguished body scholarship of Australian feminist researchers such as Elizabeth Grosz (Grosz & Probyn, 1995), Elspeth Probyn (1993), and Moira Gatens (1996). In this chapter I provide glimpses of the processes of meaning making of four emerging contemporary Australian scholars whose research work is feminist, arts-inspired, interdisciplinary, embodied.

These four works illuminate the complex challenges to conventional research practices that continue to characterize much arts-inspired women's studies research, through providing examples, in turn, of the use of reflexivity to comment on the politics of knowledge making (McLaren, 2001); the use of performance to explore connections to place and space (Somerville, 1999), the use of embodied aesthetic engagement and re-membering in the autobiographical endeavor (Williams, 2003), and the use of fanciful imaginings and patterns of thought that brood rather than argue (Modjeska, 1990, p. 308) to explore embodied ways of knowing (Hopkins, 2001).

◆ Menopause, Art, and the Body

A recent example of Australian arts-based inquiry into a subject of central importance to women's studies is in Rosie McLaren's (2001) work *Menopause, Art, and the Body: Contemporary Tales From the Daughters of Hysteria*. This work emerges from McLaren's study of the ways women's art work changes during menopause. She rereads the discourses of hysteria through a process she calls a *conversational mapping* of the textual and visual representations of menopause. This glimpse of her work provides an example of the use of reflexivity to comment on the politics of knowledge making.

McLaren is an artist and psychotherapist whose work explores the visual and textual experience of menopause of 12 women artists. In an intricately woven and delicately nuanced text, McLaren draws on the art work, visual diaries, interview transcripts, phone conversations, journals, creative writing, and self-reflections of her participants to depict the lived experience of menopause as they reimagine their

memories and the experiences that informed their changing sense of self and the lived body. Together, in an intense and often intimate collaboration, McLaren and each of her participants explore the ways in which their artistic modes of self-expression are negotiated and influenced by contemporary cultural meanings of femininity, sexuality, and identity. In situating her work epistemologically, McLaren has cast her net wide: She draws on discourses of feminist poststructuralism, phenomenology, narrative inquiry, art, and medicine.

Rather than focus on the work of her participants, though, it is my intention here to focus on the processes of meaning making that McLaren foregrounds as she weaves her intricate text. From the outset she positions her work in resistance to mainstream knowledge making, citing Lorri Neilsen to justify her intense interest in reflexivity as an integral part of her research process.

> Reflexivity, telling stories about our researcher roles, is often considered to be self-serving, arrogant, even irresponsible. And yet, it is worth asking whether the charge of narcissistic self-absorption against such inquiry is, in large part, a function of an academic culture which is fearful of passion, emotion, gritty details, unpleasant smells, pillow-biting mistakes, sensuality and sexuality, sharp noises and messy processes. . . . To many, telling the stories that account for why we research and what really happens in the process of research is beyond the boundaries of good taste: it is akin to flashing in a faculty meeting, or having to explain away one's tipsy aunt in the hallway. (Neilsen, 1998, p. 269)

Rosie McLaren's work begins with an amplification of the battle that she, like many feminist researchers before her, fought for recognition of the embodied and subjective nature of meaning making. This excerpt provides glimpses of McLaren's (2001) creativity in weaving works of art, poetized reflections, and fragments of theoretical writings into the fabric of her research work, and draws attention to the multiple sites of engagement with the body and with lived experience that characterize her work. The two drawings included here are McLaren's own (McLaren, 2001, pp. 9–11).

Mid semester, first term.
It is hot and sultry.
I am giving a tutorial to undergraduate
and masters' students
on my choice of research topic.
Standing in the classroom
I note the male lecturer seated to my right.
I have brought four drawings.
Images of my tentative attempts
to make sense of my disruptive body
as I begin this journey called menopause.
I am proud of them.
I am nervous also.
They are childlike and innocent.
I have drawn myself naked—Picasso style—
with my genitals exposed.
These are drawings about my body,
about desire,
about sexuality.
About not knowing who I was.
I have drawn an image of myself
and my beloved dog Jimmy,
a symbol of the keeper of my soul.
We are looking at our bodies.
At our sex.
The caption reads
Is this what love is?
I tell the students of my recent reading of
    Germaine Greer's book
The Change, and how in part,
she examined the historical writings of women,
and the ways in which they wrote in coded
    metaphor to speak of menopause.
I explain how my interest was aroused
and how this led me to the question:
How did women artists articulate this experience?

Figure 47.1   Are You Looking for Love?

SOURCE: McLaren, R. (2001). *Menopause, Art and the Body. Contemporary Tales From the Daughters of Hysteria*. Flaxton, Queensland, Australia: Post Press. Copyright © Rosie McLaren. Reprinted with permission.

The lecturer interjects and says
Would you just get to the theory that is inform-
    ing your work?
Your personal story is of no interest to anyone
    here.
I stand transfixed to the floor.
I stop breathing.
I feel a hot flush rising
I hope no one can see.
My heart races.
My tongue feels like it is moving.
No sounds emerge.
I look around the room
into the eyes of women
and to the young men looking at me
and my body in the drawings.
There is silence.
My eyes implore

where are your voices?
Why don't you say
but the personal IS political?
Why are you colluding in this negation of my
   story?
I feel betrayed.
The heat in my body turns to rage.
It tears open my tear ducts.
I feel a hot stinging in my eyes.
Please God don't let me cry.
Deep breath.
I want to cry out
Why can't you people
you women who call yourselves feminists
and you young men who think you are embrac-
   ing our ideals
see that my life HAS been given agency by my
   organic body.
It is the awakening of my critical conscious-
   ness.
This IS the basis for my methodology.
The absence of blood and raging hormones
has impelled me to a different space.
I am no longer making art.
My practice has changed.
I am a becoming writer struggling with words.
I feel my body collapsing
Spiralling down to my gut
Shrinking.

Familiar feeling this.
Speaking out—then censure—then shame.
My utterance, my personal anecdote
of fractures and openings
falls like a dead leaf into the drawer of memory
marked Acts of Resistance—Action Pending.
I sit down,
and with head bowed
read text
like dry oatmeal off the page.*

SOURCE: *McLaren, R. (2001). *Menopause, art
and the body. Contemporary tales from the
daughters of hysteria.* Flaxton: Post Press. Copyright
© Rosie McLaren. Reprinted with permission.

Here written text and drawings can be
seen to work together to evoke the complex
interplay of gender, academic status, generational politics, and bodily knowing in the
battle over competing research paradigms.
The bold, powerful, intensely subjective
drawings attest to the researcher's deep certainty, clearly articulated in the written
text, that the menopausal body is the
ground on which her research practice is
built. These images contrast strongly with
the other image that arises from the written
text, of the vulnerable, crushed novice

Figure 47.2   Dog Dying

SOURCE: McLaren, R. (2001). *Menopause, Art and the Body. Contemporary Tales From the Daughters of
Hysteria.* Flaxton, Queensland, Australia: Post Press. Copyright © Rosie McLaren. Reprinted with permission.

researcher, whose body collapses and shrinks, and who "sit[s] down /and with head bowed/read[s] text/like dry oatmeal off the page." Strength and vulnerability sit side by side. The dichotomous conceptual order is subverted, and complexity uncovered. Rather than providing a rationale for using embodied, arts-based research data such as this, the passage works to foreground the very processes of such embodied, subjective meaning making.   ◆

◆ *Body/Landscape Journals*

I turn now to the work of Margaret Somerville, whose book *Body/Landscape Journals* was published by Spinifex Press in 1999. This glimpse of her work highlights her use of performance to explore bodily connections to place and space, and provides a subjective account of the bodily impact of her kind of knowledge making. Somerville sets out in her work to explore the connections between body and landscape by remembering six sets of experiences from her own life, each of which is conceived of as a performance.

These six performances occur in Australia in a range of landscapes: We move from a couple of sites in the red dust of the Central Desert at the heart of this vast land to the lush tropics of the cassowary country on the far northeast coast of Queensland, via the rolling temperate inland tableland country of Northern New South Wales, and back again. All six performances grapple with the liminal spaces between being and becoming as they reenact Somerville's own embodiment in landscape. All six performances involve connections with women: the women of the antinuclear protest camp at Pine Gap in the Central Australian desert in 1983; the indigenous women camped in the middle of Pitjantjatara Lands, 600

kilometres south west of Alice Springs; the old indigenous women of the tableland country in Northern New South Wales; the indigenous Emily celebrating the Queen, high on a mountain toward the Warrambungles; the cassowary women who campaign for the preservation of these huge birds in North Queensland; the women of home.

To create her text Somerville uses a combination of genres: poetry, prose, photographs, excerpts from interview transcripts, songs; she draws, too, on a range of literary sources (Modjeska, Rich, Trinh) and feminist theoretical sources (Irigaray, Cixous, Davies, Probyn) to explore her bodily immersion in landscape. Meaning accrues; theoretical insights emerge. As with McLaren's work, the impact on the reader is bodily. Layer upon layer of meaning suggests itself as one becomes more and more immersed in her text. In an attempt to amplify the collaborative nature of meaning making and the affective responses evoked by such a research text, I include here an extract from my own research journal, written after spending the day reading, for perhaps the fourth time, Somerville's work.

I have spent the day up here in my aerie, reading M's Body/Landscape journals. This isn't the first time I've read them, of course, but this time they make my heart sing. This time I'm reading closely for process, for insights into when, how, how long, this part of the narration took. . . . Along the way I get delicious glimpses of her daily life, her friends, her habits, her daughter's presence in her life, her absent husband, her dead but present mother, her Aboriginal women friends, families, stretching from the Central Desert in a wide web of interconnecting threads, enmeshing her daily patterns in the web of story and practice. I glimpse too the networks of cassowary women she finds in the tropical rainforests, and I become acutely aware of the webs she then spins herself, linking cassowary women through verandas to forests and in to an understanding of Liz Ferrier's postcolonial architectural work, and from here to spatial discourses spun by Paul Carter and some man called Turner whose work I do not know.

I think cloth and see washing on lines, and see billowing calico curtains in houses she has made; I think houses and see nests shaped by the breast and beak of tiny birds; I think tiny birds and see huge cassowaries both visible and invisible, both real and imagined. I think houses and see the recipe for mud bricks: at first you play by the rules but later you just know how to do it; later the knowing is yours, you do it by feel. I think recipes and I see all those cakes and salads and brown rice plain lunches and special truffle sauced beef for a feast day, and see whole pigs and sheep cooked in the earth oven, and jellies kept cold in great tubs of ice from the iceworks, and a movable feast open to all the family who straggle in for a week or more at Christmas: There's always a place at Aunty Someone's table for anyone who comes for a week around Christmas.

I think story and I see Trinh and Irigaray and Cixous hold hands to dance with M as she creates her performance. I think story and I see the performance in the Desert, the stories told about the Queen, the family stories, the stories of displacement, of finding the self, of creating the self as Elspeth Probyn says at the outer limits of our knowing. I think of her struggles to narrate her self into existence, and I feel connected with her through seeing, connected with her through imagining her life, filling in the gaps and spaces. I think of the whole project and understand, finally, why it had to be a performance in landscape before ever it could move to the interior, the

house home we build. Her embodiment in landscape is more profoundly practised in this text than any other I have read, I think. I picture her clearly as a small child escaping always into the bush. I understand with my body, out of an experience which is never and cannot be mine, but which I know from the body nevertheless, what it is to be anchored in landscape, what it is to be deeply connected with other liminal figures in reciprocal love of, understanding of, landscape.

In taking me on this journey with her, she has gifted me with the ability to know enmeshment with the world of tree and mud and cave and icy river; of sea and sand, central desert and liminal beach. Today I have grasped the enormity of the country, this Australia, this landscape, as never before. Today I have seen into someone's soul. My gut churns with it. It is exciting, new, wondrous, and calming, deeply satisfying. It is like coming home.

◆ *Feminine Fictions*

Another highly original recent Australian research project is Rose Williams's *Feminine Fictions* (2003). This glimpse of her work amplifies contemporary arts-based research in women's studies by foregrounding Williams's use of embodied aesthetic engagement and remembering in the autobiographical endeavor. This work sets out to navigate feminine embodied ontology with/in aesthetic autography via a performance/installation that took place in the shell of the former Fremantle Prison, in Fremantle, Western Australia, on December 8, 2002, and via an exegesis presented as a CD-ROM in Web-page format.

Rose Williams draws upon a wide range of theoretical texts and a wealth of lived experience to create three sets of 15 creative texts (15 life stories written in different locations, 15 installation texts written at the sites of the developed installation work based on these texts, and 15 theoretical texts drawn from theoretical reading underpinning the project), which together formed the basis for the series of 15 installations within the prison, metaphorically based on 15 stations of the cross. The concluding communal performance that took place among the installations at the prison brought together 55 members of what Williams calls her epistemic community. The exegesis, presented as a CD-ROM in Web-page format, extends her proposal of embodied ontology into cyberspace. Installation, performance, and exegesis work together to extend, dislodge, disrupt, re-member, and read afresh the knowledges from which they spring.

This is work of a vast scale that engages deeply with contemporary feminist theory. Rose Williams works with some of the most complex and intricate of contemporary feminist theoretical concepts—Irigaray's notion of the feminine divine (Grosz, 1989) and Trinh's (1989) explorations of the connections of infinity with divinity; Cixous's (1991) concept of embodied inscription and Kristeva's feminine semiotics; the complexly different body scholarship of Elizabeth Grosz (1989), Bronwyn Davies (1994), Iris Marion Young (1990), and Donna Harraway (1990)—and attempts through her installation/performance not simply to embody this suite of theoretical concepts but to re-embody, re-member them through the process of enactment.

For the performance/installation event, a vast number of objects and art works were installed in three floors of the prison. They included paintings, sculptures, drawings, found objects, photographs, a range of textiles, videos, written texts, soundscapes, and cyberscapes. Against this backdrop, the space was prepared for performance with the installation of sound equipment, lighting equipment, and stage props. At the center of it all was the body: the immediate living body of Rose the performer, decorated, inscribed, prepared for performance; the filmed body of Rose the theorist, speaking theoretical insights onto videotape; the remembered body of Rose the child/woman, glimpsed through a range of stories, photographs, films, and artworks.

The eclectic range of artistic genres, from the high art of painting and sculpture to the kitch of recreated domestic 1980s paraphernalia, demanded a visceral, embodied response from those of us invited to participate in this installation and performance. Here was a text as messy, fragmented, incoherent, and sensuous, as unmapped and illogical as the raw experience of lived life, a text onto which we must track our own journeys, through which we must negotiate our own bodily response. It was impossible to negotiate this space without being alternately physically jolted, moved, shocked, delighted, and sometimes just plain confused. At times the need to think through the body (e.g., in negotiating a space with dismembered chicken carcasses) was confronting and uncomfortable. At other times, my sheer delight in recognizing the feminist theoretical play in the use of light, sound, mirror, and text to illuminate the iconic photographs of her grandmother shifted to horror mixed with a sense of curious wonderment, as the installation text took me into the seductive realms of murder, suicide, imprisonment, and death.

The performance space itself had its own bodily impact. I found it impossible to forget that this space had, until recently, been a prison. The hollow clanking noises as people trudged up and down metal staircases; the loud clanging bangs as objects were dropped or tripped on; the competing, echoing musical soundtracks emanating from the various performance spaces jerked and jarred the body, reminding me constantly of the impossibility of escape. At one stage during the performance in a scene when the audience was gathered on a mezzanine floor above the three performers, looking down onto the sterile hospital bed where the anorexic child engages with the stories of the child in the bed next to hers, the anguish of the performance combined with the anguish of the prison space itself created in me a kind of vertigo that left me feeling faint.

Underpinning the entire installation/performance was an intricate grappling with the notion of breaking through into new theoretical territory, working with embodied aesthetic engagement to uncover Irigaray's notion of the feminine as a site of difference, and to explore what this might mean for contemporary feminisms. In Irigaray's terms (Grosz, 1989), it is work that links the terrestrial with the celestial. I have found it to be work that is both starlit and earthbound.

◆ *Finding Voice*

Finally, I turn to my own research on restorying the self, linking contemporary feminist knowledges of the body, sexuality, narrative, and textual representations of femininities to feminist activist practice (Hopkins, 2001). Conceptually this work explores the ways we might work with poststructuralist notions of subjectivity and power to enact feminist activist practice. It draws specifically on Drusilla Modjeska's (1990) fictionalized biography, *Poppy,* to explore the ways Modjeska views the processes of finding voice, of giving life to a story and story to a life. In writing the text, I have attempted to use narrative strategies similar to those used in *Poppy* (collage, dislocated chronologies linking linear stories, moments of lyric

stasis) to reflect on the journey toward feminist activism of my central participant, a former women's studies student called Sandy Newby. To amplify Sandy's and my own respective journeys toward feminist activism, I intertwine many different kinds of writing, including poetry, prose, story, theoretical analysis, journal writing, transcript of interview, fanciful imaginings, and a process of circular reflection that echoes Modjeska's own.

I provide here a brief example of the shift from fanciful imagining to reflective theorizing that specifically calls on Modjeska's (1990) technique of using "patterns of thought that brood rather than argue"(p. 308) to explore embodied ways of knowing:

> In wrestling with the problem of how someone as articulate and capable as Sandy came to be silenced. . . I have a dream. In the dream, Sandy and I are in India together, but I know this is a different visit from the one we have already made. Our auras are different. We both seem pale, dejected. We're standing on the paved area in front of the ferry terminal in Mumbai harbour. A snake charmer sits cross legged on the paving in front of us. His weird mysterious music spins a thin blue smoky thread which winds its way around us both. Ever so gently, the music envelops us. Our bodies become smoke, each lifting separately off the ground, mine to the right, Sandy's to the left.
>
> Looking down from on high, I see that millions of snakes infest these smoky bodies. Slowly the music changes, and the snakes disappear. But they have left their tails. I know this because I can see them lurking in the shadows from on high. When I return to my body, the snake tails are hidden, and I am glowing

with a different light. Sandy is too. The snake charmer has gone, his bag of snakes with him. I am dreamily happy. But I know that somehow, somewhere, danger lurks in shadows. I wake feeling troubled. My heart is heavy.

* * *

Memories of this dream return to me now as I'm pulled up short in my attempts to narrate the story of Sandy and her life at the union. My own experience of uncovering a (not very well hidden) desire for the triumphant conclusion to Sandy's story and, in my academic life, a triumphant conclusion to the story of a decade of feminist activism, has reminded me of the tendency of old discourses to lurk, like the tails of discarded snakes, often unbidden, within the psyche which has willingly taken on newer or different ways of seeing/reading the world.

I understand intuitively and intellectually that epistemologies and ontologies are inextricably linked. Do the tails of these old discourses also linger in the body. . . . If voice is born of the interstices of epistemologies and ontologies, so too, surely, is silence? My experience and Sandy's suggests that the imagination has to be very strong in order to over-ride the pull into bleakness and despair which the pain-filled body will insist on. Can the body's own bleakness sabotage one's capacity to re-read and re-story events? (Hopkins, 2001, pp. 182–183)

The power of this narrative technique lies in its conceptual resonance. In the final section of the *Poppy* text, called *Friends*, the narrator, Lalage, indicates that she has moved into the conceptual territory beyond binary oppositions with her reference to a conversation with her father about the writing of this biography, where "I talked about

patterns of thought that brood rather than argue, and of the fictional paradox of truthfulness"(Modjeska, 1990, p. 308).

Lalage's emphasis on the circularity and stillness implicit in the notion of "patterns of thought which brood" rather than on the linearity and forward thrusting movement on those that *argue* suggests a desire to communicate to her father that she has moved beyond masculinist ways of thinking (which would allow her only to favor rationality/linearity/argument) and into the territory where the boundaries between fiction and truthfulness merge and blur.

Such thinking resonates within the feminist epistemological canon. Hovering around the desire to think beyond binary oppositions is the image of Irigaray's two sets of two lips, drawn from a metaphor whose simultaneity "defies binary categories and forms of classification, being undecidedly inside and outside, one and two, genital and oral" (Grosz, 1989, p. 116).

◆ Conclusion

I began this chapter with the claim that three characteristics of much research in women's studies—its interdisciplinarity, its highly political nature, and, at times, its occupation of the margins of academia—have implications for the ways it is conducted. The four examples of contemporary feminist scholarship I have provided here are not intended to be representative of the body of Australian women's studies scholarship, or, indeed, of women's studies scholarship occurring elsewhere around the globe. Rather, they are recent works with which I am familiar, and that mobilize the arts to generate new, embodied ways of seeing, of knowing, of making meaning in the social sciences.

What, then, is the future of arts-based or arts-informed research in creating knowledges within the broader field of women's studies? The major international journals (*Signs: A Journal of Women in Culture and Society, Women's Studies International Forum, Feminist Review*) and their Australian counterparts (*Australian Feminist Studies, Hecate, Violence Against Women*) continue to publish work that is innovative, exciting, rich, disturbing, and politically necessary. Some of it draws explicitly on the arts to make knowledge; some does not. The tensions for women's studies scholars are perhaps generated not so much by the divide between arts-based or non-arts-based research (if there ever is such a divide) but, rather, by the recognition that much women's studies scholarship creates and grows out of new ways of seeing: It is frequently groundbreaking, rulebreaking research. Perhaps most significantly of all, being able to draw on the arts allows a sensory, bodily engagement with the research endeavor. As researchers we thread our ways around and through, up and under, reading and rereading, accumulating insights, gathering wisdoms, connecting myth with contemporary story, connecting explorations of ways of knowing with ways of reading, ways of living, ways of loving, ways of being, to open the way for further journeys.

In the words of Cixous (1991), "Heed. Need. Woman does not stop at woman, doesn't stop. Flows, writes herself in parataxes of liquid light, tears, and her style is Aqua Viva, the stream of life" (p. 166).

◆ References

Chicago, J. (1979). *The dinner party*. Stanford, CT: Sandak.

Cixous, H. (1991). *Coming to writing and other essays* (D. Jensen, Ed.). Cambridge, MA: Harvard University Press.

Cixous, H., & Calle-Guber, M. (1997). *Rootprints: Memory and life writing*. London: Routledge.

Curti, L. (1998). *Female stories female bodies: Narrative, identity, and representation*. London: Macmillan.

Davies, B. (1994). *Poststructuralist theory and classroom practice*. Geelong, Victoria, Australia: Deakin University Press.

Diprose, R. (2002). *Corporeal generosity: On giving with Nietzsche, Merleau-Ponty, and Levinas*. Albany: State University of New York Press.

Gatens, M. (1996). *Imaginary bodies: Ethics, power, and corporeality*. London: Routledge.

Greene, G., & Kahn, C. (Eds.). (1993). *Changing subjects*. London: Routledge.

Grosz, E. (1989). *Sexual subversions: Three French feminists*. Melbourne, Victoria, Australia: Oxford University Press.

Grosz, E., & Probyn, E. (Eds.). (1995). *Sexy bodies: The strange carnalities of feminism*. London: Routledge.

Haraway, D. (1990). A manifesto for cyborgs: Science, technology, and socialist feminism in the 1980s. In L. Nicholson (Ed.), *Feminism/Postmodernism* (pp. 190–233). New York: Routledge.

Hopkins, L. (2001). *Finding voice: Giving life to a story and story to a life—A temporal and spatial mapping of the creation of the feminist activist self in contemporary Australia*. Unpublished doctoral thesis, James Cook University, Townsville, Queensland, Australia.

Jaggar, A., & Bordo, S. (1989) *Gender/body/knowledge: Feminist reconstructions of being and knowing*. New Brunswick, NJ: Rutgers University Press.

McLaren, R. (2001). *Menopause, art, and the body. Contemporary tales from the daughters of hysteria*. Flaxton, Queensland, Australia: Post Pressed.

Modjeska, D. (1990). *Poppy*. Ringwood, Victoria, Australia: McPhee Gribble.

Neilsen, L. (1998). *Knowing her place: Research literacies and feminist occasions*. San Francisco & Halifax, Nova Scotia, Canada: Caddo Gap Press & Backalong Books.

Price, J., & Shildrick, M. (1999). *Feminist theory and the body: A reader*. Edinburgh, UK: Edinburgh University Press.

Probyn, E. (1993). *Sexing the self*. London: Routledge.

Somerville, M. (1999). *Body/landscape journals: A politics and practice of space.* North Melbourne, Victoria, Australia: Spinifex Press.

Trinh, T. M. (1989). *Woman, native, other.* Bloomington: Indiana University Press.

Williams, R. (2003). *Feminine fictions.* Unpublished doctoral thesis, Edith Cowan University, Perth, Australia.

Young, I. M. (1990). *Throwing like a girl and other essays in feminist philosophy and social theory.* Bloomington: Indiana University Press.

48

A HISTORY OF THE ARTS IN EDUCATIONAL RESEARCH

A Postmodern Guide for Readers-Flâneurs

◆ Christine van Halen-Faber
and C. T. Patrick Diamond

History is far from concerned with mere literal facts. . . . [It has] an essentially mythological shape, which reveals itself most clearly in fiction and provides the basic conceptual structure for history.

—Butler, 2002, pp. 34–35

An aesthetic experience, the work of art in its actuality, is perception. . . . Perception is more than just looking and recognizing, it is a way to make sense of what one senses, to partake of its meaning. . . . What is perceived are meanings rather than just events or circumstances.

—Jackson, 1998, p. 57

◆ Our History

First the sight-/guidelines that we see as informing "the allegorical gaze" (Frisby, 2002, p. 33) that we cast over the events that caught our eye while we were imagining a history of the arts in educational research: Using the indifferent, "perceptive" mode of a pair of watchful postmodern or neo-*flâneurs*,[1] we see postmodernism as a condition of our time in which there has been a loss of belief in any one account of history. No longer privileged as a "truth-telling" meta-narrative and with even its very sense being challenged (Jameson, 1991), history has become another form of fiction making in which the play of assorted metaphors and nomadic randomness is freely courted. To form our situated mini-narrative, we un/enfolded and reshuffled fragments of preexisting texts as in a series of heightened literary collages spilling from these pages into the cyberspace of the *Handbook's* accompanying Web site (see Figures 48.1–48.5 and www.sagepub.com/knowlessupplement); paper and screen text together producing "a citational hybridity" (Butler, 2002, p. 89); word-crowds, associations, borrowings, and tropes haunt our account of a history aesthetically observed.

Even though there is no synoptic picture to be had, "a postmodern position allows us to know something without claiming to know everything" (Richardson, 1994, p. 518). We know, for example, that the importance of the arts, like their spread, is far reaching. The arts are being acknowledged and celebrated in social science research, including history and education. What we offer here is not a conventional nonfiction outline told from a single authorial perspective, twisted to conform to one "main thesis" or argument determining its development. Our chapter is an essay in (re)presenting a history of the arts in educational research perceived as a set

of floor plans supported (or undermined) by postmodernism. Realized as a series of (non)conceptual montages and throughlines (Pinar, 2004), we mount our history so that it does not merely speak *about* the arts in research but actually shows the arts *being used* in research, providing a collaborative, three-dimensional, and ambulatory guide.

We see the arts as an organizing cluster of principles that both constructs and is constructed by postmodernism. Within the crisis of representation, the work of the arts is to present different ways of documenting efforts to evoke and reflect on experience. In this postreconceptualist time, we see (and later display) the arts in research in three interrelated ways: as a preoccupation with imaginative experience and with the liberating power that proceeds from them (Diamond & Mullen, 1999); as a free-wheeling, *flâneur*-like "form of theoretical research [that applies] concepts from the arts, humanities . . . social sciences" (Pinar, Reynolds, Slattery, & Taubman, 1996, p. 62) and architecture to inquiry; and as a means for (re)viewing research, self-identity, and social issues through blending postmodern, literary, visual, and text-based approaches. We use a collection of citations borrowed from a large number of arts-based authors who, over time, have guided our understandings of what it might mean to perceive and proceed as arts-based inquirers. As authors-collectors-archivists-curators, we "frame" these quotations and display them for you, our reader-viewers, as if in a museum-gallery (see Figures 48.3–48.5, and link it all to www.sagepub.com/knowlessupplement).

We do not award these text fragments or their authors any kind of privileged "collector status." Nor do we mean to suggest that those not chosen for display have failed to meet some set of predetermined criteria for determining "winners and losers." For us, the act of collecting, curating, and displaying is a nonjuried move: a sharing of ourselves as arts-based inquirers who acknowledge that herein "lies the whole miracle of collecting. For it is invariably *oneself* that one collects" (Baudrillard, 1994, p. 12). In artful inquiry, "who we are is invariably related to who others are, as well as to who we have been and want to become" (Pinar, 1994, pp. 243–244). As subjects of our own perceptions, we partake of the meaning making and sense ourselves doing so, like Surrealist photographers catching their own outlines reflected in their ex/interior images.

A postmodern, arts-based form of inquiry entails a struggle to represent experience as it is directly experienced. This requires the deployment of artful ways of bringing experience to form and then encouraging reader-viewers to continue its reconstruction, all proceeding by arts-informed touch. Inquirers do "not produce a work [of artful inquiry] and then give it a twist by inserting devices and techniques here and there like acupuncture needles. The work itself is the device" (Dillard, 1982, p. 29), just as ours is the series of figures below.

We use image- and text-based ways of pursuing our arts-based inquiry into the meaning and structures of some of the past events (authors and their publications) that we awoke to as constituting our history, a three-storied plan among many others. As reader-viewers, you will hear us worrying about the difficulties of the task. But then, the arts in educational research will self-consciously draw attention to their status as artifacts in order to pose questions about the relationship between experience and art, especially about the ways in which their forms can be (re)configured; a reflexive turn. In providing a critique of their own methods of construction, artful inquiries explore the fictional nature of multiple "realities" and our places in them. While some impatient critics may prefer more matter with less art, a postmodern work/inquiry

with all its quotations from the past and intimations of the future recalls features of postmodern architecture—redundantly abundant, maximalist, and neo-eclectic.

Our reader-viewers will have to be "satisfied with swirls, confluxions, and inconstant connections. . . . What we can construct, if we keep [curatorial] notes and survive, are *hindsight accounts of the connectedness of things that seem to have happened: pieced-together patternings* [italics added], after the fact" (Geertz, 1995, p. 2). Or as in a dream.

In sharing our curatorial notes and citations as hindsight accounts, we can offer only a confused ordering of arts-based works and a sense of their relationship that must remain open to rearrangement and reinterpretation. We place similar glimpses in conjunction with one another, relying on intuition and imagination to provide access to forms of felt knowledge not able to be encountered as "sensibly" through nonaesthetic means.

◆ Giving Arts-Based Inquiry a Figure and a Place in Time

In our chapter-text history we (re)present the abstractions and effects of this contested research tradition by imagining a way into the events and circumstances that we see as surrounding it. Such approaches have previously been aggregated and known, through a series of appropriations or renovations, as the arts and/in education, or as aesthetic, a/r/tographic, arts-centered, arts-informed, arts-based inquiry. These constructs and practices have left us with a store of material ready for (re-)citing. In this chapter and its companion Web site (www.sagepub.com/ knowlessupplement), we describe and illustrate our history through placing together selections from our own artful inquiry holdings. We use the Musée d'Orsay, a refurbished train station-as-museum in Paris, to house and display our arranged citations. Like curators using a postmodern approach, we structure our exhibition of artifacts/fragments by listing and thematically clustering the holdings rather than ordering them in a conventional, periodized display. In this museum setting, we cast our reader-viewers in the role of visitors who are invited to wander *flâneur*-like through our virtual world of artful inquiry. Recalling Walter Benjamin's methodological procedures as a literary critic-artist-historian, we look carefully at, decipher, and produce our history as a hybridized text.

Like Benjamin, who inquired into the origins of modernity through (re)viewing the architecture of Paris (see Frisby, 2002), we assumed the role of then-collectors but now-museum-guides as we prepared this exhibition catalog for you, our reader-viewers. Although you might begin with our guide, feel free to make your own way through the display. We retrace the contours of our working models, of *flânerie* and the d'Orsay, to locate as much as we can in the time and space of our chapter. We hope that you will allow yourselves to become lost in our museum-gallery-based maze. But remembering that to do so—"as one loses oneself in a forest—calls for quite a different schooling" (Benjamin, 1932/1986a, p. 8) or gaze. Our inquiry is positioned in galleries and rooms for you to make your own sense of what we have sensed (see Figures 48.3–48.5). So, please imagine and wander through our history as a series of rooms—as Benjamin did through Paris—arranged for your viewing pleasure.

Even as Paris created the *flâneur*, that ambiguous urban figure used the city in turn as an aid to historical memory. The fundamental experience of the *flâneur* revolves around "the sensational phenomenon of space" (Frisby, 2002, p. 39). A glance at a city map reveals its arrangement into 20 *arrondissements*, with each claiming a place in history. For our history we might have reimagined this city map, with its clockwise spiraling from the first to the last *arrondissement*, as symbolic of the emergence of different forms of arts-based inquiry within the development of educational research, both as a more recent arrival and as a reworking of older traditions. But that metaphoric line of inquiry does not suit our disposition.

We stroll along the Seine quayside to the Musée d'Orsay art gallery, in the 6th district, to gaze at its *belle epoche* ex/interior clock—only to be reminded in our mind's eye of Wolcott's (1990) display in which qualitative or descriptive studies are depicted as a baker's pie.[2] We next (re)present this graph as a second clock face showing his 14 research approaches, with equal time allocated to each (see Figure 48.1). Beginning at 12:00 and moving clockwise, they include: the ethnography of communication, ethnomethodology, field study, participant observation, oral history, phenomenology, case study, connoisseurship/criticism, investigative journalism, nonparticipant observation, human ethnology, natural history, ethnology, and back again to ethnography just before midnight/early daylight. All as ways of showcasing collections of experiences, figures, and objects. For us, Eisner's (1979) paradigm-altering construct of connoisseurship/criticism appears as the segment for *flânerie* just past 6 o'clock.

In an (re)imaging move, we next superimpose Wolcott's nonchronological clock face on that of the *fin-de-siècle* clock of the Musée d'Orsay to situate and foreshadow our inquiry, showing how in research, as in history, vision can outlive changing times and purposes. The Gare d'Orsay was originally designed as the architectural centerpiece for the Universal Exhibition of 1900. Its light-filled vault of glass panels and wrought iron tracery gave the station the air of a palace of the Beaux-Arts. It served as a mark of

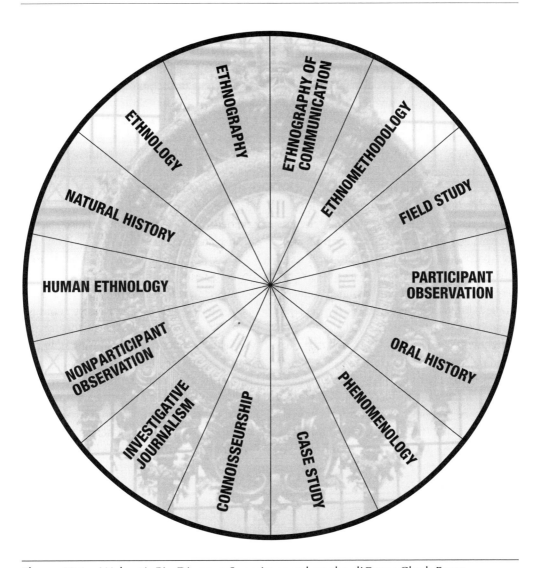

Figure 48.1 Wolcott's Pie Diagram Superimposed on the d'Orsay Clock Faces

SOURCE: From H. F. Wolcott (1990). *Writing up Qualitative Research*. Sage Publications, Inc. Reprinted with permission.

French progress that burgeoned only to fade. However, that vision and the building were reinvented as the Musée d'Orsay.

Not unlike securing a place for the arts in academic research, the museum's conception and (re)birth involved battles over history, cultural policy, and layout. Architectural teams, mayors, cultural ministers, and presidents quarreled over the project. These tensions were overlaid with the subtle but commanding views of museum curators and gallery directors.

As we now see it, the role of a historian (or curator) is not merely to be "a chronicler, displaying art as a record of past society," but to aspire to become "a connoisseur . . . who relies on aesthetic judgment" (Kupfer Schneider, 1998, p. 102)—a discerning but unassuming *flâneur*. This led us to ask questions about the function of a museum or a history: Is it to provide "a temple of contemplation" (p. 103) in which deliberately placed works of art may be savored by knowing viewers? Or is it to act as "an educator" whose purpose is "to humanize, to educate, and to refine" (p. 104) more casual others while still engaging the scholars in dialogue? Might it possibly do both?

Such issues must have confronted Gae Aulenti, the Italian architect who was selected to reconcile the cavernous d'Orsay train station space with its new purpose: to serve as a multiform space to display works of art. In her postmodern interior design, Aulenti worked closely with the curators to create separate rooms and galleries to highlight the collected works. Her blend of architectural, curatorial, and aesthetic adaptations to a difficult space resulted in a form that, unlike a bustling train station, offers a haven where time can be well spent, and not just passed through. Using the rededicated museum (see Figure 48.2), we seek to display a postmodern interior (the arts) within a possibly constraining shell (educational research), with a main hall announcing itself with dramatic works of sculpture—offset by intimate inner rooms and multilevel galleries, corridors and concourses. Even as there are always "educational/aesthetic messages conveyed by the [museum] building . . . [and reader-]visitors are quite aware of the experiential impact of their surroundings" (Vallance, 2005, p. 82), we seek to provide our viewers with experiences of arresting calm and disturbance, surprise and estrangement.

We connect the past of this station-museum with the then–now in the history of the arts in research to provide a guide for our reader-viewers and not just to confuse them with indirections. The history of the Musée d'Orsay reflects the shifting political/inquiry landscape of different times and claims. It also re-presents the seemingly conflicting in/external segments that can find their place within a broadly inclusive postmodern worldview. Coexistence. After deciding to use the Gare/Musée d'Orsay

Gare d'Orsay then. . .   . . .Musée d'Orsay now.

Figure 48.2   Side-by-Side Photos of d'Orsay as Station [then] and as Museum [now]

as the guiding image for our confluxions, we awoke to the many ways in which our experiences paralleled those of designing and (re)structuring a then-train-station-now-museum. Next, we share moments from our joint history of designing and (re)arranging this chapter space.

◆ *Our Search in/for Time and Space: We Are in Our History*

Even as the symbolism of literary art (poetry, short stories, novels, and plays) is figurative and realized mainly in terms of metaphor and tropes, so too the symbolism of much arts-based inquiry, like visual, graphic art (painting, drawing, sculpture, design), is spatial and realized mainly in terms of association and distance. We present our history as an interior consisting of floor plans and gallery layouts, offering indices, subject lists, and directories, as if borrowed from a museum guide that is posted beside the entrance (to this chapter) and gestures from beyond (the *Handbook* Web site). As a "work of [post]modern scholarship [ours] is intended to be [viewed and] read like a catalogue" (Benjamin, 1928/1986b, p. 79). Like an audio-wand replaying how we found/lost our way, sharing with you, our reader-viewers, the problems of our inquiry at the same time that it was being conducted.

Arts-in-research approaches are themselves proliferating metaphors and different positions at a dizzying rate. For some time now in our writing alone together, we have waited on our intuition and imagination to suggest the metaphor that might provide the basic conceptual (the iron) and artful structure (the glass) for each of our inquiries. For us as educational researchers-writers,

the "right" metaphor makes public and accessible the personal and the ineffable. "Metaphoric precision [has become] the central vehicle for revealing the qualitative aspects of life" (Eisner, 1991, p. 227).

We begin our collaborative inquiries by searching literary works, exchanging (auto)biographies, novels, reviews, and articles, penciling in and sharing our annotations or daydreams about our inquiry. While we know that there will always be more than one way of proceeding, our starting point (and that of return) is usually found in one of the multidimensional forms of self–other study. As *flâneurs,* we typically approach the vast interiors of self–other through writing as citation, our version of coinhabiting the inquiry—a detective or investigative team delving into assorted visuals and texts for hard-earned clues. We next resort to a series of lifts and borrowings, piling up traces or remembrances of things past, at first losing ourselves in details without restraint.

Recently, our reading (like much of our writing) has been (mis)shaped by Benjamin, and we dedicate this museum inquiry to him. He developed his own method of self-definition as *a form of antisubjective historical criticism,* borrowing from literary figures. Like a critical *feuilletonist,* he used shorter prose forms such as aphorisms, dreams, letters, reviews, asides, fragments, essays, and footnotes, steadfastly preferring to explore his ideas through the analysis of those of others. In 1927, he embarked on what would become his monumental opus, *The Arcades Project.* For over 13 years, Benjamin collected a vast number of quotations from which he built his emerging understandings of Paris, his place in time. But his notes were not securely anchored, remaining ready to be re-sensed through his and the self-insertion of others. After his suicide, Benjamin's precious collection of quotations and thought traces languished for 40 years in the

Bibliothèque Nationale de France where he had felt that, while working, he was actually in the historical Arcades. The world appeared to him only as reflected by his own inwardness. The first edition of his unfinished manuscript was not edited and published until 1982 as *The Arcades Project* (*Das Passagenwerk*), an epic poem cobbled together out of fragments.

The collecting model that Benjamin used did not center on theorizing about and settling things once and for all time by using exclusively conceptual or explanatory means but rather on riding with the accumulation of things as in building an eccentric collection. He sought to replace concrete conclusions with spirals of possibility and the release of emotional responses. Abandoning the isolation of literal "facts" to rely on the chance companionship of a myriad of intimate details, he evoked memory and history as "the capacity for endless interpolations into what has been" (Benjamin, 1932/1986a, p. 16), pouring details into the void.

Using the glass-and-iron montage construction of the Parisian Arcades as his central metaphoric organizer, Benjamin wrote that the city taught him the art of straying, of losing himself in endless *flâneries*. A city in which observers might be observed, Paris offered a reconstructed home in which the montage of the most brittle and strong materials, glass and iron, heralded a new form of inquiry. Its hybrid construction now allows the light to flood in through the sweeping arches of the atrium of our d'Orsay train station-now-museum to illuminate and shadow the viewer-*flâneurs*. Looking down from the stairs, ramps and catwalks at the collections on display, they too may embody self–other consciousness.

With Benjamin as our shadow guide, we experienced our own coincidences during the framing of this history: In the summer of 2004, Patrick revisited and took digital snapshots of the d'Orsay. These were later transformed by Christine as watermark imprints in our text as we sought to (re)present our transforming roles as collectors-curators of fragments. In the summer of 2005, Christine found the announcement of the Art Gallery of Ontario (AGO) about its two latest exhibitions: *Favorites: Your Choices From Our Collection and the Transformative Power of Art*. It read: "Due to our transformative construction project, our collections on view are constantly changing" ("Favorites," 2005, p. R15). Both incidents prefigured our searching for, collecting, selecting, and now displaying our artifacts as a history.

Always wanting more documents than can ever really be used, we finally had to agree to "close" and search our collection of arts-based references, including those acquired from other handbooks, themed issues of journals, and arts-based inquiry projects. Without meaning to monumentalize our partial understandings of the history, in the end and as a way forward, we each made an arbitrary listing of "100 Artful Inquiry Quotes" from all our choices. Next, we placed our lists side by side and together eliminated overlap and doubling, paring it all down to a third 100. This last inventory provided the fragments for us to curate and display. We then sorted through our joint register, developing tentative juxtapositions while sensing other patterns in the mosaic as we went on. We assigned the text fragments to possible rooms, corridors, and galleries in ways similar (but not identical) to those in the present Musée d'Orsay.

For ease of retrieval we listed the citations within each grouping (which are shown in Figures 48.3–48.5) in alphabetical order by author. We pursued our inquiry in this way so as "to create the particular meanings we wish[ed] to display or experience" (Eisner, 1993, p. 6)—*those of flânerie* as a fundamental inquiry disposition, proceeding not unlike Benjamin with his never-quite-finished text montage: He copied his quotations on "426 loose sheets of yellowish paper, each folded in half . . . gathered into 36 sheafs [or *Konvoluts*] in accordance with a set of themes mysteriously keyed to the letters of the alphabet [a–z, and a–r, with c, e, f, h, n, o, and q missing]" (Eiland & McLaughlin, 1982/2002, p. 958). M for *flâneur* (pp. 416–455).

Less architecturally, we might have simply used an alphabetized list of our 100 references to indicate a (dis)ordering of the arts in research—under erasure. While the random effect of using only the last names of the authors could have been construed as a subversive move, the multiple entries attributed to some "authorities" might have seemed to promote a history written as the sum total of a few outstanding biographies, privileging the contributions of superstars, perpetuating the "great person" theory of history.

Or then again we might have reordered our reference list from the earliest to latest year of publication to suggest a linear relationship among successive works—forming an annal or a chronicle. This could then have been divided into a well-defined past, present, and future (works submitted), predicated on a long view as of development or progression from one stage to another, suggestive of cause and effect. But from a postmodern point of view, a history is dedicated neither to telling the story of a few individual geniuses nor to providing a record of change that continues to unfold. As now, history has not always had any fixed sense attributed to it. But even this admission might seem to suggest some kind of cyclical view of the overarching sweep of history. Nothing new under the sun.

In our museum as a-history-housed-in-a-postmodern-chapter, we present nine rooms (organized over three floors) selected to commemorate the nine Muses who evoked memory and history, the sciences and the arts (poetry and literature), song and dance, comedy and tragedy, and astronomy. Inspired by the Muses and their museum home, our alluding to and borrowing from the revisited d'Orsay for our chapter form emphasizes that its composition and reimagined readings are meant to constitute an aesthetic experience. As Dewey (1934/1980) insisted, "aesthetic art . . . does something different from leading to an experience. It constitutes one" (p. 85). Our use of the Musée d'Orsay for our architectural or "mythological shape" is meant to enhance the probability of our history becoming a performative text whenever experience of it *in* and *as* inquiry is realized—a *flânerie* under a dome of glass and iron.

In mounting our room-based testimony to the arts in inquiry, we do not mean to polarize the field (poststructuralists, contextualists, constructivists, narrativists, affirmative and negative postmodernists, arts-based/informed inquirers, and practicing artists) with yet more oppositions (Classicists and Neoclassicists, for example) but to overturn them. We present our guide to the labyrinth as an architectural-literary image, (re)presenting the historical time period covering the accumulating work of the first generation of arts-based researchers and recent developments. We are now witnessing changes in relative influence with newer forms of arts-based research not just being eulogized but now being practiced in universities, schools, prisons, hospitals, and other sites such as museums, and being reported on by a second generation. There is increasing agreement that "experimentation . . . with inquiry methods should be promoted and encouraged [partly because] legitimate and important non-scientific purposes and uses associated with arts-based research have long been marginalized" (Barone, 1995, pp. 171–172)—no longer to be relegated to the *Salon des Refusés*.

◆ *How to Use This Guide*

We structured our inquiry through the uses of mosaic-like, multileveled forms of representation:

Via a community of quotations, didactics, reflections and images, we intended some clustering that sets up resonances [and dissonances] to move readers toward thinking about meaning in history within the crisis of representation. Following Benjamin's textual practice of an assemblage of fragments, a methodical, continuous experiment of conjunction, we jammed ideas, texts, traditions and procedures together. (Lather, 2003)

Using different levels of existence and experience, we present our museum floor plan-catalog-map as spilling over into cyberspace. Even within that framework we still wondered how best to display/complicate our collection and how reader-*flâneurs* might take up our invitation and wander away on their own, "open[ing] the fan of memory [that] never comes to the end of its segments" (Benjamin, 1932/1986a, p. 8).

In preparation for our fragment sorting and display, we carefully attended to the interior of the d'Orsay and its traffic flow. At each turn, we asked: "(How) might this parallel (or not) the way in which we might arrange our cited works of art?" "How might we best (high)light our selections?" and "How might our arrangement facilitate the reader-visitors' engagement with the work and lead to an experience of arts-based inquiry as *flânerie?*" We wished to present an exhibition that would (re)member the needs of our reader-visitors, increasing the probability that it would be "the aesthetic dimensions of our professional [or curatorial] choices that [they would] respond to and remember most strongly" (Vallance, 2005,

p. 78). We wanted to involve the visitor-readers of this chapter (and the entire *Handbook*) in ways we could not control. By choosing and navigating their own paths, they can become increasingly self-directed and transformative. We invite our reader-visitors to stroll casually through our museum-text concourses and corridors.

The *flâneur* is "that aimless stroller who loses him[/her]self in the crowd, who has no destination and goes wherever caprice or curiosity directs his or her steps" (White, 2001, p. 16). The authentic *flâneur* is never a gaping tourist in search of the 10 major sights as in a potted history. Rather, the *flâneur* is content to become lost in search of the unknown. Roaming and circulating, seeing and being seen. A passionate observer and open-minded advocate of ambiguity. A hunter on the lookout for troubling experience rather than a passive receiver of settled knowledge.

An aimless sauntering or *flânerie* through our artful text arti-facts is meant to evoke something of the pieced-together patterning of "the arts in educational research," and of our inquiry into them. Our open floor plan does not dictate a predetermined or one-way traffic flow but rather invites quiet contemplation in separate pockets/rooms of stillness. In this spirit, our display avoids any "linear unfolding of information that builds towards a sense of 'being on top' of a situation through knowledge" (Lather, 1997, p. 287)—even on the third floor. Each inquiry or entry in our museum-chapter seeks to "permit . . . a lived experience, the vivid present of watching and hearing a . . . moment" (Paget, 1990, p. 141), seeking the lightning flash of a historical re-sensing.

We lay down our history as a fabricated room and movement arrangement that we then superimpose on the Musée d'Orsay blueprint. We indicate only a limited number of rooms and sample of quotations to evoke the overall weight and thrust of the exhibits that might find a home there. And we invite our reader-visitors to rearrange it all and to (re)inscribe spaces not yet filled. Gesturing toward the *flâneur* who knew all the Parisian "studios by heart and could recite the sequence of signs without omitting a single one" (Benjamin, 1982/2002, p. 451), we have placed a door sign over each exhibition area. As in the d'Orsay brochures, we suggest that visitor-readers enter the main space on the ground level (or not), then proceed directly to the third level, next to the second level, and back through the main space sculpture hall, via the bookstore to the exit or begin another ramble.

Arranged in architectural and alphabetical order, *Appendix A* serves as a summary guide to the sources of the works on display. A detailed view of the artful citation exhibits introduced as Figures 48.3–48.5, including their provenance and bibliographic information offered in alphabetical order by artist/author, may be experienced more fully in cyberspace at www.sagepub.com/knowlessupplement.

Upon entering the main floor exhibition space (see Figure 48.3), we hope that reader-viewers will be immediately waylaid by its soaring height and spaciousness—room for all. Our *Sculpture and Installations Gallery* contains studies of "self–other." Its entry is flanked by two female sculptures: one a body-casting (Cole, 2000), the other a shop mannequin (re)covered with body-writing (Finley, 2001). Both pieces (like Mantas, 2004) use layered forms to testify to the complexity of artful educational inquiry into self(ves)–others—forms that inform and beckon the reader-*flâneurs* to pass between them so that the other three-dimensional works may be viewed from all sides to reveal new meanings, (re)sensed like the Rodin-Claudel sculptural pieces in the d'Orsay.

Our arts-based forms include single/collaborative, multimedia art installations (Cole & McIntyre, 2004; Slattery, 2001;

Weber & Mitchell, 2005) that incorporate (re)cycled, (re)cast, (re)used, and (re)positioned pieces. Slattery's (2001) installation interrogates the regulation of the human body and sexuality as in a Roman Catholic junior high school in the 1960s. Other works highlight the textile and fabric arts: quilted artwork (Wilson, 2002), batik panels (van Halen-Faber, 2004), and cloth collages (Springgay, 2003). In yet another area, we position those who dance their data (Janesick, 2000; Snowber, 2002)—dancers-frozen-in-time like Degas bronzes.

Off on the side, within one of the large rooms (see Figure 48.3), we (re)discover *The Classicists,* those artist-scholars whose pioneering works continue to influence the history of the arts in educational and in social science research: past and present voices found in text fragments borrowed from Barone (1995), Bergson (1946/1992), Bullough and Pinnegar (2001), de Saint-Exupéry (1943/2000), Dewey (1934/1980), Eisner (1991, 1993), Gadamer (1975/1986), Greene (1988, 1995), Grumet (1987, 1988), Heaney (1995), Jackson (1998), Johnson (1987), Langer (1957), Marcuse (1977), Pinar (1976), Proust (1951/1999), and Shelley (1821/1990). The timelessness of their inquiry approaches forms a platform from which other arts-inspired inquirers can launch and return from their artistic (re)searches.

Next, as in the d'Orsay catalog-guide, we invite reader-*flâneurs* to climb to the third level of the museum-gallery (see Figure 48.4). Here we house the works of our *Impressionists and Surrealists.* Under the glass dome, light and darkness, beauty and horror are distinguished only by a fine, heartfelt line. Their door signs read as *Postmodernists and Wild Chimeras* (Diamond, 1999; Diamond & Mullen, 1999; Freire, 1996; Jipson & Paley, 1997; Krase, 2001; Lyotard cited in Baker, 2000; Sansom, 1973; Slattery, 1997; van Halen-Faber & Diamond, 2001) and *Room of Anguish and Cautionary Tales* (Crowe,

Sculpture and Installations Gallery

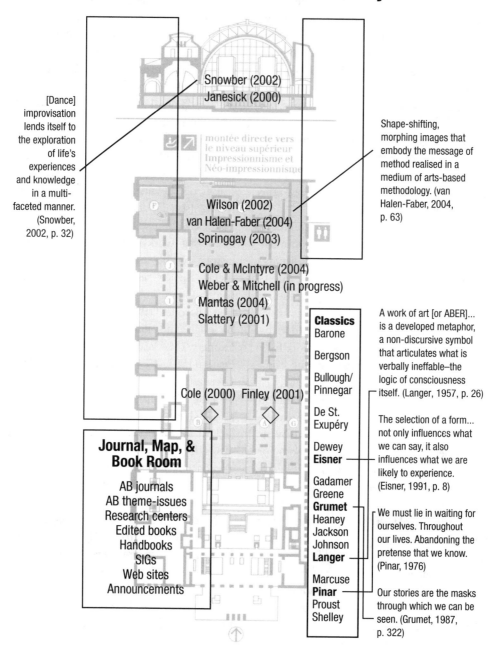

[Dance] improvisation lends itself to the exploration of life's experiences and knowledge in a multi-faceted manner. (Snowber, 2002, p. 32)

Snowber (2002)
Janesick (2000)

Shape-shifting, morphing images that embody the message of method realised in a medium of arts-based methodology. (van Halen-Faber, 2004, p. 63)

Wilson (2002)
van Halen-Faber (2004)
Springgay (2003)

Cole & McIntyre (2004)
Weber & Mitchell (in progress)
Mantas (2004)
Slattery (2001)

Cole (2000) Finley (2001)

Classics
Barone
Bergson
Bullough/Pinnegar
De St. Exupéry
Dewey
Eisner
Gadamer
Greene
Grumet
Heaney
Jackson
Johnson
Langer
Marcuse
Pinar
Proust
Shelley

A work of art [or ABER]... is a developed metaphor, a non-discursive symbol that articulates what is verbally ineffable–the logic of consciousness itself. (Langer, 1957, p. 26)

The selection of a form... not only influences what we can say, it also influences what we are likely to experience. (Eisner, 1991, p. 8)

We must lie in waiting for ourselves. Throughout our lives. Abandoning the pretense that we know. (Pinar, 1976)

Our stories are the masks through which we can be seen. (Grumet, 1987, p. 322)

Journal, Map, & Book Room

AB journals
AB theme-issues
Research centers
Edited books
Handbooks
SIGs
Web sites
Announcements

Figure 48.3   Main-Level Exhibition Space Superimposed on d'Orsay Ground-Level Floor Plan

2004; Davis-Halifax, 2002; Mullen, 1999; Mullen, Buttignol, & Diamond, 2005; Paz, 1990; Paz cited in Taylor, 1990; Reid-Patton, 2005; Shelley, 1821/1990; Stewart, 1998; Veale, 2001). A third room on this floor is reserved for an exhibition-on-loan and is marked as *Installation in Progress*. Here we display works of student-artists-in-residence who form the avant-garde in artful research and who are waiting to outrage and be "hung." Our exhibit features a small sampling or *inventarium* of Canadian doctoral dissertation inquiries defended successfully in postmodern ivory towers where research artistry is honored.

In keeping with the sequence of the d'Orsay guide map, the last round of our virtual museum tour brings reader-*flâneurs* to the middle floor (see Figure 48.5). Here, too, we have selected three rooms. Situated directly above *The Classicists* on the main floor are *The Neoclassicists* (Barone, 2001; Barone & Eisner, 1988/1997; Blumenfeld-Jones, 2004; Borges, 1984; Clifford, 1988; Eisner, 2002; Gadamer, 1975/1986; Greene, 1995; Irwin, 2005; James, 1884/1957; Lather, 1997; Pinar, 1975; Vallance, 1985; van Halen-Faber & Diamond, 2004). Next to them, in a salon-style room arrangement, we feature *The Narrativists* (Byatt, 2000; Clandinin & Connelly, 2000; Connelly & Clandinin, 1999; Craig, 2002; Geertz, 1995; Matthews, 2005) and some of their long-term and current projects. In a separate alcove, we display works that represent inquiry artists as *Photographers and (Multicultural) Portraitists* (Anzaldúa, 1987; Bach, 2001; Bautista, 2004; E. Chan, 2004; F. N. Chan, 2004; He, 1999; Holm, 1997; Knowles & Thomas, 2002; Lawrence-Lightfoot, 1997; Mitchell, 2004; Phillion, 1999; Poon, 2004; Wong, 2005). On the other side of the second level, we place the *"Poets, Storytellers, Musicians, Novelists, and Playwrights"* (Buttignol, 1998; Damelin, 2002; de Freitas, 2003; Goldstein, 2001;

Gosse, 2005; Gray, 2004; Greene, 1988; Leggo, 2004; Neilsen, 2004; Norris, 2001; Richardson, 1994, 1997; Sullivan, 2000; Vinall-Cox, 2004) in a large performance space—all single voices.

On the way toward the exit, reader-*flâneurs* may make their way once more to the sculpture and installation garden, lingering to view the works from yet more angles. Then they may browse the final space designated as *The Journal, Map, and Book Room*. This offers a vital collection of journals (including electronic ones such as the *International Journal of Education and the Arts*), real and cyberspace maps indicating Canadian university–based projects, special interest groups, posted announcements, handbooks, and other (non)synoptic texts, edited books, and the prints of all the works by the author-artists displayed in the rooms. Collecting these items may allow the effects of the museum-gallery to extend beyond the confines of this exhibition, which like our gaze must always be under "transformative construction."

◆ *Other Ways*

This chapter's sight-/guidelines inform and are informed by our perceived ways of making sense of what we (two collaborative authors and their readers) make of the arts in educational research. We wanted to show/hide more than we could say. We acted on Eisner's (1997) advice that "there is an intimate relationship between our conception of what the products of research are to look like and the way we go about doing research" (p. 5). We began our image-based research on the history of the arts in educational research by *imagining* the research and by *following* our inquiry wherever it led. Medium-like, we sought to let the research reveal itself: finding its own form, showing "new possibilities for

Impressionists and Surrealists

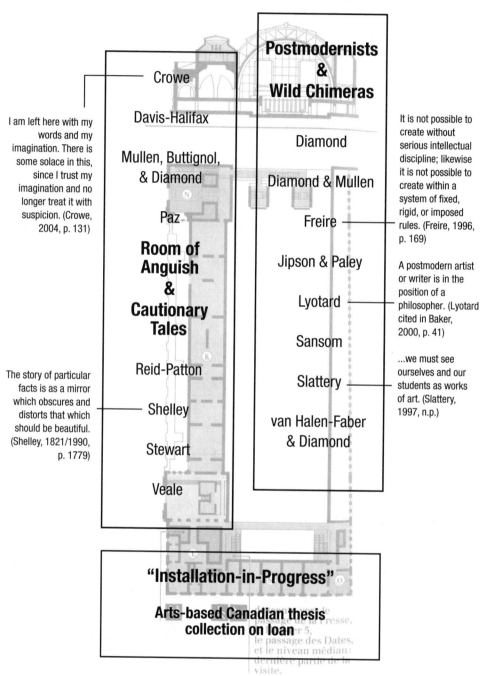

Crowe

Davis-Halifax

Mullen, Buttignol, & Diamond

Paz

Room of Anguish & Cautionary Tales

Reid-Patton

Shelley

Stewart

Veale

Postmodernists & Wild Chimeras

Diamond

Diamond & Mullen

Freire

Jipson & Paley

Lyotard

Sansom

Slattery

van Halen-Faber & Diamond

"Installation-in-Progress"

Arts-based Canadian thesis collection on loan

I am left here with my words and my imagination. There is some solace in this, since I trust my imagination and no longer treat it with suspicion. (Crowe, 2004, p. 131)

The story of particular facts is as a mirror which obscures and distorts that which should be beautiful. (Shelley, 1821/1990, p. 1779)

It is not possible to create without serious intellectual discipline; likewise it is not possible to create within a system of fixed, rigid, or imposed rules. (Freire, 1996, p. 169)

A postmodern artist or writer is in the position of a philosopher. (Lyotard cited in Baker, 2000, p. 41)

...we must see ourselves and our students as works of art. (Slattery, 1997, n.p.)

Figure 48.4 Third-Level Exhibition Space Superimposed on d'Orsay Upper-Level Floor Plan

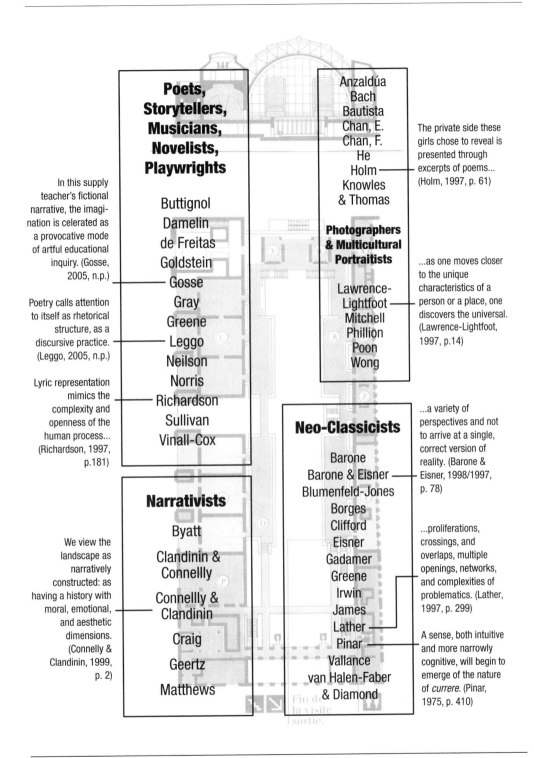

In this supply teacher's fictional narrative, the imagination is celerated as a provocative mode of artful educational inquiry. (Gosse, 2005, n.p.)

Poetry calls attention to itself as rhetorical structure, as a discursive practice. (Leggo, 2005, n.p.)

Lyric representation mimics the complexity and openness of the human process... (Richardson, 1997, p.181)

Poets, Storytellers, Musicians, Novelists, Playwrights

Buttignol
Damelin
de Freitas
Goldstein
Gosse
Gray
Greene
Leggo
Neilson
Norris
Richardson
Sullivan
Vinall-Cox

Anzaldúa
Bach
Bautista
Chan, E.
Chan, F.
He
Holm
Knowles
& Thomas

The private side these girls chose to reveal is presented through excerpts of poems... (Holm, 1997, p. 61)

Photographers & Multicultural Portraitists

Lawrence-Lightfoot
Mitchell
Phillion
Poon
Wong

...as one moves closer to the unique characteristics of a person or a place, one discovers the universal. (Lawrence-Lightfoot, 1997, p.14)

We view the landscape as narratively constructed: as having a history with moral, emotional, and aesthetic dimensions. (Connelly & Clandinin, 1999, p. 2)

Narrativists

Byatt
Clandinin & Connellly
Connellly & Clandinin
Craig
Geertz
Matthews

Neo-Classicists

Barone
Barone & Eisner
Blumenfeld-Jones
Borges
Clifford
Eisner
Gadamer
Greene
Irwin
James
Lather
Pinar
Vallance
van Halen-Faber
& Diamond

...a variety of perspectives and not to arrive at a single, correct version of reality. (Barone & Eisner, 1998/1997, p. 78)

...proliferations, crossings, and overlaps, multiple openings, networks, and complexities of problematics. (Lather, 1997, p. 299)

A sense, both intuitive and more narrowly cognitive, will begin to emerge of the nature of *currere*. (Pinar, 1975, p. 410)

Figure 48.5 Middle-Level Exhibition Space Superimposed on d'Orsay Middle-Level Floor Plan

matters of representation," enlisting "our imaginative capacities," and generating yet other "forms of experience that would otherwise not exist" (Eisner, 2004, p. 8).

More precisely, we relied on documentary, "imagistically concrete and [even] nonconceptual" (Pinar, 2004, p. 15) means to create out of our positionality a public space with different floors and rooms. We present our museum-sourced history as one of those "endeavors of the imagination [that] employ an imaginative rationality" (Lakoff & Johnson, 1980, p. 193). We learned, however, that understanding "as a form of life [or inquiry] . . . and convincing others that you have indeed done so, involves more than the assembly of telling particulars or the imposition of general narratives" or gaze. "It involves bringing figure and ground, the passing occasion and the long story, into coincident" (Geertz, 1995, p. 51) and even accidental view. By suggesting a wider relevance for the *flâneur* as illuminating significant aspects of arts-based investigation, we hoped to house insignificant details and seemingly fortuitous events within a meaningful context. We trust that we have not sounded too obscure a note or valorized too North American– or Toronto-centric a perspective. Existing buildings of that city like the AGO (Art Gallery of Ontario) are being (re)visited by celebrity-based, architectural retrofits.

We close/open with a handing on, inviting you, our intergenerational groups of reader-*flâneurs*, to wander through the other chapters of this *Handbook* where a complex interplay of other treatments of the arts in different areas of social science research awaits. May you perceive yet more ways as you partake for yourselves of the meanings shaped by the word-crowds, associations, borrowings, and tropes that haunt inquiry aesthetically observed. As you pause and gaze awhile on our shared experience of the arts in educational research, may you sense shifting positions within and dream of fresh "throughlines" across it all—finding and seeking, placing your imprint on such inquiry spaces by developing the art of walking through them.

◆ Notes

1. While we use the more usual form of *flâneur,* no disrespect or exclusion of *flâneuse* is intended. This is only to disencumber the text. Both mid-19th century figures forever sought alternative ways of looking. As did Walt Whitman, one of the greatest *flâneurs,* in Manhattan. The *flâneur* was also a recurring motif of many Impressionist painters who were self-avowed *flâneurs.* Surrealism, a literary/visual production of *flânerie,* is based on a belief in certain forms of neglected associations and in the dreamlike play of thought.

2. Like the *feuilletonist,* the *flâneur* leafed through experience like pages in a book, rolling and folding it all together like a pastry chef.

◆ Appendix

References arranged alphabetically by exhibition area.

ENTRANCE LEVEL—SCULPTURE AND INSTALLATIONS GALLERY AND CLASSICISTS

SCULPTURE AND INSTALLATIONS GALLERY

Cole, A. L. (with Mantas, K., Rice, D., & Knowles, J. G.). (2000). *Bodies of knowledge, knowledge of bodies* [body casting as data video]. Unpublished paper presented at the Scholartistry Day (Colloquium Series), Centre for Arts-Informed Research, the Ontario Institute for Studies in Education of the University of Toronto, Ontario, Canada.

Cole, A. L., & McIntyre, M. (2004, December). Research as aesthetic contemplation: The role of the audience in research interpretation. *Educational Insights, 9*(1). Retrieved January 4, 2007, from http://www.ccfi.educ.ubc.ca/publication/insights/v09n01/articles/cole.html

Finley, S. (2001). Painting life histories. *Journal of Curriculum Theorizing, 7*(3), 13–26.

Janesick, V. J. (2000). The choreography of qualitative research design: Minuets, improvisations, and crystallization. In N. K. Denzin & Y. S. Lincoln (Eds.), *Handbook of qualitative research* (2nd ed.; pp. 379–400). Thousand Oaks, CA: Sage.

Mantas, K. (2004). *Becoming AIR-BORNe: Women co-creating, ex-pressing, and informing our lives.* Unpublished doctoral thesis, Ontario Institute for Studies in Education of the University of Toronto, Ontario, Canada.

Slattery, P. (2001). *Knowledge (de)constructed and (re)embodied: An art installation that disrupts regulation of the body in classroom practices. An art installation that explores religion and sexuality in the curriculum.* Retrieved January 4, 2007, from http://education.wsu.edu/journal/patrick.htm

Snowber, C. (2002). Bodydance: Enfleshing soulful inquiry through improvisation. In C. Bagley & M. B. Cancienne (Eds.), *Dancing the data* (pp. 20–33). New York: Peter Lang.

Springgay, S. (2003, November 25). Cloth as intercorporeality: Touch, fantasy, and performance and the construction of body knowledge. *International Journal of Education and the Arts, 4*(5). Retrieved January 4, 2007, from http://ijea.asu.edu/v4n5/

van Halen-Faber, C. (2004). *Seeing through apples: An arts-based exploration into the ethics and aesthetics of a teacher-educator-researcher's arts-based beginnings.* Unpublished doctoral thesis, Ontario Institute for Studies in Education of the University of Toronto, Ontario, Canada.

Weber, S., & Mitchell, C. (2005). *What are you wearing to the dance?* Manuscript in preparation. Retrieved June 5, 2007, from http://www.iirc.mcgill.ca/txp/index.php?id=71

Wilson, S. (2002). Collecting rocks, leaves, and seeds: a journey through loss. *Educational Insights, 7*(1). Retrieved January 4, 2007, from http://ccfi.educ.ubc.ca/publication/insights/v07n01/contextualexplorations/wilson/

CLASSICISTS

Barone, T. (1995). The purposes of arts-based educational research. *International Journal of Educational Research, 23*(2), 169–180.

Bergson, H. (1992). *The creative mind.* New York: Carol Publishing Group. (Original work published 1946)

Bullough, R., Jr., & Pinnegar, S. (2001). Guideline for quality of autobiographical forms of self-study. *Educational Researcher, 30*(3), 13–21.

de Saint-Exupéry, A. (2000). *The little prince* (R. Howard, Trans.). San Diego: Harcourt. (Original work published 1943)

Dewey, J. (1980). *Art as experience.* New York: Perigee Books. (Original work published 1934)

Eisner, E. W. (1991). *The enlightened eye: Qualitative inquiry and the enhancement of educational practice.* New York: Macmillan Publishing.

Eisner, E. W. (1993). Forms of understanding and the future of educational research. *Educational Researcher, 22*(7), 5–11.

Gadamer, H. G. (1986). *Truth and method.* New York: The Crossroad Publishing Company. (Original work published 1975)

Greene, M. (1988). *The dialectic of freedom.* New York: Teachers College Press.

Greene, M. (1995). *Releasing the imagination. Essays on education, the arts, and social change.* San Francisco: Jossey-Bass.

Grumet, M. (1987). The politics of personal knowledge. *Curriculum Inquiry, 17*(3), 319–329.

Grumet, M. R. (1988). *Bitter milk: Women and teaching.* Amherst: University of Massachusetts Press.

Heaney, S. (1995). *The redress of poetry: Oxford lectures.* London: Faber & Faber.

Jackson, P. W. (1998). *John Dewey and the lessons of art*. New Haven, CT: Yale University Press.

Johnson, M. (1987). *The body in the mind: The bodily basis of meaning, imagination, and reason*. Chicago: University of Chicago Press.

Langer, S. K. (1957). *Problems of art: Ten philosophical lectures*. New York: Charles Scribner's.

Marcuse, H. (1977). *The aesthetic dimension: Toward a critique of Marxist aesthetics*. Boston: Beacon Press.

Pinar, W. F. (1976). [Epigraph to introduction]. In W. F. Pinar & M. R. Grumet, *Toward a poor curriculum*. Dubuque, IA: Kendall/Hunt.

Proust, M. (1999). *Time regained: In search of lost time* (Vol. 6, A. Mayor & T. Kilmartin, Trans.). New York: The Modern Library. (Original work published 1951)

Shelley, P. B. (1990). A defence of poetry. In M. H. Abrams (Gen. Ed.), *The Norton Anthology of English Literature* (7th ed., pp. 1769–1781). New York: W.W. Norton. (Original work published 1821)

THIRD LEVEL—IMPRESSIONISTS AND SURREALISTS

POSTMODERNISTS AND WILD CHIMERAS

Baker, S. (2000). *The postmodern animal*. London: Reaktion.

Diamond, C. T. P. (1999). Reciting and reviewing the educator self: An exhibition of five self-works. In C. T. P. Diamond & C. A. Mullen (Eds.), *The postmodern educator. Arts-based inquiries and teacher development* (pp. 191–221). New York: Peter Lang.

Diamond, C. T. P., & Mullen, C. A. (1999). A quest: Birthing the postmodern individual. In C. T. P. Diamond & C. A. Mullen (Eds.), *The postmodern educator: Arts-based inquiries and teacher development* (pp. 449–463). New York: Peter Lang.

Freire, P. (1996). *Letters to Cristina: Reflections on my life and work*. New York: Routledge.

Jipson, J. A., & Paley, N. (1997). Curriculum and its unconsciousness. In J. A. Jipson & N. Paley (Eds.), *Daredevil research: Re-creating analytic practice* (pp. 110–135). New York: Peter Lang.

Krase, A. (2001). Essay: Archive of visions, inventory of things. In H. C. Adam (Ed.), *Eugène Atget: Paris* (pp. 25–29). Paris: Taschen.

Sansom, W. (1973). *Proust*. London: Thames & Hudson.

Slattery, P. (1997). *Postmodern curriculum research and alternative forms of data presentation*. Public seminar/occasional paper presented to the Curriculum and Pedagogy Institute of the University of Alberta, Canada, September 29, 1997. Retrieved January 4, 2007, from http://www.quasar.ualberta.ca/cpin/cpinfolder/papers/slattery.htm

van Halen-Faber, C., & Diamond, C. T. P. (2001). Doing an arts-based dissertation inquiry: An inclusive nebula of spiraling pebbles. In S. T. Poetter, C. Haerr, M. Hayes, C. Higgins, & K. Wilson Baptist (Eds.), *In(Ex)clusion: (Re)Visioning the democratic ideal* (pp. 47–63). Troy, NY: Educator's International Press.

ROOM OF ANGUISH AND CAUTIONARY TALES

Crowe, R. (2004). Crafting tales of trauma. In A. L. Cole, L. Nielsen, J. G. Knowles, & T. C. Luciani (Eds.), *Provoked by art: Theorizing arts-informed research* (pp. 123–133). Halifax, Nova Scotia, Canada: Backalong Books.

Davis-Halifax, N. V. (2002). *Of rose petals and sutures, marks on a woman's body: An aesthetic and oblique inquiry into dys-body, solace, and vulnerability*. Unpublished doctoral thesis, Ontario Institute for Studies in Education of the University of Toronto, Ontario, Canada.

Mullen, C. A. (1999). Carousel: A metaphor for spinning inquiry in prison and education. In C. T. P. Diamond & C. A. Mullen (Eds.), *The postmodern educator: Arts-based inquiries and teacher development* (pp. 281–314). New York: Peter Lang.

Mullen, C. A., Buttignol, M., & Diamond, C. T. P. (2005, July 29). Flyboy: Using the arts and theater to assist suicidal adolescents. *International Journal of Education & the*

Arts, 6(5). Retrieved January 4, 2007, from http://ijea.asu.edu/v6n5/

Paz, O. (1990). *In search of the present* [Nobel lecture]. Retrieved January 4, 2007, from http://www.nobel.se/literature/laureates/1990/paz-lecture-e.html

Reid-Patton, V. (2005). *The inward journey: Sacred spaces and stories of becoming.* Unpublished doctoral thesis, Ontario Institute for Studies in Education of the University of Toronto, Ontario, Canada.

Shelley, P. B. (1990). A defence of poetry. In M. H. Abrams (Gen. Ed.), *The Norton Anthology of English Literature* (7th ed., pp. 1769–1781). New York: W. W. Norton. (Original work published 1821)

Stewart, M. (1998). *The experience of extreme intrafamilial violence: A personal story of recovery.* Unpublished doctoral thesis, Ontario Institute for Studies in Education of the University of Toronto, Ontario, Canada.

Taylor, R. (1990, October 12). Octavio Paz invents his own reality. *The Boston Globe,* p. 29. Retrieved January 4, 2007, from http://www.boston.com/globe/search/stories/nobel/1990/1990n.html

Veale, B. (2001). *Teaching at-risk adolescent girls: Stories of silence and voice.* Unpublished doctoral thesis, Ontario Institute for Studies in Education of the University of Toronto, Ontario, Canada.

SECOND LEVEL—NEOCLASSICISTS, NARRATIVISTS, PHOTOGRAPHERS, AND (MULTICULTURAL) PORTRAITISTS, AND "POETS, STORYTELLERS, MUSICIANS, NOVELISTS, AND PLAYWRIGHTS"

NEOCLASSICISTS

Barone, T. (2001). *Touching eternity: The enduring outcome of teaching.* New York: Teachers College Press.

Barone, T., & Eisner, E. W. (1997). Arts-based educational research. In R. M. Jaeger (Ed.), *Complementary methods for research in education* (2nd ed., pp. 73–99). Washington, DC: American Educational Research Association. (Original work published 1988)

Blumenfeld-Jones, D. S. (2004). Hogan dreams. *Qualitative Inquiry, 10*(3), 316–338.

Borges, J. L. (1984). *Twenty conversations with Borges, including a selection of poems: Interviews by Roberto Alifano, 1981–1983.* Housatonic, MA: Lascaux Publishers.

Clifford, J. (1988). *The predicament of culture: Twentieth century ethnography, literature, art.* Cambridge, MA: Harvard University Press.

Eisner, E. W. (2002). *The arts and the creation of mind.* New Haven, CT: Yale University Press.

Gadamer, H. G. (1986). *Truth and method.* New York: The Crossroad Publishing Company. (Original work published 1975)

Greene, M. (1995). *Releasing the imagination: Essays on education, the arts, and social change.* San Francisco, CA: Jossey-Bass.

Irwin, R. (2005). *A/r/tography.* Retrieved January 4, 2007, from http://cust.educ.ubc.ca/faculty/irwin.html

James, H. (1957). The art of fiction. In L. Edel (Ed.), *The house of fiction: Essays on the novel by Henry James.* London: Rupert Hart-Davis. (Original work published 1884)

Lather, P. (1997). Drawing the line at angels: Working the ruins of feminist ethnography. *Qualitative Studies in Education, 10*(3), 285–304.

Pinar, W. (1975). Currere: Toward reconceptualization. In W. Pinar (Ed.), *Curriculum theorizing: The reconceptualists* (pp. 396–413). Berkeley, CA: McCutchan.

Vallance, E. (1985). Ways of knowing and curricular conceptions: Implications for program planning. In E. W. Eisner (Ed.), *Learning and teaching the ways of knowing* (pp. 199–217). Chicago: University of Chicago Press.

van Halen-Faber, C., & Diamond, C. T. P. (2004). "Catch us if you can": Arts-based interplay. *Journal of Curriculum and Pedagogy, 1*(2), 84–88.

NARRATIVISTS

Byatt, A. S. (2000). *On histories and stories: Selected essays.* Cambridge, MA: Harvard University Press.

Clandinin, D. J., & Connelly, F. M. (2000). *Narrative inquiry: Experience and story in qualitative research*. San Francisco: Jossey-Bass.

Connelly, F. M., & Clandinin, D. J. (Eds.). (1999). *Shaping a professional identity: Stories of educational practice*. New York: Teachers College Press.

Craig, C. J. (2002). The shadows of New York: A continuing inquiry into the school as parkland metaphor. *International Journal of Education and the Arts, 3*(4). Retrieved January 4, 2007, from http://ijea.asu.edu/v3n4/

Geertz, C. (1995). *After the fact: Two countries, four decades, one anthropologist*. Cambridge MA: Harvard University Press.

Matthews, G. (2005). The arts as a metaphor for learning about self: Four stories in a teacher narrative. *Journal of the Canadian Association for Curriculum Studies, 3*(1), 75–92.

PHOTOGRAPHERS AND (MULTICULTURAL) PORTRAITISTS

Anzaldúa, G. (1987). *Borderlands/La frontera: The new mestiza*. San Francisco: Spinsters/ Aunt Lute.

Bach, H. (2001). *The place of the photograph in visual narrative research—Project statement. Afterimage, Nov.–Dec. 2001*. Retrieved January 4, 2007, from http://www.findarticles .com/p/articles/mi_m2479/is_3_29/ai_80 757500

Bautista, D. (2004). *Estorya Sa (the story of) Mid-Air: From an artist of diversity towards a teacher for peace*. Unpublished doctoral thesis, Ontario Institute for Studies in Education of the University of Toronto, Ontario, Canada.

Chan, E. (2004). *Narratives of ethnic identity: Experiences of first generation Chinese Canadian students*. Unpublished doctoral thesis, Ontario Institute for Studies in Education of the University of Toronto, Ontario, Canada.

Chan, F. N. (2004). *Crossing the border: Identity and education—A narrative self study*. Unpublished doctoral thesis, Ontario Institute for Studies in Education of the University of Toronto, Ontario, Canada.

He, M. F. (1999). A life-long inquiry forever flowing between China and Canada: Crafting a composite auto/biographical narrative method to represent three Chinese women teachers' cultural experiences. *Journal of Critical Inquiry Into Curriculum and Instruction, 1*(2), 5–29.

Holm, G. (1997). Teenage motherhood: Public posing and private thoughts. In J. Jipson & N. Paley (Eds.), *Daredevil research* (pp. 61–81). New York: Peter Lang.

Knowles, J. G., & Thomas, S. M. (2002). Artistry, inquiry, and sense-of-place: Secondary school students portrayed in context. In C. Bagley & M. B. Cancienne (Eds.), *Dancing the data* (pp. 121–132). New York: Peter Lang.

Lawrence-Lightfoot, S. (1997). A view of the whole. In S. Lawrence-Lightfoot & J. Hoffman Davis (Eds.), *The art and science of portraiture* (pp. 3–16). San Francisco: Jossey-Bass.

Mitchell, C. (2004). *Visual studies and democratic spaces: Textual evidence and educational research*. Retrieved January 4, 2007, from: http://www.cepd.org.za/content/ conferences%20PDF%20files/EPU% Conference/phot02.pdf

Phillion, J. (1999). Reflections on Ming Fang He's aesthetic narrative work. *Journal of Critical Inquiry Into Curriculum and Instruction, 1*(2), 29.

Poon, H. (2004). *Teachers' experiences of caring: Stories and images of arts-based teacher development*. Unpublished doctoral thesis, Ontario Institute for Studies in Education of the University of Toronto, Ontario, Canada.

Wong, G. (2005). *An inquiry into an arts-based curriculum in preservice early childhood teacher education*. Unpublished doctoral thesis, Ontario Institute for Studies in Education of the University of Toronto, Ontario, Canada.

POETS, STORYTELLERS, MUSICIANS, NOVELISTS, AND PLAYWRIGHTS

Buttignol, M. F. (1998). *Colouring outside the lines: Transformative experiences of creativity and teacher-selves*. Unpublished doctoral thesis, Ontario Institute for Studies in Education of the University of Toronto, Ontario, Canada.

Damelin, A. (2002). *Walking barefoot: A storyteller's arts-based inquiry.* Unpublished doctoral thesis, Ontario Institute for Studies in Education of the University of Toronto, Ontario, Canada.

de Freitas, E. (2003). Contested positions: How fiction informs empathic research. *International Journal of Education and the Arts, 4*(7). Retrieved January 4, 2007, from http://ijea.asu .edu/v4n7/

Goldstein, T. (2001). Hong Kong, Canada: A one-act ethnographic play for critical teacher education. *Journal of Curriculum Theorizing, 17*(2), 97–110.

Gosse, D. (2005). My arts-informed narrative inquiry into homophobia in elementary schools as a supply teacher. *International Journal of Education and the Arts, 6*(7). Retrieved January 4, 2007, from http://ijea. asu.edu/v6n7/

Gray, R. E. (2004). Performing for whom? Spotlight on the audience. In A. L. Cole, L. Nielsen, J. G. Knowles, & T. C. Luciani (Eds.), *Provoked by art: Theorizing arts-informed research* (pp. 238–250). Halifax, Nova Scotia, Canada: Backalong Books.

Greene, M. (1988). *The dialectic of freedom.* New York: Teachers College Press.

Leggo, C. (2004). Living poetry: Five ruminations. *Language & Literacy, 6*(2). Retrieved January 4, 2007, from http://www.langandlit.ualberta.ca/Fa112004/Leggo.html

Neilsen, L. (2004). Aesthetics and knowing: Ephemeral principles for a groundless theory. In A. L. Cole, L. Nielsen, J. G. Knowles, & T. C. Luciani (Eds.), *Provoked by art: Theorizing arts-informed research,* (pp. 44–49). Halifax, Nova Scotia, Canada: Backalong Books.

Norris, J. (2001). What can we do? A performance workshop on bullying and managing anger. *Journal of Curriculum Theorizing, 17*(2), 111–128.

Richardson, L. (1994). Writing: A method of inquiry. In N. K. Denzin & Y. S. Lincoln (Eds.), *Handbook of qualitative research* (pp. 516–529). Thousand Oaks, CA: Sage.

Richardson, L. (1997). *Fields of play: Constructing an academic life.* New Brunswick, NJ: Rutgers University Press.

Sullivan, A. M. (2000). Notes from a marine biologist's daughter: On the art and science of attention. *Harvard Educational Review, 72*(2), 211–227.

Vinall-Cox, J. (2004). *Threading the story: A technological and arts-based inquiry.* Unpublished doctoral thesis, Ontario Institute for Studies in Education of the University of Toronto, Ontario, Canada.

◆ References

Barone, T. (1995). The purpose of arts-based educational research. *International Journal of Educational Research, 23*(2), 169–180.

Baudrillard, J. (1994). The system of collecting. In J. Elsner & R. Cardinal (Eds.), *The cultures of collecting* (pp. 7–24). Cambridge, MA: Harvard University Press.

Benjamin, W. (1986a). A Berlin chronicle. In P. Demetz (Ed.) & E. Jephcott (Trans.), *Reflections: Walter Benjamin—Essays, aphorisms, autobiographical writings* (pp. 3–60). New York: Schocken Books. (Original work published 1932)

Benjamin, W. (1986b). One-way street [Selection]. In P. Demetz (Ed.) & E. Jephcott (Trans.), *Reflections: Walter Benjamin— Essays, aphorisms, autobiographical writings* (pp. 61–94). New York: Schocken Books. (Original work published 1928)

Benjamin, W. (2002). Convolutes. In R. Tiedemann (Ed.) & H. Eiland & K. McLaughlin (Trans.), *The Arcades Project: Walter Benjamin* (pp. 27–824). Cambridge, MA: Belknap Press of Harvard University Press. (Original work published 1982)

Butler, C. (2002). *Postmodernism: A very short introduction.* Oxford, UK: Oxford University Press.

Dewey, J. (1980). *Art as experience.* New York: Perigee Books. (Original work published 1934)

Diamond, C. T. P., & Mullen, C. A. (Eds.). (1999). *The postmodern educator: Arts-based inquiries and teacher development.* New York: Peter Lang.

Dillard, A. (1982). *Living by fiction.* New York: Harper & Row.

Eiland, H., & McLaughlin, K. (Trans.). (2002). Translators' notes. In R. Tiedemann (Ed.), *The Arcades Project: Walter Benjamin* (pp. 955–1015). Cambridge, MA: Belknap Press of Harvard University Press. (Original work published 1982)

Eisner, E. W. (1979). *The educational imagination: On the design and evaluation of school programs.* New York: MacMillan.

Eisner, E. W. (1991). *The enlightened eye: Qualitative inquiry and the enhancement of educational practice.* New York: Macmillan Publishing.

Eisner, E. W. (1993). Forms of understanding and the future of educational research. *Educational Researcher, 22*(7), 5–11.

Eisner, E. W. (1997). The promise and perils of alternative forms of data representation. *Educational Researcher, 26*(6), 4–10.

Eisner, E. W. (2004). What can education learn from the arts about the practice of education? *International Journal of Education and the Arts, 5*(4). Retrieved January 4, 2007, from http://ijea.asu.edu/v5n4/

Favorites: Your choices from our collection and the transformative power of art. (2005, September 3). *Globe and Mail,* p. R15.

Frisby, D. (2002). *Cityscapes of modernity: Critical explorations.* Cambridge, UK: Polity Press.

Geertz, C. (1995). *After the fact: Two countries, four decades, one anthropologist.* Cambridge, MA: Harvard University Press.

Jackson, P. W. (1998). *John Dewey and the lessons of art.* New Haven, CT: Yale University Press.

Jameson, F. (1991). *Postmodernism, or the cultural logic of late capitalism.* Durham, NC: Duke University Press.

Kupfer Schneider, A. (1998). *Creating the Musée d'Orsay: The politics of culture in France.*

University Park: Pennsylvania State University Press.

Lakoff, G., & Johnson, M. (1980). *Metaphors we live by.* Chicago: University of Chicago Press.

Lather, P. (1997). Creating a multilayered text: Women, AIDS, and angels. In W. G. Tierney & Y. S. Lincoln (Eds.), *Representation and the text: Re-framing the narrative voice* (pp. 233–258). New York: State University of New York.

Lather, P. (2003). *Applied Derrida: (Mis)reading the work of mourning in educational research.* Paper presented at the American Educational Research Association, Chicago. Retrieved January 4, 2007, from http://www.coe.ohio-state.edu/plather/pdf/conferences/derridaaera03.pdf

Paget, M. A. (1990). Performing the text. *Journal of Contemporary Ethnography, 19,* 136–155.

Pinar, W. F. (1994). *Autobiography, politics, and sexuality: Essays in curriculum theory, 1972–1992.* New York: Peter Lang.

Pinar, W. F. (2004). The synoptic text today. *Journal of Curriculum Theorizing, 20*(1), 7–22.

Pinar, W. F., Reynolds, W. M., Slattery, P., & Taubman, P. M. (Eds.). (1996). *Understanding curriculum: An introduction to the study of historical and contemporary curriculum discourses.* New York: Peter Lang.

Richardson, L. (1994). Writing: A method of inquiry. In N. K. Denzin & Y. S. Lincoln (Eds.), *Handbook of qualitative research* (pp. 516–529). Thousand Oaks, CA: Sage.

Vallance, E. (2005). Educational criticism, museum education, and novice critics. In P. B. Uhrmacher & J. Matthews (Eds.), *Intricate palette: Working the ideas of Elliot Eisner* (pp. 75–89). Upper Saddle River, NJ: Pearson.

White, E. (2001). *The flâneur: A stroll through the paradoxes of Paris.* London: Bloomsbury.

Wolcott, H. F. (1990). *Writing up qualitative research.* Newbury Park, CA: Sage.

49

SOCIAL WORK AND THE ARTS

Critical Imagination

◆ Adrienne Chambon

S ocial work is in the midst of a significant shift in its historical terrain, and a palpable sense of urgency has reawakened in the discipline. Faced with the dismantling of institutional arrangements that
have supported social welfare and the notion of public space, the field
of social work seeks a renewed definition in education and a different
implication in society (Chambon, 2007a). It is in that breach, and at
that point of a *bifurcation* of the discipline (Wallerstein, 2004), that
new perspectives can make a difference. The acute wish for critical
imaginings has moved me to engage with art works in relation to social
work training and research. It is in this context that I have developed a
program of inquiry that turns to practices of art for redefinition of the
discipline.

Social work has relied significantly on rational modes of operation,
even when questioning and contesting dominant representations and
knowledge in society (e.g., Leonard, 1997; Rossiter, 2000, 2005; Saleebey

Author's Note: I wish to thank the Social Sciences and Humanities Research
Council of Canada for supporting this inquiry through its Standard Grants
Program.

& Witkin, 2007; Witkin, 1999). The pursuit after evidence-based criteria of professional performance remain highly rationalistic, within a positivist or a postpositivist approach. The critical theory literature on *governmentality* (a Foucauldian approach that reveals the minute mechanisms of power) equally defers to a standard form of rationality in constructing its arguments—in a manner that the writings of Foucault himself generally do not. Thus, alternative ways of questioning and of representing (Witkin, 2000), no less reasoned but in a nonrationalistic perspective, are needed in social work. Stated otherwise, how can the critical reflexivity advocated in feminist writings implicate our subjectivities? What can embodied forms of knowledge, as much as they are advocated (Peile, 1998; Tangenberg & Kemp, 2002), look like?

Few disciplines are uniform, and social work is no different. It tells different stories about itself. Side by side with expert systems, performance indicators, and increased normalization, other responses have grown. A couple of examples: Jane Gorman's (1993) often cited article on postmodern research in social work conveyed the sense of physical and emotional resonance that a social worker encounters when working with fragile clients in a mental health setting. Martha Kuwee Kumsa (2004) proposes a politically informed hermeneutics to elicit the layered meanings held by young African immigrants toward significant material and symbolic possessions (such as a photograph, a necklace, or a song) that awaken their sense(s) of identity, their "longing-to-belong," as indicated in the title of her work, *Sieves and Reeds: Identity, Cohesion, and Be-longing in a Glocalizing Space—Young Oromos in Toronto.*

The approach taken in Anglo-American cultural studies offers some routes to grapple with clients' and workers' cultural entanglements (Denzin, 2002), as the field relies a lot on popular forms of expression and circulation. One of Denzin's suggestions that he formulated precisely toward social work is to bring the discipline closer to the arts. A "poetics of social work" has not been much pursued. This direction has lesser known historical roots in the discipline, as Ken Moffatt (2000) has shown. He writes about Dorothy Livesay, a Canadian social worker, poet, and radical activist. Over the years, the most adamant social work scholar, Howard Goldstein (1990, 1998), repeatedly clamored for an explicit convergence between social work, the humanities, and the arts. Others followed suit, such as Gorman (1993) and Chambon, Irving, and Epstein (1999).

It is from the realm of words and texts (interviews, case records, procedural forms, and policies, cf. Smith, 1999) that social work has tried to explore alternatives. Thus, the writings by Allan Irving (e.g., 1999) draw on the words of Samuel Beckett to give social work a different sensibility. Save in rare instances, social work has had little to do with visual or other plastic modes of representation. The exhibit created by Kathryn Church (2001) on the stitching of wedding dresses in rural Canada is a wonderful exception, a way of telling through material means of a women's world and a mother–daughter relationship.

In my own quest, I first explored the processes of narrative and the fine mechanics of discourses (drawing on linguistics and literary theory). I then pursued a project on Michel Foucault and social work, a different yet still text-based way of stepping outside the home discipline. At present, I focus on practices of art as a source of social work knowledge (Chambon, 2005, 2007a, 2007b; Chambon & Irving, 2003). *The Heuristics of Art Practices* is an epistemological project (Chambon, 2002) in which I examine alternatives to the modernist tradition in which social work has been steeped (Epstein, 1994). I concentrate on historical periods characterized by deep social transformations, turmoil, and uncertainty. The project is grounded in art forms that belong either to premodern or to contemporary practices.

In this chapter, I draw on two works by contemporary Canadian video, Web, and installation artist Vera Frenkel, and comment on the specificity and relevance of that work and art practices more broadly, for social work. On the surface, the works by Frenkel are not about social work. Yet a number of parallels can be drawn between the questions she poses and those that we raise, independently, in social work. Consistent themes in her works include multiplicity in channels of communication; the workings of collective memory; loss, migration, and displacement; and the machineries of bureaucratic institutions. The contextual body of her work points to compatibilities with social work inquiry.

An internationally recognized artist, Frenkel's projects have been seen in multiple venues, including Documenta IX in Kassel, the Offenes Kulturhaus in Linz, the Setagaya Museum in Tokyo, the National Gallery of Canada in Ottawa, the Museum of Modern Art in New York, and the Biennale di Venezia. Her numerous awards include the Canada Council Molson Prize (1989), the Bell Canada Award in Video Art (2001), and the Canadian Governor General's Award in Visual and Media Arts (2006).

Created in 1994, *BodyMissing*, a Web-video-photo project, was exhibited in Scandinavia and in Germany, and the more recent site-specific versions were installed during 2001–2003 at the Goethe-Institut in Toronto, the Canadian Cultural Centre in Paris, the Georg Kargl Gallery in Vienna, and the Freud Museum in London. Another project, *The Institute*™ *or What We Do for Love* (2000–ongoing), an installation and Web-based work (hereafter, *The Institute*; www.the-national-institute.org), was developed and shown at the Banff Centre for the Arts in Canada and the University of Leeds

Centre for Cultural Analysis (during her stays as artist in residence). It was exhibited at the World Wide Video and New Media Festival in Amsterdam in 2001, and in Canada again at the Art Gallery of Sudbury, the J. M. Barnickle and Hart House Galleries of the University of Toronto, Carleton University Art Gallery, and the Agnes Etherington Art Centre at Queens University. The work is still in expansion.

◆ *BodyMissing*, a Star-Shaped, Fractured Text

Not only the context or pretext of Frenkel's work points to compatibilities with social work, but the manner in which she presents her "findings" is also germane to the concerns of the profession. A process of discovery, of making sense, is offered. Moments of meaning are deliberately achieved in a process of query through associations—step by step, fragment by fragment, moment by moment. Starting in the present and from the local site, the "here and now" (as social workers would say), she takes us by the hand and works backwards to trace various pathways. She does not tell us where to go. It is a search that combines documentation and imagination into a careful architecture, fold onto folds. She seeks and gathers existing documents, archives of texts, pictures, letters, and legislations, in a manner not unlike textual practices in social work (Smith, 1999). Documents of the search are created by introducing characters, questions, moments of doubt and resolution. A record is produced of minute steps—bureaucratic, personal, collegial, relations of friendship. In social work alike, the "content" and "the process" of the search are always documented. All along, what is shown is the porousness of each decision and of its consequences:

The story is questioned and subverted even as it unfolds. I'm interested in how we got from there to here, or how we arrived at the story that seems to explain this to us. Narrative is just one way of sustaining a network of tensions that invite the viewer to question what's being presented. (Frenkel & Tuer, 1993, p. 41)

BodyMissing originated in an invitation to create a site-specific work for an exhibit in the city of Linz in Austria. The video opens with contemporary photographs of the city's sculptures. We are told of its fine chocolate industry. A question is posed: What is less known and less claimed about the city of Linz? The Web site has a fictional narrative beginning. The Transit Bar, an imagined bar stemming from a previous installation on displacement and migration (. . . *From the Transit Bar*), has become the setting for a hushed meeting between friends and acquaintances who whisper about the Missing Works of Art that were stolen during the war upon orders of Hitler and stored in the salt mines close to the city. This looted collection was to become the core of Hitler's art museum. When the crates were opened at the end of the war, many works were missing. So the story begins. The video and the Web site, the photographs and documented fiction, the present and the memory retrievals, all function as overlaid voices.

◆ Bodily Knowledge as Evidence

Evidence-based research is one of the current trends in social work as in the health sciences more generally. Frenkel's work is rooted in a sense of physical evidence that keeps the viewer grounded in the materiality of the documents and the eventfulness of the encounter, grasping, breathing. It is the physical forms of knowing that connect the realms of the documentary and of fantasy:

. . . to say we live in invented reality is a way of saying that we live in metaphor, but it's an invention that's just air without the evidence of the body and that evidence, in turn, concrete as it seems, has not meaning outside some form of narrative. (Frenkel & Tuer, 1993, p. 41)

Even when you, or the archaeologist, arrive at a sort of narrative, the ambiguities in the evidence move you beyond the story back into the physical. The *physicality* of piecing together of the evidence got to me. (p. 42)

The *BodyMissing* video shows a group of people striding in an empty hallway. We see their legs and feet and the tips of their shoes as they come up upon a tile in the floor. They stop and we look "down" with them. The group is standing around a single tile adorned with the reverse design of a swastika, one of many such tiles that once covered the floor of this building and other buildings years past, an echo of that other, now silent, form. The action of walking has been interrupted by a discovery that runs through one's body from the tip of the shoe along one's spine. In a variant sequence, one person steps on the design, intent at covering it, if not crushing it. And the haunting German *Maikäfer* lullaby, *Ladybird Fly Away*, keeps returning in the sound track and on the walls of the installation, alternating with the *Black Bird* song, its English equivalent. It sings of war, of destruction, of flight, of parents and children (Frenkel, Schade, & Schmidt, 1996).

The image of a staircase is recurrent: stairs that go down to the storage rooms, up into a building, seeking, retrieving. Black and white photographs show the dark corridors and the damp storage spaces that hid the paintings in the salt mines. The monumental crates contrast with the size of the people who stand around them, looking for the paintings. We see list after list of the documented stolen or disappeared art works: different kinds of lists, fragmentary lists that provide glimpses into people's circumstances and are silent about their lives. Lists that mark absence and loss. Volumes of lists that show intense bureaucratic practices and exemplify the peculiar "poetics of bureaucracies" (cf. Legge, 2003).

The artist is seen here to practice, in Elspeth Probyn's (1996) words, a "sociology of the skin," a way of knowing through the personal and the social body. A way of grasping at something not yet named. A "skin sense" of uncertainties at the edge of an experience that is still unworded. A practice that favors emergence, the way associations come to rest on apparently small examples, articulating cultural links through hinges in ordinary experiences: "the necessity of getting at the minuteness of movement that occurs in the everyday processes of articulation" (Probyn, 1996, p. 6).

"Like the processes of articulation which involve making evident the movement together of different distinct elements, I seek here to mobilize different levels of phenomena: words and things, sounds and sensations, theories and fiction" (pp. 6–7). A video sequence shows a young woman carrying and balancing overflowing archives in her arms. The tilt of her head and the swing in her step express joy and tenderness. Other times, she walks with great caution, as if the mass of papers might slip out of her reach and disperse like leaves on the ground.

◆ A Plural Text

The features of "serious play" and multiple pathways run deep in the work. They are essential to it. Only in this manner does the work harbor a plural text. In Barthes's words: "The more plural the text, the less it is written before I read it" (Barthes, 1974, p. 10).

> The one text is not an (inductive) access to a Model, but entrance into a network with a thousand entrances; to take this entrance is to aim, ultimately, not at a legal structure of norms and departures, a narrative or poetic Law, but at a perspective (of fragments, of voices from other texts, other codes) whose vanishing point is nonetheless ceaselessly pushed back, mysteriously opened. (Barthes, 1974, p. 12)

As for the reader, she or he is not more unitary than the text itself (Carpentiers, 1999). Readers too bring their own plurality to the act of reading:

> I is not an innocent subject, anterior to the text, one which will subsequently deal with the text as it would an object to dismantle or a site to occupy. This "I" which approaches the text is already itself a plurality of other texts, of codes which are infinite, or more precisely, lost (whose origin is lost). (Barthes, 1974, p. 10)

When we think of the social worker as a reader, her task becomes one of highlighting and expanding the plurality and potentialities of the supporting (re)quest, rather than imposing an artificial unity unto it. She approaches this quest as a *star-shaped, fractured text*. "The tutor text will ceaselessly be broken, interrupted" (Barthes, 1974, p. 15); "the step-by-step commentary . . . stars the text instead of assembling it" (p. 13).

The composite image that Nancy Davis Halifax and I put together is an attempt to juxtapose several entrance points into the *BodyMissing* work, to show its fragmentary nature and the openness of discovery. The format is inspired by a series of photomontages displayed on the walls of the exhibits and reproduced in a postcard format. This particular composition that accompanies this text is of our making and should not be taken to be Frenkel's. We thank Vera Frenkel for her permission to use her own work to our ends. (See the Vermeer painting in the postcard in Figure 49.1 and 49.2).

The map of the Web site, made of handwritten phrases, indicates various locations and points of connection. As in social work, the unfolding of sets of relationships and understandings is fundamental. Viewers encounter multiple choices and choose their own pathways. The viewer is a participant, and her decisions make a difference. The act of reading, the moves of interpretation, the "working through" of an issue in social work terms do not respond to a ready-made sequence, to directories of resources, but resemble instead a process of intercepting codes, recognizing crossing routes through gradual moves, in a step-by-step fashion.

◆ The Story Is Partial

The work enters into a dialogue with each of its contexts. In each location (Paris,

Figure 49.1 Composite image from Vera Frenkel (1994–5) *BodyMissing* sources (Details) Read from left to right, clockwise. 1. The Art of Painting, detail, Vermeer, c. 1666–8, kunsthistorisches Museum, Vienna; screen capture. 2. Storages spaces, screen capture. 3. Song in English and German. 4. Aule, Akademie der bildende Künste; video still. 5. *BodyMissing*, site map; screen capture.

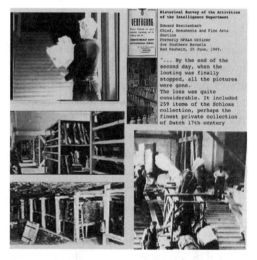

Figure 49.2 Composite image from *BodyMissing*. Read from left to right, clockwise. 1. Girl climbing stairs; video still. 2. Historical survey; screen capture. 3. Rescuing art from the Louvre; screen capture. 4. Storage spaces, detail; screen capture.

SOURCE: All screen captures retrieved February 21, 2005, from http://www.yorku.ca/BodyMissing. Video captures from *Of Memory and Displacement, Vera Frenkel: Collected Works, 2005*. Reproduced, courtesy of Vera Frenkel, with thanks also to Vtape, Toronto, ON.

Vienna, London), the exhibit has taken on a different form. Over time, these traces have been incorporated into the moving work. In social work terms, each context invites a different configuration, another set of relations through the pliability of the materials to the person and persons (or subjectivity/ies) that engage with it, alongside the long-standing imprints of the institution and the range of responses. Each intervention is contextual and multiply shaped.

In one of my classes on Intersecting Narratives, I had asked students to prepare at home a personal pathway into the Web site and present it to the class. I wanted to spark a discussion on narrative authorship. I wished to explore multiple entrances into the work and the students' direct engagement with it. Each student made singular choices, reached out to particular images and statements and avoided others. One student felt most attuned with the images of the missing art works and the process of their reconstruction. The task, she explained, was *not* to reproduce the works but to address their absence. A group of contemporary artists had each developed a response to one missing work of art and to that artist. They had done so on their own terms.

Another student, who wished to avoid the dark side of the video, as she scrolled an official record, was faced, jarringly, with the handwritten signature of Adolf Hitler at the top of her screen. What she had most avoided was staring at her open-eyed in its indifference. She called out to her friend to come and stand beside her so she would not face this discovery alone. In class, she communicated some of her disarray, and added that earlier visits she had made to Holocaust museums in Israel and in the United States had never moved her the way this encounter had. The image had reached her in her bedroom, uninvited, yet she had played a part in eliciting it through the moves she had made. Part of the class

bristled at the intensity of her talk. My own physiological response was an intense feeling of cold. The installation was reaching me anew through her.

Several of us could not retrace out steps and reproduce the path we had initially created for ourselves in the work. Strict reiteration was not possible. Each itinerary expanded on the previous one and with it, our interpretations.

The impression is of an approach that thrives on suspending meaning, a choreography of fragments. Social work and other professions in health and education routinely engage with fragments of information, events that rupture previous claims. Shifting material crystallizes into an understanding "for now" in the context of a particular purpose and set of circumstances. Interpretations are provisional (Frenkel & Tuer, 1993). They are temporary until another develops.

◆ Neoliberalism and The Institute

The work operates by derivatives and slippages and through "side-glances"—a notion that art theorist Irit Rogoff (2002) has proposed to critically engage with contemporary culture from within by deploying tactics of "critical embeddedness."

The starting point for *The Institute*™ or *What We Do for Love* is the demolition of the large state hospitals in Canada as a result of national and regional policy. These institutional structures, which seemed eternal providers of services and organizations of caring, were targeted for destruction. Their disappearance is taking place swiftly, though the debates flow on. Archival footage shows the Calgary hospital crashing down and the site turning to dust within minutes. Watching this monumental act of erasure of a building, we are left to ponder about what it stands for, and the length of time it took to establish such arrangements as opposed to the brief moment of their annihilation. As a senior social worker, Betty Touzel, the first director of welfare services in Ottawa, and the primary author behind the welfare principles, cried out in the mid-1990s: "Don't let them take away what we fought for all these years!" Meanwhile, the Canada Arts Council, the public resource that funds artists, is also dismantled according to the same logic.

These two architectural, institutional, and sociopolitical undoings are transposed in the realistic fantasy of the *Institute.* The remaining hospitals have been restructured into group homes for retired artists, run by staff from the former Arts Council. In the spirit of change, corporate terminology imbues the residence's mission statement, rules, and regulations. The work centers on the malaise of the institution. Residents and staff members, with their profiles and idiosyncrasies, play out the procedural terrors and errors, celebrations, appeals, and arguments. Daily quandaries and controversies, gossip and procedural complications

accompany the emergence of the new social form. The personae that inhabit the work move effortlessly between imagined and real life people, because they have been created from the options available in society. Peer artists in real life have negotiated their personal statement of a resident profile. Live authors have contributed critical writings to the "guest speaker series" posted on the Web site. Individuals from the public at large have even inquired into applying to one of the network's residencies.

The words sung in the "chorus of the bureaucrat": "No One's in Charge," "It's a Job, That's All," "We Have No Power," "Which Gives Us Endless Authority" (*The Staff Speaks—Chant-Rant from Artists in Residence,* in Frenkel, 2003) are far from fictitious. Backed by an upbeat musical accompaniment, the phrases sound outrageously real. The managerial wording, which the artist has lifted from her correspondence with bureaucracies, is all too familiar. This work shares with the previous one a seething perspective on the rational management of society. Dissecting the dehumanizing consequences of the bureaucratic logic attached to

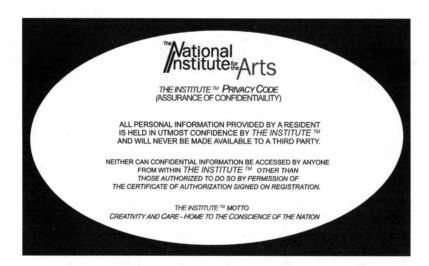

Figure 49.3   Vera Frenkel, *The Institute™: Or, What We Do for Love* (2003 and ongoing). Frame Capture From Web Site (www.the-national-institute.org). One of the Policy Plaques (Privacy Code)

Figure 49.4 Vera Frenkel, *The Institute*™. Frame Capture From Web Site (see Fig. 3). Calgary General Hospital Demolishment

modernity, it converges with the scathing critique worded by Bauman:

> I suggest that it was the spirit of instrumental rationality, and its modern, bureaucratic form of institutionalization, which had made the Holocaust-style solutions not only possible, but eminently "reasonable"—and increased the probability of their choice. (Bauman, 1989, p. 18)

Neoliberalism has further expanded the potential of hyperrationality by fostering segmented practices. By removing the decision points from the outcomes, these variations of rationalism have resulted in the "social production of moral invisibility" (Bauman, 1989, p. 24).

We need to take stock of the evidence that the civilizing process is, among other things, a process of divesting the use and deployment of violence from moral calculus, and of emancipating the desiderata of rationality from interference of ethical norms or moral inhibitions. (p. 28)

Viewers of Frenkel's works do not remain bystanders. The viewer's stance becomes one of partial participation, alternating between delight and unease. Positioned as contemporaries of the hospital demolition shown as a *fait accompli*, viewers participate in displacing the trace and the memory of a social arrangement. They also laugh at the daily gestures of institutions. The humor in the work, like Freud's *Witz*, rests on a play of words and images that reveals ambiguities and contradictions. These acts of mischief have a strong affiliation to the German *Eulenspiegel* character, the jester who resorts to jest as a commentary on society. Serious mischief shows us what most of the public, professionals included, would rather *not* be reminded of—what we wish to be shielded from.

Through the interactive features of the Web site, visitors can pose questions to a resident of their choosing and obtain some form of answer. Seeking personalized responses to their queries, they may fill in the residency eligibility questionnaire and assess their resulting creativity score. By playful implication and through mischievous stagings, viewers, as partial participants, start to face these events and these words that are of our time.

◆ A View of Social Work

What is it about the nature of that work that is so deeply relevant to social work and to society? Quite a few of the main themes are germane to social work. As a mediated activity, social work operates on the fine hinges between micro-events and historical, political, and cultural circumstances, and relies on everyday processes of articulation. Social work mobilizes different levels of reality. It requires precise, careful documentation and simultaneously rests on personal and collective imagery and memory. Social work, as a field, is made of material conditions and social imagination.

What would it mean to "star" a case, a family or a policy case in social work? It would be to open and perform its social tensions and logics. To see beyond classification systems that group cases into "kinds" (Good-Gingrich, 2003)—young street people, internationally adopted children, welfare recipients—as the basis for intervention. It would examine the personal-social-cultural hinges that constitute these life situations historically as societal possibilities. This would mean the representations and institutional arrangements, the personal ways of living, the codes and values of the market, the various forms of capital, the fantasies and imaginings, the forms of memory, gendered, transnational, on the question of "poverty" or "immigration." It would explore the "circuits of culture" (Denzin, 2002) and examine the social constructions that the social work field dispenses and distills (Witkin, 1999). To star a case would imply to invite the words that the person uses, to listen to the language that social workers rely on, to peer at the mission statements, rules, and regulations that implicate us (Rossiter, 2005).

Social work as a deliberate activity that aims to critique, to show, to question can benefit from encounters with practices of art to the extent that such practices can point to and question what is perceived as "natural" ways of relating in society—homelessness, precarious living conditions, unequal access to various forms of capital, appropriation of and exercising knowledge. In social work education, the introduction of art practices

and reflexivity using art-like modalities dissolves the person–society split that is pervasive in the field. I say this based on my own experiments in teaching. Such an approach breaks up the tendency for dividing lines between social workers and clients that create a large misunderstanding. We are all implicated in the societal arrangements, though we are positioned differently.

Italian philosopher Mario Perniola (2004) has urged us to resort to practices that counter the dominant forms of representation produced by contemporary capitalism and neoliberalism, that is, forms that rely on entertainment and escapism, that foreclose options, that suture and saturate. "Only through the filter of memory and of poetic imagination can the astonishing reality of life become capable of eliciting interest and amazement" (p. 79). Insisting on a notion of *surnaturalism* (developed in the literary field) as distinct from realism or from transparency, Perniola advances an aesthetic that is not meant to be pleasant or comforting but aims to enhance and to reveal sites of tension, an aesthetic to serve for opening possibilities, an aesthetic understood as thought, as sensitivity, and as action. Perniola's words hearken back to the work of Vera Frenkel. Could social work resemble Frenkel's work more?

◆ References

Barthes, R. (1974). *S/Z: An essay* (R. Miller, Trans.). New York: Farrar, Straus and Giroux. (Original work published 1970)

Bauman, Z. (1989). *Modernity and the Holocaust.* Ithaca, NY: Cornell University Press.

Carpentiers, N. (1999). *La lecture selon Barthes* [Reading according to Barthes]. Paris: L'Harmattan.

Chambon, A. (2002, October). *A heuristics of art practices for social work.* Unpublished research proposal submitted to the Social Sciences and Humanities Research Council of Canada, General Grants Program.

Chambon, A. (2005). Social work practices of art [Electronic version]. *Critical Social Work Journal, 6*(1).

Chambon, A. (2007a). Art works: Between social critique and active re-enchantment. In D. Saleebey & S. Witkin (Eds.), *Social work dialogues: Transforming the canon in inquiry, practice, and education* (pp. 203–226). Alexandria, VA: Council of Social Work Education Publications.

Chambon, A. (2007b). Transplanted knowledge: Uncertain visitors at an exhibit. In J. G. Knowles, A. L. Cole, L. Neilsen, & T. C. Luciani (Eds.), *The art of visual inquiry* (pp. 235–250). Halifax, Nova Scotia, Canada: Backalong Books.

Chambon, A., & Irving, A. (2003). "They give reason a responsibility which it simply can't bear": Ethics, care of the self, and caring knowledge. *Journal of Medical Humanities, 24*(3/4), Winter, 265–278.

Chambon, A., Irving, A., & Epstein, L., (Eds.). (1999). *Reading Foucault for social work.* New York: Columbia University Press.

Church, K. (2001, January–February). *Fabrications: Stitching our lives together* [Exhibit]. Toronto, Ontario, Canada: The Textile Museum.

Denzin, N. K. (2002). Social work in the seventh moment. *Qualitative Social Work, I*(1), 25–38.

Epstein, L. (1994). The therapeutic idea in contemporary society. In A. Chambon & A. Irving (Eds.), *Essays on postmodernism and social work* (pp. 3–18). Toronto, Ontario, Canada: Canadian Scholars' Press.

Frenkel, V. (1994; 2001–2003). *BodyMissing.* Retrieved June 25, 2007, from www.yorku .ca/BodyMissing

Frenkel, V. (2000–ongoing). *The Institute*™ *or what we do for love.* Retrieved June 25, 2007 from www.the-national-institute.org/ theinst/Frenkel, V. (2003). *The Institute*™ *or what we do for love* [Exhibit catalogue]. Toronto, Ontario, Canada: Hart House, University of Toronto.

Frenkel, V., Schade, S., & Schmidt, E. (1996). *Vera Fenkel: BodyMissing* [Exhibit catalogue]. Bremen, Germany: Gesellschaft für Aktuelle Kunst.

Frenkel, V., & Tuer, D. (1993). Interview. In *Vera Frenkel: Raincoats, suitcases, palms* (pp. 40–57). Toronto, Ontario, Canada: Authors.

Goldstein, H. (1990). The knowledge base of social work practice: Theory, wisdom, analogue or art? *Families in Society, 71,* 32–43.

Goldstein, H. (1998). Education for ethical dilemmas in social work practice. *Families in Society, 79*(3), 241–253.

Good-Gingrich, L. (2003). Social exclusion as an individual kind. *Canadian Review of Social Policy, 52*(Fall–Winter), 93–115.

Gorman, J. (1993). Postmodernism and the conduct of inquiry in social work. *Affilia, 8*(3), 247–264.

Irving, A. (1999). Waiting for Foucault: Social work and the multitudinous truth(s) of life. In A. Chambon, A. Irving, & L. Epstein (Eds.), *Reading Foucault for social work* (pp. 27–50). New York: Columbia University Press.

Kumsa, M. K. (2004). *Sieves and reeds: Identity, cohesion, and be-longing in a glocalizing space—Young Oromos in Toronto.* Unpublished doctoral thesis, University of Toronto, Ontario, Canada.

Legge, E. (2003). A bureaucratic poetics. In V. Frenkel, *The Institute*™ *or what we do for love* [Exhibit catalogue] (pp. 36–42). Toronto, Ontario, Canada: Hart House, University of Toronto.

Leonard, P. (1997). *Postmodern welfare: Reconstructing an emancipatory project.* London: Sage.

Moffatt, K. (2000). *The poetics of social work.* Toronto, Ontario, Canada: University of Toronto Press.

Peile, C. (1998). Emotional and embodied knowledge: Implications for critical practice. *Journal of Sociology and Social Welfare, 25,* 39–59.

Perniola, M. (2004). *Contro la comunicazione.* Torino, Italy: Guilio Einaudi Editore.

Probyn, E. (1996). *Outside belongings.* London: Routledge.

Rogoff, I. (2002). *Looking away: Participations in visual culture.* Paper presented at the Museums after Modernism Conference.

Toronto, Ontario, Canada, Art Gallery of Ontario.

Rossiter, A. (2000). The postmodern feminist condition. In B. Fawcett, B. Featherstone, J. Fook, & Rossiter, A. (Eds.), *Practice and research in social work: Postmodern feminist perspectives* (pp. 24–37). London: Routledge.

Rossiter, A. (2005). Discourse analysis in critical social work: From apology to question. *Critical Social Work, 6*(1), 14–25.

Saleebey, D., & Witkin, S. (Eds.). (2007). *Social work dialogues: Transforming the canon in inquiry, practice, and education.* Alexandria, VA: Council of Social Work Education Publications.

Smith, D. E. (1999). *Writing the social: Critique, theory, and investigations.* Toronto, Ontario, Canada: University of Toronto Press.

Tangenberg, K. M., & Kemp, S. (2002). Embodied practice: Claiming the body's experience, agency, and knowledge for social work. *Social Work, 47*(1), 9–18.

Wallerstein, I. (2004). *The uncertainties of knowledge.* Philadelphia: Temple University Press.

Witkin, S. L. (1999) Social construction and social work [Editorial]. *Social Work, 44*(1), 5–8.

Witkin, S. L. (2000). Writing social work [Editorial]. *Social Work, 45*(5), 389–394.

50

NURSING RESEARCH AND THE TRANSFORMATIVE VALUE OF ART

◆ Vangie Bergum and
Dianne Godkin

Art is integral to the experience of being human. Both active involvement in artistic expression and the appreciation of art produced by others facilitate self-expression, understanding the human-environment mutual process, and finding meaning in varied life experiences.

—Malinski, 2005, p. 105

During nursing's history, in its development as a profession, the art of nursing has at times been overshadowed and its importance devalued by an overarching emphasis on science. However, the artfulness of nursing is reclaiming a position of worth alongside the scientific, and the boundaries between art and science are disappearing (Mitchell & Halifax, 2005; Newman, 2003). These changes are evidenced by the growing body of work in this area by nursing scholars and researchers. Given the importance of art for understanding others and recognizing what we already know as discussed in earlier sections of this *Handbook*, in this chapter we explore the transformative value of art in nursing research. We propose that the value of art within our research environments is found in the intermediate space (Behar, 1996) or relational space (Bergum & Dossetor, 2005) that exists *between* the researcher and the researched, between the question that is asked and the answer that evolves, between the research done by the researcher and the public for whose benefit the research is carried out. This significant space is one of opportunity where something new is possible—where disruption occurs and the new begins. The new is not found in the research itself, the art itself, or the public as such.

Newness, new knowledge and insight, is found in the space between research, art, and the public, in the "immediate communal experience of what we are and how things stand with us in the vital interchange between player and onlooker" (Gadamer, 1986, p. 65). The nursing enterprise has at its heart a desire to understand persons in their wholeness and in relation to the world around them, so we believe that artful nursing research is well suited to this goal.

In this chapter, we explore various art forms and ways in which art has been incorporated in nursing research and point to potential implications for nursing. We describe our own experiences of using art (theatre) and storytelling (narrative) as ways to disseminate research. Our experience of research has been toward understanding events of real life and appreciating the embedded ethical complexities: Bergum exploring issues at the beginning of life and mothering (Bergum, 1989, 1997) and relational ethics (Bergum & Dossetor, 2005) and Godkin exploring issues at the end of life and preparing advance directives (Godkin, 2002). The goal of our research is to inspire ethical action, and little did we know when we began our work the impact that art (play, symbol, festival) would have on our research or how our research might impact art. Nor did we, as researchers, anticipate the ways in which we would be changed in the process. In writing this chapter, we want to show how works of art can transform

fleeting experiences into stable and lasting forms of an independent and internally coherent creation. "It does so in such a way that we go beyond ourselves by penetrating deeper into the work" (Gadamer, 1986, p. 53).

◆ The Role of Art in Nursing Research

In this chapter, we cannot possibly capture the diversity and depth of innovative, artful nursing research in which nurses have been engaged. Instead we show that art has been utilized within the nursing research enterprise and reported in the literature from the point of conception of the research question through to the dissemination of research findings. We highlight the application of art within nursing research in five general areas that cover a wide spectrum of possibilities: art as inspiration, art as method, art as intervention, art as data, and art as dissemination tool. The categories are not discrete, and the boundaries between them are fluid; however, they do provide a structure for describing the role of art in nursing research and nursing research's artful potential. Building upon the accounts of others and our own experiences, we touch upon the synergy between artful nursing research and nursing practice and point to some of the specific challenges one might encounter.

ART AS INSPIRATION

While traveling in England, one nursing researcher, Young-Mason (1998), happened upon Rodin's sculpture of *The Burghers of Calais* and was immediately captivated by its portrayal of fear and suffering. The sculpture depicts the forms of six prominent citizens of the town of Calais who offered themselves as permanent hostages in return for the safe keeping of the remaining citizens of Calais. The emotional anguish that the men felt as they were separated from family and home is dramatically and permanently captured in the bronze sculptures. Intuiting that there was much to learn by examining the sculpture more closely and by studying the life of the sculptor, Young-Mason took a series of photographs showing various angles of the sculpture from different vantage points.

The sculpture served as a jumping off point for an exploration of the concept of sacrifice, a concept that is relevant in nursing. By examining the photographs of the sculpture, the researcher sought a deeper understanding of the nature of sacrifice through the phenomena of corporeality, relationality, spatiality, and temporality. She examined the spatial relationships of each man to the others; she contemplated their emotional states through their facial expressions and the ways in which they held their bodies, and she explored how others responded to the sculpture, stating that "I have never seen anyone pass them without stopping. Everyone is drawn to them, usually circling the work counter-clockwise and then returning to a Burgher whose state of soul corresponds in that moment with their own" (Young-Mason, 1998, p. 109). Young-Mason's aesthetic research method was inspired by Rodin's sculpture and has been since incorporated into nursing curriculum at the undergraduate and graduate level.

ART AS METHOD

A number of nursing researchers have incorporated art as a method for eliciting data and have found that it often yields rich and meaningful information. To study the perceptions of nurses, nursing students, and the elderly about the experience of living with a chronic illness, Hodges, Keeley, and Grier (2001) selected a number of images of masterworks of art. The images were chosen as they illustrated some aspect of chronicity and aging. The researchers suggest that

> works of visual art provide a means of engagement with images and subjects that may sensitize the viewer to human experiences depicted by the artist. It is this engagement that fosters recognition, understanding, and the potential for shared meaning. Clinically the image bridges the gap between the limitations of language and experience. (Hodges et al., 2001, p. 390)

Phenomenological research is a particularly useful example of the way in which art is used by researchers in their attempt to grasp in a thematic way the essence of some experience (van Manen, 1997). In concert with van Manen's approach to phenomenological research, Bergum and Dossetor (2005) used artistic expressions such as videos, photographs, and art, as well as personal and family narratives, to explore issues in healthcare ethics. The concrete examples included *Dax's Case,* a video about a severely burned person who was treated against his will; *A Choice for K'aila,* a video about parents whose infant son risked apprehension by social welfare because the parents would not consent to a liver transplant for him; *Allison's Story,* a personal account by three family members of a family's decision to remove the feeding tube of a comatose daughter and sister, and *Who Should Decide?* a video about the choices facing parents following an unexpected and worrisome prenatal diagnosis.

Photographs and paintings are useful because of their ability to sharpen visual senses, generate new insights and understandings, create interpretive understandings, and promote ethical awareness (Darbyshire, 1993). Through exploring ethical concerns experienced in everyday life, it becomes clear that both the heart (through artistic expression) and mind (through theoretical and analytic deliberation) must be stimulated. Neither rationality nor emotional response is adequate. Using artistic expression as method assisted in capturing the themes of the relational ethic: engagement, embodiment, environment, uncertainty, and mutual respect (Bergum & Dossetor, 2005).

ART AS DATA

In a number of studies, research participants have been asked to photograph, draw, or videotape images related to their perceptions or experiences. One particularly poignant example is that of a small group of persons who, against insurmountable odds, survived an infection with the Ebola virus. These individuals were asked by a team of researchers to draw images of their experience (Locsin, Barnard, Matua, & Bongomin, 2003). In follow-up interviews, participants were asked to explain the meaning the illustrations held for them. From these images and stories, four ways of understanding the experience emerged: escape in peaceful awareness, hope for a world outside of fear, persistence in defying death, and constant fear of dying. The researchers believed participation in the research was transformative for both participants and researchers. They concurred with Dewey's (1934/1980) statement that "not only are people changed by their appreciation of art but the making of art also involves a process of self-expression" (p. 302).

Zucker (2000) used classic pieces of literature as a way of introducing nursing students to death and dying. Following discussion of the literature, the students were asked to create an image that depicted their perception of death and dying. The

researcher found that, through their pictures, the nursing students were able to capture an abstract concept in a language (the language of art) that was universal. In another study, operating room nurses were asked to take pictures of their work environment (Riley & Manias, 2003). The photographs were used as a way of exploring governance in the operating room and were used as a jumping off point to stimulate discussion of the topic of interest. The researchers describe this method of data generation as "photo-voice." In a subsequent article, Riley and Manias (2004) describe the use of photography in nursing research as falling into three general categories: (1) to evoke responses from participants (as was the case in the preceding example), (2) to promote empowerment, and (3) to establish the validity of nursing assessment tools.

ART AS INTERVENTION

A variety of art forms, ranging from photography to theatre to tai chi, have been hypothesized to be potentially beneficial nursing interventions. Chen and Snyder (1999) found that tai chi had a number of positive health effects for elderly persons, including improved balance, enhanced cardiovascular and pulmonary function, and reduction of pain. The role of photographs in assisting bereaved parents through the grieving process was explored by Riches and Dawson (1998), who conclude that

> photographs and other artifacts arising from their children's living can be perceived as the illustrations of a developing story in which previous and present relationships may be represented and interrogated for meaning. [They argue] that visual representations of children's lives, no matter how brief are a crucial feature of the process of coming to terms

with both the fact of the loss and the reality of the life that has been lived. (p. 121)

In another study, Kemp (2003) found that a drama-based education initiative was an effective strategy for promoting the emotional well-being of young people. Theatre has also been used in participatory action research in North America and in developing countries such as in Africa. Kalipeni and Kamlongera (1996) used interactive dramatic techniques to assist two rural communities in Africa to assess their health needs and develop grassroots-based solutions.

In a novel venture, Tognoni (1990) describes how bringing an interactive circus whose program incorporated health teaching about nutrition and hygiene to 15,000 people in remote communities in Brazil impacted child death rates in the area. The circus was entitled *Health and Merriment* and included characters such as Larimunda, the housewife; Salim, the druggist; and three clowns: Banziero, Xulex, and Primentinha. Although the researchers conclude that measuring the "effect of laughter and mirth on changing one's mindset" as this circus sought to do is difficult, in the 12 months that followed its performance, there was not a single instance of child death from diarrhea or malnutrition.

Walsh, Chang, Schmidt, and Yoepp (2005) describe a research project utilizing art as an intervention that was undertaken with two very different goals in mind: (1) an educational vehicle to teach principles of research to nursing students and (2) an intervention for lowering stress of nursing students. As part of an undergraduate nursing research course, consent from students to participate in a research study was obtained. Students were actively involved in all phases of the project as both participants and coresearchers. The intervention was comprised of four creative arts activities; some were completed individually, and others were undertaken in small or large groups. Reports by the students at the end of the course indicated that participation in the research project enhanced their knowledge and enthusiasm about research. Additionally, using several different instruments, it was found that their overall level of stress was reduced following the intervention.

ART AS DISSEMINATION TOOL

Many researchers realize that the academic text is not the only appropriate way to disseminate research that explores human experience. A number have engaged personal stories (narrative, poetry), images (photographs, art), and drama as ways of disseminating research findings to audiences of healthcare professionals and the general public. Gray, Fitch, Labrecque, and Greenberg (2003), for example, produced a drama that depicted the experiences of men with prostate cancer. Those who viewed the play entitled *No Big Deal?* reported an enhanced awareness of the issues facing prostate cancer patients and that they planned to make changes in their practice to reflect what they had learned.

Other nurse researchers have used the medium of theatre to explore the experience of living with Alzheimer's disease. The play *I'm Still Here*, by Christine Jonas-Simpson (Brooke, 2005), was built upon over 10 years of nursing research in the area of quality of life and dementia. As one reporter who attended a performance wrote in *The Jewish Tribune* (an online weekly newspaper), "It provides a telling, yet moving glimpse into the frustration, sorrow and sometimes little joys that inhabit the world of dementia" (Brooke, 2005). Simpson, when asked to comment on her research, said, "It gets down to the core of being human and how we can all react to this in different ways. I think that's the power of theatre too" (Brooke, 2005).

Creating a video as part of the research dissemination plan was felt by Bergum and Dossetor's (2005) research team to be a way to keep the conversation about relational ethics ongoing, allowing for the ideas from the research to continually grow through public involvement. Three nurse researchers, Carol McDonald, Marjorie McIntyre, and Lyn Davis, also used public performance (speaking different voices from McDonald's 2004 research on lesbian experiences of disclosure). Public performance enhanced understanding of the health and social needs of lesbian women and the experiences of lesbians with health care providers. The effort to deconstruct essentializing categories (considering the historical evolution of the binary categories of heterosexual/homosexual women and the multiplicity of subcategories that have evolved within the term lesbian) in an oral poetic performance is a provocative way of destabilizing the categories and opening them to new understandings. This work is itself an intersection of the multiple ways in which lesbians live their lives as academics, as activists, and as people blurring the boundaries of what it is to stand under the sign of lesbian.

Godkin (2002), in her doctoral dissertation, used narrative to describe the older adult's experience of preparing an advance directive. She created the character of Alice to represent an amalgam of the individuals that she interviewed in her study and had encountered during her own clinical nursing practice. Her goal in writing Alice's story was to blend the voices of many into one coherent and articulate voice that showed the experience of preparing an advance directive as fully as language allows. By creating Alice and giving a personal voice to the older adult's experience of preparing an advance directive, it was hoped that readers would come closer to this experience than

they might have otherwise. Ultimately, the nurse researcher sought to evoke in readers a sense of wonder about their own end of life. Along the way through the various phases of this study from conception to completion, the researcher found that her own attempts to apprehend death in a meaningful way continued alongside those of the fictional Alice.

What follows is a discussion of the way Bergum (1989, 1997) used theatre to present themes and experiences of women who become mothers through pregnancy, birth, and early mothering. Beginning with a phenomenological method, she engaged in conversations with women who birthed their child and women who adopted, as well as women who placed their child for adoption. The research with teen mothers and their decision whether to place their baby for adoption or raise the child themselves was particularly interesting and challenging. Subsequently Bergum, in collaboration with Jeffrey Nisker, an obstetrician and in vitro fertilization specialist, created *A Child on Her Mind: A Play* (Nisker & Bergum, 1999) based on Bergum's research with mothers and Nisker's clinical experiences with reproductive technology.

The play examines issues about mothering, ethics, and reproductive technologies through the characters of six women in a hospital's obstetrical unit. In the following excerpt from the play (Nisker & Bergum, 1999) we ask readers to imagine what it might be like for Jane, an infertile woman seeking to adopt a baby, and Jeannine, a teen mom who gives her baby up for adoption. In the play, these women are talking to the audience and not to each other but notice the symmetry of their experiences.

Jane: Finally they told us we could take the baby home. When my husband brought the car seat up we both lost it.

Jeannine: I could see them through the window of the nursery. I watched them leaving with her. I watched them go into the elevator. I went into the nursery. My baby's crib was still warm.

Jane: It was so cold outside. We bundled her up. She was so precious.

Jeannine: I went back to my room and looked out the window. I saw her waiting for the car. The last thing I saw was her fixing the blanket on *my* baby, making sure she was comfortable.

Jane: When we got her home I thought, okay, now it's all just a technicality. We just have to wait the month.

Jeannine: Everyone wanted me to give my baby up, so I did. But it was so hard. I just kept telling myself, "Do the right thing. Do the right thing. Don't be selfish. Do the right thing."

Jane: That month, I felt like I was at everyone's mercy, not just the birthmother's, everyone's. And then the lawyer called and said that the teenager had changed her mind. The lawyer felt maybe if she came to our house and saw the child was being well looked after, she might rethink her decision. So they asked her to pick the child up at our house. She brought a friend with her. And when she saw the child she cried and kept saying that she was so sorry, she was so sorry.

Jeannine: I did what I was supposed to do. I did the right thing.

Jane: It was as if my child had died.

Jeannine: My child is almost nine months old. I haven't seen her since she left the hospital. I wonder what she looks like, what she's doing. What she's feeling. I know she's being cared for, being loved. But she calls someone else "Mummy." Yet, I'm her mummy, too. I'll always be her mummy.

Jane: I couldn't go through adoption again. (Scene 13, pp. 23–24)

The beauty and complexity of becoming a mother amid the challenges of societal pressures and socioeconomic and age differences, as well as the availability of new reproductive technologies, give this play its widespread appeal. The play, aimed at stimulating thought around provocative issues in mothering and reproductive ethics, is also an opportunity to explore pedagogical issues regarding dealing with emotionally and socially difficult moral issues. While entertaining, it is not merely entertainment. It is like a festival where there is opportunity for actors and audiences to find out something new—beyond the research, beyond the art, toward individual experience. The play offers an opportunity for research to reach us in ways that posters or papers cannot.

An added dimension of the Nisker and Bergum (1999) theatre production of *A Child on Her Mind* is that, in the initial performances, the actors were university students and staff (nursing, medicine, law). These students (not professional actors, but health care professionals and lawyers in training) took on the roles of women whose life circumstances were often very unlike their own. During rehearsals and postrehearsal discussions, the actors explored their feelings and connections with the characters they were playing, with one another, and with the playwrights. The actors who portrayed the two teen mothers, in particular, acknowledged how playing these roles had changed the way they thought about and responded to teen mothers they encountered on the street or in their practice, from being quick to judge and perhaps even condemn, to a more open stance. They were now more likely to wonder: "What is her experience?" "What is she going through?" or "How will she make decisions about her baby?" In playing the roles of women deciding on how and when to have children in their lives, the students began to experience themselves the choices, the difficulties, and the ethical decision making that is involved in mothering. Using the mother–child experience is a particularly vibrant metaphor to explore these moral issues and our relationships with each other as human beings.

The vibrancy and potential of the relational, intermediate space that art opens was experienced in a telling moment during the performance of *A Child on Her Mind*. During a poignant dialogue where the teen mothers are struggling with the decision of whether to give their babies up for adoption or raise the babies themselves, a young woman in the audience rushed out of the theatre in gulping sobs. As researchers (and nurses) we followed. The woman shared her experience with us and to our surprise it was not what we expected. The relational space allows for people to come to their own understandings, often ones that cannot be anticipated. The relational space offers the possibility for people to learn knowledge that helps them live their own lives—and sometimes it is knowledge that "breaks your heart" (Behar, 1996). The postperformance discussions became as important a part of the research dissemination process as the performance itself.

◆ Concluding Thoughts

According to the Canadian Nurses' Association *Code of Ethics for Registered Nurses* (2002), "nurses value health promotion and well-being and assisting persons to achieve their optimum level of health in situations of normal health, illness, injury, disability or at the end of life" (p. 8). Artful nursing research can play an integral role in living out this value in the everyday practice of nursing. As the examples we have used illustrate, the impact can be explicit and implicit, direct and indirect. The direct impact of art on specific individuals has been demonstrated in many studies that have shown objective and subjective health benefits. We have shared a few of these examples in the art as intervention section of this chapter. Less direct but incredibly important benefits have been realized through the use of art as method, data, and dissemination tool in expanding nursing's knowledge base and communicating that knowledge within and outside of the nursing discipline. Many art forms such as photographs, paintings, and written stories leave behind a lasting legacy through which we can continue to come to know, understand, and share the experience of others and ourselves.

Art is a powerful tool for nursing research. Art is engaging and entertaining. Art can evoke an empathic response; it can be used to inspire ethical action. But as with any powerful tool, one must be cautious in its application. Art can evoke painful and difficult memories; art can be intrusive. Thus, its use requires nurse researchers to be phronetic, to exercise practical wisdom. Through art we experience the reality of the need for mutual respect as we realize that we are fundamentally connected to one another. Because an understanding of the differences between people (e.g., power, knowledge, beliefs and values, experience, attitudes) does not come easily, there is a need to use all the resources of our community (both art and science) to help us understand the human experience. Art engages people in exploring something together, and creates the possibility of gaining an "imaginative grasp of the relevant webs of interdependency [where] . . . concepts like sufficiency, wholeness, health, participation, diversity, possibility, creativity become the keywords, instead of privation, rationing, authority, centralization, rationalization, downsizing, inevitability, and management" (Peacock, 1999, pp. 705, 710). Perhaps the ultimate reality and transformative value of artful nursing research is to enhance our own understanding of ourselves, as human beings. Through that self-knowledge and openness we can genuinely begin to care for and assist others to achieve their optimum level of health and well-being.

◆ References

Behar, R. (1996). *The vulnerable observer: Anthropology that breaks your heart.* Boston: Beacon Press.

Bergum, V. (1989). *Woman to mother: A transformation.* Granly, MA: Bergin & Garvey.

Bergum, V. (1997). *A child on her mind: The experience of becoming a mother.* Westport, CT: Bergin & Garvey.

Bergum, V., & Dossetor, J. (2005). *Relational ethics: The full meaning of respect.* Hagerstown, MD: University Publishing Group.

Brooke, S. (2005). Play uses research to show truths about dementia sufferers. *The Jewish Tribune.* Retrieved March 30, 2005, from http://www.jewishtribune.ca

Canadian Nurses Association. (2002). *Code of ethics for registered nurses.* Ottawa, Ontario: Canadian Nurses Association.

Chen, K. M., & Snyder, M. (1999). A research-based use of tai chi/movement therapy as a nursing intervention. *Journal of Holistic Nursing, 17*(3), 267–279.

Darbyshire, P. (1993). Understanding caring through photography. In N. L. Diekelmann & M. L. Rather (Eds.), *Transforming RN education: Dialogue and debate* (pp. 275–290). New York: National League for Nursing Press.

Dewey, J. (1980). *Art as experience.* New York: G. P. Putnam's Sons. (Original work published 1934)

Gadamer, H. G. (1986). *The relevance of the beautiful and other essays.* Cambridge, UK: Cambridge University Press.

Godkin, M. D. (2002). *Apprehending death: The older adult's experience of preparing an advance directive.* Unpublished doctoral dissertation, University of Alberta, Edmonton, Alberta, Canada.

Gray, R. E., Fitch, M. I., Labrecque, M., & Greenberg, M. (2003). Reactions of health professionals to a research-based theatre production. *Journal of Cancer Education, 18*(4), 223–229.

Hodges, H. F., Keeley, A. C., & Grier, E. C. (2001). Masterworks of art and chronic illness experiences in the elderly. *Journal of Advanced Nursing, 36*(3), 389–398.

Kalipeni, E., & Kamlongera, C. (1996). The role of "Theatre for Development" in mobilising rural communities for primary health care: The case of Liwonde PHC Unit in southern Malawi. *Journal of Social Development of Africa, 11*(1), 53–78.

Kemp, M. (2003). Acting out: A qualitative evaluation of a mental health promotion project for young people. *Journal of Mental Health Promotion, 2*(3), 20–31.

Locsin, R. C., Barnard, A., Matua, A. G., & Bongomin, B. (2003). Surviving Ebola: Understanding experience through artistic expression. *International Nursing Review, 50*(3), 156–166.

Malinski, V. M. (2005). Art in nursing research. *Nursing Science Quarterly, 18*(2), 105.

McDonald, C. (2004). *There's something I wanted to tell you: Interpretations of lesbian disclosure.* Unpublished doctoral dissertation, University of Calgary, Calgary, Alberta, Canada.

Mitchell, G. J., & Halifax, N. D. (2005). Feeling respected–not respected: The embedded artist in Parse method research. *Nursing Science Quarterly, 18*(2), 105–112.

Newman, M. A. (2003). A world of no boundaries. *Advances in Nursing Science, 26*(4), 240–245.

Nisker, J., & Bergum, V. (1999). *A child on her mind: A play.* Unpublished play, Ontario, Canada: University of Western Ontario.

Peacock, K. A. (1999). Symbiosis and the ecological role of philosophy. *Dialogue, 38,* 703.

Riches, G., & Dawson, P. (1998). Lost children, living memories: The role of photographs in processes of grief and adjustment among bereaved parents. *Death Studies, 22*(2), 121–140.

Riley R., & Manias, E. (2003). Snap-shots of live theatre: The use of photography to research governance in operating room nursing. *Nursing Inquiry, 10*(2), 81–90.

Riley, R. G., & Manias, E. (2004). The uses of photography in clinical nursing practice and research: A literature review. *Journal of Advanced Nursing, 48*(4), 397–405.

Tognoni, G. (1990). Circuses and clowns: Experimental contribution to nursing methodology [English abstract]. *Riv Inferm, 9*(1), 14–18.

van Manen, M. (1997). *Researching lived experience: Human science for an action sensitive pedagogy.* London, Ontario, Canada: Althouse Press.

Walsh, S. M., Chang, C. Y., Schmidt, L. A., & Yoepp, J. H. (2005). Lowering stress while teaching research: A creative arts intervention in the classroom. *Journal of Nursing Education, 44*(7), 330–333.

Young-Mason, J. (1998). Aesthetic research: Sculpture. *Clinical Nurse Specialist, 12*(3), 108–110.

Zucker, D. M. (2000). Depicting death: Lessons on writing and professional development in nursing. *Journal of Nursing Education, 39*(3), 142–144.

51

HEALTH-POLICY RESEARCH AND THE POSSIBILITIES OF THEATER

◆ Jeff Nisker

It is only with the heart that one can see rightly for what is essential is invisible to the eye.

—Antoine de Saint-Exupéry, *The Little Prince*

Engagement of large numbers of citizens of many perspectives is required for fair policy development (Nisker, Martin, Bluhm, & Daar, 2006; Webler & Renn, 1995). Strategies for citizen participation in policy research, such as focus groups and citizens' juries, are limited by lack of opportunity to engage large numbers of participants (Lenaghan, 1999; Nisker, Martin, et al., 2006; Rowe & Frewer, 2000). Strategies, such as public opinion polls, are limited by lack of opportunity for citizens to receive relevant information prior to offering their concerns, opinions, and experiences (Coleman & Gøtze, 2001; Einsiedel & Eastlick, 2000; Lenaghan, 1999; Nisker, Martin, et al., 2006; Rowe & Frewer, 2000; Webler & Renn, 1995). Thus, there has been a call from both policy researchers and scholars of the democratic process for the development of new instruments of citizen participation in policy development (Brunger & Cox, 2000; Coleman & Gøtze, 2001; Einsiedel & Eastlick, 2000; Lenaghan, 1999; Nisker, Martin, et al., 2006; Rowe & Frewer, 2000; Webler & Renn, 1995). Theater can be such an instrument, as it is able to engage, cognitively and emotionally, large numbers of citizens of diverse perspectives, provide them relevant information prior to their formulating opinions, and provide a forum where citizens are able to air and debate their opinions for policy research purposes (Nisker, Martin, et al., 2006).

◆ History of Theater and Policy Development

For millennia theater, like most narrative forms, has been integral to understanding events and issues, and to learning about how to behave as moral beings (Burrell & Hauerwas, 1977; Greenhalgh & Hurwitz, 1998; Nelson, 2001; Nisker, 2004b). Unlike other narrative forms, however, theater "can heighten the intensity of the moral experience" by subjecting the audience to "sensorial impact" through sets, costumes, music, vocal characterizations, facial expressions, and other theatrical strategies that convey characters' emotions and better communicate their feelings (Winston, 1999, p. 463). Ann Hunsaker Hawkins (1997) writes that "moral choice is an act of the whole person: it should involve all our mental faculties—reason, intuition, emotion, imagination—working in concert" (p. 154). Moral choice is essential for policy development and, through theatre audience members, as Nussbaum (2001) writes, make "sense of the suffering by recognizing that one might oneself encounter such a reversal" (p. 316). Boal (1998) describes theater as "our capacity to observe ourselves in action" (p. 7).

Although theater has engaged the public in moral, social, and political issues from the first time plays were performed (Batley

& Bradby, 2001; Gergen & Gergen, 2000; McGrath, 2001; Nussbaum, 2001; Reinelt, 2001), the origins of theater for policy development likely lie in the work of Greek dramatists, such as Euripides and Sophocles (Winston, 1999), with the restriction that only citizens (and indeed male citizens) could participate in policy development and vote. Indeed, Plato worried about the power of theater and other narrative forms to influence thought, and banned poets from his "Republic" (Plato, 1974) under the auspices of their detrimental effects upon the citizenry (Scott, 1998, p. 155).

Shakespeare explored political, moral, and social issues in plays such as *Julius Caesar, Hamlet,* and *Macbeth* (Evans, 1974). Schiller assisted in the democratization of Germany with his play *Wilhelm Tell* (Batley & Bradby, 2001). Theater significantly contributed to explorations of morality in the French Romantic Period (1815–1840), largely due to the value placed on writers as educators, their contact with the populace, and their acknowledged "social, political and religious mission" (Busst, 2001, p. 143). Whitton (2001) describes how theater, "inspired by principles of social justice," was important in France in the 1890s in the socialist workers' theater movement and, indeed, existed in France until 1968 as the "National People's Theater" and other public theaters (p. 53). He draws attention to Vilar (1975), who believed that theater should be treated as a "public service exactly like gas, water, or electricity" (Whitton, 2001, p. 54). Boal's innovative theatrical forms encouraged Brazilians in the 1960s and Europeans in the 1970s and 1980s to become active in democratic policy development (Boal, 1995, 1998, 2001; Nisker, Martin, et al., 2006). In the United States, playwrights criticized government policy, such as the McCarthy-era communist witch hunts in *The Crucible* by Arthur Miller (1957). Also in the United States, theater took on pervasive policy issues, such as in *Angels in America* by Tony Kushner (1995), which challenged perceptions and policies regarding gay relationships and HIV/AIDS.

◆ *Theater and Health Policy Development*

Sandra Jovchelovitch and Martin Bauer (2000) write that "Narratives have become a widespread research method in the social sciences" and are "particularly useful in projects investigating specific events, especially 'hot' issues . . . projects where different 'voices' are at stake" (p. 67). Theatrical productions, focusing on the persons at the center of a health care issue, can bring all who ought to be responsible for its policy development (e.g., patients, their family members, the general public, health professionals) to a better understanding of the new scientific possibilities, ethical issues, and, most important, the persons immersed therein (Nisker, 2004b; Nisker, Martin, et al., 2006).

Recently, several theater-based initiatives have been created specifically for health policy development, such as two in which I was a researcher/scriptwriter. *Sarah's Daughters* (Nisker, 2001b, 2004c), directed by Kayla Gordon, explored policy issues regarding adult predictive genetic testing (Nisker & Daar, 2006; Nisker, Martin, et al., 2006), and *Orchids* (Nisker, 2001a), directed by Liza Balkan, was used for a national citizen deliberation on the testing of in vitro embryos for genetic markers[1] (Nisker, Cox, & Kazubowski-Houston, 2006). The *Sarah's Daughters* project also explored the ethical issues inherent in using theater for health-policy research (Nisker, Martin, et al., 2006). The project (Susan Cox, coprincipal investigator), funded by the Canadian Institutes of Health Research

and Health Canada, also studied the concept of theater as a health policy research tool. These projects will be described below.

As poverty is a major social determinant of health, I include here *Practicing Democracy,* a 20-minute play and interactive discussion on poverty issues, "written and performed by people who have experienced poverty first hand" in Vancouver (Diamond, 2004). In Great Britain, *Mind the Gap,* a play on "mental illness," was written by Abi Bown (2004), directed by Nigel Townsend, and performed by Y Touring Theater Company. This play was supported by the Wellcome Trust—an organization with a long history of funding theater projects to inform the public regarding health issues.

Many more plays, although not specifically created or funded for the development of health policy, affect health policy through the knowledge of the issue they bring to the general public and, directly or indirectly, to policy makers. The research for these plays may be considered health-policy research. For example, in the United States, plays such as *Angels in America* (Kushner, 1995) and *Miss Evers' Boys* (Feldshuh, 1990), through altering public perceptions, have changed health policy regarding HIV/AIDS and research participants. Ross Gray and Christine Sinding (2002), with director and scriptwriter Vrenia Ivonoffski and a theater troupe that included cancer patients, developed *Handle With Care* (Ivonoffski & Gray, 1998), based on the experiences of women with breast cancer, and *No Big Deal?* (Ivonoffski & Gray, 2001), based on the experiences of men with prostate cancer. Gail Mitchell and Christine Jonas-Simpson, again with writer and director Ivonoffski, took their research-based theater on dementia and dementia care to the public in *I'm Still Here* (Mitchell, Jonas-Simpson, & Ivonoffski, 2006). Ardra Cole and Maura McIntyre's (2006) play *Love Stories About*

Caregiving and Alzheimer's Disease, created from data gathered in a large-scale study, and performed by Cole and McIntyre, shows how "ordinary" Canadians respond to the extraordinary demands of caregiving for loved ones with Alzheimer's disease. Vangie Bergum and I wove our research—hers on experiences of birthing and mothering (Bergum, 1997) and mine on justice issues in reproductive and genetic technologies (Nisker, 1996, 1997; Rodgers et al., 1997)—into the play *A Child on Her Mind* (Nisker & Bergum, 1999). *Un jeu de société ou pourquoi se gêner* (Bédard, 2004), a play on genomics, was initiated by a research team led by Hubert Doucet and Isabelle Gareau and directed by Michel Cormier. Similar theater-based health-policy initiatives are rapidly emerging worldwide.

◆ Illustrations

The process of using theater for health-policy research may begin with either a contract policy developer hiring a playwright or director, as was the case for the Wellcome Trust commissioning *Mind the Gap* (Bown, 2004), or a playwright or director, with insight into a health-policy issue, seeking funding for health-policy research. The latter is how the *Sarah's Daughters* project (Nisker, Martin, et al., 2006) and the *Orchids* project (Nisker, 2001a; Nisker, Cox, et al., 2006) came into being. Both *Sarah's Daughters* and *Orchids* are 70-minute plays. Each performance was followed by a one-hour facilitated audience discussion that was taped and transcribed for qualitative analysis. In the *Sarah's Daughters* project this occurred in the theater auditorium whereas, in the *Orchids* project, break-out focus groups occurred simultaneously with the theater

auditoria discussions (Nisker, Cox, et al., 2006).

Sarah's Daughters is a two-woman (one actor and one cellist) play. Based on 12 key informant interviews, *Sarah's Daughters* conveys the concerns of a 38-year-old woman with a strong family history of breast cancer occurring in 30- to 45-year-old women, and her difficulty in accessing genetic counseling. The play presented audience members the social, psychological, scientific, and clinical facts cogent to adult predictive genetic testing (BRCA gene in particular) prior to inviting their opinions in the audience discussion. The play opens with Joanne sharing her psychological and social situation through her lived experience, as she talks about her mother:

> [Who] lived with the knowledge it would happen to her,
>
> Knowledge more felt than understood,
>
> Knowledge gleaned from intuition that could not be confessed,
>
> Knowledge that always lived but would never rest.
>
> She lived with the knowledge it would happen to her,
>
> Woke each day to the knowledge it would happen to her,
>
> That what happened to *her* mother would happen to her.
>
> She wondered only when it would happen,
>
> When it would end. (Nisker, 2004c; Nisker, Martin, et al., 2006)

The scientific and clinical information is presented in scenes that take the form of conversations shared by the actor with the audience, in television news reports, and even in a short mock lecture.

Sarah's Daughters engaged more than 1,300 Canadians in six script readings for key informants and communities (284 citizens) that were staged to inform the accuracy of the script and to ensure sensitivity of the communities portrayed. Twelve productions (1,065 citizens) in nine cities were staged to glean citizens' opinions on the health policy issue (Nisker, Martin, et al., 2006). The number of citizens engaged exceeded that generally surveyed through public opinion polls and was many times more than the number of citizens engaged in citizen participation strategies that educate citizens prior to soliciting their opinions, such as citizens' juries (Lenaghan, 1999; Rowe & Frewer, 2000), and at less cost per citizen engaged (Nisker, Martin, et al., 2006).

Audience members' comments indicated that citizens engaged by theater could provide informed opinions on health-policy issues, including resource allocation, patenting of genetic tests, research policy, insurance discrimination, and public education (Nisker, Martin, et al., 2006). For example,

regarding resource allocation, a theme that surfaced in almost all audience discussions, audience members were divided as to whether public funding should be directed toward access to genetic counseling and testing for women at high risk of developing BRCA gene-related cancer (Nisker, Martin, et al, 2006). Most audience members, who commented from the perspective of either having breast cancer or being at increased risk for breast cancer, believed in public funding and rapid access. For example, one woman said, "I am living daily with the consequences of knowing women who cannot get the BRCA testing in British Columbia [pause], I think we really need some serious public policy on this." Another shared that she "had breast cancer twice" and did not agree with public funding because, "people will go and spend $2000 on a tooth at the dentist, people will spend megabucks on a car, [so] why is it that the Canadians don't want to spend any money on their health care?" Some audience members, who indicated that they were involved in policy development, were

Figure 51.1   Performing *Sarah's Daughters*

supportive of public funding in their comments, such as: "We can also make an economic argument that it's incredibly expensive to die of breast cancer." Others, however, expressed concern that "we keep putting more money and resources into the genes and still fail to do something about the socioeconomic or environmental conditions. It's like, you know, again health care and health science and technology is kind of a Pacman" (Nisker, Martin, et al., 2006).

The *Orchids* project (Nisker, 2001a; Nisker, Cox, et al., 2006) was my first experience working directly with a contracting policy development body (Health Canada). The storyline in *Orchids* is based on the real-life inevitability that two women carrying a gene marker for the same condition will meet in an infertility clinic waiting room: one wanting in vitro fertilization (IVF) to bypass her blocked fallopian tubes in order to have a child (who may or may not carry the gene), and the other wanting IVF for preimplantation genetic diagnosis (PGD) in order to prevent having a child with the gene. The other two lead characters are physician-scientists: one enamored by the potential of genetic science to assist patients in their desires for genetic testing through PGD, the other increasingly concerned with the effect that embryo selection through PGD will have on persons living with disabilities.

Audience members acquired the social, psychological, and scientific information necessary to inform policy opinions from the dialogue between the characters, and between the characters and the audience *qua* orchid cultivators or students (Nisker, 2001a). *Orchids* engaged 741 citizens in 16 performances in Vancouver, Toronto, and in French-language performances and discussion in Montreal. The audience members' comments illustrated the complexity of the issues regarding the genetic testing of embryos and scientific "progress"

in general. Audience members were often concerned with drawing a line between acceptable and unacceptable uses of PGD and who will decide where the line is drawn. In addition, "many audience members were concerned regarding the responsibility that all citizens bear in shaping future society by making individual choices that have collective effects and by making collective choices that will also have individual effects" (Nisker, Cox, et al., 2006).

As summarized in Figure 51.2 (Nisker, Martin, et al., 2006), through this model of theater-based policy research, audience members participated in multidirectional learning (Coleman & Gøtze, 2001; Freire, 2003). Audience members received information from the script and from the comments of other audience members, and had the opportunity to respond to the play and the comments of other audience members with their own comments and questions (to which other audience members could also respond). In addition, the contracting policy body (government in this case) asked questions of the researchers *qua* script developers in the script development and, through its performance, asked questions of the audience members in the discussions following (Nisker, Cox, et al., 2006). It is important that the researchers can ask questions of and respond to questions of the contracting policy developers as occurred in this project (Nisker, Cox, et al., 2006).

◆ Tips for Using Theater as a Policy Research Tool

SCRIPT DEVELOPMENT

Research for the script should include interviews with persons immersed in the health issue, their family and community

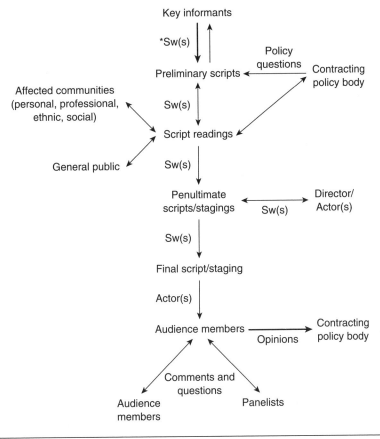

Figure 51.2 Multidirectional Learning in Theater-Based Health Policy Research

SOURCE: Copyright © Jeff Nisker.

*Sw(s) - Scriptwriter(s)

members, scientists (including social scientists), and health professionals. These key informants should read drafts of the script and attend script readings to provide "reality check[s]," "counter-perspective[s]" (Newell, 1998, p. 173), and assurance of the representations. Script readings should also be arranged for the general public to uncover any areas of inadequate or confusing information. Although always maintaining a high degree of independence from the contracting policy body in the presentation of the information derived from key informants, the scriptwriter(s) need to be open to suggestions from the contracting policy development body regarding points essential to the policy development.

PRODUCTION

Because audience members can be engaged emotionally and cognitively without large casts, elaborate props, or extraordinary lighting, low production costs can promote maximum citizen engagement. I also recommend that the play not exceed 70 minutes, in order to leave time for a one-hour audience discussion. A short break preceding the audience discussion provides time for audience members to gain some emotional distance from the play before offering opinions (Nisker, Martin, et al., 2006). This time also allows audience members who do not wish to participate in the discussion to leave less conspicuously.

RECRUITMENT OF AUDIENCE MEMBERS

As all citizen participation strategies privilege an "intelligent, motivated, self-interested and unrepresentative elite" (Rowe & Frewer, 2000, p. 12), the general public should be recruited through posters in malls, community centers, and public transport locations, as well as through advertisements in newspapers (Nisker, Martin, et al., 2006). Members of communities of particular importance to the policy issue can be recruited through additional strategies, such as posters in specific community centers and healthcare institutions, as well as community newsletters and Listservs (Nisker, Martin, et al., 2006).

INFORMED CHOICE TO PARTICIPATE

Participation in policy research insists the same choices and protections as for other areas of research with attention to particular contextual sensitivities (Newell, 1998; Nisker, 2004b; Nisker & Daar, 2006; Sinding, Gray, & Nisker, Chapter 38 in this volume; Smythe & Murray, 2000). Participants, whether key informants for the script or audience members, may be in a negative power differential with the researchers, analogous to when patients are asked by their physician to be research participants (Kenny, 1994; Nisker, 2004a; Nisker & Daar, 2006; Sherwin, 1992, 1998). This is of particular concern in health-policy research because persons identified as "good" key informants may be "provided" by physicians (Nisker, 2004a; Nisker & Daar, 2006) or national advocacy groups, and may feel obligated to comply. Recruitment information should include the purpose of the research, the content of the play, and the nature of the audience discussion, as well as information about informed consent, anonymity, and

voluntary participation (Nisker, Martin, et al., 2006).

AUDIENCE DISCUSSION

Facilitated audience discussions should occur simultaneously in the theater-auditorium and in focus group formats in break-out rooms. Although powerful voices, such as those of scientists, clinicians, and representatives of patient advocacy groups should generally be sequestered, health-policy research also benefits from cross-pollination of the general public with people who have personal or professional lived experience relevant to the policy issue. Thus, some "mixed" focus groups can be informative (Nisker, Cox, et al., 2006; Nisker, Martin, et al., 2006). Audience members in both venues should be reminded about the importance of anonymity and informed about how their responses and comments will be used. Touch pad technology (Schackow, Chavez, Loya, & Friedman, 2004) may also be useful (Nisker, Martin, et al., 2006).

POSTPERFORMANCE COUNSELING AND OPPORTUNITIES FOR FURTHER INFORMATION

Emotional support from health providers or counselors may be required for audience members who experience distress during the performance or audience discussion. Access to additional information, including counseling, regarding the health issue under deliberation should be available to audience members.

DISSEMINATION AND IMPLEMENTATION OF RESULTS

A summary of the policy discussion analysis may be printed in newspapers, posted on Listservs and on community center bulletin boards (particularly community centers frequented by those affected by the potential policy) along with information about how to access a full report on the research (Nisker, Cox, et al., 2006; Nisker, Martin, et al., 2006). Town-hall and community center meetings may also be useful, not only to disseminate the results, but to receive feedback. These dissemination strategies, as well as the open, broad, and diverse recruiting strategies, will raise the profile of the policy research to the media and, through the media, to a greater number of citizens. In this way, it will be more difficult for the policy developer to ignore the result of the research if it is politically problematic.

◆ Note

1. The genetic testing of embryos created through in vitro fertilization (IVF) is called preimplantation genetic diagnosis (PGD) (Handyside, Kontogianni, Hardy, & Winston, 1990; Mykitiuk & Nisker, in press; Nisker & Gore-Langton, 1995). The embryos are assessed genetically, through polymerase chain reaction (PCR) (Mullis & Faloona, 1987) or fluorescent in situ hybridization (FISH) (Delahanty et al., 1993).

◆ References

Batley, E., & Bradby, D. (2001). *Morality and justice: The challenge of European theatre. European studies.* Amsterdam: Rodopi Bv Editions.

Bédard, R. (2004). *Un jeu de société ou pourquoi se gèner.* Unpublished play.

Bergum, V. (1997). *A child on her mind: The experience of becoming a mother.* Westport, CT: Bergin & Garvey.

Boal, A. (1995). *The rainbow of desire: The Boal method of theatre and therapy.* London: Routledge.

Boal, A. (1998). *Legislative theatre: Using performance to make politics.* London: Routledge.

Boal, A. (2001). *Hamlet and the baker's son: My life in theatre and politics.* London: Routledge.

Bown, A. (2004). *Mind the gap.* Unpublished play.

Brunger, F., & Cox, S. M. (2000). Ethics and genetics: The need for transparency. In F. Miller (Ed.), *The gender of genetic futures: The Canadian biotechnology strategy, women, and health* (pp. 27–32). Toronto, Ontario, Canada: York University, National Network on Environments and Women's Health Working Paper Series.

Burrell, D., & Hauerwas, S. (1977). From system to story: An alternative pattern for rationality in ethics. In H. T. Englehardt, Jr., & D. Callahan (Eds.), *The foundation of ethics and its relationship to science: Knowledge, value, and belief* (pp. 111–152). Hastings-on-Hudson, NY: Hastings Center.

Busst, A. J. L. (2001). Moralizing and the stage: French Romanticism's uneasy marriage. In E. Batley & D. Bradby (Eds.), *Morality and justice: The challenge of European theatre* (pp. 143–158). Amsterdam: Editions Rodopi.

Canadian Institutes of Health Research, Natural Sciences and Engineering Research Council of Canada, Social Sciences and Humanities Research Council of Canada. (1998). *Tricouncil policy statement: Ethical conduct for research involving humans (with 2000, 2002, and 2005 amendments).* Retrieved August 29, 2006, from http://www.pre.ethics.gc.ca/english

Cole, A., & McIntyre, M. (2006). *Love stories about caregiving and Alzheimer's disease* [DVD]. Available from http://www.oise.utoronto.ca/research/mappingcare

Coleman, S., & Gøtze, J. (2001). *Bowling together: Online public engagement in policy deliberation.* London: Hansard Society.

Delhanty, J. D. E., Griffen, D. K., Handyside, A. H., Harper, J., Atkinson, G. H. G., Poiters, M. H. E. C., et al. (1993). Detection of aneuploidy and chromosomal mosaicism in human embryos during preimplantation sex determination by fluorescent in situ hybridization (FISH). *Human Molecular Genetics, 2*(1), 183–185.

Diamond, D. (2004). *Practicing democracy.* Unpublished play.

Einsiedel, E. F., & Eastlick, D. L. (2000). Consensus conferences as deliberative democracy: A communications perspective. *Science Communication, 21,* 323–343.

Evans, G. B. (Ed.). (1974). *The Riverside Shakespeare.* Boston: Houghton Mifflin.

Feldshuh, D. (1990). Miss Evers' boys. *American Theater, 7*(8).

Freire, P. (2003). *Pedagogy of the oppressed.* New York: The Continuum International Publishing Group.

Gergen, M., & Gergen, K. (2000). Qualitative inquiry: Tensions and transformations. In N. K. Denzin & Y. S. Lincoln (Eds.), *Handbook of qualitative research* (2nd ed.; pp. 1025–1046). Thousand Oaks: Sage.

Gray, R., & Sinding, C. (2002). *Standing ovation: Performing social science research about cancer.* Walnut Creek: AltaMira Press.

Greenhalgh, T., & Hurwitz, B. (1998). Why study narrative? In T. Greenhalgh & B. Hurwitz (Eds.), *Narrative based medicine: Dialogue and discourse in clinical practice* (pp. 3–16). London: BMJ Books.

Handyside, A. H., Kontogianni, E. H., Hardy, K., & Winston, R. M. (1990). Pregnancies from biopsied human preimplantation embryos sexed by Y-specific DNA amplification. *Nature, 344*(6268), 768–770.

Hawkins, A. H. (1997). Medical ethics and the epiphanic dimension of narrative. In H. L. Nelson (Ed.), *Stories and their limits: Narrative approaches to bioethics* (pp. 153–170). New York: Routledge.

Ivonoffski, V., & Gray, R. (1998). *Handle with care? Women living with metastatic breast cancer* [Performance script]. Toronto, Ontario, Canada: Psychosocial and Behavioural Research Unit at Toronto Sunnybrook Regional Cancer Centre.

Ivonoffski, V., & Gray, R. E. (2000). *No big deal?* [Performance script]. Toronto, Ontario, Canada: Toronto Sunnybrook Regional Cancer Centre.

Jovchelovitch, S., & Bauer, M. W. (2000). Narrative interviewing. In M. W. Bauer & G. Gaskell (Eds.), *Qualitative researching with text, image, and sound: A practical handbook* (pp. 57–74). London: Sage.

Kenny, N. P. (1994). The ethics of care and the patient-physician relationship. *Annals of the Royal College of Physicians and Surgeons of Canada, 17,* 356–358.

Kushner, T. (1995). *Angels in America.* New York: Theater Communications Group.

Lenaghan, J. (1999). Involving the public in rationing decisions. The experience of citizens' juries. *Health Policy, 49,* 45–61.

McGrath, J. (2001). Theatre and democracy. In E. Batley & D. Bradby (Eds.), *Morality and justice: The challenge of European theatre* (pp. 19–35). Amsterdam: Rodopi Bv Editions.

Miller, A. (1957). *The crucible: Arthur Miller's collected plays.* New York: Viking Press.

Mitchell, G. J., Jonas-Simpson, C., & Ivonoffski, V. (2006). Research-based theatre: The making of "I'm Still Here." *Nursing Science Quarterly, 19,* 198–206.

Mullis, K. B., & Faloona, F. A. (1987). Specific synthesis of DNA in vitro via a polymerase-catalyzed chain reaction. *Methods in Enzymology, 155,* 335–350.

Mykitiuk, R., & Nisker, J. (in press). Assisted reproduction. In P. Singer, J. Lantos, & A. Viens (Eds.), *Bioethics for clinicians.* Cambridge, UK: Cambridge University Press.

Nelson, H. L. (2001). *Damaged identities: Narrative repair.* Ithaca, NY: Cornell University Press.

Newell, C. (1998). The ethics of narrative ethics: Some teaching reflections. *Health Care Analysis, 6,* 171–174.

Nisker, J. A. (1996). Rachel's ladders, or how societal situation determines reproductive therapy. *Human Reproduction, 11,* 162–1167.

Nisker, J. A. (1997). In quest of the perfect analogy for using in vitro fertilization patients as oocyte donors. *Women's Health Issues, 7,* 241–247.

Nisker, J. A. (2001a). Orchids: Not necessarily a gospel. In J. Murray (Ed.), *Mappa mundi:*

Mapping culture/mapping the world (pp. 61–109). Windsor, Ontario, Canada: University of Windsor Press.

Nisker J. A. (2001b). *Sarah's daughters* [Premier]. Warehouse Theatre, Winnipeg, Manitoba, Canada.

Nisker, J. A. (2004a). Ethical issues of "case" reports: What can we learn from case studies? *Journal of Obstetrics and Gynaecology Canada, 26,* 7–9.

Nisker, J. A. (2004b). Narrative ethics in health care. In J. Storch, P. Rodney, & R. Starzomski (Eds.), *Toward a moral horizon* (pp. 285–309). Toronto, Ontario, Canada: Pearson Education Canada.

Nisker, J. A. (2004c). She lived with the knowledge. *Ars Medica, 1*(1), 75–80.

Nisker, J. A., & Bergum, V. (1999). *A child on her mind* [Premier]. Canadian Bioethics Society Annual Conference, Edmonton, Alberta, Canada.

Nisker, J., Cox, S., & Kazubowski-Houston, M. (2006). *Citizen deliberation on preimplantation genetic diagnosis.* Unpublished manuscript.

Nisker, J., & Daar, A. S. (2006). Moral presentation of genetics-based narratives for public understanding of genetic science and its implications. *Public Understanding of Science, 15,* 113–123.

Nisker, J. A., & Gore-Langton, R. E. (1995). Pre-implantation genetic diagnosis: A model of progress and concern. *Canadian Journal of Obstetrics & Gynaecology, 17*(3), 247–262.

Nisker, J. A., Martin, D., Bluhm, R., & Daar, A. (2006). Theatre as a public engagement tool for health-policy research. *Health Policy, 78*(2–3), 258–271.

Nussbaum, M. C. (2001). *Upheavals of thought: The intelligence of emotions.* Cambridge, UK: Cambridge University Press.

Plato (1974). *The Republic.* Harmondsworth, UK: Penguin.

Reinelt, J. (2001). Performing justice for the future of our time. In E. Batley & D. Bradby (Eds.), *Morality and justice: The challenge of European theatre* (pp. 37–51). Amsterdam: Rodopi Bv Editions.

Rodgers, S., Baylis, F., Lippman, A., MacMillan, J., Parish, B., & Nisker, J. (1997). Preconception arrangements. *Canadian Journal of Obstetricians and Gynaecology, 19*(4), 393–399.

Rowe, G., & Frewer, L. J. (2000). Public participation methods: A framework for evaluation. *Science, Technology, & Human Values, 25,* 3–29.

Schackow, T. E., Chavez, M., Loya, L., & Friedman, M. (2004). Audience response system: Effect on learning in family medicine residents. *Family Medicine, 36,* 496–504.

Scott, P. A. (1998). Nursing, narrative, and the moral imagination. In T. Greenhalgh & B. Hurwitz (Eds.), *Narrative based medicine: Dialogue and discourse in clinical practice* (pp. 149–158). London: BMJ Books.

Sherwin S. (1992). *No longer patient: Feminist ethics and health care.* Philadelphia: Temple University Press.

Sherwin, S. (1998). A relational approach to autonomy in health care. In S. Sherwin (Ed.), *The politics of women's health* (pp. 19–47). Philadelphia: Temple University Press.

Smythe, W. E., & Murray, M. J. (2000). Owning the story: Ethical considerations in narrative research. *Ethics & Behavior, 10,* 311–336.

Vilar, J. (1975). *Le théâtre: Service public.* Paris: Gallimard.

Webler, T., & Renn, O. (1995). A brief primer on participation: Philosophy and practice. In O. Renn, T. Webler, & P. Wiedemann (Eds.), *Fairness and competence in citizen participation: Evaluating models for environmental discourse* (pp. 17–33). Dordrecht, Netherlands: Kluwer Academic Publishers.

Whitton, D. (2001). Whatever happened to théâtre populaire? The unfinished history of people's theatre in France. In E. Batley & D. Bradby (Eds.), *Morality and justice: The challenge of European theatre* (pp. 53–71). Amsterdam: Editions Rodopi.

Winston, J. (1999). Theorising drama as moral education. *Journal of Moral Education, 28,* 459–471.

52

DISABILITY STUDIES AND THE TIES AND TENSIONS WITH ARTS-INFORMED INQUIRY

One More Reason to Look Away?

◆ Esther Ignagni and
Kathryn Church

We feel like imposters. Neither of us has intentionally set out to conduct an explicitly arts-informed inquiry. Indeed, we could not. Such a methodological positioning has not been readily available within disability studies—the field, roughly speaking, within which our research is located. Yet we have each found ourselves drawing on the arts extensively throughout our work. We have sought out arts-informed literature, attended seminars, registered for conferences—generally trying to locate ourselves within this emerging methodological tradition. As researchers possessing considerable lived and academic experience with disability and difference, we have not always found this a comfortable task.

Disabled people have had an ambivalent relationship with research and with the arts. Each of these endeavors has contributed to a disturbing tradition of normalization and social exclusion. For disabled people, it is hardly relevant whether the inquiring gaze is motivated by aesthetics or a desire for knowledge. Either way, it is one more instance in which the doubled practice of "the look" occurs.[1] Disabled people are looked at as sites of inspiration, curiosity, and exploration.[2] And this only invites the corollary practice of "looking away"—a practice of exclusion. Thus, writing a chapter about the role of arts-informed inquiry in disability studies is inevitably treacherous.

Our stance is emancipatory. However, we are uncertain whether arts-informed researchers see themselves as part of an activist project. We are attracted by the possibilities of arts-informed inquiry—particularly by its efforts to broaden the relations of knowledge production. But we remain mindful that all researchers, including ourselves, work within existing power relations; it is impossible to "step outside" these relations. Thus, our work in disability studies remains haunted by the very representational practices disabled people have fought to leave behind.

We begin the chapter with an overview of disability studies that traces its theoretical shifts and the consequences these have for research practice. We then consider how the arts have been incorporated into knowledge production about (and for) disabled people. We argue that the arts have been used in ways roughly intersecting with the major theoretical approaches to the study of disability.

Throughout, we inject our experiences of bringing together arts-informed methods with our investigations of disability. Esther (Ignagni, 2007) draws on her doctoral research, an experiment in video-arts action research called *The Poster Child Shoots Back*. Kathryn draws on a long period of community-based research in which she grappled with problems of building knowledge/s with and for psychiatric survivor activists and their organizations. We conclude by considering the contribution—realized and

potential—of arts-informed inquiry to future disability studies scholarship.

◆ Tracing Disability Theory and Practice[3]

Disability studies emerged in the mid-1970s from the work of academics, many of whom had disabilities and had developed theoretical insights through grassroots activism. An interdisciplinary field, its project is a radical recasting of disability from a biological given to a socially created system of representation with material and social effects (Thomson, 2002). Prior to this development, disability was largely the academic terrain of medicine and health-related disciplines such as rehabilitation, psychology, and nursing. Scholars in the United Kingdom proposed an alternative "social model" in which the task was to document, critique, and transform the material conditions of disabled people's lives. This approach has since broadly informed disability studies, dovetailing with a concurrent disability rights movement.

Although it helped loosen medicine's grip on disability, the social model has given rise to other problems. Its heavy reliance on historical materialism and its analysis of disabling environments has contributed to a neglect of experiences of impairment (Thomas, 1999), of bodies (Hughes & Paterson, 1997), and of intersections between disability and other social relationships: gender, race, sexual orientation, and class (Asch, 2004; Ghai, 2002; Shakespeare, 1998; Thomas & Corker, 2002; Vernon, 1999). Scholars who have approached disability studies from a phenomenological (Titchkosky, 2003) or postconventional orientation (Corker & Shakespeare, 2002; Davis, 1997, 2002; Shildrick & Price, 1999) have sought redress by deepening the challenge to what we think disability is and how we can study or understand it.

New traditions of inquiry and exploration require new languages for bodies, difference, and disability. American scholar Paul Longmore (1995) argues that, while the disability rights movement began in legal and political spheres with the quest for inclusion and equal opportunity, it has now entered a second phase through the exploration and creation of a disability culture. Art and imagery are imperative in culture and cannot, without debilitating consequences, be controlled by those outside of the disability rights movement (Wood, 1991). Disabled artists and performers seek to reclaim the ways in which images of disability are constructed and delivered, to control the words, images, and ideas that have historically worked against them (Abbas, Church, Frazee, & Panitch, 2004).

Disability culture aims to transform representations of disability. By reimagining artwork-artist-audience relations, proponents imagine a political community based on accessibility. Disability culture inspires and compels audiences to adopt new emotional responses. It encourages audiences "to incorporate rather than to reject unfamiliar ideas and physical forms, to tolerate mixtures of greater varieties and kinds, and to broaden their understanding of human beings and their behavior" (Siebers, 2003, p. 196). Disability culture blurs the boundaries between "us and them," transforming the social relationships of disability and creating worlds more inclusive of difference.[4]

◆ Artistry in Inquiry

What is the relationship between disability culture and arts-informed inquiry into disability? We would argue that the answers to this question are only beginning to form and be articulated. Clearly, there is a resonance between the two. There are also crucial distinctions—beginning with the observation that disability culture lacks an explicit concern with traditional method.

As interpretive researchers, we want to produce work that does something more— or different—than foster artistic or cultural display/performance. We want to work through and with artistic/cultural forms to ask questions, generate data, theorize, and/or communicate findings to a range of audiences. For our purposes, an arts-informed inquiry of disability would be concerned less with past and possible representations of disability than with investigating disability through the arts.

Our assumptions about the nature of disability and how we can come to know it shapes the direction of our artistic inquiry. Because of this, we now turn our attention to how the epistemological and ontological assumptions about disability shape the ways in which the arts are drawn into inquiry.

◆ Art as Repair: "Fixing" Disability

"Art as repair" mediates relationships of disability as potentially "fixable." Rather than inquire or discover, "art as repair" restores well-known normativities of mind and body.

ESTHER: THE POSTER CHILD SHOOTS BACK

Looking and not seeing: It happens several times at the poster session that day. I review the methodology from my dissertation—a video action research project in which disabled youth created videos about their experiences with home and community supports.

There is little interest in the substantive content: That youth conceive of support in ways that diverge sharply from the broader disability rights community appears of little relevance; that youth want better access to transportation, leisure activities, and real educational opportunities goes unnoticed as far as I can tell. Passers-by do appear interested in the use of video and photography. They seem drawn to the images and perhaps to the idea of the images. One after another, conference-goers share stories about art therapy programs in their home communities. Each time I explain that this is not a "therapeutic" project but a participatory action research project with clearly defined political aims. One by one each visitor nods and resumes their discussion of the therapeutic merit of the project. They inquire about the individual outcomes. Did self-esteem improve? Did I observe a greater acceptance of and coping with disability? Our conversation trails as I am unable to answer their questions. One by one, they thank me and politely excuse themselves.

Over the past decade, practitioners of biomedicine have taken an interest in using the arts and humanities to extend their practice (e.g., Nelson, 1997). One striking illustration is the work of the Society for Arts in Healthcare (http://www.societyartshealth care.org). A visit to their Web site reveals projects that utilize the arts to enhance the work of medicine. Drama, visual arts, narrative, and poetry are deployed to facilitate the healing process, to enhance health care delivery, to heighten patient understanding and acceptance of various disorders, to enhance professional education, and so forth. Much of the society's research agenda focuses on evaluating the effectiveness of the arts in the biomedical project. Calls for clearly measurable evidence regarding the capacity of art to achieve a set of well-defined outcomes reveal a strongly positivist orientation.

One link on the society's Web site brings readers to the summary of a recent conference exploring the use of arts in diabetes care. A quotation by its keynote speaker exemplifies the overall tone of the society's activities:

> Can we . . . direct [the arts] to help us tackle some of the challenges posed by this disease? If so, we may provide a valuable arrow in the quiver of tools for doctors, nurses, educators, behaviourists, patients and their families to fight diabetes. (Wikoff, 2004)

Art serves the interests of medicine and of researchers involved in arts-based clinical practice. It does not broaden the narrow epistemic terrain of biomedical knowledge production in the ways suggested by arts-informed inquiry or critical disability theory. "Art" is positioned as a tool for biomedicine. It is incorporated into biomedicine's teleological narrative in which the body is "fixed" in every sense. Art is a means of repair, rehabilitation, and reconstitution of "broken" bodies. Art erases (or contains) disability, rather than facilitates or enables diverse ways of sensing, moving through, or otherwise being in and relating to the world. Such an approach maintains the disability/ability binary in which disability is produced as a wholly biological relation.

◆ The Narrative "Fix"

Narrative and storytelling are powerful tools for the exploration of disability. The "storytelling movement" strives to include the voices of disabled people in public debates and accounting of their lives (Booth & Booth, 1996). One popular approach involves telling stories of "self-change" (Couser, 2000). This approach allows people to articulate their new bodily awareness, and the threats to self and biography posed by impairment and illness (Bury, 2001; Charmaz, 1995; Frank, 1991).

Stories of self-change take many forms but primarily strive to reconstitute the "broken" self and resume a sense of biographic continuity. On the surface this appears consistent with at least some of the aims of disability studies. Through storytelling, disabled people can reclaim our experiences from medical hegemony. We can create unique ways of working through or within the material or ontological "anxiety" wrought by the intrusions on normative embodiment (Frank, 1995).

Yet many self-change stories begin in the experience of newly acquired illness and impairment. Disability remains a biomedical problem, constituted as inherent and addressable within the individual. Experiences of living through and with disability as an everyday, taken-for-granted practice are not well represented within this genre. By focusing on disruptions of self, body. and life story incurred by impairment and illness, storytelling can remain consistently inside the dominant construction of "disability as personal tragedy."[5] As Lennard Davis (1997) cautions "by narrativizing impairment, one tends to sentimentalize it, and link it to the bourgeois sensibility of individualism and the drama of an individual story, with a hero or victim" (p. 4). Within this model, storytelling is at best an individual achievement.

Stories of self-change are easily subsumed within therapeutic or rehabilitation processes through which people come to terms with disruptions to their lives and bodies by "storying" them. Moreover, the coherence and closure of the reconstituted life story reinforces normative discourse. Narrators' impairments/illnesses are overcome; they regain use of their bodies, or "broken" bodies are transcended.[6] Narrative continuity privileges a smooth and steady physical *and* biographical state.

We caution that there are as many approaches to storytelling within disability

studies as there are stories of disability. Critical stories and political autobiographical work by disabled people are a valuable resource for political organizing and cultural critique. It is to the arts as "voice"—arts as implicated in the political process—that we now turn.

◆ Art as Voice: Politicizing Disability

Referring specifically to life stories, Couser (2000) notes that arts and culture can invalidate dominant cultural narratives of disability. Counter discursive arts and imagery can challenge the multitude of one-dimensional disability portraits that proliferate in mainstream arts and popular culture: disability as evil or innocent, as heroic or pitiful, as asexual or sexually deviant (Crow, 2000; Hevey, 1992; Mitchell & Snyder, 2000; Pointon & Davies, 1997).

KATHRYN: IN WHOSE VOICE? FOR WHICH AUDIENCE?

The purpose of the research was to investigate community economic development (CED) done by marginalized people in downtown Toronto. The process was alive with issues of participation and access. I felt them most sharply around "working up" the data. What forms would best reach "readers" who carried labels of deviance and histories of impoverishment? On cultural grounds alone, academic writing was out of the question. A more "indigenous" rendering was necessary. Halfway through the study, we created a ring-bound booklet comprised of five "tales" drawn from focus groups with key informants (Church & Creal, 1995). My editing preserved the spoken language and analysis of these groups and, with their permission, the actual names of the main characters. I drew titles from group dialogue and created text boxes that highlighted the most potent stories from each discussion. We paired the booklet with a short video that also featured stories, and marketed the two as a package called "Voices of Experience." These unusual materials circulated widely, but the strong use of narrative made the research appear "soft" to policy makers. Still, it had some impact through strategic presentation to targets in the provincial bureaucracy. I never found the (paid) time to translate these products for academic publication and credit.

Like Kathryn, Dan Goodley and Michelle Moore were charged with developing an accessible evaluation, in this instance, of a grassroots theatre project involving intellectually disabled performers. They produced a plain language report comprised of "cartoon" drawings and minimal text. This format responded to the fact that the disability academic and activist movements have been inhospitable to their own constituencies, most particularly to people with intellectual impairments (Matysiak, 2001; Traustadottir & Johnson, 2000; Walmsley, 2001).

Goodley and Moore's (2000) work offers a concrete example of how academic texts can be more accessible and inclusive. Moreover, the unique format of the report—published in full in the scholarly journal *Disability & Society*—captured and held the attention of readers more readily than a traditional format.[7] Their format brought the voices of project participants to a more diverse audience, including academics, policymakers, and members of the disability community. In Goodley and Moore's work—as in Kathryn's—drawing on the arts became a means of inclusion that afforded greater participation within the knowledge production process. An outcome such as this is consistent with the core tenets of disability studies.

But while an artistic format may capture and hold audience attention, we know little of how those audiences interpret the artwork. Minimalist drawings and texts might be more easily committed to memory; cartoon-like drawings might inspire satirical or transgressive readings. However, the genre introduces new risks. For example, audiences might inadvertently essentialize project participants; viewers/readers might slip into available interpretive frames that foster constructions of intellectual disability as childlike and cute. Representing the project through "cartoons" might lead audiences to regard the project and the evaluation findings as "trivial" or "soft."

If we are committed to fostering accessibility and inclusion, we must ask how using artistic forms affects the content of our representations. Unconventional forms can force audiences to make their own sense of the content.

KATHRYN: CHALLENGING NEGATIVE IMAGES?

Several years later, I was embroiled once again in a participatory project with a handful of survivor leaders. Inspired by our earlier work with the Voices of Experience video, we wanted to create a broadcast quality film for public television. We wanted a product that would put a different "face" to the psychiatric survivor community by foregrounding its knowledge/s and identity/ies—for a change. After 2 years of collaboration with a pair of independent filmmakers, we had in hand a vivid portrait of six psychiatric survivors working in three survivor-run businesses. What would happen when we screened *Working Like Crazy* across Ontario? We soon discovered that audiences interpreted the film in unique and unpredictable ways—some of which utterly contradicted its intended message. Humour was taken up quite differently by survivor and nonsurvivor audiences. Professional audiences often viewed the content of the video as overtly hostile toward psychiatry: "outdated" and "one-sided." Other audiences missed almost completely the film's agenda for emancipatory community organizing. This is not to say that the film failed to realize its political aims. It has been well received in Canada and internationally. It has inspired survivor groups and been instrumental in connecting them with their allies. Perhaps most integral to the project of disability studies, it has humanized psychiatric survivors. And this time, I made sure to analyze and document the work for academic publication (Church, 2006).

Working Like Crazy is just one example of a broader tradition of participatory uses of photography and video (Bing-Canar & Zerkel, 1998; Krogh, 2001; Wong, 2000; Young & Barrett, 2001). The intent is to privilege the perspective of the "marginalized" or subjugated other by enabling members of these groups to direct the camera's gaze. What is offered is a critical, alternative perspective, not necessarily singular, but definitely within the control of those who have been subject to demeaning and diminishing gazes.

Using art forms in these ways gives voice to a silenced and marginalized group with greater authenticity than disability studies usually affords. Artistic and other unconventional forms of inquiry further praxis in this field. But we are seeking not only other ways to be heard and seen. We are seeking ways to evoke and provoke moments of epiphany, solidarity, and even frustration.

◆ Art as Trouble: Destabilizing Relations of Disability

Art can sometimes be used to trouble the embedded and taken-for-granted relations of disability. Drawing on the arts can force us to relate radically to disability in ways not easily available to us in our everyday lives.

ESTHER: THE DANGERS OF VOYEURISM

Isabella presented the video—a DIY[8] entitled *The 411 on Sex and Disability*—to a large group of university students. We expected a subdued reaction by now—audiences were having a hard time with the videos—and this one was controversial. This class sank to our expectations. Few questions came from the group, despite our considerable preparation for the presentation. Finally one woman spoke up—irritated—from the middle of the group.

"I'm not sure why you presented sexuality in this way."

"What way?" asked Isabella.

"Like just sex. It's such a narrow way to look at sexuality. Like the scene with the two people . . ."

"Oh, yeah. That's from this great video."

Isabella went on to describe how much the video, *Sexuality Reborn*, had taught her. But the student was not diverted from her initial comment.

"To me that's just crass. I mean it's just two people fucking. What are we supposed to learn from that?"

I watched, shaking, as Isabella leaned heavily forward in her chair, flung her hair off her face, setting her chin into her hand. Her eyes narrow, she looked directly and coldly at the student.

"You are not my target audience," she hissed. (Field notes, July 2004)

Placing themselves in front of the camera's lens—or at least placing "disability" on the big screen—opened up participants and disabled people in general to "the stare." Davis (2002) describes the stare as "that telling glance directed toward people with physical differences" (p. 35) in which humanity is stripped from the disabled person and they are turned into an object of curiosity. Youth who participated in Esther's study knew far too well how their humanity could disintegrate with a single glance. They had learned to defy the stare—at least in their talk. As one young woman asserted, "Look at me and I'll give you something to look at!" However until Isabella created her video, it was not always apparent that the youth "walked" their talk. Isabella took stereotypes—ingrained ways of "seeing" disability—and fed them back to audiences in ways they could not anticipate. She showed disability as it rarely is seen in public: disabled people naked, making love, in interracial and same-sex relationships. Yet disrupting these stereotypes drew boundaries between herself and the audience—and within the audience itself.

Mairian Corker (1999) suggests that to play with stereotypes, to feed them back to able-bodied audiences, is to create boundaries that are "impudent," not quite transgressive, and "positively generative." The "in-your-face" quality of Isabella's video clearly shocked the audience—and produced all kinds of other boundaries. Confronted with open sexuality, some audiences received not an enhanced or more humanized view of disability but one more reason to "look away." At the same time, the sexually explicit content of the video was "sensational." It became the object of the kind of curiosity that invites stolen glances and eventually closer examination. Curiosity, then, is not necessarily totally objectifying, but an act of moving closer, asking questions, and possibly learning.

In her discussion of the freak show, Thomson (1997, 1998) claims that the disabled figure—the freak—had a doubled effect of filling the audience with dread and attraction. While the sight of the disabled person warned the audience of its own potential fragility, "it" also represented the

possibility of freedom from the relentless homogeneity of the crowd. Appreciating this "double effect" helps us regard the boundary between disability and ability as far less rigid than in modernist categories. This brings us to the work of Alexa Wright.

In her photographic essay "I," Alexa Wright (2001) digitally manipulates her own image, shifting the morphology of her body so that she appears alternately intellectually disabled, limb deficient, little, and so forth. Her photographs redirect our gaze inward, impelling us to confront the universal, unspoken fear we experience at the sight of difference. Wright works from a phenomenological orientation in which bodies matter because the self is irreducibly embodied, and thus vulnerable. She uses art as a source of theorizing and to provoke her audience into producing new relations of (dis)ability in their moment of seeing.

Rather than attempt to offer "a" perspective, artistic representations invite viewers to imagine diverse embodiments. Audiences are not directed toward any specific emancipatory goal; the artistic images invite a more reflexive and emotional process of contemplation—and perhaps blurring the binary categories of disability/ability.

◆ Possibilities

We began this chapter by foregrounding our ambivalence: drawn to arts-informed inquiry yet pondering its limitations for the emancipatory project of disability studies. We want to conclude in a more hopeful vein. In this section, we identify four fruitful directions that emerge from the conjuncture of an emergent methodology with a field of study.

CREATING NEW LANGUAGES

Simi Linton (1998) speculates that explorations of disability risk individualizing and essentializing the experiences of impairment. Shot through with normative assumptions, our language is not up to the task. Take, for instance, the metaphor of sight and the "ocular-centricity of western philosophy" (Kleege, 2005; Michalko, 2002). In Western cultures, "sight" signifies understanding, awareness, even truth. We "focus" on important issues—blocking out extraneous and distracting details. If we are "blinded" to alternative explanations, we are left with incomplete knowledge, missing what might otherwise be obvious—often because of our inability "to see." Similar metaphors exist for movement, speech, cognition, and other "abilities."

Drawing on the arts may provide new ways to "language" the experience of disability—ways that allow for engagement across physical, sensory, and cognitive difference, rather than merely reproducing these differences. Thoughtful use of arts-informed inquiry might foster an aesthetics of disability that is less contingent upon wholeness, integrity, continuity, or coherence. Experimental and abstract art forms may be particularly effective at challenging normative aesthetics. Appeals to a range of emotion—surprise, anger, and belligerence, in addition to worn-out dispositions such as pathos, sympathy, and kindness—could open new relationships between audiences and disabled subjects.

ILLUMINATING DISABLING CONTEXTS

Arts-informed researchers may be motivated to reflexively consider how their own practices and assumptions reproduce ableist relations. Thinking about the sociopolitical context as creating disability, for instance, pushes researchers to reconsider the genres that inform their inquiry. Economic and political interests enable and constrain how artistic forms such as dance, painting,

music, and video are produced in particular ways in particular contexts.

In her discussion of disability dance, Joyce Sherlock (1996) argues that even transgressive cultural products cannot conflict significantly with the interests and functioning of consumer culture. Dance privileges the clean and smooth lines of a "strong and beautiful body." Cartoons invoke innocence. Video and documentary suggest "eyewitness testimony." We may wish to challenge these interests, but we cannot fully escape them in our work. Instead, we can rely on disability studies' critique of powerful interests to illuminate the ways in which the genres used in arts-informed inquiry reproduce and submit to disabling environments.

EXPANDING ACCESSIBILITY

Goodley and Moore (2000) and others (Duckett & Pratt, 2001; Walmsley, 2001) have shown that many disabled people have been excluded from full participation in knowledge production about their lives— even within disability studies. The recent turn to postmodern, queer, and postcolonial theories in the field has sought to bring more diverse perspectives to bear; yet these theories are characterized by increasingly specialized and elite languages that may exclude the very "subjects" they aim to embrace (D. Gosse, personal communication, February 2003). The same could be said of the planning, implementation, and analysis of research projects. These processes, too, exclude people without fairly high levels of literacy, who are inexperienced with pedagogical settings or who lack other forms of social capital (Church, 1995).

Arts-informed methods may enable disability studies to more fully democratize knowledge production. They offer more and different opportunities for a greater diversity of disabled people to participate in the research process. Beyond that, they may enhance their access to the research results. By the same token, greater attention to disability studies may help broaden the "accessibility" claims made by arts-informed practitioners. All participatory methodologies, including those that are arts-informed, are confronted by issues of accommodation. For example, a researcher planning to create an installation would need to consider wheelchair accessibility, or visual materials in alternative formats. But we must go beyond ensuring that projects meet legislated standards.

For "accessibility" to fully enrich our inquiry, we need to closely inspect the values inherent within the arts, and our genre in particular. We can reflect critically on our methods of data collection, our analyses, the ways in which audiences can interact with our products, and the venues in which our results appear. We can push ourselves to think about the different ways our work can be represented and the consequences this has for audience education, interaction, and engagement, regardless of ability "status."

BRIDGING CULTURE AND SCHOLARSHIP

The history that we outline in this chapter positions disability culture as integral to both the disability rights movement and the related field of disability studies. Over the past decade, scholars have published several books and many journal articles dedicated to disability culture (Crutchfield & Epstein, 2000; Frazee, 1998; Kuppers, 2003; Peters, 2000). Yet few disability theorists have incorporated this work into their research agendas, and particularly into their research designs. As a consequence, disability culture has yet to be explicitly linked with knowledge production in disability studies.

Arts-informed inquiry has the potential to bridge this divide. Its methods decenter academic expertise by creating opportunities for learning through "epiphany," empathy, and engagement. "Decentering" is certainly consistent with the stated intention of disability culture and scholarship. However, paradoxically, just as dominant representations of disability are challenged, so too are more radical/political representations.

Although some are emancipatory, many models of disability remain grounded in the binary thinking that has produced the categories of able-bodied/disabled and mad/sane. Arts-informed inquiry, at its most effective, tends to evade such binary categorizations, tending toward a more hermeneutic or phenomenological orientation to its "subjects" (see, for example, *The Art of Writing Inquiry*, by Neilsen, Cole, & Knowles, 2001, or *Provoked by Art*, by Cole, Neilsen, Knowles, & Luciani, 2004). These "takes" on disability add valuable insight and, as we have suggested, offer new ways to conceptualize and represent it. However, they are not always amenable to emancipatory goals. As such, some of the more explicitly activist projects may not find a wholly arts-informed method congruent with the aims of their work.

◆ Conclusion

We are left with a troubling question. What are the implications of producing representations of disability that cannot displace their "official" counterparts, especially those promulgated by medicine, technology, neoliberal economics, or religion? If our work is always both critical and complicitous (Hutcheon, 1989), what is to prevent audiences from reading our research representations through the "official text" (Bakhtin, 1981) rather than against it?

As Kathryn's work demonstrates, even cultural forms used for protest or resistance inevitably invoke what they wish to challenge. Similarly, some audience members saw

Esther's project as a testament to the heroism of the youth—who in turn found this to be patronizing. At the other extreme, some audience members refused to believe that youth could have created their videos without considerable assistance—thus persisting in viewing disabled youth as incompetent.

All of us tend to read and see through the frames that have been most widely available to us, since those are most familiar, most comfortable (Butler, 2004). Although disability studies, disability culture, *and* arts-informed inquiry seek to de-center them, the familiar frames of disability remain remarkably durable. In the end, one has to get comfortable with simply "letting go" of one's research. For a scholarly discipline whose roots are so tightly bound with political activism, "letting go" is not always easy.

◆ Notes

1. We depart here from Foucauldian notions of "the gaze" in which subjecthood is produced through practices of surveillance. We follow in the tradition of disability theorists who have explored the practice of staring and looking-at as dehumanizing disabled people (Davis, 2002; Titchkosky, 2003).

2. Disabled people have been looked to in many other ways—for instance, as sites of pity, objectification, and exploitation. One of the key practices of eugenics was to look differently at the bodies of those deemed "disabled" in order to justify their institutionalization, sterilization, and in some cases extermination (Dowbiggin, 1999; Mitchell & Snyder, 1998).

3. In this chapter we follow the United Kingdom tradition, which views the field of disability studies as developing in the late 1970s and early 1980s in conjunction with the rise of the independent living movement and the disability rights movements. In contrast, disability theorists in the United States have made a distinction between critical disability studies, which is similar to the United Kingdom model, and

disability studies, which refers to the activities of the allied health professions (see Linton, 1998). In a Canadian and European context, disability studies has been critical from the outset.

4. From its inception, disability culture has had strong ties with the academic community. A primary example is the growing interest from cultural and literary studies in analyses of cultural products that address or invoke disability—including from within arts and culture (Sherlock, 1996). Conference programs from the annual meeting of the Society for Disability Studies, the 2002 Narratives of Disease, Disability, and Trauma Conference in Vancouver, and many others encouraged submissions from artists. The peer-reviewed journal *Disability Studies Quarterly* accepts submissions in poetry, narrative, and visual art format. *Body and Society*, the *Journal of Contemporary Ethnography, Public Cultures*, and *Gay and Lesbian Quarterly* all welcomed artistic submissions in special issues dedicated to disability.

5. The expression "disability as personal tragedy" is closely associated with medical definitions of disability and has been strongly critiqued by social model proponents.

6. See for instance the recent documentary *Murderball* (Rubin & Shapiro, 2005) or *The Body Silent* (Murphy, 1987).

7. In e-mail correspondence, Dan Goodley remarked that this was the "hit" paper of the *Disability & Society* journal that year.

8. Do it yourself—a style of grassroots production, for example, zines, blogs, or YouTube videos.

◆ References

Abbas, J., Church, K., Frazee, C., & Panitch, M. (2004). *Lights . . . camera . . . attitude! Introducing disability arts and culture.* Toronto, Ontario, Canada: Ryerson RBC Institute for Disability Studies Research and Education.

Asch, A. (2004). Critical race theory, feminism, and disability: Reflections on social justice and personal identity. In B. G. Smith & B. Hutchison (Eds.), *Gendering disability* (pp. 9–44). New Brunswick, NJ: Rutgers University Press.

Bakhtin, M. M. (1981). *The dialogic imagination.* Austin: University of Texas Press.

Barnes, C., Oliver, M., & Barton, L. (2002). *Disability studies today.* Cambridge, UK: Polity Press.

Bing-Canar, J., & Zerkel, M. (1998). Reading the media and myself: Experiences in critical media literacy with young Arab-American women. *Signs: Journal of Women in Culture and Society, 23*(3), 735–743.

Booth, T., & Booth, W. (1996). Sounds of silence: Narrative research with inarticulate subjects. *Disability and Society, 11*(1), 55–69.

Bury, M. (2001). Illness narratives: Fact or fiction? *Sociology of Health & Illness, 23*(3), 263–285.

Butler, J. (2004). *Precarious life: The powers of mourning and violence.* New York: Verso.

Charmaz, K. (1995). *Good days, bad days: The self in chronic illness and time.* New Brunswick, NJ: Rutgers.

Church, K. (1995). *Forbidden narratives: Critical autobiography as social science.* London: Routledge.

Church, K. (2006). Working like crazy on "Working Like Crazy": Imag(in)ing CED practice through documentary film. In E. Shragge & M. Toye (Eds.), *Community economic development: Building for social change* (pp. 169–182). Sydney, Nova Scotia, Canada: University College of Cape Breton.

Church, K., & Creal, L. (1995). *Voices of experience: Five tales of community economic development in Toronto* [Book and video]. Available from K. Church at k3church@ryerson.ca

Cole, A. L., Neilsen, L., Knowles, J. G., & Luciani, T. (Eds.). (2004). *Provoked by art: Theorizing arts-informed research.* Halifax, Nova Scotia, Canada: Backalong Books.

Corker, M. (1999). Disability: The unwelcome ghost at the banquet . . . and the conspiracy of "normality." *Body & Society, 5*(4), 75–83.

Corker, M., & Shakespeare, T. (2002). *Disability/postmodernity: Embodying disability theory.* New York: Continuum.

Couser, G. T. (2000). *Recovering bodies: Illness, disability, and life writing.* Madison: University of Wisconsin Press.

Crow, L. (2000). Helen Keller: Rethinking a problematic icon. *Disability & Society, 16*(5), 845–859.

Crutchfield, S., & Epstein, M. (2000). *Points of contact: Disability, art, and culture.* Ann Arbor: University of Michigan Press.

Davis, L. (1997). Constructing normalcy: The bell curve, the novel, and the invention of the disabled body in the nineteenth century. In L. Davis (Ed.), *The disability studies reader* (pp. 9–29). New York: Routledge.

Davis, L. (2002). *Bending over backwards: Disability, dismodernism, and other difficult positions.* New York: New York Press.

Dowbiggin, I. R. (1999). *Keeping America sane: Psychiatry and eugenics in the United States and Canada, 1880–1940.* Ithaca, NY: Cornell University Press.

Duckett, P. S., & Pratt, R. (2001). The researched opinions on research: Visually impaired people and visual impairment research. *Disability & Society, 16*(6), 815–835.

Frank, A. (1991). *At the will of the body: Reflections on an illness.* Boston: Houghton Mifflin.

Frank, A. (1995). *The wounded storyteller: Body, illness, and ethics.* Chicago: University of Chicago Press.

Frazee, C. (1998). Prideful culture. *Entourage, 10*(2), 3–4.

Ghai, A. (2002). Disability in the Indian context: Post colonial perspectives. In M. Corker & T. Shakespeare (Eds.), *Disability/postmodernity* (pp. 88–100). London: Continuum.

Goodley, D., & Moore, M. (2000). Doing disability research: Activist lives and the academy. *Disability & Society, 15*(6), 861–882.

Hevey, D. (1992). *The creatures that time forgot.* London: Routledge.

Hughes, B., & Paterson, K. (1997). The social model of disability and the disappearing body. *Disability & Society, 12*(3), 325–340.

Hutcheon, L. (1989). *The politics of postmodernism.* New York: Routledge.

Ignagni, E. (2007). *The poster child shoots back: The hidden labour of negotiating and maintaining home support.* Doctoral thesis, University of Toronto, Ontario, Canada. Manuscript in preparation.

Kleege, G. (2005). Blindness and visual culture: An eyewitness account. *Journal of Visual Culture, 4*(2), 179–190.

Krogh, K. S. (2001). *Beyond four walls*. Toronto, Ontario, Canada: Ryerson University. Unpublished report.

Kuppers, P. (2003). *Disability and contemporary performance: Bodies on the edge*. New York: Routledge.

Linton, S. (1998). *Claiming disability*. New York: New York University Press.

Longmore, P. K. (1995, September/October). The second phase: From disability rights to disability culture. *The Disability Rag & ReSource*, 3–11.

Matysiak, B. (2001). Interpretive research and people with intellectual disabilities: Politics and practicalities. *Research in Social Science and Disability, 2*, 185–207.

Michalko, R. (2002). *The difference that disability makes*. Philadelphia: Temple University Press.

Mitchell, D. T., & Snyder, S. L. (Directors). (1998). World without bodies. Chicago: Brace Yourself Productions.

Mitchell, D. T., & Snyder, S. L. (2000). Talking about *Talking Back*: Afterthoughts on the making of the disability documentary *Vital signs: Crip culture talks back*. In S. Crutchfield & M. Epstein (Eds.), *Points of contact: Disability, art, and culture* (pp. 197–217). Ann Arbor: University of Michigan Press.

Murphy, R. (1987). *The body silent*. New York: Harry Holt.

Neilsen, L., Cole, A. L., & Knowles, J. G. (Eds.). (2001). *The art of writing inquiry*. Halifax, Nova Scotia, Canada: Centre for Arts-Informed Research/Backalong Books.

Nelson, H. L. (1997). *Stories and their limits: Narrative approaches to bioethics*. New York: Routledge.

Peters, S. (2000). Is there a disability culture? A syncretization of three possible world views. *Disability & Society, 15*(4), 583–601.

Pointon, A., & Davies, C. (1997). *Framed: Interrogating disability in the media*. London: British Film Institute.

Rubin, H. A., & Shapiro, D. A. (Directors). (2005). *Murderball*. United States: Paramount Pictures.

Shakespeare, T. (1998). Out on the edge: The exclusion of disabled people from the British gay and lesbian community. *Disability Studies Quarterly, 19*(3), 169–174.

Sherlock, J. (1996). Dance and the culture of the body: Where is the grotesque? *Women's Studies International Forum, 19*(5), 525–533.

Shildrick, M., & Price, J. (1999). Breaking the boundaries of the broken body. In J. Price & M. Shildrick (Eds.), *Feminist theory and the body* (pp. 432–444). New York: Routledge.

Siebers, T. (2003, Fall). What can disability studies learn from the culture wars? *Cultural Critique, 55*, 182–216.

Society of Disability Studies. (2004). *Critical disability studies*. Retrieved June 1, 2004, from http://www.sds.org

Thomas, C. (1999). *Female forms: Experiencing and understanding disability*. Milton Keynes, UK: Open University Press.

Thomas, C., & Corker, M. (2002). A journey around the social model. In M. Corker & T. Shakespeare (Eds.), *Disability/postmodernity* (pp. 18–31), London: Continuum.

Thomson, R. G. (1997). *Extraordinary bodies: Figuring physical disability in American culture and literature*. New York: Columbia University Press.

Thomson, R. G. (1998). The beauty and the freak. *Michigan Quarterly Review, 37*(3), 459–474.

Thomson, R.G. (2002). Integrating disability, transforming feminist theory. *NWSA Journal, 14*(3), 1–32.

Titchkosky, T. (2003). *Disability, self, and society*. Toronto, Ontario, Canada: University of Toronto Press.

Traustadottir, R., & Johnson, K. (Eds.). (2000). *Women with intellectual disabilities: Finding a place in the world*. Philadelphia: Jessica Kingsley Publishers.

Vernon, A. (1999). The dialectics of multiple disabilities and the disabled people's movement. *Disability & Society, 14*(3), 335–348.

Walmsley, J. (2001). Normalization, emancipatory research, and inclusive research in learning disability. *Disability & Society, 16*(2), 187–205.

Wikoff, N. (2004). [Quotation on the conference Web site]. Society for Arts in Health Care, Edmonton, Alberta, Canada. Retrieved January 2005 from https://www1074 .ssldomain.com/thesah/template/page.cfm? page_id=2

Wong, C. H. Y. (2000, Fall). Who makes the media? Looking at grassroots videography and social action. *Social Policy, 4,* 26–32.

Wood, R. (1991, November 20). *Introduction to the seminar.* Transcript of a disability arts and culture seminar. Retrieved March 21, 2004, from http://www.leeds.ac.uk/disability-studies/archiveuk/archframe.htm

Wright, A. (2001). "I." *Public Culture, 13*(3), 506–510.

Young, L., & Barrett, H. (2001). Adapting visual methods: Action research with Kampala street children. *Area, 33*(2), 141–152.

53

BUSINESS STUDIES

Vivifying Data and Experience Through Artful Approaches

◆ Laura Brearley and Lotte Darsø

There are some experiences in organizational life that are so intense and multilayered that traditional forms of densely referenced academic text cannot adequately evoke their texture and complexity. Artful approaches complement existing qualitative research methods by inviting us to develop insights that would otherwise be inaccessible, because these approaches encourage us to see more clearly and feel more deeply as well as to express ourselves in multiple and diverse ways. When we describe the work we do as "aesthetic" or "artful," we mean that it is vital, relational, multivocal, and multisensory.

This chapter is an exemplar of aesthetic research in business studies. Within it, we tell stories about using artful approaches in our research and in our professional practice. Our intention is to demonstrate that the arts in business studies offer new types of interventions that integrate cognitive and emotional experiences and have the potential to be transformative.

Working in artful ways in business studies requires courage, confidence, and a willingness to work at the edge. This is not mainstream work, and it is not always safe. Pioneering work of this kind, particularly in conservative contexts, requires a heightened sensitivity to contexts and a sound knowledge of one's own strengths and limitations, combined with strong theoretical underpinnings.

Within this chapter, we deploy a number of different voices. Sometimes we write from our individual perspectives, and sometimes we use our collective voice. We include stories and poems as well as the more conventional forms of academically referenced text and analytic models.

◆ What Is Aesthetic or Artful Research in an Organizational Context?

We begin this chapter with some ideas generated from a global conversation currently occurring between academics, artists, and organizational practitioners within a research network called AACORN (Art, Aesthetics, Creativity, and Organizational Research Network). We feel that these ideas reflect the essence of the field of aesthetic and artful organizational research.

The original context of these ideas was an e-mail conversation. To present them here, we have linked connected ideas, distilled concepts to their essence, and shaped them into the form of poetic text. The names of the people from the AACORN network who have expressed these ideas are listed at the end of each untitled poem.

Aesthetic research seeks truths that we each
    connect to
And make our own in different ways

It explores sense-making
As the product of all of our senses
It challenges the slick way of editing reality
Of making quick decisions in a historical void

Of applying managerialist technology
To processes we do not really understand

Of choosing a strategy
And pretending we can make it come true

Aesthetic research challenges the core
Of our economically colonized society

> —*Pierre Guillet de Monthoux*
> *Nanette Monin*
> *Miha Pogacnik*
> *Steve Taylor*

Artists are an endangered species

What do they offer?
Criticism
Experience and insight

Sensory knowing
An extended epistemology
Narratives that capture the hard-to-say

The basis for the search
Of a worldview

> —*David Barry*
> *Pierre Guillet de Monthoux*
> *Miha Pogacnik*
> *Steve Taylor*

Linger longer
In spaces and ideas that are attractive
Not explanatory

Spend some time
Exploring the relationship
Between art and what it is to be fully human

Linger longer
Points that can only be felt
Emerge long after the first encounter

> —*David Barry*
> *Ken Friedman*

It may not be possible
To articulate ideas
In a dominant language

Sometimes the best theories
Are wisely woven
Into a beautiful story or play or poem

> —*David Cowan*
> *Pierre Guillet de Monthoux*

Aesthetic research restores continuity
Between artistic intensity and the everyday

It honors the integral nature of theory and practice
It seeks divergent generalizability

The logic of the senses
The ecology of the senses

The organic process of
Decomposing and recomposing

> —*Ralph Bathurst*
> *Sue Copas*
> *Nanette Monin*
> *Miha Pogacnik*
> *Steve Taylor*

◆ *Theoretical Overview*

Arts and aesthetics in organizational research are increasingly attracting the attention of scholars and organizational practitioners. Explorations of how an organization feels (Strati, 2000a), how it is experienced on a day-to-day basis (Ramirez, 1996), and its aesthetic impact on identity (Linstead & Hopfl, 2000) provide a critical, sensual, and human-centered perspective on business studies.

The use of metaphors to describe organizations (Grant & Oswick, 1996; Morgan 1986, 1996) has brought to conscious and direct sensory awareness the constructs that we use to frame organizations (Taylor, 2004; Taylor & Hansen, 2005). Metaphoric and artistic explorations of organizations draw on other fields of professional practice to reveal the nature of organizational life, such

as improvisational jazz (Hatch, 1998; Mirvis, 1998), organizational theatre (Nissley, Taylor, & Houden, 2004), performance art (Guillet de Monthoux, 1996, 2000, 2004), and architecture (Cairns, 2002), as well as storytelling, poetry, song, and visual art (Barry, 1996, 1997; Boje 1994, 1995; Brearley, 2000, 2001b, 2002; Cowan, 1995; Linstead, 2000; Nissley, Taylor, & Butler, 2002; Strati, 2000b).

The nature of scholarship is changing and opening up to new forms and voices. A growing body of literature is challenging the voice of the researcher as omniscient academic observer and advocating for greater reflexivity and subjectivity within research (Erdunder, 1993; Jantsch, 1975; Lakoff, 1987). The epistemological underpinnings of this exploration come from the literature of representation, from ethnographic (Banks & Banks, 1998; Haarsager, 1998; Jipson & Paley, 1997; Morgan, 1996; Richardson, 1997, 2000; Tierney & Lincoln, 1997;) and phenomenological perspectives (Brearley, 2000, 2001a; Ellis, 1997; Ellis & Flaherty, 1992; van Manen, 1997), as well as from the field of educational research (Barone & Eisner, 1997; Cole & Knowles, 2001; Eisner, 1998; Lather, 1991; Lather & Smithies, 1997). These writers are exploring creative forms of representation, which reflect richness and complexity of data and invite new and multiple levels of engagement that are both cognitive and emotional.

The aesthetic representation and analysis of research data "vivifies" rather than "proves" (Lather, 1991, p. 91). The strength of the data is in its ambiguity and potential for multiple interpretations and levels of engagement. Challenging the voice of the omniscient academic observer disturbs the very basis of epistemological assumptions, as articulated by Jipson and Paley (1997):

> What counts as research? What matters as data? What procedures are considered

legitimate for the production of knowledge? What forms shape the making of explanations? What constitutes proof? (Jipson & Paley, 1997, p. 2)

◆ Application in Business Studies

In business studies, some widely used approaches are action research (Argyris, 1992; Argyris, Putnam, & Smith, 1985; Reason, 1994; Reason & Bradbury, 2001) and clinical research (Schein, 1987). Both focus on initiating change in organizations. Theories of organization inspired by complexity theory (Stacey, 2001; Stacey, Griffin, & Shaw, 2000; Wheatley, 1999) and living systems (Wheatley & Kellner-Rogers, 1996) argue that change starts by changing the conversations in organizations (Barry, 1997; Shaw, 2002; Wheatley, 2002). Organizational Theatre (Meisiek & Dawids, 2003; Nissley, Taylor, & Houden, 2004) and Forum Theatre (Boal, 2000) are

newer approaches that aim at provoking conversations leading to change.

The current discourse in organizational life of valuing creativity and enrichment is impacting how business studies are conducted, as explored in *The Experience Economy* (Pine & Gilmore, 1999), *The Rise of the Creative Class* (Florida, 2002), and *Artful Creation* (Darsø, 2004). According to the latter, artistic approaches improve communication and enable profound changes in individuals and organizations. The following model illustrates the different ways that art can influence us (inspired by the framework on improvisation by Crossan & Sorrenti, 2002). (See Table 53.1).

The vertical axis represents the presence or absence of cognitive change, and the horizontal axis equally represents the presence or absence of emotional change. When both are absent, there is indifference. A person could have been invited to participate in some artistic process, but was not affected by it. It made no impression. Another individual exposed to the same process could be influenced cognitively, at least for a moment, but

Table 53.1 Cognitive-Emotional Change

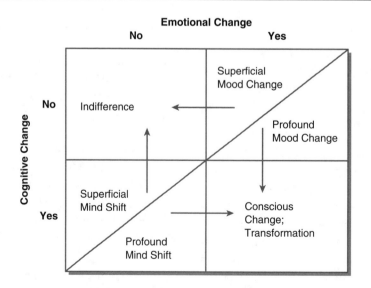

SOURCE: Brearley and Darsø, 2005.

(a) quickly the old schemas took over and in reality no change happened (Festinger, 1964), or (b) the person might have an experience that provoked a real mind shift. This type of shift can give rise to innovation (e.g., in Darsø, 2004, pp. 77–82).

As for emotional change (the top right part of the model), this can be superficial, which means that it could be a change in mood that might evaporate as soon as the person left the place, or it could cross the threshold and become a more permanent change. Music has the quality that it can affect feelings and mood. At times music can affect people so deeply that they experience an inner spiritual transformation (Darsø, 2004, p. 63). It might still be a feeling, though grounded in the body. When this feeling is accompanied by a cognitive shift, we label it conscious change and integrated learning (bottom right corner). Integrated learning thus happens when cognition is accompanied by sensing (emotion) and when emotional experience is followed by reflection or dialogue (cognition).

Integrated learning can be experienced at different levels of consciousness, and the term "artful creation" (Darsø, 2004, p. 146), which we refer to several times in this text, implies a profound change of consciousness combined with vision, passion, and will.

◆ Applications of Artful Organizational Research

In *Artful Creation* (Darsø, 2004) there are many examples of how artful approaches can help to build relations and culture, start meaningful conversations leading to change, provoke cognitive mind shifts, and bring out hidden talents in organizations. The arts can offer powerful and expressive vehicles for researchers as well as for people working in organizations. Through the use of the arts, business studies can encompass both verbal and nonverbal forms of understanding and expression, appealing to diverse cultures and revealing comprehensive knowledge and insights into organizational life. The use of artistic forms or "presentational knowledge" (Heron, 1981; Reason, 1994; Taylor, 2004) encourages multiple ways of sensing, experiencing, expressing, and learning.

The arts can also bring out hidden talents in organizations. In a case study (Darsø, 2004, pp. 108–123) on organizational transformation through the arts, it was found that artistic processes, involving multiple types of art, could work as "catalysts" for new ways of seeing and sensing and new ways of dealing with complexity (preparation, improvisation, and performance), as well as new vehicles for communication and expression. At the strategic level the purpose was to develop an "enterprise culture." At the pragmatic level, apart from the immediately visible effects, there was a spin-off effect in the sense that hidden talents emerged (e.g., in photography, creative writing, poetry) that enriched both the individuals and the organization.

◆ Artful Approaches— Lotte's Experience

I have worked for many years on the innovation process both as a researcher and as a consultant in organizations. In my research in this field, I found it impossible to define the innovation process and even more difficult to form a hypothesis regarding what was involved. I could have done what most researchers do—interview people who had been successful in innovating (e.g., Collins & Porras, 1994; Nonaka & Takeuchi, 1995; Trott, 1998)—but I felt that I had to observe and experience it firsthand in order to fully understand it. My choice of methodology was to conduct my research mainly in Mode 2 (Gibbons et al., 1994) as a combination of action research (Argyris, 1992; Argyris, Putnam, & Smith, 1985; Reason, 1994) and clinical research (Schein, 1987).

Another important choice was to do prospective instead of retrospective research. Retrospective studies look back at the process *after* the innovation, which involves "hindsight bias" (Weick, 1995, p. 30) or the "ex post facto fact" fallacy (Shotter, 1993, p. 85). Prospective research is explorative; it means to study something "in the making" (Latour & Woolgar, 1986) that involves a situation and a context that is "open" (vs. "closed"; Shotter, 1993).

The real challenge for me was, however, to find a way to express my findings that would be both accurate and dynamic. I struggled with this for almost 3 years. It came as a cognitive shift of perspective in relation to a model that I had been using throughout my research, and as this is the bridge to understand how my interest grew for involving the arts in my research, I give a brief description of the model. (See Figure 53.1)

The Diamond of Innovation offers a language for innovation processes in heterogeneous groups and should be understood as a dynamic field (Wheatley, 1999) that encompasses four dimensions: knowledge, relations, ignorance, and concepts. These aspects are all important for innovation to spark, but it turned out that it is the type and quality of the relations between the participants that is crucial for the group to really explore the area of ignorance (Darsø, 2001), which, according to my findings, makes innovation more likely to occur. Also, the quality and sharpness of the questions turned out to be imperative, and as experts were usually too "plugged in," I pondered on who would be able to ask these types of questions. Artists, of course. Thus, I became interested in finding out how artists would work with the four dimensions of the model. But why artists? What is their contribution and why is this important for business studies?

The answer to the first question came soon after, when I was involved in an educational program for artists. I presented my research findings and explained the dimensions of the innovation model. For many of the artists this was an "Aha" experience, and one of them exclaimed: "Suddenly I see where I have my strength and my potential. It is in the area of ignorance."

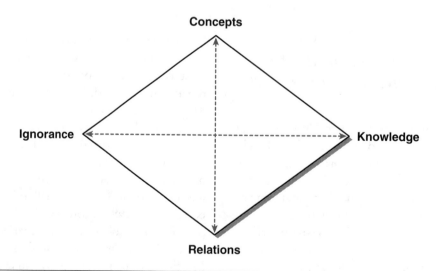

Figure 53.1   The Diamond of Innovation

Later I worked with an artist in an organizational setting. Usually when I explain the model to people, I do it the normal way of academics: I talk. The artist used a different method. She had developed a simple nonverbal drawing exercise in which the participants could experience the difference between knowledge and ignorance, between certainty and uncertainty. Afterward, when I asked the participants to share their thoughts, she asked how it felt in the body. Both aspects are central and illustrate how important the experience is, because it involves inner sensations, feelings, and thinking. The learning from this small exercise was enforced by some other exercises that explored where courage was situated in the body. Afterward the participants were invited to draw courage, the point being that it takes courage to deal with uncertainty and ignorance. At the end of the session one of the participants said: "My body has been more engaged here; normally our meetings are head, head, head."

In 2005 I started a research project, ACT! (Artful Change and Transformation), which involves the Danish Ministry of Tax and a public consultancy. The focus is on the classical problem of anchoring change in organizations. There is a tendency that organizations start one change process after the other and continue with new changes without ever stopping to find out if the interventions actually worked. In this project the top management team decided to collaborate with researchers on anchoring important changes that have taken place by trying out artful approaches. The methodology is CoLLab, a Collaborative Learning Lab, which is a learning and experimental partnership between organizations, researchers, and artists. The participants are considered coresearchers, and together with the research team, they design approaches to transfer the change process into their part of the organization. The researchers document and analyze the process. The CoLLab method is inspired by Gibbons et al.'s work on Mode 2 (1994), Donald Schön's (1983) *The Reflective Practitioner*, Heron and Reason's (2001) research "with" rather than "on" people, and Robert K. Yin's (1994) case study and quasi-experimental approach. The idea is to create a safe space for organizational discovery, experimentation, and innovation through artful intervention and to produce actionable, practical knowledge that is grounded in real-world organizational needs and interests.

Another example of artful creation in a business context involves a leadership program in which we introduced painting in teams during the first module. The purpose of the painting process was to build relationships of trust and respect from the start (in accordance with the Diamond of Innovation). The process was carefully designed with painting intervals accompanied by classical music and no talking, and intervals of stepping back from the painting to talk about it. When words were not an option, people began to use their senses more vividly and to notice new things about their teammates. Relying on nonverbal communication invited people to express themselves in colors, figures, and lines, which allowed new images to emerge—sometimes as cocreation.

From the above examples and other stories about organizational transformation through the arts (Darsø, 2004), it is apparent that artistic approaches are effective for "catalyzing" new ways of seeing and sensing, for creating new ways of dealing with complexity and change, and as new vehicles for reflection, communication, and expression. The research field is obviously still in its early phases and more research is needed.

◆ Artful Approaches— Laura's Experience

Some years ago, I undertook a major study on the nature of managers' experiences of transition in turbulent organizations. I worked with a group of 10 managers who were going through an amalgamation that resulted in three organizational restructures in 2 years. Over this 2-year period, the managers participated in my research project, drawing images of what the experience felt like for them. Their drawings revealed deep questioning about issues of meaning, identity, responsibility, and belonging. From the data, I developed a number of creative resources, including songs, poems, and multimedia tracks. I then used these resources in my work with other managers experiencing similar organizational upheavals.

Two experiences of presenting this material stand out as exemplars of the richness and the risks of using the arts in business studies. I remember one of the first times I presented this material at a university conference. I had pages of notes brimming with theory, multimedia tracks, images drawn by the managers, and some poetic text distilled from transcripts of interviews with them. I was anxious.

The audience was sitting in rows in a darkened auditorium. I began the presentation with Shakespeare's words from Hamlet:

This above all: to thine own self be true.

I was talking to myself really. As the presentation went on, I felt more and more comfortable about telling the truth of who I was, and of inviting deeper levels of engagement with the stories of the managers' experiences. Toward the end of the session, I darkened the auditorium and showed one of the multimedia tracks. I could hear people crying in the darkness. I had thought, when the lights returned, we would talk about the issue of data representation, which had been the focus of the session. To my surprise, the discussion centered on the trauma of the experience of organizational change as represented in the data. They spoke of their own vulnerability and crises of meaning.

People were sitting in rows in a lecture theatre at a research conference talking about their existential issues.

Afterward, I felt exposed but safe. The feedback from the participants after the session was affirming and deeply moving. I knew I was on to something and I also realized that the work had the potential to trigger something powerful that needed to be handled with care.

Not long after this experience, I gave another presentation. This time, instead of feeling elation after it was over, I felt shaken to the core. This was when I fully realized how risky this work could be.

In this presentation, I was not in an auditorium, but in a sun-filled classroom. With the help of two colleagues, I had covered the walls with examples of poems, quotes, and enlarged images drawn by the managers. Chairs for participants were placed in a circle around some brightly colored fabric that held more research data in the form of managers' quotes and images. In one corner stood a guitar and a flute in readiness for a live performance of one of the songs based on managers' experiences.

I saw people coming to the door. Some continued through it and others looked at what was in the room and continued down the corridor to join another session. One woman, when seeing the room and the circle of chairs said loudly: "Oh my God," but she stayed.

I began to see how it was being perceived. I realized I had made many assumptions. I had assumed that people would find the data and their colorful presentation interesting and dynamic. I had assumed that in being immersed and surrounded by the data, they would be drawn to engage.

My anxiety level about the decoration of the room was by now very high, and to compensate, I began the presentation with some solid theoretical underpinnings on a safe and secure overhead projector. I tried to demonstrate the academic rigor of the work, but I could hear it coming across as apologetic self-justification.

I read out a poem from one of the managers. I picked the one that I thought had the greatest emotional charge. I tried to read it with feeling, even though my anxiety level was high. In the middle of reading it, I noticed that a participant was flicking through the reference pages of the academic paper I had left on the chairs. I felt embarrassed and a bit melodramatic.

I then sang a song drawn from the transcripts of interviews. Two colleagues accompanied me. Even though it was unamplified, the music seemed very loud in the small room. It all felt too much—too much volume, too much data, too much emotion. I felt awful. Why had it been received so differently from the other presentation?

After the session, unexpected things started to happen. One woman approached me in tears and said that the stories of transition in the session had matched her own experience. She had come to Australia to study in an attempt to heal herself from the trauma she had experienced in her home country. The man who had been flicking through the research paper while I was reading the poem also approached me. He had been an army officer for many years and began to talk about the posttraumatic stress of soldiers after active combat.

From the feedback, I gradually began to build up a different picture of the presentation. It had not been a total disaster, as I had thought. There were, however, some significant learnings for me about inviting engagement and also taking care of myself.

I looked at the issue of vulnerability and exposure, both mine and the participants'. In the first presentation, people had sat in rows in semidarkness, which had provided a cloak of protection and anonymity. The circle was much more demanding. There was nowhere to hide and no choice about being seen or not.

My own issues about being judged by a potentially punitive and disapproving academy were played out more in the second presentation. Stretching the boundaries of what is considered acceptable and scholarly to the gatekeepers of academic rigor makes me overcompensate. Sometimes, I judge myself more harshly than any external body.

Doing more with less was another learning from the second presentation. Less data around the room would probably have invited people in more. Less data and less talking from me would have been helpful. More silence and more time to reflect were also needed.

I also came to realize that people experience the same presentation in different ways and in different timeframes. I hoped that I could create a safe place for sharing within a period of less than an hour nestled in the middle of a research conference. I had unrealistic expectations.

I have come to learn, and continue to learn, that the paradox and the power of the work is to be present enough and trusting enough to get out of the way and to allow what is emerging in the moment to be fully expressed and felt.

◆ Complexities of Undertaking Aesthetic Organizational Research

Challenging the shape and appearance of research simultaneously opens doors and creates barriers. Inherent in this contradiction are issues of authority, legitimacy, responsibility, and power, which go to the very core of how we view the world and what we value.

The complexities involve knowing the rules *and* challenging assumptions, being creative *and* maintaining rigor, and honoring content *and* exploring form. These sets of paired ideas are not dualities, but can be true simultaneously. It is the process of holding the differences together that, in our experience, has provided the challenge and the creative possibilities of exploring aesthetic forms of organizational research. Here are some questions that emerge from this interplay:

Knowing the rules AND challenging assumptions

- How can we work within a recognized framework of scholarship and challenge its assumptions about form?

- How can we stretch the edges of a recognized form and retain its strengths?

- How can we move beyond compliance to an authentic originality?

Being creative AND maintaining rigor

- How can we invite emotional engagement with data and avoid sentimentality and self-indulgence?

- How can we invite intellectual engagement and avoid pomposity and emotional absence?

- How can we integrate our creativity and our rationality?

Honoring content AND exploring form

- How can we reflect the substance of research content in a congruent creative form?

- How can we avoid the form subsuming and eclipsing the content?

- How can we creatively enliven content while responsibly honoring the original voices?

Awareness of these paradoxes helps the richness of the voices of research participants to emerge as cleanly as possible and helps in developing our own voices as researchers.

Using creative forms of research in business studies and in organizational contexts requires political awareness, sensitivity, and, above all, courage.

◆ Conclusion

Creative forms of research and organizational interventions extend an invitation to engage with experience in new ways. They invite us to transcend the limitations of our usual frames of reference and beliefs, so that new patterns of association can be brought into play (van Maanen, 1983). Engagement of this kind can generate levels of awareness that combine cognitive, emotional, and creative aspects of our being.

The arts have always had the potential of reaching beyond, and obviously the current and potential role of the arts in business studies could have far-reaching and long-term effects, because corporations have such a far-reaching impact in our global society. These new approaches open up a rich resource for the study of business and for organizational research.

Our aim in this chapter has been to demonstrate that the role of the arts in business studies is currently increasing the potential of both research and organizational practices. By integrating the arts into our study and our work, we are able to include multiple voices and languages. These practices help facilitate change and transformation processes that span the continuum of cognitive and emotional insights.

The perspective of involving emotions in business studies does, however, raise new questions of ethics, as emotional and personal involvement can, in some contexts, be experienced as manipulative. Researchers and consultants, therefore, have to be aware of the risks and sensitivities involved when applying the arts. It is extremely important that people who undertake activities involving artistic approaches do so on a voluntary basis and that the facilitator guides the session in a sensitive and respectful manner.

The use of artistic forms or "presentational knowledge" (Heron, 1981; Reason, 1994; Taylor, 2004) encourages multiple ways of sensing, experiencing, expressing, and learning. Through the use of the arts, business studies can encompass both verbal and nonverbal forms of understanding and expression, appealing to diverse cultures and revealing comprehensive knowledge and insights into organizational life. Those who engage can become cocreators of meaning. As articulated by Wolfgang Iser, "The reader receives it by composing it" (Iser in Bruner, 1986, p. 24).

Winnicot (1982) frames the creative act as a political one, claiming that without the creative links between inner and outer, we can become submissive and resigned to the demands of our environment. Exploring creative forms of expression within the academy, and particularly in business studies, is a political act. We believe it has the potential to both enrich the practice of scholarship and deepen our understanding of what it means to be human.

To finish (and maybe to begin something new), we would like to invite you into an experience of directly engaging with an aesthetic text about the nature of creativity itself. This text is in the form of a song that we have cocreated. To hear us singing this song and to read about our experience of collaboratively developing it from raw data, you can go to the Sage Publications Web site at www.sagepub.com/knowlessupplement.

We will therefore conclude this chapter with the lyrics of the song:

— **Knowing** —

There was a time when I would doubt
My sense of what was true
I'd let the shadows of my fear
Cloud my point of view

I'd walk my questions to the sea
And shout them loud and clear
There may have been some answers there
But nothing I could hear
I struggled hard to make things fit
A framework bright and bold
I could not grasp the open space
It felt too much to hold

But all things change and now I trust
That something will be born
It comes from somewhere deep in me
And something far beyond

There was a time when I would doubt
My sense of what was true
Now I see that all along
I already knew

◆ References

Argyris, C. (1992). *On organizational learning.* Malden, MA: Blackwell Publishers.

Argyris, C., Putnam, R., & Smith, D. M. (1985). *Action science: Concepts, methods, and skills for research and intervention.* San Francisco: Jossey-Bass.

Banks, A., & Banks, S. (Eds.). (1998). *Fiction and social research: By ice or fire.* Thousand Oaks, CA: Sage.

Barry, D. (1996). Artful inquiry: A symbolic constructivist approach to social science research. *Qualitative Inquiry, 2*(4), 411–438.

Barry, D. (1997). Telling changes: From narrative family therapy to organizational change and development. *Journal of Organizational Change Management, 10*(1), 30–46.

Barone, T., & Eisner, E. (1997). *Arts-based educational research in complementary methods for research in education* (R. Jaeger, Ed.). Washington, DC: American Education Research Association.

Bjorkvold, J. (1992). *Creativity and communication, song and play from childhood through maturity.* New York: HarperCollins.

Boal, A. (2000). *Theater of the oppressed.* London: Pluto Press.

Boje, D. M. (1994). Organizational storytelling: The struggles of premodern, modern, and postmodern organizational learning discourses. *Management Learning, 25*(3), 433–461.

Boje, D. M. (1995). Stories of the storytelling organization: A postmodern analysis of Disney as Tamara-land. *Academy Of Management Journal, 38*(4), 997–1035.

Brearley, L. (2000). Exploring the creative voice in an academic context. *The Qualitative Report, 5*(3 & 4). Retrieved June 12, 2007, from http://www.nova.edu/ssss/QR/QR5-3/brearley.html

Brearley, L. (2001a). Exploring creative forms within phenomenological research. In R. Barnacle (Ed.), *Phenomenology* (pp. 74–87). Melbourne, Australia: RMIT University Press.

Brearley, L. (2001b). Foot in the air: An exploration of the experience of transition in organizational life. In C. Boucher & R. Holian (Eds.), *Emerging forms of representing qualitative data* (pp. 151–184). Melbourne, Australia: RMIT University Press.

Brearley, L. (2002). What is the matter? *Journal of Management Inquiry, 11*(3), 298.

Bruner, J. (1986). *Actual minds, possible worlds.* Cambridge, MA: Harvard University Press.

Cairns, G. (2002). Aesthetics, morality and power: Design as espoused freedom and implicit control. *Human Relations, 55*(7), 799–820.

Cole, A. L., & Knowles, J. G. (2001). *Lives in context: The art of life history research.* Walnut Creek, CA: AltaMira Press.

Collins, J. B., & Porras, J. I. (1994). *Built to last: Successful habits of visionary companies.* New York: HarperCollins.

Cowan, D. (1995). Rhythms of learning: Patterns that integrate individuals and organizations, *Journal of Management Inquiry,* 4(3), 222–246.

Coyle, S. (1998). Dancing with the chameleon. In A. Banks & S. Banks (Eds.), *Fiction and social research: By ice or fire* (pp. 147–163). Thousand Oaks, CA: Sage.

Crossan, M. M., & Sorrenti, M. (2002). Making sense of improvisation. In K. N. Kamoche, M. Pina e Cunha, & J. Vieira da Cunha (Eds.), *Organizational improvisation* (pp. 29–57). New York: Routledge.

Darsø, L. (2001). *Innovation in the making.* Frederiksberg, Denmark: Samfundslitteratur.

Darsø, L. (2004). *Artful creation: Learning-tales of arts-in-business.* Frederiksberg, Denmark: Samfundslitteratur.

Eisner, E. (1998). *The enlightened eye: Qualitative inquiry and the enhancement of educational practice.* Upper Saddle River, NJ: Prentice Hall.

Ellis, C. (1997). Evocative autoethnography: Writing emotionally about our lives. In W. Tierney & T. Lincoln (Eds.), *Representation and the text: Reframing the narrative voice* (pp. 115–139). Albany: State University of New York Press.

Ellis, C., & Flaherty, M. (Eds.). (1992). *Investigating subjectivity: Research on lived experience.* Newbury Park, CA: Sage.

Erdunder, D. (1993). *Doing naturalistic inquiry: A guide to methods.* Newbury Park, CA: Sage.

Festinger, L. (1964). *Conflict, decision, and dissonance.* Stanford, CA: Stanford University Press.

Florida, R. (2002). *The rise of the creative class.* New York: Basic Books.

Gibbons, M., Limoges, C., Nowotny, H., Schwartzman, S., Scott, P., & Trow, M. (1994). *The new production of knowledge: The dynamics of science and research in contemporary societies.* London: Sage.

Grant, D., & Oswick, C. (Eds.). (1996). *Metaphor and organizations.* London: Sage.

Guillet de Monthoux, P. (1996). The theatre of war: Art, organization, and the aesthetics of strategy. *Studies in Cultures, Organizations, and Societies, 2,* 147–160.

Guillet de Monthoux, P. (2000). Performing the absolute. Marina Abramovic organizing the unfinished business of Arthur Schopenhauer. *Organization Studies, 21*(0), 29–51.

Guillet de Monthoux, P. (2004). *The art firm: Aesthetic management and metaphysical marketing.* Stanford, CA: Stanford Business Books.

Haarsager, S. (1998). Stories that tell it like it is? Fiction techniques and prize-winning journalism. In A. Banks & S. Banks (Eds.), *Fiction and social research: By ice or fire* (pp. 51–66). Thousand Oaks, CA: Sage.

Hatch, M. J. (1998). Jazz as a metaphor for organizing in the 21st century. *Organization Science, 9*(5), 556–557.

Heron, J. (1981). Philosophical basis for a new paradigm. In P. Reason & J. Rowan (Eds.), *Human inquiry. A sourcebook of new paradigm research* (pp. 19–35). Chichester, UK: John Wiley & Sons.

Heron, J., & Reason, P. (2001). The practice of co-operative inquiry: Research "with" rather than "on" people. In P. Reason & H. Bradbury (Eds.), *Handbook of action research: Participative inquiry and practice* (pp. 179–188). London: Sage.

Jantsch, E. (1975). *Design for evolutions: Self-organization and planning in the life of human systems.* New York: George Braziller.

Jipson, J., & Paley, N. (Eds.). (1997). *Daredevil research: Re-creating analytic practice.* New York: Peter Lang.

Lakoff, G. (1987). *Women, fire, and dangerous things: What categories reveal about the mind.* Chicago: University of Chicago Press.

Lather, P. (1991). *Getting smart: Feminist research and pedagogy with/in the postmodern.* New York: Routledge.

Lather, P., & Smithies, C. (1997). *Troubling the angels: Women living with HIV/AIDS.* Boulder, CO: Westview Press.

Latour, B., & Woolgar, S. (1986). *Laboratory life: The construction of scientific facts.* Princeton, NJ: Princeton University Press.

Linstead, S. (2000). Ashes and madness: The play of negativity and the poetics of organization. In S. Linstead & H. Hopfl (Eds.), *The aesthetics of organization* (pp. 61–92). London: Sage.

Linstead, S., & Hopfl, H. (Eds.). (2000). *The aesthetics of organizations.* London: Sage.

Meisiek, S., & Dawids, M. (2003). *"I carry with a smile"*: Spectators' post-performance perception of organization theatre. Working paper presented at workshop of the European Institute for Advance Studies in Management, Gattières, France.

Mirvis, P. H. (1998). Practice improvisation. *Organization Science, 9*(5), 586–592.

Morgan, G. (1986). *Images of organization.* Beverly Hills, CA: Sage.

Morgan, G. (1996). An afterword: Is there anything more to be said about metaphor? In D. Grant & C. Oswick (Eds.), *Metaphor and organizations* (pp. 227–240). London: Sage.

Nissley, N., Taylor, S. S., & Butler, O. (2002). The power of organizational song: An organizational discourse and aesthetic expression for organizational culture. *Tamara: Journal of Critical Postmodern Organization Science, 2*(1), 47–62.

Nissley, N., Taylor, S. S., & Houden, L. (2004). The politics of performance in organizational theatre-based training and interventions. *Organization Studies, 25*(5), 817–839.

Nonaka, I., & Takeuchi, H. (1995). *The knowledge-creating company: How Japanese companies create the dynamics of innovation.* New York: Oxford University Press.

Oswick, C., & Grant, D. (1996). The organization of metaphors and the metaphors of organization: Where are we and where do we go from here? In D. Grant & C. Oswick (Eds.), *Metaphor and organizations* (pp. 201–213). London: Sage.

Pine, J. B., II, & Gilmore, J. H. (1999). *The experience economy: Work is theatre and every business a stage.* Boston: Harvard Business School Press.

Ramirez, R. (1996). Wrapping form and organizational beauty. *Organization, 3*(2), 233–242.

Reason, P. (Ed.). (1994). *Participation in human inquiry.* London: Sage.

Reason, P., & Bradbury, H. (Eds.). (2001). *Handbook of action research: Participative inquiry and practice.* London: Sage.

Richardson, L. (1997). *Fields of play: Constructing an academic life.* New Brunswick, NJ: Rutgers University Press.

Richardson, L. (2000). Writing a method of inquiry. In Y. Lincoln & N. Denzin (Eds.), *Handbook of qualitative research* (2nd ed.) (pp. 923–948). Thousand Oaks, CA: Sage.

Schein, E. (1987). The clinical perspective in fieldwork. *Qualitative Research Methods, Series 5.* Newbury Park, CA: Sage.

Schön, D. A. (1983). *The reflective practitioner: How professionals think in action.* New York: Basic Books.

Shakespeare, W. (1993). Hamlet, Act 1, Scene 3, L. 76. In A. Partington (Ed.), *The concise Oxford dictionary of quotations* (3rd ed., p. 274). Oxford, UK: Oxford University Press.

Shaw, P. (2002). *Changing conversations in organizations: A complexity approach to change.* London: Routledge.

Shotter, J. (1993). *Conversational realities: Constructing life through language.* Newbury Park, CA: Sage.

Stacey, R. (2001). *Complex responsive processes in organizations: Learning and knowledge creation.* London: Routledge.

Stacey, R., Griffin, D., & Shaw, P. (2000). *Complexity and management: Fad or radical challenge to systems thinking?* London: Routledge.

Strati, A. (2000a). The aesthetic approach to organization studies. In H. Hopfl (Ed.), *The aesthetics of organization* (pp. 13–34). London: Sage.

Strati, A. (2000b). Putting people in the picture: Art and aesthetics in photography and in understanding organizational life. *Organization Studies, 21*(0), 53–69.

Taylor, S. S. (2004). Presentational form in first person research: Off-line collaborative reflection using art. *Action Research, 2*(1), 71–88.

Taylor, S. S., & Hansen, H. (2005). Finding form: Looking at the field of organizational aesthetics. *Journal of Management Studies, 42*(6), 1211–1232.

Tierney, W., & Lincoln, T. (1997). *Representation and the text: Reframing the narrative Voice.* Albany: State University of New York Press.

Trott, P. (1998). *Innovation management and new product development.* London: Financial Times Pitman Publishing.

van Maanen, J. (1983). *Qualitative methodology.* Beverly Hills, CA: Sage.

van Manen, M. (1997). From meaning to method. *Qualitative Health Research, 7*(3), 345–369.

Weick, K. E. (1995). *Sensemaking in organizations: Foundations for organizational science.* Thousand Oaks, CA: Sage.

Wheatley, M. J. (1999). *Leadership and the new science. Discovering order in a chaotic world.* San Francisco: Berrett-Kohler Publishers.

Wheatley, M. J. (2002). *Turning to one another: Simple conversations to restore hope to the future.* San Francisco: Berrett-Kohler Publishers.

Wheatley, M. J., & Kellner-Rogers, M. (1996). *A simpler way.* San Francisco: Berrett-Kohler Publishers.

Winnicott, D. W. (1982). *Playing and reality.* London: Routledge.

Yalom, I. D. (1980). *Existential psychotherapy.* New York: Basic Books.

Yalom, I. D. (1991). *Love's executioner and other tales of psychotherapy.* London: Penguin.

Yin, R. K. (1994). Case study research: Design and methods. *Applied Social Research Methods Series, Vol. 5.* Thousand Oaks, CA: Sage.

54

SPORT AND PHYSICAL EDUCATION

Embracing New Forms of Representation

◆ Andrew C. Sparkes

The practices of sport and physical education (SPE) are informed by a knowledge base that draws on a range of disciplines and communities of interest. These include sport sociology, sport psychology, exercise psychology, sport pedagogy, physical education, exercise physiology, and biomechanics. Historically, SPE has drawn its inspiration from the successes of the natural biological sciences and quantitative social sciences. It remains strongly influenced by the philosophical assumptions of positivism and postpositivism, and adopts nomothetic methodologies that serve the technical interests of prediction and control. The dominant research tradition or paradigm remains "quantitative" in nature, and the findings are reported using the conventions of the standard "scientific tale" (Sparkes, 2002c). Here, it is assumed that the data "speak for themselves" and the researcher is an externally privileged reporter who simply *presents* rather than *(re)presents* "the findings." With regard to this kind of tale, the *Publication Manual of the American Psychological Association* (1994) states that scientific prose and creative writing serve different purposes:

Devices that are often found in creative writing—for example, setting up ambiguity, inserting the unexpected, omitting the expected, and suddenly shifting the topic, tense, or person—can confuse or disturb readers of scientific prose. Therefore, you should avoid these devices and aim for clear and logical communication. (p. 25)

In the early 1980s scholars began making the case for utilizing qualitative research in SPE, and toward the end of this decade a number of debates were conducted in leading journals regarding the merits of "qualitative versus quantitative" research. Since then, influenced by various strands of feminism, critical theory, postmodernism, and poststructuralism, qualitative research within SPE has developed along a number of different avenues to gain a level of acceptance within this domain. Qualitative researchers, however, remain in the minority. For example, in their review of a decade of research in sport psychology journals, Culver, Gilbert, and Trudel (2003) point out that over 80% of studies published between 1990 and 1999 are quantitative in nature. They also note that qualitative researchers generally limit themselves to the interview method of data collection. Culver and colleagues might have added that the findings of these qualitative studies have been represented using the conventions of the "realist" tale as described by van Maanen (1988). These are characterized by experiential authority, the participant's point of view, and interpretive omnipotence. Similarly, while the proportion of quantitative to qualitative publications in other SPE related journals might differ, the dominance of the realist tale does not.

In the early 1990s, influenced by the dual crises of representation and legitimation in the social sciences, questions were raised regarding the dominance of the realist and scientific tale within SPE and the limitations these impose on understanding and communication. For example, from a sociological perspective, Cole (1991) drew attention to the politics of cultural representation in sport. Likewise, Foley (1992) and Sparkes (1992) made early attempts to focus attention on writing practices and the textual construction of realities in SPE. Sparkes (1995) made a call to explore new writing practices as a different way of knowing about and expressing lived experience, and he outlined the possible uses of a range of tales. Bruce (1998), Duncan (1998), and Tomlinson (1999) also discussed the possibilities of generating new insights by writing differently and more creatively in sport sociology.

Against this backdrop, there has been a small but significant amount of work by qualitative researchers within SPE that openly acknowledges and celebrates the impressionistic, literary, and artistic aspects of their endeavors. Following Richardson (2000), they recognize that form matters, that form and content cannot be separated, that the form of representation one uses shapes the form of understanding one secures, and that writing is a form of analysis. These researchers in SPE work from an orientation that, according to Ellis (2004), blends the practices and emphases of social science with the aesthetic sensibility and expressive forms of art. For her, these researchers seek to tell stories and show bodily, cognitive, emotional, and spiritual experience: "The goal is to practice an artful, poetic, and empathetic social science in which readers can keep in their minds and feel in their bodies the complexities of concrete moments of lived experience" (p. 30). As part of this emerging venture within SPE, there are some significant markers that are worthy of attention.

◆ *Significant Markers*

In a special edition of the *International Review for the Sociology of Sport* in 1994, a group of Scandinavian scholars focused on "narrative sociology" and use "memory-work" to explore a range of sporting experiences. They explicitly make connections to artistic forms of expression and ways of knowing to explore their own subjectivities. Reflecting on the contributions to this special edition, the guest editor Eichberg (1994) comments, "Narrative discourses will be taxed for their literary value. They grow in quality by the development of their aesthetic expression. They are a form of poetry, forming a new world out of rhythmical and metaphorical language material" (p. 110).

An edited volume by Sparkes and Silvennoinen (1999) entitled *Talking Bodies: Men's Narratives of the Body and Sport* draws on "nothing but stories." Here, contributors use autoethnography, poetic representation, and ethnographic fiction in an evocative fashion to explore the intimate, subjective experiences of men, their multiple senses of self and shifting identities, and the relationships they form with their bodies and the bodies of others over time through their involvement in sporting practices. Shortly after this, a special issue of the *Sociology of Sport Journal* in 2000 focused on imagining sociological narratives in sport. In their introduction, the guest editors, Denison and Rinehart (2000), state that the motivations behind the project are to create a space for sport sociologists who have turned to more evocative ways of writing than standard practices, and to help legitimize the use of fiction and stories as nuanced ways to write experimental ethnography. This special volume provides examples of autoethnography, ethnographic fiction, and creative fiction in action and illustrates how in the hands of skilled authors, these genres can bring a critical yet creative sensibility to issues in SPE.

Further enticements for those wishing to explore new forms of representation are offered by Sparkes (2002c) in his book

Telling Tales in Sport and Physical Activity: A Qualitative Journey. He encourages researchers in SPE to think of themselves as storytellers, to acquire and nurture their own voices, and to view writing as a process of discovery, understanding, and analysis. Having explored the conventions and rhetorical features of the scientific and realist tales, Sparkes focuses on a range of alternative genres, such as confessional tales, autoethnography, poetic representations, ethnodrama, and fictional representations that draw on more artistic and literary ways of knowing. The potential and strengths of each genre to understand the world of SPE in different ways are highlighted, and scholars are asked to make reflexive, disciplined, principled, and strategic choices regarding their use of genre. A strong case is made for expanding the repertoire of representational possibilities in this domain as part of an emerging research community in SPE that is spoken, written, performed, and experienced from many sites.

The edited book by Denison and Markula (2003) titled *Moving Writing: Crafting Movement in Sport Research* calls for researchers in sport to move away from traditional practices of representation and experiment more freely with content, form, and style. The contributors provide examples of autoethnography and ethnographic fiction in sport research as evocative writing practices that can portray movement in a rounder, richer, more expressive way that both stirs the imagination and enlarges our appreciation of movement in our own and others' lives.

These publications are significant markers and provide a resource for others who wish to engage with experimental forms of writing and new modes of representation that embrace artistic ways of knowing. Within SPE various strands of experimentation have developed that cohere around the use of specific genres. Some examples within each genre will now be provided to give a flavor of how they have been used.

◆ *Autoethnography*

According to Richardson (2000) autoethnographies are "highly personalized, revealing texts in which authors tell stories about their own lived experiences, relating the personal to the cultural" (p. 931). In this form of evocative writing, Ellis (2004) suggests, multiple layers of consciousness are displayed as systematic sociological introspection and emotional recall are used to try and understand the experiences the author has lived through. Readers are invited into the intimate, embodied world of the other in a way that stimulates them to reflect on their own lives in relation to that of the author. Within sport sociology and physical education, in particular, a number of scholars have produced autoethnographies that explore issues relating to sporting body–self relationships over time with regard to identity construction, gender, sexuality, disability, race, and ethnicity (see Sparkes, 2002c). They have called upon a variety of forms, such as personal essays, short stories, photographic essays, poetry, fragmented and layered writing, and social science prose.

Over time, as confidence has grown, there has been a gradual shift in the balance from telling to showing experience or a mixing of both. *Telling* occurs when writers intervene in the narrative and suggest how they and we might feel about characters or interpret events. In contrast, *showing* involves the author's effacement, so that characters act out the story and reveal things about themselves without the author proposing interpretations.

Early examples that tell about experience include the work of Kosonen (1993) who focuses on memories of her own running body as a young woman growing up in Finland to explore issues of femininity, sexuality, the social norms of surveillance that constrain women's bodies, and

how they might be challenged. Likewise, Kaskisaari (1994) draws upon her personal experiences of growing up as an athletic girl, and her "rhythmbody," to focus on lesbianism as a female experience that allows some athletes to resolve the conflict between traditional female roles and their own sexual identity.

More recent autoethnographies that focus on the women's experience of SPE include the work of Tsang (2000), an elite international rower and an Olympian. Mixing telling and showing, Tsang combines experiential, inner, and academic voices to explore, via five short stories, the nuanced ways in which she comes to know her self and constructs different identities in and through sport as, for example, a woman, an academic, and a heterosexual Chinese-Anglo feminist. Duncan (2000) utilizes a series of nonfictional vignettes based on autobiographical recollections of her body for herself, and in relation to others, over time and in different physical activity contexts. The stories show rather than tell and take the reader first into the remembered world of Duncan as a 4-year-old girl learning to swim, before moving on to other epiphanic moments associated with physicality, such as acquiring muscles at 11 years of age, and later as an academic, feminist, mother, and wife becoming a martial artist and a member of an aerobics class. Finally, Parrott (2003) examines her own and her family's involvement in the joy, sadness, conflicts, and contradictions of the sport of polo via a story that shows her relationship with, and connection to, a horse, and the heartbreak she feels when it is eventually sold for commercial reasons.

With regard to the range of men's experiences of SPE, a number of autoethnographies have explored the construction of specific forms of masculinity. Again, over time there has been a shift from telling to showing or a mixing of both. For example, Tinning (1998) and Fernandez-Balboa (1998) tell stories that draw on their own experiences to illustrate how the social practices involved in SPE shaped their developing masculinities and understandings of their own embodiment. Silvennoinen (1993, 1994, 1999) undertakes a similar task by engaging in memory work of his childhood and adolescence to explore the dynamics of masculine identity construction within Finnish culture. Tiihonen (1994) develops this theme by drawing upon memories of his own sporting involvement and body experiences as a Finnish boy and how they were shaped in relation to his intensely colored experiences of asthma. In writing through these experiences, he produces a multilayered text that is able to draw the reader into his story world while simultaneously thematizing the body as anxious, instrumental, male, ambivalent, disciplined, and released via its inscription within hegemonic masculinity. Furthermore, as the emotional experiences that Tiihonen gained in sport unfold in the stories he tells, we begin to understand how sport has contributed to his own learning about social class, power, authority, social bonding, gender relations, and sexuality.

Autoethnographies have also been used by male scholars to explore the identity dilemmas associated with serious injury. For example, Pringle (2001) tells of the tensions and contradictions he lived with growing up as a "rugby boy" to both problematize the ways in which this sport encourages the giving and taking of pain, and to illustrate how the realization of this led him to reject hypermasculine values. In similar fashion, Gilbourne (2002) explores his past sporting experiences and a career-ending injury, to reflect upon his current life experiences. The story he tells captures the benefits and the "legacies" associated with his participation in sport and provides insights into how sport and sports injury influenced, and still influence to this day, Gilbourne's relationship with his family

and the connections he makes between his lived body and senses of self.

In contrast, Denison (1999) provides a story that draws on moments with his family and friends to show when he began to realize that his running career was over due to an injury. Sparkes (1996, 2003a, 2003b) mixes showing and telling to produce a multilayered text as he reflects on a "failed," problematic, middle-aged body following three surgical operations on his lumbar spine and his ongoing experience of chronic back pain. This is set against memories of a younger, elite, nonproblematic, sport-performing body in order to raise issues regarding the social construction of specific class-related masculine identities and the multiple meanings of impairment in this process.

◆ Poetic Representations

Poets have often focused their attention on sport and physical activity. For example, a special issue of the journal *Quest* in 1989 was dedicated to poetry and art in sport and movement. The contents of this special issue illustrate how poets and artists are able to synthesize, assemble, and compose images that make connections to the subjective world of feelings and emotions. Likewise, athletes and nonathletes have often used poetry to communicate the significance of sport in their lives. For example, poems and short stories are called on in Bandy and Darden's (1999) international anthology of women's experiences in sport called *Crossing Boundaries*. Other volumes of poems and short stories by women, such as those edited by Sandoz and Winans (1999) in *Whatever It Takes: Women on Women's Sport* and by Sandoz (1997) in *A Whole New Ball Game,* make further contributions to an understanding of women's unique experiences in sport and physical education.

In the examples above, the poems are intended and presented as poems per se, as poetry for its own sake. In contrast, some scholars in SPE have used poetry as a practical and powerful method for analyzing social worlds and as an evocative way of communicating their research findings. This allows both the researcher and the audience to see and feel the world in different ways, touching both where they live, in their bodies (Richardson, 2000). Here, poetry is used as a vehicle to represent the data to an audience.

Poems by Jackson (1999), which explore how his masculine senses of self were constructed via school sport and physical activity, appear in an edited volume on men's narratives of the body and sport (Sparkes & Silvennoinen, 1999). In the same volume, Swan (1999) includes a poetic representation within a multilayered text that explores his experiences of coming to understand the complexities, oppression, and ironies of masculinity, via reflections on his own body and the bodies of other Australian men/boys in the spaces provided by change rooms in sport centers. The poetic representation he produces, called *Changing (for) Bryan,* draws upon a study in an Australian Catholic secondary school and focuses on the abuse and harassment experienced by one boy in the change room after physical education classes. Talking of his use of this kind of representation, Swan notes how he uses forms of verse to allow the reader to feel the emotional contexts of the data and to produce a story that ruptures the tranquility of assumed relationships.

More recently, Sparkes, Nilges, Swan, and Dowling (2003) provide insider views on, and rationales for, the production of poetic representations in SPE before presenting examples that explore the student teaching experience in physical education, surviving oppression in PE, and the circularity of a career in this subject area. Sparkes

(2003b) also uses a poetic representation within a multilayered autoethnographic text to explore the connectedness of masculinities and memories of the flesh through three generations (grandfather, father, and son) via the sporting body in action.

◆ *Ethnodrama*

The process of ethnodrama involves transforming data into theatrical scripts and performance pieces. When done well, ethnodrama has the ability to give voice to what may be unspoken, and to more accurately give voice to those who consider themselves without power. It is also better able to represent lived experience, from multiple and contested perspectives, to a much wider audience than normal. Furthermore, ethnodrama can often do this in ways that are more authentic, evocative, and engaging than other forms of representation. This being the case, it is surprising to note that scholars in SPE have made little use of this genre.

Rare examples include the work of Brown (1998), who looks at the world of physical education teacher education (PETE) students. For Brown, the purpose of her play, called *Boys' Training,* is to provide a "creative but empirically grounded" (p. 84) insight into the negotiation, social positioning, and identity construction process that occurs for many young males entering into PETE. It attempts to highlight issues relating to hegemonic masculinity within PETE and, in particular, to illuminate the processes by which certain values and characteristics are celebrated and how becoming an "in" male physical educator is legitimized and reproduced.

More recently, in 2000, based on her life history research with "queer," "lesbian," "bisexual," and "gay male" physical education teachers, and in collaboration with two actors/drama educators, Sykes produced an ethnodrama in the form of a 25-minute play called *Wearing the Secret Out*. This play, which can be performed live by actors or screened as a video, has been presented to a wide range of audiences and at a variety of academic conferences specializing in physical education (e.g., American Alliance for Health, Physical Education, Recreation, and Dance conferences in 2001 and 2002), education (e.g., American Educational Research Association conferences in 2001 and 2002), and sport sociology (e.g., North American Society for the Sociology of Sport conferences in 2001 and 2002). The performance raises a number of issues about homophobia (and homoeroticism) that teachers face when teaching physical education. It is a creative way of assisting teacher education students to understand how homophobia operates in schools and assists them to engage with the issues in a complex yet thoughtful way (Chapman, Swedberg, & Sykes, 2003; 2005; Sykes & Goldstein, 2004).

Robinson performed (read) a two-act play called *FrontRunners* at the North American Society for the Sociology of Sport conference in 2003 that explores the experiences of 10 indigenous runners in Canada. These men had been good runners and students in 1967 when Winnipeg hosted the Pan-Am Games and had been selected to run 800 kilometers with the torch from St. Paul, Minnesota, to Winnipeg. However, just before entering the stadium, the torch was taken from them and given to a non-Aboriginal runner. Against this backdrop, the play examines the systemic racism perpetrated against Aboriginal people in Canada.

In 2004, Gilbourne, Richardson, Littlewood (all sport psychologists), and Merkin (a drama specialist) considered the use of ethnodrama to applied practice in sport psychology. In collaboration with student actors they wrote, produced, and performed a play called *Get Out the Car Park!* This explores the experiences of a young, anxious, naïve, and idealistic sport psychologist who shadows a more seasoned sport psychologist who has been working full-time with a professional football team for several years. The play locates these experiences provocatively, humorously, and evocatively within the dynamic relationships of the players, the coach, and the manager in the build-up to a crucial game. It reveals the multilayered complexities of this culture and the dilemmas facing those who try to enter into it.

◆ Fictional Representations

With regard to rendering lived experience, a small number of scholars in SPE have utilized what can loosely be described as *ethnographic fiction* and *creative fiction* as described by Sparkes (2002a, 2002b) to represent their research findings in the form of short stories. For him, calling on a variety of fictional techniques, the authors of these stories seek to evoke the emotions, enabling a wide range of audiences to viscerally inhabit and understand different worlds in ways that convey complexity and ambiguity without producing closure.

According to Denison and Rinehart (2000) ethnographic fictions are works "grounded in everyday, concrete, and specific events and research protocols, utilizing fictional strategies to make their conclusions more explicit" (p. 3). In this genre, acts of imagination are brought to bear via various realms or settings that have been studied ethnographically, and the purpose of the fiction is to express the writer's visions of social-scientific truths within sports. Sparkes (2002c) suggests that in making it clear that their stories are based on real events and people along with the collection of data from the field via, for example, participant observation or interviews, authors signal that their work is grounded in the tradition of literary nonfiction or creative nonfiction.

An early example of an ethnographic fiction in SPE is provided by Lyons (1992) who draws on data generated by a 3-year study to develop two short stories that explore the teaching of Physical Education (PE). In a similar fashion, Rinehart (1995) generates three short stories that focus on the issue of ethics in youth sports and, in particular, the ethics between adult sport-providers and child consumers of sport. Rinehart (1998a, 1998b) produces two short stories to explore the ethical place of the researcher in personal stories about sport, and he also uses short stories in a number of chapters in his book *Players All: Performances in Contemporary Sport*. Another early example is provided by Denison (1996) who, having collected interview data on the retirement experiences of elite athletes, presents his findings in the form of three short stories. These stories illuminate the problems athletes face in finding another way to feel good about themselves when their career is over and the fans stop cheering.

In the domain of PE, Nilges (2001) presents her findings from 14 weeks of fieldwork by condensing them into a story contained within the fictive time span of one school day. This story explores the physical and social alienation experienced by one girl in the context of her gender-integrated PE class. The work of Halas (2001) also focuses on the value of PE and physical activity for troubled youth. Here, 24 vignettes are used to create a running narrative of the experiences of young people attending an active living program at an adolescent treatment center/school.

More recently, ethnographic fictions have been produced by Rowe (2003), who offers a highly charged stylization of football fanaticism that of necessity locates women on the fringes. Bruce (2003) explores sexual identity in sport via a story about women's basketball that draws attention to the struggles female athletes encounter on and off the court as they try to come to terms with various relations and expectations that encompass gender, sexuality, and identity. Likewise, an ethnographic fiction is used by Rinehart (2003) to take us into the world of displaced youngsters on the fringes of "real" sport who are engaged in skateboarding. In contrast, Silvennoinen (2003) connects movement to nature and culture via stories of snow and ski jumping to provide a fascinating vision of a "nationalized" body in the making.

With regard to scholars in SPE experimenting with creative fiction, there appear to be two strands of development. The first is where a creative fiction is presented with a commentary by the author that signals the nature and purpose of the work. Examples include the work of Duncan (1998), who explores how stigmatized bodies are constructed and the feeling worlds embedded in this process, and Sparkes (1997), who generates insights into the experiences of a young, male, gay PE teacher and sportsman in a homophobic and heterosexist culture and school environment. These are not based on the systematic collection of data, but they do include some events that happened, or that the authors think happened, in their pasts. These remembered events form the basis of the stories that weave in events that did not happen or might happen.

In contrast, other scholars in SPE have chosen to present a creative fiction in the form of a story that does not include any commentary or "academic" interpretation and no references to other literature. Indeed, no claim is made to the author having "been there" or that the events on which the story is based actually happened at all. Examples of this narrative imagination at work include the following: the story by Bethanis (2000) that describes an adolescent boy learning what it is to become a man and discovering his place in his father's world, Christensen's (2000) poignant and desperate story of corruption and exploitation in collegiate sport, Denison's (2000) tale that casts doubt on just how wonderful it really is for a young person to have the "gift" of sport, and the finely layered story of Wood (2000) who evokes the hopelessness of subjugation before using this as a springboard to explore eating- and exercise-disordered behaviors and ways that empowerment might be achieved.

◆ Comment

The use of new forms of representation by a small group of qualitative researchers in SPE, with those of a sociological orientation leading the way, suggests an emerging connection to artistic ways of knowing within this domain. Experimentation with new writing practices, however, is not a commonplace activity in SPE. The sixth (postexperimental) and seventh (the future) moments described by Denzin and Lincoln (2000), in which fictional ethnographies, ethnographic poetry, and multimedia texts are taken for granted, have yet to arrive.

Despite the many potential benefits for researchers in SPE using new forms of representation, particularly in terms of communicating their findings to a diverse range of audiences (e.g., members of the general public, students, academic colleagues, athletes, teachers, coaches, policy makers, and health professionals), those who attempt to do so often feel like artistic intruders. Their work tends to be greeted with suspicion, even hostility, and questions are raised as to whether it constitutes legitimate or "proper" research (see Sparkes, 2002a). Publication outlets and opportunities are harder to find when compared to those available to tellers

of scientific or realist tales. In part, as Sparkes (1998, 2000) points out, this is because many in SPE hold a prejudiced and narrow view of what constitutes research, making them prone to apply inappropriate foundational, epistemic criteria when judging new writing practices and novel forms of inquiry. When this happens, the danger is that such work is by definition dismissed, trivialized, and deemed unworthy of attention. Given these circumstances, engaging with experimental forms of representation in SPE carries both personal and professional risks that may be off-putting to both novitiates and experienced researchers alike.

For artistic ways of knowing to be given a fair chance and a just hearing in SPE, according to Sparkes (2002c), there needs to be a shift toward incorporating literary and artistic forms of judgment that are nonfoundational in nature. Here, the more traditional concerns regarding validity and reliability are replaced by concerns with, for example, verisimilitude, coherence, evocation, empathy, fidelity, believability, plausibility, expansiveness, interpretive insight, relevance, rhetorical force, beauty, and texture of argument. Such criteria, when operating as characterizing traits rather than universal standards against which to make judgment, can act as starting points and guiding ideals for considering different forms of representation.

Various criteria in list form, therefore, can be used to judge a certain kind of tale. However, these need not all be applied on all occasions. That is, other criteria can be added to or subtracted from any given list depending on intentions, purposes, circumstances, and context. These lists are challenged, changed, and modified in their application to actual inquiries and actual writing practices. As such, the limits of modification are a *practical* matter that allows not only old criteria to be combined in novel ways, but allows different criteria to emerge.

It also encourages the creation of new criteria for choosing criteria in SPE and the social sciences in general.

In the coming years it is likely that scientific tales will remain the chosen genre for quantitative researchers and realist tales will continue to dominate for qualitative researchers. These tales will not be replaced and nor should they be, as each makes its own contribution to our understanding of SPE. However, perhaps they might be displaced and relocated as a greater range of representational forms become available and gradually prove their worth. That there *are* scholars who engage with experimental writing within SPE and that their work *does* get published and performed is a cause for celebration. The debate regarding the contribution of artistic ways of knowing in SPE will certainly continue to play a part in expanding the horizons of this domain in the future.

◆ References

American Psychological Association. (1994). *Publication manual of the American Psychological Association* (4th ed.). Washington, DC: Author.

Bandy, S., & Darden, A. (Eds.). (1999). *Crossing boundaries.* Champaign, IL: Human Kinetics.

Bethanis, P. (2000). The shadowboxer. *Sociology of Sport Journal, 17*(1), 81–82.

Brown, L. (1998). "Boys' training": The inner sanctum. In C. Hickey, L. Fitzclarence, & R. Matthews (Eds.), *Where the boys are: Masculinity sport and education* (pp. 83–96). Geelong, Australia: Deakin University Press.

Bruce, T. (1998). Postmodernism and the possibilities for writing "vital" sports texts. In G. Rail (Ed.), *Sport and postmodern times* (pp. 3–19). New York: State University of New York Press.

Bruce, T. (2003). Pass. In J. Denison & P. Markula (Eds.), *Moving writing: Crafting movement in sport research* (pp. 133–150). New York: Peter Lang.

Chapman, J., Swedberg, A., & Sykes, H. (2003). Wearing the secret out: Performing stories of sexual identities. *Youth Theatre Journal, 17*, 27–37.

Chapman, J., Swedberg, A., & Sykes, H. (2005). Wearing the secret out. In J. Saldaña (Ed.), *Ethnodrama: An anthology of reality theatre* (pp. 106–120). Walnut Creek, CA: AltaMira Press.

Christensen, P. (2000). Believing. *Sociology of Sport Journal, 17*(1), 83–94.

Cole, C. (1991). The politics of cultural representation: Visions of fields/fields of visions. *International Review for the Sociology of Sport, 26*(1), 36–49.

Culver, D., Gilbert, W., & Trudel, P. (2003). A decade of qualitative research in sport psychology journals: 1990–1999. *The Sport Psychologist, 17*(1), 1–15.

Denison, J. (1996). Sport narratives. *Qualitative Inquiry, 2*(3), 351–362.

Denison, J. (1999). Boxed in. In A. Sparkes & M. Silvennoinen (Eds.), *Talking bodies: Men's narratives of the body and sport* (pp. 29–36). Jyvaskyla, Finland: SoPhi.

Denison, J. (2000). Gift. *Sociology of Sport Journal, 17*(1), 98–99.

Denison, J., & Markula, P. (Eds.). (2003). *Moving writing: Crafting movement in sport research.* New York: Peter Lang.

Denison, J., & Rinehart, R. (2000). Introduction: Imagining sociological narratives. *Sociology of Sport Journal, 17*(1), 1–4.

Denzin, N. K., & Lincoln, Y. S. (2000). Introduction: The discipline and practice of qualitative inquiry. In N. K. Denzin & Y. S. Lincoln (Eds.), *Handbook of qualitative research* (2nd ed., pp. 1–29). London: Sage.

Duncan, M. (1998). Stories we tell ourselves about ourselves. *Sociology of Sport Journal, 15*, 95–108.

Duncan, M. (2000). Reflex: Body as memory. *Sociology of Sport Journal, 17*(10), 60–68.

Eichberg, H. (1994). The narrative, the situational, the biographical: Scandinavian sociology of the body culture trying a third way. *International Review for the Sociology of Sport, 29*(1), 99–115.

Ellis, C. (2004). *The ethnographic I*. Walnut Creek, CA: AltaMira Press.

Fernandez-Balboa, J. (1998). Transcending masculinities: Linking personhood and pedagogy. In C. Hickey, L. Fitzclarence, & R. Matthews (Eds.), *Where the boys are: Masculinity, sport, and education* (pp. 121–139). Deakin, Australia: Deakin University Press.

Foley, D. (1992). Making the familiar strange: Writing critical sports narratives. *Sociology of Sport Journal, 9*(1), 36–47.

Gilbourne, D. (2002). Sports participation, sports injury, and altered images of self: An autobiographical narrative of a lifelong legacy. *Reflective Practice, 3*(1), 71–88.

Gilbourne, D., Richardson, D., Littlewood, M., & Merkin, R. (2004). *Dramatic representations of applied practice in sport psychology*. The First International Conference for Qualitative Research in Sport and Exercise, Liverpool John Moores University, Liverpool, England.

Halas, J. (2001). Shooting hoops at the treatment center: Sport stories. *Quest, 53*, 77–96.

Jackson, D. (1999). Boxing glove. In A. Sparkes & M. Silvennoinen (Eds.), *Talking bodies: Men's narratives of the body and sport* (p. 48). Jyvaskyla, Finland: SoPhi.

Kaskisaari, M. (1994). The rhythmbody. *International Review for the Sociology of Sport, 29*(1), 15–23.

Kosonen, U. (1993). A running girl: Fragments of my body history. In L. Laine (Ed.), *On the fringes of sport* (pp. 16–25). St. Augustin, Germany: Akademia Verlag.

Lyons, K. (1992). Telling stories from the field? A discussion of an ethnographic approach to researching the teaching of physical education. In A. Sparkes (Ed.), *Research in physical education and sport: Exploring alternative visions* (pp. 248–270). London: Falmer Press.

Nilges, L. (2001). The twice told tale of Alice's physical life in Wonderland: Writing qualitative research in the 21st century. *Quest, 53*, 231–259.

Parrott, K. (2003). Initiation. In J. Denison & P. Markula (Eds.), *Moving writing: Crafting movement and sport research* (pp. 87–112). New York: Peter Lang.

Pringle, R. (2001). Competing discourses: Narratives of a fragmented self, manliness, and rugby union. *International Review for the Sociology of Sport, 36*(4), 425–439.

Richardson, L. (2000). Writing: A method of inquiry. In N. K. Denzin & Y. S. Lincoln (Eds.), *Handbook of qualitative research* (2nd ed., pp. 923–948). London: Sage.

Rinehart, R. (1995). Pentecostal aquatics: Sacrifice, redemption, and secrecy at camp. *Studies in Symbolic Interaction, 19*, 109–121.

Rinehart, R. (1998a). Born-again sport: Ethics in biographical research. In G. Rail (Ed.), *Sport and postmodern times* (pp. 33–46). New York: State University of New York Press.

Rinehart, R. (1998b). *Players all: Performances in contemporary sport*. Bloomington: Indiana University Press.

Rinehart, R. (2003). On 'Sk8ing': Reflections on method. In J. Denison & P. Markula (Eds.), *Moving writing: Crafting movement in sport research* (pp. 151–166). New York: Peter Lang.

Robinson, L. (2003, November). *FrontRunners*. Performance presented at the annual conference of the North American Society for the Sociology of Sport, Montreal, Canada.

Rowe, D. (2003). A fan's life: Lost and found. In J. Denison & P. Markula (Eds.), *Moving writing: Crafting movement in sport research* (pp. 115–131). New York: Peter Lang.

Sandoz, J. (Ed.). (1997). *A whole new ball game: Women's literature on women's sport*. New York: The Noonday Press.

Sandoz, J., & Winans, J. (Eds.). (1999). *Whatever it takes: Women on women's sport*. New York: Farrar, Straus and Giroux.

Silvennoinen, M. (1993). A model for a man: Tracing a personal history of body awareness. In L. Laine (Ed.), *On the fringes of sport* (pp. 26–31). St. Augustin, Germany: Akademia Verlag.

Silvennoinen, M. (1994). To childhood heroes. *International Review for the Sociology of Sport, 29*(1), 25–30.

Silvennoinen, M. (1999). My body as metaphor. In A. Sparkes & M. Silvennoinen (Eds.), *Talking bodies: Men's narratives of the body and sport* (pp. 163–175). Jyvaskyla, Finland: SoPhi.

Silvennoinen, M. (2003). Ecstasy on skis. In J. Denison & P. Markula (Eds.), *Moving writing: Crafting movement in sport research* (pp. 167–179). New York: Peter Lang.

Sparkes, A. (1992). Writing and the textual constructions of reality: Some challenges for alternative paradigms research in physical education. In A. Sparkes (Ed.), *Research in physical education and sport: Exploring alternative visions* (pp. 271–297). London: Falmer Press.

Sparkes, A. (1995). Writing people: Reflections on the dual crises of representation and legitimation in qualitative inquiry. *Quest, 47,* 158–195.

Sparkes, A. (1996). The fatal flaw: A narrative of the fragile body-self. *Qualitative Inquiry, 2*(4), 463–494.

Sparkes, A. (1997). Ethnographic fiction and representing the absent Other. *Sport, Education, and Society, 2*(1), 25–40.

Sparkes, A. (1998). Validity in qualitative inquiry and the problem of criteria: Implications for sport psychology. *The Sport Psychologist, 12*(4), 363–386.

Sparkes, A. (2000). Autoethnographies and narratives of self: Reflections on criteria in action. *Sociology of Sport Journal, 17*(1), 21–43.

Sparkes, A. (2002a). Autoethnography: Self-indulgence or something more? In A. Bochner & C. Ellis (Eds.), *Ethnographically speaking: Autoethnography, literature, and aesthetics* (pp. 209–232). Walnut Creek, CA: AltaMira Press.

Sparkes, A. (2002b). Fictional representations: On difference, choice, and risk. *Sociology of Sport Journal, 19*(1), 1–24.

Sparkes, A. (2002c). *Telling tales in sport and physical Activity: A qualitative journey.* Champaign, IL: Human Kinetics.

Sparkes, A. (2003a). Bodies, identities, selves: Autoethnographic fragments and reflections. In J. Denison & P. Markula (Eds.), *Moving writing: Crafting movement in sport research* (pp. 51–76). New York: Peter Lang.

Sparkes, A. (2003b). From performance to impairment: A patchwork of embodied memories. In J. Evans, B. Davies, & J. Wright (Eds.), *Body knowledge and control* (pp. 157–172). London: Routledge.

Sparkes, A., & Silvennoinen, M. (Eds.). (1999). *Talking bodies: Men's narratives of the body and sport.* Jyvaskyla, Finland: SoPhi.

Sparkes, A., Nilges, L., Swan, P., & Dowling, F. (2003). Poetic representations in sport and physical education: Insider perspectives. *Sport, Education, and Society, 8*(2), 153–177.

Swan, P. (1999). Three ages of changing. In A. Sparkes & M. Silvennoinen (Eds.), *Talking bodies: Men's narratives of the body and sport* (pp. 37–47). Jyvaskyla, Finland: SoPhi.

Sykes, H., & Goldstein, T. (2004). From performing to performed ethnography: Translating life history research into anti-homophobia curriculum for a teacher education program. *Teaching Education, 15*(1), 41–61.

Tiihonen, A. (1994). Asthma: The construction of the masculine body. *International Review for the Sociology of Sport, 29*(1), 51–62.

Tinning, R. (1998). "What position do you play?" A narrative about sport, physical education, and masculinities. In C. Hickey, L. Fitzclarence, & R. Matthews (Eds.), *Where the boys are: Masculinity, sport, and education* (pp. 109–120). Geelong, Victoria, Australia: Deakin University Press.

Tomlinson, A. (1999). *The game's up: Essays in the cultural analysis of leisure and popular culture.* Aldershot, England: Ashgate.

Tsang, T. (2000). Let me tell you a story: A narrative exploration of identity in high-performance sport. *Sociology of Sport Journal, 17*(10), 44–59.

van Maanen, J. (1988). *Tales of the field: On writing ethnography.* Chicago: University of Chicago Press.

Wood, M. (2000). Disappearing. *Sociology of Sport Journal, 17*(1), 100–102.

ABOUT THE EDITORS

J. Gary Knowles and **Ardra L. Cole** are both professors of creative inquiry and adult learning within the Program of Adult Education and Community Development at the Ontario Institute for Studies in Education of the University of Toronto. They also are codirectors of the Centre for Arts-Informed Research (CAIR) in the Department of Adult Education and Counselling Psychology.

Gary and Ardra have published extensively on life history, reflexive, and arts-informed research, as well as in the area of teacher education and development. Their coauthored books include: *Through Preservice Teachers' Eyes: Exploring Field Experiences Through Narrative and Inquiry*, *Researching Teaching: Exploring Teacher Development Through Reflexive Inquiry*, *The Heart of the Matter: Teacher Educators and Teacher Education Reform*, and *Lives in Context: The Art of Life History Research*. They are coeditors of *The Arts-Informed Inquiry Series* (Series Editor, J. Gary Knowles), which includes *The Art of Writing Inquiry* (2001), *Provoked by Art* (2004), *The Art of Visual Inquiry* (2007), and *Creating Scholartistry* (2007).

Gary and Ardra have each helped many graduate students complete arts-informed doctoral and master's degree theses. Graduates furnished work embodying poetic, fictional, performative, and visual arts inquiry processes and forms in addressing educational and social issues. Some of Gary's other coauthored books include *Emerging as a Teacher* and *Home Schooling: Parents as Educators*. More recent inquiry work involves high school students from Ontario and Newfoundland, Canada, portraying experiences of school and community through photography and narrative.

Gary is a water media visual artist drawn to subject matter that enables him to explore experiences and notions of self-in-context. Recent work is large scale and mural-like, focusing on the plight of the Atlantic fishery, for instance. He has exhibited in several South Pacific countries, as well as in the United States and Canada. In the 1990s Gary codirected a contemporary art gallery in Toronto that exhibited "autobiographical work situated in place." In an earlier life in Australasia (Aotearoa New Zealand, Australia, and Papua New Guinea) and the South Pacific, he worked first in architecture and later in outdoor education. He continues to enjoy and explore the out-of-doors and is passionate about modern architecture.

Ardra has published extensively in conventional and nonconventional academic prose and in alternative, scholarly, nonprint media throughout her career as a teacher educator and qualitative research methodologist. Ardra's ongoing research (with Maura McIntyre) on care and caregiving and Alzheimer's disease involves multimedia installation—*Living and Dying With Dignity: The Alzheimer's Project;* performance—*Love Stories About Caregiving and Alzheimer's Disease;* and the World Wide Web—*Putting Care on the Map* (www.oise.utoronto.ca/research/mappingcare). Her current writing projects include a series of research-based novellas about the teacher education professoriate, *But I Want to Make a Difference* and *Of Dogs and Dissertations: Notes on Writing and Life.* As she moves through life in the company of dogs, Ardra continues to learn about the meaning of love, loyalty, and living in the moment.

ABOUT THE CONTRIBUTORS

Susann Allnutt is a doctoral candidate in the Department of Integrated Studies in Education in the Faculty of Education at McGill University, with an educational background in communications and women's studies. Her research interests center around visual studies, linking photography, remembered and current spaces, and the curriculum of public space.

Jo-ann Archibald, Q'um Q'um Xiiem, from the Sto:lo Nation in southwestern British Columbia, is the associate dean for indigenous education, acting director of the Native Indian Teacher Education Program (NITEP), and associate professor in the University of British Columbia Faculty of Education. Jo-ann received a Bachelor of Education (BEd) degree from the University of British Columbia, and a Master's of Education (MEd) degree and Doctor of Philosophy (PhD) degree from Simon Fraser University. She is an editor of the *Canadian Journal of Native Education*. Formerly director of the First Nations House of Learning at UBC, she has also worked as a public school teacher and school district Aboriginal education coordinator. Her research interests relate to Indigenous knowledge systems, oral tradition, transformative education, teacher education, working with Indigenous Elders, and Indigenous methodologies. In 2000, she received a Canadian national award for her work in education from the National Aboriginal Achievement Foundation.

Helen K. Ball, PhD, is assistant professor in the School of Social Work, Memorial University of Newfoundland, St. John's, Newfoundland and Labrador. Her research interests include feminist methodologies, language and power in clinical practice, and social constructionist family therapy. Feminist methodologies define her scholarly work and clinical practice. All of her free time is spent watching whales in the North Atlantic.

Stephen Banks is professor at the University of Idaho, where he directs the Communication Studies Program. His research on communication and the construction of identity has appeared in many academic journals, and he has published short stories and poems in regional literary magazines. He is author or editor of three books, including *Fiction and Social Research: By Ice or Fire* (with Anna Banks, 1998). His current research focuses on the narrative construction of identities among expatriate U.S. and Canadian retirees who live in Mexico. He also is at work on a biography of the American adventurer–travel writer Neill James. Banks earned his PhD at the University of Southern California.

Deborah Barndt has engaged in participatory research, popular education, and community arts with social movements in the United States, Canada, and Latin America over the past 40 years. She has published and exhibited widely, around issues ranging from women, food, and globalization to popular education and arts as cultural resistance. She currently teaches in the Faculty of Environmental Studies at York University. Her most recent edited volume, *Wild Fire: Art as Activism,* is a collection of essays by former students, linking art, activism, and academics.

Tom Barone is professor of education at Arizona State University. Over 25 years ago, Barone's dissertation at Stanford University explored the possibilities of literary nonfiction within educational inquiry. Since then he has explored, conceptually and through examples, a variety of narrative and arts-based approaches to contextualizing and theorizing about significant educational issues. Barone is the author of *Aesthetics, Politics, and Educational Inquiry: Essays and Examples* (2000) and *Touching Eternity: The Enduring Outcomes of Teaching* (2001). He is also coeditor (with Liora Bresler) of the online *International Journal of Education and the Arts.* Barone currently teaches courses in curriculum studies and qualitative research methods in the ASU College of Education.

Ruth Behar is the recipient of a MacArthur "genius" Award, a John Simon Guggenheim Fellowship, and a Distinguished Alumna Award from Wesleyan University. Her books include *The Presence of the Past in a Spanish Village, Translated Woman: Crossing the Border With Esperanza's Story,* and *The Vulnerable Observer: Anthropology That Breaks Your Heart.* Behar is coeditor of *Women Writing Culture* and editor of *Bridges to Cuba.* Her essay "Juban América" appeared in *King David's Harp: Autobiographical Essays by Jewish Latin American Writers,* and her short story "La Cortada" was selected by Joyce Carol Oates for inclusion in *Telling Stories: An Anthology for Writers.* Behar's poems have been published in *Burnt Sugar [Caña Quemada]: Contemporary Cuban Poetry in English and Spanish, Sephardic American Voices: Two Hundred Years of a Literary Legacy,* and *Little Havana Blues: A Cuban-American Literature Anthology.* Behar wrote, directed, and produced a feature-length documentary, *Adio Kerida [Goodbye Dear Love]: A Cuban Sephardic Journey.* Her forthcoming book, *An Island Called Home: A Return to Jewish Cuba,* is a blend of creative nonfiction and photography. She is professor of anthropology at the University of Michigan. www.ruthbehar.com.

Vangie Bergum is professor emeritus at the University of Alberta. From a background in childbirth education and public health nursing, Vangie came to the field of healthcare ethics, where she worked for almost 20 years. She has published four books, numerous papers, and book chapters in areas of ethics and mothering from her research approach of hermeneutic phenomenology. Vangie completed her 5-year term as director of the Dossetor Health Ethics Centre, University of Alberta, in 2002. Her latest book, *Motherlife: Studies of Mothering Experience* (with Jeanne Van Zalm, 2007), includes both research studies and artistic presentations. In her retirement she continues to write, taking inspiration from the mountains and river and sustenance in living close to grandchildren.

Donald Blumenfeld-Jones is the Lincoln Associate Professor for Ethics and Education at Arizona State University. Prior to teaching curriculum studies, he spent 20 years as a professional modern dancer, studying and dancing with the Phyllis Lamhut Dance company for 7 years, and with Alwin Nikolais, Murray Louis, and Hanya Holm, and teaching dance at Duke University, Columbia College, and University of North Carolina–Greensboro, where he earned his MFA in dance and EdD in curriculum studies. He specializes in arts-based education research, ethics, hermeneutics, and critical social theory, and has published articles and book chapters in many journals and in such books as *Daredevil Research* (1997) and *Dancing the Data* (2002). He has recently published two handbook chapters on dance: "Aesthetics Consciousness and Dance Curriculum: Liberation Possibilities for Inner-City Schools" in *Encyclopedia of Urban Education* (2006) and "Dance Curriculum Research" (with Sheaun-Yann Liang) in *International Handbook of Research in Arts Education* (2007).

Laura Brearley is senior lecturer in the School of Education at RMIT University, Victoria, Australia, and is also a singer and songwriter. She specializes in creative approaches to research and incorporates multimedia, poetry, art, and music into her own research and into her presentations and performances. Laura coordinates the Koori Cohort of Researchers at RMIT in which a large group of Indigenous students are undertaking degrees at the master's and doctoral levels. Laura also coordinates the Creative Research Methods course at RMIT, which brings together postgraduate research students from the Schools of Education, Art, Creative Media, and Architecture and Design. Laura is the managing editor of the *Creative Approaches to Research Journal,* which incorporates multiple forms of text. She is currently coediting a book entitled *Creative Arts Research: Narratives of Methodologies and Practice.*

Liora Bresler is professor at the College of Education at the University of Illinois at Champaign and affiliate professor in the School of Music. Most recently, she has edited the *International Handbook of Research in Arts Education* (2007), received the Ziegfeld USSEA Award (2006/7), and received the University of Illinois Award for Excellence in Graduate teaching at the University of Illinois. Bresler serves as an editor for the book series *Landscapes: Aesthetics, Arts, and Education.* She is the cofounder and coeditor of the *International Journal for Arts and Education* (with Tom Barone, 1999–). Bresler has written about 100 papers and chapters in leading journals of arts and education, including the *Educational Researcher, Studies in Art Education,* and *Music Education Research.* She has been invited to give keynote speeches on six continents, and has given invited talks, seminars, and short courses in thirty-some universities in Europe, Asia, North and South America, and Australia.

Catherine Burke is senior lecturer in education at the School of Education, University of Leeds, UK. She has taught, researched, and published in the area of children's perspectives on education and is especially interested in the material culture of childhood in educational contexts. Her publications include *The School I'd Like: Children and Young People's Reflections on an Education for the 21st Century,* coauthored with Ian Grosvenor. She was coinvestigator alongside Jon Prosser and Judy Torrington (Sheffield University, UK) of the "View of the Child" Design 21 Research Cluster, funded by the AHRC/EPSRC in 2005.

Lynn Butler-Kisber, BEd and MEd (McGill), EdD (Harvard), is associate professor in the Department of Integrated Studies in Education at McGill University in Montreal. She is currently the director of the Centre for Educational Leadership and of the Graduate Certificate Programs in Educational Leadership. She teaches courses on language arts, qualitative research, and teacher education. Her research and development activities focus on literacy, student engagement, leadership, professional development, and qualitative methodologies. She is particularly interested in feminist/equity issues and the role of arts-informed analysis and representation in qualitative research.

Mary Beth Cancienne is assistant professor at James Madison University in the Department of Middle, Secondary, and Mathematics Education. She earned a PhD in curriculum and instruction from the University of Virginia. She prepares pre-service teachers by teaching courses in English methods, action research, and diversity. Her research interests and publications are in the fields of teacher education and arts-based research. She recently coedited a book and CD-ROM titled *Dancing the Data and Dancing the Data Too* (2002). Her other publications are located in journals such as *Qualitative Inquiry, The Journal of Curriculum Theorizing,* and *Sex Education.*

Cynthia Chambers is professor of education at the University of Lethbridge where she teaches curriculum studies with specializations in Indigenous education and literacy. Her research focuses on Canadian curriculum studies and what has been absent in those discourses, particularly Indigenous perspectives and relationship to place, and at what cost. Her essays and stories perform a praxis of métissage, (re)tracing the biography of ideas through personal memoir/story/events as well as collective memory/history at particular places or sites of Canadian topography. Her work appears online in *Educational Insights* and *Journal of American Association for Curriculum Studies,* as well as in print in *JCT: An Interdisciplinary Journal of Curriculum Studies* and *Canadian Journal of Education.* She contributed an essay on curriculum research in Canada to W. Pinar's *International Handbook on Curriculum Research* (2003).

Adrienne Chambon is professor at the University of Toronto's Faculty of Social Work. She teaches courses on intersecting narratives and on social exclusion. She has written on critical theory. She coedited *Essays on Postmodernism and Social Work* with Allan Irving and *Reading Foucault for Social Work* with Allan Irving and Laura Epstein. Her research has focused on the transformation of narrative in the therapeutic dialogue and discursive strategies in policy texts. In her current research project, "The Heuristics of Art Practices for Social Work," she explores ways in which premodern and contemporary art practices can be articulated with social work, how art forms can expand social sciences' understanding of public space and the space of relations, the movement between documentary and fictional practices, and strategies of critique. She has also done research regarding refugees.

Kathryn Church is associate professor in the School of Disability Studies at Ryerson University in Toronto. She teaches courses in community organizing and research methods and directs the school's affiliated research program through the Ryerson-RBC Institute for Disability Studies Research and Education. Kathryn uses interpretive methods that are sensitive to the subjectivities of researcher and researched, and is attentive to insider/outsider relations across identities and communities. Her practice is an experiment in fusing (institutional) ethnographic studies of ruling with arts-informed methods of writing (narrative, autobiography) and knowledge dissemination (installation.)

Lotte Darsø, associate professor at Learning Lab Denmark at the Danish University of Education, is researcher, consultant, lecturer, and author. Her main areas of interest are creativity and innovation as well as arts-in-business. She designs and develops Collaborative Learning Labs (CoLLabs) with public and private organizations doing "Mode 2" research on the learning potential of the interplay between arts and organizations. Lotte is cocreator of the master's degree program LAICS: Leadership and Innovation in Complex Systems (see www.laics.net) and is part of the core faculty. She also works as advisor for several indus-trial PhD students within the areas of creativity, innovation, design, and change processes. Lotte has published two books, *Innovation in the Making* (2001) and *Artful Creation: Learning-Tales of Arts-in-Business* (2004). In May, 2000, she was awarded the Danish indus-trial PhD prize, and in 2004 she was invited to the World Economic Forum meeting in Davos as a discussion leader and panelist.

Alex F. de Cosson, PhD (University of British Columbia), has worked as a professional sculp-tor exhibiting nationally and internationally for over 25 years. Alex has an MFA from York University and was on the faculty at The Ontario College of Art and Design between 1989 and 2006; he currently teaches at The Emily Carr Institute of Art + Design and is presently artist-in-residence and artist coordinator for the Teaching From the Heart Cohort and sessional instructor at the University of British Columbia, where he has taught in the Curriculum Studies Department since 1999. In 2004 he was coeditor, with Dr. Rita L. Irwin, of *A/r/tography: Ren-dering Self Through Arts-Based Living Inquiry*. He has been awarded numerous grants, including The Canada Council, The Ontario Arts Council, and The BC Arts Council. Alex was awarded the Gordon and Marion Smith Award for Excellence in Art Education, from UBC's Curriculum Studies Department, in 2003.

Elizabeth de Freitas teaches in the Ruth S. Ammon School of Education at Adelphi University and in the Faculty of Education at the University of Prince Edward Island. She has published papers in *Educational Studies in Mathematics, Teaching Education, The International Journal of Education and the Arts, Language and Literacy: A Canadian Educational E-journal, The Journal of the Canadian Association of Curriculum Studies,* and *Interchange: A Quarterly Review of Education.* She has also contributed a number of chapters to books about arts-informed research practices. Her current research interests include critical mathematics edu-cation, theories of identity, and research methodology.

Norman K. Denzin is professor of communications, sociology, and humanities at the University of Illinois, Urbana-Champaign. Editor of *Studies in Symbolic Interaction: A Research Journal* and *The Sociological Quarterly*, Dr. Denzin is the author of numerous books. He is the recipient of two awards from the Society for the Study of Symbolic Interaction: The Cooley Award in 1988 and the George Herbert Mead Award for lifetime contribution to the study of human behavior in 1997.

C. T. Patrick Diamond is professor emeritus, Ontario Institute for Studies in Education, University of Toronto. Pat was involved with 90 dissertations on arts-based narrative inquiry, teacher educator development, and qualitative research, and led arts-based insti-tutes in Canada, Brazil, Jamaica, and Hong Kong. Pat has published many works, includ-ing the books *Teacher Education as Transformation* (1991) and *The Postmodern Educator* (with C. A. Mullen, 1999). He was an associate editor for *Curriculum Inquiry*. Christine van Halen-Faber and he were founding coeditors for its Special Series on Arts-Based Educational Research. Pat has returned to Australia where he had spent a sabbatical year at the University of Sydney. He has an appointment at Griffith University (Brisbane) where he is a research consultant for the publications and grant applications of the Faculty of Education. He was a member of its external review team in 2006.

Dwayne Donald is a PhD candidate in secondary education at the University of Alberta. His work focuses on Aboriginal curriculum perspectives and their intersection with Western perspectives.

June Yennie Donmoyer, a National Board certified teacher, taught in middle and secondary schools for 19 years. Currently, she is helping teachers in an Austin, Texas, high school design and implement action research initiatives. In the late 1990s, she was the only classroom teacher selected by the Indonesian Ministry of Education to serve on a team of international scholars set up to explore the potential of using collaborative action research in Indonesian schools. She coauthored *The International Handbook of Action Research for Indonesian Educators.* June also has served as a literacy consultant in the San Diego city schools and on the Navajo reservation in Monument Valley, Utah. With her husband and coauthor for the chapter included in this volume, June has explored the potential of using readers' theater both as a pedagogical technique and as a method for displaying qualitative research data. She has written about the technique in papers published in such journals as *Educational Inquiry* and *The International Journal of Qualitative Studies in Education.*

Robert Donmoyer is currently professor of leadership studies and the codirector for the Center for Applied Nonprofit Research at the University of San Diego. Previously he served for 20 years as a professor and administrator at Ohio State University. His scholarship has focused on issues related to research utilization and the implications of the postpositivist critique for using empirical research in policymaking and practice. His research agenda has included developing and/or exploring various strategies for collecting, analyzing, and displaying qualitative data, including the readers' theater data display technique discussed in the chapter he coauthored for this volume. His paper "Take my Paradigm . . . Please! The Legacy of Kuhn's Construct in Educational Research" was recently published by *The International Journal of Qualitative Research,* and he authored chapters on qualitative methods and research utilization issues for the most recent editions of two American Educational Research Association handbooks, one focused on research teaching and the other on research on educational administration.

Elliot Eisner is the Lee Jacks Professor of Education and professor emeritus of art at Stanford University. He was trained as a painter at the School of the Art Institute of Chicago, and studied design at the Illinois Institute of Technology's School of Design. He received his PhD from the University of Chicago. Professor Eisner has long been interested in the relationship of the arts to the development of human intelligence. He has advanced the argument that qualitative considerations pervade not only what we call the fine arts, but the events that populate our daily activities, thus cultivating what can be regarded as a qualitative form of intelligence ought to be a high priority in our schools. Professor Eisner has served as president of the John Dewey Society, the American Educational Research Association, the International Society for Education through Art, and the National Society for the Study of Education. He is a fellow of the Norwegian Society of Arts and Letters and a fellow of the Royal Academy in the United Kingdom. In the United States, he is a member of the National Academy of Education. He is the recipient of six honorary doctorates, two of which were awarded by foreign universities.

Carolyn Ellis is professor of communication and sociology at the University of South Florida. She is the author of *Fisher Folk: Two Communities on Chesapeake Bay, Final Negotiations: A Story of Love, Loss, and Chronic Illness, The Ethnographic I: A Methodological Novel About Autoethnography,* and numerous edited collections and articles. Carolyn is interested in interpretive and artistic representations of qualitative research, in particular personal narratives. When she's not writing or teaching, she usually can be found sitting on the deck of her North Carolina mountain cabin or hiking in the woods with her partner, Art Bochner, and their dogs, Buddha and Sunya.

Susan Finley is associate professor of education at Washington State University and director of the At Home At School (AHAS) Program. She makes her home at the Vancouver campus of WSU, near Portland, Oregon. She bases her pedagogy and inquiry in arts-based approaches to understanding social and cultural issues in educational contexts. She is an activist who has implemented educational efforts with people living in tent communities, street youths, and economically poor children and their families, housed and unhoused. Her research has taken the forms of drama, poetry, and collage and includes presentations in numerous events and exhibits. She is author of more than 30 scholarly articles and book chapters that address issues of representation in qualitative inquiry. Recent projects include creation of the interactive At Home At School multimedia toolkit (Digital video/DVD-ROM).

Dianne Godkin has worked as a clinical ethicist with the Centre for Clinical Ethics (a shared service of Providence Healthcare, St. Joseph's Health Centre, and St. Michael's Hospital) since completing a postgraduate Clinical Ethics Fellowship with the University of Toronto Joint Centre for Bioethics in August 2003. Her role includes consultation, education, policy, and research ethics. Her prior education includes doctoral and master's degrees in nursing from the University of Alberta and a bachelor of science in nursing from the University of Western Ontario. Dianne has a particular research interest in end-of-life decision making and advance care planning in the older adult population that grew out of her clinical experiences in acute and long-term care settings. Outside of the work environment, her passions include music, travel, spending time with family, and playing with her two cats, Clio and Calliope.

Ross Gray is a consultant psychologist and social scientist at Sunnybrook Health Sciences Centre in Toronto, as well as associate professor in the Faculty of Medicine at the University of Toronto. He has worked with people with cancer for the past 20 years. Known as an innovator in the representation of qualitative social science research, Ross has developed research-based dramas and storytelling performances about cancer experiences and issues.

Erika Hasebe-Ludt is associate professor of teacher education in the areas of language and literacy education (English Language and English as a Second/Other Language) and curriculum theory and practice in the Faculty of Education, University of Lethbridge, Alberta, Canada. Her background is in interdisciplinary studies in linguistics, literature, and cultural studies. Her current teaching and research focus on local and global literacies and discourses of teaching. Collaboratively and individually, she investigates questions about the place of life writing and other auto/biographical texts in cosmopolitan educational settings. She uses interpretive hermeneutical frameworks to better understand the role of languages and cultures in education and the social sciences. She works with teachers to investigate their own practices and to advocate inclusive discourses for communicating across and between languages and cultures, genres, and disciplines. She is coeditor of *Curriculum Intertext: Place/Language/Pedagogy* (2003).

Graham E. Higgs is associate professor of psychology and education at Columbia College of Missouri where he finds great joy in teaching and engaging with colleagues and students in critical and creative thinking. He has been involved in qualitative research and the arts for many years, using the arts in therapy, in the classroom, and in valuing creative processes as emancipatory and transformative. Professor Higgs creates cross-disciplinary courses and applies creative research methods in teaching and evaluating learning outcomes. He has an abiding interest in ethics and in the deliberative democratic process of creating community agreements and has found that the arts can play an important role in finding meaningful and authentic solutions to human dilemmas.

Lekkie Hopkins is a feminist scholar and coordinator of women's studies in the School of International, Cultural, and Community Studies at Edith Cowan University in Perth, Australia. She is an oral historian, archivist, and literary critic, with research interests in the history of social protest, collective biography, feminist pedagogy, and feminist research methodologies.

Wanda Hurren is a researcher/poet/photographer/mapmaker who writes "snapshots" of everyday life, with a focus on notions of place and identity. Her mapwork has been published in *Gender, Place, and Culture: A Journal of Feminist Geography, Canadian Women's Studies, Canadian Journal of Prairie Literature,* and in *Fast Forward: Saskatchewan's New Poets.* She is the author of *Line Dancing: An Atlas of Geography, Curriculum, and Poetic Possibilities* (2003) and a coeditor of *Curriculum Intertext: Place/Language/Pedagogy.* She is associate professor of curriculum studies at the University of Victoria in British Columbia, Canada.

Esther Ignagni is assistant professor in the School of Disability Studies at Ryerson University, Toronto, Canada, and is completing her doctorate in public health sciences at the University of Toronto. Her research and teaching in the area of disability, the body, and youth extensively draw on arts-informed methodologies. She is interested in how dialogue works as a form of knowledge production, especially in inquiry and writing processes. Esther especially appreciates the creative expressions of others.

Rita L. Irwin is professor of curriculum studies and art education and associate dean of teacher education at the University of British Columbia, Vancouver, Canada. Prior to becoming associate dean in 2005, she was the head of the Department of Curriculum Studies for 6 years. Her research interests have spanned in-service art education, teacher education, sociocultural issues, and curriculum practices across K-12 and informal learning settings. Rita publishes widely, exhibits her artworks, and has secured a range of research grants, including a number of Social Science and Humanities Research Council of Canada grants to support her work in Canada, Australia, and Taiwan. Her most recent coedited books include *Curriculum in a New Key: The Collected Works of Ted T. Aoki* (coedited with William F. Pinar), *StARTing With . . .* (coedited with Kit Grauer), and *A/r/tography: Rendering Self Through Arts-Based Living Inquiry* (coedited with Alex de Cosson).

Valerie J. Janesick, PhD, is professor of educational leadership and policy studies, University of South Florida, Tampa. She teaches classes in qualitative research methods, curriculum theory and inquiry, foundations of curriculum, ethics and educational leadership, and program evaluation. She has recently completed the text *Authentic Assessment: A Primer* (2006). *Oral History for the Qualitative Researcher: Choreographing the Story* will be published in 2007. Her text *Stretching Exercises for Qualitative Researchers* (2004) uses dance as a metaphor for understanding the design and interpretation of qualitative methods.

Janice Jipson is professor of interdisciplinary studies in curriculum at National Louis University. She is one of the founders of the Reconceptualizing Early Childhood Education Special Interest Group and is editor of the series *Rethinking Childhood Education.* She has written extensively about narrative and arts-based research, including several books: *Daredevil Research: Re-Creating Analytic Practice* with Nicholas Paley, *Resistance and Representation: Rethinking Early Childhood Education* with Richard Johnson, and *Questions of You and the Struggle of Collaborative Life,* also with Nicholas Paley. Her professional interests include curriculum theory, the history of early childhood education, and research issues related to identity, intersubjectivity, and research representation.

Kelli Jo Kerry-Moran received her BA and MA in theatre arts from Brigham Young University and her PhD in Education from Iowa State University, where she completed an arts-based dissertation. Former positions include coordinator of institutional research for Eastern Arizona College and adjunct faculty for Northern Arizona University. Kelli is assistant professor in the Professional Studies in Education Department of Indiana University of Pennsylvania and the coordinator of an urban-focus collaborative elementary education program between Indiana University of Pennsylvania and the Community College of Allegheny County. Her primary research interests include creative drama, arts integration, and research methodology.

Sylvia Kind is a recent PhD graduate and instructor in the Department of Curriculum Studies at the University of British Columbia. She is an artist, researcher, and teacher interested in artistic practice as inquiry, the autobiographical text of teaching, and in the silent and inarticulate spaces of curriculum.

Thomas King holds a PhD in English/American studies from the University of Utah and has taught Native studies at universities in Utah, California, Minnesota, and Alberta for the past 25 years. He is currently associate professor of English (teaching Native literature and creative writing) at the University of Guelph, Ontario, Canada. His widely acclaimed novels include *Medicine River, Green Grass, Running Water,* and *Truth and Bright Water,* and he has been nominated for the Governor General's Award as well as the Commonwealth Writer's Prize. He is the editor of *All My Relations: An Anthology of Contemporary Canadian Native Fiction* and coeditor of *The Native in Literature: Canadian and Comparative Perspectives.* He's also well known as the creator and writer of the very popular Canadian Broadcasting Corporation radio series *The Dead Dog Café.* Thomas King's father was Cherokee, his mother is Greek, and he is the first scholar of Native descent to deliver the prestigious Massey Lecture Series at the University of Toronto.

Carl Leggo is a poet and professor in the Department of Language and Literacy Education at the University of British Columbia, where he teaches courses in English language arts education, creative writing, narrative research, and postmodern critical theory. In addition to degrees in English literature, education, and theology, he has a master's degree in creative writing. His poetry and fiction and scholarly essays have been published in many journals in North America and around the world. He is the author of three collections of poems: *Growing Up Perpendicular on the Side of a Hill, View From My Mother's House,* and *Come-By-Chance,* as well as a book about reading and teaching poetry: *Teaching to Wonder: Responding to Poetry in the Secondary Classroom.*

Troy R. Lovata earned a doctorate in anthropology from the University of Texas, with a focus on the visual presentation of archaeological research and the public presentation of prehistory in comic books. He was senior lecturer in the University of Texas's Technology, Literacy, and Culture Program and is now assistant professor in the University Honors Program at the University of New Mexico. Dr. Lovata also serves by appointment of the mayor on the Albuquerque Public Arts Board, the entity that oversees the city's extensive collection of public art. His recent book, *Inauthentic Archaeologies: Public Uses and Abuses of the Past,* is available from Left Coast Press and he has produced two short, animated films about the work of archaeology for The Archaeology Channel/The Archaeological Legacy Institute.

Maura McIntyre is adjunct professor at the Ontario Institute for Studies in Education of the University of Toronto. She is a founding member of the Centre for Arts-Informed Research at OISE/UT and has published and presented in a variety of alternative representative forms.

Together with Ardra Cole, Maura is working on a large-scale program of research about care and caregiving and Alzheimer's disease. Information about the current project, *Putting Care on the Map: Portraits of Care and Caregiving Across Canada,* can be found at www.oise.utoronto.ca/research/mappingcare. Maura makes her home on the Toronto Islands with her family.

Christine McKenzie is a doctoral student in adult education and community development at the Ontario Institute for Studies in Education. She teaches qualitative research methods part-time at the Faculty of Environmental Studies at York University and conducts community-based research training workshops at the Wellesley Institute in Toronto. She is a research collaborator in York University's Social Sciences and Humanities Research Council participatory action research project on popular arts and social change in the Americas, where her work focuses on training artists to engage communities in knowledge production and action. Her work has appeared in *Wild Fire: Art as Activism* and journals such as *Convergence* and *WANI.* In her current research she focuses on women's critical learning in nonformal education programs.

Shaun McNiff, the dean of Lesley College and university professor at Lesley University in Cambridge, Massachusetts, is an internationally recognized figure in the areas of the arts and healing and the author of many books that include *Art Heals; Trust the Process: An Artist's Guide to Letting Go; Art as Medicine; Creating With Others: The Practice of Imagination in Life, Art, and the Workplace; Art-Based Research; Depth Psychology of Art;* and *The Arts and Psychotherapy.* Dr. McNiff is a past president of the American Art Therapy Association, and he has published widely on art-based research after studying with Rudolf Arhheim in the early 1970s. He teaches and lectures throughout the United States, Canada, Europe, and Israel, and is considered by many to be the founder of integrated expressive arts therapy, having established the first graduate program in this area and then supporting the development of other programs throughout the world.

Jim Mienczakowski's research has involved the exploration of arts-informed qualitative research as a means of deepening and widening the impacts of qualitative (ethnographic) narrative methodologies. Working with transdisciplinary teams of psychologists, nurse educators, and theatre and arts practitioners, he has established a multidimensional approach to both education and reflexive ethnography through ethnodrama. Jim has taught in the UK, West Indies, and Australia and has been a deputy vice-chancellor (academic and research) in two Australian universities. He is currently Head of Higher Education at the Abu Dhabi Education Council, United Arab Emirates.

Claudia Mitchell is a James McGill Professor in the Faculty of Education, McGill University. Her research interests include girlhood studies, teacher identity, and youth participation in the context of HIV and AIDS. She is a cofounder of the Centre for Visual Methodologies for Social Change at the University of KwaZulu-Natal, South Africa.

Teresa Moore is senior lecturer in the Faculty of Arts, Humanities, and Education at Central Queensland University (CQU). She has a number of postgraduate doctoral and master's degree students. Her PhD, completed in 2004, was a transdisciplinary study concerning the changing nature of the academic workplace where issues of globalization, gender, and technology influenced workplace interaction. Dr. Moore also provided executive research support for the Chair of the Ministerial Advisory Committee for Education Renewal (MACER) in Queensland, Australia. She is a member of the CQU Human Ethics Research

Committee. Her research interests include the contemporary workplace, identity, and performance and the "regional/rural" space.

Lorri Neilsen (who also publishes as Lorri Neilsen Glenn) is professor of education at Mount Saint Vincent University in Halifax, Nova Scotia, Canada. The author, editor, and coeditor of six scholarly books on literacy and research, she is also author of two books of poetry and a chapbook. Neilsen's courses in feminist inquiry, lyric inquiry, and ethnography have been held at her home university, as well as in settings across Canada, and in Australia, New Zealand, and Ireland. Neilsen Glenn's poetry and research have earned North American and international awards. She is currently completing a book of essays on grief and loss, and editing a collection of women's writing. She lives in Halifax where she is serving a 4-year term as Halifax poet laureate.

Jeff Nisker is professor of obstetrics-gynaecology and oncology and coordinator of health ethics and humanities in the Schulich School of Medicine and Dentistry, University of Western Ontario. His research interests center on the use of theatre as a citizen deliberation tool for health policy development, particularly regarding reproductive and genetic technologies, and their impact on concepts of "health" and "disease." Jeff has written many scientific articles and book chapters, as well as six plays and many short stories to explore ethical issues and promote compassionate health care. He has also edited or coedited collections of stories, poems, and plays of health care students and professionals to this end. His national positions have included cochair of Health Canada's Advisory Committee on Reproductive and Genetic Technology, Executive Canadian Bioethics Society, National Council of Ethics in Human Research, Royal College of Physicians and Surgeons' Ethics and Equity Committee, and editor-in-chief of the *Journal of Obstetrics and Gynaecology Canada.*

Antoinette Oberg taught graduate courses in curriculum theory and interpretive inquiry at the University of Victoria (British Columbia) for three decades. An independent scholar since 2005, Dr. Oberg continues her research on imaginative, personal, and reflective narrative writing and its value for both her own and students' inquiries. Dr. Oberg was awarded the University of Victoria's Alumni Teaching Award (1995) and the Canadian Association for Curriculum Studies Ted T. Aoki Award for Distinguished Service within the Field of Curriculum Studies (2005). Her articles and essays appear in periodicals such as *Educational Insights, Curriculum Inquiry, Journal of Curriculum Studies, Journal of Curriculum and Supervision, Phenomenology + Pedagogy, JCT: An Interdisciplinary Journal of Curriculum Studies, Peabody Journal of Education,* and *Theory Into Practice,* as well as in Wanda Hurren and Erika Hasebe-Ludt's *Curriculum Inter-Text.*

Nicholas Paley is professor of curriculum and educational foundations and an honors professor in the liberal arts at George Washington University. His books include *Finding Art's Place: Experiments in Contemporary Education and Culture, Daredevil Research: Re-Creating Analytic Practice* (with Janice Jipson), and *The Period of Self-Education and the Arts: Projects, Essays, Interviews* (with Tadashi Kawamata and Takaaki Kumakura). He is the author of numerous articles on literature and curriculum, artistic practice and collaboration, and representation and self-representation in educational life.

Ronald J. Pelias teaches performance studies in the Department of Speech Communication at Southern Illinois University, Carbondale. His most recent books are *Writing Performance: Poeticizing the Researcher's Body* and *A Methodology of the Heart: Evoking Academic and Daily Life.*

Sara Promislow, PhD, is an independent scholar and member of the Centre for Arts-Informed Research at the Ontario Institute for Studies in Education of the University of Toronto. She is editor of *arts-informed,* the Centre's online publication, and coeditor of the fourth volume of the arts-informed inquiry series *Creating Scholartistry: Imagining the Arts-Informed Thesis or Dissertation* (in press). Sara is a collage scholartist and educational researcher. Her research explores the immigrant and refugee experience in and through languages, cultures and identities, minority bilingualism and biculturalism, and arts-informed research methods.

Jon Prosser is director of international education management at Leeds University, UK. He is also director of the Building Capacity in Visual Methods project, which is part of the Researcher Development Initiative (ESRC) and a coapplicant of Real Life Methods, a Node of the National Centre for Research Methods (ESRC).

Janice Rahn is interdisciplinary in her research and teaching. She writes about the poetics and politics of popular culture with implications for education. Her book *Painting Without Permission: An Ethnographic Study of Hip Hop Graffiti Culture* was published in 2002. She made five documentary videos about the many subcultures within hip-hop culture. Rahn published several articles about media and the social construction of identity and new media as an art material. She collaborated on artist-in-the-school projects and made videos about the process. Rahn's art practice has been mainly audio/video art installations that have been shown across Canada in places such as the Banff Centre, Edmonton, and Ottawa art galleries. She teaches courses in the Education and Fine Arts Faculties at the University of Lethbridge. She is currently editing a book on new media, writing chapters on video artists, and teaching video sketchbook.

Robert Runte is associate professor in the Faculty of Education at the University of Lethbridge where he teaches courses in student evaluation, sociology, and research methodologies. His current research interests include the impact of emergent communication technologies on youth culture, on avocational subcultures, on work/family balance of professional level labor, and on research methodology. For example, he is currently investigating the nature and salience of references to schooling in adolescent blogs, and is collaborating with his wife, Dr. Mary Runte, on how cell phones and the Internet have contributed to long hours culture and the blurring of the work/home boundary. He is also editing a university text on Canadian science fiction and fantasy that will illustrate the various theoretical approaches to English literature. Dr. Runte's Web page is http://www.edu.uleth.ca/~runte.

Johnny Saldaña is professor of theatre and associate director for the School of Theatre and Film in the Katherine K. Herberger College of Fine Arts at Arizona State University (ASU) where he has taught since 1981. His books include *Longitudinal Qualitative Research: Analyzing Change Through Time* (2003), a research methods book and recipient of the 2004 Outstanding Book Award from the National Communication Association's Ethnography Division; and an edited collection of plays, *Ethnodrama: An Anthology of Reality Theatre* (2005). His ethnodramatic adaptation *Finding My Place: The Brad Trilogy* appears in Harry F. Wolcott's *Sneaky Kid and Its Aftermath: Ethics and Intimacy in Fieldwork* (2002). Saldaña is a recipient of the American Alliance for Theatre and Education's 1996 and 2001 Research Awards, and the ASU Herberger College of Fine Arts Distinguished Teacher of the Year Award in 1995 and Research Award in 2005.

Karen Scott-Hoy is an independent scholar who resides in the beautiful wine district of the Barossa Valley, South Australia. Combining her love of the arts with her desire to always "dig deeper" into issues she encounters in her work as a health educator, mother, and rural community member, she uses the medium of painting to re-enter, explore, and portray her experiences, developing an evocative arts-based autoethnography that seeks to challenge, inspire, and ask new questions.

Christina Sinding is assistant professor at McMaster University, jointly appointed to the Department of Health, Aging, and Society and the School of Social Work. Her research and teaching focus on health and social justice (or, more accurately and more often, illness and social injustice). Her current research is with and about people with cancer and their families and supporters. She works in interpretive and critical traditions, foregrounding the meanings research participants assign to their experiences and examining their accounts with reference to health and social systems. She is interested in innovative—particularly arts-informed—knowledge exchange (both doing it, and taking it as an object of study).

Andrew C. Sparkes is professor of social theory and director of the Qualitative Research Unit in the School of Health and Sport Sciences, Exeter University, Exeter, England. Research interests include performing bodies, identities, and selves; interrupted body projects and the narrative reconstruction of self; sporting auto/biographies; and the lives of marginalized individuals and groups. He is drawn toward qualitative methodologies as a way of exploring these interests and seeks to represent his findings using multiple genres.

Stephanie Springgay is assistant professor of art education and women's studies at Penn State University. Her research and artistic explorations focus on the body and in particular on issues of *relationality* and *an ethics of embodiment*. In addition, as a multidisciplinary artist working with installation and video-based art, she investigates the relationship between artistic practices and methodologies of educational research through a/r/tography. She recently coedited the book *Curriculum and the Cultural Body* with Debra Freedman.

Graeme Sullivan is chair of the Department of Arts and Humanities, Teachers College, Columbia University and associate professor of art education. His research focuses on the investigation of critical-reflexive thinking processes and creative methods of inquiry in the visual arts. These ideas are described in his book *Art Practice as Research: Inquiry in the Visual Arts* (2005). He has published widely in the field of art education, and in 1990 he was awarded the Manual Barkan Memorial Award by the National Art Education Association (NAEA) for his scholarly writing, and he received the 2007 Lowenfeld Award for distinguished contribution to art education. Graeme is the former senior editor of *Studies in Art Education,* the research journal of the NAEA. He maintains an active art practice, and his Streetworks have been installed in several international cities and sites over the past 10 years (www.streetworksart.com).

Christine van Halen-Faber is principal of Covenant Canadian Reformed Teachers College, Hamilton, Ontario, and works as an independent scholar out of the Center for Teacher Development, Ontario Institute for Studies in Education, University of Toronto. Her research interests focus on arts-based narrative inquiry, teacher(-educator) development, and forms of qualitative research. She is particularly intrigued by the presence of architectural elements in writing. Christine pursues artful pathways of inquiry into self/other using visual and literary forms, and derives much sustaining joy and inspiration from exploring museums, art galleries, and libraries. Her PhD dissertation, *Seeing Through Apples: An Arts-Based Exploration Into the Ethics and Aesthetics of a Teacher-Educator-Researcher's Arts-Based Beginnings,* was awarded the Canadian Association for Teacher Education 2004 Dissertation Award. Christine has published numerous book chapters and peer-reviewed articles, including editorials in *Curriculum*

Inquiry. C. T. Patrick Diamond and she were founding coeditors for its Special Series on Arts-Based Educational Research.

Sandra Weber is professor of education at Concordia University, Montreal, where she teaches courses on image-based research methodologies, children's toys and popular culture, media literacy, gender, and everyday uses of digital technologies. Codirector and founder of the Image and Identity Research Collective (see http://www.iirc.mcgill.ca), her passions include arts-based visual methods, the roles and significance of clothing and the body, and searching for ways to involve children more actively in research. One of her primary goals is to make research less hierarchical, more interdisciplinary, and more accessible to the public through film, performance, art installations, and collaborations with others. Dr. Weber is author or coeditor of five books: *That's Funny, You Don't Look Like A Teacher: Interrogating Images and Identity in Popular Culture; Reinventing Ourselves as Teachers: Beyond Nostalgia; Just Who Do We Think We Are? Arts-Based Methodologies for Self-Study; Not Just Any Dress: Explorations of Dress, Identity, and the Body;* and *Growing Up Online: Children and Technology,* as well as over a hundred articles and book chapters.

INDEX